Core Rulebook III v.3.5

Based on the original DUNGEONS & DRAGONS game
created by E. Gary Gygax and Dave Arneson

U.S., CANADA,
ASIA, PACIFIC, & LATIN AMERICA
Wizards of the Coast, Inc.
P.O. Box 707
Renton WA 98057-0707
QUESTIONS? 1-800-324-6496

EUROPEAN HEADQUARTERS
Wizards of the Coast, Belgium
T Hosfveld 6d
1702 Groot-Bijgaarden
Belgium
+322- 467- 3360

620-17755-001-EN   9 8 7 6 5 4 3 2 1
First Printing: July 2003

Visit our website at www.wizards.com/dnd

CREDITS

MONSTER MANUAL DESIGN
Skip Williams

MONSTER MANUAL D&D DESIGN TEAM
Monte Cook, Jonathan Tweet, Skip Williams

ADDITIONAL DESIGN
Peter Adkison, Richard Baker, Jason Carl, William W. Connors, Sean K Reynolds

EDITORS
Jennifer Clarke Wilkes, Jon Pickens

EDITORIAL ASSITANCE
Julia Martin, Jeff Quick, Rob Heinsoo, David Noonan, Penny Williams

MANAGING EDITOR
Kim Mohan

CORE D&D CREATIVE DIRECTOR
Ed Stark

DIRECTOR OF RPG R&D
Bill Slavicsek

VISUAL CREATIVE DIRECTOR
Jon Schindehette

ART DIRECTOR
Dawn Murin

D&D CONCEPTUAL ARTISTS
Todd Lockwood, Sam Wood

D&D LOGO DESIGN
Matt Adelsperger, Sherry Floyd

COVER ART
Henry Higginbotham

INTERIOR ARTISTS
Glen Angus, Carlo Arellano, Daren Bader, Tom Baxa, Carl Critchlow, Brian Despain, Tony Diterlizzi, Larry Elmore, Scott Fischer, Rebecca Guay, Paul Jaquays, Michael Kaluta, Dana Knutson, Todd Lockwood, David Martin, Matthew Mitchell, Monte Moore, rk post, Adam Rex, Wayne Reynolds, Richard Sardinha, Brian Snoddy, Mark Tedin, Anthony Waters

GRAPHIC DESIGNER
Sean Glenn, Sherry Floyd

TYPOGRAPHERS
Erin Dorries, Angelika Lokotz, Nancy Walker

PHOTOGRAPHER
Craig Cudnohufsky

BRAND MANAGER
Ryan Dancey

CATEGORY MANAGER
Keith Strohm

PROJECT MANAGERS
Larry Weiner, Josh Fischer

DIGI-TECH SPECIALIST
Joe Fernandez

PRODUCTION MANAGER
Chas DeLong

SPECIAL THANKS
Cindi Rice, Jim Lin, Richard Garfield, Skaff Elias, Andrew Finch

MONSTER MANUAL REVISION
Rich Baker, Skip Williams

D&D REVISION TEAM
Rich Baker, Andy Collins, David Noonan, Rich Redman, Skip Williams

ADDITIONAL DEVELOPMENT
David Eckelberry, Jennifer Clarke Wilkes, Gwendolyn F.M. Kestrel, Bill Slavicsek

PROOFREADER
Penny Williams

MANAGING EDITOR
Kim Mohan

D&D CREATIVE DIRECTOR
Ed Stark

DIRECTOR OF RPG R&D
Bill Slavicsek

ART DIRECTOR
Dawn Murin

COVER ART
Henry Higginbotham

INTERIOR ARTISTS
Glen Angus, Carlo Arellano, Daren Bader, Tom Baxa, Carl Critchlow, Brian Despain, Tony Diterlizzi, Scott Fischer, Rebecca Guay-Mitchell, Jeremy Jarvis, Paul Jaquays, Michael Kaluta, Dana Knutson, Todd Lockwood, David Martin, Raven Mimura, Matthew Mitchell, Monte Moore, Adam Rex, Wayne Reynolds, Richard Sardinha, Brian Snoddy, Mark Tedin, Anthony Waters, Sam Wood

GRAPHIC DESIGNER
Dawn Murin

GRAPHIC PRODUCTION SPECIALISTS
Erin Dorries, Angelika Lokotz

PHOTOGRAPHER
Craig Cudnohufsky

VICE PRESIDENT OF PUBLISHING
Mary Kirchoff

CATEGORY MANAGER
Anthony Valterra

PROJECT MANAGER
Martin Durham

PRODUCTION MANAGER
Chas DeLong

OTHER WIZARDS OF THE COAST R&D CONTRIBUTORS
Paul Barclay, Michele Carter, Bruce Cordell, Mike Donais, Skaff Elias, Andrew Finch, Jeff Grubb, Rob Heinsoo, Christopher Perkins, Charles Ryan, Michael Selinker, Jonathan Tweet, James Wyatt

SPECIAL THANKS
Mary Elizabeth Allen, Jefferson Dunlap, Stephen Radney-McFarland, Liz Schuh, Andy Smith, Mat Smith, Alex Weitz

TABLE OF CONTENTS

ALPHABETICAL LISTING OF MONSTERS

MONSTERS BY TYPE (AND SUBTYPE)

Aberration: aboleth, athach, beholders, carrion crawler, choker, chuul, cloaker, delver, destrachan, drider, ethereal filcher, ettercap, gauth, ghaur, gibbering mouther, grick, mimic, mind flayer, nagas, otyugh, phasm, rust monster, skum, umber hulk, will-o'-wisp.

(Air): air mephit, arrowhawk, cloud giant, dust mephit, green dragon, ice mephit, will-o'-wisp.

Animal: animals, bat swarm, dinosaurs, dire animals, rat swarm, roc.

(Aquatic): aboleth, aquatic elf, chuul, dire shark, dragon turtle, giant octopus, kraken, kuo-toa, locathah, merfolk, merrow, octopus, sahuagin, sea cat, sea hag, sharks, skum, squids, water naga.

(Cold): cryohydra, frost giant, frost worm, ice mephit, silver dragon, white dragon, winter wolf.

Construct: animated objects, golems, homunculus, inevitables, retriever, shield guardian.

Dragon: dragons, dragon turtle, pseudodragon, wyvern.

(Earth): blue dragon, copper dragon, earth mephit, gargoyle, salt mephit, stone giant.

Elemental: belker, elementals, invisible stalker, magmin, thoqqua.

Elemental (Air): belker, air elementals, invisible stalker.

Elemental (Earth): earth elementals, thoqqua.

Elemental (Fire): fire elementals, magmin, thoqqua.

Elemental (Water): water elementals.

Fey: dryad, grig, nixie, nymph, pixie, satyr.

(Fire): azer, brass dragon, fire giant, fire mephit, gold dragon, magma mephit, pyrohydra, red dragon, steam mephit.

Giant: ettin, giants, ogre, ogre mage, troll.

TABLE OF CONTENTS

INTRODUCTION

This is the DUNGEONS & DRAGONS® Roleplaying Game, the game that defines the genre and has set the standard for fantasy roleplaying for more than 30 years.

Specifically, this is the *Monster Manual*. This book contains entries for hundreds of creatures, both hostile and benign, for use in DUNGEONS & DRAGONS adventures. This book, the *Player's Handbook*, and the *Dungeon Master's Guide* comprise the core rules for the D&D® game.

This introduction explains how to read each creature's write-up. It often refers to the Glossary, located in Chapter 7 at the back of this book (starting on page 305), for more details on attack forms and the special qualities associated with monsters.

A list of monsters organized by Challenge Rating appears on pages 318 and 319 to make it easy for the Dungeon Master to tailor encounters to the party level of the player characters.

READING THE ENTRIES

Each monster description is organized in the same general format, as outlined below. For complete information about the characteristics of monsters, consult Chapter 7: Glossary (starting on page 305), the *Player's Handbook*, or the *Dungeon Master's Guide*.

STATISTICS BLOCK

This portion of a monster description contains basic game information on the creature.

Name

This is the name by which the creature is generally known. The descriptive text may provide other names.

Size and Type

This line describes the creature's size (Huge, for example). Size categories are defined in the Glossary. A size modifier applies to the creature's Armor Class (AC) and attack bonus, as well as to certain skills. A creature's size also determines how far it can reach to make a melee attack and how much space it occupies in a fight (see Space/Reach, below).

The size and type line continues with the creature's type (giant, for example). Type determines how magic affects a creature; for example, the *hold animal* spell affects only creatures of the animal type. Type determines certain features, such as Hit Dice size, base attack bonus, base saving throw bonuses, and skill points. For quick reference, the Glossary gives a full description of the features and traits of each type and subtype.

Hit Dice

This line gives the creature's number and type of Hit Dice, and lists any bonus hit points. A parenthetical note gives the average hit points for a creature of the indicated number of Hit Dice.

A creature's Hit Dice total is also treated as its level for determining how spells affect the creature, its rate of natural healing, and its maximum ranks in a skill.

Initiative

This line gives the creature's modifier on initiative checks.

Speed

This line gives the creature's tactical speed on land (the amount of distance it can cover in one move action). If the creature wears armor that reduces its speed, the creature's base land speed follows.

If the creature has other modes of movement, these are given after (or in place of) the land speed. Unless noted otherwise, modes of movement are natural (not magical). See the Glossary for information on movement modes.

Armor Class

The Armor Class line gives the creature's AC for normal combat and includes a parenthetical mention of the modifiers contributing to it (usually size, Dexterity, and natural armor). The creature's touch and flat-footed ACs follow the combat-ready AC.

A creature's armor proficiencies (if it has any) depend on its type, but in general a creature is automatically proficient with any kind of armor it is described as wearing (light, medium, or heavy), and with all lighter kinds of armor.

Base Attack/Grapple

The number before the slash on this line is the creature's base attack bonus (before any modifiers are applied). The DM usually won't need this number, but it can be handy sometimes, especially if the creature has the Power Attack or Combat Expertise feats.

The number after the slash is the creature's grapple bonus, which

---

continued from page 4

(Goblinoid): bugbear, goblin, hobgoblin.

Humanoid: bugbear, dwarf, elf, githyanki, githzerai, gnoll, gnome, goblin, halfling, hobgoblin, kobold, lizardfolk, locathah, merfolk, orc, troglodyte.

(Incorporeal): allip, ghost, shadow, spectre, wraith.

(Lawful): inevitable.

Magical Beast: ankheg, aranea, basilisk, behir, bulette, blink dog, chimera, cockatrice, darkmantle, digester, displacer beast, dragonne, ethereal marauder, fiendish dire rat, frost worm, giant eagle, giant owl, girallon, gorgon, gray render, griffon, hellwasp swarm, hippogriff, hydras, kraken, krenshar, lamia, lammasu, manticore, owlbear, pegasus, phase spider, purple worm, remorhaz, roper, shocker lizard, sea cat, sphinxes, spider eater, stirge, tarrasque, unicorn, winter wolf, worg, yrthak.

Monstrous Humanoid: centaur, derro, doppelganger, gargoyle, grimlock, hags, harpy, kuo-toa, medusa, minotaur, sahuagin, yuan-ti.

Ooze: black pudding, gelatinous cube, gray ooze, ochre jelly.

Outsider: ravid.

Outsider (Air): air mephit, arrowhawk, djinni, dust mephit, ice mephit.

Outsider (Chaotic): chaos beast, demons, eladrins, howler, lillend, slaadi, titan.

Outsider (Evil): achaierai, barghest, demons, devils, hell hound, howler, night hag, nightmare, rakshasa, shadow mastiff, vargouille, xill, yeth hound.

Outsider (Earth): earth mephit, salt mephit, xorn.

Outsider (Fire): azer, efreeti, hell hound, fire mephit, magma mephit, steam mephit, rast, salamanders.

Outsider (Good): angels, archons, eladrins, guardinals, lillend, titan.

Outsider (Lawful): achaierai, archons, barghest, devils, formians, hell hound, rakshasa, xill.

Outsider (Native): aasimar, couatl, janni, tiefling, rakshasa, triton.

Outsider (Water): ooze mephit, water mephit, tojanidas, triton.

Plant: assassin vine, phantom fungus, shambling mound, shrieker, tendriculos, treant, violet fungus.

(Reptilian): kobold, lizardfolk, troglodyte.

(Shapechanger): aranea, barghest, doppelganger, lycanthropes, mimic, phasm.

Undead: allip, bodak, devourer, ghast, ghost, ghoul, lich, mohrg, mummy, nightshades, shadow, skeletons, spectre, vampire, vampire spawn, wight, wraith, zombie.

Vermin: centipede swarm, giant insects, locust swarm, monstrous centipedes, monstrous scorpions, monstrous spiders, spider swarm.

(Water): black dragon, bronze dragon, ooze mephit, water mephit.

is used when the creature makes a grapple attack or when someone tries to grapple the creature. The grapple bonus includes all modifiers that apply to the creature's grapple checks (base attack bonus, Strength modifier, special size modifier, and any other applicable modifier, such as a racial bonus on grapple checks).

Attack

This line shows the single attack the creature makes with an attack action. In most cases, this is also the attack the creature uses when making an attack of opportunity as well. The attack line provides the weapon used (natural or manufactured), attack bonus, and form of attack (melee or ranged). The attack bonus given includes modifications for size and Strength (for melee attacks) or Dexterity (for ranged attacks). A creature with the Weapon Finesse feat can use its Dexterity modifier on melee attacks.

If the creature uses natural attacks, the natural weapon given here is the creature's primary natural weapon (see the Glossary).

If the creature has several different weapons at its disposal, the alternatives are shown, with each different attack separated by the word "or."

A creature can use one of its secondary natural weapons (see the Glossary) when making an attack action, but if it does it takes an attack penalty, as noted in the Full Attack section below.

The damage that each attack deals is noted parenthetically. Damage from an attack is always at least 1 point, even if a subtraction from a die roll reduces the result to 0 or lower.

Full Attack

This line shows all the physical attacks the creature makes when it uses a full-round action to make a full attack. It gives the number of attacks along with the weapon, attack bonus, and form of attack (melee or ranged). The first entry is for the creature's primary weapon, with an attack bonus including modifications for size and Strength (for melee attacks) or Dexterity (for ranged attacks). A creature with the Weapon Finesse feat can use its Dexterity modifier on melee attacks.

The remaining weapons are secondary, and attacks with them are made with a –5 penalty to the attack roll, no matter how many there are. Creatures with the Multiattack feat (see page 304) take only a –2 penalty on secondary attacks.

The damage that each attack deals is noted parenthetically. Damage from an attack is always at least 1 point, even if a subtraction from a die roll reduces the result to 0 or lower.

A creature's primary attack damage includes its full Strength modifier (1-1/2 times its Strength bonus if the attack is with the creature's sole natural weapon) and is given first. Secondary attacks add only 1/2 the creature's Strength bonus and are given second in the parentheses.

If any attacks also have some special effect other than damage (poison, disease, energy drain, and so forth), that information is given here.

Unless noted otherwise, creatures using natural weapons deal double damage on critical hits.

Manufactured Weapons: Creatures that use swords, bows, spears, and the like follow the same rules as characters do. The bonus for attacks with two-handed weapons is 1-1/2 times the creature's Strength modifier (if it is a bonus), and is given first. Off-hand weapons add only 1/2 the Strength bonus and are given second in the parentheses.

Space/Reach

This line describes how much space the creature takes up on the battle grid and thereby needs to fight effectively, as well as how close it has to be to threaten an opponent. The number before the slash is the creature's space, or how many feet one side of the creature occupies (refer to the *Dungeon Master's Guide* for additional details). For example, a creature with a space of 15 feet occupies a 3-square-by-3-square space on the battle grid. The number after the slash is the creature's natural reach. If the creature has exceptional reach due to a weapon, tentacle, or the like, the extended reach and its source are noted in parentheses at the end of the line.

Special Attacks and Special Qualities

Many creatures have unusual abilities, which can include special attack forms, resistance or vulnerability to certain types of damage, and enhanced senses, among others. A monster entry breaks these abilities into special attacks and special qualities. The latter category includes defenses, vulnerabilities, and other special abilities that are not modes of attack. A special ability is either extraordinary (Ex), spell-like (Sp), or supernatural (Su). See the Glossary for definitions of special abilities. Additional information (when needed) is provided in the creature's descriptive text.

When a special ability allows a saving throw, the kind of save and the save DC is noted in the descriptive text. Most saving throws against special abilities have DCs calculated as follows: 10 + 1/2 the attacker's racial Hit Dice + the relevant ability modifier. The save DC is given in the creature's description along with the ability on which the DC is based.

Saves

This line gives the creature's Fortitude, Reflex, and Will save modifiers.

Abilities

This line lists the creature's ability scores, in the customary order: Str, Dex, Con, Int, Wis, Cha. Except where noted otherwise, each

WHY A REVISION?

The new DUNGEONS & DRAGONS game debuted in 2000. In the three years since the d20 game system energized the RPG industry, we've gathered tons of data on how the game is being played. We consider D&D to be a living game that constantly evolves as it is played. Using the gathered feedback, we've retooled the game from the ground up and incorporated everyone's suggestions to improve the game and this product.

If this is your first experience with D&D, we welcome you to a wonderful world of adventure and imagination. If you played the prior version of this book, rest assured that this revision is a testament to our dedication to continuous product improvement and innovation. We've updated errata, clarified rules, polished the presentation, and made the game better than it was. This is an upgrade of the d20 System, not a new edition of the game. This revision is compatible with existing products, and these products can be used with the revision with only minor adjustments.

What's new in the revised *Monster Manual*? The entire book has been

polished and refined, all in response to your feedback and to reflect the way the game is actually being played. We've reorganized the group monster entries into easier-to-use, single-entry formats. New monsters have been added to this larger book. Advanced versions of some monsters have been included to challenge higher-level characters. New monster feats have been added, and all monster abilities are detailed in the glossary for easy reference. Monsters that can be used as player characters have level adjustments and other information to expedite such play, and we've reworked all monsters so that they gain feats and skills the same way that player characters do. We've added extensive information on how to advance, customize, and design monsters. And there are other improvements throughout, such as first-glance descriptions of monsters, typical spell lists for spellcasting monsters, additional statistics to speed up play (including grapple bonus and full attack routines), and ready-to-play entries for all monster types.

Take a look, play the game. We think you'll like how everything turned out.

creature is assumed to have the standard array of ability scores before racial adjustments (all 11s and 10s). To determine any creature's racial ability adjustments, subtract 10 from any even-numbered ability score and subtract 11 from any odd-numbered score. (Exceptions are noted in the Combat section of a creature's descriptive text.) Humanoid warriors are generally built using the nonelite array: 13, 12, 11, 10, 9, 8. Advanced creatures (such as the hound archon hero) are built using the elite array: 15, 14, 13, 12, 10, 8.

Most abilities work as described in Chapter 1 of the *Player's Handbook*, with exceptions given below.

Strength: As noted on page 162 of the *Player's Handbook*, quadrupeds can carry heavier loads than bipeds can. Any creature with four or more motive limbs can carry a load as a quadruped, even if it does not necessarily use all the limbs at once. For example, dragons carry loads as quadrupeds.

Intelligence: A creature can speak all the languages mentioned in its description, plus one additional language per point of Intelligence bonus. Any creature with an Intelligence score of 3 or higher understands at least one language (Common, unless noted otherwise).

Nonabilities: Some creatures lack certain ability scores. These creatures do not have an ability score of 0—they lack the ability altogether. The modifier for a nonability is +0. Other effects of nonabilities are detailed in the Glossary.

Skills

This line gives the creature's skills, along with each skill's modifier (including adjustments for ability scores, armor check penalties, and any bonuses from feats or racial traits). All listed skills are class skills, unless the creature has a character class (noted in the entry). A creature's type and Intelligence score determine the number of skill points it has.

The Skills section of the creature's description recaps racial bonuses and other adjustments to skill modifiers for the sake of clarity; these bonuses should not be added to the listed skill modifiers. An asterisk (*) beside the relevant score and in the Skills section of the descriptive text indicates a conditional adjustment, one that applies only in certain situations (for instance, a gargoyle gets an additional +8 bonus on Hide checks when it is concealed against a background of worked stone).

Natural Tendencies: Some creatures simply aren't made for certain types of physical activity. Elephants, despite their great Strength scores, are terrible at jumping. Giant crocodiles, despite their high Strength scores, don't climb well. Horses can't walk tightropes. If it seems clear to you that a particular creature simply is not made for a particular physical activity, you can say that the creature takes a –8 penalty on skill checks that defy its natural tendencies. In extreme circumstances (a porpoise attempting a Climb check, for instance) you can rule that the creature fails the check automatically.

Feats

The line gives the creature's feats. A monster gains feats just as a character does—one for its first Hit Die, a second feat if it has at least 3 HD, and an additional feat for every additional 3 HD. (For example, a 9 HD creature is entitled to four feats.)

Sometimes a creature has one or more bonus feats, marked with a superscript B (^{B}). Creatures often do not have the prerequisites for a bonus feat. If this is so, the creature can still use the feat. If you wish to customize the creature with new feats, you can reassign its other feats, but not its bonus feats. A creature cannot have a feat that is not a bonus feat unless it has the feat's prerequisites.

Environment

This line gives a type of climate and terrain where the creature is typically found. This describes a tendency, but is not exclusionary. A great wyrm gold dragon, for instance, has an environment entry of warm plains, but could also be encountered underground, in cold hills, or even on another plane of existence. See Chapter 3 of the *Dungeon Master's Guide* for more on terrain types and climate.

Organization

This line describes the kinds of groups the creature might form. A range of numbers in parentheses indicates how many combat-ready adults are in each type of group. Many groups also have a number of noncombatants, expressed as a percentage of the fighting population. Noncombatants can include young, the infirm, slaves, or other individuals who are not inclined to fight. A creature's Society section may include more details on noncombatants.

If the organization line contains the term "domesticated," the creature is generally found only in the company of other creatures, whom it serves in some capacity.

Challenge Rating

This shows the average level of a party of adventurers for which one creature would make an encounter of moderate difficulty. Assume a party of four fresh characters (full hit points, full spells, and equipment appropriate to their levels). Given reasonable luck, the party should be able to win the encounter with some damage but no casualties. For more information about Challenge Ratings, see pages 36 and 48 of the *Dungeon Master's Guide*.

Treasure

This line reflects how much wealth the creature owns and refers to Table 3–5: Treasure on page 52 of the *Dungeon Master's Guide*. In most cases, a creature keeps valuables in its home or lair and has no treasure with it when it travels. Intelligent creatures that own useful, portable treasure (such as magic items) tend to carry and use these, leaving bulky items at home. See the glossary for more details on using the Treasure line of each monster entry.

Alignment

This line gives the alignment that the creature is most likely to have. Every entry includes a qualifier that indicates how broadly that alignment applies to the species as a whole. See the Glossary for details.

Advancement

This book usually describes only the most commonly encountered version of a creature (though some entries for advanced monsters can be found). The advancement line shows how tough a creature can get, in terms of extra Hit Dice. (This is not an absolute limit, but exceptions are extremely rare.) Often, intelligent creatures advance by gaining a level in a character class instead of just gaining a new Hit Die.

Level Adjustment

This line is included in the entries of creatures suitable for use as player characters or as cohorts (usually creatures with Intelligence scores of at least 3 and possessing opposable thumbs). Add this number to the creature's total Hit Dice, including class levels, to get the creature's effective character level (ECL). A character's ECL affects the experience the character earns, the amount of experience the character must have before gaining a new level, and the character's starting equipment. See pages 172, 199, and 209 of the *Dungeon Master's Guide* for more information.

DESCRIPTIVE TEXT

The body of each entry opens with a sentence or two that describes what the player characters might see on first encountering a monster, followed by a short description of the creature: what it does, what it looks like, and what is most noteworthy about it. Special sections describe how the creature fights and give details on special attacks, special qualities, skills, and feats.

CHAPTER 1:
MONSTERS A TO Z

This book contains hundreds of creatures for use in any DUNGEONS & DRAGONS game. Refer to the Glossary, starting on page 305, for definitions of common features and abilities of individual monsters. In most cases, a monster entry describes a typical individual of the kind in question, which is the most common version encountered by characters on adventures. The DM can modify these entries, create advanced or weaker versions, or alter any statistics to play a monster against type and surprise the player characters.

And now, let's meet the monsters. . . .

ABOLETH

The cool, refreshing water suddenly erupts in a storm of reaching, grasping tentacles. The tentacles connect to a primeval fish, 20 feet in length from its bulbous head to its crescent-shaped tail. Three slit-shaped eyes, protected by bony ridges, are set one atop the other in the front of its head, which remains just beneath the surface as it attacks.

The aboleth is a revolting fishlike amphibian found primarily in subterranean lakes and rivers. It despises all nonaquatic creatures and attempts to destroy them on sight.

An aboleth has a pink belly. Four pulsating blue-black orifices line the bottom of its body and secrete gray slime that smells like rancid grease. It uses its tail for propulsion in the water and drags itself along with its tentacles on land. An aboleth weighs about 6,500 pounds.

Aboleths are cruel and highly intelligent, making them dangerous predators. They know many ancient and terrible secrets, for they inherit their parents' knowledge at birth and assimilate the memories of all they consume.

Aboleths are smart enough to refrain from immediately attacking land dwellers who draw near. Instead they hang back, hoping their prey will enter the water, which they often make appear cool, clear, and refreshing with their powers of illusion. Aboleths also use their psionic abilities to enslave individuals for use against their own companions.

Aboleths have both male and female reproductive organs. They breed in solitude, laying 1d3 eggs every five years. These eggs grow for another five years before hatching into full-grown aboleths. Although the young are physically mature, they remain with their parent for some ten years, obeying the older creature utterly.

Aboleths speak their own language, as well as Undercommon and Aquan.

COMBAT

An aboleth attacks by flailing with its long, slimy tentacles, though it prefers to fight from a distance using its illusion powers.

Enslave (Su): Three times per day, an aboleth can attempt to enslave any one living creature within 30 feet. The target must succeed on a DC 17 Will save or be affected as though by a *dominate person* spell (caster level 16th). An enslaved creature obeys the aboleth's telepathic commands until freed by *remove curse*, and can attempt a new Will save every 24 hours to break free. The control is also broken if the aboleth dies or travels more than 1 mile from its slave. The save DC is Charisma-based.

Psionics (Sp): At will—*hypnotic pattern* (DC 15), *illusory wall* (DC 17), *mirage arcana* (DC 18), *persistent image* (DC 18), *programmed*

image (DC 19), *project image* (DC 20), *veil* (DC 19). Effective caster level 16th. The save DCs are Charisma-based.

Slime (Ex): A blow from an aboleth's tentacle can cause a terrible affliction. A creature hit by a tentacle must succeed on a DC 19 Fortitude save or begin to transform over the next 1d4+1 minutes, the skin gradually becoming a clear, slimy membrane. An afflicted creature must remain moistened with cool, fresh water or take 1d12 points of damage every 10 minutes. The slime reduces the creature's natural armor bonus by 1 (but never to less than 0). The save DC is Constitution-based.

A *remove disease* spell cast before the transformation is complete will restore an afflicted creature to normal. Afterward, however, only a *heal* or *mass heal* spell can reverse the affliction.

Mucus Cloud (Ex): An aboleth underwater surrounds itself with a viscous cloud of mucus roughly 1 foot thick. Any creature coming into contact with and inhaling this substance must succeed on a DC 19 Fortitude save or lose the ability to breathe air for the next 3 hours. An affected creature suffocates in 2d6 minutes if removed from the water. Renewed contact with the mucus cloud and failing another Fortitude save continues the effect for another 3 hours. The save DC is Constitution-based.

Skills: An aboleth has a +8 racial bonus on any Swim check to perform some special action or avoid a hazard. It can always choose to take 10 on a Swim check, even if distracted or endangered. It can use the run action while swimming, provided it swims in a straight line.

Aboleth

ABOLETH MAGE

Among the watery tombs and dungeons they inhabit, the lords of the aboleths focus their efforts to achieve dominion through their study of wizardry. Their great power marks them as among the lords of all subterranean creatures. Still, these creatures, devoted to their arcane scholarship, spend most of their long lives alone.

Combat

The save DC for the aboleth mage's transformation tentacle attack (DC 21) and its mucus cloud (DC 21) are adjusted for its higher Constitution score. The save DC for its enslave ability (DC 16) is adjusted for its lower Charisma score, as are the save DCs for its psionic abilities: *Hypnotic pattern* (DC 14), *illusory wall* (DC 16), *mirage arcana* (DC 17), *persistent image* (DC 17), *programmed image* (DC 18), *project image* (DC 19), *veil* (DC 18). Effective caster level 16th.

The aboleth mage uses a number of spells, such as *displacement*, *greater invisibility*, and *wall of force*, to protect itself while seizing control of its foes with spells and innate abilities.

Typical Wizard Spells Prepared (4/6/5/4/4/3; save DC 15 + spell level): 0—*daze, detect magic* (2), *resistance*; 1st—*alarm, charm person, color spray, mage armor, magic missile* (2); 2nd—*blur, bull's strength, darkness, fox's cunning, see invisibilty*; 3rd—*dispel magic, displacement,*

	Aboleth Huge Aberration (Aquatic)	Aboleth Mage, 10th-Level Wizard Huge Aberration (Aquatic)
Hit Dice:	8d8+40 (76 hp)	8d8+56 plus 10d4+70 (177 hp)
Initiative:	+1	+7
Speed:	10 ft. (2 squares), swim 60 ft.	10 ft. (2 squares), swim 60 ft.
Armor Class:	16 (−2 size, +1 Dex, +7 natural), touch 9, flat-footed 15	18 (−2 size, +3 Dex, +7 natural), touch 11, flat-footed 15
Base Attack/Grapple:	+6/+22	+11/+28
Attack:	Tentacle +12 melee (1d6+8 plus slime)	Tentacle +18 melee (1d6+9 plus slime)
Full Attack:	4 tentacles +12 melee (1d6+8 plus slime)	4 tentacles +18 melee (1d6+9 plus slime)
Space/Reach:	15 ft./10 ft.	15 ft./10 ft.
Special Attacks:	Enslave, psionics, slime	Enslave, psionics, slime, spells
Special Qualities:	Aquatic subtype, darkvision 60 ft., mucus cloud	Aquatic subtype, darkvision 60 ft., mucus cloud, summon familiar
Saves:	Fort +7, Ref +3, Will +11	Fort +15, Ref +10, Will +15
Abilities:	Str 26, Dex 12, Con 20, Int 15, Wis 17, Cha 17	Str 28, Dex 16, Con 24, Int 20, Wis 16, Cha 14
Skills:	Concentration +16, Knowledge (any one) +13, Listen +16, Spot +16, Swim +8	Bluff +13, Concentration +25, Decipher Script +15, Diplomacy +6, Disguise +2 (+4 acting), Intimidate +4, Knowledge (arcana) +15, Knowledge (dungeoneering) +25, Knowledge (history) +15, Knowledge (the planes) +15, Listen +15, Search +10, Sense Motive +15, Spellcraft +20, Spot +17, Survival +3 (+5 following tracks, on other planes, and underground), Swim +8
Feats:	Alertness, Combat Casting, Iron Will	Combat Casting, Empower Spell, Eschew Materials, Great Fortitude, Improved Initiative, Lightning Reflexes, Scribe Scroll, Spell Focus (illusion), Spell Focus (enchantment), Spell Penetration
Environment	Underground	Underground
Organization:	Solitary, brood (2–4), or slaver brood (1d3+1 plus 7–12 skum)	Solitary
Challenge Rating:	7	17
Treasure:	Double standard	Double standard
Alignment:	Usually lawful evil	Usually lawful evil
Advancement:	9–16 HD (Huge); 17–24 HD (Gargantuan)	By character class
Level Adjustment:	—	

fly, lightning bolt; 4th—*greater invisibility, phantasmal killer, scrying, stoneskin*; 5th—*hold monster,* empowered *lightning bolt, wall of force.*

ACHAIERAI

Large Outsider (Evil, Extraplanar, Lawful)
Hit Dice: 6d8+12 (39 hp)
Initiative: +1
Speed: 50 ft. (10 squares)
Armor Class: 20 (−1 size, +1 Dex, +10 natural), touch 10,
   flat-footed 19
Base Attack/Grapple: +6/+14
Attack: Claw +9 melee (2d6+4)
Full Attack: 2 claws +9 melee (2d6+4) and bite +4 melee (4d6+2)
Space/Reach: 10 ft./10 ft.
Special Attacks: Black cloud
Special Qualities: Darkvision 60 ft., spell resistance 19
Saves: Fort +7, Ref +6, Will +7
Abilities: Str 19, Dex 13, Con 14, Int 11, Wis 14, Cha 16
Skills: Balance +10, Climb +13, Diplomacy +5, Hide +6,
   Jump +21, Listen +11, Move Silently +10, Sense Motive +11,
   Spot +11
Feats: Dodge, Mobility, Spring Attack
Environment: Infernal Battlefield of Acheron
Organization: Solitary or flock (5–8)
Challenge Rating: 5
Treasure: Double standard
Alignment: Always lawful evil
Advancement: 7–12 HD (Large); 13–18 HD (Huge)
Level Adjustment: —

Achaierai

A large creature stands on four stiltlike legs. It has a birdlike body, round and plump, about the size of a small pony, balanced atop its legs. Feathers that range in color from brown to red cover its body, and its terrible claws and beak glint like burnished metal.

Achaierais are massive, 15-foot-tall flightless birds that inhabit the plane of Acheron and are only occasionally encountered elsewhere. They are evil, clever, and predatory, with a distinct taste for torture.

Achaierais speak Infernal. They weigh about 750 pounds.

COMBAT

In close combat, an achaierai lashes out with two of its four legs and snaps with its powerful beak. It makes frequent use of its Spring Attack feat to strike quickly and then retreat out of range before an enemy can counterattack.

An achaierai's natural weapons, as well as any weapons it wields, are treated as evil-aligned and lawful-aligned for the purpose of overcoming damage reduction.

Black Cloud (Ex): Up to three times per day an achaierai can release a choking, toxic black cloud. Those other than achaierai within 10 feet instantly take 2d6 points of damage. They must also succeed on a DC 15 Fortitude save or be affected for 3 hours as though by an *insanity* spell (caster level 16th). The save DC is Constitution-based.

An allip is the spectral remains of someone driven to suicide by a madness that afflicted it in life. It craves only revenge and unrelentingly pursues those who tormented it in life and pushed it over the brink. An allip cannot speak intelligibly.

COMBAT

An allip is unable to cause physical harm, although it doesn't appear to know that. It keeps flailing away at enemies, yet it inflicts no wounds.

Babble (Su): An allip constantly mutters and whines to itself, creating a hypnotic effect. All sane creatures within 60 feet of the allip must succeed on a DC 16 Will save or be affected as though by a *hypnotism* spell for 2d4 rounds. This is a sonic mind-affecting compulsion effect. Creatures that successfully save cannot be affected by the same allip's babble for 24 hours. The save DC is Charisma-based.

Madness (Su): Anyone targeting an allip with a thought detection, mind control, or telepathic ability makes direct contact with its tortured mind and takes 1d4 points of Wisdom damage.

Wisdom Drain (Su): An allip causes 1d4 points of Wisdom drain each time it hits with its incorporeal touch attack. On each such successful attack, it gains 5 temporary hit points.

ALLIP

Medium Undead (Incorporeal)

Hit Dice: 4d12 (26 hp)

Initiative: +5

Speed: Fly 30 ft. (perfect) (6 squares)

Armor Class: 15 (+1 Dex, +4 deflection), touch 15, flat-footed 14

Base Attack/Grapple: +2/—

Attack: Incorporeal touch +3 melee (1d4 Wisdom drain)

Full Attack: Incorporeal touch +3 melee (1d4 Wisdom drain)

Space/Reach: 5 ft./5 ft.

Special Attacks: Babble, madness, Wisdom drain

Special Qualities: Darkvision 60 ft., incorporeal traits, +2 turn resistance, undead traits

Saves: Fort +1, Ref +4, Will +4

Abilities: Str —, Dex 12, Con —, Int 11, Wis 11, Cha 18

Skills: Hide +8, Intimidate +7, Listen +7, Search +4, Spot +7, Survival +0 (+2 following tracks)

Feats: Improved Initiative, Lightning Reflexes

Environment: Any

Organization: Solitary

Challenge Rating: 3

Treasure: None

Alignment: Always neutral evil

Advancement: 5–12 HD (Medium)

Level Adjustment: —

The creature that floats before you is like a thing out of nightmare. It has a vaguely humanoid shape, but it's a shape without features that has been distorted and bristles with madness. From the waist down, it trails away into vaporous nothingness, leaving a faint trace of fog behind it as it moves.

Allip

ANGEL

Angels are a race of celestials, beings who live on the good-aligned Outer Planes. Celestials positively drip with goodness—every fiber of their bodies and souls is suffused with it. They are the natural enemies of demons and devils (creatures of the infernal realms).

Angels can be of any good alignment. Lawful good angels hail from the plane of Celestia, neutral good angels from the plane of Elysium or the Beastlands, and chaotic good angels from plane of Arborea. Regardless of their alignment, angels never lie, cheat, or steal. They are impeccably honorable in all their dealings and often prove the most trustworthy and diplomatic of all the celestials.

All angels are blessed with comely looks, though their actual appearances vary widely.

Angels speak Celestial, Infernal, and Draconic, though they can speak with almost any creature because of their tongues ability.

COMBAT

Though they are honorable and good, angels don't hesitate to back up their arguments with their weapons and other powers when necessary. Though they do not relish combat, they do not hesitate to take the battle to the enemy. In combat, most angels make full use of their mobility and their ability to attack at a distance.

Angel Traits: An angel possesses the following traits (unless otherwise noted in a creature's entry).

—Darkvision out to 60 feet and low-light vision.

—Immunity to acid, cold, and petrification.

—Resistance to electricity 10 and fire 10.

—+4 racial bonus on saves against poison.

—*Protective Aura (Su):* Against attacks made or effects created by evil creatures, this ability provides a +4 deflection bonus to AC and a

+4 resistance bonus on saving throws to anyone within 20 feet of the angel. Otherwise, it functions as a *magic circle against evil* effect and a *lesser globe of invulnerability*, both with a radius of 20 feet (caster level equals angel's HD). This aura can be dispelled, but the angel can create it again as a free action on its next turn. (The defensive benefits from the circle are not included in an angel's statistics block.)

—*Tongues* (Su): All angels can speak with any creature that has a language, as though using a *tongues* spell (caster level equal to angel's Hit Dice). This ability is always active.

ANGEL, ASTRAL DEVA

Medium Outsider (Angel, Extraplanar, Good)
Hit Dice: 12d8+48 (102 hp)
Initiative: +8
Speed: 50 ft. (10 squares), fly 100 ft. (good)
Armor Class: 29 (+4 Dex, +15 natural), touch 14, flat-footed 25
Base Attack/Grapple: +12/+18
Attack: +3 *heavy mace of disruption* +21 melee (1d8+12 plus stun) or slam +18 melee (1d8+9)
Full Attack: +3 *heavy mace of disruption* +21/+16/+11 melee (1d8+12 plus stun) or slam +18 melee (1d8+9)
Space/Reach: 5 ft./5 ft.
Special Attacks: Spell-like abilities, stun
Special Qualities: Damage reduction 10/evil, darkvision 60 ft., low-light vision, immunity to acid, cold, and petrification, protective aura, resistance to electricity 10 and fire 10, spell resistance 30, tongues, uncanny dodge
Saves: Fort +14 (+18 against poison), Ref +12, Will +12
Abilities: Str 22, Dex 18, Con 18, Int 18, Wis 18, Cha 20
Skills: Concentration +19, Craft or Knowledge (any three) +19, Diplomacy +22, Escape Artist +19, Hide +19, Intimidate +20, Listen +23, Move Silently +19, Sense Motive +19, Spot +23, Use Rope +4 (+6 with bindings)
Feats: Alertness, Cleave, Great Fortitude, Improved Initiative, Power Attack
Environment: Any good-aligned plane
Organization: Solitary, pair, or squad (3–5)
Challenge Rating: 14
Treasure: No coins; double goods; standard items
Alignment: Always good (any)
Advancement: 13–18 HD (Medium); 19–36 HD (Large)
Level Adjustment: +8

A beautiful, extremely tall, humanlike creature with long, feathery wings and a very supple and lithe body glows with an inner power that makes it hard to look directly at the creature.

Astral devas watch over lesser beings of good alignment and help when they can. In particular, they are patrons of planar travelers and powerful creatures undertaking good causes.

An astral deva is about 7-1/2 feet tall and weighs about 250 pounds.

Combat

An astral deva is not afraid to enter melee combat. It takes a fierce joy in bashing evil foes with its powerful +3 *heavy mace of disruption*.

An astral deva's natural weapons, as well as any weapons it wields, are treated as good-aligned for the purpose of overcoming damage reduction.

Spell-Like Abilities: At will—*aid, continual flame, detect evil, discern lies* (DC 19), *dispel evil* (DC 20), *dispel magic, holy aura* (DC 23), *holy smite* (DC 19), *holy word* (DC 22), *invisibility* (self only), *plane shift* (DC 22), *polymorph* (self only), *remove curse* (DC 18), *remove disease* (DC 18), *remove fear* (DC 16); 7/day—*cure light wounds* (DC 16), *see invisibility*; 1/day—*blade barrier* (DC 21), *heal* (DC 21). Caster level 12th. The save DCs are Charisma-based.

Stun (Su): If an astral deva strikes an opponent twice in one round with its mace, that creature must succeed on a DC 22 Fortitude save or be stunned for 1d6 rounds. The save DC is Strength-based.

Uncanny Dodge (Ex): An astral deva retains its Dexterity bonus to AC when flat-footed, and it cannot be flanked except by a rogue of at least 16th level. It can flank characters with the uncanny dodge ability as if it were a 12th-level rogue.

ANGEL, PLANETAR

Large Outsider (Angel, Extraplanar, Good)
Hit Dice: 14d8+70 (133 hp)
Initiative: +8
Speed: 30 ft. (6 squares), fly 90 ft. (good)
Armor Class: 32 (–1 size, +4 Dex, +19 natural), touch 13, flat-footed 28
Base Attack/Grapple: +14/+25
Attack: +3 *greatsword* +23 melee (3d6+13/19–20) or slam +20 melee (2d8+10)
Full Attack: +3 *greatsword* +23/+18/+13 melee (3d6+13/19–20) or slam +20 melee (2d8+10)
Space/Reach: 10 ft./10 ft.
Special Attacks: Spell-like abilities, spells
Special Qualities: Damage reduction 10/evil, darkvision 60 ft., low-light vision, immunity to acid, cold, and petrification, protective aura, regeneration 10, resistance to electricity 10 and fire 10, spell resistance 30, tongues
Saves: Fort +14 (+18 against poison), Ref +13, Will +15
Abilities: Str 25, Dex 19, Con 20, Int 22, Wis 23, Cha 22
Skills: Concentration +22, Craft or Knowledge (any four) +23, Diplomacy +25, Escape Artist +21, Hide +17, Intimidate +23, Listen +23, Move Silently +21, Sense Motive +23, Search +23, Spot +23, Use Rope +4 (+6 with bindings)
Feats: Blind-Fight, Cleave, Improved Initiative, Improved Sunder, Power Attack
Environment: Any good-aligned plane
Organization: Solitary or pair
Challenge Rating: 16
Treasure: No coins; double goods; standard items
Alignment: Always good (any)
Advancement: 15–21 HD (Large); 22–42 HD (Huge)
Level Adjustment: —

The creature resembles a massively muscular and tall human with smooth emerald skin, white-feathered wings, and a bald head.

Planetars serve as mighty generals of celestial armies. They also help powerful mortals on missions of good, particularly those that involve battles with fiends. A planetar is nearly 9 feet tall and weighs about 500 pounds.

Combat

Despite their vast array of magical powers, planetars are likely to wade into melee with their +3 *greatswords*. They particularly enjoy fighting fiends.

A planetar's natural weapons, as well as any weapons it wields, are treated as good-aligned for the purpose of overcoming damage reduction.

Regeneration: A planetar takes damage from evil-aligned weapons and from spells and effects with the evil descriptor.

Spell-Like Abilities: At will—*continual flame, dispel magic, holy smite* (DC 20), *invisibility* (self only), *lesser restoration* (DC 18), *remove curse* (DC 19), *remove disease* (DC 19), *remove fear* (DC 17), *speak with dead* (DC 19); 3/day—*blade barrier* (DC 22), *flame strike* (DC 21), *polymorph* (self only), *power word stun, raise dead, waves of fatigue*; 1/day—*earthquake* (DC 24), *greater restoration* (DC 23), *mass charm monster* (DC 24), *waves of exhaustion*. Caster level 17th. The save DCs are Charisma-based.

Illus. by J. Jarvis

The following abilities are always active on the planetar's person, as the spells (caster level 17th): *detect evil, detect snares and pits, discern lies* (DC 20), *see invisibility,* and *true seeing.* They can be dispelled, but the planetar can reactivate them as a free action.

Spells: Planetars can cast divine spells as 17th-level clerics. A planetar has access to two of the following domains: Air, Destruction, Good, Law, or War (plus any others from its deity). The save DCs are Wisdom-based.

Typical Cleric Spells Prepared (6/8/8/7/7/6/6/4/3/2; save DC 16 + spell level): 0—*create water, detect magic, guidance, resistance* (2), *virtue;* 1st—*bless* (2), *cause fear, divine favor* (2), *entropic shield, inflict light wounds*, shield of faith;* 2nd—*aid*, align weapon, bear's endurance, bull's strength* (2), *consecrate, eagle's splendor, hold person;* 3rd—*contagion*, daylight, invisibility purge, prayer* (2), *summon monster III, wind wall;* 4th—*death ward, dismissal, inflict critical wounds*, neutralize poison* (2), *summon monster IV;* 5th—*break enchantment, circle of doom*, dispel evil, mark of justice, plane shift, righteous might;* 6th—*banishment, greater dispel magic, harm*, heal, heroes' feast, mass cure moderate wounds;* 7th—*dictum, disintegrate*, holy word, regenerate;* 8th—*holy aura*, mass cure critical wounds, shield of law;* 9th—*implosion, summon monster IX (good)*.*

*Domain spell. Domains: Destruction and Good.

ANGEL, SOLAR

Large Outsider (Angel, Extraplanar, Good)
Hit Dice: 22d8+110 (209 hp)
Initiative: +9
Speed: 50 ft. (10 squares), fly 150 ft. (good)
Armor Class: 35 (–1 size, +5 Dex, +21 natural), touch 14, flat-footed 30
Base Attack/Grapple: +22/+35
Attack: +5 dancing greatsword +35 melee (3d6+18/19–20) or +2 composite longbow (+5 Str bonus) +28 ranged (2d6+7/×3 plus slaying) or slam +30 melee (2d8+13)
Full Attack: +5 dancing greatsword +35/+30/+25/+20 melee (3d6+18/19–20) or +2 composite longbow (+5 Str bonus) +28/+23/+18/+13 ranged (2d6+7/×3 plus slaying) or slam +30 melee (2d8+13)
Space/Reach: 10 ft./10 ft.
Special Attacks: Spell-like abilities, spells
Special Qualities: Damage reduction 15/epic and evil, darkvision 60 ft., low-light vision, immunity to acid, cold, and petrification, protective aura, regeneration 15, resistance to electricity 10 and fire 10, spell resistance 32, tongues
Saves: Fort +18 (+22 against poison), Ref +18, Will +20
Abilities: Str 28, Dex 20, Con 20, Int 23, Wis 25, Cha 25
Skills: Concentration +30, Craft or Knowledge (any five) +33, Diplomacy +34, Escape Artist +30, Hide +26, Listen +32, Move Silently +30, Search +31, Sense Motive +32, Spellcraft +31, Spot +32, Survival +7 (+9 following tracks), Use Rope +5 (+7 with bindings)

Feats: Cleave, Dodge, Great Cleave, Improved Initiative, Improved Sunder, Mobility, Power Attack, Track
Environment: Any good-aligned plane
Organization: Solitary or pair
Challenge Rating: 23
Treasure: No coins; double goods; standard items
Alignment: Always good (any)
Advancement: 23–33 HD (Large); 34–66 HD (Huge)
Level Adjustment: —

Solar

Planetar

Astral deva

The creature resembles a towering, powerfully built human with brilliant topaz eyes, silvery (or golden) skin, and gleaming white wings.

Solars are the greatest of the angels, usually close attendants to a deity or champions of some cosmically beneficent task (such as eliminating a particular type of wrongdoing).

A solar has a deep and commanding voice, and stands about 9 feet tall. It weighs about 500 pounds.

Combat

Solars are puissant champions of good. Only the most powerful fiends approach their power. Even more fearsome than their +5 dancing greatswords are their +2 composite longbows that create any sort of *slaying arrow* when drawn.

A solar's natural weapons, as well as any weapons it wields, are treated as good-aligned and epic for the purpose of overcoming damage reduction.

Regeneration (Ex): A solar takes normal damage from epic evil-aligned weapons, and from spells or effects with the evil descriptor.

Spell-Like Abilities: At will—*aid, animate objects, commune, continual flame, dimensional anchor, greater dispel magic, holy smite* (DC 21), *imprisonment* (DC 26), *invisibility* (self only), *lesser restoration* (DC 19), *polymorph* (self only) *power word stun, remove curse* (DC 20), *remove disease* (DC 20), *remove fear* (DC 18), *resist energy, summon monster VII, speak with dead* (DC 20), *waves of fatigue;* 3/day—*blade barrier* (DC 23), *earthquake* (DC 25), *heal* (DC 23), *mass charm monster* (DC 25), *permanency, resurrection, waves of exhaustion;* 1/day—*greater restoration* (DC 24), *power word blind, power word kill, power word stun, prismatic spray* (DC 24), *wish.* Caster level 20th. The save DCs are Charisma-based.

The following abilities are always active on a solar's person, as the spells (caster level 20th): *detect evil, detect snares and pits, discern lies* (DC 21), *see invisibility, true seeing.* They can be dispelled, but the solar can reactivate them as a free action.

Spells: Solars can cast divine spells as 20th-level clerics. A solar has access to two of the following domains: Air, Destruction, Good, Law, or War (plus any others from its deity). The save DCs are Wisdom-based.

Typical Cleric Spells Prepared (6/8/8/8/7/7/6/6/5/5; save DC 17 + spell level): 0—*create water, detect magic, guidance* (2), *resistance*

(2); 1st—*bless* (2), *cause fear*, *divine favor* (2), *entropic shield*, *obscuring mist**, *shield of faith*; 2nd—*align weapon*, *bear's endurance* (2), *bull's strength* (2), *consecrate*, *eagle's splendor*, *spiritual weapon**; 3rd—*daylight*, *invisibility purge*, *magic circle against evil*, *magic vestment**, *prayer* (2), *protection from energy*, *wind wall*; 4th—*death ward* (2), *dismissal* (2), *divine power**, *neutralize poison* (2); 5th—*break enchantment*, *control winds**, *dispel evil*, *plane shift*, *righteous might* (2), *symbol of pain*; 6th—*banishment*, *chain lightning**, *heroes' feast*, *mass cure moderate wounds*, *undeath to death*, *word of recall*; 7th—*control weather**, *destruction*, *dictum*, *ethereal jaunt*, *holy word*, *regenerate*; 8th—*fire storm*, *holy aura*, *mass cure critical wounds* (2), *whirlwind**; 9th—*etherealness*, *elemental swarm (air)**, *mass heal*, *miracle*, *storm of vengeance*.

*Domain spell. Domains: Air and War.

ANIMATED OBJECT

Animated objects come in all sizes, shapes, and colors. They owe their existence as creatures to spells such as *animate objects* or similar supernatural abilities.

COMBAT

Animated objects fight only as directed by the animator. They follow orders without question and to the best of their abilities. Since they do not need to breathe and never tire, they can be extremely capable minions.

An animated object can have one or more of the following special abilities, depending on its form.

Blind (Ex): A sheetlike animated object such as a carpet or tapestry can grapple an opponent up to three sizes larger than itself. The object makes a normal grapple check. If it wins, it wraps itself around the opponent's head, causing that creature to be blinded until removed.

Animated object

Constrict (Ex): A flexible animated object such as a rope, vine, or rug deals damage equal to its slam damage value plus 1-1/2 times its Strength bonus with a successful grapple check against a creature up to one size larger than itself.

An object of at least Large size can make constriction attacks against multiple creatures at once, if they all are at least two sizes smaller than the object and can fit under it.

Hardness (Ex): An animated object has the same hardness it had before it was animated (see Table 9–9 and Table 9–11, page 166 of the *Player's Handbook*, for the hardness of some common substances and objects).

Improved Speed (Ex): The base land speed given in the statistics block assume that an animated object lurches, rocks, or slithers along. Objects with two legs (statues, ladders) or a similar shape that allows faster movement have a +10 foot bonus to speed. Objects with multiple legs (tables, chairs) have a +20 foot bonus to speed. Wheeled objects have a +40 foot bonus to speed.

Objects might have additional modes of movement. A wooden object can float and has a swim speed equal to half its land speed. A rope or similar sinuous object has a climb speed equal to half its land speed. A sheetlike object can fly (clumsy maneuverability) at half its normal speed.

Trample (Ex): An animated object of at least Large size and with a hardness of at least 10 can trample creatures two or more sizes smaller than itself, dealing damage equal to the object's slam damage + 1-1/2 times its Strength bonus. Opponents who do not

	Animated Object, Tiny Tiny Construct	Animated Object, Small Small Construct	Animated Object, Medium Medium Construct
Hit Dice:	1/2 d10 (2 hp)	1d10+10 (15 hp)	2d10+20 (31 hp)
Initiative:	+2	+1	+0
Speed:	40 ft. (8 squares); 50 ft. legs, 60 ft. multiple legs; 80 ft. wheels	30 ft. (6 squares); 40 ft. legs, 50 ft. multiple legs; 70 ft. wheels	30 ft. (6 squares); 40 ft. legs, 50 ft. multiple legs; 70 ft. wheels
Armor Class:	14 (+2 size, +2 Dex), touch 14, flat-footed 12	14 (+1 size, +1 Dex, +2 natural), touch 12, flat-footed 13	14 (+4 natural), touch 10, flat-footed 14
Base Attack/Grapple:	+0/−9	+0/−4	+1/+2
Attack:	Slam +1 melee (1d3−1)	Slam +1 melee (1d4)	Slam +2 melee (1d6+1)
Full Attack:	Slam +1 melee (1d3−1)	Slam +1 melee (1d4)	Slam +2 melee (1d6+1)
Space/Reach:	2-1/2 ft./0 ft.	5 ft./5 ft.	5 ft./5 ft.
Special Attacks:	See text	See text	See text
Special Qualities:	Construct traits, darkvision 60 ft., low-light vision; also see text	Construct traits, darkvision 60 ft., low-light vision; also see text	Construct traits, darkvision 60 ft., low-light vision; also see text
Saves:	Fort +0, Ref +2, Will −5	Fort +0, Ref +1, Will −5	Fort +0, Ref +0, Will −5
Abilities:	Str 8, Dex 14, Con —, Int —, Wis 1, Cha 1	Str 10, Dex 12, Con —, Int —, Wis 1, Cha 1	Str 12, Dex 10, Con —, Int —, Wis 1, Cha 1
Skills:	—	—	—
Feats:	—	—	—
Environment:	Any	Any	Any
Organization:	Group (4)	Pair	Solitary
Challenge Rating:	1/2	1	2
Treasure:	None	None	None
Alignment:	Always neutral	Always neutral	Always neutral
Advancement:	—	—	—
Level Adjustment:	—	—	—

	Animated Object, Large Large Construct	Animated Object, Huge Huge Construct	Animated Object, Gargantuan Gargantuan Construct
Hit Dice:	4d10+30 (52 hp)	8d10+40 (84 hp)	16d10+60 (148 hp)
Initiative:	+0	−1	−2
Speed:	20 ft. (4 squares); 30 ft. legs, 40 ft. multiple legs, 60 ft. wheels	20 ft. (4 squares); 30 ft. legs, 40 ft. multiple legs, 60 ft. wheels	10 ft. (2 squares); 20 ft. legs, 30 ft. multiple legs, 50 ft. wheels
Armor Class:	14 (−1 size, +5 natural), touch 9, flat-footed 14	13 (−2 size, −1 Dex, +6 natural), touch 7, flat-footed 13	12 (−4 size, −2 Dex, +8 natural), touch 4, flat-footed 12
Base Attack/Grapple:	+3/+10	+6/+19	+12/+31
Attack:	Slam +5 melee (1d8+4)	Slam +9 melee (2d6+7)	Slam +15 melee (2d8+10)
Full Attack:	Slam +5 melee (1d8+4)	Slam +9 melee (2d6+7)	Slam +15 melee (2d8+10)
Space/Reach:	10 ft./5 ft. (long) 10 ft./10 ft. (tall)	15 ft./10 ft. (long) 15 ft./15 ft. (tall)	20 ft./15 ft. (long) 20 ft./20 ft. (tall)
Special Attacks:	See text	See text	See text
Special Qualities:	Construct traits, darkvision 60 ft., low-light vision; also see text	Construct traits, darkvision 60 ft., low-light vision; also see text	Construct traits, darkvision 60 ft., low-light vision; also see text
Saves:	Fort +1, Ref +1, Will −4	Fort +2, Ref +1, Will −3	Fort +5, Ref +3, Will +0
Abilities:	Str 16, Dex 10, Con —, Int —, Wis 1, Cha 1	Str 20, Dex 8, Con —, Int —, Wis 1, Cha 1	Str 24, Dex 6, Con —, Int —, Wis 1, Cha 1
Skills:	—	—	—
Feats:	—	—	—
Environment:	Any	Any	Any
Organization:	Solitary	Solitary	Solitary
Challenge Rating:	3	5	7
Treasure:	None	None	None
Alignment:	Always neutral	Always neutral	Always neutral
Advancement:	—	—	—
Level Adjustment:	—	—	—

	Animated Object, Colossal Colossal Construct
Hit Dice:	32d10+80 (256 hp)
Initiative:	−3
Speed:	10 ft. (2 squares); 20 ft. legs, 30 ft. multiple legs, 50 ft. wheels
Armor Class:	11 (−8 size, −3 Dex, +12 natural), touch −1, flat-footed 11
Base Attack/Grapple:	+24/+49
Attack:	Slam +25 melee (4d6+13)
Full Attack:	Slam +25 melee (4d6+13)
Space/Reach:	30 ft./20 ft. (long) 30 ft./30 ft. (tall)
Special Attacks:	See text
Special Qualities:	Construct traits, darkvision 60 ft., low-light vision; also see text
Saves:	Fort +10, Ref +7, Will +5
Abilities:	Str 28, Dex 4, Con —, Int —, Wis 1, Cha 1
Skills:	—
Feats:	—
Environment:	Any
Organization:	Solitary
Challenge Rating:	10
Treasure:	None
Alignment:	Always neutral
Advancement:	—
Level Adjustment:	—

ANKHEG

Large Magical Beast
Hit Dice: 3d10+12 (28 hp)
Initiative: +0
Speed: 30 ft. (6 squares), burrow 20 ft.
Armor Class: 18 (−1 size, +9 natural), touch 9, flat-footed 18
Base Attack/Grapple: +3/+12
Attack: Bite +7 melee (2d6+7 plus 1d4 acid)
Full Attack: Bite +7 melee (2d6+7 plus 1d4 acid)
Space/Reach: 10 ft./5 ft.
Special Attacks: Improved grab, spit acid
Special Qualities: Darkvision 60 ft., low-light vision, tremorsense 60 ft.
Saves: Fort +6, Ref +3, Will +2
Abilities: Str 21, Dex 10, Con 17, Int 1, Wis 13, Cha 6
Skills: Climb +8, Listen +6, Spot +3
Feats: Alertness, Toughness
Environment: Warm plains
Organization: Solitary or cluster (2–4)
Challenge Rating: 3
Treasure: None
Alignment: Always neutral
Advancement: 4 HD (Large); 5–9 HD (Huge)
Level Adjustment: —

A huge segmented insect with slender legs, each ending in a sharp claw, emerges from the ground in a burst of rock and dirt. A tough chitinous brown shell covers its entire body, and glistening black eyes stare out from above powerful mandibles.

make attacks of opportunity against the object can attempt Reflex saves (DC 10 + 1/2 object's HD + object's Str modifier) to halve the damage.

The ankheg is a burrowing monster with a taste for fresh meat.

An ankheg has six legs, and some specimens are yellow rather than brown. It is about 10 feet long and weighs about 800 pounds.

An ankheg burrows with legs and mandibles. A burrowing ankheg usually does not make a usable tunnel, but can construct a tunnel; it burrows at half speed when it does so. It often digs a winding tunnel up to 40 feet below the surface in the rich soil of forests or farmlands. The tunnel is 5 feet tall and wide, and from 60 to 150 feet long ([1d10 + 5] × 10). The hollowed ends of the tunnel serve as temporary lairs for sleeping, eating, or hibernating.

An ankheg can eat decayed organic matter but prefers fresh meat. Though a hungry ankheg might kill a farmer, the creature is quite beneficial to farmland. Its tunnel system laces the soil with passages for air and water, while its wastes add rich nutrients.

COMBAT

An ankheg usually lies 5 to 10 feet below the surface until its antennae detect the approach of prey. It then burrows up to attack. (Treat this as a charge, even though the ankheg does not need to move 10 feet before attacking.)

Clusters of ankhegs share the same territory but do not cooperate. If several attack, each tries to grab a different foe. If there aren't enough targets, two might grab the same creature in a tug-of-war.

Improved Grab (Ex): To use this ability, an ankheg must hit with its bite attack. It can then attempt to start a grapple as a free action without provoking an attack of opportunity. If the ankheg is damaged after grabbing its prey, it retreats backward down its tunnel at its land speed (not its burrow speed), dragging the victim with it.

Spit Acid (Ex): 30-ft. line, once every 6 hours; damage 4d4 acid, Reflex DC 14 half. One such attack depletes the ankheg's acid supply for 6 hours. It cannot spit acid or deal acid damage during this time. The save DC is Constitution-based.

An ankheg does not use this ability unless it is desperate or frustrated. It most often spits acid when reduced to fewer than half its full normal hit points or when it has not successfully grabbed an opponent.

Ankheg

ARANEA

Medium Magical Beast (Shapechanger)
Hit Dice: 3d10+6 (22 hp)
Initiative: +6
Speed: 50 ft. (10 squares), climb 25 ft.
Armor Class: 13 (+2 Dex, +1 natural), touch 12, flat-footed 11
Base Attack/Grapple: +3/+3
Attack: Bite +5 melee (1d6 plus poison) or web +5 ranged
Full Attack: Bite +5 melee (1d6 plus poison) or web +5 ranged
Space/Reach: 5 ft./5 ft.
Special Attacks: Poison, spells, web
Special Qualities: Change shape, darkvision 60 ft., low-light vision
Saves: Fort +5, Ref +5, Will +4
Abilities: Str 11, Dex 15, Con 14, Int 14, Wis 13, Cha 14
Skills: Climb +14, Concentration +8, Escape Artist +5, Jump +13, Listen +6, Spot +6

Feats: Improved Initiative, Iron Will[B], Weapon Finesse
Environment: Temperate forests
Organization: Solitary or colony (3–6)
Challenge Rating: 4
Treasure: Standard coins; double goods; standard items
Alignment: Usually neutral
Advancement: By character class
Level Adjustment: +4

The creature appears to be a monstrous spider, but it has two small humanlike arms below its mandibles.

An aranea is an intelligent, shapechanging spider with sorcerous powers. In its natural form, an aranea resembles a big spider, with a humpbacked body a little bigger than a human torso. It has fanged mandibles like a normal spider. Two small arms, each about 2 feet long, lie below the mandibles. Each arm has a hand with four many-jointed fingers and a double-jointed thumb.

An aranea weighs about 150 pounds. The hump on its back houses its brain.

Araneas speak Common and Sylvan.

COMBAT

An aranea avoids physical combat and uses its webs and spells when it can. In a battle, it tries to immobilize or distract the most aggressive opponents first. Araneas often subdue opponents for ransom.

Poison (Ex): Injury, Fortitude DC 13, initial damage 1d6 Str, secondary damage 2d6 Str. The save DC is Constitution-based.

Spells: An aranea casts spells as a 3rd-level sorcerer. It prefers illusions and enchantments and avoids fire spells.

Typical Sorcerer Spells Known (6/6; save DC 12 + spell level): 0—*daze, detect magic, ghost sound, light, resistance;* 1st—*mage armor, silent image, sleep.*

Web (Ex): In spider or hybrid form (see below), an aranea can throw a web up to six times per day. This is similar to an attack with a net but has a maximum range of 50 feet, with a range increment of 10 feet, and is effective against targets of up to Large size. The web anchors the target in place, allowing no movement.

An entangled creature can escape with a DC 13 Escape Artist check or burst the web with a DC 17 Strength check. The check DCs are Constitution-based, and the Strength check DC includes a +4 racial bonus. The web has 6 hit points, hardness 0, and takes double damage from fire.

Change Shape (Su): An aranea's natural form is that of a Medium monstrous spider. It can assume two other forms. The first is a unique Small or Medium humanoid; an aranea in its humanoid form always assumes the same appearance and traits, much as a lycanthrope would. In humanoid form, an aranea cannot use its bite attack, webs, or poison.

The second form is a Medium spider–humanoid hybrid. In hybrid form, an aranea looks like a Medium humanoid at first glance, but a DC 18 Spot check reveals the creature's fangs and spinnerets. The aranea retains its bite attack, webs, and poison in this form, and can also wield weapons or wear armor. When in hybrid form, an aranea's speed is 30 feet (6 squares).

Aranea

An aranea remains in one form until it chooses to assume a new one. A change in form cannot be dispelled, nor does an aranea revert to its natural form when killed. A *true seeing* spell, however, reveals its natural form if it is in humanoid or hybrid form.

Skills: Araneas have a +2 racial bonus on Jump, Listen, and Spot checks. They have a +8 racial bonus on Climb checks and can always choose to take 10 on Climb checks even if rushed or threatened.

ARCHON

Archons are celestials from the plane of Celestia. They have charged themselves with the protection of the plane, and also consider themselves guardians of all who are innocent or free of evil. They are the natural enemies of fiends (creatures of the lower planes), particularly demons.

Archons speak Celestial, Infernal, and Draconic, but can speak with almost any creature because of their tongues ability.

COMBAT

Archons never attack without provocation (though their overwhelming lawful goodness often makes them easily provoked). They avoid harming other good creatures if they can, using nondamaging spells or weapon attacks that deal nonlethal damage if possible. An angry archon can be vengeance itself, however, no matter what the foe's alignment is.

Archons generally prefer to meet a foe head-on if it is prudent to do so, but if outmatched, they do what they can to even the odds (usually by employing hit-and run tactics or standing off and engaging a foe with magic before moving into melee).

Archon Traits: An archon possesses the following traits (unless otherwise noted in a creature's entry).

—Darkvision out to 60 feet and low-light vision.

—*Aura of Menace (Su):* A righteous aura surrounds archons that fight or get angry. Any hostile creature within a 20-foot radius of an archon must succeed on a Will save to resist its effects. The save DC varies with the type of archon, is Charisma-based, and includes a +2 racial bonus. Those who fail take a –2 penalty on attacks, AC, and saves for 24 hours or until they successfully hit the archon that generated the aura. A creature that has resisted or broken the effect cannot be affected again by the same archon's aura for 24 hours.

—Immunity to electricity and petrification.

—+4 racial bonus on saves against poison.

—*Magic Circle against Evil (Su):* A magic circle against evil effect always surrounds an archon (caster level equals the archon's Hit Dice). (The defensive benefits from the circle are not included in an archon's statistics block.)

—*Teleport (Su):* Archons can use greater teleport at will, as the spell (caster level 14th), except that the creature can transport only itself and up to 50 pounds of objects.

—*Tongues (Su):* All archons can speak with any creature that has a language, as though using a *tongues* spell (caster level 14th). This ability is always active.

LANTERN ARCHON

Small Outsider (Archon, Extraplanar, Good, Lawful)
Hit Dice: 1d8 (4 hp)
Initiative: +4
Speed: Fly 60 ft. (perfect) (12 squares)
Armor Class: 15 (+1 size, +4 natural), touch 11, flat-footed 15
Base Attack/Grapple: +1/–8
Attack: Light ray +2 ranged touch (1d6)
Full Attack: 2 light rays +2 ranged touch (1d6)
Space/Reach: 5 ft./5 ft.
Special Attacks: Spell-like abilities
Special Qualities: Aura of menace, damage reduction 10/evil and magic, darkvision 60 ft., immunity to electricity and petrification, magic circle against evil, teleport, tongues
Saves: Fort +2 (+6 against poison), Ref +2, Will +2
Abilities: Str 1, Dex 11, Con 10, Int 6, Wis 11, Cha 10
Skills: Concentration +4, Diplomacy +4, Knowledge (the planes) +2, Listen +4, Sense Motive +4, Spot +4
Feats: Improved Initiative
Environment: Seven Mounting Heavens of Celestia
Organization: Solitary, pair, or squad (3–5)
Challenge Rating: 2
Treasure: None
Alignment: Always lawful good
Advancement: 2–4 HD (Small)
Level Adjustment: —

A ball of glowing light floats toward you.

Lantern archons appear as floating balls of light that glow about as brightly as a torch. Only their destruction can extinguish the glow, though they can try to hide it.

Lantern archons are very friendly and usually eager to give what assistance they can. However, their bodies are just gaseous globes, and they are much too weak to render any material aid. Lantern archons speak in soft, musical voices.

Combat

A lantern archon has little reason to get within melee range. It usually hovers just close enough to bring the enemy within its aura of menace, then blasts away with its light rays. Lantern archons prefer to concentrate on a single opponent, seeking to reduce enemy numbers quickly.

Aura of Menace (Su): Will DC 12 negates.

Light Ray (Ex): A lantern archon's light rays have a range of 30 feet. This attack overcomes damage reduction of any type.

Spell-Like Abilities: At will—*aid, detect evil, continual flame.* Caster level 3rd.

HOUND ARCHON

A powerfully built humanoid with the head of a dog appears both serene and ready for action, with a greatsword strapped across its broad back and an expression that indicates intelligence and protectiveness.

Hound archons look like well-muscled humans with canine heads. They seek to defend the innocent and the helpless against evil.

Their broad shoulders and meaty fists mark hound archons as able combatants. Likewise, their strong legs indicate that fleeing enemies won't get very far.

	Hound Archon Medium Outsider (Archon, Extraplanar, Good, Lawful)	Hound Archon Hero, 11th-Level Paladin Medium Outsider (Archon, Extraplanar, Good, Lawful)
Hit Dice:	6d8+6 (33 hp)	6d8+18 plus 11d10+33 (143 hp)
Initiative:	+4	+4
Speed:	40 ft. (8 squares)	30 ft. in full plate armor (6 squares); base speed 40 ft.
Armor Class:	19 (+9 natural), touch 10, flat-footed 19	30 (+9 natural, +11 +3 full plate armor), touch 10, flat-footed 30
Base Attack/Grapple:	+6/+8	+17/+22
Attack:	Bite +8 melee (1d8+2) or greatsword +8 melee (2d6+3/19–20)	+2 cold iron greatsword +25 melee (2d6+9/19–20) or bite +22 melee (1d8+5)
Full Attack:	Bite +8 melee (1d8+2) and slam +3 melee (1d4+1); or greatsword +8/+3 melee (2d6+3/19–20) and bite +3 melee (1d8+1)	+2 cold iron greatsword +25/+20/+15/+10 melee (2d6+9/19–20) and bite +17 melee (1d8+2); or bite +22 melee (1d8+5) and slam +17 melee (1d4+2)
Space/Reach:	5 ft./5 ft.	5 ft./5 ft.
Special Attacks:	Spell-like abilities	Smite evil, spells, spell-like abilities, turn undead 6/day
Special Qualities:	Aura of menace, change shape, damage reduction 10/evil, darkvision 60 ft., immunity to electricity and petrification, magic circle against evil, scent, spell resistance 16, teleport, tongues	Aura of menace, change shape, damage reduction 10/evil, darkvision 60 ft., immunity to electricity and petrification, magic circle against evil, paladin abilities, scent, spell resistance 27, teleport, tongues
Saves:	Fort +6 (+10 against poison), Ref +5, Will +6	Fort +18 (+22 against poison), Ref +11, Will +13
Abilities:	Str 15, Dex 10, Con 13, Int 10, Wis 13, Cha 12	Str 21, Dex 10, Con 16, Int 8, Wis 14, Cha 16
Skills:	Concentration +10, Diplomacy +3, Hide +9*, Jump +15, Listen +10, Move Silently +9, Sense Motive +10, Spot +10, Survival +10* (+12 following tracks)	Concentration +20, Diplomacy +19, Hide +2*, Jump +0, Listen +10, Ride +14, Sense Motive +19, Spot +10, Survival +2*
Feats:	Improved Initiative, Power Attack, Track	Improved Initiative, Leadership, Mounted Combat, Ride-By Attack, Track, Weapon Focus (greatsword)
Environment:	Seven Mounting Heavens of Celestia	Seven Mounting Heavens of Celestia
Organization:	Solitary, pair, or squad (3–5)	Solitary or with juvenile bronze dragon
Challenge Rating:	4	16
Treasure:	No coins; double goods; standard items	Standard
Alignment:	Always lawful good	Always lawful good
Advancement:	7–9 HD (Medium); 10–18 HD (Large)	By character class
Level Adjustment:	+5	+5

Combat

Hound archons always fight with a will. They prefer to attack with their natural weapons but occasionally use greatswords.

A hound archon's natural weapons, as well as any weapons it wields, are treated as good-aligned and lawful-aligned for the purpose of overcoming damage reduction.

Spell-Like Abilities: At will—aid, continual flame, detect evil, message. Caster level 6th.

Aura of Menace (Su): Will DC 16 negates.

Change Shape (Su): A hound archon can assume any canine form of Small to Large size. While in canine form, the hound archon loses its bite, slam, and greatsword attacks, but gains the bite attack of the form it chooses. For the purposes of this ability, canines include any doglike or wolflike animal of the animal type.

Skills: *While in canine form, a hound archon gains a +4 circumstance bonus on Hide and Survival checks.

HOUND ARCHON HERO

The hound archon hero is a mighty champion of justice, devoted to the pursuit and destruction of evil in all its forms.

Combat

Hound archon heroes have over time developed a love for their weapons. They prefer to use their holy greatswords over their bite and slam attacks.

Spell-Like Abilities: At will—aid, continual flame, detect evil, message. Caster level 6th.

Aura of Menace (Su): The save DC for the hound archon hero's aura of menace (DC 18) is adjusted for its higher Charisma score.

Smite Evil (Su): Three times per day a hound archon hero can make a normal melee attack with a +3 bonus that deals an extra 11 points of damage against an evil foe.

Change Shape (Su): A hound archon hero can assume any canine form of Small to Large size. While in canine form, the hound archon loses its bite, slam, and greatsword attacks, but gains the bite attack of the form it chooses. For the purposes of this ability, canines include any doglike or wolflike animal of the animal type.

Skills: *While in canine form, a hound archon hero gains a +4 circumstance bonus on Hide and Survival checks.

Paladin Abilities: Aura of courage, aura of good, detect evil, divine grace, divine health, lay on hands (33 points/day), remove disease 2/week, special mount (juvenile bronze dragon).

Typical Paladin Spells Prepared (2/2; save DC 12 + spell level): 1st—divine favor, protection from evil; 2nd—bull's strength, eagle's splendor.

Possessions: +3 full plate armor, +2 cold iron greatsword.

Hound Archon Hero Mounts

In the course of their adventures, many hound archon heroes befriend bronze dragons, which may come to serve as their mounts. The relationship between these mounts and their celestial riders goes beyond even the special bond between paladin and mount. The dragon and the archon are naturally allies and friends, as can be expected of two powerful servants of cosmic justice. The juvenile bronze dragon mount gains 2 additional HD, 4 points of Strength, an additional 4 points of natural armor, improved evasion, and +10 feet to speed in all its movement forms. The dragon cannot, however, command other creatures of its type as other kinds of paladin mounts can.

TRUMPET ARCHON
Medium Outsider (Archon, Extraplanar, Good, Lawful)
Hit Dice: 12d8+72 (126 hp)

Initiative: +7
Speed: 40 ft. (8 squares), fly 90 ft. (good)
Armor Class: 27 (+3 Dex, +14 natural), touch 13, flat-footed 24
Base Attack/Grapple: +12/+17
Attack: +4 greatsword +21 melee (2d6+11/19–20)
Full Attack: +4 greatsword +21/+16/+11 melee (2d6+11/19–20)
Space/Reach: 5 ft./5 ft.
Special Attacks: Spell-like abilities, spells, trumpet
Special Qualities: Aura of menace, damage reduction 10/evil, darkvision 60 ft., immunity to electricity and petrification, magic circle against evil, spell resistance 29, teleport, tongues
Saves: Fort +14 (+18 against poison), Ref +11, Will +11
Abilities: Str 20, Dex 17, Con 23, Int 16, Wis 16, Cha 16
Skills: Concentration +21, Diplomacy +20, Escape Artist +18, Handle Animal +18, Knowledge (any one) +18, Listen +18, Move Silently +18, Perform (wind instruments) +18, Ride +20, Sense Motive +18, Spot +18, Use Rope +3 (+5 with bindings)
Feats: Blind-Fight, Cleave, Combat Reflexes, Improved Initiative, Power Attack
Environment: Seven Mounting Heavens of Celestia
Organization: Solitary, pair, or squad (3–5)
Challenge Rating: 14
Treasure: No coins; double goods; standard items
Alignment: Always lawful good
Advancement: 13–18 HD (Medium); 19–36 HD (Large)
Level Adjustment: +8

Appearing as a green, winged elf of supernatural goodness and beauty, the creature raises a massive silver trumpet and sounds a blast of piercing, soul-wrenching music.

Trumpet archons serve as celestial messengers and heralds, though their martial skills are considerable. Each carries a gleaming silver trumpet about 6 feet long.

Combat

A trumpet archon usually disdains physical combat, preferring to obliterate foes with spells quickly and return to its duties. If forced into an extended battle, it sounds its trumpet and attacks with a vengeance.

A trumpet archon's natural weapons, as well as any weapons it wields, are treated as good-aligned and lawful-aligned for the purpose of overcoming damage reduction.

Spell-Like Abilities: At will—*detect evil, continual flame, message.* Caster level 12th.

Aura of Menace (Su): Will DC 21 negates.

Hound Archons as Characters

Hound archon characters possess the following racial traits.

— +4 Strength, +2 Constitution, +2 Wisdom, +2 Charisma.

—Medium size.

—A hound archon's base land speed is 40 feet.

—Racial Hit Dice: A hound archon begins with six levels of outsider, which provide 6d8 Hit Dice, a base attack bonus of +6, and base saving throw bonuses of Fort +5, Ref +5, and Will +5.

—Racial Skills: A hound archon's outsider levels give it skill points equal to 9 × (8 + Int modifier). Its class skills are Concentration, Hide, Jump, Listen, Move Silently, Sense Motive, Spot, and Survival.

—Racial Feats: A hound archon's outsider levels give it three feats.

— +9 natural armor bonus.

—Natural Weapons: Bite (1d8) and slam (1d4).

—Archon Traits (see page 16): Darkvision 60 ft., low-light vision, aura of menace (Will DC 15 + character's Cha modifier), immunity to electricity and petrification, +4 racial bonus on saves against poison, magic circle against evil, teleport, tongues.

—Special Attacks: Spell-like abilities.

—Special Qualities: Change shape, damage reduction 10/evil, scent, spell resistance equal to 16 + class levels.

—Automatic Languages: Celestial. Bonus Languages: Common, Draconic, Infernal.

—Favored class: Ranger.

—Level adjustment +5.

Lantern archon

Hound archon

Trumpet archon

W&N 03

Spells: Trumpet archons can cast divine spells as 14th-level clerics. A trumpet archon has access to two of the following domains: Air, Destruction, Good, Law, or War (plus any others from its deity). The save DCs are Wisdom-based.

Typical Cleric Spells Prepared (6/7/7/6/5/4/4/3; DC 13 + spell level): 0—*detect magic, light, purify food and drink, read magic, resistance* (2); 1st—*bless* (2), *divine favor* (2), *protection from chaos*, sanctuary, shield of faith*; 2nd—*aid*, bull's strength* (2), *consecrate, lesser restoration, owl's wisdom* (2); 3rd—*daylight, invisibility purge, magic circle against chaos*, magic vestment, protection from energy* (2); 4th—*dismissal, divine power, holy smite*, neutralize poison, spell immunity*; 5th—*dispel evil*, mass cure light wounds, plane shift, raise dead*; 6th—*blade barrier*, banishment, heal, undeath to death*; 7th—*dictum*, holy word, mass cure serious wounds.*

*Domain spell. Domains: Good and Law.

Trumpet (Su): An archon's trumpet produces music of utter clarity, piercing beauty, and, if the trumpet archon wills it, paralyzing awe. All creatures except archons within 100 feet of the blast must succeed on a DC 19 Fortitude save or be paralyzed for 1d4 rounds. The save DC is Charisma-based. The archon can also command its trumpet to become a +4 greatsword as a free action.

If a trumpet is ever stolen, it becomes a chunk of useless metal until the owner can recover it. Woe betide any thief caught with one.

The creature has a sinuous, snakelike body with a long neck and tail. Two pairs of feathered wings extend from the body, one on the top and another on the bottom. Most of the body is covered with iridescent blue scales, with tufts of yellow feathers at the base of the neck and the tail. The head has a black, toothed beak and four eyes, one pair above the beak and the other below.

An arrowhawk is a predator and scavenger from the Elemental Plane of Air. It is a consummate flier that spends its entire life on the wing.

An arrowhawk is always in motion while it lives. It can fly from the moment it hatches, and it eats, sleeps, and mates without ever touching ground. By twisting its body and varying the cadence of its wingbeats, an arrowhawk can fly at top speed in any direction.

Arrowhawk eggs have an innate levitation ability. Females lay clutches of 2d4 eggs in midair and leave them to float until they hatch. The female guards the eggs and collects them if the wind scatters them, but otherwise leaves them alone.

A juvenile arrowhawk (1 to 10 years old) is about 5 feet long from beak to tail, with the body accounting for about one-third of that length. Its wingspan is about 7 feet, and it weighs about 20 pounds.

An adult (11 to 40 years old) is about 10 feet long from beak to tail, with a wingspan of about 15 feet and a weight of about 100 pounds.

	Juvenile Arrowhawk Small Outsider (Air, Extraplanar)	**Adult Arrowhawk** Medium Outsider (Air, Extraplanar)	**Elder Arrowhawk** Large Outsider (Air, Extraplanar)
Hit Dice:	3d8+3 (16 hp)	7d8+7 (38 hp)	15d8+45 (112 hp)
Initiative:	+5	+5	+5
Speed:	Fly 60 ft. (perfect) (12 squares)	Fly 60 ft. (perfect) (12 squares)	Fly 60 ft. (perfect) (12 squares)
Armor Class:	20 (+1 size, +5 Dex, +4 natural), touch 16, flat-footed 15	21 (+5 Dex, +6 natural), touch 15, flat-footed 16	22 (−1 size, +5 Dex, +8 natural), touch 14, flat-footed 17
Base Attack/Grapple:	+3/+0	+7/+9	+15/+25
Attack:	Electricity ray +9 ranged touch (2d6) or bite +9 melee (1d6+1)	Electricity ray +12 ranged touch (2d8) or bite +12 melee (1d8+3)	Electricity ray +19 ranged touch (2d8) or bite +21 melee (2d6+9)
Full Attack:	Electricity ray +9 ranged touch (2d6) or bite +9 melee (1d6+1)	Electricity ray +12 ranged touch (2d8) or bite +12 melee (1d8+3)	Electricity ray +19 ranged touch (2d8) or bite +20 melee (2d6+9)
Space/Reach:	5 ft./5 ft.	5 ft./5 ft.	10 ft./5 ft.
Special Attacks:	Electricity ray	Electricity ray	Electricity ray
Special Qualities:	Darkvision 60 ft., immunity to acid, electricity, and poison, resistance to cold 10 and fire 10	Darkvision 60 ft., immunity to acid, electricity, and poison, resistance to cold 10 and fire 10	Darkvision 60 ft., immunity to acid, electricity, and poison, resistance to cold 10 and fire 10
Saves:	Fort +4, Ref +8, Will +4	Fort +6, Ref +10, Will +6	Fort +12, Ref +14, Will +10
Abilities:	Str 12, Dex 21, Con 12, Int 10, Wis 13, Cha 13	Str 14, Dex 21, Con 12, Int 10, Wis 13, Cha 13	Str 22, Dex 21, Con 16, Int 10, Wis 13, Cha 13
Skills:	Diplomacy +3, Escape Artist +11, Knowledge (the planes) +6, Listen +7, Move Silently +11, Search +6, Sense Motive +7, Spot +7, Survival +7 (+9 following tracks, +9 Plane of Air), Use Rope +5 (+7 with bindings)	Diplomacy +3, Escape Artist +15, Knowledge (the planes) +10, Listen +11, Move Silently +15, Search +10, Sense Motive +11, Spot +11, Survival +11 (+13 following tracks, +13 Plane of Air), Use Rope +5 (+7 with bindings)	Diplomacy +3, Escape Artist +23, Knowledge (the planes) +18, Listen +21, Move Silently +23, Search +18, Sense Motive +19, Spot +21, Survival +19 (+21 following tracks, +21 Plane of Air), Use Rope +5 (+7 involving bindings)
Feats:	Dodge, Weapon Finesse	Dodge, Flyby Attack, Weapon Finesse	Alertness, Blind-Fight, Combat Reflexes, Dodge, Flyby Attack, Weapon Finesse, Weapon Focus (bite)[B]
Environment:	Elemental Plane of Air	Elemental Plane of Air	Elemental Plane of Air
Organization:	Solitary or clutch (2–4)	Solitary or clutch (2–4)	Solitary or clutch (2–4)
Challenge Rating:	3	5	8
Treasure:	None	None	None
Alignment:	Always neutral	Always neutral	Always neutral
Advancement:	4–6 HD (Small)	8–14 HD (Medium)	16–24 HD (Large); 25–32 HD (Gargantuan)
Level Adjustment:	—	—	—

An elder arrowhawk (41 to 75 years old) is about 20 feet long with a wingspan of 30 feet and a weight of about 800 pounds.

Arrowhawks speak Auran, but they are not usually talkative creatures.

COMBAT

Arrowhawks are extremely territorial and always hungry. They attack almost any other creature they meet, seeking a meal or trying to drive away a rival. The primary mode of attack is an electricity ray, fired from the tail. The creature also bites, but it prefers to stay out of reach.

Electricity Ray (Su): An arrowhawk can fire this ray once per round, with a range of 50 feet.

Arrowhawk

A mature plant consists of a main vine, about 20 feet long. Smaller vines up to 5 feet long branch off from the main vine about every 6 inches. These small vines bear clusters of leaves, and in late summer they produce bunches of small fruits that resemble wild grapes. The fruit is tough and has a hearty but bitter flavor. Assassin vine berries make a heady wine.

An assassin vine can move about, albeit very slowly, but usually stays put unless it needs to seek prey in a new vicinity. A subterranean version of the assassin vine grows near hot springs, volcanic vents, and other sources of thermal energy. These plants have thin, wiry stems and gray leaves shot through with silver, brown, and white veins so that they resemble mineral deposits. An assassin vine growing underground usually generates enough offal to support a thriving colony of mushrooms and other fungi, which spring up around the plant and help conceal it.

ASSASSIN VINE

Large Plant
Hit Dice: 4d8+12 (30 hp)
Initiative: +0
Speed: 5 ft. (1 square)
Armor Class: 15 (–1 size, +6 natural), touch 9, flat-footed 15
Base Attack/Grapple: +3/+12
Attack: Slam +7 melee (1d6+7)
Full Attack: Slam +7 melee (1d6+7)
Space/Reach: 10 ft./10 ft. (20 ft. with vine)
Special Attacks: Constrict 1d6+7, entangle, improved grab
Special Qualities: Blindsight 30 ft., camouflage, immunity to electricity, low-light vision, plant traits, resistance to cold 10 and fire 10
Saves: Fort +7, Ref +1, Will +2
Abilities: Str 20, Dex 10, Con 16, Int —, Wis 13, Cha 9
Environment: Temperate forests
Organization: Solitary or patch (2–4)
Challenge Rating: 3
Treasure: 1/10th coins; 50% goods; 50% items
Alignment: Always neutral
Advancement: 5–16 HD (Huge); 17–32 HD (Gargantuan); 33+ HD (Colossal)
Level Adjustment: —

This vine has a fibrous stem covered with brown, stringy bark and as thick as a human's forearm. Its leaves are shaped like human hands.

The assassin vine is a semimobile plant that collects its own grisly fertilizer by grabbing and crushing animals and depositing the carcasses near its roots.

COMBAT

An assassin vine uses simple tactics: It lies still until prey comes within reach, then attacks. It uses its entangle ability both to catch prey and to deter counterattacks.

Constrict (Ex): An assassin vine deals 1d6+7 points of damage with a successful grapple check.

Entangle (Su): An assassin vine can animate plants within 30 feet of itself as a free action (Ref DC 13 partial). The effect lasts until the vine dies or decides to end it (also a free action). The save DC is Wisdom-based. The ability is otherwise similar to *entangle* (caster level 4th).

Improved Grab (Ex): To use this ability, an assassin vine must hit with its slam attack. It can then attempt to start a grapple as a free action without provoking an attack of opportunity. If it wins the grapple check, it establishes a hold and can constrict.

Blindsight (Ex): Assassin vines have no visual organs but can ascertain all foes within 30 feet using sound, scent, and vibration.

Camouflage (Ex): Since an assassin vine looks like a normal plant when at rest, it takes a DC 20 Spot check to notice it before it attacks. Anyone with ranks in Survival or Knowledge (nature) can use one of those skills instead of Spot to notice the plant. Dwarves can use stonecunning to notice the subterranean version.

Assassin vine

Arrowhawk illus. by T. Lockwood

ATHACH

Huge Aberration

Hit Dice: 14d8+70 (133 hp)

Initiative: +1

Speed: 35 ft. in hide armor (7 squares); base speed 50 ft.

Armor Class: 20 (–2 size, +1 Dex, +3 hide armor, +8 natural), touch 9, flat-footed 19

Base Attack/Grapple: +10/+26

Attack: Morningstar +16 melee (3d6+8) or rock +9 ranged (2d6+8)

Full Attack: Morningstar +12/+7 melee (3d6+8), and 2 morningstars +12 melee (3d6+4), and bite +12 melee (2d8+4 plus poison); or rock +5 ranged (2d6+8), and 2 rocks +5 ranged (2d6+4)

Space/Reach: 15 ft./15 ft.

Special Attacks: Poison

Special Qualities: Darkvision 60 ft.

Saves: Fort +9, Ref +5, Will +10

Abilities: Str 26, Dex 13, Con 21, Int 7, Wis 12, Cha 6

Skills: Climb +9, Jump +18, Listen +7, Spot +7

Feats: Alertness, Cleave, Multiweapon Fighting, Power Attack, Weapon Focus (bite)

Environment: Temperate hills

Organization: Solitary, gang (2–4), or tribe (7–12)

Challenge Rating: 8

Treasure: 1/2 coins; double goods; standard items

Alignment: Often chaotic evil

Advancement: 15–28 HD (Huge)

Level Adjustment: +5

The creature looks like a portly giant dressed in shabby rags and furs. It has a third arm growing from its chest. Its wide, slobbering mouth has curving tusks that jut from its lower jaw. It has tiny eyes, a small nose, and lopsided ears—one huge and one tiny.

The athach is a hulking, misshapen biped. Immensely strong, an athach can hammer most opponents to gory paste.

An athach rarely bathes, and smells particularly foul. An adult stands some 18 feet tall and weighs about 4,500 pounds.

Athachs are fond of gems and crystals of all types. They often jam bracelets on their chubby fingers, necklaces around their fat wrists, and wear other jewelry where they can. They have been known to sit for hours, polishing and admiring their jewels. The only other things athachs tend to be passionate about are food and violence. They despise hill giants and, unless outnumbered, attack them on sight. They fear other giants and most other Huge creatures.

Athachs speak a crude dialect of Giant.

COMBAT

Athachs charge into melee combat unless their opponents are out of reach, in which case they throw rocks. They sometimes try to overrun armored opponents to reach unarmored opponents in back ranks. With its first few melee attacks, an athach tends to flail about indiscriminately. After a few rounds, it concentrates on foes that have been hitting it most often and uses its bite on whoever has dealt it the most damage.

Poison (Ex): Injury, Fortitude DC 22, initial damage 1d6 Str, secondary damage 2d6 Str. The save DC is Constitution-based.

AZER

Medium Outsider (Extraplanar, Fire)

Hit Dice: 2d8+2 (11 hp)

Initiative: +1

Speed: 20 ft. in scale mail (4 squares); base speed 30 ft.

Armor Class: 23 (+1 Dex, +6 natural, +4 scale mail, +2 heavy shield), touch 11, flat-footed 22

Base Attack/Grapple: +2/+3

Attack: Warhammer +3 melee (1d8+1/×3 plus 1 fire) or shortspear +3 ranged (1d6+1 plus 1 fire)

Full Attack: Warhammer +3 melee (1d8+1/×3 plus 1 fire) or shortspear +3 ranged (1d6+1 plus 1 fire)

Space/Reach: 5 ft./5 ft.

Special Attacks: Heat

Special Qualities: Darkvision 60 ft., immunity to fire, spell resistance 13, vulnerability to cold

Saves: Fort +4, Ref +4, Will +4

Abilities: Str 13, Dex 13, Con 13, Int 12, Wis 12, Cha 9

Skills: Appraise +6, Climb +0, Craft (any two) +6, Hide +0, Jump –6, Listen +6, Search +6, Spot +6

Feats: Power Attack

Environment: Elemental Plane of Fire

Organization: Solitary, pair, team (3–4), squad (11–20 plus 2 3rd-level sergeants and 1 leader of 3rd–6th level), or clan (30–100 plus 50% noncombatants plus 1 3rd-level sergeant per 20 adults, 5 5th-level lieutenants, and 3 7th-level captains)

Challenge Rating: 2

Treasure: Standard coins; double goods (nonflammables only); standard items (nonflammables only)

Alignment: Always lawful neutral

Advancement: By character class

Level Adjustment: +4

The creature resembles a dwarf with hair of fire and a beard of flames. It has brass-colored skin and appears to have been forged from fire and metal.

Athach

Azers are dwarflike beings native to the Elemental Plane of Fire. They wear kilts of brass, bronze, or copper, and speak Ignan and Common.

COMBAT

Azers use broad-headed spears or well-crafted hammers in combat. When unarmed, they attempt to grapple foes.

Although unfriendly and taciturn, azers rarely provoke a fight except to relieve a foe of gems, which they love. If threatened, they fight to the death, but they see the value of taking prisoners themselves.

Heat (Ex): An azer's body is intensely hot, so its unarmed attacks deal extra fire damage. Its metallic weapons also conduct this heat.

AZER SOCIETY

Azers maintain a tightly regimented society in which every member has a specific place. The state always takes precedence over the individual. Azer nobles are prodigiously strong and wield absolute power. Azers dwell within bronze fortresses on their home plane, only rarely visiting other planes to gather gems. They hate efreet, with whom they wage an eternal war for territory and slaves.

AZERS AS CHARACTERS

Rare among their well-ordered kind, a few azers leave behind the absolute rule of their kin. These explorers tend to be fierce warriors, quick to take offense.

Azer characters possess the following racial traits.

— +2 Strength, +2 Dexterity, +2 Constitution, +2 Intelligence, +2 Wisdom, –2 Charisma.

—Medium size.

—An azer's base land speed is 30 feet.

—Darkvision: Azers can see in the dark up to 60 feet.

—Racial Hit Dice: An azer begins with two levels of outsider, which provide 2d8 Hit Dice, a base attack bonus of +2, and base saving throw bonuses of Fort +3, Ref +3, and Will +3.

—Racial Skills: An azer's outsider levels give it skill points equal to 5 × (8 + Int modifier). Its class skills are Appraise, Climb, Craft, Hide, Jump, Listen, Search, and Spot.

Azer

—Racial Feats: An azer's outsider levels give it one feat.

— +6 natural armor bonus.

—Special Attacks (see above): Heat.

—Special Qualities (see above): Immunity to fire, spell resistance equal to 13 + class levels, vulnerability to cold.

—Automatic Languages: Common, Ignan. Bonus Languages: Abyssal, Aquan, Auran, Celestial, Infernal, Terran.

—Favored Class: Fighter.

—Level adjustment +4.

Barghest illus. by S. Wood

BARGHEST

A horrifying wolflike monster with blue-tinged fur, long sharp claws, and a fiendish glint of intelligence in its hateful, glowing eyes darts out of the shadows.

A barghest is a lupine fiend that can take the shape of a wolf or a goblin. In its natural form, it resembles a goblin–wolf hybrid with terrible jaws and sharp claws. Barghests come into the world to feed on blood and souls and thus grow stronger.

As whelps, barghests are nearly indistinguishable from wolves, except for their size and claws. As they grow larger and stronger, their skin darkens to bluish-red and eventually becomes blue altogether. A full-grown barghest,

Barghest

such as the one described here, is about 6 feet long and weighs 180 pounds. A barghest's eyes glow orange when the creature becomes excited.

Barghests speak Goblin, Worg, and Infernal.

COMBAT

Barghests can claw and bite, no matter what their form, and usually disdain weapons. Though they love killing, they have little stomach for direct combat and attack from ambush whenever possible. Barghests start a combat by using *crushing despair* and *charm monster* to keep opponents off balance. They try to stay away from the enemy's main strength.

A barghest's natural weapons, as well as any weapons it wields, are treated as evil-aligned and lawful-aligned for the purpose of overcoming damage reduction. Its natural weapons are treated as magic weapons for the purpose of overcoming damage reduction.

Spell-Like Abilities: At will—*blink, levitate, misdirection* (DC 14), *rage* (DC 15); 1/day—*charm monster* (DC 16), *crushing despair* (DC 16), *dimension door*. Caster level equals the barghest's HD. The save DCs are Charisma-based.

Feed (Su): When a barghest slays a humanoid opponent, it can feed on the corpse, devouring both flesh and life force, as a full-round action. Feeding destroys the victim's body and prevents any form of raising or resurrection that requires part of the corpse. There is a 50% chance that a *wish, miracle,* or *true resurrection* spell can restore a devoured victim to life. Check once for each destroyed creature. If the check fails, the creature cannot be brought back to life by mortal magic.

A barghest advances in Hit Dice by consuming corpses in this fashion. For every three suitable corpses a barghest devours, it gains 1 Hit Die, and its Strength, Constitution, and natural armor increase by +1. Its attack bonus and saves improve as normal for an outsider of its Hit Dice, and it gains skill points, feats, and ability score improvements normally. The barghest only advances by consuming the corpses of creatures whose Hit Dice or levels are equal to or greater than its own current total. A barghest that reaches 9 Hit Dice through feeding immediately becomes a greater barghest upon completion of the act.

Change Shape (Su): A barghest can assume the shape of a goblin or a wolf as a standard action. In goblin form, a barghest cannot use its natural weapons but can wield weapons and

	Barghest Medium Outsider (Evil, Extraplanar, Lawful, Shapechanger)	Greater Barghest Large Outsider (Evil, Extraplanar, Lawful, Shapechanger)
Hit Dice:	6d8+6 (33 hp)	9d8+27 (67 hp)
Initiative:	+6	+6
Speed:	30 ft. (6 squares)	40 ft. (8 squares)
Armor Class:	18 (+2 Dex, +6 natural), touch 12, flat-footed 16	20 (−1 size, +2 Dex, +9 natural), touch 11, flat-footed 18
Base Attack/Grapple:	+6/+9	+9/+18
Attack:	Bite +9 melee (1d6+3)	Bite +13 melee (1d8+5)
Full Attack:	Bite +9 melee (1d6+3) and 2 claws +4 melee (1d4+1)	Bite +13 melee (1d8+5) and 2 claws +8 melee (1d6+2)
Space/Reach:	5 ft./5 ft.	10 ft./5 ft.
Special Attacks:	Spell-like abilities, feed	Spell-like abilities, feed
Special Qualities:	Change shape, damage reduction 5/magic, darkvision 60 ft., scent	Change shape, damage reduction 10/magic, darkvision 60 ft., scent
Saves:	Fort +6, Ref +7, Will +7	Fort +9, Ref +8, Will +10
Abilities:	Str 17, Dex 15, Con 13, Int 14, Wis 14, Cha 14	Str 20, Dex 15, Con 16, Int 18, Wis 18, Cha 18
Skills:	Bluff +11, Diplomacy +6, Disguise +2 (+4 acting), Hide +11*, Intimidate +13, Jump +12, Listen +11, Move Silently +10, Search +11, Sense Motive +11, Spot +11, Survival +11 (+13 following tracks)	Bluff +16, Climb +17, Concentration +15, Diplomacy +8, Disguise +4 (+6 acting), Hide +10*, Intimidate +18, Jump +21, Listen +16, Move Silently +14, Sense Motive +16, Spot +16 Survival +16 (+18 following tracks), Tumble +16
Feats:	Combat Reflexes, Improved Initiative, Track	Combat Casting, Combat Reflexes, Improved Initiative, Track
Environment	Bleak Eternity of Gehenna	Bleak Eternity of Gehenna
Organization:	Solitary or pack (3–6)	Solitary or pack (3–6)
Challenge Rating:	4	5
Treasure:	Double standard	Double standard
Alignment:	Always lawful evil	Always lawful evil
Advancement:	Special (see below)	Special (see below)
Level Adjustment:	—	—

wear armor. In wolf form, a barghest loses its claw attacks but retains its bite attack.

Pass Without Trace (Ex): A barghest in wolf form can use pass without trace (as the spell) as a free action.

Skills: *A barghest in wolf form gains a +4 circumstance bonus on Hide checks.

GREATER BARGHEST

A barghest that reaches 9 Hit Dice through feeding becomes a greater barghest. These creatures can change shape into a goblinlike creature of Large size (about 8 feet tall and 400 pounds) or a dire wolf. In goblin form, a greater barghest cannot use its natural weapons but can wield weapons and wear armor. In dire wolf form, a greater barghest loses its claw attacks but retains its bite attack.

A greater barghest can reach a maximum of 18 Hit Dice through feeding.

Spell-Like Abilities: In addition to the spell-like abilities all barghests possess, a greater barghest gains the following abilities. At will—*invisibility sphere*; 1/day—*mass bull's strength, mass enlarge*. Caster level equals the greater barghest's HD.

Combat

Occasionally, a greater barghest uses a magic two-handed weapon in combat instead of its claws, giving it multiple attacks (attack bonus +13/+8). It can also make one bite attack (attack bonus +8) each round. The save DC against a greater barghest's spell-like abilities is 14 + spell level.

BASILISK

The creature looks like a thick-bodied reptile with eight legs. Rows of bony spines jut from its back, and its eyes glow with an eerie, pale green incandescence.

A basilisk is a reptilian monster that petrifies living creatures with a mere gaze. Surviving a fight with a basilisk requires either careful preparation or considerable good fortune.

Basilisks are found in nearly every climate, and often in underground areas as well. They tend to lair in shallow burrows, caves, or other sheltered areas. The entrance to a basilisk lair is sometimes distinguished by lifelike stone statues or carvings, which are actually creatures that ran afoul of the creature's gaze. Basilisks are omnivorous and able to consume their petrified victims. They make effective guardians, if one has the magical or monetary

Basilisk

	Basilisk Medium Magical Beast	Abyssal Greater Basilisk Large Outsider (Augmented Magical Beast, Extraplanar)
Hit Dice:	6d10+12 (45 hp)	18d10+90 (189 hp)
Initiative:	−1	−1
Speed:	20 ft. (4 squares)	20 ft. (4 squares)
Armor Class:	16 (−1 Dex, +7 natural), touch 9, flat-footed 16	17 (−1 Dex, −1 size, +9 natural) touch 8, flat-footed 17
Base Attack/Grapple:	+6/+8	+18/+29
Attack:	Bite +8 melee (1d8+3)	Bite +25 melee (2d8+10)
Full Attack:	Bite +8 melee (1d8+3)	Bite +25 melee (2d8+10)
Space/Reach:	5 ft./5 ft.	10 ft./5 ft.
Special Attacks:	Petrifying gaze	Petrifying gaze, smite good
Special Qualities:	Darkvision 60 ft., low-light vision	Resistance to cold 10 and fire 10, damage reduction 10/magic, darkvision 60 ft., low-light vision, spell resistance 23
Saves:	Fort +9, Ref +4, Will +3	Fort +18, Ref +12, Will +8
Abilities:	Str 15, Dex 8, Con 15, Int 2, Wis 12, Cha 11	Str 24, Dex 8, Con 21, Int 3, Wis 10, Cha 15
Skills:	Hide +0*, Listen +7, Spot +7	Hide +0*, Listen +10, Spot +10
Feats:	Alertness, Blind-Fight, Great Fortitude	Alertness, Blind-Fight, Great Fortitude, Iron Will, Improved Natural Attack (bite), Lightning Reflexes, Weapon Focus (bite)
Environment:	Warm deserts	Infinite Layers of the Abyss
Organization:	Solitary or colony (3–6)	Solitary or colony (3–6)
Challenge Rating:	5	12
Treasure:	None	Standard
Alignment:	Always neutral	Always chaotic evil
Advancement:	7–10 HD (Medium); 11–18 HD (Large)	—
Level Adjustment:	—	—

resources to capture and contain them.

A basilisk usually has a dull brown body with a yellowish underbelly. Some specimens sport a short, curved horn atop the nose. An adult basilisk's body grows to about 6 feet long, not including its tail, which can reach an additional length of 5 to 7 feet. The creature weighs about 300 pounds.

COMBAT

A basilisk relies on its gaze attack, biting only when opponents come within reach. Though it has eight legs, its slow metabolism renders it relatively sluggish, so it does not expend energy unnecessarily. Intruders who flee a basilisk rather than fight can expect, at best, a halfhearted pursuit.

These creatures tend to spend most of their time lying in wait for prey, which includes small mammals, birds, reptiles, and similar creatures. When not hunting, basilisks are usually sleeping off their latest meal in their lairs. Basilisks sometimes gather in small colonies for mating or for mutual defense in unusually hostile terrain, and a colony will attack intruders in concert.

Abyssal greater basilisk

LOCKWOOD

Petrifying Gaze (Su): Turn to stone permanently, range 30 feet; Fortitude DC 13 negates. The save DC is Charisma-based.

Skills: *The basilisk's dull coloration and its ability to remain motionless for long periods of time grant it a +4 racial bonus on Hide checks in natural settings.

ABYSSAL GREATER BASILISK

Adventurers are likely to encounter these fiends of the underworld either in their native environment, barren wastelands of the Abyss, or summoned to the employ of some dark sorcerer. Servants of the demon lords make good use of the greater basilisk as guards and escorts.

Combat

The save DC for the abyssal greater basilisk's petrifying gaze (DC 21) is adjusted for its greater Hit Dice and higher Charisma score.

An abyssal greater basilisk's natural weapons are treated as magic weapons for the purpose of overcoming damage reduction.

Smite Good (Su): Once per day an abyssal greater basilisk can make a normal melee attack to deal an extra 18 points of damage against a good foe.

BEHIR

Huge Magical Beast
Hit Dice: 9d10+45 (94 hp)
Initiative: +1
Speed: 40 ft. (8 squares), climb 15 ft.
Armor Class: 20 (–2 size, +1 Dex, +11 natural), touch 9,
  flat-footed 19
Base Attack/Grapple: +9/+25
Attack: Bite +15 melee (2d4+12)
Full Attack: Bite +15 melee (2d4+12)
Space/Reach: 15 ft./10 ft.
Special Attacks: Breath weapon, constrict 2d8+8, improved
  grab, rake 1d4+4, swallow whole
Special Qualities: Can't be tripped, darkvision 60 ft., immunity
  to electricity, low-light vision, scent
Saves: Fort +11, Ref +7, Will +5
Abilities: Str 26, Dex 13, Con 21, Int 7, Wis 14, Cha 12
Skills: Climb +16, Hide +5, Listen +4, Spot +4, Survival +2
Feats: Alertness, Cleave, Power Attack, Track
Environment: Warm hills
Organization: Solitary or pair
Challenge Rating: 8
Treasure: Standard
Alignment: Often neutral
Advancement: 10–13 HD (Huge); 14–27 HD (Gargantuan)
Level Adjustment: —

*At first the creature appears as a huge armored snake, slithering across the
ground at great speed. Then, without slowing, it unfolds a dozen legs from
its serpentine body and runs forward to strike.*

The behir is a serpentine monster that can slither like a snake or
use its dozen legs to move with considerable speed.

A behir is about 40 feet long and weighs about 4,000 pounds. It
can fold its limbs close to its long, narrow body and slither in
snake fashion if it desires. The coloration of behirs ranges from
ultramarine to deep blue with bands of gray-brown. The belly is
pale blue. The two large horns curving back over the head look
dangerous but are actually used for preening the creature's scales,
not for fighting.

Behirs are never friendly with dragonkind and won't coexist
with any type of dragon. If a dragon enters a behir's territory, the
behir does everything it can to drive the dragon out. If the behir
fails, it moves off to find a new home. A behir never knowingly
enters the territory of a dragon.
Behirs speak Common.

Behir

COMBAT

A behir usually bites and grabs its prey first, then either swallows
or constricts the opponent. It can employ its claws only against
foes caught in its coils. If beset by a large number of foes, it uses its
breath weapon.

Breath Weapon (Su): 20-foot line, once every 10 rounds,
damage 7d6 electricity, Reflex DC 19 half. The save DC is
Constitution-based.

Constrict (Ex): A behir deals 2d8+8 points of damage with
a successful grapple check. It can make six rake attacks against
a grappled foe as well.

Improved Grab (Ex): To use this ability, a behir must hit a creature of any size with its bite attack. It can then attempt to start a
grapple as a free action without provoking an attack of opportunity. If it wins the grapple check, it it establishes a hold and can
attempt to constrict the opponent or swallow the opponent in the
following round.

Rake (Ex): Six claws, attack bonus +15 melee, damage 1d4+4.

Swallow Whole (Ex): A behir can try to swallow a grabbed Medium or smaller opponent by making a successful grapple check.
A behir that swallows an opponent can use its Cleave feat to bite
and grab another opponent.

A swallowed creature takes 2d8+8 points of bludgeoning
damage and 8 points of acid damage per round from the behir's
gizzard. A swallowed creature can cut its way out by using a
light slashing or piercing weapon to deal 25 points of damage to
the gizzard (AC 15). Once the creature exits, muscular action
closes the hole; another swallowed opponent must cut its own
way out.

A behir's gizzard can hold 2 Medium, 8 Small, 32 Tiny, or 128
Diminutive or smaller opponents.

Skills: Behirs have a +8 racial bonus on Climb checks and can
always choose to take 10 on Climb checks, even if rushed or
threatened.

BEHOLDER

*It floats before you, a bulbous body with a central, unblinking eye, and a
large maw filled with daggerlike teeth. Smaller eyes, attached to wriggling
stalks, sprout from the top of the orblike body.*

Beholders are the stuff of nightmares. These creatures, also called
the "spheres of many eyes" or "eye tyrants," are deadly adversaries.
Beholders speak their own language and Common.

COMBAT

The primary weapon of both the gauth and the beholder is a series
of deadly eye rays.

Eye Rays (Su): Each of a beholder's small eyes can produce
a magical ray once per round as a free action. During a single
round, a creature can aim only two eye rays (gauth) or three eye
rays (beholder) at targets in any one 90-degree arc (up, forward,
backward, left, right, or down). The remaining eyes must aim at
targets in other arcs, or not at all. A beholder can tilt and pan its
body each round to change which rays it can bring to bear in any
given arc.

Each eye's effect resembles a spell (caster level 8th level for a
gauth, or 14th for a beholder), but follows the rules for a ray (see
Aiming a Spell, page 175 of the *Player's Handbook*).

All-Around Vision (Ex): Beholders are exceptionally alert and
circumspect. Their many eyes give them a +4 racial bonus on Spot
and Search checks, and they can't be flanked.

Flight (Ex): A beholder's body is naturally buoyant. This
buoyancy allows it to fly at a speed of 20 feet. This buoyancy also
grants it a permanent feather fall effect (as the spell) with personal range.

Illus. by M. Tedin after T. Lockwood

GAUTH

Medium Aberration
Hit Dice: 6d8+18 (45 hp)
Initiative: +6
Speed: 5 ft. (1 square), fly 20 ft. (good)
Armor Class: 19 (+2 Dex, +7 natural), touch 12, flat-footed 17
Base Attack/Grapple: +4/+3
Attack: Eye rays +6 ranged touch and bite –2 melee (1d6–1)
Full Attack: Eye rays +6 ranged touch and bite –2 melee (1d6–1)
Space/Reach: 5 ft./5 ft.
Special Attacks: Eye rays, stunning gaze
Special Qualities: All-around vision, darkvision 60 ft., flight
Saves: Fort +5, Ref +4, Will +9
Abilities: Str 8, Dex 14, Con 16, Int 15, Wis 15, Cha 13
Skills: Hide +11, Knowledge (arcana) +11, Listen +4, Search +15, Spot +17, Survival +2 (+4 following tracks)
Feats: Alertness[B], Flyby Attack, Improved Initiative, Iron Will
Environment: Cold hills
Organization: Solitary, pair, or cluster (3–6)
Challenge Rating: 6
Treasure: Standard
Alignment: Usually lawful evil
Advancement: 7–12 HD (Medium); 13–18 HD (Large)
Level Adjustment: —

The gauth, sometimes known as the lesser beholder, is a 4-foot wide orb dominated by a central eye. Six smaller eyes on stalks sprout from the top of its body. It is a rapacious and tyrannical creature that seeks to exact tribute from anything weaker than itself, and often attacks adventurers simply to acquire their wealth.

Eye Rays (Su): Each of a gauth's six eye rays resembles a spell cast by an 8th-level caster. Each eye ray has a range of 100 feet and a save DC of 14. The save DCs are Charisma-based. The six eye rays include:

Sleep: This works like the spell, except that it affects one creature with any number of Hit Dice (Will negates). Gauths like to use this ray against warriors and other physically powerful creatures.

Inflict Moderate Wounds: This works like the spell, causing 2d8+8 points of damage (Will half).

Dispel Magic: This works like the targeted dispel function of the spell. The gauth's dispel check is 1d20+8.

Scorching Ray: This works like the spell, dealing 4d6 points of fire damage (no save). A gauth creates only one fiery ray per use of this ability.

Paralysis: The target must succeed on a Fortitude save or be paralyzed for 2d10 minutes.

Exhaustion: This works like the spell *ray of exhaustion* (no save).

Stunning Gaze (Su): Stun for 1 round, 30 feet, Will DC 14 negates. The save DC is Charisma-based. Any creature meeting the gaze of the gauth's central eye

is subject to its stunning gaze attack. Since the gauth can use its eye-rays as a free action, the creature can use a standard action to focus its stunning gaze on an opponent and attack with all eye rays that bear on its foes at the same time.

BEHOLDER

Large Aberration
Hit Dice: 11d8+44 (93 hp)
Initiative: +6
Speed: 5 ft. (1 square), fly 20 ft. (good)
Armor Class: 26 (–1 size, +2 Dex, +15 natural), touch 11, flat-footed 24
Base Attack/Grapple: +8/+12
Attack: Eye rays +9 ranged touch and bite +2 melee (2d4)
Full Attack: Eye rays +9 ranged touch and bite +2 melee (2d4)
Space/Reach: 10 ft./5 ft.
Special Attacks: Eye rays
Special Qualities: All-around vision, antimagic cone, darkvision 60 ft., flight
Saves: Fort +9, Ref +5, Will +11
Abilities: Str 10, Dex 14, Con 18, Int 17, Wis 15, Cha 15
Skills: Hide +12, Knowledge (arcana) +17, Listen +18, Search +21, Spot +22, Survival +2 (+4 following tracks)
Feats: Alertness[B], Flyby Attack, Great Fortitude, Improved Initiative, Iron Will
Environment: Cold hills
Organization: Solitary, pair, or cluster (3–6)
Challenge Rating: 13
Treasure: Double standard
Alignment: Usually lawful evil
Advancement: 12–16 HD (Large); 17–33 HD (Huge)
Level Adjustment: —

Beholder

A beholder is an 8-foot-wide orb dominated by a central eye and a large, toothy maw. Ten smaller eyes on stalks sprout from the top of the orb.

Combat

Beholders often attack without provocation. Though not powerful physically, they often plow right into groups of opponents to use as many of their eyes as they can. When closing with an enemy, a beholder tries to cause as much disruption and confusion as possible.

Eye Rays (Su): Each of a beholder's ten eye rays resembles a spell cast by a 13th-level caster. Each eye ray has a range of 150 feet and a save DC of 17. The save DCs are Charisma-based. The ten eye rays include:

Charm Monster: The target must succeed on a Will save or be affected as though by the spell. Beholders use this ray to confuse the opposition, usually employing it early in a fight. The beholder generally instructs a *charmed* target to either restrain a comrade or stand aside.

Charm Person: The target must succeed on a Will save or be affected as though by the spell. Beholders use this ray in the same manner as the *charm monster* ray.

Disintegrate: The target must succeed on a Fortitude save or be affected as though by the spell. The beholder likes to use this ray on any foe it considers a real threat.

Fear: This works like the spell, except that it targets one creature. The target must succeed on a Will save or be affected as though by the spell. Beholders like to use this ray against warriors and other powerful creatures early in a fight, to break up the opposition.

Finger of Death: The target must succeed on a Fortitude save or be slain as though by the spell. The target takes 3d6+13 points of damage if its saving throw succeeds. Beholders use this ray to eliminate dangerous foes quickly.

Flesh to Stone: The target must succeed on a Fortitude save or be affected as though by the spell. Beholders like to aim this ray at enemy spellcasters. They also use it on any creature whose appearance they find interesting. (After the fight, the beholder takes the statue to its lair as a decoration.)

Inflict Moderate Wounds: This works like the spell, causing 2d8+10 points of damage (Will half).

Sleep: This works like the spell, except that it affects one creature with any number of Hit Dice (Will negates). Beholders like to use this ray against warriors and other physically powerful creatures. They know their foes can quickly awaken the sleepers, but they also know that doing so takes time and can delay an effective counterattack.

Slow: This works like the spell, except that it affects one creature. The target can make a Will save to negate the effect. Beholders often use this ray against the same creature targeted by their *disintegrate, flesh to stone,* or *finger of death* ray. If one of the former rays fails to eliminate the foe, this ray might at least hamper it.

Telekinesis: A beholder can move objects or creatures that weigh up to 325 pounds, as though with a *telekinesis* spell. Creatures can resist the effect with a successful Will save.

Antimagic Cone (Su): A beholder's central eye continually produces a 150-foot cone of antimagic. This functions just like *antimagic field* (caster level 13th). All magical and supernatural powers and effects within the cone are suppressed—even the beholder's own eye rays. Once each round, during its turn, the beholder decides whether the antimagic cone is active or not (the beholder deactivates the cone by shutting its central eye).

Beholder Society

Beholders are hateful, aggressive, and avaricious, attacking or dominating others whenever they can get away with it. They exhibit a xenophobic intolerance, hating all creatures not like themselves. The basic body type comprises a great variety of beholder subspecies. Some are covered with overlapping chitinous plates; some have smooth hides or snakelike eye tentacles; some have crustacean joints. But even a difference as small as hide color or size of the central eye can make two groups of beholders sworn enemies. Every beholder declares its own unique form to be the "true ideal of beholderhood," the others being nothing but ugly replicas fit only to be eliminated.

Beholders usually carve out underground lairs for themselves using their *disintegrate* rays. Beholder architecture emphasizes the vertical, and a lair usually has a number of parallel tubes, with chambers stacked on top of each other. Beholders prefer inaccessible locations that earthbound foes can reach only with difficulty.

BELKER

Large Elemental (Air, Extraplanar)
Hit Dice: 7d8+7 (38 hp)
Initiative: +5
Speed: 30 ft. (6 squares), fly 50 ft. (perfect)
Armor Class: 22 (–1 size, +5 Dex, +8 natural), touch 14, flat-footed 17
Base Attack/Grapple: +5/+11
Attack: Wing +9 melee (1d6+2)
Full Attack: 2 wings +9 melee (1d6+2) and bite +4 melee (1d4+1) and 2 claws +4 melee (1d3+1)
Space/Reach: 10 ft./10 ft.
Special Attacks: Smoke claws
Special Qualities: Darkvision 60 ft., elemental traits, smoke form
Saves: Fort +3, Ref +10, Will +2
Abilities: Str 14, Dex 21, Con 13, Int 6, Wis 11, Cha 11
Skills: Listen +7, Move Silently +9, Spot +7
Feats: Alertness, Multiattack, Weapon Finesse
Environment: Elemental Plane of Air
Organization: Solitary, pair, or clutch (3–4)
Challenge Rating: 6
Treasure: None
Alignment: Usually neutral evil
Advancement: 8–10 HD (Large); 11–21 HD (Huge)
Level Adjustment: —

Belker

A mass of dark smoke moves against the breeze, shifting shape as it comes closer. Cloudlike, roiling, it suddenly explodes into a demonic creature of smoke and wind, with large bat wings, clawed tendrils, and a biting maw.

Belkers are creatures from the Plane of Air. They are composed primarily of smoke. Although undeniably evil, they are very reclusive and usually have no interest in the affairs of others.

A belker's winged shape makes it look distinctly demonic. Because of its semigaseous nature, however, it shifts and changes shape with every puff of wind. It is about 7 feet long and weighs about 8 pounds.

Belkers speak Auran.

COMBAT

In most cases, a belker fights with its nasty claws and painful bite.

Smoke Claws (Ex): A belker in smoke form (see below) can engulf opponents by moving on top of them. It fills the air around one Medium or smaller opponent without provoking an attack of opportunity. The target must succeed on a DC 14 Fortitude save or inhale part of the creature. The save DC is Constitution-based. Smoke inside the victim solidifies into a claw and begins to rip at the surrounding organs, dealing 3d4 points of damage per round. An affected creature can attempt another Fortitude save each subsequent round to cough out the semivaporous menace.

Smoke Form (Su): Most of the time a belker is more or less solid, but at will it can assume smoke form. It can switch forms once per round as a free action and can spend up to 20 rounds per day in smoke form. A belker in smoke form can fly at a speed of 50 feet (perfect). The ability is otherwise similar to a *gaseous form* spell (caster level 7th).

Skills: Belkers have a +4 racial bonus on Move Silently checks.

BLINK DOG

Medium Magical Beast
Hit Dice: 4d10 (22 hp)
Initiative: +3
Speed: 40 ft. (8 squares)
Armor Class: 16 (+3 Dex, +3 natural), touch 13, flat-footed 13
Base Attack/Grapple: +4/+4
Attack: Bite +4 melee (1d6)
Full Attack: Bite +4 melee (1d6)
Space/Reach: 5 ft./5 ft.
Special Attacks: —
Special Qualities: Blink, darkvision 60 ft., dimension door, low-light vision, scent
Saves: Fort +4, Ref +7, Will +4
Abilities: Str 10, Dex 17, Con 10, Int 10, Wis 13, Cha 11
Skills: Hide +3, Listen +5, Sense Motive +3, Spot +5, Survival +4
Feats: Iron Will, Run, Track[B]
Environment: Temperate plains
Organization: Solitary, pair, or pack (7–16)
Challenge Rating: 2
Treasure: None
Alignment: Usually lawful good
Advancement: 5–7 HD (Medium); 8–12 HD (Large)
Level Adjustment: +2 (cohort)

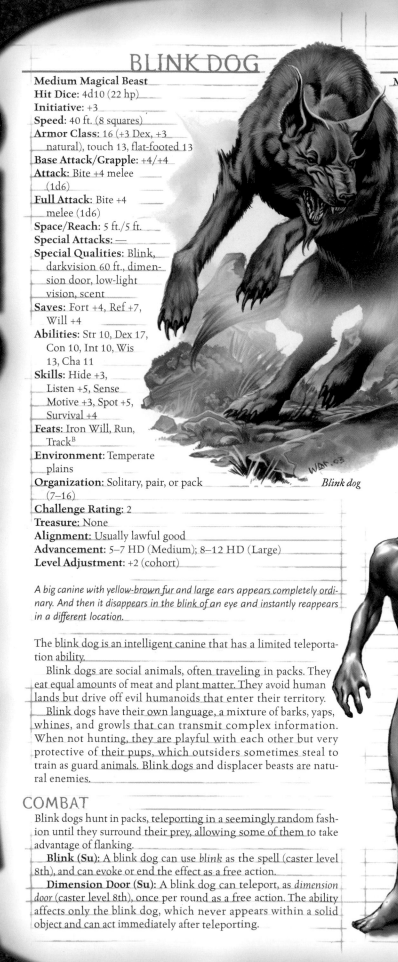

Blink dog

A big canine with yellow-brown fur and large ears appears completely ordinary. And then it disappears in the blink of an eye and instantly reappears in a different location.

The blink dog is an intelligent canine that has a limited teleportation ability.

Blink dogs are social animals, often traveling in packs. They eat equal amounts of meat and plant matter. They avoid human lands but drive off evil humanoids that enter their territory.

Blink dogs have their own language, a mixture of barks, yaps, whines, and growls that can transmit complex information. When not hunting, they are playful with each other but very protective of their pups, which outsiders sometimes steal to train as guard animals. Blink dogs and displacer beasts are natural enemies.

COMBAT

Blink dogs hunt in packs, teleporting in a seemingly random fashion until they surround their prey, allowing some of them to take advantage of flanking.

Blink (Su): A blink dog can use *blink* as the spell (caster level 8th), and can evoke or end the effect as a free action.

Dimension Door (Su): A blink dog can teleport, as *dimension door* (caster level 8th), once per round as a free action. The ability affects only the blink dog, which never appears within a solid object and can act immediately after teleporting.

BODAK

Medium Undead (Extraplanar)
Hit Dice: 9d12 (58 hp)
Initiative: +6
Speed: 20 ft. (4 squares)
Armor Class: 20 (+2 Dex, +8 natural), touch 12, flat-footed 18
Base Attack/Grapple: +4/+5
Attack: Slam +6 melee (1d8+1)
Full Attack: Slam +6 melee (1d8+1)
Space/Reach: 5 ft./5 ft.
Special Attacks: Death gaze
Special Qualities: Damage reduction 10/cold iron, darkvision 60 ft., immunity to electricity, resistance to acid 10 and fire 10, undead traits, vulnerability to sunlight
Saves: Fort +3, Ref +5, Will +7
Abilities: Str 13, Dex 15, Con —, Int 6, Wis 12, Cha 12
Skills: Listen +11, Move Silently +10, Spot +11
Feats: Alertness, Dodge, Improved Initiative, Weapon Focus (slam)
Environment: Infinite Layers of the Abyss
Organization: Solitary or gang (2–4)
Challenge Rating: 8
Treasure: None
Alignment: Always chaotic evil
Advancement: 10–13 HD (Medium); 14–27 HD (Large)
Level Adjustment: —

This creature is a gray-fleshed, hairless humanoid with an elongated skull-like head, noseless face, and white, empty eyes.

Bodaks are the undead remnants of humanoids who have been destroyed by the touch of absolute evil.

A bodak retains fleeting memories of its past life and can speak Common (or some other humanoid language).

COMBAT

Bodaks love to approach their opponents at a leisurely pace, letting their gaze do its work before closing.

Death Gaze (Su): Death, range 30 feet, Fortitude DC 15 negates. Humanoids who die from this attack are transformed into bodaks 24 hours later. The save DC is Charisma-based.

Vulnerability to Sunlight (Ex): Bodaks loathe sunlight, for its merest touch burns their impure flesh. Each round of exposure to the direct rays of the sun deals 1 point of damage to the creature.

Bodak

BUGBEAR

Medium Humanoid (Goblinoid)

Hit Dice: 3d8+3 (16 hp)

Initiative: +1

Speed: 30 ft. (6 squares)

Armor Class: 17 (+1 Dex, +3 natural, +2 leather armor, +1 light wooden shield), touch 11, flat-footed 16

Base Attack/Grapple: +2/+4

Attack: Morningstar +5 melee (1d8+2) or javelin +3 ranged (1d6+2)

Full Attack: Morningstar +5 melee (1d8+2) or javelin +3 ranged (1d6+2)

Space/Reach: 5 ft./5 ft.

Special Attacks: —

Special Qualities: Darkvision 60 ft., scent

Saves: Fort +2, Ref +4, Will +1

Abilities: Str 15, Dex 12, Con 13, Int 10, Wis 10, Cha 9

Skills: Climb +3, Hide +4, Listen +4, Move Silently +6, Spot +4

Feats: Alertness, Weapon Focus (morningstar)

Environment: Temperate mountains

Organization: Solitary, gang (2–4), or band (11–20 plus 150% noncombatants plus 2 2nd-level sergeants and 1 leader of 2nd–5th level)

Challenge Rating: 2

Treasure: Standard

Alignment: Usually chaotic evil

Advancement: By character class

Level Adjustment: +1

This muscular, savage humanoid stands 7 feet tall. Coarse hair covers most of its body. Its mouth is full of long, sharp fangs, and its nose is much like that of a bear.

The biggest and strongest of the goblinoids, bugbears are more aggressive than their smaller relatives. They live by hunting any creature weaker than themselves.

The bugbear's nose is the cause of its name, though the creature is not related to bears. Its hide and sharp claws also resemble those of bears. A bugbear's hands are far more dexterous than a bear's paws, however, and its claws are too small to make effective weapons.

Bugbears speak Goblin and Common.

COMBAT

Bugbears prefer to ambush opponents whenever possible. When hunting, they normally send scouts ahead of the main group that, if they spy prey, return to report and bring up reinforcements. Bugbear attacks are coordinated, and their tactics are sound if not brilliant.

Skills: Bugbears have a +4 racial bonus on Move Silently checks.

BUGBEAR SOCIETY

Bugbears prefer to dwell in temperate, mountainous regions with many caves, living in small tribal units. A single bugbear, usually the biggest and meanest, leads each tribe. A tribe has as many young as it has adults. Children do not join the adults in the hunt, but they will fight to protect themselves or their lairs.

Bugbears have only two genuine goals in life: food and treasure. Prey and intruders are considered a valuable source of both. These extremely greedy creatures prize anything shiny, including arms and armor. They never miss an opportunity to increase their hoards through theft, plunder, and ambush. On rare occasions they parley with other beings if they believe something can be gained, but they are not skilled negotiators, losing their patience quickly if such encounters run overlong.

They are sometimes found commanding goblins and hobgoblins, whom they bully mercilessly.

Bugbears survive primarily by hunting, and they eat whatever they can bring down. Any creature is a legitimate source of food, including monsters and even their own smaller kin. When game is scarce, bugbears turn to raiding and ambush to fill their stewpots.

Most bugbears revere a deity named Hruggek, who delights in ambushes followed by furious combat.

BUGBEARS AS CHARACTERS

Most bugbear leaders are fighters or fighter/rogues. Bugbear clerics worship Hruggek and can choose any two of the following domains: Chaos, Evil, Trickery, and War.

Bugbear characters possess the following racial traits.

— +4 Strength, +2 Dexterity, +2 Constitution, –2 Charisma.

—Medium size.

—A bugbear's base land speed is 30 feet.

—Darkvision out to 60 feet.

—Racial Hit Dice: A bugbear begins with three levels of humanoid, which provide 3d8 Hit Dice, a base attack bonus of +2, and base saving throw bonuses of Fort +1, Ref +3, and Will +1.

—Racial Skills: A bugbear's humanoid levels give it skill points equal to 6 × (2 + Int modifier). Its class skills are Climb, Hide, Listen, Move Silently, Search, and Spot.

—Racial Feats: A bugbear's humanoid levels give it two feats.

— +3 natural armor bonus.

— +4 racial bonus on Move Silently checks.

—Automatic Languages: Common, Goblin. Bonus Languages: Draconic, Elven, Giant, Gnoll, Orc.

—Favored Class: Rogue.

—Level adjustment +1.

Bugbear

WAY. 2000

BULETTE

Huge Magical Beast
Hit Dice: 9d10+45 (94 hp)
Initiative: +2
Speed: 40 ft. (8 squares), burrow 10 ft.
Armor Class: 22 (–2 size, +2 Dex, +12 natural), touch 10, flat-footed 20
Base Attack/Grapple: +9/+25
Attack: Bite +16 melee (2d8+8)
Full Attack: Bite +16 melee (2d8+8) and 2 claws +10 melee (2d6+4)
Space/Reach: 15 ft./10 ft.
Special Attacks: Leap
Special Qualities: Darkvision 60 ft., low-light vision, scent, tremorsense 60 ft.
Saves: Fort +11, Ref +8, Will +6
Abilities: Str 27, Dex 15, Con 20, Int 2, Wis 13, Cha 6
Skills: Jump +18, Listen +9, Spot +3
Feats: Alertness, Iron Will, Track, Weapon Focus (bite)
Environment: Temperate hills
Organization: Solitary or pair
Challenge Rating: 7
Treasure: None
Alignment: Always neutral
Advancement: 10–16 HD (Huge); 17–27 HD (Gargantuan)
Level Adjustment: —

Bulette

The ground shakes and rolls and then bursts open to reveal a terrible, armor-plated, bullet-shaped creature with a huge snapping maw and short, powerful legs.

Also known as the landshark, the bulette is a terrifying predator that lives only to eat. It is universally shunned, even by other monsters. Fortunately for the rest of the world, the bulette is a solitary animal, although mated pairs (very rare) might share the same territory. Since its appetite is so voracious, each bulette has a large territory that can range up to 30 square miles. Other predators rarely share territory with one, for fear of being eaten. A bulette has no lair, preferring to wander above and below ground; it burrows beneath the soil to rest.

A bulette totally consumes its victims—clothing, weapons, and all. Its powerful stomach acid quickly destroys armor, weapons, and even magic items. It is not above nibbling on chests or sacks of coins either. When it has eaten everything in its territory, a bulette moves on. The sole criterion for a suitable territory is availability of food, so bulettes occasionally locate themselves near human settlements and terrorize the residents.

COMBAT

A bulette attacks anything it regards as edible, choosing the easiest or closest prey first. The only creatures it refuses to eat are elves (and it dislikes the taste of dwarves). When burrowing underground, a landshark relies on its tremorsense ability to detect prey. When it senses something edible (that is, senses movement), it breaks to the surface, crest first, and begins its attack.

The bulette has a foul temperament—stupid, mean, and fearless. The size, strength, and number of its opponents mean nothing.

Leap (Ex): A bulette can jump into the air during combat. This allows it to make four claw attacks instead of two, each with a +15 attack bonus, but it cannot bite.

CARRION CRAWLER

Large Aberration
Hit Dice: 3d8+6 (19 hp)
Initiative: +2
Speed: 30 ft. (6 squares), climb 15 ft.
Armor Class: 17 (–1 size, +2 Dex, +6 natural), touch 11, flat-footed 15
Base Attack/Grapple: +2/+8
Attack: Tentacle +3 melee (paralysis)
Full Attack: 8 tentacles +3 melee (paralysis) and bite –2 melee (1d4+1)
Space/Reach: 10 ft./5 ft.
Special Attacks: Paralysis
Special Qualities: Darkvision 60 ft., scent
Saves: Fort +3, Ref +3, Will +5
Abilities: Str 14, Dex 15, Con 14, Int 1, Wis 15, Cha 6
Skills: Climb +12, Listen +6, Spot +6
Feats: Alertness[B], Combat Reflexes, Track
Environment: Underground
Organization: Solitary, pair, or cluster (3–5)
Challenge Rating: 4
Treasure: None
Alignment: Always neutral
Advancement: 4–6 HD (Large); 7–9 HD (Huge)
Level Adjustment: —

The stink of rotten meat surrounds this multilegged creature with a segmented, 10-foot-long body. Eight writhing tentacles protrude from its head, growing directly from below its clacking mandibles and tooth-filled maw.

Carrion crawlers are aggressive subterranean scavengers, greatly feared for their paralyzing attacks. They scour their underground territory for dead and decaying flesh but won't hesitate to attack and kill living creatures.

Each of a carrion crawler's tentacles is about 2 feet long and secretes a sticky, paralyzing substance. Like so many hybrid monsters, the carrion crawler may well be the result of arcane experimentation. A carrion crawler weighs about 500 pounds.

COMBAT

Carrion crawlers use their senses of sight and smell to detect carcasses and potential prey. When attacking, a crawler lashes out

Illus. by T. Lockwood

with its tentacles and tries to paralyze its victim. The tentacles deal no other damage. The creature then kills the paralyzed victim with its bite and devours the flesh. Multiple crawlers do not fight in concert, but each paralyzes as many opponents as possible. The unintelligent creature continues to attack as long as it faces any moving opponents.

Paralysis (Ex): Those hit by a carrion crawler's tentacle attack must succeed on a DC 13 Fortitude save or be paralyzed for 2d4 rounds. The save DC is Constitution-based.

Skills: Carrion crawlers have a +8 racial bonus on Climb checks and can always choose to take 10 on Climb checks, even if rushed or threatened.

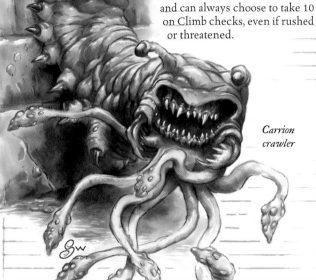

Carrion crawler

CELESTIAL CREATURE

Celestial creatures dwell on the upper planes, the realms of good, although they resemble beings found on the Material Plane. They are more regal and more beautiful than their earthly counterparts.

Celestial creatures often come in metallic colors (usually silver, gold, or platinum). They can be mistaken for half-celestials, more powerful creatures that are created when a celestial mates with a noncelestial creature.

SAMPLE CELESTIAL CREATURE

Celestial Lion
Large Magical Beast (Augmented Animal, Extraplanar)
Hit Dice: 5d8+10 (32 hp)
Initiative: +3
Speed: 40 ft. (8 squares)
Armor Class: 15 (–1 size, +3 Dex, +3 natural), touch 12, flat-footed 12
Base Attack/Grapple: +3/+12
Attack: Claw +7 melee (1d4+5)
Full Attack: 2 claws +7 melee (1d4+5) and bite +2 melee (1d8+2)
Space/Reach: 10 ft./5 ft.
Special Attacks: Improved grab, pounce, rake 1d4+2, smite evil
Special Qualities: Damage reduction 5/magic, darkvision 60 ft., resistance to acid 5, cold 5, and electricity 5, spell resistance 10
Saves: Fort +6, Ref +7, Will +2
Abilities: Str 21, Dex 17, Con 15, Int 3, Wis 12, Cha 6
Skills: Balance +7, Hide +3*, Listen +5, Move Silently +11, Spot +5

Feats: Alertness, Run
Environment: Seven Mounting Heavens of Celestia
Organization: Solitary, pair, or pride (6–10)
Challenge Rating: 4
Treasure: None
Alignment: Always good (any)
Advancement: 6–8 HD (Large)
Level Adjustment: —

Combat
A celestial lion's natural weapons are treated as magic weapons for the purpose of overcoming damage reduction.

Improved Grab (Ex): To use this ability, a celestial lion must hit with its bite attack. It can then attempt to start a grapple as a free action without provoking an attack of opportunity. If it wins the grapple check, it establishes a hold and can rake.

Pounce (Ex): If a celestial lion charges, it can make a full attack, including two rake attacks.

Rake (Ex): Attack bonus +7 melee, damage 1d4+2.

Skills: Celestial lions have a +4 racial bonus on Balance, Hide, and Move Silently checks. *In areas of tall grass or heavy undergrowth, the Hide bonus improves to +8.

CREATING A CELESTIAL CREATURE
"Celestial" is an inherited template that can be added to any corporeal animal, aberration, animal, dragon, fey, giant, humanoid, magical beast, monstrous humanoid, plant, or vermin of good or neutral alignment (referred to hereafter as the base creature).

A celestial creature uses all the base creature's statistics and abilities except as noted here. Do not recalculate the creature's Hit Dice, base attack bonus, saves, or skill points if its type changes.

Size and Type: Animals or vermin with this template become magical beasts, but otherwise the creature type is unchanged. Size is unchanged. Celestial creatures encountered on the Material Plane have the extraplanar subtype.

Special Attacks: A celestial creature retains all the special attacks of the base creature and also gains the following attack.

Smite Evil (Su): Once per day a celestial creature can make a normal melee attack to deal extra damage equal to its HD (maximum of +20) against an evil foe.

Special Qualities: A celestial creature retains all the special qualities of the base creature and also gains the following qualities.
—Darkvision out to 60 feet.
—Damage reduction (see the table below).
—Resistance to acid, cold, and electricity (see the table below).
—Spell resistance equal to HD + 5 (maximum 25).

Hit Dice	Resistance to Acid, Cold, Electricity	Damage Reduction
1–3	5	—
4–7	5	5/magic
8–11	10	5/magic
12 or more	10	10/magic

If the base creature already has one or more of these special qualities, use the better value.

If a celestial creature gains damage reduction, its natural weapons are treated as magic weapons for the purpose of overcoming damage reduction.

Abilities: Same as the base creature, but Intelligence is at least 3.

Environment: Any good-aligned plane.

Challenge Rating: HD 3 or less, as base creature; HD 4 to 7, as base creature +1; HD 8 or more, as base creature +2.

Alignment: Always good (any).

Level Adjustment: Same as the base creature +2.

CENTAUR

Large Monstrous Humanoid
Hit Dice: 4d8+8 (26 hp)
Initiative: +2
Speed: 50 ft. (10 squares)
Armor Class: 14 (–1 size, +2 Dex, +3 natural), touch 11, flat-footed 12
Base Attack/Grapple: +4/+12
Attack: Longsword +7 melee (2d6+6/19–20) or composite longbow (+4 Str bonus) +5 ranged (2d6+4/×3)
Full Attack: Longsword +7 melee (2d6+6/19–20) and 2 hooves +3 melee (1d6+2); or composite longbow (+4 Str bonus) +5 ranged (2d6+4/×3)
Space/Reach: 10 ft./5 ft.
Special Attacks: —
Special Qualities: Darkvision 60 ft.
Saves: Fort +3, Ref +6, Will +5
Abilities: Str 18, Dex 14, Con 15, Int 8, Wis 13, Cha 11
Skills: Listen +3, Move Silently +4, Spot +3, Survival +2
Feats: Dodge, Weapon Focus (hoof)
Environment: Temperate forests
Organization: Solitary, company (5–8), troop (8–18 plus 1 leader of 2nd–5th level), or tribe (20–150 plus 30% noncombatants plus 10 3rd-level sergeants, 5 5th-level lieutenants, and 1 leader of 5th–9th level)
Challenge Rating: 3
Treasure: Standard
Alignment: Usually neutral good
Advancement: By character class
Level Adjustment: +2

The creature gallops out of the trees, its thundering hooves echoing throughout the forest. It has the upper torso, arms, and head of a humanoid, and the lower body of a large horse. It carries a longbow, drawn and nocked, ready to loose an arrow at the first hint of danger.

Centaur

Centaurs are woodland beings who shun the company of strangers. They are deadly archers and even more fearsome in melee.

A centaur is as big as a heavy horse, but much taller and slightly heavier. A centaur is about 7 feet tall and weighs about 2,100 pounds.

Centaurs speak Sylvan and Elven.

COMBAT

Although generally mild-tempered, centaurs are always armed. Their favorite melee weapon is the longsword. When scouting or hunting, they carry composite longbows. A centaur employing a lance deals double damage when it charges, just as a rider on a mount does.

Centaurs usually don't provoke a fight. Their normal response to aggression is swift retreat, perhaps after launching a few arrows to discourage pursuit. Against creatures powerful enough to pose danger to the tribe, they appear to use this same tactic, except that about half of the "retreating" centaurs will circle around to lie in ambush or attack the foe from the rear.

CENTAUR SOCIETY

Among their own kind, centaurs are sociable creatures, but they have been known to become rowdy, boorish, and aggressive when under the influence of alcohol.

Solitary centaurs are usually out hunting or scouting. Companies and troops are usually hunting or scouting in force. Most of the members of a centaur tribe remain near their lair. Most of the centaurs in the tribal lair are female; while the males are out hunting and scouting, the females lead and administer the tribe. A third of a tribe's population is young.

The typical centaur lair is located deep within a forest. It consists of a large hidden glade and pastures, with a good supply of running water. Depending on the climate, the lair may contain huts or lean-tos to shelter individual families. Hearths for cooking and warmth are in an open area, away from the trees.

Centaurs are skilled in horticulture and may cultivate useful plants near their lair. In dangerous, monster-infested areas they plant thick barriers of thorn bushes around their lair, dig pits, and set snares.

Centaurs survive through a mixture of hunting, foraging, fishing, agriculture, and trade. Though they shun dealings with humans, centaurs do trade with elves, especially for food and wine. The elves are paid from the tribe's treasury, which consists of the booty of slain monsters.

The size of a centaur tribe's territory varies with its population and the nature of the area it inhabits. Centaurs do not object to sharing territory with elves. The attitude of a centaur toward a stranger in its territory depends on the visitor. Humans and dwarves are politely asked to leave, halflings or gnomes are tolerated, and elves are welcomed. Centaurs deal with monsters according to how much of a threat they are to the welfare and survival of the tribe: If a giant or dragon were to enter a tribe's territory, the centaurs would relocate, but they would attempt to kill trolls, orcs, and the like.

Most centaurs revere a deity named Skerrit, who is a god of nature and community.

CENTAURS AS CHARACTERS

Centaurs sometimes become bards, rangers, or druids. Centaur rangers often choose magical beasts or some variety of humanoid as their favored enemy. A centaur druid is usually a tribe's designated leader and speaker. Centaur clerics (who are rare) worship Skerrit and can choose any two of the following domains: Animal, Good, or Plant.

Centaur characters possess the following racial traits.

— +8 Strength, +4 Dexterity, +4 Constitution, –2 Intelligence, +2 Wisdom.

—Large size. –1 penalty to Armor Class, –1 penalty on attack rolls, –4 penalty on Hide checks, +4 bonus on grapple checks, lifting and carrying limits double those of Medium characters.

—Space/Reach: 10 feet/5 feet.

—A centaur's base land speed is 50 feet.

—Darkvision out to 60 feet.

—Racial Hit Dice: A centaur begins with four levels of monstrous humanoid, which provide 4d8 Hit Dice, a base attack bonus of +4, and base saving throw bonuses of Fort +1, Ref +4, and Will +4.

—Racial Skills: A centaur's monstrous humanoid levels give it skill points equal to $7 \times (2 + $ Int modifier). Its class skills are Listen, Move Silently, Spot, and Survival.

—Racial Feats: A centaur's monstrous humanoid levels give it two feats.

— +3 natural armor bonus.

— Automatic Languages: Sylvan, Elven. Bonus Languages: Common, Gnome, Halfling.

—Favored Class: Ranger.

—Level adjustment +2.

CHAOS BEAST

Medium Outsider (Chaotic, Extraplanar)
Hit Dice: 8d8+8 (44 hp)
Initiative: +5
Speed: 20 ft. (4 squares)
Armor Class: 16 (+1 Dex, +5 natural), touch 11, flat-footed 15
Base Attack/Grapple: +8/+10
Attack: Claw +10 melee (1d3+2 plus corporeal instability)
Full Attack: 2 claws +10 melee (1d3+2 plus corporeal instability)
Space/Reach: 5 ft./5 ft.
Special Attacks: Corporeal instability
Special Qualities: Darkvision 60 ft., immunity to critical hits and transformation, spell resistance 15
Saves: Fort +7, Ref +7, Will +6
Abilities: Str 14, Dex 13, Con 13, Int 10, Wis 10, Cha 10
Skills: Climb +13, Escape Artist +12, Hide +12, Jump +9, Listen +11, Search +11, Spot +11, Survival +0 (+2 following tracks), Tumble +14, Use Rope +1 (+3 with bindings)
Feats: Dodge, Improved Initiative, Mobility
Environment: Ever-Changing Chaos of Limbo
Organization: Solitary
Challenge Rating: 7
Treasure: None
Alignment: Always chaotic neutral
Advancement: 9–12 HD (Medium); 13–24 HD (Large)
Level Adjustment: —

Foul and terrible, the creature before you has no set form. It constantly melts and reforms, apparently drawing each shape from every nightmare that has ever plagued humankind. It chaotically shifts through a dozen monstrous forms before shaping itself into a bulbous thing with ten eyes swimming in a viscous sac at the top of a body that's surrounded by a ring of smacking mouths.

The horrific creatures known as chaos beasts have mutable, ever-changing forms. Their deadly touch can make opponents melt into formless goo.

There's no telling what a chaos beast will look like. One moment it might be a towering horror of hooks and fangs, all pulpy flesh and exposed veins, and the next a slithering mass of ropy, vermilion-tipped tentacles. Then it become a mighty creature, all muscle and fury A chaos beast's dimensions vary, but it always weighs about 200 pounds.

Chaos beasts do not speak.

COMBAT

How many different attacks can a creature capable of any form have? In this case, only two.

For all its fearsome appearances, whether it has claws, fangs, pincers, tentacles, or spines, a chaos beast does little physical harm. Regardless of form, the creature seems unable to manage more than two attacks per round. Its continual transmutations prevent the coordination needed to do more.

A chaos beast's claw attacks, as well as any weapons it wields, are treated as chaotic-aligned for the purpose of overcoming damage reduction.

Corporeal Instability (Su): A blow from a chaos beast against a living creature can cause a terrible transformation. The creature must succeed on a DC 15 Fortitude save or become a spongy, amorphous mass. Unless the victim manages to control the effect (see below), its shape melts, flows, writhes, and boils. The save DC is Constitution-based.

An affected creature is unable to hold or use any item. Clothing, armor, rings, and helmets become useless. Large items worn or carried—armor, backpacks, even shirts—hamper more than help, reducing the victim's Dexterity score by 4. Soft or misshapen feet and legs reduce speed to 10 feet or one-quarter normal, whichever is less. Searing pain courses along the nerves, so strong that the victim cannot act coherently. The victim cannot cast spells or use magic items, and it attacks blindly, unable to distinguish friend from foe (–4 penalty on attack rolls and a 50% miss chance, regardless of the attack roll).

Each round the victim spends in an amorphous state causes 1 point of Wisdom drain from mental shock. If the victim's Wisdom score falls to 0, it becomes a chaos beast. A victim can regain its own shape by taking a standard action to attempt a DC 15 Charisma check (this check DC does not vary for a chaos beast with different Hit Dice or ability scores). A success reestablishes the creature's normal form for 1 minute. On a failure, the victim can still repeat this check each round until successful.

Corporeal instability is not a disease or a curse and so is hard to remove. A *shapechange* or *stoneskin* spell does not cure an afflicted creature but fixes its form for the duration of the spell. A *restoration*, *heal*, or *greater restoration* spell removes the affliction (a separate *restoration* is necessary to restore any drained points of Wisdom).

Immunity to Transformation (Ex): No mortal magic can permanently affect or fix a chaos beast's form. Effects such as polymorphing or petrification force the creature into a new shape, but at the start of its next turn it immediately returns to its mutable form as a free action.

Chaos beast

LOCKWOOD

CHIMERA

Large Magical Beast
Hit Dice: 9d10+27 (76 hp)
Initiative: +1
Speed: 30 ft. (6 squares), fly 50 ft. (poor)
Armor Class: 19 (−1 size, +1 Dex, +9 natural), touch 10, flat-footed 18
Base Attack/Grapple: +9/+17
Attack: Bite +12 melee (2d6+4)
Full Attack: Bite +12 melee (2d6+4) and bite +12 melee (1d8+4) and gore +12 melee (1d8+4) and 2 claws +10 melee (1d6+2)
Space/Reach: 10 ft./5 ft.
Special Attacks: Breath weapon
Special Qualities: Darkvision 60 ft., low-light vision, scent
Saves: Fort +9, Ref +7, Will +6
Abilities: Str 19, Dex 13, Con 17, Int 4, Wis 13, Cha 10
Skills: Hide +1*, Listen +9, Spot +9
Feats: Alertness, Hover, Iron Will, Multiattack
Environment: Temperate hills
Organization: Solitary, pride (3–5), or flight (6–13)
Challenge Rating: 7
Treasure: Standard
Alignment: Usually chaotic evil
Advancement: 10–13 HD (Large); 14–27 HD (Huge)
Level Adjustment: +2 (cohort)

This creature has the hindquarters of a big goat and the forequarters of a great lion. It has dragon wings and three heads: a horned goat, a maneless lion, and a fierce dragon.

The chimera is a bizarre predator that hunts on the ground and on the wing. It can defeat even the hardiest opponent with a flurry of claws and fangs.

A chimera is about 5 feet tall at the shoulder, nearly 10 feet long, and weighs about 4,000 pounds. A chimera's dragon head might be black, blue, green, red, or white.

Chimeras can speak Draconic but seldom bother to do so, except when toadying to more powerful creatures.

COMBAT

A deadly foe, the chimera prefers to surprise prey. It often swoops down from the sky or lies concealed until it charges. The dragon head can loose a breath weapon instead of biting. Several chimeras attack in concert.

Breath Weapon (Su): A chimera's breath weapon depends on the color of its dragon head, as summarized on the table below.

Chimera

Regardless of its type, a chimera's breath weapon is usable once every 1d4 rounds, deals 3d8 points of damage, and allows a DC 17 Reflex save for half damage. The save DC is Constitution-based.

To determine a chimera's head color and breath weapon randomly, roll 1d10 and consult the table below.

1d10	Head Color	Breath Weapon
1–2	Black	40-foot line of acid
3–4	Blue	40-foot line of lightning
5–6	Green	20-foot cone of gas (acid)
7–8	Red	20-foot cone of fire
9–10	White	20-foot cone of cold

Skills: A chimera's three heads give it a +2 racial bonus on Spot and Listen checks.

*In areas of scrubland or brush, a chimera gains a +4 racial bonus on Hide checks.

Carrying Capacity: A light load for a chimera is up to 348 pounds; a medium load, 349–699 pounds, and a heavy load, 700–1,050 pounds.

CHOKER

Small Aberration
Hit Dice: 3d8+3 (16 hp)
Initiative: +6
Speed: 20 ft. (4 squares), climb 10 ft.
Armor Class: 17 (+1 size, +2 Dex, +4 natural), touch 13, flat-footed 15
Base Attack/Grapple: +2/+5
Attack: Tentacle +6 melee (1d3+3)
Full Attack: 2 tentacles +6 melee (1d3+3)
Space/Reach: 5 ft./10 ft.
Special Attacks: Improved grab, constrict 1d3+3
Special Qualities: Darkvision 60 ft., quickness
Saves: Fort +2, Ref +5, Will +4
Abilities: Str 16, Dex 14, Con 13, Int 4, Wis 13, Cha 7
Skills: Climb +13, Hide +10, Move Silently +6
Feats: Improved Initiative[B], Lightning Reflexes, Stealthy
Environment: Underground
Organization: Solitary
Challenge Rating: 2
Treasure: 1/10 coins; 50% goods; 50% items
Alignment: Usually chaotic evil
Advancement: 4–6 HD (Small); 7–12 HD (Medium)
Level Adjustment: —

A creature perches in the shadows, near the ceiling, in a corner of the chamber. Its body resembles that of a naked halfling with mottled flesh, but its limbs are incredibly spindly and long. It hisses, showing sharp, large teeth an instant before one of its limbs snaps out like a whip.

These vicious little predators lurk underground, grabbing whatever prey happens by.

A choker's skull, spine, and rib cage are bony, but its limbs are really tentacles with multiple knobby joints of cartilage. Thus, it appears bowlegged, and its movements seem peculiar and fluid. Its hands and feet have spiny pads that help the choker grip almost any surface. The creature weighs about 35 pounds. Chokers speak Undercommon.

COMBAT

A choker likes to perch near the ceiling, often at intersections, archways, wells, or staircases, and reach down to attack its prey.

A choker attacks creatures of almost any size, but prefers lone prey of its size or larger. If one is very hungry, it may attack a group, but it waits to grab the last creature in line.

Illus. by C. Critchlow

Chokers are greedy. Quick-thinking characters who spot one before it attacks might be able to bribe a choker with food and question it about the area around its lair.

Constrict (Ex): A choker deals 1d3+3 points of damage with a successful grapple check against a Large or smaller creature. Because it seizes its victim by the neck, a creature in the choker's grasp cannot speak or cast spells with verbal components.

Improved Grab (Ex): To use this ability, a choker must hit a Large or smaller opponent with a tentacle attack. It can then attempt to start a grapple as a free action without provoking an attack of opportunity. If it wins the grapple check, it establishes a hold and can constrict. Chokers receive a +4 racial bonus on grapple checks, which is already included in the statistics block.

Quickness (Su): Although not particularly dexterous, a choker is supernaturally quick. It can take an extra standard action or move action during its turn each round.

Skills: A chokers has a +8 racial bonus on Climb checks and can always choose to take 10 on Climb checks, even if rushed or threatened.

Choker

Chuul illus. by D. Knutson

Like some large insect or *monstrous crustacean, the creature rises from the still pool, its pincerlike claws snapping angrily as torchlight reflects off its mottled, armored carapace. Its small dark eyes fix you with a hungry stare, and the tentacles dripping from its mouth squirm excitedly as it emerges from the water.*

A horrible mix of crustacean, insect, and serpent, the chuul is an abomination that lurks submerged or partially submerged, awaiting intelligent prey to devour.

Although amphibious, chuuls are not good swimmers and actually prefer to be on land or in very shallow water when they attack. They love to prey on lizardfolk. Chuuls are known to collect trophies from their kills. Although unable to use weapons, armor, or most other belongings, chuuls keep these items in their lairs. If a victim has no interesting possessions, the chuul takes its skull.

Most chuuls live in swamps and jungles, but some have adapted to subterranean life, hunting in and near underground streams and lakes. These underground varieties often prey on troglodytes and unwary drow. They are sometimes found as thralls of beholders or mind flayers.

A chuul is about 8 feet long and weighs 650 pounds.

Chuuls speak Common (or Undercommon, for the underground variety).

CHUUL

Large Aberration (Aquatic)
Hit Dice: 11d8+44 (93 hp)
Initiative: +7
Speed: 30 ft. (6 squares), swim 20 ft.
Armor Class: 22 (–1 size, +3 Dex, +10 natural), touch 12, flat-footed 19
Base Attack/Grapple: +8/+17
Attack: Claw +12 melee (2d6+5)
Full Attack: 2 claws +12 melee (2d6+5)
Space/Reach: 10 ft./5 ft.
Special Attacks: Constrict 3d6+5, improved grab, paralytic tentacles
Special Qualities: Amphibious, darkvision 60 ft., immunity to poison
Saves: Fort +7, Ref +6, Will +9
Abilities: Str 20, Dex 16, Con 18, Int 10, Wis 14, Cha 5
Skills: Hide +13, Listen +11, Spot +11, Swim +13
Feats: Alertness, Blind-Fight, Combat Reflexes, Improved Initiative
Environment: Temperate marshes
Organization: Solitary, pair, or pack (3–5)
Challenge Rating: 7
Treasure: 1/10th coins; 50% goods; standard items
Alignment: Usually chaotic evil
Advancement: 12–16 HD (Large); 17–33 HD (Huge)
Level Adjustment: —

Chuul

COMBAT

A chuul prefers to wait by the shore, submerged in murky water, until it hears nearby prey (in or out of the water) that it can attack with surprise.

A chuul grabs with its claws and constricts its foe, then passes the opponent to its paralytic tentacles. It tries to always have one claw free, so if it faces a large number of opponents, it drops a paralyzed or dead victim and continues attempting to grab, constrict, and paralyze the rest.

Constrict (Ex): On a successful grapple check, a chuul deals 3d6+5 points of damage.

Improved Grab (Ex): To use this ability, a chuul must hit with a claw attack. It can then attempt to start a grapple as a free action without provoking an attack of opportunity. If it wins the grapple check, it establishes a hold and can constrict or on its next turn transfer a grabbed opponent to its tentacles.

Paralytic Tentacles (Ex): A chuul can transfer grabbed victims from a claw to its tentacles as a move action. The tentacles grapple with the same strength as the claw but deal no damage. However, they exude a paralytic secretion. Anyone held in the tentacles must succeed on a DC 19 Fortitude save each round on the chuul's turn or be paralyzed for 6 rounds. The save DC is Constitution-based. While held in the tentacles, paralyzed or not, a victim automatically takes 1d8+2 points of damage each round from the creature's mandibles.

Amphibious (Ex): Although chuuls are aquatic, they can survive indefinitely on land.

Skills: A chuul has a +8 racial bonus on any Swim check to perform some special action or avoid a hazard. It can always choose to take 10 on a Swim check, even if distracted or endangered. It can use the run action while swimming, provided it swims in a straight line.

CLOAKER

Large Aberration

Hit Dice: 6d8+18 (45 hp)
Initiative: +7
Speed: 10 ft. (2 squares), fly 40 ft. (average)
Armor Class: 19 (–1 size, +3 Dex, +7 natural), touch 12, flat-footed 16
Base Attack/Grapple: +4/+13
Attack: Tail slap +8 melee (1d6+5)
Full Attack: Tail slap +8 melee (1d6+5) and bite +3 melee (1d4+2)
Space/Reach: 10 ft./10 ft. (5 ft. with bite)
Special Attacks: Moan, engulf
Special Qualities: Darkvision 60 ft., shadow shift
Saves: Fort +5, Ref +5, Will +7
Abilities: Str 21, Dex 16, Con 17, Int 14, Wis 15, Cha 15
Skills: Hide +8, Listen +13, Move Silently +12, Spot +13
Feats: Alertness, Combat Reflexes, Improved Initiative
Environment: Underground
Organization: Solitary, mob (3–6), or flock (7–12)
Challenge Rating: 5
Treasure: Standard
Alignment: Usually chaotic neutral
Advancement: 7–9 HD (Large); 10–18 HD (Huge)
Level Adjustment: —

A long black cloak hangs from the cave wall. Suddenly, the cloak slips from the wall and catches a breeze moving through the cavern. Then it unfolds, the cloak becoming dark wings and a bony, whiplike tail unfurling to stretch out behind it. It flies forward, revealing a toothy maw and piercing red eyes deep in the shadows of its raylike body.

Cloakers are bizarre creatures that lurk in dark places far beneath the surface. They kill intruders without remorse or pause, except to plan cruel amusement.

When resting or lying in wait, these creatures are almost impossible to distinguish from common black cloaks (the cloaker's ivory claws look very much like bone clasps). Only when it unfurls does the horrific nature of the creature become apparent.

Cloakers pursue their own mysterious goals. While they are certainly intelligent, their minds work in a way so alien that few humans have ever been able to make meaningful contact with one.

Cloaker

A cloaker has a wingspan of about 8 feet. It weighs about 100 pounds.

Cloakers speak Undercommon.

COMBAT

Cloakers usually lie still, watching and listening for prey. If facing a single opponent, a cloaker uses its engulf attack. Against multiple foes, it lashes with its tail in concert with its moan and shadow shift abilities to reduce the opposition's numbers, then engulfs a survivor. Multiple cloakers usually split up, leaving one or two behind to use special abilities while the rest make melee attacks.

Moan (Ex): A cloaker can emit a dangerous subsonic moan as a standard action. By changing the frequency, the cloaker can cause one of four effects. Cloakers are immune to these sonic, mind-affecting attacks. Unless otherwise specified, a creature that successfully saves against one of these effects cannot be affected by the same moan effect from the same cloaker for 24 hours. All save DCs for moan effects are Charisma-based.

Unnerve: Anyone within a 60-foot spread automatically takes a –2 penalty on attack and damage rolls. Those forced to hear the moan for more than 6 consecutive rounds must succeed on a DC 15 Will save or enter a trance, unable to attack or defend themselves until the moaning stops.

Fear: Anyone within a 30-foot spread must succeed on a DC 15 Will save or become panicked for 2 rounds.

Nausea: Anyone in a 30-foot cone must succeed on a DC 15 Fortitude save or be overcome by nausea and weakness. Affected characters fall prone and become nauseated for 1d4+1 rounds.

Stupor: A single creature within 30 feet of the cloaker must succeed on a DC 15 Fortitude save or be affected as though by a *hold monster* spell for 5 rounds. Even after a successful save, the creature must repeat the save if the cloaker uses this effect again.

Engulf (Ex): A cloaker can try to wrap a Medium or smaller creature in its body as a standard action. The cloaker attempts a grapple that does not provoke an attack of opportunity. If it wins the grapple check, it establishes a hold and bites the engulfed victim with a +4 bonus on its attack roll. It can still use its whiplike tail to strike at other targets.

Attacks that hit an engulfing cloaker deal half their damage to the monster and half to the trapped victim.

Shadow Shift (Su): A cloaker can manipulate shadows. This ability is effective only in shadowy areas and has three possible effects.

Obscure Vision: The cloaker gains concealment (20% miss chance) for 1d4 rounds.

Dancing Images: This effect duplicates a *mirror image* spell (caster level 6th).

Silent Image: This effect duplicates a *silent image* spell (DC 15, caster level 6th). The save DC is Charisma-based.

Illus. by T. Lockwood

COCKATRICE

Small Magical Beast
Hit Dice: 5d10 (27 hp)
Initiative: +3
Speed: 20 ft. (4 squares), fly 60 ft. (poor)
Armor Class: 14 (+1 size, +3 Dex), touch 14, flat-footed 11
Base Attack/Grapple: +5/−1
Attack: Bite +9 melee (1d4−2 plus petrification)
Full Attack: Bite +9 melee (1d4−2 plus petrification)
Space/Reach: 5 ft./5 ft.
Special Attacks: Petrification
Special Qualities: Darkvision 60 ft., low-light vision
Saves: Fort +4, Ref +7, Will +2
Abilities: Str 6, Dex 17, Con 11, Int 2, Wis 13, Cha 9
Skills: Listen +7, Spot +7
Feats: Alertness, Dodge, Weapon Finesse[B]
Environment: Temperate plains
Organization: Solitary, pair, flight (3–5), or flock (6–13)
Challenge Rating: 3
Treasure: None
Alignment: Always neutral
Advancement: 6–8 HD (Small); 9–15 HD (Medium)
Level Adjustment: —

This avian creature is about the size of a large goose or turkey. It has the head and body of a cockerel, bat wings, and the long tail of a lizard. Its eyes glow with a dangerous-looking crimson sheen.

The cockatrice is an eerie, repulsive hybrid. It is infamous for its ability to turn flesh to stone.

A male cockatrice has wattles and a comb, just like a rooster. Females, much rarer than males, differ only in that they have no wattles or comb. A cockatrice weighs about 25 pounds.

COMBAT

A cockatrice fiercely attacks anything that it deems a threat to itself or its lair. Flocks of cockatrices do their utmost to overwhelm and confuse their foes, and sometimes fly directly into their opponents' faces.

Petrification (Su): Creatures hit by a cockatrice's bite attack must succeed on a DC 12 Fortitude save or instantly turn to stone. The save DC is Constitution-based.

Cockatrices have immunity to the petrification ability of other cockatrices, but other petrification attacks affect them normally (a medusa's gaze, gorgon's breath, a *flesh to stone* spell, or the like).

Cockatrice

COUATL

Large Outsider (Native)
Hit Dice: 9d8+18 (58 hp)
Initiative: +7
Speed: 20 ft. (4 squares), fly 60 ft. (good)
Armor Class: 21 (−1 size, +3 Dex, +9 natural), touch 12, flat-footed 18
Base Attack/Grapple: +9/+17
Attack: Bite +12 melee (1d3+6 plus poison)
Full Attack: Bite +12 melee (1d3+6 plus poison)
Space/Reach: 10 ft./5 ft.
Special Attacks: Constrict 2d8+6, improved grab, poison, psionics, spells
Special Qualities: Darkvision 60 ft., ethereal jaunt, telepathy 90 ft.
Saves: Fort +8, Ref +9, Will +10
Abilities: Str 18, Dex 16, Con 14, Int 17, Wis 19, Cha 17
Skills: Concentration +14, Diplomacy +17, Jump +0, Knowledge (any two) +15, Listen +16, Search +15, Sense Motive +16, Spellcraft +15 (+17 scrolls), Spot +16, Survival +4 (+6 following tracks), Tumble +15, Use Magic Device +15 (+17 scrolls)
Feats: Dodge, Empower Spell, Eschew Materials[B], Hover, Improved Initiative
Environment: Warm forests
Organization: Solitary, pair, or flight (3–6)
Challenge Rating: 10
Treasure: Standard
Alignment: Always lawful good
Advancement: 10–13 HD (Large); 14–27 HD (Huge)
Level Adjustment: +7

This great serpent with rainbow-feathered wings appears confident, powerful, and totally aware of everything around it.

The couatl is legendary for its sheer beauty, vast magical powers, and unwavering virtue. Its intelligence and goodness have made it an object of reverence in the regions it inhabits.

A couatl is about 12 feet long, with a wingspan of about 15 feet. It weighs about 1,800 pounds.

Couatls speak Celestial, Common, and Draconic, and also have the power of telepathy (see below).

COMBAT

A couatl seldom attacks without provocation, though it always attacks evildoers caught red-handed. It uses its *detect thoughts* ability on any creature that arouses its suspicions. Since it is highly intelligent, a couatl usually casts spells from a distance before closing. If more than one couatl is involved, they discuss their strategy before a battle.

Constrict (Ex): A couatl deals 2d8+6 points of damage with a successful grapple check.

Improved Grab (Ex): To use this ability, a couatl must hit a creature of up to two size categories larger with its bite attack. It can then attempt to start a grapple as a free action without provoking an attack of opportunity. If it wins the grapple check, it establishes a hold and can constrict.

Poison (Ex): Injury, Fortitude DC 16, initial damage 2d4 Str, secondary damage 4d4 Str. The save DC is Constitution-based.

Psionics (Sp): At will—*detect chaos, detect evil, detect good, detect law, detect thoughts* (DC 15), *invisibility, plane shift* (DC 20), *polymorph* (self only). Effective caster level 9th. The save DCs are Charisma-based.

Spells: A couatl casts spells as a 9th-level sorcerer. It can choose its spells known from the sorcerer list, the cleric list, and from the lists for the Air, Good, and Law domains. The cleric spells and domain spells are considered arcane spells for a couatl, meaning that the creature does not need a divine focus to cast them.

Typical Spells Known (6/7/7/7/4; save DC 13 + spell level): 0—*cure minor wounds, daze, disrupt undead, light, obscuring mist, ray of frost, read magic, resistance;* 1st—*endure elements, mage armor, protection from chaos, true strike, wind wall;* 2nd—*cure moderate wounds, eagle's splendor, scorching ray, silence;* 3rd—*gaseous form, magic circle against evil, summon monster III;* 4th—*charm monster, freedom of movement.*

Ethereal Jaunt (Su): This ability works like the *ethereal jaunt* spell (caster level 16th).

Telepathy (Su): A couatl can communicate telepathically with any creature within 90 feet that has an Intelligence score. The creature can respond to the couatl if it wishes—no common language is needed.

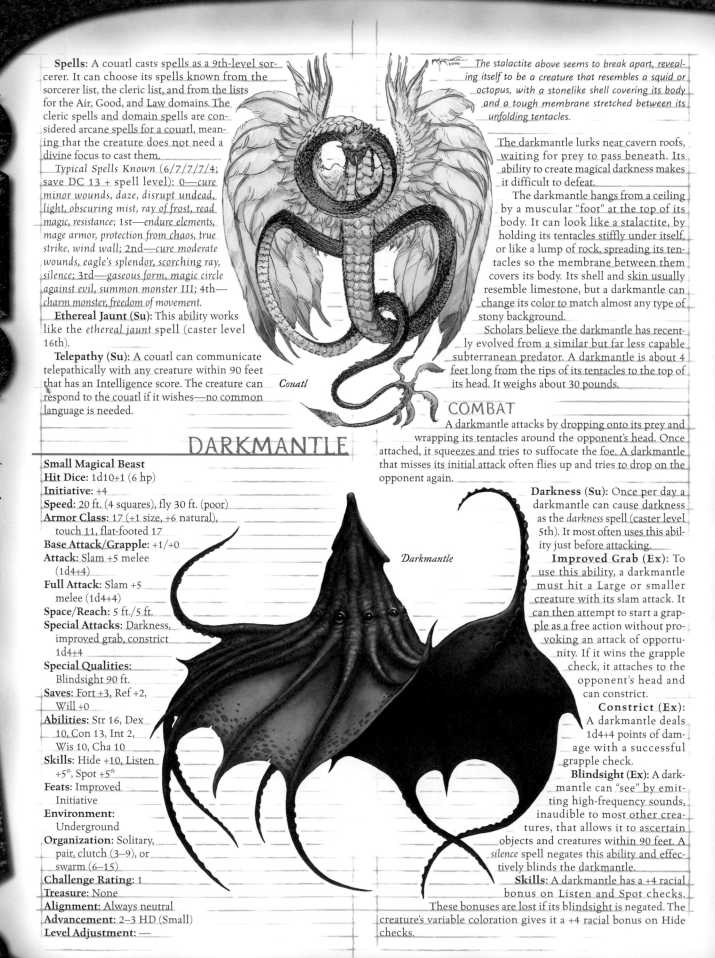

Couatl

The stalactite above seems to break apart, revealing itself to be a creature that resembles a squid or octopus, with a stonelike shell covering its body and a tough membrane stretched between its unfolding tentacles.

The darkmantle lurks near cavern roofs, waiting for prey to pass beneath. Its ability to create magical darkness makes it difficult to defeat.

The darkmantle hangs from a ceiling by a muscular "foot" at the top of its body. It can look like a stalactite, by holding its tentacles stiffly under itself, or like a lump of rock, spreading its tentacles so the membrane between them covers its body. Its shell and skin usually resemble limestone, but a darkmantle can change its color to match almost any type of stony background.

Scholars believe the darkmantle has recently evolved from a similar but far less capable subterranean predator. A darkmantle is about 4 feet long from the tips of its tentacles to the top of its head. It weighs about 30 pounds.

COMBAT

A darkmantle attacks by dropping onto its prey and wrapping its tentacles around the opponent's head. Once attached, it squeezes and tries to suffocate the foe. A darkmantle that misses its initial attack often flies up and tries to drop on the opponent again.

DARKMANTLE

Small Magical Beast
Hit Dice: 1d10+1 (6 hp)
Initiative: +4
Speed: 20 ft. (4 squares), fly 30 ft. (poor)
Armor Class: 17 (+1 size, +6 natural), touch 11, flat-footed 17
Base Attack/Grapple: +1/+0
Attack: Slam +5 melee (1d4+4)
Full Attack: Slam +5 melee (1d4+4)
Space/Reach: 5 ft./5 ft.
Special Attacks: Darkness, improved grab, constrict 1d4+4
Special Qualities: Blindsight 90 ft.
Saves: Fort +3, Ref +2, Will +0
Abilities: Str 16, Dex 10, Con 13, Int 2, Wis 10, Cha 10
Skills: Hide +10, Listen +5*, Spot +5*
Feats: Improved Initiative
Environment: Underground
Organization: Solitary, pair, clutch (3–9), or swarm (6–15)
Challenge Rating: 1
Treasure: None
Alignment: Always neutral
Advancement: 2–3 HD (Small)
Level Adjustment: —

Darkmantle

Darkness (Su): Once per day a darkmantle can cause darkness as the *darkness* spell (caster level 5th). It most often uses this ability just before attacking.

Improved Grab (Ex): To use this ability, a darkmantle must hit a Large or smaller creature with its slam attack. It can then attempt to start a grapple as a free action without provoking an attack of opportunity. If it wins the grapple check, it attaches to the opponent's head and can constrict.

Constrict (Ex): A darkmantle deals 1d4+4 points of damage with a successful grapple check.

Blindsight (Ex): A darkmantle can "see" by emitting high-frequency sounds, inaudible to most other creatures, that allows it to ascertain objects and creatures within 90 feet. A *silence* spell negates this ability and effectively blinds the darkmantle.

Skills: A darkmantle has a +4 racial bonus on Listen and Spot checks. These bonuses are lost if its blindsight is negated. The creature's variable coloration gives it a +4 racial bonus on Hide checks.

DELVER

Huge Aberration
Hit Dice: 15d8+78 (145 hp)
Initiative: +5
Speed: 30 ft. (6 squares), burrow 10 ft.
Armor Class: 24 (–2 size, +1 Dex, +15 natural), touch 9, flat-footed 23
Base Attack/Grapple: +11/+27
Attack: Slam +17 melee (1d6+8 plus 2d6 acid)
Full Attack: 2 slams +17 melee (1d6+8 plus 2d6 acid)
Space/Reach: 15 ft./10 ft.
Special Attacks: Corrosive slime
Special Qualities: Darkvision 60 ft., immunity to acid, stone shape, tremorsense 60 ft.
Saves: Fort +12, Ref +6, Will +11
Abilities: Str 27, Dex 13, Con 21, Int 14, Wis 14, Cha 12
Skills: Knowledge (dungeoneering) +14, Knowledge (nature) +4, Listen +20, Move Silently +17, Spot +20, Survival +14 (+16 underground)
Feats: Alertness, Blind-Fight, Great Fortitude, Improved Initiative, Power Attack, Toughness
Environment: Underground
Organization: Solitary
Challenge Rating: 9
Treasure: None
Alignment: Usually neutral
Advancement: 16–30 HD (Huge); 31–45 HD (Gargantuan)
Level Adjustment: —

A huge creature burrows through the solid rock wall. Its teardrop-shaped, rocky body glistens with slime, and it uses the blunt claws of its two great appendages to clear away the debris.

The delver is a bizarre creature that lives in the depths of the earth, burrowing through solid stone with the help of a corrosive slime it secretes from its rocklike skin.

Delvers are shy and mostly inoffensive, but rogue specimens with murderous streaks are not unknown. They feed on stone and may even devour creatures such as xorns and earth elementals. A delver burrowing through stone leaves behind a usable tunnel about 10 feet in diameter.

The slime covering a delver's body is highly corrosive. The creature feeds by dissolving rock with its slime and shoving the resulting goo under its body, the underside of which is almost all mouth.

A delver eats rock but enjoys various nonmetallic minerals as seasonings in the same way that a human enjoys spices. Adventurers might secure information and assistance from a delver by offering it tasty minerals (usually gems) or pick-me-ups (such as coins). Metal is an intoxicant to delvers. Some delvers become addicted to metal and are a menace to miners and anyone who carries metal equipment.

A delver is about 15 feet long and 10 feet wide. It weighs about 6,000 pounds.

Delvers speak Terran and Undercommon.

COMBAT

A delver prefers to fight from its tunnel, which it uses to protect its flanks while lashing out with its flippers.

A delver expecting trouble may honeycomb an area with tunnels, leaving most closed with layers of stone 1 or 2 inches thick. The delver can quickly dissolve the stone cover and pop up to attack unexpectedly.

Corrosive Slime (Ex): A delver produces a mucuslike slime that contains a highly corrosive substance. The slime is particularly effective against stone.

A delver's mere touch deals 2d6 points of acid damage to organic creatures or objects. Against metallic creatures or objects, a delver's slime deals 4d8 points of damage, and against stony creatures (including earth elementals) or objects it deals 8d10 points of damage. A slam attack by a delver leaves a patch of slime that deals 2d6 points of damage on contact and another 2d6 points of damage in each of the next 2 rounds. A large quantity (at least a quart) of water or weak acid, such as vinegar, washes off the slime.

An opponent's armor and clothing dissolve and become useless immediately unless the wearer succeeds on a DC 22 Reflex save. Weapons that strike a delver also dissolve immediately unless the wielder succeeds on a DC 22 Reflex save.

A creature attacking a delver with natural weapons takes damage from its slime each time an attack hits unless the creature succeeds on a DC 22 Reflex save. These save DCs are Constitution-based.

Stone Shape (Ex): A delver can alter its slime to temporarily soften stone instead of dissolving it. Once every 10 minutes, a delver can soften and shape up to 25 cubic feet of stone, as a *stone shape* spell (caster level 15th).

Delver

DEMON

Demons are a race of creatures native to the Abyss, a plane of endless evil. They are ferocity personified and will attack any creature just for the sheer fun of it—even other demons. They enjoy terrifying their victims before slaying them and often devour the slain. Many demons, not satisfied with their own iniquity, take pleasure in tempting mortals to become as depraved as they are.

A number of demons belong to a race (and subtype) known as the tanar'ri. The tanar'ri form the largest and most diverse group of demons, and they are the unchallenged masters of the Abyss.

Tanar'ri Traits: A tanar'ri possesses the following traits (unless otherwise noted in a creature's entry).

—Immunity to electricity and poison.

—Resistance to acid 10, cold 10, and fire 10.

—*Summon* (Sp): Tanar'ri share the ability to summon others of their kind (the success chance and type of tanar'ri summoned are noted in each monster description). However, between their arrogance and disdain for owing favors to one another, tanar'ri are often reluctant to use this power until in obvious peril or extreme circumstances.

—Telepathy.

Except where otherwise noted, demons speak Abyssal, Celestial, and Draconic.

BABAU

Medium Outsider (Chaotic, Extraplanar, Evil, Tanar'ri)
Hit Dice: 7d8+35 (66 hp)
Initiative: +1
Speed: 30 ft. (6 squares)
Armor Class: 19 (+1 Dex, +8 natural), touch 11, flat-footed 18
Base Attack/Grapple: +7/+12
Attack: Claw +12 melee (1d6+5)
Full Attack: 2 claws +12 melee (1d6+5) and bite +7 melee (1d6+2)
Space/Reach: 5 ft./5 ft.
Special Attacks: Sneak attack +2d6, spell-like abilities, *summon tanar'ri*
Special Qualities: Damage reduction 10/cold iron or good, darkvision 60 ft., immunity to electricity and poison, protective slime, resistance to acid 10, cold 10, and fire 10, spell resistance 14, telepathy 100 ft.
Saves: Fort +10, Ref +6, Will +6
Abilities: Str 21, Dex 12, Con 20, Int 14, Wis 13, Cha 16
Skills: Climb +15, Disable Device +12, Disguise +13, Escape Artist +11, Hide +19, Listen +19, Move Silently +19, Open Lock +11, Search +20, Sleight of Hand +11, Survival +1 (+3 following tracks), Use Rope +1 (+3 with bindings)
Feats: Cleave, Multiattack, Power Attack
Environment: Infinite Layers of the Abyss
Organization: Solitary or gang (3–6)
Challenge Rating: 6
Treasure: Standard
Alignment: Always chaotic evil
Advancement: 8–14 HD (Large); 15–21 HD (Huge)
Level Adjustment: —

Reeking of decay, this gaunt humanoid is covered in black, leathery skin. Behind its pointed ears, a large curved horn rises out of the back of its skull. A mouth of jagged teeth takes up half of the foul creature's head.

Babaus serve as assassins that strike with a sudden ferocity. They are devious, forming careful plans before going into plans—always making sure that they do not have to engage in a fair fight. Almost every demon lord has a number of babaus employed as spies and killers.

A babau is about 6 feet tall and weighs about 140 pounds.

Combat

Babaus are sneaky and sly. They attack the most powerful foe first, hoping to eliminate the true threats quickly and then toy with the rest. When ambushing their opponents, they make excellent use of the combination of multiple attacks and sneak attacks.

A babau's natural weapons, as well as any weapons it wields, are treated as chaotic-aligned and evil-aligned for the purpose of overcoming damage reduction.

Sneak Attack (Ex): A babau can make a sneak attack like a rogue, dealing an extra 2d6 points of damage whenever a foe is denied his or her Dexterity bonus, or when the babau is flanking.

Spell-Like Abilities: At will—*darkness, dispel magic, see invisibility, greater teleport* (self plus 50 pounds of objects only). Caster level 7th.

Protective Slime (Su): A slimy red jelly coats the babau's skin. Any weapon that touches it takes 1d8 points of acid damage from the corrosive goo, and the weapon's hardness does not reduce this damage. A magic weapon may attempt a DC 18 Reflex save to avoid taking this damage. A creature who strikes the babau with an unarmed attack, unarmed strike, touch spell, or natural weapon takes this damage as well but can negate the damage with a DC 18 Reflex save. The save DCs are Constitution-based.

Summon Tanar'ri (Sp): Once per day a babau can attempt to summon 1 babau with a 40% chance of success. This ability is the equivalent of a 3rd-level spell.

Skills: Babaus have a +8 racial bonus on Hide, Listen, Move Silently, and Search checks.

BALOR

Large Outsider (Chaotic, Extraplanar, Evil, Tanar'ri)
Hit Dice: 20d8+200 (290 hp)
Initiative: +11
Speed: 40 ft. (8 squares), fly 90 ft. (good)
Armor Class: 35 (–1 size, +7 Dex, +19 natural), touch 16, flat-footed 28
Base Attack/Grapple: +20/+36
Attack: +1 *vorpal longsword* +33 melee (2d6+8/19–20)
Full Attack: +1 *vorpal longsword* +31/+26/+21/+16 melee (2d6+8/19–20) and +1 *flaming whip* +30/+25 melee (1d4+4 plus 1d6 fire plus entangle); or 2 slams +31 melee (1d10+7)
Space/Reach: 10 ft./10 ft. (20 ft. with +1 *flaming whip*)
Special Attacks: Death throes, entangle, spell-like abilities, *summon tanar'ri, vorpal sword*
Special Qualities: Damage reduction 15/cold iron and good, darkvision 60 ft., flaming body, immunity to electricity, fire, and poison, resistance to acid 10 and cold 10, spell resistance 28, telepathy 100 ft., true seeing
Saves: Fort +22, Ref +19, Will +19
Abilities: Str 35, Dex 25, Con 31, Int 24, Wis 24, Cha 26
Skills: Bluff +31, Concentration +33, Diplomacy +35, Disguise +8 (+10 acting), Hide +26, Intimidate +33, Knowledge (any two) +30, Listen +38, Move Silently +30, Search +30, Sense Motive +30, Spellcraft +30 (+32 scrolls), Spot +38, Survival +7 (+9 following tracks), Use Magic Device +31 (+33 scrolls)
Feats: Cleave, Improved Initiative, Improved Two-Weapon Fighting, Power Attack, Quicken Spell-Like Ability (*telekinesis*), Two-Weapon Fighting, Weapon Focus (longsword)
Environment: Infinite Layers of the Abyss
Organization: Solitary or troupe (1 balor, 1 marilith, and 2–5 hezrous)
Challenge Rating: 20
Treasure: Standard coins; double goods; standard items, plus +1 *vorpal greatsword* and +1 *flaming whip*
Alignment: Always chaotic evil
Advancement: 21–30 HD (Large); 31–60 HD (Huge)
Level Adjustment: —

Balor

Marilith

A dark aura of power surrounds this towering humanoid with huge bat wings. Lurid flames dance over its skin. In one of its massive clawed hands, this creature bears a sword that looks sharp enough to cut even to the soul. In its other hand, it bears a whip licked by tongues of fire.

Balors stand among the greatest and most terrible of the underworld creatures. They rule as generals over demonic armies. They are the masterminds of schemes to seize power and destroy the innocent. Even among their own kind, balors are feared, as they motivate their kindred to spread terror and misery.

A balor stands about 12 feet tall. Its skin is usually dark red. It weighs about 4,500 pounds.

Combat

Balors love to join battle armed with their swords and whips. If they face stiff resistance, they may teleport away to loose a few spell-like effects at the foe.

A balor's +1 *flaming whip* is a long, flexible weapon with many tails tipped with hooks, spikes, and balls. The weapon deals bludgeoning and slashing damage, in addition to fire damage.

A balor's natural weapons, as well as any weapons it wields, are treated as chaotic-aligned and evil-aligned for the purpose of overcoming damage reduction.

Death Throes (Ex): When killed, a balor explodes in a blinding flash of light that deals 100 points of damage to anything within 100 feet (Reflex DC 30 half). This explosion automatically destroys any weapons the balor is holding. The save DC is Constitution-based.

Entangle (Ex): A balor's +1 *flaming whip* entangles foes much like an attack with a net. The whip has 20 hit points. The whip needs no folding. If it hits, the target and the balor immediately make opposed Strength checks; if the balor wins, it drags the target against its flaming body (see below). The target remains anchored against the balor's body until it escapes the whip.

Spell-Like Abilities: At will—*blasphemy* (DC 25), *dominate monster* (DC 27), *greater dispel magic, greater teleport* (self plus 50 pounds of objects only), *insanity* (DC 25), *power word stun, telekinesis* (DC 23), *unholy aura* (DC 26); 1/day—*fire storm* (DC 26), *implosion* (DC 27). Caster level 20th. The save DCs are Charisma-based.

Vorpal Sword (Su): Every balor carries a +1 *vorpal longsword* that looks like a flame or a bolt of lightning.

Summon Tanar'ri (Sp): Once per day a balor can automatically summon 4d10 dretches, 1d4 hezrous, or one nalfeshnee, glabrezu, marilith, or balor. This ability is the equivalent of a 9th-level spell.

Flaming Body (Su): The body of a balor is wreathed in flame. Anyone grappling a balor takes 6d6 points of fire damage each round.

True Seeing (Su): Balors have a continuous true seeing ability, as the spell (caster level 20th).

Skills: Balors have a +8 racial bonus on Listen and Spot checks.

Tactics Round-by-Round

The balor is most effective as a ranged combatant, using its spell-like abilities to attack from a distance.

Prior to combat: Unholy aura.

Round 1: Fire storm or implosion and quickened telekinesis, or summon additional demons. If the balor does not deem itself seriously threatened, it conserves abilities usable only once per day and uses blasphemy instead.

Round 2: Insanity or power word stun.

DEMONS BY CHALLENGE RATING

A quick overview of the demons that follow over the next few pages:

CR 2	Dretch	Petty demon that attacks in mobs.
CR 2	Quasit	Clever imp that aids evil mortals.
CR 6	Babau	Tall, gaunt assassin with teeth.
CR 7	Succubus	Seductive temptress that can take many forms.
CR 9	Vrock	Savage, vulturelike warrior that delights in battle.
CR 10	Bebilith	Hulking spiderlike horror that hunts demons and mortals both.
CR 11	Hezrou	Froglike demon with incapacitating stench and the goal of tempting mortals to ruin.
CR 11	Retriever	Demonic spiderlike construct with deadly eye rays.
CR 13	Glabrezu	Towering giant demon that tempts mortals with power.
CR 14	Nalfeshnee	Bloated apelike judge of the damned, with a deadly smite ability.
CR 17	Marilith	Six-armed serpent demon queen, general of abyssal battalions.
CR 20	Balor	Mighty fire-demon lord with a vorpal sword and terrifying spell-like abilities.

Illus. by D. Knutson

Round 3: Full melee attack with weapons, including entangle with whip.

Round 4: Teleport or fly away with entangled foe to reestablish range; repeat round 1 and continue.

A balor who wants to drive off or neutralize a party without slaying its foes avoids lethal attacks.

Prior to combat: Unholy aura.
Round 1: Dominate monster.
Round 2: Power word stun.
Round 3: Insanity or *telekinesis* to incapacitate or repel a dangerous opponent.
Round 4: Teleport or fly away to reestablish range; repeat round 1 and continue.

BEBILITH

Huge Outsider (Chaotic, Extraplanar, Evil)
Hit Dice: 12d8+96 (150 hp)
Initiative: +5
Speed: 40 ft. (8 squares), climb 20 ft.
Armor Class: 22 (–2 size, +1 Dex, +13 natural), touch 9, flat-footed 21
Base Attack/Grapple: +12/+29
Attack: Bite +19 melee (2d6+9 plus poison) or web +11 ranged
Full Attack: Bite +19 melee (2d6+9 plus poison) and 2 claws +14 melee (2d4+4); or web +11 ranged
Space/Reach: 15 ft./10 ft.
Special Attacks: Poison, rend armor, web
Special Qualities: Damage reduction 10/good, darkvision 60 ft., plane shift, scent, telepathy 100 ft.
Saves: Fort +16, Ref +9, Will +9
Abilities: Str 28, Dex 12, Con 26, Int 11, Wis 13, Cha 13
Skills: Climb +24, Diplomacy +3, Hide +16, Jump +28, Listen +16, Move Silently +16, Search +15, Sense Motive +16, Spot +16, Survival +1 (+3 following tracks)
Feats: Cleave, Improved Initiative, Improved Grapple, Power Attack, Track
Environment: Infinite Layers of the Abyss
Organization: Solitary
Challenge Rating: 10
Treasure: None
Alignment: Always chaotic evil
Advancement: 13–18 HD (Huge); 19–36 HD (Gargantuan)
Level Adjustment: —

An enormous, misshapen spider stalks out of the darkness. Its forelegs end in wicked barbs, and globs of foul goo drip from its fanged mouth.

Bebiliths are enormous, predatory, arachnid demons that hunt other demons. While they favor preying upon other demons, they aren't picky—they will stalk and attack any type of creature.

A bebilith has a body the size of a plow horse, with legs spanning more than 14 feet. It weighs more than two tons.

Bebiliths understand but do not speak Abyssal. Their telepathy allows them to communicate silently with one another.

COMBAT

A bebilith attacks any creature it sees. It usually picks one target and concentrates its attacks on that opponent, using its webs to isolate the target from its comrades. Should the bebilith become overwhelmed by tougher opponents, it often attempts to bite one or more of its victims and retreats, allowing its poison to do its work.

Bebilith

A bebilith's natural weapons, as well as any weapons it wields, are treated as chaotic-aligned and evil-aligned for the purpose of overcoming damage reduction.

Poison (Ex): Injury, Fortitude DC 24, initial damage 1d6 Con, secondary damage 2d6 Con.

Bebilith venom is highly perishable, losing its potency and becoming inert, foul-smelling goo almost as soon as it comes into contact with air. The save DC is Constitution-based.

Rend Armor (Ex): If a bebilith hits with both claw attacks, it pulls apart any armor worn by its foe. This attack deals 4d6+18 points of damage to the opponent's armor. Creatures not wearing armor are unaffected by this special attack. Armor reduced to 0 hit points is destroyed. Damaged armor may be repaired with a successful Craft (armorsmithing) check.

Web (Ex): A bebilith can throw a web up to four times per day. This is similar to an attack with a net but has a maximum range of 30 feet, with a range increment of 10 feet. This attack is effective against targets of up to Gargantuan size. The web anchors the target in place, allowing no movement.

An entangled creature can escape with a DC 24 Escape Artist check or burst the web with a DC 24 Strength check. The check DCs are Constitution-based. The web has 14 hit points and hardness 0. There is a 75% chance that the webbing will not burn if any sort of fire is applied to it (check each round).

Plane Shift (Su): This ability affects only the bebilith. It is otherwise similar to the spell (caster level 12th).

Skills: A bebilith has mottled coloration that gives it a +8 racial bonus on Hide checks.

DRETCH

Small Outsider (Chaotic, Extraplanar, Evil, Tanar'ri)
Hit Dice: 2d8+4 (13 hp)
Initiative: +0
Speed: 20 ft. (4 squares)
Armor Class: 16 (+1 size, +5 natural), touch 11, flat-footed 16
Base Attack/Grapple: +2/–1
Attack: Claw +4 melee (1d6+1)
Full Attack: 2 claws +4 melee (1d6+1) and bite +2 melee (1d4)
Space/Reach: 5 ft./5 ft.
Special Attacks: Spell-like abilities, *summon tanar'ri*
Special Qualities: Damage reduction 5/cold iron or good, darkvision 60 ft., immunity to electricity and poison, resistance to acid 10, cold 10, and fire 10, telepathy 100 ft.
Saves: Fort +5, Ref +3, Will +3
Abilities: Str 12, Dex 10, Con 14, Int 5, Wis 11, Cha 11
Skills: Hide +9, Listen +5, Move Silently +5, Spot +5, Search +2, Survival +0 (+2 following tracks)
Feats: Multiattack
Environment: Infinite Layers of the Abyss
Organization: Solitary, pair, gang (3–5), crowd (6–15), or mob (10–40)
Challenge Rating: 2
Treasure: None
Alignment: Always chaotic evil

Advancement: 3–6 HD (Small)
Level Adjustment: +2

This humanoid-looking *creature has a squat and blubbery, almost hairless body, with pale, sickly flesh and a slack mouth full of small fangs.*

Dretches are pathetic but wicked creatures that spend most of their time milling about in mobs or serving as rank-and-file troops in tanar'ri armies.

A dretch is about 4 feet tall and weighs about 60 pounds.

Dretches cannot speak but can communicate telepathically.

Combat

Dretches are slow, stupid, and not very effective combatants. In one-on-one combat, they rely on their damage reduction to keep them alive. In groups, they depend on sheer numbers to overcome foes and immediately summon other dretches to improve the odds in battle. They flee at the first sign of adversity unless more powerful demons are present to intimidate them into fighting. Dretches' fear of their greater kin is stronger then even their fear of death.

A dretch's natural weapons, as well as any weapons it wields, are treated as chaotic-aligned and evil-aligned for the purpose of overcoming damage reduction.

Spell-Like Abilities: 1/day—*scare* (DC 12), *stinking cloud* (DC 13). Caster level 2nd. The save DCs are Charisma-based.

Summon Tanar'ri (Sp): Once per day a dretch can attempt to summon another dretch with a 35% chance of success. This ability is the equivalent of a 1st-level spell.

Telepathy (Su): Dretches can communicate telepathically with creatures within 100 feet that speak Abyssal.

GLABREZU

Huge Outsider (Chaotic, Extraplanar, Evil, Tanar'ri)
Hit Dice: 12d8+120 (174 hp)
Initiative: +0
Speed: 40 ft. (8 squares)
Armor Class: 27 (–2 size, +19 natural) touch 8, flat-footed 27
Base Attack/Grapple: +12/+30
Attack: Pincers +20 melee (2d8+10)
Full Attack: 2 pincers +20 melee (2d8+10) and 2 claws +18 melee (1d6+5) and bite +18 melee (1d8+5)
Space/Reach: 15 ft./15 ft.
Special Attacks: Improved grab, spell-like abilities, *summon tanar'ri*
Special Qualities: Damage reduction 10/good, darkvision 60 ft., immunity to electricity and poison, resistance to acid 10, cold 10, and fire 10, spell resistance 21, telepathy 100 ft., true seeing
Saves: Fort +18, Ref +8, Will +11
Abilities: Str 31, Dex 10, Con 31, Int 16, Wis 16, Cha 20
Skills: Bluff +22, Concentration +25, Diplomacy +9, Disguise +5 (+7 acting), Intimidate +24, Knowledge (any two) +18, Listen +26, Move Silently +18, Search +18, Sense Motive +18, Spellcraft +18, Spot +26, Survival +3 (+5 following tracks)
Feats: Cleave, Great Cleave, Multiattack, Persuasive, Power Attack
Environment: Infinite Layers of the Abyss
Organization: Solitary or troupe (1 glabrezu, 1 succubus, and 2–5 vrocks)

Challenge Rating: 13
Treasure: Standard coins; double goods; standard items
Alignment: Always chaotic evil
Advancement: 13–18 HD (Huge); 19–36 HD (Gargantuan)
Level Adjustment: —

This creature is as tall as a giant, with a broad, muscular body. Its four arms end in weapons—two with clawed hands, two with powerful pincers. Its doglike head is topped with horns, and its muzzle drips with sharp fangs. Its eyes have a cold, dark, penetrating quality that suggests cunning and intelligence.

Like succubi, glabrezu tempt victims into ruin, but they lure their prey with power or wealth rather than passion.

Glabrezu have penetrating violet eyes, and their skin color ranges from deep russet to pitch black. A glabrezu stands about 15 feet tall and weighs about 5,500 pounds.

Combat

Glabrezu prefer subterfuge to combat. However, if their attempts to entice or deceive fail, these enormous demons attack with a vengeance. They follow a *confusion* attack with melee attacks, hoping to finish off wounded foes with *chaos hammer* or *unholy blight.*

A glabrezu's natural weapons, as well as any weapons it wields, are treated as chaotic-aligned and evil-aligned for the purpose of overcoming damage reduction.

Hezrou

Babau

Dretch

Improved Grab (Ex): To use this ability, a glabrezu must hit a Medium or smaller opponent with a pincer attack. It can then attempt to start a grapple as a free action without provoking an attack of opportunity.

Spell-Like Abilities: At will—*chaos hammer* (DC 19), *confusion* (DC 19), *dispel magic, mirror image, reverse gravity* (DC 22), *greater teleport* (self plus 50 pounds of objects only), *unholy blight* (DC 19); 1/day—*power word stun.* Caster level 14th. The save DCs are Charisma-based.

Once per month, a glabrezu can fulfill a *wish* for a mortal humanoid. The demon can use this ability to offer a mortal whatever he or she desires—but unless the *wish* is used to create pain and suffering in the world, the glabrezu demands either terrible evil acts or great sacrifice as compensation.

Summon Tanar'ri **(Sp):** Once per day a glabrezu can attempt to summon 4d10 dretches or 1d2 vrocks with a 50% chance of success, or another glabrezu with a 20% chance of success. This ability is the equivalent of a 4th-level spell.

True Seeing (Su): Glabrezu continuously use true seeing as the spell (caster level 14th).

Skills: Glabrezu have a +8 racial bonus on Listen and Spot checks.

HEZROU

Large Outsider (Chaotic, Extraplanar, Evil, Tanar'ri)
Hit Dice: 10d8+93 (138 hp)
Initiative: +0
Speed: 30 ft. (6 squares)
Armor Class: 23 (−1 size, +14 natural) touch 9, flat-footed 23
Base Attack/Grapple: +10/+19
Attack: Bite +14 melee (4d4+5)
Full Attack: Bite +14 melee (4d4+5) and 2 claws +9 melee (1d8+2)
Space/Reach: 10 ft./10 ft.
Special Attacks: Spell-like abilities, stench, improved grab, *summon tanar'ri*
Special Qualities: Damage reduction 10/good, darkvision 60 ft., immunity to electricity and poison, resistance to acid 10, cold 10, and fire 10, spell resistance 19, telepathy 100 ft.
Saves: Fort +16, Ref +7, Will +9
Abilities: Str 21, Dex 10, Con 29, Int 14, Wis 14, Cha 18
Skills: Climb +18, Concentration +22, Hide +13, Escape Artist +13, Intimidate +17, Listen +23, Move Silently +13, Search +15, Spellcraft +15, Spot +23, Survival +2 (+4 following tracks), Use Rope +0 (+2 with bindings)
Feats: Blind-Fight, Cleave, Power Attack, Toughness
Environment: Infinite Layers of the Abyss
Organization: Solitary or gang (2–4)
Challenge Rating: 11
Treasure: Standard
Alignment: Always chaotic evil
Advancement: 11–15 HD (Large); 16–30 HD (Huge)
Level Adjustment: +9

This creature looks like a massive, roughly humanoid toad with arms in place of forelegs. Its wide mouth has rows of blunt, powerful teeth, and long spines run down the length of its back.

Hezrou are demonic sergeants, overseeing the formation of armies and commanding units in battle. They don't have the scheming instincts of the more powerful demons, but hezrou are cunning in battle.

A hezrou can walk both upright and on all fours, but it always fights standing up.

A hezrou is about 8 feet tall and weighs about 750 pounds.

Combat

Hezrous enjoy melee combat even more than vrocks do. They eagerly press an attack deep into the heart of enemy forces, so their stench can take effect as quickly as possible. They enter most battles by using *blasphemy,* and follow it with an occasional *chaos hammer* or *unholy blight,* depending on the alignment of their opponents.

A hezrou's natural weapons, as well as any weapons it wields, are treated as chaotic-aligned and evil-aligned for the purpose of overcoming damage reduction.

Improved Grab (Ex): To use this ability, a hezrou must hit with both claw attacks. It can then attempt to start a grapple as a free action without provoking an attack of opportunity.

Spell-Like Abilities: At will—*chaos hammer* (DC 18), *greater teleport* (self plus 50 pounds of objects only), *unholy blight* (DC 18); 3/day—*blasphemy* (DC 21), *gaseous form.* Caster level 13th. The save DCs are Charisma-based.

Stench (Ex): A hezrou's skin produces a foul-smelling, toxic liquid whenever it fights. Any living creature (except other demons) within 10 feet must succeed on a DC 24 Fortitude save or be nauseated for as long as it remains within the affected area and for 1d4 rounds afterward. Creatures that successfully save are sickened for as long as they remain in the area. A creature that successfully saves cannot be affected again by the same hezrou's stench for 24 hours. A *delay poison* or *neutralize poison* spell removes either condition from one creature. Creatures that have immunity to poison are unaffected, and creatures resistant to poison receive their normal bonus on their saving throws.. The save DC is Constitution-based.

Summon Tanar'ri **(Sp):** Once per day a hezrou can attempt to summon 4d10 dretches or another hezrou with a 35% chance of success. This ability is the equivalent of a 4th-level spell.

Skills: Hezrous have a +8 racial bonus on Listen and Spot checks.

MARILITH

Large Outsider (Chaotic, Extraplanar, Evil, Tanar'ri)
Hit Dice: 16d8+144 (216 hp)
Initiative: +4
Speed: 40 ft. (8 squares)
Armor Class: 29 (−1 size, +4 Dex, +16 natural), touch 13, flat-footed 25
Base Attack/Grapple: +16/+29
Attack: Longsword +25 melee (2d6+9/19–20) or slam +24 melee (1d8+9) or tail slap +24 melee (4d6+9)
Full Attack: Primary longsword +25/+20/+15/+10 melee (2d6+9/19–20) and 5 longswords +25 melee (2d6+4/19–20) and tail slap +22 melee (4d6+4); or 6 slams +24 melee (1d8+9) and tail slap +22 melee (4d6+4)
Space/Reach: 10 ft./10 ft.
Special Attacks: Constrict 4d6+13, improved grab, spell-like abilities, *summon tanar'ri*
Special Qualities: Damage reduction 10/good and cold iron, darkvision 60 ft., immunity to electricity and poison, resistance to acid 10, cold 10, and fire 10, spell resistance 25, telepathy 100 ft.
Saves: Fort +19, Ref +14, Will +14
Abilities: Str 29, Dex 19, Con 29, Int 18, Wis 18, Cha 24
Skills: Bluff +26, Concentration +28, Diplomacy +30, Disguise +7 (+9 acting), Hide +19, Intimidate +28, Listen +31, Move Silently +23, Search 23, Sense Motive +23, Spellcraft +23 (+25 scrolls), Spot +31, Survival +4 (+6 following tracks), Use Magic Device +26 (+28 scrolls)
Feats: Combat Expertise, Combat Reflexes, Multiattack, Multiweapon Fighting, Power Attack, Weapon Focus (longsword)
Environment: Infinite Layers of the Abyss
Organization: Solitary or pair
Challenge Rating: 17
Treasure: Standard coins; double goods; standard items, plus 1d4 magic weapons
Alignment: Always chaotic evil
Advancement: 17–20 HD (Large); 21–48 HD (Huge)
Level Adjustment: —

This large, otherworldly entity appears to be an attractive female human with six arms—at least from her head to her waist. From the waist down, the creature has the body of a massive snake with green, scaly coils.

Mariliths are generals and tacticians, often rivaling balors in sheer brilliance and cunning. Some also serve as chief lieutenants for major demon royalty.

A marilith usually holds a longsword in each of its six hands and wears many bangles and jewels.

A marilith stands about 9 feet tall and measures about 20 feet from head to tip of tail. It weighs about 4,000 pounds.

Combat

Though mariliths thrive on grand strategy and army-level tactics, they love physical combat and never pass up an opportunity to fight. Each of a marilith's six arms can wield a weapon, and the creature gets an additional three weapon attacks with its primary arm. Mariliths seldom rush headlong into battle, however, preferring to hang back and size up the situation first. They always seek to gain the best possible advantage from the local terrain, obstacles, and any vulnerability or weakness in their opponents.

A marilith's natural weapons, as well as any weapons it wields, are treated as chaotic-aligned and evil-aligned for the purpose of overcoming damage reduction.

Constrict (Ex): A marilith deals 4d6+13 points of damage with a successful grapple check. The constricted creature must succeed on a DC 27 Fortitude save or lose consciousness for as

Nalfeshnee

Quasit

Succubus

long as it remains in the coils and for 2d4 rounds thereafter. The save DC is Strength-based.

Improved Grab (Ex): To use this ability, a marilith must hit with its tail slap attack. It can then attempt to start a grapple as a free action without provoking an attack of opportunity. If it succeeds on the grapple check, it can constrict.

Spell-Like Abilities: At will—*align weapon, blade barrier* (DC 23), *magic weapon, project image* (DC 23), *polymorph, see invisibility, telekinesis* (DC 22), *greater teleport* (self plus 50 pounds of objects only), *unholy aura* (DC 25). Caster level 16th. The save DCs are Charisma-based.

Summon Tanar'ri (Sp): Once per day a marilith can attempt to summon 4d10 dretches, 1d4 hezrou, or one nalfeshnee with a 50% chance of success, or one glabrezu or another marilith with a 20% chance of success. This ability is the equivalent of a 5th-level spell.

True Seeing (Su): Mariliths continuously use this ability, as the spell (caster level 16th).

Skills: Mariliths have a +8 racial bonus on Listen and Spot checks.

Feats: In combination with its natural abilities, a marilith's Multiweapon Fighting feat allows it to attack with all its arms at no penalty.

NALFESHNEE

Huge Outsider (Chaotic, Extraplanar, Evil, Tanar'ri)
Hit Dice: 14d8+112 (175 hp)
Initiative: +1
Speed: 30 ft. (6 squares), fly 40 ft. (poor)
Armor Class: 27 (−2 size, +1 Dex, +18 natural) touch 9, flat-footed 26
Base Attack/Grapple: +14/+29
Attack: Bite +20 melee (2d8+7)
Full Attack: Bite +20 melee (2d8+7) and 2 claws +17 melee (1d8+3)
Space/Reach: 15 ft./15 ft.
Special Attacks: Smite, spell-like abilities, *summon tanar'ri*
Special Qualities: Damage reduction 10/good, darkvision 60 ft., immunity to electricity and poison, resistance to acid 10, cold 10, and fire 10, spell resistance 22, telepathy 100 ft., true seeing
Saves: Fort +17, Ref +10, Will +15
Abilities: Str 25, Dex 13, Con 27, Int 22, Wis 22, Cha 20
Skills: Bluff +22, Concentration +25, Diplomacy +26, Disguise +5 (+7 acting), Hide +10, Intimidate +22, Knowledge (arcana) +23, Listen +31, Move Silently +18, Search +23, Sense Motive +23, Spellcraft +25 (+27 scrolls), Spot +31, Survival +6 (+8 following tracks), Use Magic Device +22 (+24 scrolls)
Feats: Cleave, Improved Bull Rush, Multiattack, Power Attack, Weapon Focus (bite)
Environment: Infinite Layers of the Abyss
Organization: Solitary or troupe (1 nalfeshnee, 1 hezrou, and 2–5 vrocks)
Challenge Rating: 14
Treasure: Standard coins; double goods; standard items
Alignment: Always chaotic evil
Advancement: 15–20 HD (Huge); 21–42 HD (Gargantuan)
Level Adjustment: —

This creature is a grotesque blending of an ape and a corpulent boar. It stands on its hind legs, rising to more than three times the height of a human. It has a pair of feathered wings that seem ridiculously small compared to the rest of its body.

These enormous demons await the arrival of doomed souls into the Abyss, where the nalfeshnees can judge them. Of course, nalfeshnees relish the chance to begin the punishment of the damned.

A nalfeshnee can fly despite its small wings.

A nalfeshnee is more than 20 feet tall and weighs 8,000 pounds.

Combat

When fulfilling their duties in the underworld, nalfeshnees usually disdain combat as being beneath them. Given the opportunity, they succumb to blood lust and do battle. They disable opponents with their smite ability and slaughter them while they can't fight back.

A nalfeshnee's natural weapons, as well as any weapons it wields, are treated as chaotic-aligned and evil-aligned for the purpose of overcoming damage reduction.

Smite (Su): Three times per day a nalfeshnee can create a nimbus of unholy light. When the demon triggers the ability, rainbow-colored beams play around its body. One round later they burst in a 60-foot radius. Any creature within this area must succeed on a DC 22 Will save or be dazed for 1d10 rounds as visions of its worst fears hound it. The creature receives its full Dexterity and shield bonuses to AC if attacked but can take no actions. Other demons are immune to this effect. The save DC is Charisma-based.

Spell-Like Abilities: At will—*call lightning* (DC 18), *feeblemind* (DC 20), *greater dispel magic*, *slow* (DC 18), *greater teleport* (self plus 50 pounds of objects only), *unholy aura* (DC 23). Caster level 12th. The save DCs are Charisma-based.

Summon Tanar'ri (Sp): Twice per day a nalfeshnee can attempt to summon 1d4 vrocks, 1d4 hezrous, or one glabrezu with a 50% chance of success, or another nalfeshnee with a 20% chance of success. This ability is the equivalent of a 5th-level spell.

True Seeing (Su): Nalfeshnees continuously use *true seeing*, as the spell (caster level 14th).

Skills: Nalfeshnees have a +8 racial bonus on Listen and Spot checks.

QUASIT

Tiny Outsider (Chaotic, Extraplanar, Evil)
Hit Dice: 3d8 (13 hp)
Initiative: +7
Speed: 20 ft. (4 squares), fly 50 ft. (perfect)
Armor Class: 18 (+2 size, +3 Dex, +3 natural), touch 15, flat-footed 15
Base Attack/Grapple: +3/–6
Attack: Claw +8 melee (1d3–1 plus poison)
Full Attack: 2 claws +8 melee (1d3–1 plus poison) and bite +3 melee (1d4–1)
Space/Reach: 2-1/2 ft./0 ft.
Special Attacks: Poison, spell-like abilities
Special Qualities: Alternate form, damage reduction 5/cold iron or good, darkvision 60 ft., fast healing 2, immunity to poison, resistance to fire 10
Saves: Fort +3, Ref +6, Will +4
Abilities: Str 8, Dex 17, Con 10, Int 10, Wis 12, Cha 10
Skills: Bluff +6, Diplomacy +2, Disguise +0 (+2 acting), Hide +17, Intimidate +2, Knowledge (any one) +6, Listen +7, Move Silently +9, Search +6, Spellcraft +6, Spot +6
Feats: Improved Initiative, Weapon Finesse
Environment: Infinite Layers of the Abyss
Organization: Solitary
Challenge Rating: 2

Treasure: None
Alignment: Always chaotic evil
Advancement: 4–6 HD (Tiny)
Level Adjustment: — (Improved Familiar)

A tiny humanoid-shaped creature with spiky horns and bat wings hovers nearby. Its hands and feet are long and slender, with long, claw-tipped digits. Warts or pustules cover its greenish skin.

Quasits are insidious demons from the Abyss. They are often found serving chaotic evil spellcasters as counselors and spies.

In its natural form, a quasit stands about 1-1/2 feet tall and weighs about 8 pounds.

Quasits speak Common and Abyssal.

Combat

Although quasits thirst for victory and power as other demons do, they are cowards at heart. They typically attack from ambush, using their alternate form ability and *invisibility* to get within reach, then try to scuttle away. When retreating, they use their *cause fear* ability to deter pursuit.

A quasit's natural weapons, as well as any weapons it wields, are treated as chaotic-aligned and evil-aligned for the purpose of overcoming damage reduction.

Poison (Ex): Injury, Fortitude DC 13, initial damage 1d4 Dex, secondary damage 2d4 Dex. The save DC is Constitution-based and includes a +2 racial bonus.

Spell-Like Abilities: At will—*detect good, detect magic,* and *invisibility* (self only); 1/day—*cause fear* (as the spell, except that its area is a 30-foot radius from the quasit, save DC 11). Caster level 6th. The save DCs are Charisma-based.

Once per week a quasit can use *commune* to ask six questions. The ability otherwise works as the spell (caster level 12th).

Alternate Form (Su): A quasit can assume other forms at will as a standard action. This ability functions as a *polymorph* spell cast on itself (caster level 12th), except that a quasit does not regain hit points for changing form, and any individual quasit can assume only one or two forms no larger than Medium. Common forms include bat, monstrous centipede, toad, and wolf. A quasit in alternate form loses its poison attack.

RETRIEVER

Huge Construct (Extraplanar)
Hit Dice: 10d10+80 (135 hp)
Initiative: +3
Speed: 50 ft. (10 squares)
Armor Class: 21 (–2 size, +3 Dex, +10 natural), touch 11, flat-footed 18
Base Attack/Grapple: +7/+25
Attack: Claw +15 melee (2d6+10) and eye ray +8 ranged touch
Full Attack: 4 claws +15 melee (2d6+10) and bite +10 melee (1d8+5) and eye ray +8 ranged touch
Space/Reach: 15 ft./10 ft.
Special Attacks: Eye rays, *find target*, improved grab
Special Qualities: Construct traits, darkvision 60 ft., fast healing 5, low-light vision
Saves: Fort +3, Ref +6, Will +3
Abilities: Str 31, Dex 17, Con —, Int —, Wis 11, Cha 1
Skills: —
Feats: —
Environment: Infinite Layers of the Abyss
Organization: Solitary
Challenge Rating: 11
Treasure: None
Alignment: Always chaotic evil
Advancement: 11–15 HD (Huge); 16–30 HD (Gargantuan)
Level Adjustment: —

Retriever

This creature looks like an enormous spider, standing twice as tall as a human. Its forelegs end in massive cleavers. Four bulbous eyes, a malevolent gleam in each one, rise out of its carapace.

A retriever specializes in recovering lost or desired objects, runaway slaves, and enemies and bringing them back to its master. Retrievers were created through foul sorcery to be warriors and servants to powerful demon nobles. Most scholars believe retrievers are built to resemble bebiliths. More powerful demons often use these mindless constructs to perform ugly tasks, or tasks they could not trust to their own scheming kind.

A retriever has a body the size of an ox, with legs spanning more than 14 feet. It weighs about 6,500 pounds.

Combat

Retrievers attack with four claws, but their eye rays are far more deadly.

Eye Rays (Su): A retriever's eyes can produce four different magical rays with a range of 100 feet. Each round, it can fire one ray as a free action. A particular ray is usable only once every 4 rounds. A retriever can fire an eye ray in the same round that it makes physical attacks. The save DC for all rays is 18. The save DC is Dexterity-based.

The four eye effects are:

Fire: Deals 12d6 points of fire damage to the target (Reflex half).
Cold: Deals 12d6 points of cold damage to the target (Reflex half).
Electricity: Deals 12d6 points of electricity damage to the target (Reflex half).
Petrification: The target must succeed on a Fortitude save or turn to stone permanently.

Find Target (Sp): When ordered to find an item or a creature, a retriever does so unerringly, as though guided by *discern location*. The being giving the order must have seen (or must have an item belonging to) the creature to be found, or must have touched the object to be located. This ability is the equivalent of an 8th-level spell.

Improved Grab (Ex): To use this ability, a retriever must hit with its bite attack. It can then attempt to start a grapple as a free action without provoking an attack of opportunity. If it wins the grapple check, it establishes a hold and grips the opponent fast in its mouth. This is the method by which it usually "retrieves" things.

SUCCUBUS

Medium Outsider (Chaotic, Extraplanar, Evil, Tanar'ri)
Hit Dice: 6d8+6 (33 hp)
Initiative: +1
Speed: 30 ft. (6 squares), fly 50 ft. (average)
Armor Class: 20 (+1 Dex, +9 natural), touch 11, flat-footed 19
Base Attack/Grapple: +6/+7
Attack: Claw +7 melee (1d6+1)
Full Attack: 2 claws +7 melee (1d6+1)
Space/Reach: 5 ft./5 ft.
Special Attacks: Energy drain, spell-like abilities, *summon tanar'ri*
Special Qualities: Damage reduction 10/cold iron or good, darkvision 60 ft., immunity to electricity and poison, resistance to acid 10, cold 10, and fire 10, spell resistance 18, telepathy 100 ft., tongues
Saves: Fort +6, Ref +6, Will +7
Abilities: Str 13, Dex 13, Con 13, Int 16, Wis 14, Cha 26
Skills: Bluff +19, Concentration +10, Diplomacy +12, Disguise +17* (+19 acting), Escape Artist +10, Hide +10, Intimidate +19, Knowledge (any one) +12, Listen +19, Move Silently +10, Search +12, Spot +19, Survival +2 (+4 following tracks), Use Rope +1 (+3 with bindings)
Feats: Dodge, Mobility, Persuasive
Environment: Infinite Layers of the Abyss
Organization: Solitary
Challenge Rating: 7
Treasure: Standard
Alignment: Always chaotic evil
Advancement: 7–12 HD (Medium)
Level Adjustment: +6

This creature is stunning, statuesque, and extraordinarily beautiful, with flawless skin and raven hair. Her form, so tempting, also has an otherworldly side. Large bat wings unfurl from her back, and her eyes glow with sinister desire.

Succubi are the most comely of the tanar'ri (perhaps of all demons), and they live to tempt mortals.

A succubus is 6 feet tall in its natural form and weighs about 125 pounds.

Combat

Succubi are not warriors. They flee combat whenever they can. If forced to fight, they can attack with their claws, but they prefer to turn foes against one another. Succubi use their *polymorph* ability to assume humanoid guise, and can maintain this deception indefinitely. Their preferred tactic when dealing with heroes is to feign friendship and create an opportunity to be alone with one of them, whereupon the succubus applies her life-draining kiss. Succubi are not above taking on the role of a damsel in distress when encountered within a dungeon.

A succubus's natural weapons, as well as any weapons it wields, are treated as chaotic-aligned and evil-aligned for the purpose of overcoming damage reduction.

Energy Drain (Su): A succubus drains energy from a mortal it lures into some act of passion, or by simply planting a kiss on the victim. If the target is not willing to be kissed, the succubus must start a grapple, which provokes an attack of opportunity. The succubus's kiss or embrace bestows one negative level. The kiss also has the effect of a *suggestion* spell, asking the victim to accept another kiss from the succubus. The victim must succeed on a DC 21 Will save to negate the effect of the *suggestion*. The DC is 21 for the Fortitude save to remove a negative level. These save DCs are Charisma-based.

Spell-Like Abilities: At will—*charm monster* (DC 22), *detect good*, *detect thoughts* (DC 20), *ethereal jaunt* (self plus 50 pounds of objects only), *polymorph* (humanoid form only, no limit on duration), *suggestion* (DC 21), *greater teleport* (self plus 50 pounds of objects only). Caster level 12th. The save DCs are Charisma-based.

Summon Tanar'ri (Sp): Once per day a succubus can attempt to summon 1 vrock with a 30% chance of success. This ability is the equivalent of a 3rd-level spell.

Tongues (Su): A succubus has a permanent tongues ability (as the spell, caster level 12th). Succubi usually use verbal communication with mortals.

Skills: Succubi have a +8 racial bonus on Listen and Spot checks.

*While using her *alter self* ability, a succubus gains a +10 circumstance bonus on Disguise checks.

Glabrezu

VROCK

Large Outsider (Chaotic, Extraplanar, Evil, Tanar'ri)
Hit Dice: 10d8+70 (115 hp)
Initiative: +2
Speed: 30 ft. (6 squares), fly 50 ft. (average)
Armor Class: 22 (–1 size, +2 Dex, +11 natural), touch 11, flat-footed 20
Base Attack/Grapple: +10/+20
Attack: Claw +15 melee (2d6+6)
Full Attack: 2 claws +15 melee (2d6+6) and bite +13 melee (1d8+3) and 2 talons +13 melee (1d6+3)
Space/Reach: 10 ft./10 ft.
Special Attacks: Dance of ruin, spell-like abilities, spores, stunning screech, *summon tanar'ri*
Special Qualities: Damage reduction 10/good, darkvision 60 ft., immunity to electricity and poison, resistance to acid 10, cold 10, and fire 10, spell resistance 17, telepathy 100 ft.
Saves: Fort +14, Ref +9, Will +10
Abilities: Str 23, Dex 15, Con 25, Int 14, Wis 16, Cha 16
Skills: Concentration +20, Diplomacy +5, Hide +11, Intimidate +16, Knowledge (any one) +15, Listen +24, Move Silently +15, Search +15, Sense Motive +16, Spellcraft +15, Spot +24, Survival +3 (+5 following tracks)
Feats: Cleave, Combat Reflexes, Multiattack, Power Attack
Environment: Infinite Layers of the Abyss
Organization: Solitary, pair, gang (3–5), or squad (6–10)
Challenge Rating: 9
Treasure: Standard
Alignment: Always chaotic evil
Advancement: 11–14 HD (Large); 15–30 HD (Huge)
Level Adjustment: +8

This creature looks like a cross between a large human and a huge vulture. It has strong, sinewy limbs covered with small gray feathers, a long neck topped with a vulture head, and vast feathered wings.

Vrocks serve as guards to more powerful demons and as flying assault troops in the abyssal wars.

A vrock is about 8 feet tall and weighs about 500 pounds.

Combat

Vrocks are vicious fighters who like to fly down into the enemy and cause as much damage as possible. They prance about in battle, taking briefly to the air and bringing their clawed feet into play. Despite their advantage in mobility, the vrocks' deep love of battle frequently leads them into melee combats against heavy odds.

A vrock's natural weapons, as well as any weapons it wields, are treated as chaotic-aligned and evil-aligned for the purpose of overcoming damage reduction.

Dance of Ruin (Su): To use this ability, a group of at least three vrocks must join hands in a circle, dancing wildly and chanting. At the end of 3 rounds of dancing, a wave of crackling energy flashes outward in a 100-foot radius. All creatures except for demons within the radius take 20d6 points of damage (Reflex DC 18 half). Stunning, paralyzing, or slaying one of the vrocks stops the dance. The save DC is Charisma-based.

Vrock

Spell-Like Abilities: At will—*mirror image*, *telekinesis* (DC 18), *greater teleport* (self plus 50 pounds of objects only); 1/day—*heroism*. Caster level 12th. The save DCs are Charisma-based.

Spores (Ex): A vrock can release masses of spores from its body once every 3 rounds as a free action. The spores automatically deal 1d8 points of damage to all creatures adjacent to the vrock. They then penetrate the skin and grow, dealing an additional 1d4 points of damage each round for 10 rounds. At the end of this time, the victim is covered with a tangle of viny growths. (The vines are harmless and wither away in 1d4 days.) A *delay poison* spell stops the spores' growth for its duration. *Bless*, *neutralize poison*, or *remove disease* kills the spores, as does sprinkling the victim with a vial of holy water.

Stunning Screech (Su): Once per hour a vrock can emit a piercing screech. All creatures except for demons within a 30-foot radius must succeed on a DC 22 Fortitude save or be stunned for 1 round. The save DC is Constitution-based.

Summon Tanar'ri (Sp): Once per day a vrock can attempt to summon 2d10 dretches or another vrock with a 35% chance of success. This ability is the equivalent of a 3rd-level spell.

Skills: Vrocks have a +8 racial bonus on Listen and Spot checks.

DERRO

Small Monstrous Humanoid
Hit Dice: 3d8+3 (16 hp)
Initiative: +6
Speed: 20 ft. (4 squares)
Armor Class: 19 (+1 size, +2 Dex, +2 natural, +3 studded leather armor, +1 buckler), touch 13, flat-footed 17
Base Attack/Grapple: +3/−1
Attack: Short sword +4 melee (1d4/19–20) or repeating light crossbow +6 ranged (1d6/19–20 plus poison)
Full Attack: Short sword +4 melee (1d4/19–20) or repeating light crossbow +6 ranged (1d6/19–20 plus poison)
Space/Reach: 5 ft./5 ft.
Special Attacks: Poison use, spell-like abilities, sneak attack +1d6
Special Qualities: Madness, spell resistance 15 vulnerability to sunlight
Saves: Fort +2, Ref +5, Will +6
Abilities: Str 11, Dex 14, Con 13, Int 10, Wis 5*, Cha 16*
Skills: Bluff +5, Hide +10, Listen +1, Move Silently +8
Feats: Blind-Fight, Improved Initiative
Environment: Underground
Organization: Team (2–4), squad (5–8 plus 1 3rd-level sorcerer), or band (11–20 plus 30% noncombatants plus 3 3rd-level sorcerers and 1 sorcerer of 5th–8th level)
Challenge Rating: 3
Treasure: Standard coins; double goods; standard items
Alignment: Usually chaotic evil
Advancement: By character class
Level Adjustment: — (+2 if sane)

A small, stocky dwarflike creature in studded leather armor titters and mumbles to himself. His skin is a pale blue-white color, and his bulbous white eyes have no irises or pupils. His hair is coarse and white, and a long mustache droops past his chin.

Derro are degenerate and evil creatures of the underground, created from dwarf and human stock by some nameless deity of darkness and madness. Incredibly cruel and murderously insane, they enjoy taking slaves and torturing surface dwellers (especially humans) to death.

Derro are afflicted by a form of racial madness, which most often manifests as delusions of grandeur coupled with an overpowering urge to inflict torment on other creatures. Derro are capable of holding their murderous impulses in check for short periods of time in order to cooperate with creatures of other races, but such arrangements rarely last more than a few weeks. Of course, no derro is capable of recognizing that he is out of his mind.

COMBAT

Derro are stealthy and bloodthirsty. They like to carefully arrange cruel traps and deadly ambushes, and strike savagely from hiding. They delight in taking captives who can be tortured to death later, and favor traps and poisons that disable without killing.

Madness (Ex): Derro use their Charisma modifier on Will saves instead of their Wisdom modifier, and have immunity to *confusion* and *insanity* effects. A derro cannot be restored to sanity by any means short of a *miracle* or *wish* spell.

*The racial madness of the derro provides a +6 bonus to their Charisma scores and a −6 penalty to their Wisdom scores. A derro restored to sanity gains 6 points of Wisdom and loses 6 points of Charisma.

Poison Use (Ex): Derro typically carry 2d4 doses of greenblood oil or Medium monstrous spider venom (see Poison, page 296 of the *Dungeon Master's Guide*), applying it to their crossbow bolts. Derro are not at risk of poisoning themselves when handling poison.

Sneak Attack (Ex): Any time a derro's opponent is denied his Dexterity bonus to AC, or if a derro flanks his opponent, he deals an extra 1d6 points of damage. This ability is just like the rogue's sneak attack and subject to the same limitations.

Spell-Like Abilities: At will—*darkness, ghost sound*; 1/day—*daze* (DC 13), *sound burst* (DC 15). Caster level 3rd. The save DCs are Charisma-based.

Vulnerability to Sunlight (Ex): A derro takes 1 point of Constitution damage for every hour it is exposed to sunlight, and it dies if its Constitution score reaches 0. Lost Constitution points are recovered at the rate of 1 per every 24-hour period spent underground or otherwise sheltered from the sun.

Skills: Derro have a +4 racial bonus on Hide and Move Silently checks.

DERRO CHARACTERS

Most derro revere Diirinka, a chaotic deity of magic and cruelty. Very few derro are clerics, but those who follow this path can choose two of the following domains: Chaos, Destruction, Evil, or Trickery.

The leaders of the derro are spellcasters called savants, whom other derro follow fanatically. Derro savants are at least 5th-level sorcerers; they have one to three Knowledge skills (usually arcana and other esoteric fields). A savant is accompanied by two lower-level students. Savants use their spells to confuse and frustrate rather than kill, preferring to make slaves of defeated foes.

DESTRACHAN

Large Aberration
Hit Dice: 8d8+24 (60 hp)
Initiative: +5
Speed: 30 ft. (6 squares)
Armor Class: 18 (−1 size, +1 Dex, +8 natural), touch 10, flat-footed 17
Base Attack/Grapple: +6/+14
Attack: Claw +9 melee (1d6+4)
Full Attack: 2 claws +9 melee (1d6+4)
Space/Reach: 10 ft./5 ft.
Special Attacks: Destructive harmonics
Special Qualities: Blindsight 100 ft., immunities, protection from sonics
Saves: Fort +5, Ref +5, Will +10
Abilities: Str 18, Dex 12, Con 16, Int 12, Wis 18, Cha 12
Skills: Hide +8, Listen +25, Move Silently +7, Survival +9
Feats: Dodge, Improved Initiative, Lightning Reflexes
Environment: Underground
Organization: Solitary or pack (3–5)
Challenge Rating: 8
Treasure: None
Alignment: Usually neutral evil
Advancement: 9–16 HD (Large); 17–24 HD (Huge)
Level Adjustment: —

The creature shambles forward on thick, taloned legs. Vaguely reptilian in form, its large, stooped frame ends in a mostly featureless head dominated by large ear structures and a gaping, toothless mouth.

The dungeon-dwelling destrachan looks like some bizarre, nonintelligent beast, but it's an incredibly evil and crafty sadist.

A destrachan has a pair of complex, three-part ears that it can adjust to be more or less sensitive to various sounds. It is blind, yet hunts with a sense of hearing more precise than most creatures' sight.

From its tubular mouth a destrachan emits carefully focused harmonics, producing sonic energy so powerful it can shatter a stone wall. So skilled is a destrachan at controlling the sounds it emits that it can choose what type of material to affect with its attack.

Destrachans feed on death and misery. They haunt inhabited underground complexes, spreading woe for evil's own sake. They can blast their way through stone well enough to travel beneath the surface as they wish. Sometimes a destrachan subdues its victims and brings them back to its lair for torture and imprisonment.

No living thing would ever willingly ally itself with this monster, although sometimes undead or evil outsiders accompany a destrachan as it attacks and slays other creatures.

A destrachan is about 10 feet long from its mouth to the tip of the tail and weighs about 4,000 pounds.

A destrachan speaks no language but understands Common. If a destrachan must communicate, it does so through action.

COMBAT

A destrachan uses its claws only as a last resort or to finish off foes weakened by its sonic attacks. It often enters battle with surprise if possible. It first focuses on destroying metal armor and weapons and then changes to harmonics that disrupt flesh.

Destructive Harmonics (Su): A destrachan can blast sonic energy in a cone up to 80 feet long. It can also use this attack to affect any creatures or objects within a 30-foot radius. It can tune the harmonics of this destructive power to affect different types of targets. All save DCs are Charisma-based.

Flesh: Disrupting tissue and rending bone, this attack deals 4d6

Destrachan

points of damage to all within the area (Reflex DC 15 half).

Nerves: A destrachan can focus its harmonics to knock out foes rather than slay them. This attack deals 6d6 points of nonlethal damage to all within the area (Reflex DC 15 half).

Material: When using this form of harmonics, a destrachan chooses wood, stone, metal, or glass. All objects made of that material within the area must succeed on a DC 15 Fortitude save or shatter. Objects (or portions of objects) that have up to 30 hit points are potentially affected by this attack.

Blindsight (Ex): A destrachan can use hearing to ascertain all foes within 100 feet as a sighted creature would.

Immunities: Destrachans have immunity to gaze attacks, visual effects, illusions, and other attack forms that rely on sight.

Protection from Sonics (Ex): While they can be affected by loud noises and sonic spells (such as *ghost sound* or *silence*), destrachans are less vulnerable to sonic attacks (+4 circumstance bonus on all saves) because they can protect their ears. A destrachan whose sense of hearing is impaired is effectively blinded, and all targets are treated as having total concealment.

Skills: A destrachan has a +10 racial bonus on Listen checks.

DEVIL

The scourge of humanity and the cosmos, devils are fiends from the Nine Hells of Baator, a lawful evil realm. Devils enjoy bullying those weaker than themselves and often attack good creatures just to gain a trophy or three. The most powerful devils occupy themselves with plots to seize power, wreck civilizations, and inflict misery upon mortals.

Many devils are surrounded by a fear aura, which they use to break up powerful groups and defeat opponents piecemeal. Devils with spell-like abilities use their illusion abilities to delude and confuse foes as much as possible. A favorite trick is to create illusory reinforcements; enemies can never be entirely sure if a threat is only a figment or real summoned devils joining the fray.

The most numerous devils are the baatezu, infamous for their strength, evil temperament, and ruthlessly efficient organization. Baatezu have a rigid caste system, in which authority derives not only from power but also from station. They occupy themselves mainly with extending their influence throughout the planes by corrupting mortals. Baatezu who further this goal are usually rewarded with improved stations.

Baatezu Traits: A baatezu possesses the following traits (unless otherwise noted in a creature's entry).
—Immunity to fire and poison.
—Resistance to acid 10 and cold 10.

DEVILS BY CHALLENGE RATING
A quick overview of the devils that follow over the next few pages:

CR 1	Lemure	Mindless, tormented creature that attacks in mobs.	CR 8	Erinyes	A fallen angel that delivers death from her fiery bow.
CR 2	Imp	Clever devil that aids evil mortals with dark counsel and trickery.	CR 9	Bone devil	Osyluth. Hateful fiend with a dangerous sting.
CR 5	Bearded devil	Barbazu. Ferocious warrior that frenzies with a saw-toothed glaive.	CR 11	Barbed devil	Hamatula. Elite infernal warrior with impaling spikes.
CR 6	Chain devil	Kyton. Murderous torturer with an infernal command of chains.	CR 13	Ice devil	Gelugon. Insectlike horror promising a cold death.
CR 7	Hellcat	Bezekira. Infernal, invisible catlike devil the size of a tiger.	CR 16	Horned devil	Cornugon. Gargoylelike fiend armed with a spiked chain.
			CR 20	Pit fiend	Lord of devils, with great strength and deadly power.

—See in Darkness (Su): All baatezu can see perfectly in darkness of any kind, even that created by a *deeper darkness* spell.

—Summon (Sp): Baatezu share the ability to summon others of their kind (the success chance and type of baatezu summoned are noted in each monster description).

—Telepathy.

Except when otherwise noted, devils speak Infernal, Celestial, and Draconic.

BARBED DEVIL (HAMATULA)
Medium Outsider (Baatezu, Evil, Extraplanar, Lawful)
Hit Dice: 12d8+72 (126 hp)
Initiative: +6
Speed: 30 ft. (6 squares)
Armor Class: 29 (+6 Dex, +13 natural) touch 16, flat-footed 23
Base Attack/Grapple: +12/+22
Attack: Claw +18 melee (2d8+6 plus fear)
Full Attack: 2 claws +18 melee (2d8+6 plus fear)
Space/Reach: 5 ft./5 ft.
Special Attacks: Fear, improved grab, impale 3d8+9, *summon baatezu*
Special Qualities: Barbed defense, damage reduction 10/good, darkvision 60 ft., immunity to fire and poison, resistance to acid 10 and cold 10, see in darkness, spell resistance 23, spell-like abilities, telepathy 100 ft.
Saves: Fort +14, Ref +14, Will +12
Abilities: Str 23, Dex 23, Con 23, Int 12, Wis 14, Cha 18
Skills: Concentration +21, Diplomacy +6, Hide +21, Intimidate +19, Knowledge (any one) +16, Listen +19, Move Silently +21, Search +16, Sense Motive +17, Spot +19, Survival +2 (+4 following tracks)
Feats: Alertness, Cleave, Improved Grapple, Iron Will, Power Attack
Environment: Nine Hells of Baator
Organization: Solitary, pair, team (3–5), or squad (6–10)
Challenge Rating: 11
Treasure: Standard
Alignment: Always lawful evil
Advancement: 13–24 (Medium); 25–36 HD (Large)
Level Adjustment: —

This creature looks like a tall humanoid covered with sharp barbs, right down to the tip of its long, meaty tail. Its eyes shift and dart about, making it appear agitated or nervous.

Barbed devils, also called hamatulas, serve as guardians of vaults and bodyguards to the most powerful denizens of the Nine Hells.

A barbed devil is about 7 feet tall and weighs about 300 pounds.

Combat
Barbed devils eagerly fight with their claws, trying to impale their opponents. They use *hold person* to immobilize those who avoid their hug attacks.

A barbed devil's natural weapons, as well as any weapons it wields, are treated as evil-aligned and lawful-aligned for the purpose of overcoming damage reduction.

Fear (Su): A creature hit by a barbed devil must succeed on a DC 20 Will save or be affected as though by *fear* (caster level 9th). Whether or not the save is successful, that creature cannot be affected by that same barbed devil's fear ability for 24 hours. The save DC is Charisma-based.

Impale (Ex): A barbed devil deals 3d8+9 points of piercing damage to a grabbed opponent with a successful grapple check.

Improved Grab (Ex): To use this ability, a barbed devil must hit with a claw attack. It can then attempt to start a grapple as a free action without provoking an attack of opportunity. If it wins the grapple check, it establishes a hold and can impale the opponent on its barbed body.

Summon Baatezu (Sp): Once per day a barbed devil can attempt to summon 1d6 bearded devils or another barbed devil with a 35% chance of success. This ability is the equivalent of a 4th-level spell.

Barbed Defense (Su): Any creature striking a barbed devil with handheld weapons or natural weapons takes 1d8+6 points of piercing and slashing damage from the devil's barbs. Note that weapons with exceptional reach, such as longspears, do not endanger their users in this way.

Spell-Like Abilities: At will—*greater teleport* (self plus 50 pounds of objects only), *hold person* (DC 16), *major image* (DC 17), *scorching ray* (2 rays only). 1/day—*order's wrath* (DC 18), *unholy blight* (DC 18). Caster level 12th. The save DCs are Charisma-based.

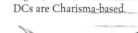

Ice devil

Imp

Lemure

Barbed devil

Horned devil

Bearded devil

Erinyes

for more powerful devils. Every bearded devil carries a saw-toothed glaive.

A bearded devil stands 6 feet tall and weighs about 225 pounds.

Combat

Bearded devils are aggressive and love to fight. They revel in their battle frenzy, spreading mayhem among their foes.

A bearded devil's natural weapons, as well as any weapons it wields, are treated as evil-aligned and lawful-aligned for the purpose of overcoming damage reduction.

Spell-Like Abilities: At will—*greater teleport* (self plus 50 pounds of objects only). Caster level 12th.

Infernal Wound (Su): The damage a bearded devil deals with its glaive causes a persistent wound. An injured creature loses 2 additional hit points each round. The wound does not heal naturally and resists healing spells. The continuing hit point loss can be stopped by a DC 16 Heal check, a *cure* spell, or a *heal* spell. However, a character attempting to cast a *cure* spell or a *heal* spell on a creature damaged by a bearded devil's glaive must succeed on a DC 16 caster level check, or the spell has no effect on the injured character. A successful Heal check automatically stops the continuing hit point loss as well as restoring hit points. The infernal wound is a supernatural ability of the bearded devil, not of the weapon. The check DC is Constitution-based.

Beard (Ex): If a bearded devil hits a single opponent with both claw attacks, it automatically hits with its beard. The affected creature takes 1d8+2 points of damage and must succeed on a DC 16 Fortitude save or be infected with a vile disease known as devil chills (incubation period 1d4 days, damage 1d4 Str). Damage is dealt each day until the afflicted creature succeeds on three consecutive Fortitude saves, the disease is cured magically, or the creature dies. The save DC is Constitution-based.

Battle Frenzy (Ex): Twice per day, a bearded devil can work itself into a battle frenzy similar to the barbarian's rage (+4 Strength, +4 Constitution, +2 morale bonus on Will saves, −2 AC penalty). The frenzy lasts for 6 rounds, and the bearded devil suffers no ill effects afterward.

Summon Baatezu (Sp): Once per day a bearded devil can attempt to summon 2d10 lemures with a 50% chance of success, or another bearded devil with a 35% chance of success. This ability is the equivalent of a 3rd-level spell.

BEARDED DEVIL (BARBAZU)

Medium Outsider (Baatezu, Evil, Extraplanar, Lawful)
Hit Dice: 6d8+18 (45 hp)
Initiative: +6
Speed: 40 ft. (8 squares)
Armor Class: 19 (+2 Dex, +7 natural) touch 12, flat-footed 17
Base Attack/Grapple: +6/+8
Attack: Glaive +9 melee (1d10+3 plus infernal wound) or claw +8 melee (1d6+2)
Full Attack: Glaive +9/+4 melee (1d10+3 plus infernal wound) or 2 claws +8 melee (1d6+2)
Space/Reach: 5 ft./5 ft. (10 ft. with glaive)
Special Attacks: Infernal wound, beard, battle frenzy, *summon baatezu*
Special Qualities: Damage reduction 5/silver or good, darkvision 60 ft., immunity to fire and poison, resistance to acid 10 and cold 10, see in darkness, spell resistance 17, telepathy 100 ft.
Saves: Fort +8, Ref +7, Will +5
Abilities: Str 15, Dex 15, Con 17, Int 6, Wis 10, Cha 10
Skills: Climb +11, Diplomacy +2, Hide +11, Listen +9, Move Silently +9, Sense Motive +9, Spot +9
Feats: Improved Initiative, Power Attack, Weapon Focus (glaive)
Environment: Nine Hells of Baator
Organization: Solitary, pair, team (3–5), or squad (6–10)
Challenge Rating: 5
Treasure: Standard
Alignment: Always lawful evil
Advancement: 7–9 HD (Medium); 10–18 HD (Large)
Level Adjustment: +6

The first thing that stands out about this creature is the massive saw-toothed glaive it carries. The creature's pointed ears and moist, scaly skin mark it as an outsider. It has a long tail, clawed hands and feet, and a snaky, disgusting beard.

Bearded devils, also called barbazu, serve as shock troops in hell's armies, spearheading attacks by masses of lemures. Between wars, they find employment as guards and sentinels

BONE DEVIL (OSYLUTH)

Large Outsider (Baatezu, Evil, Extraplanar, Lawful)
Hit Dice: 10d8+50 (95 hp)
Initiative: +9
Speed: 40 ft. (8 squares)
Armor Class: 25 (−1 size, +5 Dex, +11 natural) touch 14, flat-footed 20
Base Attack/Grapple: +10/+19

Attack: Bite +14 melee (1d8+5)

Full Attack: Bite +14 melee (1d8+5) and 2 claws +12 melee (1d4+2) and sting +12 melee (3d4+2 plus poison)

Space/Reach: 10 ft./10 ft.

Special Attacks: Spell-like abilities, fear aura, poison, *summon baatezu*

Special Qualities: Damage reduction 10/good, darkvision 60 ft., immunity to fire and poison, resistance to acid 10 and cold 10, see in darkness, spell resistance 21, telepathy 100 ft.

Saves: Fort +12, Ref +12, Will +11

Abilities: Str 21, Dex 21, Con 21, Int 14, Wis 14, Cha 14

Skills: Bluff +15, Concentration +18, Diplomacy +6, Disguise +2 (+4 acting), Hide +14, Intimidate +17, Knowledge (any one) +15, Listen +17, Move Silently +18, Search +15, Sense Motive +15, Spot +17, Survival +2 (+4 following tracks)

Feats: Alertness, Improved Initiative, Iron Will, Multiattack

Environment: Nine Hells of Baator

Organization: Solitary, team (2–4), or squad (6–10)

Challenge Rating: 9

Treasure: Standard

Alignment: Always lawful evil

Advancement: 11–20 HD (Large); 21–30 HD (Huge)

Level Adjustment: —

This tall creature looks skeletal and wretched, almost a husk of a humanoid form, with dried skin stretched so tight as to outline and emphasize every bone. It has a fearsome, skull-like head and a tail like a scorpion's, and a foul odor of decay hangs in the air around it.

Bone devils, also called osyluths, often serve as the police and informers of the Nine Hells, monitoring other devils' activities and reporting on their service.

Bone devils stand about 9 feet tall and weigh about 500 pounds.

Combat

Bone devils hate all other creatures and attack ruthlessly. They freely use *wall of ice* to keep the enemy divided.

A bone devil's natural weapons, as well as any weapons it wields, are treated as evil-aligned and lawful-aligned for the purpose of overcoming damage reduction.

Fear Aura (Su): Bone devils can radiate a 5-foot-radius fear aura as a free action. Affected creatures must succeed on a DC 17 Will save or be affected as though by a *fear* spell (caster level 7th). A creature that successfully saves cannot be affected again by the same bone devil's aura for 24 hours. Other baatezu are immune to the aura. The save DC is Charisma-based.

Poison (Ex): Injury, Fortitude DC 20, initial damage 1d6 Str, secondary damage 2d6 Str. The save DC is Constitution-based.

Spell-Like Abilities: At will—*greater teleport* (self plus 50 pounds of objects only), *dimensional anchor, fly, invisibility* (self only), *major image* (DC 15), *wall of ice*. Caster level 12th. The save DC is Charisma-based.

Summon Baatezu (Sp): Once per day a bone devil can attempt to summon 2d10 lemures with a 50% chance of success, or another bone devil with a 35% chance of success. This ability is the equivalent of a 4th-level spell.

Chain devil

CHAIN DEVIL (KYTON)

Medium Outsider (Evil, Extraplanar, Lawful)

Hit Dice: 8d8+16 (52 hp)

Initiative: +6

Speed: 30 ft. (6 squares)

Armor Class: 20 (+2 Dex, +8 natural), touch 12, flat-footed 18

Base Attack/Grapple: +8/+10

Attack: Chain +10 melee (2d4+2/19–20)

Full Attack: 2 chains +10 melee (2d4+2/19–20)

Space/Reach: 5 ft./5 ft. (10 ft. with chains)

Special Attacks: Dancing chains, unnerving gaze

Special Qualities: Damage reduction 5/silver or good, darkvision 60 ft., immunity to cold, regeneration 2, spell resistance 18

Saves: Fort +8, Ref +8, Will +6

Abilities: Str 15, Dex 15, Con 15, Int 6, Wis 10, Cha 12

Skills: Climb +13, Craft (blacksmithing) +17, Escape Artist +13, Intimidate +12, Listen +13, Spot +13, Use Rope +2 (+4 with bindings)

Feats: Alertness, Improved Critical (chain), Improved Initiative

Environment: Nine Hells of Baator

Organization: Solitary, gang (2–4), band (6–10), or mob (11–20)

Challenge Rating: 6

Treasure: Standard

Alignment: Always lawful evil

Advancement: 9–16 HD (Medium)

Level Adjustment: +6

The clank and rattle of chains announces the arrival of this creature. It appears human in shape and size, but chains wrap it like a shroud, every length ending in a hook or a blade or a heavy ball. The chains seem to slither and slide over the creature's form, almost as if they were alive.

These chain-shrouded beings, also called kytons, are often mistaken for undead by those who liken them to the traditional shackle-rattling ghost. Kytons are humanlike devils, wrapped in chains instead of clothing.

A chain devil is 6 feet tall and weighs about 300 pounds, chains included.

Chain devils speak Infernal and Common.

Combat

A chain devil attacks by flailing away with the spiked chains that serve as its clothing, armor, and weapons. Chain devils savor fear and terror so much that they may stalk victims for hours, building dread and panic prior to attacking.

A chain devil's natural weapons, as well as any weapons it wields, are treated as evil-aligned and lawful-aligned for the purpose of overcoming damage reduction.

Dancing Chains (Su): A chain devil's most awesome attack is its ability to control up to four chains within 20 feet as a standard action, making the chains dance or move as it wishes. In addition, a chain devil can increase these chains' length by up to 15 feet and cause them to sprout razor-edged barbs. These chains attack as effectively as the devil itself. If a chain is in another creature's possession, the creature can attempt a DC 15 Will save to break the chain devil's power over that chain. If the save is successful, the kyton cannot attempt to control that particular chain again for 24 hours or until the chain leaves the creature's possession. The save DC is Charisma-based.

A chain devil can climb chains it controls at its normal speed without making Climb checks.

Unnerving Gaze (Su): Range 30 ft., Will DC 15 negates. A chain devil can make its face resemble one of an opponent's departed loved ones or bitter enemies. Those who fail their saves take a –2 penalty on attack rolls for 1d3 rounds. The save DC is Charisma-based.

Regeneration (Ex): Chain devils take normal damage from silvered weapons, good-aligned weapons, and spells or effects with the good descriptor.

A chain devil that loses a piece of its body regrows it in 2d6×10 minutes. Holding the severed member against the stump enables it to reattach instantly.

Skills: Chain devils have a +8 racial bonus on Craft checks involving metalwork.

ERINYES

Medium Outsider (Baatezu, Evil, Extraplanar, Lawful)
Hit Dice: 9d8+45 (85 hp)
Initiative: +5
Speed: 30 ft. (6 squares), fly 50 ft. (good)
Armor Class: 23 (+5 Dex, +8 natural) touch 15, flat-footed 18
Base Attack/Grapple: +9/+14
Attack: Longsword +14 melee (1d8+5/19–20) or +1 flaming composite longbow (+5 Str bonus) +15 ranged (1d8+6/×3 plus 1d6 fire) or rope +14 ranged (entangle)
Full Attack: Longsword +14/+9 melee (1d8+5/19–20) or +1 flaming composite longbow (+5 Str bonus) +15/+10 ranged (1d8+6/×3 plus 1d6 fire) or rope +14 ranged (entangle)
Space/Reach: 5 ft./5 ft.
Special Attacks: Entangle, spell-like abilities, summon baatezu
Special Qualities: Damage reduction 5/good, darkvision 60 ft., immunity to fire and poison, resistance to acid 10 and cold 10, see in darkness, spell resistance 20, telepathy 100 ft., true seeing
Saves: Fort +11, Ref +11, Will +10
Abilities: Str 21, Dex 21, Con 21, Int 14, Wis 18, Cha 20
Skills: Concentration +17, Diplomacy +7, Escape Artist +17, Hide +17, Knowledge (any two) +14, Listen +16, Move Silently +17, Search +14, Sense Motive +16, Spot +16, Survival +4 (+6 following tracks), Use Rope +5 (+7 with bindings)
Feats: Dodge[B], Mobility[B], Point Blank Shot, Precise Shot, Rapid Shot, Shot on the Run
Environment: Nine Hells of Baator
Organization: Solitary
Challenge Rating: 8
Treasure: Standard, plus rope and +1 flaming composite longbow (+5 Str bonus)
Alignment: Always lawful evil
Advancement: 10–18 HD (Medium)
Level Adjustment: +7

A fierce and beautiful woman, with a statuesque build and flawless skin, stands nearby. She has large, feathery wings and red, glowing eyes. She wields a longsword, and a shining red bow is strapped across her back.

Rumor in the underworld tells that the first erinyes were angels who fell from their lofty heights because of some temptation or misdeed. Now, the skies of the Nine Hells are litterered with their descendants. Erinyes serve as scouts, servants, and even concubines for powerful devils. Unlike other devils, erinyes appear attractive to humans, resembling very comely women or men. They're not above taking advantage of being mistaken for the celestials that legend says they once were.

An erinyes stands about 6 feet tall and weighs about 150 pounds. Erinyes speak Infernal, Celestial, and Draconic.

Combat

Erinyes prefer to engage in combat from a distance. They use *charm monster* to distract or disorganize their opponents, then rain down fiery arrows from above.

An erinyes's natural weapons, as well as any weapons it wields, are treated as evil-aligned and lawful-aligned for the purpose of overcoming damage reduction.

Entangle (Ex): Each erinyes carries a stout rope some 50 feet long that entangles opponents of any size as an *animate rope* spell (caster level 16th). An erinyes can hurl its rope 30 feet with no range penalty. Typically, an erinyes entangles a foe, lifts it into the air, and drops it from a great height.

Spell-Like Abilities: At will—*greater teleport* (self plus 50 pounds of objects only), *charm monster* (DC 19), *minor image* (DC 17), *unholy blight* (DC 19). Caster level 12th. The save DCs are Charisma-based.

Summon Baatezu (Sp): Once per day an erinyes can attempt to summon 2d10 lemures or 1d4 bearded devils with a 50% chance of success. This ability is the equivalent of a 3rd-level spell.

True Seeing (Su): Erinyes continuously use *true seeing*, as the spell (caster level 14th).

HELLCAT (BEZEKIRA)

Large Outsider (Evil, Extraplanar, Lawful)
Hit Dice: 8d8+24 (60 hp)
Initiative: +9
Speed: 40 ft. (8 squares)
Armor Class: 21 (–1 size, +5 Dex, +7 natural), touch 14, flat-footed 16
Base Attack/Grapple: +8/+18
Attack: Claw +13 melee (1d8+6)
Full Attack: 2 claws +13 melee (1d8+6) and bite +8 melee (2d8+3)
Space/Reach: 10 ft./5 ft.
Special Attacks: Improved grab, pounce, rake 1d8+3
Special Qualities: Damage reduction 5/good, darkvision 60 ft., invisible in light, resistance to fire 10, scent, spell resistance 19, telepathy 100 ft.
Saves: Fort +9, Ref +11, Will +8
Abilities: Str 23, Dex 21, Con 17, Int 10, Wis 14, Cha 10
Skills: Balance +16, Climb +17, Hide +13, Jump +21, Listen +17, Move Silently +20, Spot +13, Swim +17
Feats: Dodge, Improved Initiative, Track
Environment: Nine Hells of Baator
Organization: Solitary, pair, or pride (6–10)
Challenge Rating: 7
Treasure: None
Alignment: Always lawful evil
Advancement: 9–10 HD (Large); 11–24 HD (Huge)
Level Adjustment: —

Silently, with grace and power, a creature emerges on the path ahead. It has the shape of an enormous lion, but its form consists of blinding light and fiery sparks, as though its body were made of energy and not flesh and bone.

These fierce devil-cats, also called bezekiras, move about almost silently, constantly on the watch for some chance to do evil. They enjoy setting ambushes and otherwise outwitting enemies. While its appearance suggests it is incorporeal, a hellcats has a corporeal body and can be harmed by physical attacks.

Hellcats use a natural telepathy to communicate with one another and those they encounter. A hellcat measures about 9 feet long and weighs about 900 pounds.

Combat

A hellcat can hold its own in combat thanks to sharp claws and wicked fangs. It prefers to leap upon opponents, just as a lion does.

A hellcat's natural weapons, as well as any weapons it wields, are treated as evil-aligned and lawful-aligned for the purpose of overcoming damage reduction.

Improved Grab (Ex): To use this ability, a hellcat must hit with its bite attack. It can then attempt to start a grapple as a free action without provoking an attack of opportunity. If it wins the grapple check, it establishes a hold and can rake.

Pounce (Ex): If a hellcat charges, it can make a full attack, including two rake attacks.

Rake (Ex): Attack bonus +13 melee, damage 1d8+3.

Invisible in Light (Ex): A hellcat is invisible in any area lit well enough for a human to see. In a darkened area, it shows up as a faintly glowing outline visible up to 30 feet away (60 feet if the viewer has low-light vision). Magical darkness smothers the glow and conceals the outline.

Skills: Hellcats have a +4 racial bonus on Listen and Move Silently checks.

Hellcat

HORNED DEVIL (CORNUGON)

Large Outsider (Baatezu, Evil, Extraplanar, Lawful)
Hit Dice: 15d8+105 (172 hp)
Initiative: +7
Speed: 20 ft. (4 squares), fly 50 ft. (average)
Armor Class: 35 (–1 size, +7 Dex, +19 natural) touch 16, flat-footed 28
Base Attack/Grapple: +15/+29
Attack: Spiked chain +25 melee (2d6+15 plus stun) or claw +24 melee (2d6+10) or tail +24 melee (2d6+10 plus infernal wound)
Full Attack: Spiked chain +25/+20/+15 melee (2d6+15 plus stun) and bite +22 melee (2d8+5) and tail +22 melee (2d6+5 plus infernal wound); or 2 claws +24 melee (2d6+10) and bite +22 melee (2d8+5) and tail +22 melee (2d6+5 plus infernal wound)
Space/Reach: 10 ft./10 ft. (20 ft. with spiked chain)
Special Attacks: Fear aura, infernal wound, spell-like abilities, stun, *summon baatezu*
Special Qualities: Damage reduction 10/good and silver, darkvision 60 ft., immunity to fire and poison, resistance to acid 10 and cold 10, regeneration 5, see in darkness, spell resistance 28, telepathy 100 ft.
Saves: Fort +16, Ref +16, Will +15
Abilities: Str 31, Dex 25, Con 25, Int 14, Wis 18, Cha 22
Skills: Bluff +24, Climb +28, Concentration +24, Diplomacy +10, Disguise +6 (+8 acting), Hide +21, Intimidate +26, Listen +22, Move Silently +23, Search +20, Sense Motive +22, Spot +22, Survival +4 (+6 following tracks)
Feats: Cleave, Improved Sunder, Iron Will, Multiattack, Power Attack, Weapon Focus (spiked chain)
Environment: Nine Hells of Baator
Organization: Solitary, team (2–4), or squad (6–10)
Challenge Rating: 16
Treasure: Standard coins; double goods; standard items
Alignment: Always lawful evil
Advancement: 16–20 HD (Large); 21–45 HD (Huge)
Level Adjustment: —

This creature is as big as an ogre, with a vaguely humanoid shape. Hideous scales sheathe its body. Huge wings and a snaking, prehensile tail add to its intimidating appearance.

Horned devils, also called cornugons, serve as elite defense forces, the soldiers supreme of the Nine Hells. They are terrible to look upon—even to other devils.

A horned devil is 9 feet tall and weighs about 600 pounds.

Combat

Horned devils are bold fighters. They rarely retreat, even against overwhelming odds. They love to fight with their spiked chains, usually singling out the most powerful foes to stun and eliminate quickly.

A horned devil's natural weapons, as well as any weapons it wields, are treated as evil-aligned and lawful-aligned for the purpose of overcoming damage reduction.

Spell-Like Abilities: At will—*dispel chaos* (DC 21), *dispel good* (DC 21), *magic circle against good, greater teleport* (self plus 50 pounds of objects only); *persistent image* (DC 21) 3/day—*fireball* (DC 19), *lightning bolt* (DC 19). Caster level 15th. The save DCs are Charisma-based.

Fear Aura (Su): A horned devil can radiate a 5-foot-radius fear aura as a free action. A creature in the area must succeed on a DC 23 Will save or be affected as though by a *fear* spell (caster level 15th). A creature that successfully saves cannot be affected again by the same horned devil's aura for 24 hours. Other baatezu are immune to the aura. The save DC is Charisma-based.

Stun (Su): Whenever a horned devil hits with a spiked chain attack, the opponent must succeed on a DC 27 Fortitude save or be stunned for 1d4 rounds. The save DC is Strength-based. This ability is a function of the horned devil, not of the spiked chain.

Infernal Wound (Su): The damage a horned devil deals with its tail attack causes a persistent wound. An injured creature loses 2 additional hit points each round. The wound does not heal naturally and resists healing spells. The continuing hit point loss can be stopped by a DC 24 Heal check, a *cure* spell, or a *heal* spell. However, a character attempting to cast a *cure* spell or a *heal* spell on a creature damaged by a horned devil's tail must succeed on a DC 24 caster level check, or the spell has no effect on the injured character. A successful Heal check automatically stops the continuing hit point loss as well as restoring hit points. The check DC is Constitution-based.

Summon Baatezu (Sp): Once per day a horned devil can attempt to summon 2d10 lemures or 1d6 bearded devils with a 50% chance of success, 1d6 barbed devils with a 35% chance of success, or another horned devil with a 20% chance of success. This ability is the equivalent of a 6th-level spell.

Regeneration (Ex): A horned devil takes normal damage from good-aligned silvered weapons, and from spells or effects with the good descriptor.

ICE DEVIL (GELUGON)

Large Outsider (Baatezu, Evil, Extraplanar, Lawful)
Hit Dice: 14d8+84 (147 hp)
Initiative: +5
Speed: 40 ft. (8 squares)
Armor Class: 32 (–1 size, +5 Dex, +18 natural) touch 14, flat-footed 27
Base Attack/Grapple: +14/+24
Attack: Spear +20 melee (2d6+9/×3 plus slow) or claw +19 melee (1d10+6)
Full Attack: Spear +20/+15/+10 melee (2d6+9/×3 plus slow) and bite +14 melee (2d6+3) and tail +14 melee (3d6+3 plus slow); or 2 claws +19 melee (1d10+6) and bite +14 melee (2d6+3) and tail +14 melee (3d6+3 plus slow)
Space/Reach: 10 ft./10 ft.
Special Attacks: Fear aura, slow, spell-like abilities, summon baatezu
Special Qualities: Damage reduction 10/good, darkvision 60 ft., immunity to fire and poison, resistance to acid 10 and cold 10, regeneration 5, see in darkness, spell resistance 25, telepathy 100 ft.
Saves: Fort +15, Ref +14, Will +15
Abilities: Str 23, Dex 21, Con 23, Int 22, Wis 22, Cha 20
Skills: Bluff +22, Climb +23, Concentration +23, Diplomacy +9, Disguise +5 (+7 acting), Intimidate +24, Jump +27, Knowledge (any three) +23, Listen +25, Move Silently +22, Search +23, Sense Motive +23, Spellcraft +23, Spot +25, Survival +6 (+8 following tracks)
Feats: Alertness, Cleave, Combat Reflexes, Power Attack, Weapon Focus (spear)
Environment: Nine Hells of Baator
Organization: Solitary, team (2–4), squad (6–10), or troupe (1–2 ice devils, 7–12 bearded devils, and 1–4 bone devils)
Challenge Rating: 13
Treasure: Standard coins; double goods; standard items
Alignment: Always lawful evil
Advancement: 15–28 HD (Large); 29–42 HD (Huge)
Level Adjustment: —

This creature looks like a tall, bipedal insect. It has clawed hands and feet, powerful mandibles, and a long, thick tail covered in razor-sharp spikes.

Ice devils, also called gelugons, serve almost exclusively as troop commanders. When found without their soldiers and minions, they display a savage brutality.

An ice devil is about 12 feet tall and weighs about 700 pounds.

Combat

An ice devil prefers to fight only when doing so serves its mission, but it never hesitates to attack when it deems a battle necessary—or likely to end in its victory.

An ice devil's natural weapons, as well as any weapons it wields, are treated as evil-aligned and lawful-aligned for the purpose of overcoming damage reduction.

Fear Aura (Su): An ice devil can radiate a 10-foot-radius fear aura as a free action. A creature in the area must succeed on a DC 22 Will save or be affected as though by a *fear* spell (caster level 13th). A creature that successfully saves cannot be affected again by the same ice devil's aura for 24 hours. Other baatezu are immune to the aura. The save DC is Charisma-based.

Slow (Su): A hit from an ice devil's tail or spear induces numbing cold. The opponent must succeed on a DC 23 Fortitude save or be affected as though by a *slow* spell for 1d6 rounds. The save DC is Constitution-based.

Spell-Like Abilities: At will—*cone of cold* (DC 20), *fly*, *ice storm* (DC 19), *greater teleport* (self plus 50 pounds of objects only), *persistent image* (DC 20), *unholy aura* (DC 23), *wall of ice* (DC 19). Caster level 13th. The save DCs are Charisma-based.

Summon Baatezu (Sp): Once per day an ice devil can attempt to summon 2d10 lemures or 1d6 bearded devils, 2d4 bone devils with a 50% chance of success, or another ice devil with a 20% chance of success. This ability is the equivalent of a 4th-level spell.

Regeneration (Ex): An ice devil takes normal damage from good-aligned weapons and from spells or effects with the good descriptor.

IMP

Tiny Outsider (Evil, Extraplanar, Lawful)
Hit Dice: 3d8 (13 hp)
Initiative: +3
Speed: 20 ft. (4 squares), fly 50 ft. (perfect)
Armor Class: 20 (+2 size, +3 Dex, +5 natural), touch 15, flat-footed 17
Base Attack/Grapple: +3/–5
Attack: Sting +8 melee (1d4 plus poison)
Full Attack: Sting +8 melee (1d4 plus poison)
Space/Reach: 2-1/2 ft./0 ft.
Special Attacks: Poison, spell-like abilities
Special Qualities: Alternate form, damage reduction 5/good or silver, darkvision 60 ft., fast healing 2, immunity to poison, resistance to fire 5
Saves: Fort +3, Ref +6, Will +4
Abilities: Str 10, Dex 17, Con 10, Int 10, Wis 12, Cha 14
Skills: Diplomacy +8, Hide +17, Knowledge (any one) +6, Listen +7, Move Silently +9, Search +6, Spellcraft +6, Spot +7, Survival +1 (+3 following tracks)
Feats: Dodge, Weapon Finesse
Environment: Nine Hells of Baator
Organization: Solitary
Challenge Rating: 2
Treasure: None
Alignment: Always lawful evil
Advancement: 4–6 HD (Tiny)
Level Adjustment: — (Improved Familiar)

A tiny humanoid with leathery batwings, a barbed tail, and sharp, twisted horns flutters at about eye level, winking into sight from out of thin air.

Imps are insidious devils. They are often found serving lawful evil spellcasters as advisors and spies.

In its natural form, an imp stands almost 2 feet tall and weighs about 8 pounds.

Combat

Imps are craven, but not so timid as to pass up an opportunity for a surprise attack using their *invisibility* and alternate form ability. In its natural form, an imp attacks with the wicked stinger on its tail. It quickly flies out of reach if a foe manages to strike back effectively.

An imp's natural weapons, as well as any weapons it wields, are treated as evil-aligned and lawful-aligned for the purpose of overcoming damage reduction.

Poison (Ex): Injury, Fortitude DC 13, initial damage 1d4 Dex, secondary damage 2d4 Dex. The save DC is Constitution-based and includes a +2 racial bonus.

Spell-Like Abilities: At will—*detect good, detect magic, invisibility* (self only); 1/day—*suggestion* (DC 15). Caster level 6th. The save DC is Charisma-based.

Once per week an imp can use *commune* to ask six questions. The ability otherwise works as the spell (caster level 12th).

Alternate Form (Su): An imp can assume other forms at will as a standard action. This ability functions as a *polymorph* spell cast on itself (caster level 12th), except that an imp does not regain hit points for changing form, and an individual imp can assume only one or two forms no larger than Medium. Common forms include monstrous spider, raven, rat, and boar.

LEMURE

Medium Outsider (Baatezu, Evil, Extraplanar, Lawful)
Hit Dice: 2d8 (9 hp)
Initiative: +0
Speed: 20 ft. (4 squares)
Armor Class: 14 (+4 natural) touch 10, flat-footed 14
Base Attack/Grapple: +2/+2
Attack: Claw +2 melee (1d4)
Full Attack: 2 claws +2 melee (1d4)
Space/Reach: 5 ft./5 ft.
Special Attacks: —
Special Qualities: Damage reduction 5/good or silver, dark-vision 60 ft., immunity to fire and poison, mindless, resistance to acid 10 and cold 10, mindless, see in darkness
Saves: Fort +3, Ref +3, Will +3
Abilities: Str 10, Dex 10, Con 10, Int —, Wis 11, Cha 5
Environment: Nine Hells of Baator
Organization: Solitary, pair, gang (3–5), swarm (6–15), or mob (10–40)
Challenge Rating: 1
Treasure: None
Alignment: Always lawful evil
Advancement: 3–6 HD (Medium)
Level Adjustment: —

The creature surges forward, not unlike a molten mass of flesh oozing across the ground. It has a human-shaped head and torso, but its body is a shape-less mass below the waist. A permanent ex-pression of anguish twists across its face.

Lemures are pathetic creatures that mainly serve as slaves and conscript troops for more powerful baatezu.

A lemure is about 5 feet tall and weighs about 100 pounds.

Lemures are mindless and cannot communicate, but they are sensitive to telepathic messages from other devils, typically obeying a devil's mental commands.

Combat

Lemures crave revenge against the universe that has made them what they are. They surge toward anything they meet and try to claw it apart. Only a telepathic command from other devils or the complete destruction of the lemures can make them stop.

A lemure's natural weapons, as well as any weapons it wields, are treated as evil-aligned and lawful-aligned for the purpose of over-coming damage reduction.

Mindless (Ex): Immunity to mind-affecting effects (charms, compulsions, phantasms, patterns, and morale effects).

PIT FIEND

Large Outsider (Baatezu, Evil, Extraplanar, Lawful)
Hit Dice: 18d8+144 (225 hp)
Initiative: +12
Speed: 40 ft. (8 squares), fly 60 ft. (average)
AC: 40 (–1 size, +8 Dex, +23 natural) touch 17, flat-footed 32
Base Attack/Grapple: +18/+35
Attack: Claw +30 melee (2d8+13)
Full Attack: 2 claws +30 melee (2d8+13) and 2 wings +28 melee (2d6+6) and bite +28 melee (4d6+6 plus poison plus disease) and tail slap +28 melee (2d8+6)
Space/Reach: 10 ft./10 ft.
Special Attacks: Constrict 2d8+26, fear aura, improved grab, spell-like abilities, *summon baatezu*
Special Qualities: Damage reduction 15/good and silver, darkvision 60 ft., immunity to fire and poison, resistance to acid 10 and cold 10, regeneration 5, see in darkness, spell resistance 32, telepathy 100 ft.
Saves: Fort +19, Ref +19, Will +21
Abilities: Str 37, Dex 27, Con 27, Int 26, Wis 26, Cha 26
Skills: Balance +10, Bluff +29, Climb +34, Concentration +29, Diplomacy +10, Disguise +29 (+31 acting), Hide +25, Intimidate +31, Jump +40, Knowledge (arcana) +29, Knowledge (nature) +10, Knowledge (the planes) +29, Knowledge (religion) +29, Listen +29, Move Silently +29, Search +29, Spellcraft +31, Spot +29, Survival +8 (+10 on other planes, +10 when tracking), Tumble +31
Feats: Cleave, Great Cleave, Improved Initiative, Iron Will, Multiattack, Power Attack, Quicken Spell-Like Ability (fire-ball)
Environment: Nine Hells of Baator
Organization: Solitary, pair, team (3–4), or troupe (1–2 pit fiends, 2–5 horned devils, and 2–5 barbed devils)
Challenge Rating: 20
Treasure: Standard coins; double goods; standard items
Alignment: Always lawful evil
Advancement: 19–36 HD (Large); 37–54 HD (Huge)
Level Adjustment: —

Bone devil

Pit fiend

Cloaked in fire and as tall as two humans, this hulking monster spreads its batlike wings and cracks its whiplike tail. Great scales cover its body like armor. It smiles, revealing large fangs that drip with a hissing venom.

Pit fiends are the undisputed lords of the baatezu, masters of creating fear in mortals and devils alike.

A pit fiend often wraps its wings around itself like a grotesque cloak, and appears wreathed in flames.

A pit fiend is 12 feet tall and weighs 800 pounds.

Combat

Pit fiends are wily and resourceful fighters, using *invisibility* to gain the upper hand and biting at foes seemingly able to see them. They don't hesitate to blanket an area with *fireballs*, and can call down the wrath of an inferno with *meteor swarm*.

A pit fiend's natural weapons, as well as any weapons it wields, are treated as evil-aligned and lawful-aligned for the purpose of overcoming damage reduction.

Constrict (Ex): A pit fiend deals 2d8+26 points of damage with a successful grapple check.

Disease (Su): A creature struck by a pit fiend's bite attack must succeed on a DC 27 Fortitude save or be infected with a vile disease known as devil chills (incubation period 1d4 days, damage 1d4 Str). The save DC is Constitution-based.

Fear Aura (Su): A pit fiend can radiate a 20-foot-radius fear aura as a free action. A creature in the area must succeed on a DC 27 Will save or be affected as though by a *fear* spell (caster level 18th). A creature that successfully saves cannot be affected again by the same pit fiend's aura for 24 hours. Other baatezu are immune to the aura. The save DC is Charisma-based.

Improved Grab (Ex): To use this ability, a pit fiend must hit with its tail slap attack. It can then attempt to start a grapple as a free action without provoking an attack of opportunity. If it wins the grapple check, it establishes a hold and can constrict.

Poison (Ex): Injury, Fortitude DC 27, initial damage 1d6 Con, secondary damage death. The save DC is Constitution-based.

Spell-Like Abilities: At will—*blasphemy* (DC 25), *create undead*, *fireball* (DC 21), *greater dispel magic*, *greater teleport* (self plus 50 pounds of objects only), *invisibility*, *magic circle against good*, *mass hold monster* (DC 27), *persistent image* (DC 23), *power word stun*, *unholy aura* (DC 26); 1/day—*meteor swarm* (DC 27). Caster level 18th. The save DCs are Charisma-based.

Once per year a pit fiend can use *wish* as the spell (caster level 20th).

Summon Baatezu (Sp): Twice per day a pit fiend can automatically summon 2 lemures, bone devils, or bearded devils, or 1 erinyes, horned devil, or ice devil. This ability is the equivalent of an 8th-level spell.

Regeneration (Ex): A pit fiend takes normal damage from good-aligned silvered weapons, and from spells or effects with the good descriptor.

Tactics Round-by-Round

A pit fiend typically opens combat by using its spell-like abilities, attempting to neutralize dangerous opponents before entering melee.

Prior to combat: Unholy aura; activate fear aura, summon baatezu.

Round 1: Quickened *fireball* and *mass hold monster* if facing three or more visible, active opponents; otherwise *power word stun* against unarmored opponent (preferably a spellcaster).

Round 2: Meteor swarm against as many foes as possible, approach worst-injured enemy.

Round 3: Full attack against injured enemy.

Round 4: Continue melee against injured enemy, or *power word stun* against annoying spellcaster.

Round 5: Repeat from round 1, or *greater teleport* to safety if endangered.

DEVOURER

Large Undead (Extraplanar)
Hit Dice: 12d12 (78 hp)
Initiative: +4
Speed: 30 ft. (6 squares)
Armor Class: 24 (–1 size, +15 natural), touch 9, flat-footed 24
Base Attack/Grapple: +6/+19
Attack: Claw +15 melee (1d6+9)
Full Attack: 2 claws +15 melee (1d6+9)
Space/Reach: 10 ft./10 ft.
Special Attacks: Energy drain, trap essence, spell-like abilities
Special Qualities: Darkvision 60 ft., spell deflection, spell resistance 21, undead traits
Saves: Fort +4, Ref +4, Will +11
Abilities: Str 28, Dex 10, Con —, Int 16, Wis 16, Cha 17
Skills: Climb +24, Concentration +18, Diplomacy +5, Jump +24, Listen +18, Move Silently +15, Search +10, Sense Motive +11, Spot +18, Survival +3 (+5 following tracks)
Feats: Blind-Fight, Combat Casting, Expertise, Improved Initiative, Weapon Focus (claw)
Environment: Any
Organization: Solitary
Challenge Rating: 11
Treasure: None
Alignment: Always neutral evil
Advancement: 13–24 HD (Large); 25–36 HD (Huge)
Level Adjustment: —

This tall, skeletal creature has strands of mummified flesh hanging from its bones. Imprisoned within the creature's rib cage is a tiny figure, clearly in agony.

Devourers are massive creatures every bit as evil as they look. They lurk on the Ethereal Plane and the Astral Plane, stalking both natives and travelers with equal sadistic glee.

The tiny figure in the rib cage is the trapped essence of a slain opponent, which is consumed like firewood to sustain the monster's unnatural life.

A devourer is about 9 feet tall and weighs 500 pounds.

Devourers speak Common.

COMBAT

Even if it had no special abilities, a devourer would be a terrible opponent, for its bony claws can flay enemies alive.

Energy Drain (Su): Living creatures hit by a devourer's claw attack or *spectral hand* ability gain one negative level. The DC is 19 for the Fortitude save to remove a negative level. The save DC is Charisma-based.

Trap Essence (Su): The devourer is named for its ability to consume an enemy's life essence. To do so, it must forgo its normal melee attacks and make a trap essence attack. This requires a normal attack roll but deals no damage. The

Illus. by C. Arellano

Devourer

affected creature must succeed on a DC 19 Fortitude save or die instantly. The save DC is Charisma-based.

A slain creature's essence is trapped within the devourer's ribs, and the tiny figure takes on that victim's features. The trapped essence cannot be raised or resurrected, but a *limited wish*, *miracle*, or *wish* spell frees it, as does destroying the devourer. A devourer can hold only one essence at a time.

The trapped essence provides a devourer with enough power to use five spell-like abilities for each Hit Die or level of the trapped creature. As this energy is expended, the twisted soul fades away until it evaporates completely. The trapped essence gains one negative level for every five times the devourer uses one of its spell-like abilities. When the essence's number of negative levels equals the creature's total Hit Dice or level, the essence is destroyed. If an essence is freed, the restored creature must succeed on a DC 19 Fortitude save for each negative level or lose that level permanently.

Spell-Like Abilities: At the start of any encounter, the trapped essence within a devourer is assumed to have 3d4+3 levels (enough fuel for thirty to seventy-five uses). Once per round, a devourer can use one of the following abilities: *confusion* (DC 17), *control undead* (DC 20), *ghoul touch* (DC 15), *lesser planar ally*, *ray of enfeeblement* (DC 14), *spectral hand*, *suggestion* (DC 16), *true seeing*. Caster level 18th. The save DCs are Charisma-based.

Spell Deflection (Su): The trapped essence provides a measure of magical protection. If any of the following spells are cast at the devourer and overcome its spell resistance, they affect the imprisoned essence instead: *banishment, chaos hammer, confusion, crushing despair, detect thoughts, dispel evil, dominate person, fear, geas/quest, holy word, hypnosis, imprisonment, magic jar, maze, suggestion, trap the soul,* or any form of charm or compulsion. In many cases, this deflection effectively neutralizes the spell (*charming* a trapped essence, for example, is useless). Some of these effects (*banishment*, for example) might eliminate the trapped essence, depriving the devourer of its spell-like abilities until it can consume another victim.

DIGESTER

Medium Magical Beast
Hit Dice: 8d10+24 (68 hp)
Initiative: +6
Speed: 60 ft. (12 squares)
Armor Class: 17 (+2 Dex, +5 natural), touch 12, flat-footed 15
Base Attack/Grapple: +8/+11
Attack: Claw +11 melee (1d8+4)
Full Attack: Claw +11 melee (1d8+4)
Space/Reach: 5 ft./5 ft.
Special Attacks: Acid spray
Special Qualities: Darkvision 60 ft., immunity to acid, low-light vision, scent

Saves: Fort +9, Ref +10, Will +3
Abilities: Str 17, Dex 15, Con 17, Int 2, Wis 12, Cha 10
Skills: Hide +9, Listen +6, Jump +21, Spot +6
Feats: Alertness, Improved Initiative, Lightning Reflexes
Environment: Warm forests
Organization: Solitary or pack (3–6)
Challenge Rating: 6
Treasure: None
Alignment: Always neutral
Advancement: 9–12 HD (Medium); 13–24 HD (Large)
Level Adjustment: —

This creature stands on two powerful hind legs. It has a long tail, but no other limbs, and a gray, pebbly hide with daggerlike markings. Its narrow head is equipped with a sucking mouth and a tubelike orifice in its forehead.

The swift predators known as digesters have a vicious acid attack that can reduce a human to a pool of glop in seconds. Digesters may lurk almost anywhere there is prey to be found, from barren deserts to steaming jungles.

A digester stands about 5 feet tall and is 7 feet long from snout to tail. It weighs about 350 pounds,

COMBAT

A digester is a hunting and eating machine. When it is not hungry (which is rarely), it lies low and avoids most other creatures. When hunting, it looks about for a likely target, then charges forth and delivers a gout of acid. If the initial attack is insufficient to kill the prey, the digester attacks with its hind feet until it can spray acid again.

Acid Spray (Ex): A digester can spray acid in a 20-foot cone, dealing 4d8 points of damage to everything in the area. Once a digester uses this ability, it can't use it again until 1d4 rounds later. The creature can also produce a concentrated stream of acid that deals 8d8 points of damage to a single target within 5 feet. In either case, a DC 17 Reflex save halves the damage. The save DC is Constitution-based.

Skills: A digester's coloration gives it a +4 racial bonus on Hide checks. It also has a +4 racial bonus on Jump checks.

Digester

DINOSAUR

Dinosaurs, or terrible lizards, are ancient beasts that may be related to dragons.

Among the traits that predatory dinosaurs share with many dragons are sharp teeth, a savage disposition, a well-developed sense of territory, and a ruthless capacity to hunt. Herbivorous dinosaurs usually are not aggressive unless wounded or defending their young, but may attack if startled or harassed.

Dinosaurs come in many sizes and shapes. Bigger varieties have drab coloration, while smaller dinosaurs have more colorful markings. Most dinosaurs have a pebbly skin texture.

Dinosaurs most often live in rugged or isolated areas that humanoids seldom visit: remote mountain valleys, inaccessible plateaus, tropical islands, and deep fens.

COMBAT

Dinosaurs take full advantage of their size and speed. The swift carnivores stalk prey, staying hidden in cover until they can get into charge range and rush to the attack. Herbivores frequently overrun and trample their opponents.

DEINONYCHUS

Large Animal
Hit Dice: 4d8+16 (34 hp)
Initiative: +2
Speed: 60 ft. (12 squares)
Armor Class: 16 (–1 size, +2 Dex, +5 natural), touch 11, flat-footed 14
Base Attack/Grapple: +3/+11
Attack: Talons +6 melee (2d6+4)
Full Attack: Talons +6 melee (2d6+4) and 2 foreclaws +1 melee (1d3+2) and bite +1 melee (2d4+2)
Space/Reach: 10 ft./5 ft.
Special Attacks: Pounce
Special Qualities: Low-light vision, scent
Saves: Fort +8, Ref +6, Will +2
Abilities: Str 19, Dex 15, Con 19, Int 2, Wis 12, Cha 10
Skills: Hide +8, Jump +26, Listen +10, Spot +10, Survival +10
Feats: Run, Track
Environment: Warm forests
Organization: Solitary, pair, or pack (3–6)
Challenge Rating: 3
Treasure: None
Alignment: Always neutral
Advancement: 5–8 HD (Large)
Level Adjustment: —

This lean, long-legged bipedal creature has wicked-looking claws on its feet and a brightly colored hide that reminds you of a tropical bird. It stands about as tall as a human, and its outstretched tail makes it least twice as long as it is tall.

This fast carnivore is sometimes called a velociraptor, though that name properly belongs to a much smaller creature.

A deinonychus is bright green along its back and flanks, with a much lighter shade of the same color on its underside. The body has darker spots or stripes. Its tail extends straight out behind itself, held aloft by an intricate structure of bony supports, thus allowing its weight to be carried entirely by the back legs. It weighs about 600 pounds.

Combat

A deinonychus uses a combination of speed, grasping forearms, large teeth, and hind legs with ripping talons. It hunts by running at prey, leaping, and ripping with its rear talons as it claws and bites. The talons count as one attack.

A deinonychus has a relatively large brain for a dinosaur, and its pack hunts with cunning tactics.

Pounce (Ex): If a deinonychus charges, it can make a full attack.

Skills: A deinonychus has a +8 racial bonus on Hide, Jump, Listen, Spot, and Survival checks.

ELASMOSAURUS

Huge Animal
Hit Dice: 10d8+66 (111 hp)
Initiative: +2
Speed: 20 ft. (4 squares), swim 50 ft.
Armor Class: 13 (–2 size, +2 Dex, +3 natural), touch 10, flat-footed 11
Base Attack/Grapple: +7/+23
Attack: Bite +13 melee (2d8+12)
Full Attack: Bite +13 melee (2d8+12)
Space/Reach: 15 ft./10 ft.
Special Attacks: —
Special Qualities: Low-light vision, scent
Saves: Fort +15, Ref +9, Will +4
Abilities: Str 26, Dex 14, Con 22, Int 2, Wis 13, Cha 9
Skills: Hide –4*, Listen +4, Spot +9, Swim +16
Feats: Dodge, Great Fortitude, Toughness (2)
Environment: Warm aquatic
Organization: Solitary, pair, or herd (5–8)
Challenge Rating: 7
Treasure: None
Alignment: Always neutral
Advancement: 11–20 HD (Huge); 21–30 HD (Gargantuan)
Level Adjustment: —

This beast has a thick, ovoid body with fins instead of legs and a very long, snaky tail and neck. Its neck makes up one-half of its total length.

Though it resides primarily in the water, an elasmosaurus only breathes air.

An elasmosaurus has a total length of some 30 feet, including a tail half as long as its entire body, and weighs about 5,000 pounds. Observers who see only its head or tail might easily mistake it for a massive snake.

Combat

An elasmosaurus is aggressive and attacks anything it notices. The creature is strong, fast, and highly maneuverable, able to turn quickly and lunge at prey. When hunting, it travels with its head out of the water, snapping down quickly to seize prey.

Skills: *An elasmosaurus has a +8 racial bonus on Hide checks in water.

MEGARAPTOR

Huge Animal
Hit Dice: 8d8+43 (79 hp)
Initiative: +2
Speed: 60 ft. (12 squares)
Armor Class: 16 (–2 size, +2 Dex, +6 natural), touch 10, flat-footed 14
Base Attack/Grapple: +6/+19
Attack: Talons +9 melee (2d8+5)
Full Attack: Talons +9 melee (2d8+5) and 2 foreclaws +4 melee (1d4+2) and bite +4 melee (2d6+2)
Space/Reach: 15 ft./10 ft.
Special Attacks: Pounce
Special Qualities: Low-light vision, scent
Saves: Fort +10, Ref +8, Will +4
Abilities: Str 21, Dex 15, Con 21, Int 2, Wis 15, Cha 10
Skills: Hide +5, Jump +27, Listen +12, Spot +12, Survival +12

Feats: Run, Toughness, Track
Environment: Warm forests
Organization: Solitary, pair, or pack (3–6)
Challenge Rating: 6
Treasure: None
Alignment: Always neutral
Advancement: 9–16 HD (Huge); 17–24 HD (Gargantuan)
Level Adjustment: —

This creature is a larger version of the deinonychus, standing about 12 feet tall with a total length of 24 feet. It has the same appearance, habits, and abilities of the smaller version.

    Pounce (Ex): If a megaraptor charges, it can make a full attack.

    Skills: A megaraptor has a +8 racial bonus on Hide, Jump, Listen, Spot, and Survival checks.

TRICERATOPS

Huge Animal
Hit Dice: 16d8+124 (196 hp)
Initiative: –1
Speed: 30 ft. (6 squares)
Armor Class: 18 (–2 size, –1 Dex, +11 natural), touch 7, flat-footed 18
Base Attack/Grapple: +12/+30
Attack: Gore +20 melee (2d8+15)
Full Attack: Gore +20 melee (2d8+15)
Space/Reach: 15 ft./10 ft.
Special Attacks: Powerful charge, trample 2d12+15
Special Qualities: Low-light vision, scent
Saves: Fort +19, Ref +9, Will +6
Abilities: Str 30, Dex 9, Con 25, Int 1, Wis 12, Cha 7
Skills: Listen +13, Spot +12
Feats: Alertness, Great Fortitude, Toughness (4)
Environment: Temperate plains
Organization: Solitary, pair, or herd (5–8)
Challenge Rating: 9
Treasure: None
Alignment: Always neutral
Advancement: 17–32 HD (Huge); 33–48 HD (Gargantuan)
Level Adjustment: —

The massive beast has a huge plate of bone protecting the front of its 6-foot-long head, from which project two great horns, while a shorter horn juts from its nose.

This massive herbivore is fairly short-tempered and aggressive.
    A triceratops has a body about 25 feet long and weighs about 20,000 pounds.

Combat

These creatures are likely to charge and skewer any creature of at least Large size that infringes on their territory. A triceratops uses its trample attack on smaller opponents.

    Powerful Charge (Ex): When a triceratops charges, its gore attack deals 4d8+20 points of damage.

    Trample (Ex): Reflex half DC 28. The save DC is Strength-based.

TYRANNOSAURUS

Huge Animal
Hit Dice: 18d8+99 (180 hp)
Initiative: +1
Speed: 40 ft. (8 squares)
Armor Class: 14 (–2 size, +1 Dex, +5 natural) touch 9, flat-footed 13
Base Attack/Grapple: +13/+30
Attack: Bite +20 melee (3d6+13)
Full Attack: Bite +20 melee (3d6+13)
Space/Reach: 15 ft./10 ft.
Special Attacks: Improved grab, swallow whole
Special Qualities: Low-light vision, scent
Saves: Fort +16, Ref +12, Will +8
Abilities: Str 28, Dex 12, Con 21, Int 2, Wis 15, Cha 10
Skills: Hide –2, Listen +14, Spot +14
Feats: Alertness, Improved Natural Attack (bite), Run, Toughness (3), Track
Environment: Warm plains
Organization: Solitary or pair
Challenge Rating: 8
Treasure: None
Alignment: Always neutral
Advancement: 19–36 HD (Huge); 37–54 HD (Gargantuan)
Level Adjustment: —

This towering predator has an enormous head and a mouth full of dagger-sized teeth. It stands on two powerful legs and has only vestigial forelimbs.

This ravenous creature is the most fearsome of all carnivorous dinosaurs.

    Despite its enormous size and 6-ton weight, a tyrannosaurus is a swift runner. Its head is nearly 6 feet long, and its teeth are from 3 to 6 inches in length. It is slightly more than 30 feet long from nose to tail.

    A tyrannosaurus eats almost anything it can sink its teeth into, and spends a great deal of its time scavenging for carrion and chasing smaller carnivores away from their kills.

Combat

A tyrannosaurus pursues and eats just about anything it sees. Its tactics are simple—charge in and bite.

    Improved Grab (Ex): To use this ability, a tyrannosaurus must hit an opponent of up to one size smaller with its bite attack. It can then attempt to start a grapple as a free action without provoking

Tyrannosaurus

an attack of opportunity. If it wins the grapple check, it establishes a hold and can try to swallow the foe the following round.

Swallow Whole (Ex): A tyrannosaurus can try to swallow a grabbed opponent of up to two sizes smaller by making a successful grapple check.

The swallowed creature takes 2d8+8 points of bludgeoning damage and 8 points of acid damage per round from the tyrannosaurus's gizzard. A swallowed creature can cut its way out by using a light slashing or piercing weapon to deal 25 points of damage to the gizzard (AC 12). Once the creature exits, muscular action closes the hole; another swallowed opponent must cut its own way out.

A Huge tyrannosaurus's gizzard can hold 2 Medium, 8 Small, 32 Tiny, or 128 Diminutive or smaller opponents.

Skills: A tyrannosaurus has a +2 racial bonus on Listen and Spot checks.

DIRE ANIMAL

Dire animals are larger, tougher, meaner versions of ordinary animals. Each kind tends to have a feral, prehistoric, or even demonic appearance.

DIRE APE

Large Animal
Hit Dice: 5d8+13 (35 hp)
Initiative: +2
Speed: 30 ft. (6 squares), climb 15 ft.
Armor Class: 15 (−1 size, +2 Dex, +4 natural), touch 11, flat-footed 13
Base Attack/Grapple: +3/+13
Attack: Claw +8 melee (1d6+6)
Full Attack: 2 claws +8 melee (1d6+6) and bite +3 melee (1d8+3)
Space/Reach: 10 ft./10 ft.
Special Attacks: Rend 2d6+9
Special Qualities: Low-light vision, scent
Saves: Fort +6, Ref +6, Will +5
Abilities: Str 22, Dex 15, Con 14, Int 2, Wis 12, Cha 7
Skills: Climb +14, Listen +5, Move Silently +4, Spot +6
Feats: Alertness, Toughness
Environment: Warm forests
Organization: Solitary or company (5–8)
Challenge Rating: 3
Treasure: None
Alignment: Always neutral
Advancement: 6–15 HD (Large)
Level Adjustment: —

This great, feral ape is about the size of an ogre, but even more muscular. It is barrel-chested, with thick, black fur, long arms, and a broad muzzle. It seems well equipped with claws and teeth.

Dire apes are territorial and apt to attack anything they see.

A dire ape stands about 9 feet tall and weighs from 800 to 1,200 pounds.

Combat

Dire apes attack anything that enters their territory, even other dire apes. If an opponent's armor foils a dire ape's attacks, the creature will attempt to grapple and pin, then rend the prone opponent.

Rend (Ex): A dire ape that hits with both claw attacks latches onto the opponent's body and tears the flesh. This attack automatically deals an extra 2d6+12 points of damage.

Skills: Dire apes have a +8 racial bonus on Climb checks and can always choose to take 10 on Climb checks, even if rushed or threatened.

DIRE BADGER

Medium Animal
Hit Dice: 3d8+15 (28 hp)
Initiative: +3
Speed: 30 ft. (6 squares), burrow 10 ft.
Armor Class: 16 (+3 Dex, +3 natural), touch 13, flat-footed 13
Base Attack/Grapple: +2/+4
Attack: Claw +4 melee (1d4+2)
Full Attack: 2 claws +4 melee (1d4+2) and bite −1 melee (1d6+1)
Space/Reach: 5 ft./5 ft.
Special Attacks: Rage
Special Qualities: Low-light vision, scent
Saves: Fort +7, Ref +6, Will +4
Abilities: Str 14, Dex 17, Con 19, Int 2, Wis 12, Cha 10
Skills: Listen +6, Spot +6
Feats: Alertness, Toughness, Track[B]
Environment: Temperate forests
Organization: Solitary or cete (2–5)
Challenge Rating: 2
Treasure: None
Alignment: Always neutral
Advancement: 4–9 HD (Large)
Level Adjustment: —

This squat, muscular creature is covered in wild, thick fur. Its stout legs end in clawed feet, and its pointed snout has a wide mouth full of sharp teeth.

These vicious creatures tolerate no intrusions. They cannot burrow into solid rock, but can move through just about any material softer than that. A dire badger usually leaves behind a usable tunnel 5 feet in diameter when burrowing unless the material it's moving through is very loose.

A dire badger is from 5 to 7 feet in length and can weigh up to 500 pounds.

Combat

Dire badgers attack with their sharp claws and teeth.

Rage (Ex): A dire badger that takes damage in combat flies into a berserk rage on its next turn, clawing and biting madly until either it or its opponent is dead. It gains +4 Strength, +4 Constitution, and −2 AC. The creature cannot end its rage voluntarily.

DIRE BAT

Large Animal
Hit Dice: 4d8+12 (30 hp)
Initiative: +6
Speed: 20 ft. (4 squares), fly 40 ft. (good)
Armor Class: 20 (−1 size, +6 Dex, +5 natural), touch 15, flat-footed 14
Base Attack/Grapple: +3/+10
Attack: Bite +5 melee (1d8+4)
Full Attack: Bite +5 melee (1d8+4)
Space/Reach: 10 ft./5 ft.
Special Attacks: —
Special Qualities: Blindsense 40 ft.
Saves: Fort +7, Ref +10, Will +6
Abilities: Str 17, Dex 22, Con 17, Int 2, Wis 14, Cha 6
Skills: Hide +4, Listen +12*, Move Silently +11, Spot +8*
Feats: Alertness, Stealthy
Environment: Temperate deserts
Organization: Solitary or colony (5–8)
Challenge Rating: 2
Treasure: None
Alignment: Always neutral
Advancement: 5–12 HD (Large)
Level Adjustment: —

This terrifying bat has a body as big as a horse's and leathery wings that spread farther than a dragon's. Shaggy fur covers most of the body, with patches of bony armor showing through here and there.

These nocturnal hunters get excited easily, and they usually try to slay or drive off any creatures they encounter.

A dire bat has a wingspan of 15 feet and weighs about 200 pounds.

Combat

Dire bats swoop down upon unsuspecting prey from above.

Blindsense (Ex): A dire bat uses echo-location to pinpoint creatures within 40 feet. Opponents still have total concealment against the bat unless it can actually see them.

Skills: Dire bats have a +4 racial bonus on Spot and Listen checks. These bonuses are lost if its blindsense is negated.

DIRE BEAR

Large Animal
Hit Dice: 12d8+51 (105 hp)
Initiative: +1
Speed: 40 ft. (8 squares)
Armor Class: 17 (−1 size, +1 Dex, +7 natural), touch 10, flat-footed 16
Base Attack/Grapple: +9/+23
Attack: Claw +19 melee (2d4+10)
Full Attack: 2 claws +19 melee (2d4+10) and bite +13 melee (2d8+5)
Space/Reach: 10 ft./5 ft.
Special Attacks: Improved grab
Special Qualities: Low-light vision, scent
Saves: Fort +12, Ref +9, Will +9
Abilities: Str 31, Dex 13, Con 19, Int 2, Wis 12, Cha 10
Skills: Listen +10, Spot +10, Swim +13
Feats: Alertness, Endurance, Run, Toughness, Weapon Focus (claw)
Environment: Cold forests
Organization: Solitary or pair
Challenge Rating: 7
Treasure: None
Alignment: Always neutral
Advancement: 13–16 HD (Large); 17–36 HD (Huge)
Level Adjustment: —

This hulking bear has bony brow ridges and claws like sickles, with a wildness and destructive gleam in its cold, piercing eyes.

The omnivorous dire bear usually does not bother creatures that try to avoid it, but will aggressively defend a kill or other source of food. It will not hesitate to rip apart anything that might contain something edible.

A typical dire bear is 12 feet long and weighs as much as 8,000 pounds.

Combat

A dire bear attacks by tearing at opponents with its claws.

Improved Grab (Ex): To use this ability, a dire bear must hit

Dire bear

with a claw attack. It can then attempt to start a grapple as a free action without provoking an attack of opportunity.

DIRE BOAR

Large Animal
Hit Dice: 7d8+21 (52 hp)
Initiative: +0
Speed: 40 ft. (8 squares)
Armor Class: 15 (−1 size, +6 natural), touch 9, flat-footed 15
Base Attack/Grapple: +5/+17
Attack: Gore +12 melee (1d8+12)
Full Attack: Gore +12 melee (1d8+12)
Space/Reach: 10 ft./5 ft.
Special Attacks: Ferocity
Special Qualities: Low-light vision, scent
Saves: Fort +8, Ref +5, Will +8
Abilities: Str 27, Dex 10, Con 17, Int 2, Wis 13, Cha 8
Skills: Listen +8, Spot +8
Feats: Alertness, Endurance, Iron Will
Environment: Temperate forests
Organization: Solitary or herd (5–8)
Challenge Rating: 4
Treasure: None
Alignment: Always neutral
Advancement: 8–16 HD (Large); 17–21 HD (Huge)
Level Adjustment: —

This giant boar has an arched back as high as a human is tall. It has spiny armor on its head and back, great, gleaming tusks, and small, furious, demon eyes.

Dire boars are omnivorous and spend most of their time rooting around, much as ordinary pigs do. They viciously attack anything that approaches them, however. Dire boars grow up to 12 feet long and weigh as much as 2,000 pounds.

Combat

A dire boar charges its opponent, trying to rip the target open with its tusks.

Ferocity (Ex): A dire boar is such a tenacious combatant that it continues to fight without penalty even while disabled or dying.

DIRE LION

Large Animal
Hit Dice: 8d8+24 (60 hp)
Initiative: +2
Speed: 40 ft. (8 squares)
Armor Class: 15 (−1 size, +2 Dex, +4 natural), touch 11, flat-footed 13
Base Attack/Grapple: +6/+17
Attack: Claw +13 melee (1d6+7)
Full Attack: 2 claws +13 melee (1d6+7) and bite +7 melee (1d8+3)
Space/Reach: 10 ft./5 ft.
Special Attacks: Improved grab, pounce, rake 1d6+3
Special Qualities: Low-light vision, scent
Saves: Fort +9, Ref +8, Will +7
Abilities: Str 25, Dex 15, Con 17, Int 2, Wis 12, Cha 10
Skills: Hide +2*, Listen +7, Move Silently +5, Spot +7
Feats: Alertness, Run, Weapon Focus (claw)
Environment: Warm plains

Organization: Solitary, pair, or pride (6–10)
Challenge Rating: 5
Treasure: None
Alignment: Always neutral
Advancement: 9–16 HD (Large); 17–24 HD (Huge)
Level Adjustment: —

This immense lion has a short mane and a spotted, tawny coat, but there ends the resemblance to a normal animal. This monstrous creature has bony protrusions around its eyes and shoulders, with spiked ridges running along the length of its back.

Dire lions are patient hunters, just like their smaller cousins, but apt to take on bigger prey.

Dire lions grow to be up to 15 feet long and weigh up to 3,500 pounds.

Combat

A dire lion attacks by running at prey, leaping, and clawing and biting as it rakes with its rear claws. It often jumps onto a creature larger than itself.

Improved Grab (Ex): To use this ability, a dire lion must hit with its bite attack. It can then attempt to start a grapple as a free action without provoking an attack of opportunity. If it wins the grapple check, it establishes a hold and can rake.

Pounce (Ex): If a dire lion charges, it can make a full attack, including two rake attacks.

Rake (Ex): Attack bonus +12 melee, damage 1d6+3.

Skills: Dire lions have a +4 racial bonus on Hide and Move Silently checks. *In areas of tall grass or heavy undergrowth, the Hide bonus improves to +8.

DIRE RAT

Small Animal
Hit Dice: 1d8+1 (5 hp)
Initiative: +3
Speed: 40 ft. (8 squares), climb 20 ft.
Armor Class: 15 (+1 size, +3 Dex, +1 natural), touch 14, flat-footed 12
Base Attack/Grapple: +0/−4
Attack: Bite +4 melee (1d4 plus disease)
Full Attack: Bite +4 melee (1d4 plus disease)
Space/Reach: 5 ft./5 ft.
Special Attacks: Disease
Special Qualities: Low-light vision, scent
Saves: Fort +3, Ref +5, Will +3
Abilities: Str 10, Dex 17, Con 12, Int 1, Wis 12, Cha 4
Skills: Climb +11, Hide +8, Listen +4, Move Silently +4, Spot +4, Swim +11
Feats: Alertness, Weapon Finesse[B]
Environment: Any
Organization: Solitary or pack (11–20)
Challenge Rating: 1/3
Treasure: None
Alignment: Always neutral
Advancement: 2–3 HD (Small); 4–6 HD (Medium)
Level Adjustment: —

This enormous rat looks bigger and more vicious than most dogs. It has coarse, spiky fur, malevolent eyes, and a long, naked tail.

Dire rats are omnivorous scavengers, but will attack to defend their nests and territories.

A dire rat can grow to be up to 4 feet long and weigh over 50 pounds.

Combat

Dire rat packs attack fearlessly, biting and chewing with their sharp incisors.

Disease (Ex): Filth fever—bite, Fortitude DC 11, incubation period 1d3 days, damage 1d3 Dex and 1d3 Con. The save DC is Constitution-based.

Skills: Dire rats have a +8 racial bonus on Swim checks.

Dire rats have a +8 racial bonus on Climb checks and can always choose to take 10 on Climb checks, even if rushed or threatened.

Dire rats use their Dexterity modifier for Climb and Swim checks.

DIRE SHARK

Huge Animal (Aquatic)
Hit Dice: 18d8+66 (147 hp)
Initiative: +2
Speed: Swim 60 ft. (12 squares)
Armor Class: 17 (−2 size, +2 Dex, +7 natural), touch 10, flat-footed 15
Base Attack/Grapple: +13/+27
Attack: Bite +18 melee (2d8+9)
Full Attack: Bite +18 melee (2d8+9)
Space/Reach: 15 ft./10 ft.
Special Attacks: Improved grab, swallow whole
Special Qualities: Keen scent
Saves: Fort +14, Ref +13, Will +12
Abilities: Str 23, Dex 15, Con 17, Int 1, Wis 12, Cha 10
Skills: Listen +12, Spot +11, Swim +14
Feats: Improved Natural Attack (bite), Toughness (4), Weapon Focus (bite)
Environment: Cold aquatic
Organization: Solitary or school (2–5)
Challenge Rating: 9
Treasure: None
Alignment: Always neutral
Advancement: 19–32 (Huge); 33–54 (Gargantuan)
Level Adjustment: —

This enormous sea monster has a streamlined body with a triangular fin atop its back, a toothy mouth set well under its long snout, and a symmetrical tail shaped like a crescent moon.

Dire sharks attack anything they perceive to be edible, even larger creatures.

This monstrous fish can grow to a length of 25 feet and weigh more than 20,000 pounds.

Combat

Dire sharks bite with their powerful jaws, swallowing smaller creatures in one gulp.

Improved Grab (Ex): To use this ability, a dire shark must hit with its bite attack. It can then attempt to start a grapple as a free action without provoking an attack of opportunity. If it wins the grapple check, it establishes a hold and can try to swallow the foe in the following round.

Swallow Whole (Ex): A dire shark can try to swallow a grabbed opponent of up to one size smaller by making a successful grapple check. Once inside, the opponent takes 2d6+6 points of bludgeoning damage plus 1d8+4 points of acid damage per round from the shark's digestive juices. A swallowed creature can cut its way out using a light slashing or piercing weapon by dealing 25 points of damage to the shark's digestive tract (AC 13). Once the creature exits, muscular action closes the hole; another swallowed opponent must cut its own way out.

A Huge dire shark's gullet can hold 2 Large, 8 Medium or Small, 32 Tiny, 128 Diminutive, or 512 Fine or smaller opponents.

Keen Scent (Ex): A dire shark can notice creatures by scent in a 180-foot radius and can detect blood in the water at a range of up to 1 mile.

Skills: A dire shark has a +8 racial bonus on any Swim check to perform some special action or avoid a hazard. It can always choose to take 10 on a Swim check, even if distracted or endangered. It can use the run action while swimming, provided it swims in a straight line.

DIRE TIGER

Large Animal
Hit Dice: 16d8+48 (120 hp)
Initiative: +2
Speed: 40 ft. (8 squares)
Armor Class: 17 (−1 size, +2 Dex, +6 natural), touch 11, flat-footed 15
Base Attack/Grapple: +12/+24
Attack: Claw +20 melee (2d4+8)
Full Attack: 2 claws +20 melee (2d4+8) and bite +14 melee (2d6+4)
Space/Reach: 10 ft./5 ft.
Special Attacks: Improved grab, pounce, rake 2d4+4
Special Qualities: Low-light vision, scent
Saves: Fort +13, Ref +12, Will +11
Abilities: Str 27, Dex 15, Con 17, Int 2, Wis 12, Cha 10
Skills: Hide +7*, Jump +14, Listen +6, Move Silently +11, Spot +7, Swim +10
Feats: Alertness, Improved Natural Attack (claw), Improved Natural Attack (bite), Run, Stealthy, Weapon Focus (claw)
Environment: Warm forests
Organization: Solitary or pair
Challenge Rating: 8
Treasure: None
Alignment: Always neutral
Advancement: 17–32 HD (Large); 33–48 (Huge)
Level Adjustment: —

This immense, monstrous feline is almost as tall at the shoulder as a human. It has a long body with bold stripes and paws the size of bucklers.

Dire tigers prey on just about anything that moves. They will patiently stalk a potential meal, striking whenever the creature lets down its guard.

Dire tigers grow to be over 12 feet long and can weigh up to 6,000 pounds.

Combat

A dire tiger attacks by running at prey, leaping, and clawing and biting as it rakes with its rear claws.

Improved Grab (Ex): To use this ability, a dire tiger must hit with its bite attack. It can then attempt to start a grapple as a free action without provoking an attack of opportunity. If it wins the grapple check, it establishes a hold and can rake.

Pounce (Ex): If a dire tiger charges, it can make a full attack, including two rake attacks.

Rake (Ex): Attack bonus +18 melee, damage 2d4+4.

Skills: Dire tigers have a +4 racial bonus on Hide and Move Silently checks. *In areas of tall grass or heavy undergrowth, the Hide bonus improves to +8.

DIRE WEASEL

Medium Animal
Hit Dice: 3d8 (13 hp)
Initiative: +4
Speed: 40 ft. (8 squares)
Armor Class: 16 (+4 Dex, +2 natural), touch 14, flat-footed 12
Base Attack/Grapple: +2/+4

Attack: Bite +6 melee (1d6+3)
Full Attack: Bite +6 melee (1d6+3)
Space/Reach: 5 ft./5 ft.
Special Attacks: Attach, blood drain
Special Qualities: Low-light vision, scent
Saves: Fort +3, Ref +7, Will +4
Abilities: Str 14, Dex 19, Con 10, Int 2, Wis 12, Cha 11
Skills: Hide +8, Listen +3, Move Silently +8, Spot +5
Feats: Alertness, Stealthy , Weapon Finesse[B]
Environment: Temperate hills
Organization: Solitary or pair
Challenge Rating: 2
Treasure: None
Alignment: Always neutral
Advancement: 4–6 HD (Medium); 7–9 HD (Large)
Level Adjustment: —

This sleek, fur-covered creature has a body longer than a human is tall. It has a wedged-shaped head crowned in short horns, four short legs, and a stumpy tail. It movements are fluid and very quick.

Dire weasels are aggressive, almost manic creatures with boundless energy.

Dire weasels grow to be up to 10 feet long and can reach a weight of 700 pounds.

Combat

Dire weasels stalk their prey in the dark and then leap on it, biting and clawing.

Attach (Ex): A dire weasel that hits with its bite attack latches onto the opponent's body with its powerful jaws. An attached dire weasel loses its Dexterity bonus to AC and thus has an AC of 12.

An attached dire weasel can be struck with a weapon or grappled itself. To remove an attached dire weasel through grappling, the opponent must achieve a pin against the creature.

Blood Drain (Ex): A dire weasel drains blood for 1d4 points of Constitution damage each round it remains attached.

DIRE WOLF

Large Animal
Hit Dice: 6d8+18 (45 hp)
Initiative: +2
Speed: 50 ft. (10 squares)
Armor Class: 14 (−1 size, +2 Dex, +3 natural), touch 11, flat-footed 12
Base Attack/Grapple: +4/+15
Attack: Bite +11 melee (1d8+10)
Full Attack: Bite +11 melee (1d8+10)
Space/Reach: 10 ft./5 ft.
Special Attacks: Trip
Special Qualities: Low-light vision, scent
Saves: Fort +8, Ref +7, Will +6
Abilities: Str 25, Dex 15, Con 17, Int 2, Wis 12, Cha 10
Skills: Hide +0, Listen +7, Move Silently +4, Spot +7, Survival +2*
Feats: Alertness, Run, Track[B], Weapon Focus (bite)
Environment: Temperate forests
Organization: Solitary or pack (5–8)
Challenge Rating: 3
Treasure: None
Alignment: Always neutral
Advancement: 7–18 HD (Large)
Level Adjustment: —

This immense gray wolf seems as big as a horse. It has fiery eyes and a thick coat of fur.

Dire wolves are efficient pack hunters that will kill anything they can catch.

Dire wolves are mottled gray or black, about 9 feet long and weighing some 800 pounds.

Combat

Dire wolves prefer to attack in packs, surrounding and flanking a foe when they can.

Trip (Ex): A dire wolf that hits with a bite attack can attempt to trip its opponent (+11 check modifier) as a free action without making a touch attack or provoking an attack of opportunity. If the attempt fails, the opponent cannot react to trip the dire wolf.

Skills: A dire wolf has a +2 racial bonus on Hide, Listen, Move Silently, and Spot checks.*It also has a +4 racial bonus on Survival checks when tracking by scent.

DIRE WOLVERINE

Large Animal

Hit Dice: 5d8+23 (45 hp)

Initiative: +3

Speed: 30 ft. (6 squares), climb 10 ft.

Armor Class: 16 (–1 size, +3 Dex, +4 natural), touch 12, flat-footed 13

Base Attack/Grapple: +3/+13

Attack: Claw +8 melee (1d6+6)

Full Attack: 2 claws +8 melee (1d6+6) and bite +3 melee (1d8+3)

Space/Reach: 10 ft./5 ft.

Special Attacks: Rage

Special Qualities: Low-light vision, scent

Saves: Fort +8, Ref +7, Will +5

Abilities: Str 22, Dex 17, Con 19, Int 2, Wis 12, Cha 10

Skills: Climb +14, Listen +7, Spot +7

Feats: Alertness, Toughness, Track[B]

Environment: Cold forests

Organization: Solitary or pair

Challenge Rating: 4

Treasure: None

Alignment: Always neutral

Advancement: 6–15 HD (Large)

Level Adjustment: —

This massive, low-slung creature has a wedge-shaped head and body covered in coarse, shaggy fur. Its legs are short and thick, and it has claws like pickaxes on its feet.

These foul-tempered creatures have been known to attack settlements, destroying both livestock and food stores. They are reputed to be utterly fearless.

Dire wolverines grow to about 12 feet in length and can weigh as much as 2,000 pounds.

Combat

Dire wolverines attack opponents wantonly, fearing no other creatures.

Rage (Ex): A dire wolverine that takes damage in combat flies into a berserk rage on its next turn, clawing and biting madly until either it or its opponent is dead. An enraged dire wolverine gains +4 Strength, +4 Constitution, and –2 AC. The creature cannot end its rage voluntarily.

Skills: A dire wolverine has a +8 racial bonus on Climb checks and can always choose to take 10 on Climb checks, even if rushed or threatened.

DISPLACER BEAST

This creature looks like an emaciated panther, with blue-black fur, six legs, and a body that is nothing but muscle and bone. A pair of tentacles sprout from its shoulders and end in horny-ridged pads.

The displacer beast is a savage and stealthy carnivore that resembles a puma in some respects.

Displacer beasts favor small game but will eat anything they can catch. They regard all other creatures as prey and tend to attack anything they meet. They have a deep-seated hatred of blink dogs, and the two attack each other ruthlessly when their paths cross. A displacer beast is the size of a Bengal tiger, about 9 feet long and weighing about 500 pounds.

Displacer beasts speak Common.

	Displacer Beast Large Magical Beast	Displacer Beast Pack Lord Huge Magical Beast
Hit Dice:	6d10+18 (51 hp)	18d10+192 (203 hp)
Initiative:	+2	+1
Speed:	40 ft. (8 squares)	40 ft. (8 squares)
Armor Class:	16 (–1 size, +2 Dex, +5 natural), touch 11, flat-footed 14	17 (–2 size, +1 Dex, +8 natural), touch 9, flat-footed 16
Base Attack/Grapple:	+6/+14	+18/+34
Attack:	Tentacle +9 melee (1d6+4)	Tentacle +25 melee (1d8+8)
Full Attack:	2 tentacles +9 melee (1d6+4) and bite +4 melee (1d8 +2)	2 tentacles +25 melee (1d8+8) and bite +19 melee (2d6+4)
Space/Reach:	10 ft./5 ft. (10 ft. with tentacles)	15 ft./10 ft. (20 ft. with tentacles)
Special Attacks:	—	—
Special Qualities:	Darkvision 60 ft., displacement, low-light vision, resistance to ranged attacks	Darkvision 60 ft., displacement, low-light vision, resistance to ranged attacks
Saves:	Fort +8, Ref +7, Will +3	Fort +16, Ref +14, Will +9
Abilities:	Str 18, Dex 15, Con 16, Int 5, Wis 12, Cha 8	Str 26, Dex 13, Con 20, Int 5, Wis 12, Cha 8
Skills:	Hide +10, Listen +5, Move Silently +7, Spot +5	Hide +11, Listen +4, Move Silently +6, Spot +10
Feats:	Alertness, Dodge, Stealthy	Alertness, Combat Reflexes, Dodge, Iron Will, Lightning Reflexes, Toughness, Weapon Focus (tentacle)
Environment:	Temperate hills	Temperate hills
Organization:	Solitary, pair, or pride (6–10)	Solitary or pair
Challenge Rating:	4	12
Treasure:	1/10 coins; 50% goods; 50% items	1/10 coins, 50% goods, standard items
Alignment:	Usually lawful evil	Usually lawful evil
Advancement:	7–9 HD (Large); 10–18 HD (Huge)	—
Level Adjustment:	+4	—

COMBAT

Displacer beasts tear at opponents with their tentacles and bite foes that get close.

Displacement (Su): A light-bending glamer continually surrounds a displacer beast, making it difficult to surmise the creature's true location. Any melee or ranged attack directed at it has a 50% miss chance unless the attacker can locate the beast by some means other than sight. A *true seeing* effect allows the user to see the beast's position, but *see invisibility* has no effect.

Resistance to Ranged Attacks (Su): A displacer beast has a +2 resistance bonus on saves against any ranged magical attack that specifically targets it (except for ranged touch attacks).

Skills: A displacer beast has a +8 racial bonus on Hide checks, thanks to its displacement ability.

DISPLACER BEAST PACK LORD

Due to the bizarre nature of their anatomy, displacer beasts are unusually likely to produce mutant offspring. These whelps can grow to tremendous size, reaching a length of 20 feet and standing almost 10 feet high at the shoulder. Pack lords, as these gigantic displacer beasts are known, frequently lead bands of their smaller fellows.

Except for their freakish size and strength, pack lords resemble normal displacer beasts.

Displacer beast

Illus. by S. Wood

DOPPELGANGER

Medium Monstrous Humanoid (Shapechanger)

Hit Dice: 4d8+4 (22 hp)
Initiative: +1
Speed: 30 ft. (6 squares)
Armor Class: 15 (+1 Dex, +4 natural), touch 11, flat-footed 14
Base Attack/Grapple: +4/+5
Attack: Slam +5 melee (1d6+1)
Full Attack: Slam +5 melee (1d6+1)
Space/Reach: 5 ft./5 ft.
Special Attacks: Detect thoughts
Special Qualities: Change shape, immunity to *sleep* and charm effects
Saves: Fort +4, Ref +5, Will +6
Abilities: Str 12, Dex 13, Con 12, Int 13, Wis 14, Cha 13
Skills: Bluff +10*, Diplomacy +3, Disguise +9* (+11 acting), Intimidate +3, Listen +6, Sense Motive +6, Spot +6
Feats: Dodge, Great Fortitude
Environment: Any
Organization: Solitary, pair, or gang (3–6)
Challenge Rating: 3
Treasure: Double standard
Alignment: Usually neutral
Advancement: By character class
Level Adjustment: +4

This gaunt, gray-skinned humanoid has long, gangly limbs and a bulbous head with large, octopoid eyes. Its face is otherwise blank and featureless.

Doppelgangers are strange beings that are able to take on the shapes of those they encounter. In its natural form, the creature looks more or less humanoid, but slender and frail, with gangly limbs and half-formed features. The flesh is pale and hairless. Its large, bulging eyes are yellow with slitted pupils.

A doppelganger's appearance is deceiving even when it's in its true form. A doppelganger is hardy, with a natural agility not in keeping with its frail appearance.

Because they can take the shape of any humanoid between 4 and 8 feet tall, doppelgangers are natural spies and assassins. They can sneak past sentries, slip into secured places, and fool even lovers or close friends. They are cunning and patient, willing to wait until an opportunity presents itself instead of attacking rashly.

Doppelgangers make excellent use of their natural mimicry to stage ambushes, bait traps, and infiltrate humanoid society. Although not usually evil, they are interested only in themselves and regard all others as playthings to be manipulated and deceived.

It is natural form a doppelganger is about 5-1/2 feet tall and weighs abut 150 pounds.

COMBAT

When in its natural form, a doppelganger strikes with its powerful fists. In the shape of a warrior or some other armed person, it attacks with whatever weapon is appropriate. In such cases, it uses its detect thoughts ability to employ the same tactics and strategies as the person it is impersonating.

Detect Thoughts (Su): A doppelganger can continuously use *detect thoughts* as the spell (caster level 18th; Will DC 13 negates). It can suppress or resume this ability as a free action. The save DC is Charisma-based.

Change Shape (Su): A doppelganger can assume the shape of any Small or Medium humanoid. In humanoid form, the doppelganger loses its natural attacks. A doppelganger can remain in its humanoid form until it chooses to assume a new one. A change in form cannot be dispelled, but a doppelganger reverts to its natural form when killed. A *true seeing* spell or ability reveals its natural form.

Doppelganger

Skills: A doppelganger has a +4 racial bonus on Bluff and Disguise checks. *When using its change shape ability, a doppelganger gets an additional +10 circumstance bonus on Disguise checks. If it can read an opponent's mind, it gets a further +4 circumstance bonus on Bluff and Disguise checks.

DOPPELGANGERS AS CHARACTERS

Spies supreme, doppelgangers infiltrate enemy territory, impersonate leaders, and probe enemies' minds for thoughts and plans.

Doppelganger characters possess the following racial traits.

— +2 Strength, +2, Dexterity, +2 Constitution, +2 Intelligence, +4 Wisdom, +2 Charisma.

—Medium size.

—A doppelganger's base land speed is 30 feet.

—Darkvision: Doppelgangers can see in the dark up to 60 feet.

—Racial Hit Dice: A doppelganger begins with four levels of monstrous humanoid, which provide 4d8 Hit Dice, a base attack bonus of +4, and base saving throw bonuses of Fort +1, Ref +4, and Will +4.

––Racial Skills: A doppelganger's monstrous humanoid levels give it skill points equal to 7 × (2 + Int modifier). Its class skills are Bluff, Diplomacy, Disguise, Intimidate, Listen, Sense Motive, and Spot.

—Racial Feats: A doppelganger's monstrous humanoid levels give it two feats.

— +4 natural armor bonus.

— +4 racial bonus on Bluff and Disguise checks. When using its change shape ability, a doppelganger gets an additional +10 circumstance bonus on Disguise checks. If it can read an opponent's mind, it gets a further +4 circumstance bonus on Bluff and Disguise checks.

—Special Attacks (see above): Detect thoughts.

—Special Qualities (see above): Change shape, immunity to *sleep* and charm effects.

—Automatic Languages: Common. Bonus Languages: Auran, Dwarven, Elven, Gnome, Halfling, Giant, Terran.

—Favored Class: Rogue.

—Level adjustment +4.

DRAGON, TRUE

True dragons are winged, reptilelike creatures of ancient lineage. They are known and feared for their size, physical prowess, and magical abilities. The oldest dragons are among the most powerful creatures in the world.

The known varieties of true dragons (as opposed to other creatures that have the dragon type) fall into two broad categories: chromatic and metallic. The chromatic dragons are black, blue, green, red, and white; they are all evil and extremely fierce. The metallic dragons are brass, bronze, copper, gold, and silver; they are all good, usually noble, and highly respected by the wise.

All true dragons gain more abilities and greater power as they age. (Other creatures that have the dragon type do not.) They range in length from several feet upon hatching to more than 100 feet after attaining the status of great wyrm. The size of a particular dragon varies according to age and variety.

Though they are fearsome predators, dragons scavenge when necessary and can eat almost anything if they are hungry enough. A dragon's metabolism operates like a highly efficient furnace and can metabolize even inorganic material. Some dragons have developed a taste for such fare.

Although goals and ideals vary among varieties, all dragons are covetous. They like to hoard wealth, collecting mounds of coins and gathering as many gems, jewels, and magic items as possible. Those with large hoards are loath to leave them for long, venturing out of their lairs only to patrol the immediate area or to get food. For dragons, there is no such thing as

DRAGON AGE CATEGORIES

	Category	Age (Years)
1	Wyrmling	0–5
2	Very young	6–15
3	Young	16–25
4	Juvenile	26–50
5	Young adult	51–100
6	Adult	101–200
7	Mature adult	201–400
8	Old	401–600
9	Very old	601–800
10	Ancient	801–1,000
11	Wyrm	1,001–1,200
12	Great wyrm	1,201 or more

enough treasure. It's pleasing to look at, and they bask in its radiance. Dragons like to make beds of their hoards, shaping nooks and mounds to fit their bodies. By the time a dragon matures to the age of great wyrm, hundreds of gems and coins may be imbedded in its hide.

All dragons speak Draconic.

COMBAT

A dragon attacks with its powerful claws and bite, and can also use a breath weapon and special physical attacks, depending on its size. It prefers to fight on the wing, staying out of reach until it has worn down the enemy with ranged attacks. Older, more intelligent dragons are adept at sizing up the opposition and eliminating the most dangerous foes first (or avoiding them while picking off weaker enemies).

The accompanying table provides space and reach statistics for dragons of various sizes, plus the natural weapons a dragon of a certain size can employ and the damage those attacks deal.

Bite: Bite attacks deal the indicated damage plus the dragon's Strength bonus. A dragon also can use its bite to snatch opponents if it has the Snatch feat (see page 304).

Claw: Claw attacks deal the indicated damage plus 1/2 the dragon's Strength bonus (round down). The dragon also can use its claws to snatch opponents if it has the Snatch feat (see page 304). Claw attacks are secondary attacks, requiring a −5 penalty on the attack roll. (Many dragons choose the Multiattack feat to lessen this penalty to −2.)

Wing: The dragon can slam opponents with its wings, even when flying. Wing attacks deal the indicated damage plus 1/2 the dragon's Strength bonus (round down) and are treated as secondary attacks.

Tail Slap: The dragon can slap one opponent each round with its tail. A tail slap deals the indicated damage plus 1-1/2 times the dragon's Strength bonus (round down) and is treated as a secondary attack.

Crush (Ex): This special attack allows a flying or jumping dragon of at least Huge size to land on opponents as a standard action, using its whole body to crush them. Crush attacks are effective only against opponents three or more size categories smaller than the dragon (though it can attempt normal overrun or grapple attacks against larger opponents).

A crush attack affects as many creatures as can fit under the dragon's body. Creatures in the affected area must succeed on a Reflex save (DC equal to that of the dragon's breath weapon) or be pinned, automatically taking bludgeoning damage during the next round unless the dragon moves off them. If the dragon chooses to maintain the pin, treat it as a normal grapple attack. Pinned opponents take damage from the crush each round if they don't escape.

A crush attack deals the indicated damage plus 1-1/2 times the dragon's Strength bonus (round down).

Tail Sweep (Ex): This special attack allows a dragon of at least Gargantuan size to sweep with its tail as a standard action. The

DRAGON SPACE/REACH, ATTACKS, AND DAMAGE

Size	Space/Reach*	1 Bite	2 Claws	2 Wings	1 Tail Slap	1 Crush	1 Tail Sweep
Tiny	2-1/2 ft./0 ft. (5 ft. with bite)	1d4	1d3	—	—	—	—
Small	5 ft./5 ft.	1d6	1d4	—	—	—	—
Medium	5 ft./5 ft.	1d8	1d6	1d4	—	—	—
Large	10 ft./5 ft. (10 ft. with bite)	2d6	1d8	1d6	1d8	—	—
Huge	15 ft./10 ft. (15 ft. with bite)	2d8	2d6	1d8	2d6	2d8	—
Gargantuan	20 ft./15 ft. (20 ft. with bite)	4d6	2d8	2d6	2d8	4d6	2d6
Colossal	30 ft./20 ft. (30 ft. with bite)	4d8	4d6	2d8	4d6	4d8	2d8

*A dragon's bite attack has reach as if the creature were one size category larger. All other attacks are made with the standard reach for the dragon's size.

sweep affects a half-circle with a radius of 30 feet (or 40 feet for a Colossal dragon), extending from an intersection on the edge of the dragon's space in any direction. Creatures within the swept area are affected if they are four or more size categories smaller than the dragon. A tail sweep automatically deals the indicated damage plus 1-1/2 times the dragon's Strength bonus (round down). Affected creatures can attempt Reflex saves to take half damage (DC equal to that of the dragon's breath weapon).

Grappling: Dragons do not favor grapple attacks, though their crush attack (and Snatch feat, if they know it) use normal grapple rules.

A dragon can always use its breath weapon while grappling, as well as its spells and spell-like or supernatural abilities, provided it succeeds on Concentration checks.

Breath Weapon (Su): Using a breath weapon is a standard action. Once a dragon breathes, it can't breathe again until 1d4 rounds later. If a dragon has more than one type of breath weapon, it still can breathe only once every 1d4 rounds. A blast from a breath weapon always starts at any intersection adjacent to the dragon and extends in a direction of the dragon's choice, with an area as noted on the table below. If the breath weapon deals damage, creatures caught in the area can attempt Reflex saves to take half damage; the DC depends on the dragon's age and variety, and is given in each individual entry. Saves against nondamaging breath weapons use the same DC; the kind of saving throw is noted in the variety descriptions. The save DC against a breath weapon is 10 + 1/2 dragon's HD + dragon's Con modifier.

Breath weapons come in two basic shapes, line and cone, whose areas vary with the dragon's size.

DRAGON BREATH WEAPONS

Dragon Size	Line* (Length)	Cone** (Length)
Tiny	30 ft.	15 ft.
Small	40 ft.	20 ft.
Medium	60 ft.	30 ft.
Large	80 ft.	40 ft.
Huge	100 ft.	50 ft.
Gargantuan	120 ft.	60 ft.
Colossal	140 ft.	70 ft.

*A line is always 5 feet high and 5 feet wide.
**A cone is as high and wide as its length.

Frightful Presence (Ex): A young adult or older dragon can unsettle foes with its mere presence. The ability takes effect automatically whenever the dragon attacks, charges, or flies overhead. Creatures within a radius of 30 feet × the dragon's age category are subject to the effect if they have fewer HD than the dragon.

A potentially affected creature that succeeds on a Will save (DC 10 + 1/2 dragon's HD + dragon's Cha modifier) remains immune to that dragon's frightful presence for 24 hours. On a failure, creatures with 4 or less HD become panicked for 4d6 rounds and those with 5 or more HD become shaken for 4d6 rounds. Dragons ignore the frightful presence of other dragons.

Spells: A dragon knows and casts arcane spells as a sorcerer of the level indicated in its variety description, gaining bonus spells for a high Charisma score. Some dragons can also cast spells from the cleric list or cleric domain lists as arcane spells.

Spell-Like Abilities: A dragon's spell-like abilities depend on its age and variety. It gains the abilities indicated for its age plus all previous ones. Its age category or its sorcerer caster level, whichever is higher, is the caster level for these abilities. The save DC is 10 + dragon's Cha modifier + spell level. All spell-like abilities are usable once per day unless otherwise noted.

Damage Reduction: Young adult and older dragons have damage reduction. Their natural weapons are treated as magic weapons for the purpose of overcoming damage reduction.

Immunities (Ex): All dragons have immunity to *sleep* and paralysis effects. Each variety of dragon has immunity to one or two additional forms of attack no matter what its age, as given in its description.

Spell Resistance (Ex): As dragons age, they become more resistant to spells and spell-like abilities, as indicated in the variety descriptions.

Blindsense (Ex): Dragons can pinpoint creatures within a distance of 60 feet. Opponents the dragon can't actually see still have total concealment against the dragon.

Keen Senses (Ex): A dragon sees four times as well a human in shadowy illumination and twice as well in normal light. It also has darkvision out to 120 feet.

Skills: All dragons have skill points equal to (6 + Int modifier, minimum 1) × (Hit Dice + 3). Most dragons purchase the following skills at the maximum ranks possible: Listen, Search, and Spot. The remaining skill points are generally spent on Concentration, Diplomacy, Escape Artist, Intimidate, Knowledge (any), Sense Motive, and Use Magic Device at a cost of 1 skill point per rank. All these skills are considered class skills for dragons. (Each dragon has other class skills as well, as noted in the variety descriptions.)

Feats: All dragons have one feat, plus an additional feat per 3 Hit Dice, just like any other creature. Dragons favor Alertness, Blind-Fight, Cleave, Flyby Attack, Hover, Improved Initiative, Improved Sunder, Power Attack, Snatch, Weapon Focus (claw or bite), Wingover, and any metamagic feat that is available and useful to sorcerers.

Dragon Overland Movement

Chromatic and metallic dragons are exceedingly strong flyers and can cover vast distances quickly. A dragon's overland flying speed is a function of its tactical fly speed, as shown on the table below.

Dragon Overland Flying Speeds

	Dragon's Fly Speed			
	100 feet	150 feet	200 feet	250 feet
One Hour				
Normal	15 miles	20 miles	30 miles	40 miles
Hustle	24 miles	40 miles	60 miles	80 miles
One Day				
Normal	120 miles	160 miles	240 miles	320 miles

Dragons do not tire as quickly as other creatures when moving overland on the ground. If a dragon attempts a hustle or a forced march, check for nonlethal damage once every 2 hours instead of every hour (see page 164 of the *Player's Handbook*).

DRAGON SOCIETY

Although all dragons are believed to have come from the same roots tens of thousands of years ago, the present varieties keep to themselves and cooperate only under extreme circumstances, such as a powerful mutual threat. Good dragons never work with evil dragons, however, though a few neutral specimens have been found with either. Gold dragons occasionally associate with silver dragons.

When evil dragons of different varieties encounter one another, they usually fight to protect their territories. Good dragons are more tolerant, though also very territorial, and usually try to work out differences in a peaceful manner.

Dragons follow a number of reproductive strategies to suit their needs and temperaments. These help assure the continuation of a dragon's bloodline, no matter what happens to the parent or the parent's lair. Young adults, particularly evil or less intelligent ones, tend to lay clutches of 1d4+1 eggs all around the countryside, leaving their offspring to fend for themselves. These hatch into clutches of dragons, usually juvenile or younger, which stick together until they can establish their own lairs.

Older and more intelligent dragons form families consisting of a mated pair and 1d4+1 young. Mated dragons are always adults or mature adults; offspring found with their parents are of wyrmling (01–10 on d%), very young (11–30), young (31–50), juvenile (51–90), or young adult (91–100) age. Shortly after a dragon reaches young adult (or rarely, juvenile) age, it leaves its parents to establish a lair of its own.

A pair of mated dragons beyond mature adult age usually splits up, independence and the lust for treasure driving them apart. Older females continue to mate and lay eggs, but only one parent stays in the lair to raise young. Often an older female lays many clutches of eggs, keeping one to tend herself and one for her mate, and leaving the rest untended. Sometimes a female dragon places an egg or a wyrmling with nondraconic foster parents.

DRAGONHIDE

Armorsmiths can work with the hides of dragons to produce armor or shields of masterwork quality (see Dragonhide under Special Materials, page 283 of the *Dungeon Master's Guide*).

CHROMATIC DRAGONS

Chromatic dragons form the evil branch of dragonkind. They are aggressive, greedy, vain, and nasty.

BLACK DRAGON

Dragon (Water)

Environment: Warm marshes

Organization: Wyrmling, very young, young, juvenile, and young adult: solitary or clutch (2–5); adult, mature adult, old, very old, ancient, wyrm, or great wyrm: solitary, pair, or family (1–2 and 2–5 offspring)

Challenge Rating: Wyrmling 3; very young 4; young 5; juvenile 7; young adult 9; adult 11; mature adult 14; old 16; very old 18; ancient 19; wyrm 20; great wyrm 22

Treasure: Triple standard

Alignment: Always chaotic evil

Advancement: Wyrmling 5–6 HD; very young 8–9 HD; young 11–12 HD; juvenile 14–15 HD; young adult 17–18 HD; adult 20–21 HD; mature adult 23–24 HD; old 26–27 HD; very old 29–30 HD; ancient 32–33 HD; wyrm 35–36 HD; great wyrm 38+ HD

Level Adjustment: Wyrmling +3; very young +3; young +3; juvenile +4; others —

The dragon's head looks decidedly like a skull thanks to its deep-socketed eyes and wide, flat nasal opening. It has forward-curving horns and a spinal crest that peaks just behind the head and tapers off about three quarters of the way down the neck. An acidic smell surrounds the dragon, whose scales are mostly dull ebony and dark gray.

Black dragons are evil-tempered, cunning, and malevolent, characteristics that are reflected in their crafty, sinister faces.

Black dragon are sometimes known as skull dragons because of their skeletal faces. Adding to the skeletal impression is the gradual deterioration of the hide around the base of the horn and the cheekbones. This deterioration increases with age and does not harm the dragon. On hatching, a black dragon's scales

Black Dragons by Age

Age	Size	Hit Dice (hp)	Str	Dex	Con	Int	Wis	Cha	Base Attack/ Grapple	Attack	Fort Save	Ref Save	Will Save	Breath Weapon (DC)	Frightful Presence DC
Wyrmling	T	4d12+4 (30)	11	10	13	8	11	8	+4/−4	+6	+5	+4	+4	2d4 (13)	—
Very young	S	7d12+7 (52)	13	10	13	8	11	8	+7/+4	+9	+6	+5	+5	4d4 (14)	—
Young	M	10d12+20 (85)	15	10	15	10	11	10	+10/+12	+12	+9	+7	+7	6d4 (17)	—
Juvenile	M	13d12+26 (110)	17	10	15	10	11	10	+13/+16	+16	+10	+8	+8	8d4 (18)	—
Young adult	L	16d12+48 (152)	19	10	17	12	13	12	+16/+24	+19	+13	+10	+11	10d4 (21)	19
Adult	L	19d12+76 (199)	23	10	19	12	13	12	+19/+29	+24	+15	+11	+12	12d4 (23)	20
Mature adult	H	22d12+110 (253)	27	10	21	14	15	14	+22/+38	+28	+18	+13	+15	14d4 (26)	23
Old	H	25d12+125 (287)	29	10	21	14	15	14	+25/+42	+32	+19	+14	+16	16d4 (27)	24
Very old	H	28d12+168 (350)	31	10	23	16	17	16	+28/+46	+36	+22	+16	+19	18d4 (30)	27
Ancient	H	31d12+186 (387)	33	10	23	16	17	16	+31/+50	+40	+23	+17	+20	20d4 (31)	28
Wyrm	G	34d12+238 (459)	35	10	25	18	19	18	+34/+58	+42	+26	+19	+23	22d4 (34)	31
Great wyrm	G	37d12+296 (536)	37	10	27	20	21	20	+37/+62	+46	+28	+20	+25	24d4 (36)	33

Black Dragon Abilities by Age

Age	Speed	Initiative	AC	Special Abilities	Caster Level	SR
Wyrmling	60 ft., fly 100 ft. (average), swim 60 ft.	+0	15 (+2 size,+3 natural), touch 12, flat-footed 15	Immunity to acid, water breathing	—	—
Very young	60 ft., fly 100 ft. (average), swim 60 ft.	+0	17 (+1 size,+6 natural) touch 11, flat-footed 17		—	—
Young	60 ft., fly 150 ft. (poor), swim 60 ft.	+0	19 (+9 natural), touch 10, flat-footed 19		—	—
Juvenile	60 ft., fly 150 ft. (poor), swim 60 ft.	+0	22 (+12 natural), touch 10, flat-footed 22	*Darkness*	—	—
Young adult	60 ft., fly 150 ft. (poor), swim 60 ft.	+0	24 (−1 size,+15 natural), touch 9, flat-footed 24	DR 5/magic	1st	17
Adult	60 ft., fly 150 ft. (poor), swim 60 ft.	+0	27 (−1 size,+18 natural), touch 9, flat-footed 27	*Corrupt water*	3rd	18
Mature adult	60 ft., fly 150 ft. (poor), swim 60 ft.	+0	29 (−2 size,+21 natural), touch 8, flat-footed 29	DR 10/magic	5th	21
Old	60 ft., fly 150 ft. (poor), swim 60 ft.	+0	32 (−2 size,+24 natural), touch 8, flat-footed 32	*Plant growth*	7th	22
Very old	60 ft., fly 150 ft. (poor), swim 60 ft.	+0	35 (−2 size,+27 natural), touch 8, flat-footed 35	DR 15/magic	9th	23
Ancient	60 ft., fly 150 ft. (poor), swim 60 ft.	+0	38 (−2 size,+30 natural), touch 8, flat-footed 38	*Insect plague*	11th	25
Wyrm	60 ft., fly 200 ft. (clumsy), swim 60 ft.	+0	39 (−4 size,+33 natural), touch 6, flat-footed 39	DR 20/magic	13th	26
Great wyrm	60 ft., fly 200 ft. (clumsy), swim 60 ft.	+0	42 (−4 size,+36 natural), touch 6, flat-footed 42	*Charm reptiles*	15th	28

are thin, small, and glossy. As the dragon ages, they become larger, thicker, and duller, helping it camouflage itself in swamps and marshes.

Black dragons lair in large, damp caves and multichambered underground caverns. They smell of rotting vegetation and foul water, with an acidic undertone. Older dragons hide the entrance to their lairs using *plant growth*. Black dragons dine primarily on fish, mollusks, and other aquatic creatures. They also hunt for red meat but like to "pickle" it by letting it lie in ponds within the lair for days before eating it.

Black dragons are especially fond of coins. Older dragons sometimes capture and question humanoids about stockpiles of gold, silver, and platinum coins before killing them.

Combat

Black dragons prefer to ambush their targets, using their surroundings as cover. When fighting in heavily forested swamps and marshes, they try to stay in the water or on the ground; trees and leafy canopies limit their aerial maneuverability. When outmatched, a black dragon attempts to fly out of sight, so as not to leave tracks, and hide in a deep pond or bog.

Breath Weapon (Su): A black dragon has one type of breath weapon, a line of acid.

Water Breathing (Ex): A black dragon can breathe underwater indefinitely and can freely use its breath weapon, spells, and other abilities while submerged.

Corrupt Water **(Sp):** Once per day an adult or older black dragon can stagnate 10 cubic feet of water, making it become still, foul, and unable to support animal life. The ability spoils liquids containing water. Magic items (such as potions) and items in a creature's possession must succeed on a Will save (DC equal to that of the dragon's frightful presence) or become fouled. This ability is the equivalent of a 1st-level spell. Its range is equal to that of the dragon's frightful presence.

Illus. by S. Wood

Black dragon

Illus. by S. Wood

Blue dragon

DRAGON

Charm Reptiles (Sp): A great wyrm black dragon can use this ability three times per day. It works as a *mass charm* spell that affects only reptilian animals. The dragon can communicate with any charmed reptiles as though casting a *speak with animals* spell. This ability is the equivalent of a 1st-level spell.

Other Spell-Like Abilities: 3/day—*darkness* (juvenile or older; radius 10 feet per age category), *insect plague* (ancient or older); 1/day—*plant growth* (old or older).

Skills: Hide, Move Silently, and Swim are considered class skills for black dragons.

Young Adult Black Dragon: CR 9; Large dragon (water); HD 16d12+48, hp 152; Init +0; Spd 60 ft., fly 150 ft. (poor), swim 60 ft.; AC 25, touch 9, flat-footed 25; Base Atk +16; Grp +24; Atk +20 melee (2d6+4, bite); Full Atk +20 melee (2d6+4, bite), +17 melee (1d8+2, 2 claws), +17 melee (1d6+2, 2 wings), +17 melee (1d8+6, tail slap); Space/ Reach 10 ft./5 ft. (bite 10 ft.); SA breath weapon, *darkness*, frightful presence, spells; SQ blind-sense 60 ft., damage reduction 5/ magic, darkvision 120 ft., immunity to acid, *sleep*, and paralysis, low-light vision, spell resistance 17, water breathing; AL CE; SV Fort +13, Ref +10, Will +11; Str 19, Dex 10, Con 17, Int 12, Wis 13, Cha 12.

Skills and Feats: Bluff +9, Climb +20, Diplomacy +10, Hide +8, Intimidate +19, Listen +17, Move Silently +16, Search +17, Speak Language 6 ranks, Spot +17, Swim +12; Improved Natural Armor, Multi-attack, Power Attack, Snatch, Weapon Focus (bite), Wingover.

Breath Weapon (Su): 80-ft. line, damage 10d4 acid, Reflex DC 21 half.

Darkness (Sp): 3/day—as *darkness*, but 50-ft. radius. Caster level 5th.

Frightful Presence (Ex): 150-ft. radius, HD 15 or less, Will DC 19 negates.

Water Breathing (Ex): Can breathe underwater indefinitely and can freely use breath weapon, spells, and other abilities underwater.

Spells: As 1st-level sorcerer.

Typical Sorcerer Spells Known (5/4; save DC 11 + spell level): 0—*daze, detect magic, ray of frost, resistance;* 1st—*mage armor, protection from good.*

BLUE DRAGON

Dragon (Earth)

Environment: Temperate deserts

Organization: Wyrmling, very young, young, juvenile, and young adult: solitary or clutch (2–5); adult, mature adult, old, very old, ancient, wyrm, or great wyrm: solitary, pair, or family (1–2 and 2–5 offspring)

Challenge Ratings: Wyrmling 3; very young 4; young 6; juvenile 8; young adult 11; adult 14; mature adult 16; old 18; very old 19; ancient 21; wyrm 23; great wyrm 25

Treasure: Triple standard

Alignment: Always lawful evil

Advancement: Wyrmling 7–8 HD; very young 10–11 HD; young 13–14 HD; juvenile 16–17 HD; young adult 19–20 HD; adult 22–23 HD; mature adult 25–26 HD; old 28–29 HD; very old 31–32 HD; ancient 34–35 HD; wyrm 37–38 HD; great wyrm 40+ HD

Level Adjustment: Wyrmling +4; very young +4; young +5; others —

The dragon has dramatic frilled ears and a single massive horn emerging from its snout. The smell of ozone lingers in the air near the dragon, whose azure-tinged scales glitter in the sun.

Blue dragons are vain and territorial. They are one of the dragon varieties best adapted to digging into sand.

A blue dragon's scales vary in color from an iridescent azure to a deep indigo, polished to a glossy finish by blowing desert sands. The size of its scales increases little as the dragon ages, although they do become thicker and harder. Its hide tends to hum and crackle faintly with built-up static electricity. These effects intensify when the dragon is angry or about to attack, giving off an odor of ozone and sand.

Their vibrant color makes blue dragons easy to spot in barren desert surroundings. However, they often burrow into the sand so only part of their heads are exposed. Blue dragons love to soar in the hot desert air, usually flying in the daytime when temperatures are highest. Some nearly match the color of the desert sky and use this coloration to their advantage.

Blue dragons lair in vast underground caverns, where they also store their treasure. Although they collect anything that looks valuable, they are most fond of gems—especially sapphires. They are sometimes are forced to eat snakes, lizards, and desert plants to sate their great hunger but especially prefer herd animals such as camels. When they get the chance, they gorge themselves on these creatures.

Combat

Typically, blue dragons attack from above or burrow beneath the sands until opponents come within 100 feet. Older dragons use their special abilities, such as *hallucinatory terrain*, in concert with these tactics to mask the land and improve their chances to surprise the target. Blue dragons run from a fight only if they are severely damaged, since they view retreat as cowardly.

Breath Weapon (Su): A blue dragon has one type of breath weapon, a line of lightning.

Create/Destroy Water (Sp): A blue dragon of any age can use this ability three times per day. It works like the *create water* spell, except that the dragon can decide to destroy water instead of creating it, which automatically spoils unattended liquids containing water. Magic items (such as potions) and items in a creature's possession must succeed on a Will save (DC equal to that of the dragon's frightful presence) or be ruined. This ability is the equivalent of a 1st-level spell.

Sound Imitation (Ex): A juvenile or older blue dragon can mimic any voice or sound it has heard, anytime it likes. Listeners must succeed on a Will save (DC equal to that of the dragon's frightful presence) to detect the ruse.

Other Spell-Like Abilities: 3/day—*ventriloquism* (adult or older); 1/day—*hallucinatory terrain* (old or older), *veil* (ancient or older), *mirage arcana* (great wyrm).

Skills: Bluff, Hide, and Spellcraft are considered class skills for blue dragons.

Mature Adult Blue Dragon: CR 16; Huge dragon (earth); HD 24d12+120, hp 276; Init +4; Spd 40 ft., burrow 20 ft., fly 150 ft. (poor); AC 31, touch 8, flat-footed 31; Base Atk +24; Grp +41; Atk +31 melee (2d8+9, bite); Full Atk +31 melee (2d8+9, bite), +29 melee (2d6+4, 2 claws), +29 melee (1d8+4, 2 wings), +29 melee (2d6+13, tail slap); Space/Reach 15 ft./10 ft. (bite 15 ft.); SA breath weapon, *create/destroy water*, crush, frightful presence, sound imitation, spell-like abilities, spells; SQ damage reduction 10/magic, darkvision 120 ft., immunity to electricity, *sleep*, and paralysis, low-light vision, spell resistance 22; AL LE; SV Fort +19, Ref +14, Will +17; Str 29, Dex 10, Con 21, Int 16, Wis 17, Cha 16.

Skills and Feats: Bluff +28, Concentration +16, Diplomacy +32, Hide +11, Intimidate +30, Knowledge (arcana) +14, Knowledge (nature) +13, Listen +30, Search +28, Sense Motive +28, Spellcraft +30, Spot +30; Ability Focus (frightful presence), Alertness, Combat Expertise, Eschew Materials, Flyby Attack, Hover, Improved Initiative, Multiattack, Power Attack.

Breath Weapon (Su): 100-ft. line, damage 14d8 electricity, Reflex DC 27 half.

Create/Destroy Water (Sp): 3/day—as *create water*, but can also be used to destroy water. Caster level 7th; Will DC 25 negates.

Crush (Ex): Area 15 ft. by 15 ft.; Small or smaller opponents take 2d8+13 points of bludgeoning damage, and must succeed on a DC 27 Reflex save or be pinned.

Frightful Presence (Ex): 210-ft. radius, HD 23 or less, Will DC 27 negates.

Sound Imitation (Ex): Can mimic any voice or sound it has heard, anytime it likes. Listeners must succeed on DC 25 Will saves to detect the ruse.

Spell-Like Abilities: 3/day—*ventriloquism*. Caster level 7th; save DC 13 + spell level.

BLUE DRAGONS BY AGE

Age	Size	Hit Dice (hp)	Str	Dex	Con	Int	Wis	Cha	Base Attack/ Grapple	Attack	Fort Save	Ref Save	Will Save	Breath Weapon (DC)	Frightful Presence DC
Wyrmling	S	6d12+6 (45)	13	10	13	10	11	10	+6/+3	+8	+6	+5	+5	2d8 (14)	—
Very young	M	9d12+18 (76)	15	10	15	10	11	10	+9/+11	+11	+8	+6	+6	4d8 (16)	—
Young	M	12d12+24 (102)	17	10	15	12	13	12	+12/+15	+15	+10	+8	+9	6d8 (18)	—
Juvenile	L	15d12+45 (142)	19	10	17	14	15	14	+15/+23	+18	+12	+9	+11	8d8 (20)	—
Young adult	L	18d12+72 (189)	23	10	19	14	15	14	+18/+28	+23	+15	+11	+13	10d8 (23)	21
Adult	H	21d12+105 (241)	27	10	21	16	17	16	+21/+37	+27	+17	+12	+15	12d8 (25)	23
Mature adult	H	24d12+120 (276)	29	10	21	16	17	16	+24/+41	+31	+19	+14	+17	14d8 (27)	25
Old	H	27d12+162 (337)	31	10	23	18	19	18	+27/+45	+35	+21	+15	+19	16d8 (29)	27
Very old	H	30d12+180 (375)	33	10	23	18	19	18	+30/+49	+39	+23	+17	+21	18d8 (31)	29
Ancient	G	33d12+231 (445)	35	10	25	20	21	20	+33/+57	+41	+25	+18	+23	20d8 (33)	31
Wyrm	G	36d12+288 (522)	37	10	27	20	21	20	+36/+61	+45	+28	+20	+25	22d8 (36)	33
Great wyrm	G	39d12+312 (565)	39	10	27	22	23	22	+39/+65	+49	+29	+21	+27	24d8 (37)	35

BLUE DRAGON ABILITIES BY AGE

Age	Speed	Initiative	AC	Special Abilities	Caster Level	SR
Wyrmling	40 ft., burrow 20 ft., fly 100 ft. (average)	+0	16 (+1 size, +5 natural), touch 11, flat-footed 16	Immunity to electricity, *create/destroy water*	—	—
Very young	40 ft., burrow 20 ft., fly 150 ft. (poor)	+0	18 (+8 natural), touch 10, flat-footed 18		—	—
Young	40 ft., burrow 20 ft., fly 150 ft. (poor)	+0	21 (+11 natural), touch 10, flat-footed 21		—	—
Juvenile	40 ft., burrow 20 ft., fly 150 ft. (poor)	+0	23 (−1 size, +14 natural), touch 9, flat-footed 23	Sound imitation	1st	—
Young adult	40 ft., burrow 20 ft., fly 150 ft. (poor)	+0	26 (−1 size, +17 natural), touch 9, flat-footed 26	DR 5/magic	3rd	19
Adult	40 ft., burrow 20 ft., fly 150 ft. (poor)	+0	28 (−2 size, +20 natural), touch 8, flat-footed 28	*Ventriloquism*	5th	21
Mature adult	40 ft., burrow 20 ft., fly 150 ft. (poor)	+0	31 (−2 size, +23 natural), touch 8, flat-footed 31	DR 10/magic	7th	22
Old	40 ft., burrow 20 ft., fly 150 ft. (poor)	+0	34 (−2 size, +26 natural), touch 8, flat-footed 34	*Hallucinatory terrain*	9th	24
Very old	40 ft., burrow 20 ft., fly 150 ft. (poor)	+0	37 (−2 size, +29 natural), touch 8, flat-footed 37	DR 15/magic	11th	25
Ancient	40 ft., burrow 20 ft., fly 200 ft. (clumsy)	+0	38 (−4 size, +32 natural), touch 6, flat-footed 38	*Veil*	13th	27
Wyrm	40 ft., burrow 20 ft., fly 200 ft. (clumsy)	+0	41 (−4 size, +35 natural), touch 6, flat-footed 41	DR 20/magic	15th	29
Great wyrm	40 ft., burrow 20 ft., fly 200 ft. (clumsy)	+0	44 (−4 size, +38 natural), touch 6, flat-footed 44	*Mirage arcana*	17th	31

*Can also cast cleric spells and those from the Air, Evil, and Law domains as arcane spells.

Spells: As 7th-level sorcerer.

Typical Sorcerer Spells Known (6/7/7/5; save DC 13 + spell level):
0—*dancing lights, detect magic, ghost sound, mage hand, ray of frost, read magic, resistance;* 1st—*alarm, command, magic missile, Nystul's magic aura, shield of faith;* 2nd—*darkness, invisibility, shatter;* 3rd—*cure serious wounds, dispel magic.*

GREEN DRAGON

Dragon (Air)

Environment: Temperate forests

Organization: Wyrmling, very young, young, juvenile, and young adult: solitary or clutch (2–5); adult, mature adult, old, very old, ancient, wyrm, or great wyrm: solitary, pair, or family (1–2 and 2–5 offspring)

Challenge Ratings: Wyrmling 3; very young 4; young 5; juvenile 8; young adult 11; adult 13; mature adult 16; old 18; very old 19; ancient 21; wyrm 22; great wyrm 24

Treasure: Triple standard

Alignment: Always lawful evil

Advancement: Wyrmling 6–7 HD; very young 9–10 HD; young 12–13 HD; juvenile 15–16 HD; young adult 18–19 HD; adult 21–22 HD; mature adult 24–25 HD; old 27–28 HD; very old 30–31 HD; ancient 33–34 HD; wyrm 36–37 HD; great wyrm 39+ HD

Level Adjustment: Wyrmling +5; very young +5; young +5; juvenile +6; others —

The dragon has a toothy, curving jaw line and rows of hornlets over its eyes. There is a cluster of hornlets at the chin. A crest begins just behind the eyes and runs the length of the body, rising to full height just behind the skull. The odor of chlorine clings to the dragon, whose scales radiate with a glowing emerald shine.

Green dragons are belligerent and tend to attack without provocation.

A wyrmling green dragon's scales are thin, very small, and a deep shade of green that appears nearly black. As the dragon ages, the scales grow larger and lighter, turning shades of forest, emerald, and olive green, which helps it blend in with its wooded surroundings.

Green dragons make their lairs in forests; the older the forest and bigger the trees, the better. They prefer caves in cliffs or hillsides and can be detected by the stinging odor of chlorine. Although they have been known to eat practically anything, including shrubs and small trees when they are hungry enough, green dragons especially prize elves and sprites.

GREEN DRAGONS BY AGE

Age	Size	Hit Dice (hp)	Str	Dex	Con	Int	Wis	Cha	Base Attack/ Grapple	Attack	Fort Save	Ref Save	Will Save	Breath Weapon (DC)	Frightful Presence DC
Wyrmling	S	5d12+5 (37)	13	10	13	10	11	10	+5/+2	+7	+5	+4	+4	2d6 (13)	—
Very young	M	8d12+16 (68)	15	10	15	10	11	10	+8/+10	+10	+8	+6	+6	4d6 (16)	—
Young	M	11d12+22 (93)	17	10	15	12	13	12	+11/+14	+14	+9	+7	+8	6d6 (17)	—
Juvenile	L	14d12+42 (133)	19	10	17	14	15	14	+14/+22	+17	+12	+9	+11	8d6 (20)	—
Young adult	L	17d12+68 (178)	23	10	19	14	15	14	+17/+27	+22	+14	+10	+12	10d6 (22)	20
Adult	H	20d12+100 (230)	27	10	21	16	17	16	+20/+36	+26	+17	+12	+15	12d6 (25)	23
Mature adult	H	23d12+115 (264)	29	10	21	16	17	16	+23/+40	+30	+18	+13	+16	14d6 (26)	24
Old	H	26d12+156 (325)	31	10	23	18	19	18	+26/+44	+34	+21	+15	+19	16d6 (29)	27
Very old	H	29d12+174 (362)	33	10	23	18	19	18	+29/+48	+38	+22	+16	+20	18d6 (30)	28
Ancient	G	32d12+224 (432)	35	10	25	20	21	20	+32/+56	+40	+25	+18	+23	20d6 (33)	31
Wyrm	G	35d12+280 (507)	37	10	27	20	21	20	+35/+60	+44	+27	+19	+24	22d6 (35)	32
Great wyrm	G	38d12+304 (551)	39	10	27	22	23	22	+38/+64	+48	+29	+21	+27	24d6 (37)	35

GREEN DRAGON ABILITIES BY AGE

Age	Speed	Initiative	AC	Special Abilities	Caster Level	SR
Wyrmling	40 ft., fly 100 ft. (average), swim 40 ft.	+0	15 (+1 size, +4 natural) touch 11, flat-footed 15	Immunity to acid, water breathing	—	—
Very young	40 ft., fly 150 ft. (poor), swim 40 ft.	+0	17 (+7 natural) touch 10, flat-footed 17		—	—
Young	40 ft., fly 150 ft. (poor), swim 40 ft.	+0	20 (+10 natural) touch 10, flat-footed 20		—	—
Juvenile	40 ft., fly 150 ft. (poor), swim 40 ft.	+0	22 (–1 size, +13 natural) touch 9, flat-footed 22		1st	—
Young adult	40 ft., fly 150 ft. (poor), swim 40 ft.	+0	25 (–1 size, +16 natural), touch 9, flat-footed 25	DR 5/magic	3rd	19
Adult	40 ft., fly 150 ft. (poor), swim 40 ft.	+0	27 (–2 size, +19 natural), touch 8, flat-footed 27	*Suggestion*	5th	21
Mature adult	40 ft., fly 150 ft. (poor), swim 40 ft.	+0	30 (–2 size, +22 natural), touch 8, flat-footed 30	DR 10/magic	7th	22
Old	40 ft., fly 150 ft. (poor), swim 40 ft.	+0	33 (–2 size, +25 natural), touch 8, flat-footed 33	*Plant growth*	9th	24
Very old	40 ft., fly 150 ft. (poor), swim 40 ft.	+0	36 (–2 size, +28 natural), touch 8, flat-footed 36	DR 15/magic	11th	25
Ancient	40 ft., fly 200 ft. (clumsy), swim 40 ft.	+0	37 (–4 size, +31 natural), touch 6, flat-footed 37	*Dominate person*	13th	27
Wyrm	40 ft., fly 200 ft. (clumsy), swim 40 ft.	+0	40 (–4 size, +34 natural), touch 6, flat-footed 40	DR 20/magic	15th	28
Great wyrm	40 ft., fly 200 ft. (clumsy), swim 40 ft.	+0	43 (–4 size, +37 natural), touch 6, flat-footed 43	*Command plants*	17th	30

Combat

Green dragons initiate fights with little or no provocation, picking on creatures of any size. If the target is intriguing or seems formidable, the dragon stalks the creature to determine the best time to strike and the most appropriate tactics to use. If the target appears weak, the dragon makes its presence known quickly—it enjoys evoking terror. Sometimes the dragon elects to control a humanoid creature through intimidation and *suggestion*. Green dragons especially like to question adventurers to learn more about their society and abilities, what is going on in the countryside, and if there is treasure nearby.

Breath Weapon (Su): A green dragon has one type of breath weapon, a cone of corrosive (acid) gas.

Water Breathing (Ex): A green dragon can breathe underwater indefinitely and can freely use its breath weapon, spells, and other abilities while submerged.

Spell-Like Abilities: 3/day—*suggestion* (adult or older), *dominate person* (ancient or older); 1/day—*plant growth* (old or older), *command plants* (great wyrm).

Skills: Bluff, Hide, and Move Silently are considered class skills for green dragons.

Adult Green Dragon: CR 13; Huge dragon (air); HD 20d12+100, hp 230; Init +0; Spd 40 ft., swim 40 ft., fly 150 ft. (poor); AC 27, touch 8, flat-footed 27; Base Atk +20; Grp +36; Atk +26 melee (3d8+8, bite), Full Atk +26 melee (3d8+8, bite), +21 melee (2d6+4, 2 claws), +21 melee (1d8+4, 2 wings), +21 melee (2d6+12, tail slap); Space/Reach 15 ft./10 ft. (bite 15 ft.); SA breath weapon, crush, frightful presence, spell-like abilities, spells; SQ damage reduction 5/magic, darkvision 120 ft., immunity to acid, *sleep*, and paralysis, low-light vision, spell resistance 21, water breathing; AL LE; SV Fort +17, Ref +12, Will +15; Str 27, Dex 10, Con 21, Int 16, Wis 17, Cha 16.

Skills and Feats: Bluff +20, Concentration +15, Diplomacy +13, Hide +0, Intimidate +25, Knowledge (arcana) +18, Knowledge (nature) +18, Listen +25, Move Silently +20, Search +23, Sense Motive +11, Spellcraft +25, Spot +25, Swim +16; Alertness, Cleave, Flyby Attack, Hover, Improved Natural Attack (bite), Power Attack, Wingover.

Breath Weapon (Su): 50-ft. cone, damage 12d6 acid, Reflex DC 25 half.

Crush (Ex): Area 15 ft. by 15 ft.; Small or smaller opponents take 2d8+12 points of bludgeoning damage, and must succeed on a DC 23 Reflex save or be pinned; grapple bonus +36.

Frightful Presence (Ex): 180-ft. radius, HD 19 or less, Will DC 21 negates.

Spell-Like Abilities: 3/day—*suggestion*. Caster level 6th; save DC 16.

Spells: As 5th-level sorcerer.

Typical Sorcerer Spells Known (6/7/5; save DC 13 + spell level): 0—arcane mark, dancing lights, detect magic, ghost sound, read magic, resistance; 1st—expeditious retreat, Nystul's undetectable aura, shield, true strike; 2nd—blur, detect thoughts.

Green dragon

Water Breathing (Ex): This dragon can breathe underwater indefinitely and can freely use its breath weapon, spells, and other abilities while submerged.

RED DRAGON

Dragon (Fire)

Environment: Warm mountains

Organization: Wyrmling, very young, young, juvenile, and young adult: solitary or clutch (2–5); adult, mature adult, old, very old, ancient, wyrm, or great wyrm: solitary, pair, or family (1–2 and 2–5 offspring)

Challenge Ratings: Wyrmling 4; very young 5; young 7; juvenile 10; young adult 13; adult 15; mature adult 18; old 20; very old 21; ancient 23; wyrm 24; great wyrm 26

Treasure: Triple standard

Alignment: Always chaotic evil

Red Dragons by Age

Age	Size	Hit Dice (hp)	Str	Dex	Con	Int	Wis	Cha	Base Attack/ Grapple	Attack	Fort Save	Ref Save	Will Save	Breath Weapon (DC)	Frightful Presence DC
Wyrmling	M	7d12+14 (59)	17	10	15	10	11	10	+7/+10	+10	+7	+5	+5	2d10 (15)	—
Very young	L	10d12+30 (95)	21	10	17	12	13	12	+10/+19	+14	+10	+7	+8	4d10 (18)	—
Young	L	13d12+39 (123)	25	10	17	12	13	12	+13/+24	+19	+11	+8	+9	6d10 (19)	—
Juvenile	L	16d12+64 (168)	29	10	19	14	15	14	+16/+29	+24	+14	+10	+12	8d10 (22)	—
Young adult	H	19d12+95 (218)	31	10	21	14	15	14	+19/+37	+27	+16	+11	+13	10d10 (24)	21
Adult	H	22d12+110 (253)	33	10	21	16	19	16	+22/+41	+31	+18	+13	+17	12d10 (26)	24
Mature adult	H	25d12+150 (312)	33	10	23	18	19	18	+25/+44	+34	+20	+14	+18	14d10 (28)	26
Old	G	28d12+196 (378)	35	10	25	20	21	20	+28/+52	+36	+23	+16	+21	16d10 (31)	29
Very old	G	31d12+248 (449)	37	10	27	22	23	22	+31/+56	+40	+25	+17	+23	18d10 (33)	31
Ancient	G	34d12+306 (527)	39	10	29	24	25	24	+34/+60	+44	+28	+19	+26	20d10 (36)	34
Wyrm	G	37d12+370 (610)	41	10	31	24	25	24	+37/+64	+48	+30	+20	+27	22d10 (38)	35
Great wyrm	C	40d12+400 (660)	45	10	31	26	27	26	+40/+73	+49	+32	+22	+30	24d10 (40)	38

RED DRAGON ABILITIES BY AGE

Age	Speed	Initiative	AC	Special Abilities	Caster Level	SR
Wyrmling	40 ft., fly 150 ft. (poor)	+0	16 (+6 natural) touch 10, flat-footed 16	Immunity to fire, vulnerability to cold	—	—
Very young	40 ft., fly 150 ft. (poor)	+0	18 (–1 size, +9 natural) touch 9, flat-footed 18		—	—
Young	40 ft., fly 150 ft. (poor)	+0	21 (–1 size, +12 natural) touch 9, flat-footed 21		1st	—
Juvenile	40 ft., fly 150 ft. (poor)	+0	24 (–1 size, +15 natural) touch 9, flat-footed 24	*Locate object*	3rd	—
Young adult	40 ft., fly 150 ft. (poor)	+0	26 (–2 size, +18 natural) touch 8, flat-footed 26	DR 5/magic	5th	19
Adult	40 ft., fly 150 ft. (poor)	+0	29 (–2 size, +21 natural) touch 8, flat-footed 29		7th	21
Mature adult	40 ft., fly 150 ft. (poor)	+0	32 (–2 size, +24 natural) touch 8, flat-footed 32	DR 10/magic	9th	23
Old	40 ft., fly 200 ft. (clumsy)	+0	33 (–4 size, +27 natural) touch 6, flat-footed 33	*Suggestion*	11th	24
Very old	40 ft., fly 200 ft. (clumsy)	+0	36 (–4 size, +30 natural) touch 6, flat-footed 36	DR 15/magic	13th	26
Ancient	40 ft., fly 200 ft. (clumsy)	+0	39 (–4 size, +33 natural) touch 6, flat-footed 39	*Find the path*	15th	28
Wyrm	40 ft., fly 200 ft. (clumsy)	+0	42 (–4 size, +36 natural) touch 6, flat-footed 42	DR 20/magic	17th	30
Great wyrm	40 ft., fly 200 ft. (clumsy)	+0	41 (–8 size, +39 natural) touch 2, flat-footed 41	*Discern location*	19th	32

*Can also cast cleric spells and those from the Chaos, Evil, and Fire domains as arcane spells.

Advancement: Wyrmling 8–9 HD; very young 11–12 HD; young 14–15 HD; juvenile 17–18 HD; young adult 20–21 HD; adult 23–24 HD; mature adult 26–27 HD; old 29–30 HD; very old 32–33 HD; ancient 35–36 HD; wyrm 38–39 HD; great wyrm 41+ HD

Level Adjustment: Wyrmling +4; very young +5; young +6; others —

The dragon has horns extending back over the neck, frilled ears, and smaller horns at the cheeks and chin, with rows of horns over the brows. The nose is beaklike and sports a small horn. A frill begins behind the head and runs to the tip of the tail. The dragon reeks of smoke and sulfur, and its scales shine with shades of crimson and scarlet.

Red dragons are the most covetous of all dragons, forever seeking to increase their treasure hoards. They are exceptionally vain, which is reflected in their proud bearing and disdainful expression.

The small scales of a wyrmling red dragon are a bright glossy scarlet, making the dragon easily spotted by predators and hunters, so it stays underground and does not venture outside until it is more able to take care of itself. Toward the end of young age, the scales turn a deeper red, and the glossy texture is replaced by a smooth, dull finish. As the dragon grows older, the scales become large, thick, and as strong as metal. The neck frill and wings are an ash blue or purple-gray toward the edges, becoming darker with age. The pupils of a red dragon fade as it ages; the oldest red dragons have eyes that resemble molten lava orbs.

Red dragons lair in large caves that extend deep into the earth, which shimmer with the heat of their bodies and are marked by a sulfurous, smoky odor. However, they always have a high perch nearby from which to haughtily survey their territory, which they consider to be everything in sight. This high perch sometimes intrudes upon the territory of a silver dragon, and for this reason red dragons and silver dragons are often enemies.

Red dragons are meat eaters by preference, and their favorite food is a human or elven youth. Sometimes they charm villagers into regularly sacrificing townsfolk to them.

Combat

Because red dragons are so confident, they seldom pause to appraise an adversary. On spotting a target, they make a snap decision whether to attack,

Red dragon

Illus. by T. Lockwood

using one of many strategies worked out ahead of time. A red dragon lands to attack small, weak creatures with its claws and bite rather than obliterating them with its breath weapon, so as not to destroy any treasure they might be carrying.

Breath Weapon (Su): A red dragon has one type of breath weapon, a cone of fire.

Locate Object (Sp): A juvenile or older red dragon can use this ability as the spell of the same name, once per day per age category.

Other Spell-Like Abilities: 3/day—*suggestion* (old or older); 1/day—*find the path* (ancient or older), *discern location* (great wyrm).

Skills: Appraise, Bluff, and Jump are considered class skills for red dragons.

Very Old Red Dragon: CR 21; Gargantuan dragon (fire); HD 31d12+248, hp 449; Init +4; Spd 40 ft., fly 200 ft. (clumsy); AC 36, touch 6, flat-footed 36; Base Atk +31; Grp +56; Atk +40 melee (4d6+13, bite); Full Atk +40 melee (4d6+13, bite), +35 melee (2d8+6, 2 claws), +35 melee (2d8+19, tail slap); Space/Reach 20 ft./15 ft. (bite 20 ft.); SA breath weapon, crush, frightful presence, snatch, spell-like abilities, spells, tail sweep; SQ damage reduction 15/magic, darkvision 120 ft., immunity to fire, *sleep,* and paralysis, low-light vision, spell resistance 25, vulnerability to cold; AL CE; SV Fort +25, Ref +19, Will +25; Str 37, Dex 10, Con 27, Int 22, Wis 23, Cha 22.

Skills and Feats: Appraise +31, Bluff +37, Concentration +28, Craft (trapmaking) +18, Hide +2, Intimidate +39, Jump +48, Knowledge (arcana) +31, Knowledge (local) +31, Knowledge (religion) +31, Listen +37, Search +37, Sense Motive +37, Spellcraft +39, Spot +37, Use Magic Device +22; Awesome Blow, Flyby Attack, Cleave, Great Cleave, Improved Bull Rush, Improved Initiative, Iron Will, Lightning Reflexes, Power Attack, Snatch, Wingover.

Breath Weapon (Su): 60-ft. cone, damage 18d10 fire, Reflex DC 33 half.

Crush (Ex): Area 20 ft. by 20 ft.; Medium or smaller opponents take 4d6+19 points of bludgeoning damage, and must succeed on a DC 33 Reflex save or be pinned; grapple bonus +56.

Frightful Presence (Ex): 270-ft. radius, HD 30 or less, Will DC 29 negates.

Snatch (Ex): Grapple bonus +56; claw against creature of Medium or smaller for 2d8+6/round, bite against Large or smaller for 4d6+13/round, or 8d6+26 if the dragon does not move; snatched creature can be flung 90 ft. for 9d6 points of damage.

Spell-Like Abilities: 9/day—*locate object*; 3/day—*suggestion.* Caster level 13th; save DC 16 + spell level.

Spells: As 13th-level sorcerer.

Typical Sorcerer Spells Known (6/8/8/7/7/7/5; save DC 16 + spell level): 0—*arcane mark, dancing lights, detect magic, ghost sound, guidance, mage hand, prestidigitation, read magic, resistance;* 1st—*alarm,* chill touch, divine favor, magic missile, shield; 2nd—*cat's grace, cure moderate wounds, darkness, detect thoughts, invisibility; 3rd—deeper darkness, dispel magic, haste, protection from elements; 4th—charm monster, emotion, restoration, spell immunity; 5th—circle of doom, feeblemind, shadow evocation; 6th—acid fog, heal.*

Tail Sweep (Ex): Half-circle 30 ft. in diameter, Small or smaller opponents take 2d6+19 points of bludgeoning damage, Reflex DC 33 half.

WHITE DRAGON

Dragon (Cold)

Environment: Cold mountains

Organization: Wyrmling, very young, young, juvenile, and young adult: solitary or clutch (2–5); adult, mature adult, old, very old, ancient, wyrm, or great wyrm: solitary, pair, or family (1–2 and 2–5 offspring)

Challenge Ratings: Wyrmling 2; very young 3; young 4; juvenile 6; young adult 8; adult 10; mature adult 12; old 15; very old 17; ancient 18; wyrm 19; great wyrm 21

Treasure: Triple standard

Alignment: Always chaotic evil

Advancement: Wyrmling 4–5 HD; very young 7–8 HD; young 10–11 HD; juvenile 13–14 HD; young adult 16–17 HD; adult 19–20 HD; mature adult 22–23 HD; old 25–26 HD; very old 28–29 HD; ancient 31–32 HD; wyrm 34–35 HD; great wyrm 37+ HD

Level Adjustment: Wyrmling +2; very young +3; young +3; juvenile +5; others —

The dragon has a beaked nose, spiny dewlaps, and a crest supported by a single, back-curving spine. A crisp, faintly chemical odor accompanies the dragon, whose scales glisten like snow.

Among the smallest and least intelligent of dragonkind, most white dragons are simply animalistic predators. Their faces express single-minded ferocity rather than the shrewdness of their more powerful kin.

The scales of a wyrmling white dragon glisten like mirrors. As the dragon ages, the sheen disappears, and by very old age, scales of pale blue and light gray are mixed in with the white.

White dragons' lairs are usually icy caves and deep underground chambers that open away from the warming rays of the sun. They store all of their treasure within the lair, preferably in caverns coated in ice, which reflect the gems. White dragons are especially fond of diamonds.

Although white dragons are able to eat nearly anything, they are very particular and will consume only food that has been frozen. Usually a dragon devours a creature killed by its breath weapon while the carcass is still stiff and frigid. It buries other kills in snowbanks until they are suitably frozen.

WHITE DRAGONS BY AGE

Age	Size	Hit Dice (hp)	Str	Dex	Con	Int	Wis	Cha	Base Attack/ Grapple	Attack	Fort Save	Ref Save	Will Save	Breath Weapon (DC)	Frightful Presence DC
Wyrmling	T	3d12+3 (22)	11	10	13	6	11	6	+3/−5	+5	+4	+3	+3	1d6 (12)	—
Very young	S	6d12+6 (45)	13	10	13	6	11	6	+6/+3	+8	+6	+5	+5	2d6 (14)	—
Young	M	9d12+18 (76)	15	10	15	6	11	6	+9/+11	+11	+8	+6	+6	3d6 (16)	—
Juvenile	M	12d12+24 (102)	17	10	15	8	11	8	+12/+15	+15	+10	+8	+8	4d6 (18)	—
Young adult	L	15d12+45 (142)	19	10	17	8	11	10	+15/+23	+18	+12	+9	+9	5d6 (20)	17
Adult	L	18d12+72 (189)	23	10	19	10	11	12	+18/+28	+23	+15	+11	+11	6d6 (23)	20
Mature adult	H	21d12+105 (241)	27	10	21	12	13	12	+21/+37	+27	+17	+12	+13	7d6 (25)	21
Old	H	24d12+120 (276)	29	10	21	12	13	12	+24/+41	+31	+19	+14	+15	8d6 (27)	23
Very old	H	27d12+162 (337)	31	10	23	14	15	14	+27/+45	+35	+21	+15	+17	9d6 (29)	25
Ancient	H	30d12+180 (375)	33	10	23	14	15	14	+30/+49	+39	+23	+17	+19	10d6 (31)	27
Wyrm	G	33d12+231 (445)	35	10	25	14	15	16	+33/+57	+41	+25	+18	+20	11d6 (33)	29
Great wyrm	G	36d12+288 (522)	37	10	27	18	19	18	+36/+61	+45	+28	+20	+24	12d6 (36)	32

White dragons' natural enemies are frost giants, who kill the dragons for food and armor and capture them to use as guards.

Combat

White dragons prefer sudden assaults, swooping down from aloft or bursting from beneath water, snow, or ice. They loose their breath weapon, then try to knock out a single opponent with a follow-up attack.

Breath Weapon (Su): A white dragon has one type of breath weapon, a cone of cold.

Icewalking (Ex): This ability works like the *spider climb* spell, but the surfaces the dragon climbs must be icy. It is always in effect.

Freezing Fog (Sp): An old or older white dragon can use this ability three times per day. It is similar to a *solid fog* spell but also causes a rime of slippery ice to form on any surface the fog touches, creating the effect of a *grease* spell. The dragon is immune to the *grease* effect because of its icewalking ability. This ability is the equivalent of a 5th-level spell.

Other Spell-Like Abilities: 3/day—*fog cloud* (juvenile or older), *gust of wind* (adult or older), *wall of ice* (ancient or older); 1/day—*control weather* (great wyrm).

Skills: Hide, Move Silently, and Swim are considered class skills for white dragons.

Young White Dragon: CR 4; Medium dragon (cold); HD 9d12+18; hp 76; Init +4; Spd 60 ft., burrow 30 ft., fly 200 ft. (poor), swim 60 ft.; AC 18, touch 10, flat-footed 18; Base Atk +9; Grp +11; Atk +11 melee (2d6+2, bite); Full Atk +11 melee (2d6+2, bite), +6 melee (1d6+1, 2 claws), +6 melee (1d4+1, 2 wings); SA Breath weapon; SQ darkvision 120 ft., icewalking, immunity to cold, *sleep*, and paralysis, low-light vision, vulnerability to fire; AL CE; SV Fort +8, Ref +6, Will +6; Str 15, Dex 10, Con 15, Int 6, Wis 11, Cha 6.

Skills and Feats: Intimidate +10, Listen +12, Search +12, Spot +12; Flyby Attack, Improved Initiative, Improved Natural Attack (bite), Wingover.

Breath Weapon (Su): 30-ft. cone, damage 3d6 cold, Reflex DC 16 half.

Icewalking (Ex): As the *spider climb* spell, but the surfaces the dragon climbs must be icy; always in effect.

White dragon

WHITE DRAGON ABILITIES BY AGE

Age	Speed	Initiative	AC	Special Abilities	Caster Level	SR
Wyrmling	60 ft., burrow 30 ft., fly 150 ft. (average), swim 60 ft.	+0	14 (+2 size, +2 natural), touch 12, flat-footed 14	Icewalking, immunity to cold, vulnerability to fire	—	—
Very young	60 ft., burrow 30 ft., fly 150 ft. (average), swim 60 ft.	+0	16 (+1 size, +5 natural), touch 11, flat-footed 16		—	—
Young	60 ft., burrow 30 ft., fly 200 ft. (poor), swim 60 ft.	+0	18 (+8 natural), touch 10, flat-footed 18		—	—
Juvenile	60 ft., burrow 30 ft., fly 200 ft. (poor), swim 60 ft.	+0	21 (+11 natural), touch 10, flat-footed 21	*Fog cloud*	—	—
Young adult	60 ft., burrow 30 ft., fly 200 ft. (poor), swim 60 ft.	+0	23 (−1 size, +14 natural), touch 9, flat-footed 23	DR 5/magic	—	16
Adult	60 ft., burrow 30 ft., fly 200 ft. (poor), swim 60 ft.	+0	26 (−1 size, +17 natural), touch 9, flat-footed 26	*Gust of wind*	1st	18
Mature adult	60 ft., burrow 30 ft., fly 200 ft. (poor), swim 60 ft.	+0	28 (−2 size, +20 natural), touch 8, flat-footed 28	DR 10/magic	3rd	20
Old	60 ft., burrow 30 ft., fly 200 ft. (poor), swim 60 ft.	+0	31 (−2 size, +23 natural), touch 8, flat-footed 31	*Freezing fog*	5th	21
Very old	60 ft., burrow 30 ft., fly 200 ft. (poor), swim 60 ft.	+0	34 (−2 size, +26 natural), touch 8, flat-footed 34	DR 15/magic	7th	23
Ancient	60 ft., burrow 30 ft., fly 200 ft. (poor), swim 60 ft.	+0	37 (−2 size, +29 natural), touch 8, flat-footed 37	*Wall of ice*	9th	24
Wyrm	60 ft., burrow 30 ft., fly 250 ft. (clumsy), swim 60 ft.	+0	38 (−4 size, +32 natural), touch 6, flat-footed 38	DR 20/magic	11th	25
Great wyrm	60 ft., burrow 30 ft., fly 250 ft. (clumsy), swim 60 ft.	+0	41 (−4 size, +35 natural), touch 6, flat-footed 41	*Control weather*	13th	27

METALLIC DRAGONS

Metallic dragons make up the good branch of dragonkind, but they are every bit as aggressive as their evil cousins when threatened or challenged. They also tend to be covetous and proud.

BRASS DRAGON

Dragon (Fire)
Environment: Warm deserts
Organization: Wyrmling, very young, young, juvenile, and young adult: solitary or clutch (2–5); adult, mature adult, old, very old, ancient, wyrm, or great wyrm: solitary, pair, or family (1–2 and 2–5 offspring)
Challenge Ratings: Wyrmling 3; very young 4; young 6; juvenile 8; young adult 10; adult 12; mature adult 15; old 17; very old 19; ancient 20; wyrm 21; great wyrm 23
Treasure: Triple standard
Alignment: Always chaotic good
Advancement: Wyrmling 5–6 HD; very young 8–9 HD; young 11–12 HD; juvenile 14–15 HD; young adult 17–18 HD; adult 20–21 HD; mature adult 23–24 HD; old 26–27 HD; very old 29–30 HD; ancient 32–33 HD; wyrm 35–36 HD; great wyrm 38+ HD
Level Adjustment: Wyrmling +2; very young +3; young +4; juvenile +4; others —

The dragon's head has a massive plate at the forehead and bladelike horns at the chin. A frill runs the length of the neck, and the dragon has manta-like wings. The dragon smells like sunbaked sand, and its scales glisten like polished brass.

Brass dragons are notoriously talkative. They may have useful information, but usually share it only after long rambling and hinting for a gift.

At birth, a brass dragon's scales are a dull, mottled brown. As the dragon gets older, the scales become more brassy until they reach a warm, burnished appearance. The grand head-plates of a brass dragon are smooth and metallic, and it sports bladed chin horns that grow sharper with age. Wings and frills are mottled green toward the edges, darkening with age. As the dragon grows older, its pupils fade until the eyes resemble molten metal orbs.

Brass dragons love intense, dry heat and spend most of their time basking in the desert sun. They are accompanied by a tangy metallic or sandy odor. They lair in high caves, preferably facing east to enjoy the morning warmth, and their territories always contain several spots where they can sunbathe and trap unwary travelers in conversation.

Brass dragons can and will eat almost anything if the need arises, but they normally consume very little. They are able to get nourishment from the morning dew, a rare commodity in their habitat, and have been seen carefully lifting it off plants with their long tongues.

Because they share similar habitats, blue dragons are brass dragons' worst enemies. The larger blues have the advantage in one-on-one confrontations, so brass dragons usually try to evade them until they can rally their neighbors for a mass attack.

Brass dragon

Combat

Brass dragons would rather talk than fight. If an intelligent creature tries to leave without engaging in conversation, the dragon might force compliance in a fit of pique, using *suggestion* or a dose of *sleep* gas. A creature put to sleep may wake to find itself pinned or buried to the neck in the sand until the dragon's thirst for small talk is slaked. When faced with real danger, younger brass dragons fly out of sight, then

BRASS DRAGONS BY AGE

Age	Size	Hit Dice (hp)	Str	Dex	Con	Int	Wis	Cha	Base Attack/ Grapple	Attack	Fort Save	Ref Save	Will Save	Breath Weapon (DC)	Frightful Presence DC
Wyrmling	T	4d12+4 (30)	11	10	13	10	11	10	+4/−4	+6	+5	+4	+4	1d6 (13)	—
Very young	S	7d12+7 (52)	13	10	13	10	11	10	+7/+4	+9	+6	+5	+5	2d6 (14)	—
Young	M	10d12+20 (85)	15	10	15	12	13	12	+10/+12	+12	+9	+7	+8	3d6 (17)	—
Juvenile	M	13d12+26 (110)	17	10	15	12	13	12	+13/+16	+16	+10	+8	+9	4d6 (18)	—
Young adult	L	16d12+48 (152)	19	10	17	14	15	14	+16/+24	+19	+13	+10	+12	5d6 (21)	20
Adult	L	19d12+76 (199)	23	10	19	14	15	14	+19/+29	+24	+15	+11	+13	6d6 (23)	21
Mature adult	H	22d12+110 (253)	27	10	21	16	17	16	+22/+38	+28	+18	+13	+16	7d6 (26)	24
Old	H	25d12+125 (287)	29	10	21	16	17	16	+25/+42	+32	+19	+14	+17	8d6 (27)	25
Very old	H	28d12+168 (350)	31	10	23	18	19	18	+28/+46	+36	+22	+16	+20	9d6 (30)	28
Ancient	H	31d12+186 (387)	33	10	23	18	19	18	+31/+50	+40	+23	+17	+21	10d6 (31)	29
Wyrm	G	34d12+238 (459)	35	10	25	20	21	20	+34/+58	+42	+26	+19	+24	11d6 (34)	32
Great wyrm	G	37d12+296 (536)	37	10	27	20	21	20	+37/+62	+46	+28	+20	+25	12d6 (36)	33

BRASS DRAGON ABILITIES BY AGE

Age	Speed	Initiative	AC	Special Abilities	Caster Level	SR
Wyrmling	60 ft., burrow 30 ft., fly 150 ft. (average)	+0	15 (+2 size, +3 natural), touch 12, flat-footed 15	Immunity to fire, *speak with animals*, vulnerability to cold	—	—
Very young	60 ft., burrow 30 ft., fly 150 ft. (average)	+0	17 (+1 size, +6 natural), touch 11, flat-footed 17		—	—
Young	60 ft., burrow 30 ft., fly 200 ft. (poor)	+0	19 (+9 natural), touch 10, flat-footed 19		1st	—
Juvenile	60 ft., burrow 30 ft., fly 200 ft. (poor)	+0	22 (+12 natural), touch 10, flat-footed 22	*Endure elements*	3rd	—
Young adult	60 ft., burrow 30 ft., fly 200 ft. (poor)	+0	24 (−1 size, +15 natural), touch 9, flat-footed 24	DR 5/magic	5th	18
Adult	60 ft., burrow 30 ft., fly 200 ft. (poor)	+0	27 (−1 size, +18 natural touch 9, flat-footed 27	*Suggestion*	7th	20
Mature adult	60 ft., burrow 30 ft., fly 200 ft. (poor)	+0	29 (−2 size, +21 natural), touch 8, flat-footed 29	DR 10/magic	9th	22
Old	60 ft., burrow 30 ft., fly 200 ft. (poor)	+0	32 (−2 size, +24 natural), touch 8, flat-footed 32	*Control winds*	11th	24
Very old	60 ft., burrow 30 ft., fly 200 ft. (poor)	+0	35 (−2 size, +27 natural), touch 8, flat-footed 35	DR 15/magic	13th	25
Ancient	60 ft., burrow 30 ft., fly 200 ft. (poor)	+0	38 (−2 size, +30 natural), touch 8, flat-footed 38	*Control weather*	15th	27
Wyrm	60 ft., burrow 30 ft., fly 250 ft. (clumsy)	+0	39 (−4 size, +33 natural), touch 6, flat-footed 39	DR 20/magic	17th	28
Great wyrm	60 ft., burrow 30 ft., fly 250 ft. (clumsy)	+0	42 (−4 size, +36 natural), touch 6, flat-footed 42	*Summon djinni*	19th	30

*Can also cast cleric spells and those from the Chaos and Knowledge domains as arcane spells.

hide by burrowing into the sand. Older dragons spurn this ploy but still prefer to have the advantage in combat.

Breath Weapon (Su): A brass dragon has two types of breath weapon, a line of fire and a cone of *sleep*. Creatures within the cone must succeed on a Will save or fall asleep, regardless of HD, for 1d6 rounds plus 1 round per age category of the dragon.

Spell-Like Abilities: At will—*speak with animals*; 3/day—*endure elements* (juvenile or older; radius 10 ft. × dragon's age category); 1/day—*suggestion* (adult or older), *control winds* (old or older), *control weather* (ancient or older).

Summon Djinni (Sp): This ability, usable by a great wyrm brass dragon, works like a *summon monster* spell, except that it summons one djinni. This ability is the equivalent of a 7th-level spell.

Skills: Bluff, Gather Information, and Survival are considered class skills for brass dragons.

Wyrmling Brass Dragon: CR 3; Tiny dragon (fire); HD 4d12+4; hp 30; Init +4; Spd 60 ft., burrow 30 ft., fly 150 ft. (average); AC 15, touch 12, flat-footed 15; Base Atk +4; Grp −4; Atk +6 melee (1d4, bite); Full Atk +6 melee (1d4, bite), +1 melee (1d3, 2 claws); Space/Reach 2-1/2 ft./0 ft. (bite 5 ft.); SA breath weapon, spell-like abilities; SQ darkvision 120 ft., immunity to fire, *sleep*, and paraly-

sis, low-light vision, vulnerability to cold; AL CG; SV Fort +5, Ref +4, Will +4; Str 11, Dex 10, Con 13, Int 10, Wis 11, Cha 10.

Skills and Feats: Hide +7, Knowledge (history) +6, Knowledge (local) +6, Knowledge (nature) +5, Listen +6, Search +6, Spot +6; Flyby Attack, Improved Initiative.

Breath Weapon (Su): 30-ft. line, damage 1d6 fire, Reflex DC 13 half; or 15-ft. cone, *sleep* 1d6+1 rounds, Will DC 13 negates.

Spell-Like Abilities: At will—*speak with animals*. Caster level 1st.

BRONZE DRAGON

Dragon (Water)
Environment: Temperate hills
Organization: Wyrmling, very young, young, juvenile, and young adult: solitary or clutch (2–5); adult, mature adult, old, very old, ancient, wyrm, or great wyrm: solitary, pair, or family (1–2 and 2–5 offspring)
Challenge Ratings: Wyrmling 3; very young 5; young 7; juvenile 9; young adult 12; adult 15; mature adult 17; old 19; very old 20; ancient 22; wyrm 23; great wyrm 25
Treasure: Triple standard
Alignment: Always lawful good

BRONZE DRAGONS BY AGE

Age	Size	Hit Dice (hp)	Str	Dex	Con	Int	Wis	Cha	Base Attack/ Grapple	Attack	Fort Save	Ref Save	Will Save	Breath Weapon (DC)	Frightful Presence DC
Wyrmling	S	6d12+6 (45)	13	10	13	14	15	14	+6/+3	+8	+6	+5	+7	2d6 (14)	—
Very young	M	9d12+18 (76)	15	10	15	14	15	14	+9/+11	+11	+8	+6	+8	4d6 (16)	—
Young	M	12d12+24 (102)	17	10	15	16	17	16	+12/+15	+15	+10	+8	+11	6d6 (18)	—
Juvenile	L	15d12+45 (142)	19	10	17	18	19	18	+15/+23	+18	+12	+9	+13	8d6 (20)	—
Young adult	L	18d12+72 (189)	23	10	19	18	19	18	+18/+28	+23	+15	+11	+15	10d6 (23)	23
Adult	H	21d12+105 (241)	27	10	21	20	21	20	+21/+37	+27	+17	+12	+17	12d6 (25)	25
Mature adult	H	24d12+120 (276)	29	10	21	20	21	20	+24/+41	+31	+19	+14	+19	14d6 (27)	27
Old	H	27d12+162 (337)	31	10	23	22	23	22	+27/+45	+35	+21	+15	+21	16d6 (29)	29
Very old	H	30d12+180 (375)	33	10	23	22	23	22	+30/+49	+39	+23	+17	+23	18d6 (31)	31
Ancient	G	33d12+231 (445)	35	10	25	24	25	24	+33/+57	+41	+25	+18	+25	20d6 (33)	33
Wyrm	G	36d12+288 (522)	37	10	27	26	27	26	+36/+61	+45	+28	+20	+28	22d6 (36)	36
Great wyrm	G	39d12+312 (565)	39	10	27	26	27	26	+39/+65	+49	+29	+21	+29	24d6 (37)	37

Advancement: Wyrmling 7–8 HD; very young 10–11 HD; young 13–14 HD; juvenile 16–17 HD; young adult 19–20 HD; adult 22–23 HD; mature adult 25–26 HD; old 28–29 HD; very old 31–32 HD; ancient 34–35 HD; wyrm 37–38 HD; great wyrm 40+ HD

Level Adjustment: Wyrmling +4; very young +4; young +6; others —

The dragon has a ribbed and fluted crest sweeping back from its cheeks and eyes. The ribs in the crests end in curving horns. The dragon also has small horns on its lower jaw and chin. It has a beaklike snout and a small head frill, as well as a tall neck frill. The scent of the sea surrounds the dragon, and its scales have a metallic, golden brown cast.

Bronze dragons are inquisitive and enjoy polymorphing into small, friendly animals to observe adventurers. They are fascinated by warfare, eagerly joining an army for a just cause—and good pay.

A bronze wyrmling's scales are yellow tinged with green, showing only a hint of bronze. As the dragon approaches adulthood, its color deepens slowly to a darker, rich bronze tone. Very old dragons develop

Bronze dragon

a blue-black tint to the edges of their scales. Powerful swimmers, they have webbed feet and smooth, flat scales. The pupils of its eyes fade as a dragon ages, until in the oldest the eyes resemble glowing green orbs.

Bronze dragons like coastal hills near deep fresh water or salt water. They often visit the depths to cool off or hunt for pearls and sunken treasure. They prefer caves that are accessible only from the water, but their lairs are always dry—they do not lay eggs, sleep, or store treasure underwater. A smell of sea spray lingers about them. Bronze dragons eat aquatic plants and some varieties of seafood. They especially prize shark meat. They also dine on the occasional pearl.

Combat

Bronze dragons dislike killing animals and would rather bribe them (perhaps with food) or force them away magically. They use *detect thoughts* to learn intelligent creatures' intentions. When attacking they blind their opponents with *fog cloud* and then charge or, if flying, snatch them up. Against seafaring opponents they conjure up a storm or use their tails to smash the vessels' hulls. If a dragon is inclined to be lenient, ships might be merely becalmed, fogbound, or broken-masted.

Breath Weapon (Su): Bronze dragons have two types of breath weapon, a line of lightning and a cone

Illus. by T. Lockwood

BRONZE DRAGON ABILITIES BY AGE

Age	Speed	Initiative	AC	Special Abilities	Caster Level	SR
Wyrmling	40 ft., fly 100 ft. (average), swim 60 ft.	+0	16 (+1 size, +5 natural), touch 11, flat-footed 16	Immunity to electricity, water breathing, *speak with animals*	—	—
Very young	40 ft., fly 150 ft. (poor), swim 60 ft.	+0	18 (+8 natural), touch 10, flat-footed 18		—	—
Young	40 ft., fly 150 ft. (poor), swim 60 ft.	+0	21 (+11 natural), touch 10, flat-footed 21	Alternate form	1st	—
Juvenile	40 ft., fly 150 ft. (poor), swim 60 ft.	+0	23 (–1 size, +14 natural), touch 9, flat-footed 23		3rd	—
Young adult	40 ft., fly 150 ft. (poor), swim 60 ft.	+0	26 (–1 size, +17 natural), touch 9, flat-footed 26	DR 5/magic	5th	20
Adult	40 ft., fly 150 ft. (poor), swim 60 ft.	+0	28 (–2 size, +20 natural), touch 8, flat-footed 28	*Create food and water, fog cloud*	7th	22
Mature adult	40 ft., fly 150 ft. (poor), swim 60 ft.	+0	31 (–2 size, +23 natural), touch 8, flat-footed 31	DR 10/magic	9th	23
Old	40 ft., fly 150 ft. (poor), swim 60 ft.	+0	34 (–2 size, +26 natural), touch 8, flat-footed 34	*Detect thoughts*	11th	25
Very old	40 ft., fly 150 ft. (poor), swim 60 ft.	+0	37 (–2 size, +29 natural), touch 8, flat-footed 37	DR 15/magic	13th	26
Ancient	40 ft., fly 200 ft. (clumsy), swim 60 ft.	+0	38 (–4 size, +32 natural), touch 6, flat-footed 38	*Control water*	15th	28
Wyrm	40 ft., fly 200 ft. (clumsy), swim 60 ft.	+0	41 (–4 size, +35 natural), touch 6, flat-footed 41	DR 20/magic	17th	29
Great wyrm	40 ft., fly 200 ft. (clumsy), swim 60 ft.	+0	44 (–4 size, +38 natural), touch 6, flat-footed 44	*Control weather*	19th	31

*Can also cast cleric spells and those from the Animal, Law, and Water domains as arcane spells.

of *repulsion* gas. Creatures within the cone must succeed on a Will save or be compelled to do nothing but move away from the dragon for 1d6 rounds plus 1 round per age category of the dragon. This is a mind-affecting compulsion enchantment effect.

Water Breathing (Ex): A bronze dragon can breathe underwater indefinitely and can freely use its breath weapon, spells, and other abilities while submerged.

Alternate Form (Su): A young or older bronze dragon can assume any animal or humanoid form of Medium size or smaller as a standard action three times per day. This ability functions as a *polymorph* spell cast on itself at its caster level, except that the dragon does not regain hit points for changing form and can only assume the form of an animal or humanoid. The dragon can remain in its animal or humanoid form until it chooses to assume a new one or return to its natural form.

Spell-Like Abilities: At will—*speak with animals*; 3/day—*create food and water* (adult or older), *fog cloud* (adult or older), *detect thoughts* (old or older), *control water* (ancient or older); 1/day—*control weather* (great wyrm).

Skills: Disguise, Swim, and Survival are considered class skills for bronze dragons.

Juvenile Bronze Dragon: CR 9; Large dragon (water); HD 15d12+45, hp 142; Init +4; Spd 40 ft., fly 150 ft. (poor), swim 60 ft.; AC 23, touch 9, flat-footed 23; Base Atk +15; Grp +23; Atk +18 melee (2d6+4, bite); Full Atk +18 melee (2d6+4, bite), +17 melee (1d8+2, 2 claws), +16 melee (1d6+2, 2 wings), +16 melee (1d8+6, tail slap); Space/Reach 10 ft./5 ft. (bite 10 ft.); SA breath weapon, spell-like abilities, spells; SQ alternate form, darkvision 120 ft., immunity to electricity, *sleep*, and paralysis, low-light vision, water breathing; AL LG; SV Fort +12, Ref +9, Will +13; Str 19, Dex 10, Con 17, Int 18, Wis 19, Cha 18.

Skills and Feats: Appraise +9, Bluff +9, Concentration +20, Diplomacy +25, Disguise +21, Hide +5, Intimidate +11, Knowledge (arcana) +9, Knowledge (local) +9, Knowledge (nature) +9, Listen +21, Search +21, Sense Motive +21, Spellcraft +23, Spot +21, Swim +8, Survival +9; Flyby Attack, Hover, Improved Initiative, Multiattack, Weapon Focus (claw), Wingover.

Alternate Form (Su): This bronze dragon can assume any animal or humanoid form of Medium size or smaller as a standard action three times per day. This ability functions as a *polymorph* spell cast on itself at its caster level, except that the dragon does not regain hit points for changing form and can only assume the form of an animal or humanoid. The dragon can remain in its animal or humanoid form until it chooses to assume a new one or return to its natural form.

Breath Weapon (Su): 60-ft. line, damage 8d6 electricity, Reflex DC 20 half; or 40-ft. cone, *repulsion* 1d6+4 rounds, Will DC 20 negates.

Spell-Like Abilities: At will—*speak with animals.* Caster level 4th.

Spells: As 3rd-level sorcerer.

Typical Sorcerer Spells Known (6/6; save DC 14 + spell level): 0—*dancing lights, detect magic, mage hand, ray of frost, read magic;* 1st—*animate rope, magic missile, shield.*

Water Breathing (Ex): This dragon can breathe underwater indefinitely and can freely use breath weapon, spells, and other abilities underwater.

COPPER DRAGON
Dragon (Earth)
Environment: Warm hills
Organization: Wyrmling, very young, young, juvenile, and young adult: solitary or clutch (2–5); adult, mature adult, old, very old, ancient, wyrm, or great wyrm: solitary, pair, or family (1–2 and 2–5 offspring)
Challenge Ratings: Wyrmling 3; very young 5; young 7; juvenile 9; young adult 11; adult 14; mature adult 16; old 19; very old 20; ancient 22; wyrm 23; great wyrm 25
Treasure: Triple standard
Alignment: Always chaotic good
Advancement: Wyrmling 6–7 HD; very young 9–10 HD; young 12–13 HD; juvenile 15–16 HD; young adult 18–19 HD; adult 21–22 HD; mature adult 24–25 HD; old 27–28 HD; very old 30–31 HD; ancient 33–34 HD; wyrm 36–37 HD; great wyrm 39+ HD
Level Adjustment: Wyrmling +2; very young +3; young +4; juvenile +4; others —

The dragon has massive thighs and shoulders, with a short face and broad, smooth brow plates jutting over the eyes. Long, flat horns extend back from the brow plates in a series of overlapping segments. The dragon also has backswept cheek ridges and frills on the backs of the lower jaws that sweep forward slightly. Layers of triangular blades point down from the chin. The dragon has an acrid odor, and its reddish scales have a metallic shine.

Copper dragons are incorrigible pranksters, joke tellers, and riddlers. Most are good-natured but also have a covetous, miserly streak. They are powerful jumpers and climbers.

At birth, a copper dragon's scales have a ruddy brown color with a metallic tint. As the dragon gets older, the scales become finer and more coppery, assuming a soft, warm gloss by young adult age. Very old dragons' scales pick up a green tint. A copper dragon's pupils fade with age, and the eyes of great wyrms resemble glowing turquoise orbs.

Copper dragons like dry, rocky uplands and hilltops. They lair in narrow caves and often conceal the entrances using *move earth* and *stone shape.* Within

Copper dragon

the lair, they construct twisting mazes with open tops that allow the dragon to fly or jump over intruders.

Copper dragons are determined hunters, considering good sport at least as important as the food. They are known to eat almost anything, including metal ore. However, they prize monstrous scorpions and other large poisonous creatures (they say the venom sharpens their wit).

Because copper dragons often inhabit hills in sight of red dragons' lairs, conflicts between the two varieties are inevitable. The smaller coppers usually run for cover until they can even the odds.

Combat

A copper dragon appreciates wit and usually doesn't harm creatures that can relate a joke, humorous story, or riddle the dragon has not heard before. It quickly gets annoyed with anyone who doesn't laugh at its jokes or accept its tricks with good humor. It likes to taunt and annoy opponents into giving up or acting foolishly.

An angry copper dragon prefers to mire foes using *transmute rock to mud*. The dragon pushes trapped opponents into the mud or snatches and carries them aloft. A copper dragon tries to draw airborne enemies into narrow, stony gorges where it can use its spider climb ability and maneuver them into colliding with the walls.

Breath Weapon (Su): A copper dragon has two types of breath weapon, a line of acid and a cone of *slow* gas. Creatures within the cone must succeed on a Fortitude save or be slowed for 1d6 rounds plus 1 round per age category of the dragon.

Spider Climb (Ex): A copper dragon can climb on stone surfaces as though using the *spider climb* spell.

Spell-Like Abilities: 2/day—*stone shape* (adult or older); 1/day—*transmute rock to mud* or *mud to rock* (old or older), *wall of stone* (ancient or older), *move earth* (great wyrm).

Skills: Bluff, Hide, and Jump are considered class skills for copper dragons.

Young Copper Dragon: CR 7; Medium dragon (earth); HD 11d12+22; hp 93; Init +0; Spd 40 ft., fly 150 ft. (poor); AC 20, touch 10, flat-footed 20; Base Atk +11; Grp +13; Atk +13 melee (1d8+2, bite); Full Atk +13 melee (1d8+2, bite), +11 melee (1d6+1, 2 claws), +11 melee (1d4+1, 2 wings); Space/Reach 5 ft./5 ft.; SA breath weapon, spells; SQ darkvision 120 ft., immunity to acid, *sleep*, and paralysis, low-light vision, spider climb; AL CG; SV Fort +9, Ref +7, Will +9; Str 15, Dex 10, Con 15, Int 14, Wis 15, Cha 14.

COPPER DRAGONS BY AGE

Age	Size	Hit Dice (hp)	Str	Dex	Con	Int	Wis	Cha	Base Attack/ Grapple	Attack	Fort Save	Ref Save	Will Save	Breath Weapon (DC)	Frightful Presence DC
Wyrmling	T	5d12+5 (37)	11	10	13	12	13	12	+5/–3	+7	+5	+4	+5	2d4 (13)	—
Very young	S	8d12+8 (60)	13	10	13	12	13	12	+8/+5	+10	+7	+6	+7	4d4 (15)	—
Young	M	11d12+22 (93)	15	10	15	14	15	14	+11/+13	+13	+9	+7	+9	6d4 (17)	—
Juvenile	M	14d12+28 (119)	17	10	15	14	15	14	+14/+17	+17	+11	+9	+11	8d4 (19)	—
Young adult	L	17d12+51 (161)	19	10	17	16	17	16	+17/+25	+20	+13	+10	+13	10d4 (21)	21
Adult	L	20d12+80 (210)	23	10	19	16	17	16	+20/+30	+25	+16	+12	+15	12d4 (24)	23
Mature adult	H	23d12+115 (264)	27	10	21	18	19	18	+23/+39	+29	+18	+13	+17	14d4 (26)	25
Old	H	26d12+130 (299)	29	10	21	18	19	18	+26/+43	+33	+20	+15	+19	16d4 (28)	27
Very old	H	29d12+174 (362)	31	10	23	20	21	20	+29/+47	+37	+22	+16	+21	18d4 (30)	29
Ancient	H	32d12+192 (400)	33	10	23	20	21	20	+32/+51	+41	+24	+18	+23	20d4 (32)	31
Wyrm	G	35d12+245 (472)	35	10	25	22	23	22	+35/+59	+43	+26	+19	+25	22d4 (34)	33
Great wyrm	G	38d12+304 (551)	37	10	27	22	23	22	+38/+63	+47	+29	+21	+27	24d4 (37)	35

COPPER DRAGON ABILITIES BY AGE

Age	Speed	Initiative	AC	Special Abilities	Caster Level	SR
Wyrmling	40 ft., fly 100 ft. (average)	+0	16 (+2 size, +4 natural), touch 12, flat-footed 16	Immunity to acid, spider climb	—	—
Very young	40 ft., fly 100 ft. (average)	+0	18 (+1 size, +7 natural), touch 11, flat-footed 18		—	—
Young	40 ft., fly 150 ft. (poor)	+0	20 (+10 natural), touch 10, flat-footed 20		1st	—
Juvenile	40 ft., fly 150 ft. (poor)	+0	23 (+13 natural), touch 10, flat-footed 23		3rd	—
Young adult	40 ft., fly 150 ft. (poor)	+0	25 (–1 size, +16 natural), touch 9, flat-footed 25	DR 5/magic	5th	19
Adult	40 ft., fly 150 ft. (poor)	+0	28 (–1 size, +19 natural), touch 9, flat-footed 28	*Stone shape*	7th	21
Mature adult	40 ft., fly 150 ft. (poor)	+0	30 (–2 size, +22 natural), touch 8, flat-footed 30	DR 10/magic	9th	23
Old	40 ft., fly 150 ft. (poor)	+0	33 (–2 size, +25 natural), touch 8, flat-footed 33	*Transmute rock to mud/mud to rock*	11th	25
Very old	40 ft., fly 150 ft. (poor)	+0	36 (–2 size, +28 natural), touch 8, flat-footed 36	DR 15/magic	13th	26
Ancient	40 ft., fly 150 ft. (poor)	+0	39 (–2 size, +31 natural), touch 8, flat-footed 39	*Wall of stone*	15th	28
Wyrm	40 ft., fly 200 ft. (clumsy)	+0	40 (–4 size, +34 natural), touch 6, flat-footed 40	DR 20/magic	17th	29
Great wyrm	40 ft., fly 200 ft. (clumsy)	+0	43 (–4 size, +37 natural), touch 6, flat-footed 43	*Move earth*	19th	31

*Can also cast cleric spells and those from the Chaos, Earth, and Trickery domains as arcane spells.

Skills and Feats: Bluff +10, Concentration +13, Diplomacy +6, Intimidate +4, Jump +17, Knowledge (geography) +10, Knowledge (nature) +9, Listen +13, Perform (oratory) +11, Search +13, Sense Motive +13, Spellcraft +13, Spot +13, Use Magic Device +14; Combat Expertise, Hover, Multiattack, Wingover.

Breath Weapon (Su): 60-ft. line, damage 6d4 acid, Reflex DC 17 half; or 30-ft. cone, slow 1d6+3 rounds, Fortitude DC 17 negates.

Spells: As 1st-level sorcerer.

Sorcerer Spells Known (5/4; save DC 12 + spell level): 0—*dancing lights, daze, detect magic, ghost sound*; 1st—*command, grease.*

Spider Climb (Ex): Can use spider climb (as the spell) on stone surfaces.

GOLD DRAGON

Dragon (Fire)
Environment: Warm plains
Organization: Wyrmling, very young, young, juvenile, and young adult: solitary or clutch (2–5); adult, mature adult, old, very old, ancient, wyrm, or great wyrm: solitary, pair, or family (1–2 and 2–5 offspring)
Challenge Ratings: Wyrmling 5; very young 7; young 9; juvenile 11; young adult 14; adult 16; mature adult 19; old 21; very old 22; ancient 24; wyrm 25; great wyrm 27
Treasure: Triple standard
Alignment: Always lawful good
Advancement: Wyrmling 9–10 HD; very young 12–13 HD; young 15–16 HD; juvenile 18–19 HD; young adult 21–22 HD; adult 24–25 HD; mature adult 27–28 HD; old 30–31 HD; very old 33–34 HD; ancient 36–37 HD; wyrm 39–40 HD; great wyrm 42+ HD
Level Adjustment: Wyrmling +4; very young +5; young +6; others —

The dragon has large, smooth, twin horns that sweep back from its nose and brow. Twin frills adorn its long neck, and whiskers around its mouth look like the barbels of a catfish. Its saillike wings start at its shoulders and trace down to the tip of its tail. The dragon smells of saffron and incense, and its scales glisten like polished gold.

Gold dragons are graceful, sinuous, and wise. They hate injustice and foul play, often embarking on self-appointed quests to promote good. A gold dragon often assumes human or animal guise.

On hatching, a gold dragon's scales are dark yellow with golden metallic flecks. The flecks get larger as the dragon matures until, at the

Gold dragon

GOLD DRAGONS BY AGE

Age	Size	Hit Dice (hp)	Str	Dex	Con	Int	Wis	Cha	Base Attack/ Grapple	Attack	Fort Save	Ref Save	Will Save	Breath Weapon (DC)	Frightful Presence DC
Wyrmling	M	8d12+16 (68)	17	10	15	14	15	14	+8/+11	+11	+8	+6	+8	2d10 (16)	—
Very young	L	11d12+33 (104)	21	10	17	16	17	16	+11/+20	+15	+10	+7	+10	4d10 (18)	—
Young	L	14d12+42 (133)	25	10	17	16	17	16	+14/+25	+20	+12	+9	+12	6d10 (20)	—
Juvenile	L	17d12+68 (178)	29	10	19	18	19	18	+17/+30	+25	+14	+10	+14	8d10 (22)	—
Young adult	H	20d12+100 (230)	31	10	21	18	19	18	+20/+38	+28	+17	+12	+16	10d10 (25)	24
Adult	H	23d12+115 (264)	33	10	21	20	21	20	+23/+42	+32	+18	+13	+18	12d10 (26)	26
Mature adult	H	26d12+156 (325)	35	10	23	20	21	20	+26/+46	+36	+21	+15	+20	14d10 (29)	28
Old	G	29d12+203 (391)	39	10	25	24	25	24	+29/+55	+39	+23	+16	+23	16d10 (31)	31
Very old	G	32d12+256 (464)	41	10	27	26	27	26	+32/+59	+43	+26	+18	+26	18d10 (34)	34
Ancient	G	35d12+315 (542)	43	10	29	28	29	28	+35/+63	+47	+28	+19	+28	20d10 (36)	36
Wyrm	C	38d12+380 (627)	45	10	31	30	31	30	+38/+71	+47	+31	+21	+31	22d10 (39)	39
Great wyrm	C	41d12+451 (717)	47	10	33	32	33	32	+41/+75	+51	+33	+22	+33	24d10 (41)	41

Gold Dragon Abilities by Age

Age	Speed	Initiative	AC	Special Abilities	Caster Level	SR
Wyrmling	60 ft., fly 200 ft. (poor), swim 60 ft	+0	17 (+7 natural) touch 10, flat-footed 17	Alternate form, immunity to fire, vulnerability to cold, water breathing	—	—
Very young	60 ft., fly 200 ft. (poor), swim 60 ft.	+0	19 (–1 size, +10 natural) touch 9, flat-footed 19		—	—
Young	60 ft., fly 200 ft. (poor), swim 60 ft.	+0	22 (–1 size, +13 natural) touch 9, flat-footed 22		1st	—
Juvenile	60 ft., fly 200 ft. (poor), swim 60 ft.	+0	25 (–1 size, +16 natural) touch 9, flat-footed 25	Bless	3rd	—
Young adult	60 ft., fly 200 ft. (poor), swim 60 ft.	+0	27 (–2 size, +19 natural) touch 8, flat-footed 27	DR 5/magic	5th	21
Adult	60 ft., fly 200 ft. (poor), swim 60 ft.	+0	30 (–2 size, +22 natural touch 8, flat-footed 30	Luck bonus	7th	23
Mature adult	60 ft., fly 200 ft. (poor), swim 60 ft.	+0	33 (–2 size, +25 natural) touch 8, flat-footed 33	DR 10/magic	9th	25
Old	60 ft., fly 250 ft. (clumsy), swim 60 ft	+0	34 (–4 size, +28 natural) touch 6, flat-footed 34	Geas/quest, detect gems	11th	27
Very old	60 ft., fly 250 ft. (clumsy), swim 60 ft.	+0	37 (–4 size, +31 natural) touch 6, flat-footed 37	DR 15/magic	13th	28
Ancient	60 ft., fly 250 ft. (clumsy), swim 60 ft.	+0	40 (–4 size, +34 natural) touch 6, flat-footed 40	Sunburst	15th	30
Wyrm	60 ft., fly 250 ft. (clumsy), swim 60 ft	+0	39 (–8 size, +37 natural) touch 2, flat-footed 39	DR 20/magic	17th	31
Great wyrm	60 ft., fly 250 ft. (clumsy), swim 60 ft.	+0	42 (–8 size, +40 natural) touch 2, flat-footed 42	Foresight	19th	33

*Can also cast cleric spells and those from the Law, Luck, and Good domains as arcane spells.

adult stage, the scales are completely golden. Gold dragons' faces are bewhiskered and sagacious; as they age, their pupils fade until the eyes resemble pools of molten gold.

Gold dragons can live anywhere. Their lairs are secluded and always made of stone, whether caves or castles. These usually have loyal guards: animals appropriate to the terrain, storm giants, or good cloud giants. Giants usually form a mutual defensive agreement with a dragon.

Gold dragons usually sustain themselves on pearls or small gems. Such gifts are well received, as long as they are not bribes.

Combat

Gold dragons usually parley before fighting. When conversing with intelligent creatures, they use Intimidate and Sense Motive to gain the upper hand. In combat, they employ *bless* and their *luck bonus*; older dragons use their *luck bonus* at the start of each day. They make heavy use of spells in combat. Among their favorites are *cloudkill, delayed blast fireball, fire shield, globe of invulnerability, maze, sleep, slow,* and *stinking cloud.*

Breath Weapon (Su): A gold dragon has two types of breath weapon, a cone of fire and a cone of weakening gas. Creatures within a cone of weakening gas must succeed on a Fortitude save or take 1 point of Strength damage per age category of the dragon.

Alternate Form (Su): A gold dragon can assume any animal or humanoid form of Medium size or smaller as a standard action three times per day. This ability functions as a *polymorph* spell cast on itself at its caster level, except that the dragon does not regain hit points for changing form and can only assume the form of an animal or humanoid. The dragon can remain in its animal or humanoid form until it chooses to assume a new one or return to its natural form.

Water Breathing (Ex): A gold dragon can breathe underwater indefinitely and can freely use its breath weapon, spells, and other abilities while submerged (the cone of fire becomes a cone of superheated steam underwater).

Luck Bonus (Sp): Once per day an adult or older gold dragon can touch a gem, usually one embedded in the dragon's hide, and enspell it to bring good luck. As long as the dragon carries the gem, it and every good creature in a 10-foot radius per age category of the dragon receives a +1 luck bonus on all saving throws and similar rolls, as for a *stone of good luck* (see the item description, page 267 of the *Dungeon Master's Guide*). If the dragon gives an enspelled gem to another creature, only that bearer gets the bonus. The effect lasts 1d3 hours plus 3 hours per age category of the dragon but ends if the gem is destroyed. This ability is the equivalent of a 2nd-level spell.

Detect Gems (Sp): An old or older gold dragon can use this ability three times per day. This is a divination effect similar to a *detect magic* spell, except that it finds only gems. The dragon can scan a 60-degree arc each round: By concentrating for 1 round it knows if there are any gems within the arc; 2 rounds of concentration reveal the exact number of gems; and 3 rounds reveal their exact location, type, and value. This ability is the equivalent of a 2nd-level spell.

Other Spell-Like Abilities: 3/day—*bless* (juvenile or older); 1/day—*geas/quest* (old or older), *sunburst* (ancient or older), *foresight* (great wyrm).

Skills: Disguise, Heal, and Swim are considered class skills for gold dragons.

Adult Gold Dragon: CR 16; Huge dragon (fire); HD 23d12+115, hp 264; Init +4; Spd 60 ft., swim 60 ft., fly 200 ft. (poor); AC 30, touch 8, flat-footed 30; Base Atk +23; Grp +42; Atk +32 melee (2d8+11, bite); Full Atk +32 melee (2d8+11, bite), +27 melee (2d6+5, 2 claws), +27 melee (1d8+5, 2 wings), +27 melee (2d6+16, tail slap); Space/Reach 15 ft./10 ft. (bite 15 ft.); SA breath weapon, crush, frightful presence, spell-like abilities, spells; SQ alternate form, damage reduction 5/magic, darkvision 120 ft., immunity to fire, *sleep,* and paralysis, low-light vision *luck bonus,* spell resistance 23, vulnerability to cold, water breathing; AL LG; SV Fort +18, Ref +13, Will +18; Str 33, Dex 10, Con 21, Int 20, Wis 21, Cha 20.

Skills and Feats: Bluff +13, Concentration +20, Diplomacy +30, Disguise +28, Hide –1, Intimidate +24, Jump +46, Knowledge (arcana) +20, Knowledge (local) +25, Knowledge (nobility and royalty) +15, Listen +30, Move Silently +7, Search +28, Sense Motive +27, Spellcraft +28, Spot +30, Swim +19; Survival +15; Alertness,

Flyby Attack, Improved Initiative, Leadership, Negotiator, Power Attack, Stealthy, Wingover.

Breath Weapon (Su): 50-ft. cone, damage 12d10 fire, Reflex DC 26 (or higher if heightened) half; or 50-ft. cone, 6 points Strength damage, Fortitude DC 26 (or higher if heightened) negates.

Crush (Ex): Area 15 ft. by 15 ft.; Small or smaller opponents take 2d8+13 points of bludgeoning damage, and must succeed on a DC 26 Reflex save or be pinned; grapple bonus +38.

Frightful Presence (Ex): 180-ft. radius, HD 22 or less, Will DC 26 negates.

Spells: As 7th-level sorcerer.

Typical Sorcerer Spells Known (6/8/7/5; save DC 15 + spell level): 0—*arcane mark, detect magic, flare, light, mage hand, prestidigitation, read magic;* 1st—*charm person, magic missile, protection from evil, shield of faith, true strike;* 2nd—*cure moderate wounds, fog cloud, resist elements;* 3rd—*searing light, suggestion.*

Spell-Like Abilities: 3/day—*bless.* Caster level 7th.

Alternate Form (Su): A gold dragon can assume any animal or humanoid form of Medium size or smaller as a standard action three times per day. This ability functions as a *polymorph* spell cast on itself at its caster level, except that the dragon does not regain hit points for changing form and can only assume the form of an animal or humanoid. The dragon can remain in its animal or humanoid form until it chooses to assume a new one or return to its natural form.

Luck Bonus (Sp): 1/day—good creatures in a 60-ft emanation gain a +1 luck bonus on all saving throws.

Water Breathing (Ex): This dragon can breathe underwater indefinitely and can freely use breath weapon, spells, and other abilities underwater.

SILVER DRAGON

Dragon (Cold)

Environment: Temperate mountains

Organization: Wyrmling, very young, young, juvenile, and young adult: solitary or clutch (2–5); adult, mature adult, old, very old, ancient, wyrm, or great wyrm: solitary, pair, or family (1–2 and 2–5 offspring)

Challenge Ratings: Wyrmling 4; very young 5; young 7; juvenile 10; young adult 13; adult 15; mature adult 18; old 20; very old 21; ancient 23; wyrm 24; great wyrm 26

Treasure: Triple standard

Alignment: Always lawful good

Advancement: Wyrmling 8–9 HD; very young 11–12 HD; young 14–15 HD; juvenile 17–18 HD; young adult 20–21 HD; adult 23–24 HD; mature adult 26–27 HD; old 29–30 HD; very old 32–33 HD; ancient 35–36 HD; wyrm 38–39 HD; great wyrm 41+ HD

Level Adjustment: Wyrmling +4; very young +4; young +5; others —

A smooth, shiny plate forms the dragon's face. It has a frill that rises high over its head and continues down the neck and back to the tip of the tail. Long spines with dark tips support the frill. It has two smooth, shiny horns, and wings that are wide and sleek. The dragon has the scent of rain, and its scales gleam like liquid metal.

Silver dragons are regal and statuesque. They cheerfully assist good creatures that are in genuine need and often take the forms of kindly old men or fair damsels when associating with humans.

A silver wyrmling's scales are blue-gray with silver highlights. As the dragon approaches adulthood, its color gradually brightens until the individual scales are scarcely visible. From a distance, these dragons look as if they have been sculpted from pure metal. Silver dragons are sometimes known as shield dragons because of the silvery plates on their heads. As a silver dragon grows older, its pupils fade until in the oldest the eyes resemble orbs of mercury.

Silver dragons prefer aerial lairs on secluded mountain peaks or amid the clouds themselves. A faint smell of rain always accompanies them. Even in clouds, though, the lair always has a magical area with a solid floor for laying eggs and storing treasure.

Silver dragons seem to prefer human form to their own, and they often have mortal companions, even forming deep friendships. Inevitably, however, a dragon resumes its true form and departs for a time. Silver dragons have a taste for human cuisine and can live on such fare indefinitely. Because they lair in similar territories, silver dragons and red dragons often come into conflict. Duels between the two varieties are furious and deadly, but silver dragons generally get the upper hand by working together against their foes, often with human allies.

Silver dragon

Combat

Silver dragons are not violent and avoid combat except when faced with highly evil or aggressive foes. If necessary, they use *fog cloud* or *control weather* to blind or confuse opponents before

SILVER DRAGONS BY AGE

Age	Size	Hit Dice (hp)	Str	Dex	Con	Int	Wis	Cha	Base Attack/ Grapple	Attack	Fort Save	Ref Save	Will Save	Breath Weapon (DC)	Frightful Presence DC
Wyrmling	S	7d12+7 (52)	13	10	13	14	15	14	+7/+4	+9	+6	+5	+7	2d8 (14)	—
Very young	M	10d12+20 (85)	15	10	15	14	15	14	+10/+12	+12	+9	+7	+9	4d8 (17)	—
Young	M	13d12+26 (110)	17	10	15	16	17	16	+13/+16	+16	+10	+8	+11	6d8 (18)	—
Juvenile	L	16d12+48 (152)	19	10	17	18	19	18	+16/+24	+19	+13	+10	+14	8d8 (21)	—
Young adult	L	19d12+76 (199)	23	10	19	18	19	18	+19/+29	+24	+15	+11	+15	10d8 (23)	23
Adult	H	22d12+110 (253)	27	10	21	20	21	20	+22/+38	+28	+18	+13	+18	12d8 (26)	26
Mature adult	H	25d12+125 (287)	29	10	21	20	21	20	+25/+42	+32	+19	+14	+19	14d8 (27)	27
Old	H	28d12+168 (350)	31	10	23	22	23	22	+28/+46	+36	+22	+16	+22	16d8 (30)	30
Very old	H	31d12+186 (387)	33	10	23	24	25	24	+31/+50	+40	+23	+17	+24	18d8 (31)	32
Ancient	G	34d12+238 (459)	35	10	25	26	27	26	+34/+58	+42	+26	+19	+27	20d8 (34)	35
Wyrm	G	37d12+333 (573)	39	10	29	28	29	28	+37/+63	+47	+29	+20	+29	22d8 (37)	37
Great wyrm	C	40d12+400 (660)	43	10	31	30	31	30	+40/+72	+48	+32	+22	+32	24d8 (40)	40

SILVER DRAGON ABILITIES BY AGE

Age	Speed	Initiative	AC	Special Abilities	Caster Level	SR
Wyrmling	40 ft., fly 100 ft. (average)	+0	17 (+1 size, +6 natural), touch 11, flat-footed 17	Alternate form, immunity to acid and cold, cloudwalking, vulnerability to fire	—	—
Very young	40 ft., fly 150 ft. (poor)	+0	19 (+9 natural), touch 10, flat-footed 19		—	—
Young	40 ft., fly 150 ft. (poor)	+0	22 (+12 natural), touch 10, flat-footed 22		1st	—
Juvenile	40 ft., fly 150 ft. (poor)	+0	24 (–1 size, +15 natural), touch 9, flat-footed 24	Feather fall	3rd	—
Young adult	40 ft., fly 150 ft. (poor)	+0	27 (–1 size, +18 natural), touch 9, flat-footed 27	DR 5/magic	5th	20
Adult	40 ft., fly 150 ft. (poor)	+0	29 (–2 size, +21 natural), touch 8, flat-footed 29	Fog cloud	7th	22
Mature adult	40 ft., fly 150 ft. (poor)	+0	32 (–2 size, +24 natural), touch 8, flat-footed 32	DR 10/magic	9th	24
Old	40 ft., fly 150 ft. (poor)	+0	35 (–2 size, +27 natural), touch 8, flat-footed 35	Control winds	11th	26
Very old	40 ft., fly 150 ft. (poor)	+0	38 (–2 size, +30 natural), touch 8, flat-footed 38	DR 15/magic	13th	27
Ancient	40 ft., fly 200 ft. (clumsy)	+0	39 (–4 size, +33 natural), touch 6, flat-footed 39	Control weather	15th	29
Wyrm	40 ft., fly 200 ft. (clumsy)	+0	42 (–4 size, +36 natural), touch 6, flat-footed 42	DR 20/magic	17th	30
Great wyrm	40 ft., fly 200 ft. (clumsy)	+0	41 (–8 size, +39 natural), touch 2, flat-footed 41	Reverse gravity	19th	32

*Can also cast cleric spells and those from the Air, Good, Law, and Sun domains as arcane spells.

attacking. When angry, they use *reverse gravity* to fling enemies helplessly into the air, where they can be snatched. Against flying opponents, a silver dragon hides in clouds (creating some with *control weather* on clear days), then jumps to the attack when it has the advantage.

Breath Weapon (Su): A silver dragon has two types of breath weapon, a cone of cold and a cone of paralyzing gas. Creatures within a cone of paralyzing gas must succeed on a Fortitude save or be paralyzed for 1d6 rounds plus 1 round per age category of the dragon.

Alternate Form (Su): A silver dragon can assume any animal or humanoid form of Medium size or smaller as a standard action three times per day. This ability functions as a *polymorph* spell cast on itself at its caster level, except that the dragon does not regain hit points for changing form and can only assume the form of an animal or humanoid. The dragon can remain in its animal or humanoid form until it chooses to assume a new one or return to its natural form.

Cloudwalking (Su): A silver dragon can tread on clouds or fog as though on solid ground. The ability functions continuously but can be negated or resumed at will.

Spell-Like Abilities: 3/day—*fog cloud* (adult or older), *control winds* (old or older); 2/day—*feather fall* (juvenile or older); 1/day—*control weather* (ancient or older), *reverse gravity* (great wyrm).

Skills: Bluff, Disguise, and Jump are considered class skills for silver dragons.

Young Adult Silver Dragon: CR 13; Large dragon (air); HD 19d12+79, hp 202; Init +0; Spd 40 ft., fly 150 ft. (poor); AC 28, touch 9, flat-footed 28; Base Atk +19; Grp +29; Atk +24 melee (2d6+6, bite); Full Atk +24 melee (2d6+6, bite), +19 melee (1d8+3, 2 claws), +19 melee (1d6+3, 2 wings), +19 melee (1d8+9, tail slap); Space/Reach 10 ft./5 ft. (bite 10 ft.); SA breath weapon, frightful presence, spell-like abilities, spells; SQ alternate form, cloudwalking, damage reduction 5/magic, darkvision 120 ft., immunity to acid, cold, *sleep*, and paralysis, low-light vision, spell resistance 20; AL LG; SV Fort +15, Ref +11, Will +15; Str 23, Dex 10, Con 19, Int 18, Wis 19, Cha 18.

Skills and Feats: Balance +7, Bluff +16, Concentration +18, Diplomacy +18, Disguise +23, Heal +15, Hide –4, Intimidate +8, Jump +29, Knowledge (arcana) +14, Knowledge (nature) +14, Listen +24, Search +24, Sense Motive +24, Spellcraft +26, Spot +24, Tumble +9;

Acrobatic, Combat Casting, Flyby Attack, Improved Natural Armor, Persuasive, Toughness, Wingover.

Breath Weapon (Su): 40-ft. cone, damage 10d8 cold, Reflex DC 23 half; or 40-ft. cone, paralysis 1d6+5 rounds, Fortitude DC 23 negates.

Frightful Presence (Ex): 150-ft. radius, HD 18 or less, Will DC 23 negates.

Spell-Like Abilities: 2/day—*feather fall.* Caster level 5th.

Spells: As 5th-level sorcerer.

Typical Sorcerer Spells Known (6/7/5; save DC 14 + spell level): 0—*dancing lights, detect magic, detect poison, mage hand, mending, prestidigitation;* 1st—*chill touch, divine favor, protection from evil, unseen servant;* 2nd—*cat's grace, cure moderate wounds.*

Cloudwalking (Su): Tread on clouds or fog as though on solid ground; functions continuously but can be negated or resumed at will.

Alternate Form (Su): A silver dragon can assume any animal or humanoid form of Medium size or smaller as a standard action three times per day. This ability functions as a *polymorph* spell cast on itself at its caster level, except that the dragon does not regain hit points for changing form and can only assume the form of an animal or humanoid. The dragon can remain in its animal or humanoid form until it chooses to assume a new one or return to its natural form.

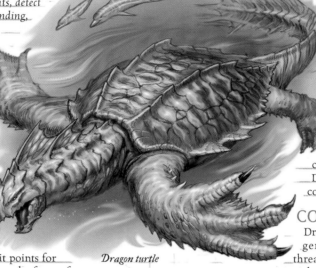

Dragon turtle

DRAGON TURTLE

Huge Dragon (Aquatic)
Hit Dice: 12d12+60 (138 hp)
Initiative: +0
Speed: 20 ft. (4 squares), swim 30 ft.
Armor Class: 25 (–2 size, +17 natural), touch 8, flat-footed 25
Base Attack/Grapple: +12/+28
Attack: Bite +18 melee (4d6+8)
Full Attack: Bite +18 melee (4d6+8) and 2 claws +13 melee (2d8+4)
Space/Reach: 15 ft./10 ft.
Special Attacks: Breath weapon, snatch, capsize
Special Qualities: Darkvision 60 ft., immunity to fire, *sleep,* and paralysis, low-light vision, scent
Saves: Fort +13, Ref +8, Will +9
Abilities: Str 27, Dex 10, Con 21, Int 12, Wis 13, Cha 12
Skills: Diplomacy +3, Hide +7*, Intimidate +16, Listen +16, Search +16, Sense Motive +16, Spot +16, Survival +16 (+18 following tracks), Swim +21
Feats: Blind-Fight, Cleave, Improved Bull Rush, Power Attack, Snatch
Environment: Temperate aquatic
Organization: Solitary
Challenge Rating: 9
Treasure: Triple standard
Alignment: Usually neutral
Advancement: 13–24 HD (Huge); 25–36 HD (Gargantuan)
Level Adjustment: —

This huge creature has a wide, streamlined shell with jagged protrusions. A long neck emerges from one end of the shell, ending in a crested head with sharp-lined jaws. Taloned flippers extend from holes along the sides of the shell, and a long tail snakes from the rear of the shell.

Dragon turtles are among the most beautiful, awesome, and feared creatures of the water. Deadly jaws, steaming breath, and a penchant for capsizing ships make them dreaded by mariners.

A surfacing dragon turtle is sometimes mistaken for the reflection of the sun or moon on the water. Its rough, deep green shell is much the same color as the deep water the monster favors, and the silver highlights that line the shell resemble light dancing on open water. The turtle's legs, tail, and head are a lighter green, flecked with golden highlights. An adult dragon turtle can measure from 20 to 30 feet from snout to tail, with a shell from 15 to 25 feet in diameter, and can weigh 8,000 to 32,000 pounds. Dragon turtles speak Aquan, Draconic, and Common.

COMBAT

Dragon turtles are fierce fighters and generally attack any creature that threatens their territory or looks like a potential meal.

Breath Weapon (Su): Cloud of superheated steam 20 feet high, 25 feet wide, and 50 feet long, once every 1d4 rounds, damage 12d6 fire, Reflex DC 21 half; effective both on the surface and underwater. The save DC is Constitution-based.

Capsize (Ex): A submerged dragon turtle that surfaces under a boat or ship less than 20 feet long capsizes the vessel 95% of the time. It has a 50% chance to capsize a vessel from 20 to 60 feet long and a 20% chance to capsize one over 60 feet long.

Skills: A dragon turtle has a +8 racial bonus on any Swim check to perform some special action or avoid a hazard. It can always choose to take 10 on a Swim check, even if distracted or endangered. It can use the run action while swimming, provided it swims in a straight line.

*Dragon turtles have a +8 racial bonus on Hide checks when submerged.

Dragonne

DRAGONNE

Large Magical Beast
Hit Dice: 9d10+27 (76 hp)
Initiative: +6
Speed: 40 ft. (8 squares), fly 30 ft. (poor)
Armor Class: 18 (−1 size, +2 Dex, +7 natural), touch 11, flat-footed 16
Base Attack/Grapple: +9/+17
Attack: Bite +12 melee (2d6+4)
Full Attack: Bite +12 melee (2d6+4) and 2 claws +7 melee (2d4+2)
Space/Reach: 10 ft./5 ft.
Special Attacks: Pounce, roar
Special Qualities: Darkvision 60 ft., low-light vision, scent
Saves: Fort +9, Ref +8, Will +4
Abilities: Str 19, Dex 15, Con 17, Int 6, Wis 12, Cha 12
Skills: Listen +11, Spot +11
Feats: Blind-Fight, Combat Reflexes, Improved Initiative, Track
Environment: Temperate deserts
Organization: Solitary, pair, or pride (5–10)
Challenge Rating: 7
Treasure: Double standard
Alignment: Usually neutral
Advancement: 10–12 HD (Large); 13–27 HD (Huge)
Level Adjustment: +4 (cohort)

Part giant lion and part dragon, the creature has a pair of small, brass-colored wings sprouting from its shoulders. It is covered with brass-colored scales, and its mane is thick and coarse.

Possessing some of the most dangerous qualities of a lion and a brass dragon, the dragonne is a vicious and deadly hunter.

Dragonnes are not necessarily aggressive toward strangers. Their reputation as remorseless devourers of helpless travelers is more the product of ignorance than well-researched fact. A dragonne almost always attacks a creature that invades its lair or threatens its territory, so adventurers who stumble across its cave or settlers who attempt to set up camp in the area are often subject to fierce and immediate retaliation. Those not threatening the dragonne's lair or simply passing through its territory are usually left alone.

Dragonnes prefer herd animals such as goats for food, especially since they don't fight back as fiercely as humanoids. They attack humanoids only if no other game is available.

A dragonne possesses huge claws and fangs, and large eyes, usually the color of its scales. A dragonne is about 12 feet long and weighs about 700 pounds.

Dragonnes speak Draconic.

COMBAT

A dragonne's wings are useful only for short flights, carrying the creature for 10 to 30 minutes at a time. Nevertheless, it uses its wings effectively in battle. If opponents attempt to charge or encircle it, the dragonne simply takes to the air and finds a more defensible position.

Pounce (Ex): If a dragonne charges, it can make a full attack in the same round.

Roar (Su): A dragonne can loose a devastating roar every 1d4 rounds. All creatures except dragonnes within 120 feet must succeed on a DC 15 Will save or become fatigued. Those within 30 feet who fail their saves become exhausted. The save DC is Charisma-based.

Skills: Dragonnes have a +4 racial bonus on Listen and Spot checks.

Carrying Capacity: A light load for a dragonne is up to 348 pounds; a medium load, 349–699 pounds, and a heavy load, 700–1,050 pounds.

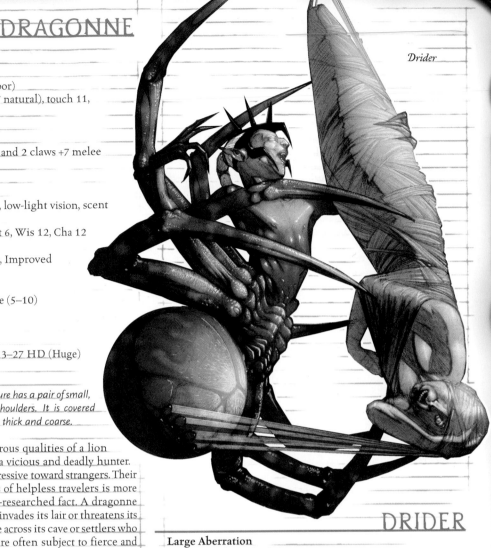

Drider

Illus. by C. Arellano

DRIDER

Large Aberration
Hit Dice: 6d8+18 (45 hp)
Initiative: +2
Speed: 30 ft. (6 squares), climb 15 ft.
Armor Class: 17 (−1 size, +2 Dex, +6 natural), touch 11, flat-footed 15
Base Attack/Grapple: +4/+10
Attack: Dagger +5 melee (1d6+2/19–20) or bite +6 melee (1d4+1 plus poison) or shortbow +5 ranged (1d8/×3)
Full Attack: 2 daggers +3 melee (1d6+2/19–20, 1d6+1/19–20) and bite +1 melee (1d4+1 plus poison); or shortbow +5 ranged (1d8/×3)
Space/Reach: 10 ft./5 ft.
Special Attacks: Spells, spell-like abilities, poison
Special Qualities: Darkvision 60 ft., spell resistance 17
Saves: Fort +5, Ref +4, Will +8
Abilities: Str 15, Dex 15, Con 16, Int 15, Wis 16, Cha 16
Skills: Climb +14, Concentration +9, Hide +10, Listen +9, Move Silently +12, Spot +9
Feats: Combat Casting, Two-Weapon Fighting, Weapon Focus (bite)
Environment: Underground
Organization: Solitary, pair, or troupe (1–2 plus 7–12 Medium monstrous spiders)
Challenge Rating: 7
Treasure: Double standard
Alignment: Always chaotic evil
Advancement: By character class
Level Adjustment: +4

This strange being has the head and torso of a dark elf and the legs and lower body of a giant spider.

Driders are bloodthirsty creatures that lurk in the depths of the earth, seeking warm-blooded prey of any kind.

Driders are created by the drow's dark goddess, Lolth. When a dark elf of above average ability reaches 6th level, the goddess may put him or her through a special test. Those who fail the test become driders.

Because they have failed their goddess's test, driders are outcasts from their own communities. Drow and driders hate one another passionately.

Driders speak Elven, Common, and Undercommon.

COMBAT

Driders seldom pass up an opportunity to attack other creatures, especially from ambush. They usually begin with a spell assault and often levitate out of the enemy's reach.

Poison (Ex): Injury, Fortitude DC 16, initial and secondary damage 1d6 Str. The save DC is Constitution based.

Spell-Like Abilities: 1/day—*dancing lights* (DC 13), *clairaudience/clairvoyance, darkness, detect good, detect law, detect magic, dispel magic, faerie fire, levitate, suggestion* (DC 16). Caster level 6th. The save DCs are Charisma-based.

Spells: Driders cast spells as 6th-level clerics, wizards, or sorcerers. Drider clerics can choose from the following domains: Chaos, Destruction, Evil, and Trickery. The typical spells prepared shown here are for a drider sorcerer.

Typical Sorcerer Spells Known (6/7/6/4, base save DC 13 + spell level): 0—*daze, detect magic, ghost sound, mage hand, ray of frost, read magic, resistance;* 1st—*mage armor, magic missile, ray of enfeeblement, silent image;* 2nd—*invisibility, web;* 3rd—*lightning bolt.*

Skills: A drider has a +4 racial bonus on Hide and Move Silently checks. It has a +8 racial bonus on Climb checks and can always choose to take 10 on a Climb check, even if rushed or threatened.

DRYAD

Medium Fey
Hit Dice: 4d6 (14 hp)
Initiative: +4
Speed: 30 ft. (6 squares)
Armor Class: 17 (+4 Dex, +3 natural), touch 14, flat-footed 13
Base Attack/Grapple: +2/+2
Attack: Dagger +6 melee (1d4/19–20) or masterwork longbow +7 ranged (1d8/×3)
Full Attack: Dagger +6 melee (1d4/19–20) or masterwork longbow +7 ranged (1d8/×3)
Space/Reach: 5 ft./5 ft.
Special Attacks: Spell-like abilities
Special Qualities: Damage reduction 5/cold iron, tree dependent, wild empathy
Saves: Fort +3, Ref +8, Will +6

Abilities: Str 10, Dex 19, Con 11, Int 14, Wis 15, Cha 18
Skills: Escape Artist +11, Handle Animal +11, Hide +11, Knowledge (nature) +11, Listen +9, Move Silently +11, Ride +6, Spot +9, Survival +9, Use Rope +4 (+6 with bindings)
Feats: Great Fortitude, Weapon Finesse
Environment: Temperate forests
Organization: Solitary or grove (4–7)
Challenge Rating: 3
Treasure: Standard
Alignment: Usually chaotic good
Advancement: By character class
Level Adjustment: —

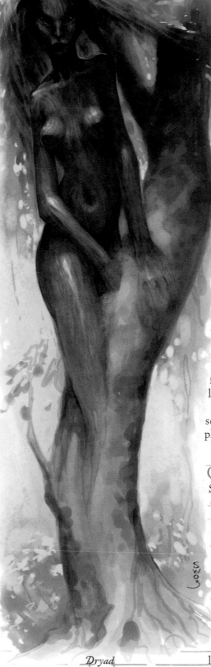

Dryad

The creature blossoms out of the bark of the ancient tree, at first appearing as a new branch before solidifying into a decidedly female shape. She has a wild, unfathomable look in her large, almond-shaped eyes, and her hair has a pronounced, leafy texture, while her skin looks like burnished wood.

Dryads are wild, mysterious entities found deep in secluded woodlands. They defend the trees from any who would fell them and sometimes come into conflict with humans and others who take wood from the forests. Dryads have been known to charm adventurers into helping them defend their homes or hunting down the forest's enemies—even if those enemies are human loggers and woodcutters.

Dryads remain something of a mystery even to other woodland beings. Tales tell of dryads who took a fancy to handsome elf or human men, charmed them, and held them captive. But since dryads rarely associate with any outside their own kind, these stories may be purely apocryphal. Dryads are more likely to ensnare intruders and then send their charmed "guests" out to deal with threats the dryads cannot handle.

A dryad's delicate features are much like a female elf's, though her flesh is like bark or fine wood, and her hair is like a canopy of leaves that changes color with the seasons. Although they are generally solitary, up to seven dryads have been encountered in one place on rare occasions.

Dryads speak Common, Elven, and Sylvan.

COMBAT

Shy, intelligent, and resolute, dryads are as elusive as they are alluring—they avoid physical combat and are rarely seen unless they wish to be. If threatened, or in need of an ally, a dryad uses *charm person* or *suggestion,* attempting to gain control of the attacker(s) who could help the most against the rest. Any attack on her tree, however, provokes the dryad into a frenzied defense.

Spell-Like Abilities: At will—*entangle* (DC 13), *speak with plants, tree shape;* 3/day—*charm person* (DC 13), *deep slumber* (DC 15), *tree stride;* 1/day—*suggestion* (DC 15). Caster level 6th. The save DCs are Wisdom-based.

Tree Dependent (Su): Each dryad is mystically bound

	Dwarf, 1st-Level Warrior Medium Humanoid (Dwarf)	Duergar, 1st-Level Warrior Medium Humanoid (Dwarf)
Hit Dice:	1d8+2 (6 hp)	1d8+5 (9 hp)
Initiative:	+0	+0
Speed:	20 ft. in scale mail (4 squares); base speed 20 ft.	20 ft. in chainmail (4 squares); base speed 20 ft.
Armor Class:	16 (+4 scale mail, +2 heavy shield), touch 10, flat-footed 16	17 (+5 chainmail, +2 heavy shield), touch 10, flat-footed 17
Base Attack/Grapple:	+1/+2	+1/+2
Attack:	Dwarven waraxe +3 melee (1d10+1/×3) or shortbow +1 ranged (1d6/×3)	Warhammer +2 melee (1d8+1/×3) or light crossbow +1 ranged (1d8/19–20)
Full Attack:	Dwarven waraxe +3 melee (1d10+1/×3) or shortbow +1 ranged (1d6/×3)	Warhammer +2 melee (1d8+1/×3) or light crossbow +1 ranged (1d8/19–20)
Space/Reach:	5 ft./5 ft.	5 ft./5 ft.
Special Attacks:	Dwarf traits	Duergar traits, spell-like abilities
Special Qualities:	Darkvision 60 ft., dwarf traits	Darkvision 60 ft., duergar traits
Saves:	Fort +4*, Ref +0*, Will −1*	Fort +4*, Ref +0*, Will −1*
Abilities:	Str 13, Dex 11, Con 14, Int 10, Wis 9, Cha 6	Str 13, Dex 11, Con 14, Int 10, Wis 9, Cha 4
Skills:	Appraise +2, Craft (blacksmithing) +2, Craft (stonemasonry) +2, Listen +2, Spot +2	Appraise +2, Craft (blacksmithing) +2, Craft (stonemasonry) +2, Listen +3, Move Silently −4, Spot +2
Feats:	Weapon Focus (dwarven waraxe)	Toughness
Environment:	Temperate mountains (Deep: Underground)	Underground
Organization:	Team (2–4), squad (11–20 plus 2 3rd-level sergeants and 1 leader of 3rd–6th level), or clan (30–100 plus 30% noncombatants plus 1 3rd-level sergeant per 10 adults, 5 5th-level lieutenants, and 3 7th-level captains)	Team (2–4), squad (9–16 plus 3 3rd-level sergeants and 1 leader of 3rd–8th level) or clan (20–80 plus 25% noncombatants plus 1 3rd-level sergeant per 5 adults, 3–6 6th-level lieutenants, and 1–4 9th-level captains)
Challenge Rating:	1/2	1
Treasure:	Standard coins; double goods; standard items	Standard coins, double goods, standard items
Alignment:	Often lawful good (Deep: Usually lawful neutral or neutral)	Often lawful evil
Advancement:	By character class	By character class
Level Adjustment:	+0	+1

to a single, enormous oak tree and must never stray more than 300 yards from it. Any who do become ill and die within 4d6 hours. A dryad's oak does not radiate magic.

Wild Empathy (Ex): This power works like the druid's wild empathy class feature, except that the dryad has a +6 racial bonus on the check.

DWARF

Stocky, broad of body and extremely muscular, the short figure before you may lack in height but not in physical strength or presence. Wrapped in metal armor and armed with a waraxe, the humanoid has light brown skin, ruddy cheeks, and bright eyes, with black hair and a long, carefully groomed beard and mustache.

Dwarves are noble warriors who excel at metalcraft, stoneworking, and war. They tend to be serious, determined, and very honorable.

Dwarves favor earth tones in their clothing and prefer simple and functional garb. The skin can be very dark, but it is always some shade of tan or brown. Hair color can be black, gray, or brown. Dwarves average 4 feet tall and weigh as much as adult humans.

Dwarves prefer to spend their time making masterpieces of stone, steel, and precious metals. They create durable weapons, craft beautiful jewelry, and cut superior gems. However, they consider it bad taste to flaunt wealth, so few wear jewelry other than one simple piece.

Dwarves speak Dwarven. Most who travel outside dwarven lands (as traders, mercenaries, or adventurers) know the Common tongue, while warriors in the dwarven cities usually learn Goblin to better interrogate and spy on those evil denizens of the deep caves.

Most dwarves encountered outside their home are warriors.

COMBAT

Dwarves are experts in combat, effectively using their environment and executing well-planned group attacks. They rarely use magic in fights, since they have few wizards or sorcerers (but dwarven clerics throw themselves into battle as heartily as their fellow warriors). If they have time to prepare, they may build deadfalls or other traps involving stone. In addition to the dwarven waraxe and thrown hammer, dwarves also use warhammers, picks, shortbows, heavy crossbows, and maces.

Dwarf Traits (Ex): Dwarves possess the following racial traits.

— +2 Constitution, −2 Charisma.

—Medium size.

—A dwarf's base land speed is 20 feet. However, dwarves can move at this speed even when wearing medium or heavy armor or when carrying a medium or heavy load.

—Darkvision out to to 60 feet.

—Stonecunning: This ability grants a dwarf a +2 racial bonus on Search checks to notice unusual stonework, such as sliding walls, stonework traps, new construction (even when built to match the old), unsafe stone surfaces, shaky stone ceilings, and the like. Something that isn't stone but that is disguised as stone also counts as unusual stonework. A dwarf who merely comes within 10 feet of unusual stonework can make a Search check as if he were actively searching, and a dwarf can use the Search skill to find stonework traps as a rogue can. A dwarf can also intuit depth, sensing his approximate depth underground as naturally as a human can sense which way is up. Dwarves have a sixth sense about stonework, an innate ability that they get plenty of opportunity to practice and hone in their underground homes.

—Weapon Familiarity: Dwarves treat dwarven waraxes and dwarven urgroshes (see Chapter 7 of the *Player's Handbook*) as martial weapons, rather than exotic weapons.

—Stability: Dwarves are exceptionally stable on their feet. A dwarf has a +4 bonus on ability checks made to resist being bull rushed or tripped when standing on the ground (but not when climbing, flying, riding, or otherwise not standing firmly on the ground).

— +2 racial bonus on saving throws against poison. *Not reflected in the saving throw numbers given here.

— +2 racial bonus on saving throws against spells and spell-like effects. *Not reflected in the saving throw numbers given here.

— +1 racial bonus on attack rolls against orcs (including half-orcs) and goblinoids (including goblins, hobgoblins, and bugbears).

— +4 dodge bonus to Armor Class against creatures of the giant type (such as ogres, trolls, and hill giants).

— +2 racial bonus on Appraise checks that are related to stone or metal items.

— +2 racial bonus on Craft checks that are related to stone or metal.

—Automatic Languages: Common, Dwarven. Bonus Languages: Giant, Gnome, Goblin, Orc, Terran, Undercommon.

—Favored Class: Fighter.

Hill dwarf

The dwarf warrior presented here had the following ability scores before racial adjustments: Str 13, Dex 11, Con 12, Int 10, Wis 9, Cha 8.

DWARF SOCIETY

Dwarves prefer living in underground cities that they build around mines (although some live on surface outposts). Carved into solid stone, these cities take centuries to complete but remain for ages. Dwarf society is organized into clans, with distinct family lines within each. A clan is led by a hereditary ruler, usually a king or queen who is a direct descendant of the clan's founder. Dwarves are strongly loyal to their family, clan, monarch, and people as a whole; in conflicts with other races, even objective dwarves tend to side with their kinfolk. These ties have helped dwarves survive generations of warfare against the evil creatures that live under the earth.

A dwarven city has noncombatant members (usually the young, elderly, and a few adults) equal to 30% of the fighting population; female dwarves are as numerous as males and are accepted in any part of dwarf society, including warriors.

Dwarf clans usually focus on one or two types of craft, such as blacksmithing, making weapons or armor, creating jewelry, engineering, or stonemasonry. To avoid becoming overspecialized, dwarves apprentice some of their young ones to other clans; this practice also helps foster unity. Since dwarves live a long time, these apprenticeships can last many years, even well into adulthood.

The chief dwarven deity is Moradin, the god who created their race and the patron of smiths and other skilled craftworkers.

SUBRACES

The information above is for hill dwarves, the most common variety. There are three other major dwarven subraces, which differ from hill dwarves as follows.

Deep Dwarf

These dwarves live far underground and tend to be more stand-offish with nondwarves.

Deep dwarves are the same height as other dwarves, but leaner. Their skin sometimes has a reddish tinge, and their large eyes lack the brightness of those of their kindred, being a washed-out blue. Their hair color ranges from bright red to straw blond. They have little contact with surface dwellers, relying on hill dwarves or mountain dwarves to trade goods for them.

Deep dwarves speak Dwarven and Goblin, and occasionally Draconic or Undercommon.

Deep Dwarf Traits (Ex): These traits are in addition to the hill dwarf traits, except where noted.

—Racial bonus on saves against spells and spell-like abilities increases to +3.

—Racial bonus on Fortitude saves against poisons increases to +3.

—Darkvision out to 90 feet.

—Light Sensitivity: Deep dwarves are dazzled in bright sunlight or within the radius of a *daylight* spell.

Duergar

Sometimes called gray dwarves, these evil beings dwell in the underground.

Most duergar are bald (even the females), and they dress in drab clothing that is designed to blend into stone. In their lairs they may wear jewelry, but it is always kept dull. They war with other dwarves, even allying with other underground creatures from time to time.

The duergar revere the deity Laduguer, a joyless god who demands constant toil.

Duergar speak Dwarven and Undercommon.

Duergar Traits (Ex): These traits are in addition to the hill dwarf traits, except where noted.

— –4 Charisma instead of –2.

—Darkvision out to 120 feet.

—Immunity to paralysis, phantasms, and poison. This trait replaces the hill dwarf's +2 racial bonus on saving throws against poison.

— +2 racial bonus on saves against spells and spell-like abilities.

—Spell-Like Abilities: 1/day—*enlarge person* and *invisibility* as a wizard of twice the duergar's class level (minimum caster level 3rd); these abilities affect only the duergar and whatever it carries.

—Light Sensitivity: Duergar are dazzled in bright sunlight or within the radius of a *daylight* spell.

— +4 racial bonus on Move Silently checks.

— +1 racial bonus on Listen and Spot checks.

—Automatic Languages: Common, Dwarven, Undercommon. Bonus Languages: Draconic, Giant, Goblin, Orc, Terran. This trait replaces the hill dwarf's automatic and bonus languages.

—Favored Class: Fighter.

—Level adjustment +1

—Unlike other dwarves, duergar do not have weapon familiarity with the dwarven waraxe and dwarven urgrosh.

The duergar warrior presented here had the following ability scores before racial adjustments: Str 13, Dex 11, Con 12, Int 10, Wis 9, Cha 8.

Challenge Rating: Duergar with levels in NPC classes have a CR equal to their character level. Duergar with levels in PC classes have a CR equal to their character level +1.

Mountain Dwarf

Mountain dwarves live deeper under the mountains than hill dwarves but generally not as far underground as deep dwarves. They average about 4-1/2 feet tall and have lighter skin and hair than hill dwarves, but the same general appearance. They claim they were the first dwarf race and that all other dwarves are descended from them, an attitude that contributes to their isolationism.

EAGLE, GIANT

Large Magical Beast
Hit Dice: 4d10+4 (26 hp)
Initiative: +3
Speed: 10 ft. (2 squares), fly 80 ft. (average)
Armor Class: 15 (–1 size, +3 Dex, +3 natural), touch 12, flat-footed 12
Base Attack/Grapple: +4/+12
Attack: Claw +7 melee (1d6+4)
Full Attack: 2 claws +7 melee (1d6+4) and bite +2 melee (1d8+2)
Space/Reach: 10 ft./5 ft.
Special Attacks: —
Special Qualities: Low-light vision, evasion
Saves: Fort +5, Ref +7, Will +3
Abilities: Str 18, Dex 17, Con 12, Int 10, Wis 14, Cha 10
Skills: Knowledge (nature) +2, Listen +6, Sense Motive +4, Spot +15, Survival +3
Feats: Alertness, Flyby Attack
Environment: Temperate mountains
Organization: Solitary, pair, or eyrie (5–12)
Challenge Rating: 3
Treasure: None
Alignment: Usually neutral good
Advancement: 5–8 HD (Large); 9–12 HD (Huge)
Level Adjustment: +2 (cohort)

Giant eagles are intelligent, keen-eyed birds of prey that sometimes associate with good creatures.

Giant eagle

Giant eagles attack creatures that appear threatening, especially those intent on raiding the eagles' nest for eggs or fledglings, which fetch a handsome price in many civilized areas. Young eagles can be trained and are prized as aerial mounts.

A typical giant eagle stands about 10 feet tall, has a wingspan of up to 20 feet, and resembles its smaller cousins in nearly every way except size. It weighs about 500 pounds.

Giant eagles speak Common and Auran.

COMBAT

A giant eagle typically attacks from a great height, diving earthward at tremendous speed. When it cannot dive, it uses its powerful talons and slashing beak to strike at its target's head and eyes.

A solitary giant eagle is typically hunting or patrolling in the vicinity of its nest and generally ignores creatures that do not appear threatening. A mated pair attacks in concert, making repeated diving attacks to drive away intruders, and fights to the death to defend their nest or hatchlings.

Evasion (Ex): With a successful Reflex save against an attack that allows a Reflex save for half damage, a giant eagle takes no damage.

Skills: Giant eagles have a +4 racial bonus on Spot checks.

TRAINING A GIANT EAGLE

Although intelligent, a giant eagle requires training before it can bear a rider in combat. To be trained, a giant eagle must have a friendly attitude toward the trainer (this can be achieved through a successful Diplomacy check). Training a friendly giant eagle requires six weeks of work and a DC 25 Handle Animal check. Riding a giant eagle requires an exotic saddle. A giant eagle can fight while carrying a rider, but the rider cannot also attack unless he or she succeeds on a Ride check.

Giant eagle eggs are worth 2,500 gp apiece on the open market, while chicks are worth 4,000 gp each. Professional trainers charge 1,000 gp to rear or train a giant eagle.

Carrying Capacity: A light load for a giant eagle is up to 300 pounds; a medium load, 301–600 pounds; and a heavy load, 601–900 pounds.

ELADRIN

The eladrins are a celestial race native to the plane of Arborea. They are knights and lords who roam the cosmos in search of good folk to aid. Eladrins are free-spirited, but they are also mighty champions of good.

COMBAT

Eladrins are deadly and resolute foes of evil, fearless and clever in battle.

Eladrin Traits: An eladrin possesses the following traits (unless otherwise noted in a creature's entry).

—Darkvision out to 60 feet and low-light vision.

—Immunity to electricity and petrification.

—Resistance to cold 10 and fire 10.

—Tongues (Su): All eladrins can speak with any creature that has a language, as though using a *tongues* spell (caster level 14th). This ability is always active.

BRALANI

Medium Outsider (Chaotic, Eladrin, Extraplanar, Good)
Hit Dice: 6d8+18 (45 hp)
Initiative: +8
Speed: 40 ft. (8 squares), fly 100 ft. (perfect)
Armor Class: 20 (+4 Dex, +6 natural), touch 14, flat-footed 16

Illus. by T. Lockwood

Base Attack/Grapple: +6/+10

Attack: +1 holy scimitar +11 melee (1d6+4/18–20) or +1 holy composite longbow (+4 Str bonus) +11 ranged (1d8+5/×3) or slam +10 melee (1d6+4)

Full Attack: +1 holy scimitar +11/+6 melee (1d6+4/18–20) or +1 holy composite longbow (+4 Str bonus) +11/+6 ranged (1d8+5/×3) or slam +10 melee (1d6+4)

Space/Reach: 5 ft./5 ft.

Special Attacks: Spell-like abilities, whirlwind blast

Special Qualities: Alternate form, damage reduction 10/cold iron or evil, darkvision 60 ft., immunity to electricity and petrification, low-light vision, resistance to cold 10 and fire 10, spell resistance 17, tongues

Saves: Fort +8, Ref +9, Will +7

Abilities: Str 18, Dex 18, Con 17, Int 13, Wis 14, Cha 14

Skills: Concentration +12, Diplomacy +4, Escape Artist +13, Handle Animal +11, Hide +13, Jump +10, Listen +13, Move Silently +13, Ride +6, Sense Motive +11, Spot +13, Tumble +13, Use Rope +4 (+6 with bindings)

Feats: Alertness, Blind-Fight, Improved Initiative

Environment: Olympian Glades of Arborea

Organization: Solitary, pair, or squad (3–5)

Challenge Rating: 6

Treasure: No coins; double goods; standard items

Alignment: Always chaotic good

Advancement: 7–12 HD (Medium); 13–18 HD (Large)

Level Adjustment: +5

The being before you resembles a short, stocky elf, broad in the shoulders but quick and nimble. Its hair is a bright silver-white, and its eyes are an ever-changing rainbow of hues.

The bralanis are the wildest and most feral of their kind, existing from heartbeat to heartbeat in a glorious, never-ending passion. In addition to their natural form, bralanis can assume the shape of a whirlwind or zephyr of dust, snow, or sand.

Bralanis speak Celestial, Infernal, and Draconic, but can communicate with almost any creature, thanks to their *tongues* ability.

Combat

Bralanis prefer the scimitar and bow, the weapons of the desert nomads they most closely resemble.

A bralani's natural weapons, as well as any weapons it wields, are treated as chaotic-aligned and good-aligned for the purpose of overcoming damage reduction.

Spell-Like Abilities: At will— *blur, charm person* (DC 13), *gust of wind* (DC 14), *mirror image, wind wall;* 2/day—*lightning bolt* (DC 15), *cure serious wounds* (DC 15).

Caster level 6th. The save DCs are Charisma-based.

Whirlwind Blast (Su): When in whirlwind form, a bralani can attack with a scouring blast of wind, dealing 3d6 points of damage in a 20-foot line (Reflex DC 16 half). The save DC is Constitution-based.

Alternate Form (Su): A bralani can shift between its humanoid and whirlwind forms as a standard action. In humanoid form, it cannot fly or use its whirlwind blast, but it can use its spell-like abilities and its weapons. In whirlwind form, it can fly, make slam attacks and whirlwind blast attacks, and use spell-like abilities.

A bralani remains in one form until it chooses to assume a new one. A change in form cannot be dispelled, nor does the bralani revert to any particular form when killed. A *true seeing* spell, however, reveals both forms simultaneously.

GHAELE

Medium Outsider (Chaotic, Eladrin, Extraplanar, Good)

Hit Dice: 10d8+20 (65 hp)

Initiative: +5

Speed: 50 ft. (10 squares), fly 150 ft. (perfect)

Armor Class: 25 (+1 Dex, +14 natural), touch 11, flat-footed 24, or 14 (+1 Dex, +3 deflection), touch 14, flat-footed 13

Base Attack/Grapple: +10/+17

Attack: +4 holy greatsword +21 melee (2d6+14/19–20) or light ray +11 ranged touch (2d12)

Full Attack: +4 holy greatsword +21/+16 melee (2d6+14/19–20) or 2 light rays +11 ranged touch (2d12)

Space/Reach: 5 ft./5 ft.

Special Attacks: Spell-like abilities, spells, gaze

Special Qualities: Alternate form, damage reduction 10/evil and cold iron, dark-

Ghaele

Bralani

vision 60 ft., immunity to electricity and petrification, low-light vision, protective aura, resistance to cold 10 and fire 10 spell resistance 28, tongues

Saves: Fort +9, Ref +8, Will +10

Abilities: Str 25, Dex 12, Con 15, Int 16, Wis 17, Cha 16

Skills: Concentration +15, Diplomacy +5, Escape Artist +14, Handle Animal +16, Hide +14, Knowledge (any two) +16, Listen +16, Move Silently +14, Ride +16, Sense Motive +16, Spot +16, Use Rope +1 (+3 with bindings)

Feats: Combat Expertise, Improved Disarm, Improved Initiative, Improved Trip

Environment: Olympian Glades of Arborea

Organization: Solitary, pair, or squad (3–5)

Challenge Rating: 13

Treasure: No coins; double goods; standard items

Alignment: Always chaotic good

Advancement: 11–15 HD (Medium); 16–30 HD (Large)

Level Adjustment: —

This creature resembles an elf with a noble bearing. It has pearly, opalescent eyes and seems to give off a radiant aura.

Ghaeles are the knights-errant of the celestials. Wherever evil and tyranny raise their ugly heads, the ghaeles respond. Working behind the scenes more than other eladrins, ghaeles quietly muster resistance and offer guidance to any of good heart with the courage to stand against their oppressors.

A ghaele can take the form of an incorporeal globe of eldritch colors, 5 feet in diameter.

A ghaele is about 6 feet tall and weighs about 170 pounds.

Ghaeles speak Celestial, Infernal, and Draconic, but can communicate with almost any creature, thanks to their *tongues* ability.

Combat

Ghaeles who enter combat prefer direct confrontation and damaging attacks to more subtle or insidious methods. They usually fight in their humanoid form, wielding incandescent +4 *holy greatswords*. If a ghaele desires mobility, it assumes its globe form and blasts the enemy with light rays.

A ghaele's natural weapons, as well as any weapons it wields, are treated as chaotic-aligned and good-aligned for the purpose of overcoming damage reduction.

Spell-Like Abilities: At will—*aid, charm monster* (DC 17), *color spray* (DC 14), *comprehend languages, continual flame, cure light wounds* (DC 14), *dancing lights, detect evil, detect thoughts* (DC 15), *disguise self, dispel magic, hold monster* (DC 18), *greater invisibility* (self only), *major image* (DC 16), *see invisibility, greater teleport* (self plus 50 pounds of objects only); 1/day—*chain lightning* (DC 19), *prismatic spray* (DC 20), *wall of force.* Caster level 12th. The save DCs are Charisma-based.

Spells: Ghaeles in humanoid form can cast divine spells as 14th-level clerics. A ghaele has access to two of the following domains: Air, Animal, Chaos, Good, or Plant (plus any others from its deity). The save DCs are Wisdom-based.

Typical Cleric Spells Prepared (6/7/7/6/5/4/4/3; save DC 13 + spell level): 0—*cure minor wounds, detect magic, guidance, light, resistance, virtue;* 1st—*bless, calm animals*, command, divine favor, obscuring mist, sanctuary, shield of faith;* 2nd—*aid, align weapon, bear's endurance, hold animal*, lesser restoration, remove paralysis, zone of truth;* 3rd—*daylight, gaseous form*, prayer, remove curse, searing light, water breathing;* 4th—*death ward, dismissal, divine power, restoration, summon nature's ally IV (animal)*;* 5th—*control winds*, flame strike, raise dead, true seeing;* 6th—*banishment, blade barrier, chain lightning*, heal;* 7th—*animal shapes*, holy word, summon monster VII.*

*Domain spell. Domains: Air and Animal.

Gaze (Su): In humanoid form—slay evil creatures of 5 or less HD, range 60 feet, Will DC 18 negates. Even if the save succeeds, the creature is affected as though by a *fear* spell for 2d10 rounds.

Nonevil creatures, and evil creatures with more than 5 HD, must succeed on a DC 18 Will save or suffer the *fear* effect. The save DCs are Charisma-based.

Light Ray (Ex): A ghaele in globe form can project light rays with a range of 300 feet. This attack overcomes damage reduction of any type.

Alternate Form (Su): A ghaele can shift between its humanoid and globe forms as a standard action. In humanoid form, it cannot fly or use its light rays, but it can use its gaze attack and spell-like abilities, make physical attacks, and cast spells. In globe form, it can fly, use its light rays, and use spell-like abilities, but it cannot cast spells or use its gaze attack. The globe form is incorporeal, and the ghaele has no Strength score while in that form.

A ghaele remains in one form until it chooses to assume a new one. A change in form cannot be dispelled, nor does the ghaele revert to any particular form when killed. A *true seeing* spell or ability, however, reveals both forms simultaneously.

Protective Aura (Su): Against attacks made or effects created by evil creatures, this ability provides a +4 deflection bonus to AC and a +4 resistance bonus on saving throws to anyone within 20 feet of the ghaele. Otherwise, it functions as a *magic circle against evil* effect and a *lesser globe of invulnerability*, both with a radius of 20 feet (caster level equals ghaele's HD). (The defensive benefits from the circle are not included in a ghaele's statistics block.)

ELEMENTAL

Elementals are incarnations of the elements that compose existence. They are as wild and dangerous as the forces that birthed them.

COMBAT

Elementals have varied combat abilities and tactics, but all have the same elemental qualities.

AIR ELEMENTAL

This creature appears to be an amorphous, shifting cloud surrounded by fast-moving currents of air. Darker bits of twirling vapor form the suggestion of two eyes and a mouth, but this could be a trick of the swirling air.

Air elementals are among the swiftest and most agile creatures in existence. They seldom leave their home plane except when summoned elsewhere by a spell.

Air elementals speak Auran, though they rarely choose to do so. The voice of an air elemental sounds like the high-pitched screech of a tornado or the low moan of a midnight storm.

Combat

Their rapid speed makes air elementals useful on vast battlefields or in extended aerial combat.

Air Mastery (Ex): Airborne creatures take a –1 penalty on attack and damage rolls against an air elemental.

Whirlwind (Su): The elemental can transform itself into a whirlwind once every 10 minutes and remain in that form for up to 1 round for every 2 HD it has. In this form, the elemental can move through the air or along a surface at its fly speed.

The whirlwind is 5 feet wide at the base, up to 30 feet wide at the top, and up to 50 feet tall, depending on the elemental's size. The elemental controls the exact height, but it must be at least 10 feet.

The elemental's movement while in whirlwind form does not provoke attacks of opportunity, even if the elemental enters the space another creature occupies. Another creature might be caught in the whirlwind if it touches or enters the whirlwind, or if the elemental moves into or through the creature's space.

Creatures one or more size categories smaller than the elemental might take damage when caught in the whirlwind (see the table below for details) and may be lifted into the air. An affected creature must succeed on a Reflex save when it comes into contact with the whirlwind or take the indicated damage. It must also succeed on a second Reflex save or be picked up bodily and held suspended in the powerful winds, automatically taking the indicated damage each round. A creature that can fly is allowed a Reflex save each round to escape the whirlwind. The creature still takes damage but can leave if the save is successful. The DC for saves against the whirlwind's effects varies with the elemental's size (see the table). The save DC is Strength based.

Creatures trapped in the whirlwind cannot move except to go where the elemental carries them or to escape the whirlwind. Creatures caught in the whirlwind can otherwise act normally, but must succeed on a Concentration check (DC 15 + spell level) to cast a spell. Creatures caught in the whirlwind take a –4 penalty to Dexterity and a –2 penalty on attack rolls. The elemental can have

	Air Elemental, Small Small Elemental (Air, Extraplanar)	Air Elemental, Medium Medium Elemental (Air, Extraplanar)	Air Elemental, Large Large Elemental (Air, Extraplanar)
Hit Dice:	2d8 (9 hp)	4d8+8 (26 hp)	8d8+24 (60 hp)
Initiative:	+7	+9	+11
Speed:	Fly 100 ft. (perfect) (20 squares)	Fly 100 ft. (perfect) (20 squares)	Fly 100 ft. (perfect) (20 squares)
Armor Class:	17 (+1 size, +3 Dex, +3 natural), touch 14, flat-footed 14	18 (+5 Dex, +3 natural), touch 15, flat-footed 13	20 (–1 size, +7 Dex, +4 natural), touch 16, flat-footed 13
Base Attack/Grapple:	+1/–3	+3/+4	+6/+12
Attack:	Slam +5 melee (1d4)	Slam +8 melee (1d6+1)	Slam +12 melee (2d6+2)
Full Attack:	Slam +5 melee (1d4)	Slam +8 melee (1d6+1)	2 slams +12 melee (2d6+2)
Space/Reach:	5 ft./5 ft.	5 ft./5 ft.	10 ft./10 ft.
Special Attacks:	Air mastery, whirlwind	Air mastery, whirlwind	Air mastery, whirlwind
Special Qualities:	Darkvision 60 ft., elemental traits	Darkvision 60 ft., elemental traits	Damage reduction 5/–, darkvision 60 ft., elemental traits
Saves:	Fort +0, Ref +6, Will +0	Fort +3, Ref +9, Will +1	Fort +5, Ref +13, Will +2
Abilities:	Str 10, Dex 17, Con 10, Int 4, Wis 11, Cha 11	Str 12, Dex 21, Con 14, Int 4, Wis 11, Cha 11	Str 14, Dex 25, Con 16, Int 6, Wis 11, Cha 11
Skills:	Listen +2, Spot +3	Listen +3, Spot +4	Listen +5, Spot +6
Feats:	Flyby Attack, Improved Initiative[B], Weapon Finesse[B]	Dodge, Flyby Attack, Improved Initiative[B], Weapon Finesse[B]	Combat Reflexes, Dodge, Flyby Attack, Improved Initiative[B], Weapon Finesse[B]
Environment:	Elemental Plane of Air	Elemental Plane of Air	Elemental Plane of Air
Organization:	Solitary	Solitary	Solitary
Challenge Rating:	1	3	5
Treasure:	None	None	None
Alignment:	Usually neutral	Usually neutral	Usually neutral
Advancement:	3 HD (Small)	5–7 HD (Medium)	9–15 HD (Large)
Level Adjustment:	—	—	—

	Air Elemental, Huge Huge Elemental (Air, Extraplanar)	Air Elemental, Greater Huge Elemental (Air, Extraplanar)	Air Elemental, Elder Huge Elemental (Air, Extraplanar)
Hit Dice:	16d8+64 (136 hp)	21d8+84 (178 hp)	24d8+96 (204 hp)
Initiative:	+13	+14	+15
Speed:	Fly 100 ft. (perfect) (20 squares)	Fly 100 ft. (perfect) (20 squares)	Fly 100 ft. (perfect) (20 squares)
Armor Class:	21 (–2 size, +9 Dex, +4 natural), touch 17, flat-footed 12	26 (–2 size, +10 Dex, +8 natural), touch 18, flat-footed 16	27 (–2 size, +11 Dex, +8 natural), touch 19, flat-footed 16
Base Attack/Grapple:	+12/+24	+15/+28	+18/+32
Attack:	Slam +19 melee (2d8+4)	Slam +23 melee (2d8+5)	Slam +27 melee (2d8+6)
Full Attack:	2 slams +19 melee (2d8+4)	2 slams +23 melee (2d8+5)	2 slams +27 melee (2d8+6)
Space/Reach:	15 ft./15 ft.	15 ft./15 ft.	15 ft./15 ft.
Special Attacks:	Air mastery, whirlwind	Air mastery, whirlwind	Air mastery, whirlwind
Special Qualities:	Damage reduction 5/–, darkvision 60 ft., elemental traits	Damage reduction 10/–, darkvision 60 ft., elemental traits	Damage reduction 10/–, darkvision 60 ft., elemental traits
Saves:	Fort +9, Ref +19, Will +5	Fort +11, Ref +22, Will +9	Fort +12, Ref +25, Will +10
Abilities:	Str 18, Dex 29, Con 18, Int 6, Wis 11, Cha 11	Str 20, Dex 31, Con 18, Int 8, Wis 11, Cha 11	Str 22, Dex 33, Con 18, Int 10, Wis 11, Cha 11
Skills:	Listen +11, Spot +12	Listen +14, Spot +14	Listen +29, Spot +29
Feats:	Alertness, Combat Reflexes, Dodge, Flyby Attack, Improved Initiative[B], Mobility, Spring Attack, Weapon Finesse[B]	Alertness, Blind-fight, Combat Reflexes, Flyby Attack, Improved Initiative[B], Iron Will, Mobility, Power Attack, Spring Attack, Weapon Finesse[B]	Alertness, Blind-fight, Cleave, Combat Reflexes, Flyby Attack, Improved Initiative[B], Iron Will, Mobility, Power Attack, Spring Attack, Weapon Finesse[B]
Environment:	Elemental Plane of Air	Elemental Plane of Air	Elemental Plane of Air
Organization:	Solitary	Solitary	Solitary
Challenge Rating:	7	9	11
Treasure:	None	None	None
Alignment:	Usually neutral	Usually neutral	Usually neutral
Advancement:	17–20 HD (Huge)	22–23 HD (Huge)	25–48 HD (Huge)
Level Adjustment:	—	—	—

only as many creatures trapped inside the whirlwind at one time as will fit inside the whirlwind's volume.

The elemental can eject any carried creatures whenever it wishes, depositing them wherever the whirlwind happens to be. A summoned elemental always ejects trapped creatures before returning to its home plane.

If the whirlwind's base touches the ground, it creates a swirling cloud of debris. This cloud is centered on the elemental and has a diameter equal to half the whirlwind's height. The cloud obscures all vision, including darkvision, beyond 5 feet. Creatures 5 feet away have concealment, while those farther away have total concealment. Those caught in the cloud must succeed on a Concentration check (DC 15 + spell level) to cast a spell.

An elemental in whirlwind form cannot make slam attacks and does not threaten the area around it.

	Earth Elemental, Small Small Elemental (Earth, Extraplanar)	Earth Elemental, Medium Medium Elemental (Earth, Extraplanar)	Earth Elemental, Large Large Elemental (Earth, Extraplanar)
Hit Dice:	2d8+2 (11 hp)	4d8+12 (30 hp)	8d8+32 (68 hp)
Initiative:	−1	−1	−1
Speed:	20 ft. (4 squares)	20 ft. (4 squares)	20 ft. (4 squares)
Armor Class:	17 (+1 size, −1 Dex, +7 natural) touch 10, flat-footed 17	18 (−1 Dex, +9 natural) touch 9, flat-footed 18	18 (−1 size, −1 Dex, +10 natural) touch 8, flat-footed 18
Base Attack/Grapple:	+1/+0	+3/+8	+6/+17
Attack:	Slam +5 melee (1d6+4)	Slam +8 melee (1d8+7)	Slam +12 melee (2d8+7)
Full Attack:	Slam +5 melee (1d6+4)	Slam +8 melee (1d8+7)	2 slams +12 melee (2d8+7)
Space/Reach:	5 ft./5 ft.	5 ft./5 ft.	10 ft./10 ft.
Special Attacks:	Earth mastery, push	Earth mastery, push	Earth mastery, push
Special Qualities:	Darkvision 60 ft., earth glide, elemental traits	Darkvision 60 ft., earth glide, elemental traits	Damage reduction 5/−, earth glide, darkvision 60 ft., elemental traits
Saves:	Fort +4, Ref −1, Will +0	Fort +7, Ref +0, Will +1	Fort +10, Ref +1, Will +2
Abilities:	Str 17, Dex 8, Con 13, Int 4, Wis 11, Cha 11	Str 21, Dex 8, Con 17, Int 4, Wis 11, Cha 11	Str 25, Dex 8, Con 19, Int 6, Wis 11, Cha 11
Skills:	Listen +3, Spot +2	Listen +4, Spot +3	Listen +6, Spot +5
Feats:	Power Attack	Cleave, Power Attack	Cleave, Great Cleave, Power Attack
Environment:	Elemental Plane of Earth	Elemental Plane of Earth	Elemental Plane of Earth
Organization:	Solitary	Solitary	Solitary
Challenge Rating:	1	3	5
Treasure:	None	None	None
Alignment:	Usually neutral	Usually neutral	Usually neutral
Advancement:	3 HD (Small)	5–7 HD (Medium)	9–15 HD (Large)
Level Adjustment:	—	—	—

	Earth Elemental, Huge Huge Elemental (Earth, Extraplanar)	Earth Elemental, Greater Huge Elemental (Earth, Extraplanar)	Earth Elemental, Elder Huge Elemental (Earth, Extraplanar)
Hit Dice:	16d8+80 (152 hp)	21d8+105 (199 hp)	24d8+120 (228 hp)
Initiative:	−1	−1	−1
Speed:	30 ft. (6 squares)	30 ft. (6 squares)	30 ft. (6 squares)
Armor Class:	18 (−2 size, −1 Dex, +11 natural) touch 7, flat-footed 18	20 (−2 size, −1 Dex, +13 natural) touch 7, flat-footed 20	22 (−2 size, −1 Dex, +15 natural) touch 7, flat-footed 22
Base Attack/Grapple:	+12/+29	+15/+33	+18/+37
Attack:	Slam +19 melee (2d10+9)	Slam +23 melee (2d10+10)	Slam +27 melee (2d10+11/19–20)
Full Attack:	2 slams +19 melee (2d10+9)	2 slams +23 melee (2d10+10)	2 slams +27 melee (2d10+11/19–20)
Space/Reach:	15 ft./15 ft.	15 ft./15 ft.	15 ft./15 ft.
Special Attacks:	Earth mastery, push	Earth mastery, push	Earth mastery, push
Special Qualities:	Damage reduction 5/−, earth glide, darkvision 60 ft., elemental traits	Damage reduction 10/−, earth glide, darkvision 60 ft., elemental traits	Damage reduction 10/−, earth glide, darkvision 60 ft., elemental traits
Saves:	Fort +15, Ref +4, Will +7	Fort +17, Ref +6, Will +9	Fort +19, Ref +7, Will +10
Abilities:	Str 29, Dex 8, Con 21, Int 6, Wis 11, Cha 11	Str 31, Dex 8, Con 21, Int 8, Wis 11, Cha 11	Str 33, Dex 8, Con 21, Int 10, Wis 11, Cha 11
Skills:	Listen +10, Spot +9	Listen +14, Spot +14	Listen +29, Spot +29
Feats:	Awesome Blow, Cleave, Great Cleave, Improved Bull Rush, Iron Will, Power Attack	Alertness, Awesome Blow, Cleave, Great Cleave, Improved Bull Rush, Improved Sunder, Iron Will, Power Attack	Alertness, Awesome Blow, Cleave, Great Cleave, Improved Bull Rush, Improved Critical (slam), Improved Sunder, Iron Will, Power Attack
Environment:	Elemental Plane of Earth	Elemental Plane of Earth	Elemental Plane of Earth
Organization:	Solitary	Solitary	Solitary
Challenge Rating:	7	9	11
Treasure:	None	None	None
Alignment:	Usually neutral	Usually neutral	Usually neutral
Advancement:	17–20 HD (Huge)	22–23 HD (Huge)	25–48 HD (Huge)
Level Adjustment:	—	—	—

AIR ELEMENTAL SIZES

Elemental	Height	Weight	Save DC	Whirlwind Damage	Whirlwind Height
Small	4 ft.	1 lb.	11	1d4	10–20 ft.
Medium	8 ft.	2 lb.	13	1d6	10–30 ft.
Large	16 ft.	4 lb.	16	2d6	10–40 ft.
Huge	32 ft.	8 lb.	22	2d8	10–50 ft.
Greater	36 ft.	10 lb.	25	2d8	10–60 ft.
Elder	40 ft.	12 lb.	28	2d8	10–60 ft.

EARTH ELEMENTAL

Like a walking hill, the creature plods nearer on two featureless legs of rock and earth, its clublike arms of jagged stone swinging at its sides, and its featureless head staring blankly in your direction.

Earth elementals are immensely strong and tough. The larger ones can pound almost anything into rubble. They seldom leave their home plane except when summoned elsewhere by a spell.

When summoned to the Material Plane, an earth elemental consists of whatever types of dirt, stones, precious metals, and gems it was conjured from.

Earth elementals speak Terran but rarely choose to do so. An earth elemental's voice sounds like an echo in a deep tunnel, the rumbling of an earthquake, or the grinding of plates of stone.

Combat

Though an earth elemental moves slowly, it is a relentless opponent. It can travel though solid ground or stone as easily as humans walk on the earth's surface. It cannot swim, however, and must either walk around a body of water or go through the ground under it. An earth elemental can move along the bottom of a body of water but prefers not to.

Earth Mastery (Ex): An earth elemental gains a +1 bonus on attack and damage rolls if both it and its foe are touching the ground. If an opponent is airborne or waterborne, the elemental takes a –4 penalty on attack and damage rolls. (These modifiers are not included in the statistics block.)

Push (Ex): An earth elemental can start a bull rush maneuver without provoking an attack of opportunity. The combat modifiers given in Earth Mastery, above, also apply to the elemental's opposed Strength checks.

Earth Glide (Ex): An earth elemental can glide through stone, dirt, or almost any other sort of earth except metal as easily as a fish swims through water. Its burrowing leaves behind no tunnel or hole, nor does it create any ripple or other signs of its presence. A *move earth* spell cast on an area containing a burrowing earth elemental flings the elemental back 30 feet, stun-

EARTH ELEMENTAL SIZES

Elemental	Height	Weight	Elemental	Height	Weight
Small	4 ft.	80 lb.	Huge	32 ft.	48,000 lb.
Medium	8 ft.	750 lb.	Greater	36 ft.	54,000 lb.
Large	16 ft.	6,000 lb.	Elder	40 ft.	60,000 lb.

ning the creature for 1 round unless it succeeds on a DC 15 Fortitude save.

FIRE ELEMENTAL

A mass of ambulatory flame races across the ground, seeming to flicker and spark from a central, humanoid-shaped conflagration. Like a living inferno, the fire-creature's burning dance of heat and flame brings it ever closer.

Fire elementals are fast and agile. The merest touch from their fiery bodies is sufficient to set many materials aflame.

A fire elemental cannot enter water or any other nonflammable liquid. A body of water is an impassable barrier unless the fire elemental can step or jump over it.

Fire elementals speak Ignan, though they rarely choose to do so. When one speaks, its voice sounds like the crackle and hiss of a great fire.

Combat

A fire elemental is a fierce opponent that attacks its enemies directly and savagely. It takes joy in burning the creatures and objects of the Material Plane to ashes.

Burn (Ex): A fire elemental's slam attack deals bludgeoning damage plus fire damage from the elemental's flaming body. Those hit by a fire elemental's slam attack also must succeed on a Reflex save or catch on fire. The flame burns for 1d4 rounds. The save DC varies with the elemental's size (see the table below). A burning creature can take a move action to put out the flame. The save DC is Constitution-based.

Earth elemental

Creatures hitting a fire elemental with natural weapons or unarmed attacks take fire damage as though hit by the elemental's attack, and also catch on fire unless they succeed on a Reflex save.

FIRE ELEMENTAL SIZES

Elemental	Height	Weight	Burn Save DC
Small	4 ft.	1 lb.	11
Medium	8 ft.	2 lb.	14
Large	16 ft.	4 lb.	17
Huge	32 ft.	8 lb.	22
Greater	36 ft.	10 lb.	24
Elder	40 ft.	12 lb.	26

WATER ELEMENTAL

A vortex of water rolls across the ground, though it never seems to crash or lose its shape. The waves cascade and storm around a central, humanoid-shaped whirlpool, with watery appendages that pound with the force of an ocean storm.

A water elemental can be as ferocious and powerful as a stormy sea.

A water elemental can't venture more than 180 feet from the body of water from which it was conjured.

Water elementals speak Aquan but rarely choose to do so. When one speaks, its voice sounds like the crashing of waves on a rocky shore or the howls of an ocean gale.

	Fire Elemental, Small Small Elemental (Fire, Extraplanar)	Fire Elemental, Medium Medium Elemental (Fire, Extraplanar)	Fire Elemental, Large Large Elemental (Fire, Extraplanar)
Hit Dice:	2d8 (9 hp)	4d8+8 (26 hp)	8d8+24 (60 hp)
Initiative:	+5	+7	+9
Speed:	50 ft. (10 squares)	50 ft. (10 squares)	50 ft. (10 squares)
Armor Class:	15 (+1 size, +1 Dex, +3 natural) touch 12, flat-footed 14	16 (+3 Dex, +3 natural) touch 13, flat-footed 13	18 (−1 size, +5 Dex, +4 natural) touch 14, flat-footed 13
Base Attack/Grapple:	+1/−3	+3/+4	+6/+12
Attack:	Slam +3 melee (1d4 plus 1d4 fire)	Slam +6 melee (1d6+1 plus 1d6 fire)	Slam +10 melee (2d6+2 plus 2d6 fire)
Full Attack:	Slam +3 melee (1d4 plus 1d4 fire)	Slam +6 melee (1d6+1 plus 1d6 fire)	2 slams +10 melee (2d6+2 plus 2d6 fire)
Space/Reach:	5 ft./5 ft.	5 ft./5 ft.	10 ft./10 ft.
Special Attacks:	Burn	Burn	Burn
Special Qualities:	Darkvision 60 ft., elemental traits, immunity to fire, vulnerability to cold	Darkvision 60 ft., elemental traits, immunity to fire, vulnerability to cold	Damage reduction 5/−, darkvision 60 ft., elemental traits, immunity to fire, vulnerability to cold
Saves:	Fort +0, Ref +4, Will +0	Fort +3, Ref +7, Will +1	Fort +5, Ref +11, Will +2
Abilities:	Str 10, Dex 13, Con 10, Int 4, Wis 11, Cha 11	Str 12, Dex 17, Con 14, Int 4, Wis 11, Cha 11	Str 14, Dex 21, Con 16, Int 6, Wis 11, Cha 11
Skills:	Listen +2, Spot +3	Listen +3, Spot +4	Listen +5, Spot +6
Feats:	Dodge, Improved Initiative[B], Weapon Finesse[B]	Dodge, Improved Initiative[B], Mobility, Weapon Finesse[B]	Dodge, Improved Initiative,[B] Mobility, Spring Attack, Weapon Finesse[B]
Environment:	Elemental Plane of Fire	Elemental Plane of Fire	Elemental Plane of Fire
Organization:	Solitary	Solitary	Solitary
Challenge Rating:	1	3	5
Treasure:	None	None	None
Alignment:	Usually neutral	Usually neutral	Usually neutral
Advancement:	3 HD (Small)	5–7 HD (Medium)	9–15 HD (Large)
Level Adjustment:	—	—	—

	Fire Elemental, Huge Huge Elemental (Fire, Extraplanar)	Fire Elemental, Greater Huge Elemental (Fire, Extraplanar)	Fire Elemental, Elder Huge Elemental (Fire, Extraplanar)
Hit Dice:	16d8+64 (136 hp)	21d8+84 (178 hp)	24d8+96 (204 hp)
Initiative:	+11	+12	+13
Speed:	60 ft. (12 squares)	60 ft. (12 squares)	60 ft. (12 squares)
Armor Class:	19 (−2 size, +7 Dex, +4 natural) touch 15, flat-footed 12	24 (−2 size, +8 Dex, +8 natural) touch 16, flat-footed 16	25 (−2 size, +9 Dex, +8 natural) touch 17, flat-footed 16
Base Attack/Grapple:	+12/+24	+15/+28	+18/+32
Attack:	Slam +17 melee (2d8+4 plus 2d8 fire)	Slam +22 melee (2d8+5 plus 2d8 fire)	Slam +26 melee (2d8+6 plus 2d8 fire)
Full Attack:	2 slams +17 melee (2d8+4 plus 2d8 fire)	2 slams +22 melee (2d8+5 plus 2d8 fire)	2 slams +26 melee (2d8+6 plus 2d8 fire)
Space/Reach:	15 ft./15 ft.	15 ft./15 ft.	15 ft./15 ft.
Special Attacks:	Burn	Burn	Burn
Special Qualities:	Damage reduction 5/−, darkvision 60 ft., elemental traits, immunity to fire, vulnerability to cold	Damage reduction 10/−, darkvision 60 ft., elemental traits, immunity to fire, vulnerability to cold	Damage reduction 10/−, darkvision 60 ft., elemental traits, immunity to fire, vulnerability to cold
Saves:	Fort +9, Ref +17, Will +7	Fort +11, Ref +20, Will +9	Fort +14, Ref +23, Will +10
Abilities:	Str 18, Dex 25, Con 18, Int 6, Wis 11, Cha 11	Str 20, Dex 27, Con 18, Int 6, Wis 11, Cha 11	Str 22, Dex 29, Con 18, Int 6, Wis 11, Cha 11
Skills:	Listen +11, Spot +12	Listen +14, Spot +14	Listen +28, Spot +29
Feats:	Alertness, Combat Reflexes, Dodge, Improved Initiative[B], Iron Will, Mobility, Spring Attack, Weapon Finesse[B]	Alertness, Blind-Fight, Combat Reflexes, Dodge, Improved Initiative[B], Iron Will, Mobility, Spring Attack, Weapon Finesse[B], Weapon Focus (slam)	Alertness, Blind-Fight, Combat Reflexes, Dodge, Improved Initiative[B], Great Fortitude, Iron Will, Mobility, Spring Attack, Weapon Finesse[B], Weapon Focus (slam)
Environment:	Elemental Plane of Fire	Elemental Plane of Fire	Elemental Plane of Fire
Organization:	Solitary	Solitary	Solitary
Challenge Rating:	7	9	11
Treasure:	None	None	None
Alignment:	Usually neutral	Usually neutral	Usually neutral
Advancement:	17–20 HD (Huge)	22–23 HD (Huge)	25–48 HD (Huge)
Level Adjustment:	—	—	—

Combat

A water elemental prefers to fight in a large body of water where it can disappear beneath the waves and suddenly swell up behind its opponents.

Water Mastery (Ex): A water elemental gains a +1 bonus on attack and damage rolls if both it and its opponent are touching water. If the opponent or the elemental is touching the ground, the elemental takes a −4 penalty on attack and damage rolls. (These modifiers are not included in the statistics block.)

A water elemental can be a serious threat to a ship that crosses its path. An elemental can easily overturn small craft (5 feet of length per Hit Die of the elemental) and stop larger vessels (10 feet long per HD). Even large ships (20 feet long per HD) can be slowed to half speed.

	Water Elemental, Small Small Elemental (Water, Extraplanar)	Water Elemental, Medium Medium Elemental (Water, Extraplanar)	Water Elemental, Large Large Elemental (Water, Extraplanar)
Hit Dice:	2d8+2 (11 hp)	4d8+12 (30 hp)	8d8+32 (68 hp)
Initiative:	+0	+1	+2
Speed:	20 ft. (4 squares), swim 90 ft.	20 ft. (4 squares), swim 90 ft.	20 ft. (4 squares), swim 90 ft.
Armor Class:	17 (+1 size, +6 natural) touch 11, flat-footed 17	19 (+1 Dex, +8 natural) touch 11, flat-footed 18	20 (−1 size, +2 Dex, +9 natural) touch 11, flat-footed 18
Base Attack/Grapple:	+1/−1	+3/+6	+6/+15
Attack:	Slam +4 melee (1d6+3)	Slam +6 melee (1d8+4)	Slam +10 melee (2d8+5)
Full Attack:	Slam +4 melee (1d6+3)	Slam +6 melee (1d8+4)	2 slams +10 melee (2d8+5)
Space/Reach:	5 ft./5 ft.	5 ft./5 ft.	10 ft./10 ft.
Special Attacks:	Water mastery, drench, vortex	Water mastery, drench, vortex	Water mastery, drench, vortex
Special Qualities:	Darkvision 60 ft., elemental traits	Darkvision 60 ft., elemental traits	Damage reduction 5/−, darkvision 60 ft., elemental traits
Saves:	Fort +4, Ref +0, Will +0	Fort +7, Ref +2, Will +1	Fort +10, Ref +4, Will +2
Abilities:	Str 14, Dex 10, Con 13, Int 4, Wis 11, Cha 11	Str 16, Dex 12, Con 17, Int 4, Wis 11, Cha 11	Str 20, Dex 14, Con 19, Int 6, Wis 11, Cha 11
Skills:	Listen +2, Spot +3	Listen +3, Spot +4	Listen +5, Spot +6
Feats:	Power Attack	Cleave, Power Attack	Cleave, Great Cleave, Power Attack
Environment:	Elemental Plane of Water	Elemental Plane of Water	Elemental Plane of Water
Organization:	Solitary	Solitary	Solitary
Challenge Rating:	1	3	5
Treasure:	None	None	None
Alignment:	Usually neutral	Usually neutral	Usually neutral
Advancement:	3 HD (Small)	5–7 HD (Medium)	9–15 HD (Large)
Level Adjustment:	—	—	—

	Water Elemental, Huge Huge Elemental (Water, Extraplanar)	Water Elemental, Greater Huge Elemental (Water, Extraplanar)	Water Elemental, Elder Huge Elemental (Water, Extraplanar)
Hit Dice:	16d8+80 (152 hp)	21d8+105 (199 hp)	24d8+120 (228 hp)
Initiative:	+4	+5	+6
Speed:	30 ft. (6 squares), swim 120 ft.	30 ft. (6 squares), swim 120 ft.	30 ft. (6 squares), swim 120 ft.
Armor Class:	21 (−2 size, +4 Dex, +9 natural), touch 12, flat-footed 17	22 (−2 size, +5 Dex, +9 natural), touch 13, flat-footed 17	23 (−2 size, +6 Dex, +9 natural), touch 14, flat-footed 17
Base Attack/Grapple:	+12/+27	+15/+31	+18/+35
Attack:	Slam +17 melee (2d10+7)	Slam +21 melee (2d10+8)	Slam +25 melee (2d10+9/19–20)
Full Attack:	2 slams +17 melee (2d10+7)	2 slams +21 melee (2d10+8)	2 slams +25 melee (2d10+9/19–20)
Space/Reach:	15 ft./15 ft.	15 ft./15 ft.	15 ft./15 ft.
Special Attacks:	Water mastery, drench, vortex	Water mastery, drench, vortex	Water mastery, drench, vortex
Special Qualities:	Damage reduction 5/−, darkvision 60 ft., elemental traits	Damage reduction 10/−, darkvision 60 ft., elemental traits	Damage reduction 10/−, darkvision 60 ft., elemental traits
Saves:	Fort +15, Ref +9, Will +7	Fort +17, Ref +14, Will +9	Fort +19, Ref +16, Will +10
Abilities:	Str 24, Dex 18, Con 21, Int 6, Wis 11, Cha 11	Str 26, Dex 20, Con 21, Int 8, Wis 11, Cha 11	Str 28, Dex 22, Con 21, Int 10, Wis 11, Cha 11
Skills:	Listen +11, Spot +12	Listen +14, Spot +14	Listen +29, Spot +29
Feats:	Alertness, Cleave, Great Cleave, Power Attack, Improved Bull Rush, Iron Will	Alertness, Cleave, Great Cleave, Improved Bull Rush, Improved Sunder, Iron Will, Lightning Reflexes, Power Attack	Alertness, Cleave, Great Cleave, Improved Critical (slam), Improved Bull Rush, Improved Sunder, Iron Will, Iron Will, Lightning Reflexes, Power Attack
Environment:	Elemental Plane of Water	Elemental Plane of Water	Elemental Plane of Water
Organization:	Solitary	Solitary	Solitary
Challenge Rating:	7	9	11
Treasure:	None	None	None
Alignment:	Usually neutral	Usually neutral	Usually neutral
Advancement:	17–20 HD (Huge)	22–23 HD (Huge)	25–48 HD (Huge)
Level Adjustment:	—	—	—

ELEMENTAL

100

Drench (Ex): The elemental's touch puts out torches, campfires, exposed lanterns, and other open flames of nonmagical origin if these are of Large size or smaller. The creature can dispel magical fire it touches as *dispel magic* (caster level equals elemental's HD).

Vortex (Su): The elemental can transform itself into a whirlpool once every 10 minutes, provided it is underwater, and remain in that form for up to 1 round for every 2 HD it has. In vortex form, the elemental can move through the water or along the bottom at its swim speed.

The vortex is 5 feet wide at the base, up to 30 feet wide at the top, and 10 feet or more tall, depending on the elemental's size. The elemental controls the exact height, but it must be at least 10 feet.

The elemental's movement while in vortex form does not provoke attacks of opportunity, even if the elemental enters the space another creature occupies. Another creature might be caught in the vortex if it touches or enters the vortex, or if the elemental moves into or through the creature's space.

Creatures one or more size categories smaller than the elemental might take damage when caught in the vortex (see the table below for details) and may be swept up by it. An affected creature must succeed on a Reflex save when it comes into contact with the vortex or take the indicated damage. It must also succeed on a second Reflex save or be picked up bodily and held suspended in the powerful currents, automatically taking damage each round. An affected creature is allowed a Reflex save each round to escape the vortex. The creature still takes damage, but can leave if the save is successful. The DC for saves against the vortex's effects varies with the elemental's size. The save DC is Strength-based.

Creatures trapped in the vortex cannot move except to go where the elemental carries them or to escape the whirlwind. Creatures caught in the whirlwind can otherwise act normally, but must make a Concentration check (DC 10 + spell level) to cast a spell. Creatures caught in the whirlwind take a –4 penalty to Dexterity and a –2 penalty on attack rolls. The elemental can have only as many creatures trapped inside the vortex at one time as will fit inside the vortex's volume.

The elemental can eject any carried creatures whenever it wishes, depositing them wherever the vortex happens to be. A summoned elemental always ejects trapped creatures before returning to its home plane.

If the vortex's base touches the bottom, it creates a swirling cloud of debris. This cloud is centered on the elemental and has a diameter equal to half the vortex's height. The cloud obscures all vision, including darkvision, beyond 5 feet. Creatures 5 feet away have concealment, while those farther away have total concealment. Those caught in the cloud must make a Concentration check (DC 15 + spell level) to cast a spell.

An elemental in vortex form cannot make slam attacks and does not threaten the area around it.

Skills: A water elemental has a +8 racial bonus on any Swim check to perform some special action or avoid a hazard. It can always choose to take 10 on a Swim check, even if distracted or endangered. It can use the run action while swimming, provided it swims in a straight line.

WATER ELEMENTAL SIZES

Elemental	Height	Weight	Save DC	Vortex Damage	Vortex Height
Small	4 ft.	34 lb.	13	1d4	10–20 ft.
Medium	8 ft.	280 lb.	15	1d6	10–30 ft.
Large	16 ft.	2,250 lb.	19	2d6	10–40 ft.
Huge	32 ft.	18,000 lb.	25	2d8	10–50 ft.
Greater	36 ft.	21,000 lb.	28	2d8	10–60 ft.
Elder	40 ft.	24,000 lb.	31	2d8	10–60 ft.

ELF

This humanoid, slender and slightly shorter than a human, has pale skin and dark hair. Pointed ears grace the sides of its elongated head. It wears armor with a natural, forest-themed design that appears organic instead of worked and crafted.

Elves are aloof guardians of the forests, studying magic and swordplay for the duration of their long lives.

Elves average 5 feet tall and typically weigh just over 100 pounds. They live on fruits and grains, though they occasionally hunt for fresh meat. Elves prefer colorful clothes, usually with a green-and-gray cloak that blends well with the colors of the forest.

They appreciate beautiful things, from elegant jewelry to attractive flowers to decorated clothing and tools.

Like dwarves, elves are craftmasters, although they work in wood and metal rather than metal and stone. Elven items are prized by other races, and many elven communities have become prosperous by trading crafted goods with other peoples in and out of the forests.

Elves speak Elven, and most also know Common and Sylvan.

Most elves encountered outside their homes are warriors; the information presented here is for one of 1st level.

COMBAT

Elves are cautious warriors and take time to analyze their opponents and the location of the fight if at all possible, maximizing their advantage by using ambushes, snipers, and camouflage. They prefer to fire from cover and retreat before they are found, repeating this maneuver until all of their enemies are dead. They prefer longbows, shortbows, rapiers, and longswords. In melee, elves are graceful and deadly, using complex maneuvers that are beautiful to observe. Their wizards often use *sleep* spells during combat because these won't affect other elves.

Elf Traits (Ex): Elves possess the following racial traits.

— +2 Dexterity, –2 Constitution.

—Medium size.

—An elf's base land speed is 30 feet.

—Immunity to *sleep* spells and effects, and a +2 racial saving throw bonus against enchantment spells or effects. (Not reflected in the saving throw modifiers given here.)

—Low-light vision.

—Weapon Proficiency: Elves are automatically proficient with the longsword, rapier, longbow, composite longbow, shortbow, and composite shortbow.

Elf

	Elf, 1st-Level Warrior Medium Humanoid (Elf)	Drow, 1st-Level Warrior Medium Humanoid (Elf)
Hit Dice:	1d8 (4 hp)	1d8 (4 hp)
Initiative:	+1	+1
Speed:	30 ft. (6 squares)	30 ft. (6 squares)
Armor Class:	15 (+1 Dex, +3 studded leather, +1 light shield), touch 11, flat-footed 14	16 (+1 Dex, +4 chain shirt, +1 light shield) touch 11, flat-footed 15
Base Attack/Grapple:	+1/+2	+1/+2
Attack:	Longsword +2 melee (1d8+1/19–20) or longbow +3 ranged (1d8/×3)	Rapier +3 melee (1d6+1/18–20) or hand crossbow +2 ranged (1d4/19–20)
Full Attack:	Longsword +2 melee(1d8+1/19–20) or longbow +3 ranged (1d8/×3)	Rapier +3 melee (1d6+1/18–20) or hand crossbow +2 ranged (1d4/19–20)
Space/Reach:	5 ft./5 ft.	5 ft./5 ft.
Special Attacks:	None	Poison, spell-like abilities
Special Qualities:	Elven traits	Drow traits, spell resistance 12
Saves:	Fort +2, Ref +1, Will –1*	Fort +2, Ref +1, Will –1*
Abilities:	Str 13, Dex 13, Con 10, Int 10, Wis 9, Cha 8	Str 13, Dex 13, Con 10, Int 12, Wis 9, Cha 10
Skills:	Hide +1, Listen +2, Search +3, Spot +2	Hide +0, Listen +2, Search +4, Spot +3
Feats:	Weapon Focus (longbow)	Weapon Focus (rapier)
Environment:	Temperate forest 　(Half-elf: Temperate forests) 　(Aquatic: Temperate aquatic) 　(Gray: Temperate mountains) 　(Wild: Warm forests) 　(Wood: Temperate forests)	Underground
Organization:	Squad (2–4), company (11–20 plus 2 3rd-level sergeants and 1 leader of 3rd–6th level), or band (30–100 plus 20% noncombatants plus 1 3rd-level sergeant per 10 adults, 5 5th-level lieutenants, and 3 7th-level captains)	Squad (2–4), patrol (5–8 plus 2 2nd-level sergeants and 1 leader of 3rd–6th level), or band (20–50 plus 10% noncombatants plus 1 2nd-level sergeant per 5 adults, 2d4 6th-level lieutenants, and 1d4 9th-level captains)
Challenge Rating:	1/2	1 (see text)
Treasure:	Standard	Standard
Alignment:	Usually chaotic good 　(Wood: Usually neutral)	Usually neutral evil
Advancement:	By character class	By character class
Level Adjustment:	+0	+2

　　— +2 racial bonus on Listen, Search, and Spot checks. An elf who merely passes within 5 feet of a secret or concealed door is entitled to a Search check to notice it as if she were actively looking for it.

　　—Automatic Languages: Common, Elven. Bonus Languages: Draconic, Gnoll, Gnome, Goblin, Orc, Sylvan.

　　—Favored Class: Wizard.

The elf warrior presented here had the following ability scores before racial adjustments: Str 13, Dex 11, Con 12, Int 10, Wis 9, Cha 8.

ELF SOCIETY

Elves believe that independence and freedom for the individual are more important than the rigid structures of civilization, so they tend to live and travel in small bands. These bands accept the loose authority of a noble, who in turn owes allegiance to an elven monarch (who rules his or her own band directly).

　　Elves live in harmony with nature, building temporary camps that blend into the trees—or are in the branches of the trees, away from prying eyes. They frequently have animal guardians or giant eagles watching their homes. An elven settlement contains noncombatants (mostly children) equal to 20% of the fighting population. Elf society is egalitarian, and males or females may be found in almost any role.

　　Their long life span gives elves a patient perspective and allows them to take pleasure in the enduring beauty of the natural world. They don't see the point in short-term gains and instead learn things that will provide joy for years to come, such as stories, music, art, and dance. Treasures such as elven music and crafts disguise the fact that elves are dedicated warriors determined to check the spread of evil in the forests.

　　Elves eat little, and although they are omnivorous, they eat more plants than meat. This is partly because of their affinity with nature (they believe a harvested plant causes less disruption to nature than a slain animal) and partly because their fondness for roving requires food that is preserved more easily.

　　The chief elf deity is Corellon Larethian, who is the creator and protector of the race.

SUBRACES

The above information describes the high elf, the most common variety. There are five other major subraces of elf, in addition to half-elves, who share enough elven characteristics to be included here.

Half-Elf

Half-elves are not truly an elf subrace, but they are often mistaken for elves. They may be outcasts from their parents' societies or welcomed into the elven or human community, depending on the attitudes the two groups have for each other. Half-elves usually inherit a good blend of their parents' physical characteristics, so a half-aquatic elf has greenish skin, a half-drow has dusky skin and light hair, and so on.

　　Half-Elf Traits (Ex): Half-elves possess the following racial traits.

　　—Medium size.

　　—A half-elf's base land speed is 30 feet.

　　—Immunity to *sleep* spells and similar magical effects, and a

+2 racial bonus on saving throws against enchantment spells or effects.

— Low-light vision.

— +1 racial bonus on Listen, Search, and Spot checks. A half-elf does not have the elf's ability to notice secret doors simply by passing near them.

— +2 racial bonus on Diplomacy and Gather Information checks: Half-elves get along naturally with all people. This bonus may not apply in situations or settings where half-elves are viewed with distrust (such as isolated human settlements), at the DM's option.

—Elven Blood: For all effects related to race, a half-elf is considered an elf. Half-elves, for example, are just as vulnerable to special effects that affect elves as their elf ancestors are, and they can use magic items that are only usable by elves.

Drow

—Automatic Languages: Common, Elven. Bonus Languages: Any (other than secret languages, such as Druidic).

—Favored Class: Any. When determining whether a multiclass half-elf takes an experience point penalty for multiclassing, her highest-level class does not count.

Aquatic Elf

This humanoid is slender and slightly shorter than a human. It has pale, greenish silver skin and emerald green hair. Its ears are pointed, and its fingers and toes are partially webbed.

Also called sea elves, these creatures are water-breathing cousins to land-dwelling elves. They cavort amid the waves and the ocean depths with allies such as dolphins and whales.

Aquatic elves fight underwater with tridents, spears, and nets.

Many aquatic elves revere Deep Sashelas, an undersea god of knowledge and beauty.

Aquatic Elf Traits (Ex): These traits are in addition to the high elf traits, except where noted.

— +2 Dexterity, –2 Intelligence. These adjustments replace the high elf's ability score adjustments.

—An aquatic elf has the aquatic subtype.

—An aquatic elf has a swim speed of 40 feet.

—Gills: Aquatic elves can survive out of the water for 1 hour per point of Constitution (after that, refer to the suffocation rules on page 304 of the *Dungeon Master's Guide*).

—Superior Low-Light Vision: Aquatic elves can see four times as far as a human in starlight, moonlight, torchlight, and similar conditions of low illumination. This trait replaces the high elf's low-light vision.

—Favored Class: Fighter. This trait replaces the high elf's favored class.

Drow

This humanoid is slender and shorter than a human. It has jet black skin and white hair.

Also known as dark elves, drow are a depraved and evil subterranean offshoot.

White is the most common hair color among drow, but almost any pale shade is possible. Drow tend to be smaller and thinner than other sorts of elves, and their eyes are often a vivid red. Their society is matriarchal and rigidly controlled by the priesthood. The drow's patron deity is the spider goddess Lolth. Female drow favor the cleric class rather than wizard and have access to two of the following domains: Chaos, Destruction, Evil, or Trickery. Drow usually coat their arrows with a potent venom.

Poison (Ex): An opponent hit by a drow's poisoned weapon must succeed on a DC 13 Fortitude save or fall unconscious. After 1 minute, the subject must succeed on another DC 13 Fortitude save or remain unconscious for 2d4 hours. A typical drow carries 1d4–1 doses of drow knock-out poison. Drow typically coat arrows and crossbow bolts with this poison, but it can also be applied to a melee weapon. Note that drow have no special ability to apply poison without risking being poisoned themselves. Since this poison is not a magical effect, drow and other elves are susceptible to it.

Drow Traits (Ex): These traits are in addition to the high elf traits, except where noted.

— +2 Intelligence, +2 Charisma.

—Darkvision out to 120 feet. This trait replaces the high elf's low-light vision.

—Spell resistance equal to 11 + class levels.

— +2 racial bonus on Will saves against spells and spell-like abilities.

—Spell-Like Abilities: Drow can use the following spell-like abilities once per day: *dancing lights, darkness, faerie fire.* Caster level equals the drow's class levels.

—Weapon Proficiency: A drow is automatically proficient with the hand crossbow, the rapier, and the short sword. This trait replaces the high elf's weapon proficiency.

—Automatic Languages: Common, Elven, Undercommon. Bonus Languages: Abyssal, Aquan, Draconic, Drow Sign Language, Gnome, Goblin, Kuo-toan. This trait replaces the high elf's automatic and bonus languages.

—Light Blindness: Abrupt exposure to bright light (such as sunlight or a *daylight* spell) blinds drow for 1 round. On subsequent rounds, they are dazzled as long as they remain in the affected area.

—Favored Class: Wizard (male) or cleric (female). This trait replaces the high elf's favored class.

—Level adjustment +2.

The drow warrior presented here had the following ability scores before racial adjustments: Str 13, Dex 11, Con 12, Int 10, Wis 9, Cha 8.

Challenge Rating: Drow with levels in NPC classes have a CR equal to their character level. Drow with levels in PC classes have a CR equal to their character level +1.

Gray Elf

This humanoid is slender and nearly as tall as a human. It is pale-skinned and dark-haired, with pointed ears.

Gray elves are the most noble and regal of all elves. Taller and grander in physical appearance than others of their race, gray elves have a reputation for being aloof and arrogant (even by elven standards). They certainly are more reclusive than high elves, living in isolated mountain citadels and allowing entry only to a select few outsiders. They have either silver hair and amber eyes or pale golden hair and violet eyes. They prefer clothing of white, silver, yellow, or gold, with cloaks of deep blue or purple.

Gray Elf Traits (Ex): These traits are in addition to the high elf traits.

— +2 Intelligence, –2 Strength.

Wild Elf

This humanoid is slender and shorter than a human. Its has dark brown skin, pointed ears, and black hair.

Wild elves, also known as grugach, are barbaric and tribal.

Wild elves' hair color ranges from black to light brown, lightening to silvery white with age. They dress in simple clothing of animal skins and basic plant weaves. Though other elves consider them savages, they contend that they are the true elves, for the rest have lost their primal elven essence in needing to build. Nomadic and rugged, wild elves favor the sorcerer class rather than wizard, although many are barbarians as well.

Wild Elf Traits (Ex): These traits are in addition to the high elf traits, except where noted.

— +2 Dexterity, –2 Intelligence. These adjustments replace the high elf's ability score adjustments.

—Favored Class: Sorcerer. This trait replaces the high elf's favored class.

Wood Elf

Also called sylvan elves, members of this subrace live deep in primordial forests. Their hair color ranges from yellow to a coppery red, and they are more muscular than other elves. Their clothing is in dark shades of green and earth tones to better blend in with their natural surroundings. Their homes are sometimes guarded by giant owls or leopards.

Wood Elf Traits (Ex): These traits are in addition to the high elf traits, except where noted.

— +2 Strength, –2 Intelligence.

—Favored Class: Ranger. This trait replaces the high elf's favored class.

ETHEREAL FILCHER

Medium Aberration
Hit Dice: 5d8 (22 hp)
Initiative: +8
Speed: 40 ft. (8 squares)
Armor Class: 17 (+4 Dex, +3 natural), touch 14, flat-footed 13
Base Attack/Grapple: +3/+3
Attack: Bite +3 melee (1d4)
Full Attack: Bite +3 melee (1d4)
Space/Reach: 5 ft./5 ft.
Special Attacks: —
Special Qualities: Darkvision 60 ft., detect magic, ethereal jaunt
Saves: Fort +1, Ref +5, Will +5
Abilities: Str 10, Dex 18, Con 11, Int 7, Wis 12, Cha 10
Skills: Listen +9, Sleight of Hand +12, Spot +9
Feats: Dodge, Improved Initiative
Environment: Underground
Organization: Solitary
Challenge Rating: 3
Treasure: No coins; standard goods; double items
Alignment: Usually neutral
Advancement: 6–7 HD (Medium); 8–15 HD (Large)
Level Adjustment: —

This bizarre creature stands nearly as tall as a human, but that's where the similarity ends. It has a baglike body that balances on a single, powerful leg that ends in a prehensile foot. Its face is located in the center of its body, with four eyes and a large mouth. Four long, multijointed arms extend from the body, each ending in long, slender fingers.

Ethereal filchers are bizarre-looking creatures with a penchant for snatching trinkets from passersby. Their ability to move quickly between the Ethereal Plane and the Material Plane makes them spectacular pickpockets.

Ethereal filcher

Ethereal filchers dwell on the Material Plane, where they stuff their lairs with all manner of refuse. They prefer secluded, inaccessible spots, such as the bottom of an abandoned well or mine shaft, an alpine cave, or the basement of a ruined building.

Ethereal filchers do not speak.

COMBAT

An ethereal filcher prowls about, using its ethereal jaunt ability to move about unseen (and often through solid objects). Upon locating a likely mark, it shifts to the Material Plane, attempting to catch its victim unaware. The creature attempts to seize an item, then retreats quickly back to the Ethereal Plane. It is not above delivering a bite to distract its target. Once it secures a trinket, it scurries back to its lair to admire its prize. When badly wounded, a filcher escapes rather than continuing the fight.

Any number of simple ruses can blunt a filcher's attack. Quick-thinking individuals often can recover a stolen item simply by snatching it back before the filcher can escape. (Use the rules for making a disarm attempt, page 155 of the *Player's Handbook*.) Others keep a few cheap baubles available for the local filcher to snatch. Filchers are known to have a nose for magic, so items enspelled with *Nystul's magic aura* or *continual flame* spells often prove irresistible, especially if they are also gaudy. Fortunately for its target, a filcher usually is satisfied with a single prize.

Detect Magic (Su): Ethereal filchers can detect magic as the spell (caster level 5th) at will.

Ethereal Jaunt (Su): An ethereal filcher can shift from the Ethereal Plane to the Material Plane as part of any move action, and shift back again as a free action. It can remain on the Ethereal Plane for 1 round before returning to the Material Plane. The ability is otherwise identical with the *ethereal jaunt* spell (caster level 15th).

Skills: Ethereal filchers have a +8 racial bonus on Sleight of Hand checks, and a +4 racial bonus on Listen and Spot checks.

Ethereal marauder

ETHEREAL MARAUDER

Medium Magical Beast (Extraplanar)
Hit Dice: 2d10 (11 hp)
Initiative: +5
Speed: 40 ft. (8 squares)
Armor Class: 14 (+1 Dex, +3 natural), touch 11, flat-footed 13
Base Attack/Grapple: +2/+4
Attack: Bite +4 melee (1d6+3)
Full Attack: Bite +4 melee (1d6+3)
Space/Reach: 5 ft./5 ft.
Special Attacks: —
Special Qualities: Darkvision 60 ft., ethereal jaunt
Saves: Fort +3, Ref +4, Will +1
Abilities: Str 14, Dex 12, Con 11, Int 7, Wis 12, Cha 10
Skills: Listen +5, Move Silently +5, Spot +4
Feats: Improved Initiative
Environment: Ethereal Plane
Organization: Solitary
Challenge Rating: 3
Treasure: None
Alignment: Always neutral
Advancement: 3–4 HD (Medium); 5–6 HD (Large)
Level Adjustment: —

This creature resembles a bipedal lizard with a sinuous tail. Its most disturbing feature is its lack of a head. Instead it has a gaping maw surrounded by three powerful mandibles; gleaming, jet-black teeth line the inner mouth. Three small eyes ring the maw, interspersed with the mandibles.

Ethereal marauders are aggressive predators that can move quickly from the Ethereal Plane to attack opponents on the Material Plane.

Ethereal marauders live and hunt on the Ethereal Plane. Their ecology and habits are obscure at best—few have observed them in their natural habitat for any length of time, and their appearances on the Material Plane are limited to those occasions when they are attacking prey. They are assumed to have no society or culture in the traditional sense, being motivated solely by the need for sustenance and survival.

Ethereal marauders' coloration ranges from bright blue to deep violet. An ethereal marauder stands about 4 feet tall, but its overall length is about 7 feet. It weighs about 200 pounds.

Ethereal marauders speak no known languages. Survivors of their attacks on the Material Plane claim that they emit an eerie, high whine that varies in pitch depending on the creature's speed and health.

COMBAT

Once a marauder locates prey, it shifts to the Material Plane to attack, attempting to catch its victim flat-footed. The creature bites its victim, then retreats quickly back to the Ethereal Plane. When badly hurt or wounded, a marauder escapes to its home plane rather than continuing the fight.

Ethereal Jaunt (Su): An ethereal marauder can shift from the Ethereal Plane to the Material Plane as a free action, and shift back again as a move action. The ability is otherwise identical with the *ethereal jaunt* spell (caster level 15th).

Skills: Ethereal marauders have a +2 racial bonus on Listen, Move Silently, and Spot checks.

ETTERCAP

Medium Aberration

Hit Dice: 5d8+5 (27 hp)

Initiative: +3

Speed: 30 ft. (6 squares), climb 30 ft.

Armor Class: 14 (+3 Dex, +1 natural), touch 13, flat-footed 11

Base Attack/Grapple: +3/+5

Attack: Bite +5 melee (1d8+2 plus poison)

Attack: Bite +5 melee (1d8+2 plus poison) and 2 claws +3 melee (1d3+1)

Space/Reach: 5 ft./5 ft.

Special Attacks: Poison, web

Special Qualities: Low-light vision

Saves: Fort +4, Ref +4, Will +6

Abilities: Str 14, Dex 17, Con 13, Int 6, Wis 15, Cha 8

Skills: Climb +10, Craft (trapmaking) +4, Hide +9, Listen +4, Spot +8

Feats: Great Fortitude, Multiattack

Environment: Warm forests

Organization: Solitary, pair, or troupe (1–2 plus 2–4 Medium monstrous spiders)

Challenge Rating: 3

Treasure: Standard

Alignment: Usually neutral evil

Advancement: 6–7 HD (Medium); 8–15 HD (Large)

Level Adjustment: +4

Ettercap

This revolting creature resembles a cross between a gangly human and a bloated spider. It has long, slender arms and legs protruding from a rounded, fleshy body. It has a spider's head with a pair of bulbous black eyes.

Although not very intelligent, ettercaps are cunning predators. Like the monstrous spiders in whose company they are often found, they are skilled hunters and trappers.

Lurking in dark shadows, ettercaps are solitary creatures that exist only to eat and breed. They often make their homes near well-traveled paths or game trails, where food is plentiful. They savor the taste of still-living flesh, often consuming incapacitated prey before it dies.

Ettercaps are very fond of spiders and often keep them as others keep bees. Some ettercaps have a number of monstrous spiders as pets, which are as loyal to it as a dog is to a human master.

An ettercap is about 6 feet tall and weighs about 200 pounds. Ettercaps speak Common.

COMBAT

Ettercaps are not brave creatures, but their cunning traps often ensure that the enemy never draws a weapon. When an ettercap does engage its enemies, it attacks with its keen-edged claws and venomous bite. It usually will not come within melee reach of any foe that is still able to move.

Poison (Ex): Injury, Fortitude DC 15, initial damage 1d6 Dex, secondary damage 2d6 Dex. The save DC is Constitution based and includes a +2 racial bonus.

Web (Ex): An ettercap can throw a web eight times per day. This is similar to an attack with a net but has a maximum range of 50 feet, with a range increment of 10 feet, and is effective against targets of up to Medium size. The web anchors the target in place, allowing no movement.

An entangled creature can escape with a DC 13 Escape Artist check or burst the web with a DC 17 Strength check. The check DCs are Constitution-based, and the Strength check DC includes a +4 racial bonus. The web has 6 hit points, hardness 0, and takes double damage from fire.

Ettercaps can also create sheets of sticky webbing from 5 to 60 feet square. They usually position these to snare flying creatures but can also try to trap prey on the ground. Approaching creatures must succeed on a DC 20 Spot check to notice a web, or they stumble into it and become trapped as though by a successful web attack. Attempts to escape or burst the webbing receive a +5 bonus if the trapped creature has something to walk on or grab while pulling free. Each 5-foot-square section has 6 hit points, hardness 0, and takes double damage from fire.

An ettercap can move across its own sheet web at its climb speed and can determine the exact location of any creature touching the web.

Skills: Ettercaps have a +4 racial bonus on Craft (trapmaking), Hide, and Spot checks. They have a +8 racial bonus on Climb checks and can always choose to take 10 on Climb checks, even if rushed or threatened.

ETTIN

Large Giant

Hit Dice: 10d8+20 (65 hp)

Initiative: +3

Speed: 30 ft. in hide armor (6 squares); base speed 40 ft.

Armor Class: 18 (–1 size, –1 Dex, +7 natural, +3 hide), touch 8, flat-footed 18

Base Attack/Grapple: +7/+17

Attack: Morningstar +12 melee (2d6+6) or javelin +5 ranged (1d8+6)

Full Attack: 2 morningstars +12/+7 melee (2d6+6) or 2 javelins +5 ranged (1d8+6)

Space/Reach: 10 ft./10 ft.
Special Attacks: —
Special Qualities: Low-light vision, superior two-weapon fighting
Saves: Fort +9, Ref +2, Will +5
Abilities: Str 23, Dex 8, Con 15, Int 6, Wis 10, Cha 11
Skills: Listen +10, Search +1, Spot +10
Feats: Alertness, Improved Initiative, Iron Will, Power Attack
Environment: Cold hills
Organization: Solitary, gang (2–4), troupe (1–2 plus 1–2 brown bears), band (3–5 plus 1–2 brown bears), or colony (3–5 plus 1–2 brown bears and 7–12 orcs or 9–16 goblins)
Challenge Rating: 6
Treasure: Standard
Alignment: Usually chaotic evil
Advancement: By character class
Level Adjustment: +5

This hulking giant has two heads. Each head has a porcine face with a shovel jaw and protruding lower canines like a boar's tusks. The rest of its teeth are large and rotten. Its stringy hair is filthy, just like the rest of the creature.

Ettins, or two-headed giants, are vicious and unpredictable hunters that stalk the night. Their two heads make them exceptionally sharp-eyed and alert. They are excellent guardians and scouts.

An ettin never bathes if it can help it, which usually leaves it so grimy and dirty its skin resembles thick, gray hide (ettins that don't smell bad are rare indeed). Adult ettins are about 13 feet tall and weigh 5,200 pounds. They live about 75 years.

Ettins have no language of their own but speak a pidgin of Orc, Goblin, and Giant. Creatures that can speak any of these languages must succeed on a DC 15 Intelligence check to communicate with an ettin. Check once for each bit of information: If the other creature speaks two of these languages, the DC is 10, and for someone who speaks all three, the DC is 5. Ettins talk among themselves without difficulty, despite their low Intelligence, and a lone ettin often whiles away the hours chatting with itself.

COMBAT

Though ettins aren't very intelligent, they are cunning fighters. They prefer to ambush their victims rather than charge into a straight fight, but once the battle has started, an ettin usually fights furiously until all enemies are dead.

Superior Two-Weapon Fighting (Ex): An ettin fights with a morningstar or javelin in each hand. Because each of its two heads controls an arm, the ettin does not take a penalty on attack or damage rolls for attacking with two weapons.

Skills: An ettin's two heads give it a +2 racial bonus on Listen, Spot, and Search checks.

Ettin

ETTIN SOCIETY

Ettins like to establish their lairs in remote, rocky areas. They dwell in dark, underground caves that stink of decaying food and offal. They tolerate other creatures, such as orcs, if these can be useful in some way. Otherwise, ettins tend to be violently isolationist, crushing trespassers without question. Ettins are generally solitary, and mated pairs stay together for only a few months after a child is born. Young ettins mature quickly. Within eight to ten months after birth, they are self-sufficient enough to go off on their own.

On rare occasions, a particularly strong ettin may gather a small group, or gang, of ettins. This gang stays together only as long as the leader is undefeated. Any major defeat shatters the leader's hold over the others, and they go their separate ways.

Ettins place little value on wealth but are smart enough to understand its value to others. They collect treasure only because it can buy them the services of goblins or orcs. These lesser creatures sometimes build traps around ettins' lairs, or help them fight off powerful opponents.

FIENDISH CREATURE

Fiendish creatures dwell on the lower planes, the realms of evil, although they resemble beings found on the Material Plane. They are more fearsome in appearance than their earthly counterparts.

Fiendish creatures are often mistaken for half-fiends, more powerful creatures that are created when a fiend mates with a noncelestial creature, or through some foul infernal breeding project.

SAMPLE FIENDISH CREATURE

Fiendish Dire Rat
Small Magical Beast (Augmented Animal, Extraplanar)
Hit Dice: 1d8+1 (5 hp)
Initiative: +3
Speed: 40 ft. (8 squares), climb 20 ft.
Armor Class: 15 (+1 size, +3 Dex, +1 natural), touch 14, flat-footed 11
Base Attack/Grapple: +0/–4
Attack: Bite +4 melee (1d4 plus disease)
Full Attack: Bite +4 melee (1d4 plus disease)
Space/Reach: 5 ft./5 ft.
Special Attacks: Disease, smite good
Special Qualities: Darkvision 60 ft., resistance to cold 5 and fire 5, scent, spell resistance 6
Saves: Fort +3, Ref +5, Will +3
Abilities: Str 10, Dex 17, Con 12, Int 3, Wis 12, Cha 4
Skills: Climb +11, Hide +8, Listen +4, Move Silently +4, Spot +4, Swim +11
Feats: Alertness, Weapon Finesse[B]
Environment: Infinite Layers of the Abyss
Organization: Solitary or pack (11–20)
Challenge Rating: 1/2
Treasure: None
Alignment: Always evil (any)
Advancement: 2–3 HD (Small); 4–6 HD (Medium)
Level Adjustment: —

Combat

Disease (Ex): Filth fever—bite, Fortitude DC 11, incubation period 1d3 days, damage 1d3 Dex and 1d3 Con. The save DC is Constitution-based.

Skills: Fiendish dire rats have a +8 racial bonus on Swim checks. They have a +8 racial bonus on Climb checks and can always choose to take 10 on Climb checks, even if rushed or threatened. They use their Dexterity modifier instead of their Strength modifier for Climb and Swim checks.

CREATING A FIENDISH CREATURE

"Fiendish" is an inherited template that can be added to any corporeal aberration, animal, dragon, fey, giant, humanoid, magical beast, monstrous humanoid, ooze, plant, or vermin of nongood alignment (referred to hereafter as the base creature).

A fiendish creature uses all the base creature's statistics and abilities except as noted here. Do not recalculate the creature's Hit Dice, base attack bonus, saves, or skill points if its type changes.

Size and Type: Animals or vermin with this template become magical beasts, but otherwise the creature type is unchanged. Size is unchanged. Fiendish creatures encountered on the Material Plane have the extraplanar subtype.

Special Attacks: A fiendish creature retains all the special attacks of the base creature and also gains the following special attack.

Smite Good (Su): Once per day the creature can make a normal melee attack to deal extra damage equal to its HD total (maximum of +20) against a good foe.

Special Qualities: A fiendish creature retains all the special qualities of the base creature and also gains the following.

—Darkvision out to 60 feet.
—Damage reduction (see the table below).
—Resistance to cold and fire (see the table below).
—Spell resistance equal to the creature's HD + 5 (maximum 25).

If the base creature already has one or more of these special qualities, use the better value.

If a fiendish creature gains damage reduction, its natural weapons are treated as magic weapons for the purpose of overcoming damage reduction.

Abilities: Same as the base creature, but Intelligence is at least 3.

Environment: Any evil-aligned plane.

Challenge Rating: HD 3 or less, as base creature; HD 4 to 7, as base creature +1; HD 8 or more, as base creature +2.

Alignment: Always evil (any).

Level Adjustment: Same as the base creature +2.

| | Resistance to | |
Hit Dice	Cold and Fire	Damage Reduction
1–3	5	—
4–7	5	5/magic
8–11	10	5/magic
12 or more	10	10/magic

FORMIAN

Formians hail from the plane of Mechanus. They seek to colonize all that they see and incorporate all living things into their hive as workers.

Expansionist in the extreme, formians are dedicated to spreading their colonies until they have taken over everything and their order is unquestioned. To further this end, they attack all other creatures, usually to put them to work building and expanding cities. Formians maintain these "conscripted" workers as well as those mentally dominated by the power of their taskmasters.

A formian resembles a cross between an ant and a centaur. All formians are covered in a brownish-red carapace; size and appearance differs for each variety.

COMBAT

Formians are generally aggressive, seeking to subdue all they encounter. If they perceive even the slightest threat to their hive-city or to their queen, they attack immediately and fight to the death. Any formian also attacks immediately if ordered to do so by a superior.

Hive Mind (Ex): All formians within 50 miles of their queen are in constant communication. If one is aware of a particular danger, they all are. If one in a group is not flat-footed, none of them are. No formian in a group is considered flanked unless all of them are.

Warrior

Myrmarch

Formians

FORMIAN SOCIETY

Formians build fabulous hive-cities in which hundreds of the creatures dwell. They are born into their station, with no ability to progress. Workers obey orders given by warriors, myrmarchs, or the queen. Warriors carry out the will of their myrmarch commanders or the queen. Myrmarchs take orders only from the queen herself, although they have different ranks depending on services rendered. These are not positions of power but of prestige. The most prestigious of the myrmarchs guard the queen. Taskmasters are equal in rank to warriors but seldom interact with other formians.

WORKER

This creature is about the size of a jackal or bulldog. It looks like an ant, but holds its head and thorax upright. It has humanlike shoulders and arms ending in rudimentary hands with blunt claws.

Workers are the lowest-ranking and most common formians. They exist only to serve, performing all the necessary, lowly tasks that the hive needs done.

While workers cannot speak, they can convey simple concepts (such as danger) by body movements. Through the hive mind, however, they can communicate just fine—although their intelligence still limits the concepts that they can grasp.

A worker is about 3 feet long and about 2-1/2 feet high at the front. It weighs about 60 pounds. Its hands are suitable only for manual labor.

Combat

Formian workers fight only to defend their hive-cities, using their mandibled bite.

A formian worker's natural weapons, as well as any weapons it wields, are treated as lawful-aligned for the purpose of overcoming damage reduction.

Cure Serious Wounds (Sp): Eight workers together can heal a creature's wounds as though using the *cure serious wounds* spell (caster level 7th). This is a full-round action for all eight workers.

Make Whole (Sp): Three workers together can repair an object as though using the *make whole* spell (caster level 7th). This is a full-round action for all three workers.

WARRIOR

This creature is about the size of a pony. It looks like an ant, but holds its head and thorax upright. Its mouth features powerful-looking mandibles. The creature has humanlike shoulders and arms ending in powerful hands with sharp claws. Its abdomen bears a stinger.

Formian warriors exist only to fight.

Warriors rank only slightly above workers. They communicate through the hive mind to convey battle plans and make reports to their commanders. They cannot speak otherwise.

A warrior is about is about 5 feet long and about 4-1/2 feet high at the front. It weighs about 180 pounds.

Combat

Warriors are wicked combatants, using claws, bite, and a poisonous sting all at once. Through the hive mind, they attack with coordinated and extremely efficient tactics.

A formian warrior's natural weapons, as well as any weapons it wields, are treated as lawful-aligned for the purpose of overcoming damage reduction.

Poison (Ex): Injury, Fortitude DC 14, initial and secondary damage 1d6 Str. The save DC is Constitution-based.

TASKMASTER

This creature is about the size of a pony. It looks like an ant, but holds its head and thorax upright. It does not appear to have a mouth. The creature has humanlike shoulders and arms ending in powerful hands with sharp claws. Its abdomen bears a stinger.

	Formian Worker Small Outsider (Lawful, Extraplanar)	Formian Warrior Medium Outsider (Lawful, Extraplanar)	Formian Taskmaster Medium Outsider (Lawful, Extraplanar)
Hit Dice:	1d8+1 (5 hp)	4d8+8 (26 hp)	6d8+12 (39 hp)
Initiative:	+2	+3	+7
Speed:	40 ft. (8 squares)	40 ft. (8 squares)	40 ft. (8 squares)
Armor Class:	17 (+1 size, +2 Dex, +4 natural), touch 13, flat-footed 15	18 (+3 Dex, +5 natural), touch 13, flat-footed 15	19 (+3 Dex, +6 natural), touch 13, flat-footed 16
Base Attack/Grapple:	+1/−2	+4/+7	+6/+10
Attack:	Bite +3 melee (1d4+1)	Sting +7 melee (2d4+3 plus poison)	Sting +10 melee (2d4+4 plus poison)
Full Attack:	Bite +3 melee (1d4+1)	Sting +7 melee (2d4+3 plus poison) and 2 claws +5 melee (1d6+1) and bite +5 melee (1d4+1)	Sting +10 melee (2d4+4 plus poison) and 2 claws +8 melee (1d6+2)
Space/Reach:	5 ft./5 ft.	5 ft./5 ft.	5 ft./5 ft.
Special Attacks:	—	Poison	Dominate monster, dominated creature, poison
Special Qualities:	*Cure serious wounds*, hive mind, immunity to poison, petrification, and cold, *make whole*, resistance to electricity 10, fire 10, and sonic 10	Hive mind, immunity to poison, petrification, and cold, resistance to electricity 10, fire 10, and sonic 10, spell resistance 18	Hive mind, immunity to poison, petrification, and cold, resistance to electricity 10, fire 10, and sonic 10, spell resistance 21, telepathy 100 ft.
Saves:	Fort +3, Ref +4, Will +2	Fort +6, Ref +7, Will +5	Fort +7, Ref +8, Will +8
Abilities:	Str 13, Dex 14, Con 13, Int 6, Wis 10, Cha 9	Str 17, Dex 16, Con 14, Int 10, Wis 12, Cha 11	Str 18, Dex 16, Con 14, Int 11, Wis 16, Cha 19
Skills:	Climb +10, Craft (any one) +5, Hide +6, Listen +4, Search +2, Spot +4	Climb +10, Hide +10, Jump +14, Listen +8, Move Silently +10, Search +7, Spot +8, Survival +1 (+3 following tracks), Tumble +12	Climb +13, Diplomacy +6, Hide +12, Intimidate +13, Listen +12, Move Silently +12, Search +9, Sense Motive +12, Spot +12, Survival +3 (+5 following tracks)
Feats:	Skill Focus (Craft [selected skill])	Dodge, Multiattack	Dodge, Improved Initiative, Multiattack
Environment:	Clockwork Nirvana of Mechanus	Clockwork Nirvana of Mechanus	Clockwork Nirvana of Mechanus
Organization:	Team (2–4) or crew (7–18)	Solitary, team (2–4), or troop (6–11)	Solitary (1 plus 1 dominated creature) or conscription team (2–4 plus 1 dominated creature per team member)
Challenge Rating:	1/2	3	7
Treasure:	None	None	Standard
Alignment:	Always lawful neutral	Always lawful neutral	Always lawful neutral
Advancement:	2–3 HD (Medium)	5–8 HD (Medium); 9–12 HD (Large)	7–9 HD (Medium); 10–12 HD (Large)
Level Adjustment:	—	—	—

	Formian Myrmarch	Formian Queen
	Large Outsider (Lawful, Extraplanar)	Large Outsider (Lawful, Extraplanar)
Hit Dice:	12d8+48 (102 hp)	20d8+100 (190 hp)
Initiative:	+8	−5
Speed:	50 ft. (10 squares)	0 ft.
Armor Class:	28 (−1 size, +4 Dex, +15 natural), touch 13, flat-footed 24	23 (−1 size, +14 natural), touch 9, flat-footed 23
Base Attack/Grapple:	+12/+20	+20/+24
Attack:	Sting +15 melee (2d4+4 plus poison) or javelin +15 ranged (1d6+4)	—
Full Attack:	Sting +15 melee (2d4+4 plus poison) and bite +13 melee (2d6+2); or javelin +15/+10 ranged (1d6+4)	—
Space/Reach:	10 ft./5 ft.	10 ft./5 ft.
Special Attacks:	Poison, spell-like abilities	Spell-like abilities, spells
Special Qualities:	Fast healing 2, hive mind, immunity to poison, petrification, and cold, resistance to electricity 10, fire 10, and sonic 10, spell resistance 25	Fast healing 2, hive mind, immunity to poison, petrification, and cold, resistance to electricity 10, fire 10, and sonic 10, spell resistance 30, telepathy
Saves:	Fort +12, Ref +12, Will +11	Fort +19, Ref —, Will +19
Abilities:	Str 19, Dex 18, Con 18, Int 16, Wis 16, Cha 17	Str —, Dex —, Con 20, Int 20, Wis 20, Cha 21
Skills:	Climb +19, Concentration +18, Diplomacy +20, Hide +15, Knowledge (any one) +18, Listen +18, Move Silently +19, Search +18, Sense Motive +18, Spot +18, Survival +3 (+5 following tracks)	Appraise +28, Bluff +28, Concentration +28, Diplomacy +32, Disguise +5 (+7 acting), Intimidate +30, Knowledge (any three) +28, Listen +30, Sense Motive +28, Spellcraft +28 (+30 scrolls), Spot +30, Use Magic Device +28 (+30 scrolls)
Feats:	Dodge, Improved Initiative, Mobility, Multiattack, Spring Attack	Alertness, Eschew Materials[B], Great Fortitude, Improved Counterspell, Iron Will, item creation feat (any one), Maximize Spell, Spell Focus (enchantment)
Environment	Clockwork Nirvana of Mechanus	Clockwork Nirvana of Mechanus
Organization:	Solitary, team (2–4), or platoon (1 plus 7–18 workers and 6–11 warriors)	Hive (1 plus 100–400 workers, 11–40 warriors, 4–7 taskmasters with 1 dominated creature each, and 5–8 myrmarchs)
Challenge Rating:	10	17
Treasure:	Standard	Double standard
Alignment:	Always lawful neutral	Always lawful neutral
Advancement:	13–18 HD (Large); 19–24 HD (Huge)	21–30 HD (Huge); 31–40 HD (Gargantuan)
Level Adjustment:	—	—

Taskmasters resemble warriors with no mandibles—no apparent mouth at all, in fact. These formians communicate only telepathically and derive sustenance from the mental energies of those they dominate.

A taskmaster's duty is to gather and control nonformians for integration into the hive. Put simply, taskmasters enslave other creatures. They do not enjoy controlling others but believe it is the only efficient way to spread the hive to all places, a desirable end for all rational creatures. If a taskmaster can manage to "conscript" a laborer without using its dominate monster ability, it will do so.

Those few souls who have escaped refer to formian hive-cities as "work pits." While formians are not cruel, they are still emotionless—and pitiless.

A taskmaster is about the same size as a warrior.

Combat

Taskmasters rely on their dominated slaves to fight for them if at all possible. If necessary, though, they can defend themselves with claws and a poison sting.

A formian taskmaster's natural weapons, as well as any weapons it wields, are treated as lawful-aligned for the purpose of overcoming damage reduction.

Dominate Monster (Su): A taskmaster can use a *dominate monster* ability as the spell from a 10th-level caster (Will DC 17 negates), although the subject may be of any kind and may be up to Large size. Creatures that successfully save cannot be affected by the same taskmaster's dominate monster ability for 24 hours. A single taskmaster can dominate up to four subjects at a time. The save DC is Charisma-based.

Dominated Creature (Ex): A taskmaster is never encountered alone. One dominated nonformian creature always accompanies it (choose or determine randomly any creature of CR 4).

Poison (Ex): Injury, Fortitude DC 15, initial and secondary damage 1d6 Str. The save DC is Constitution-based.

MYRMARCH

This creature is about the size of a light horse. It looks like an ant, but holds its head and thorax upright. Its mouth features powerful-looking mandibles, and it wears an elaborate bronze helmet. The creature has humanlike shoulders and arms ending in humanlike hands. Its abdomen bears a stinger.

Myrmarchs are the elite of formian society. Much more than those beneath them, these creatures are individuals, with goals, desires, and creative thought. Very rarely do these thoughts conflict with the wishes of the queen, though—most myrmarchs are still very loyal to her.

Myrmarchs are commanders in formian armies and leaders in formian communities. They are the hands of the queen, carrying out her direct orders and making sure everything goes as she desires. Myrmarchs also have a secondary role: stamping out chaos wherever and whenever they can. Those who foment disorder, and particularly creatures that revere or exemplify it (such as slaadi), are the hated foes of myrmarchs.

A myrmarch is about 7 feet long and about 5-1/2 feet high at the front. It weighs about 1,500 pounds. Its claws are capable of fine manipulation, like human hands. Each myrmarch wears a bronze helm to signify its position (the more elaborate the helm, the more prestigious the position).

Myrmarchs speak Formian and Common.

Combat

Myrmarchs' claws are like hands and thus serve no combat purpose. Myrmarchs occasionally employ javelins for ranged attacks, coated with poison from their own stingers.

They fight intelligently, aiding those under them (if any such are present) and commanding them through the hive mind. If chaotic creatures are present, however, a myrmarch is single-minded in its quest to destroy them.

A formian myrmarch's natural weapons, as well as any weapons it wields, are treated as lawful-aligned for the purpose of overcoming damage reduction.

Poison (Ex): Injury, Fortitude DC 20, initial and secondary damage 2d6 Dex. The save DC is Constitution-based.

Spell-Like Abilities: At will—*charm monster* (DC 17), *clairaudience/clairvoyance, detect chaos, detect thoughts* (DC 15), *magic circle against chaos, greater teleport*; 1/day—*dictum* (DC 20), *order's wrath* (DC 17). Caster level 12th. The save DCs are Charisma-based.

QUEEN

This creature looks like a gigantic, bloated ant. Its legs seem atrophied and nonfunctional.

The formian queen sits at the center of the hive-city, her bloated form never moving from the royal chamber. She is served and guarded by the most loyal myrmarchs.

The formian queen cannot move. With her telepathic abilities, though, she can send instructions to and get reports from any formian within her range. She is about 10 feet long, perhaps 4 feet high, and weighs about 3,500 pounds.

The queen speaks Formian and Common, although she can communicate with any creature telepathically.

Combat

The queen does not fight. She has no ability to move. If necessary, a team of workers and myrmarchs (or dominated slaves) haul her enormous bulk to where she needs to go. This sort of occurrence is very rare, however, and most of the time the queen remains within her well-defended chambers.

Despite her utter lack of physical activity, the queen can cast spells and use spell-like abilities to great effect in her own defense as well as the defense of the hive-city.

Spells: The queen casts arcane spells as a 17th-level sorcerer.

Typical Sorcerer Spells Known (6/8/7/7/7/7/6/6/4, base save DC 15 + spell level): 0—*acid splash, arcane mark, daze, detect magic, light, mage hand, read magic, resistance, touch of fatigue;* 1st—*comprehend languages, identify, mage armor, magic missile, shield;* 2nd—*hypnotic pattern, invisibility, protection from arrows, resist energy, scorching ray;* 3rd—*dispel magic, heroism, nondetection, slow;* 4th—*confusion, detect scrying, Evard's black tentacles, scrying;* 5th—*cone of cold, dismissal, teleport, wall of force;* 6th—*analyze dweomer, geas/quest,*

repulsion; 7th—*summon monster VII, vision, waves of exhaustion;* 8th—*prismatic wall, temporal stasis.*

Spell-Like Abilities: At will—*calm emotions* (DC 17), *charm monster* (DC 19), *clairaudience/clairvoyance, detect chaos, detect thoughts, dictum* (DC 22), *divination, hold monster* (DC 20), *magic circle against chaos, order's wrath* (DC 19), *shield of law* (DC 23), *true seeing.* Caster level 17th. The save DCs are Charisma-based.

Telepathy (Su): The queen can communicate telepathically with any intelligent creature within 50 miles whose presence she is aware of.

FROST WORM

Huge Magical Beast (Cold)
Hit Dice: 14d10+70 (147 hp)
Initiative: +4
Speed: 30 ft. (6 squares), burrow 10 ft.
Armor Class: 18 (–2 size, +10 natural), touch 8, flat-footed 18
Base Attack/Grapple: +14/+30
Attack: Bite +21 melee (2d8+12 plus 1d8 cold)
Full Attack: Bite +21 melee (2d8+12 plus 1d8 cold)
Space/Reach: 15 ft./10 ft.
Special Attacks: Trill, cold, breath weapon
Special Qualities: Darkvision 60 ft., death throes, immunity to cold, low-light vision, vulnerability to fire
Saves: Fort +14, Ref +9, Will +6
Abilities: Str 26, Dex 10, Con 20, Int 2, Wis 11, Cha 11
Skills: Hide +3*, Listen +5, Spot +5
Feats: Alertness, Improved Initiative, Improved Natural Attack (bite), Iron Will, Weapon Focus (bite)
Environment: Cold plains
Organization: Solitary
Challenge Rating: 12
Treasure: None
Alignment: Usually neutral
Advancement: 15–21 HD (Huge); 22–42 HD (Gargantuan)
Level Adjustment: —

Frost worm

This long, blue-white creature has huge mandibles and a strange nodule atop its head from which it generates a trilling sound.

Terror of the frozen lands, the frost worm spends most of its life burrowing through the ice, snow, and even the frozen earth. It surfaces only to attack its prey. Frost worms eat yaks, polar bears, walruses, seals, moose, and mammoths.

Sages cannot agree whether this horrible monster is related to the purple worm or to the remorhaz. Perhaps the answer is neither. It is true that frost worms hate remorhazes and attack them on sight in a colossal battle that might very well lay waste to a large area. Remorhazes are frequently the victors in such battles.

A frost worm cannot burrow through stone, but can manage ice and frozen earth. When moving through such hard materials it leaves behind a usable tunnel about 5 feet in diameter.

Frost worms lay eggs that to the untrained observer appear to be simply oval-shaped ice formations. Hatchling frost worms must immediately fend for themselves, growing to maturity in three to five years. Tribesfolk of the cold wastes can sometimes train young frost worms to help protect the community and even to be ridden using magic, cold-resistant saddles.

A frost worm is about 40 feet long, 5 feet in diameter, and weighs about 8,000 pounds.

COMBAT

Frost worms lurk under the snow, waiting for prey to come near. They begin an attack with a trill and then set upon helpless prey with their bite.

Trill (Su): A frost worm can emit a noise that forces its prey to stand motionless. This sonic mind-affecting compulsion affects all creatures other than frost worms within a 100-foot radius. Creatures must succeed on a DC 17 Will save or be stunned for as long as the worm trills and for 1d4 rounds thereafter, even if they are attacked. However, if attacked or violently shaken (a full-round action), a victim is allowed another saving throw. Once a creature has resisted or broken the effect, it cannot be affected again by that same frost worm's trill for 24 hours. The effect's caster level is 14th. The save DC is Charisma-based.

Cold (Ex): A frost worm's body generates intense cold, causing opponents to take an extra 1d8 points of cold damage every time the creature succeeds on a bite attack. Creatures attacking a frost worm unarmed or with natural weapons take this same cold damage each time one of their attacks hits.

Breath Weapon (Su): 30-foot cone, once per hour, damage 15d6 cold, Reflex DC 22 half. Opponents held motionless by the frost worm's trill get no saving throw. The save DC is Constitution-based.

Death Throes (Ex): When killed, a frost worm turns to ice and shatters in an explosion that deals 12d6 points of cold damage and 8d6 points of piercing damage to everything within 100 feet (Reflex half DC 22). The save DC is Constitution-based.

Skills: *A frost worm, due to its coloration and its affinity for burying itself in the snow, has a +10 racial bonus on Hide checks in its native environment.

FUNGUS

Unlike ordinary kinds of fungus, which are harmless to other living creatures, the two specimens described here—the shrieker and the violet fungus—can be dangerous to unwary adventurers.

A fungus lacks chlorophyll, a true stem, roots, or leaves. Incapable of photosynthesis, it exists as a parasite, breaking down organic matter slowly. While both of the creatures described here occur individually, shriekers and violet fungi often coexist in the same environment.

Violet fungus

	Shrieker	Violet Fungus
	Medium Plant	Medium Plant
Hit Dice:	2d8+2 (11 hp)	2d8+6 (15 hp)
Initiative:	−5	−1
Speed:	0 ft.	10 ft. (2 squares)
Armor Class:	8 (−5 Dex, +3 natural), touch 5, flat-footed 8	13 (−1 Dex, +4 natural), touch 9, flat-footed 13
Base Attack/Grapple:	+1/−4	+1/+3
Attack:	—	Tentacle +3 melee (1d6+2 plus poison)
Full Attack:	—	4 tentacles +3 melee (1d6+2 plus poison)
Space/Reach:	5 ft./0 ft.	5 ft./10 ft.
Special Attacks:	Shriek	Poison
Special Qualities:	Low-light vision, plant traits	Low-light vision, plant traits
Saves:	Fort +4, Ref —, Will −4	Fort +6, Ref −1, Will +0
Abilities:	Str —, Dex —, Con 13, Int —, Wis 2, Cha 1	Str 14, Dex 8, Con 16, Int —, Wis 11, Cha 9
Skills:	—	—
Feats:	—	—
Environment:	Underground	Underground
Organization:	Solitary or patch (3–5)	Solitary, patch (2–4), or mixed patch (2–4 violet fungi and 3–5 shriekers)
Challenge Rating:	1	3
Treasure:	None	None
Alignment:	Always neutral	Always neutral
Advancement:	3 HD (Medium)	3–6 HD (Medium)
Level Adjustment:	—	—

COMBAT

Shriekers and violet fungi often work together to attract and kill prey. When the shriekers' hellish racket attracts a curious creature, the violet fungus tries to kill it. Both creatures enjoy the fruits of a successful hunt.

SHRIEKER

This creature looks like a human-sized mushroom.

A shrieker is a stationary fungus that emits a loud noise to attract prey or when disturbed. Shriekers live in dark, subterranean places, often in the company of violet fungi, whose poison they are immune to.

Shriekers come in of shades of purple.

Combat

A shrieker has no means of attack. Instead, it lures prey to its vicinity by emitting a loud noise.

Shriek (Ex): Movement or a light source within 10 feet of a shrieker causes the fungus to emit a piercing sound that lasts for 1d3 rounds. The sound attracts nearby creatures that are disposed to investigate it. Some creatures that live near shriekers come to learn that the fungus's noise means there is food nearby.

VIOLET FUNGUS

This human-sized mushroom has four tendrillike tentacles and a mass of small, rootlike feelers at its base that enable it to move slowly.

Violet fungi resemble shriekers and are often found growing among them.

A violet fungi's coloration ranges from purple overall to dull gray or violet covered with purple spots.

Combat

A violet fungus flails about with its tentacles at living creatures that come within its reach.

Poison (Ex): Injury, Fortitude DC 14, initial and secondary damage 1d4 Str and 1d4 Con. The save DC is Constitution-based.

GARGOYLE

Medium Monstrous Humanoid (Earth)
Hit Dice: 4d8+19 (37 hp)
Initiative: +2
Speed: 40 ft. (8 squares), fly 60 ft. (average)
Armor Class: 16 (+2 Dex, +4 natural), touch 12, flat-footed 14
Base Attack/Grapple: +4/+6
Attack: Claw +6 melee (1d4+2)
Full Attack: 2 claws +6 melee (1d4+2) and bite +4 melee (1d6+1) and gore +4 melee (1d6+1)
Space/Reach: 5 ft./5 ft.
Special Attacks: —
Special Qualities: Damage reduction 10/magic, darkvision 60 ft., freeze
Saves: Fort +5, Ref +6, Will +4
Abilities: Str 15, Dex 14, Con 18, Int 6, Wis 11, Cha 7
Skills: Hide +7*, Listen +4, Spot +4
Feats: Multiattack, Toughness

Environment: Any
Organization: Solitary, pair, or wing (5–16)
Challenge Rating: 4
Treasure: Standard
Alignment: Usually chaotic evil
Advancement: 5–6 HD (Medium); 7–12 HD (Large)
Level Adjustment: +5

This creature looks like a grotesque, winged humanoid with a horned head and a stony hide.

A gargoyle is a vicious flying predator that enjoys torturing creatures weaker than itself.

Gargoyles often appear to be winged stone statues, for they can perch indefinitely without moving and use this disguise to surprise their foes. They require no food, water, or air, but often eat their fallen foes out of fondness for inflicting pain. When not enjoying their favorite pastime, a wing of gargoyles can be found waiting silently for prey or bragging among themselves.

Gargoyles speak Common and Terran.

COMBAT

Gargoyles either remain still, then suddenly attack, or dive onto their prey.

A gargoyle's natural weapons are treated as magic weapons for the purpose of overcoming damage reduction.

Freeze (Ex): A gargoyle can hold itself so still it appears to be a statue. An observer must succeed on a DC 20 Spot check to notice the gargoyle is really alive.

Skills: Gargoyles have a +2 racial bonus on Hide, Listen, and Spot checks. *The Hide bonus increases by +8 when a gargoyle is concealed against a background of stone.

Gargoyle

WAR 2000

KAPOACINTH

These cousins of the gargoyle have the aquatic subtype. They have a base land speed of 40 feet and a swim speed of 60 feet (no fly speed) and are found only in aquatic environments.

GARGOYLES AS CHARACTERS

Gargoyles make excellent scouts, spies, and fighters. Able to soar aloft at a moment's notice, they can ravage their landbound foes and take aloft to the air.

Gargoyle characters possess the following racial traits.

— +4 Strength, +4 Dexterity, +8 Constitution, –4 Intelligence, –4 Charisma.

—Medium size.

—A gargoyle's base land speed is 40 feet. It also has a fly speed of 60 feet (average).

—Darkvision out to 60 feet.

—Racial Hit Dice: A gargoyle begins with four levels of monstrous humanoid, which provide 4d8 Hit Dice, a base attack bonus of +4, and base saving throw bonuses of Fort +1, Ref +4, and Will +4.

—Racial Skills: A gargoyle's monstrous humanoid levels give it skill points equal to 7 × (2 + Int modifier). Its class skills are Hide, Listen, and Spot. A gargoyle has a +2 racial bonus on Hide, Listen, and Spot checks, and an additional +8 bonus on Hide checks when it is concealed against a background of stone.

—Racial Feats: A gargoyle's monstrous humanoid levels give it two feats.

— +4 natural armor bonus.

—Special Qualities (see above): Damage reduction 10/magic, freeze.

—Automatic Languages: Common. Bonus Languages: Auran, Dwarven, Elven, Gnome, Halfling, Giant, Terran.

—Favored Class: Fighter.

—Level adjustment +5.

GENIE

Genies are humanlike beings who dwell on the elemental planes. They are famous for their strength, guile, and skill with illusion magic.

Genies sometimes use the Material Plane as a neutral ground for meeting (or fighting) others of their kind or collecting goods not readily available on their home planes.

COMBAT

Genies prefer to outmaneuver and outthink their foes. They are not too proud to flee if it means they'll live to fight another day. If trapped, they bargain, offering treasure or favors in return for their lives and freedom.

Plane Shift (Sp): A genie can enter any of the elemental planes, the Astral Plane, or the Material Plane. This ability transports the genie and up to eight other creatures, provided they all link hands with the genie. It is otherwise similar to the spell of the same name (caster level 13th).

DJINNI

Large Outsider (Air, Extraplanar)
Hit Dice: 7d8+14 (45 hp)
Initiative: +8
Speed: 20 ft. (4 squares), fly 60 ft. (perfect)
Armor Class: 16 (–1 size, +4 Dex, +3 natural), touch 13, flat-footed 12
Base Attack/Grapple: +7/+15
Attack: Slam +10 melee (1d8+4)
Full Attack: 2 slams +10 melee (1d8+4)
Space/Reach: 10 ft./10 ft.
Special Attacks: Air mastery, spell-like abilities, whirlwind
Special Qualities: Darkvision 60 ft., immunity to acid, *plane shift*, telepathy 100 ft.
Saves: Fort +7, Ref +9, Will +7
Abilities: Str 18, Dex 19, Con 14, Int 14, Wis 15, Cha 15
Skills: Appraise +12, Concentration +12, Craft (any one) +12, Diplomacy +4, Escape Artist +14, Knowledge (any one) +12, Listen +12, Move Silently +14, Sense Motive +12, Spellcraft +12, Spot +12, Use Rope +4 (+6 with bindings)
Feats: Combat Casting, Combat Reflexes, Dodge, Improved Initiative[B]
Environment: Elemental Plane of Air
Organization: Solitary, company (2–4), or band (6–15)
Challenge Rating: 5 (noble 8)
Treasure: Standard
Alignment: Always chaotic good
Advancement: 8–10 HD (Large); 11–21 (Huge)
Level Adjustment: +6

The being looks like a well-formed human with a dark complexion, but nearly twice as tall.

The djinn (singular djinni) are genies from the Elemental Plane of Air. They live on floating islands of earth and rock, anywhere from 3,000 feet to several miles across, crammed with buildings, courtyards, gardens, fountains, and sculptures. Each island is ruled by a local sheik.

The structure of djinn society is based on rule by a caliph served by various nobles and officials (viziers, beys, amirs, sheiks, sharifs, and maliks). A caliph rules all djinn estates within two days' travel and is advised by six viziers who help maintain the balance of the landholds.

If a large force attacks a landhold, a messenger (usually the youngest djinni) is sent to the next landhold, which sends aid and dispatches two more messengers to warn the next landholds, thus alerting the entire nation.

A djinni is about 10-1/2 feet tall and weighs about 1,000 pounds. Djinn speak Auran, Celestial, Common, and Ignan.

Combat

Djinn disdain physical combat, preferring to use their magical powers and aerial abilities against foes. A djinni overmatched in combat usually takes flight and becomes a whirlwind to harass those who follow.

Air Mastery (Ex): Airborne creatures take a –1 penalty on attack and damage rolls against a djinni.

Spell-Like Abilities: At will—*invisibility* (self only); 1/day—*create food and water, create wine* (as *create water*, but wine instead), *major creation* (created vegetable matter is permanent), *persistent image* (DC 17), *wind walk*. Once per day, a djinni can assume *gaseous form* (as the spell) for up to 1 hour. Caster level 20th. The save DCs are Charisma-based.

Whirlwind (Su): A djinni can transform itself into a whirlwind once every 10 minutes and remain in that form for up to 7 rounds. In this form, it can move through the air or along a surface at its fly speed.

The whirlwind is 5 feet wide at the base, up to 30 feet wide at the top and up to 50 feet tall. The djinni controls the exact height, but it must be at least 10 feet.

A djinni's movement while in whirlwind form does not provoke attacks of opportunity, even if the djinni enters the space another creature occupies. Another creature might be caught in the whirlwind if it touches or enters the whirlwind, or if the djinni moves into or through the creature's space.

Creatures one or more size categories smaller than the djinni might take damage when caught in the whirlwind and be lifted into the air. An affected creature must succeed on a DC 20 Reflex save when it comes into contact with the whirlwind or take 3d6 points of damage. It must also succeed on a second DC 20 Reflex save or be picked up bodily and held suspended in the powerful winds, automatically taking 1d8 points of damage each round. A creature with a fly speed is allowed a DC 20 Reflex save each round to escape the whirlwind. The creature still takes damage but can leave if the save is successful. The save DC is Strength-based and includes a +3 racial adjustment.

Creatures trapped in the whirlwind cannot move except to go where the djinni carries them or to escape the whirlwind. Creatures caught in the whirlwind can otherwise act normally, but must make a Concentration check (DC 15 + spell level) to cast a spell. Creatures caught in the whirlwind take a –4 penalty to Dexterity and a –2 penalty on attack rolls. The djinni can have only as many trapped inside a whirlwind at one time as will fit inside the whirlwind's volume.

The djinni can eject any carried creatures whenever it wishes, depositing them wherever the whirlwind happens to be.

If the whirlwind's base touches the ground, it creates a swirling cloud of debris. This cloud is centered on the djinni and has a diameter equal to half the whirlwind's height. The cloud obscures all vision, including darkvision, beyond 5 feet. Creatures 5 feet away have concealment, while those farther away have total concealment. Those caught in the cloud must succeed on a Concentration check (DC 15 + spell level) to cast a spell.

A djinni in whirlwind form cannot make melee attacks and does not threaten the area around it.

Noble Djinn

Some djinn (1% of the total population) are noble. A noble djinni can grant three *wishes* to any being (nongenies only) who captures it. Noble djinn perform no other services and, upon granting the third *wish*, are free of their servitude. Noble djinn are as strong as efreet (see below), with 10 Hit Dice.

EFREETI

Large Outsider (Extraplanar, Fire)

Hit Dice: 10d8+20 (65 hp)
Initiative: +7
Speed: 20 ft. (4 squares), fly 40 ft. (perfect)
Armor Class: 18 (–1 size, +3 Dex, +6 natural), touch 12, flat-footed 15
Base Attack/Grapple: +10/+20
Attack: Slam +15 melee (1d8+6 plus 1d6 fire)
Full Attack: 2 slams +15 melee (1d8+6 plus 1d6 fire)
Space/Reach: 10 ft./ 10 ft.
Special Attacks: *Change size, heat, spell-like abilities*
Special Qualities: Darkvision 60 ft., immunity to fire, *plane shift*, telepathy 100 ft., vulnerability to cold
Saves: Fort +9, Ref +10, Will +9
Abilities: Str 23, Dex 17, Con 14, Int 12, Wis 15, Cha 15
Skills: Bluff +15, Craft (any one) +14, Concentration +15, Diplomacy +6, Disguise +2 (+4 acting), Intimidate +17, Listen +15, Move Silently +16, Sense Motive +15, Spellcraft +14, Spot +15
Feats: Combat Casting, Combat Reflexes, Dodge, Improved Initiative[B], Quicken Spell-Like Ability (*scorching ray*)
Environment: Elemental Plane of Fire
Organization: Solitary, company (2–4), or band (6–15)
Challenge Rating: 8
Treasure: Standard coins; double goods; standard items
Alignment: Always lawful evil
Advancement: 11–15 HD (Large); 16–30 HD (Huge)
Level Adjustment: —

Djinni

Efreeti

This being looks like a mighty giant with brick-red skin, fiery eyes, small horns, and jutting tusks.

The efreet (singular efreeti) are genies from the Elemental Plane of Fire. They are said to be made of basalt, bronze, and congealed flames.

Efreet are infamous for their hatred of servitude, desire for revenge, cruel nature, and ability to beguile and mislead. Their primary home is the fabled City of Brass, but there are many efreet outposts throughout the Elemental Plane of Fire, military stations for watching or harassing others on the plane. Efreet are enemies of the djinn and attack them whenever they meet.

The efreet are ruled by a grand sultan who makes his home in the City of Brass. He is advised by a variety of beys, amirs, and maliks concerning actions on the plane, and by six great pashas who deal with efreet business on the Material Plane.

The City of Brass is a huge citadel that is home to the majority of efreet. It hovers in the hot regions of the plane and is bordered by seas and lakes of glowing magma. The city sits upon a hemisphere of glowing brass some 40 miles in diameter. From the upper towers rise the minarets of the great bastion of the sultan's palace, which is said to hold vast riches. The city's population far outnumbers that of any of the great cities of the Material Plane.

An efreeti stands about 12 feet tall and weighs about 2,000 pounds.

Efreet speak Auran, Common, Ignan, and Infernal.

Combat

Efreet love to mislead, befuddle, and confuse their foes. They do so for enjoyment as well as a battle tactic.

Change Size (Sp): Twice per day, an efreeti can magically change a creature's size. This works just like an *enlarge person* or *reduce person* spell (the efreeti chooses when using the ability), except that the ability can work on the efreeti. A DC 13 Fortitude save negates the effect. The save DC is Charisma-based. This is the equivalent of a 2nd-level spell.

Heat (Ex): An efreeti's red-hot body deals 1d6 points of extra fire damage whenever it hits in melee, or in each round it maintains a hold when grappling.

Spell-Like Abilities: At will—*detect magic, produce flame, pyrotechnics* (DC 14), *scorching ray* (1 ray only); 3/day—*invisibility, wall of fire* (DC 16); 1/day—grant up to three *wishes* (to nongenies only), *gaseous form, permanent image* (DC 18), *polymorph* (self only). Caster level 12th. The save DCs are Charisma-based.

JANNI

Medium Outsider (Native)

Hit Dice: 6d8+6 (33 hp)

Initiative: +6

Speed: 20 ft. (4 squares), fly 15 ft. (perfect) in chainmail; base land speed 30 ft., base fly speed 20 ft. (perfect)

Armor Class: 18 (+2 Dex, +1 natural, +5 chainmail), touch 12, flat-footed 16

Base Attack/Grapple: +6/+9

Attack: Scimitar +9 melee (1d6+4/18–20) or longbow +8 ranged (1d8/×3)

Full Attack: Scimitar +9/+4 melee (1d6+4/18–20) or longbow +8/+3 ranged (1d8/×3)

Space/Reach: 5 ft./5 ft.

Special Attacks: *Change size,* spell-like abilities

Special Qualities: Darkvision 60 ft., elemental endurance, *plane shift,* resistance to fire 10, telepathy 100 ft.

Saves: Fort +6, Ref +7, Will +7

Abilities: Str 16, Dex 15, Con 12, Int 14, Wis 15, Cha 13

Skills: Appraise +11, Concentration +10, Craft (any two) +11, Diplomacy +3, Escape Artist +6, Listen +11, Move Silently +6, Ride +11, Sense Motive +11, Spot +11, Use Rope +2 (+4 with bindings)

Feats: Combat Reflexes, Dodge, Improved Initiative[B], Mobility

Environment: Warm deserts

Organization: Solitary, company (2–4), or band (6–15)

Challenge Rating: 4

Treasure: Standard

Alignment: Usually neutral

Advancement: 7–9 HD (Medium); 10–18 HD (Large)

Level Adjustment: +5

This creature looks like a tall human. It stands proudly, with a regal bearing that is almost palpable.

The jann (singular janni) are the weakest of the genies. Jann are formed out of all four elements and must therefore spend most of their time on the Material Plane. They favor forlorn deserts and hidden oases, where they have both privacy and safety.

Jann society is very open, treating males and females as equals. Each tribe is ruled by a sheik and one or two viziers. Exceptionally powerful sheiks are given the title of amir, and in times of need they gather and command large forces of jann (and sometimes allied humans).

Many jann bands are nomadic, traveling with herds of camels, goats, or sheep from oasis to oasis. These itinerant jann are often mistaken for humans—until they are attacked. The territory of a jann tribe can extend for hundreds of miles.

Jann speak Common, one elemental language (Aquan, Auran, Ignan, or Terran) and one alignment language (Abyssal, Celestial, or Infernal).

Combat

Jann are physically strong and courageous, and do not take kindly to insult or injury. If they meet a foe they cannot defeat in a stand-up fight, they use flight and *invisibility* to regroup and maneuver to a more advantageous position.

Change Size (Sp): Twice per day, a janni can magically change a creature's size. This works just like an *enlarge person* or *reduce person* spell (the janni chooses when using the ability), except that the ability can work on the janni. A DC 13 Fortitude save negates the effect. The save DC is Charisma-based. This is the equivalent of a 2nd-level spell.

Spell-Like Abilities: 3/day—*invisibility* (self only), *speak with animals.* Caster level 12th. Once per day a janni can *create food and water* (caster level 7th) and can use *ethereal jaunt* (caster level 12th) for 1 hour. The save DCs are Charisma-based.

Elemental Endurance (Ex): Jann can survive on the Elemental Planes of Air, Earth, Fire, or Water for up to 48 hours. Failure to return to the Material Plane before that time expires causes a janni to take 1 point of damage per additional hour spent on the elemental plane, until it dies or returns to the Material Plane.

Jann as Characters

Janni characters possess the following racial traits.

— +6 Strength, +4 Dexterity, +2 Constitution, +4 Intelligence, +4 Wisdom, +2 Charisma.

—Medium size.

—A janni's base land speed is 30 feet. It also has a fly speed of 20 feet (perfect).

—Darkvision out to 60 feet.

—Racial Hit Dice: A janni begins with six levels of outsider, which provide 6d8 Hit Dice, a base attack bonus of +6, and base saving throw bonuses of Fort +5, Ref +5, and Will +5.

—Racial Skills: A janni's outsider levels give it skill points equal to 9 × (8 + Int modifier). Its class skills are Appraise, Concentration, Craft (any), Escape Artist, Listen, Move Silently, Ride, Sense Motive, and Spot.

—Racial Feats: A janni's outsider levels give it three feats. A janni receives Improved Initiative as a bonus feat.

— +1 natural armor bonus.

—Special Attacks (see above): *Change size,* spell-like abilities.

—Special Qualities (see above): Elemental endurance, *plane shift,* resistance to fire 10, telepathy 100 ft.

—Automatic Languages: Common. Bonus Languages: Abyssal, Aquan, Auran, Celestial, Ignan, Infernal, Terran.

—Favored Class: Rogue.

—Level adjustment +5.

GHOST

Ghosts are the spectral remnants of intelligent beings who, for one reason or another, cannot rest easily in their graves.

Some ghosts go about their business with little or no interest in the living. Others, however, are malevolent spirits who loathe all life and seek to destroy it whenever possible. Although ghosts can often be driven off or destroyed, they return again and again until they deal with the reason for their existence.

A ghost greatly resembles its corporeal form in life, but in some cases the spiritual form is somewhat altered. Some ghosts look angelic and sweet, while others are twisted and horrible things, showing clearly the agony of the undead. There is often—but not always—a correlation between a ghost's appearance and its alignment. Assumptions are dangerous.

A ghost's behavior usually matches its life. The spirit of a miserly person, for example, might continue to hoard wealth even though it has no use for such treasures. Similarly, a ghost is generally tied to the place where it died. If the aforementioned miser had died in a robbery, the ghost might remain in the counting house, tormenting the new owner and all who do business there. This is not a hard and fast rule, though—many ghosts wander freely.

SAMPLE GHOST

This creature appears to be a human soldier or guardsman, outfitted with heavy armor and a shield. The image is hazy and translucent, suggesting something not natural.

This example ghost uses a 5th-level human fighter as the base creature.

Ghost 5th-Level Human Fighter
Medium Undead (Augmented Humanoid) (Incorporeal)
Hit Dice: 5d12 (32 hp)
Initiative: +5
Speed: Fly 30 ft. (perfect) (6 squares)
Armor Class: 12 (+1 Dex, +1 deflection), touch 12, flat-footed 11, or 21 (+1 Dex, +8 full plate, +2 heavy shield), touch 11, flat-footed 20
Base Attack/Grapple: +5/+8
Attack: Incorporeal touch +6 melee or +8 against ethereal foes (1d6 or 1d6+3 against ethereal foes); or masterwork bastard sword +10 melee (1d10+3/19–20); or masterwork shortbow +7 ranged (1d6/×3)
Full Attack: Incorporeal touch +6 melee or +8 against ethereal foes (1d6 or 1d6+3 against ethereal foes); or masterwork bastard sword +10 melee (1d10+3/19–20); or masterwork shortbow +7 ranged (1d6/×3)
Space/Reach: 5 ft./5 ft.
Special Attacks: Corrupting touch, malevolence, manifestation
Special Qualities: Darkvision 60 ft., incorporeal traits, rejuvenation, +4 turn resistance, undead traits
Saves: Fort +4, Ref +2, Will +2
Abilities: Str 16, Dex 13, Con —, Int 10, Wis 12, Cha 12
Skills: Climb +1, Hide –1, Listen +11, Ride +9, Search +8, Spot +11
Feats: Blind-Fight, Cleave, Exotic Weapon Proficiency (bastard sword), Improved Initiative, Power Attack, Weapon Focus (bastard sword)
Environment: Temperate plains
Organization: Solitary, gang (2–4), or mob (7–12)
Challenge Rating: 7
Treasure: None
Alignment: Any
Level Adjustment: +5

The Will save DC is 16 against this ghost's malevolence.

Ghosts

CREATING A GHOST

"Ghost" is an acquired template that can be added to any aberration, animal, dragon, giant, humanoid, magical beast, monstrous humanoid, or plant. The creature (referred to hereafter as the base creature) must have a Charisma score of at least 6.

A ghost uses all the base creature's statistics and special abilities except as noted here.

Size and Type: The creature's type changes to undead. Do not recalculate the creature's base attack bonus, saves, or skill points. It gains the incorporeal subtype. Size is unchanged.

Hit Dice: All current and future Hit Dice become d12s.

Speed: Ghosts have a fly speed of 30 feet, unless the base creature has a higher fly speed, with perfect maneuverability.

Armor Class: Natural armor is the same as the base creature's but applies only to ethereal encounters. When the ghost manifests (see below), its natural armor bonus is +0, but it gains a deflection bonus equal to its Charisma modifier or +1, whichever is higher.

Attack: A ghost retains all the attacks of the base creature, although those relying on physical contact do not affect creatures that are not ethereal.

Full Attack: A ghost retains all the attacks of the base creature, although those relying on physical contact do not affect creatures that are not ethereal.

Damage: Against ethereal creatures, a ghost uses the base creature's damage values. Against non-ethereal creatures, the ghost usually cannot deal physical damage at all but can use its special attacks, if any, when it manifests (see below).

Special Attacks: A ghost retains all the special attacks of the base creature, although those relying on physical contact do not affect nonethereal creatures. The ghost also gains a manifestation ability plus one to three other special attacks as described below. The save DC against a special attack is equal to 10 + 1/2 ghost's HD + ghost's Cha modifier unless otherwise noted.

Corrupting Gaze (Su): A ghost can blast living beings with a glance, at a range of up to 30 feet. Creatures that meet the ghost's gaze must succeed on a Fortitude save or take 2d10 points of damage and 1d4 points of Charisma damage.

Corrupting Touch (Su): A ghost that hits a living target with its incorporeal touch attack deals 1d6 points of damage. Against ethereal opponents, it adds its Strength modifier to attack and damage rolls. Against nonethereal opponents, it adds its Dexterity modifier to attack rolls only.

Draining Touch (Su): A ghost that hits a living target with its incorporeal touch attack drains 1d4 points from any one ability score it selects. On each such successful attack, the ghost heals

5 points of damage to itself. Against ethereal opponents, it adds its Strength modifier to attack rolls only. Against nonethereal opponents, it adds its Dexterity modifier to attack rolls only.

Frightful Moan (Su): A ghost can emit a frightful moan as a standard action. All living creatures within a 30-foot spread must succeed on a Will save or become panicked for 2d4 rounds. This is a sonic necromantic mind-affecting fear effect. A creature that successfully saves against the moan cannot be affected by the same ghost's moan for 24 hours.

Horrific Appearance (Su): Any living creature within 60 feet that views a ghost must succeed on a Fortitude save or immediately take 1d4 points of Strength damage, 1d4 points of Dexterity damage, and 1d4 points of Constitution damage. A creature that successfully saves against this effect cannot be affected by the same ghost's horrific appearance for 24 hours.

Malevolence (Su): Once per round, an ethereal ghost can merge its body with a creature on the Material Plane. This ability is similar to a *magic jar* spell (caster level 10th or the ghost's Hit Dice, whichever is higher), except that it does not require a receptacle. To use this ability, the ghost must be manifested and it must try move into the target's space; moving into the target's space to use the malevolence ability does not provoke attacks of opportunity. The target can resist the attack with a successful Will save (DC 15 + ghost's Cha modifier). A creature that successfully saves is immune to that same ghost's malevolence for 24 hours, and the ghost cannot enter the target's space. If the save fails, the ghost vanishes into the target's body.

Manifestation (Su): Every ghost has this ability. A ghost dwells on the Ethereal Plane and, as an ethereal creature, it cannot affect or be affected by anything in the material world. When a ghost manifests, it partly enters the Material Plane and becomes visible but incorporeal on the Material Plane. A manifested ghost can be harmed only by other incorporeal creatures, magic weapons, or spells, with a 50% chance to ignore any damage from a corporeal source. A manifested ghost can pass through solid objects at will, and its own attacks pass through armor. A manifested ghost always moves silently.

A manifested ghost can strike with its touch attack or with a ghost touch weapon (see Ghostly Equipment, below). A manifested ghost remains partially on the Ethereal Plane, where is it not incorporeal. A manifested ghost can be attacked by opponents on either the Material Plane or the Ethereal Plane. The ghost's incorporeality helps protect it from foes on the Material Plane, but not from foes on the Ethereal Plane.

When a spellcasting ghost is not manifested and is on the Ethereal Plane, its spells cannot affect targets on the Material Plane, but they work normally against ethereal targets. When a spellcasting ghost manifests, its spells continue to affect ethereal targets and can affect targets on the Material Plane normally unless the spells rely on touch. A manifested ghost's touch spells don't work on nonethereal targets.

A ghost has two home planes, the Material Plane and the Ethereal Plane. It is not considered extraplanar when on either of these planes.

Telekinesis (Su): A ghost can use *telekinesis* as a standard action (caster level 12th or equal to the ghost's HD, whichever is higher). When a ghost uses this power, it must wait 1d4 rounds before using it again.

Special Qualities: A ghost has all the special qualities of the base creature as well as those described below.

Rejuvenation (Su): In most cases, it's difficult to destroy a ghost through simple combat: The "destroyed" spirit will often restore itself in 2d4 days. Even the most powerful spells are usually only temporary solutions. A ghost that would otherwise be destroyed returns to its old haunts with a successful level check (1d20 + ghost's HD) against DC 16. As a rule, the only way to get rid of a ghost for sure is to determine the reason for its existence and set right whatever prevents it from resting in peace. The exact means varies with each spirit and may require a good deal of research.

Turn Resistance (Ex): A ghost has +4 turn resistance.

Abilities: Same as the base creature, except that the ghost has no Constitution score, and its Charisma score increases by +4.

Skills: Ghosts have a +8 racial bonus on Hide, Listen, Search, and Spot checks. Otherwise same as the base creature.

Environment: Any, often as base creature.

Organization: Solitary, gang (2–4), or mob (7–12).

Challenge Rating: Same as the base creature +2.

Treasure: None.

Alignment: Any.

Level Adjustment: Same as the base creature +5.

Ghostly Equipment

When a ghost forms, all its equipment and carried items usually become ethereal along with it. In addition, the ghost retains 2d4 items that it particularly valued in life (provided they are not in another creature's possession). The equipment works normally on the Ethereal Plane but passes harmlessly through material objects or creatures. A weapon of +1 or better magical enhancement, however, can harm material creatures when the ghost manifests, but any such attack has a 50% chance to fail unless the weapon is a ghost touch weapon (just as magic weapons can fail to harm the ghost).

The original material items remain behind, just as the ghost's physical remains do. If another creature seizes the original, the ethereal copy fades away. This loss invariably angers the ghost, who stops at nothing to return the item to its original resting place.

GHOUL

This foul creature appears more or less humanoid, but has mottled, decaying flesh drawn tight across clearly visible bones. It is mostly hairless and has a carnivore's sharp teeth. Its eyes burn like hot coals in their sunken sockets.

Ghouls haunt graveyards, battlefields, and other places rich with the carrion they hunger for. These terrible creatures lurk wherever the stench of death hangs heavy, ready to devour the unwary.

Ghouls are said to be created upon the death of a living man or woman who savored the taste of the flesh of people. This assertion may or may not be true, but it does explain the disgusting behavior of these anthropophagous undead. Some believe that anyone of exceptional debauchery and wickedness runs the risk of becoming a ghoul. The transformation from living beings into fell things of the night has warped their minds, making them cunning and feral.

Ghouls speak the languages they spoke in life (usually Common).

COMBAT

Ghouls try to attack with surprise whenever possible. They strike from behind tombstones and burst from shallow graves.

Ghoul Fever (Su): Disease—bite, Fortitude DC 12, incubation period 1 day, damage 1d3 Con and 1d3 Dex. The save DC is Charisma-based.

An afflicted humanoid who dies of ghoul fever rises as a ghoul at the next midnight. A humanoid who becomes a ghoul in this way retains none of the abilities it possessed in life. It is not under the control of any other ghouls, but it hungers for the flesh of the living and behaves like a normal ghoul in all respects. A humanoid of 4 Hit Dice or more rises as a ghast, not a ghoul.

Paralysis (Ex): Those hit by a ghoul's bite or claw attack must succeed on a DC 12 Fortitude save or be paralyzed for 1d4+1 rounds. Elves have immunity to this paralysis. The save DC is Charisma-based.

LACEDON

These cousins of the ghoul have the aquatic subtype. They lurk near hidden reefs or other places where ships are likely to meet their end. They have a base land speed of 30 feet and a swim speed of 30 feet and are found only in aquatic environments.

GHAST

Although these creatures look just like their lesser kin, they are far more deadly and cunning.

Combat

Ghoul Fever (Su): Disease—bite, Fortitude DC 15, incubation period 1 day, damage 1d3 Con and 1d3 Dex. The save DC is Charisma-based.

Paralysis (Ex): Those hit by a ghast's bite or claw attack must succeed on a DC 15 Fortitude save or be paralyzed for 1d4+1 rounds. Even elves can be affected by this paralysis. The save DC is Charisma-based.

Stench (Ex): The stink of death and corruption surrounding these creatures is overwhelming. Living creatures within 10 feet must succeed on a DC 15 Fortitude save or be sickened for 1d6+4 minutes. A creature that successfully saves

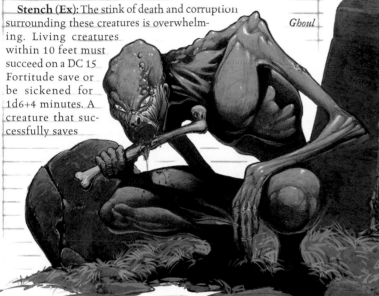

Ghoul

cannot be affected again by the same ghast's stench for 24 hours. A *delay poison* or *neutralize poison* spell removes the effect from a sickened creature. Creatures with immunity to poison are unaffected, and creatures resistant to poison receive their normal bonus on their saving throws. The save DC is Charisma-based.

GIANT

Giants combine great size with great strength, giving them an unparalleled ability to wreak destruction upon anyone or anything unfortunate enough to get in their way.

Giants have a reputation for crudeness and stupidity that is not undeserved, especially among the evil varieties. Most rely on their tremendous strength to solve problems, reasoning that any difficulty that won't succumb to brute force isn't worth worrying about. Giants usually subsist by hunting and raiding, taking what they like from creatures weaker than themselves.

All giants speak Giant. Those with Intelligence scores of 10 or higher also speak Common.

COMBAT

Giants relish melee combat. They favor massive two-handed weapons and wield them with impressive skill. They have enough cunning to soften up a foe with ranged attacks first, if they can. A giant's favorite ranged weapon is a big rock.

Rock Throwing (Ex): Adult giants are accomplished rock throwers and receive a +1 racial bonus on attack rolls when throwing rocks. A giant of at least Large size can hurl rocks weighing 40 to 50 pounds each (Small objects) up to five range increments. The size of the range increment varies with the giant's variety. A Huge giant can hurl rocks of 60 to 80 pounds (Medium objects).

Rock Catching (Ex): A giant of at least Large size can catch Small, Medium, or Large rocks (or projectiles of similar shape). Once per round, a giant that would normally be hit by a rock can

Illus. by B. Snoddy

	Ghoul	Ghast
	Medium Undead	Medium Undead
Hit Dice:	2d12 (13 hp)	4d12+3 (29 hp)
Initiative:	+2	+3
Speed:	30 ft. (6 squares)	30 ft. (6 squares)
Armor Class:	14 (+2 Dex, +2 natural), touch 12, flat-footed 12	17 (+3 Dex, +4 natural), touch 12, flat-footed 14
Base Attack/Grapple:	+1/+2	+2/+5
Attack:	Bite +2 melee (1d6+1 plus paralysis)	Bite +5 melee (1d8+3 plus paralysis)
Full Attack:	Bite +2 melee (1d6+1 plus paralysis) and 2 claws +0 melee (1d3 plus paralysis)	Bite +5 melee (1d8+3 plus paralysis) and 2 claws +3 melee (1d4+1 plus paralysis)
Space/Reach:	5 ft./5 ft.	5 ft./5 ft.
Special Attacks:	Ghoul fever, paralysis	Ghoul fever, paralyis, stench
Special Qualities:	Darkvision 60 ft., undead traits, +2 turn resistance	Darkvision 60 ft., undead traits, +2 turn resistance
Saves:	Fort +0, Ref +2, Will +5	Fort +1, Ref +4, Will +6
Abilities:	Str 13, Dex 15, Con —, Int 13, Wis 14, Cha 12	Str 17, Dex 17, Con —, Int 13, Wis 14, Cha 16
Skills:	Balance +6, Climb +5, Hide +6, Jump +5, Move Silently +6, Spot +7	Balance +7, Climb +9, Hide +8, Jump +9, Move Silently +8, Spot +8
Feats:	Multiattack	Multiattack, Toughness
Environment:	Any (Lacedon: Any aquatic)	Any
Organization:	Solitary, gang (2–4), or pack (7–12)	Solitary, gang (2–4), or pack (2–4 plus 7–12 ghouls)
Challenge Rating:	1	3
Treasure:	None	Standard
Alignment:	Always chaotic evil	Always chaotic evil
Advancement:	3 HD (Medium)	5–8 HD (Medium)
Level Adjustment:	—	—

make a Reflex save to catch it as a free action. The DC is 15 for a Small rock, 20 for a Medium one, and 25 for a Large one. (If the projectile provides a magical bonus on attack rolls, the DC increases by that amount.) The giant must be ready for and aware of the attack in order to make a rock catching attempt.

GIANT SOCIETY

Solitary giants are often young adults striking out on their own. Gangs are usually made up of young adults who hunt or raid (or both) together. Giant bands are usually large or extended families. Sometimes a band contains unrelated young adults that the band has taken in as mates, servants, or guards.

Giant tribes are similar to bands but have more members, plus contingents of guard creatures and nongiant servants. Hunting and raiding parties include guard creatures and may be made up of giants from different tribes working together.

About a third of the giants in a band or tribe are giant children, who can be formidable creatures in their own right. When a group of giants includes children, roll d% for each child to determine maturity: 01–25 = infant (no combat ability); 26–50 = juvenile (two sizes smaller than an adult, 8 fewer HD, –8 Strength, –8 Constitution, and 1 rank in each skill that an adult has); and 51–100 = adolescent (one size smaller than an adult, 4 fewer HD, –4 Strength, –4 Constitution, and 2, 3, or 4 ranks in each skill that an adult has). Giant children can throw rocks if they meet the minimum size requirement (see above). Except when otherwise noted, giant children are identical with adults of their variety.

CLOUD GIANT

Huge Giant (Air)
Hit Dice: 17d8+102 (178 hp)
Initiative: +1
Speed: 50 ft. (10 squares)
Armor Class: 25 (–2 size, +1 Dex, +12 natural, +4 chain shirt), touch 9, flat-footed 24
Base Attack/Grapple: +12/+32
Attack: Gargantuan morningstar +22 melee (4d6+18) or slam +22 melee (1d6+12) or rock +12 ranged (2d8+12)
Full Attack: Gargantuan morningstar +22/+17/+12 melee (4d6+18) or 2 slams +22 melee (1d6+12) or rock +12 ranged (2d8+12)
Space/Reach: 15 ft./15 ft.
Special Attacks: Rock throwing, spell-like abilities
Special Qualities: Low-light vision, oversized weapon, rock catching, scent
Saves: Fort +16, Ref +6, Will +10
Abilities: Str 35, Dex 13, Con 23, Int 12, Wis 16, Cha 13
Skills: Climb +19, Craft (any one) +11, Diplomacy +3, Intimidate +11, Listen +15, Perform (harp) +2, Sense Motive +9, Spot +15
Feats: Awesome Blow, Cleave, Improved Bull Rush, Improved Overrun, Iron Will, Power Attack
Environment: Temperate mountains
Organization: Solitary, gang (2–4), family (2–4 plus 35% noncombatants plus 1 sorcerer or cleric of 4th–7th level plus 2–5 griffons or 2–8 dire lions), or band (6–9 plus 1 sorcerer or cleric of 4th–7th level plus 2–5 griffons or 2–8 dire lions)
Challenge Rating: 11
Treasure: Standard coins; double goods; standard items
Alignment: Usually neutral good or neutral evil
Advancement: By character class
Level Adjustment: —

This giant has a muscular humanoid build and handsome, well-defined features. Its skin is milky white tinged with blue, and it has silvery white hair.

Cloud giants consider themselves above all others, except storm giants, whom they regard as equals. They are creative, appreciate fine things, and are master strategists in battle.

Cloud giants' skin ranges in color from milky white to light sky blue. Their hair is silvery white or brass, and their eyes are iridescent blue. Adult males are about 18 feet tall and weigh about 5,000 pounds. Females are slightly shorter and lighter. Cloud giants can live to be 400 years old.

Cloud giants dress in the finest clothing available and wear jewelry. To many, appearance indicates station: The better the clothes and the finer the jewelry, the more important the wearer. They also appreciate music, and most can play one or more instruments (the harp is a favorite).

Unlike most other giant varieties, cloud giants leave their treasure in their lairs. A could giant's bag contains food, 1d4+1 throwing rocks, 3d4 mundane items, a modest amount of cash (no more

GIANTS' BAGS

Most giants carry big leather shoulder sacks to hold their personal possessions. It is a common myth that giants' bags are stuffed with gold (always at least 1,000 gp, by some accounts). In truth, they usually hold a few battered and smelly personal items, a supply of throwing rocks, some less than fresh rations, and a few trinkets. However, giants sometimes carry magic treasures that are too small for them to use, and many adventurers find looting a giant's bag to be worthwhile. The table below shows typical mundane items; roll d% or choose from the list. The number of items in a bag varies according to the giant variety (see each description).

d%	Item
01–02	Berries or fruit
03–08	Bowl and spoon
09–10	Candles (1d6)
11–14	Hand-held chopper
15–16	Sticks of charcoal (1d6) or quills and ink
17–18	Chunk of cheese
19–20	Chunk of wood, whittled or carved
21–23	Cup or tankard
24–27	Cloak

d%	Item
28–29	Comb or brush
30–31	Cooking pot
32–33	Container of grease or grease paint
34–35	Drinking horn
36–37	Bag of flour or meal (5 pounds)
38–39	Piece of fur or hide
40–41	Hairpins
42–47	Knife
48–53	Knucklebones or dice
54–57	Haunch of meat
58–59	Incense or dried animal dung
60–65	100 to 200 feet of strong rope
66–67	Bag of salt (1 pound)
68–73	Shoes, sandals, or boots
74–76	Sewing needle
77–81	String or thread
82–86	Beads, stones, teeth, or tusks
87–93	Tinderbox (flint, steel, and tinder)
94–96	Lump of wax
97–100	Whetstone

than 10d10 coins), and a musical instrument. A cloud giant's possessions are usually well made and maintained.

Combat

Cloud giants fight in well-organized units, using carefully developed battle plans. They prefer to fight from a position above their opponents. A favorite tactic is to circle the enemies, barraging them with rocks while the giants with magical abilities confound them with spells.

Rock Throwing (Ex): The range increment is 140 feet for a cloud giant's thrown rocks.

Oversized Weapon (Ex): A cloud giant wields a great, two-handed morningstar (big enough for Gargantuan creatures) without penalty.

Spell-Like Abilities: 3/day—*levitate* (self plus 2,000 pounds), *obscuring mist*; 1/day—*fog cloud*. Caster level 15th.

Cloud Giant Society

The majority of cloud giants dwell on cloud-shrouded mountain peaks, making their lairs in crude castles. They live in small groups but know the location of 1d8 other groups and come together with some of these other tribes for celebrations, battles, or trade.

Good-aligned cloud giants trade with humanoid communities for food, wine, jewelry, and cloth. Some establish such good relations that they come to a community's aid if it is endangered. Evil-aligned cloud giants raid communities to get what they want.

Legends tell of rare cloud giants that build castles on magical cloud islands isolated even from other cloud giants.

Cloud islands are reputed to be fantastic places with giant-sized gardens of fruit trees.

Cloud Giant Characters

Most cloud giant groups include a sorcerer or a cleric. Good-aligned clerics have access to two of the following domains: Good, Healing, Strength, or Sun. Evil-aligned clerics have access to two of the following domains: Death, Evil, or Trickery.

FIRE GIANT

Large Giant (Fire)
Hit Dice: 15d8+75 (142 hp)
Initiative: –1
Speed: 30 ft. in half-plate armor (6 squares); base speed 40 ft.
Armor Class: 23 (–1 size, –1 Dex, +8 natural, +7 half-plate armor) touch 8, flat-footed 23
Base Attack/Grapple: +11/+25
Attack: Greatsword +20 melee (3d6+15) or slam +20 melee (1d4+10) or rock +10 ranged (2d6+10 plus 2d6 fire)
Full Attack: Greatsword +20/+15/+10 melee (3d6+15) or 2 slams +20 melee (1d4+10) or rock +10 ranged (2d6+10 plus 2d6 fire)
Space/Reach: 10 ft./10 ft.
Special Attacks: Rock throwing

Special Qualities: Immunity to fire, low-light vision, rock catching, vulnerability to cold
Saves: Fort +14, Ref +4, Will +9
Abilities: Str 31, Dex 9, Con 21, Int 10, Wis 14, Cha 11
Skills: Climb +9, Craft (any one) +6, Intimidate +6, Jump +9, Spot +14
Feats: Cleave, Great Cleave, Improved Overrun, Improved Sunder, Iron Will, Power Attack
Environment: Warm mountains
Organization: Solitary, gang (2–5), band (6–9 plus 35% noncombatants plus 1 adept or cleric of 1st or 2nd level), hunting/raiding party (6–9 plus 1 adept or sorcerer of 3rd–5th level plus 2–4 hell hounds and 2–3 trolls or ettins), or tribe (21–30 plus 1 adept, cleric, or sorcerer of 6th or 7th level plus 12–30 hell hounds, 12–22 trolls, 5–12 ettins, and 1–2 young red dragons)
Challenge Rating: 10
Treasure: Standard
Alignment: Often lawful evil
Advancement: By character class
Level Adjustment: +4

This giant resembles a mammoth dwarf with coal-black skin, flaming red hair, and a prognathous jaw that reveals dirty ivory teeth.

Fire giants are brutal, ruthless, and militaristic.

Some fire giants have bright orange hair. An adult male is 12 feet tall, has a chest that measures 9 feet around, and weighs about 7,000 pounds. Females are slightly shorter and lighter. Fire giants can live to be 350 years old.

Fire giants wear sturdy cloth or leather garments colored red, orange, yellow, or black. Warriors wear helmets and half-plate armor of blackened steel.

A typical fire giant's bag contains 1d4+1 throwing rocks, 3d4 mundane items, a tinderbox, and the giant's personal wealth. Everything a fire giant owns is battered, dirty, and often singed by heat.

Combat

Fire giants heat their rocks in a nearby fire, geyser, or lava pools, so that they deal extra fire damage. They favor magic flaming swords in melee (when they can get them). They are also fond of grabbing smaller opponents and tossing them somewhere very hot.

Rock Throwing (Ex): The range increment is 120 feet for a fire giant's thrown rocks.

Fire Giant Society

Fire giants dwell only in hot places. They prefer volcanic regions or areas with hot springs. They live in well-organized military groups, occupying large castles or caverns. Tribal leaders refer to themselves as "king" or "queen." Fire giants usually engage in ongoing military campaigns to subjugate the areas around them and often receive tribute from creatures living nearby.

Fire giants like to take captives. For each ten adult giants in a tribe, there is a 30% chance

Fire giant   Storm giant   Frost giant

	Frost Giant Large Giant (Cold)	Frost Giant Jarl, 8th-Level Blackguard Large Giant (Cold)
Hit Dice:	14d8+70 (133 hp)	14d8+84 plus 8d10+48 (231 hp)
Initiative:	−1	+5
Speed:	40 ft. (8 squares)	30 ft. in +2 *full plate armor* (6 squares); base speed 40 ft.
Armor Class:	21 (−1 size, −1 Dex, +9 natural, +4 chain shirt) touch 8, flat-footed 21	29 (−1 size, +1 Dex, +9 natural, +10 +2 *full plate armor*) touch 10, flat-footed 28
Base Attack/Grapple:	+10/+23	+18/+33
Attack:	Greataxe +18 melee (3d6+13/×3) or slam +18 melee (1d4+9) or rock +9 ranged (2d6+9)	+2 *frost greataxe* +30 melee (3d6+18/×3 plus 1d6 cold) or slam +28 melee (1d4+11) or rock +18 ranged (2d6+11)
Full Attack:	Huge greataxe +18/+13 melee (3d6+13/×3) or 2 slams +18 melee (1d4+9) or rock +9 ranged (2d6+9)	+2 *frost greataxe* +30/+25/+20/+15 melee (3d6+18/×3 plus 1d6 cold) or 2 slams +28 melee (1d4+11) or rock +18 ranged (2d6+11)
Space/Reach:	10 ft./10 ft.	10 ft./10 ft.
Special Attacks:	Rock throwing	Rock throwing, smite good, sneak attack +2d6
Special Qualities:	Immunity to cold, low-light vision, rock catching, vulnerability to fire	Aura of despair, aura of evil, command undead, dark blessing, *detect good*, immunity to cold, low-light vision, poison use, resistance to fire 10, rock catching, vulnerability to fire
Saves:	Fort +14, Ref +3, Will +6	Fort +25, Ref +13, Will +13
Abilities:	Str 29, Dex 9, Con 21, Int 10, Wis 14, Cha 11	Str 32, Dex 12, Con 22, Int 10, Wis 12, Cha 18
Skills:	Climb +13, Craft (any one) +6, Intimidate +6, Jump +17, Spot +12	Climb +17, Hide +2, Jump +17, Knowledge (religion) +2, Ride +11, Spot +5
Feats:	Cleave, Great Cleave, Improved Overrun, Improved Sunder, Power Attack	Cleave, Great Cleave, Improved Initiative, Improved Sunder, Iron Will, Lightning Reflexes, Power Attack, Quick Draw
Environment	Cold mountains	Cold mountains
Organization:	Solitary, gang (2–5), band (6–9 plus 35% noncombatants plus 1 adept or cleric of 1st or 2nd level), hunting/raiding party (6–9 plus 35% noncombatants plus 1 adept or sorcerer of 3rd–5th level plus 2–4 winter wolves and 2–3 ogres), or tribe (21–30 plus 1 adept, cleric, or sorcerer of 6th or 7th level plus 12–30 winter wolves, 12–22 ogres, and 1–2 young white dragons)	Solitary or with tribe
Challenge Rating:	9	17
Treasure:	Standard	Standard
Alignment:	Often chaotic evil	Always chaotic evil
Advancement:	By character class	By character class
Level Adjustment:	+4	—

that the lair has 1d2 captives. These prisoners can be any sort of creature.

Fire Giant Characters

Most groups of fire giants include clerics. A fire giant cleric has access to two of the following domains: Evil, Law, Trickery, or War (most choose Trickery or War, some choose both).

FROST GIANT

This giant looks like a beefy, muscular human with snow-white skin and light blue hair and eyes.

Frost giants are justifiably feared as brutal and wantonly destructive raiders.

A frost giant's hair can be light blue or dirty yellow, and its eyes usually match its hair color. Frost giants dress in skins and pelts, along with any jewelry they own. Frost giant warriors add chain shirts and metal helmets decorated with horns or feathers.

An adult male is about 15 feet tall and weighs about 2,800 pounds. Females are slightly shorter and lighter, but otherwise identical with males. Frost giants can live to be 250 years old.

A frost giant's bag usually contains 1d4+1 throwing rocks, 3d4 mundane items, and the giant's personal wealth. Everything in a frost giant's bag is old, worn, dirty, and smelly, making the identification of any valuable items difficult.

Combat

Frost giants usually start combat at a distance, throwing rocks until they run out of ammunition or the opponent closes, then wading in with their enormous battleaxes.

A favorite tactic is to lay an ambush by hiding buried in the snow at the top of an icy or snowy slope, where opponents will have difficulty reaching them.

Rock Throwing (Ex): The range increment is 120 feet for a frost giant's thrown rocks.

Frost Giant Society

Frost giants live in frigid, arctic lands of glaciers and heavy snowfall. They make their lairs in crude castles or frigid caverns. Tribal leaders call themselves "jarl." Frost giant groups depend on hunting and raiding, though they sometimes make trading and defensive alliances with neighboring giants.

Frost giants like to take captives. For each ten adult giants in a tribe, there is a 20% chance that the lair has 1d2 captives. These prisoners can be any sort of creature.

Frost Giant Characters

Many groups of frost giants include clerics. A frost giant cleric has access to two of the following domains: Chaos, Destruction, Evil, or War (most choose Destruction or War, some choose both).

Frost Giant Jarl

A frost giant leader is often a barbarian, cleric, fighter, or sorcerer, but some of the most evil and ruthless frost giants become blackguards. Ambitious and domineering, they quickly rise to rule their tribes, and then lead their fellows further and further into cruelty and wickedness.

The frost giant jarl described here has all the qualities and abilities of a typical frost giant, as well as other abilities (see the statistics block) from being a blackguard. Details on some of these abilities follow.

Aura of Despair (Su): This jarl radiates a malign aura that causes enemies within 10 feet of him to take a –2 penalty on all saving throws.

Aura of Evil (Ex): This jarl radiates a strong aura of evil (see the *detect evil* spell) as an 8th-level cleric of an evil deity.

Command Undead (Su): This jarl can command and rebuke undead as a 6th-level cleric.

Dark Blessing (Su): This jarl applies his Charisma modifier as a bonus on all saving throws.

Detect Good (Sp): At will, this jarl can use *detect good* as a spell-like ability, duplicating the effect of the *detect good* spell.

Poison Use: Blackguards are skilled in the use of poison and never risk accidentally poisoning themselves when applying poison to a blade.

Smite Good (Su): Twice per day, this jarl may attempt to smite good with one normal melee attack. He adds his +4 Charisma modifier to his attack roll and deals 8 points of extra damage (1 per blackguard level) if the attack hits. If he accidentally smites a creature that is not good, the smite has no effect but it is still used up for that day.

Typical Blackguard Spells Prepared (3/1; save DC 11 + spell level): 1st—cause fear, doom, magic weapon; 2nd—bull's strength.

Possessions: +2 frost greataxe, +2 full plate armor, cloak of Charisma +2, ring of minor energy resistance (fire), 2 doses of bloodroot poison. (Benefits of these items are included in the statistics block.)

HILL GIANT

Large Giant
Hit Dice: 12d8+48 (102 hp)
Initiative: –1
Speed: 30 ft. in hide armor (6 squares); base speed 40 ft.
Armor Class: 20 (–1 size, –1 Dex, +9 natural, +3 hide armor), touch 8, flat-footed 20
Base Attack/Grapple: +9/+20

Attack: Greatclub +16 melee (2d8+10) or slam +15 melee (1d4+7) or rock +8 ranged (2d6+7)
Full Attack: Greatclub +16/+11 melee (2d8+10) or 2 slams +15 melee (1d4+7) or rock +8 ranged (2d6+7)
Space/Reach: 10 ft./10 ft.
Special Attacks: Rock throwing
Special Qualities: Low-light vision, rock catching
Saves: Fort +12, Ref +3, Will +4
Abilities: Str 25, Dex 8, Con 19, Int 6, Wis 10, Cha 7
Skills: Climb +7, Jump +7, Listen +3, Spot +6
Feats: Cleave, Improved Bull Rush, Power Attack, Improved Sunder, Weapon Focus (greatclub)
Environment: Temperate hills
Organization: Solitary, gang (2–5), band (6–9 plus 35% noncombatants), hunting/raiding party (6–9 plus 2–4 dire wolves), or tribe (21–30 plus 35% noncombatants plus 12–30 dire wolves, 2–4 ogres, and 12–22 orcs)
Challenge Rating: 7
Treasure: Standard
Alignment: Often chaotic evil
Advancement: By character class
Level Adjustment: +4

Cloud giant

This giant has an oddly simian appearance, with overlong arms, stooped shoulders, low foreheads, and thick, powerful limbs.

Hill giants are selfish, cunning brutes who survive through hunting and raiding.

Skin color among hill giants ranges from light tan to deep ruddy brown. Their hair is brown or black, with eyes the same color. Hill giants wear layers of crudely prepared hides with the fur left on. They seldom wash or repair their garments, preferring to simply add more hides as their old ones wear out.

Stone giant

Adults are about 10-1/2 feet tall and weigh about 1,100 pounds. Hill giants can live to be 200 years old.

A hill giant's bag usually contains 2d4 throwing rocks, 1d4+4 mundane items, and the giant's personal wealth. These possessions tend to be well worn, filthy, and stinky. The items are usually crude and often jury-rigged or salvaged from some similar item. Examples include a hand chopper made from a broken battleaxe head, a wooden bowl and spoon, or a drinking cup made from a big gourd or a skull.

Hill giant

Combat

Hill giants prefer to fight from high, rocky outcroppings, where they can pelt opponents with rocks and boulders while limiting the risk to themselves.

Hill giants love to make overrun attacks against smaller creatures when they first join battle. Thereafter, they stand fast and swing away with their massive clubs.

Rock Throwing (Ex): The range increment is 120 feet for a hill giant's thrown rocks.

Hill Giant Society

Although hill giants prefer temperate areas, they can be found in practically any climate where there is an abundance of hills and mountains. Individuals and bands tend to be aggressive and prefer taking what they want over trading. Tribes (and some bands) often trade with other giants or with groups of ogres or orcs to get foodstuffs, trinkets, and servants.

Hill Giants as Characters

Reckless brutes of incredible strength but little wit, hill giant characters are never truly accepted into society. Yet they do well on its edges and frontiers, forging a strong and profitable existence. Despite their rugged appearance and great size, their basically humanoid shape makes it easy for them to relate with more civilized folk.

Hill giant characters possess the following racial traits.

— +14 Strength, –2 Dexterity, +8 Constitution, –4 Intelligence, –4 Charisma.

—Large size. –1 penalty to Armor Class, –1 penalty on attack rolls, –4 penalty on Hide checks, +4 bonus on grapple checks, lifting and carrying limits double those of Medium characters.

—Space/Reach: 10 feet/10 feet.

—A hill giant's base land speed is 40 feet.

—Low-light vision.

—Racial Hit Dice: A hill giant begins with twelve levels of giant, which provide 12d8 Hit Dice, a base attack bonus of +8, and base saving throw bonuses of Fort +8, Ref +4, and Will +4.

—Racial Skills: A hill giant's giant levels give it skill points equal to 15 × (2 + Int modifier). Its class skills are Climb, Jump, Listen, and Spot.

—Racial Feats: A hill giant's giant levels give it five feats.

— +9 natural armor bonus.

—Special Attacks (see above): Rock throwing.

—Special Qualities (see above): Rock catching.

—Weapon and Armor Proficiency: A hill giant is automatically proficient with simple weapons, martial weapons, light and medium armor, and shields.

—Automatic Languages: Giant. Bonus Languages: Common, Draconic, Elven, Goblin, Orc.

—Favored Class: Barbarian.

—Level adjustment +4.

STONE GIANT

Large Giant (Earth)
Hit Dice: 14d8+56 (119 hp)
Initiative: +2
Speed: 30 ft. in hide armor (6 squares); base speed 40 ft.
Armor Class: 25 (–1 size, +2 Dex, +11 natural, +3 hide), touch 11, flat-footed 23
Base Attack/Grapple: +10/+22
Attack: Greatclub +17 melee (2d8+12) or slam +17 melee (1d4+8) or rock +11 ranged (2d8+12)
Full Attack: Greatclub +17/+12 melee (2d8+12) or 2 slams +17 melee (1d4+8) or rock +11 ranged (2d8+12)
Space/Reach: 10 ft./10 ft.
Special Attacks: Rock throwing
Special Qualities: Darkvision 60 ft., low-light vision, rock catching
Saves: Fort +13, Ref +6, Will +7
Abilities: Str 27, Dex 15, Con 19, Int 10, Wis 12, Cha 11
Skills: Climb +11, Hide +6*, Jump +11, Spot +12

Feats: Combat Reflexes, Iron Will, Point Blank Shot, Power Attack, Precise Shot
Environment: Temperate mountains
Organization: Solitary, gang (2–5), band (6–9 plus 35% noncombatants), hunting/raiding/trading party (6–9 plus 1 elder), or tribe (21–30 plus 35% noncombatants plus 1–3 elders and 3–6 dire bears)
Challenge Rating: 8 (elder 9)
Treasure: Standard
Alignment: Usually neutral
Advancement: By character class
Level Adjustment: +4 (elder +6)

This giant resembles a lean, muscular human. Its hard, hairless flesh is smooth and gray. It has gaunt facial features and deep-sunken, black eyes that makes it seem grim.

Stone giants have a largely undeserved reputation as rock-throwing hooligans. In fact, they tend to be somewhat shy around strangers.

Stone giants prefer thick leather garments, dyed in shades of brown and gray to match the stone around them.

Adults are about 12 feet tall and weigh about 1,500 pounds. Stone giants can live to be 800 years old.

Stone giants may tend to be shy around strangers, but they are by no means timid. Many stone giants have an artistic streak. Some draw and paint scenes of their lives on the walls of their lairs and on tanned hide scrolls. Some are fond of music and play stone flutes and drums. Others make simple jewelry, fashioning painted stone beads into necklaces.

Most stone giants are playful, especially at night. They are fond of rock-throwing contests and other games that test their might. Groups of giants often gather to toss rocks at each other, the losing side being those who are hit more often. Travelers' reports of such contests have given stone giants their reputation for wildness.

A stone giant's bag usually contains 2d12 throwing rocks, 1d4+6 mundane items, and the giant's personal wealth. A stone giant's possessions are neither particularly clean nor particularly dirty, but most of them are made from stone.

Combat

Stone giants fight from a distance whenever possible, but if they can't avoid melee, they use gigantic clubs chiseled out of stone.

A favorite tactic of stone giants is to stand nearly motionless, blending in with the background, then move forward to throw rocks and surprise their foes.

Rock Throwing (Ex): The range increment is 180 feet for a stone giant's thrown rocks. It uses both hands when throwing a rock.

Rock Catching (Ex): A stone giant gains a +4 racial bonus on its Reflex save when attempting to catch a thrown rock.

Skills: *A stone giant gains a +8 racial bonus on Hide checks in rocky terrain.

Stone Giant Elders

Some stone giants develop special abilities related to their environment. These giant elders have Charisma scores of at least 15 and spell-like abilities, which they use as 10th-level sorcerers. Once per day they can use *stone shape*, *stone tell*, and either *transmute rock to mud* or *transmute mud to rock* (DC 17). The save DC is Charisma-based. One in ten elders is a sorcerer, usually of 3rd to 6th level.

Stone Giant Society

Stone giants prefer to dwell in deep caves high on rocky, storm-swept mountains. Usually, groups live fairly close together (no more than a day's travel apart) for a sense of community and protection. Most stone giant lairs have 2d4 neighboring lairs. Some older stone giants choose to live in solitude, meditating and creating artwork. Many of them become elders after several decades.

Most groups of stone giants subsist by hunting, gathering, and herding mountain animals such as sheep or goats. They trade with any other nearby communities, exchanging foodstuffs and stone goods for cloth, pottery, and manufactured items. Groups of evil giants often go raiding or extort tolls from mountain travelers.

Stone Giants as Characters

Strong, silent loners, stone giant characters are a rare sight in human lands.

Stone giant characters possess the following racial traits.

— +16 Strength, +4 Dexterity, +8 Constitution, +2 Wisdom.

—Large size. –1 penalty to Armor Class, –1 penalty on attack rolls, –4 penalty on Hide checks, +4 bonus on grapple checks, lifting and carrying limits double those of Medium characters.

—Space/Reach: 10 feet/10 feet.

—A stone giant's base land speed is 40 feet.

—Darkvision out to 60 feet and low-light vision.

—Racial Hit Dice: A stone giant begins with fourteen levels of giant, which provide 14d8 Hit Dice, a base attack bonus of +10, and base saving throw bonuses of Fort +9, Ref +4, and Will +4.

—Racial Skills: A stone giant's giant levels give it skill points equal to 17 × (2 + Int modifier). Its class skills are Climb, Hide, Listen, and Spot. A stone giant has a +8 racial bonus on Hide checks in rocky terrain.

—Racial Feats: A stone giant's giant levels give it five feats.

— +11 natural armor bonus.

—Special Attacks (see above): Rock throwing.

—Special Qualities (see above): Rock catching.

—Automatic Languages: Giant. Bonus Languages: Common, Draconic, Elven, Goblin, Orc.

—Favored Class: Barbarian.

—Level adjustment +4.

STORM GIANT

Huge Giant
Hit Dice: 19d8+114 (199 hp)
Initiative: +2
Speed: 35 ft. (7 squares), swim 30 ft. (6 squares) in breastplate; base speed 50 ft., swim 40 ft.
Armor Class: 27 (–2 size, +2 Dex, +12 natural, +5 breastplate) touch 10, flat-footed 25
Base Attack/Grapple: +14/+36
Attack: Greatsword +26 melee (4d6+21/19–20) or slam +26 melee (1d6+14) or composite longbow (+14 Str bonus) +14 ranged (3d6+14/×3)
Full Attack: Greatsword +26/+21/+16 melee (4d6+21/19–20) or 2 slams +26 melee (1d6+14) or composite longbow (+14 Str bonus) +14/+9/+4 ranged (3d6+14/×3)
Space/Reach: 15 ft./15 ft.
Special Attacks: Spell-like abilities
Special Qualities: Freedom of movement, immunity to electricity, low-light vision, rock catching, water breathing
Saves: Fort +17, Ref +8, Will +13
Abilities: Str 39, Dex 14, Con 23, Int 16, Wis 20, Cha 15
Skills: Climb +20, Concentration +26, Craft (any one) +13, Diplomacy +4, Intimidate +12, Jump +24, Listen +15, Perform (sing) +12, Sense Motive +15, Spot +25, Swim +18*
Feats: Awesome Blow, Cleave, Combat Reflexes, Improved Bull Rush, Improved Sunder, Iron Will, Power Attack
Environment: Warm mountains
Organization: Solitary or family (2–4 plus 35% noncombatants plus 1 sorcerer or cleric of 7th–10th level plus 1–2 rocs, 2–5 griffons, or 2–8 sea cats)

Challenge Rating: 13
Treasure: Standard coins; double goods; standard items
Alignment: Often chaotic good
Advancement: By character class
Level Adjustment: —

This giant resembles a well-formed human of enormous proportions. It has light green skin, dark green hair, and glittering emerald eyes.

Storm giants are gentle and reclusive. They are usually tolerant of others but can be very dangerous when angry.

Very rarely, storm giants have violet skin. Violet-skinned storm giants have deep violet or blue-black hair with silvery gray or purple eyes. Adults are about 21 feet tall and weigh about 12,000 pounds. Storm giants can live to be 600 years old.

Storm giants' garb is usually a short, loose tunic belted at the waist, sandals or bare feet, and a headband. They wear a few pieces of simple but finely crafted jewelry, anklets (favored by barefoot giants), rings, or circlets being most common. They live quiet, reflective lives and spend their time musing about the world, composing and playing music, and tilling their land or gathering food.

Storm giants usually carry their bags attached to their belts instead of as shoulder sacks. Each of these bags holds a simple musical instrument (usually a pan pipe or harp) and 2d4 mundane items. Other than the jewelry they wear, they prefer to leave their wealth in their lairs. A storm giant's possessions are usually simple (if not downright primitive), but well crafted and maintained.

Combat

Storm giants use weapons and spell-like abilities instead of throwing rocks. Their composite longbows have a range increment of 180 feet.

Spell-Like Abilities: 1/day—*call lightning* (DC 15), *chain lightning* (DC 18). Caster level 15th. 2/day—*control weather*, *levitate*. Caster level 20th. The save DCs are Charisma-based.

Freedom of Movement (Su): Storm giants have a continuous freedom of movement ability as the spell (caster level 20th). The effect can be dispelled, but the storm giant can create it again on its next turn as a free action.

Water Breathing (Ex): Storm giants can breathe underwater indefinitely and can freely use their spell-like abilities while submerged.

Skills: A storm giant has a +8 racial bonus on any Swim check to perform some special action or avoid a hazard. It can always choose to take 10 on a Swim check, even if distracted or endangered. It can use the run action while swimming, provided it swims in a straight line. *Storm giants ignore all weight penalties for gear carried when swimming.

Storm Giant Society

Storm giants live in castles built on mountain peaks or underwater. They live off the land in the immediate vicinity of their lairs. If the natural harvest is not enough to sustain them, they create and carefully till large gardens, fields, and vineyards. They do not keep animals for food, preferring to hunt. Land-dwelling storm giants usually are on good terms with neighboring copper dragons and good-aligned cloud giants, and cooperate with them for mutual defense. Water-dwelling storm giants have similar relationships with merfolk and bronze dragons.

Storm Giant Characters

About 20% of adult storm giants are sorcerers or clerics. A storm giant cleric has access to two of the following domains: Chaos, Good, Protection, or War.

GIBBERING MOUTHER

Medium Aberration
Hit Dice: 4d8+24 (42 hp)
Initiative: +1
Speed: 10 ft. (2 squares), swim 20 ft.
Armor Class: 19 (+1 Dex, +8 natural), touch 11, flat-footed 18
Base Attack/Grapple: +3/+3
Attack: Bite +4 melee (1) or spittle +4 ranged touch (1d4 acid plus blindness)
Full Attack: 6 bites +4 melee (1) and spittle +4 ranged touch (1d4 acid plus blindness)
Space/Reach: 5 ft./5 ft.
Special Attacks: Gibbering, spittle, improved grab, blood drain, engulf, ground manipulation
Special Qualities: Amorphous, damage reduction 5/bludgeoning, darkvision 60 ft.
Saves: Fort +7, Ref +4, Will +5
Abilities: Str 10, Dex 13, Con 22, Int 4, Wis 13, Cha 13
Skills: Listen +4, Spot +9, Swim +8
Feats: Lightning Reflexes, Weapon Finesse
Environment: Underground
Organization: Solitary
Challenge Rating: 5
Treasure: None
Alignment: Usually neutral
Advancement: 5–12 HD (Large)
Level Adjustment: —

This unwholesome creature has a body with the form and fluidity of an amoeba. Its surface has the color, but not the consistency, of human flesh. Countless eyes and toothy mouths constantly form and disappear all over the creature, often retreating into its body even as they become apparent.

A gibbering mouther is a horrible creature seemingly drawn from a lunatic's nightmares. Although not evil, it thirsts after bodily fluids and seems to prefer the blood of intelligent creatures.

Sometimes the arrangement of eyes and mouths on a gibbering mouther's body a resembles a face, but just as often they have no relationship to one another.

A gibbering mouther is about 3 feet across and 3 to 4 feet high. It weighs about 200 pounds.

Gibbering mouthers can speak Common, but seldom say anything other than gibberish.

COMBAT

A gibbering mouther attacks by shooting out strings of protoplasmic flesh, each ending in one or more eyes and a mouth that bites at the enemy. A mouther can send out a total of six such members in any round.

Gibbering (Su): As soon as a mouther spots something edible, it begins a constant gibbering as a free action. All creatures (other than mouthers) within a 60-foot spread must succeed on a DC 13 Will save or be affected as though by a *confusion* spell for 1d2 rounds. This is a sonic mind-affecting compulsion effect. A creature that successfully saves cannot be affected by the same gibbering mouther's gibbering for 24 hours. The save DC is Charisma-based.

Spittle (Ex): As a free action every round, a gibbering mouther fires a stream of spittle at one opponent within 30 feet. The mouther makes a ranged touch attack; if it hits, it deals 1d4 points of acid damage, and the target must succeed on a DC 18 Fortitude save or be blinded for 1d4 rounds. Eyeless creatures are immune to the blinding effect, but are still subject to the acid damage. The save DC is Constitution-based.

Improved Grab (Ex): To use this ability, a gibbering mouther must hit with a bite attack. It can then attempt to start a grapple as a free action without provoking an attack of opportunity.

Blood Drain (Ex): On a successful grapple check after grabbing, that mouth attaches to the opponent. It automatically deals bite damage and drains blood, dealing 1 point of Constitution damage each round. A mouth can be ripped off (dealing 1 point of damage) with a DC 12 Strength check or severed by a successful sunder attempt (the mouth has 2 hit points). A severed mouth continues to bite and drain blood for 1d4 rounds after such an attack. A creature whose Constitution is reduced to 0 is killed.

Engulf (Ex): A gibbering mouther can try to engulf a Medium or smaller opponent grabbed by three or more mouths. The opponent must succeed on a DC 14 Reflex save or fall and be engulfed. In the next round, the mouther makes twelve bite attacks instead of six (each with a +4 attack bonus). An engulfed creature cannot attack the mouther from within. The previously attached mouths are now free to attack others. The save DC is Strength-based and includes a +2 racial bonus.

Ground Manipulation (Su): At will, as a standard action, a gibbering mouther can cause stone and earth in all adjacent squares to become a morass akin to quicksand. Softening earth, sand, or the like takes 1 round, while stone takes 2 rounds. Anyone other than the mouther in that area must take a move-equivalent action to avoid becoming mired (treat as being pinned).

Amorphous (Ex): A gibbering mouther is not subject to critical hits. It cannot be flanked.

Skills: Thanks to their multiple eyes, gibbering mouthers have a +4 racial bonus on Spot checks.

A gibbering mouther has a +8 racial bonus on any Swim check to perform some special action or avoid a hazard. It always can choose to take 10 on a Swim check, even if distracted or endangered. It can use the run action while swimming, provided it swims in a straight line.

Gibbering mouther

GIRALLON

Large Magical Beast
Hit Dice: 7d10+20 (58 hp)
Initiative: +3
Speed: 40 ft. (8 squares), climb 40 ft.
Armor Class: 16 (–1 size, +3 Dex, +4 natural), touch 12, flat-footed 15
Base Attack/Grapple: +7/+17
Attack: Claw +12 melee (1d4+6)
Full Attack: 4 claws +12 melee (1d4+6) and bite +7 melee (1d8+3)
Space/Reach: 10 ft./10 ft.

Special Attacks: Rend 2d4+9
Special Qualities: Darkvision 60 ft., low-light vision, scent
Saves: Fort +7, Ref +8, Will +5
Abilities: Str 22, Dex 17, Con 14, Int 2, Wis 12, Cha 7
Skills: Climb +14, Move Silently +8, Spot +6
Feats: Iron Will, Toughness (2)
Environment: Warm forests
Organization: Solitary or company (5–8)
Challenge Rating: 6
Treasure: None
Alignment: Always neutral
Advancement: 8–10 HD (Large); 11–21 HD (Huge)
Level Adjustment: —

At first glance, this creature looks like an albino gorilla, but it has four arms. It also has razor-sharp teeth and long claws.

Girallons are savage, magical cousins of the gorilla. They are aggressive, bloodthirsty, highly territorial, and incredibly strong.

When moving on the ground, a girallon walks on its legs and lower arms. An adult girallon is about 8 feet tall, broad-chested, and covered in thick, pure white fur. It weighs about 800 pounds.

COMBAT

Girallons attack anything that enters their territory, even others of their kind. Their senseless belligerence is the one characteristic that keeps their numbers in check. Still, the creatures show some cunning.

A solitary girallon usually conceals itself in the branches of a tree or under a pile of leaves and brush, with only its nose showing. When it spots or scents prey, it charges to the attack. A girallon picks up prey that is small enough to carry and withdraws, often vanishing into the trees before the victim's companions can do anything to retaliate. Against larger foes, a girallon seeks to tear a single opponent to bits as quickly as it can.

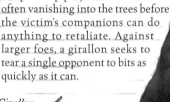

Girallon

Rend (Ex): A girallon that hits with two or more claw attacks latches onto the opponent's body and tears the flesh. This attack automatically deals an extra 2d4+12 points of damage.

Skills: A girallon has a +8 racial bonus on Climb checks and can always choose to take 10 on a Climb check, even if rushed or threatened.

Githyanki, 1st-Level Warrior
Medium Humanoid (Extraplanar)
Hit Dice: 1d8+2 (6 hp)
Initiative: +1
Speed: 20 ft. in breastplate (4 squares); base speed 30 ft.
Armor Class: 16 (+1 Dex, +5 breastplate), touch 11, flat-footed 15
Base Attack/Grapple: +1/+2
Attack: Masterwork greatsword +4 melee (2d6+1/19–20) or composite longbow (+1 Str bonus) +2 ranged (1d8+1/×3)
Full Attack: Masterwork greatsword +4 melee (2d6+1/19–20) or composite longbow (+1 Str bonus) +2 ranged (1d8+1/×3)
Space/Reach: 5 ft./5 ft.
Special Attacks: Psionics
Special Qualities: Darkvision 60 ft., psionics, spell resistance 6
Saves: Fort +4, Ref +1, Will –2
Abilities: Str 13, Dex 13, Con 14, Int 10, Wis 7, Cha 8
Skills: Craft (armorsmithing or weaponsmithing) +2, Intimidate +1, Spot +1
Feats: Weapon Focus (greatsword)
Environment: Astral Plane
Organization: Company (2–4 3rd-level fighters), squad (11–20 3rd-level fighters, plus 2 7th-level sergeants, 1 9th-level captain, and 1 young red dragon), or regiment (30–100 3rd-level fighters, plus 1 7th-level sergeant per 10 members, 5 7th-level lieutenants, 3 9th-level captains, 1 16th-level supreme leader, and 1 adult red dragon per 30 members)
Challenge Rating: 1
Treasure: Standard
Alignment: Usually evil (any)
Advancement: By character class
Level Adjustment: +2

This tall, gaunt humanoid has rough, yellow skin and russet hair pulled into a pair of topknots. Its eyes have a sinister gleam, and its ears are pointed and serrated in back.

Githyanki are an ancient line of humanlike beings residing on the Astral Plane, filling their armories for their next skirmish, raid, or war.

Githyanki are gaunt, averaging a little over 6 feet tall and typically weighing around 170 pounds. They enjoy elaborate dress and baroque armor. In fact, they revere weapons and armor, and it is not uncommon for a githyanki to show more regard for panoply of possessions than for its mate.

Like dwarves, githyanki are craftmasters, although they focus exclusively on items of warfare. Their items are distinctive, and nongithyanki who acquire them run the risk of immediate retribution should they encounter githyanki.

Githyanki speak their own secret tongue, but most also know Common and Draconic.

The statistics block describes a 1st-level warrior. Most githyanki encountered outside their homes are fighters. However, wizards (called warlocks) and multiclass githyanki (called gish) are also found.

COMBAT

Githyanki are seasoned combatants, familiar with the tactical use of ambush, cover, and psionic sniper attacks from afar. However, they prefer to engage their enemies in hand-to-hand combat so they can bring their devastating melee weapons to bear. Githyanki weapons are usually greatswords, bastard swords, and other particularly large-bladed weapons of special githyanki manufacture, all masterwork and each distinctively decorated and named. Githyanki wizards direct their powers with pinpoint accuracy to support their comrades in melee.

Psionics (Sp): 3/day—*daze* (DC 9), *mage hand*. In addition, githyanki of 3rd level or higher can use *blur* three times per day, githyanki of 6th level or higher can use *dimension door* three times per day, and githyanki of 9th level or higher can use *telekinesis* (DC 14) three times per day and *plane shift* (DC 16) once per day. Effective caster level equals the githyanki's class levels. The save DCs are Charisma-based.

Spell Resistance (Ex): A githyanki has spell resistance equal to its class levels + 5.

The githyanki warrior presented here had the following ability scores before racial adjustments: Str 13, Dex 11, Con 12, Int 10, Wis 9, Cha 8.

Challenge Rating: Githyanki with levels in NPC classes have a CR equal to their character level. Githyanki with levels in PC classes have a CR equal to their character level +1.

Githyanki Silver Swords

These impressive weapons are typically carried by githyanki combatants of 9th level and higher. Of githyanki make, a *silver sword* is a +1 silvered greatsword that looks much like a standard weapon while still in its sheath. But when drawn, the *silver sword* transforms into a column of silvery liquid, altering the weapon's balance round by round as the blade's shape flows and shimmers. A *silver sword* has the additional quality of reaching into the minds of the foes it strikes, disrupting their psionic powers. A target hit by the weapon must succeed on a DC 17 Fortitude save or lose any psionic abilities for 1d4 rounds.

High-level githyanki often take the Improved Sunder feat, using their *silver swords* to attack astral travelers' silver cords (see the *astral projection* spell, page 201 of the *Player's Handbook*). The normally insubstantial cord is treated as a tangible object with the owner's AC, hardness 10, and 20 hit points.

It is rumored that each githyanki warrior has but one *silver sword*, and if the weapon is lost or stolen, the githyanki must seek it out at all costs or be killed by its superiors. That may be only a legend, but githyanki have been known to exact terrible revenge upon those who steal their *silver swords* or win them in battle.

Some *silver swords* (belonging to particularly high-level githyanki) have additional enhancements. Enhancing a *silver sword* is just like working with any other weapon that has existing abilities. A normal githyanki *silver sword* is treated as having a +2 enhancement for this purpose: +1 for its bonus on attack and damage rolls and another +1 for the sword's antipsionic ability.

Githyanki

GITHYANKI SOCIETY

In eons past, the mind flayers enslaved entire races, including the forerunners of the githyanki. Centuries of captivity bred hatred, nurtured resolve, and finally instilled psionic powers into these slaves. With mental armaments of their own and a powerful leader to rally behind (the legendary Gith), the slaves instigated a cross-planar struggle that, in the end, threw down the mind flayer empire, bringing freedom to the surviving slaves. However, these survivors soon split into the racially distinct githyanki and their mortal enemies, the githzerai (see the Githzerai entry, below). Each constantly attempts the extinction of the other. This animosity has burned through the centuries, warping the githyanki into the evil, militaristic creatures they are today. Both creatures' hatred of mind flayers knows no bounds, though, and they will break off hostilities to slay illithids if the opportunity presents itself.

Githyanki live within massive fortresses adrift in the Astral Plane. Here they conduct commerce, manufacture goods, grow food, and live out their lives. Family dwellings are nonexistent, since most githyanki prefer their own abode; however, githyanki are often found in groups, honing their fighting skills. A fortress contains noncombatants (mostly children) equal to 20% of the fighting population. Githyanki males and females may be found in almost any role or class.

The githyanki have no deity but instead pay homage to a lich-queen. A jealous and paranoid overlord, she devours the essence of any githyanki that rises above 16th level. In addition to eliminating a potential rival, the lich-queen enhances her power with the stolen life essence.

Red Dragon Pact: Githyanki have a racial pact with red dragons, which sometimes serve githyanki as mounts. Individually, githyanki have a +4 racial bonus on Diplomacy checks when dealing with red dragons. In large groups, they can make temporary alliances with red dragons at the option of the Dungeon Master.

GITHYANKI AS CHARACTERS

Most githyanki are fighters. Some of the most powerful githyanki warlords are blackguards. Githyanki are never clerics, unless they have forsworn the dreaded lich-queen (which is a perilous and ultimately lethal decision).

Githyanki characters possess the following racial traits.

— +2 Dexterity, +2 Constitution, –2 Wisdom.
—Medium size.
—A githyanki's base land speed is 30 feet.
—Darkvision out to 60 feet.
—Racial Feats: A githyanki character gains feats according to its character class.
—Special Attacks (see above): Psionics.
—Special Qualities (see above): Psionics, spell resistance equal to class levels +5.
—Automatic Languages: Githyanki. Bonus Languages: Common, Infernal, Draconic, Undercommon.
—Favored Class: Fighter.
—Level adjustment +2.

GITHZERAI

Githzerai, 1st-Level Warrior
Medium Humanoid (Extraplanar)

Hit Dice: 1d8+1 (5 hp)
Initiative: +3
Speed: 30 ft. (6 squares)
Armor Class: 17 (+3 Dex, +4 *inertial armor*), touch 13, flat-footed 14
Base Attack/Grapple: +1/+2
Attack: Masterwork short sword +5 melee (1d6+1/19–20) or composite longbow (+1 Str bonus) +4 ranged (1d8+1/×3)
Full Attack: Masterwork short sword +5 melee (1d6+1/19–20) or composite longbow (+1 Str bonus) +4 ranged (1d8+1/×3)
Space/Reach: 5 ft./5 ft.
Special Attacks: —
Special Qualities: Darkvision 60 ft., psionics, *inertial armor*, spell resistance 6
Saves: Fort +3, Ref +3, Will +0
Abilities: Str 13, Dex 17, Con 12, Int 8, Wis 11, Cha 8
Skills: Concentration +1, Spot +2
Feats: Weapon Finesse
Environment: Ever-Changing Chaos of Limbo
Organization: Fellowship (3–12 3rd-level students), sect (12–24 3rd-level students, plus 2 7th-level teachers and 1 9th-level mentor), or order (30–100 3rd-level students, plus 1 7th-level teacher per 10 adults, 5 9th-level mentors, 2 13th-level masters, and 1 16th-level sensei)
Challenge Rating: 1
Treasure: Standard
Alignment: Any neutral
Advancement: By character class
Level Adjustment: +2

This creature is a thin and tall humanoid with sharp features, a somber face, and yellow eyes.

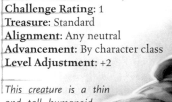

Githzerai

Githzerai are a hard-hearted, humanlike people who dwell on the plane of Limbo, secure in the protection of their hidden monasteries.

Githzerai average more than 6 feet tall and weigh about 160 pounds. Some have gray eyes instead of yellow. All of them dress in drab, unadorned clothing.

As a rule, githzerai are close-mouthed, keep their own counsel, and trust few outside their own kind.

They speak their own language (similar enough to the tongue of the githyanki that either could understand the other if they chose to speak instead of fight), but many also speak Common.

The statistics block describes a 1st-level warrior. Many githzerai are monks; however, sorcerers, rogues, and multiclass githzerai (called zerths) are also indispensable members of a monastery.

COMBAT

Able to fight without weapons and armor, githzerai monks yearn to bring the "good fight" to their enemies, the githyanki and the mind flayers. In melee, githzerai sorcerers often use their powers to enhance the monks, warriors, and rogues.

Psionics (Sp): 3/day—*daze* (DC 9), *feather fall, shatter* (DC 11). A githzerai of 11th level or higher can use *plane shift* (DC 16) once per day. Effective caster level equals the githzerai's class levels. The save DCs are Charisma-based.

Inertial Armor (Sp): Githzerai can use psychic force to block an enemy's blows. This ability gives them a +4 armor bonus to AC as long as they remain conscious. This is the equivalent of a 1st-level spell.

Spell Resistance (Ex): A githzerai has spell resistance equal to its class levels + 5.

The githzerai warrior presented here had the following ability scores before racial adjustments: Str 13, Dex 11, Con 12, Int 10, Wis 9, Cha 8.

Challenge Rating: Githzerai with levels in NPC classes have a CR equal to their character level. Githzerai with levels in PC classes have a CR equal to their character level +1.

GITHZERAI SOCIETY

The githzerai forerunners united under the command of the rebel Gith (see the Githyanki entry, above) and threw down the plane-spanning empire of the mind flayers. Once free, the former slaves split ideologically and eventually racially, becoming the githzerai and their foes, the githyanki. The githzerai's history of imprisonment was the foundation of their monastic lifestyle, in which all githzerai learn from childhood how to eradicate potential oppressors and enemies (anyone not a githzerai).

Githzerai live within self-contained, fortresslike monasteries hidden deep in the swirling chaos of Limbo. While disorder rules outside, stability holds sway inside. Each monastery is ultimately under the control of a sensei, a monk of at least 16th level, and follows a strict schedule of chants, meals, martial arts training, and devotions, according to a particular sensei's philosophy. A monastery contains noncombatants (mostly children) equal to 15% of the fighting population. Githzerai males and females may be found in almost any role or class.

Rrakkma: As a special devotion, githzerai sometimes organize mind flayer hunting parties called rrakkma. A rrakkma consists of 4–5 githzerai of 8th level and 1–2 of 11th level, mainly monks, but also containing at least one sorcerer and possibly a rogue. A rrakkma does not return to its home monastery before slaying at least as many illithids as its membership.

GITHZERAI AS CHARACTERS

Githzerai characters possess the following racial traits.

— +6 Dexterity, –2 Intelligence, +2 Wisdom.

—Medium size.

—A githzerai's base land speed is 30 feet.

—Darkvision out to 60 feet.

—Racial Feats: A githzerai gains feats according to its character class.

—Special Qualities (see above): Psionics, *inertial armor*, spell resistance equal to class levels + 5.

—Automatic Languages: Githzerai. Bonus Languages: Common, Slaad, Undercommon.

—Favored Class: Monk.

—Level adjustment +2.

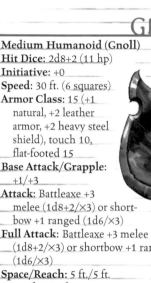

GNOLL

Medium Humanoid (Gnoll)

Hit Dice: 2d8+2 (11 hp)

Initiative: +0

Speed: 30 ft. (6 squares)

Armor Class: 15 (+1 natural, +2 leather armor, +2 heavy steel shield), touch 10, flat-footed 15

Base Attack/Grapple: +1/+3

Attack: Battleaxe +3 melee (1d8+2/×3) or shortbow +1 ranged (1d6/×3)

Full Attack: Battleaxe +3 melee (1d8+2/×3) or shortbow +1 ranged (1d6/×3)

Space/Reach: 5 ft./5 ft.

Special Attacks: —

Special Qualities: Darkvision 60 ft.

Saves: Fort +4, Ref +0, Will +0

Abilities: Str 15, Dex 10, Con 13, Int 8, Wis 11, Cha 8

Skills: Listen +2, Spot +3

Feats: Power Attack

Environment: Warm plains

Organization: Solitary, pair, hunting party (2–5 and 1–2 hyenas), band (10–100 plus 50% noncombatants plus 1 3rd-level sergeant per 20 adults and 1 leader of 4th–6th level and 5–8 hyenas), or tribe (20–200 plus 1 3rd-level sergeant per 20 adults, 1 or 2 lieutenants of 4th or 5th level, 1 leader of 6th–8th level, and 7–12 hyenas; underground lairs also have 1–3 trolls)

Challenge Rating: 1

Treasure: Standard

Alignment: Usually chaotic evil

Advancement: By character class

Level Adjustment: +1

Gnoll

This humanoid is slightly taller than a human. It has gray skin, a furry body, and a head like a hyena's, with a reddish-gray mane.

Gnolls are hyena-headed, evil humanoids that wander in loose tribes.

Most gnolls have dirty yellow or reddish-brown fur.

A gnoll is a nocturnal carnivore, preferring intelligent creatures for food because they scream more. Gnolls tend to think with their stomachs, and any alliances they make (usually with bug-bears, hobgoblins, ogres, orcs, or trolls) often fall apart when the gnolls get hungry. They dislike giants and most other humanoids, and they disdain manual labor.

A gnoll is about 7-1/2 feet tall and weighs 300 pounds.

Gnolls speak Gnoll.

COMBAT

Gnolls like to attack when they have the advantage of numbers, using horde tactics and their physical strength to overwhelm and knock down their opponents. They show little discipline when fighting unless they have a strong leader; at such times, they can maintain ranks and fight as a unit. While they do not usually prepare traps, they do use ambushes and try to attack from a flanking position. Because of its shield, a gnoll's modifier on Hide checks (untrained) is –2, which means gnolls always take special care to seek favorable conditions when laying ambushes (such as darkness, cover, or some other form of advantageous terrain).

GNOLL SOCIETY

A tribe of gnolls is ruled by its strongest member, who uses fear, intimidation, and strength to remain in power. If a chieftain is killed, the stronger members of the tribe fight to be the new chieftain; if these combats take too long or several combatants die, the tribe may break up into a number of bands that go their separate ways. Gnolls revere the phases of the moon, but most tribes have no true clerics.

A band or tribe includes as many noncombatant young as there are adults. Gnoll lairs are fortified surface encampments or underground complexes. Gnolls take prisoners for use as slaves, and any lair will have at least one slave for every ten adults. Slaves (usually humans, orcs, or hobgoblins) suffer a high attrition rate because of the gnolls' appetite.

Their special patron is the demon lord Yeenoghu, who looks like a gaunt gnoll. Most gnolls serve and revere Yeenoghu rather than worshiping a deity.

GNOLL CHARACTERS

Gnoll leaders are usually rangers. Gnoll clerics usually worship Erythnul, deity of slaughter. A gnoll cleric has access to two of the following domains: Chaos, Evil, Trickery, or War (favored weapon morningstar).

GNOLLS AS CHARACTERS

Relentless hunters, gnoll characters often begin their adventures by tracking a quarry into the world of humankind. There, they take up the role of bounty hunters and mercenaries.

Gnoll characters possess the following racial traits.

—Strength +4, Constitution +2, Intelligence –2, Charisma –2.

—Size Medium.

—A gnoll's base land speed is 30 feet.

—Darkvision out to 60 feet.

—Racial Hit Dice: A gnoll begins with two levels of humanoid, which provide 2d8 Hit Dice, a base attack bonus of +1, and base saving throw bonuses of Fort +3, Ref +0, and Will +0.

—Racial Skills: A gnoll's humanoid levels give it skill points equal to 5 × (2 + Int modifier). Its class skills are Listen and Spot.

—Racial Feats: A gnoll's humanoid levels give it one feat.
— +1 natural armor bonus.
—Automatic Languages: Gnoll. Bonus Languages: Common, Draconic, Elven, Goblin, Orc.
—Favored Class: Ranger.
—Level adjustment +1.

GNOME

This humanoid stands a little more than half as high as a human. It has a compact build, dark tan skin, fair hair, and large eyes.

Gnomes are inveterate explorers, tricksters, and inventors. They have a knack for both illusion and alchemy.

Gnomes stand 3 to 3-1/2 feet tall and weigh 40 to 45 pounds. Their skin color ranges from dark tan to woody brown, their hair is fair, and their eyes can be any shade of blue. Gnome males prefer short, carefully trimmed beards. Gnomes generally wear leather or earth tones, though they decorate their clothes with intricate stitching or fine jewelry. Gnomes reach adulthood at about age 40, and they live about 350 years, though some can live almost 500 years.

Gnomes are inquisitive. They love to learn by personal experience. At times they're even reckless. Their curiosity makes them skilled engineers, as they are always trying new ways to build things. Sometimes a gnome pulls a prank just to see how the individuals involved will react.

Gnomes speak their own language, Gnome. Most gnomes who travel outside gnome lands (as traders, tinkers, or adventurers) know Common, while warriors in gnome settlements usually learn Goblin.

Most gnomes encountered outside their home are warriors; the information in the statistics block is for one of 1st level.

COMBAT

Gnomes prefer misdirection and deception over direct confrontation. They would rather befuddle or embarrass foes (other than goblinoids or kobolds) than kill them. Gnomes make heavy use of illusion magic and carefully prepared ambushes and traps whenever they can.

Gnome Traits (Ex): Gnomes possess the following racial traits.
— +2 Constitution, –2 Strength.
—Small size. +1 bonus to Armor Class, +1 bonus on attack rolls, +4 bonus on Hide checks, –4 penalty on grapple checks, lifting and carrying limits 3/4 those of Medium characters.
—A gnome's base land speed is 20 feet.
—Low-light vision.
—Weapon Familiarity: Gnomes may treat gnome hooked hammers (see Chapter 7 of the *Player's Handbook*) as martial weapons rather than exotic weapons.

Rock gnome

LOCKWOOD

— +2 racial bonus on saving throws against illusions.
—Add +1 to the Difficulty Class for all saving throws against illusion spells cast by gnomes. This adjustment stacks with those from similar effects, such as the Spell Focus feat.
— +1 racial bonus on attack rolls against kobolds and goblinoids (including goblins, hobgoblins, and bugbears).
— +4 dodge bonus to Armor Class against creatures of the giant type (such as ogres, trolls, and hill giants).
— +2 racial bonus on Listen checks.
— +2 racial bonus on Craft (alchemy) checks.
—Automatic Languages: Common, Gnome. Bonus Languages: Draconic, Dwarven, Elven, Giant, Goblin, Orc.
—Spell-Like Abilities: 1/day—*speak with animals* (burrowing mammal only, duration 1 minute). A gnome with a Charisma score of at least 10 also has the following spell-like abilities: 1/day—*dancing lights, ghost sound, prestidigitation.* Caster level 1st; save DC 10 + gnome's Cha modifier + spell level.
—Favored Class: Bard.

The gnome warrior presented here had the following ability scores before racial adjustments: Str 13, Dex 11, Con 12, Int 10, Wis 9, Cha 8.

GNOME SOCIETY

Gnomes get along well with dwarves, who share their love of precious things, their curiosity about mechanical devices, and their hatred of goblins and giants. They enjoy the company of halflings, especially those who are easygoing enough to put up with pranks and jests. Most gnomes are a little suspicious of the taller races—humans, elves, half-elves, and half-orcs—but they are rarely hostile or malicious.

Gnomes make their homes in hilly, wooded lands. They live underground but get more fresh air than dwarves, enjoying the natural, living world on the surface whenever they can. Their homes are well hidden, both by clever construction and illusions. Those who come to visit and are welcome are ushered into the bright, warm burrows. Those who are not welcome never find the burrows in the first place.

The chief gnome deity is Garl Glittergold, the Watchful Protector. His clerics teach that gnomes are to cherish and support their communities. Pranks, for example, are seen as ways to lighten spirits and to keep gnomes humble, not ways for pranksters to triumph over those they trick.

SUBRACES

The information above is for rock gnomes, the most common variety. There are two other major gnome subraces, which differ from rock gnomes as follows.

	Gnome, 1st-Level Warrior Small Humanoid (Gnome)	Svirfneblin, 1st-Level Warrior Small Humanoid (Gnome)
Hit Dice:	1d8+2 (6 hp)	1d8+4 (8 hp)
Initiative:	+0	+1
Speed:	20 ft. (4 squares)	15 ft. in banded mail armor (3 squares); base speed 20 ft.
Armor Class:	16 (+1 size, +4 chain shirt, +1 light shield), touch 11, flat-footed 16	23 (+1 size, +1 Dex, +4 dodge, +6 banded mail, +1 buckler), touch 16, flat-footed 18
Base Attack/Grapple:	+1/−3	+1/−3
Attack:	Longsword +2 melee (1d6/19–20) or light crossbow +3 ranged (1d6/19–20)	Heavy pick +2 melee (1d4/×4) or light crossbow +3 ranged (1d6/19–20)
Full Attack:	Longsword +2 melee (1d6/19–20) or light crossbow +3 ranged (1d6/19–20)	Heavy pick +2 melee (1d4/×4) or light crossbow +3 ranged (1d6/19–20)
Space/Reach:	5 ft./5 ft.	5 ft./5 ft.
Special Attacks:	—	Spell-like abilities
Special Qualities:	Gnome traits	Gnome traits, svirfneblin traits, spell resistance 12
Saves:	Fort +4, Ref +0, Will −1	Fort +5, Ref +3, Will +2
Abilities:	Str 11, Dex 11, Con 14, Int 10, Wis 9, Cha 8	Str 11, Dex 13, Con 12, Int 10, Wis 11, Cha 4
Skills:	Hide +3, Listen +1, Spot +1	Hide +2, Listen +2, Spot +2
Feats:	Weapon Focus (light crossbow)	Toughness
Environment:	Temperate hills (Forest gnomes: Temperate forests)	Underground
Organization:	Company (2–4), squad (11–20 plus 1 leader of 3rd–6th level and 2 3rd-level lieutenants), or band (30–50 plus 1 3rd-level sergeant per 20 adults, 5 5th-level lieutenants, 3 7th-level captains, and 2–5 dire badgers)	Company (2–4), squad (11–20 plus 1 leader of 3rd–6th level and 2 3rd-level lieutenants), or band (30–50 plus 1 3rd-level sergeant per 20 adults, 5 5th-level lieutenants, 3 7th-level captains, and 2–5 Medium earth elementals)
Challenge Rating:	1/2	1
Treasure:	Standard	Standard
Alignment:	Usually neutral good	Usually neutral
Advancement:	By character class	By character class
Level Adjustment:	+0	+3

Svirfneblin

This humanoid stands a little more than half as tall as a human. It has a wiry, gnarled physique, stone-colored skin, and large gray eyes. It is bald.

Also called deep gnomes, svirfneblin are said to dwell in great cities deep underground. They keep the location of these cities secret to protect them from their deadly foes: drow, kuo-toa, and mind flayers.

A svirfneblin has wiry, rock-colored skin usually medium brown to brownish gray. Only males are bald; females have stringy gray hair. The average svirfneblin lifespan is 250 years.

Svirfneblin speak Gnome, Common, and Undercommon.

Svirfneblin Traits (Ex): These traits are in addition to the rock gnome traits, except where noted.

— −2 Strength, +2 Dexterity, +2 Wisdom, −4 Charisma. These adjustments replace the rock gnome's ability score adjustments.

—Stonecunning: This ability grants deep gnomes a +2 racial bonus on Search checks to notice unusual stonework. A deep gnome who merely comes within 10 feet of unusual stonework can make a Search check as though actively searching, and can use the Search skill to find stonework traps as a rogue can. A svirfneblin can also intuit depth, sensing the approximate distance underground as naturally as a human can sense which way is up.

—Darkvision out to 120 feet and low-light vision.

—Spell resistance equal to 11 + class levels.

— +2 racial bonus on all saving throws (figured into the statistics for the character presented here). This trait replaces the rock gnome's racial bonus on saving throws against illusions.

—Add +1 to the Difficulty Class for all saving throws against illusion spells cast by svirfneblin. This adjustment stacks with those from similar effects, such as the Spell Focus feat.

— +1 racial bonus on attack rolls against kobolds and goblinoids.

— +4 dodge bonus to Armor Class against all creatures (figured into the statistics for the character presented here). This trait replaces the rock gnome's dodge bonus against giants.

—Automatic Languages: Undercommon, Gnome, Common. Bonus Languages: Dwarven, Elven, Giant, Goblin, Orc, Terran. This trait replaces the rock gnome's automatic and bonus languages.

—Spell-Like Abilities: 1/day—*blindness/deafness* (typical save DC 13), *blur, disguise self.* Caster level equals the svirfneblin's class levels. The save DC is Charisma-based and include a +4 racial modifier. This trait replaces the rock gnome's spell-like abilities.

—Nondetection (Su): A svirfneblin has a continuous nondetection ability as the spell (caster level equal to class levels).

— +2 racial bonus on Craft (alchemy) and Listen checks.

— +2 racial bonus on Hide checks, which improves to +4 underground.

—Favored Class: Rogue.

—Level adjustment +3.

The svirfneblin warrior presented here had the following ability scores before racial adjustments: Str 13, Dex 11, Con 12, Int 10, Wis 9, Cha 8.

Challenge Rating: Svirfneblin with levels in NPC classes have a CR equal to their character level. Svirfneblin with levels in PC classes have a CR equal to their character level +1.

Forest Gnome

This exceptionally small humanoid has moss-colored skin, dark hair, and brown eyes.

Shy and elusive, forest gnomes shun contact with other races except when dire emergencies threaten their beloved homes. They are the smallest of all the gnomes, averaging 2 to 2-1/2 feet in height, but look just like regular gnomes except with bark-colored or gray-green skin, and eyes that can be brown or green as well as blue. A very long-lived people, forest gnomes have an average life expectancy of 500 years.

Forest Gnome Traits (Ex): These traits are in addition to the rock gnome traits, except where noted.

—*Pass without Trace* (Su): A forest gnome has the innate ability to use *pass without trace* (self only, as a free action) as the spell cast by a druid of the forest gnome's class levels.

— +1 racial bonus on attack rolls against kobolds, goblinoids, orcs, and reptilian humanoids.

—Automatic Languages: Gnome, Elven, Sylvan, and a simple language that enables them to communicate on a very basic level with forest animals (this replaces the rock gnome's *speak with animals* ability). Bonus Languages: Common, Draconic, Dwarven, Giant, Goblin, Orc. This trait replaces the rock gnome's automatic and bonus languages.

— +4 racial bonus on Hide checks, which improves to +8 in a wooded area.

GOBLIN

Goblin, 1st-Level Warrior
Small Humanoid (Goblinoid)
Hit Dice: 1d8+1 (5 hp)
Initiative: +1
Speed: 30 ft. (6 squares)
Armor Class: 15 (+1 size, +1 Dex, +2 leather armor, +1 light shield), touch 12, flat-footed 14
Base Attack/Grapple: +1/−3
Attack: Morningstar +2 melee (1d6) or javelin +3 ranged (1d4)
Full Attack: Morningstar +2 melee (1d6) or javelin +3 ranged (1d4)
Space/Reach: 5 ft./5 ft.
Special Attacks: —
Special Qualities: Darkvision 60 ft.
Saves: Fort +3, Ref +1, Will −1
Abilities: Str 11, Dex 13, Con 12, Int 10, Wis 9, Cha 6
Skills: Hide +5, Listen +2, Move Silently +5, Ride +4, Spot +2
Feats: Alertness
Environment: Temperate plains
Organization: Gang (4–9), band (10–100 plus 100% noncombatants plus 1 3rd-level sergeant per 20 adults and 1 leader of 4th–6th level), warband (10–24 with worg mounts), or tribe (40–400 plus 100% noncombatants plus 1 3rd-level sergeant per 20 adults, 1 or 2 lieutenants of 4th or 5th level, 1 leader of 6th–8th level, 10–24 worgs, and 2–4 dire wolves)
Challenge Rating: 1/3
Treasure: Standard
Alignment: Usually neutral evil
Advancement: By character class
Level Adjustment: +0

This little humanoid has a flat face, broad nose, pointed ears, wide mouth, and small, sharp fangs. It walks upright, but its arms hang down almost to its knees.

Goblins are small humanoids that many consider little more than a nuisance. However, if they are unchecked, their great numbers, rapid reproduction, and evil disposition enable them to overrun and despoil civilized areas.

A goblin stands 3 to 3-1/2 feet tall and weigh 40 to 45 pounds. Its eyes are usually dull and glazed, varying in color from red to yellow. A goblin's skin color ranges from yellow through any shade of orange to a deep red; usually all members of a single tribe are about the same color. Goblins wear clothing of dark leather, tending toward drab, soiled-looking colors.

Goblins speak Goblin; those with Intelligence scores of 12 or higher also speak Common.

Most goblins encountered outside their homes are warriors; the information in the statistics block is for one of 1st level.

COMBAT

Being bullied by bigger, stronger creatures has taught goblins to exploit what few advantages they have: sheer numbers and malicious ingenuity. The concept of a fair fight is meaningless in their society. They favor ambushes, overwhelming odds, dirty tricks, and any other edge they can devise.

Goblins have a poor grasp of strategy and are cowardly by nature, tending to flee the field if a battle turns against them. With proper supervision, though, they can implement reasonably complex plans, and in such circumstances their numbers can be a deadly advantage.

Skills: Goblins have a +4 racial bonus on Move Silently and Ride checks. Goblin cavalry (mounted on worgs) usually select the Mounted Combat feat in place of the Alertness feat, which reduces their Spot and Listen check modifiers from +3 to +1.

Challenge Rating: Goblins with levels in NPC classes have a CR equal to their character level −2.

GOBLIN SOCIETY

Goblins are tribal. Their leaders are generally the biggest, strongest, or sometimes the smartest of the group. They have almost no concept of privacy, living and sleeping in large common areas; only the leaders live separately. Goblins survive by raiding and stealing (preferably from those who cannot defend themselves easily), sneaking into lairs, villages, and even towns by night to take what they can. They are not above waylaying travelers on the road or in forests and stripping them of all possessions, up to and including the clothes on their backs. Goblins sometimes capture slaves to perform hard labor in the tribe's lair or camp.

Goblin

These creatures live wherever they can, from dank caves to dismal ruins, and their lairs are always smelly and filthy due to an utter lack of sanitation. Goblins often settle near civilized areas to raid for food, livestock, tools, weapons, and supplies. Once a tribe has despoiled a locale, it simply packs up and moves on to the next convenient area. Hobgoblins and bugbears are sometimes found in the company of goblin tribes, usually as bullying leaders. Some goblin tribes form alliances with worgs, which carry them into combat.

Goblin bands and tribes have noncombatant young equal in number to the adults.

The chief goblin deity is Maglubiyet, who urges his worshipers to expand their numbers and overwhelm their competitors.

GOBLINS AS CHARACTERS

Goblin leaders tend to be rogues or fighter/rogues. Goblin clerics worship Maglubiyet. A goblin cleric has access to two of the following domains: Chaos, Evil, or Trickery. Most goblin spellcasters are adepts. Goblin adepts favor spells that fool or confuse enemies.

Goblin characters possess the following racial traits.

— –2 Strength, +2 Dexterity, –2 Charisma.

—Small size: +1 bonus to Armor Class, +1 bonus on attack rolls, +4 bonus on Hide checks, –4 penalty on grapple checks, lifting and carrying limits 3/4 those of Medium characters.

—A goblin's base land speed is 30 feet.

—Darkvision out to 60 feet.

— +4 racial bonus on Move Silently and Ride checks.

—Automatic Languages: Common, Goblin. Bonus Languages: Draconic, Elven, Giant, Gnoll, Orc.

—Favored Class: Rogue.

The goblin warrior presented here had the following ability scores before racial adjustments: Str 13, Dex 11, Con 12, Int 10, Wis 9, Cha 8.

GOLEM

Golems are magically created automatons of great power. Constructing one involves the employment of mighty magic and elemental forces.

The animating force for a golem is a spirit from the Elemental Plane of Earth. The process of creating the golem binds the unwilling spirit to the artificial body and subjects it to the will of the golem's creator.

COMBAT

Golems are tenacious in combat and prodigiously strong as well. Being mindless, they do nothing without orders from their creators. They follow instructions explicitly and are incapable of any strategy or tactics. They are emotionless in combat and cannot be provoked.

A golem's creator can command it if the golem is within 60 feet and can see and hear its creator. If uncommanded, a golem usually follows its last instruction to the best of its ability, though if attacked it returns the attack. The creator can give the golem a simple command to govern its actions in his or her absence, such as "Remain in an area and attack all creatures that enter" (or only a specific type of creature), "Ring a gong and attack," or the like. The golem's creator can order the golem to obey the commands of another person (who might in turn place the golem under someone else's control, and so on), but the golem's creator can always resume control over his creation by commanding the golem to obey him alone.

Since golems do not need to breathe and are immune to most forms of energy, they can press an attack against an opponent almost anywhere, from the bottom of the sea to the frigid top of the tallest mountain.

Immunity to Magic (Ex): Golems have immunity to most magical and supernatural effects, except when otherwise noted.

CONSTRUCTION

The cost to create given for each golem includes the cost of the physical body and all the materials and spell components that are consumed or become a permanent part of the golem. Creating a golem is essentially similar to creating any sort of magic item (see page 282 of the *Dungeon Master's Guide*). However, a golem's body

includes costly material components that may require some extra preparation. The golem's creator can assemble the body or hire someone else to do the job. The builder must have the appropriate skill, which varies with the golem variety.

Completing the golem's creation drains the appropriate XP from the creator and requires casting any spells on the final day. The creator must cast the spells personally, but they can come from outside sources, such as scrolls.

The characteristics of a golem that come from its nature as a magic item (caster level, prerequisite feats and spells, market price, cost to create) are given in summary form at the end of each golem's description, in the same format used in Chapter 7 of the *Dungeon Master's Guide*.

Note: The market price of an advanced golem (a golem with more Hit Dice than the typical golem described in each entry) is increased by 5,000 gp for each additional Hit Die, and increased by an additional 50,000 gp if the golem's size increases. The XP cost for creating an advanced golem is equal to 1/25 the advanced golem's market price minus the cost of the special materials required.

CLAY GOLEM

Large Construct
Hit Dice: 11d10+30 (90 hp)
Initiative: –1
Speed: 20 ft. (4 squares)
Armor Class: 22 (–1 size, –1 Dex, +14 natural), touch 8, flat-footed 22
Base Attack/Grapple: +8/+19
Attack: Slam +14 melee (2d10+7 plus cursed wound)
Full Attack: 2 slams +14 melee (2d10+7 plus cursed wound)
Space/Reach: 10 ft./10 ft.
Special Attacks: Berserk, cursed wound
Special Qualities: Construct traits, damage reduction 10/adamantine and bludgeoning, darkvision 60 ft., haste, immunity to magic, low-light vision
Saves: Fort +3, Ref +2, Will +3
Abilities: Str 25, Dex 9, Con —, Int —, Wis 11, Cha 1
Skills: —
Feats: —
Environment: Any
Organization: Solitary or gang (2–4)
Challenge Rating: 10
Treasure: None
Alignment: Always neutral
Advancement: 12–18 HD (Large); 19–33 HD (Huge)
Level Adjustment: —

This automaton has been sculpted from soft clay. It's about 18 inches taller than a normal human, and its features are grossly distorted from the human norm. Its chest is overly large, with arms attached by thick knots of muscle at the shoulder, hanging down to its knees, and ending in short, stubby fingers. It has no neck, and the large head has broad, flat features. Its legs are short and bowed, ending in wide, flat feet. It smells faintly of clay.

This golem has a humanoid body made from clay.

A clay golem wears no clothing except for a metal or stiff leather garment around its hips.

A clay golem golem cannot speak or make any vocal noise. It walks and moves with a slow, clumsy gait. It weighs around 600 pounds.

Combat

Clay golems are frightening combatants, thanks to their immunities and their haste ability.

Berserk (Ex): When a clay golem enters combat, there is a cumulative 1% chance each round that its elemental spirit breaks free and the golem goes berserk. The uncontrolled golem goes on a rampage, attacking the nearest living creature or smashing some object smaller than itself if no creature is within reach, then moving on to spread more destruction. Once a clay golem goes berserk, no known method can reestablish control.

Cursed Wound (Ex): The damage a clay golem deals doesn't heal naturally and resists healing spells. A character attempting to cast a conjuration (healing) spell on a creature damaged by a clay golem must succeed on a DC 26 caster level check, or the spell has no effect on the injured character.

Immunity to Magic (Ex): A clay golem is immune to any spell or spell-like ability that allows spell resistance. In addition, certain spells and effects function differently against the creature, as noted below.

A *move earth* spell drives the golem back 120 feet and deals 3d12 points of damage to it.

A *disintegrate* spell slows the golem (as the *slow* spell) for 1d6 rounds and deals 1d12 points of damage.

An *earthquake* spell cast directly at a clay golem stops it from moving on its next turn and deals 5d10 points of damage. The golem gets no saving throw against any of these effects.

Any magical attack against a clay golem that deals acid damage heals 1 point of damage for every 3 points of damage it would otherwise deal. If the amount of healing would cause the golem to exceed its full normal hit points, it gains any excess as temporary hit points. For example, a clay golem hit by the breath weapon of a black dragon heals 7 points of damage if the attack would have dealt 22 points of damage. A clay golem golem gets no saving throw against magical attacks that deal acid damage.

Haste (Su): After it has engaged in at least 1 round of combat, a clay golem can haste itself once per day as a free action. The effect lasts 3 rounds and is otherwise the same as the spell.

Construction

A clay golem's body must be sculpted from a single block of clay weighing at least 1,000 pounds, treated with rare oils and powders worth 1,500 gp. Creating the body requires a DC 15 Craft (sculpting) check or a DC 15 Craft (pottery) check.

CL 11th; Craft Construct (see page 303), *animate objects, commune, resurrection*, caster must be at least 11th level; Price 40,000 gp; Cost 21,500 gp + 1,540 XP.

Iron golem

Flesh golem

WAR. 2000

FLESH GOLEM

Large Construct
Hit Dice: 9d10+30 (79 hp)
Initiative: –1
Speed: 30 ft. (6 squares)
Armor Class: 18 (–1 size, –1 Dex, +10 natural), touch 8, flat-footed 18
Base Attack/Grapple: +6/+15
Attack: Slam +10 melee (2d8+5)
Full Attack: 2 slams +10 melee (2d8+5)
Space/Reach: 10 ft./10 ft.
Special Attacks: Berserk
Special Qualities: Construct traits, damage reduction 5/adamantine, darkvision 60 ft., immunity to magic, low-light vision
Saves: Fort +3, Ref +2, Will +3
Abilities: Str 21, Dex 9, Con —, Int —, Wis 11, Cha 1
Skills: —
Feats: —
Environment: Any
Organization: Solitary or gang (2–4)
Challenge Rating: 7
Treasure: None
Alignment: Always neutral
Advancement: 10–18 HD (Large); 19–27 HD (Huge)
Level Adjustment: —

This automaton looks as though it was constructed from a grisly assortment of decaying human body parts, stitched and bolted together into a form taller than a living man. It smells faintly of freshly dug earth and dead flesh.

A flesh golem is a ghoulish collection of stolen humanoid body parts, stitched together into a single composite form.

No natural animal willingly tracks a flesh golem. The golem wears whatever clothing its creator desires, usually just a ragged pair of trousers. It has no possessions and no weapons. It stands 8 feet tall and weighs almost 500 pounds.

A flesh golem golem cannot speak, although it can emit a hoarse roar of sorts. It walks and moves with a stiff-jointed gait, as if not in complete control of its body.

Combat

Flesh golems often fare poorly in combat thanks to their fairly low Armor Class, though they can easily crush foes that lack adamantine weaponry. A flesh golem supported by an ally that can launch electricity attacks is fearsome indeed.

Berserk (Ex): When a flesh golem enters combat, there is a cumulative 1% chance each round that its elemental spirit breaks free and the golem goes berserk. The uncontrolled golem goes on a rampage, attacking the nearest living creature or smashing some object smaller than itself if no creature is within reach, then moving on to spread more destruction. The golem's creator, if within 60 feet, can try to regain control by speaking firmly and persuasively to the golem, which requires a DC 19 Charisma check. It takes 1 minute of inactivity by the golem to reset the golem's berserk chance to 0%.

Immunity to Magic (Ex): A flesh golem is immune to any spell or spell-like ability that allows spell resistance. In addition, certain spells and effects function differently against the creature, as noted below.

A magical attack that deals cold or fire damage slows a flesh golem (as the *slow* spell) for 2d6 rounds, with no saving throw.

A magical attack that deals electricity damage breaks any *slow* effect on the golem and heals 1 point of damage for every 3 points of damage the attack would otherwise deal. If the amount of healing would cause the golem to exceed its full normal hit points, it gains any excess as temporary hit points. For example, a flesh golem hit by a *lightning bolt* heals 3 points of damage if the attack would have dealt 11 points of damage. A flesh golem golem gets no saving throw against attacks that deal electricity damage.

Construction

The pieces of a flesh golem must come from normal human corpses that have not decayed significantly. Assembly requires a minimum of six different bodies—one for each limb, the torso (including head), and the brain. In some cases, more bodies may be necessary. Special unguents and bindings worth 500 gp are also required. Note that creating a flesh golem requires casting a spell with the evil descriptor.

Assembling the body requires a DC 13 Craft (leatherworking) check or a DC 13 Heal check.

CL 8th; Craft Construct (see page 303), *animate dead*, *bull's strength*, *geas/quest*, *limited wish*, caster must be at least 8th level; Price 20,000 gp; Cost 10,500 gp + 780 XP.

IRON GOLEM

Large Construct
Hit Dice: 18d10+30 (129 hp)
Initiative: −1
Speed: 20 ft. (4 squares)
Armor Class: 30 (−1 size, −1 Dex, +22 natural) touch 8, flat-footed 30
Base Attack/Grapple: +12/+28
Attack: Slam +23 melee (2d10+11)
Full Attack: 2 slams +23 melee (2d10+11)
Space/Reach: 10 ft./10 ft.
Special Attacks: Breath weapon
Special Qualities: Construct traits, damage reduction 15/adamantine, darkvision 60 ft., immunity to magic, low-light vision
Saves: Fort +6, Ref +5, Will +6
Abilities: Str 33, Dex 9, Con —, Int —, Wis 11, Cha 1
Skills: —
Feats: —
Environment: Any
Organization: Solitary or gang (2–4)
Challenge Rating: 13
Treasure: None
Alignment: Always neutral
Advancement: 19–24 HD (Large); 25–54 HD (Huge)
Level Adjustment: —

This metallic automaton is twice the height of a normal human and resembles an armored giant.

This golem has a humanoid body made from iron.

An iron golem can be fashioned in any manner, just like a stone golem (see below), although it almost always displays armor of some sort. Its features are much smoother than those of a stone golem. Iron golems sometimes carry a short sword in one hand.

An iron golem is 12 feet tall and weighs about 5,000 pounds.

An iron golem cannot speak or make any vocal noise, nor does it have any distinguishable odor. It moves with a ponderous but smooth gait. Each step causes the floor to tremble unless it is on a thick, solid foundation.

Combat

Iron golems are mighty combatants. They strike with deadly accuracy and incredible force. Their bodies are nearly invulnerable but can be reduced to piles of rubbish by rust monsters.

Breath Weapon (Su): 10-foot cube, cloud of poisonous gas lasting 1 round, free action once every 1d4+1 rounds; initial damage 1d4 Con, secondary damage 3d4 Con, Fortitude DC 19 negates. The save DC is Constitution-based.

	Stone Golem	Greater Stone Golem
	Large Construct	Huge Construct
Hit Dice:	14d10+30 (107 hp)	42d10+40 (271 hp)
Initiative:	−1	−2
Speed:	20 ft. (4 squares)	20 ft. (4 squares)
Armor Class:	26 (−1 size, −1 Dex, +18 natural), touch 8, flat-footed 26	27 (−2 size, −2 Dex, +21 natural), touch 6, flat-footed 27
Base Attack/Grapple:	+10/+23	+31/+52
Attack:	Slam +18 melee (2d10+9)	Slam +42 melee (4d8+13)
Full Attack:	2 slams +18 melee (2d10+9)	2 slams +42 melee (4d8+13)
Space/Reach:	10 ft (4 squares)./10 ft.	15 ft./15 ft.
Special Attacks:	Slow	Slow
Special Qualities:	Construct traits, damage reduction 10/adamantine, darkvision 60 ft., immunity to magic, low-light vision	Construct traits, damage reduction 10/adamantine, darkvision 60 ft., immunity to magic, low-light vision
Saves:	Fort +4, Ref +3, Will +4	Fort +14, Ref +12, Will +14
Abilities:	Str 29, Dex 9, Con —, Int —, Wis 11, Cha 1	Str 37, Dex 7, Con —, Int —, Wis 11, Cha 1
Skills:	—	—
Feats:	—	—
Environment:	Any	Any
Organization:	Solitary or gang (2–4)	Solitary or gang (2–4)
Challenge Rating:	11	16
Treasure:	None	None
Alignment:	Always neutral	Always neutral
Advancement:	15–21 HD (Large); 22–42 (Huge)	—
Level Adjustment:	—	—

Immunity to Magic (Ex): An iron golem is immune to any spell or spell-like ability that allows spell resistance. In addition, certain spells and effects function differently against the creature, as noted below.

A magical attack that deals electricity damage slows an iron golem (as the *slow* spell) for 3 rounds, with no saving throw.

A magical attack that deals fire damage breaks any *slow* effect on the golem and heals 1 point of damage for each 3 points of damage the attack would otherwise deal. If the amount of healing would cause the golem to exceed its full normal hit points, it gains any excess as temporary hit points. For example, an iron golem hit by a *fireball* gains back 6 hit points if the damage total is 18 points. An iron golem gets no saving throw against fire effects.

An iron golem is affected normally by rust attacks, such as that of a rust monster or a *rusting grasp* spell.

Construction

An iron golem's body is sculpted from 5,000 pounds of pure iron, smelted with rare tinctures and admixtures costing at least 10,000 gp. Assembling the body requires a DC 20 Craft (armorsmithing) check or a DC 20 Craft (weaponsmithing) check.

CL 16th; Craft Construct (see page 303), *cloudkill, geas/quest, limited wish, polymorph any object,* caster must be at least 16th level; Price 150,000 gp; Cost 80,000 gp + 5,600 XP.

STONE GOLEM

This automaton has been cut from stone. It is half again as tall as a normal human and resembles a roughly chiseled statue of a soldier.

This golem has a humanoid body made from stone.

A stone golem is 9 feet tall and weighs around 2,000 pounds. Its body is frequently stylized to suit its creator. For example, it might look like it is wearing armor, with a particular symbol carved on the breastplate, or have designs worked into the stone of its limbs.

Combat

Stone golems are formidable opponents, being physically powerful and difficult to harm.

Slow (Su): A stone golem can use a slow effect, as the spell, as a free action once every 2 rounds. The effect has a range of 10 feet and a duration of 7 rounds, requiring a DC 17 Will save to negate. The save DC is Constitution-based.

Immunity to Magic (Ex): A stone golem is immune to any spell or spell-like ability that allows spell resistance. In addition, certain spells and effects function differently against the creature, as noted below.

A *transmute rock to mud* spell slows a stone golem (as the *slow* spell) for 2d6 rounds, with no saving throw, while *transmute mud to rock* heals all of its lost hit points.

A *stone to flesh* spell does not actually change the golem's structure but negates its damage reduction and immunity to magic for 1 full round.

Construction

A stone golem's body is chiseled from a single block of hard stone, such as granite, weighing at least 3,000 pounds. The stone must be of exceptional quality, and costs 5,000 gp. Assembling the body requires a DC 17 Craft (sculpting) check or a DC 17 Craft (stonemasonry) check.

CL 14th; Craft Construct (see page 303), *antimagic field, geas/quest, symbol of stunning,* caster must be at least 14th level; Price 90,000 gp; Cost 50,000 gp + 3,400 XP.

Greater Stone Golem

A greater stone golem is a colossus of granite, the largest and most fearsome stone golem commonly created. These immensely powerful constructs are most often used to guard royal tombs, magical armories, and similar places of ancient power.

A greater stone golem is 18 feet tall and weighs around 32,000 pounds. It resembles a typical stone golem in all respects, except that the Will save DC is 31 against its slow ability.

CL 14th; Craft Construct (see page 303), *antimagic field, geas/quest, symbol of stunning,* caster must be at least 14th level; Price 196,000 gp; Cost 105,000 gp + 7,640 XP.

GORGON

Gorgon

Large Magical Beast
Hit Dice: 8d10+40 (85 hp)
Initiative: +4
Speed: 30 ft. (6 squares)
Armor Class: 20 (–1 size, +11 natural), touch 9, flat-footed 20
Base Attack/Grapple: +8/+17
Attack: Gore +12 melee (1d8+7)
Full Attack: Gore +12 melee (1d8+7)
Space/Reach: 10 ft./5 ft.
Special Attacks: Breath weapon, trample 1d8+7
Special Qualities: Darkvision 60 ft., low-light vision, scent
Saves: Fort +11, Ref +6, Will +5
Abilities: Str 21, Dex 10, Con 21, Int 2, Wis 12, Cha 9
Skills: Listen +9, Spot +8
Feats: Alertness, Improved Initiative, Iron Will
Environment: Temperate plains
Organization: Solitary, pair, pack (3–4), or herd (5–13)
Challenge Rating: 8
Treasure: None
Alignment: Always neutral
Advancement: 9–15 HD (Large); 16–24 HD (Huge)
Level Adjustment: —

Dusky, metallic scales cover this creature's bull-like body. It has silver horns.

Gorgons guard their territory fiercely. They are fond of rocky areas, especially underground labyrinths.

A typical gorgon stands over 6 feet tall at the shoulder and measures 8 feet from snout to tail. It weighs about 4,000 pounds.

Gorgons are nothing if not aggressive. They attack intruders on sight, attempting to trample, gore, or petrify them. There is no way to calm these furious creatures, and they are impossible to domesticate.

COMBAT

Whenever possible, a gorgon begins an encounter by charging at its opponents.

Breath Weapon (Su): 60-foot cone, once every 1d4 rounds (but no more than five times per day), turn to stone permanently, Fortitude DC 19 negates. The save DC is Constitution-based.

Trample (Ex): Reflex DC 19 half. The save DC is Strength-based.

GRAY RENDER

Large Magical Beast
Hit Dice: 10d10+70 (125 hp)
Initiative: +0
Speed: 30 ft. (6 squares)
Armor Class: 19 (–1 size, +10 natural), touch 9, flat-footed 19
Base Attack/Grapple: +10/+20
Attack: Bite +15 melee (2d6+6)
Full Attack: Bite +15 melee (2d6+6); 2 claws +10 melee (1d6+3)
Space/Reach: 10 ft./10 ft.
Special Attacks: Improved grab, rend 2d6+9
Special Qualities: Darkvision 60 ft., low-light vision, scent
Saves: Fort +14, Ref +7, Will +4
Abilities: Str 23, Dex 10, Con 24, Int 3, Wis 12, Cha 8
Skills: Hide +2, Spot +10, Survival +3
Feats: Cleave, Power Attack, Improved Bull Rush, Track
Environment: Temperate marshes
Organization: Solitary
Challenge Rating: 8
Treasure: None
Alignment: Usually neutral
Advancement: 11–15 HD (Large); 16–30 HD (Huge)
Level Adjustment: +5 (cohort)

This hulking biped has the mass of a giant. It has a stooped frame, a gray, hairless body, and broad shoulders. Its arms are long and sinewy, and its clawed hands scrape along the ground as it walks. Its sloped forehead bears six small, yellowish eyes. Its mouth is wide and powerful-looking, filled with black teeth.

Bestial and savage, the gray render is a deadly predator found in remote wilderness areas.

These beasts are thought to be composed of dense muscle and bone, granting them the strength and stamina of a giant. A gray render stands about 9 feet tall in spite of its hunched posture and is about 4 feet wide. It weighs about 4,000 pounds.

Rangers have reported seeing renders uproot trees 3 feet in diameter with their jaws and tear them into splinters in just minutes.

Gray renders are never found in groups. Each of these asexual creatures produces one offspring and carries it for a time in a pouch, but thereafter the young render must fend for itself.

A unique quality of the gray render is its tendency to bond with, protect, and provide for another creature (or group of creatures) native to its surroundings. This strange behavior seems contrary to its otherwise savage nature, yet gray renders have been found with wolves, lions, horses, displacer beasts, owlbears, unicorns, hippogriffs, and occasionally even humanoid groups. Whether accepted or not, the render always attempts to remain fairly close, watching over its adopted charge(s) and daily bringing an offering of meat. It never willingly harms adopted creatures and retreats if they attack it. Most adopted creatures quickly begin to appreciate having such a powerful ally and accept and even rely on the gray render.

COMBAT

A gray render attacks to kill, whether to bring down prey or to protect itself or those it has adopted. When hunting, it sometimes attempts to hide and wait for prey to wander close.

Improved Grab (Ex): To use this ability, a gray render must hit with its bite attack. It can then attempt to start a grapple as a free action without provoking an attack of opportunity.

Rend (Ex): A gray render that wins a grapple check after a successful bite attack establishes a hold, latching onto the opponent's body and tearing the flesh. This attack automatically deals 2d6+9 points of damage.

Skills: Gray renders have a +4 racial bonus on Spot checks due to their six keen eyes.

Gray render

138

Grick

Gricks lair in any sheltered space that can accommodate their bodies, including holes, burrows, ledges, and crevices. They do not collect treasure, but their lairs are likely to contain the uneaten possessions of their victims. When prey is scarce, gricks venture aboveground and hunt in the wilderness, using tactics similar to those they employ underground. These creatures are not comfortable under the open sky, however, and return to the subterranean world as quickly as possible.

COMBAT

Gricks attack when hungry or threatened. They hunt by holing up near high-traffic areas, using their natural coloration to blend into convenient shadows. When prey (virtually anything that moves) ventures near, they lash out with their tentacles. A grick's rubbery body seems to shed blows of any kind. Its jaws are relatively small and weak compared to its body mass, so rather than consume its kill immediately, a grick normally drags its victim back to its lair to be eaten at its leisure.

A grick's natural weapons are treated as magic weapons for the purpose of overcoming damage reduction.

Multiple gricks do not fight in concert. Each attacks the prey closest to it, and breaks off the fight as soon as it can drag dead or unconscious prey away.

Skills: A grick has a +8 racial bonus on Climb checks and can always choose to take 10 on a Climb check, even if rushed or threatened.

*Their coloration affords gricks a +8 racial bonus on Hide checks when in natural rocky areas.

GRICK

Medium Aberration
Hit Dice: 2d8 (9 hp)
Initiative: +2
Speed: 30 ft. (6 squares), climb 20 ft.
Armor Class: 16 (+2 Dex, +4 natural), touch 12, flat-footed 14
Base Attack/Grapple: +1/+3
Attack: Tentacle +3 melee (1d4+2)
Full Attack: 4 tentacles +3 melee (1d4+2); bite −2 melee (1d3+1)
Space/Reach: 5 ft./5 ft.
Special Attacks: —
Special Qualities: Damage reduction 10/magic, darkvision 60 ft., scent
Saves: Fort +0, Ref +2, Will +5
Abilities: Str 14, Dex 14, Con 11, Int 3, Wis 14, Cha 5
Skills: Climb +10, Hide +3*, Listen +6, Spot +6
Feats: Alertness, Track[B]
Environment: Underground
Organization: Solitary or cluster (2–4)
Challenge Rating: 3
Treasure: 1/10 coins; 50% goods; 50% items
Alignment: Usually neutral
Advancement: 3–4 HD (Medium); 5–6 HD (Large)
Level Adjustment: —

This wormlike monster has a body as long as a man is tall, with four tentacles a little longer than human forearms. The tentacles, located on its head along either side of its jaws, are segmented, as is the body itself.

Gricks are stealthy underground predators that infest dungeons, caves, and other shadowed places under the earth, waiting patiently for prey to come within reach.

An adult grick is about 8 feet long from the tips of its tentacles to the end of its body and weighs some 200 pounds. Its body coloration is uniformly dark, with a pale underbelly.

GRIFFON

Large Magical Beast
Hit Dice: 7d10+21 (59 hp)
Initiative: +2
Speed: 30 ft. (6 squares), fly 80 ft. (average)
Armor Class: 17 (−1 size, +2 Dex, +6 natural), touch 11, flat-footed 15
Base Attack/Grapple: +7/+15
Attack: Bite +11 melee (2d6+4)
Full Attack: Bite +11 melee (2d6+4) and 2 claws +8 melee (1d4+2)
Space/Reach: 10 ft./5 ft.
Special Attacks: Pounce, rake 1d6+2
Special Qualities: Darkvision 60 ft., low-light vision, scent
Saves: Fort +8, Ref +7, Will +5
Abilities: Str 18, Dex 15, Con 16, Int 5, Wis 13, Cha 8
Skills: Jump +8, Listen +6, Spot +10
Feats: Iron Will, Multiattack, Weapon Focus (bite)
Environment: Temperate hills
Organization: Solitary, pair, or pride (6–10)
Challenge Rating: 4
Treasure: None
Alignment: Always neutral
Advancement: 8–10 HD (Large); 11–21 HD (Huge)
Level Adjustment: +3 (cohort)

This beast's body resembles that of a muscular lion. Its head and front legs are those of a great eagle, and it has a pair of large, golden wings.

Griffons are powerful, majestic creatures with the characteristics of both lions and eagles. They hunt all manner of prey but favor the flesh of horses above all else.

From nose to tail, an adult griffon can measure as much as 8 feet. Neither males nor females are endowed with a mane. A pair of broad, golden wings emerge from the creature's back and span 25 feet or more. A griffon weighs about 500 pounds.

Griffons make their homes in high places, swooping down with a shrill, eaglelike cry to attack their prey. Although both aggressive and territorial, they are also intelligent enough to avoid obviously powerful enemies. They almost always attack horses, however, and any who attempt to protect horses from a hungry griffon often end up on the menu themselves.

A griffon cannot speak, but understands Common.

COMBAT

Griffons prefer to pounce on their prey, either diving to the attack or leaping from above.

Pounce (Ex): If a griffon dives upon or charges a foe, it can make a full attack, including two rake attacks.

Rake (Ex): Attack bonus +8 melee, damage 1d6+2.

Skills: Griffons have a +4 racial bonus on Jump and Spot checks.

TRAINING A GRIFFON

Although intelligent, a griffon requires training before it can bear a rider in combat. To be trained, a griffon must have a friendly attitude toward the trainer (this can be achieved through a successful Diplomacy check). Training a friendly griffon requires six weeks of work and a DC 25 Handle Animal check. Riding a griffon requires an exotic saddle. A griffon can fight while carrying a rider, but the rider cannot also attack unless he or she succeeds on a Ride check.

Griffon eggs are worth 3,500 gp apiece on the open market, while young are worth 7,000 gp each. Professional trainers charge 1,500 gp to rear or train a griffon.

Carrying Capacity: A light load for a griffon is up to 300 pounds; a medium load, 301–600 pounds; and a heavy load, 601–900 pounds.

Illus. by A. Waters

Griffon

GRIMLOCK

Medium Monstrous Humanoid
Hit Dice: 2d8+2 (11 hp)
Initiative: +1
Speed: 30 ft. (6 squares)
Armor Class: 15 (+1 Dex, +4 natural), touch 11, flat-footed 14
Base Attack/Grapple: +2/+4
Attack: Battleaxe +4 melee (1d8+3/×3)
Full Attack: Battleaxe +4 melee (1d8+3/×3)
Space/Reach: 5 ft./5 ft.
Special Attacks: —
Special Qualities: Blindsight 40 ft., immunities, scent
Saves: Fort +1, Ref +4, Will +2
Abilities: Str 15, Dex 13, Con 13, Int 10, Wis 8, Cha 6
Skills: Climb +4, Hide +3*, Listen +5, Spot +3
Feats: Alertness, Track[B]
Environment: Underground
Organization: Gang (2–4), pack (10–20), tribe (10–60 plus 1 leader of 3rd–5th level per 10 adults), or cult (10–80 plus 1 leader of 3rd–5th level per 10 adults and 1 mind flayer or medusa)
Challenge Rating: 1
Treasure: Standard coins; standard goods (gems only); standard items
Alignment: Often neutral evil
Advancement: By character class
Level Adjustment: +2

This muscular humanoid is about as tall as a human. It has thick, gray, scaly skin and blank, eyeless eye sockets.

Grimlocks are natives of the deep places beneath the earth but come to the surface to raid for slaves and pillage. While there, they lurk in mountainous terrain, which hides them well. They prefer raw, fresh meat—preferably human.

Extremely xenophobic, grimlocks are normally encountered in small patrols or packs on the surface. Underground, they may form larger communities that are led by powerful grimlocks or by some more intelligent creature, such as a medusa or a mind flayer.

Grimlocks speak their own language and Common.

COMBAT

Grimlocks are blind, but their exceptional senses of smell and hearing allow them to notice foes nearby. As a result, they usually shun ranged weapons and rush to the attack, brandishing their stone battleaxes.

Blindsight (Ex): Grimlocks can sense all foes within 40 feet as a sighted creature would. Beyond that range, they treat all targets as having total concealment. Grimlocks are susceptible to sound- and scent-based attacks, however, and are affected normally by loud noises and sonic spells (such as *ghost sound* or *silence*) and overpowering odors (such as *stinking cloud* or incense-heavy air). Negating a grimlock's sense of smell or hearing reduces this ability to normal Blind-Fight (as the feat). If both these senses are negated, a grimlock is effectively blinded.

Immunities: Grimlocks are immune to gaze attacks, visual effects, illusions, and other attack forms that rely on sight.

Skills: *A grimlock's dull gray skin helps it hide in its native terrain, conferring a +10 racial bonus on Hide checks when in mountains or underground.

GRIMLOCKS AS CHARACTERS

Independent groups of grimlocks are usually led by barbarians, while those in the service of a mind flayer are often rangers.

Grimlock characters possess the following racial traits.

— +4 Strength, +2 Dexterity, +2 Constitution, –2 Wisdom, –4 Charisma.

—Medium size.

—A grimlock's base land speed is 30 feet.

—Racial Hit Dice: A grimlock begins with two levels of monstrous humanoid, which provide 2d8 Hit Dice, a base attack bonus of +2, and base saving throw bonuses of Fort +0, Ref +3, and Will +3.

—Racial Skills: A grimlock's monstrous humanoid levels give it skill points equal to 5 × (2 + Int modifier, minimum 1). Its class skills are Climb, Hide, Listen, and Spot. Grimlocks gain a +10 racial bonus on Hide checks in mountain or underground settings.

—Racial Feats: A grimlock's monstrous humanoid levels give it one feat.

—Weapon Proficiency: A grimlock is automatically proficient with the battle-axe.

— +4 natural armor bonus.

—Special Qualities (see above): Blindsight 40 ft., immunities, scent.

—Automatic Languages: Common, Grimlock. Bonus Languages: Draconic, Dwarven, Gnome, Terran, Undercommon.

—Favored Class: Barbarian.

Grimlock

—Level adjustment +2.

GUARDINAL

Guardinals are a celestial race native to the plane of Elysium. When at home, they are among the most peaceful of creatures, quick to laugh and slow to anger. They show a very different face when away from Elysium, however—they have no tolerance for evil and often rove the cosmos looking for evil to confront.

Guardinals speak Celestial, Infernal, and Draconic, but can speak with almost any creature, thanks to their *tongues* ability.

Guardinal Traits: A guardinal possesses the following traits (unless otherwise noted in a creature's entry).

—Darkvision out to 60 feet and low-light vision.

—Immunity to electricity and petrification.

—Resistance to cold 10 and sonic 10.

—Lay on Hands (Su): As the paladin class feature, except that each day, a guardinal can heal an amount of damage equal to its full normal hit points.

— +4 racial bonus on saves against poison.

—Speak with Animals (Su): This ability works like *speak with animals* (caster level 8th) but is a free action and does not require sound.

AVORAL

Medium Outsider (Extraplanar, Good, Guardinal)
Hit Dice: 7d8+35 (66 hp)
Initiative: +6
Speed: 40 ft. (8 squares), fly 90 ft. (good)
Armor Class: 24 (+6 Dex, +8 natural), touch 16, flat-footed 18
Base Attack/Grapple: +7/+9
Attack: Claw +13 melee (2d6+2) or wing +13 melee (2d8+2)
Full Attack: 2 claws +13 melee (2d6+2) or 2 wings +13 melee (2d8+2)
Space/Reach: 5 ft./5 ft.
Special Attacks: Spell-like abilities, fear aura
Special Qualities: Damage reduction 10/evil or silver, darkvision 60 ft., immunity to electricity and petrification, lay on hands, low-light vision, resistance to cold 10 and sonic 10, speak with animals, spell resistance 25, true seeing
Saves: Fort +10 (+14 against poison), Ref +11, Will +8
Abilities: Str 15, Dex 23, Con 20, Int 15, Wis 16, Cha 16
Skills: Bluff +13, Concentration +15, Diplomacy +7, Disguise +3 (+5 acting), Handle Animal +13, Hide +16, Intimidate +5, Knowledge (any one) +12, Listen +13, Move Silently +16, Ride +8, Sense Motive +13, Spellcraft +12, Spot +21
Feats: Empower Spell-Like Ability (*magic missile*), Flyby Attack, Weapon Finesse
Environment: Blessed Fields of Elysium
Organization: Solitary, pair, or squad (3–5)
Challenge Rating: 9
Treasure: No coins; double goods; standard items
Alignment: Always neutral good
Advancement: 8–14 HD (Medium); 15–21 HD (Large)
Level Adjustment: —

This creature has the body of a tall, muscular human, but with long, powerful wings instead of arms. The face is more human than avian, but the hair resembles a feathery cowl, and the eyes are bright gold. The legs have strong talons and feathery vanes.

An avoral's bones are strong but hollow, so even the largest specimens weigh no more than 120 pounds. An avoral is about 7 feet tall.

Each of an avoral's wings has a small hand at the midpoint. When the wings are folded, these appendages are about where human hands would be and can do nearly anything hands can do.

An avoral's visual acuity is virtually unmatched: It can see detail on objects up to 10 miles away and is said to be able to discern the color of a creature's eyes at 200 paces.

Combat

On the ground, an avoral can lash out with its wings to deliver punishing blows. However, it prefers to meet its foes in the air, where it can employ its talons and make full use of its aerial speed and agility. It can't make wing attacks while flying, however.

An avoral's natural weapons, as well as any weapons it wields, are treated as good-aligned for the purpose of overcoming damage reduction.

Spell-Like Abilities: At will—*aid, blur* (self only), *command* (DC 14), *detect magic, dimension door, dispel magic, gust of wind* (DC 15), *hold person* (DC 16), *light, magic circle against evil* (self only), *magic missile, see invisibility;* 3/day—*lightning bolt* (DC 16). Caster level 8th. The save DCs are Charisma-based.

Fear Aura (Su): Once per day an avoral can create an aura of fear in a 20-foot radius. It is otherwise identical with *fear* from an 8th-level caster (save DC 17). The save DC is Charisma-based.

True Seeing (Su): This ability is identical with *true seeing* (caster level 14th), except that it has personal range and the avoral must concentrate for 1 full round before it takes effect. Thereafter the ability remains in effect as long as the avoral concentrates on it.

Skills: An avoral's sharp eyes give it a +8 racial bonus on Spot checks.

LEONAL

Medium Outsider (Extraplanar, Good, Guardinal)
Hit Dice: 12d8+60 (114 hp)
Initiative: +3
Speed: 60 ft. (12 squares)
Armor Class: 27 (+3 Dex, +14 natural)
Base Attack/Grapple: +12/+20
Attack: Claw +20 melee (1d6+8)
Full Attack: 2 claws +20 melee (1d6+8) and bite +15 melee (1d8+4)
Space/Reach: 5 ft./5 ft.
Special Attacks: Roar, pounce, improved grab, rake 1d6+8, spell-like abilities
Special Qualities: Damage reduction 10/evil and silver, darkvision 60 ft., immunity to electricity and petrification, lay on hands, low-light vision, protective aura, resistance to cold 10 and sonic 10, speak with animals, spell resistance 28
Saves: Fort +13 (+17 against poison), Ref +11, Will +10
Abilities: Str 27, Dex 17, Con 20, Int 14, Wis 14, Cha 15
Skills: Balance +22, Concentration +12, Diplomacy +4, Hide +22, Intimidate +10, Jump +35, Knowledge (any) +17, Listen +17, Move Silently +22, Sense Motive +17, Spot +17, Survival +17
Feats: Ability Focus (roar), Dodge, Mobility, Spring Attack, Track
Environment: Blessed Fields of Elysium
Organization: Solitary or pride (4–9)
Challenge Rating: 12
Treasure: No coins; double goods; standard items
Alignment: Always neutral good
Advancement: 13–18 HD (Medium); 19–36 HD (Large)
Level Adjustment: —

This creature looks like a powerful humanoid about 6 feet tall, covered in short, golden fur. Its head is leonine in appearance, with a short muzzle and a lush, dark gold mane. Its arms end in powerful claws, and its mouth holds rows of long, sharp teeth.

One of the most powerful guardinal forms, a leonal is every bit as regal as a lion of the Material Plane. As a foe, it can be just as terrifying, bellowing mighty roars and slashing with razor-sharp claws.

Avoral

Leonal

Combat

Leonals like their battles as straightforward as can be. They begin with a roar to put their foes off balance, then follow up with a frenzy of claw and bite attacks. They closely coordinate with others in their pride, watching one another's flanks and setting up devastating attacks.

A leonal's natural weapons, as well as any weapons it wields, are treated as good-aligned for the purpose of overcoming damage reduction.

Roar (Su): A leonal can roar up to three times per day. Each roar releases a blast in a 60-foot cone that duplicates the effects of a *holy word* spell and deals an extra 2d6 points of sonic damage (Fortitude DC 20 negates). The save DC is Charisma-based.

Pounce (Ex): If a leonal charges a foe, it can make a full attack, including two rake attacks.

Improved Grab (Ex): To use this ability, a leonal must hit with its bite attack. It can then attempt to start a grapple as a free action without provoking an attack of opportunity. If it wins the grapple check, it establishes a hold and can rake.

Rake (Ex): Attack bonus +20 melee, damage 1d6+8.

Spell-Like Abilities: At will—*detect thoughts, fireball* (DC 15), *hold monster* (DC 17), *polymorph, wall of force;* 3/day—*cure critical wounds* (DC 16), *neutralize poison, remove disease;* 1/day—*heal* (DC 18). Caster level 10th. The save DCs are Charisma-based.

Protective Aura (Su): Against attacks made or effects created by evil creatures, this ability provides a +4 deflection bonus to AC and a +4 resistance bonus on saving throws to anyone within 20 feet of the leonal. Otherwise, it functions as a *magic circle against evil* effect and a *lesser globe of invulnerability,* both with a radius of 20 feet (caster level equals leonal's HD). (The defensive benefits from the circle are not included in a leonal's statistics block.)

Skills: Leonals have a +4 racial bonus on Balance, Hide, and Move Silently checks.

HAG

Hags are horrible creatures whose love of evil is equaled only by their ugliness.

Although they often plot and scheme for power or some malevolent end, hags also appear to do evil for its own sake. They may use their dark magic and knowledge of fell things to serve a more powerful evil being, but they are seldom faithful. They may turn on their master if they see a chance to seize power for themselves.

Although different hags are unique in appearance and mannerism, they have many aspects in common. All take the form of crones whose bent shapes belie their fierce power and swiftness. Despite faces cracked by wrinkles and heavy with cruelty, their eyes shine with villainy and cunning. Their long nails have the strength of steel and are as keen as any knife.

Hags speak Giant and Common.

COMBAT

Hags are tremendously strong. They are naturally resistant to spells and can cast magic of their own. Hags often gather to form coveys. A covey, usually containing one hag of each type, can use powers beyond those of the individual members.

ANNIS

Large Monstrous Humanoid
Hit Dice: 7d8+14 (45 hp)
Initiative: +1
Speed: 40 ft. (8 squares)
Armor Class: 20 (−1 size, +1 Dex, +10 natural), touch 10, flat-footed 19
Base Attack/Grapple: +7/+18
Attack: Claw +13 melee (1d6+7)
Full Attack: 2 claws +13 melee (1d6+7) and bite +8 melee (1d6+3)
Space/Reach: 10 ft./10 ft.
Special Attacks: Improved grab, rake 1d6+7, rend 2d6+10, spell-like abilities
Special Qualities: Damage reduction 2/bludgeoning, darkvision 60 ft., spell resistance 19
Saves: Fort +6, Ref +6, Will +6
Abilities: Str 25, Dex 12, Con 14, Int 13, Wis 13, Cha 10
Skills: Bluff +8, Diplomacy +2, Disguise +0 (+2 acting), Hide +5, Intimidate +2, Listen +10, Spot +10
Feats: Alertness, Blind-Fight, Great Fortitude
Environment: Cold marshes
Organization: Solitary or covey (3 hags of any kind plus 1–8 ogres and 1–4 evil giants)
Challenge Rating: 6
Treasure: Standard
Alignment: Usually chaotic evil
Advancement: By character class
Level Adjustment: —

This creature looks like an ancient female human, but impossibly tall. It has deep blue skin and filthy black hair.

The dreaded annis may be the most horrible of hags. An annis commonly uses its *disguise self* ability to take the form of an exceptionally tall human, a fair giant, or an ogre.

An annis stands some 8 feet tall and weighs about 325 pounds.

Combat

Though physically powerful, these hags do not favor simple assaults but try to divide and confuse their foes before combat. They love to pose as commoners or gentlefolk to lull their victims into a sense of false security before they attack.

Improved Grab (Ex): To use this ability, an annis must hit a Large or smaller opponent with a claw attack. It can then attempt to start a grapple as a free action without provoking an attack of opportunity.

Rake (Ex): Attack bonus +13 melee, damage 1d6+7. An annis can attack a grappled foe with both claws at no penalty.

Rend (Ex): An annis that hits with both claw attacks latches onto the opponent's body and tears the flesh. This attack automatically deals an extra 2d6+10 points of damage.

Spell-Like Abilities: 3/day—*disguise self, fog cloud.* Caster level 8th.

GREEN HAG

Medium Monstrous Humanoid
Hit Dice: 9d8+9 (49 hp)
Initiative: +1
Speed: 30 ft. (6 squares), swim 30 ft.
Armor Class: 22 (+1 Dex, +11 natural), touch 11, flat-footed 21
Base Attack/Grapple: +9/+13
Attack: Claw +13 melee (1d4+4)
Full Attack: 2 claws +13 melee (1d4+4)
Space/Reach: 5 ft./5 ft.
Special Attacks: Spell-like abilities, weakness, mimicry
Special Qualities: Darkvision 90 ft., spell resistance 18
Saves: Fort +6, Ref +7, Will +7
Abilities: Str 19, Dex 12, Con 12, Int 13, Wis 13, Cha 14
Skills: Concentration +7, Craft or Knowledge (any one) +7, Hide +9, Listen +11, Spot +11 Swim +12
Feats: Alertness, Blind-Fight, Combat Casting, Great Fortitude
Environment: Temperate marshes
Organization: Solitary or covey (3 hags of any kind plus 1–8 ogres and 1–4 evil giants)
Challenge Rating: 5
Treasure: Standard
Alignment: Usually chaotic evil
Advancement: By character class
Level Adjustment: —

This creature looks like a very old female human. It has a sickly green complexion with dark, tangled hair that looks almost like a twisted vine.

Green hags are found in desolate swamps and dark forests.

A green hag is about the same height and weight as a female human.

Combat

Green hags prefer to attack from hiding, usually after distracting foes. They often use darkvision to their advantage by attacking during moonless nights.

Spell-Like Abilities: At will—*dancing lights, disguise self, ghost sound* (DC 12), *invisibility, pass without trace, tongues, water breathing.* Caster level 9th. The save DC is Charisma-based.

Weakness (Su): A green hag can weaken a foe by making a special touch attack. The opponent must succeed on a DC 16 Forti-

Green hag

tude save or take 2d4 points of Strength damage. The save DC is Charisma-based.

Mimicry (Ex): A green hag can imitate the sounds of almost any animal found near its lair.

Skills: A green hag has a +8 racial bonus on any Swim check to perform some special action or avoid a hazard. It can always choose to take 10 on a Swim check, even if distracted or endangered. It can use the run action while swimming, provided it swims in a straight line.

SEA HAG

Medium Monstrous Humanoid (Aquatic)
Hit Dice: 3d8+6 (19 hp)
Initiative: +1
Speed: 30 ft. (6 squares), swim 40 ft.
Armor Class: 14 (+1 Dex, +3 natural), touch 11, flat-footed 13
Base Attack/Grapple: +3/+7
Attack: Claw +7 melee (1d4+4)
Full Attack: 2 claws +7 melee (1d4+4)
Space/Reach: 5 ft./5 ft.
Special Attacks: Horrific appearance, evil eye
Special Qualities: Amphibious, spell resistance 14
Saves: Fort +2, Ref +4, Will +4
Abilities: Str 19, Dex 12, Con 12, Int 10, Wis 13, Cha 14
Skills: Craft or Knowledge (any one) +3, Hide +4, Listen +6, Spot +6, Swim +12
Feats: Alertness, Toughness
Environment: Temperate aquatic
Organization: Solitary or covey (3 hags of any kind plus 1–8 ogres and 1–4 evil giants)
Challenge Rating: 4
Treasure: Standard
Alignment: Usually chaotic evil
Advancement: By character class
Level Adjustment: —

This creature looks like an old female human. Its flesh is sickly and yellow, covered with warts and oozing sores. Its long, filthy hair resembles rotting seaweed.

Perhaps the most wretched of hags, the sea hag is found in the water of seas or overgrown lakes.

A sea hag is about the same height and weight as a female human.

Combat

Sea hags are not subtle and prefer a direct approach to combat. They usually remain in hiding until they can affect as many foes as possible with their horrific appearance.

Horrific Appearance (Su): The sight of a sea hag is so revolting that anyone (other than another hag) who sets eyes upon one must succeed on a DC 13 Fortitude save or instantly be weakened, taking 2d6 points of Strength damage. This damage cannot reduce a victim's Strength score below 0, but anyone reduced to Strength 0 is helpless. Creatures that are affected by this power or that successfully save against it cannot be affected again by the same hag's horrific appearance for 24 hours. The save DC is Charisma-based.

Evil Eye (Su): Three times per day, a sea hag can cast its dire gaze upon any single creature within 30 feet. The target must succeed on a DC 13 Will save or be dazed for three days, although *remove curse* or *dispel evil* can restore sanity sooner. In addition, an affected creature must succeed on a DC 13 Fortitude save or die from fright. Creatures with immunity to fear effects are not affected by the sea hag's evil eye. The save DCs are Charisma-based.

Amphibious (Ex): Although sea hags are aquatic, they can survive indefinitely on land.

Skills: A sea hag has a +8 racial bonus on any Swim check to perform some special action or avoid a hazard. It can always choose to take 10 on a Swim check, even if distracted or endangered. It can use the run action while swimming, provided it swims in a straight line.

HAG COVEY

From time to time, a trio of hags gathers as a covey. Usually this foul triune includes one hag of each type, but this is not always the case.

Combat

Hags in a covey rely on deception and their boosted magical abilities in combat.

A covey of hags is 80% likely to be guarded by 1d8 ogres and 1d4 evil giants who do their bidding. These minions are often disguised with a *veil* spell to appear less threatening and sent forth as spies. Such minions often (60%) carry magic stones known as *hag eyes* (see below).

Spell-Like Abilities: 3/day—*animate dead, bestow curse* (DC 17), *control weather, dream, forcecage, mind blank, mirage arcana* (DC 18), *polymorph, veil* (DC 19), *vision*. Caster level 9th. The save DCs are based on a Charisma score of 16. To use one of these abilities (which requires a full-round action), all three hags must be within 10 feet of one another, and all must participate.

Once per month, a covey that does not have a *hag eye* can create one from a gem worth at least 20 gp (see below).

Hag Eye

A *hag eye* is a magic gem created by a covey. It appears to be nothing more than a semiprecious stone, but a *gem of seeing* or other such effect reveals it as a disembodied eye. Often, a *hag eye* is worn as a ring, brooch, or other adornment. Any of the three hags who created the *hag eye* can see through it whenever they wish, so long as it is on the same plane of existence as the hag. A *hag eye* has hardness 5 and 10 hit points. Destroying a *hag eye* deals 1d10 points of damage to each member of the covey and causes the one who sustained the greatest damage to be blinded for 24 hours.

HALF-CELESTIAL

A celestial's magical nature allows it to breed with virtually any creature. The offspring of the resulting unions, half-celestials, are glorious and wonderful beings.

To carry out their responsibilities, celestials sometimes spend great amounts of time in mortal realms. Being devoted and kind, they occasionally fall in love with mortals: humans, elves, unicorns, and similar creatures. The objects of celestial affection are never evil and are always intelligent. They always return the love of their immortal paramour and willingly conceive the child, usually caring for it since the celestial has other duties.

No matter the form, half-celestials are always comely and delightful to the senses, having golden skin, sparkling eyes, angelic wings, or some other sign of their higher nature.

Though noble and compassionate, half-celestials are often dismayed at the evil among their kin and take a stern, sometimes harsh, view of base instincts or malevolent actions. Never truly fitting into any mortal society, half-celestials are usually loners and wanderers attempting to right wrongs wherever they can.

SAMPLE HALF-CELESTIAL

This noble knight seems human, but he has golden eyes, and a large pair of white-feathered wings spreads from his shoulders.

This example uses a 9th-level human paladin as the base creature.

Half-Celestial 9th-Level Human Paladin

Medium Outsider (Augmented Humanoid, Native)
Hit Dice: 9d10+36 (90 hp)
Initiative: +1
Speed: 30 ft. (6 squares), fly 60 ft. (good)
Armor Class: 24 (+1 Dex, +2 natural, +11 *+2 mithral breastplate* and *+2 heavy steel shield*), touch 11, flat-footed 23
Base Attack/Grapple: +9/+14
Attack: *+2 bastard sword* +17 melee (1d10+7/19–20) or masterwork composite longbow (+4 Str bonus) +11 ranged (1d8+4/×3)
Full Attack: *+2 bastard sword* +17/+12 melee (1d10+7/19–20) or masterwork composite longbow (+4 Str bonus) +11/+6 ranged (1d8+4/×3)
Space/Reach: 5 ft./5 ft.
Special Attacks: Daylight, smite evil, spells, spell-like abilities, turn undead 7/day
Special Qualities: Aura of courage, aura of good, damage reduction 5/magic, darkvision 60 ft., *detect evil*, divine grace, divine health, immunity to disease, lay on hands, resistance to acid 10, cold 10, and electricity 10, *remove disease* 2/week, spell resistance 19, turn undead 7/day
Saves: Fort +14 (+18 against poison), Ref +8, Will +10
Abilities: Str 20, Dex 12, Con 18, Int 10, Wis 16, Cha 18
Skills: Concentration +13, Diplomacy +13, Ride +11, Spot +7
Feats: Exotic Weapon Proficiency (bastard sword), Flyby Attack, Improved Natural Armor, Power Attack, Weapon Focus (bastard sword)
Environment: Temperate plains
Organization: Solitary
Challenge Rating: 11
Treasure: Standard
Alignment: Always lawful good
Advancement: By character class
Level Adjustment: +4

The half-celestial paladin is a champion of good, a roving knight whose courage in the face of danger is legendary.

Combat

The half-celestial paladin strives to meet his foes in blade-to-blade combat, resorting to flyby attacks only when confronted by a number of dangerous foes. Against a powerful evil creature, the half-celestial paladin readies himself for close combat with his spells and spell-like abilities, and then makes good use of his ability to smite evil.

Daylight (Su): Half-celestials can use *daylight* (as the spell) at will as a standard action.

Smite Evil (Su): Twice per day, this half-celestial paladin may attempt to smite evil with one normal melee attack. He adds his +4 Charisma modifier to his attack roll and deals 9 points of extra damage (1 per paladin level) if the attack hits. If he accidentally smites a creature that is not evil, the smite has no effect but it is still used up for that day.

Also, once per day this half-celestial paladin can make a normal melee attack with no additional bonus to deal 9 points of extra damage against an evil foe (this is a benefit of the half-celestial template).

Spell-Like Abilities (Half-Celestial): 3/day—*protection from evil*; 1/day—*aid, bless, cure serious wounds* (DC 17), *dispel evil* (DC 19), *holy smite* (DC 18), *neutralize poison, remove disease.* Caster level 9th. The save DCs are Charisma-based.

Turn Undead (Su): This paladin turns undead as a 6th-level cleric.

Aura of Courage (Su): This paladin has immunity to fear (magical or otherwise). Each ally within 10 feet of him gains a +4 morale bonus on saving throws against fear effects.

Aura of Good (Ex): This half-celestial paladin radiates a strong aura of good (see the *detect good* spell) as the 9th-level cleric of a good deity.

Detect Evil (Sp): At will, this paladin can use *detect evil*, as the spell.

Divine Grace (Su): This paladin applies his Charisma modifier as a bonus on all saving throws.

Divine Health (Ex): This paladin has immunity to all diseases, including supernatural and magical diseases (such as mummy rot and lycanthropy).

Lay on Hands (Su): This paladin can cure up to 36 points of damage per day.

Remove Disease (Sp): Half-celestial paladins can use *remove disease* twice per week as a spell-like ability (this is the paladin's class feature). A half-celestial also has the ability to use *remove disease* as a half-celestial spell-like ability (see above).

Typical Paladin Spells Prepared (2/1; save DC 13 + spell level): 1st—*bless weapon, divine favor;* 2nd—*bull's strength.*

Possessions: +2 mithral breastplate, +2 large steel shield, +2 bastard sword, masterwork composite longbow (+4 Str bonus), 10 silvered arrows, 10 cold iron arrows. (Different half-celestials may have different possessions.)

CREATING A HALF-CELESTIAL

"Half-celestial" is an inherited template that can be added to any living, corporeal creature with an Intelligence score of 4 or higher and nonevil alignment (referred to hereafter as the base creature).

A half-celestial uses all the base creature's statistics and special abilities except as noted here.

Size and Type: The creature's type changes to outsider. Do not recalculate the creature's Hit Dice, base attack bonus, or saves. Size is unchanged. Half-celestials are normally native outsiders.

Speed: A half-celestial has feathered wings and can fly at twice the base creature's base land speed (good maneuverability). If the base creature has a fly speed, use that instead.

Armor Class: Natural armor improves by +1 (this stacks with any natural armor bonus the base creature has).

Special Attacks: A half-celestial retains all the special attacks of the base creature and also gains the following special abilities.

Daylight (Su): Half-celestials can use a *daylight* effect (as the spell) at will.

Smite Evil (Su): Once per day a half-celestial can make a normal melee attack to deal extra damage equal to its HD (maximum of +20) against an evil foe.

Spell-Like Abilities: A half-celestial with an Intelligence or Wisdom score of 8 or higher has two or more spell-like abilities, depending on its Hit Dice, as indicated on the table below. The abilities are cumulative; a half-celestial wyrmling brass dragon (4 HD) can use *protection from evil* and *bless* as well as *aid* and *detect evil.* Unless otherwise noted, an ability is usable once per day. Caster level equals the creature's HD, and the save DC is Charisma-based.

HD	Abilities
1–2	*Protection from evil* 3/day, *bless*
3–4	*Aid, detect evil*
5–6	*Cure serious wounds, neutralize poison*
7–8	*Holy smite, remove disease*
9–10	*Dispel evil*
11–12	*Holy word*
13–14	*Holy aura* 3/day, *hallow*
15–16	*Mass charm monster*
17–18	*Summon monster IX* (celestials only)
19–20	*Resurrection*

Special Qualities: A half-celestial has all the special qualities of the base creature, plus the following special qualities.

—Darkvision out to 60 feet.

—Immunity to disease.

—Resistance to acid 10, cold 10, and electricity 10.

—Damage reduction: 5/magic (if HD 11 or less) or 10/magic (if HD 12 or more).

—A half-celestial's natural weapons are treated as magic weapons for the purpose of overcoming damage reduction.

—Spell resistance equal to creature's HD + 10 (maximum 35).

— +4 racial bonus on Fortitude saves against poison.

Abilities: Increase from the base creature as follows: Str +4, Dex +2, Con +4, Int +2, Wis +4, Cha +4.

Skills: A half-celestial gains skill points as an outsider and has skill points equal to (8 + Int modifier) × (HD +3). Do not include Hit Dice from class levels in this calculation—the half-celestial gains outsider skill points only for its racial Hit Dice, and gains the normal amount of skill points for its class levels. Treat skills from the base creature's list as class skills, and other skills as cross-class.

Challenge Rating: HD 5 or less, as base creature +1; HD 6 to 10, as base creature +2; HD 11 or more, as base creature +3.

Alignment: Always good (any).

Level Adjustment: Same as base creature +4.

HALF-CELESTIAL CHARACTERS

Half-celestial humanoids often have a character class, preferring bard, cleric, fighter, and paladin. Nonhumanoids are also sometimes clerics or paladins. Half-celestial clerics serve good deities such as Ehlonna, Heironeous, Kord, or Pelor.

HALF-DRAGON

A dragon's magical nature allows it to breed with virtually any creature. Conception usually occurs while the dragon has changed its shape; it then abandons the crossbreed offspring.

Half-dragon creatures are always more formidable than others of their kind that do not have dragon blood, and their appearance betrays their nature—scales, elongated features, reptilian eyes, and exaggerated teeth and claws. Sometimes they have wings.

SAMPLE HALF-DRAGON

This powerful humanoid has black, scaled skin, sharp claws and fangs, and a pair of forward-curving horns above its eyes.

Here is an example of a half-dragon using a 4th-level human fighter as the base creature and a black dragon as the nonhuman parent.

Half-Black Dragon 4th-Level Human Fighter
Medium Dragon (Augmented Humanoid)
Hit Dice: 4d10+16 (43 hp)
Initiative: +1
Speed: 20 ft. in full plate armor (4 squares); base speed 30 ft.
Armor Class: 24 (+1 Dex, +4 natural, +9 *+1 full plate armor*), touch 11, flat-footed 23
Base Attack/Grapple: +4/+10
Attack: Masterwork two-bladed sword +12 melee (1d8+11/19–20) or javelin +5 ranged (1d6+6)
Full Attack: Masterwork two-bladed sword +10 melee/+10 melee (1d8+8/19–20, 1d8+5/19–20) and bite +5 melee (1d6+3); or 2 claws +10 melee (1d4+6) and bite +5 melee (1d6+3); or javelin +5 ranged (1d6+6)
Space/Reach: 5 ft./5 ft.
Special Attacks: Breath weapon
Special Qualities: Darkvision 60 ft., immunity to acid, *sleep*, and paralysis, low-light vision
Saves: Fort +8, Ref +2, Will +4

Abilities: Str 22, Dex 13, Con 18, Int 10, Wis 12, Cha 12
Skills: Climb +5, Intimidate +4, Jump –1, Listen +3, Spot +4
Feats: Exotic Weapon Proficiency (two-bladed sword), Iron Will, Power Attack, Two Weapon Fighting, Weapon Focus (two-bladed sword), Weapon Specialization (two-bladed sword)
Environment: Temperate plains
Organization: Solitary
Challenge Rating: 6
Treasure: Standard
Alignment: Often chaotic evil
Advancement: By character class
Level Adjustment: +3

This half-dragon is based on a 4th-level human fighter with the following ability scores: Str 14, Dex 13, Con 16, Int 8, Wis 12, Cha 10.

Combat

Half-black dragon fighters use two-handed (often exotic) weapons. Aggressive and temperamental, they're usually itching for a battle. They often lead other evil warriors, but fight as individuals.

Breath Weapon (Su): 30-foot line, once per day, damage 6d8 acid, Reflex DC 14 half. The save DC is Constitution-based.

Possessions: +1 full plate armor, masterwork two-bladed sword, 2 javelins.

CREATING A HALF-DRAGON

"Half-dragon" is an inherited template that can be added to any living, corporeal creature (referred to hereafter as the base creature).

A half-dragon uses all the base creature's statistics and special abilities except as noted here.

Size and Type: The creature's type changes to dragon. Size is unchanged. Do not recalculate base attack bonus or saves.

Hit Dice: Increase base creature's racial HD by one die size, to a maximum of d12. Do not increase class HD.

Speed: A half-dragon that is Large or larger has wings and can fly at twice its base land speed (maximum 120 ft.) with average maneuverability. A half-dragon that is Medium or smaller does not have wings.

Armor Class: Natural armor improves by +4.

Attack: A half-dragon has two claw attacks and a bite attack, and the claws are the primary natural weapon. If the base creature can use weapons, the half-dragon retains this ability. A half-dragon fighting without weapons uses a claw when making an attack action. When it has a weapon, it usually uses the weapon instead.

Full Attack: A half-dragon fighting without weapons uses both claws and its bite when making a full attack. If armed with a weapon, it usually uses the weapon as its primary attack and its bite as a natural secondary attack. If it has a hand free, it uses a claw as an additional natural secondary attack.

Damage: Half-dragons have bite and claw attacks. If the base creature does not have these attack forms, use the damage values in the table below. Otherwise, use the values below or the base creature's damage values, whichever are greater.

Size	Bite Damage	Claw Damage
Fine	1	—
Diminutive	1d2	1
Tiny	1d3	1d2
Small	1d4	1d3
Medium	1d6	1d4
Large	1d8	1d6
Huge	2d6	1d8
Gargantuan	3d6	2d6
Colossal	4d6	3d6

Special Attacks: A half-dragon retains all the special attacks of the base creature and gains a breath weapon based on the dragon variety (see the table below), usable once per day. A half-dragon's breath weapon deals 6d8 points of damage. A successful Reflex save (DC 10 + 1/2 half-dragon's racial HD + half-dragon's Con modifier) reduces damage by half.

Dragon Variety	Breath Weapon
Black	60-foot line of acid
Blue	60-foot ine of lightning
Green	30-foot cone of corrosive (acid) gas
Red	30-foot cone of fire
White	30-foot cone of cold
Brass	60-foot line of fire
Bronze	60-foot line of lightning
Copper	60-foot line of acid
Gold	30-foot cone of fire
Silver	30-foot cone of cold

Special Qualities: A half-dragon has all the special qualities of the base creature, plus darkvision out to 60 feet and low-light vision. A half-dragon has immunity to *sleep* and paralysis effects, and an additional immunity based on its dragon variety.

Dragon Variety	Immunity	Dragon Variety	Immunity
Black	Acid	Brass	Fire
Blue	Electricity	Bronze	Electricity
Green	Acid	Copper	Acid
Red	Fire	Gold	Fire
White	Cold	Silver	Cold

Abilities: Increase from the base creature as follows: Str +8, Con +2, Int +2, Cha +2.

Skills: A half-dragon gains skill points as a dragon and has skill points equal to (6 + Int modifier) × (HD + 3). Do not include Hit Dice from class levels in this calculation—the half-dragon gains dragon skill points only for its racial Hit Dice, and gains the normal amount of skill points for its class levels. Treat skills from the base creature's list as class skills, and other skills as cross-class.

Environment: Same as either the base creature or the dragon variety.

Challenge Rating: Same as the base creature + 2 (minimum 3).

Alignment: Same as the dragon variety.

Level Adjustment: Same as base creature +3.

HALF-FIEND

A fiend's magical nature allows it to breed with virtually any creature. Spawned deep in the dark, nether planes, these fiendish offspring are abominations that plague mortal creatures.

Demons and devils bring their progeny along to the Material Plane and loose them upon the world. Sometimes, however, fiends force themselves on mortal creatures to create evil half-breeds. The more depraved creatures are sometimes even willing to participate. Although half-fiend offspring are usually destroyed at birth, some survive to become grotesque mockeries of their mortal parents. All too rarely, though, one learns from and takes on the characteristics of its nonfiendish parent, turning from its evil heritage.

No matter its form, a half-fiend is always hideous to behold, having dark scales, horns, glowing red eyes, bat wings, a fetid odor, or some other obvious sign that it is tainted with evil.

Never truly fitting into any mortal society, half-fiends are usually loners. On the lower planes, they are mistreated and derided because of their impure nature. Among nonfiends, they are outcasts, hated corruptions of the natural order. Humanoid half-fiends are sometimes called cambions. They often serve more powerful fiends or lead evil creatures on the Material Plane.

SAMPLE HALF-FIEND

This winged humanoid has claws, fangs, and short horns. Its eyes glow red, and it reeks of brimstone.

This example uses a 7th-level human cleric of Erythnul as the base creature.

Half-Fiend 7th-Level Human Cleric
Medium Outsider (Augmented Humanoid) (Native)
Hit Dice: 7d8+14 (49 hp)
Initiative: +7
Speed: 20 ft. in breastplate (4 squares), fly 20 ft. (average) in breastplate; base speed 30 ft., fly 30 ft. (average)
Armor Class: 24 (+3 Dex, +1 natural, +10 *+2 breastplate* and *+1 heavy shield*), touch 13, flat-footed 21
Base Attack/Grapple: +5/+9
Attack: *+1 morningstar* +11 melee (1d8+5) or claw +9 melee (1d4+4) or masterwork light crossbow +9 ranged (1d8/19–20)
Full Attack: *+1 morningstar* +11 melee (1d8+5) and bite +4 melee (1d6+2); 2 claws +9 melee (1d4+4) and bite +4 melee (1d6+2); or masterwork light crossbow +9 ranged (1d8/19–20)
Space/Reach: 5 ft./5 ft.
Special Attacks: Smite good, spells, spell-like abilities, rebuke undead 8/day

Half-dragon

Half-fiend

Special Qualities: Damage reduction 5/magic, darkvision 60 ft., immunity to poison, resistance to acid 10, cold 10, electricity 10, and fire 10, spell resistance 17

Saves: Fort +7, Ref +5, Will +9

Abilities: Str 18, Dex 17, Con 14, Int 12, Wis 18, Cha 12

Skills: Concentration +12, Diplomacy +6, Knowledge (arcana) +6, Knowledge (religion) +6, Heal +9, Spellcraft +3, Spot +9

Feats: Combat Casting, Extra Turning, Flyby Attack, Improved Initiative, Weapon Focus (morningstar)[B]

Environment: Temperate plains

Organization: Solitary

Challenge Rating: 9

Treasure: Double standard

Alignment: Always evil (any)

Advancement: By character class

Level Adjustment: +4

Half-fiend spellcasters such as the one described here are usually found as the leaders of dark cults or evil temples.

Combat

Half-fiends attack with aggressiveness and battle lust, using their ability to fly to best advantage by casting spells from the air. They enjoy torturing any enemies unfortunate enough to fall into their hands.

Smite Good (Su): Once per day this half-fiend can make a normal melee attack to deal 7 points of extra damage against a good foe.

Spell-Like Abilities: 3/day—*darkness, poison* (DC 15); 1/day—*desecrate, unholy blight* (DC 15). Caster level 7th. The save DCs are Charisma-based.

Typical Cleric Spells Prepared (6/6/5/4/3; save DC 14 + spell level): 0—*cure minor wounds, detect magic, guidance, light, read magic, resistance;* 1st—*command, cure light wounds, divine favor, doom, protection from good*, shield of faith;* 2nd—*bear's endurance, bull's strength, hold person, sound burst, spiritual weapon*;* 3rd—*bestow curse, cure serious wounds, dispel magic, magic vestment*;* 4th—*cure critical wounds, summon monster IV, unholy blight*.*

*Domain spell. Deity: Erythnul. Domains: Evil (cast evil spells at +1 caster level) and War (Weapon Focus bonus feat).

Possessions: +2 breastplate, +1 large steel shield, +1 morningstar, periapt of Wisdom +2, potion of haste. (Different half-fiends may have different possessions.)

CREATING A HALF-FIEND

"Half-fiend" is an inherited template that can be added to any living, corporeal creature with an Intelligence score of 4 or more and nongood alignment (referred to hereafter as the base creature).

A half-fiend uses all the base creature's statistics and special abilities except as noted here.

Size and Type: The creature's type changes to outsider. Do not recalculate Hit Dice, base attack bonus, or saves. Size is unchanged. Half-fiends are normally native outsiders.

Speed: A half-fiend has bat wings. Unless the base creature has a better fly speed, the creature can fly at the base creature's base land speed (average maneuverability).

Armor Class: Natural armor improves by +1 (this stacks with any natural armor bonus the base creature has).

Attack: A half-fiend has two claw attacks and a bite attack, and the claws are the primary natural weapon. If the base creature can use weapons, the half-fiend retains this ability. A half-fiend fighting without weapons uses a claw when making an attack action. When it has a weapon, it usually uses the weapon instead.

Full Attack: A half-fiend fighting without weapons uses both claws and its bite when making a full attack. If armed with a weapon, it usually uses the weapon as its primary attack and its bite as a natural secondary attack. If it has a hand free, it uses a claw as an additional natural secondary attack.

Damage: Half-fiends have bite and claw attacks. If the base creature does not have these attack forms, use the damage values in the table below. Otherwise, use the values below or the base creature's damage values, whichever are greater.

	Bite	Claw
Size	Damage	Damage
Fine	1	—
Diminutive	1d2	1
Tiny	1d3	1d2
Small	1d4	1d3
Medium	1d6	1d4
Large	1d8	1d6
Huge	2d6	1d8
Gargantuan	3d6	2d6
Colossal	4d6	3d6

Special Attacks: A half-fiend retains all the special attacks of the base creature and gains the following special attack.

Smite Good (Su): Once per day the creature can make a normal melee attack to deal extra damage equal to its HD (maximum of +20) against a good foe.

Spell-Like Abilities: A half-fiend with an Intelligence or Wisdom score of 8 or higher has spell-like abilities depending on its Hit Dice, as indicated on the table below. The abilities are cumulative; a half-fiend with 4 HD can use *darkness* as well as *desecrate*. Unless otherwise noted, an ability is usable once per day. Caster level equals the creature's HD, and the save DC is Charisma-based.

HD	Abilities
1–2	*Darkness 3/day*
3–4	*Desecrate*
5–6	*Unholy blight*
7–8	*Poison 3/day*
9–10	*Contagion*
11–12	*Blasphemy*
13–14	*Unholy aura 3/day, unhallow*
15–16	*Horrid wilting*
17–18	*Summon monster IX (fiends only)*
19–20	*Destruction*

Special Qualities: A half-fiend has all the special qualities of the base creature, plus the following special qualities.

—Darkvision out to 60 feet.

—Immunity to poison.

—Resistance to acid 10, cold 10, electricity 10, and fire 10.

—Damage reduction: 5/magic (if HD 11 or less) or 10/magic (if HD 12 or more).

—A half-fiend's natural weapons are treated as magic weapons for the purpose of overcoming damage reduction.

—Spell resistance equal to creature's HD + 10 (maximum 35).

Abilities: Increase from the base creature as follows: Str +4, Dex +4, Con +2, Int +4, Cha +2.

Skills: A half-fiend gains skill points as an outsider and has skill points equal to (8 + Int modifier) × (HD + 3). Do not include Hit Dice from class levels in this calculation—the half-fiend gains outsider skill points only for its racial Hit Dice, and gains the normal amount of skill points for its class levels. Treat skills from the base creature's list as class skills, and other skills as cross-class.

Challenge Rating: HD 4 or less, as base creature +1; HD 5 to 10, as base creature +2; HD 11 or more, as base creature +3.

Alignment: Always evil (any).

Level Adjustment: +4.

HALF-FIEND CHARACTERS

Humanoid half-fiends often have a character class, preferring cleric, fighter, rogue, and sorcerer. Rogues and fighters frequently take levels in the assassin and blackguard prestige classes, respectively. Nonhumanoids are also sometimes clerics or sorcerers.

Half-fiend clerics serve evil deities such as Erythnul, Gruumsh, Hextor, Nerull, and Vecna.

HALFLING

Halfling, 1st-Level Warrior
Small Humanoid (Halfling)
Hit Dice: 1d8+1 (5 hp)
Initiative: +1
Speed: 20 ft. (4 squares)
Armor Class: 16 (+1 size, +1 Dex, +3 studded leather, +1 light shield), touch 12, flat-footed 15
Base Attack/Grapple: +1/–3
Attack: Longsword +3 melee (1d6/19–20) or light crossbow +3 ranged (1d6/19–20)
Full Attack: Longsword +3 melee (1d6/19–20) or light crossbow +3 ranged (1d6/19–20)
Space/Reach: 5 ft./5 ft.
Special Attacks: Halfling traits
Special Qualities: Halfling traits
Saves: Fort +4, Ref +2, Will +0
Abilities: Str 11, Dex 13, Con 12, Int 10, Wis 9, Cha 8
Skills: Climb +2, Hide +4, Jump –4, Listen +3, Move Silently +1
Feats: Weapon Focus (longsword)
Environment: Warm plains
  (Deep halfling: Warm hills)
  (Tallfellow: Temperate forests)
Organization: Company (2–4), squad (11–20 plus 2 3rd-level sergeants and 1 leader of 3rd–6th level), or band (30–100 plus 100% noncombatants plus 1 3rd-level sergeant per 20 adults, 5 5th-level lieutenants, 3 7th-level captains, 6–10 dogs, and 2–5 riding dogs)
Challenge Rating: 1/2
Treasure: Standard
Alignment: Usually neutral
Advancement: By character class
Level Adjustment: +0

This humanoid stands about half as high as a human. It has an athletic build, ruddy skin, straight black hair, and dark eyes.

Halflings are cunning, resourceful survivors and opportunists who find room for themselves wherever they can. They might be reliable, hard-working citizens or thieves just waiting for their big chance.

Halflings stand about 3 feet tall and usually weigh between 30 and 35 pounds. They have brown or black eyes. Halfling men often have long sideburns, but beards are rare among them and mustaches almost unseen. Halflings prefer simple, comfortable, and practical clothes. Unlike members of most races, they prefer actual comfort to shows of wealth. Halflings reach adulthood in their early twenties and generally live into the middle of their second century.

Halflings speak Halfling and Common.

Most halflings encountered outside their home are warriors; the information in the statistics block is for one of 1st level.

Halfling

COMBAT

Halflings prefer to fight defensively, usually hiding and launching ranged attacks as the foe approaches. Their tactics are very much like those of elves but place more emphasis on cover and concealment and less on mobility.

Halfling Traits (Ex): Halflings possess the following racial traits.

— +2 Dexterity, –2 Strength.

—Small size. +1 bonus to Armor Class, +1 bonus on attack rolls, +4 bonus on Hide checks, –4 penalty on grapple checks, lifting and carrying limits 3/4 those of Medium characters.

—A halfling's base land speed is 20 feet.

— +2 racial bonus on Climb, Jump, and Move Silently checks.

— +1 racial bonus on all saving throws.

— +2 morale bonus on saving throws against fear. This bonus stacks with the halfling's +1 bonus on saving throws in general.

— +1 racial bonus on attack rolls with thrown weapons and slings.

— +2 racial bonus on Listen checks.

—Automatic Languages: Common, Halfling. Bonus Languages: Dwarven, Elven, Gnome, Goblin, Orc.

—Favored Class: Rogue.

The halfling warrior presented here had the following ability scores before racial adjustments: Str 13, Dex 11, Con 12, Int 10, Wis 9, Cha 8.

HALFLING SOCIETY

Halflings try to get along with everyone else. They are adept at fitting into communities of humans, dwarves, elves, or gnomes and making themselves valuable and welcome. Since human society changes more frequently than the societies of the longer-lived races, it most frequently offers opportunities to exploit, and halflings are often found in or around human lands.

Halflings often form tight-knit communities in human or dwarven cities. While they work readily with others, they often make friends only among themselves. Halflings also settle into secluded places where they set up self-reliant villages.

Halfling communities are known to pick up and move en masse to a place that offers some new opportunity, such as where a new mine has opened up or to a land where a devastating war has made skilled workers hard to find. If these opportunities are temporary, a community may pick up and move again once the opportunity is gone, or once a better one presents itself. If the opportunity is lasting, the halflings settle and form a new village. Some communities, on the other hand, take to traveling as a way of life, driving wagons or guiding boats from place to place, with no permanent home.

The chief halfling deity is Yondalla, the Blessed One, protector of the halflings. Yondalla promises blessings and protection to those who heed her guidance, defend their clans, and cherish their families.

SUBRACES

The information above is for the lightfoot halfling, the most common halfling variety. There are two other major halfling subraces, which differ from lightfoot halflings as follows.

Tallfellow

This humanoid stands a little more than half as high as a human. It has a slim but athletic build, fair skin, and fair hair.

Tallfellows are somewhat rare among halfling folk.

Tallfellows are 4 feet tall or more and weigh between 30 and 35 pounds. They generally speak Elven in addition to Common and Halfling, and they greatly enjoy the company of elves.

Tallfellow Traits (Ex): These traits are in addition to the lightfoot halfling traits, except where noted.

— +2 racial bonus on Search, Spot, and Listen checks. Like an elf, a tallfellow who merely passes within 5 feet of a secret or concealed door is entitled to a Search check as though actively looking for it. This trait replaces the lightfoot's +2 bonus on Listen checks.

—Tallfellows are less athletic than lightfoot halflings and do not have a racial bonus on Climb, Jump, and Move Silently checks.

Deep Halfling

This humanoid stands a little less than half as high as a human. It has a stocky but athletic build, ruddy skin, straight black hair, and dark eyes.

These halflings are shorter and stockier than the more common lightfeet.

Deep halflings are about 2-1/2 tall and weigh between 30 and 35 pounds. Deep halflings take great pleasure in gems and fine masonry, often working as jewelers or stonecutters. They rarely mix with humans and elves but enjoy the company of dwarves and speak Dwarven fluently.

Deep Halfling Traits (Ex): These traits are in addition to the lightfoot halfling traits, except where noted.

—Darkvision out to 60 feet.

—Stonecunning: Like dwarves, deep halflings have a +2 racial bonus on checks to notice unusual stonework. Something that isn't stone but that is disguised as stone also counts as unusual stonework. A deep halfling who merely comes within 10 feet of unusual stonework can make a check as though actively searching and can use the Search skill to find stonework traps as a rogue can. A deep halfling can also intuit depth, sensing the approximate distance underground as naturally as a human can sense which way is up.

— +2 racial bonus on Appraise checks and Craft checks that are related to stone or metal.

—Deep halflings are less athletic than lightfoot halflings and do not have a racial bonus on Climb, Jump, and Move Silently checks.

HARPY

This creature looks like an evil-faced old human with the lower body, legs, and wings of a reptilian monster. Its hair is tangled, filthy, and crusted with blood.

A more malignant and wretched creature than the harpy is difficult to imagine. Taking great glee in causing suffering and death, the sadistic harpy is always watching for new victims.

A harpy's coal-black eyes clearly reflect its evil soul, as do the wicked talons on its knotty fingers. These vile creatures wear no clothing and often wield large, heavy bones as though they were clubs.

Harpies like to entrance hapless travelers with their magical songs and lead them to unspeakable torments. Only when a harpy has finished playing with its new "toys" will it release them from suffering by killing and consuming them.

COMBAT

When a harpy engages in battle, it prefers to use Flyby Attack and strike with a melee weapon.

Captivating Song (Su): The most insidious ability of the harpy is its song. When a harpy sings, all creatures (other than harpies) within a 300-foot spread must succeed on a DC 16 Will save or become captivated. This is a sonic mind-affecting charm effect. A creature that successfully saves cannot be affected again by the same harpy's song for 24 hours. The save DC is Charisma-based.

A captivated victim walks toward the harpy, taking the most direct route available. If the path leads into a dangerous area (through flame, off a cliff, or the like), that creature gets a second saving throw. Captivated creatures can take no actions other than to defend themselves. (Thus, a fighter cannot run away or attack but takes no defensive penalties.) A victim within 5 feet of the harpy stands there and offers no resistance to the monster's attacks. The effect continues for as long as the harpy sings and for 1 round thereafter. A bard's countersong ability allows the captivated creature to attempt a new Will save.

Skills: Harpies have a +4 racial bonus on Bluff and Listen checks.

HARPY ARCHER

A cruel hunter and roaming brigand, the harpy archer has trained as a fighter specializing in ranged combat. Harpy archers often become mercenaries, selling their services to the highest bidder. When not employed, they make ends meet as highway robbers, forcing merchant caravans to pay protection money.

Combat

Captivating Song (Su): Will DC 17 negates.

Possessions: +3 studded leather, +1 frost composite longbow (+1 Str bonus), 10 cold iron arrows, 10 silvered arrows, 5 +2 arrows, lesser bracers of archery, potion of cure moderate wounds, potion of cat's grace, cloak of resistance +2, ring of protection +1. (Different harpy archers may have different possessions.)

Harpy

	Harpy Medium Monstrous Humanoid	Harpy Archer, 7th-Level Fighter Medium Monstrous Humanoid
Hit Dice:	7d8 (31 hp)	7d8 + 7d10 + 28 (103 hp)
Initiative:	+2	+9
Speed:	20 ft. (4 squares), fly 80 ft. (average)	20 ft. (4 squares), fly 80 ft. (average)
Armor Class:	13 (+2 Dex, +1 natural), touch 12, flat-footed 11	AC 23 (+5 Dex, +1 natural, +6 *+3 studded leather*, +1 *ring of protection +1*), touch 16, flat-footed 18
Base Attack/Grapple:	+7/+7	+14/+15
Attack:	Club +7 melee (1d6)	*+1 frost composite longbow* (+1 Str bonus) +22 ranged (1d8+4/19–20/×3 plus 1d6 cold) or claw +15 melee (1d3+1)
Full Attack:	Club +7/+2 melee (1d6) and 2 claws +2 melee (1d3)	*+1 frost composite longbow* (+1 Str bonus) +22/+17/+12 ranged (1d8+4/19–20/×3 plus 1d6 cold) or 2 claws +15 melee (1d3+1)
Space/Reach:	5 ft./5 ft.	5 ft./5 ft.
Special Attacks:	Captivating song	Captivating song
Special Qualities:	Darkvision 60 ft.	Darkvision 60 ft.
Saves:	Fort +2, Ref +7, Will +6	Fort +11, Ref +14, Will +11
Abilities:	Str 10, Dex 15, Con 10, Int 7, Wis 12, Cha 17	Str 12, Dex 20, Con 14, Int 6, Wis 11, Cha 19
Skills:	Bluff +11, Intimidate +7, Listen +7, Perform (oratory) +5, Spot +3	Bluff +11, Intimidate +5, Listen +7, Perform (oratory) +10, Spot +5
Feats:	Dodge, Flyby Attack, Persuasive	Alertness, Improved Critical (composite longbow), Improved Initiative, Iron Will, Manyshot, Point Blank Shot, Rapid Shot, Weapon Focus (composite longbow), Weapon Specialization (composite longbow)
Environment:	Temperate marshes	Temperate marshes
Organization:	Solitary, pair, or flight (7–12)	Solitary
Challenge Rating:	4	11
Treasure:	Standard	Standard (including equipment)
Alignment:	Usually chaotic evil	Usually chaotic evil
Advancement:	By character class	By character class
Level Adjustment:	+3	+3

HELL HOUND

The creature resembles a big, powerfully built dog with short, rust-red fur; its markings, teeth, and tongue are sooty black. It has red, glowing eyes.

Hell hounds are aggressive, fire-breathing canines from the plane of Acheron. Specimens are frequently brought to the Material Plane to serve evil beings, and many have established indigenous breeding populations.

A typical hell hound stands 4-1/2 feet high at the shoulder and weighs 120 pounds.

Hell hounds do not speak but understand Infernal.

COMBAT

Hell hounds are efficient hunters. A favorite pack tactic is to surround prey quietly, then attack with one or two hounds, driving it toward the rest with their fiery breath. If the prey doesn't run, the pack closes in. Hell hounds track fleeing prey relentlessly.

A hell hound's natural weapons, as well as any weapons it wields, are treated as evil-aligned and lawful-aligned for the purpose of overcoming damage reduction.

Breath Weapon (Su): 10-foot cone, once every 2d4 rounds, damage 2d6 fire, Reflex DC 13 half. The save DC is Constitution-based.

Fiery Bite (Su): A hell hound deals an extra 1d6 points of fire damage every time it bites an opponent, as if its bite were a flaming weapon.

Skills: Hell hounds have a +5 racial bonus on Hide and Move Silently checks.

*They also receive a +8 racial bonus on Survival checks when tracking by scent, due to their keen sense of smell.

NESSIAN WARHOUND

The Lords of the Nine, the great devil princes who rule over the Nine Hells, keep vast kennels of hell hounds. From the fiery pits beneath the palace of Asmodeus in Nessus, the lowest of the Nine Hells, come the Nessian warhounds, a terrifying breed of hell hound. Nessian warhounds are coal-black mastiffs the size of draft horses, often fitted with shirts of infernal chainmail.

Nessian warhounds resemble hell hounds, except as otherwise noted.

Breath Weapon (Su): 10-foot cone, once every 2d4 rounds, damage 3d6 fire, Reflex DC 21 half. The save DC is Constitution-based.

Fiery Bite (Su): A Nessian warhound deals an extra 1d8 points of fire damage every time it bites an opponent, as if its bite were a flaming weapon.

Hell hound

	Hell Hound Medium Outsider (Evil, Extraplanar, Fire, Lawful)	Nessian Warhound Large Outsider (Evil, Extraplanar, Fire, Lawful)
Hit Dice:	4d8+4 (22 hp)	12d8+60 (114 hp)
Initiative:	+5	+6
Speed:	40 ft. (8 squares)	40 ft. (8 squares)
Armor Class:	16 (+1 Dex, +5 natural), touch 11, flat-footed 15	24 (−1 size, +2 Dex, +7 natural, +6 +2 chain shirt barding), touch 11, flat-footed 22
Base Attack/Grapple:	+4/+5	+12/+24
Attack:	Bite +5 melee (1d8+1 plus 1d6 fire)	Bite +20 melee (2d6+12/19–20 plus 1d8 fire)
Full Attack:	Bite +5 melee (1d8+1 plus 1d6 fire)	Bite +20 melee (2d6+12/19–20 plus 1d8 fire)
Space/Reach:	5 ft./5 ft.	10 ft./10 ft.
Special Attacks:	Breath weapon, fiery bite	Breath weapon, fiery bite
Special Qualities:	Darkvision 60 ft., immunity to fire, scent, vulnerability to cold	Darkvision 60 ft., immunity to fire, scent, vulnerability to cold
Saves:	Fort +5, Ref +5, Will +4	Fort +13, Ref +10, Will +9
Abilities:	Str 13, Dex 13, Con 13, Int 6, Wis 10, Cha 6	Str 26, Dex 14, Con 20, Int 4, Wis 12, Cha 6
Skills:	Hide +13, Jump +12, Listen +7, Move Silently +13, Spot +7, Survival +7*	Hide +17, Jump +19, Listen +18, Move Silently +21, Spot +18, Survival +8*, Tumble +3
Feats:	Improved Initiative, Run, Track[B]	Alertness, Improved Critical (bite), Improved Initiative, Track, Weapon Focus (bite)
Environment:	Nine Hells of Baator	Nine Hells of Baator (Nessus)
Organization:	Solitary, pair, or pack (5–12)	Solitary, pair, or pack (1–2 Nessian warhounds and 5–12 hell hounds)
Challenge Rating:	3	9
Treasure:	None	+2 chain shirt barding
Alignment:	Always lawful evil	Always lawful evil
Advancement:	5–8 HD (Medium); 9–12 HD (Large)	13–17 HD (Large); 18–24 HD (Huge)
Level Adjustment:	+3 (cohort)	+4 (cohort)

HIPPOGRIFF

Large Magical Beast
Hit Dice: 3d10+9 (25 hp)
Initiative: +2
Speed: 50 ft. (10 squares), fly 100 ft. (average)
Armor Class: 15 (−1 size, +2 Dex, +4 natural), touch 11, flat-footed 13
Base Attack/Grapple: +3/+11
Attack: Claw +6 melee (1d4+4)
Full Attack: 2 claws +6 melee (1d4+4) and bite +1 melee (1d8+2)
Space/Reach: 10 ft./5 ft.
Special Attacks: —
Special Qualities: Darkvision 60 ft., low-light vision, scent
Saves: Fort +6, Ref +5, Will +2
Abilities: Str 18, Dex 15, Con 16, Int 2, Wis 13, Cha 8
Skills: Listen +4, Spot +8
Feats: Dodge, Wingover
Environment: Temperate hills
Organization: Solitary, pair, or flight (7–12)
Challenge Rating: 2
Treasure: None
Alignment: Always neutral
Advancement: 4–6 HD (Large); 7–9 HD (Huge)
Level Adjustment: —

This beast has the torso and hindquarters of a horse and the forelegs, wings, and head of a giant eagle.

Hippogriffs are aggressive flying creatures that combine features of horses and giant eagles. Voracious omnivores, hippogriffs will hunt humanoids as readily as any other meal.

These beasts are very territorial, defending their preferred hunting and grazing areas against intruders with unusual ferocity. Their range usually extends about 5d10 miles from their nest, in which the young remain while the adults hunt. Hippogriffs never leave their young undefended, however: Discovering a hippogriff nest always means encountering adult creatures.

A typical hippogriff is 9 feet long, has a wingspan of 20 feet, and weighs 1,000 pounds.

COMBAT

Hippogriffs dive at their prey and strike with their clawed forelegs. When they cannot dive, they slash with claws and beak.

Mated pairs and flights of these creatures attack in concert, diving repeatedly to drive away or kill intruders. Hippogriffs fight to the death to defend their nests and their hatchlings, which are prized as aerial mounts and fetch a handsome price in many civilized areas.

Skills: Hippogriffs have a +4 racial bonus on Spot checks.

TRAINING A HIPPOGRIFF

A hippogriff requires training before it can bear a rider in combat. Training a hippogriff requires six weeks of work and a DC 25 Handle Animal check. Riding a hippogriff requires an exotic saddle. A hippogriff can fight while carrying a rider, but the rider cannot also attack unless he or she succeeds on a Ride check.

Hippogriff eggs are worth 2,000 gp apiece on the open market, while young ones are worth 3,000 gp each. Professional trainers charge 1,000 gp to rear or train a hippogriff.

Carrying Capacity: A light load for a hippogriff is up to 300 pounds; a medium load, 301–600 pounds; and a heavy load, 601–900 pounds.

HOBGOBLIN

Hobgoblin, 1st-Level Warrior
Medium Humanoid (Goblinoid)
Hit Dice: 1d8+2 (6 hp)
Initiative: +1
Speed: 30 ft. (6 squares)
Armor Class: 15 (+1 Dex, +3 studded leather, +1 light shield), touch 11, flat-footed 14
Base Attack/Grapple: +1/+2
Attack: Longsword +2 melee (1d8+1/19–20) or javelin +2 ranged (1d6+1)
Full Attack: Longsword +2 melee (1d8+1/19–20) or javelin +2 ranged (1d6+1)
Space/Reach: 5 ft./5 ft.
Special Attacks: —
Special Qualities: Darkvision 60 ft.
Saves: Fort +4, Ref +1, Will –1
Abilities: Str 13, Dex 13, Con 14, Int 10, Wis 9, Cha 8
Skills: Hide +3, Listen +2, Move Silently +3, Spot +2
Feats: Alertness
Environment: Warm hills
Organization: Gang (4–9), band (10–100 plus 50% noncombatants plus 1 3rd-level sergeant per 20 adults and 1 leader of 4th–6th level), warband (10–24), or tribe (30–300 plus 50% noncombatants plus 1 3rd-level sergeant per 20 adults, 1 or 2 lieutenants of 4th or 5th level, 1 leader of 6th–8th level, 2–4 dire wolves, and 1–4 ogres or 1–2 trolls)
Challenge Rating: 1/2
Treasure: Standard
Alignment: Usually lawful evil
Advancement: By character class
Level Adjustment: +1

Hippogriff

Hobgoblins' hair color ranges from dark reddish-brown to dark gray. They have dark orange or red-orange skin. Large males have blue or red noses. Hobgoblins' eyes are yellowish or dark brown, while their teeth are yellow. Their garments tend to be brightly colored, often blood red with black-tinted leather. Their weaponry is kept polished and in good repair.

Hobgoblins speak Goblin and Common.

Most hobgoblins encountered outside their homes are warriors; the information in the statistics block is for one of 1st level.

COMBAT

These creatures have a strong grasp of strategy and tactics and are capable of carrying out sophisticated battle plans. Under the leadership of a skilled strategist or tactician, their discipline can prove a deciding factor. Hobgoblins hate elves and attack them first, in preference to other opponents.

Skills: Hobgoblins have a +4 racial bonus on Move Silently checks.

The hobgoblin warrior presented here had the following ability scores before racial adjustments: Str 13, Dex 11, Con 12, Int 10, Wis 9, Cha 8.

HOBGOBLIN SOCIETY

Hobgoblins are a military breed: They live for war and believe strongly in strength and martial prowess as the most desirable qualities for individuals and leaders alike. A hobgoblin leader is likely to be the biggest and strongest in the group, maintaining authority by enforcing strict discipline. Hobgoblins are often leaders among tribes of goblins and orcs, whom they bully and treat as inferiors. Hobgoblin mercenaries sometimes enter the service of wealthy evil humanoids.

Hobgoblin

This burly humanoid stands about 6-1/2 feet tall. It has hairy skin, feral eyes, and a flat nose and chin.

Hobgoblins are larger cousins of goblins. They are far more aggressive and organized than their smaller relatives and wage a perpetual war with other humanoids, particularly elves.

Hobgoblin illus. by S. Wood

Hobgoblin society is organized into tribal bands, each intensely jealous of its reputation and status. Meetings between rival bands are likely to erupt in violence if the troops are not restrained. Only an exceptionally powerful leader can force them to cooperate for any length of time. Each band has a distinctive battle standard that it carries into combat to inspire, rally, and signal the troops. Hobgoblin gangs and warbands are almost exclusively male. Bands and tribes include females who help with defense. Noncombatant hobgoblins are children too young to fight effectively.

These creatures usually make lairs in places that either boast natural defenses or can be fortified. Cavern complexes, dungeons, ruins, and forests are among their favorites. Typical lair defenses include ditches, fences, gates, guard towers, pit traps, and crude catapults or ballistas.

Most hobgoblins revere Maglubiyet, who is also the patron deity of goblins.

HOBGOBLIN CHARACTERS

Hobgoblin leaders tend to be fighters or fighter/rogues. Hobgoblin clerics worship Maglubiyet. A hobgoblin cleric has access to two of the following domains: Evil, Destruction, or Trickery. Most hobgoblin spellcasters, however, are adepts. Hobgoblin adepts favor spells that deal damage.

Hobgoblin characters possess the following racial traits.
— +2 Dexterity, +2 Constitution.
—A hobgoblin's base land speed is 30 feet.
—Darkvision out to 60 feet.
— +4 racial bonus on Move Silently checks.
—Automatic Languages: Common, Goblin. Bonus Languages: Draconic, Dwarven, Infernal, Giant, Orc.
—Favored Class: Fighter.
—Level adjustment +1.

HOMUNCULUS

Tiny Construct
Hit Dice: 2d10 (11 hp)
Initiative: +2
Speed: 20 ft. (4 squares), fly 50 ft. (good)
Armor Class: 14 (+2 Dex, +2 size), touch 14, flat-footed 12
Base Attack/Grapple: +1/−8
Attack: Bite +2 melee (1d4−1 plus poison)
Full Attack: Bite +2 melee (1d4−1 plus poison)
Space/Reach: 2-1/2 ft./0 ft.
Special Attacks: Poison
Special Qualities: Construct traits, darkvision 60 ft., low-light vision
Saves: Fort +0, Ref +4, Will +1
Abilities: Str 8, Dex 15, Con —, Int 10, Wis 12, Cha 7
Skills: Hide +14, Listen +4, Spot +4
Feats: Lightning Reflexes
Environment: Any
Organization: Solitary
Challenge Rating: 1
Treasure: None
Alignment: Any (same as creator)
Advancement: 3–6 HD (Tiny)
Level Adjustment: —

Homunculus

This creature has a vaguely humanoid form. It stands about 18 inches tall and has wings spanning about 2 feet. Its skin looks rough and warty, and it has a mouth full of needlelike teeth.

A homunculus is a miniature servant created by a wizard. These creatures are weak combatants but make effective spies, messengers, and scouts.

A homunculus's creator determines its precise features.

Homunculi are little more than tools designed to carry out assigned tasks. They are extensions of their creators, sharing the same alignment and basic nature. A homunculus cannot speak, but the process of creating one links it telepathically with its creator. It knows what its master knows and can convey to him or her everything it sees and hears, out to a distance of 1,500 feet. A homunculus never travels beyond this range willingly, though it can be removed forcibly. If this occurs, the creature does everything in its power to regain contact with its master. An attack that destroys a homunculus deals 2d10 points of damage to its master. If the creature's master is slain, the homunculus also dies, and its body swiftly melts away into a pool of ichor.

COMBAT

Homunculi land on their victims and bite with their venomous fangs.

Poison (Ex): Injury, Fortitude DC 13, initial damage sleep for 1 minute, secondary damage sleep for another 5d6 minutes. The save DC is Constitution-based and includes a +2 racial bonus.

CONSTRUCTION

A homunculus is shaped from a mixture of clay, ashes, mandrake root, spring water, and one pint of the creator's own blood. The materials cost 50 gp. The creature's master may assemble the body or hire someone else to do the job. Creating the body requires a DC 12 Craft (sculpting) check or a DC 12 Craft (pottery) check. After the body is sculpted, it is animated through an extended magical ritual that requires a specially prepared laboratory or workroom, similar to an alchemist's laboratory and costing 500 gp to establish. If the creator is personally constructing the creature's body, the building and ritual can be performed together.

A homunculus with more than 2 Hit Dice can be created, but each additional Hit Die adds +2,000 gp to the cost to create.

Craft Construct (see page 303), *arcane eye, mirror image, mending,* caster must be at least 4th level; Price — (never sold); Cost 1,050 gp + 78 XP.

HOWLER

Large Outsider (Chaotic, Evil, Extraplanar)
Hit Dice: 6d8+12 (39 hp)
Initiative: +7
Speed: 60 ft. (12 squares)
Armor Class: 17 (−1 size, +3 Dex, +5 natural), touch 12, flat-footed 14
Base Attack/Grapple: +6/+15
Attack: Bite +10 melee (2d8+5)
Full Attack: Bite +10 melee (2d8+5) and 1d4 quills +5 melee (1d6+2)
Space/Reach: 10 ft./5 ft.
Special Attacks: Quills, howl
Special Qualities: Darkvision 60 ft.
Saves: Fort +7, Ref +8, Will +7
Abilities: Str 21, Dex 17, Con 15, Int 6, Wis 14, Cha 8
Skills: Climb +14, Hide +8, Listen +13, Move Silently +12, Search +7, Spot +13, Survival +2 (+4 following tracks)
Feats: Alertness, Combat Reflexes, Improved Initiative

Environment: Windswept Depths of Pandemonium
Organization: Solitary, gang (2–4), or pack (6–10)
Challenge Rating: 3
Treasure: None
Alignment: Always chaotic evil
Advancement: 7–9 HD (Large); 11–18 HD (Huge)
Level Adjustment: +3 (cohort)

This creature looks like some gaunt, bestial hound or feline, with a mane of bristling quills.

Howlers live on planes where chaos and evil hold sway; they originate on the plane of Pandemonium. These beasts hunt in packs, racing through caverns to wear down their prey and rend it to bits.

A howler is about 8 feet long and weighs about 2,000 pounds.

Although they are surprisingly intelligent, howlers do not speak—they only howl. If there is a language within the howls, as some have suggested, even spells cannot decipher it. Howlers understand Abyssal.

COMBAT

Howlers attack in groups, for they are cowardly and cruel. They prefer to charge into combat, race out, and then charge in again.

A howler's natural weapons, as well as any weapons it wields, are treated as chaotic-aligned and evil-aligned for the purpose of overcoming damage reduction.

Quills (Ex): A howler's neck bristles with long quills. While biting, the creature thrashes about, striking with 1d4 of them. An opponent hit by a howler's quill attack must succeed on a DC 16 Reflex save or have the quill break off in his or her flesh. Lodged quills impose a –1 penalty on attacks, saves, and checks per quill. The save DC is Dexterity-based.

A quill can be removed safely with a DC 20 Heal check; otherwise, removing a quill deals an extra 1d6 points of damage.

Howl (Ex): All beings other than outsiders that hear the creature's howling for an hour or longer are subject to its effect, though it does not help the howler in combat. Anyone within hearing range of a howler for a full hour must succeed on a DC 12 Will save or take 1 point of Wisdom damage. The save DC is Charisma-based. The save must be repeated for each hour of exposure. This is a sonic mind-affecting effect.

TRAINING A HOWLER

Small and Medium infernal creatures such as quasits, abyssal orcs, and even succubi sometimes use howlers as mounts or pack animals. Larger and more powerful demons use them like hunting dogs.

Although intelligent, a howler requires training before it can bear a rider in combat. To be trained, a howler must have a friendly attitude toward the trainer (this can be achieved through a successful Diplomacy check). Training a friendly howler requires six weeks of work and a DC 25 Handle Animal check. Riding a howler requires an exotic saddle. A howler can fight while carrying a rider, but the rider cannot also attack unless he or she succeeds on a Ride check.

Carrying Capacity: A light load for a howler is up to 460 pounds; a medium load, 461–920 pounds; and a heavy load, 921–1,380 pounds. A howler can drag 6,900 pounds.

Howler

HYDRA

This beast resembles some great reptile with a veritable forest of heads on long, slender necks.

Hydras are reptilelike monsters with multiple heads; they can quickly tear apart all but the most well-armored foes.

A hydra is gray-brown to dark brown, with a light yellow or tan underbelly. The eyes are amber and the teeth are yellow-white. It is about 20 feet long and weighs about 4,000 pounds.

Hydras do not speak.

COMBAT

Hydras can attack with all their heads at no penalty, even if they move or charge during the round.

A hydra can be killed either by severing all its heads or by slaying its body. To sever a head, an opponent must make a successful sunder attempt with a slashing weapon. (The player should declare where the attack is aimed before making the attack roll.) Making a sunder attempt provokes an attack of opportunity unless the foe has the Improved Sunder feat. An opponent can strike at a hydra's heads from any position in which he could strike at the hydra itself, because the hydra's head writhe and whip about in combat. An opponent can ready an action to attempt to sunder a hydra's head when the creature bites at him.

Each of a hydra's heads has hit points equal to the creature's full normal hit point total, divided by its original number of heads. For example, if a five-headed hydra has 52 hit points, 10 or more points of damage severs a head (52 ÷ 5 = 10.4, rounded down to 10). Losing a head deals damage to the body equal to half the head's full normal hit points. A natural reflex seals the neck shut to prevent further blood loss. A hydra can no longer attack with a severed head but takes no other penalties.

Each time a head is severed, two new heads spring from the stump in 1d4 rounds. A hydra can never have more than twice its original number of heads at any one time, and any extra heads it gains beyond its original number wither and die within a day. To prevent a severed head from growing back into two heads, at least 5 points of fire or acid damage must be dealt to the stump.

BEHIND THE CURTAIN: HYDRAS

Hydras are intended to be monsters that are difficult to defeat by conventional means. Characters without the Improved Sunder feat will find it difficult and dangerous to attack by lopping off the monster's heads, and the hydra's fast healing ability means that damage directed at its body is quickly restored. The hydra rewards characters who have the Improved Sunder feat and parties who learn to coordinate their attacks effectively.

(a touch attack to hit) before the new heads appear. A flaming weapon (or similar effect) deals its energy damage to the stump in the same blow in which a head is severed. Fire or acid damage from an area effect (such as a *fireball* spell or dragon breath) may burn multiple stumps in addition to dealing damage to the hydra's body. A hydra does not die from losing its heads until all its heads have been cut off and the stumps seared by fire or acid.

A hydra's body can be slain just like any other creature's, but hydras possess fast healing (see below) and are difficult to defeat in this fashion. Any attack that is not (or cannot be) an attempt to sunder a head affects the body. For example, area effects deal damage to a hydra's body, not to its heads. Targeted magical effects cannot sever a hydra's heads (and thus must be directed at the body) unless they deal slashing damage and could be used to make sunder attempts.

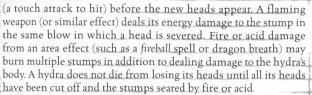

Hydra

Fast Healing (Ex): Each round, a hydra heals damage equal to 10 + the number of its original heads.

Skills: Hydras have a +2 racial bonus on Listen and Spot checks, thanks to their multiple heads.

A hydra has a +8 racial bonus on any Swim check to perform some special action or avoid a hazard. It can always choose to take 10 on a Swim check, even if distracted or endangered. It can use the run action while swimming, provided it swims in a straight line.

Feats: A hydra's Combat Reflexes feat allows it to use all its heads for attacks of opportunity.

PYROHYDRA
Huge Magical Beast (Fire)
These reddish hydras can breathe jets of fire 10 feet high, 10 feet wide, and 20 feet long. All heads breathe once every 1d4 rounds. Each jet deals 3d6 points of fire damage per head. A successful Reflex save halves the damage. The save DC is 10 + 1/2 hydra's original number of heads + hydra's Con modifier.

	Five-Headed Hydra Huge Magical Beast	Six-Headed Hydra Huge Magical Beast	Seven-Headed Hydra Huge Magical Beast
Hit Dice:	5d10+28 (55 hp)	6d10+33 (66 hp)	7d10+38 (77 hp)
Initiative:	+1	+1	+1
Speed:	20 ft. (4 squares), swim 20 ft.	20 ft. (4 squares), swim 20 ft.	20 ft. (4 squares), swim 20 ft.
Armor Class:	15 (−2 size, +1 Dex, +6 natural), touch 9, flat-footed 14	16 (−2 size, +1 Dex, +7 natural), touch 9, flat-footed 15	17 (−2 size, +1 Dex, +8 natural), touch 9, flat-footed 16
Base Attack/Grapple:	+5/+16	+6/+17	+7/+19
Attack:	5 bites +6 melee (1d10+3)	6 bites +8 melee (1d10+3)	7 bites +10 melee (1d10+4)
Full Attack:	5 bites +6 melee (1d10+3)	6 bites +8 melee (1d10+3)	7 bites +10 melee (1d10+4)
Space/Reach:	15 ft./10 ft.	15 ft./10 ft..	15 ft./10 ft.
Special Attacks:	—	—	—
Special Qualities:	Darkvision 60 ft., fast healing 15, low-light vision, scent	Darkvision 60 ft., fast healing 16, low-light vision, scent	Darkvision 60 ft., fast healing 17, low-light vision, scent
Saves:	Fort +9, Ref +5, Will +3	Fort +10, Ref +6, Will +4	Fort +10, Ref +6, Will +4
Abilities:	Str 17, Dex 12, Con 20, Int 2, Wis 10, Cha 9	Str 17, Dex 12, Con 20, Int 2, Wis 10, Cha 9	Str 19, Dex 12, Con 20, Int 2, Wis 10, Cha 9
Skills:	Listen +6, Spot +6, Swim +11	Listen +6, Spot +7, Swim +11	Listen +7, Spot +7, Swim +12
Feats:	Combat Reflexes[B], Iron Will, Toughness	Combat Reflexes[B], Iron Will, Toughness, Weapon Focus (bite)	Combat Reflexes[B], Iron Will, Toughness, Weapon Focus (bite)
Environment:	Temperate marshes (Pyro: Warm marshes) (Cryo: Cold marshes)	Temperate marshes (Pyro: Warm marshes) (Cryo: Cold marshes)	Temperate marshes (Pyro: Warm marshes) (Cryo: Cold marshes)
Organization:	Solitary	Solitary	Solitary
Challenge Rating:	4 (normal); 6 (pyro- or cryo-)	5 (normal); 7 (pyro- or cryo-)	6 (normal); 8 (pyro- or cryo-)
Treasure:	1/10 coins; 50% goods; 50% items	1/10 coins; 50% goods; 50% items	1/10 coins; 50% goods; 50% items
Alignment:	Usually neutral	Usually neutral	Usually neutral
Advancement:	—	—	—
Level Adjustment:	—	—	—

	Eight-Headed Hydra Huge Magical Beast	Nine-Headed Hydra Huge Magical Beast	Ten-Headed Hydra Huge Magical Beast
Hit Dice:	8d10+43 (87 hp)	9d10+48 (97 hp)	10d10+53 (108 hp)
Initiative:	+1	+1	+1
Speed:	20 ft. (4 squares), swim 20 ft.	20 ft. (4 squares), swim 20 ft.	20 ft. (4 squares), swim 20 ft.
Armor Class:	18 (−2 size, +1 Dex, +9 natural), touch 9, flat-footed 17	19 (−2 size, +1 Dex, +10 natural), touch 9, flat-footed 18	20 (−2 size, +1 Dex, +11 natural), touch 9, flat-footed 19
Base Attack/Grapple:	+8/+20	+9/+22	+10/+23
Attack:	8 bites +11 melee (1d10+4)	9 bites +13 melee (1d10+5)	10 bites +14 melee (1d10+5)
Full Attack:	8 bites +11 melee (1d10+4)	9 bites +13 melee (1d10+5)	10 bites +14 melee (1d10+5)
Space/Reach:	15 ft./10 ft.	15 ft./10 ft.	15 ft./10 ft.
Special Attacks:	—	—	—
Special Qualities:	Darkvision 60 ft., fast healing 18, low-light vision, scent	Darkvision 60 ft., fast healing 19, low-light vision, scent	Darkvision 60 ft., fast healing 20, low-light vision, scent
Saves:	Fort +11, Ref +7, Will +4	Fort +11, Ref +7, Will +5	Fort +12, Ref +8, Will +3
Abilities:	Str 19, Dex 12, Con 20, Int 2, Wis 10, Cha 9	Str 21, Dex 12, Con 20, Int 2, Wis 10, Cha 9	Str 21, Dex 12, Con 20, Int 2, Wis 10, Cha 9
Skills:	Listen +7, Spot +8, Swim +12	Listen +8, Spot +8, Swim +13	Listen +8, Spot +9, Swim +13
Feats:	Combat Reflexes[B], Iron Will, Toughness, Weapon Focus (bite)	Blind-Fight, Combat Reflexes[B], Iron Will, Toughness, Weapon Focus (bite)	Blind-Fight, Combat Reflexes[B], Iron Will, Toughness, Weapon Focus (bite)
Environment:	Temperate marshes (Pyro: Warm marshes) (Cryo: Cold marshes)	Temperate marshes (Pyro: Warm marshes) (Cryo: Cold marshes)	Temperate marshes (Pyro: Warm marshes) (Cryo: Cold marshes)
Organization:	Solitary	Solitary	Solitary
Challenge Rating:	7 (normal); 9 (pyro- or cryo-)	8 (normal); 10 (pyro- or cryo-)	9 (normal); 11 (pyro- or cryo-)
Treasure:	1/10 coins; 50% goods; 50% items	1/10 coins; 50% goods; 50% items	1/10 coins; 50% goods; 50% items
Alignment:	Usually neutral	Usually neutral	Usually neutral
Advancement:	—	—	—
Level Adjustment:	—	—	—

	Eleven-Headed Hydra Huge Magical Beast	Twelve-Headed Hydra Huge Magical Beast
Hit Dice:	11d10+58 (118 hp)	12d10+63 (129 hp)
Initiative:	+1	+1
Speed:	20 ft. (4 squares), swim 20 ft.	20 ft. (4 squares), swim 20 ft.
Armor Class:	21 (−2 size, +1 Dex, +12 natural), touch 9, flat-footed 20	22 (−2 size, +1 Dex, +13 natural), touch 9, flat-footed 21
Base Attack/Grapple:	+11/+25	+12/+26
Attack:	11 bites +16 melee (1d10+6)	12 bites +17 melee (2d8+6)
Full Attack:	11 bites +16 melee (1d10+6)	12 bites +17 melee (2d8+6)
Space/Reach:	15 ft./10 ft.	15 ft./10 ft.
Special Attacks:	—	—
Special Qualities:	Darkvision 60 ft., fast healing 21, low-light vision, scent	Darkvision 60 ft., fast healing 22, low-light vision, scent
Saves:	Fort +12, Ref +8, Will +5	Fort +13, Ref +9, Will +6
Abilities:	Str 23, Dex 12, Con 20, Int 2, Wis 10, Cha 9	Str 23, Dex 12, Con 20, Int 2, Wis 10, Cha 9
Skills:	Listen +9, Spot +9, Swim +14	Listen +9, Spot +10, Swim +14
Feats:	Blind-Fight, Combat Reflexes[B], Iron Will, Toughness, Weapon Focus (bite)	Blind-Fight, Combat Reflexes[B], Improved Natural Attack (bite), Iron Will, Toughness, Weapon Focus (bite)
Environment:	Temperate marshes (Pyro: Warm marshes) (Cryo: Cold marshes)	Temperate marshes (Pyro: Warm marshes) (Cryo: Cold marshes)
Organization:	Solitary	Solitary
Challenge Rating:	10 (normal); 12 (pyro- or cryo-)	11 (normal); 13 (pyro- or cryo-)
Treasure:	1/10 coins; 50% goods; 50% items	1/10 coins; 50% goods; 50% items
Alignment:	Usually neutral	Usually neutral
Advancement:	—	—
Level Adjustment:	—	—

Fire attacks cannot prevent a pyrohydra's stump from growing new heads (since a pyrohydra has immunity to fire), but 5 points of cold damage does.

CRYOHYDRA

Huge Magical Beast (Cold)

These purplish hydras can breathe jets of frost 10 feet high, 10 feet wide, and 20 feet long. All heads breathe once every 1d4 rounds. Each jet deals 3d6 points of cold damage per head. A successful Reflex save halves the damage. The save DC is 10 + 1/2 hydra's original number of heads + hydra's Con modifier.

Cold attacks cannot prevent a cryohydra's stump from growing new heads (since a cryohydra has immunity to cold), but 5 points of fire damage does.

INEVITABLE

Hailing from the lawful neutral plane of Mechanus, inevitables are constructs whose sole aim is to enforce the natural laws of the universe.

Each type of inevitable is designed to find and punish a particular kind of transgression, hunting down a person or group that has violated a fundamental principle, such as "The guilty should be punished," "Bargains should be kept," or "Everyone dies eventually." When an inevitable is created, it receives its first mission, then finds the transgressors and metes out appropriate punishment. The sentence is usually death, although some inevitables insist on compensation to the wronged party instead, using *geas* and *mark of justice* to ensure compliance. From its first step, an inevitable focuses totally on its target. It continues its efforts no matter how cold the trail or hopeless the task. If unable to cross an ocean any other way, inevitables have been known to walk into the waves, traversing the seabed to emerge on another continent months later.

Inevitables are single-minded in pursuit of their quarry, but they are under orders to leave innocents alone. Accomplices to their prey are fair game, however, which sometimes creates conflicts within their programming. Even the most effective inevitables are periodically recalled to Mechanus for reprogramming.

Inevitables gladly sacrifice themselves to complete a mission, but they aren't suicidal. Faced with impending defeat, they are likely to withdraw and seek a way to even the odds. They are determined but patient foes. They ally with others if that helps accomplish their mission, but they have a hard time keeping allies for long. It's apparent to anyone who spends much time with one that an inevitable would sacrifice an ally to fulfill its purpose without a second thought.

When an inevitable completes its task, it wanders the landscape and passively observes life around it. When it discerns another transgression of the principle it is dedicated to, it has a new mis-

sion. Inevitables tend to stick out in a crowd while they're in observation mode, but they seem oblivious to the attention. Those in the know who hear about a 12-foot-tall, golden-armored statue roaming the countryside might seek out the inevitable and present a case, hoping it will take on the alleged transgressor. The decision is based on the idiosyncrasies of the inevitable's programming, so there's no guarantee.

Their forms vary, but all inevitables are gold-and-silver clockwork creatures, with gears and pistons where muscles would be on flesh-and-blood creatures. Their eyes glow with a golden radiance.

Note that unlike most constructs, inevitables have an Intelligence score and can think, learn, and remember.

Inevitables speak Abyssal, Celestial, Infernal, and the native language of their first target.

COMBAT

Unless their very existence is threatened, inevitables focus completely on the transgressor they've been assigned to, ignoring other combatants completely. An inevitable might attack anyone who hinders its progress, but it won't tarry beyond the point where it can reengage its quarry.

Zelekhut

Kolyarut

Marut

Inevitables take self-defense very seriously; anyone who attacks an inevitable with what the creature perceives as deadly force is met with deadly force in return. An inevitable's natural weapons, as well as any weapons it wields, are treated as lawful-aligned for the purpose of overcoming damage reduction.

Fast Healing (Ex): An inevitable heals a certain amount of damage each round (specified in each variety's description) as long as it has at least 1 hit point. However, damage dealt by chaotic weapons heals at the normal rate.

KOLYARUT

Medium Construct (Extraplanar, Lawful)
Hit Dice: 13d10+20 (91 hp)
Initiative: +1
Speed: 20 ft. in banded mail (4 squares); base speed 30 ft.
Armor Class: 27 (+1 Dex, +10 natural, +6 banded mail) touch 11, flat-footed 26
Base Attack/Grapple: +9/+11
Attack: Vampiric touch +11 melee touch (5d6) or enervation ray +10 ranged touch (as spell) or +2 longsword +13 melee (1d8+5/19–20) or slam +11 melee (1d6+3)
Full Attack: Vampiric touch +11/+6 melee touch (5d6) or enervation ray +10 ranged touch (as spell) or +2 longsword +13/+8 melee (1d8+5/19–20) or slam +11/+6 melee (1d6+3)
Space/Reach: 5 ft./5 ft.
Special Attacks: Enervation ray, spell-like abilities, vampiric touch
Special Qualities: Construct traits, damage reduction 10/chaotic, darkvision 60 ft., fast healing 5, low-light vision, spell resistance 22
Saves: Fort +6, Ref +7, Will +7
Abilities: Str 14, Dex 13, Con —, Int 10, Wis 17, Cha 16
Skills: Diplomacy +5, Disguise +12, Gather Information +12, Listen +11, Search +5, Sense Motive +12, Spot +11, Survival +3 (+5 following tracks)
Feats: Alertness, Combat Casting, Great Fortitude, Lightning Reflexes, Quickened Spell-Like Ability (suggestion)
Environment: Clockwork Nirvana of Mechanus
Organization: Solitary
Challenge Rating: 12
Treasure: None
Alignment: Always lawful neutral
Advancement: 14–22 HD (Medium); 23–39 HD (Large)
Level Adjustment: —

This creature looks like a red-skinned humanoid made up of mechanical parts. It is dressed in ornate golden armor and a flowing golden robe. It carries a gleaming sword and wears banded mail.

Kolyaruts represent the ultimate enforcement clause in a contract—they mete out punishment to those who break bargains and oaths. Originally sent from Mechanus to avenge major betrayals, once on the Material Plane they hunt down everyone from unscrupulous merchants to army deserters. Anyone who reneges on a deal could draw the ire of a kolyarut, although the creature usually ignores inconsequential deals and rashly sworn oaths.

Before beginning a mission against a deal-breaker, a kolyarut learns as much about the contract or oath as possible. It's not interested in those who break deals accidentally or against their will—only those who willingly break contracts violate the principle that kolyaruts are created to uphold. If a written contract was broken, the kolyarut typically carries a copy of the contract with it.

Kolyaruts are the most talkative of the inevitables, making credible attempts at social niceties such as proper greetings before getting down to the matter at hand. They can use *disguise self* to appear as almost any kind of humanoid—useful if they need to go undercover to catch their quarry.

Combat

Like all inevitables, a kolyarut is patient enough to study a target before striking. It has a good idea of the deal-breaker's abilities and defenses before it enters battle. When it fights, it tries to get the conflict over as soon as possible, minimizing excess bloodshed and mayhem. It doesn't let concern for innocents delay or endanger its mission, however.

A kolyarut's favorite tactic is to use *invisibility* or *disguise self* to sneak close, then eliminate the quarry with its vampiric touch ability before it can react. A kolyarut has no compunctions about using its vampiric touch ability on allies to increase its own power, if doing so helps it complete its mission.

A kolyarut's natural weapons, as well as any weapons it wields, are treated as lawful-aligned for the purpose of overcoming damage reduction.

Enervation Ray (Su): A kolyarut can fire a black enervation ray at targets within 200 feet. The effect is identical with the *enervation* spell (caster level 13th).

Spell-Like Abilities: At will—*discern lies* (DC 17), *disguise self, fear* (DC 17), *hold person* (DC 16), *invisibility, locate creature, suggestion* (DC 16); 1/day—*hold monster* (DC 17), *mark of justice;* 1/week—*geas/quest.* Caster level 13th. The save DCs are Charisma-based.

Vampiric Touch (Su): As a melee touch attack, a kolyarut can steal life force from its foe, as the *vampiric touch* spell (caster level 13th).

Skills: A kolyarut has a +4 racial bonus on Disguise, Gather Information, and Sense Motive checks.

MARUT

Large Construct (Extraplanar, Lawful)
Hit Dice: 15d10+30 (112 hp)
Initiative: +1
Speed: 30 ft. in full plate armor (6 squares); base speed 40 ft.
Armor Class: 34 (–1 size, +1 Dex, +16 natural, +8 full plate armor), touch 10, flat-footed 33
Base Attack/Grapple: +11/+27
Attack: Slam +22 melee (2d6+12 plus 3d6 sonic or 3d6 electricity)
Full Attack: 2 slams +22 melee (2d6+12 plus 3d6 sonic or 3d6 electricity)
Space/Reach: 10 ft./10 ft.
Special Attacks: Fists of thunder and lightning, spell-like abilities
Special Qualities: Construct traits, damage reduction 15/chaotic, darkvision 60 ft., fast healing 10, low-light vision, spell resistance 25
Saves: Fort +7, Ref +6, Will +8
Abilities: Str 35, Dex 13, Con —, Int 12, Wis 17, Cha 18
Skills: Concentration +13, Diplomacy +6, Knowledge (religion) +10, Listen +16, Search +10, Sense Motive +12, Spot +16, Survival +3 (+5 following tracks)
Feats: Ability Focus (fists), Awesome Blow, Combat Casting, Great Fortitude, Improved Bull Rush, Power Attack
Environment: Clockwork Nirvana of Mechanus
Organization: Solitary
Challenge Rating: 15
Treasure: None
Alignment: Always lawful neutral
Advancement: 16–28 HD (Large); 29–45 HD (Huge)
Level Adjustment: —

This creature, outfitted in golden armor over an onyx-colored body, is humanoid in shape but much larger than a human and seems to be made of mechanical parts. It carries no weapons or other equipment.

Maruts represent the inevitability of death. They confront those who would try to deny the grave itself.

Any who use unnatural means to extend their life span (such as a lich) could be targeted by a marut. Those who take extraordinary measures to cheat death in some other way (such as sacrificing hundreds of others to keep oneself safe from a plague) might be labeled transgressors as well. Those who use magic to reverse death (*raise dead* spells, for example) aren't worthy of a marut's attention unless they do so repeatedly or on a massive scale.

When a marut has identified its target, it walks surely and implacably toward the foe, never resting.

Combat

Once it has found its target, a marut brings it the death it has been trying to avoid. Those who defile death through necromancy may instead receive a *geas* and/or *mark of justice* to enforce proper respect. It typically uses *wall of force* to shut off any escape routes, then opens up with *chain lightning* while it closes to melee range. Once there, it strikes with its massive fists, using *circle of death* if beset by numbers of defenders. It hits spellcasting opponents with repeated uses of *greater dispel magic*, and it uses *dimension door* and *locate creature* to track down foes who flee.

A marut's natural weapons, as well as any weapons it wields, are treated as lawful-aligned for the purpose of overcoming damage reduction.

Fists of Thunder and Lightning (Su): A marut's left fist delivers a loud thunderclap whenever it hits something, dealing an extra 3d6 points of sonic damage and causing the target to be deafened for 2d6 rounds (Fortitude DC 31 negates the deafness). Its right fist delivers a shock for an extra 3d6 points of electricity damage, and the flash of lightning causes the target to be blinded for 2d6 rounds (Fortitude DC 31 negates the blindness). The save DCs are Strength-based and include the marut's Ability Focus feat.

Spell-Like Abilities: At will—*air walk, dimension door, fear* (DC 18), *greater command* (DC 19), *greater dispel magic, mass inflict light wounds* (DC 19), *locate creature, true seeing;* 1/day—*chain lightning* (DC 20), *circle of death* (DC 20), *mark of justice, wall of force;* 1/week—*earthquake* (DC 22), *geas/quest, plane shift* (DC 21). Caster level 14th. The save DCs are Charisma-based.

Skills: A marut has a +4 racial bonus on Concentration, Listen, and Spot checks.

ZELEKHUT

Large Construct (Extraplanar, Lawful)
Hit Dice: 8d10+30 (74 hp)
Initiative: +0
Speed: 35 ft. in plate barding (7 squares), fly 40 ft. (average) in plate barding (8 squares); base speed 50 ft., fly 60 ft. (average)
Armor Class: 27 (–1 size, +10 natural, +8 plate barding), touch 9, flat-footed 27
Base Attack/Grapple: +6/+15
Attack: Spiked chain +10 melee (2d6+5 plus 1d6 electricity)
Full Attack: 2 spiked chains +10 melee (2d6+5 plus 1d6 electricity)
Space/Reach: 10 ft./10 ft.
Special Attacks: Spell-like abilities
Special Qualities: Construct traits, damage reduction 10/chaotic, darkvision 60 ft., fast healing 5, low-light vision, spell resistance 20
Saves: Fort +4, Ref +2, Will +5
Abilities: Str 21, Dex 11, Con —, Int 10, Wis 17, Cha 15
Skills: Diplomacy +4, Listen +9, Search +9, Sense Motive +12, Spot +9, Survival +3 (+5 following tracks)
Feats: Great Fortitude, Ride-By Attack, Spirited Charge
Environment: Clockwork Nirvana of Mechanus
Organization: Solitary
Challenge Rating: 9
Treasure: None
Alignment: Always lawful neutral
Advancement: 9–16 HD (Large); 17–24 HD (Huge)
Level Adjustment: +7

This clockwork creature resembles a centaur in shape. It wears ornate golden armor over alabaster skin. It carries no weapons or other equipment.

Zelekhuts are charged with hunting down those who would deny justice—especially those who flee to escape punishment. Expert trackers, they use a combination of natural skill and magic to find fugitives wherever they may hide.

A zelekhut may initially appear rather nonthreatening—but when it is about to enter combat, it can cause two spiked chains to spring forth from its forearms as a free action. In similar fashion, it can cause a pair of golden metallic wings to emerge from its back. Retracting the chains or the wings is also a free action.

Combat

Once it has found its fugitive, a zelekhut uses its speed and its spell-like abilities to cover the most likely escape routes. Then it immobilizes any defenders while attempting to protect any innocent bystanders. Finally, it apprehends the fugitive with its spiked chains, tripping or disarming the foe as needed. If the sentence is death, the zelekhut carries it out with little fuss or fanfare.

A zelekhut's natural weapons, as well as any weapons it wields, are treated as lawful-aligned for the purpose of overcoming damage reduction.

Spell-Like Abilities: At will—*clairaudience/clairvoyance, dimensional anchor, dispel magic, fear* (DC 16), *hold person* (DC 15), *locate creature, true seeing;* 3/day—*hold monster* (DC 17), *mark of justice;* 1/week—*lesser geas* (DC 16). Caster level 8th. The save DCs are Charisma-based.

Skills: A zelekhut has a +4 racial bonus on Search and Sense Motive checks.

Feats: Due to its centaurlike construction, a zelekhut qualifies for feats as if it had the Mounted Combat feat.

INVISIBLE STALKER

Large Elemental (Air, Extraplanar)
Hit Dice: 8d8+16 (52 hp)
Initiative: +8
Speed: 30 ft. (6 squares), fly 30 ft. (perfect)
Armor Class: 17 (–1 size, +4 Dex, +4 natural), touch 13, flat-footed 13
Base Attack/Grapple: +6/+14
Attack: Slam +10 melee (2d6+4)
Full Attack: 2 slams +10 melee (2d6+4)
Space/Reach: 10 ft./10 ft.
Special Attacks: —
Special Qualities: Darkvision 60 ft., elemental traits, natural invisibility, improved tracking
Saves: Fort +4, Ref +10, Will +4
Abilities: Str 18, Dex 19, Con 14, Int 14, Wis 15, Cha 11
Skills: Listen +13, Move Silently +15, Search +13, Spot +13, Survival +2 (+4 following tracks)
Feats: Combat Reflexes, Improved Initiative, Weapon Focus (slam)
Environment: Elemental Plane of Air
Organization: Solitary
Challenge Rating: 7
Treasure: None
Alignment: Usually neutral
Advancement: 9–12 HD (Large); 13–24 HD (Huge)
Level Adjustment: —

Invisible stalkers are creatures native to the Elemental Plane of Air. They sometimes serve wizards and sorcerers, who summon them to perform specific tasks.

A summoned invisible stalker undertakes whatever task the summoner commands, even if the task sends it hundreds or thousands of miles away. The creature follows a command until the task is completed and obeys only the summoner. However, it resents protracted missions or complex tasks and seeks to pervert its instructions accordingly.

Invisible stalkers have an amorphous form. A *see invisibility* spell shows only a dim outline of a cloud, while a *true seeing* spell reveals a roiling cloud of vapor.

These creatures speak only Auran but can understand Common.

Invisible stalker

COMBAT

An invisible stalker attacks by using the air itself as a weapon. It creates a sudden, intense blast of wind that pounds a single target on the same plane as the creature.

An invisible stalker can be killed only when it is on the Elemental Plane of Air. When performing a task elsewhere, it automatically returns to its home plane when it takes damage sufficient to destroy it.

Natural Invisibility (Su): This ability is constant, allowing a stalker to remain invisible even when attacking. This ability is inherent and not subject to the *invisibility purge* spell.

Improved Tracking (Ex): An invisible stalker is a consummate tracker and makes Spot checks instead of the usual Survival checks to trace a creature's passage.

KOBOLD

Kobold, 1st-Level Warrior
Small Humanoid (Reptilian)
Hit Dice: 1d8 (4 hp)
Initiative: +1
Speed: 30 ft. (6 squares)
Armor Class: 15 (+1 size, +1 Dex, +1 natural, +2 leather), touch 12, flat-footed 14
Base Attack/Grapple: +1/−4
Attack: Spear +1 melee (1d6−1/×3) or sling +3 ranged (1d3)
Full Attack: Spear +1 melee (1d6−1/×3) or sling +3 ranged (1d3)
Space/Reach: 5 ft./5 ft.
Special Attacks: —
Special Qualities: Darkvision 60 ft., light sensitivity
Saves: Fort +2, Ref +1, Will −1
Abilities: Str 9, Dex 13, Con 10, Int 10, Wis 9, Cha 8

Kobold

Skills: Craft (trapmaking) +2, Hide +6, Listen +2, Move Silently +2, Profession (miner) +2, Search +2, Spot +2
Feats: Alertness
Environment: Temperate forests
Organization: Gang (4–9), band (10–100 plus 100% noncombatants plus 1 3rd-level sergeant per 20 adults and 1 leader of 4th–6th level), warband (10–24 plus 2–4 dire weasels), tribe (40–400 plus 1 3rd-level sergeant per 20 adults, 1 or 2 lieutenants of 4th or 5th level, 1 leader of 6th–8th level, and 5–8 dire weasels)
Challenge Rating: 1/4
Treasure: Standard
Alignment: Usually lawful evil
Advancement: By character class
Level Adjustment: +0

This humanoid is about the size of a gnome or halfling. It has a scaly hide, a naked tail like that of a rat, and a doglike head with two small horns.

Kobolds are short, reptilian humanoids with cowardly and sadistic tendencies.

A kobold's scaly skin ranges from dark rusty brown to a rusty black color. It has glowing red eyes. Its tail is nonprehensile. Kobolds wear ragged clothing, favoring red and orange.

Kobolds usually consume plants or animals but are not averse to eating intelligent beings. They spend most of their time fortifying the land around their lairs with traps and warning devices (such as spiked pits, tripwires attached to crossbows, and other mechanical contraptions).

Kobolds hate almost every other sort of humanoid or fey, especially gnomes and sprites.

A kobold is 2 to 2-1/2 feet tall and weighs 35 to 45 pounds.

Kobolds speak Draconic with a voice that sounds like that of a yapping dog.

COMBAT

Kobolds like to attack with overwhelming odds—at least two to one—or trickery; should the odds fall below this threshold, they usually flee. However, they attack gnomes on sight if their numbers are equal.

They begin a fight by slinging bullets, closing only when they can see that their foes have been weakened. Whenever they can, kobolds set up ambushes near trapped areas. They aim to drive enemies into the traps, where other kobolds wait to pour flaming oil over them, shoot them, or drop poisonous vermin onto them.

Light Sensitivity (Ex): Kobolds are dazzled in bright sunlight or within the radius of a *daylight* spell.

Skills: Kobolds have a +2 racial bonus on Craft (trapmaking), Profession (miner), and Search checks.

The kobold warrior presented here had the following ability scores before racial adjustments: Str 13, Dex 11, Con 12, Int 10, Wis 9, Cha 8.

Challenge Rating: Kobolds with levels in NPC classes have a CR equal to their character level −3.

KOBOLD SOCIETY

Kobolds live in dark places, usually underground locations and overgrown forests. They are good miners and often live in the mines they are developing. A kobold tribe sends out warbands

Invisible stalker illus. by T. Lockwood

that patrol within a 10-mile radius from the lair, attacking any intelligent creatures that enter their territory. Kobolds usually kill prisoners for food but occasionally sell some of them as slaves. Their nasty habits and their distrust of most other beings mean that they have many enemies.

A kobold lair has one noncombatant child and one egg per ten adults.

The patron deity of the kobolds is Kurtulmak, who despises all living creatures except kobolds.

KOBOLD CHARACTERS

Kobold characters possess the following racial traits.

—–4 Strength, +2 Dexterity, –2 Constitution.

—Small size: +1 bonus to Armor Class, +1 bonus on attack rolls, +4 bonus on Hide checks, –4 penalty on grapple checks, lifting and carrying limits 3/4 those of Medium characters.

—A kobold's base land speed is 30 feet.

—Darkvision out to 60 feet.

—Racial Skills: A kobold character has a +2 racial bonus on Craft (trapmaking), Profession (miner), and Search checks.

—Racial Feats: A kobold character gains feats according to its character class.

— +1 natural armor bonus.

—Special Qualities (see above): Light sensitivity.

—Automatic Languages: Draconic. Bonus Languages: Common, Undercommon.

—Favored Class: Sorcerer.

—Level adjustment +0.

KRAKEN

Gargantuan Magical Beast (Aquatic)
Hit Dice: 20d10+180 (290 hp)
Initiative: +4
Speed: Swim 20 ft. (4 squares)
Armor Class: 20 (–4 size, +14 natural), touch 6, flat-footed 20
Base Attack/Grapple: +20/+44
Attack: Tentacle +28 melee (2d8+12/19–20)
Full Attack: 2 tentacles +28 melee (2d8+12/19–20) and 6 arms +23 melee (1d6+6) and bite +23 melee (4d6+6)
Space/Reach: 20 ft./15 ft. (60 ft. with tentacle, 30 ft. with arm)
Special Attacks: Improved grab, constrict 2d8+12 or 1d6+6
Special Qualities: Darkvision 60 ft., ink cloud, jet, low-light vision, spell-like abilities
Saves: Fort +21, Ref +12, Will +13
Abilities: Str 34, Dex 10, Con 29, Int 21, Wis 20, Cha 20
Skills: Concentration +21, Diplomacy +7, Hide +0, Intimidate +16, Knowledge (geography) +17, Knowledge (nature) +16, Listen +30, Search +28, Sense Motive +17, Spot +30, Survival +5 (+7 following tracks), Swim +20, Use Magic Device +16
Feats: Alertness, Blind-Fight, Expertise, Improved Critical (tentacle), Improved Initiative, Improved Trip, Iron Will
Environment: Temperate aquatic
Organization: Solitary
Challenge Rating: 12
Treasure: Triple standard
Alignment: Usually neutral evil
Advancement: 21–32 HD (Gargantuan); 33–60 HD (Colossal)
Level Adjustment: —

This creature resembles an immense squid, with a streamlined body, two staring eyes, and a mass of tentacles. Its body is approximately 30 feet long and protected by layers of thick muscle.

Aggressive, cruel, and highly intelligent, krakens rule entire undersea regions. Though these behemoths are rarely seen on the surface, stories tell of ships dragged under and islands scoured of life by these monsters.

Krakens make their lairs thousands of feet below the ocean surface. They frequently inhabit huge cavern complexes that include sections filled with breathable air, where they imprison and breed humanoid slaves to serve and feed them.

Six of the beast's tentacles are shorter arms about 30 feet long; the remaining two are nearly 60 feet long and covered with barbs. Its beaklike mouth is located where the tentacles meet the lower portion of its body.

Krakens speak Common and Aquan.

COMBAT

Krakens strike their opponents with their barbed tentacles, then grab and crush with their arms or drag victims into their huge jaws. An opponent can make sunder attempts against a kraken's tentacles or arms as if they were weapons. A kraken's tentacles have 20 hit points, and its arms have 10 hit points. If a kraken is currently grappling a target with one tentacle or arm, it usually uses another limb to make its attack of opportunity against the sunder attempt. Severing a kraken's tentacle or arm deals damage to the kraken equal to half the limb's full normal hit points. A kraken usually withdraws from combat if it loses both tentacles or three of its arms. A kraken regrows severed limbs in 1d10+10 days.

Improved Grab (Ex): To use this ability, the kraken must hit with an arm or tentacle attack. It can then attempt to start a grapple as a free action without provoking an attack of opportunity. If it wins the grapple check, it establishes a hold and can constrict.

Constrict (Ex): A kraken deals automatic arm or tentacle damage with a successful grapple check.

Jet (Ex): A kraken can jet backward once per round as a full-round action, at a speed of 280 feet. It must move in a straight line, but does not provoke attacks of opportunity while jetting.

Kraken

SARDINHA

Ink Cloud (Ex): A kraken can emit a cloud of jet-black ink in an 80-foot spread once per minute as a free action. The cloud provides total concealment, which the kraken normally uses to escape a fight that is going badly. Creatures within the cloud are considered to be in darkness.

Spell-Like Abilities: 1/day—*control weather, control winds, dominate animal* (DC 18), *resist energy*. Caster level 9th. The save DC is Charisma-based.

Skills: A kraken has a +8 racial bonus on any Swim check to perform some special action or avoid a hazard. It can always choose to take 10 on a Swim check, even if distracted or endangered. It can use the run action while swimming, provided it swims in a straight line.

KRENSHAR

Medium Magical Beast
Hit Dice: 2d10 (11 hp)
Initiative: +2
Speed: 40 ft. (8 squares)
Armor Class: 15 (+2 Dex, +3 natural), touch 12, flat-footed 13
Base Attack/Grapple: +2/+2
Attack: Bite +2 melee (1d6)
Full Attack: Bite +2 melee (1d6) and 2 claws +0 melee (1d4)
Space/Reach: 5 ft./5 ft.
Special Attacks: Scare
Special Qualities: Darkvision 60 ft., low-light vision, scent
Saves: Fort +3, Ref +5, Will +1
Abilities: Str 11, Dex 14, Con 11, Int 6, Wis 12, Cha 13
Skills: Hide +4, Jump +9, Listen +3, Move Silently +6
Feats: Multiattack, Track[B]
Environment: Temperate forests
Organization: Solitary, pair, or pride (6–10)
Challenge Rating: 1
Treasure: None
Alignment: Usually neutral
Advancement: 3–4 HD (Medium); 5–8 HD (Large)
Level Adjustment: +2

This creature seems to combine the worst features of a wolf and a hyena. It has a shaggy, spotted coat, a bristling mane along its spine, and a long, bushy tail.

The krenshar is a strange, catlike carnivore with extremely flexible skin on its head.

A typical krenshar measures 4 or 5 feet in length with a long, narrow head. It weighs about 175 pounds. Males and females hunt together, preferring herd animals for food but attacking humanoids when game becomes scarce. Krenshars are very social among their own kind, and occasional attempts to domesticate cubs have produced fierce and loyal companions. They otherwise behave much like mundane great cats. A lair contains cubs numbering half the adult total.

COMBAT

Krenshars use solitary scouts to drive prey into the waiting clutches of the pride. The scout appears from hiding, uses its scare ability, then chases the fleeing target to join the attack.

Scare (Ex or Su): As a standard action, a krenshar can pull the skin back from its head, revealing the musculature and bony structures of its skull. This alone is usually sufficient to scare away foes (treat as a Bluff check with a +3 bonus).

Combining this scare ability with a loud screech produces an unsettling effect that works like a *scare* spell from a 3rd-level caster (Will DC 13 partial). A creature that successfully saves cannot be affected again by the same krenshar's scare ability for 24 hours. The shriek does not affect other krenshars. This is a supernatural, sonic mind-affecting fear effect. The save DC is Charisma-based.

Skills: Krenshars have a +4 racial bonus on Jump and Move Silently checks.

KUO-TOA

Medium Monstrous Humanoid (Aquatic)
Hit Dice: 2d8+2 (11 hp)
Initiative: +0
Speed: 20 ft. (4 squares), swim 50 ft.
Armor Class: 16 (+6 natural) or 18 (+6 natural, +2 heavy wooden shield), touch 10, flat-footed 16 or 18
Base Attack/Grapple: +2/+3
Attack: Shortspear +3 melee (1d6+1) or bite +3 melee (1d4+1)
Full Attack: Shortspear +3 melee (1d6+1) and bite −2 melee (1d4)
Space/Reach: 5 ft./5 ft.
Special Attacks: Lightning bolt, pincer staff
Special Qualities: Adhesive, amphibious, immunity to poison and paralysis, keen sight, light blindness, resistance to electricity 10, slippery
Saves: Fort +3, Ref +3, Will +5
Abilities: Str 13, Dex 10, Con 13, Int 13, Wis 14, Cha 8
Skills: Craft or Knowledge (any one) +4, Escape Artist +8, Listen +7, Move Silently +3, Search +8, Spot +11, Swim +9
Feats: Alertness[B], Great Fortitude
Environment: Temperate aquatic
Organization: Patrol (2–4 plus 1 3rd-level whip), squad (6–11 plus 1 or 2 3rd-level whips, 1 or 2 4th-level monitors, and 1 8th-level fighter), band (20–50 plus 100% noncombatants plus 2 3rd-level whips, 2 8th-level fighters, and 1 10th-level fighter), or tribe (40–400 plus 1 3rd-level whip per 20 adults, 1 4th-level monitor, 4 8th-level fighters, 1 10th-level whip, and 2 10th-level fighters)
Challenge Rating: 2
Treasure: Standard
Alignment: Often neutral evil
Advancement: By character class
Level Adjustment: +3

Krenshar

This humanoid is a little shorter than a human. Its rounded body is covered with fine scales, giving it the appearance of being pudgy or bloated. The arms and legs are slender, almost willowy, ending in broad hands and distended feet that look much like flippers. Its fishlike, bullet-shaped head has bulging, silver-black eyes and a wide mouth full of sharp teeth.

Kuo-toa

The kuo-toas are an ancient line of aquatic humanoids noted for their sinister nature and diabolical tendencies.

Although most individuals shun contact with these loathsome creatures, sometimes avoiding them is simply not possible. Kuo-toas know much about long-forgotten, ancient evils dwelling in the deepest parts of the ocean.

An average kuo-toa stands roughly 5 feet tall and weighs about 160 pounds.

Although kuo-toas are generally a silver-gray color, their pigmentation changes with their mood. An angry kuo-toa is dark red, while a frightened one becomes pale gray or even white. The air around a kuo-toa carries a strong odor of rotting fish.

Kuo-toas speak Kuo-Toan, Undercommon, and Aquan.

COMBAT

Kuo-toa tactics and weapons vary greatly depending upon the training and skills of the individual encountered. A group of kuo-toa fighters usually fights in formation, throwing spears before closing to melee range.

Lightning Bolt (Su): Two or more kuo-toa clerics (known as whips) operating together can generate a stroke of lightning every 1d4 rounds. The whips must join hands to launch the bolt but need merely be within 30 feet of one another while it builds. The lightning bolt deals 1d6 points of electricity damage per whip, but a successful Reflex save (DC 13 + number of whips) halves this amount.

Pincer Staff: Many kuo-toa fighters and all whips of 7th level or higher carry this Large exotic weapon. A pincer staff deals 1d10 points of bludgeoning damage, threatens a critical hit on a natural 20, and deals double damage on a critical hit. It has a 10-foot reach and cannot be used against an adjacent opponent. A wielder that hits an opponent of at least Small but no larger than Large size can attempt to start a grapple as a free action without provoking an attack of opportunity. If the wielder wins the grapple check, the staff establishes a hold and grabs the opponent, dealing 1d10 points of damage each round the hold is maintained.

Adhesive (Ex): Kuo-toas use their own body oil and other materials to give their shields a finish almost like flypaper, holding fast any creatures or items touching them. Anyone who makes an unsuccessful melee attack against a kuo-toa must succeed on a DC 14 Reflex save, or the attacker's weapon sticks to the shield and is yanked out of the wielder's grasp. Creatures using natural weapons are automatically grappled if they get stuck.

A kuo-toa requires 1 hour and special materials costing 20 gp to coat a shield with adhesive. The adhesive remains good for up to three days or until it actually catches someone or something (in which case the shield can trap no additional items, since the adhesive is used up). Pulling a stuck weapon or limb from a shield requires a DC 20 Strength check.

Amphibious (Ex): Although kuo-toas breathe by means of gills, they can survive indefinitely on land.

Keen Sight (Ex): Kuo-toas have excellent vision thanks to their two independently focusing eyes. Their eyesight is so keen that they can spot a moving object or creature even if it is invisible or ethereal. Only by remaining perfectly still can such objects or creatures avoid their notice.

Light Blindness (Ex): Abrupt exposure to bright light (such as sunlight or a *daylight* spell) blinds kuo-toas for 1 round. On subsequent rounds, they are dazzled while operating in bright light.

Slippery (Ex): All kuo-toas secrete an oily film that makes them difficult to grapple or snare. Webs, magical or otherwise, don't affect kuo-toas, and they usually can wriggle free from most other forms of confinement.

Skills: Kuo-toas have a +8 racial bonus on Escape Artist checks and a +4 racial bonus on Spot and Search checks.

A kuo-toa has a +8 racial bonus on any Swim check to perform some special action or avoid a hazard. It can always choose to take 10 on a Swim check, even if distracted or endangered. It can use the run action while swimming, provided it swims in a straight line.

KUO-TOA SOCIETY

Kuo-toas dwell in subterranean communities that are well supplied with pools for recreation and breeding. They spawn as fish do, raising their young in special pools until their amphibian qualities develop (about a year after hatching).

Thanks to the efforts of the whips, virtually all kuo-toas are devoted worshipers of the goddess Blibdoolpoolp, whom they refer to as the Sea Mother. Every kuo-toa community has at least one shrine to the Sea Mother. Larger communities with major temples serve as hubs for clusters of smaller settlements. These are also centers for intergroup trade and politics. Virtually all kuo-toa communities are open to drow and their servants, who provide useful goods and services, although the drow are both feared and hated by the kuo-toas. This enmity leads to many minor skirmishes and frequent kidnappings between the two societies.

Lamia

KUO-TOA CHARACTERS

A kuo-toa's favored class is rogue. Most kuo-toa leaders are cleric/rogues or clerics (whips). Kuo-toa clerics worship Blib-doolpoolp. A kuo-toa cleric has access to two of the following domains: Destruction, Evil, or Water. Kuo-toa monks, called monitors, also exist.

LAMIA

Large Magical Beast
Hit Dice: 9d10+9 (58 hp)
Initiative: +2
Speed: 60 ft. (12 squares)
Armor Class: 18 (–1 size, +2 Dex, +7 natural), touch 11, flat-footed 16
Base Attack/Grapple: +9/+17
Attack: Touch +12 melee (1d4 Wisdom drain) or dagger +12 melee (1d6+4/19–20) or claw +12 melee (1d4+4)
Full Attack: Touch +12 melee (1d4 Wisdom drain); or dagger +12/+7 melee (1d6+4/19–20) and 2 claws +7 melee (1d4+2)
Space/Reach: 10 ft./5 ft.
Special Attacks: Spell-like abilities, Wisdom drain
Special Qualities: Darkvision 60 ft., low-light vision
Saves: Fort +7, Ref +8, Will +7
Abilities: Str 18, Dex 15, Con 12, Int 13, Wis 15, Cha 12
Skills: Bluff +14, Concentration +10, Diplomacy +3, Disguise +1 (+3 acting), Hide +11, Intimidate +3, Spot +11
Feats: Dodge, Iron Will, Mobility, Spring Attack
Environment: Temperate deserts
Organization: Solitary, pair, or gang (3–4)
Challenge Rating: 6
Treasure: Standard
Alignment: Usually chaotic evil
Advancement: 10–13 HD (Large); 14–27 HD (Huge)
Level Adjustment: +4

This creature seems to be a cross between a stunningly attractive human and a sleek lion. It looks human from the waist up, with the body of a lion below that.

Lamias are evil and cruel creatures that take pleasure in causing suffering. They particularly target those who serve the cause of good.

A typical lamia is about 8 feet long and weighs about 700 pounds.

COMBAT

Though a lamia is powerful and dangerous in close combat, it has no stomach for a fair fight. It uses its illusion abilities to lure heroes into perilous situations, and then uses its Spring Attack feat to bound out of the shadows and drain Wisdom from its opponents. When it has sapped the will of its victim, it uses its enchantment abilities to beguile and ensnare the unfortunate soul. A lamia forced into physical combat attacks with a dagger in one of its human hands and a pair of lionlike claws.

Spell-Like Abilities: At will—*disguise self, ventriloquism;* 3/day—*charm monster* (DC 15), *major image* (DC 14), *mirror image, suggestion* (DC 14); 1/day—*deep slumber* (DC 14). Caster level 9th. The save DCs are Charisma-based.

Wisdom Drain (Su): A lamia drains 1d4 points of Wisdom each time it hits with its melee touch attack. (Unlike with other kinds of ability drain attacks, a lamia does not heal any damage when it uses its Wisdom drain.) Lamias try to use this power early in an encounter to make foes more susceptible to *charm monster* and *suggestion.*

Skills: Lamias have a +4 racial bonus on Bluff and Hide checks.

LAMMASU

This creature has the golden-brown body of a lion, the wings of a giant eagle, and the face of a human.

Lammasus are noble creatures that are concerned with the welfare and safety of all good beings.

These creatures dwell most often in old, abandoned temples and ruins located in remote areas, where they contemplate how best to combat the influence of evil in the world. Adventurers sometimes seek them out to gain the benefit of their wisdom and their knowledge of ancient mysteries. Lammasus receive good beings and creatures cordially and usually offer assistance if the visitor is directly combating evil. They tolerate neutral beings but watch them carefully. They do not tolerate the presence of evil beings, attacking them on sight.

The demeanor of a lammasu is noble and stern, but these creatures can be quite compassionate.

Lammasu

A typical lammasu is about 8 feet long and weighs about 500 pounds.

Lammasus speak Common, Draconic, and Celestial.

COMBAT

A lammasu attacks with spells or its razor-sharp claws. It almost always enters combat if it observes a good creature being threatened by evil.

Spells: A lammasu casts spells as a 7th-level cleric, and can choose spells from the cleric spell list, plus any two of the following domains: Good, Healing, Knowledge, or Law.

Typical Cleric Spells Prepared (6/6/5/4/2; save DC 13 + spell level): 0—*detect magic, guidance* (2), *light, read magic, resistance;* 1st—*bless* (2), *detect evil, divine favor, entropic shield, protection from evil*;* 2nd—*aid*, bear's endurance, bull's strength, lesser restoration, resist energy;* 3rd—*daylight, dispel magic, magic circle against evil*, remove curse;* 4th—*holy smite*, neutralize poison.*

*Domain spell. Domains: Good and Healing.

Magic Circle against Evil (Su): A lammasu radiates a continuous magic circle against evil that affects a 20-foot radius.

Spell-Like Abilities: 2/day—*greater invisibility* (self only); 1/day—*dimension door.* Caster level 7th.

Pounce (Ex): If a lammasu charges a foe, it can make a full attack, including two rake attacks.

Rake (Ex): Attack bonus +12 melee, damage 1d6+3.

Skills: Lammasus have a +2 racial bonus on Spot checks.

Breath Weapon (Su): 30-foot cone, 1/day, damage 6d8 fire, Reflex DC 21 half.

	Lammasu	Golden Protector (Celestial Half-Dragon Lammasu)
	Large Magical Beast	Large Dragon
Hit Dice:	7d10+21 (59 hp)	10d12+60 (125 hp)
Initiative:	+1	+3
Speed:	30 ft. (6 squares), fly 60 ft.(average)	30 ft. (6 squares), fly 60 ft.(average)
Armor Class:	20 (−1 size, +1 Dex, +10 natural), touch 10, flat-footed 19	29 (−1 size, +3 Dex, +14 natural, +2 *bracers of armor +2*, +1 *ring of protection +1*), touch 13, flat-footed 26
Base Attack/Grapple:	+7/+17	+10/+23
Attack:	Claw +12 melee (1d6+6)	Claw +19 melee (1d6+9)
Full Attack:	2 claws +12 melee (1d6+6)	Claw +19 melee (1d6+9) and bite +13 melee (1d8+4)
Space/Reach:	10 ft./5 ft.	10 ft./5 ft.
Special Attacks:	Pounce, rake 1d6+3, spells	Breath weapon, pounce, smite evil, rake 1d6+4, spells
Special Qualities:	Darkvision 60 ft., low-light vision, magic circle against evil, spell-like abilities	Damage reduction 5/magic, darkvision 60 ft., immunity to fire, *sleep*, and paralysis, low-light vision, magic circle against evil, resistance to acid 10, cold 10, and electricity 10, spell-like abilities, spell resistance 15
Saves:	Fort +8, Ref +8, Will +7	Fort +13, Ref +12, Will +10
Abilities:	Str 23, Dex 12, Con 17, Int 16, Wis 17, Cha 14	Str 28, Dex 17, Con 22, Int 18, Wis 20, Cha 18
Skills:	Concentration +13, Diplomacy +4, Knowledge (arcana) +13, Listen +13, Sense Motive +13, Spot +15	Concentration +19, Diplomacy +19, Knowledge (arcana) +17, Knowledge (the planes) +17, Listen +18, Search +17, Sense Motive +18, Spellcraft +19, Spot +20, Survival +18 (+20 other planes and tracking)
Feats:	Blind-Fight, Iron Will, Lightning Reflexes	Blind-Fight, Iron Will, Lightning Reflexes, Weapon Focus (claw)
Environment:	Temperate deserts	Seven Mounting Heavens of Celestia
Organization:	Solitary	Solitary
Challenge Rating:	8	13
Treasure:	Standard	Standard
Alignment:	Always lawful good	Always lawful good
Advancement:	8–10 HD (Large); 11–21 HD (Huge)	11–30 HD (Huge)
Level Adjustment:	+5	+10

GOLDEN PROTECTOR (CELESTIAL HALF-DRAGON LAMMASU)

Child of a celestial lammasu and a gold dragon, the golden protector has migrated to the Material Plane to more actively combat evil.

Combat

The golden protector's natural weapons are treated as magic weapons for the purpose of overcoming damage reduction.

Breath Weapon (Su): 30-foot cone, 1/day, damage 6d8 fire, Reflex DC 21 half.

Smite Evil (Su): Once per day a golden protector can make a normal melee attack to deal an extra 10 points of damage against an evil opponent.

Typical Cleric Spells Prepared (6/7/5/4/3; save DC 15 + spell level): 0—*detect magic, guidance* (2), *light, read magic, resistance*; 1st—*bless* (2), *detect evil, divine favor* (2), *entropic shield, protection from evil**; 2nd—*aid**, *bear's endurance, bull's strength, lesser restoration, resist energy*; 3rd—*daylight, dispel magic, magic circle against evil**, *remove curse*; 4th—*dismissal, holy smite**, *neutralize poison*.

*Domain spell. Domains: Good and Healing.

Rake (Ex): Attack bonus +19 melee, damage 1d6+4.

Possessions: Bracers of armor +2, ring of protection +1. (Different golden protectors may have different possessions.)

LICH

A lich is an undead spellcaster, usually a wizard or sorcerer but sometimes a cleric or other spellcaster, who has used its magical powers to unnaturally extend its life.

As a rule, these creatures are scheming and, some say, insane. They hunger for ever greater power, long-forgotten knowledge, and the most terrible of arcane secrets. Because the shadow of death does not hang over them, they often conceive plans taking years, decades, or even centuries to come to fruition.

A lich is a gaunt and skeletal humanoid with withered flesh stretched tight across horribly visible bones. Its eyes have long ago been lost to decay, but bright pinpoints of crimson light burn on in the empty sockets. Even the least of these creatures was a powerful person in life, so they often are draped in once-grand clothing. Multiclass fighters or clerics may still bear the armor of a warrior. Like its body, however, the garb of a lich shows all too well the weight of years. Decay and corruption are its constant companion.

Liches speak Common plus any other languages they knew in life.

SAMPLE LICH

This skeletal creature wears the rotting, rich robes of a mighty wizard long dead. Hateful crimson light dances in its empty eye sockets.

This example uses an 11th-level human wizard as the character.

Lich, 11th-Level Human Wizard
Medium Undead (Augmented Humanoid)
Hit Dice: 11d12+3 (74 hp)
Initiative: +3
Speed: 30 ft. (6 squares)
Armor Class: 23 (+3 Dex, +5 natural, +4 *bracers of armor +4*, +1 *ring of protection*), touch 14, flat-footed 20
Base Attack/Grapple: +5/+5
Attack: Touch +5 melee (1d8+5 negative energy plus paralysis) or quarterstaff +5 melee (1d6) or dagger +5 melee (1d4/19–20) or masterwork light crossbow +9 ranged (1d8/19–20)
Full Attack: Touch +5 melee (1d8+5 negative energy plus paralysis) or quarterstaff +5 melee (1d6) or dagger +5 melee (1d4/19–20) or masterwork light crossbow +9 ranged (1d8/19–20)
Space/Reach: 5 ft./5 ft.
Special Attacks: Damaging touch, fear aura, paralyzing touch, spells
Special Qualities: +4 turn resistance, damage reduction

15/bludgeoning and magic, darkvision 60 ft., immunity to cold, electricity, polymorph, and mind-affecting effects, undead traits

Saves: Fort +4, Ref +7, Will +10 (*cloak of resistance +1*)
Abilities: Str 10, Dex 16, Con —, Int 19, Wis 14, Cha 13
Skills: Concentration +15, Decipher Script +14, Hide +15, Knowledge (arcana) +18, Listen +12, Move Silently +16, Search +16, Sense Motive +10, Spellcraft +20, Spot +12
Feats: Combat Casting, Craft Wondrous Item, Quicken Spell, Scribe Scroll, Silent Spell, Spell Focus (evocation), Still Spell, Toughness
Environment: Temperate plains
Organization: Solitary
Challenge Rating: 13
Treasure: Standard coins; double goods; double items
Alignment: Neutral evil
Advancement: By character class
Level Adjustment: +4

Combat

A lich's natural weapons are treated as magic weapons for the purpose of overcoming damage reduction.

The Will save against this lich's fear aura and damaging touch, and the Fortitude save against its paralyzing touch, have a DC of 16.

Wizard Spells Prepared (4/5/5/5/4/2/1; save DC 14 + spell level): 0—*acid splash, detect magic, ray of frost*, touch of fatigue;* 1st—*expeditious retreat, magic missile (3), ray of enfeeblement;* 2nd—*mirror image, protection from arrows, scorching ray*, spectral hand, web;* 3rd—*dispel magic, fireball*, haste, lightning bolt*, vampiric touch;* 4th—*enervation, fear, ice storm*, shout*;* 5th—*cone of cold*, teleport;* 6th—*disintegrate.*

*Because of Spell Focus (evocation), the save DC for these spells is 15 + spell level.

Possessions: Bracers of armor +4, cloak of resistance +1, potion of gaseous form, ring of protection +1, scroll of summon monster IV (8th level), wand of magic missile (50 charges, 9th level).

CREATING A LICH

"Lich" is an acquired template that can be added to any humanoid creature (referred to hereafter as the base creature), provided it can create the required phylactery; see The Lich's Phylactery, below. (Liches of other kinds of creatures, such as dragons, exist, but use different templates.)

A lich has all the base creature's statistics and special abilities except as noted here.

Size and Type: The creature's type changes to undead. Do not recalculate base attack bonus, saves, or skill points. Size is unchanged.

Hit Dice: Increase all current and future Hit Dice to d12s.

Armor Class: A lich has a +5 natural armor bonus or the base creature's natural armor bonus, whichever is better.

Attack: A lich has a touch attack that it can use once per round. If the base creature can use weapons, the lich retains this ability. A creature with natural weapons retains those natural weapons. A lich fighting without weapons uses either its touch attack or its primary natural weapon (if it has any). A lich armed with a weapon uses its touch or a weapon, as it desires.

Lich

Full Attack: A lich fighting without weapons uses either its touch attack (see above) or its natural weapons (if it has any). If armed with a weapon, it usually uses the weapon as its primary attack along with a touch as a natural secondary attack, provided it has a way to make that attack (either a free hand or a natural weapon that it can use as a secondary attack).

Damage: A lich without natural weapons has a touch attack that uses negative energy to deal 1d8+5 points of damage to living creatures; a Will save (DC 10 + 1/2 lich's HD + lich's Cha modifier) halves the damage. A lich with natural weapons can use its touch attack or its natural weaponry, as it prefers. If it chooses the latter, it deals 1d8+5 points of extra damage on one natural weapon attack.

Special Attacks: A lich retains all the base creature's special attacks and gains those described below. Save DCs are equal to 10 + 1/2 lich's HD + lich's Cha modifier unless otherwise noted.

Fear Aura (Su): Liches are shrouded in a dreadful aura of death and evil. Creatures of less than 5 HD in a 60-foot radius that look at the lich must succeed on a Will save or be affected as though by a *fear* spell from a sorcerer of the lich's level. A creature that successfully saves cannot be affected again by the same lich's aura for 24 hours.

Paralyzing Touch (Su): Any living creature a lich hits with its touch attack must succeed on a Fortitude save or be permanently paralyzed. *Remove paralysis* or any spell that can remove a curse can free the victim (see the *bestow curse* spell description, page 203 of the *Player's Handbook*). The effect cannot be dispelled. Anyone paralyzed by a lich seems dead, though a DC 20 Spot check or a DC 15 Heal check reveals that the victim is still alive..

Spells: A lich can cast any spells it could cast while alive.

Special Qualities: A lich retains all the base creature's special qualities and gains those described below.

Turn Resistance (Ex): A lich has +4 turn resistance.

Damage Reduction (Su): A lich's undead body is tough, giving the creature damage reduction 15/bludgeoning and magic. Its natural weapons are treated as magic weapons for the purpose of overcoming damage reduction.

Immunities (Ex): Liches have immunity to cold, electricity, polymorph (though they can use polymorph effects on themselves), and mind-affecting attacks.

Abilities: Increase from the base creature as follows: Int +2, Wis +2, Cha +2. Being undead, a lich has no Constitution score.

Skills: Liches have a +8 racial bonus on Hide, Listen, Move Silently, Search, Sense Motive, and Spot checks. Otherwise same as the base creature.

Organization: Solitary or troupe (1 lich, plus 2–4 vampires and 5–8 vampire spawn).

Challenge Rating: Same as the base creature + 2.

Treasure: Standard coins; double goods; double items.

Alignment: Any evil.

Advancement: By character class.

Level Adjustment: Same as the base creature +4.

LICH CHARACTERS

The process of becoming a lich is unspeakably evil and can be undertaken only by a willing character. A lich retains all class abilities it had in life.

THE LICH'S PHYLACTERY

An integral part of becoming a lich is creating a magic phylactery in which the character stores its life force. As a rule, the only way to get rid of a lich for sure is to destroy its phylactery. Unless its phylactery is located and destroyed, a lich reappears 1d10 days after its apparent death.

Each lich must make its own phylactery, which requires the Craft Wondrous Item feat. The character must be able to cast spells and have a caster level of 11th or higher. The phylactery costs 120,000 gp and 4,800 XP to create and has a caster level equal to that of its creator at the time of creation.

The most common form of phylactery is a sealed metal box containing strips of parchment on which magical phrases have been transcribed. The box is Tiny and has 40 hit points, hardness 20, and a break DC of 40. Other forms of phylacteries can exist, such as rings, amulets, or similar items.

LILLEND

Large Outsider (Chaotic, Extraplanar, Good)

Hit Dice: 7d8+14 (45 hp)

Initiative: +3

Speed: 20 ft. (4 squares), fly 70 ft. (average)

Armor Class: 17 (−1 size, +3 Dex, +5 natural), touch 12, flat-footed 14

Base Attack/Grapple: +7/+16

Attack: Short sword +11 melee (1d8+5/19–20)

Full Attack: Short sword +11/+6 melee (1d8+5/19–20) and tail slap +6 melee (2d6+2)

Space/Reach: 10 ft./10 ft.

Special Attacks: Constrict 2d6+5, improved grab, spells, spell-like abilities

Special Qualities: Darkvision 60 ft., immunity to poison, resistance to fire 10

Saves: Fort +7, Ref +10, Will +8

Abilities: Str 20, Dex 17, Con 15, Int 14, Wis 16, Cha 18

Skills: Appraise +12, Concentration +12, Diplomacy +16, Knowledge (arcana) +12, Listen +13, Perform (any one) +14, Sense Motive +13, Spellcraft +14, Spot +13, Survival +17

Feats: Combat Casting, Extend Spell, Lightning Reflexes

Environment: Heroic Domains of Ysgard

Organization: Solitary or covey (2–4)

Challenge Rating: 7

Treasure: Standard

Alignment: Always chaotic good

Advancement: 8–10 HD (Large); 11–21 HD (Huge)

Level Adjustment: +6

The creature looks like a female human or elf with the lower torso of a multicolored serpent and huge, strikingly patterned wings like a bird's.

Lillends are mysterious visitors from the plane of Ysgard. Many are skilled in one or more forms of artistic expression.

Lillends are lovers of music and art. Gold, even food, means little to them, while a song, story, or piece of artwork holds great value. The destruction of art and the ill treatment of artists enrages them. They are infamous for holding grudges, and they are often encountered seeking violent retribution against enemies of their favorite arts.

Lillends also have a great love of unspoiled wilderness. The wilds remind them of the natural beauty of their home plane, and they occasionally visit and enjoy similar regions. A lillend is as protective of its chosen wilderness as it is of the arts. These beings sometimes form temporary alliances with rangers, druids, and bards to defend their favorite retreats against the encroachment of civilization. Sometimes a covey of lillends adopts a tract of wilderness, using any means necessary to drive off despoilers.

A typical lillend's coils are 20 feet long. The creature weighs about 3,800 pounds. A few lillends have male torsos.

Lillends speak Celestial, Infernal, Abyssal, and Common.

COMBAT

Lillends are generally peaceful unless they intend vengeance against someone they believe guilty of harming, or even threatening, a favored art form, artwork, or artist. Then they become implacable foes. They use their spells and spell-like abilities to confuse and weaken opponents before entering combat. A covey of lillends usually discusses strategy before a battle.

A lillend's natural weapons, as well as any weapons it wields, are treated as chaotic-aligned and good-aligned for the purpose of overcoming damage reduction.

Constrict (Ex): A lillend deals 2d6+5 points of damage with a successful grapple check. Constricting uses the entire lower portion of its body, so it cannot take any move actions when constricting, though it can still attack with its sword.

Improved Grab (Ex): To use this ability, a lillend must hit with its tail slap attack. It can then attempt to start a grapple as a free action without provoking an attack of opportunity. If it wins the grapple check, it establishes a hold and can constrict.

Spells: A lillend casts arcane spells as a 6th-level bard.

Typical Bard Spells Known (3/4/3; save DC 14 + spell level): 0—dancing lights, daze, detect magic, lullaby, mage hand, read magic; 1st—charm person, cure light wounds, identify, sleep; 2nd—hold person, invisibility, sound burst.

Spell-Like Abilities: 3/day—*darkness, hallucinatory terrain* (DC 18), *knock, light;* 1/day—*charm person* (DC 15), *speak with animals, speak with plants.* Caster level 10th. The save DCs are Charisma-based.

A lillend also has the bardic music ability as a 6th-level bard.

Skills: Lillends have a +4 racial bonus on Survival checks.

Lillend

LIZARDFOLK

Medium Humanoid (Reptilian)
Hit Dice: 2d8+2 (11 hp)
Initiative: +0
Speed: 30 ft. (6 squares)
Armor Class: 15 (+5 natural) or 17 (+5 natural, +2 heavy shield), touch 10, flat-footed 15 or 17
Base Attack/Grapple: +1/+2
Attack: Claw +2 melee (1d4+1) or club +2 melee (1d6+1) or javelin +1 ranged (1d6+1)
Full Attack: 2 claws +2 melee (1d4+1) and bite +0 melee (1d4); or club +2 melee (1d6+1) and bite +0 melee (1d4); or javelin +1 ranged (1d6+1)
Special Attacks: —
Special Qualities: Hold breath
Space/Reach: 5 ft./5 ft.
Saves: Fort +1, Ref +3, Will +0
Abilities: Str 13, Dex 10, Con 13, Int 9, Wis 10, Cha 10
Skills: Balance +4, Jump +5, Swim +2
Feats: Multiattack
Environment: Temperate marshes
Organization: Gang (2–3), band (6–10 plus 50% noncombatants plus 1 leader of 3rd–6th level), or tribe (30–60 plus 2 lieutenants of 3rd–6th level and 1 leader of 4th–10th level)
Challenge Rating: 1
Treasure: 50% coins; 50% goods; 50% items
Alignment: Usually neutral
Advancement: By character class
Level Adjustment: +1

This tall humanoid looks like a cross between a powerfully built human and a lizard. It has clawed hands, a long tail, and toothy jaws.

Lizardfolk are primitive reptilian humanoids that can be very dangerous if provoked.

Although they are omnivores, lizardfolk prefer meat; popular lore holds that lizardfolk prefer humanoid flesh, but this charge is largely unfounded (though some tribes do eat captives or slain foes). Some more advanced tribes build huts and use a variety of weapons and shields; leaders of these tribes may have equipment stolen from or obtained in trade with other intelligent creatures.

A lizardfolk is usually 6 to 7 feet tall with green, gray, or brown scales. Its tail is used for balance and is 3 to 4 feet long. A lizardfolk can weigh from 200 to 250 pounds.

Lizardfolk speak Draconic.

COMBAT

Lizardfolk fight as unorganized individuals. They prefer frontal assaults and massed rushes, sometimes trying to force foes into the water, where the lizardfolk have an advantage. If outnumbered or if their territory is being invaded, they set snares, plan ambushes, and make raids to hinder enemy supplies. Advanced tribes use more sophisticated tactics and have better traps and ambushes.

Hold Breath: A lizardfolk can hold its breath for a number of rounds equal to four times its Constitution score before it risks drowning (see page 304 of the *Dungeon Master's Guide*).

Skills: Because of their tails, lizardfolk have a +4 racial bonus on Jump, Swim, and Balance checks. The skill modifiers given in the statistics block include a –2 armor check penalty (–4 on Swim checks) for carrying a heavy shield.

LIZARDFOLK SOCIETY

Lizardfolk have a patriarchal society in which the most powerful member rules the others. Shamans offer advice but rarely become leaders themselves. Survival is the utmost concern of lizardfolk, and a threatened or starving tribe will go to incredible lengths (even committing deeds considered abominable by other humanoids) to ensure its continued existence.

Most tribes live in swamps, but about a third of the population lives in underwater air-filled caves. Local tribes often unite against a greater threat (including hostile lizardfolk tribes) and occasionally make alliances with locathahs or serve more powerful creatures such as nagas or dragons. In isolated areas they survive by fishing, gathering, and scavenging, while those that live near other humanoids make raids for food, supplies, and slaves. A lizardfolk lair has half as many noncombatant hatchlings as adults, and one egg per ten adults.

The patron deity of lizardfolk is Semuanya, whose chief concern is the survival and propagation of its charges.

LIZARDFOLK AS CHARACTERS

Most lizardfolk leaders are barbarians or druids. Lizardfolk clerics (shamans) worship Semuanya. A lizardfolk cleric has access to two of the following domains: Animal, Plant, or Water.

Lizardfolk characters possess the following racial traits.

— +2 Strength, +2 Constitution, –2 Intelligence.

—Medium size.

—A lizardfolk's base land speed is 30 feet.

—Racial Hit Dice: A lizardfolk begins with two levels of humanoid, which provide 2d8 Hit Dice, a base attack bonus of +1, and base saving throw bonuses of Fort +0, Ref +3, and Will +0.

—Racial Skills: A lizardfolk's humanoid levels give it skill points equal to 5 × (2 + Int modifier, minimum 1). Its class skills are Balance, Jump, and Swim. Lizardfolk have a +4 racial bonus on Balance, Jump, and Swim checks.

—Racial Feats: A lizardfolk's humanoid levels give it one feat.

—Weapon and Armor Proficiency: A lizardfolk is automatically proficient with simple weapons and shields.

— +5 natural armor bonus.

—Natural Weapons: 2 claws (1d4) and bite (1d4).

—Special Qualities (see above): Hold breath.

—Automatic Languages: Common, Draconic. Bonus Languages: Aquan, Goblin, Gnoll, Orc.

—Favored Class: Druid.

—Level adjustment +1.

Lizardfolk

LOCATHAH

Medium Humanoid (Aquatic)
Hit Dice: 2d8 (9 hp)
Initiative: +1
Speed: 10 ft. (2 squares), swim 60 ft.
Armor Class: 14 (+1 Dex, +3 natural), touch 11, flat-footed 13
Base Attack/Grapple: +1/+1
Attack: Longspear +2 melee (1d8/×3) or light crossbow +2 ranged (1d8/19–20)
Full Attack: Longspear +2 melee (1d8/×3) or light crossbow +2 ranged (1d8/19–20)
Space/Reach: 5 ft./5 ft.

Saves: Fort +3, Ref +1, Will +1
Special Attacks: —
Special Qualities: —
Abilities: Str 10, Dex 12, Con 10, Int 13, Wis 13, Cha 11
Skills: Craft (any one) +6, Listen +6, Spot +6, Swim +8
Feats: Weapon Focus (longspear)
Environment: Warm aquatic
Organization: Company (2–4), patrol (11–20 plus 2 3rd-level sergeants and 1 leader of 3rd–6th level), or tribe (30–100 plus 100% noncombatants plus 1 3rd-level sergeant per 10 adults, 5 5th-level lieutenants, and 3 7th-level captains)
Challenge Rating: 1/2
Treasure: Standard
Alignment: Usually neutral
Advancement: By character class
Level Adjustment: +1

This humanoid is slender and a little shorter than a human. It has fine, yellow-green scales and large fins on its arms and legs.

The nomadic locathahs dwell in warm coastal waters, hunting fish and gathering crustaceans for food. Although humanoid in shape, they are clearly more fish than human.

Locathahs are not particularly aggressive but do not trust surface dwellers—far too many of their kind have been swept up in fishing nets.

The average locathah stands 5 feet tall and weighs 175 pounds. Females and males look very much alike, although the former can be recognized by the two ochre stripes marking their egg sacs.

Locathahs speak Aquan.

COMBAT

Any battle with locathahs usually begins with the creatures loosing volleys of bolts from their crossbows; underwater, their crossbows have a range increment of 20 feet. If they have managed to set up an ambush or other trap, they continue to employ crossbows for as long as possible. Otherwise, they close to bring their longspears into play. Although primarily used for fishing, these spears make formidable weapons.

Locathahs lack teeth, claws, and other natural weapons, so they are not especially dangerous if unarmed. A weaponless locathah will generally turn and flee.

Skills: A locathah has a +8 racial bonus on any Swim check to perform some special action or avoid a hazard. It can always choose to take 10 on a Swim check, even if distracted or endangered. It can use the run action while swimming, provided it swims in a straight line.

LOCATHAH SOCIETY

Locathah tribes usually move with each change of season, going where they can find food. They make their encampments in caves, rocky areas, or seaweed beds—locales that afford some concealment and protection. Patrols are usually hunting parties after small game, but they also keep a lookout for enemies trespassing in the tribe's hunting area. Larger patrols of locathah are sometimes found tracking big animals or engaged in similar activities. Entire tribes come together to trade or hold council.

Locathahs revere the deity Eadro, who created both them and the merfolk.

LOCATHAH CHARACTERS

A locathah's favored class is barbarian, and most locathah leaders are barbarians. Most locathah spellcasters are adepts. Locathah clerics worship Eadro. A locathah cleric has access to two of the following domains: Animal, Protection, or Water.

LYCANTHROPE

Lycanthropes are humanoids or giants who can transform themselves into animals. In its natural form, a lycanthrope looks like any other members of its kind, though natural lycanthropes and those who have been afflicted for a long time tend to have or acquire features reminiscent of their animal forms, such as thick, shaggy hair, pointed teeth, or long, strong fingers. In animal form, a lycanthrope resembles a powerful version of the normal animal, but on close inspection, its eyes (which often glow red in the dark) show a faint spark of unnatural intelligence.

Evil lycanthropes often hide among normal folk, emerging in animal form at night (especially under a full moon) to spread terror and bloodshed. Good lycanthropes tend to be reclusive individuals, uncomfortable around large numbers of people. They often live alone in wilderness areas, far from villages and towns.

Lycanthropy can be spread like a disease. Sometimes a lycanthrope begins life as a normal humanoid or giant who subsequently contracts lycanthropy after being wounded by a lycanthrope. Such a creature is called an afflicted lycanthrope. Other lycanthropes are born as lycanthropes, and are known as natural lycanthropes.

Combat

A lycanthrope in its humanoid (or giant) form uses whatever tactics and weapons are favored by others of its kind, though it tends to be slightly more aggressive. A lycanthrope possesses the senses of its animal form, including scent and low-light vision, and it has a deep empathy for (and ability to communicate with) animals of its animal form. An afflicted lycanthrope damaged in combat may be overwhelmed by rage, causing it to change to its animal form involuntarily.

A lycanthrope in animal form fights like the animal it resembles, although its bite carries the disease of lycanthropy. It is preternaturally cunning and strong, and possesses damage reduction that is overcome only by silvered weapons.

Finally, a natural lycanthrope (or an afflicted lycanthrope that has become aware of its affliction) can assume a hybrid form that is a mix of its humanoid and animal forms. A hybrid has hands and can use weapons, but it can also attack with its teeth and claws. A hybrid can spread lycanthropy with its bite, and it has the same damage reduction that its animal form possesses.

WEREBEAR

This hulking humanoid is covered in shaggy brown fur and has long claws and a bearlike face. It carries a greataxe in one paw.

Locathah

	Werebear, Human Form Medium Humanoid (Human, Shapechanger)	Werebear, Bear Form Large Humanoid (Human, Shapechanger)	Werebear, Hybrid Form Large Humanoid (Human, Shapechanger)
Hit Dice:	1d8+1 plus 6d8+30 (62 hp)	1d8+1 plus 6d8+30 (62 hp)	1d8+1 plus 6d8+30 (62 hp)
Initiative:		+0	+1 +1
Speed:	30 ft. (6 squares)	40 ft. (8 squares)	30 ft. (6 squares)
Armor Class:	15 (+2 natural, +3 studded leather armor), touch 10, flat-footed 15	17 (−1 size, +1 Dex, +7 natural), touch 10, flat-footed 16	17 (−1 size, +1 Dex, +7 natural) touch 10, flat-footed 16
Base Attack/Grapple:	+5/+6	+5/+18	+5/+18
Attack:	Greataxe +6 melee (1d12+1/×3) or throwing axe +5 ranged (1d6+1)	Claw +13 melee (1d8+9)	Greataxe +11 melee (1d12+13/×3); or claw +13 melee (1d6+9)
Full Attack:	Greataxe +6 melee (1d12+1/×3) or throwing axe +5 ranged (1d6+1)	2 claws +13 melee (1d8+9) and bite +11 melee (2d6+4)	Claw +13 melee (1d6+9) and greataxe +9 melee (1d12+4/×3) and bite +11 melee (1d8+4) or 2 claws +13 melee (1d6+9) and bite +11 melee (1d8+4)
Space/Reach:	5 ft./5 ft.	10 ft./5 ft.	10 ft./10 ft.
Special Attacks:	—	Improved grab, curse of lycanthropy	Curse of lycanthropy
Special Qualities:	Alternate form, bear empathy, low-light vision, scent damage reduction 10/silver,	Alternate form, bear empathy, damage reduction 10/silver, low-light vision, scent	Alternate form, bear empathy, low-light vision, scent
Saves:	Fort +8, Ref +5, Will +4	Fort +12, Ref +6, Will +4	Fort +12, Ref +6, Will +4
Abilities:	Str 13, Dex 11, Con 12 Int 10, Wis 11, Cha 8	Str 29, Dex 13, Con 20, Int 10, Wis 11, Cha 8	Str 29, Dex 13, Con 20, Int 10, Wis 11, Cha 8
Skills:	Handle Animal +3, Listen +4, Spot +4, Swim +1	Handle Animal +3, Listen +4, Spot +4, Swim +13	Handle Animal +3, Listen +4, Spot +5, Swim +9
Feats:	Endurance, Iron Will[B], Multiattack, Power Attack, Run, Track[B]	(same as human form)	(same as human form)
Environment:	Cold forests	Cold forests	Cold forests
Organization:	Solitary, pair, family (3–4), or troupe (2–4 plus 1–4 brown bears)	(same as human form)	(same as human form)
Challenge Rating:	5	5	5
Treasure:	Standard	Standard	Standard
Alignment:	Always lawful good	Always lawful good	Always lawful good
Advancement:	By character class	By character class	By character class
Level Adjustment:	+3	+3	+3

Werebears in humanoid form tend to be stout, well-muscled, and hairy. Their brown hair is thick, and males usually wear beards. They may have reddish, blond, ivory, or black hair, matching the color of the ursine form. They dress in simple cloth and leather garments that are easy to remove, repair, or replace. In their animal form, werebears are moody and grumpy. They desire only their own company and seek out evil creatures to slay.

Combat

Werebears fight just as brown bears do in animal form. In humanoid or hybrid form, they favor large, heavy weapons such as greataxes or greatswords. The werebear's greataxe is a Medium weapon, so it can wield the axe in one hand in hybrid form.

Alternate Form (Su): A werebear can assume the form of a brown bear or a bear-humanoid hybrid.

Bear Empathy (Ex): Communicate with bears and dire bears, and +4 racial bonus on Charisma-based checks against bears and dire bears.

Curse of Lycanthropy (Su): Any humanoid or giant hit by a werebear's bite attack in animal or hybrid form must succeed on a DC 15 Fortitude save or contract lycanthropy.

Improved Grab (Ex): To use this ability, a werebear must be in bear form and must hit with a claw attack. It can then attempt to start a grapple as a free action without provoking an attack of opportunity.

Skills: Werebears have a +4 racial bonus on Swim checks in any bear form.

The werebear presented here is a 1st-level human warrior and natural lycanthrope, using the following base ability scores: Str 13, Dex 11, Con 12, Int 10, Wis 9, Cha 8.

WEREBOAR

Stocky and powerful, this fierce humanoid is covered in short, stiff fur and has boarlike tusks.

A wereboar in humanoid form tends to be a stocky, muscular individual of average height. It dresses in simple garments that are easy to remove, repair, or replace.

Combat

In any form, wereboars are as ferocious as normal boars. When in hybrid form, they fight with a weapon and their dangerous gore attack.

Alternate Form (Su): A wereboar can assume the form of a boar or a boar-humanoid hybrid.

Boar Empathy (Ex): Communicate with boars and dire boars, and +4 racial bonus on Charisma-based checks against boars and dire boars.

Curse of Lycanthropy (Su): Any humanoid or giant hit by the wereboar's gore attack in animal or hybrid form must succeed on a DC 15 Fortitude save or contract lycanthropy.

Ferocity (Ex): A wereboar is such a tenacious combatant that it continues to fight without penalty even while disabled or dying.

The wereboar presented here is a 1st-level human warrior and natural lycanthrope, using the following base ability scores: Str 13, Dex 11, Con 12, Int 10, Wis 9, Cha 8.

WERERAT

Quick and feral, this humanoid is covered with matted brown fur and has a long, hairless tail. It carries a rapier in its paw, and its face is distinctly ratlike.

	Wereboar, Human Form Medium Humanoid (Human, Shapechanger)	Wereboar, Boar Form Medium Humanoid (Human, Shapechanger)	Wereboar, Hybrid Form Medium Humanoid (Human, Shapechanger)
Hit Dice:	1d8+4 plus 3d8+12 (34 hp)	1d8+4 plus 3d8+12 (34 hp)	1d8+4 plus 3d8+12 (34 hp)
Initiative:	+0	+0	+0
Speed:	20 ft. in scale mail (4 squares); base speed 30 ft.	40 ft. (8 squares)	30 ft. (6 squares)
Armor Class:	18 (+2 natural, +4 scale mail, +2 heavy shield) touch 10, flat-footed 18	18 (+8 natural) touch 10, flat-footed 18	18 (+8 natural) touch 10, flat-footed 18
Base Attack/Grapple:	+3/+4	+3/+6	+3/+6
Attack:	Battleaxe +4 melee (1d8+1/×3) or javelin +3 ranged (1d6+1)	Gore +6 melee (1d8+4)	Battleaxe +6 melee (1d8+4/×3) or claw +6 melee (1d4+3)
Full Attack:	Battleaxe +4 melee (1d8+1/×3) or	Gore +6 melee (1d8+4) javelin +3 ranged (1d6+1)	Battleaxe +6 melee (1d8+4/×3) and gore +1 melee (1d6+1); or 2 claws +6 melee (1d4+3) and gore +1 melee (1d6+1)
Space/Reach:	5 ft./5 ft.	5 ft./5 ft.	5 ft./5 ft.
Special Attacks:	—	Curse of lycanthropy	Curse of lycanthropy
Special Qualities:	Alternate form, boar empathy, ferocity, low-light vision, scent	Alternate form, boar empathy, damage reduction 10/silver, ferocity, low-light vision, scent	Alternate form, boar empathy, damage reduction 10/silver, ferocity, low-light vision, scent
Saves:	Fort +6, Ref +3, Will +3	Fort +9, Ref +3, Will +3	Fort +9, Ref +3, Will +3
Abilities:	Str 13, Dex 11, Con 12 Int 10, Wis 11, Cha 8	Str 17, Dex 11, Con 18, Int 10, Wis 11, Cha 8	Str 17, Dex 11, Con 18, Int 10, Wis 11, Cha 8
Skills:	Handle Animal +3, Intimidate +3, Listen +5, Spot +4	Handle Animal +3, Intimidate +3, Listen +5, Spot +4	Handle Animal +3, Intimidate +3, Listen +5, Spot +4
Feats:	Alertness[B], Improved Bull Rush, Iron Will[B], Power Attack, Toughness	(same as human form)	(same as human form)
Environment:	Temperate forests	Temperate forests	Temperate forests
Organization:	Solitary, pair, brood (3–4), or troupe (2–4 plus 1–4 boars)	(same as human form)	(same as human form)
Challenge Rating:	4	4	4
Treasure:	Standard	Standard	Standard
Alignment:	Always neutral	Always neutral	Always neutral
Advancement:	By character class	By character class	By character class
Level Adjustment:	+3	+3	+3

A wererat in humanoid form tends to be a thin, wiry individual of shorter than average height. The eyes constantly dart around, and the nose and mouth may twitch if he or she is excited. Males often have thin, ragged mustaches.

Combat

In animal form, wererats avoid combat, preferring to use their dire rat shape for skulking and spying. In hybrid form, a wererat fights with a rapier and light crossbow.

Alternate Form (Su): A wererat can assume a bipedal hybrid form or the form of a dire rat.

Curse of Lycanthropy (Su): Any humanoid or giant hit by a wererat's bite attack in animal or hybrid form must succeed on a DC 15 Fortitude save or contract lycanthropy.

Disease (Ex): Filth fever; bite, Fortitude DC 12, incubation period 1d3 days, damage 1d3 Dex and 1d3 Con. The save DC is Constitution-based.

Rat Empathy (Ex): Communicate with rats and dire rats, and +4 racial bonus on Charisma-based checks against rats and dire rats.

Skills: A wererat in rat or hybrid form uses its Dexterity modifier for Climb or Swim checks. It has a +8 racial bonus on Climb checks and can always choose to take 10 on a Climb check, even if rushed or threatened.

Wererats have a +8 racial bonus on Swim checks from their dire rat form.

Feats: Wererats gain Weapon Finesse as a bonus feat.

The wererat presented here is based on a 1st-level human warrior who is a natural lycanthrope, using the following base ability scores: Str 13, Dex 11, Con 12, Int 10, Wis 9, Cha 8.

WERETIGER

Sleek and powerful, this humanoid has tawny, striped fur and deadly claws and teeth. It stands more than 8 feet tall.

Weretigers in humanoid form tend to be sleekly muscular, taller than average, and very agile.

Combat

Weretigers can assume a hybrid form as well as an animal form. In tiger form, they can pounce and grab just as normal tigers do. In hybrid form, they rely on their deadly claws.

Alternate Form (Su): A weretiger can assume a bipedal hybrid form or the form of a tiger.

Curse of Lycanthropy (Su): Any humanoid or giant hit by a weretiger's bite attack in animal or hybrid form must succeed on a DC 15 Fortitude save or contract lycanthropy.

Improved Grab (Ex): To use this ability, a weretiger in tiger form must hit with a claw or bite attack. It can then attempt to start a grapple as a free action without provoking an attack of opportunity. If it wins the grapple check, it establishes a hold and can rake.

Pounce (Ex): If a weretiger in tiger form charges an opponent, it can make a full attack, including two rake attacks.

Rake (Ex): Attack bonus +9 melee, damage 1d8+3.

Tiger Empathy (Ex): Communicate with tigers and dire tigers, and +4 racial bonus on Charisma-based checks against tigers and dire tigers.

Skills: In any form, weretigers have a +4 bonus on Balance, Hide, and Move Silently checks. *In areas of tall grass or heavy undergrowth, the Hide bonus improves to +8 in the tiger form.

The weretiger presented here is a 1st-level human warrior and natural lycanthrope, using the following base ability scores: Str 13, Dex 11, Con 12, Int 10, Wis 9, Cha 8.

Wererat

Werebear

Werewolf

WEREWOLF

Short, gray fur covers this lean, feral humanoid. It has sharp claws and a wolflike muzzle.

Werewolves in humanoid form have no distinguishing traits.

Combat

In wolf form, a werewolf can trip just as a normal wolf does. A werewolf in hybrid form usually dispenses with weapon attacks, though it can wield a weapon and use its bite as a secondary natural attack.

Alternate Form (Su): A werewolf can assume a bipedal hybrid form or the form of a wolf.

Curse of Lycanthropy (Su): Any humanoid or giant hit by a werewolf's bite attack in animal or hybrid form must succeed on a DC 15 Fortitude save or contract lycanthropy.

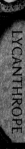

	Wererat, Human Form Medium Humanoid (Human, Shapechanger)	Wererat, Dire Rat Form Small Humanoid (Human, Shapechanger)	Wererat, Hybrid Form Medium Humanoid (Human, Shapechanger)
Hit Dice:	1d8+1 plus 1d8+2 (12 hp)	1d8+1 plus 1d8+2 (12 hp)	1d8+1 plus 1d8+2 (12 hp)
Initiative:	+0	+3	+3
Speed:	30 ft. (6 squares)	40 ft. (8 squares), climb 20 ft.	30 ft. (6 squares)
Armor Class:	15 (+2 natural, +2 leather, +1 buckler) touch 10, flat-footed 15	17 (+1 size, +3 Dex, +3 natural), touch 14, flat-footed 14	16 (+3 Dex, +3 natural) touch 13, flat-footed 13
Base Attack/Grapple:	+1/+2	+1/−2	+1/+2
Attack:	Rapier +2 melee (1d6+1/18–20) or light crossbow +1 ranged (1d8/19–20)	Bite +6 melee (1d4+1 plus disease)	Rapier +5 melee (1d6+1/18–20) or light crossbow +4 ranged (1d8/19–20)
Full Attack:	Rapier +2 melee (1d6+1/18–20) or light crossbow +1 ranged (1d8/19–20)	Bite +6 melee (1d4+1 plus disease)	Rapier +4 melee (1d6+1/18–20) and bite −1 melee (1d6 plus disease); or light crossbow +4 ranged (1d8/19–20)
Space/Reach:	5 ft./5 ft.	5 ft./5 ft.	5 ft./5 ft.
Special Attacks:	—	Curse of lycanthropy, disease	Curse of lycanthropy, disease
Special Qualities:	Alternate form, rat empathy, low-light vision, scent	Alternate form, rat empathy, damage reduction 10/silver, low-light vision, scent	Alternate form, rat empathy, damage reduction 10/silver, low-light vision, scent
Saves:	Fort +5, Ref +2, Will +4	Fort +6, Ref +5, Will +4	Fort +6, Ref +5, Will +4
Abilities:	Str 13, Dex 11, Con 12 Int 10, Wis 11, Cha 8	Str 13, Dex 17, Con 14 Int 10, Wis 11, Cha 8	Str 13, Dex 17, Con 14 Int 10, Wis 11, Cha 8
Skills:	Climb +0, Handle Animal +3, Hide +1, Listen +4, Move Silently +0, Spot +4, Swim +9	Climb +11, Handle Animal +3, Hide +8, Listen +4, Move Silently +4, Spot +4, Swim +11	Climb +4, Handle Animal +3, Hide +5, Listen +4, Move Silently +4, Spot +4, Swim +9
Feats:	Alertness, Dodge, Iron Will[B], Weapon Finesse[B]	(same as human form)	(same as human form)
Environment:	Any	Any	Any
Organization:	Solitary, pair, pack (6–10), or troupe (2–5 plus 5–8 dire rats)	(same as human form)	(same as human form)
Challenge Rating:	2	2	2
Treasure:	Standard	Standard	Standard
Alignment:	Always lawful evil	Always lawful evil	Always lawful evil
Advancement:	By character class	By character class	By character class
Level Adjustment:	+3	+3	+3

Trip (Ex): A werewolf in animal form that hits with a bite attack can attempt to trip the opponent (+2 check modifier) as a free action without making a touch attack or provoking an attack of opportunity. If the attempt fails, the opponent cannot react to trip the werewolf.

Wolf Empathy (Ex): Communicate with wolves and dire wolves, and +4 racial bonus on Charisma-based checks against wolves and dire wolves.

Skills: *A werewolf in hybrid or wolf form gains a +4 racial bonus on Survival checks when tracking by scent.

The werewolf presented here is based on a 1st-level human warrior and natural lycanthrope, using the following base ability scores: Str 13, Dex 11, Con 12, Int 10, Wis 9, Cha 8.

LYCANTHROPE, WEREWOLF LORD

Feral and powerful, this humanoid is covered in gray fur and armed with sharp claws and teeth. It stands as tall as an ogre, and it has a wolflike muzzle and hateful eyes.

Stronger, hardier, and more deadly than its lesser fellows, the werewolf lord is a murderous beast that delights in wreaking havoc.

The werewolf lord presented here is a 10th-level human fighter and natural lycanthrope, using the following base ability scores: Str 16, Dex 14, Con 14, Int 10, Wis 10, Cha 12.

Combat

Werewolf lords can assume a hybrid form as well as an animal form. In dire wolf form, they can trip just as normal wolves do. In hybrid form, they can wield weapons or fight with their claws.

Alternate Form (Su): A werewolf lord can assume a bipedal hybrid form or the form of a dire wolf.

Curse of Lycanthropy (Su): Any humanoid or giant hit by a werewolf lord's bite attack in wolf or hybrid form must succeed on a DC 15 Fortitude save or contract lycanthropy.

Trip (Ex): A werewolf lord in dire wolf form that hits with a bite attack can attempt to trip the opponent (+15 check modifier) as a free action without making a touch attack or provoking an attack of opportunity. If the attempt fails, the opponent cannot react to trip the werewolf lord.

Wolf Empathy (Ex): Communicate with wolves and dire wolves, and +4 racial bonus on Charisma-based checks against wolves and dire wolves.

Skills: *A werewolf lord in hybrid or wolf form gains a +4 racial bonus on Survival checks when tracking by scent.

Possessions: +2 mithral chain shirt, +3 heavy shield, +2 bastard sword, gauntlets of ogre power, cloak of resistance +2, masterwork composite longbow (+4 Str bonus). (Different werewolf lords may have different possessions.)

HILL GIANT DIRE WEREBOAR

This giant is covered in short, bristly fur and has sharp claws. Its head is piglike, with jutting tusks and small, angry red eyes.

	Weretiger, Human Form Medium Humanoid (Human, Shapechanger)	Weretiger, Tiger Form Large Humanoid (Human, Shapechanger)	Weretiger, Hybrid Form Large Humanoid (Human, Shapechanger)
Hit Dice:	1d8+1 plus 6d8+18 (50 hp)	1d8+1 plus 6d8+18 (50 hp)	1d8+1 plus 6d8+18 (50 hp)
Initiative:	+4	+6	+6
Speed:	20 ft. in breastplate (4 squares); base speed 30 ft.	40 ft. (8 squares)	30 ft. (6 squares)
Armor Class:	17 (+2 natural, +5 breastplate) touch 10, flat-footed 17	16 (−1 size, +2 Dex, +5 natural), touch 11, flat-footed 14	16 (−1 size, +2 Dex, +5 natural), touch 11, flat-footed 14
Base Attack/Grapple:	+5/+6	+5/+16	+5/+16
Attack:	Glaive +6 melee (1d10+1/×3) or composite longbow (+1 Str bonus) +5 ranged (1d8+1/×3)	Claw +11 melee (1d8+7)	Claw +11 melee (1d8+7)
Full Attack:	Glaive +6 melee (1d10+1/×3) or composite longbow (+1 Str bonus) +5 ranged (1d8+1/×3)	2 claws +11 melee (1d8+7) and bite +6 melee (2d6+3)	2 claws +11 melee (1d8+7) and bite +6 melee (2d6+3)
Space/Reach:	5 ft./5 ft. (10 ft. with glaive)	10 ft./5 ft.	10 ft./10 ft.
Special Attacks:	—	Pounce, improved grab, rake, curse of lycanthropy	Curse of lycanthropy
Special Qualities:	Alternate form, tiger empathy, low-light vision, scent	Alternate form, tiger empathy, damage reduction 10/silver, low-light vision, scent	Alternate form, tiger empathy, damage reduction 10/silver, low-light vision, scent
Saves:	Fort +8, Ref +5, Will +4	Fort +10, Ref +7, Will +4	Fort +10, Ref +7, Will +4
Abilities:	Str 13, Dex 11, Con 12 Int 10, Wis 11, Cha 8	Str 25, Dex 15, Con 16 Int 10, Wis 11, Cha 8	Str 25, Dex 15, Con 16 Int 10, Wis 11, Cha 8
Skills:	Balance +0, Climb +1, Handle Animal +3, Hide +0, Listen +6, Move Silently +0, Spot +6	Balance +6, Climb +12, Handle Animal +3, Hide +2*, Listen +6, Move Silently +12, Spot +6	Balance +6, Climb +12, Handle Animal +3, Hide +2, Listen +6, Move Silently +12, Spot +6
Feats:	Alertness[B], Combat Reflexes, Improved Initiative, Improved Natural Attack (bite, claw), Iron Will[B]	(same as human form)	(same as human form)
Environment:	Warm forests	Warm forests	Warm forests
Organization:	Solitary or pair	(same as human form)	(same as human form)
Challenge Rating:	5	5	5
Treasure:	Standard	Standard	Standard
Alignment:	Always neutral	Always neutral	Always neutral
Advancement:	By character class	By character class	By character class
Level Adjustment:	+3	+3	+3

	Werewolf, Human Form Medium Humanoid (Human, Shapechanger)	Werewolf, Wolf Form Medium Humanoid (Human, Shapechanger)	Werewolf, Hybrid Form Medium Humanoid (Human, Shapechanger)
Hit Dice:	1d8+1 plus 2d8+6 (20 hp)	1d8+1 plus 2d8+6 (20 hp)	1d8+1 plus 2d8+6 (20 hp)
Initiative:	+4	+6	+6
Speed :	30 ft. (6 squares)	50 ft. (10 squares)	30 ft. (6 squares)
Armor Class:	17 (+2 natural, +4 chain shirt, +1 light shield) touch 10, flat-footed 17	16 (+2 Dex, +4 natural), touch 12, flat-footed 14	16 (+2 Dex, +4 natural), touch 12, flat-footed 14
Base Attack/Grapple:	+2/+3	+2/+4	+2/+4
Attack:	Longsword +3 melee (1d8+1/19–20) or Bite +5 melee (1d6+3) light crossbow +2 ranged (1d8/19–20)		Claw +4 melee (1d4+2)
Full Attack:	Longsword +3 melee (1d8+1/19–20) or Bite +5 melee (1d6+3) light crossbow +2 ranged (1d8/19–20)		2 claws +4 melee (1d4+2) and bite +0 melee (1d6+1)
Space/Reach:	5 ft./5 ft.	5 ft./5 ft.	5 ft./5 ft.
Special Attacks:	—	Curse of lycanthropy, trip	Curse of lycanthropy
Special Qualities:	Alternate form, wolf empathy, low-light vision, scent	Alternate form, wolf empathy, damage reduction 10/silver, low-light vision, scent	Alternate form, wolf empathy, damage reduction 10/silver, low-light vision, scent
Saves:	Fort +6, Ref +3, Will +2	Fort +8, Ref +5, Will +2	Fort +8 Ref +5, Will +2
Abilities:	Str 13, Dex 11, Con 12, Int 10, Wis 11, Cha 8	Str 15, Dex 15, Con 16, Int 10, Wis 11, Cha 8	Str 15, Dex 15, Con 16, Int 10, Wis 11, Cha 8
Skills:	Handle Animal +1, Hide +1, Listen +1, Move Silently +2, Spot +1, Survival +2	Handle Animal +1, Hide +6, Listen +1, Move Silently +6, Spot +1, Survival +2*	Handle Animal +1, Hide +6, Listen +1, Move Silently +6, Spot +1, Survival +2*
Feats:	Improved Initiative, Iron Will[B], Stealthy, Track[B], Weapon Focus (bite)	(same as human form)	(same as human form)
Environment:	Temperate forests	Temperate forests	Temperate forests
Organization:	Solitary, pair, pack (6–10), or troupe (2–5 plus 5–8 wolves)	(same as human form)	(same as human form)
Challenge Rating:	3	3	3
Treasure:	Standard	Standard	Standard
Alignment:	Always chaotic evil	Always chaotic evil	Always chaotic evil
Advancement:	By character class	By character class	By character class
Level Adjustment:	+3	+3	+3

Dire wereboars in giant form look much like normal hill giants, though slightly stockier, and with coarser, stiffer hair and stiff.

The dire wereboar described here is based on a hill giant and natural lycanthrope with normal ability scores for a hill giant.

Combat

Dire wereboars anger quickly. They usually begin a battle in giant form, then switch to hybrid form to take advantage of their immense strength in that shape. They like to use their Improved Bull Rush and Improved Sunder feats to shove opponents around and smash their weapons and shields.

Alternate Form (Su): A dire wereboar can assume a bipedal hybrid form or the form of a dire boar.

Boar Empathy (Ex): Communicate with boars and dire boars, and +4 racial bonus on Charisma-based checks against boars and dire boars.

Curse of Lycanthropy (Su): Any humanoid or giant hit by a dire wereboar's bite attack in animal or hybrid form must succeed on a DC 15 Fortitude save or contract lycanthropy.

Ferocity (Ex): A dire wereboar is such a tenacious combatant that it continues to fight without penalty even while disabled or dying.

CREATING A LYCANTHROPE

"Lycanthrope" is a template that can be added to any humanoid or giant (referred to hereafter as the base creature). The lycanthrope template can be inherited (for natural lycanthropes) or acquired (for afflicted lycanthropes). Becoming a lycanthrope is very much like multiclassing as an animal and gaining the appropriate Hit Dice.

Size and Type: The base creature's type does not change, but the creature gains the shapechanger subtype. The lycanthrope takes on the characteristics of some type of carnivorous or omnivorous crea-ture of the animal type (referred to hereafter as the base animal). This animal can be any predator, scavenger, or omnivore whose size is within one size category of the base creature's size (Small, Medium, or Large for a Medium base creature). Lycanthropes can also adopt a hybrid shape that combines features of the base crea-ture and the base animal. A lycanthrope's hybrid form is the same size as the base animal or the base creature, whichever is larger.

A lycanthrope uses either the base creature's or the base animal's statistics and special abilities in addition to those described here.

Hit Dice and Hit Points: Same as the base creature plus those of the base animal. To calculate total hit points, apply Constitution modifiers according to the score the lycanthrope has in each form. For example, a human commoner with a Constitution score of 11 as a human and a Constitution score of 15 as a wolf has 1d4 plus 2d8+4 hit points.

Speed: Same as the base creature or base animal, depending on which form the lycanthrope is using. Hybrids use the base crea-ture's speed.

Armor Class: The base creature's natural armor bonus increases by +2 in all forms. In hybrid form, the lycanthrope's natural armor bonus is equal to the natural armor bonus of the base animal or the base creature, whichever is better.

Base Attack/Grapple: Add the base attack bonus for the base animal to the base attack bonus for the base creature. The lycan-thrope's grapple bonus uses its attack bonus and modifiers for Strength and size depending on the lycanthrope's form.

Attacks: Same as the base creature or base animal, depending on which form the lycanthrope is using. A lycanthrope in hybrid form gains two claw attacks and a bite attack as natural weapons. These weapons deal damage based on the hybrid form's size. A hy-brid may attack with a weapon and a bite, or may attack with its natural weapons. The bite attack of a hybrid is a secondary attack.

	Werewolf Lord, Human Form Medium Humanoid (Human, Shapechanger)	Werewolf Lord, Dire Wolf Form Large Humanoid (Human, Shapechanger)	Werewolf Lord, Hybrid Form Large Humanoid (Human, Shapechanger)
Hit Dice:	10d10+20 plus 6d8+30 (132 hp)	10d10+20 plus 6d8+30 (132 hp)	10d10+20 plus 6d8+30 (132 hp)
Initiative:	+2	+4	+4
Speed :	30 ft. (6 squares)	40 ft. (8 squares)	30 ft. (6 squares)
Armor Class:	26 (+2 Dex, +3 natural, +6 +2 *mithral chain shirt*, +5 +3 *heavy shield*) touch 12, flat-footed 24	19 (−1 size, +4 Dex, +6 natural), touch 13, flat-footed 15	19 (−1 size, +4 Dex, +6 natural), touch 13, flat-footed 15
Base Attack/Grapple:	+14/+18	+14/+29	+14/+27
Attack:	+2 *bastard sword* +21 melee (1d10+8/17–20) or masterwork composite longbow (+4 Str bonus) +17 ranged (1d8+4/×3)	Bite +25 melee (2d6+16/19–20)	Claw +24 melee (1d6+11) or +2 *bastard sword* +27 melee (2d8+15/17–20)
Full Attack:	+2 *bastard sword* +21/+16/+11 melee (1d10+8/17–20) or masterwork composite longbow (+4 Str bonus) +17/+12/+7ranged (1d8+4/×3)	Bite +25 melee (2d6+16/19–20)	2 claws +24 melee (1d6+11) and bite +20 melee (2d6+5/19–20); or +2 *bastard sword* +27/+22/+17 melee (2d8+15/17–20) and bite +20 melee (2d6+5/19–20)
Space/Reach:	5 ft./5 ft.	10 ft./5 ft.	10 ft./10 ft.
Special Attacks:	—	Curse of lycanthropy, trip	Curse of lycanthropy
Special Qualities:	Alternate form, wolf empathy, low-light vision, scent	Alternate form, wolf empathy, damage reduction 10/silver, low-light vision, scent	Alternate form, wolf empathy, damage reduction 10/silver, low-light vision, scent
Saves:	Fort +16, Ref +12, Will +13	Fort +17, Ref +12, Will +11	Fort +17, Ref +12, Will +11
Abilities:	Str 18, Dex 14, Con 14 Int 10, Wis 12, Cha 12	Str 32, Dex 18, Con 20 Int 10, Wis 12, Cha 12	Str 32, Dex 18, Con 20 Int 10, Wis 12, Cha 12
Skills:	Handle Animal +4, Hide +6, Listen +9, Move Silently +8, Spot +13, Survival +5	Handle Animal +4, Hide +6, Listen +9, Move Silently +12, Spot +13, Survival +5*	Handle Animal +4, Hide +6, Listen +9, Move Silently +12, Spot +13, Survival +5*
Feats:	Alertness, Cleave, Combat Reflexes, Exotic Weapon Proficiency (bastard Sword), Improved Critical (bastard sword), Improved Critical (bite), Improved Natural Armor, Improved Natural Attack (bite), Iron Will[B], Power Attack, Run, Stealthy, Track[B], Weapon Focus (bastard sword), Weapon Focus (bite), Weapon Specialization (bastard sword)	(same as human form)	(same as human form)
Environment:	Temperate forests	Temperate forests	Temperate forests
Organization:	Solitary, pair, or pack (1–2 werewolf lords plus 2–4 werewolves plus 5–8 wolves)	(same as human form)	(same as human form)
Challenge Rating:	14	14	14
Treasure:	Standard	Standard	Standard
Alignment:	Always chaotic evil	Always chaotic evil	Always chaotic evil
Advancement:	By character class	By character class	By character class
Level Adjustment:	+3	+3	+3

Hybrid Size	Claw	Bite
Small	1d3	1d4
Medium	1d4	1d6
Large	1d6	1d8
Huge	2d4	2d6

Damage: Same as the base creature or base animal, depending on which form the lycanthrope is in.

Special Attacks: A lycanthrope retains the special attacks of the base creature or base animal, depending on which form it is using, and also gains the special attacks described below.

A lycanthrope's hybrid form does not gain any special attacks of the base animal. A lycanthrope spellcaster cannot cast spells with verbal, somatic, or material components while in animal form, or spells with verbal components while in hybrid form.

Curse of Lycanthropy (Su): Any humanoid or giant hit by a natural lycanthrope's bite attack in animal or hybrid form must succeed on a DC 15 Fortitude save or contract lycanthropy. If the victim's size is not within one size category of the lycanthrope (for example, a hill giant bitten by a wererat), the victim cannot contract lycanthropy from that lycanthrope. Afflicted lycanthropes cannot pass on the curse of lycanthropy.

Special Qualities: A lycanthrope retains all the special qualities of the base creature and the base animal, and also gains those described below.

Alternate Form (Su): A lycanthrope can shift into animal form as though using the *polymorph* spell on itself, though its gear is not affected, it does not regain hit points for changing form, and only the specific animal form indicated for the lycanthrope can be assumed. It does not assume the ability scores of the animal, but instead adds the animal's physical ability score modifiers to its own ability scores. A lycanthrope also can assume a bipedal hybrid form with prehensile hands and animalistic features.

Changing to or from animal or hybrid form is a standard action. A slain lycanthrope reverts to its humanoid form, although it remains dead. Separated body parts retain their animal form, however. Afflicted lycanthropes find this ability difficult to control (see Lycanthropy as an Affliction, below), but natural lycanthropes have full control over this power.

Damage Reduction (Ex): An afflicted lycanthrope in animal or hybrid form has damage reduction 5/silver. A natural lycanthrope in animal or hybrid form has damage reduction 10/silver.

Lycanthropic Empathy (Ex): In any form, lycanthropes can communicate and empathize with normal or dire animals of their animal form. This gives them a +4 racial bonus on checks when influencing the animal's attitude and allows the communication of simple concepts and (if the animal is friendly) commands, such as "friend," "foe," "flee," and "attack."

Low-Light Vision (Ex): A lycanthrope has low-light vision in any form.

Scent (Ex): A lycanthrope has the scent ability in any form.

Base Save Bonuses: Add the base save bonuses of the base animal to the base save bonuses of the base creature.

Abilities: All lycanthropes gain +2 to Wisdom. In addition, when in animal form, a lycanthrope's physical ability scores improve according to its kind, as set out in the table below. These adjustments are equal to the animal's normal ability scores –10 or –11. For example, a werecrocodile (Str 19, Dex 12, Con 17) would add Str +8, Dex +2, and Con +6 to its normal ability scores when it takes crocodile form. A lycanthrope in hybrid form modifies its physical ability scores by the same amount.

In addition, a lycanthrope may also gain an additional ability score increase by virtue of its extra Hit Dice.

Skills: A lycanthrope gains skill points equal to (2 + Int modifier, minimum 1) per Hit Die of its animal form, as if it had multiclassed into the animal type. (Animal is never its first Hit Die, though, and it does not gain quadruple skill points for any animal Hit Die.) Any skill given in the animal's description is a class skill for the lycanthrope's animal levels. In any form, a lycanthrope also has any racial skill bonuses of the base creature and of the base animal, although conditional skill bonuses, such as a weretiger's camouflage bonus on Hide checks, only apply in the associated form.

Feats: Add the base animal's feats to the base creature's. If this results in a lycanthrope having the same feat twice, the lycanthrope gains no additional benefit unless the feat normally can be taken more once, in which case the duplicated feat works as noted in the feat description. This process may give the lycanthrope more feats than a character of its total Hit Dice would normally be entitled to; if this occurs, any "extra" feats are denoted as bonus feats.

It's possible that a lycanthrope cannot meet the prerequisites for all its feats when in humanoid form. If this occurs, the lycanthrope still has the feats, but cannot use them when in humanoid form. A lycanthrope receives Iron Will as a bonus feat.

Environment: Same as either the base creature or base animal.

Organization: Solitary or pair, sometimes family (3–4), pack (6–10), or troupe (family plus related animals).

Challenge Rating: By class level or base creature, modified according to the HD of the base animal: 1 HD or 2 HD, +2; 3 HD to 5 HD, +3; 6 HD to 10 HD, +4; 11 HD to 20 HD, +5; 21 or more HD, +6.

Treasure: Standard.

	Hill Giant Dire Wereboar Giant Form Large Giant (Shapechanger)	Hill Giant Dire Wereboar Dire Boar Form Large Giant (Shapechanger)	Hill Giant Dire Wereboar Hybrid Boar Form Large Giant (Shapechanger)
Hit Dice:	12d8+51 plus 7d8+49 (185 hp)	12d8+51 plus 7d8+49 (185 hp)	12d8+51 plus 7d8+49 (185 hp)
Initiative:	–1	–1	–1
Speed:	30 ft. in hide armor (6 squares); base speed 40 ft.	40 ft. (8 squares)	40 ft. (8 squares)
Armor Class:	22 (–1 size, –1 Dex, +11 natural, +3 hide armor), touch 8, flat-footed 22	16 (–1 size, –1 Dex, +8 natural), touch 8, flat-footed 16	19 (–1 size, –1 Dex, +11 natural), touch 8, flat-footed 19
Base Attack/Grapple:	+14/+25	+14/+33	+14/+33
Attack:	Greatclub +21 melee (2d8+10) or slam +20 melee (1d4+7) or rock +12 ranged (2d6+7)	Gore +28 melee (1d8+22)	Greatclub +29 melee (2d8+22) or claw +28 melee (1d6+15)
Full Attack:	Greatclub +21/+16 melee (2d8+10) or 2 slams +20 melee (1d4+7) or rock +12 ranged (2d6+7)	Gore +28 melee (1d8+22)	Greatclub +29 melee (2d8+22) and gore +23 melee (1d8+7); or 2 claws +28 melee (1d6+15) and gore +23 melee (1d8+7)
Space/Reach:	10 ft./10 ft.	10 ft./5 ft.	10 ft./10 ft.
Special Attacks:	Rock throwing	Curse of lycanthropy	Curse of lycanthropy
Special Qualities:	Alternate form, boar empathy, ferocity, low-light vision, rock catching, scent	Alternate form, boar empathy, damage reduction 10/silver, ferocity, low-light vision, scent	Alternate form, boar empathy, damage reduction 10/silver, ferocity, low-light vision, scent
Saves:	Fort +17, Ref +8, Will +12	Fort +20, Ref +8, Will +12	Fort +20, Ref +8, Will +12
Abilities:	Str 25, Dex 8, Con 19, Int 6, Wis 12, Cha 7	Str 41, Dex 8, Con 25, Int 6, Wis 12, Cha 7	Str 41, Dex 8, Con 25, Int 6, Wis 12, Cha 7
Skills:	Climb +10, Jump +10, Listen +10, Spot +12	Climb +18, Jump +22, Listen +10, Spot +12	Climb +18, Jump +22, Listen 10, Spot +12
Feats:	Alertness[B], Cleave, Endurance, Improved Bull Rush, Improved Sunder, Iron Will[B], Power Attack, Weapon Focus (greatclub)	(same as giant form)	(same as giant form)
Environment:	Temperate hills	Temperate hills	Temperate hills
Organization:	Solitary, pair, brood (3–4), or troupe (2–4 plus 1–4 dire boars)	(same as giant form)	(same as giant form)
Challenge Rating:	11	11	11
Treasure:	Standard	Standard	Standard
Alignment:	Always neutral	Always neutral	Always neutral
Advancement:	By character class	By character class	By character class
Level Adjustment:	+7	+7	+7

Alignment: Any. Noble creatures such as bears, eagles, and lions tend to produce good-aligned lycanthropes. Sinister creatures such as rats, snakes, and wolves tend to produce evil-aligned lycanthropes. This is a reflection of how these animals are perceived, not any innate quality of the animal itself, so the Dungeon Master can arbitrarily assign the alignment of the animal form.

Advancement: By character class.

Level Adjustment: Same as the base creature +2 (afflicted) or +3 (natural). In addition, a lycanthrope's character level is increased by the number of racial Hit Dice the base animal has.

COMMON LYCANTHROPES

Name	Animal Form	Animal or Hybrid Form Ability Modifiers	Preferred Alignment
Werebear	Brown bear	Str +16, Dex +2, Con +8	Lawful good
Wereboar	Boar	Str +4, Con +6	Neutral
Wererat	Dire rat	Dex +6, Con +2	Chaotic evil
Weretiger	Tiger	Str +12, Dex +4, Con +6	Neutral
Werewolf	Wolf	Str +2, Dex +4, Con +4	Chaotic evil
Dire wereboar	Dire boar	Str +16, Con +6	Neutral

LYCANTHROPY AS AN AFFLICTION

When a character contracts lycanthropy through a lycanthrope's bite (see above), no symptoms appear until the first night of the next full moon. On that night, the afflicted character involuntarily assumes animal form and forgets his or her own identity, temporarily becoming an NPC under the DM's control. The character remains in animal form, assuming the appropriate alignment, until the next dawn.

The character's actions during this first episode are dictated by the alignment of its animal form. Good-aligned lycanthropes seek to avoid settlements or travelers and nonnatural environments, seeking out wilderness environs. They may hunt the natural prey of their kind, but avoid attacking good and neutral intelligent creatures. Evil-aligned lycanthropes seek to murder as many intelligent creatures as possible, often killing their own family members and friends. They generally seek out places where such victims may be found. Neutral creatures seek remote areas and avoid contact with civilization, but might attack travelers or other folk abroad in the wilderness if the travelers are few in number. However, the attack is driven by natural ferocity and hunger, not malice. In any case, the character remembers nothing about the entire episode (or subsequent episodes) unless he succeeds on a DC 15 Wisdom check, in which case he becomes aware of his lycanthropic condition.

Thereafter, the character is subject to involuntary transformation under the full moon and whenever damaged in combat. He or she feels an overwhelming rage building up and must succeed on a Control Shape check (see page 303) to resist changing into animal form. Any player character not yet aware of his or her lycanthropic condition temporarily becomes an NPC under the DM's control during an involuntary change, and acts as described above depending on the alignment of his or her animal form.

A character with awareness of his condition retains his identity and does not lose control of his actions if he changes. However, each time he changes to his animal form, he must make a Will save (DC 15 + number of times he has been in animal form) or permanently assume the alignment of his animal form in all shapes. An evil lycanthrope who is aware of his actions in animal form is not compelled to murder and kill indiscriminately, but he delights in bloodshed and will certainly seek out opportunities to slaughter intelligent beings, preferably those of his own race.

Once a character becomes aware of his affliction, he can now voluntarily attempt to change to animal or hybrid form, using the appropriate Control Shape check DC (see page 303). An attempt is a standard action and can be made each round. Any voluntary change to animal or hybrid form immediately and permanently changes the character's alignment to that of the appropriate lycanthrope.

Changing Form

Changing form is a standard action. If the change is involuntary, the character performs the change on his next turn following the triggering event. Changing to animal or hybrid form ruins the character's armor and clothing (including any items worn) if the new form is larger than the character's natural form; carried items are simply dropped. Characters can hastily doff clothing while changing, but not armor. Magic armor survives the change if it succeeds on a DC 15 Fortitude save. An afflicted character who is not aware of his condition remains in animal form until the next dawn. An afflicted character who is aware of his or her condition (see above) can try to resume humanoid form following a change (voluntary or involuntary) with a Control Shape check, but if he fails his check, he remains in animal (or hybrid) form until the following dawn.

Curing Lycanthropy

An afflicted character who eats a sprig of belladonna (also called wolfsbane) within 1 hour of a lycanthrope's attack can attempt a DC 20 Fortitude save to shake off the affliction. If a healer administers the herb, use the character's save bonus or the healer's Heal modifier, whichever is higher. The character gets only one chance, no matter how much belladonna is consumed. The belladonna must be reasonably fresh (picked within the last week).

However, fresh or not, belladonna is toxic. The character must succeed on a DC 13 Fortitude save or take 1d6 points of Strength damage. One minute later, the character must succeed on a second DC 13 save or take an additional 2d6 points of Strength damage.

A *remove disease* or *heal* spell cast by a cleric of 12th level or higher also cures the affliction, provided the character receives the spell within three days of the lycanthrope's attack.

The only other way to remove the affliction is to cast *remove curse* or *break enchantment* on the character during one of the three days of the full moon. After receiving the spell, the character must succeed on a DC 20 Will save to break the curse (the caster knows if the spell works). If the save fails, the process must be repeated. Characters undergoing this cure are often kept bound or confined in cages until the cure takes effect.

Only afflicted lycanthropes can be cured of lycanthropy.

LYCANTHROPES AS CHARACTERS

Since they live in the wilderness, most lycanthropes become barbarians or rangers. Wererats tend to become rogues. Becoming a lycanthrope does not change a character's favored class but usually changes alignment (see above). This alignment change may cause characters of certain classes to lose some of their class features, as noted in Chapter 3 of the *Player's Handbook*.

Lycanthrope characters possess the following racial traits.

— +2 Wisdom. Physical abilities are increased by the animal form's ability modifiers when a lycanthrope changes to its hybrid or animal forms.

—Size same as the base creature or the base animal form.

—Low-light vision in any form.

—Scent in any form.

—Racial Hit Dice: A lycanthrope adds the Hit Dice of its animal form to its base Hit Dice for race, level, and class. These additional Hit Dice modify the lycanthrope's base attack bonus and base saving throw bonuses accordingly.

—Racial Skills: A lycanthrope adds skill points for its animal Hit Dice much as if it had multiclassed into the animal type. It gains skill points equal to (2 + Int modifier, minimum 1) per Hit Die of the animal form. Any skills that appear in the animal's description are treated as class skills for the lycanthrope's animal levels. The lycanthrope's maximum skill ranks are equal to its animal form Hit Dice + its racial Hit Dice (if any) + its class levels + 3. Any racial skill adjustments of the lycanthrope's base race and its animal form (but not conditional adjustments) are added to its skill modifiers in any form.

—Racial Feats: Add the animal's Hit Dice to the base character's own Hit Dice to determine how many feats the character has. All lycanthropes gain Iron Will as a bonus feat.

— +2 natural armor bonus in any form.

—Special Qualities (see above): Alternate form, lycanthropic empathy, curse of lycanthropy (in animal or hybrid form only).

—Afflicted lycanthrope: damage reduction 5/silver (in animal or hybrid form only).

—Natural lycanthrope: damage reduction 10/silver (in animal or hybrid form only).

—Automatic Languages: As base creature.

—Favored Class: Same as the base creature.

—Level adjustment: Same as the base creature +2 (afflicted) or +3 (natural).

MAGMIN

Small Elemental (Fire, Extraplanar)
Hit Dice: 2d8+2 (11 hp)
Initiative: +0
Speed: 30 ft. (6 squares)
Armor Class: 17 (+1 size, +6 natural), touch 11, flat-footed 17
Base Attack/Grapple: +1/−1
Attack: Burning touch +4 melee touch (1d8 fire plus combustion) or slam +4 melee (1d3+3 plus combustion)
Full Attack: Burning touch +4 melee touch (1d8 fire plus combustion) or slam +4 melee (1d3+3 plus combustion)
Space/Reach: 5 ft./5 ft.
Special Attacks: Combustion, fiery aura
Special Qualities: Damage reduction 5/magic, darkvision 60 ft., elemental traits, immunity to fire, melt weapons, vulnerability to cold
Saves: Fort +3, Ref +3, Will +0
Abilities: Str 15, Dex 11, Con 13, Int 8, Wis 10, Cha 10
Skills: Climb +4, Spot +3
Feats: Great Fortitude
Environment: Elemental Plane of Fire
Organization: Solitary, gang (2–4), or squad (6–10)
Challenge Rating: 3
Treasure: Standard coins; standard goods (nonflammables only); standard items (nonflammables only)
Alignment: Always chaotic neutral
Advancement: 3–4 HD (Small); 5–6 HD (Medium)
Level Adjustment: —

This glowing, humanoid creature looks like a stumpy human sculpted from fire and flowing lava. It radiates heat like a small bonfire, and it has a gleeful, almost malicious smile on its face.

Magmin

Magmins are small, human-shaped beings from the Elemental Plane of Fire that radiate intense heat and are wreathed in an aura of searing flames.

Although not evil, these fiery creatures are extremely mischievous. They like to watch things burn, perhaps lacking the ability to understand that flames are painful or even deadly to other creatures.

A typical magmin is 4 feet tall and weighs 400 pounds. Magmins speak Ignan.

COMBAT

Although small, magmins are dangerous opponents. Their touch is effective against those who lack protection or immunity from heat and flames, but if faced with opponents who have immunity to fire, magmins rely on their slam attack. In any case, magmins are not valiant fighters. They usually flee if injured, although often only far enough to set up a fiery ambush for their enemies.

A magmin's natural weapons are treated as magic weapons for the purpose of overcoming damage reduction.

Combustion (Ex): Anyone a magmin touches must succeed on a DC 12 Reflex save or take an extra 1d8 points of fire damage as clothes ignite or armor becomes searing hot. The damage continues for another 1d4+2 rounds after the magmin's last successful attack. Magmins can also ignite flammable materials with a touch. The save DC is Constitution-based.

Fiery Aura (Ex): Anyone within 20 feet of a magmin must succeed on a DC 12 Fortitude save or take 1d6 points of heat damage per round from the intense heat. The save DC is Constitution-based.

Melt Weapons (Ex): Any metal weapon that strikes a magmin must succeed on a DC 12 Fortitude save or melt away into slag. The save DC is Constitution-based.

MANTICORE

Large Magical Beast
Hit Dice: 6d10+24 (57 hp)
Initiative: +2
Speed: 30 ft. (6 squares), fly 50 ft. (clumsy)
Armor Class: 17 (−1 size, +2 Dex, +6 natural), touch 11, flat-footed 15
Base Attack/Grapple: +6/+15
Attack: Claw +10 melee (2d4+5) or 6 spikes +8 ranged (1d8+2/19–20)
Full Attack: 2 claws +10 melee (2d4+5) and bite +8 melee (1d8+2); or 6 spikes +8 ranged (1d8+2/19–20)
Space/Reach: 10 ft./5 ft.
Special Attacks: Spikes
Special Qualities: Darkvision 60 ft., low-light vision, scent
Saves: Fort +9, Ref +7, Will +3
Abilities: Str 20, Dex 15, Con 19, Int 7, Wis 12, Cha 9
Skills: Listen +5, Spot +9, Survival +1
Feats: Flyby Attack, Multiattack, Track[B], Weapon Focus (spikes)
Environment: Warm marshes
Organization: Solitary, pair, or pride (3–6)
Challenge Rating: 5
Treasure: Standard
Alignment: Usually lawful evil
Advancement: 7–16 HD (Large); 17–18 HD (Huge)
Level Adjustment: +3 (cohort)

179

Illus. by C. Arelano

This creature is a monster in every sense of the word. It has the head of a vaguely humanoid beast, the body of a lion, and the wings of a dragon. The creature's back is set with curved barbs, and its long tail ends in a cluster of deadly spikes.

Manticore

Manticores are fierce creatures that hunt widely for living flesh. They are cunning and evil. A manticore can be a deadly enemy or a powerful ally.

A typical manticore is about 10 feet long and weighs about 1,000 pounds.

Manticores speak Common.

COMBAT

A manticore begins most attacks with a volley of spikes, then closes. In the outdoors, it often uses its powerful wings to stay aloft during battle.

Spikes (Ex): With a snap of its tail, a manticore can loose a volley of six spikes as a standard action (make an attack roll for each spike). This attack has a range of 180 feet with no range increment. All targets must be within 30 feet of each other. The creature can launch only twenty-four spikes in any 24-hour period.

Skills: *Manticores have a +4 racial bonus on Spot checks.

MEDUSA

Medium Monstrous Humanoid

Hit Dice: 6d8+6 (33 hp)
Initiative: +2
Speed: 30 ft. (6 squares)
Armor Class: 15 (+2 Dex, +3 natural), touch 12, flat-footed 13
Base Attack/Grapple: +6/+6
Attack: Shortbow +8 ranged (1d6/×3) or dagger +8 melee (1d4/19–20) or snakes +8 melee (1d4 plus poison)
Full Attack: Shortbow +8/+3 ranged (1d6/×3); or dagger +8/+3 melee (1d4/19–20) and snakes +3 melee (1d4 plus poison)
Space/Reach: 5 ft./5 ft.
Special Attacks: Petrifying gaze, poison
Special Qualities: Darkvision 60 ft.
Saves: Fort +3, Ref +7, Will +6
Abilities: Str 10, Dex 15, Con 12, Int 12, Wis 13, Cha 15
Skills: Bluff +9, Diplomacy +4, Disguise +9 (+11 acting), Intimidate +4, Move Silently +8, Spot +8
Feats: Point Blank Shot, Precise Shot, Weapon Finesse
Environment: Temperate marshes

Organization: Solitary or covey (2–4)
Challenge Rating: 7
Treasure: Double standard
Alignment: Usually lawful evil
Advancement: By character class
Level Adjustment: —

Though at first glance this creature appeared to be a well-proportioned human, a closer look reveals a hideous face crowned with a mass of writhing, hissing snakes instead of hair, eyes glowing a deep, feral red, and scaly, earth-colored skin.

The medusa is a hateful, repulsive creature that petrifies living beings with its gaze. It prizes art objects, fine jewelry, and wealth. Its activities often revolve around obtaining these items.

A medusa is indistinguishable from a normal human at distances greater than 30 feet (or closer, if its face is concealed). The creature often wears garments that enhance its body while hiding its face behind a hood or veil.

Medusas are found in nearly every climate. Some dwell in large cities, becoming active in the criminal underworld to gain their desires. A few medusas have formed robbery rings or organized smuggling cabals.

A typical medusa is 5 to 6 feet tall and about the same weight as a human.

Medusas speak Common.

COMBAT

A medusa tries to disguise its true nature until the intended victim is within range of its petrifying gaze, using subterfuge and bluffing games to convince the target that there is no danger. It uses normal weapons to attack those who avert their eyes or survive its gaze, while its poisonous snakes strike at adjacent opponents.

Petrifying Gaze (Su): Turn to stone permanently, 30 feet, Fortitude DC 15 negates. The save DC is Charisma-based.

Poison (Ex): Injury, Fortitude DC 14, initial damage 1d6 Str, secondary damage 2d6 Str. The save DC is Constitution-based.

MEPHIT

Mephits are minor creatures from the elemental planes. They are more curious than evil, though each individual's nature varies depending on the essence of the element that birthed it.

All mephits appear as small, winged creatures with more or less humanoid features. While they are often described as impish, their elemental origins are apparent at first glance.

COMBAT

All mephits fight by biting and clawing or by using a breath weapon, the nature and effects of which vary from creature to creature.

A mephit's natural weapons are treated as magic weapons for the purpose of overcoming damage reduction.

Breath Weapon (Su): A mephit can use its breath weapon once every 1d4 rounds as a standard action. See the individual descriptions for details.

Spell-Like Abilities: All mephits have one or more spell-like abilities (save DC 12 + spell level). See the individual descriptions for details.

Summon Mephit (Sp): Once per day, a mephit can attempt to summon another mephit of the same variety, much as though casting a *summon monster* spell, but with only a 25% chance of success. Roll d%: On a failure, no creature answers the summons that day. A mephit that has just been summoned cannot use its own summon ability for 1 hour. This ability is the equivalent of a 2nd-level spell.

Fast Healing (Ex): Mephits heal 2 points of damage each round, provided they are still alive and certain other conditions are met. See the individual descriptions for details.

MEPHIT GANGS AND MOBS

Groups of similar mephits (for example, water, ooze, and ice) sometimes congregate in any locale they all find comfortable.

AIR MEPHIT

Small Outsider (Air, Extraplanar)
Hit Dice: 3d8 (13 hp)
Initiative: +7
Speed: 30 ft. (6 squares), fly 60 ft. (perfect)
Armor Class: 17 (+1 size, +3 Dex, +3 natural), touch 14, flat-footed 14
Base Attack/Grapple: +3/−1
Attack: Claw +4 melee (1d3)
Full Attack: 2 claws +4 melee (1d3)
Space/Reach: 5 ft./5 ft.
Special Attacks: Breath weapon, spell-like abilities, *summon mephit*
Special Qualities: Damage reduction 5/magic, darkvision 60 ft., fast healing 2
Saves: Fort +3, Ref +6, Will +3
Abilities: Str 10, Dex 17, Con 10, Int 6, Wis 11, Cha 15
Skills: Bluff +8, Escape Artist +9, Hide +13, Diplomacy +4, Disguise +2 (+4 acting), Intimidate +4, Listen +6, Move Silently +9, Spot +6, Use Rope +3 (+5 with bindings)
Feats: Dodge, Improved Initiative
Environment: Elemental Plane of Air
Organization: Solitary (1), gang (2–4 mephits of mixed types), or mob (5–12 mephits of mixed types)
Challenge Rating: 3
Treasure: Standard
Alignment: Usually neutral
Advancement: 4–6 HD (Small); 7–9 HD (Medium)
Level Adjustment: +3 (cohort)

Medusa

This winged creature looks like a short, cloud-white human with a whirlwind where its legs should be.

Air mephits come from the Elemental Plane of Air.

An air mephit is about 4 feet tall and weighs about 1 pound.

Air mephits speak Common and Auran.

Combat

Breath Weapon (Su): 15-foot cone of dust and grit, damage 1d8, Reflex DC 12 half. The save DC is Constitution-based and includes a +1 racial bonus.

Spell-Like Abilities: Once per hour an air mephit can surround itself with vapor, duplicating the effect of a *blur* spell (caster level 3rd). Once per day it can use *gust of wind* (DC 14, caster level

6th) . The save DC is Charisma-based.

Fast Healing (Ex): An air mephit heals only if exposed to moving air, be it a breeze, a draft, a spell effect, or even the mephit fanning itself.

DUST MEPHIT

Small Outsider (Air, Extraplanar)
Hit Dice: 3d8 (13 hp)
Initiative: +7
Speed: 30 ft. (6 squares), fly 50 ft. (perfect)
Armor Class: 17 (+1 size, +3 Dex, +3 natural), touch 14, flat-footed 14
Base Attack/Grapple: +3/−1
Attack: Claw +4 melee (1d3)
Full Attack: 2 claws +4 melee (1d3)
Space/Reach: 5 ft./5 ft.
Special Attacks: Breath weapon, spell-like abilities, *summon mephit*
Special Qualities: Damage reduction 5/magic, darkvision 60 ft., fast healing 2
Saves: Fort +3, Ref +6, Will +3
Abilities: Str 10, Dex 17, Con 10, Int 6, Wis 11, Cha 15
Skills: Bluff +8, Escape Artist +9, Hide +13, Diplomacy +4, Disguise +2 (+4 acting), Intimidate +4, Listen +6, Move Silently +9, Spot +6, Use Rope +3 (+5 with bindings)
Feats: Dodge, Improved Initiative
Environment: Elemental Plane of Air
Organization: Solitary (1), gang (2–4 mephits of mixed types), or mob (5–12 mephits of mixed types)
Challenge Rating: 3
Treasure: Standard
Alignment: Usually neutral
Advancement: 4–6 HD (Small); 7–9 HD (Medium)
Level Adjustment: +3 (cohort)

This winged creature looks like a short, gaunt human with gray, flaky skin and a sorrowful expression.

Dust mephits come from the Elemental Plane of Air.

A dust mephit is about 4 feet tall and weighs about 2 pounds. Dust mephits speak Common and Auran.

Combat

Breath Weapon (Su): 10-foot cone of irritating particles, damage 1d4, Reflex DC 12 half. Living creatures that fail their saves are tormented by itching skin and burning eyes. This effect imposes a −4 penalty to AC and a −2 penalty on attack rolls for 3 rounds. The save DC is Constitution-based and includes a +1 racial bonus.

Spell-Like Abilities: Once per hour, a dust mephit can surround itself with a plume of dust, duplicating the effect of a *blur* spell (caster level 3rd). Once per day it can create a mass of roiling dust that duplicates the effect of *wind wall* (DC 15, caster level 6th). The save DC is Charisma-based.

Fast Healing (Ex): A dust mephit heals only if in an arid, dusty environment.

EARTH MEPHIT

Small Outsider (Earth, Extraplanar)
Hit Dice: 3d8+6 (19 hp)
Initiative: −1
Speed: 30 ft. (6 squares), fly 40 ft. (average)
Armor Class: 16 (+1 size, −1 Dex, +6 natural), touch 10, flat-footed 16
Base Attack/Grapple: +3/+2
Attack: Claw +7 melee (1d3+3)
Full Attack: 2 claws +7 melee (1d3+3)
Space/Reach: 5 ft./5 ft.
Special Attacks: Breath weapon, spell-like abilities, *summon mephit*
Special Qualities: Change size, damage reduction 5/magic, darkvision 60 ft., fast healing 2
Saves: Fort +4, Ref +2, Will +3
Abilities: Str 17, Dex 8, Con 13, Int 6, Wis 11, Cha 15
Skills: Bluff +8, Escape Artist +5, Hide +9, Diplomacy +4, Disguise +2 (+4 acting), Intimidate +4, Listen +6, Move Silently +5, Spot +6, Use Rope −1 (+1 with bindings)
Feats: Power Attack, Toughness
Environment: Elemental Plane of Earth
Organization: Solitary (1), gang (2–4 mephits of mixed types), or mob (5–12 mephits of mixed types)
Challenge Rating: 3
Treasure: Standard
Alignment: Usually neutral
Advancement: 4–6 HD (Small); 7–9 HD (Medium)
Level Adjustment: +3 (cohort)

This winged creature looks like a stony, rugged, mostly hairless dwarf.

Earth mephits come from the Elemental Plane of Earth.
  An earth mephit is about 4 feet tall and weighs about 80 pounds.
  Earth mephits speak Common and Terran.

Combat

Breath Weapon (Su): 15-foot cone of rock shards and pebbles, damage 1d8, Reflex DC 13 half. The save DC is Constitution-based and includes a +1 racial bonus.

Spell-Like Abilities: 1/day—*soften earth and stone.* Caster level 6th.

Change Size (Sp): Once per hour, an earth mephit can magically change its size. This works just like an *enlarge person* spell, except that the power works only on the earth mephit. This is the equivalent of a 2nd-level spell.

Fast Healing (Ex): An earth mephit heals only if it is underground or buried up to its waist in earth.

FIRE MEPHIT

Small Outsider (Extraplanar, Fire)
Hit Dice: 3d8 (13 hp)
Initiative: +5
Speed: 30 ft. (6 squares), fly 50 ft. (average)
Armor Class: 16 (+1 size, +1 Dex, +4 natural), touch 12, flat-footed 15
Base Attack/Grapple: +3/−1
Attack: Claw +4 melee (1d3 and 1d4 fire)
Full Attack: 2 claws +4 melee (1d3 and 1d4 fire)
Space/Reach: 5 ft./5 ft.
Special Attacks: Breath weapon, spell-like abilities, *summon mephit*
Special Qualities: Damage reduction 5/magic, darkvision 60 ft., immunity to fire, fast healing 2, vulnerability to cold
Saves: Fort +3, Ref +4, Will +3
Abilities: Str 10, Dex 13, Con 10, Int 6, Wis 11, Cha 15
Skills: Bluff +8, Escape Artist +7, Hide +11, Listen +6, Diplomacy +4, Disguise +2 (+4 acting), Move Silently +7, Spot +6, Use Rope +1 (+3 with bindings)
Feats: Dodge, Improved Initiative
Environment: Elemental Plane of Fire
Organization: Solitary (1), gang (2–4 mephits of mixed types), or mob (5–12 mephits of mixed types)
Challenge Rating: 3
Treasure: Standard
Alignment: Usually neutral
Advancement: 4–6 HD (Small); 7–9 HD (Medium)
Level Adjustment: +3 (cohort)

This winged creature looks like a miniature devil, wreathed in flame and cackling with mischief.

Fire mephits come from the Elemental Plane of Fire.
  A fire mephit is about 4 feet tall and weighs about 1 pound.
  Fire mephits speak Common and Ignan.

Combat

Breath Weapon (Su): 15-foot cone, damage 1d8 fire, Reflex half DC 12. The save DC is Constitution-based and includes a +1 racial adjustment.

Spell-Like Abilities: 1/hour—*scorching ray* (DC 14) as the spell cast by a 3rd-level sorcerer; 1/day—*heat metal* (DC 14). Caster level 6th. The save DC is Charisma-based.

Fast Healing (Ex): A fire mephit heals only if it is touching a flame at least as large as a torch.

ICE MEPHIT

Small Outsider (Air, Cold, Extraplanar)
Hit Dice: 3d8 (13 hp)
Initiative: +7
Speed: 30 ft. (6 squares), fly 50 ft. (perfect)
Armor Class: 18 (+1 size, +3 Dex, +4 natural), touch 14, flat-footed 15
Base Attack/Grapple: +3/−1
Attack: Claw +4 melee (1d3 plus 1d4 cold)
Full Attack: 2 claws +4 melee (1d3 plus 1d4 cold)
Space/Reach: 5 ft./5 ft.
Special Attacks: Breath weapon, spell-like abilities, *summon mephit*
Special Qualities: Damage reduction 5/magic, darkvision 60 ft., fast healing 2, immunity to cold, vulnerability to fire
Saves: Fort +3, Ref +6, Will +3
Abilities: Str 10, Dex 17, Con 10, Int 6, Wis 11, Cha 15
Skills: Bluff +8, Escape Artist +9, Hide +13, Listen +6, Diplomacy +4, Disguise +2 (+4 acting), Move Silently +9, Spot +6, Use Rope +3 (+5 with bindings)
Feats: Dodge, Improved Initiative
Environment: Elemental Plane of Air
Organization: Solitary (1), gang (2–4 mephits of mixed types), or mob (5–12 mephits of mixed types)
Challenge Rating: 3
Treasure: Standard
Alignment: Usually neutral
Advancement: 4–6 HD (Small); 7–9 HD (Medium)
Level Adjustment: +3 (cohort)

This winged creature looks like a miniature human made of snow and ice. It has translucent skin.

Ice mephits come from the Elemental Plane of Air.
  Ice mephits have a cold, aloof demeanor. Each one is about 4 feet tall and weighs about 30 pounds.
  Ice mephits speak Common and Auran.

Combat

Breath Weapon (Su): 10-foot cone of ice shards, damage 1d4 cold, Reflex DC 12 half. Living creatures that fail their saves are tormented by frostbitten skin and frozen eyes unless they have immunity to cold or are otherwise protected. This effect imposes a –4 penalty to AC and a –2 penalty on attack rolls for 3 rounds. The save DC is Constitution-based and includes a +1 racial bonus.

Spell-Like Abilities: 1/hour—*magic missile* (caster level 3rd); 1/day—*chill metal* (DC 14, caster level 6th). The save DC is Charisma-based.

Fast Healing (Ex): An ice mephit heals only if it is touching a piece of ice of at least Tiny size or if the ambient temperature is 32°F. or below.

MAGMA MEPHIT

Small Outsider (Fire, Extraplanar)
Hit Dice: 3d8 (13 hp)
Initiative: +5
Speed: 30 ft. (6 squares), fly 50 ft. (average)
Armor Class: 16 (+1 size, +1 Dex, +4 natural), touch 12, flat-footed 15
Base Attack/Grapple: +3/–1
Attack: Claw +4 melee (1d3 plus 1d4 fire)
Full Attack: 2 claws +4 melee (1d3 plus 1d4 fire)
Space/Reach: 5 ft./5 ft.
Special Attacks: Breath weapon, spell-like abilities, *summon mephit*
Special Qualities: Damage reduction 5/magic, darkvision 60 ft., fast healing 2, immunity to fire, vulnerability to cold
Saves: Fort +3, Ref +4, Will +3
Abilities: Str 10, Dex 13, Con 10, Int 6, Wis 11, Cha 15
Skills: Bluff +8, Escape Artist +7, Hide +11, Listen +6, Diplomacy +4, Disguise +2 (+4 acting), Move Silently +7, Spot +6, Use Rope +1 (+3 with bindings)
Feats: Dodge, Improved Initiative
Environment: Elemental Plane of Fire
Organization: Solitary (1), gang (2–4 mephits of mixed types), or mob (5–12 mephits of mixed types)
Challenge Rating: 3
Treasure: Standard
Alignment: Usually neutral
Advancement: 4–6 HD (Small); 7–9 HD (Medium)
Level Adjustment: +3 (cohort)

This winged creature looks like a brutish, miniature human made of molten stone and glowing lava.

Magma mephits come from the Elemental Plane of Fire.

Magma mephits are slow-witted and brutish. Each one is about 4 feet tall and weighs about 60 pounds.

Magma mephits speak Common and Ignan.

Combat

Breath Weapon (Su): 10-foot cone of magma, damage 1d4 fire, Reflex DC 12 half.

Living creatures that fail their saves are tormented by burned skin and seared eyes unless they have immunity to fire or are otherwise protected. This effect imposes a –4 penalty to AC and a –2 penalty on attack rolls for 3 rounds. The save DC is Constitution-based and includes a +1 racial bonus.

Spell-Like Abilities: Once per hour, a magma mephit can use *shapechange* to take the form of a pool of lava 3 feet in diameter and 6 inches deep. The mephit's damage reduction improves to 20/magic when in this form. The mephit can't attack while in lava form but can use other spell-like abilities. It can move at a speed of 10 feet, but it can't run. In this form the mephit can pass through small holes or narrow openings, even mere cracks. The pool's touch ignites flammable materials such as paper, straw, or dry wood.

Once per day a magma mephit can use *pyrotechnics* (DC 14). It can use itself as the fire source without harm. Caster level 6th. The save DC is Charisma-based.

Fast Healing (Ex): A magma mephit heals only if it is touching magma, lava, or a flame at least as large as a torch.

OOZE MEPHIT

Small Outsider (Extraplanar, Water)
Hit Dice: 3d8+6 (19 hp)
Initiative: +0
Speed: 30 ft. (6 squares), fly 40 ft. (average), swim 30 ft.
Armor Class: 16 (+1 size, +5 natural), touch 11, flat-footed 16
Base Attack/Grapple: +3/+1
Attack: Claw +6 melee (1d3+2)
Full Attack: 2 claws +6 melee (1d3+2)
Space/Reach: 5 ft./5 ft.
Special Attacks: Breath weapon, spell-like abilities, *summon mephit*
Special Qualities: Damage reduction 5/magic, darkvision 60 ft., fast healing 2
Saves: Fort +4, Ref +3, Will +3
Abilities: Str 14, Dex 10, Con 13, Int 6, Wis 11, Cha 15
Skills: Bluff +8, Escape Artist +6, Hide +10, Listen +6, Diplomacy +4, Disguise +2 (+4 acting), Move Silently +6, Spot +6, Swim +10, Use Rope +0 (+2 with bindings)
Feats: Power Attack, Toughness
Environment: Elemental Plane of Water
Organization: Solitary (1), gang (2–4 mephits of mixed types), or mob (5–12 mephits of mixed types)
Challenge Rating: 3
Treasure: Standard
Alignment: Usually neutral
Advancement: 4–6 HD (Small); 7–9 HD (Medium)
Level Adjustment: +3 (cohort)

This loathsome, winged creature looks like a miniature human composed of muck and filth. The creature has a terribly offensive odor, and slime dribbles from its body.

Ooze mephits come from the Elemental Plane of Water.

An ooze mephit is about 4 feet tall and weighs about 30 pounds.

Ooze mephits speak Common and Aquan.

Combat

Breath Weapon (Su): 10-foot cone of caustic liquid, damage 1d4 acid, Reflex DC 13 half. Living creatures that fail their saves are tormented by itching skin and burning eyes unless they have immunity to acid or are otherwise protected. This effect imposes a –4 penalty to AC and a –2 penalty on attack rolls for 3 rounds. The save DC is Constitution-based and includes a +1 racial bonus.

Spell-Like Abilities: Once per hour an ooze mephit can hurl an acidic blob that functions like *Melf's acid arrow* (caster level 3rd). Once per day it can create a mass of smelly fog that duplicates the effect of *stinking cloud* (DC 15, caster level 6th). The save DC is Charisma-based.

Fast Healing (Ex): An ooze mephit heals only if in a wet or muddy environment.

Skills: An ooze mephit has a +8 racial bonus on any Swim check to perform some special action or avoid a hazard. It can always choose to take 10 on a Swim check, even if distracted or endangered. It can use the run action while swimming, provided it swims in a straight line.

SALT MEPHIT

Salt Mephit
Small Outsider (Earth, Extraplanar)
Hit Dice: 3d8+6 (19 hp)
Initiative: –1
Speed: 30 ft. (6 squares), fly 40 ft. (average)
Armor Class: 16 (+1 size, –1 Dex, +6 natural), touch 10, flat-footed 16
Base Attack/Grapple: +3/+2
Attack: Claw +7 melee (1d3+3)
Full Attack: 2 claws +7 melee (1d3+3)
Space/Reach: 5 ft./5 ft.
Special Attacks: Breath weapon, spell-like abilities, *summon mephit*
Special Qualities: Damage reduction 5/magic, darkvision 60 ft., fast healing 2
Saves: Fort +4, Ref +2, Will +3
Abilities: Str 17, Dex 8, Con 13, Int 6, Wis 11, Cha 15
Skills: Bluff +8, Escape Artist +5, Hide +9, Listen +6, Diplomacy +4, Disguise +2 (+4 acting), Move Silently +5, Spot +6, Use Rope –1 (+1 with bindings)
Feats: Power Attack, Toughness
Environment: Elemental Plane of Earth
Organization: Solitary (1), gang (2–4 mephits of mixed types), or mob (5–12 mephits of mixed types)
Challenge Rating: 3
Treasure: Standard
Alignment: Usually neutral
Advancement: 4–6 HD (Small); 7–9 HD (Medium)
Level Adjustment: +3 (cohort)

This winged creature looks like a miniature human with bleary red eyes and crystalline flesh.

Salt mephits come from the Elemental Plane of Earth.

Salt mephits are sarcastic creatures who loathe water and moisture of any kind. Each one is about 4 feet tall and weighs about 80 pounds. Salt mephits speak Common and Terran.

Combat

Breath Weapon (Su): 10-foot cone of salt crystals, damage 1d4, Reflex DC 13 half. Living creatures that fail their saves are tormented by itching skin and burning eyes. This effect imposes a –4 penalty to AC and a –2 penalty on attack rolls for 3 rounds. The save DC is Constitution-based and includes a +1 racial bonus.

Spell-Like Abilities: Once per hour a salt mephit can use *glitterdust* (DC 14, caster level 3rd).

Once per day it can draw the moisture from an area in a 20-foot radius centered on itself. Living creatures within range take 2d8 points of damage (Fortitude DC 14 half; caster level 6th). This effect is especially devastating to plant creatures and aquatic creatures, which take a –2 penalty on their saving throws. This ability is the equivalent of a 2nd-level spell. The save DCs are Charisma-based.

Fast Healing (Ex): A salt mephit heals only if in an arid environment.

STEAM MEPHIT

Small Outsider (Extraplanar, Fire)
Hit Dice: 3d8 (13 hp)
Initiative: +5
Speed: 30 ft. (6 squares), fly 50 ft. (average)
Armor Class: 16 (+1 size, +1 Dex, +4 natural), touch 12, flat-footed 15
Base Attack/Grapple: +3/–1
Attack: Claw +4 melee (1d3 plus 1d4 fire)
Full Attack: 2 claws +4 melee (1d3 plus 1d4 fire)
Space/Reach: 5 ft./5 ft.
Special Attacks: Breath weapon, spell-like abilities, *summon mephit*
Special Qualities: Damage reduction 5/magic, darkvision 60 ft., fast healing 2, immunity to fire, vulnerability to cold
Saves: Fort +3, Ref +4, Will +3
Abilities: Str 10, Dex 13, Con 10, Int 6, Wis 11, Cha 15
Skills: Bluff +8, Escape Artist +7, Hide +11, Listen +6, Diplomacy +4, Disguise +2 (+4 acting), Move Silently +7, Spot +6, Use Rope +1 (+3 with bindings)
Feats: Dodge, Improved Initiative
Environment: Elemental Plane of Fire
Organization: Solitary (1), gang (2–4 mephits of mixed types), or mob (5–12 mephits of mixed types)
Challenge Rating: 3
Treasure: Standard
Alignment: Usually neutral
Advancement: 4–6 HD (Small); 7–9 HD (Medium)
Level Adjustment: +3 (cohort)

This winged creature looks like a miniature human with pale skin and wisps of vapor rising from its nose, mouth, and ears. It sheds drops of steaming water when it moves.

Steam mephits come from the Elemental Plane of Fire.

Steam mephits are bossy creatures who consider themselves the lords of all their kind. Each one is about 4 feet tall and weighs about 2 pounds.

Steam mephits speak Common and Ignan.

Combat

Unlike other mephits, steam mephits rush into combat eagerly, driven by an oversized ego.

Breath Weapon (Su): 10-foot cone of steam, damage 1d4 fire, Reflex DC 12 half. Living creatures that fail their saves are tormented by burned skin and seared eyes unless they have immunity to fire or are otherwise protected. This effect imposes a –4 penalty to AC and a –2 penalty on attack rolls for 3 rounds. The save DC is Constitution-based and includes a +1 racial bonus.

Spell-Like Abilities: Once per hour a steam mephit can surround itself with a plume of vapor, duplicating the effect of a *blur* spell (caster level 3rd). Once per day it can create a rainstorm of boiling water that affects a 20-foot-square area. Living creatures caught in the storm take 2d6 points of fire damage (Reflex DC 14 half; caster level 6th). This ability is the equivalent of a 2nd-level spell. The save DCs are Charisma-based.

Fast Healing (Ex): A steam mephit heals only if it is touching boiling water or is in a hot, humid area.

184

WATER MEPHIT

Small Outsider (Extraplanar, Water)
Hit Dice: 3d8+6 (19 hp)
Initiative: +0
Speed: 30 ft. (6 squares), fly 40 ft. (average) , swim 30 ft.
Armor Class: 16 (+1 size, +5 natural), touch 11, flat-footed 16
Base Attack/Grapple: +3/+1
Attack: Claw +6 melee (1d3+2)
Full Attack: 2 claws +6 melee (1d3+2)
Space/Reach: 5 ft./5 ft.
Special Attacks: Breath weapon, spell-like abilities, *summon mephit*
Special Qualities: Damage reduction 5/magic, darkvision 60 ft., fast healing 2
Saves: Fort +4, Ref +3, Will +3
Abilities: Str 14, Dex 10, Con 13, Int 6, Wis 11, Cha 15
Skills: Bluff +8, Escape Artist +6, Hide +10, Listen +6, Diplomacy +4, Disguise +2 (+4 acting), Move Silently +6, Spot +6, Swim +10, Use Rope +0 (+2 with bindings)
Feats: Power Attack, Toughness
Environment: Elemental Plane of Water
Organization: Solitary (1), gang (2–4 mephits of mixed types), or mob (5–12 mephits of mixed types)
Challenge Rating: 3
Treasure: Standard
Alignment: Usually neutral
Advancement: 4–6 HD (Small); 7–9 HD (Medium)
Level Adjustment: +3 (cohort)

This winged creature looks like a miniature fish-person. It is covered with scales and views the world through black, bulbous eyes.

Water mephits come from the Elemental Plane of Water.

Water mephits are jaunty creatures with an unflagging sense of humor who quickly get on the nerves of everyone around them. Each one is about 4 feet tall and weighs about 30 pounds.

Water mephits speak Common and Aquan.

Combat

Breath Weapon (Su): 15-foot cone of caustic liquid, damage 1d8 acid, Reflex DC 13 half. The save DC is Constitution-based and includes a +1 racial bonus.

Spell-Like Abilities: Once per hour a water mephit can hurl an acidic blob that functions like *Melf's acid arrow* (caster level 3rd). Once per day it can create a mass of smelly fog that duplicates the effect of a *stinking cloud* spell (DC 15, caster level 6th). The save DC is Charisma-based.

Fast Healing (Ex): A water mephit heals only if it is exposed to rain or submerged up to its waist in water.

Skills: A water mephit has a +8 racial bonus on any Swim check to perform some special action or avoid a hazard. It can always choose to take 10 on a Swim check, even if distracted or endangered. It can use the run action while swimming, provided it swims in a straight line.

Merfolk

MERFOLK

Merfolk, 1st-Level Warrior
Medium Humanoid (Aquatic)
Hit Dice: 1d8+2 (6 hp)
Initiative: +1
Speed: 5 ft. (1 square), swim 50 ft.
Armor Class: 13 (+1 Dex, +2 leather), touch 11, flat-footed 12
Base Attack/Grapple: +1/+2
Attack: Trident +2 melee (1d8+1) or heavy crossbow +2 ranged (1d10/19–20)
Full Attack: Trident +2 melee (1d8+1) or heavy crossbow +2 ranged (1d10/19–20)
Space/Reach: 5 ft./5 ft.
Special Attacks: —
Special Qualities: Amphibious, low-light vision
Saves: Fort +4, Ref +1, Will –1
Abilities: Str 13, Dex 13, Con 14, Int 10, Wis 9, Cha 10
Skills: Listen +3, Spot +3, Swim +9
Feats: Alertness
Environment: Temperate aquatic
Organization: Company (2–4), patrol (11–20 plus 2 3rd-level lieutenants and 1 leader of 3rd–6th level), or band (30–60 plus 1 3rd-level sergeant per 20 adults, 5 5th-level lieutenants, 3 7th-level captains, and 10 porpoises)
Challenge Rating: 1/2
Treasure: Standard
Alignment: Usually neutral
Advancement: By character class
Level Adjustment: +1

This being has the upper body, arms, and head of a fair-featured human. Instead of legs, however, it has the scaled tail of a great fish.

The merfolk are playful, marine-dwelling people. Although wary of surface dwellers, they are not usually hostile: They prefer sunning themselves on rocks to engaging in warfare.

Both male and female merfolk decorate themselves with shells, coral, and other underwater adornments.

Adventurers who encounter merfolk are often the victims of pranks and mischief. The sport of merfolk can be cruel, although they are not actually evil. Should surface dwellers do them harm, however, these creatures can be formidable enemies.

A merfolk is about 8 feet long from the top of the head to the end of the tail, and weighs about 400 pounds.

Merfolk speak Common and Aquan.

Most merfolk encountered outside their home are warriors; the information in the statistics block is for one of 1st level.

COMBAT

Merfolk favor heavy crossbows of shell and coral that fire bolts fashioned from blowfish spines, with an underwater range increment of 30 feet. Merfolk often barrage their enemies before closing, when they resort to tridents.

Amphibious (Ex): Merfolk can breathe both air and water, although they rarely travel more than a few feet from the water's edge.

Skills: A merfolk has a +8 racial bonus on any Swim check to perform some special action or avoid a hazard. It can always choose to take 10 on a Swim check, even if distracted or endangered. It can use the run action while swimming, provided it swims in a straight line.

The merfolk warrior presented here had the following ability scores before racial adjustments: Str 13, Dex 11, Con 12, Int 10, Wis 9, Cha 8.

MERFOLK SOCIETY

Merfolk live in semipermanent communities located near choice fishing and hunting areas. They often keep company with porpoises. Surface dwellers who come face to face with merfolk commonly encounter a scouting or hunting patrol.

The merfolk revere the deity Eadro, who created both them and the locathahs.

MERFOLK CHARACTERS

A merfolk's favored class is bard; most merfolk leaders are bards. Merfolk spellcasters who are not bards are generally adepts. Merfolk clerics worship Eadro. A merfolk cleric has access to two of the following domains: Animal, Protection, or Water.

MIMIC

Large Aberration (Shapechanger)

Hit Dice: 7d8+21 (52 hp)
Initiative: +1
Speed: 10 ft. (2 squares)
Armor Class: 15 (–1 size, +1 Dex, +5 natural), touch 10, flat-footed 15
Base Attack/Grapple: +5/+13
Attack: Slam +9 melee (1d8+4)
Full Attack: 2 slams +9 melee (1d8+4)
Space/Reach: 10 ft./10 ft.
Special Attacks: Adhesive, crush
Special Qualities: Darkvision 60 ft., immunity to acid, mimic shape
Saves: Fort +5, Ref +5, Will +6
Abilities: Str 19, Dex 12, Con 17, Int 10, Wis 13, Cha 10
Skills: Climb +9, Disguise +13, Listen +8, Spot +8
Feats: Alertness, Lightning Reflexes, Weapon Focus (slam)
Environment: Underground
Organization: Solitary
Challenge Rating: 4
Treasure: 1/10th coins; 50% goods; 50% items
Alignment: Usually neutral
Advancement: 8–10 HD (Large); 11–21 HD (Huge)
Level Adjustment: —

What originally appeared to be an object now shows signs of organic life as the creature sprouts a lashing pseudopod.

The mimic is a strange and deadly creature that can change its pigmentation and shape. It uses this ability to lure hapless victims close enough to slay them.

Mimic

It is said that mimics are not natural creatures but were created long ago by a now-forgotten wizard. Ever since, these terrible things have served to guard treasures.

A mimic can have almost any dimensions, but usually is not more than 10 feet long. A typical mimic has a volume of 150 cubic feet (5 feet by 5 feet by 6 feet) and weighs about 4,500 pounds. Mimics speak Common.

COMBAT

A mimic often surprises an unsuspecting adventurer, lashing out with a heavy pseudopod. The creature does not necessarily fight to the death if it can succeed in extorting treasure or food from a party.

Adhesive (Ex): A mimic exudes a thick slime that acts as a powerful adhesive, holding fast any creatures or items that touch it. An adhesive-covered mimic automatically grapples any creature it hits with its slam attack. Opponents so grappled cannot get free while the mimic is alive without removing the adhesive first.

A weapon that strikes an adhesive-coated mimic is stuck fast unless the wielder succeeds on a DC 16 Reflex save. A successful DC 16 Strength check is needed to pry it off.

Strong alcohol dissolves the adhesive, but the mimic still can grapple normally. A mimic can dissolve its adhesive at will, and the substance breaks down 5 rounds after the creature dies.

Crush (Ex): A mimic deals 1d8+4 points of damage with a successful grapple check.

Mimic Shape (Ex): A mimic can assume the general shape of any object that fills roughly 150 cubic feet (5 feet by 5 feet by 6 feet), such as a massive chest, a stout bed, or a wide door frame. The creature cannot substantially alter its size, though. A mimic's body is hard and has a rough texture, no matter what appearance it might present. Anyone who examines the mimic can detect the ruse with a successful Spot check opposed by the mimic's Disguise check. Of course, by this time it is generally far too late.

Skills: A mimic has a +8 racial bonus on Disguise checks.

MIND FLAYER

This strange humanoid-shaped being stands about as tall as a human. Its flesh is rubbery and greenish-mauve, glistening with slime. The creature's head looks rather like a four-tentacled octopus, made all the more horrible by a pair of bloated white eyes.

Mind flayers, also called illithids, are so insidious, diabolical, and powerful that all denizens of the dark fear them. They bend others to their will and shatter enemies' minds.

A mind flayer's mouth, a revolting thing shaped like a lamprey's maw, constantly drips an oily slime when it is not siphoning out the brains of living prey.

In addition to being highly intelligent, wholly evil, and terribly sadistic, mind flayers are utterly self-serving. If an encounter turns against the creature, it flees at once, caring nothing for the fate of its companions or servitors.

A mind flayer is about the same height and weight as a human.

Mind flayers speak Undercommon but prefer to communicate telepathically.

COMBAT

Mind flayers like to fight from a distance, using their psionic abilities, particularly *mind blast*. If pressed into melee combat, a mind flayer lashes its enemies with the tentacles ringing its mouth.

Mind Blast (Sp): This psionic attack is a cone 60 feet long. Anyone caught in this cone must succeed on a DC 17 Will save or be stunned for 3d4 rounds. Mind flayers often hunt using this power and then drag off one or two of their stunned victims to feed upon. The save DC is Charisma-based. This ability is the equivalent of a 4th-level spell.

Psionics (Sp): At will—*charm monster* (DC 17), *detect thoughts* (DC 15), *levitate*, *plane shift*, *suggestion* (DC 16). Effective caster level 8th. The save DCs are Charisma-based.

Improved Grab (Ex): To use this ability, a mind flayer must hit a Small, Medium, or Large creature with its tentacle attack. It can then attempt to start a grapple as a free action without provoking an attack of opportunity. If it wins the grapple check, it establishes a hold and attaches the tentacle to the opponent's head. A mind flayer can grab a Huge or larger creature, but

Mindflayer

only if it can somehow reach the foe's head. If a mind flayer begins its turn with at least one tentacle attached, it can try to attach its remaining tentacles with a single grapple check. The opponent can escape with a single successful grapple check or an Escape Artist check, but the mind flayer gets a +2 circumstance bonus for every tentacle that was attached at the beginning of the opponent's turn.

Extract (Ex): A mind flayer that begins its turn with all four tentacles attached and that makes a successful grapple check automatically extracts the opponent's brain, instantly killing that creature. This power is useless against constructs, elementals, oozes, plants, and undead. It is not instantly fatal to foes with multiple heads, such as ettins and hydras.

MIND FLAYER SORCERER

While many mind flayers train as wizards and grow mighty in the arcane arts along that disciplined path, some of the most fearsome of the illithids are sorcerers, whose mastery of magic seems almost instinctual.

Combat

The save DCs for this mind flayer sorcerer's *mind blast* (DC 21) and its psionics (*charm monster* DC 21, *detect thoughts* DC 19, *suggestion* DC 20) are adjusted for its higher Charisma score. The mind flayer sorcerer uses its spells to protect itself from attack (*greater invisibil-*

Illus. by T. Lockwood

	Mind Flayer Medium Aberration	Mind Flayer, 9th-Level Sorcerer Medium Aberration
Hit Dice:	8d8+8 (44 hp)	8d8+24 plus 9d4+27 (109 hp)
Initiative:	+6	+8
Speed:	30 ft. (6 squares)	30 ft. (6 squares)
Armor Class:	15 (+2 Dex, +3 natural), touch 12, flat-footed 13	24 (+4 Dex, +3 natural, +5 *+1 mithral chain shirt*, +2 *ring of protection +2*), touch 16, flat-footed 20
Base Attack/Grapple:	+6/+7	+10/+10
Attack:	Tentacle +8 melee (1d4+1)	Tentacle +15 melee (1d4)
Full Attack:	4 tentacles +8 melee (1d4+1)	4 tentacles +15 melee (1d4)
Space/Reach:	5 ft./5 ft.	5 ft./5 ft.
Special Attacks:	*Mind blast*, psionics, improved grab, extract	*Mind blast*, psionics, improved grab, extract, spells
Special Qualities:	Spell resistance 25, telepathy 100 ft.	Spell resistance 34, telepathy 100 ft.
Saves:	Fort +3, Ref +4, Will +9	Fort +8, Ref +9, Will +16
Abilities:	Str 12, Dex 14, Con 12, Int 19, Wis 17, Cha 17	Str 10, Dex 18, Con 16, Int 18, Wis 18, Cha 24
Skills:	Bluff +11, Concentration +11, Diplomacy +7, Disguise +3 (+5 acting), Hide +10, Intimidate +9, Knowledge (any) +12, Listen +11, Move Silently +10, Sense Motive +7, Spot +11	Bluff +14, Concentration +22, Craft (alchemy) +13, Diplomacy +11, Disguise +7 (+9 acting), Hide +11, Intimidate +21, Knowledge (arcana) +20, Knowledge (the planes) +15, Listen +13, Move Silently +11, Spellcraft +13, Spot +13, Survival +4 (+6 planes)
Feats:	Combat Casting, Improved Initiative, Weapon Finesse	Alertness, Combat Casting, Dodge, Improved Initiative, Weapon Finesse, Weapon Focus (tentacle)
Environment:	Underground	Underground
Organization:	Solitary, pair, inquisition (3–5), or cult (3–5 plus 6–10 grimlocks)	Solitary, inquisition (1 plus 2–4 mind flayers), or cult (2 plus 2–4 mind flayers and 6–10 grimlocks)
Challenge Rating:	8	17
Treasure:	Double standard	Double standard (including *ring of protection +2*, *+1 mithral chain shirt*, and *cloak of Charisma +2*)
Alignment:	Usually lawful evil	Usually lawful evil
Advancement:	By character class	By character class
Level Adjustment:	+7	+7

ity, stoneskin, resist energy, mage armor) and improve its own effectiveness in combat (haste, see invisibility), and only secondarily to supplement its own innate attacks with magical ones (ray of exhaustion, suggestion, touch of idiocy).

Typical Sorcerer Spells Known: (6/8/8/8/5; save DC 17 + spell level, 10% arcane spell failure chance): 0—arcane mark, daze, detect magic, disrupt undead, flare, ghost sound, light, read magic; 1st—chill touch, mage armor, magic missile, ray of enfeeblement, shocking grasp; 2nd—minor image, resist energy, see invisibility, touch of idiocy; 3rd—fly, haste, ray of exhaustion; 4th—greater invisibility, stoneskin.

MIND FLAYER SOCIETY

Mind flayers congregate in underground cities of 200 to 2,000 inhabitants, plus at least two slaves for each resident. Slaves obey their masters without question. The center of a community is its elder brain, a pool of briny fluid that contains the brains of the city's deceased mind flayers.

Although they constantly vie for power, mind flayers are quite willing to work together. A small group of these creatures, known as an inquisition, often forms to root out some dark and terrible secret. In many ways, a mind flayer inquisition is not unlike a party of adventurers, with each member contributing its own skills and knowledge to the group.

When a task is too great for an inquisition to handle, mind flayers generally form a cult. A pair of illithids commands the group, each struggling for supremacy.

MIND FLAYERS AS CHARACTERS

Most mind flayers with class levels are sorcerers or wizards.

Mind flayer characters possess the following racial traits.

— +2 Strength, +4 Dexterity, +2 Constitution, +8 Intelligence, +6 Wisdom, +6 Charisma.

—A mind flayer's base land speed is 30 feet.

—Darkvision out to 60 feet.

—Racial Hit Dice: A mind flayer begins with eight levels of aberration, which provide 8d8 Hit Dice, a base attack bonus of +6, and base saving throw bonuses of Fort +2, Ref +2, and Will +6.

—Racial Skills: A mind flayer's aberration levels give it skill points equal to $11 \times (2 + $ Int modifier). Its class skills are Bluff, Concentration, Hide, Intimidate, Knowledge (any), Listen, Move Silently, and Spot.

—Racial Feats: A mind flayer's aberration levels give it three feats.

— +3 natural armor bonus.

—Natural Weapons: 4 tentacles (1d4).

—Special Attacks (see above): Mind blast, psionics, improved grab, extract.

—Special Qualities (see above): Spell resistance equal to 25 + class levels, telepathy 100 ft.

—Automatic Languages: Common, Undercommon. Bonus Languages: Abyssal, Aquan, Draconic, Dwarven, Elven, Gnome, Infernal, Terran.

—Favored Class: Wizard.

—Level adjustment +7.

Tactics Round-by-Round

A mind flayer is most effective as a ranged combatant, using its spell-like abilities to attack from a distance.

Prior to combat: Use detect thoughts to scout foes and determine threat potential. (Highly intelligent creatures are considered most dangerous; creatures of lower intelligence are potential pawns and food.)

Round 1: Mind blast.

Round 2: If most of the party is stunned, use charm monster on a remaining foe. If most of the party is not stunned, maintain distance and use mind blast again.

Round 3: If fewer than two foes remain unstunned, order any charmed foes to protect you. Grapple a stunned foe with tentacles. If a majority of the party remains unstunned, flee using levitate or, if necessary, plane shift.

Round 4: If still in a position of strength, start eating brains. Use charmed foes to guard you. If in a position of weakness, use plane shift, perhaps with grappled foe.

A mind flayer works well as a "boss monster." If it has minions, it varies its tactics to suit the situation, as follows.

Prior to combat: Dispatch minions with orders to assault foes from one side of the battlefield. Use levitate and cover to take a safe command position, preferably out of obvious sight.

Round 1: Order minions into optimal positions using telepathy. If the opportunity presents itself, use mind blast on foes (without hitting minions if possible—but they're all expendable). If the battlefield is too congested, use charm monster or suggestion to sow confusion in foes.

Round 2: Identify enemy spellcasters and order minions telepathically to assault them at all costs. Focus spell-like abilities on lesser foes.

Round 3: Order charmed foes toward you (telepathically). Grapple them. Have minions keep uncharmed, unstunned foes busy.

Round 4: Eat brains.

Mind flayer sorcerer

MINOTAUR

Large Monstrous Humanoid

Hit Dice: 6d8+12 (39 hp)

Initiative: +0

Speed: 30 ft. (6 squares)

Armor Class: 14 (–1 size, +5 natural), touch 9, flat-footed — (see text)

Base Attack/Grapple: +6/+14

Attack: Greataxe +9 melee (3d6+6/×3) or gore +9 melee (1d8+4)

Full Attack: Greataxe +9/+4 melee (3d6+6/×3) and gore +4 melee (1d8+2)

Space/Reach: 10 ft./10 ft.

Special Attacks: Powerful charge 4d6+6

Special Qualities: Darkvision 60 ft., natural cunning, scent

Saves: Fort +6, Ref +5, Will +5

Abilities: Str 19, Dex 10, Con 15, Int 7, Wis 10, Cha 8

Skills: Intimidate +2, Listen +7, Search +2, Spot +7

Feats: Great Fortitude, Power Attack, Track

Environment: Underground

Organization: Solitary, pair, or gang (3–4)

Challenge Rating: 4

Treasure: Standard

Alignment: Usually chaotic evil

Advancement: By character class

Level Adjustment: +2

The creature looks like an incredibly tall, powerfully muscled human, covered in shaggy fur, with the head of a bull. The dark eyes of the brute gleam with savage fury.

Minotaurs are strong, fiercely territorial creatures often found in vast underground labyrinths.

A minotaur's natural cunning and feral instincts enable it to find its way easily through even the most confusing tunnel complexes —an ability it puts to great use in hunting, tormenting, and ultimately destroying intruders.

A minotaur stands more than 7 feet tall and weighs about 700 pounds.

Minotaurs speak Giant.

Minotaur

COMBAT

Minotaurs prefer melee combat, where their great strength serves them well.

Powerful Charge (Ex): A minotaur typically begins a battle by charging at an opponent, lowering its head to bring its mighty horns into play. In addition to the normal benefits and hazards of a charge, this allows the beast to make a single gore attack with a +9 attack bonus that deals 4d6+6 points of damage.

Natural Cunning (Ex): Although minotaurs are not especially intelligent, they possess innate cunning and logical ability. This gives them immunity to *maze* spells, prevents them from ever becoming lost, and enables them to track enemies. Further, they are never caught flat-footed.

Skills: Minotaurs have a +4 racial bonus on Search, Spot, and Listen checks.

MINOTAURS AS CHARACTERS

Minotaur characters possess the following racial traits.

— +8 Strength, +4 Constitution, –4 Intelligence (minimum 3), –2 Charisma.

—Large size. –1 penalty to Armor Class, –1 penalty on attack rolls, –4 penalty on Hide checks, +4 bonus on grapple checks, lifting and carrying limits double those of Medium characters.

—Space/Reach: 10 feet/10 feet.

—A minotaur's base land speed is 30 feet.

—Darkvision out to 60 feet.

—Racial Hit Dice: A minotaur begins with six levels of monstrous humanoid, which provide 6d8 Hit Dice, a base attack bonus of +6, and base saving throw bonuses of Fort +2, Ref +5, and Will +5.

—Racial Skills: A minotaur's monstrous humanoid levels give it skill points equal to 9 × (2 + Int modifier, minimum 1). Its class skills are Intimidate, Jump, Listen, Search, and Spot. Minotaurs have a +4 racial bonus on Search, Spot, and Listen checks.

—Racial Feats: A minotaur's monstrous humanoid levels give it three feats.

—Weapon Proficiency: A minotaur is proficient with the greataxe and all simple weapons.

— +5 natural armor bonus.

—Natural Weapons: Gore (1d8).

—Special Attacks (see above): Powerful charge.

—Special Qualities (see above): Natural cunning, scent.

—Automatic Languages: Common, Giant. Bonus Languages: Orc, Goblin, Terran.

—Favored Class: Barbarian.

—Level adjustment +2.

MOHRG

Medium Undead

Hit Dice: 14d12 (91 hp)

Initiative: +9

Speed: 30 ft. (6 squares)

Armor Class: 23 (+4 Dex, +9 natural), touch 14, flat-footed 14

Base Attack/Grapple: +7/+12

Attack: Slam +12 melee (1d6+7) or tongue +12 melee touch (paralysis)

Full Attack: Slam +12 melee (1d6+7) and tongue +12 melee touch (paralysis)

Space/Reach: 5 ft./5 ft.

Special Attacks: Improved grab, paralyzing touch, create spawn

Special Qualities: Darkvision 60 ft., undead traits

Saves: Fort +4, Ref +10, Will +9

Abilities: Str 21, Dex 19, Con —, Int 11, Wis 10, Cha 10

Skills: Climb +13, Hide +21, Listen +11, Move Silently +21, Spot +15, Swim +9

Feats: Alertness, Dodge, Improved Initiative, Lightning Reflexes, Mobility

Environment: Any

Organization: Solitary, gang (2–4), or mob (2–4 plus 5–10 zombies)

Challenge Rating: 8

Treasure: None

Alignment: Always chaotic evil

Advancement: 15–21 HD (Medium); 22–28 HD (Large)

Level Adjustment: —

This creature looks like a gaunt, nearly skeletal corpse, its rib cage filled with horrid, writhing viscera. The creature's tongue is its most noteworthy feature—long, cartilaginous, and clawed.

Mohrgs are the animated corpses of mass murderers or similar villains who died without atoning for their crimes. Tortured by an all-consuming hatred of living things, they long to live again.

Most mohrgs are 5 to 6 feet tall and weigh about 120 pounds.

Mohrg illus. by B. Snoddy

MOHRG

Mohrg

COMBAT

Like zombies, mohrgs attack by slamming enemies with their fists. They often catch opponents flat-footed, for they move much faster than zombies.

Improved Grab (Ex): To use this ability, a mohrg must hit a creature of its size or smaller with its slam attack. It can then attempt to start a grapple as a free action without provoking an attack of opportunity.

Paralyzing Touch (Su): A mohrg lashes out with its tongue in combat. An opponent the tongue touches must succeed on a DC 17 Fortitude save or become paralyzed for 1d4 minutes. The save DC is Charisma-based.

Create Spawn (Su): Creatures killed by a mohrg rise after 1d4 days as zombies under the morhg's control. They do not possess any of the abilities they had in life.

MUMMY

This creature looks like a withered and desiccated corpse, with features hidden beneath centuries-old funereal wrappings. It moves with a slow, shambling gait and groans with the weight of the ages.

Mummies are preserved corpses animated through the auspices of dark desert gods best forgotten. They usually inhabit great tombs or temple complexes, maintaining a timeless vigil and destroying would-be grave robbers.

These horrid creatures are often marked with symbols of the dire gods they serve. While other undead often stink of carrion, the herbs and powders

Mummy

used to create a mummy give off a sharp, pungent odor like that of a spice cabinet.

Mummies attack intruders without pause or mercy. They never attempt to communicate with their enemies and never retreat. An encounter with a mummy can end only with the destruction of one combatant or the other (unless the mummy's foe elects to retreat).

Most mummies are 5 to 6 feet tall and weigh about 120 pounds. Mummies can speak Common, but seldom bother to do so.

COMBAT

In melee combat, a mummy delivers a powerful blow. Even if it had no other abilities, its great strength and grim determination would make it a formidable opponent.

Despair (Su): At the mere sight of a mummy, the viewer must succeed on a DC 16 Will save or be paralyzed with fear for 1d4 rounds. Whether or not the save is successful, that creature cannot be affected again by the same mummy's despair ability for 24 hours. The save DC is Charisma-based.

Mummy Rot (Su): Supernatural disease—slam, Fortitude DC 16, incubation period 1 minute; damage 1d6 Con and 1d6 Cha. The save DC is Charisma-based.

Unlike normal diseases, mummy rot continues until the victim reaches Constitution 0 (and dies) or is cured as described below.

	Mummy Medium Undead	Mummy Lord, 10th-Level Cleric Medium Undead
Hit Dice:	8d12+3 (55 hp)	8d12 plus 10d8 (97 hp)
Initiative:	+0	+5
Speed:	20 ft. (4 squares)	15 ft. in half-plate armor (3 squares); base speed 20 ft.
Armor Class:	20 (+10 natural), touch 10, flat-footed 20	30 (+1 Dex, +10 natural, +9 +2 *half-plate armor*), touch 11, flat-footed 29
Base Attack/Grapple:	+4/+11	+11/+19
Attack:	Slam +11 melee (1d6+10 plus mummy rot)	Slam +20 melee (1d6+12/19–20 plus mummy rot)
Full Attack:	Slam +11 melee (1d6+10 plus mummy rot)	Slam +20 melee (1d6+12/19–20 plus mummy rot)
Space/Reach:	5 ft./5 ft.	5 ft./5 ft.
Special Attacks:	Despair, mummy rot	Despair, mummy rot, rebuke undead, spells
Special Qualities:	Damage reduction 5/—, darkvision 60 ft., undead traits, vulnerability to fire	Damage reduction 5/—, darkvision 60 ft., resistance to fire 10, undead traits, vulnerability to fire
Saves:	Fort +4, Ref +2, Will +8	Fort +13, Ref +8, Will +20
Abilities:	Str 24, Dex 10, Con —, Int 6, Wis 14, Cha 15	Str 26, Dex 12, Con —, Int 8, Wis 20, Cha 17
Skills:	Hide +7, Listen +8, Move Silently +7, Spot +8	Concentration +8, Knowledge (religion) +4, Listen +18, Move Silently +5, Spot +18
Feats:	Alertness, Great Fortitude, Toughness	Alertness, Combat Casting, Great Fortitude, Improved Critical (slam), Improved Initiative, Weapon Focus (slam)
Environment:	Any	Any
Organization:	Solitary, warden squad (2–4), or guardian detail (6–10)	Solitary or tomb guard (1 mummy lord and 6–10 mummies)
Challenge Rating:	5	15
Treasure:	Standard	Standard plus possessions noted below
Alignment:	Usually lawful evil	Usually lawful evil
Advancement:	9–16 HD (Medium); 17–24 HD (Large)	By character class
Level Adjustment:	—	—

Mummy rot is a powerful curse, not a natural disease. A character attempting to cast any conjuration (healing) spell on a creature afflicted with mummy rot must succeed on a DC 20 caster level check, or the spell has no effect on the afflicted character.

To eliminate mummy rot, the curse must first be broken with *break enchantment* or *remove curse* (requiring a DC 20 caster level check for either spell), after which a caster level check is no longer necessary to cast healing spells on the victim, and the mummy rot can be magically cured as any normal disease.

An afflicted creature who dies of mummy rot shrivels away into sand and dust that blow away into nothing at the first wind.

MUMMY LORD

Unusually powerful or evil individuals preserved as mummies sometimes rise as greater mummies after death. A mummy lord resembles its lesser fellows, but often wears or carries equipment it used in life—ancient bronze armor, a rune-marked sword, or a magic staff.

Mummy lords are often potent spellcasters. They are found as guardians of the tombs of high lords, priests, and mages. Most are sworn to defend for eternity the resting place of those whom they served in life, but in some cases a mummy lord's unliving state is the result of a terrible curse or rite designed to punish treason, infidelity, or crimes of an even more abhorrent nature. A mummy lord of this sort is usually imprisoned in a tomb that is never meant to be opened again.

Despair (Su): The save DC against this mummy lord's despair is 17.

Mummy Rot (Su): The save DC against this mummy lord's mummy rot is 17.

Typical Cleric Spells Prepared (6/7/6/5/5/4; save DC 15 + spell level): 0 —*detect magic* (2), *guidance, read magic, resistance, virtue*; 1st—*bane, command, deathwatch, divine favor, doom, sanctuary*, shield of faith*; 2nd—*bull's strength, death knell*, hold person, resist energy, silence, spiritual weapon*; 3rd—*animate dead*, deeper darkness, dispel magic, invisibility purge, searing light*; 4th—*air walk, dismissal, divine power, giant vermin, spell immunity**; 5th—*insect plague, slay living*, spell resistance, symbol of pain*.

*Domain Spell. Domains: Death and Protection.

Possessions: +2 half-plate armor, cloak of resistance +2, ring of minor elemental resistance (fire), brooch of shielding. (Different mummy lords may have different possessions.)

NAGA

Nagas are highly intelligent creatures with a variety of magical powers. They are natural masters of those around them, using subtle wards and clever traps to keep intruders from disturbing their peace.

All nagas have long, snakelike bodies covered with glistening scales, and more or less human faces. They range in length from 10 to 20 feet and weigh from 200 to 500 pounds. The eyes of a naga are bright and intelligent, burning with an almost hypnotic inner light.

COMBAT

Nagas favor spells over other forms of combat. Because they are almost always found in the lairs they guard and know well, they can arrange most encounters to suit their wishes.

Mummy lord

DARK NAGA

Large Aberration
Hit Dice: 9d8+18 (58 hp)
Initiative: +2
Speed: 40 ft. (8 squares)
Armor Class: 14 (–1 size, +2 Dex, +3 natural), touch 11, flat-footed 12
Base Attack/Grapple: +6/+12
Attack: Sting +7 melee (2d4+2 plus poison)
Full Attack: Sting +7 melee (2d4+2 plus poison) and bite +2 melee (1d4+1)
Space/Reach: 10 ft./5 ft.
Special Attacks: Poison, spells
Special Qualities: Darkvision 60 ft., detect thoughts, guarded thoughts, immunity to poison, resistance to charm
Saves: Fort +5, Ref +7, Will +8
Abilities: Str 14, Dex 15, Con 14, Int 16, Wis 15, Cha 17
Skills: Bluff +9, Concentration +13, Diplomacy +7, Disguise +5 (+7 acting), Intimidate +5, Listen +11, Sense Motive +8, Spellcraft +12, Spot +11
Feats: Alertness, Combat Casting, Dodge, Eschew Materials[B], Lightning Reflexes
Environment: Temperate hills
Organization: Solitary or nest (2–4)
Challenge Rating: 8
Treasure: Standard
Alignment: Usually lawful evil
Advancement: 10–13 HD (Large); 14–27 HD (Huge)
Level Adjustment: —

This snakelike creature has a deep purple body covered in fine scales, making it look rather like a great eel. Its tail ends in a barbed stinger. Its head resembles an eel's but has a humanlike visage.

Dark nagas are infamous plotters and schemers. They often form alliances with other evil creatures so as to more efficiently gather prey and wealth.

Dark nagas speak Common and Infernal.

Combat

Dark nagas prefer to fight from an elevated position where they get a good view of the battlefield while also staying out of reach.

Poison (Ex): Injury, Fortitude DC 16 or lapse into a nightmare-haunted sleep for 2d4 minutes. The save DC is Constitution-based.

Spells: Dark nagas cast spells as 7th-level sorcerers.

Typical Sorcerer Spells Known (6/7/7/5; save DC 13 + spell level): 0—*daze, detect magic, light, mage hand, open/close, ray of frost, read magic;* 1st—*expeditious retreat, magic missile, ray of enfeeblement, shield, silent image;* 2nd—*cat's grace, invisibility, scorching ray;* 3rd—*displacement, lightning bolt.*

Resistance to *Charm*: Dark nagas have a +2 racial bonus on saving throws against all *charm* effects (not included in the statistics block).

Detect Thoughts (Su): A dark naga can continuously use *detect thoughts* as the spell (caster level 9th; Will DC 15 negates). This ability is always active. The save DC is Charisma-based.

Guarded Thoughts (Ex): Dark nagas are immune to any form of mind reading.

GUARDIAN NAGA

Large Aberration
Hit Dice: 11d8+44 (93 hp)
Initiative: +2
Speed: 40 ft. (8 squares)
Armor Class: 18 (–1 size, +2 Dex, +7 natural), touch 11, flat-footed 16
Base Attack/Grapple: +8/+17
Attack: Bite +12 melee (2d6+7 plus poison) or spit +9 ranged touch (poison)
Full Attack: Bite +12 melee (2d6+7 plus poison) or spit +9 ranged touch (poison)
Space/Reach: 10 ft./5 ft.
Special Attacks: Poison, spit, spells
Special Qualities: Darkvision 60 ft.
Saves: Fort +7, Ref +7, Will +11
Abilities: Str 21, Dex 14, Con 19, Int 16, Wis 19, Cha 18
Skills: Bluff +18, Concentration +19, Listen +13, Diplomacy +8, Disguise +4 (+6 acting), Intimidate +6, Sense Motive +18, Spellcraft +17, Spot +13
Feats: Alertness, Combat Casting, Dodge, Eschew Materials[B], Lightning Reflexes
Environment: Temperate plains
Organization: Solitary or nest (2–4)
Challenge Rating: 10
Treasure: Standard
Alignment: Usually lawful good
Advancement: 12–16 HD (Large); 17–33 HD (Huge)
Level Adjustment: —

This beautiful creature looks like a snake with a human face and green-gold scales. A golden frill runs from the top of its head to the tip of its tail. The sweet scent of flowers accompanies the creature.

Wise and good, guardian nagas often protect sacred places or maintain a lookout against evil deeds.

A guardian naga tends to raise its crest when it becomes angry.

Guardian nagas speak Celestial and Common.

Combat

Guardian nagas usually warn off intruders before attacking. If the warning is ignored, they may begin a spell assault or spit poison.

Poison (Ex): Injury or contact, Fortitude DC 19, initial and secondary damage 1d10 Con. The save DC is Constitution-based.

Spit (Ex): A guardian naga can spit its venom up to 30 feet as a

standard action. This is a ranged touch attack with no range increment. Opponents hit by this attack must make successful saves (see above) to avoid the effect.

Spells: Guardian nagas cast spells as 9th-level sorcerers, and can also cast spells from the cleric list and from the Good and Law domains. The cleric spells and domain spells are considered arcane spells for a guardian naga, meaning that the creature does not need a divine focus to cast them.

Typical Spells Known (6/7/7/7/5; save DC 14 + spell level): 0—*cure minor wounds, daze, detect magic, light, mage hand, open/close, ray of frost, read magic;* 1st—*cure light wounds, divine favor, expeditious retreat, mage armor, magic missile;* 2nd—*detect thoughts, lesser restoration, see invisibility, scorching ray;* 3rd—*cure serious wounds, dispel magic, lightning bolt;* 4th—*divine power, greater invisibility.*

SPIRIT NAGA

Large Aberration
Hit Dice: 9d8+36 (76 hp)
Initiative: +1
Speed: 40 ft. (8 squares)
Armor Class: 16 (–1 size, +1 Dex, +6 natural), touch 10, flat-footed 15
Base Attack/Grapple: +6/+14
Attack: Bite +9 melee (2d6+6 plus poison)
Full Attack: Bite +9 melee (2d6+6 plus poison)
Space/Reach: 10 ft./5 ft.
Special Attacks: Charming gaze, poison, spells
Special Qualities: Darkvision 60 ft.
Saves: Fort +7, Ref +6, Will +9
Abilities: Str 18, Dex 13, Con 18, Int 12, Wis 17, Cha 17
Skills: Concentration +13, Listen +14, Spellcraft +10, Spot +14
Feats: Ability Focus (charming gaze), Alertness, Combat Casting, Eschew Materials[B], Lightning Reflexes
Environment: Temperate marshes
Organization: Solitary or nest (2–4)
Challenge Rating: 9
Treasure: Standard
Alignment: Usually chaotic evil
Advancement: 10–13 HD (Large); 14–27 HD (Huge)
Level Adjustment: —

This loathsome serpent has a black body banded in swaths of bright crimson. Its head is vaguely human, with stringy hair. The odor of carrion hangs heavy in the air about it.

Spirit Naga

Spirit nagas are named for their habit of inhabiting ruined and dismal places; they are thoroughly evil and seek to do harm whenever they can.

Spirit nagas speak Abyssal and Common.

Combat

Spirit nagas meet foes boldly so as to use their gaze attacks to best effect. They quickly slither forward to bite foes that avert their eyes.

Charming Gaze (Su): As *charm person*, 30 feet, Will DC 19 negates. The save DC is Charisma-based.

Poison (Ex): Injury, Fortitude DC 18, initial and secondary damage 1d8 Con. The save DC is Constitution-based.

Spells: Spirit nagas cast spells as 7th-level sorcerers, and can also cast spells from the cleric spell list and from the Chaos and Evil domains as arcane spells. The cleric spells and domain spells are considered arcane spells for a spirit naga, meaning that the creature does not need a divine focus to cast them.

Typical Spells Known (6/7/7/5; save DC 13 + spell level): 0—*cure minor wounds, daze, detect magic, mage hand, open/close, ray of frost, read magic;* 1st—*charm person, cure light wounds, divine favor, magic missile, shield of faith;* 2nd—*cat's grace, invisibility, summon swarm;* 3rd—*displacement, fireball.*

WATER NAGA

Large Aberration (Aquatic)
Hit Dice: 7d8+28 (59 hp)
Initiative: +1
Speed: 30 ft. (6 squares), swim 50 ft.
Armor Class: 15 (–1 size, +1 Dex, +5 natural), touch 10, flat-footed 14
Base Attack/Grapple: +5/+12
Attack: Bite +7 melee (2d6+4 plus poison)
Full Attack: Bite +7 melee (2d6+4 plus poison)
Space/Reach: 10 ft./5 ft.
Special Attacks: Poison, spells
Special Qualities: Darkvision 60 ft.
Saves: Fort +6, Ref +5, Will +8
Abilities: Str 16, Dex 13, Con 18, Int 10, Wis 17, Cha 15
Skills: Concentration +12, Listen +7, Spellcraft +8, Spot +7, Swim +11
Feats: Alertness, Combat Casting, Eschew Materials[B], Lightning Reflexes
Environment: Temperate aquatic
Organization: Solitary, pair, or nest (3–4)
Challenge Rating: 7
Treasure: Standard
Alignment: Usually neutral
Advancement: 8–10 HD (Large); 11–21 HD (Huge)
Level Adjustment: —

This beautiful creature looks like a snake with a faintly human head and reticulated emerald-green patterns running the length of its body. Fiery red and orange spines jut from its backbone.

Water nagas often prove bad-tempered or mischievous, though they usually do not attack to kill unless they feel threatened.

A water naga's spines rise like hackles when the naga becomes angry.

Water nagas speak Aquan and Common.

Combat

Water nagas prefer to stay mostly concealed in a body of water while they launch a spell attack.

Poison (Ex): Injury, Fortitude DC 17, initial and secondary damage 1d8 Con. The save DC is Constitution-based.

Spells: Water nagas cast spells as 7th-level sorcerers but never use fire spells.

Typical Sorcerer Spells Known (6/7/7/4; save DC 12 + spell level): 0—*acid splash, daze, detect magic, light, mage hand, open/close, read magic;* 1st—*expeditious retreat, magic missile, obscuring mist, shield, true strike;* 2nd—*invisibility, Melf's acid arrow, mirror image;* 3rd—*protection from energy, suggestion.*

Skills: A water naga has a +8 racial bonus on any Swim check to perform some special action or avoid a hazard. It can always choose to take 10 on a Swim check, even if distracted or endangered. It can use the run action while swimming, provided it swims in a straight line.

NIGHT HAG

Medium Outsider (Evil, Extraplanar)
Hit Dice: 8d8+32 (68 hp)
Initiative: +1
Speed: 20 ft. (4 squares)
Armor Class: 22 (+1 Dex, +11 natural), touch 11, flat-footed 21
Base Attack/Grapple: +8/+12
Attack: Bite +12 melee (2d6+6 plus disease)
Full Attack: Bite +12 melee (2d6+6 plus disease)
Space/Reach: 5 ft./5 ft.
Special Attacks: Spell-like abilities, dream haunting
Special Qualities: Damage reduction 10/cold iron and magic, immunity to fire, cold, charm, *sleep*, and fear, spell resistance 25
Saves: Fort +12*, Ref +9*, Will +10*
Abilities: Str 19, Dex 12, Con 18, Int 11, Wis 15, Cha 12
Skills: Bluff +12, Concentration +15, Diplomacy +5, Disguise +1 (+3 acting), Intimidate +14, Listen +15, Ride +12, Sense Motive +13, Spellcraft +11, Spot +15
Feats: Alertness, Combat Casting, Mounted Combat
Environment: Gray Waste of Hades
Organization: Solitary, mounted (1, on nightmare), or covey (3, on nightmares)
Challenge Rating: 9
Treasure: Standard
Alignment: Always neutral evil
Advancement: 9–16 HD (Medium)
Level Adjustment: —

Night hag

This being looks like a hideously ugly human woman. Its flesh is the blue-violet of a deep bruise and covered with warts, blisters, and open sores. It has straggly jet-black hair and jagged, yellow teeth The eyes burn like hot coals, throwing out a thick, red radiance.

Merciless and utterly evil, night hags are creatures from the plane of Hades that constantly hunger for the flesh and souls of innocent men and women.

A night hag is about the same height and weight as a female human. Night hags speak Abyssal, Celestial, Common, and Infernal.

COMBAT

Night hags attack good creatures on sight if the odds of success seem favorable.

These creatures rip through armor and flesh with their deadly teeth. They love to use *sleep* and then strangle those who are overcome by it.

A night hag's natural weapons, as well as any weapons it wields, are treated as evil-aligned for the purpose of overcoming damage reduction. Its natural weapons are treated as magic weapons for the purpose of overcoming damage reduction.

Disease (Ex): Demon fever—bite, Fortitude DC 18, incubation period 1 day, damage 1d6 Con. Each day after the first, on a failed save, an afflicted creature must immediately succeed on another DC 18 Fortitude save or take 1 point of Constitution drain. The save DC is Constitution based.

Spell-Like Abilities: At will—*detect chaos, detect evil, detect good, detect law, detect magic, magic missile, polymorph* (self only), *ray of enfeeblement* (DC 12), *sleep* (DC 12). Caster level 8th. A night hag can use *etherealness* at will (caster level 16th) so long as it possesses its *heartstone* (see below). The save DCs are Charisma-based.

Dream Haunting (Su): Night hags can visit the dreams of chaotic or evil individuals by using a special periapt known as a *heartstone* to become ethereal, then hovering over the creature. Once a hag invades someone's dreams, it rides on the victim's back until dawn. The sleeper suffers from tormenting dreams and takes 1 point of Constitution drain upon awakening. Only another ethereal being can stop these nocturnal intrusions, by confronting and defeating the night hag.

HEARTSTONE

All night hags carry a periapt known as a *heartstone*, which instantly cures any disease contracted by the holder. In addition, a *heartstone* provides a +2 resistance bonus on all saving throws (this bonus is included in the statistics block). A night hag that loses this charm can no longer use *etherealness* until it can manufacture another (which takes one month). Creatures other than the hag can benefit from the *heartstone*'s powers, but the periapt shatters after ten uses (any disease cured or saving throw affected counts as a use) and it does not bestow *etherealness* to a bearer that is not a night hag. If sold, an intact *heartstone* brings 1,800 gp.

NIGHTMARE

At first glance, this creature looks like a large, powerful horse with a jet-black coat. A closer look, however, reveals its true nature. Flames wreathe its steely hooves, trail from its flared nostrils, and smolder in the depths of its dark eyes.

Nightmares are proud equine creatures with hearts as black and evil as the dark abysses from which they come. They dwell on the plane of Hades.

A nightmare is a wild and restless creature. It roams the world doing evil and haunting the dreams of all who dare cross it. Although it has no wings, the creature can fly with great speed. It seldom allows anyone to ride it, but particularly powerful and evil creatures have been known to make mounts of nightmares.

A nightmare is about the size of a light war horse.

COMBAT

A nightmare does battle by biting with its viperish fangs and kicking with its powerful legs. A nightmare can fight while carrying a rider, but the rider cannot also fight unless he or she succeeds on a Ride check.

	Nightmare Large Outsider (Evil, Extraplanar)	Nightmare, Cauchemar Huge Outsider (Evil, Extraplanar)
Hit Dice:	6d8+18 (45 hp)	15d8+105 (172 hp)
Initiative:	+6	+6
Speed:	40 ft. (8 squares), fly 90 ft. (good)	40 ft. (8 squares), fly 90 ft. (good)
Armor Class:	24 (−1 size, +2 Dex, +13 natural), touch 11, flat-footed 22	26 (−2 size, +2 Dex, +16 natural), touch 10, flat-footed 24
Base Attack/Grapple:	+6/+14	+15/+33
Attack:	Hoof +9 melee (1d8+4 plus 1d4 fire)	Hoof +23 melee (2d6+10 plus 1d4 fire)
Full Attack:	2 hooves +9 melee (1d8+4 plus 1d4 fire) and bite +4 melee (1d8+2)	2 hooves +23 melee (2d6+10 plus 1d4 fire) and bite +18 melee (2d6+5)
Space/Reach:	10 ft./5 ft.	15 ft./10 ft.
Special Attacks:	Flaming hooves, smoke	Flaming hooves, smoke
Special Qualities:	Astral projection, darkvision 60 ft., etherealness	Astral projection, darkvision 60 ft., etherealness
Saves:	Fort +8, Ref +7, Will +6	Fort +16, Ref +11, Will +10
Abilities:	Str 18, Dex 15, Con 16, Int 13, Wis 13, Cha 12	Str 31, Dex 14, Con 24, Int 16, Wis 12, Cha 12
Skills:	Concentration +12, Diplomacy +3, Intimidate +10, Knowledge (the planes) +10, Listen +12, Move Silently +11, Search +10, Sense Motive +10, Spot +12, Survival +10 (+12 on other planes and following tracks)	Bluff +19, Concentration +25, Diplomacy +5, Disguise +1 (+3 acting), Intimidate +21, Knowledge (arcana) +21, Knowledge (the planes) +21, Listen +21, Move Silently +20, Search +21, Sense Motive +19, Spot +21, Survival +19 (+21 on other planes and following tracks)
Feats:	Alertness, Improved Initiative, Run	Alertness, Cleave, Improved Initiative, Power Attack, Run, Track
Environment:	Gray Waste of Hades	Gray Waste of Hades
Organization:	Solitary	Solitary
Challenge Rating:	5	11
Treasure:	None	None
Alignment:	Always neutral evil	Always neutral evil
Advancement:	7–10 HD (Large); 11–18 HD (Huge)	—
Level Adjustment:	+4 (cohort)	+4 (cohort)

A nightmare's natural weapons, as well as any weapons it wields, are treated as evil-aligned for the purpose of overcoming damage reduction.

Flaming Hooves (Su): A blow from a nightmare's hooves sets combustible materials alight.

Smoke (Su): During the excitement of battle, a nightmare snorts and neighs with rage. This snorting fills a 15-foot cone with a hot, sulfurous smoke that chokes and blinds opponents. Anyone in the cone must succeed on a DC 16 Fortitude save or take a –2 penalty on all attack and damage rolls until 1d6 minutes after leaving the cone. The cone lasts 1 round, and the nightmare uses it once as a free action during its turn each round. The save DC is Constitution-based.

Because of the smoke it gives off, a nightmare has concealment against creatures 5 feet away and total concealment against creatures 10 feet or farther away. The smoke does not obscure the nightmare's vision at all.

Astral Projection and Etherealness (Su): These abilities function just like the spells of the same names (caster level 20th); a nightmare can use either at will.

Carrying Capacity: A light load for a nightmare is up to 300 pounds; a medium load, 301–600 pounds; and a heavy load, 601–900 pounds.

CAUCHEMAR

The cauchemar is a horrible, especially malevolent version of a nightmare. The sight of one of these great horrors bearing down is enough to shake the heart of the boldest champion.

Combat

The save DC for the cauchemar's smoke attack (DC 24) is adjusted for its greater number of Hit Dice and higher Constitution score.

Carrying Capacity: A light load for a cauchemar is up to 612 pounds; a medium load, 613–1,224 pounds; and a heavy load, 1,225–1,840 pounds.

NIGHTSHADE

Nightshades are powerful undead composed of equal parts darkness and absolute evil. Their chilling malevolence hangs heavily about them, along with the smell of an open grave on a winter's morning.

Nightshades can read and understand all forms of communication; however, they communicate with others by telepathy.

COMBAT

Each of the three known varieties of nightshade is a terrible creature with unique powers and abilities. Their tactics vary according to their abilities, but they all make liberal use of *haste*.

Nightshade Abilities

All nightshades have the following special abilities.

Aversion to Daylight (Ex): Nightshades are creatures of utter darkness and loathe all light. If exposed to natural daylight (not merely a *daylight* spell), they take a –4 penalty on all attack rolls, saving throws, and skill checks.

Desecrating Aura (Su): All nightshades give off a 20-foot-radius emanation of utter desecration, imbuing their surroundings with negative energy. This ability works much like a *desecrate* spell, except that the nightshade's evil is so great that it is treated as the shrine of an evil power. All undead within 20 feet of the nightshade (including the creature itself) gain a +2 profane bonus on attack rolls, damage rolls, and saving throws, and +2 hit points per HD. (The nightshade Hit Dice, attack, and save entries given here include these profane bonuses.) Charisma checks made to turn undead within this area take a –6 penalty.

A nightshade's desecrating aura cannot be dispelled except by a *dispel evil* spell or similar effect. If the effect is dispelled, the nightshade can resume it as a free action on its next turn. Its desecrating aura is suppressed if a nightshade enters a *consecrated* or *hallowed* area, but the nightshade's presence also suppresses the *consecrated* or *hallowed* effect for as long as it remains in the area.

Illus. by T. Lockwood

NIGHTCRAWLER

Gargantuan Undead (Extraplanar)
Hit Dice: 25d12+50 (212 hp)
Initiative: +4
Speed: 30 ft. (6 squares), burrow 60 ft.
Armor Class: 35 (–4 size, +29 natural), touch 6, flat-footed 35
Base Attack/Grapple: +12/+45
Attack: Bite +29 melee (4d6+21)
Full Attack: Bite +29 melee (4d6+21/19–20) and sting +24 melee (2d8+11/19–20 plus poison)
Space/Reach: 20 ft./15 ft.
Special Attacks: Desecrating aura, energy drain, spell-like abilities, poison, summon undead, swallow whole
Special Qualities: Aversion to daylight, damage reduction 15/silver and magic, darkvision 60 ft., immunity to cold, spell resistance 31, telepathy 100 ft., tremorsense 60 ft., undead traits
Saves: Fort +12, Ref +10, Will +23
Abilities: Str 48, Dex 10, Con —, Int 20, Wis 20, Cha 18
Skills: Concentration +32, Diplomacy +6, Hide +16, Knowledge (arcana) +33, Listen +33, Move Silently +28, Search +33, Sense Motive +23, Spellcraft +35, Spot +33, Survival +5 (+7 following tracks)
Feats: Blind-Fight, Combat Casting, Great Fortitude, Improved Critical (bite), Improved Critical (sting), Improved Initiative, Iron Will, Power Attack, Quicken Spell-Like Ability (*cone of cold*)
Environment: Plane of Shadow
Organization: Solitary or pair
Challenge Rating: 18
Treasure: Standard
Alignment: Always chaotic evil
Advancement: 26–50 HD (Colossal)
Level Adjustment: —

This creature looks like an immense worm covered with plates of dead black, chitinous armor. Its toothy maw is wider than a human is tall, and its teeth and gullet are black, too.

A nightcrawler is a massive behemoth similar to a purple worm, though utterly black in color.

A nightcrawler measures about 7 feet in diameter and is 100 feet long from its toothy maw to the tip of its stinging tail. It weighs about 55,000 pounds.

Combat

A nightcrawler attacks by burrowing through the ground and emerging to strike.

A nightcrawler's natural weapons are treated as magic weapons for the purpose of overcoming damage reduction.

Energy Drain (Su): Living creatures inside a nightcrawler's gizzard gain one negative level each round. The DC is 26 for the Fortitude save to remove a negative level. The save DC is Charisma-based. For each such negative level bestowed, the nightcrawler gains 5 temporary hit points.

Improved Grab (Ex): To use this ability, a nightcrawler must hit with its bite attack. It can then attempt to start a grapple as a free action without provoking an attack of opportunity. If it wins the grapple check, it establishes a hold and can try to swallow the opponent in the following round.

Poison (Ex): Injury, Fortitude DC 22, initial and secondary damage 2d6 Str. The save DC is Constitution-based.

Spell-Like Abilities: At will—*contagion* (DC 18), *deeper darkness, detect magic, greater dispel magic, haste, invisibility, see invisibility, unholy blight* (DC 18); 3/day—*cone of cold* (DC 19), *confusion* (DC 18), *hold monster* (DC 19); 1/day—*finger of death* (DC 21), *mass hold monster* (DC 23), *plane shift* (DC 21). Caster level 25th. The save DCs are Charisma-based.

Summon Undead (Su): A nightcrawler can summon undead creatures once per night: 9–16 shadows, 3–6 greater shadows, or 2–4 dread wraiths. The undead arrive in 1d10 rounds and serve for 1 hour or until released.

Swallow Whole (Ex): A nightcrawler can try to swallow a grabbed opponent of Huge or smaller size by making a successful grapple check. Once inside, the opponent takes 2d8+12 points of bludgeoning damage plus 12 points of acid damage per round from the nightcrawler's gizzard and is subject to the creature's energy drain. A swallowed creature can cut its way out by using a light slashing or piercing weapon to deal 35 points of damage to the gizzard (AC 21). Once the creature exits, muscular action closes the hole; another swallowed opponent must cut its own way out.

A nightcrawler's interior can hold 2 Huge, 8 Large, 32 Medium, 128 Small, 512 Tiny or smaller opponents.

NIGHTWALKER

Huge Undead (Extraplanar)
Hit Dice: 21d12+42 (178 hp)
Initiative: +6
Speed: 40 ft (8 squares)., fly 20 ft. (poor)
Armor Class: 32 (–2 size, +2 Dex, +22 natural), touch 10, flat-footed 30
Base Attack/Grapple: +10/+34
Attack: Slam +24 melee (2d6+16)
Full Attack: 2 slams +24 melee (2d6+16)
Space/Reach: 15 ft./15 ft.
Special Attacks: Crush item, desecrating aura, evil gaze, spell-like abilities, summon undead
Special Qualities: Aversion to daylight, damage reduction 15/silver and magic, darkvision 60 ft., immunity to cold, spell resistance 29, telepathy 100 ft., undead traits
Saves: Fort +11, Ref +11, Will +19
Abilities: Str 38, Dex 14, Con —, Int 20, Wis 20, Cha 18
Skills: Concentration +28, Diplomacy +6, Hide +18*, Knowledge (arcana) +29, Listen +29, Move Silently +26, Search +29, Sense Motive +29, Spellcraft +31, Spot +29, Survival +5 (+7 following tracks)
Feats: Cleave, Combat Expertise, Combat Reflexes, Great Fortitude, Improved Disarm, Improved Initiative, Power Attack, Quicken Spell-Like Ability (*unholy blight*)
Environment: Plane of Shadow
Organization: Solitary, pair, or gang (3–4)
Challenge Rating: 16
Treasure: Standard
Alignment: Always chaotic evil
Advancement: 22–31 HD (Huge); 32–42 HD (Gargantuan)
Level Adjustment: —

The creature looks like a humanoid giant, taller than a house and composed of pure darkness. It wears no clothing and has smooth, hairless skin and a genderless body.

Nightwalkers are human-shaped horrors that haunt the darkness.

A nightwalker is about 20 feet tall and weighs about 12,000 pounds.

Combat

Nightwalkers lurk in dark areas where they can almost always surprise the unwary.

A nightwalker's natural weapons are treated as magic weapons for the purpose of overcoming damage reduction.

Crush Item (Su): A nightwalker can destroy any weapon or item of Large size or smaller (even magic ones, but not artifacts) by picking it up and crushing it between its hands. The nightwalker must make a successful disarm attempt to grab an item held by an opponent. The item is entitled to a DC 34 Fortitude save to resist destruction. The save DC is Strength-based.

Evil Gaze (Su): Fear, 30 feet. A creature that meets the nightwalker's gaze must succeed on a DC 24 Will save or be paralyzed

Nightwalker

with fear for 1d8 rounds. Whether or not the save is successful, that creature cannot be affected again by the same nightshade's gaze for 24 hours. This is a mind-affecting fear effect. The save DC is Charisma-based.

Spell-Like Abilities: At will—*contagion* (DC 18), *deeper darkness, detect magic, greater dispel magic, haste, see invisibility*, and *unholy blight* (DC 18); 3/day—*confusion* (DC 18), *hold monster* (DC 19), *invisibility*; 1/day—*cone of cold* (DC 19), *finger of death* (DC 21), *plane shift* (DC 21). Caster level 21st. The save DCs are Charisma-based.

Summon Undead (Su): A nightwalker can summon undead creatures once per night: 7–12 shadows, 2–5 greater shadows, or 1–2 dread wraiths. The undead arrive in 1d10 rounds and serve for 1 hour or until released.

Skills: *When hiding in a dark area, a nightwalker gains a +8 racial bonus on Hide checks.

Tactics Round-by-Round

The nightwalker is an exceedingly intelligent foe that makes the best use of all its abilities. It favors using its spell-like abilities to divide and disable its enemies, then closing to melee with opponents it has isolated from their allies.

Prior to combat: The nightwalker keeps its *see invisibility* power active most of the time. It uses *haste* and *invisibility* to prepare for battle.

Round 1: Move to within 30 feet to make use of gaze attack and strike with *confusion* or *hold monster*, coupled with a quickened *unholy blight*.

Round 2: Hit a spellcaster with *finger of death* and another quickened *unholy blight*.

Round 3: Move up to engage the enemy and attempt to disarm an enemy fighter.

Round 4: Crush the disarmed weapon (or use gaze attack if disarm attempt failed).

Round 5: Full attack against the unarmed foe (or on a nearby spellcaster).

NIGHTWING

Huge Undead (Extraplanar)
Hit Dice: 17d12+34 (144 hp)
Initiative: +8
Speed: 20 ft. (4 squares), fly 60 ft. (good)
Armor Class: 30 (–2 size, +4 Dex, +18 natural) touch 12, flat-footed 26
Base Attack/Grapple: +8/+28
Attack: Bite +18 melee (2d6+17/19–20 plus magic drain)
Full Attack: Bite +18 melee (2d6+17/19–20 plus magic drain)
Space/Reach: 15 ft./10 ft.
Special Attacks: Desecrating aura, magic drain, spell-like abilities, summon undead
Special Qualities: Aversion to daylight, damage reduction 15/silver and magic, darkvision 60 ft., immunity to cold, spell resistance 27, telepathy 100 ft., undead traits
Saves: Fort +9, Ref +11, Will +17
Abilities: Str 31, Dex 18, Con —, Int 18, Wis 20, Cha 18
Skills: Concentration +24, Diplomacy +6, Hide +16*, Listen +25, Move Silently +24, Search +24, Sense Motive +25, Spellcraft +24, Spot +25, Survival +5 (+7 following tracks)
Feats: Combat Reflexes, Dodge, Flyby Attack, Great Fortitude, Improved Critical (bite), Improved Initiative
Environment: Plane of Shadow
Organization: Solitary, pair, or flock (3–6)
Challenge Rating: 14
Treasure: Standard
Alignment: Always chaotic evil
Advancement: 18–25 HD (Huge); 26–34 HD (Gargantuan)
Level Adjustment: —

The creature seems to be nothing but a mass of utter darkness shaped like a monstrous bat.

Nightwings are batlike flyers that hunt on the wing.

A nightwing has a wingspan of about 40 feet and weighs about 4,000 pounds.

Combat

Nightwings prowl the night sky and dive onto their victims. They are all but invisible, detectable only because of the stars they obscure in their passing.

A nightwing's natural weapons are treated as magic weapons for the purpose of overcoming damage reduction.

Magic Drain (Su): A nightwing can weaken magic armor, weapons, and shields by making a successful touch attack. The targeted item must succeed on a DC 22 Fortitude save or lose 1 point of its enhancement bonus (for example, a +2 *sword* becomes a +1 *sword*). The save DC is Charisma-based. An item that loses its entire enhancement bonus becomes merely a masterwork item and loses any special abilities (such as flaming) as well. Casting *dispel evil* upon the item reverses the effect of the magic drain, provided this occurs within a number of days after the attack equal to the caster's level and the caster succeeds on a DC 29 caster level check.

Spell-Like Abilities: At will—*contagion* (DC 18), *deeper darkness, detect magic, haste, see invisibility, unholy blight* (DC 18); 3/day—*confusion* (DC 18), *greater dispel magic, hold monster* (DC 19), *invisibility*; 1/day—*cone of cold* (DC 19), *finger of death* (DC 21), *plane shift* (DC 21). Caster level 17th. The save DCs are Charisma-based.

Summon Undead (Su): A nightwing can summon undead creatures once per night: 5–12 shadows, 2–4 greater shadows, or 1 dread wraith. The undead arrive in 1d10 rounds and serve for 1 hour or until released.

Skills: *When hiding in a dark area or flying in a dark sky, a nightwing gains a +8 racial bonus on Hide checks.

NYMPH

Medium Fey
Hit Dice: 6d6+6 (27 hp)
Initiative: +3
Speed: 30 ft. (6 squares), swim 20 ft.
Armor Class: 17 (+3 Dex, +4 deflection), touch 17, flat-footed 14
Base Attack/Grapple: +3/+3
Attack: Dagger +6 melee (1d4/19–20)
Full Attack: Dagger +6 melee (1d4/19–20)
Space/Reach: 5 ft./5 ft.
Special Attacks: Blinding beauty, spells, spell-like abilities, stunning glance
Special Qualities: Damage reduction 10/cold iron, low-light vision, unearthly grace, wild empathy
Saves: Fort +7, Ref +12, Will +12
Abilities: Str 10, Dex 17, Con 12, Int 16, Wis 17, Cha 19
Skills: Concentration +10, Diplomacy +6, Escape Artist +12, Handle Animal +13, Heal +12, Hide +12, Listen +12, Move Silently +12, Ride +5, Sense Motive +12, Spot +12, Swim +8, Use Rope +3 (+5 with bindings)
Feats: Combat Casting, Dodge, Weapon Finesse
Environment: Temperate forests
Organization: Solitary
Challenge Rating: 7
Treasure: Standard
Alignment: Usually chaotic good
Advancement: 7–12 HD (Medium)
Level Adjustment: +7

This being's beauty exceeds mere words; she is captivating and dangerous because of the emotions she inspires. She has long, copper hair, perfect skin, large eyes, and long, swept-back ears.

Nymphs are nature's embodiment of physical beauty, and the guardians of the sacred places of the wild. They are so unbearably lovely that even a glimpse of one can blind an onlooker. Nymphs hate evil and any who would despoil the wilds for any reason.

A nymph's demeanor is wild and mercurial. Like nature itself, she embodies both great beauty and fearsome danger. She can be kind and graceful to mortals who revere the wild places of the world, but is also quick to strike against mortals who take more than they need or who treat nature thoughtlessly. Animals of all types flock to a nymph, ignoring the presence of natural enemies; injured beasts know that the nymph will tend their wounds.

A nymph is about the height and weight of a female elf.

Nymphs speak Sylvan and Common.

COMBAT

A nymph usually avoids contact with nonfey, but she often has a place she holds sacred and defends against all intrusion—a grove, a pool, or sometimes a hilltop or peak. She uses her spells and animal allies to drive intruders away from the spot she defends, preferring to use nonlethal attacks first and resorting to deadly attacks only when faced by evil creatures or intruders who reply to her efforts with deadly attacks of their own.

Nymphs are better disposed toward elves, half-elves, and druids, individuals they recognize as friends of nature. They are likely to offer such people a chance to explain their presence instead of driving them away. Nymphs have also been known to aid good heroes who approach them in a courteous and respectful manner.

Blinding Beauty (Su): This ability affects all humanoids within 30 feet of a nymph. Those who look directly at a nymph must succeed on a DC 17 Fortitude save or be blinded permanently as though by the *blindness* spell. A nymph can suppress or resume this ability as a free action. The save DC is Charisma-based.

Spell-Like Abilities: 1/day—*dimension door*. Caster level 7th.

Spells: A nymph casts divine spells as a 7th-level druid.

Typical Druid Spells Prepared (6/5/4/3/1, save DC 13 + spell level): 0—*cure minor wounds, detect magic, flare, guidance, light, resistance;* 1st—*calm animal, cure light wounds, entangle, longstrider, speak with animals;* 2nd—*barkskin, heat metal, lesser restoration, tree shape;* 3rd—*call lightning, cure moderate wounds, protection from energy;* 4th—*rusting grasp.*

Stunning Glance (Su): As a standard action, a wrathful nymph can stun a creature within 30 feet with a look. The target creature

must succeed on a DC 17 Fortitude save or be stunned for 2d4 rounds. The save DC is Charisma-based.

Unearthly Grace (Su): A nymph adds her Charisma modifier as a bonus on all her saving throws, and as a deflection bonus to her Armor Class. (The statistics block already reflects these bonuses).

Wild Empathy (Ex): This power works like the druid's wild empathy class feature, except that a nymph has a +6 racial bonus on the check.

Skills: A nymph has a +8 racial bonus on any Swim check to perform some special action or avoid a hazard. She can always choose to take 10 on a Swim check, even if distracted or endangered. She can use the run action while swimming, provided she swims in a straight line.

Nymph

OGRE

This hulking brute appears to be at least 9 feet tall. It has a thick hide covered in dark, warty bumps, it wears smelly skins, and its hair is long, unkempt, and greasy.

Ogres are big, ugly, greedy creatures that live by raiding and scavenging. They join other monsters to prey on the weak and associate freely with ogre mages, giants, and trolls.

Lazy and bad-tempered, ogres solve problems by smashing them; what they can't smash, they either ignore or flee. Dwelling in small tribal groups, ogres occupy any convenient location and eat nearly anything they can catch, steal, or slay. Ogres sometimes accept mercenary service with other evil humanoids (including humans).

Adult ogres stand 9 to 10 feet tall and weigh 600 to 650 pounds. Their skin color ranges from dull yellow to dull brown. Their clothing consists of poorly cured furs and hides, which add to their naturally repellent odor.

Ogres speak Giant, and those specimens who boast Intelligence scores of at least 10 also speak Common.

Combat

Ogres favor overwhelming odds, sneak attacks, and ambushes over a fair fight. They are intelligent enough to fire ranged weapons first to soften up their foes before closing, but ogre gangs and bands fight as unorganized individuals.

OGRE BARBARIAN

Their inherent bent toward chaos combines with their size and strength to make ogres natural barbarians. Indeed, their leaders are almost always barbarians of low to middle level, monstrous brutes whose fury in battle is truly fearsome. A raging ogre barbarian is an inspiration to other ogres.

Combat

Marginally more intelligent than his brutish fellows, an ogre barbarian is slightly more likely to enter a fair fight, but in general prefers the brutish tactics common to all its kind.

Rage (Ex): Twice per day, an ogre barbarian can enter a state of fierce rage that last for 9 rounds. The following changes are in effect as long as he rages: AC 17 (touch 8, flat-footed 17); hp 95; Atk +18/+13 melee (2d6+16, +1 *greatclub*); SV Fort +14, Will +4; Str 30, Con 22; Climb +15, Jump +16. At the end of his rage, the ogre barbarian is fatigued for the duration of the encounter.

Trap Sense (Ex): An ogre barbarian has a +1 bonus on Reflex saves made to avoid traps. He also has a +1 bonus to his AC against attacks by traps.

Uncanny Dodge (Ex): An ogre barbarian retains his Dex bonus to AC regardless of being caught flat-footed or attacked by an invisible opponent. His Dex bonus to AC is +0, but this means that he is not subject to a rogue's sneak attack in these circumstances.

MERROW

These cousins of the ogre have the aquatic subtype. They dwell in freshwater lakes and rivers. They have a base land speed of 30 feet and a swim speed of 40 feet and are found only in aquatic environments. Instead of the typical ogre's greatclub, they prefer to use longspears in melee (attack +8 melee, damage 1d8+7).

Ogre

OGRES AS CHARACTERS

Most exceptional ogres are barbarians or fighters.

Ogre characters possess the following racial traits.

— +10 Strength, –2 Dexterity, +4 Constitution, –4 Intelligence, –4 Charisma.

—Large size. –1 penalty to Armor Class, –1 penalty on attack rolls, –4 penalty on Hide checks, +4 bonus on grapple checks, lifting and carrying limits double those of Medium characters.

—Space/Reach: 10 feet/10 feet.

—An ogre's base land speed is 40 feet.

—Darkvision out to 60 feet.

—Racial Hit Dice: An ogre begins with four levels of giant, which provide 4d8 Hit Dice, a base attack bonus of +3, and base saving throw bonuses of Fort +4, Ref +1, and Will +1.

—Racial Skills: An ogre's giant levels give it skill points equal to 7 × (2 + Int modifier, minimum 1). Its class skills are Climb, Listen, and Spot.

—Racial Feats: An ogre's giant levels give it two feats.

—Weapon and Armor Proficiency: An ogre is automatically proficient with simple weapons, martial weapons, light and medium armor, and shields.

— +5 natural armor bonus.

	Ogre	Ogre, 4th-Level Barbarian
	Large Giant	Large Giant
Hit Dice:	4d8+11 (29 hp)	4d8+19 plus 4d12+16 (79 hp)
Initiative:	–1	+0
Speed:	30 ft. in hide armor (6 squares); base speed 40 ft.	40 ft. in hide armor (8 squares); base speed 50 ft.
Armor Class:	16 (–1 size, –1 Dex, +5 natural, +3 hide armor), touch 8, flat-footed 16	19 (–1 size, +5 natural, +4 *+1 hide armor, ring of protection +1*), touch 10, flat-footed 19
Base Attack/Grapple:	+3/+12	+7/+19
Attack:	Greatclub +8 melee (2d8+7) or javelin +1 ranged (1d8+5)	+1 *greatclub* +16 melee (2d8+13) or javelin +6 ranged (1d8+8)
Full Attack:	Greatclub +8 melee (2d8+7) or javelin +1 ranged (1d8+5)	+1 *greatclub* +16/+11 melee (2d8+13) or javelin +6 ranged (1d8+8)
Space/Reach:	10 ft./10 ft.	10 ft./10 ft.
Special Attacks:	—	Rage 2/day
Special Qualities:	Darkvision 60 ft., low-light vision	Darkvision 60 ft., low-light vision, trap sense +1, uncanny dodge
Saves:	Fort +6, Ref +0, Will +1	Fort +12, Ref +2, Will +2
Abilities:	Str 21, Dex 8, Con 15, Int 6, Wis 10, Cha 7	Str 26, Dex 11, Con 18, Int 8, Wis 10, Cha 4
Skills:	Climb +5, Listen +2, Spot +2	Climb +13, Hide –6, Jump +17, Listen +6, Spot +2
Feats:	Toughness, Weapon Focus (greatclub)	Power Attack, Toughness, Weapon Focus (greatclub)
Environment:	Temperate hills (Merrow: Temperate aquatic)	Temperate hills
Organization:	Solitary, pair, gang (3–4), or band (5–8)	Solitary, pair, gang (1 plus 1–3 ogres), or band (1 plus 4–7 ogres)
Challenge Rating:	3	7
Treasure:	Standard	Standard (including +1 hide armor, +1 greatclub, and ring of protection +1)
Alignment:	Usually chaotic evil	Usually chaotic evil
Advancement:	By character class	By character class
Level Adjustment:	+2	+2

—Automatic Languages: Common, Giant. Bonus Languages: Dwarven, Orc, Goblin, Terran.
—Favored Class: Barbarian.
—Level adjustment +2.

OGRE MAGE

Large Giant
Hit Dice: 5d8+15 (37 hp)
Initiative: +4
Speed: 40 ft. (8 squares), fly 40 ft. (good)
Armor Class: 18 (–1 size, +5 natural, +4 chain shirt), touch 9, flat-footed 18
Base Attack/Grapple: +3/+12
Attack: Greatsword +7 melee (3d6+7/19–20) or longbow +2 ranged (2d6/×3)
Full Attack: Greatsword +7 melee (3d6+7/19–20) or longbow +2 ranged (2d6/×3)
Space/Reach: 10 ft./10 ft.
Special Attacks: Spell-like abilities
Special Qualities: Darkvision 90 ft., low-light vision, regeneration 5, spell resistance 19
Saves: Fort +7, Ref +1, Will +3
Abilities: Str 21, Dex 10, Con 17, Int 14, Wis 14, Cha 17
Skills: Concentration +11, Listen +10, Spellcraft +10, Spot +10
Feats: Combat Expertise, Improved Initiative
Environment: Cold hills
Organization: Solitary, pair, or troupe (1–2 plus 2–4 ogres)
Challenge Rating: 8
Treasure: Double standard
Alignment: Usually lawful evil
Advancement: By character class
Level Adjustment: +7

This creature looks like a big, demonic human. It has green skin, dark hair, and a pair of short ivory horns protruding from its forehead. The eyes are dark with strikingly white pupils, and its teeth and claws are jet black.

The ogre mage is a more intelligent and dangerous variety of its mundane cousin. Rapacious and cruel by nature, ogre mages often lead organized raids for slaves, treasure, and food.

These creatures dwell in fortified structures or underground lairs, usually living alone or with a small group of ogre followers. Status among ogre mages is measured by wealth. While they do not generally associate with their own kind, they often undertake raids and schemes in competition with one another to amass the most riches.

An ogre mage stands about 10 feet tall and weighs up to 700 pounds. Its skin varies in color from light green to light blue, and its hair is black or very dark brown. Ogre mages favor loose, comfortable clothing and lightweight armor.

Ogre mages speak Giant and Common.

Combat

Ogre mages rely on their spell-like abilities, resorting to physical combat only when necessary. When faced with obviously superior forces, they prefer to retreat using *gaseous form* rather than fight a losing battle. Ogre mages hold deep, abiding grudges, however, and the unwise person who crosses one would do well to keep looking over one's shoulder.

Spell-Like Abilities: At will—*darkness, invisibility;* 1/day—*charm person* (DC 14), *cone of cold* (DC 18), *gaseous form, polymorph, sleep* (DC 14). Caster level 9th. The save DCs are Charisma-based.

Flight (Su): An ogre mage can cease or resume flight as a free action. While using *gaseous form* it can fly at its normal speed and has perfect maneuverability.

Regeneration (Ex): Fire and acid deal normal damage to an ogre mage.

Ogre mage

An ogre mage that loses a limb or body part can reattach it by holding the severed member to the stump. Reattachment takes 1 minute. If the head or some other vital organ is severed, it must be reattached within 10 minutes or the creature dies. An ogre mage cannot regrow lost body parts.

OGRE MAGES AS CHARACTERS

Ogre mage characters possess the following racial traits.

— +10 Strength, +6 Constitution, +4 Intelligence, +4 Wisdom, +6 Charisma.

—Large size. –1 penalty to Armor Class, –1 penalty on attack rolls, –4 penalty on Hide checks, +4 bonus on grapple checks, lifting and carrying limits double those of Medium characters.

—Space/Reach: 10 feet/10 feet.

—An ogre mage's base land speed is 40 feet. It also has a fly speed of 40 feet (good).

—Darkvision: Ogre mages can see in the dark up to 60 feet.

—Racial Hit Dice: An ogre mage begins with five levels of giant, which provide 5d8 Hit Dice, a base attack bonus of +3, and base saving throw bonuses of Fort +4, Ref +1, and Will +1.

—Racial Skills: An ogre mage's giant levels give it skill points equal to 8 × (2 + Int modifier [minimum 1]). Its class skills are Concentration, Listen, Spellcraft, and Spot.

—Racial Feats: An ogre mage's giant levels give it two feats.

— +5 natural armor bonus..

—Special Attacks (see above): Spell-like abilities.

—Special Qualities (see above): Regeneration 5, spell resistance 19.

—Automatic Languages: Common, Giant. Bonus Languages: Dwarven, Goblin, Infernal, Orc.

—Favored Class: Sorcerer.

—Level adjustment +7.

OOZE

Oozes are amorphous creatures that live only to eat. They inhabit underground areas throughout the world, scouring caverns, ruins, and dungeons in search of organic matter—living or dead.

COMBAT

Oozes attack any creatures they encounter. They lash out with pseudopods or simply engulf opponents with their bodies, which secrete acids that help them catch or digest their prey.

Blindsight (Ex): An ooze's entire body is a primitive sensory organ that can ascertain prey by scent and vibration within 60 feet.

BLACK PUDDING

This creature resembles nothing so much as a roundish blob of inky black goo.

Black puddings slither and undulate along underground terrain seeking sustenance.

The typical black pudding measures 15 feet across and 2 feet thick. It weighs about 18,000 pounds.

Combat

A black pudding attacks by grabbing and squeezing their prey.

Acid (Ex): The creature secretes a digestive acid that dissolves organic material and metal quickly, but does not affect stone. Any melee hit or constrict attack deals acid damage, and the opponent's armor and clothing dissolve and become useless immediately unless they succeed on DC 21 Reflex saves. A metal or wooden weapon that strikes a black pudding also dissolves immediately unless it succeeds on a DC 21 Reflex save. The save DCs are Constitution-based.

The pudding's acidic touch deals 21 points of damage per round to wooden or metal objects, but the ooze must remain in contact with the object for 1 full round to deal this damage.

Constrict (Ex): A black pudding deals automatic slam and acid damage with a successful grapple check. The opponent's clothing and armor take a –4 penalty on Reflex saves against the acid.

Improved Grab (Ex): To use this ability, a black pudding must hit with its slam attack. It can then attempt to start a grapple as a free action without provoking an attack of opportunity. If it wins the grapple check, it establishes a hold and can constrict.

Split (Ex): Slashing and piercing weapons deal no damage to a black pudding. Instead the creature splits into two identical puddings, each with half of the original's current hit points (round down). A pudding with 10 hit points or less cannot be further split and dies if reduced to 0 hit points.

Skills: A black pudding has a +8 racial bonus on Climb checks and can always choose to take 10 on a Climb check, even if rushed or threatened.

ELDER BLACK PUDDING

The most ancient black puddings are vast pools of inky death.

Gelatinous cube

Combat

The save DC for the elder black pudding's acid attack (DC 29) is adjusted for its additional Hit Dice and higher Constitution score.

GELATINOUS CUBE

Huge Ooze
Hit Dice: 4d10+32 (54 hp)
Initiative: –5
Speed: 15 ft. (3 squares)
Armor Class: 3 (–2 size, –5 Dex), touch 3, flat-footed 3
Base Attack/Grapple: +3/+11
Attack: Slam +1 melee (1d6 plus 1d6 acid)

Illus. by T. Lockwood

	Black Pudding Huge Ooze	Elder Black Pudding Gargantuan Ooze
Hit Dice:	10d10+60 (115 hp)	20d10+180 (290 hp)
Initiative:	–5	–5
Speed:	20 ft. (4 squares), climb 20 ft.	20 ft. (4 squares), climb 20 ft.
Armor Class:	3 (–2 size, –5 Dex), touch 3, flat-footed 3	1 (–4 size, –5 Dex), touch 1, flat-footed 1
Base Attack/Grapple:	+7/+18	+15/+35
Attack:	Slam +8 melee (2d6+4 plus 2d6 acid)	Slam +19 melee (3d6+12 plus 3d6 acid)
Full Attack:	Slam +8 melee (2d6+4 plus 2d6 acid)	Slam +19 melee (3d6+12 plus 3d6 acid)
Space/Reach:	15 ft./10 ft.	20 ft./20 ft.
Special Attacks:	Acid, constrict 2d6+4 plus 2d6 acid, improved grab	Acid, constrict 2d8+12 plus 2d6 acid, improved grab
Special Qualities:	Blindsight 60 ft., split, ooze traits	Blindsight 60 ft., split, ooze traits
Saves:	Fort +9, Ref –2, Will –2	Fort +15, Ref +1, Will +1
Abilities:	Str 17, Dex 1, Con 22, Int —, Wis 1, Cha 1	Str 26, Dex 1, Con 28, Int —, Wis 1, Cha 1
Skills:	Climb +11	Climb +16
Feats:	—	—
Environment:	Underground	Underground
Organization:	Solitary	Solitary
Challenge Rating:	7	12
Treasure:	None	None
Alignment:	Always neutral	Always neutral
Advancement:	11–15 HD (Huge); 16–30 HD (Gargantuan)	—
Level Adjustment:	—	—

OOZE

Full Attack: Slam +1 melee (1d6 plus 1d6 acid)
Space/Reach: 15 ft./10 ft.
Special Attacks: Acid, engulf, paralysis
Special Qualities: Blindsight 60 ft., immunity to electricity, ooze traits, transparent
Saves: Fort +9, Ref –4, Will –4
Abilities: Str 10, Dex 1, Con 26, Int —, Wis 1, Cha 1
Skills: —
Feats: —
Environment: Underground
Organization: Solitary
Challenge Rating: 3
Treasure: 1/10th coins, 50% goods (no nonmetal or nonstone), 50% items (no nonmetal or nonstone)
Alignment: Always neutral
Advancement: 5–12 HD (Huge); 13–24 HD (Gargantuan)
Level Adjustment: —

This creature looks like a thick wall of quivering, transparent protoplasm.

The nearly transparent gelatinous cube travels slowly along dungeon corridors and cave floors, absorbing carrion, creatures, and trash. Inorganic material remains trapped and visible inside the cube's body.

A typical gelatinous cube is 15 feet on a side and weighs about 50,000 pounds, though much larger specimens are not unknown.

Combat

A gelatinous cube attacks by slamming its body into its prey. It is capable of lashing out with a pseudopod, but usually engulfs foes.

Acid (Ex): A gelatinous cube's acid does not harm metal or stone.

Engulf (Ex): Although it moves slowly, a gelatinous cube can simply mow down Large or smaller creatures as a standard action. It cannot make a slam attack during a round in which it engulfs. The gelatinous cube merely has to move over the opponents, affecting as many as it can cover. Opponents can make opportunity attacks against the cube, but if they do so they are not entitled to a saving throw. Those who do not attempt attacks of opportunity must succeed on a DC 13 Reflex save or be engulfed; on a success, they are pushed back or aside (opponent's choice) as the cube moves forward. Engulfed creatures are subject to the cube's paralysis and acid, and are considered to be grappled and trapped within its body. The save DC is Strength-based and includes a +1 racial bonus.

Paralysis (Ex): A gelatinous cube secretes an anesthetizing slime. A target hit by a cube's melee or engulf attack must succeed on a DC 20 Fortitude save or be paralyzed for 3d6 rounds. The cube can automatically engulf a paralyzed opponent. The save DC is Constitution-based.

Transparent (Ex): Gelatinous cubes are hard to see, even under ideal conditions, and it takes a DC 15 Spot check to notice one. Creatures who fail to notice a cube and walk into it are automatically engulfed.

GRAY OOZE

Medium Ooze
Hit Dice: 3d10+15 (31 hp)
Initiative: –5
Speed: 10 ft. (2 squares)
Armor Class: 5 (–5 Dex), touch 5, flat-footed 5
Base Attack/Grapple: +2/+3
Attack: Slam +3 melee (1d6+1 plus 1d6 acid)
Full Attack: Slam +3 melee (1d6+1 plus 1d6 acid)
Space/Reach: 5 ft./5 ft.
Special Attacks: Acid, constrict 1d6+1 plus 1d6 acid, improved grab

Special Qualities: Blindsight 60 ft., immunity to cold and fire, ooze traits, transparent
Saves: Fort +6, Ref –4, Will –4
Abilities: Str 12, Dex 1, Con 21, Int —, Wis 1, Cha 1
Skills: —
Feats: —
Environment: Cold marshes
Organization: Solitary
Challenge Rating: 4
Treasure: None
Alignment: Always neutral
Advancement: 4–6 HD (Medium); 7–9 HD (Large)
Level Adjustment: —

What seemed to be just a puddle of water is in fact a slimy horror that moves and flows like some giant protozoan.

A gray ooze appears to be a harmless puddle of water, a patch of wet sand, or a section of damp stone—until it moves or strikes.

A gray ooze can grow to a diameter of up to 10 feet and a thickness of about 6 inches. A typical specimen weighs about 700 pounds.

Combat

A gray ooze strikes like a snake, slamming opponents with its body.

Acid (Ex): A gray ooze secretes a digestive acid that quickly dissolves organic material and metal, but not stone. Any melee hit or constrict attack deals acid damage. Armor or clothing dissolves and becomes useless immediately unless it succeeds on a DC 16 Reflex save. A metal or wooden weapon that strikes a gray ooze also dissolves immediately unless it succeeds on a DC 16 Reflex save. The save DCs are Constitution-based.

The ooze's acidic touch deals 16 points of damage per round to wooden or metal objects, but the ooze must remain in contact with the object for 1 full round to deal this damage.

Constrict (Ex): A gray ooze deals automatic slam and acid damage with a successful grapple check. The opponent's clothing and armor take a –4 penalty on Reflex saves against the acid.

Improved Grab (Ex): To use this ability, a gray ooze must hit with its slam attack. It can then attempt to start a grapple as a free action without provoking an attack of opportunity. If it wins the grapple check, it establishes a hold and can constrict.

Transparent (Ex): A gray ooze is hard to identify, even under ideal conditions, and it takes a DC 15 Spot check to notice one. Creatures who fail to notice a gray ooze and walk into it are automatically hit with a melee attack for slam and acid damage.

OCHRE JELLY

Large Ooze
Hit Dice: 6d10+36 (69 hp)
Initiative: –5
Speed: 10 ft. (2 squares), climb 10 ft.
Armor Class: 4 (–1 size, –5 Dex), touch 4, flat-footed 4
Base Attack/Grapple: +4/+10
Attack: Slam +5 melee (2d4+3 plus 1d4 acid)
Full Attack: Slam +5 melee (2d4+3 plus 1d4 acid)
Space/Reach: 10 ft./5 ft.
Special Attacks: Acid, constrict 2d4+3 plus 1d4 acid, improved grab
Special Qualities: Blindsight 60 ft., split, ooze traits
Saves: Fort +8, Ref –3, Will –3
Abilities: Str 15, Dex 1, Con 22, Int —, Wis 1, Cha 1
Skills: Climb +10
Feats: —
Environment: Temperate marshes
Organization: Solitary

Challenge Rating: 5

Treasure: None

Alignment: Always neutral

Advancement: 7–9 HD (Large); 10–18 HD (Huge)

Level Adjustment: —

This creature resembles a giant, dark yellow amoeba.

An ochre jelly seeps along floors, walls, and ceilings with ease, squeezing its malleable body under doors and through cracks in search of meals.

An ochre jelly can grow to a diameter of about 15 feet and a thickness of about 6 inches, but can compress its body to fit into cracks as small as 1 inch wide. A typical specimen weighs about 5,600 pounds.

Combat

An ochre jelly attempts to envelop and squeeze its prey.

Acid (Ex): An ochre jelly secretes a digestive acid that dissolves only flesh. Any melee hit or constrict attack deals acid damage.

Constrict (Ex): An ochre jelly deals automatic slam and acid damage with a successful grapple check.

Improved Grab (Ex): To use this ability, an ochre jelly must hit with its slam attack. It can then attempt to start a grapple as a free action without provoking an attack of opportunity. If it wins the grapple check, it establishes a hold and can constrict.

Split (Ex): Slashing and piercing weapons and electricity attacks deal no damage to an ochre jelly. Instead the creature splits into two identical jellies, each with half of the original's current hit points (round down). A jelly with 10 hit points or less cannot be further split and dies if reduced to 0 it points.

Skills: An ochre jelly has a +8 racial bonus on Climb checks and can always choose to take 10 on a Climb check, even if rushed or threatened.

ORC

Orc, 1st-Level Warrior

Medium Humanoid (Orc)

Hit Dice: 1d8+1 (5 hp)

Initiative: +0

Speed: 30 ft. (6 squares)

Armor Class: 13 (+3 studded leather armor), touch 10, flat-footed 13

Base Attack/Grapple: +1/+4

Attack: Falchion +4 melee (2d4+4/18–20) or javelin +1 ranged (1d6+3)

Full Attack: Falchion +4 melee (2d4+4/18–20) or javelin +1 ranged (1d6+3)

Space/Reach: 5 ft./5 ft.

Special Attacks: —

Special Qualities: Darkvision 60 ft., light sensitivity

Saves: Fort +3, Ref +0, Will –2

Abilities: Str 17, Dex 11, Con 12, Int 8, Wis 7, Cha 6

Skills: Listen +1, Spot +1

Feats: Alertness

Environment: Temperate hills

Organization: Gang (2–4), squad (11–20 plus 2 3rd-level sergeants and 1 leader of 3rd–6th level), or band (30–100 plus 150% noncombatants plus 1 3rd-level sergeant per 10 adults, 5 5th-level lieutenants, and 3 7th-level captains)

Challenge Rating: 1/2

Treasure: Standard

Alignment: Often chaotic evil

Advancement: By character class

Level Adjustment: +0

This creature looks like a primitive human with gray skin and coarse hair. It has a stooped posture, low forehead, and a piglike face with prominent lower canines that resemble a boar's tusks.

Orcs are aggressive humanoids that raid, pillage, and battle other creatures. They have a hatred of elves and dwarves that began generations ago, and often kill such creatures on sight.

An orc's hair usually is black. It has lupine ears and reddish eyes. Orcs prefer wearing vivid colors that many humans would consider unpleasant, such as blood red, mustard yellow, yellow-green, and deep purple. Their equipment is dirty and unkempt. An adult male orc is a little over 6 feet tall and weighs about 210 pounds. Females are slightly smaller.

When not actually fighting other creatures, orcs are usually planning raids or practicing their fighting skills.

The language an orc speaks varies slightly from tribe to tribe, but any orc is understandable by someone else who speaks Orc. Some orcs know Goblin or Giant as well.

Most orcs encountered away from their homes are warriors; the information in the statistics block is for one of 1st level.

COMBAT

Orcs are proficient with all simple weapons, preferring those that cause the most damage in the least time. Many orcs who take up the warrior or fighter class also gain proficiency with the falchion or the greataxe as a martial weapon. They enjoy attacking from concealment and setting ambushes, and they obey the rules of war (such as honoring a truce) only as long as it is convenient for them.

Light Sensitivity (Ex): Orcs are dazzled in bright sunlight or within the radius of a *daylight* spell.

Orc

ORC SOCIETY

Orcs believe that to survive, they must conquer as much territory as possible, which puts them at odds with all intelligent creatures that live near them. They are constantly warring with or preparing to war with other humanoids, including other orc tribes. They can ally with other humanoids for a time but quickly rebel if not commanded by orcs. Their deities teach them that all other beings are inferior and that all worldly goods rightfully belong to the orcs, having been stolen by the others. Orc spellcasters are ambitious, and rivalries between them and warrior leaders sometimes tear a tribe apart.

Orc society is patriarchal: Females are prized possessions at best and chattel at worst. Male orcs pride themselves on the number of females they own and male children they sire, as well as their battle prowess, wealth, and amount of territory. They wear their battle scars proudly and ritually scar themselves to mark significant achievements and turning points in their lives.

An orc lair may be a cave, a series of wooden huts, a fort, or even a large city built above and below ground. A tribe includes females (as many as there are males), young (half as many as there are females), and slaves (about one for every ten males).

The chief orc deity is Gruumsh, a one-eyed god who tolerates no sign of peaceability among his people.

ORCS AS CHARACTERS

Orc leaders tend to be barbarians. Orc clerics worship Gruumsh. An orc cleric has access to two of the following domains: Chaos, Evil, Strength, or War (favored weapon: any spear). Most orc spellcasters are adepts. Orc adepts favor spells that deal damage.

Orc Traits (Ex): Orcs possess the following racial traits.

— +4 Strength, –2 Intelligence, –2 Wisdom, –2 Charisma.

—An orc's base land speed is 30 feet.

—Darkvision out to 60 feet.

—Light Sensitivity: Orcs are dazzled in bright sunlight or within the radius of a *daylight* spell.

—Automatic Languages: Common, Orc. Bonus Languages: Dwarven, Giant, Gnoll, Goblin, Undercommon.

—Favored Class: Barbarian.

The orc warrior presented here had the following ability scores before racial adjustments: Str 13, Dex 11, Con 12, Int 10, Wis 9, Cha 8.

HALF-ORCS

These orc–human crossbreeds can be found in either orc or human society (where their status varies according to local sentiments), or in communities of their own. Half-orcs usually inherit a good blend of the physical characteristics of their parents. They are as tall as humans and a little heavier, thanks to their muscle. They have greenish pigmentation, sloping foreheads, jutting jaws, prominent teeth, and coarse body hair. Half-orcs who have lived among or near orcs have scars, in keeping with orcish tradition.

Half-Orc Traits (Ex): Half-orcs possess the following racial traits.

— +2 Strength, –2 Intelligence, –2 Charisma.

—Medium size.

—A half-orc's base land speed is 30 feet.

—Darkvision: Half-orcs can see in the dark up to 60 feet.

—Orc Blood: For all effects related to race, a half-orc is considered an orc. Half-orcs, for example, are just as vulnerable to special effects that affect orcs as their orc ancestors are, and they can use magic items that are only usable by orcs.

—Automatic Languages: Common, Orc. Bonus Languages: Draconic, Giant, Gnoll, Goblin, Abyssal.

—Favored Class: Barbarian.

OTYUGH

Large Aberration
Hit Dice: 6d8+9 (36 hp)
Initiative: +0
Speed: 20 ft. (4 squares)
Armor Class: 17 (–1 size, +8 natural), touch 9, flat-footed 17
Base Attack/Grapple: +4/+8
Attack: Tentacle +4 melee (1d6)
Full Attack: 2 tentacles +4 melee (1d6) and bite –2 melee (1d4)
Space/Reach: 10 ft./10 ft. (15 ft. with tentacle)
Special Attacks: Constrict 1d6, disease, improved grab
Special Qualities: Darkvision 60 ft., scent
Saves: Fort +3, Ref +2, Will +6
Abilities: Str 11, Dex 10, Con 13, Int 5, Wis 12, Cha 6
Skills: Hide –1*, Listen +6, Spot +6
Feats: Alertness, Toughness, Weapon Focus (tentacle)
Environment: Underground
Organization: Solitary, pair, or cluster (3–4)
Challenge Rating: 4
Treasure: Standard
Alignment: Usually neutral
Advancement: 7–8 HD (Large); 9–18 HD (Huge)
Level Adjustment: —

This creature looks like a bloated ovoid covered with a rocklike skin. A vinelike stalk about 2 feet long rises from the top of the disgusting body and bears the two eyes. Its mouth—little more than a wide gash filled with razor-sharp teeth—is in the center of the mass. The creature shuffles about on three thick, sturdy legs and has two long tentacles covered in rough, thorny protrusions. The tentacles end in leaflike appendages covered in more thorny growths.

Otyugh

Illus. by T. Lockwood

Otyughs are grotesque subterranean monsters that lurk within heaps of refuse. Although primarily scavengers that can eat almost any kind of refuse, they never object to a meal of fresh meat when the opportunity presents itself.

An otyugh spend most of its time within its lair, which it keeps filled with carrion, offal, and all manner of similar trash. An otyugh usually covers itself with this vile stuff, leaving only its sensory stalk exposed (the stack also carries the otyugh's olfactory organ) and lies there for hours, shoveling food into its mouth. Intelligent subterranean beings sometimes coexist with otyughs, which they regard as convenient garbage disposals: They dump their refuse in the lair of the otyugh, which generally refrains from attacking them.

A typical otyugh has a body 8 feet in diameter and weighs about 500 pounds.

Otyughs speak Common.

COMBAT

An otyugh attacks living creatures if it feels threatened or if it is hungry; otherwise it is content to remain hidden. Otyughs slash and squeeze opponents with their tentacles, which they also use to drag prey into their mouths.

Constrict (Ex): An otyugh deals automatic tentacle damage with a successful grapple check.

Disease (Ex): Filth fever—bite, Fortitude DC 14, incubation period 1d3 days; damage 1d3 Dex and 1d3 Con. The save DC is Constitution-based.

Improved Grab (Ex): To use this ability, an otyugh must hit with a tentacle attack. It can then attempt to start a grapple as a free action without provoking an attack of opportunity. If it wins the grapple check, it establishes a hold and can constrict.

Skills: *An otyugh has a +8 racial bonus on Hide checks when in its lair, due to its natural coloration.

OWL, GIANT

Large Magical Beast
Hit Dice: 4d10+4 (26 hp)
Initiative: +3
Speed: 10 ft. (2 squares), fly 70 ft. (average)
Armor Class: 15 (–1 size, +3 Dex, +3 natural), touch 12, flat-footed 12
Base Attack/Grapple: +4/+12
Attack: Claw +7 melee (1d6+4)
Full Attack: 2 claws +7 melee (1d6+4) and bite +2 melee (1d8+2)
Space/Reach: 10 ft./5 ft.
Special Attacks: —
Special Qualities: Superior low-light vision
Saves: Fort +5, Ref +7, Will +3
Abilities: Str 18, Dex 17, Con 12, Int 10, Wis 14, Cha 10
Skills: Knowledge (nature) +2, Listen +17, Move Silently +8*, Spot +10
Feats: Alertness, Wingover
Environment: Temperate forests
Organization: Solitary, pair, or company (3–5)

Challenge Rating: 3
Treasure: None
Alignment: Usually neutral good
Advancement: 5–8 HD (Large); 9–12 HD (Huge)
Level Adjustment: +2 (cohort)

Giant owls are nocturnal birds of prey, feared for their ability to hunt and attack in near silence. They are intelligent, and though naturally suspicious, sometimes associate with good creatures.

They attack creatures that appear threatening, especially those intent on raiding the owls' nest for eggs or fledglings, which fetch a handsome price in many civilized areas. Young owls can be trained and are prized as aerial mounts.

A typical giant owl stands about 9 feet tall, has a wingspan of up to 20 feet, and resembles its smaller cousins in nearly every way except size.

Giant owls speak Common and Sylvan.

COMBAT

A giant owl attacks by gliding silently just a few feet above its prey and plunging to strike when directly overhead.

A solitary giant owl is typically hunting or patrolling in the vicinity of its nest and generally ignores creatures that do not appear threatening. A mated pair of giant owls will attack in concert and fight to the death to defend their nest. Several giant owls sometimes operate as a company for some specific purpose, such as driving away a group of evil humanoids.

Giant owl

Superior Low-Light Vision (Ex): A giant owl can see five times as far as a human can in dim light.

Skills: Giant owls have a +8 racial bonus on Listen checks and a +4 racial bonus on Spot checks.

*When in flight, giant owls gain a +8 bonus on Move Silently checks.

TRAINING A GIANT OWL

Although intelligent, a giant owl requires training before it can bear a rider in combat. To be trained, a giant owl must have a friendly attitude toward the trainer (this can be achieved through a successful Diplomacy check). Training a friendly giant owl requires six weeks of work and a DC 25 Handle Animal check. Riding a giant owl requires an exotic saddle. A giant owl can fight while carrying a rider, but the rider cannot also attack unless he or she succeeds on a Ride check.

Giant owl eggs are worth 2,500 gp apiece on the open market, while chicks are worth 4,000 gp each. Professional trainers charge 1,000 gp to rear or train a giant owl.

Carrying Capacity: A light load for a giant owl is up to 300 pounds; a medium load, 301–600 pounds; and a heavy load, 601–900 pounds.

OWLBEAR

Large Magical Beast
Hit Dice: 5d10+25 (52 hp)
Initiative: +1
Speed: 30 ft. (6 squares)
Armor Class: 15 (–1 size, +1 Dex, +5 natural), touch 10, flat-footed 14
Base Attack/Grapple: +5/+14
Attack: Claw +9 melee (1d6+5)
Full Attack: 2 claws +9 melee (1d6+5) and bite +4 melee (1d8+2)
Space/Reach: 10 ft./5 ft.
Special Attacks: Improved grab
Special Qualities: Scent
Saves: Fort +9, Ref +5, Will +2
Abilities: Str 21, Dex 12, Con 21, Int 2, Wis 12, Cha 10
Skills: Listen +8, Spot +8
Feats: Alertness, Track
Environment: Temperate forests
Organization: Solitary, pair, or pack (3–8)
Challenge Rating: 4
Treasure: None
Alignment: Always neutral
Advancement: 6–8 HD (Large); 9–15 HD (Huge)
Level Adjustment: —

This creature has a thick, shaggy coat of feathers and fur. Its body is like a bear's, but it has an avian head with big, round eyes and a hooked beak.

Owlbear

Owlbears are extraordinarily vicious predators with a reputation for ferocity, aggression, and sheer ill temper. They tend to attack nearly anything that moves without provocation.

Scholars have long debated the origins of the owlbear. The most common theory is that a demented wizard created the first specimen by crossing a giant owl with a bear. An owlbear's coat ranges in color from brown-black to yellowish brown; its beak is a dull ivory color. A full-grown male can stand as tall as 8 feet and weigh up to 1,500 pounds. Adventurers who have survived encounters with the creature often speak of the bestial madness they glimpsed in its red-rimmed eyes.

Owlbears inhabit wilderness areas, making their lairs within tangled forests or in shallow underground caverns. They can be active during the day or night, depending on the habits of the available prey. Adults live in mated pairs and hunt in packs, leaving their young in the lair. A lair usually has 1d6 young, fetching a price of 3,000 gp each in many civilized areas. While owlbears cannot be domesticated, they can still be placed in strategically important areas as free-roaming guardians. Professional trainers charge 2,000 gp to rear or train an owlbear (DC 23 for a young creature, DC 30 for an adult).

COMBAT

Owlbears attack prey—any creature bigger than a mouse—on sight, always fighting to the death. They slash with claws and beak, trying to grab their prey and rip it apart.

Improved Grab (Ex): To use this ability, an owlbear must hit with a claw attack. It can then attempt to start a grapple as a free action without provoking an attack of opportunity.

PEGASUS

Large Magical Beast
Hit Dice: 4d10+12 (34 hp)
Initiative: +2
Speed: 60 ft. (12 squares), fly 120 ft. (average)
Armor Class: 14 (–1 size, +2 Dex, +3 natural), touch 11, flat-footed 12
Base Attack/Grapple: +4/+12
Attack: Hoof +7 melee (1d6+4)
Full Attack: 2 hooves +7 melee (1d6+4) and bite +2 melee (1d3+2)
Space/Reach: 10 ft./5 ft.
Special Attacks: —
Special Qualities: Darkvision 60 ft., low-light vision, scent, spell-like abilities
Saves: Fort +7, Ref +6, Will +4
Abilities: Str 18, Dex 15, Con 16, Int 10, Wis 13, Cha 13
Skills: Diplomacy +3, Listen +8, Sense Motive +9, Spot +8
Feats: Flyby Attack, Iron Will
Environment: Temperate forests
Organization: Solitary, pair, or herd (6–10)
Challenge Rating: 3
Treasure: None
Alignment: Usually chaotic good
Advancement: 5–8 HD (Large)
Level Adjustment: +2 (cohort)

This creature looks like a horse but has two large, feathered wings. Its coat and wings are pure white.

The pegasus is a magnificent winged horse that sometimes serves the cause of good. Though highly prized as aerial steeds, pegasi are wild and shy creatures not easily tamed.

Pegasi mate for life, building their nests in high, remote locations. A mated pair have either 1–2 eggs or 1–2 young in their nest.

A typical pegasus stands 6 feet high at the shoulder, weighs 1,500 pounds, and has a wingspan of 20 feet. Rumors tell of some specimens that are brown or black instead of white.

Pegasi cannot speak, but they understand Common.

COMBAT

Pegasi attack with their sharp hooves and powerful bite. Mated pairs and herds attack as a team, fighting to the death to defend their eggs and young.

Spell-Like Abilities: At will—*detect good* and *detect evil* within a 60-foot radius. Caster level 5th.

Skills: Pegasi have a +4 racial bonus on Listen and Spot checks.

TRAINING A PEGASUS

Although intelligent, a pegasus requires training before it can bear a rider in combat. To be trained, a pegasus must have a friendly attitude toward the trainer (this can be achieved through a successful Diplomacy check). Training a friendly pegasus requires six weeks of work and a DC 25 Handle Animal check. Riding a pegasus requires an exotic saddle. A pegasus can fight while carrying a rider, but the rider cannot also attack unless he or she succeeds on a Ride check.

Pegasus eggs are worth 2,000 gp each on the open market, while young are worth 3,000 gp per head. Pegasi mature at the same rate

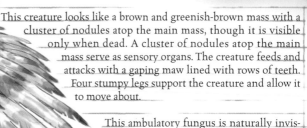

This creature looks like a brown and greenish-brown mass with a cluster of nodules atop the main mass, though it is visible only when dead. A cluster of nodules atop the main mass serve as sensory organs. The creature feeds and attacks with a gaping maw lined with rows of teeth. Four stumpy legs support the creature and allow it to move about.

This ambulatory fungus is naturally invisible, making it a feared predator among subterranean inhabitants.

COMBAT

A phantom fungus usually roams quietly, hunting for prey. It attacks lone individuals almost anywhere, but when tackling groups it prefers an open space where it has a better chance.

Greater Invisibility (Su): This ability is constant, allowing a phantom fungus to remain invisible even when attacking. It works like *greater invisibility* (caster level 12th) and lasts as long as the phantom fungus is alive. This ability is not subject to the *invisibility purge* spell. A phantom fungus becomes visible 1 minute after it is killed.

Skills: A phantom fungus has a +5 racial bonus on Move Silently checks.

Pegasus

as horses. Professional trainers charge 1,000 gp to rear or train a pegasus, which serves a good or neutral master with absolute faithfulness for life.

Carrying Capacity: A light load for a pegasus is up to 300 pounds; a medium load, 301–600 pounds; and a heavy load, 601–900 pounds.

PHANTOM FUNGUS

Medium Plant
Hit Dice: 2d8+6 (15 hp)
Initiative: +0
Speed: 20 ft. (4 squares)
Armor Class: 14 (+4 natural), touch 10, flat-footed 14
Base Attack/Grapple: +1/+3
Attack: Bite +3 melee (1d6+3)
Full Attack: Bite +3 melee (1d6+3)
Space/Reach: 5 ft./5 ft.
Special Attacks: —
Special Qualities: Low-light vision, plant traits, greater invisibility
Saves: Fort +6, Ref +0, Will +0
Abilities: Str 14, Dex 10, Con 16, Int 2, Wis 11, Cha 9
Skills: Listen +4, Move Silently +6, Spot +4
Feats: Alertness
Environment: Underground
Organization: Solitary
Challenge Rating: 3
Treasure: None
Alignment: Always neutral
Advancement: 3–4 HD (Medium); 5–6 HD (Large)
Level Adjustment: —

Soft, squelching footfalls and a strange, moldy odor indicate that some creature is nearby—but nothing can be seen.

Phantom fungus

PHASE SPIDER

Large Magical Beast
Hit Dice: 5d10+15 (42 hp)
Initiative: +7
Speed: 40 ft. (8 squares), climb 20 ft.
Armor Class: 15 (–1 size, +3 Dex, +3 natural), touch 12, flat-footed 12
Base Attack/Grapple: +5/+12
Attack: Bite +7 melee (1d6+4 plus poison)
Full Attack: Bite +7 melee (1d6+4 plus poison)
Space/Reach: 10 ft./5 ft.
Special Attacks: Poison
Special Qualitiy: Darkvision 60 ft., ethereal jaunt, low-light vision
Saves: Fort +7, Ref +7, Will +2
Abilities: Str 17, Dex 17, Con 16, Int 7, Wis 13, Cha 10
Skills: Climb +11, Move Silently +11, Spot +4
Feats: Ability Focus (poison), Improved Initiative
Environment: Warm hills
Organization: Solitary or cluster (2–5)
Challenge Rating: 5
Treasure: None
Alignment: Always neutral
Advancement: 6–8 HD (Large); 9–15 HD (Huge)
Level Adjustment: —

Phantom fungus illus. by C. Crichlow

This creature resembles a giant wolf spider, except with a larger head and variegated markings in white, gray, and blue over the legs and back. Its eight eyes are silver-white.

Phase spiders are aggressive predators that can move quickly from the Ethereal Plane to attack opponents on the Material Plane.

A typical phase spider's body is 8 feet long. It weighs about 700 pounds.

Phase spiders cannot speak.

COMBAT

Phase spiders dwell and hunt on the Material Plane. Once a spider locates prey, however, it shifts to the Ethereal Plane to attack, attempting to catch its victim flat-footed. The spider shifts in, bites its victim, and retreats quickly back to the Ethereal Plane.

Ethereal Jaunt (Su): A phase spider can shift from the Ethereal Plane to the Material Plane as a free action, and shift back again as a move action (or during a move action). The ability is otherwise identical with *ethereal jaunt* (caster level 15th).

Poison (Ex): Injury, Fortitude DC 17, initial and secondary damage 1d8 Con. The save DC is Constitution-based.

Skills: A phase spider has a +8 racial bonus on Climb checks and can always choose to take 10 on a Climb check, even if rushed or threatened.

This creature looks like a slithering blob of multicolored goo perhaps 5 feet wide and a little less than half that high.

A phasm is an amorphous creature that can assume the guise of almost any other creature or object.

Its shapeshifting ability frees a phasm from most material needs, which usually leads it to a life of exploration, hedonism, or philosophical contemplation. There's no telling where a phasm will turn up, nor what it will do if discovered. They are natural spies but notoriously unreliable, since they feel no particular need to report what they learn. They have an affinity for doppelgangers and sometimes ally themselves with groups of them for security—or just for the fun of it.

Phase spider

A phasm in its natural form is about 5 feet in diameter and 2 feet high at the center. Swirls of color indicate sensory organs. In this form, a phasm slithers about like an ooze and can attack with a pseudopod. It weighs about 400 pounds.

Phasms can speak Common but prefer telepathic communication.

COMBAT

When faced with potential danger, a phasm is equally likely to retreat, parley, or attack, as its fancy strikes. Phasms value new experiences: fresh scents and tastes, obscure facts, gossip, odd bric-a-brac, and the like. Those who offer a phasm such things stand a good chance of avoiding a fight.

If pursued or harassed, a phasm transforms into the most fearsome creature it knows, such as an adult white dragon or a fire giant, and attacks. When seriously hurt, it changes to some fast or agile form and tries to escape.

Amorphous (Ex): A phasm in its natural form has immunity to poison, *sleep*, paralysis, polymorph, and stunning effects. It is not subject to critical hits and, having no clear front or back, cannot be flanked.

Resilient (Ex): A phasm has a +4 racial bonus on Fortitude and Reflex saves (included in the statistics block).

Alternate Form (Su): A phasm can assume any form of Large size or smaller as a standard action. This ability functions as a *polymorph* spell cast on itself (caster level 15th), except that the phasm does not regain hit points for changing form. A phasm can remain in its alternate form until it chooses to assume a new one or return to its natural form.

Tremorsense (Ex): A phasm can automatically sense the location of anything within 60 feet that is in contact with the ground, so long as it is touching the ground itself.

Skills: *When using shapechange, a phasm gains a +10 circumstance bonus on Disguise checks.

PHASM

Medium Aberration (Shapechanger)
Hit Dice: 15d8+30 (97 hp)
Initiative: +6
Speed: 30 ft. (6 squares)
Armor Class: 17 (+2 Dex, +5 natural), touch 12, flat-footed 15
Base Attack/Grapple: +11/+12
Attack: Slam +12 melee (1d3+1)
Full Attack: Slam +12 melee (1d3+1)
Space/Reach: 5 ft./5 ft.
Special Attacks: —
Special Qualities: Alternate form, amorphous, resilient, scent, telepathy 100 ft., tremorsense 60 ft.
Saves: Fort +11, Ref +11, Will +11
Abilities: Str 12, Dex 15, Con 15, Int 16, Wis 15, Cha 14
Skills: Bluff +20, Climb +7, Craft (any one) +12, Diplomacy +12, Disguise +20 (+22 acting)*, Intimidate +4, Knowledge (any one) +18, Listen +12, Spot +12, Survival +8
Feats: Alertness, Blind-Fight, Combat Reflexes, Dodge, Improved Initiative, Mobility
Environment: Underground
Organization: Solitary
Challenge Rating: 7
Treasure: Standard
Alignment: Usually chaotic neutral
Advancement: 15–21 HD (Huge); 22–45 HD (Gargantuan)
Level Adjustment: —

Phasm

PLANETOUCHED

Planetouched is a general word to describe someone who can trace his or her bloodline back to an outsider, usually a fiend or celestial.

The effects of having a supernatural being in one's heritage last for many generations. Although not as dramatically altered as a half-celestial or a half-fiend, planetouched still retain some special qualities.

The two planetouched varieties described here are the most common. Aasimars are humans with some trace of celestial blood in their veins, and tieflings have some fiendishness in their family tree.

There is no "typical" aasimar or tiefling. They do not have their own societies or cultures, instead blending into existing ones. Many have character classes.

AASIMAR

Aasimar, 1st-Level Warrior
Medium Outsider (Native)
Hit Dice: 1d8+1 (5 hp)
Initiative: +4
Speed: 20 ft. in scale mail (4 squares); base speed 30 ft.
Armor Class: 16 (+4 scale mail, +2 heavy shield), touch 10, flat-footed 16
Base Attack/Grapple: +1/+2
Attack: Longsword +2 melee (1d8+1/19–20) or light crossbow +1 ranged (1d8/19–20)
Full Attack: Longsword +2 melee (1d8+1/19–20) or light crossbow +1 ranged (1d8/19–20)
Space/Reach: 5 ft./5 ft.
Special Attacks: Daylight
Special Qualities: Darkvision 60 ft., resistance to acid 5, cold 5, and electricity 5
Saves: Fort +3, Ref +0, Will +0
Abilities: Str 13, Dex 11, Con 12, Int 10, Wis 11, Cha 10
Skills: Heal +4, Knowledge (religion) +1, Listen +3, Ride +1, Spot +3
Feats: Improved Initiative
Environment: Temperate plains
Organization: Solitary, pair, or team (3–4)
Challenge Rating: 1/2
Treasure: Standard
Alignment: Usually good (any)
Advancement: By character class
Level Adjustment: +1

This being looks like a beautiful human, with calm, serene features and an inner radiance that shines from its face.

Graced with a touch of the holy, aasimars are usually tall, good-looking, and generally pleasant. Some have a minor physical trait suggesting their heritage, such as silver hair, golden eyes, or an unnaturally intense stare.

Most aasimars are decidedly good-aligned. They fight against evil causes and attempt to sway others to do the right thing. Occasionally they take on the vengeful, judgmental aspect of their celestial ancestor, but this is rare. They are rarely found in leadership positions and often live as loners due to their absolute dedication to goodness. Others are less fanatical and fit seamlessly into normal human society.

Combat

Aasimars usually like a fair, straightforward contest. Against a particularly evil foe, however, they fight with utter conviction and to the death.

Daylight (Sp): An aasimar can use *daylight* once per day as a 1st-level caster or a caster of his class levels, whichever is higher.

Skills: An aasimar has a +2 racial bonus on Spot and Listen checks.

The aasimar warrior presented here had the following ability scores before racial adjustments: Str 13, Dex 11, Con 12, Int 10, Wis 9, Cha 8.

Aasimar as Characters

Aasimar characters possess the following racial traits.

— +2 Wisdom, +2 Charisma.

—Medium size.

—An aasimar's base land speed is 30 feet.

—Darkvision: Aasimars can see in the dark up to 60 feet.

—Racial Skills: Aasimars have a +2 racial bonus on Spot and Listen checks.

—Racial Feats: An aasimar gains feats according to its class levels.

—Special Attacks (see above): *Daylight.*

—Special Qualities (see above): Resistance to acid 5, cold 5, and electricity 5.

—Automatic Languages: Common, Celestial. Bonus Languages: Draconic, Dwarven, Elven, Gnome, Halfling, Sylvan.

—Favored Class: Paladin.

—Level adjustment +1.

Aasimar

TIEFLING

Tiefling, 1st-Level Warrior
Medium Outsider (Native)
Hit Dice: 1d8+1 (5 hp)
Initiative: +1
Speed: 30 ft. (6 squares)
Armor Class: 15 (+1 Dex, +3 studded leather, +1 light shield), touch 11, flat-footed 14
Base Attack/Grapple: +1/+2
Attack: Rapier +3 melee (1d6+1/18–20) or light crossbow +2 ranged (1d8/19–20)
Full Attack: Rapier +3 melee (1d6+1/18–20) or light crossbow +2 ranged (1d8/19–20)
Space/Reach: 5 ft./5 ft.
Special Attacks: Darkness
Special Qualities: Darkvision 60 ft., resistance to cold 5, electricity 5, and fire 5
Saves: Fort +3, Ref +1, Will –1
Abilities: Str 13, Dex 13, Con 12, Int 12, Wis 9, Cha 6

Tiefling

Planetouched

Skills: Bluff +4, Hide +5, Move Silently +1, Sleight of Hand +1
Feats: Weapon Focus (rapier)
Environment: Temperate plains
Organization: Solitary, pair, or gang (3–4)
Challenge Rating: 1/2
Treasure: Standard
Alignment: Usually evil (any)
Advancement: By character class
Level Adjustment: +1

This being looks like a human, but it has a faintly disturbing demeanor about it and a wicked gleam in its eyes. Short horns sprout from its forehead.

Twisted, devious, and untrustworthy, tieflings more often than not follow their inherent tendencies and heed the call to evil. A few defy their nature, but still must fight against popular opinion (if their nature is known) or the feeling of otherworldly "wrongness" that seems to follow them wherever they go.

Aside from a demeanor that many find disturbing, many tieflings are indistinguishable from humans. Others have small horns, pointed teeth, red eyes, a whiff of brimstone about them, or even cloven feet. No two tieflings are the same.

In most human societies, tieflings maintain a low profile, operating as thieves, assassins, or spies. Occasionally one rises to a position of power, but when its nature is revealed it quickly becomes an outcast.

Combat

Tieflings are sneaky, subtle, and generally conniving. They prefer to strike from ambush and usually avoid a fair fight if they can.

Darkness (Sp): A tiefling can use *darkness* once per day (caster level equal to class levels).

Skills: A tiefling has a +2 racial bonus on Bluff and Hide checks.

The tiefling warrior presented here had the following ability scores before racial adjustments: Str 13, Dex 11, Con 12, Int 10, Wis 9, Cha 8.

Tieflings as Characters

Tiefling characters possess the following racial traits.

— +2 Dexterity, +2 Intelligence, –2 Charisma.
— Medium size.
— A tiefling's base land speed is 30 feet.
— Darkvision out to 60 feet.
— Racial Skills: Tieflings have a +2 racial bonus on Bluff and Hide checks.
— Racial Feats: A tiefling gains feats according to its class levels.
— Special Attacks (see above): *Darkness.*
— Special Qualities (see above): Resistance to cold 5, electricity 5, and fire 5.
— Automatic Languages: Common, Infernal. Bonus Languages: Draconic, Dwarven, Elven, Gnome, Goblin, Halfling, Orc.
— Favored Class: Rogue.
— Level adjustment +1.

PSEUDODRAGON

Tiny Dragon
Hit Dice: 2d12+2 (15 hp)
Initiative: +2
Speed: 15 ft. (3 squares), fly 60 ft. (good)
Armor Class: 18 (+2 size, +2 Dex, +4 natural), touch 14, flat-footed 16
Base Attack/Grapple: +2/–8
Attack: Sting +4 melee (1d3–2 plus poison)
Full Attack: Sting +4 melee (1d3–2 plus poison) and bite –1 melee (1)
Space/Reach: 2-1/2 ft./0 ft. (5 ft. with tail)
Special Attacks: Poison
Special Qualities: Blindsense 60 ft., darkvision 60 ft., immunity to *sleep* and paralysis, low-light vision, spell resistance 19, telepathy 60 ft.
Saves: Fort +4, Ref +5, Will +4
Abilities: Str 6, Dex 15, Con 13, Int 10, Wis 12, Cha 10
Skills: Diplomacy +2, Hide +20*, Listen +7, Search +6, Sense Motive +7, Spot +7, Survival +1 (+3 following tracks)
Feats: Weapon Finesse
Environment: Temperate forests
Organization: Solitary, pair, or clutch (3–5)
Challenge Rating: 1
Treasure: None
Alignment: Always neutral good
Advancement: 3–4 HD (Tiny)
Level Adjustment: +3

This creature resembles a miniature red dragon, slightly smaller than a housecat. It is red-brown in color rather than deep red. It has fine scales and sharp horns and teeth. Its tail is about twice as long as its body, barbed, and very flexible.

Pseudodragons are tiny, playful members of the dragon family. A pseudodragon has a body about 1 foot long, with a 2-foot tail. It weights about 7 pounds.

A pseudodragon can communicate telepathically and can also vocalize animal noises, such as a rasping purr (pleasure), a hiss (unpleasant surprise), a chirp (desire), or a growl (anger).

Pseudodragon

COMBAT

A pseudodragon can deliver a vicious bite, but its principal weapon is its sting-equipped tail.

Poison (Ex): Injury, Fortitude DC 14, initial damage sleep for 1 minute, secondary damage sleep for 1d3 hours. The save DC is Constitution-based and includes a +2 racial bonus.

Blindsense (Ex): A pseudodragon can locate creatures within 60 feet by nonvisual means (mostly hearing and scent, but also by noticing vibration and other environmental clues). Opponents the pseudodragon can't actually see still have total concealment against the pseudodragon.

Telepathy (Su): Pseudodragons can communicate telepathically with creatures that speak Common or Sylvan, provided they are within 60 feet.

Skills: Pseudodragons have a chameleonlike ability that grants them a +4 racial bonus on Hide checks. *In forests or overgrown areas, this bonus improves to +8.

PSEUDODRAGON COMPANIONS

A pseudodragon may very rarely seek humanoid companionship. It stalks a candidate silently for days, reading his or her thoughts and judging his or her deeds. If it finds the candidate promising, the pseudodragon presents itself as a potential companion and observes the other's reaction. If the candidate seems delighted and promises to take very good care of it, the pseudodragon accepts. Otherwise, it flies away.

A pseudodragon's personality has been described as catlike. At times the creature seems arrogant, demanding, and less than helpful. It is willing to serve—provided that it is well fed and groomed, and receives lots of attention. The companion must pamper it and make it feel like the most important thing in his or her life. If the pseudodragon is mistreated or insulted, it will leave— or worse, play pranks when least expected. Pseudodragons particularly dislike cruelty and will not serve cruel masters.

A pseudodragon egg can fetch a price of up to 10,000 gp, and a hatchling as much as 20,000 gp. Pseudodragons have a life span of 10 to 15 years. Like dragons, they are attracted to bright, shiny objects.

PURPLE WORM

Gargantuan Magical Beast
Hit Dice: 16d10+112 (200 hp)
Initiative: –2
Speed: 20 ft. (4 squares), burrow 20 ft., swim 10 ft.
Armor Class: 19 (–4 size, –2 Dex, +15 natural), touch 4, flat-footed 19
Base Attack/Grapple: +16/+40
Attack: Bite +25 melee (2d8+12)
Full Attack: Bite +25 melee (2d8+12) and sting +20 melee (2d6+6 plus poison)
Space/Reach: 20 ft./15ft.
Special Attacks: Improved grab, swallow whole, poison
Special Qualities: Tremorsense 60 ft.
Saves: Fort +17, Ref +8, Will +4
Abilities: Str 35, Dex 6, Con 25, Int 1, Wis 8, Cha 8
Skills: Listen +18, Swim +20
Feats: Awesome Blow, Cleave, Improved Bull Rush, Power Attack, Weapon Focus (bite), Weapon Focus (sting)
Environment: Underground
Organization: Solitary
Challenge Rating: 12
Treasure: No coins, 50% goods (stone only), no items
Alignment: Always neutral
Advancement: 16–32 HD (Gargantuan); 33–48 HD (Colossal)
Level Adjustment: —

This creature looks like a massive worm covered with plates of dark purple, chitinous armor. Its toothy maw is as wide as a human is tall.

These massive scavengers attempt to consume any organic material they find. Purple worms are feared for swallowing their prey whole: Entire groups of adventurers have vanished down their gullets, one member after the other.

The body of a mature purple worm is 5 feet in diameter and 80 feet long, weighing about 40,000 pounds. The creature has a poisonous stinger in its tail.

A purple worm consumes great quantities of dirt and rock when tunneling. Its gizzard may hold gems and other acid-resistant items. In mineral-rich areas, purple worm castings might contain unrefined ores.

COMBAT

In battle, a purple worm forms into a coil 20 feet in diameter, biting and stinging anything within reach.

Improved Grab (Ex): To use this ability, a purple worm must hit with its bite attack. It can then attempt to start a grapple as a free action without provoking an attack of opportunity. If it wins the grapple check, it establishes a hold and can attempt to swallow the foe the following round.

Poison (Ex): Injury, Fortitude DC 25, initial damage 1d6 Str, secondary damage 2d6 Str. The save DC is Constitution-based.

Swallow Whole (Ex): A purple worm can try to swallow a grabbed opponent of a smaller size than itself by making a successful grapple check. Once inside, the opponent takes 2d8+12 points of crushing damage plus 8 points of acid damage per round from the worm's gizzard. A swallowed creature can cut its way out by using a light slashing or piercing weapon to deal 25 points of damage to the gizzard (AC 17). Once the creature exits, muscular action closes the hole; another swallowed opponent must cut its own way out. A Gargantuan worm's interior can hold 2 Large, 8 Medium, 32 Small, 128 Tiny, or 512 Diminutive or smaller opponents.

Skills: A purple worm has a +8 racial bonus on any Swim check to perform some special action or avoid a hazard. It can always choose to take 10 on a Swim check, even if distracted or endangered. It can use the run action while swimming, provided it swims in a straight line.

Purple worm

RAKSHASA

Medium Outsider (Native)
Hit Dice: 7d8+21 (52 hp)
Initiative: +2
Speed: 40 ft. (8 squares)
Armor Class: 21 (+2 Dex, +9 natural), touch 12, flat-footed 19
Base Attack/Grapple: +7/+8
Attack: Claw +8 melee (1d4+1)
Full Attack: 2 claws +8 melee (1d4+1) and bite +3 melee (1d6)
Space/Reach: 5 ft./5 ft.
Special Attacks: Detect thoughts, spells
Special Qualities: Change shape, damage reduction 15/good and piercing, darkvision 60 ft., spell resistance 27
Saves: Fort +8, Ref +7, Will +6
Abilities: Str 12, Dex 14, Con 16, Int 13, Wis 13, Cha 17

Skills: Bluff +17*, Concentration +13, Diplomacy +7, Disguise +17 (+19 acting)*, Intimidate +5, Listen +13, Move Silently +13, Perform (oratory) +13, Sense Motive +11, Spellcraft +11, Spot +11

Feats: Alertness, Combat Casting, Dodge

Environment: Warm marshes

Organization: Solitary

Challenge Rating: 10

Treasure: Standard coins; double goods; standard items

Alignment: Always lawful evil

Advancement: By character class

Level Adjustment: +7

This being looks like a humanoid tiger garbed in expensive clothes. The body seems mostly human except for a luxurious coat of tiger's fur and its tiger head.

Some say rakshasas are the very embodiment of evil. Few beings are more malevolent.

A closer look at a rakshasa reveals that the palms of its hands are where the backs of the hands would be on a human. While this doesn't detract from the creature's manual dexterity, it makes a rakshasa look very disturbing to those unfamiliar with the creature.

A rakshasa is about the same height and weight as a human. Rakshasas speak Common, Infernal, and Undercommon.

COMBAT

In close combat, which a rakshasa disdains as ignoble, it employs its sharp claws and powerful bite. Whenever possible, it uses its other abilities to make such encounters unnecessary.

Detect Thoughts (Su): A rakshasa can continuously use detect thoughts as the spell (caster level 18th; Will DC 15 negates). It can suppress or resume this ability as a free action. The save DC is Charisma-based.

Spells: A rakshasa casts spells as a 7th-level sorcerer.

Typical Sorcerer Spells Known (6/7/7/5; save DC 13 + spell level): 0—*detect magic, light, mage hand, message, read magic, resistance, touch of fatigue;* 1st—*charm person, mage armor, magic missile, shield, silent image;* 2nd—*bear's endurance, invisibility, Melf's acid arrow;* 3rd—*haste, suggestion.*

Change Shape (Su): A rakshasa can assume any humanoid form, or revert to its own form, as a standard action. In humanoid form, a rakshasa loses its claw and bite attacks (although it often equips itself with weapons and armor instead). A rakshasa remains in one form until it chooses to assume a new one. A change in form cannot be dispelled, but the rakshasa reverts to its natural form when killed. A *true seeing* spell reveals its natural form.

Skills: A rakshasa has a +4 racial bonus on Bluff and Disguise checks.

*When using change shape, a rakshasa gains an additional +10 circumstance bonus on Disguise checks. If reading an opponent's mind, its circumstance bonus on Bluff and Disguise checks increases by a further +4.

RAKSHASAS AS CHARACTERS

Rakshasa characters possess the following racial traits.

— +2 Strength, +4 Dexterity, +6 Constitution, +2 Intelligence, +2 Wisdom, +6 Charisma.

—Medium size.

—A rakshasa's base land speed is 40 feet.

—Darkvision out to 60 feet.

—Racial Hit Dice: A rakshasa begins with seven levels of outsider, which provide 7d8 Hit Dice, a base attack bonus of +7, and base saving throw bonuses of Fort +5, Ref +5, and Will +5.

—Racial Skills: A rakshasa's outsider levels give it skill points equal to 10 × (8 + Int modifier). Its class skills are Bluff, Disguise, Listen, Move Silently, Perform, Sense Motive, and Spot. A rakshasa has a +4 racial bonus on Bluff and Disguise checks, and it can gain further bonuses by using change shape (+10 on Disguise checks) and detect thoughts (+4 on Bluff and Disguise checks).

—Racial Feats: A rakshasa's outsider levels give it three feats.

— +9 natural armor bonus.

—Natural Weapons: Bite (1d6) and 2 claws (1d4).

—Detect Thoughts (Su): The save DC is 13 + the character's Cha modifier.

—Spells: A rakshasa character casts spells as a 7th-level sorcerer. If the character takes additional levels of sorcerer, these levels stack with the rakshasa's base spellcasting ability for spells known, spells per day, and other effects dependent on caster level. For example, a rakshasa 2nd-level sorcerer has the same spells known, spells per day, and caster level as any other 9th-level sorcerer. A rakshasa character likewise uses the sum of its racial spellcasting levels and class levels to determine the abilities of its familiar.

—Special Qualities (see above): Change shape, damage reduction 15/good and piercing, spell resistance equal to 27 + class levels.

—Automatic Languages: Common, Infernal. Bonus Languages: Sylvan, Undercommon.

—Favored Class: Sorcerer.

—Level adjustment +7.

Rakshasa

RAST

Medium Outsider (Extraplanar, Fire)

Hit Dice: 4d8+7 (25 hp)
Initiative: +5
Speed: 5 ft. (1 square), fly 60 ft. (good)
Armor Class: 15 (+1 Dex, +4 natural), touch 11, flat-footed 14
Base Attack/Grapple: +4/+6
Attack: Claw +6 melee (1d4+2) or bite +6 melee (1d8+3)
Full Attack: 4 claws +6 melee (1d4+2) or bite +6 melee (1d8+3)
Space/Reach: 5 ft./5 ft.
Special Attacks: Paralyzing gaze, improved grab, blood drain
Special Qualities: Darkvision 60 ft., flight, immunity to fire, vulnerability to cold
Saves: Fort +5, Ref +5, Will +5
Abilities: Str 14, Dex 12, Con 13, Int 3, Wis 13, Cha 12
Skills: Hide +8, Listen +8, Move Silently +8, Spot +8
Feats: Improved Initiative, Toughness
Environment: Elemental Plane of Fire
Organization: Solitary, pair, or cluster (3–6)
Challenge Rating: 5
Treasure: None
Alignment: Usually neutral
Advancement: 5–6 HD (Medium); 7–12 HD (Large)
Level Adjustment: —

This vile creature must have at least a dozen long, spindly claws that hang from its bulbous, floating body. Its round head is almost all mouth, and its mouth is almost all teeth.

Rasts swarm in isolated pockets on distant planes, particularly the Elemental Plane of Fire. Floating, fleshy sacks of teeth and claws, these insatiable creatures eat almost continuously.

At its heart, a rast is a creature of ash and cinder, but it feasts on blood with a lust that would shame most normal beasts. A rast has anywhere from ten to fifteen claws, though it can only use four at once.

A rast has a body about the size of a large dog's, with a head almost as large as the body. It weighs about 200 pounds.

Rast

Fisch IIID
2000

COMBAT

Rasts attack with a frightening, brutal cunning. The creatures paralyze as many of their foes as possible, then attack any that are still moving. A rast can claw or bite, but cannot do both during the same round.

Paralyzing Gaze (Su): Paralysis for 1d6 rounds, 30 feet, Fortitude DC 13 negates. The save DC is Charisma-based.

Improved Grab (Ex): To use this ability, a rast must hit with its bite attack. It can then attempt to start a grapple as a free action without provoking an attack of opportunity.

Blood Drain (Ex): A rast drains blood from a grabbed opponent, dealing 1 point of Constitution damage each round it maintains the hold.

Flight (Su): A rast can cease or resume flight as a free action. A rast that loses this ability falls and can perform only a single action (either a move action or an attack action) each round.

RAVID

Medium Outsider (Extraplanar)

Hit Dice: 3d8+3 (16 hp)
Initiative: +4
Speed: 20 ft. (4 squares), fly 60 ft. (perfect)
Armor Class: 25 (+15 natural), touch 10, flat-footed 25
Base Attack/Grapple: +3/+4
Attack: Tail slap +4 melee (1d6+1 plus positive energy) or tail touch +4 melee touch (positive energy)
Full Attack: Tail slap +4 melee (1d6+1 plus positive energy) and claw +2 melee (1d4 plus positive energy); or tail touch +4 melee touch (positive energy) and claw touch +2 melee touch (positive energy)
Space/Reach: 5 ft./5 ft.
Special Attacks: Positive energy lash, animate objects
Special Qualities: Darkvision 60 ft., flight, immunity to fire
Saves: Fort +4, Ref +3, Will +4
Abilities: Str 13, Dex 10, Con 13, Int 7, Wis 12, Cha 14
Skills: Escape Artist +6, Hide +6, Listen +7, Move Silently +6, Spot +7, Survival +7, Use Rope +0 (+2 with bindings)
Feats: Improved Initiative, Multiattack
Environment: Positive Energy Plane
Organization: Solitary (1 plus at least 1 animated object)
Challenge Rating: 5
Treasure: None
Alignment: Always neutral
Advancement: 4 HD (Medium); 5–9 HD (Large)
Level Adjustment:

This creature has a long, serpentine body that trails away as it floats effortlessly through the air, and a single claw that juts forward near its head.

Ravids are creatures from the Positive Energy Plane. These bizarre entities imbue creatures with energy by their touch and animate lifeless objects around them.

Ravids that make their way to the Material Plane wander about aimlessly, followed by the objects to which they have given life.

A ravid is about 7 feet long and weighs about 75 pounds.

COMBAT

Ravids fight only in self-defense. A ravid itself is not very powerful but is always accompanied by at least one animated object that defends it.

Positive Energy Lash (Su): A ravid can make a touch attack or hit with a claw or tail slap attack to infuse a target with positive energy. The energy produces an unpleasant tingle in living creatures, and against undead foes (even incorporeal ones) it deals 2d10 points of damage.

Animate Objects (Su): Once per round, a random object within 20 feet of a ravid animates as though by the spell *animate objects* (caster level 20th). These objects defend the ravid to the best of their ability, but the ravid isn't intelligent enough to employ elaborate tactics with them.

Flight (Su): A ravid can cease or resume flight as a free action. A rast that loses this ability falls and can perform only a single action (either a move action or an attack action) each round.

Feats: A ravid has the Multiattack feat even through it does not have the requisite three natural weapons.

Ravid

Skills: Listen +8, Spot +8

Feats: Awesome Blow, Improved Bull Rush, Power Attack

Environment: Cold desert

Organization: Solitary

Challenge Rating: 7

Treasure: None

Alignment: Usually neutral

Advancement: 8–14 HD (Huge); 15–21 HD (Gargantuan)

Level Adjustment: —

REMORHAZ

Huge Magical Beast

Hit Dice: 7d10+35 (73 hp)

Initiative: +1

Speed: 30 ft. (6 squares), burrow 20 ft.

Armor Class: 20 (–2 size, +1 Dex, +11 natural), touch 9, flat-footed 19

Base Attack/Grapple: +7/+23

Attack: Bite +13 melee (2d8+12)

Full Attack: Bite +13 melee (2d8+12)

Space/Reach: 15 ft./10 ft.

Special Attacks: Improved grab, swallow whole

Special Qualities: Darkvision 60 ft., heat, low-light vision, tremorsense 60 ft.

Saves: Fort +10, Ref +6, Will +3

Abilities: Str 26, Dex 13, Con 21, Int 5, Wis 12, Cha 10

The beast looks like a huge worm with dozens of insectoid legs, faceted eyes, and a wide mouth brimming with jagged teeth. The back of the head bristles with a pair of winglike fins.

The remorhaz is an arctic monster, an aggressive predator that burrows through ice and earth.

Although wild remorhazes prey on frost giants (as well as polar bears, elk, and deer), the giants occasionally train or entice these beasts to guard their lairs.

A remorhaz is whitish-blue in color but pulses with a reddish glow from the heat its body produces. The creature is a little more than 20 feet long, with a body about 5 feet wide. It weighs about 10,000 pounds.

Remorhazes cannot speak.

COMBAT

Remorhazes hide under the snow and ice until they hear movement above them, then attack from below and surprise prey.

Improved Grab (Ex): To use this ability, a remorhaz must hit an opponent least one size category smaller than itself with its bite attack. It can then attempt to start a grapple as a free action without provoking an attack of opportunity. If it wins the grapple check, it establishes a hold and can attempt to swallow the opponent the following round.

Swallow Whole (Ex): When a remorhaz begins its turn with a grappled opponent in its mouth, it can swallow that opponent with a successful grapple check. Once inside, the opponent takes 2d8+12 points of bludgeoning damage plus 8d6 points of fire damage per round from the remorhaz's gizzard. A swallowed creature can cut its way out by using a light slashing or piercing weapon to deal 25 points of damage to the gizzard (AC 15). Once the creature exits, muscular action closes the hole; another swallowed opponent must cut its own way out.

A Huge remorhaz's interior can hold 2 Large, 4 Medium, 8 Small, 32 Tiny, 128 Diminutive, or 512 Fine or smaller opponents.

Heat (Ex): An enraged remorhaz generates heat so intense that anything touching its body takes 8d6 points of fire damage. Creatures striking a remorhaz with natural attacks or unarmed attacks are subject to this damage, but creatures striking with melee weapons do not take damage from the remorhaz's heat. This heat can melt or char weapons; any weapon that strikes a

Remorhaz

remorhaz is allowed a DC 18 Fortitude save to avoid destruction. The save DC is Constitution-based.

Skills: Remorhazes have a +4 racial bonus on Listen checks.

ROC

Gargantuan Animal
Hit Dice: 18d8+126 (207 hp)
Initiative: +2
Speed: 20 ft. (4 squares), fly 80 ft. (average)
Armor Class: 17 (–4 size, +2 Dex, +9 natural), touch 8, flat-footed 15
Base Attack/Grapple: +13/+37
Attack: Talon +21 melee (2d6+12)
Full Attack: 2 talons +21 melee (2d6+12) and bite +19 melee (2d8+6)
Space/Reach: 20 ft./15 ft.
Special Attacks: —
Special Qualities: Low-light vision
Saves: Fort +18, Ref +13, Will +9
Abilities: Str 34, Dex 15, Con 24, Int 2, Wis 13, Cha 11
Skills: Hide –3, Listen +10, Spot +14
Feats: Alertness, Flyby Attack, Iron Will, Multiattack, Power Attack, Snatch, Wingover
Environment: Warm mountains
Organization: Solitary or pair
Challenge Rating: 9
Treasure: None
Alignment: Always neutral
Advancement: 19–32 HD (Gargantuan); 33–54 (Colossal)
Level Adjustment: —

This creature is an enormous bird, easily the size of a building.

Almost too big to be believed, rocs are huge birds of prey that dwell in warm mountainous regions and are known for carrying off large animals (cattle, horses, even elephants).

A roc's plumage is either dark brown or golden from head to tail. In a few rare instances, red, black, or white rocs are sighted, but they are often considered bad omens. These enormous creatures are 30 feet long from the beak to the base of the tail, with wingspans as wide as 80 feet. A roc weighs about 8,000 pounds.

Rocs lair in vast nests made from trees, branches, lumber, and the like. They prefer to dwell high in the mountains, far from other rocs, to avoid straining their food supply; they hunt within a radius of about 10 miles around their nests.

COMBAT

A roc attacks from the air, swooping earthward to snatch prey in its powerful talons and carry it off for itself and its young to devour. A solitary roc is typically hunting and will attack any Medium or larger creature that appears edible. A mated pair of rocs attack in concert, fighting to the death to defend their nests or hatchlings.

Skills: Rocs have a +4 racial bonus on Spot checks.

Roc

ROPER

Large Magical Beast
Hit Dice: 10d10+30 (85 hp)
Initiative: +5
Speed: 10 ft. (2 squares)
Armor Class: 24 (–1 size, +1 Dex, +14 natural), touch 10, flat-footed 23
Base Attack/Grapple: +10/+18
Attack: Strand +11 ranged touch (drag) or bite +13 melee (2d6+6)
Full Attack: 6 strands +11 ranged touch (drag) and bite +13 melee (2d6+6)
Space/Reach: 10 ft./10 ft. (50 ft. with strand)
Special Attacks: Drag, strands, weakness
Special Qualities: Darkvision 60 ft., immunity to electricity, low-light vision, resistance to cold 10, spell resistance 30, vulnerability to fire
Saves: Fort +10, Ref +8, Will +8
Abilities: Str 19, Dex 13, Con 17, Int 12, Wis 16, Cha 12
Skills: Climb +12, Hide +10*, Listen +13, Spot +13
Feats: Alertness, Improved Initiative, Iron Will, Weapon Focus (strand)
Environment: Underground
Organization: Solitary, pair, or cluster (3–6)
Challenge Rating: 12
Treasure: No coins; 50% goods (stone only); no items
Alignment: Usually chaotic evil
Advancement: 11–15 HD (Large); 16–30 HD (Huge)
Level Adjustment: —

This creature looks much like a natural stalagmite about 10 feet tall. Its great, gaping maw lined with crystalline teeth suggests it is a meat eater.

Ropers are hideous creatures that lurk in the deep caverns of the world. They are altogether evil and far more intelligent than most people would judge by their appearance.

Roper

A roper stands some 9 feet tall and tapers from 3 or 4 feet in diameter at the base to 1 foot across at the top. It weighs 2,200 pounds. A roper's coloration and temperature change to match the features of the surrounding cave.

Ropers speak Terran and Undercommon.

COMBAT

A roper hunts by standing very still and imitating a bit of rock. This tactic often allows it to attack with surprise. When prey comes within reach, it lashes out with its strands. In melee, it bites adjacent opponents with its powerful maw.

Drag (Ex): If a roper hits with a strand attack, the strand latches onto the opponent's body. This deals no damage but drags the stuck opponent 10 feet closer each subsequent round (provoking no attack of opportunity) unless that creature breaks free, which requires a DC 23 Escape Artist check or a DC 19 Strength check. The check DCs are Strength-based, and the Escape Artist DC includes a +4 racial bonus. A roper can draw in a creature within 10 feet of itself and bite with a +4 attack bonus in the same round.

A strand has 10 hit points and can be attacked by making a successful sunder attempt. However, attacking a roper's strand does not provoke an attack of opportunity. If the strand is currently attached to a target, the roper takes a –4 penalty on its opposed attack roll to resist the sunder attempt. Severing a strand deals no damage to a roper.

Strands (Ex): Most encounters with a roper begin when it fires strong, sticky strands. The creature can have up to six strands at once, and they can strike up to 50 feet away (no range increment). If a strand is severed, the roper can extrude a new one on its next turn as a free action.

Weakness (Ex): A roper's strands can sap an opponent's strength. Anyone grabbed by a strand must succeed on a DC 18 Fortitude save or take 2d8 points of Strength damage. The save DC is Constitution-based.

Skills: *Ropers have a +8 racial bonus on Hide checks in stony or icy areas.

thick, lumpy hide. Its tail is covered with armor plates and ends in a bony projection that looks like a double-ended paddle. The creature sports two long antennae on its head, one beneath each eye.

Most fighters would rather face an army of orcs than confront a rust monster. These creatures corrode and eat metal objects and have ruined the armor, shields, and weapons of countless adventurers.

The hide of these creatures varies in color from a yellowish tan underside to a rust-red upper back. A rust monster's prehensile antennae can rust metals on contact.

The typical rust monster measures 5 feet long and 3 feet high, weighing 200 pounds.

COMBAT

A rust monster can scent a metal object from up to 90 feet away. When it detects one, it dashes toward the source and attempts to strike it with its antennae. The creature is relentless, chasing characters over long distances if they still possess intact metal objects but usually ceasing its attacks to devour a freshly rusted meal. A clever (or desperate) character can often distract a hungry rust monster by tossing it some metal objects, then fleeing while it consumes them.

The creature targets the largest metal object available, striking first at armor, then at shields and smaller items. It prefers ferrous metals (steel or iron) over precious metals (such as gold or silver) but will devour the latter if given the opportunity.

Rust (Ex): A rust monster that makes a successful touch attack with its antennae causes the target metal to corrode, falling to pieces and becoming useless immediately. The touch can destroy up to a 10-foot cube of metal instantly. Magic armor and weapons, and other magic items made of metal, must succeed on a DC 17 Reflex save or be dissolved. The save DC is Constitution-based and includes a +4 racial bonus.

A metal weapon that deals damage to a rust monster corrodes immediately. Wooden, stone, and other nonmetallic weapons are unaffected.

RUST MONSTER

Medium Aberration
Hit Dice: 5d8+5 (27 hp)
Initiative: +3
Speed: 40 ft. (8 squares)
Armor Class: 18 (+3 Dex, +5 natural), touch 13, flat-footed 15
Base Attack/Grapple: +3/+3
Attack: Antennae touch +3 melee (rust)
Full Attack: Antennae touch +3 melee (rust) and bite –2 melee (1d3)
Space/Reach: 5 ft./5 ft.
Special Attacks: Rust
Special Qualities: Darkvision, scent
Saves: Fort +2, Ref +4, Will +5
Abilities: Str 10, Dex 17, Con 13, Int 2, Wis 13, Cha 8
Skills: Listen +7, Spot +7
Feats: Alertness, Track
Environment: Underground
Organization: Solitary or pair
Challenge Rating: 3
Treasure: None
Alignment: Always neutral
Advancement: 6–8 HD (Medium); 9–15 HD (Large)
Level Adjustment: —

This creature seems to be about the size of a pony. It has four insectlike legs and a squat, humped body protected by a

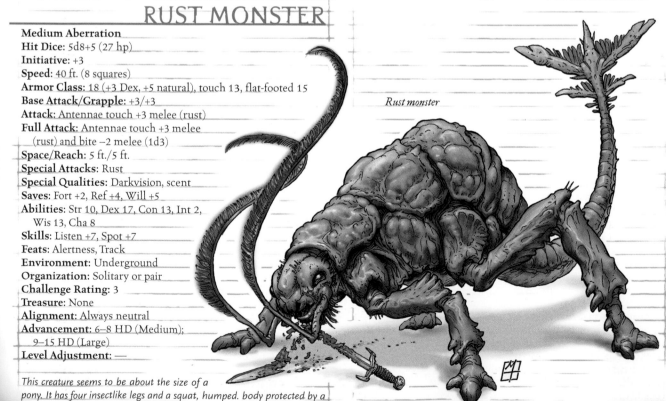

Rust monster

SAHUAGIN

Medium Monstrous Humanoid (Aquatic)

Hit Dice: 2d8+2 (11 hp)

Initiative: +1

Speed: 30 ft. (6 squares), swim 60 ft.

Armor Class: 16 (+1 Dex, +5 natural), touch 11, flat-footed 15

Base Attack/Grapple: +2/+4

Attack: Talon +4 melee (1d4+2) or trident +4 melee (1d8+3) or heavy crossbow +3 ranged (1d10/19–20)

Full Attack: Trident +4 melee (1d8+3) and bite +2 melee (1d4+1); or 2 talons +4 melee (1d4+2) and bite +2 melee (1d4+1); or heavy crossbow +3 ranged (1d10/19–20)

Space/Reach: 5 ft./5 ft.

Special Attacks: Blood frenzy, rake 1d4+1

Special Qualities: Blindsense 30 ft., darkvision 60 ft., freshwater sensitivity, light blindness, speak with sharks, water dependent

Saves: Fort +3, Ref +4, Will +4

Abilities: Str 14, Dex 13, Con 12, Int 14, Wis 13, Cha 9

Skills: Handle Animal +4*, Hide +6*, Listen +6*, Profession (hunter) +1*, Ride +3, Spot +6*, Survival +1*

Feats: Great Fortitude, Multiattack[B]

Environment: Warm aquatic

Organization: Solitary, pair, team (5–8), patrol (11–20 plus 1 3rd-level lieutenant and 1–2 sharks), band (20–80 plus 100% noncombatants plus 1 3rd-level lieutenant and 1 4th-level chieftain per 20 adults plus 1–2 sharks), or tribe (70–160 plus 100% noncombatants plus 1 3rd-level lieutenant per 20 adults, 1 4th-level chieftain per 40 adults, 9 4th-level guards, 1–4 underpriestesses of 3rd–6th level, 1 7th-level priestess, and 1 baron of 6th–8th level plus 5–8 sharks)

Challenge Rating: 2

Treasure: Standard

Alignment: Usually lawful evil

Advancement: 3–5 HD (Medium), 6–10 HD (Large), or by character class

Level Adjustment: +2 (+3 if four-armed)

This humanoid has scaly skin with webbed fingers and toes, and sharp fangs fill its mouth. It has a long tail ending in a curved fin, and it has fins on its arms, back, and head. Its great, staring eyes are deep black.

Sahuagin are marine predators superbly adapted to undersea hunting. Also known as sea devils, these beings dwell in coastal waters, forming organized groups that raid shore communities.

Most sahuagin feature green coloration, darker along the back and lighter on the belly. Many have dark stripes, bands, or spots, but these tend to fade with age. An adult male sahuagin stands roughly 6 feet tall and weighs about 200 pounds.

Sahuagin are the natural enemy of aquatic elves. The two cannot coexist peacefully: Wars between them are prolonged, bloody affairs that sometimes interfere with shipping and maritime trade. Sahuagin have an only slightly less vehement hatred for tritons.

Sahuagin speak their own language, Sahuagin. Thanks to their high Intelligence scores, most sahuagin also speak two bonus languages, usually Common and Aquan.

COMBAT

Sahuagin are savage fighters, asking for and giving no quarter. When swimming, a sahuagin tears with its feet as it strikes with its talons or a weapon. About half of any group of sahuagin are also armed with nets.

When sahuagin raid surface dwellers' communities, they venture ashore on dark, moonless nights to slaughter the inhabitants and livestock for food. They attack ships by swarming up from all sides, leaving a portion of their forces in the water as reinforcements or to deal with opponents the raiders throw into the sea.

Blindsense (Ex): A sahuagin can locate creatures underwater within a 30-foot radius. This ability works only when the sahuagin is underwater.

Blood Frenzy: Once per day a sahuagin that takes damage in combat can fly into a frenzy in the following round, clawing and biting madly until either it or its opponent is dead. It gains +2 Constitution and +2 Strength, and takes a –2 penalty to Armor Class. A sahuagin cannot end its frenzy voluntarily.

Rake (Ex): Attack bonus +2 melee, damage 1d4+1. A sahuagin also gains two rake attacks when it attacks while swimming.

Freshwater Sensitivity (Ex): A sahuagin fully immersed in fresh water must succeed on a DC 15 Fortitude save or become fatigued. Even on a success, it must repeat the save attempt every 10 minutes it remains immersed.

Light Blindness (Ex): Abrupt exposure to bright light (such as sunlight or a *daylight* spell) blinds sahuagin for round. On subsequent rounds, they are dazzled while operating in bright light.

Speak with Sharks (Ex): Sahuagin can communicate telepathically with sharks up to 150 feet away. The communication is limited to fairly simple concepts such as "food," "danger," and "enemy." Sahuagin can use the Handle Animal skill to befriend and train sharks.

Water Dependent (Ex): Sahuagin can survive out of the water for 1 hour per 2 points of Constitution (after that, refer to the drowning rules on page 304 of the *Dungeon Master's Guide*).

Skills: A sahuagin has a +8 racial bonus on any Swim check to perform some special action or avoid a hazard. It can always choose to take 10 on a Swim check, even if distracted or endangered. It can use the run action while swimming, provided it swims in a straight line.

*Underwater, a sahuagin has a +4 racial bonus on Hide, Listen, and Spot checks.

Sahuagin

Illus. by P. Jaquays

*A sahuagin has a +4 racial bonus on Survival and Profession (hunter) checks within 50 miles of its home.

*A sahuagin has a +4 racial bonus on Handle Animal checks when working with sharks.

SAHUAGIN MUTANTS

About one in two hundred sahuagin has four arms. Such creatures can make four claw attacks or use extra weapons, in addition to the claw and bite attacks.

If a community of aquatic elves is located within 100 miles of a sahuagin community, about one in one hundred sahuagin looks just like an aquatic elf. These creatures, called malenti, have a swim speed of 40 feet, can remain out of water for 1 hour per point of Constitution, and have freshwater sensitivity and light sensitivity (dazzled in bright light). Malenti have no natural attacks. They are otherwise identical with sahuagin.

SAHUAGIN SOCIETY

The sea devils live by a code of ritualized behavior developed over millennia. Every member of a sahuagin community knows its place well—and remains there. The sahuagin pride themselves on self-sufficiency and strict adherence to their social code. Unfortunately for others, one of their core beliefs is that the survival of the sahuagin depends on ruthlessly eradicating anything that is not sahuagin.

Sahuagin dwell in communities of varying sizes, from villages to cities, built of stone and other natural materials deep beneath the ocean waves. The creatures employ a variety of defenses, both passive (such as seaweed camouflage) and active (such as traps and tame sharks), to protect their communities. Elite groups of senior males (especially the four-armed ones) rule each community: A baron governs a village, while a prince rules approximately twenty villages. Sahuagin kings rule much larger territories and dwell within cities having as many as six thousand inhabitants. A sahuagin kingdom generally covers an entire seacoast, with villages and towns at least 100 miles apart. Sahuagin clerics function as teachers and keepers of lore, controlling religious life in their communities. Despite the presence of these priestesses within their society, the superstitious sea devils distrust and fear magic.

The patron deity of sahuagin is Sekolah, a great devil shark.

SAHUAGIN CHARACTERS

A male sahuagin's favored class is ranger, and most sahuagin leaders are rangers. Most sahuagin rangers choose humanoids (elves) as their favored enemy. Female sahuagin favor the cleric class. Sahuagin clerics worship Sekolah. A sahuagin cleric has access to two of the following domains: Evil, Law, Strength, or War (favored weapon: trident).

SALAMANDER

This being has a muscular humanoid upper body with a hawkish face. Its body is serpentine from the waist down, and is covered in red and black scales. Flame-shaped spines sprout form the creature's spine, arms, and head.

The Elemental Plane of Fire is home to many strange creatures, including the fearsome legions of the salamanders. These serpentine beings dwell in metal cities glowing with supernatural heat.

Salamanders are selfish and cruel, and they enjoy tormenting others. They are rarely encountered without their heated metal spears, but sometimes wield other weapons.

When summoned to the Material Plane, salamanders often assist forge workers and smiths. Their ability to work metal while it's still in the fire makes them some of the best metalsmiths known anywhere.

Salamanders reproduce asexually, each producing a single larva every ten years and incubating the young in fire pits until they reach maturity. Flamebrothers and average salamanders are actually different species, while nobles rise from the ranks of the average.

Salamanders speak Ignan. Some average salamanders and all nobles also speak Common.

Salamander

COMBAT

Salamanders use metal spears heated red-hot by their own furnacelike bodies. Bloodthirsty and sadistic, they are quick to attack. They prefer to take on those who appear strongest first, saving weaker enemies for slower, agonizing treatment later.

If a salamander has damage reduction, its natural weapons are treated as magic weapons for the purpose of overcoming damage reduction.

Constrict (Ex): A salamander deals automatic tail slap damage (including fire damage) with a successful grapple check. A noble salamander can constrict multiple creatures simultaneously, provided they are all at least two sizes smaller than it.

Heat (Ex): A salamander generates so much heat that its mere touch deals additional fire damage. Salamanders' metallic weapons also conduct this heat.

Improved Grab (Ex): To use this ability, a salamander must hit a creature of up to one size larger than itself with its tail slap attack. It can then attempt to start a grapple as a free action without provoking an attack of opportunity. If it wins the grapple check, it establishes a hold and can constrict.

Spell-Like Abilities: (Noble salamanders only) 3/day—*burning hands* (DC 13), *fireball* (DC 15), *flaming sphere* (DC 14), *wall of fire* (DC 16); 1/day—*dispel magic*, *summon monster VII* (Huge fire elemental). Caster level 15th. The save DCs are Charisma-based.

Skills: Salamanders have a +4 racial bonus on Craft (blacksmithing) checks.

	Flamebrother Salamander Small Outsider (Extraplanar, Fire)	Average Salamander Medium Outsider (Extraplanar, Fire)	Noble Salamander Large Outsider (Extraplanar, Fire)
Hit Dice:	4d8+8 (26 hp)	9d8+18 (58 hp)	15d8+45 (112 hp)
Initiative:	+1	+1	+1
Speed:	20 ft. (4 squares)	20 ft. (4 squares)	20 ft. (4 squares)
Armor Class:	19 (+1 size, +1 Dex, +7 natural), touch 12, flat-footed 18	18 (+1 Dex, +7 natural), touch 11, flat-footed 17	18 (−1 size, +1 Dex, +8 natural), touch 10, flat-footed 17
Base Attack/Grapple:	+4/+1	+9/+11	+15/+25
Attack:	Spear +6 melee (1d6+1/×3 plus 1d6 fire)	Spear +11 melee (1d8+3/×3 plus 1d6 fire)	+3 *longspear* +23 melee (1d8+9/×3 plus 1d8 fire)
Full Attack:	Spear +6 melee (1d6+1/×3 plus 1d6 fire) and tail slap +4 melee (1d4 plus 1d6 fire)	Spear +11/+6 melee (1d8+3/×3 plus 1d6 fire) and tail slap +9 melee (2d6+1 plus 1d6 fire)	+3 *longspear* +23/+18/+13 melee (1d8+9/×3 plus 1d8 fire) and tail slap +18 melee (2d8+3 plus 1d8 fire)
Space/Reach:	5 ft./5 ft.	5 ft./5 ft. (10 ft. with tail)	10 ft./10 ft. (20 ft. with tail or longspear)
Special Attacks:	Constrict 1d4 plus 1d6 fire, heat, improved grab	Constrict 2d6+1 plus 1d6 fire, heat, improved grab	Constrict 2d8+3 plus 1d8 fire, heat, improved grab, spell-like abilities
Special Qualities:	Darkvision 60 ft., immunity to fire, vulnerability to cold	Damage reduction 10/magic, darkvision 60 ft., immunity to fire, vulnerability to cold	Damage reduction 15/magic, darkvision 60 ft., immunity to fire, vulnerability to cold
Saves:	Fort +6, Ref +5, Will +6	Fort +8, Ref +7, Will +8	Fort +12, Ref +10, Will +11
Abilities:	Str 12, Dex 13, Con 14, Int 14, Wis 15, Cha 13	Str 14, Dex 13, Con 14, Int 14, Wis 15, Cha 13	Str 22, Dex 13, Con 16, Int 16, Wis 15, Cha 15
Skills:	Craft (blacksmithing) +8, Hide +12, Listen +11, Move Silently +6, Spot +11	Bluff +11, Craft (blacksmithing) +19, Diplomacy +3, Disguise +1 (+3 acting), Hide +11, Intimidate +3, Listen +8, Move Silently +11, Search +12, Spot +8	Bluff +19, Craft (blacksmithing) +25, Diplomacy +4, Hide +15, Intimidate +4, Listen +13, Move Silently +17, Spot +13
Feats:	Alertness, Multiattack	Alertness, Multiattack, Power Attack	Alertness, Cleave, Great Cleave, Multiattack, Power Attack, Skill Focus (Craft [blacksmithing])
Environment:	Elemental Plane of Fire	Elemental Plane of Fire	Elemental Plane of Fire
Organization:	Solitary, pair, or cluster (3–5)	Solitary, pair, or cluster (3–5)	Solitary, pair, or noble party (9–14)
Challenge Rating:	3	6	10
Treasure:	Standard (nonflammables only)	Standard (nonflammables only)	Double standard (nonflammables only) and +3 *longspear*
Alignment:	Usually evil (any)	Usually evil (any)	Usually evil (any)
Advancement:	4–6 HD (Small)	8–14 HD (Medium)	16–21 HD (Large); 22–45 HD (Huge)
Level Adjustment:	+4	+5	—

Feats: Salamanders have the Multiattack feat even though they do not have the requisite three natural weapons.

SALAMANDER SOCIETY

Flamebrothers, the smallest of the salamanders, are barbaric and tribal. Often more sophisticated salamanders force their civilization upon their smaller kin. Salamander nobility make a point of traveling through the planes, learning secrets to further their power. These experienced creatures eventually return to master their own kind and raise mighty kingdoms.

In a mixed society, status is determined by size and power—flamebrothers are the lowest class and the front ranks of salamander armies. Average salamanders are the middle class and the main fighting force, while noble salamanders are commanders.

Salamander nations do their best to resist the mighty elemental lords on their plane, and they disdain the azers, efreet, and other inhabitants. They often fail, though, and are enslaved by other fiery masters or conscripted into elemental armies.

SALAMANDER CHARACTERS

Flamebrothers have no favored class. They sometimes become adepts or warriors. Average or noble salamanders may be clerics, sorcerers, or fighters (their favored class).

SATYR

Medium Fey
Hit Dice: 5d6+5 (22 hp)
Initiative: +1
Speed: 40 ft. (8 squares)
Armor Class: 15 (+1 Dex, +4 natural), touch 11, flat-footed 14
Base Attack/Grapple: +2/+2
Attack: Head butt +2 melee (1d6) or shortbow +3 ranged (1d6/×3)
Full Attack: Head butt +2 melee (1d6) and dagger −3 melee (1d4/19–20); or shortbow +3 ranged (1d6/×3)
Space/Reach: 5 ft./5 ft.
Special Attacks: Pipes
Special Qualities: Damage reduction 5/cold iron, low-light vision
Saves: Fort +2, Ref +5, Will +5
Abilities: Str 10, Dex 13, Con 12, Int 12, Wis 13, Cha 13
Skills: Bluff +9, Diplomacy +3, Disguise +1 (+3 acting), Hide +13, Intimidate +3, Knowledge (nature) +9, Listen +15, Move Silently +13, Perform (wind instruments) +9, Spot +15, Survival +1 (+3 aboveground)
Feats: Alertness[B], Dodge, Mobility
Environment: Temperate forests
Organization: Solitary, pair, band (3–5), or troop (6–11)
Challenge Rating: 2 (without pipes) or 4 (with pipes)

Treasure: Standard
Alignment: Usually chaotic neutral
Advancement: 6–10 HD (Medium)
Level Adjustment: +2

This being might best be described as a horned man with the legs of a goat.

Satyrs, also known as fauns, are hedonistic creatures that frolic in the wild places of the world. They love fine food, strong drink, and passionate romance.

A satyr's hair is red or chestnut brown, while its hooves and horns are jet black.

A satyr is far more likely to be carrying musical instruments or bottles of wine than weapons. For the most part, satyrs leave travelers alone. They are, however, more than a little mischievous and often seek fun at the expense of those who wander too near their woodland homes.

A satyr is about as tall and heavy as a half-elf.

Satyrs speak Sylvan, and most also speak Common.

COMBAT

The keen senses of a satyr make it almost impossible to surprise one in the wild. Conversely, with their own natural grace and agility, satyrs can sneak up on travelers who are not carefully watching the surrounding wilderness.

Once engaged in battle, an unarmed satyr attacks with a powerful head butt. A satyr expecting trouble is likely to be armed with a bow and a dagger and typically looses arrows from hiding, weakening an enemy before closing.

Pipes (Su): Satyrs can play a variety of magical tunes on their pan pipes. Usually, only one satyr in a group carries pipes. When it plays, all creatures within a 60-foot spread (except satyrs) must succeed on a DC 13 Will save or be affected by *charm person*, *sleep*, or *fear* (caster level 10th; the satyr chooses the tune and its effect). In the hands of other beings, these pipes have no special powers. A creature that successfully saves against any of the pipe's effects cannot be affected by the same set of pipes for 24 hours. The save DC is Charisma-based.

A satyr often uses its pipes to charm and seduce especially comely women or to put a party of adventurers to sleep and then steal their valuables.

Skills: Satyrs have a +4 racial bonus on Hide, Listen, Move Silently, Perform, and Spot checks.

SATYRS AS CHARACTERS

Satyr characters possess the following racial traits.

—+2 Dexterity, +2 Constitution, +2 Intelligence, +2 Wisdom, +2 Charisma.

—Medium size.
—A satyr's base land speed is 40 feet.
—Low-light vision.
—Racial Hit Dice: A satyr begins with five levels of fey, which provide 5d8 Hit Dice, a base attack bonus of +2, and base saving throw bonuses of Fort +1, Ref +4, and Will +4.
—Racial Skills: A satyr's fey levels give it skill points equal to 8 × (6 + Int modifier). Its class skills are Bluff, Hide, Knowledge (nature), Listen, Move Silently, Perform, and Spot. Satyrs have a +4 racial bonus on Hide, Listen, Move Silently, Perform, and Spot checks.
—Racial Feats: A satyr's fey levels give it two feats. A satyr receives Alertness as a bonus feat.
— +4 natural armor bonus.
—Natural Weapons: Head butt (1d6).
—Special Attacks (see above): Pipes.
—Special Qualities (see above): Damage reduction 5/cold iron.
—Automatic Languages: Sylvan. Bonus Languages: Common, Elven, Gnome.
—Favored Class: Bard.
—Level adjustment +2.

SEA CAT

Large Magical Beast
Hit Dice: 6d10+18 (51 hp)
Initiative: +1
Speed: 10 ft. (2 squares), swim 40 ft.
Armor Class: 18 (–1 size, +1 Dex, +8 natural), touch 10, flat-footed 17
Base Attack/Grapple: +6/+14
Attack: Claw +9 melee (1d6+4)
Full Attack: 2 claws +9 melee (1d6+4) and bite +4 melee (1d8+2)
Space/Reach: 10 ft./5 ft.
Special Attacks: Rend 2d6+6
Special Qualities: Darkvision 60 ft., hold breath, low-light vision, scent
Saves: Fort +8, Ref +6, Will +5
Abilities: Str 19, Dex 12, Con 17, Int 2, Wis 13, Cha 10
Skills: Listen +8, Spot +7, Swim +12
Feats: Alertness, Endurance, Iron Will
Environment: Temperate aquatic
Organization: Solitary, pair, or pride (5–12)
Challenge Rating: 4
Treasure: None
Alignment: Always neutral
Advancement: 7–9 HD (Large); 10–18 HD (Huge)
Level Adjustment: —

This creature has a body like that of a porpoise or a small whale, with a leonine head and forepaws. A ruff of silky hair runs from the top of its head all the way to its tail flukes.

The sea cat is a fearsome aquatic predator.

Sea cats inhabit shallow coastal waters, making their lairs in undersea caves or in the wreckage of ships. They hunt for fish, aquatic mammals, sea birds, and anything else they can catch and kill.

Satyr

A typical sea cat is 12 feet long and weighs 800 pounds.

COMBAT

Sea cats attack on sight, either for food or to defend their territory, and use both claws and teeth to grab and rend their prey. They display tremendous courage, always fighting to the death, even against creatures many times their size. Pairs and prides of sea cats attack in concert, trying to wear the opponent down until one beast can dispatch it.

Hold Breath (Ex): A sea cat can hold its breath for a number of rounds equal to 6 × its Constitution score before it risks drowning.

Rend (Ex): A sea cat that hits with both claw attacks latches onto the opponent's body and tears the flesh. This automatically deals an extra 2d6+6 points of damage.

Skills: A sea cat has a +8 racial bonus on any Swim check to perform some special action or avoid a hazard. It can always choose to take 10 on a Swim check, even if distracted or endangered. It can use the run action while swimming, provided it swims in a straight line.

Sea cat

Sea cats are aggressively territorial, attacking any creature, regardless of size, that enters their domain. Their chief enemies and competitors are sharks, and sea cats go out of their way to attack them. Sometimes they form temporary prides to deal with particularly dangerous or resistant intruders. Their normal pride structure is much like that of terrestrial lions.

SHADOW

This creature seems to be nothing but a patch of mobile gloom, more or less humanoid in shape.

Shadows are creatures of sentient darkness, hating life and light with equal fervor. Their touch bestows the painful chill of nonexistence, making them very dangerous opponents.

A shadow can be difficult to see in dark or gloomy areas but stands out starkly in brightly illuminated places.

Natural enemies of all that live, shadows are aggressive and predatory. They are quick to strike and make short work of those unprepared to deal with them.

A shadow is 5 to 6 feet tall and is weightless.

Shadows cannot speak intelligibly.

COMBAT

Shadows lurk in dark places, waiting for living prey to happen by.

Strength Damage (Su): The touch of a shadow deals 1d6 points of Strength damage to a living foe. A creature reduced to Strength 0 by a shadow dies. This is a negative energy effect.

	Shadow	Greater Shadow
	Medium Undead (Incorporeal)	Medium Undead (Incorporeal)
Hit Dice:	3d12 (19 hp)	9d12 (58 hp)
Initiative:	+2	+2
Speed:	Fly 40 ft. (good) (8 squares)	Fly 40 ft. (good) (8 squares)
Armor Class:	13 (+2 Dex, +1 deflection), touch 13, flat-footed 11	14 (+2 Dex, +2 deflection), touch 14, flat-footed 12
Base Attack/Grapple:	+1/—	+4/—
Attack:	Incorporeal touch +3 melee (1d6 Str)	Incorporeal touch +6 melee (1d8 Str)
Full Attack:	Incorporeal touch +3 melee (1d6 Str)	Incorporeal touch +6 melee (1d8 Str)
Space/Reach:	5 ft./5 ft.	5 ft./5 ft.
Special Attacks:	Create spawn, strength damage	Create spawn, strength damage
Special Qualities:	Darkvision 60 ft., incorporeal traits, +2 turn resistance, undead traits	Darkvision 60 ft., incorporeal traits, +2 turn resistance, undead traits
Saves:	Fort +1, Ref +3, Will +4	Fort +3, Ref +5, Will +7
Abilities:	Str —, Dex 14, Con —, Int 6, Wis 12, Cha 13	Str —, Dex 15, Con —, Int 6, Wis 12, Cha 14
Skills:	Hide +8*, Listen +7, Search +4, Spot +7	Hide +14*, Listen +9, Search +6, Spot +9
Feats:	Alertness, Dodge	Alertness, Dodge, Mobility, Spring Attack
Environment:	Any	Any
Organization:	Solitary, gang (2–5), or swarm (6–11)	Solitary
Challenge Rating:	3	8
Treasure:	None	None
Alignment:	Always chaotic evil	Always chaotic evil
Advancement:	4–9 HD (Medium)	—
Level Adjustment:	—	—

Create Spawn (Su): Any humanoid reduced to Strength 0 by a shadow becomes a shadow under the control of its killer within 1d4 rounds.

Skills: Shadows have a +2 racial bonus on Listen and Spot checks and a +4 racial bonus on Search checks.

*A shadow gains a +4 racial bonus on Hide checks in areas of shadowy illumination. In brightly lit areas, it takes a −4 penalty on Hide checks.

GREATER SHADOW

Although no more intelligent than an average shadow, a greater shadow is more fearsome because of its increased damage and its hit-and-run tactics.

Combat

A greater shadow uses stealth and cunning in combat. A favorite tactic is to lie in wait, almost completely concealed by walls or floor, then swoop out, make an incorporeal touch attack, and retreat back into a solid object without allowing a return attack.

Strength Damage (Su): The touch of a greater shadow deals 1d8 points of Strength damage to a living foe.

Shadow

SHADOW MASTIFF

Medium Outsider (Extraplanar)
Hit Dice: 4d8+12 (30 hp)
Initiative: +5
Speed: 50 ft. (10 squares)
Armor Class: 14 (+1 Dex, +3 natural), touch 11, flat-footed 13
Base Attack/Grapple: +4/+7
Attack: Bite +7 melee (1d6+4)
Full Attack: Bite +7 melee (1d6+4)
Space/Reach: 5 ft./5 ft.
Special Attacks: Bay, trip
Special Qualities: Darkvision 60 ft., shadow blend, scent
Saves: Fort +7, Ref +5, Will +5
Abilities: Str 17, Dex 13, Con 17, Int 4, Wis 12, Cha 13
Skills: Hide +8, Listen +8, Move Silently +8, Spot +8, Survival +8*
Feats: Dodge, Improved Initiative, Track[B]
Environment: Plane of Shadow
Organization: Solitary, pair, or pack (5–12)
Challenge Rating: 5
Treasure: None
Alignment: Always neutral evil
Advancement: 5–6 HD (Medium); 7–12 HD (Large)
Level Adjustment: +3 (cohort)

This creature has the body of a large dog, with a smooth black coat and a mouth full of sharp teeth.

Shadow mastiffs are great hounds that prowl the night, seeking any prey they can find. Their native plane is a place of eternal shadow.

A shadow mastiff is slightly more than 2 feet high at the shoulder and weighs about 200 pounds. Shadow mastiffs cannot speak, but they understand Common.

Illus. by S. Wood

COMBAT

Shadow mastiffs prefer fighting in shadows or dark conditions, which gives them a great advantage. If a magical light source negates the shadows around them, shadow mastiffs are cunning enough to either move out of the light or back off and break up the opposition with their baying. They have been known to seize and carry off items enspelled with *daylight* spells.

Bay (Su): When a shadow mastiff howls or barks, all creatures except evil outsiders within a 300-foot spread must succeed on a DC 13 Will save or become panicked for 2d4 rounds. This is a sonic mind-affecting fear effect. Whether or not the save is successful, an affected creature is immune to the same mastiff's bay for 24 hours. The save DC is Charisma-based.

Trip (Ex): A shadow mastiff that hits with its bite attack can attempt to trip the opponent as a free action (+3 check modifier) without making a touch attack or provoking an attack of opportunity. If the attempt fails, the opponent cannot react to trip the shadow mastiff.

Shadow Blend (Su): In any condition of illumination other than full daylight, a shadow mastiff can disappear into the shadows, giving it total concealment. Artificial illumination, even a *light* or *continual flame* spell, does not negate this ability. A *daylight* spell, however, will.

Skills: *A shadow mastiff has a +4 racial bonus on Survival checks when tracking by scent.

SHAMBLING MOUND

Large Plant
Hit Dice: 8d8+24 (60 hp)
Initiative: +0
Speed: 20 ft. (4 squares), swim 20 ft.
Armor Class: 20 (−1 size, +11 natural), touch 9, flat-footed 20
Base Attack/Grapple: +6/+15
Attack: Slam +11 melee (2d6+5)
Full Attack: 2 slams +11 melee (2d6+5)
Space/Reach: 10 ft./10 ft.
Special Attacks: Improved grab, constrict 2d6+7
Special Qualities: Darkvision 60 ft., immunity to electricity, low-light vision, plant traits, resistance to fire 10
Saves: Fort +9, Ref +2, Will +4
Abilities: Str 21, Dex 10, Con 17, Int 7, Wis 10, Cha 9
Skills: Hide +3*, Listen +8, Move Silently +8
Feats: Iron Will, Power Attack, Weapon Focus (slam)
Environment: Temperate marshes
Organization: Solitary
Challenge Rating: 6
Treasure: 1/10th coins; 50% goods; 50% items
Alignment: Usually neutral
Advancement: 9–12 HD (Large); 13–24 HD (Huge)
Level Adjustment: +6

Shadow mastiff

Shambine mound

grasp or *lightning bolt*) used against a shambler temporarily grants it 1d4 points of Constitution. The shambler loses these points at the rate of 1 per hour.

Skills: Shamblers have a +4 racial bonus on Hide, Listen, and Move Silently checks. *They have a +12 racial bonus on Hide checks when in a swampy or forested area.

SHIELD GUARDIAN

Large Construct
Hit Dice: 15d10+30 (112 hp)
Initiative: +0
Speed: 30 ft. (6 squares)
Armor Class: 24 (–1 size, +15 natural), touch 9, flat-footed 24
Base Attack/Grapple: +11/+21
Attack: Slam +16 melee (1d8+6)
Full Attack: 2 slams +16 melee (1d8+6)
Space/Reach: 10 ft./10 ft.
Special Attacks: —
   Special Qualities: Construct traits, darkvision 60 ft., fast healing 5, find master, guard, low-light vision, *shield other, spell storing*
Saves: Fort +5, Ref +5, Will +5
Abilities: Str 22, Dex 10, Con —, Int —, Wis 10, Cha 1
Environment: Any
Organization: Solitary
Challenge Rating: 8
Treasure: None
Alignment: Always neutral
Advancement: 16–24 HD (Large); 25–45 HD (Huge)
Level Adjustment: —

Shield guardian

This creature looks like a mass of leaves and vines with a generally human-like form. It has a barrel-shaped body with ropy arms and stumpy legs. It doesn't seem to have a head.

Shambling mounds, also called shamblers, appear to be heaps of rotting vegetation. They are actually intelligent, carnivorous plants.

A shambler's brain and sensory organs are located in its upper body.

A shambler is almost totally silent and invisible in its natural surroundings, often catching opponents flat-footed. It may lie partially submerged in a shallow bog, waiting patiently for some creature to walk onto it. Shamblers move easily through water as well, and they have been known to sneak into the camps of unsuspecting travelers at night.

Adventurers tell stories of shamblers moving about during intense electrical storms without so much as flinching from direct lightning strikes.

A shambler's body has an 8-foot girth and is about 6 feet tall when the creature stands erect. It weighs about 3,800 pounds.

COMBAT

A shambling mound batters or constricts its opponents with two huge, armlike appendages.

Improved Grab (Ex): To use this ability, a shambler must hit with both slam attacks. It can then attempt to start a grapple as a free action without provoking an attack of opportunity. If it wins the grapple check, it establishes a hold and can constrict.

Constrict (Ex): A shambler deals 2d6+7 points of damage with a successful grapple check.

Immunity to Electricity (Ex): Shamblers take no damage from electricity. Instead, any electricity attack (such as *shocking*

223

This massive conglomeration of stone, wood, and metal is the size of an ogre and resembles a giant stick figure with stony appendages.

Created by spellcasters to be bodyguards, shield guardians are constructs that protect their masters with spells and stamina.

When it is fashioned, a shield guardian is keyed to a particular magical amulet. Henceforth, it regards the wearer of that amulet to be its master, protecting and following that individual everywhere (unless specifically commanded not to do so).

A shield guardian obeys its master's verbal commands to the best of its ability, although it is not good for much beyond combat and possibly simple manual labor. It can also be keyed to perform specific tasks at specific times or when certain conditions are met. The wearer of the amulet can call the shield guardian from any distance, and it will come as long as it is on the same plane.

A shield guardian is some 9 feet tall and weighs more than 1,200 pounds.

Shield guardians cannot speak, but they understand commands given in any language.

COMBAT

Shield guardians are straightforward in battle, bashing with their heavy stone fists. They are made for defense and are not particularly impressive on offense.

Find Master (Su): As long as a shield guardian and its amulet are on the same plane, the shield guardian can find the amulet wearer (or just the amulet, if it is removed after the guardian is called).

Guard (Ex): If ordered to do so, a shield guardian moves swiftly to defend the wearer of its amulet, blocking blows and disrupting foes. All attacks against the amulet wearer take a −2 penalty when the shield guardian is adjacent to its master.

Shield Other **(Sp):** The wearer of a shield guardian's amulet can activate this defensive ability if within 100 feet of the shield guardian. Just as the spell of the same name, this ability transfers to the shield guardian half the damage that would be dealt to the amulet wearer (this ability does not provide the spell's AC or save bonuses).

Spell Storing **(Sp):** A shield guardian can store one spell of 4th level or lower that is cast into it by another creature. It "casts" this spell when commanded to do so or when a predefined situation arises. Once this spell is used, the shield guardian can store another spell (or the same spell again).

CONSTRUCTION

A shield guardian is built from wood, bronze, stone, and steel. The materials cost 5,000 gp. The creature's master may assemble the body or hire someone else to do the job. Creating the body requires a DC 16 Craft (blacksmithing) or Craft (carpentry) check. The keyed amulet is fashioned at the same time, and its cost (20,000 gp) is included in the cost of the guardian. After the body is sculpted, the shield guardian is animated through an extended magical ritual that requires a specially prepared laboratory or workroom, similar to an alchemist's laboratory and costing 500 gp to establish. If the creator is personally constructing the creature's body, the building and the ritual can be performed together.

A shield guardian with more than 15 Hit Dice can be created, but each additional Hit Die adds +5,000 gp to the market price, and the price increases by +20,000 gp if the creature's size increases to Huge, modifying the cost to create accordingly.

CL 15th; Craft Construct (see page 303), *limited wish, discern location, shield, shield other,* caster must be at least 15th level; Price 120,000 gp; Cost 65,000 gp + 4,600 XP.

AMULET

If a shield guardian's amulet is destroyed, the guardian ceases to function until a new one is created. If the wearer dies but the amulet is intact, the shield guardian carries out the last command it was given.

SHOCKER LIZARD

Small Magical Beast
Hit Dice: 2d10+2 (13 hp)
Initiative: +6
Speed: 40 ft. (8 squares), climb 20 ft., swim 20 ft.
Armor Class: 16 (+1 size, +2 Dex, +3 natural), touch 13, flat-footed 14
Base Attack/Grapple: +2/−2
Attack: Bite +3 melee (1d4)

Shocker lizard

SARDINHA

Full Attack: Bite +3 melee (1d4)

Space/Reach: 5 ft./5 ft.

Special Attacks: Stunning shock, lethal shock

Special Qualities: Darkvision 60 ft., electricity sense, immunity to electricity, low-light vision

Saves: Fort +4, Ref +5, Will +1

Abilities: Str 10, Dex 15, Con 13, Int 2, Wis 12, Cha 6

Skills: Climb +11, Hide +11, Jump +7, Listen +4, Spot +4, Swim +10

Feats: Improved Initiative

Environment: Warm marshes

Organization: Solitary, pair, clutch (3–5), or colony (6–11)

Challenge Rating: 2

Treasure: 1/10 coins; 50% goods; 50% items

Alignment: Always neutral

Advancement: 3–4 HD (Small); 5–6 HD (Medium)

Level Adjustment: —

This little lizard is about the size of a terrier, It has a bullet-shaped head sporting a large pair of horns that sweep back from the sides like spiky ears. A similar structure appears on the tip of the tail.

The shocker lizard is a sleek reptilelike creature whose body can generate intense electrical shocks.

A shocker lizard has a pale gray or blue underside, shading to a darker hue on its back. It has blue-black markings along its back and tail.

Shocker lizards prefer warm and damp conditions, and often lurk in swamps, shaded riverbanks, and water-filled caves. They hunt fish, reptiles, and small animals, but also scavenge or take larger prey from time to time. They spend most of their time hiding and waiting for prey to happen by.

A shocker lizard is about 1 foot tall at the shoulder and weighs about 25 pounds.

COMBAT

Unless it is very hungry, a shocker lizard dislikes fighting creatures larger than itself and usually tries to warn off intruders by emitting a series of rapid clicks. The sound is actually a low-power electrical discharge, and living creatures within 10 feet can feel the current tickling their skins and scalps. If the warning fails, the lizard raises its horns and tail to administer stunning shocks.

A shocker lizard relies on its electricity abilities in combat. A lizard tends to bite only after its shock has rendered an opponent unconscious or when the shock seems to have no effect at all. A solitary lizard flees once it delivers its shocks, but if other shocker lizards are nearby, they all home in on their comrade's discharges and attempt to administer their shocks to the foe.

Stunning Shock (Su): Once per round, a shocker lizard can deliver an electrical shock to a single opponent within 5 feet. This attack deals 2d8 points of nonlethal damage to living opponents (Reflex DC 12 half). The save DC is Constitution-based.

Lethal Shock (Su): Whenever two or more shocker lizards are within 20 feet of each other, they can work together to create a lethal shock. This effect has a radius of 20 feet, centered on any one contributing lizard. The shock deals 2d8 points of electricity damage for each lizard contributing to it, to a maximum of 12d8. A Reflex save (DC 10 + number of lizards contributing) reduces the damage by half.

Electricity Sense (Ex): Shocker lizards automatically detect any electrical discharges within 100 feet.

Skills: Shocker lizards have a +4 racial bonus on Hide checks due to their coloration. Shocker lizards have a +2 racial bonus on Listen and Spot checks.

Shocker lizards use their Dexterity modifier instead of their Strength modifier for Climb and Jump checks.

A shocker lizard has a +8 racial bonus on Climb checks and can always choose to take 10 on a Climb check, even if rushed or threatened.

A shocker lizard has a +8 racial bonus on any Swim check to perform some special action or avoid a hazard. It can always choose to take 10 on a Swim check, even if distracted or endangered. It can use the run action while swimming, provided it swims in a straight line.

SKELETON

This creature appears to be nothing but a set of animated bones. Pinpoints of red light smolder in its empty eye sockets.

Skeletons are the animated bones of the dead, mindless automatons that obey the orders of their evil masters.

A skeleton is seldom garbed in anything more than the rotting remnants of any clothing or armor it was wearing when slain. A skeleton does only what it is ordered to do. It can draw no conclusions of its own and takes no initiative. Because of this limitation, its instructions must always be simple, such as "Kill anyone who enters this chamber." A skeleton attacks until destroyed, for that is what it was created to do. The threat posed by a group of skeletons depends primarily on its size.

Skeleton

Illus. by B. Snoddy

CREATING A SKELETON

"Skeleton" is an acquired template that can be added to any corporeal creature (other than an undead) that has a skeletal system (referred to hereafter as the base creature).

Size and Type: The creature's type changes to undead. It retains any subtype except for alignment subtypes (such as good) and subtypes that indicate kind (such as goblinoid or reptilian). It does not gain the augmented subtype. It uses all the base creature's statistics and special abilities except as noted here.

Hit Dice: Drop any Hit Dice gained from class levels (to a minimum of 1) and raise remaining Hit Dice to d12s. If the creature has more than 20 Hit Dice, it can't be made into a skeleton by the *animate dead* spell.

Speed: Winged skeletons can't use their wings to fly. If the base creature flew magically, so can the skeleton.

	Human Warrior Skeleton Medium Undead	Wolf Skeleton Medium Undead	Owlbear Skeleton Large Undead
Hit Dice:	1d12 (6 hp)	2d12 (13 hp)	5d12 (32 hp)
Initiative:	+5	+7	+6
Speed:	30 ft. (6 squares)	50 ft. (10 squares)	30 ft. (6 squares)
Armor Class:	15 (+1 Dex, +2 natural, +2 heavy steel shield), touch 11, flat-footed 14	15 (+3 Dex, +2 natural), touch 13, flat-footed 12	13 (−1 size, +2 Dex, +2 natural), touch 11, flat-footed 11
Base Attack/Grapple:	+0/+1	+1/+2	+2/+11
Attack:	Scimitar +1 melee (1d6+1/18–20) or claw +1 melee (1d4+1)	Bite +2 melee (1d6+1)	Claw +6 melee (1d6+5)
Full Attack:	Scimitar +1 melee (1d6+1/18–20) or 2 claws +1 melee (1d4+1)	Bite +2 melee (1d6+1)	2 claws +6 melee (1d6+5) and bite +1 melee (1d8+2)
Space/Reach:	5 ft./5 ft.	5 ft./5 ft.	10 ft./5 ft.
Special Attacks:	—	—	—
Special Qualities:	Damage reduction 5/bludgeoning, darkvision 60 ft., immunity to cold, undead traits	Damage reduction 5/bludgeoning, darkvision 60 ft., immunity to cold, undead traits	Damage reduction 5/bludgeoning, darkvision 60 ft., immunity to cold, undead traits
Saves:	Fort +0, Ref +1, Will +2	Fort +0, Ref +3, Will +3	Fort +1, Ref +3, Will +4
Abilities:	Str 13, Dex 13, Con —, Int —, Wis 10, Cha 1	Str 13, Dex 17, Con —, Int —, Wis 10, Cha 1	Str 21, Dex 14, Con —, Int —, Wis 10, Cha 1
Feats:	Improved Initiative	Improved Initiative	Improved Initiative
Environment:	Temperate plains	Temperate forests	Temperate forests
Organization:	Any	Any	Any
Challenge Rating:	1/3	1	2
Treasure:	None	None	None
Alignment:	Always neutral evil	Always neutral evil	Always neutral evil
Advancement:	—	3 HD (Medium); 4–6 HD (Large)	6–8 HD (Large); 9–15 HD (Huge)
Level Adjustment:	—	—	—

Armor Class: Natural armor bonus changes to a number based on the skeleton's size:

Tiny or smaller	+0
Small	+1
Medium or Large	+2
Huge	+3
Gargantuan	+6
Colossal	+10

Attacks: A skeleton retains all the natural weapons, manufactured weapon attacks, and weapon proficiencies of the base creature, except for attacks that can't work without flesh (such as a mind flayer's tentacle attacks). A creature with hands gains one claw attack per hand; the skeleton can strike with each of its claw attacks at its full attack bonus. A skeleton's base attack bonus is equal to 1/2 its Hit Dice.

Damage: Natural and manufactured weapons deal damage normally. A claw attack deals damage depending on the skeleton's size. (If the base creature already had claw attacks with its hands, use the skeleton claw damage only if it's better.)

Diminutive or Fine	1
Tiny	1d2
Small	1d3
Medium	1d4
Large	1d6
Huge	1d8
Gargantuan	2d6
Colossal	2d8

Special Attacks: A skeleton retains none of the base creature's special attacks.

Special Qualities: A skeleton loses most special qualities of the base creature. It retains any extraordinary special qualities that improve its melee or ranged attacks. A skeleton gains the following special qualities.

Immunity to Cold (Ex): Skeletons are not affected by cold.

Damage Reduction 5/Bludgeoning: Skeletons lack flesh or internal organs.

Saves: Base save bonuses are Fort +1/3 HD, Ref +1/3 HD, and Will +1/2 HD + 2.

Abilities: A skeleton's Dexterity increases by +2, it has no Constitution or Intelligence score, its Wisdom changes to 10, and its Charisma changes to 1.

Skills: A skeleton has no skills.

Feats: A skeleton loses all feats of the base creature and gains Improved Initiative.

Environment: Any, usually same as base creature.

Organization: Any.

Challenge Rating: Depends on Hit Dice, as follows:

Hit Dice	Challenge Rating
1/2	1/6
1	1/3
2–3	1
4–5	2
6–7	3
8–9	4
10–11	5
12–14	6
15–17	7
18–20	8

Treasure: None.

Alignment: Always neutral evil.

Advancement: As base creature (or — if the base creature advances by character class).

Level Adjustment: —

	Troll Skeleton	Chimera Skeleton	Ettin Skeleton
	Large Undead	Large Undead	Large Undead
Hit Dice:	6d12 (39 hp)	9d12 (58 hp)	10d12 (65 hp)
Initiative:	+7	+6	+4
Speed:	30 ft. (6 squares)	30 ft. (6 squares)	40 ft. (8 squares)
Armor Class:	14 (+3 Dex, −1 size, +2 natural) touch 12, flat-footed 11	13 (+2 Dex, −1 size, +2 natural), touch 11, flat-footed 11	11 (−1 size, +2 natural) touch 9, flat-footed 11
Base Attack/Grapple:	+3/+13	+4/+12	+5/+15
Attack:	Claw +8 melee (1d6+6)	Bite +7 melee (2d6+4)	Morningstar +10 melee (2d6+6) or claw +10 melee (1d6+6) or javelin +4 ranged (1d8+6)
Full Attack:	2 claws +8 melee (1d6+6) and bite +3 melee (1d6+3)	Bite +7 melee (2d6+4) and bite+7 melee (1d8+4) and gore +7 melee (1d8+4) and 2 claws +2 melee (1d6+2)	2 morningstars +10 melee (2d6+6) or 2 claws +10 melee (1d6+6) or 2 javelins +4 ranged (1d8+6)
Space/Reach:	10 ft./10 ft	10 ft./5 ft	10 ft./10 ft.
Special Attacks:	—	—	—
Special Qualities:	Damage reduction 5/bludgeoning, darkvision 60 ft., immunity to cold, undead traits	Damage reduction 5/bludgeoning, darkvision 60 ft., immunity to cold, undead traits	Damage reduction 5/bludgeoning, darkvision 60 ft., immunity to cold, superior two-weapon fighting, undead traits
Saves:	Fort +2, Ref +5, Will +5	Fort +3, Ref +5, Will +6	Fort +3, Ref +3, Will +7
Abilities:	Str 23, Dex 16, Con —, Int —, Wis 10, Cha 1	Str 19, Dex 15, Con —, Int —, Wis 10, Cha 1	Str 23, Dex 10, Con —, Int —, Wis 10, Cha 1
Feats:	Improved Initiative	Improved Initiative	Improved Initiative
Environment:	Cold mountains	Temperate hills	Cold hills
Organization:	Any	Any	Any
Challenge Rating:	3	4	5
Treasure:	None	None	None
Alignment:	Always neutral evil	Always neutral evil	Always neutral evil
Advancement:	—	10–13 HD (Large); 14–27 HD (Huge)	—
Level Adjustment:	—	—	—

	Advanced Megaraptor Skeleton	Cloud Giant Skeleton	Young Adult Red Dragon Skeleton
	Huge Undead	Huge Undead	Huge Undead (Fire)
Hit Dice:	12d12 (78 hp)	17d12 (110 hp)	19d12 (123 hp)
Initiative:	+7	+6	+5
Speed:	60 ft. (12 squares)	50 ft. (10 squares)	40 ft. (8 squares)
Armor Class:	14 (−2 size, +3 Dex, +3 natural), touch 11, flat-footed 11	13 (−2 size, +2 Dex, +3 natural), touch 10, flat-footed 11	12 (−2 size, +1 Dex, +3 natural), touch 9, flat-footed 11
Base Attack/Grapple:	+6/+19	+8/+28	+9/+27
Attack:	Talons +9 melee (2d8+5)	Gargantuan morningstar +18 melee (4d6+18) or claw +18 melee (1d8+12) or rock +8 ranged (2d8+12)	Bite +17 melee (2d8+10)
Full Attack:	Talons +9 melee (2d8+5) and 2 claws +4 melee (1d8+2) and bite +4 melee (2d6+2)	Gargantuan morningstar +18/+13 melee (4d6+18) or 2 claws +18 melee (1d8+12) or rock +8 ranged (2d8+12)	Bite +17 melee (2d8+10) and 2 claws +12 melee (2d6+5) and 2 wings +12 melee (1d8+5) and tail slap +12 melee (2d6+15)
Space/Reach:	15 ft./10 ft.	15 ft./15 ft.	15 ft./10 ft.
Special Attacks:	—	—	—
Special Qualities:	Damage reduction 5/bludgeoning, darkvision 60 ft., immunity to cold, undead traits	Damage reduction 5/bludgeoning, darkvision 60 ft., immunity to cold, oversize weapon, undead traits	Damage reduction 5/bludgeoning, darkvision 60 ft., immunity to cold and fire, undead traits
Saves:	Fort +4, Ref +7, Will +8	Fort +5, Ref +7, Will +10	Fort +6, Ref +7, Will +8
Abilities:	Str 21, Dex 17, Con —, Int —, Wis 10, Cha 1	Str 35, Dex 15, Con —, Int —, Wis 10, Cha 1	Str 31, Dex 12, Con —, Int —, Wis 10, Cha 1
Feats:	Improved Initiative	Improved Initiative	Improved Initiative
Environment:	Warm forests	Temperate mountains	Warm mountains
Organization:	Any	Any	Any
Challenge Rating:	6	7	8
Treasure:	None	None	None
Alignment:	Always neutral evil	Always neutral evil	Always neutral evil
Advancement:	13–16 HD (Huge); 17–20 HD (Gargantuan)	—	20 HD (Huge)
Level Adjustment:	—	—	—

Medium Aberration (Aquatic)
Hit Dice: 2d8+2 (11 hp)
Initiative: +1
Speed: 20 ft. (4 squares), swim 40 ft.
Armor Class: 13 (+1 Dex, +2 natural), touch 11, flat-footed 12
Base Attack/Grapple: +1/+5
Attack: Bite +5 melee (2d6+4)
Full Attack: Bite +5 melee (2d6+4) and 2 claws +0 melee (1d4+2)
Space/Reach: 5 ft./5 ft.
Special Attacks: Rake 1d6+2
Special Qualities: Darkvision 60 ft., amphibious
Saves: Fort +1, Ref +1, Will +3
Abilities: Str 19, Dex 13, Con 13, Int 10, Wis 10, Cha 6
Skills: Hide +6*, Listen +7*, Move Silently +6, Spot +7*, Swim +12
Feats: Alertness
Environment: Underground
Organization: Brood (2–5) or pack (6–15)
Challenge Rating: 2
Treasure: None
Alignment: Usually lawful evil
Advancement: 3–4 HD (Medium); 5–6 HD (Large)
Level Adjustment: +3

This creature looks like an abominable crossbreed of human and fish. Its fins have grown into twisted arms and legs, and its bent back is crowned with a long, spiny frill. It has a slender, muscular tail and bulbous eyes.

Skum

Skum are misbegotten creatures created by aboleths to serve as beasts of burden and slaves. They are derived from human stock, making them even more loathsome.

A skum is about the same height and weight as a human.

Skum speak Aquan.

COMBAT

In the water, skum are dangerous enemies who attack by biting, clawing, and raking with their rear legs. Skum serving an aboleth are sometimes trained to fight with weapons, usually two-handed melee weapons with reach (such as longspears) and simple ranged weapons such as javelins, tridents, or slings.

Rake (Ex): Attack bonus +0 melee, damage 1d6+2. A skum also gains two rake attacks when it attacks while swimming.

Skills: *Skum have a +4 racial bonus on Hide, Listen, and Spot checks underwater.

A skum has a +8 racial bonus on any Swim check to perform some special action or avoid a hazard. It can always choose to take 10 on a Swim check, even if distracted or endangered. It can use the run action while swimming, provided it swims in a straight line.

The chaotic planes seethe and roil with random energy and bits of matter. Weaving their way amid this cacophony of light and sound are the slaadi.

Creatures of chaos, slaadi have been likened to humanoid toads, but that description belies their agility and fearsome fighting prowess.

All slaadi speak their own language, Slaad. Green, gray, and death slaadi also speak Common, and in addition death slaadi can communicate telepathically.

COMBAT

Slaadi generally attack with their claws and bite. They relish melee combat but are savvy enough to use their summoning and other spell-like abilities to good effect. A slaad's natural weapons, as well as any weapons it wields, are treated as chaotic-aligned for the purpose of overcoming damage reduction.

All slaadi have resistance to acid 5, cold 5, electricity 5, and fire 5, and immunity to sonic damage.

Summon Slaad (Sp): Slaadi can summon other slaadi much as though casting a *summon monster* spell, but they have only a limited chance of success. Roll d%: On a failure, no slaadi answer the summons. Summoned creatures automatically return whence they came after 1 hour. A slaad that has just been summoned cannot use its own summon ability for 1 hour.

Most slaadi do not use this ability lightly, since they are generally distrustful and fearful of one another. In general, they use it only when necessary to save their own lives.

SLAADI CHARACTERS

Slaadi rarely have the focus to devote themselves to a character class. Grays sometimes become sorcerers, and the most powerful death slaadi train as rogues to take the assassin class.

RED SLAAD

Large Outsider (Chaotic, Extraplanar)
Hit Dice: 7d8+21 (52 hp)
Initiative: +2
Speed: 30 ft. (6 squares)
Armor Class: 19 (–1 size, +2 Dex, +8 natural), touch 11, flat-footed 17
Base Attack/Grapple: +7/+16
Attack: Bite +11 melee (2d8+5)
Full Attack: Bite +11 melee (2d8+5) and 2 claws +9 melee (1d4+2 plus implant)
Space/Reach: 10 ft./10 ft.
Special Attacks: Pounce, implant, stunning croak, *summon slaad*
Special Qualities: Darkvision 60 ft., fast healing 5, immunity to sonic, resistance to acid 5, cold 5, electricity 5, and fire 5
Saves: Fort +8, Ref +7, Will +3
Abilities: Str 21, Dex 15, Con 17, Int 6, Wis 6, Cha 8

Skills: Climb +15, Hide +8, Jump +15, Listen +8, Move Silently +12, Spot +8

Feats: Dodge, Mobility, Multiattack

Environment: Ever-Changing Chaos of Limbo

Organization: Solitary, pair, gang (3–5), or pack (6–10)

Challenge Rating: 7

Treasure: Standard

Alignment: Usually chaotic neutral

Advancement: 8–10 HD (Large); 11–21 HD (Huge)

Level Adjustment: +6

This creature looks like a roughly humanoid, red-skinned toad with almost no neck and a massive, flat head. It is bipedal, with clawed hands and feet. The hands and the digits on them are particularly large. A human would stand only about as high as the creature's shoulders.

Weakest of the slaadi, the reds wander about individually, often establishing secret lairs on other planes. Most seek to escape from the other more powerful and sometimes cruel slaadi.

A red slaad is about 8 feet tall and weighs about 650 pounds. As its name suggests, a red slaad is mostly red, darker along the back and paler around the belly.

Red slaadi are found in groups only when working for some greater power that somehow has mastered them. Even then, they don't coordinate actions well.

Combat

Red slaadi usually attack only when hungry or riled. Once aroused, however, a red slaad fights to the death.

Pounce (Ex): If a red slaad charges, it can make a full attack in the same round.

Implant (Ex): A red slaad that hits with a claw attack can inject an egg pellet into the opponent's body. The affected creature must succeed on a DC 16 Fortitude save to avoid implantation. The save DC is Constitution-based.

Often the slaad implants an unconscious or otherwise helpless creature (which gets no saving throw). The egg gestates for one week before hatching into a blue slaad that eats its way out, killing the host. Twenty-four hours before the egg fully matures, the victim falls extremely ill (–10 to all ability scores, to a minimum of 1). A *remove disease* spell rids a victim of the pellet, as does a DC 25 Heal check. If the check fails, the healer can try again, but each attempt (successful or not) deals 1d4 points of damage to the patient.

If the host is an arcane spellcaster, the egg pellet instead hatches into a green slaad.

Stunning Croak (Su): Once per day a red slaad can emit a loud croak. Every creature (except slaadi) within 20 feet must succeed on a DC 16 Fortitude save or be stunned for 1d3 rounds. The save DC is Constitution-based.

Summon Slaad (Sp): Once per day a red slaad can attempt to summon another red slaad with a 40% chance of success. This ability is the equivalent of a 3rd-level spell.

BLUE SLAAD

Large Outsider (Chaotic, Extraplanar)

Hit Dice: 8d8+32 (68 hp)

Initiative: +2

Speed: 30 ft. (6 squares)

Armor Class: 20 (–1 size, +2 Dex, +9 natural), touch 11, flat-footed 18

Base Attack/Grapple: +8/+18

Attack: Claw +13 melee (2d6+6)

Full Attack: 4 claws +13 melee (2d6+6) and bite +11 melee (2d8+3 plus disease)

Space/Reach: 10 ft./10 ft.

Special Attacks: Spell-like abilities, slaad fever, *summon slaad*

Special Qualities: Darkvision 60 ft., fast healing 5, immunity to sonic, resistance to acid 5, cold 5, electricity 5, and fire 5

Saves: Fort +10, Ref +8, Will +4

Abilities: Str 23, Dex 15, Con 19, Int 6, Wis 6, Cha 10

Skills: Climb +17, Hide +9, Jump +17, Listen +9, Move Silently +13, Spot +9

Feats: Dodge, Mobility, Multiattack

Environment: Ever-Changing Chaos of Limbo

Organization: Solitary, pair, gang (3–5), or pack (6–10)

Challenge Rating: 8

Treasure: Standard

Alignment: Usually chaotic neutral

Advancement: 9–12 HD (Large); 13–24 HD (Huge)

Level Adjustment: +6

This hulking creature looks like a strapping blue-skinned humanoid toad, as big as an ogre, with almost no neck and a massive, flat head. It is bipedal, with clawed hands and feet. It has wicked-looking, bony hooks on the backs of its hands.

Blue slaadi gather to wage horrific battles against other societies and their own. They are bullies that value only strength and power.

A blue slaad is about 10 feet tall and very broad. It weighs about 1,000 pounds. As its name suggests, a blue slaad is mostly blue, darker along the back and paler around the belly.

Blue slaadi are most often found in groups and work well together—at least, better than red slaadi.

Blue Slaad

Death slaad

Combat

Blue slaadi are quick to anger, and inclined to attack most other creatures on sight to prove their strength. The bone hooks on the backs of its hands give a blue slaad four claw attacks each round when it makes a full attack.

Spell-Like Abilities: At will—*hold person* (DC 13), *passwall*, *telekinesis* (DC 15); 1/day—*chaos hammer* (DC 14). Caster level 8th. The save DCs are Charisma-based.

Slaad Fever (Su): Supernatural disease—bite, Fortitude DC 18, incubation period 1 day, damage 1d3 Dex and 1d3 Cha. The save DC is Constitution-based.

An afflicted humanoid reduced to Charisma 0 by slaad fever immediately transforms into a red slaad. It retains none of the features, traits, memories, or abilities of its former self, and is a normal red slaad in all respects.

If the infected being is an arcane spellcaster, the disease instead produces a green slaad.

Green slaad

Gray slaad

Red slaad

Summon Slaad (Sp): Once per day a blue slaad can attempt to summon another blue slaad with a 40% chance of success. This ability is the equivalent of a 4th-level spell.

GREEN SLAAD

Large Outsider (Chaotic, Extraplanar)
Hit Dice: 9d8+36 (76 hp)
Initiative: +5
Speed: 30 ft. (6 squares)
Armor Class: 23 (−1 size, +1 Dex, +13 natural), touch 10, flat-footed 22
Base Attack/Grapple: +9/+19
Attack: Claw +14 melee (1d6+6)
Full Attack: 2 claws +14 melee (1d6+6) and bite +12 melee (2d8+3)
Space/Reach: 10 ft./10 ft.
Special Attacks: Spell-like abilities, *summon slaad*
Special Qualities: Change shape, darkvision 60 ft., fast healing 5, immunity to sonic, resistance to acid 5, cold 5, electricity 5, and fire 5
Saves: Fort +10, Ref +7, Will +6
Abilities: Str 23, Dex 13, Con 19, Int 10, Wis 10, Cha 12
Skills: Climb +18, Concentration +10, Hide +9, Jump +18, Listen +12, Move Silently +13, Search +12, Spot +12, Survival +6 (+8 following tracks)
Feats: Cleave, Improved Initiative, Multiattack, Power Attack
Environment: Ever-Changing Chaos of Limbo
Organization: Solitary or gang (2–5)
Challenge Rating: 9
Treasure: Standard

Alignment: Usually chaotic neutral
Advancement: 10–15 HD (Large); 16–27 HD (Huge)
Level Adjustment: +7

This tall, gangly creature looks like a cross between an ogre and a frog. Its skin is a mottled green, and it has long, sharp claws and a wide mouth.

If a red slaad's egg pellet or a blue slaad's disease infects an arcane spellcaster, that host produces a green slaad.

A green slaad is about 10 feet tall and very broad. It weighs about 1,000 pounds. As its name suggests, a green slaad is mostly green, darker along the back and paler around the belly.

Green slaadi are self-centered, arrogant louts that think only of themselves. They lust after magical power, eventually transforming into grays (see below) if they find it.

Green slaadi work in groups if doing so suits their immediate needs.

Combat

Green slaadi prefer to use spell-like abilities over physical combat but aren't afraid to attack with tooth and claw if they must. They never fight to the death, though, if they can avoid it.

Spell-Like Abilities: At will— *chaos hammer* (DC 15), *detect magic*, *detect thoughts* (DC 13), *fear* (DC 15), *protection from law*, *see invisibility*, *shatter* (DC 13); 3/day— *dispel law* (DC 16), *deeper darkness*, *fireball* (DC 14). Caster level 9th. The save DCs are Charisma-based.

Change Shape (Su): A green can assume any Medium or Large humanoid form as a standard action. In humanoid form, a green slaad cannot use its natural weapons (although a slaad can equip itself with weapons and armor appropriate to its appearance). A green slaad remains in one form until it chooses to assume a new one. A change in form cannot be dispelled, but the slaad reverts to its natural form when killed. A *true seeing* spell reveals its natural form.

Summon Slaad (Sp): Twice per day a green slaad can attempt to summon another green slaad with a 40% chance of success. This ability is the equivalent of a 5th-level spell.

Illus. by J. Jarvis

GRAY SLAAD

Medium Outsider (Chaotic, Extraplanar)
Hit Dice: 10d8+50 (95 hp)
Initiative: +7
Speed: 30 ft. (6 squares)
Armor Class: 24 (+3 Dex, +11 natural), touch 13, flat-footed 21
Base Attack/Grapple: +10/+14
Attack: Claw +15 melee (2d4+4)
Full Attack: 2 claws +15 melee (2d4+4) and bite +12 melee (2d8+2)
Space/Reach: 5 ft./5 ft.
Special Attacks: Spell-like abilities, *summon slaad*
Special Qualities: Change shape, damage reduction 10/lawful, darkvision 60 ft., fast healing 5, immunity to sonic, resistance to acid 5, cold 5, electricity 5, and fire 5
Saves: Fort +12, Ref +10, Will +9
Abilities: Str 19, Dex 17, Con 21, Int 14, Wis 14, Cha 14
Skills: Climb +17, Concentration +15, Hide +16, Jump +17, Knowledge (arcana) +15, Listen +15, Move Silently +16, Search +15, Spellcraft +17, Spot +15, Survival +5 (+7 following tracks)
Feats: Multiattack, Improved Initiative, Weapon Focus (claw), item creation feat (any one)
Environment: Ever-Changing Chaos of Limbo
Organization: Solitary or pair
Challenge Rating: 10
Treasure: Double standard
Alignment: Usually chaotic neutral
Advancement: 11–15 HD (Medium); 16–30 HD (Large)
Level Adjustment: +6

Lean and quick-looking, this humanoid resembles a two-legged frog. Its skin is a dappled gray color, and its fingers are long and clawed. It stands as tall as a human.

A green slaad that survives for more than a century retreats into isolation for at least a year. It returns as a smaller, leaner gray slaad and devotes most of its time and attention to magical study. Gray slaadi enjoy crafting magic items to further their own power.

Combat

Gray slaadi prefer to fight from a distance, using their spell-like abilities, although they don't shy away from melee.

Spell-Like Abilities: At will—*chaos hammer* (DC 16), *deeper darkness, detect magic, identify, invisibility, lightning bolt* (DC 15), *magic circle against law, see invisibility, shatter* (DC 14); 3/day—*animate objects, dispel law* (DC 17), *fly*; 1/day— *power word stun.* Caster level 10th. The save DCs are Charisma-based.

Change Shape (Su): A gray slaad can assume any humanoid form as a standard action. In humanoid form, a gray slaad cannot use its natural weapons (although a slaad can equip itself with weapons and armor appropriate to its appearance). A gray slaad remains in one form until it chooses to assume a new one. A change in form cannot be dispelled, but the slaad reverts to its natural form when killed. A *true seeing* spell reveals its natural form.

Summon Slaad **(Sp):** Twice per day a gray slaad can attempt to summon 1–2 red slaadi or 1 blue slaad with a 60% chance of success, or 1 green slaad with a 40% chance of success. This ability is the equivalent of a 5th-level spell.

DEATH SLAAD

Medium Outsider (Chaotic, Extraplanar)
Hit Dice: 15d8+75 (142 hp)
Initiative: +10
Speed: 30 ft. (6 squares)
Armor Class: 28 (+6 Dex, +12 natural), touch 16, flat-footed 22
Base Attack/Grapple: +15/+20
Attack: Claw +20 melee (3d6+5 plus stun)
Full Attack: 2 claws +20 melee (3d6+5 plus stun) and bite +18 melee (2d10+2)
Space/Reach: 5 ft./5 ft.
Special Attacks: Stun, spell-like abilities, *summon slaad*
Special Qualities: Change shape, damage reduction 10/lawful, darkvision 60 ft., fast healing 5, immunity to sonic, resistance to acid 5, cold 5, electricity 5, and fire 5, telepathy 100 ft.
Saves: Fort +14, Ref +15, Will +13
Abilities: Str 21, Dex 23, Con 21, Int 18, Wis 18, Cha 18
Skills: Climb +23, Concentration +15, Escape Artist +24, Hide +24, Intimidate +22, Jump +23, Knowledge (any two) +22, Listen +22, Move Silently +24, Search +22, Spot +22, Survival +12 (+14 when tracking), Use Rope +6 (+8 with bindings)
Feats: Cleave, Great Cleave, Improved Initiative, Improved Sunder, Multiattack, Power Attack
Environment: Ever-Changing Chaos of Limbo
Organization: Solitary or pair
Challenge Rating: 13
Treasure: Double standard
Alignment: Usually chaotic evil
Advancement: 16–22 HD (Medium); 23–45 HD (Large)
Level Adjustment: —

Lean and quick-looking, this humanoid resembles a two-legged frog. Its skin is a dappled gray color, and its fingers are long and clawed. It stands as tall as a human.

Death slaadi are grays that undergo some mysterious ritual that transforms them into veritable killing machines. Although they have spell-like abilities like gray slaadi, death slaadi focus more on killing than on magical power. They look exactly like gray slaadi.

All slaadi obey the command of a death slaad, out of fear more than anything else. Death slaadi represent a corruption of pure chaos by evil rather than true exemplars of it.

Combat

Although its prowess with its natural weapons is fearsome, a death slaad enjoys wielding a magic weapon if available.

Stun (Ex): Three times per day, a death slaad can attempt to stun its opponent on an attack with one of its natural weapons. If the opponent fails a DC 21 Fortitude save, it is stunned for 1 round in addition to taking normal damage from the attack. The save DC is Wisdom-based.

Spell-Like Abilities: At will—*animate objects, chaos hammer* (DC 18), *deeper darkness, detect magic, dispel law* (DC 19), *fear* (DC 18), *finger of death* (DC 21), *fireball* (DC 17), *fly, identify, invisibility, magic circle against law, see invisibility, shatter* (DC 16); 3/day—*circle of death* (DC 20), *cloak of chaos* (DC 22), *word of chaos* (DC 21); 1/day—*implosion* (DC 23), *power word blind.* Caster level 15th. The save DCs are Charisma-based.

Change Shape (Su): A death slaad can assume any humanoid form as a standard action. In humanoid form, a death slaad cannot use its natural weapons (although a slaad can equip itself with weapons and armor appropriate to its appearance). A death slaad remains in one form until it chooses to assume a new one. A change in form cannot be dispelled, but the slaad reverts to its natural form when killed. A *true seeing* spell reveals its natural form.

Summon Slaad **(Sp):** Twice per day a death slaad can attempt to summon 1–2 red or blue slaadi with a 60% chance of success, or 1–2 green slaadi with a 40% chance of success. This ability is the equivalent of a 6th-level spell.

SPECTRE

Medium Undead (Incorporeal)

Hit Dice: 7d12 (45 hp)
Initiative: +7
Speed: 40 ft. (8 squares), fly 80 ft. (perfect)
Armor Class: 15 (+3 Dex, +2 deflection), touch 15, flat-footed 13
Base Attack/Grapple: +3/—
Attack: Incorporeal touch +6 melee (1d8 plus energy drain)
Full Attack: Incorporeal touch +6 melee (1d8 plus energy drain)
Space/Reach: 5 ft./5 ft.
Special Attacks: Energy drain, create spawn
Special Qualities: Darkvision 60 ft., incorporeal traits, +2 turn resistance, sunlight powerlessness, undead traits, unnatural aura
Saves: Fort +2, Ref +5, Will +7
Abilities: Str —, Dex 16, Con —, Int 14, Wis 14, Cha 15
Skills: Hide +13, Intimidate +12, Knowledge (religion) +12, Listen +14, Search +12, Spot +14, Survival +2 (+4 following tracks)
Feats: Alertness, Blind-Fight, Improved Initiative
Environment: Any land and underground
Organization: Solitary, gang (2–4), or swarm (6–11)
Challenge Rating: 7
Treasure: None
Alignment: Always lawful evil
Advancement: 8–14 HD (Medium)
Level Adjustment: —

This entity looks like a human, but with a diaphanous and faintly luminous body.

Spectres are incorporeal undead often mistaken for ghosts. They haunt the places where they died, retaining their sentience but now hating all living things.

A spectre looks much as it did in life and can be easily recognized by those who knew the individual or have seen the individual's face in a painting or a drawing. In many cases, the evidence of a violent death is visible on its body. The chill of death lingers in the air around spectres and in the places they haunt.

A spectre is roughly human-sized and is weightless.

Spectre

COMBAT

In close combat a spectre attacks with its numbing, life-draining touch. It makes full use of its incorporeal nature, moving through walls, ceilings, and floors as it attacks.

Energy Drain (Su): Living creatures hit by a spectre's incorporeal touch attack gain two negative levels. The DC is 15 for the Fortitude save to remove a negative level. The save DC is Charisma-based. For each such negative level bestowed, the spectre gains 5 temporary hit points.

Create Spawn (Su): Any humanoid slain by a spectre becomes a spectre in 1d4 rounds. Spawn are under the command of the spectre that created them and remain enslaved until its death. They do not possess any of the abilities they had in life.

Unnatural Aura (Su): Animals, whether wild or domesticated, can sense the unnatural presence of a spectre at a distance of 30 feet. They do not willingly approach nearer than that and panic if forced to do so; they remain panicked as long as they are within that range.

Sunlight Powerlessness (Ex): Spectres are powerless in natural sunlight (not merely a *daylight* spell) and flee from it. A spectre caught in sunlight cannot attack and can take only a single move or attack action in a round.

SPHINX

Sphinxes are enigmatic creatures with great, feathery wings and leonine bodies. All sphinxes are territorial, but the more intelligent ones can differentiate between deliberate intrusion and temporary or inadvertent trespass.

A typical sphinx is about 10 feet long and weighs about 800 pounds.

Sphinxes speak Sphinx, Common, and Draconic.

Combat

Most sphinxes fight on the ground, using their wings to help them pounce much as lions do. If outnumbered by earthbound creatures, a sphinx takes wing and attacks on the fly.

Pounce (Ex): If a sphinx charges a foe, it can make a full attack, including two rake attacks.

Rake (Ex): A sphinx that pounces onto a creature can make two rake attacks with its hind legs. Each sphinx's description provides its attack bonus and damage.

ANDROSPHINX

Large Magical Beast

Hit Dice: 12d10+48 (114 hp)
Initiative: +0
Speed: 50 ft. (10 squares), fly 80 ft. (poor)
Armor Class: 22 (–1 size, +13 natural), touch 9, flat-footed 22
Base Attack/Grapple: +12/+23
Attack: Claw +18 melee (2d4+7)
Full Attack: 2 claws +18 melee (2d4+7)
Space/Reach: 10 ft./5 ft.
Special Attacks: Pounce, rake 2d4+3, roar, spells
Special Qualities: Darkvision 60 ft., low-light vision
Saves: Fort +12, Ref +8, Will +7
Abilities: Str 25, Dex 10, Con 19, Int 16, Wis 17, Cha 17
Skills: Intimidate +17, Knowledge (any one) +18, Listen +18, Spot +18, Survival +18
Feats: Alertness, Cleave, Great Cleave, Flyby Attack, Power Attack, Track
Environment: Warm deserts
Organization: Solitary
Challenge Rating: 9
Treasure: Standard
Alignment: Always chaotic good
Advancement: 13–18 HD (Large); 19–36 HD (Huge)
Level Adjustment: +5 (cohort)

This creature is bigger than a riding horse and has a tawny lion body, great falcon wings, and a humanoid face.

These sphinxes are always male. Androsphinxes are clever and generally good-natured, but they can be savage opponents.

Though outwardly gruff and bad-tempered, androsphinxes have noble hearts, and are a little bit shy. They appreciate small courtesies, but seldom admit it, and praise makes them feel uncomfortable.

Combat

In battle, an androsphinx rips apart enemies with its razor-sharp claws. It relies on its natural weapons in a fight, employing its spells for defense or healing.

Rake (Ex): Attack bonus +18 melee, damage 2d4+3.

Roar (Su): Three times per day an androsphinx can loose a mighty roar. The first time it does this, all creatures within 500 feet must succeed on a DC 19 Will save or be affected as though by a *fear* spell for 2d6 rounds.

If the sphinx roars a second time during the same encounter, all creatures within 250 feet must succeed on a DC 19 Fortitude save or be paralyzed for 1d4 rounds, and all those within 90 feet are deafened for 2d6 rounds (no save).

If it roars a third time during the same encounter, all those within 250 feet must succeed on a DC 19 Fortitude save or take 2d4 points of Strength damage for 2d4 rounds. In addition, any Medium or smaller creature within 90 feet must succeed on a DC 19 Fortitude save or be thrown to the ground and take 2d8 points of damage. The force of this roar is so great that it deals 50 points of damage to any stone or crystalline object within 90 feet. Magic items and held or carried items can avoid damage with a DC 19 Reflex save.

Other androsphinxes are immune to these effects. The save DCs are Charisma-based.

Spells: An androsphinx casts divine spells as a 6th-level cleric from the cleric spell list and from the Good, Healing, and Protection domains.

Typical Cleric Spells Prepared (5/5/5/4; save DC 13 + spell level): 0—*cure minor wounds, detect magic, guidance, light, resistance;* 1st—*divine favor, protection from evil*, shield of faith, remove fear, summon monster I;* 2nd—*bull's strength, remove paralysis, resist energy, shield other*, summon monster II;* 3rd—*cure serious wounds*, daylight, invisibility purge, searing light.*

*Domain spell. Domains: Good and Healing.

CRIOSPHINX

Large Magical Beast
Hit Dice: 10d10+30 (85 hp)
Initiative: +0
Speed: 30 ft. (6 squares), fly 60 ft. (poor)
Armor Class: 20 (–1 size, +11 natural), touch 9, flat-footed 20
Base Attack/Grapple: +10/+20
Attack: Gore +15 melee (2d6+6)
Full Attack: Gore +15 melee (2d6+6) and 2 claws +10 melee (1d6+3)
Space/Reach: 10 ft./5 ft.
Special Attacks: Pounce, rake 1d6+3
Special Qualities: Darkvision 60 ft., low-light vision
Saves: Fort +10, Ref +7, Will +3
Abilities: Str 23, Dex 10, Con 17, Int 10, Wis 11, Cha 11
Skills: Intimidate +8, Listen +11, Spot +1
Feats: Alertness, Cleave, Flyby Attack, Power Attack
Environment: Warm deserts
Organization: Solitary
Challenge Rating: 7
Treasure: Standard
Alignment: Always neutral

Advancement: 11–15 HD (Large); 16–30 HD (Huge)
Level Adjustment: +3 (cohort)

This creature is bigger than a horse and has a tawny lion body, great falcon wings, and a ram's head.

These sphinxes are always male. Neither good nor evil, they lack the intelligence of the androsphinx.

Criosphinxes constantly seek gynosphinxes, but if they cannot find one, they pursue wealth above all else. The best deal an adventurer can hope to strike with a criosphinx is safe passage in exchange for all of his or her treasure.

Combat

Criosphinxes attack with their claws, as do their kin, but they can also butt with their horns. They don't cast spells and employ only the most simple battle tactics.

Rake (Ex): Attack bonus +15 melee, damage 1d6+3.

GYNOSPHINX

Large Magical Beast
Hit Dice: 8d10+8 (52 hp)
Initiative: +5
Speed: 40 ft. (8 squares), fly 60 ft. (poor)
Armor Class: 21 (–1 size, +1 Dex, +11 natural), touch 10, flat-footed 20
Base Attack/Grapple: +8/+16
Attack: Claw +11 melee (1d6+4)
Full Attack: 2 claws +11 melee (1d6+4)
Space/Reach: 10 ft./5 ft.
Special Attacks: Pounce, rake 1d6+2, spell-like abilities
Special Qualities: Darkvision 60 ft., low-light vision
Saves: Fort +7, Ref +7, Will +8
Abilities: Str 19, Dex 12, Con 13, Int 18, Wis 19, Cha 19
Skills: Bluff +15, Concentration +12, Diplomacy +8, Disguise +4 (+6 acting), Intimidate +13, Listen +17, Sense Motive +15, Spot +17
Feats: Combat Casting, Improved Initiative, Iron Will
Environment: Warm deserts
Organization: Solitary or covey (2–4)
Challenge Rating: 8
Treasure: Double standard
Alignment: Always neutral
Advancement: 9–12 HD (Large); 13–24 HD (Huge)
Level Adjustment: +4 (cohort)

This creature is bigger than a horse and has a tawny lion body, great falcon wings, and the head of a female humanoid.

These sphinxes are the female counterparts of androsphinxes.

Gynosphinxes often are willing to bargain for treasure or service. They constantly seek out new intellectual challenges—riddles, puzzles, and other such tests delight them to no end. They find criosphinxes and hieracosphinxes detestable.

Combat

In close combat, gynosphinxes use their powerful claws to flay the flesh from their enemies. Despite their deadly nature, they prefer to avoid combat whenever possible.

Gynosphinx

Rake (Ex): Attack bonus +11 melee, damage 1d6+2.

Spell-Like Abilities: 3/day—*clairaudience/clairvoyance, detect magic, read magic, see invisibility;* 1/day—*comprehend languages, locate object, dispel magic, remove curse* (DC 18), *legend lore.* Caster level 14th. The save DC is Charisma-based.

Once per week a gynosphinx can create a *symbol of death,* a *symbol of fear,* a *symbol of insanity,* a *symbol of pain,* a *symbol of persuasion,* a *symbol of sleep,* and a *symbol of stunning* as the spells (caster level 18th), except that all save DCs are 22 and each symbol remains a maximum of one week once scribed. The save DCs are Charisma-based.

HIERACOSPHINX

Large Magical Beast
Hit Dice: 9d10+18 (67 hp)
Initiative: +2
Speed: 30 ft. (6 squares), fly 90 ft. (poor)
Armor Class: 19 (–1 size, +2 Dex, +8 natural), touch 11, flat-footed 17
Base Attack/Grapple: +9/+18
Attack: Bite +13 melee (1d10+5)
Full Attack: Bite +13 melee (1d10+5) and 2 claws +8 melee (1d6+2)
Space/Reach: 10 ft./5 ft.
Special Attacks: Pounce, rake 1d6+2
Special Qualities: Darkvision 60 ft., low-light vision
Saves: Fort +8, Ref +8, Will +5
Abilities: Str 21, Dex 14, Con 15, Int 6, Wis 15, Cha 10
Skills: Listen +10, Spot +14
Feats: Alertness, Cleave, Flyby Attack, Power Attack
Environment: Warm deserts
Organization: Solitary, pair, or flock (4–7)
Challenge Rating: 5
Treasure: None
Alignment: Always chaotic evil
Advancement: 10–14 HD (Large); 15–27 HD (Huge)
Level Adjustment: +3 (cohort)

This creature is bigger than a horse and has a tawny lion body, great falcon wings, and the head of a falcon.

Of all the sphinxes, only these creatures are evil at heart. They are always male. They spend much of their time searching for a gynosphinx but are generally just as happy to maul someone.

Combat

Hieracosphinxes can make short work of even the most dangerous opponents with their claws. They are not particularly intelligent, but are cunning enough to dive at their enemies from above with their flying ability.

Rake (Ex): Attack bonus +13 melee, damage 1d6+2.
Skills: Hieracosphinxes have a +4 racial bonus on Spot checks.

SPIDER EATER

Large Magical Beast
Hit Dice: 4d10+20 (42 hp)
Initiative: +1
Speed: 30 ft. (6 squares), fly 60 ft. (good)
Armor Class: 14 (–1 size, +1 Dex, +4 natural), touch 10, flat-footed 13
Base Attack/Grapple: +4/+13

Attack: Sting +8 melee (1d8+5 plus poison)
Full Attack: Sting +8 melee (1d8+5 plus poison) and bite +3 melee (1d8+2)
Space/Reach: 10 ft./5 ft.
Special Attacks: Implant, poison
Special Qualities: Darkvision 60 ft., freedom of movement, low-light vision, scent
Saves: Fort +9, Ref +5, Will +2
Abilities: Str 21, Dex 13, Con 21, Int 2, Wis 12, Cha 10
Skills: Listen +10, Spot +11
Feats: Alertness, Dodge
Environment: Temperate forests
Organization: Solitary
Challenge Rating: 5
Treasure: None
Alignment: Always neutral
Advancement: 5–12 HD (Huge)
Level Adjustment: —

Spider eater

This beast resembles an enormous, two-legged hornet with a pair of small forelimbs and huge bat wings.

A spider eater has a temperament that matches its nasty appearance. Nevertheless, these predators are valued as flying steeds. A company of bandits mounted on spider eaters is fearsome indeed. The creature gets its name from its ability to shrug off webs and its habit of laying eggs in the paralyzed bodies of enormous creatures, often arachnids.

A spider eater is about 10 feet long and 4 feet high, and has a wingspan of about 20 feet. It weighs about 4,000 pounds.

COMBAT

A spider eater attacks with its venomous sting and powerful mandibles. Its usual tactic is to deliver a sting, then back off, hovering out of reach until the venom takes effect. Spider eaters do not like to give up their prey, and foes who harry them with spells or ranged attacks provoke a determined counterattack.

Implant (Ex): Female spider eaters lay their eggs inside paralyzed creatures of Large or larger size. The young emerge about six weeks later, literally devouring the host from inside.

Poison (Ex): Injury, Fortitude DC 17, initial damage none, secondary damage paralysis for 1d8+5 weeks. The save DC is Constitution-based.

Freedom of Movement (Su): Spider eaters have a continuous freedom of movement ability as the spell (caster level 12th). When the spider eater serves as a mount, this effect does not extend to its rider.

Skills: Spider eaters have a +4 racial bonus on Listen and Spot checks.

TRAINING A SPIDER EATER

A spider eater requires training before it can bear a rider in combat. Training a spider eater requires six weeks of work and a DC 25 Handle Animal check. Riding a spider eater requires an exotic saddle. A spider eater can fight while carrying a rider, but the rider cannot also attack unless he or she succeeds on a Ride check.

Spider eater eggs are worth 2,000 gp apiece on the open market, while young are worth 3,000 gp each. Professional trainers charge 3,000 gp to rear or train a spider eater.

Carrying Capacity: A light load for a spider eater is up to 306 pounds; a medium load, 307–612 pounds; and a heavy load, 613–920 pounds.

SPRITE

Sprites are reclusive fey. They go out of their way to fight evil and ugliness and to protect their homelands. Legend claims that sprites die only through injury or disease.

Combat

Sprites fight their opponents with spell-like abilities and pint-sized weaponry. They prefer ambushes and other trickery over direct confrontation.

Skills: All sprites have a +2 racial bonus on Search, Spot, and Listen checks.

GRIG

Tiny Fey
Hit Dice: 1/2 d6+1 (2 hp)
Initiative: +4
Speed: 20 ft. (4 squares), fly 40 ft. (poor)
Armor Class: 18 (+2 size, +4 Dex, +2 natural), touch 16, flat-footed 16
Base Attack/Grapple: +0/−11
Attack: Short sword +6 melee (1d3−3/19−20) or longbow +6 ranged (1d4−3/×3)
Full Attack: Short sword +6 melee (1d3−3/19−20) or longbow +6 ranged (1d4−3/×3)
Space/Reach: 2-1/2 ft./0 ft.
Special Attacks: Spell-like abilities, fiddle
Special Qualities: Damage reduction 5/cold iron, low-light vision, spell resistance 17
Saves: Fort +1, Ref +6, Will +3
Abilities: Str 5, Dex 18, Con 13, Int 10, Wis 13, Cha 14
Skills: Craft (any one) +4, Escape Artist +8, Hide +16, Jump +3, Listen +3, Move Silently +8*, Perform (string instruments) +6, Search +2, Spot +3
Feats: Dodge[B], Weapon Finesse
Environment: Temperate forests
Organization: Gang (2–4), band (6–11), or tribe (20–80)
Challenge Rating: 1
Treasure: No coins; 50% goods; 50% items
Alignment: Always neutral good
Advancement: 1–3 HD (Tiny)
Level Adjustment: +3

This tiny being has a humanoid head, torso, and arms, with the wings, antennae, and legs of a cricket.

Grigs are mischievous and lighthearted. They have no fear of larger creatures and delight in playing tricks on them. Favorite pranks include stealing food, collapsing tents, and using *ventriloquism* to make objects talk.

Grigs can leap great distances. They have light blue skin, forest-green hair, and brown hairy legs, and usually wear tunics or brightly colored vests with buttons made from tiny gems.

A grig stands 1-1/2 feet tall and weighs about 1 pound.

Grigs speak Sylvan. Some also speak Common.

Combat

Grigs are fierce by sprite standards, attacking opponents fearlessly with bow and dagger.

Spell-Like Abilities: 3/day—*disguise self*, *entangle* (DC 13), *invisibility* (self only), *pyrotechnics* (DC 14), *ventriloquism* (DC 13). Caster level 9th. The save DCs are Charisma-based.

Fiddle (Su): One grig in each band carries a tiny, grig-sized fiddle. When the fiddler plays, any nonsprite within 30 feet of the instrument must succeed on a DC 12 Will save or be affected as though by *Otto's irresistible dance* for as long as the playing continues. The save DC is Charisma-based.

Skills: Grigs have a +8 racial bonus on Jump checks.
*They also have a +5 racial bonus on Move Silently checks in a forest setting.

NIXIE

Small Fey (Aquatic)
Hit Dice: 1d6 (3 hp)
Initiative: +3
Speed: 20 ft. (4 squares), swim 30 ft.
Armor Class: 14 (+1 size, +3 Dex), touch 14, flat-footed 11
Base Attack/Grapple: +0/−6
Attack: Short sword +4 melee (1d4−2/19−20) or light crossbow +4 ranged (1d6/19−20)
Full Attack: Short sword +4 melee (1d4−2/19−20) or light crossbow +4 ranged (1d6/19−20)
Space/Reach: 5 ft./5 ft.
Special Attacks: *Charm person*
Special Qualities: Amphibious, damage reduction 5/cold iron, low-light vision, spell resistance 16, *water breathing*, wild empathy
Saves: Fort +0, Ref +5, Will +3
Abilities: Str 7, Dex 16, Con 11, Int 12, Wis 13, Cha 18
Skills: Bluff +8, Craft (any one) +5, Escape Artist +6, Handle Animal +8, Hide +7*, Listen +6, Perform (sing) +7, Search +3, Sense Motive +5, Spot +6, Swim +6
Feats: Dodge[B], Weapon Finesse
Environment: Temperate aquatic
Organization: Gang (2–4), band (6–11), or tribe (20–80)
Challenge Rating: 1
Treasure: No coins; 50% goods (metal or stone only); 50% items (no scrolls)
Alignment: Always neutral
Advancement: 2–3 HD (Small)
Level Adjustment: +3

This being looks something like a small elf. It has green skin, webbed fingers and toes, pointed ears, and wide silver eyes.

Nixies are aquatic sprites who dwell in and protect pristine ponds and lakes. They are even more reclusive than most fey and tend to treat intruders with suspicion and hostility.

Most nixies are slim and comely, with lightly scaled, pale green skin and dark green hair. Females often twine shells and pearl strings in their hair and dress in wraps woven from colorful seaweed. Males wear loincloths of the same materials. Nixies prefer not to leave their lakes.

A nixie stands about 4 feet tall and weighs about 45 pounds.

Nixies speak Aquan and Sylvan. Some also speak Common.

Combat

Nixies rely on their *charm person* ability to deter enemies, entering combat only to protect themselves and their territory.

Charm Person **(Sp):** A nixie can use *charm person* three times per day as the spell (caster level 4th). Those affected must succeed on a DC 15 Will save or be *charmed* for 24 hours. Most *charmed* crea-

Nixie

Pixie

Grig

tures are used to perform heavy labor, guard duty, and other oner-
ous tasks for the nixie community. Shortly before the effect wears
off, the nixie escorts the *charmed* creature away and orders it to
keep walking. The save DC is Charisma-based.

Amphibious (Ex): Although nixies are aquatic, they can survive indefinitely on land.

Water Breathing (Sp): Once per day a nixie can use *water breathing* as the spell (caster level 12th). Nixies usually bestow this effect
on those they have *charmed*.

Wild Empathy (Ex): This ability works like the druid's wild
empathy class feature, except that a nixie has a +6 racial bonus on
the check.

Skills: A nixie has a +8 racial bonus on any Swim check to perform some special action or avoid a hazard. It can always choose to
take 10 on a Swim check, even if distracted or endangered. It can
use the run action while swimming, provided it swims in a
straight line.

*Nixies have a +5 racial bonus on Hide checks when in the
water.

PIXIE

Small Fey

Hit Dice: 1d6 (3 hp)

Initiative: +4

Speed: 20 ft. (4 squares), fly 60 ft. (good)

Armor Class: 16 (+1 size, +4 Dex, +1 natural), touch 15,
flat-footed 12

Base Attack/Grapple: +0/–6

Attack: Short sword +5 melee (1d4–2/19–20) or longbow +5
ranged (1d6–2/×3)

Full Attack: Short sword +5 melee (1d4–2/19–20) or longbow
+5 ranged (1d6–2)/×3

Space/Reach: 5 ft./5 ft.

Special Attacks: Spell-like abilities, special arrows

Special Qualities: Damage reduction 10/cold iron, greater
invisibility, low-light vision, spell resistance 15

Saves: Fort +0, Ref +6, Will +4

Abilities: Str 7, Dex 18, Con 11, Int 16, Wis 15, Cha 16

Skills: Bluff +7, Concentration +4, Escape Artist +8, Hide +8,
Listen +8, Move Silently +8, Ride +8, Search +9, Sense Motive
+6, Spot +8

Feats: Dodge[B], Weapon Finesse

Environment: Temperate forests

Organization: Gang (2–4), band (6–11), or tribe (20–80)

Challenge Rating: 4 (5 with *Otto's irresistible dance*)

Treasure: No coins; 50% goods; 50% items

Alignment: Always neutral good

Advancement: 2–3 HD (Small)

Level Adjustment: +4 (+6 with *Otto's irresistible dance*)

*This being resembles a very small elf, but with longer ears and gossamer
wings.*

Pixies are merry pranksters that love to lead travelers astray. They
can, however, be roused to surprising ire when dealing with evil
creatures.

These sprites love to trick misers out of their wealth. They do
not covet treasure themselves but use it to taunt and frustrate
greedy folk. If a victim of pixie pranks exhibits no greed or
demonstrates a good sense of humor, the tricksters may allow the
individual to choose a reward from their hoard.

Pixies wear bright clothing, often including a cap and shoes
with curled and pointed toes.

A pixie stands about 2-1/2 feet tall and weighs about 30 pounds.

Pixies speak Sylvan and Common, and may know other languages as well.

Combat

The normally carefree pixies ferociously attack evil creatures and
unwanted intruders. They take full advantage of their invisibility
and other abilities to harass and drive away opponents.

Greater Invisibility (Su): A pixie remains invisible even when
it attacks. This ability is constant, but the pixie can suppress or resume it as a free action.

Spell-Like Abilities: 1/day—*lesser confusion* (DC 14), *dancing
lights, detect chaos, detect good, detect evil, detect law, detect thoughts* (DC
15), *dispel magic, entangle* (DC 14), *permanent image* (DC 19; visual
and auditory elements only), *polymorph* (self only). Caster level
8th. The save DCs are Charisma-based.

One pixie in ten can use *Otto's irresistible dance* (caster level 8th)
once per day.

Special Arrows (Ex): Pixies sometimes employ arrows that
deal no damage but can erase memory or put a creature to sleep.

Memory Loss: An opponent struck by this arrow must succeed on
a DC 15 Will save or lose all memory. The save DC is Charisma-
based and includes a +2 racial bonus. The subject retains skills, languages, and class abilities but forgets everything else until he or
she receives a *heal* spell or memory restoration with *limited wish,
wish,* or *miracle.*

Sleep: Any opponent struck by this arrow, regardless of Hit Dice,
must succeed on a DC 15 Fortitude save or be affected as though
by a *sleep* spell. The save DC is Charisma-based and includes a +2
racial bonus.

Pixies as Characters

A pixie character exchanges its 1 HD of fey for its first class level,
so a 1st-level pixie sorcerer has a d4 Hit Die, a +0 base attack bonus,
the base save bonuses of a sorcerer, and the sorcerer's skill points
and class skills.

Pixie characters possess the following racial traits.

— –4 Strength, +8 Dexterity, +6 Intelligence, +4 Wisdom, +6
Charisma.

—Small size. +1 bonus to Armor Class, +1 bonus on attack rolls,
+4 bonus on Hide checks, –4 penalty on grapple checks, lifting
and carrying limits 3/4 those of Medium characters.

—A pixie's base land speed is 20 feet. It also has a fly speed of 60
feet (good).

—Low-light vision.

—Skills: Pixies have a +2 racial bonus on Listen, Search, and
Spot checks.

—Racial Feats: A pixie receives Dodge as a bonus feat.

— +1 natural armor bonus.

—Special Attacks (see above): Spell-like abilities.

—Special Qualities (see above): Damage reduction 10/cold
iron, greater invisibility, spell resistance equal to 15 + class levels.

—Automatic Languages: Common, Sylvan. Bonus Languages:
Elven, Gnome, Halfling.

—Favored Class: Sorcerer.

—Level adjustment +4 (+6 if the pixie can use *Otto's irresistible
dance*).

STIRGE

Tiny Magical Beast

Hit Dice: 1d10 (5 hp)

Initiative: +4

Speed: 10 ft (2 squares), fly 40 ft. (average)

Armor Class: 16 (+2 size, +4 Dex), touch 16, flat-footed 12

Base Attack/Grapple: +1/–11 (+1 when attached)

Attack: Touch +7 melee (attach)

Full Attack: Touch +7 melee (attach)

Space/Reach: 2-1/2 ft./0 ft.

Special Attacks: Attach, blood drain

Special Qualities: Darkvision 60 ft., low-light vision

236

Saves: Fort +2, Ref +6, Will +1
Abilities: Str 3, Dex 19, Con 10, Int 1, Wis 12, Cha 6
Skills: Hide +14, Listen +4, Spot +4
Feats: Alertness, Weapon Finesse [B]
Environment: Warm marshes
Organization: Colony (2–4), flock (5–8), or storm (9–14)
Challenge Rating: 1/2
Treasure: None
Alignment: Always neutral
Advancement: —
Level Adjustment: —

This nasty-looking creature seems to be a cross between a bat and a giant mosquito. It has membranous bat wings, a short furry body, eight jointed legs that end in sharp pincers, and a needlelike proboscis.

Stirges are batlike creatures that feed on the blood of living beings. While just one poses little danger to most adventurers, multiple stirges can be a formidable threat.

A stirge's coloration ranges from rust-red to reddish-brown, with a dirty yellow underside. The proboscis is pink at the tip, fading to gray at its base.

A stirge's body is about 1 foot long, with a wingspan of about 2 feet. It weighs about 1 pound.

COMBAT

A stirge attacks by landing on a victim, finding a vulnerable spot, and plunging its proboscis into the flesh. This is a touch attack and can target only Small or larger creatures.

Attach (Ex): If a stirge hits with a touch attack, it uses its eight pincers to latch onto the opponent's body. An attached stirge is effectively grappling its prey. The stirge loses its Dexterity bonus to AC and has an AC of 12, but holds on with great tenacity. Stirges have a +12 racial bonus on grapple checks (already figured into the Base Attack/Grapple entry above).

An attached stirge can be struck with a weapon or grappled itself. To remove an attached stirge through grappling, the opponent must achieve a pin against the stirge.

Blood Drain (Ex): A stirge drains blood, dealing 1d4 points of Constitution damage in any round when it begins its turn attached to a victim. Once it has dealt 4 points of Constitution damage, it detaches and flies off to digest the meal. If its victim dies before the stirge's appetite has been sated, the stirge detaches and seeks a new target.

SWARM

Swarms are dense masses of Fine, Diminutive, or Tiny creatures that would not be particularly dangerous in small groups, but can be terrible foes when gathered in sufficient numbers. While a single cloud of locusts might actually be hundreds of feet across, for game purposes a swarm is defined as a single creature with a space of 10 feet—gigantic hordes of bats or locusts are actually composed of dozens of swarms in close proximity. A swarm has a single pool of Hit Dice and hit points, a single initiative modifier, a single speed, and a single Armor Class. It makes saving throws as a single creature.

Many different creatures can mass as swarms; bat swarms, centipede swarms, hellwasp swarms, locust swarms, rat swarms, and spider swarms are described here. The swarm's type varies with the nature of the component creature (most are animals or vermin), but all swarms have the swarm subtype.

A swarm of Tiny creatures consists of 300 nonflying creatures or 1,000 flying creatures. A swarm of Diminutive creatures consists of 1,500 nonflying creatures or 5,000 flying creatures. A swarm of Fine creatures consists of 10,000 creatures, whether they are flying or not. Swarms of nonflying creatures include many more creatures than could normally fit in a 10-foot square based on their normal space, because creatures in a swarm are packed tightly together and generally crawl over each other and their prey when moving or attacking. Larger swarms are represented by multiples of single swarms. A large swarm is completely shapeable, though it usually remains contiguous.

COMBAT

In order to attack, a single swarm moves into opponents' spaces, which provokes an attack of opportunity. It can occupy the same space as a creature of any size, since it crawls all over its prey, but remains a creature with a 10-foot space. Swarms never make attacks of opportunity, but they can provoke attacks of opportunity.

Unlike other creatures with a 10-foot space, a swarm is shapeable. It can occupy any four contiguous squares, and it can squeeze through any space large enough to contain one of its component creatures (for example, a bat swarm can squeeze through a space that a Tiny creature could squeeze through).

Vulnerabilities of Swarms

Swarms are extremely difficult to fight with physical attacks. However, they have a few special vulnerabilities, as follows:

A lit torch swung as an improvised weapon deals 1d3 points of fire damage per hit.

A weapon with a special ability such as flaming or frost deals its full energy damage with each hit, even if the weapon's normal damage can't affect the swarm.

A lit lantern can be used as a thrown weapon, dealing 1d4 points of fire damage to all creatures in squares adjacent to where it breaks.

BAT SWARM

Diminutive Animal (Swarm)
Hit Dice: 3d8 (13 hp)
Initiative: +2
Speed: 5 ft. (1 square), fly 40 ft. (good)
Armor Class: 16 (+4 size, +2 Dex), touch 14, flat-footed 12
Base Attack/Grapple: +2/—
Attack: Swarm (1d6)
Full Attack: Swarm (1d6)
Space/Reach: 10 ft./0 ft.
Special Attacks: Distraction, wounding
Special Qualities: Blindsense 20 ft., half damage from slashing and piercing, low-light vision, swarm traits
Saves: Fort +3, Ref +7, Will +3
Abilities: Str 3, Dex 15, Con 10, Int 2, Wis 14, Cha 4
Skills: Listen +11, Spot +11
Feats: Alertness, Lightning Reflexes
Environment: Temperate deserts
Organization: Solitary, flight (2–4 swarms), or colony (11–20 swarms)
Challenge Rating: 2

Stirge

Treasure: None
Alignment: Always neutral
Advancement: None
Level Adjustment: —

A whirring mass of quick, darting shadows sweeps closer. Hundreds of high-pitched squeaks fill the air.

A bat swarm is a mass of small, fierce carnivorous bats with a thirst for the blood of any creature unfortunate enough to cross their path.

A bat swarm is nocturnal, and is never found aboveground in daylight.

Combat

A bat swarm seeks to surround and attack any warm-blooded prey it encounters. The swarm deals 1d6 points of damage to any creature whose space it occupies at the end of its move.

Distraction (Ex): Any living creature that begins its turn with a swarm in its space must succeed on a DC 11 Fortitude save or be nauseated for 1 round. The save DC is Constitution-based.

Wounding (Ex): Any living creature damaged by a bat swarm continues to bleed, losing 1 hit point per round thereafter. Multiple wounds do not result in cumulative bleeding loss. The bleeding can be stopped by a DC 10 Heal check or the application of a *cure* spell or some other healing magic.

Blindsense (Ex): A bat swarm notices and locates creatures within 20 feet. Opponents still have total concealment against the bat swarm (but swarm attacks ignore concealment).

Skills: A bat swarm has a +4 racial bonus on Listen and Spot checks. These bonuses are lost if its blindsense is negated.

CENTIPEDE SWARM

Diminutive Vermin (Swarm)
Hit Dice: 9d8–9 (31 hp)
Initiative: +4
Speed: 20 ft. (4 squares), climb 20 ft.
Armor Class: 18 (+4 size, +4 Dex), touch 18, flat-footed 14
Base Attack/Grapple: +6/—
Attack: Swarm (2d6 plus poison)
Full Attack: Swarm (2d6 plus poison)
Space/Reach: 10 ft./0 ft.
Special Attacks: Distraction, poison
Special Qualities: Darkvision 60 ft., immune to weapon damage, swarm traits, tremorsense 30 ft., vermin traits
Saves: Fort +5, Ref +7, Will +3
Abilities: Str 1, Dex 19, Con 8, Int —, Wis 10, Cha 2
Skills: Climb +12, Spot +4
Feats: Weapon Finesse[B]
Environment: Underground
Organization: Solitary, tangle (2–4 swarms), or colony (7–12 swarms)
Challenge Rating: 4
Treasure: None
Alignment: Always neutral
Advancement: None
Level Adjustment: —

A glistening, squirming mass of blue-black insects advances like a venomous army.

A centipede swarm is a crawling mass of voracious centipedes that can climb over obstacles to get at prey.

Combat

A centipede swarm seeks to surround and attack any living prey it encounters. A swarm deals 2d6 points of damage to any creature whose space it occupies at the end of its move.

Distraction (Ex): Any living creature that begins its turn with a centipede swarm in its space must succeed on a DC 13 Fortitude save or be nauseated for 1 round. The save DC is Constitution-based.

Poison (Ex): Injury, Fortitude DC 13, initial and secondary damage 1d4 Dex. The save DC is Constitution-based.

Skills: A centipede swarm has a +4 racial bonus on Spot checks and a +8 racial bonus on Climb checks, and uses its Dexterity modifier instead of its Strength modifier for Climb checks.

A centipede swarm has a +8 racial bonus on Climb checks and can always choose to take 10 on a Climb check, even if rushed or threatened.

HELLWASP SWARM

Diminutive Magical Beast (Extraplanar, Evil, Swarm)
Hit Dice: 12d10+27 (93 hp)
Initiative: +10
Speed: 5 ft. (1 square), fly 40 ft.
Armor Class: 20 (+4 size, +6 Dex), touch 20, flat-footed 14
Base Attack/Grapple: +12/—
Attack: Swarm (3d6 plus poison)
Full Attack: Swarm (3d6 plus poison)
Space/Reach: 10 ft./0 ft.
Special Attacks: Distraction, inhabit, poison
Special Qualities: Damage reduction 10/magic, darkvision 60 ft., hive mind, immune to weapon damage, resistance to fire 10, low-light vision, swarm traits
Saves: Fort +10, Ref +14, Will +7
Abilities: Str 1, Dex 22, Con 14, Int 6, Wis 13, Cha 9
Skills: Hide +19, Listen +10, Spot +10
Feats: Ability Focus (poison), Alertness, Improved Initiative, Iron Will, Toughness
Environment: Bleak Eternity of Gehenna
Organization: Solitary, fright (2–4 swarms), or terror (5–8 swarms)
Challenge Rating: 8
Treasure: None
Alignment: Always lawful evil
Advancement: None
Level Adjustment: —

An angry buzz fills the air around a darting cloud of thousands of ruby-red insects.

Hellwasps are vicious, foul-tempered magical insects from the infernal planes. A single hellwasp resembles a thumb-sized normal wasp, except its carapace is gleaming black with ruby-red stripes, and its compound eyes are an iridescent green. In swarms, hellwasps form a collective hive mind intelligence with infernal cunning and bloodlust.

Combat

Like any swarm, a hellwasp swarm seeks to surround and attack any living prey it encounters. A swarm deals 3d6 points of damage to any creature whose space it occupies at the end of its move. The swarm can take over the bodies of its prey and infest both the living and the dead, using them as horrible living (or unliving) puppets to accomplish acts of wickedness that a swarm of insects could never attempt.

A hellwasp swarm's attack is treated as an evil-aligned weapon and a magic weapon for the purpose of overcoming damage reduction.

Distraction (Ex): Any living creature that begins its turn with a hellwasp swarm in its space must succeed on a DC 18 Fortitude save or be nauseated for 1 round. The save DC is Constitution-based.

Inhabit (Ex): A hellwasp swarm can enter the body of a helpless or dead creature by crawling into its mouth and other orifices. Inhabiting requires 1 minute, and the victim must be Small, Medium, or Large (although four swarms working together can inhabit a Huge creature). The swarm can abandon the body at any time, although doing this takes 1 full round. Any attack against the host deals half damage to the hellwasp swarm as well, although the swarm's resistances and immunities may negate some or all of this damage.

If a hellwasp swarm inhabits a dead body, it can restore animation to the creature and control its movements, effectively transforming it into a zombie of the appropriate size for as long as the swarm remains inside. If a hellwasp swarm inhabits a living victim, it can neutralize the effects of its own poison and control the victim's movement and actions as if using *dominate monster* on the victim. The hellwasps quickly consume a living victim, dealing 2d4 points of Constitution damage per hour they inhabit a body. A body reduced to Constitution 0 is dead.

A hellwasp-inhabited creature is relatively easy to spot, since its skin crawls with the forms of insects inside. The swarm is intelligent enough to attempt to hide beneath loose clothing or a large cloak to keep its presence from being detected. The swarm can attempt a Disguise check to conceal its inhabitation of a host, with a –4 penalty if currently inhabiting a Small host.

A *remove disease* or *heal* spell cast on an inhabited victim forces the hellwasp swarm to abandon its host.

Poison (Ex): Injury, Fortitude DC 18, initial and secondary damage 1d6 Dex. The save DC is Constitution-based.

Hive Mind (Ex): Any hellwasp swarm with at least 1 hit point per Hit Die (or 12 hit points, for a standard hellwasp swarm) forms a hive mind, giving it an Intelligence of 6. When a hellwasp swarm is reduced below this hit point threshold, it becomes mindless.

LOCUST SWARM

Diminutive Vermin (Swarm)
Hit Dice: 6d8–6 (21 hp)
Initiative: +4
Speed: 10 ft. (2 squares), fly 30 ft. (poor)
Armor Class: 18 (+4 size, +4 Dex), touch 18, flat-footed 14
Base Attack/Grapple: +4/—
Attack: Swarm (2d6)
Full Attack: Swarm (2d6)
Space/Reach: 10 ft./0 ft.
Special Attacks: Distraction
Special Qualities: Darkvision 60 ft., immune to weapon damage, swarm traits, vermin traits
Saves: Fort +4, Ref +6, Will +2
Abilities: Str 1, Dex 19, Con 8, Int —, Wis 10, Cha 2
Skills: Listen +4, Spot +4
Feats: —
Environment: Temperate plains
Organization: Solitary, cloud (2–7 swarms), or plague (11–20 swarms)
Challenge Rating: 3
Treasure: None
Alignment: Always neutral
Advancement: None
Level Adjustment: —

A whirling, clacking cloud of voracious, grasshopperlike insects flutters closer, filling the air with a high-pitched buzz.

A locust swarm is a cloud of thousands of winged vermin that devours any organic material in its path.

Combat

A locust swarm surrounds and attacks any living prey it encounters. A swarm deals 2d6 points of damage to any creature whose space it occupies at the end of its move.

Distraction (Ex): Any living creature that begins its turn with a locust swarm in its space must succeed on a DC 12 Fortitude save

or be nauseated for 1 round. The save DC is Constitution-based.

Skills: A locust swarm has a +4 racial bonus on Listen and Spot checks.

RAT SWARM

Tiny Animal (Swarm)
Hit Dice: 4d8 (13 hp)
Initiative: +2
Speed: 15 ft. (3 squares), climb 15 ft.
Armor Class: 14 (+2 size, +2 Dex), touch 14, flat-footed 12
Base Attack/Grapple: +3/—
Attack: Swarm (1d6 plus disease)
Full Attack: Swarm (1d6 plus disease)
Space/Reach: 10 ft./0 ft.
Special Attacks: Disease, distraction
Special Qualities: Half damage from slashing and piercing, low-light vision, scent, swarm traits
Saves: Fort +4, Ref +6, Will +2
Abilities: Str 2, Dex 15, Con 10, Int 2, Wis 12, Cha 2
Skills: Balance +10, Climb +10, Hide +14, Listen +6, Spot +7, Swim +10
Feats: Alertness, Weapon Finesse
Environment: Any
Organization: Solitary, pack (2–4 swarms), or infestation (7–12 swarms)
Challenge Rating: 2
Treasure: None
Alignment: Always neutral
Advancement: None
Level Adjustment: —

A squirming, squeaking horde of feral rats surges closer, teeth glistening in their slavering jaws.

A rat swarm is a mass of teeming, famished, disease-ridden rats. A swarm is composed of individuals very much like the rat described on page 278, but in such great numbers, rats can become implacable hunters capable of killing a human with hundreds of bites.

A rat swarm sometimes can be found in the sewers and foundations of human cities.

Combat

A rat swarm seeks to surround and attack any warm-blooded prey it encounters. A swarm deals 1d6 points of damage to any creature whose space it occupies at the end of its move.

Disease (Ex): Filth fever—swarm attack, Fortitude DC 12, incubation period 1d3 days, damage 1d3 Dex and 1d3 Con. The save DC is Constitution-based.

Distraction (Ex): Any living creature that begins its turn with a swarm in its square must succeed on a DC 12 Fortitude save or be nauseated for 1 round. The save DC is Constitution-based.

Skills: A rat swarm has a +4 racial bonus on Hide and Move Silently checks, and a +8 racial bonus on Balance, Climb, and Swim checks. A rat swarm can always choose to take 10 on all Climb checks, even if rushed or threatened.

A rat swarm uses its Dexterity modifier instead of its Strength modifier for Climb and Swim checks.

A rat swarm has a +8 racial bonus on any Swim check to perform some special action or avoid a hazard. It can always choose to take 10 on a Swim check, even if distracted or endangered. It can use the run action while swimming, provided it swims in a straight line.

SPIDER SWARM

Diminutive Vermin (Swarm)
Hit Dice: 2d8 (9 hp)
Initiative: +3
Speed: 20 ft. (4 squares), climb 20 ft.

Armor Class: 17 (+4 size, +3 Dex), touch 17, flat-footed 14
Base Attack/Grapple: +1/—
Attack: Swarm (1d6 plus poison)
Full Attack: Swarm (1d6 plus poison)
Space/Reach: 10 ft./0 ft.
Special Attacks: Distraction, poison
Special Qualities: Darkvision 60 ft., swarm traits, tremorsense 30 ft., vermin traits
Saves: Fort +3, Ref +3, Will +0
Abilities: Str 1, Dex 17, Con 10, Int —, Wis 10, Cha 2
Skills: Climb +11, Listen +4, Spot +4
Environment: Warm forests
Organization: Solitary, tangle (2–4 swarms), or colony (7–12 swarms)
Challenge Rating: 1
Treasure: None
Alignment: Always neutral
Advancement: None
Level Adjustment: —

A horrible, scuttling army of hand-sized spiders scrambles forward.

A spider swarm is a scuttling horde of venomous spiders.

Combat

A spider swarm seeks to surround and attack any living prey it encounters. A swarm deals 1d6 points of damage to any creature whose space it occupies at the end of its move.

Distraction (Ex): Any living creature that begins its turn with a spider swarm in its space must succeed on a DC 11 Fortitude save or be nauseated for 1 round. The save DC is Constitution-based.

Poison (Ex): Injury, Fortitude DC 11, initial and secondary damage 1d3 Str. The save DC is Constitution-based.

Skills: A spider swarm has a +4 racial bonus on Hide and Spot checks and a +8 racial bonus on Climb checks. It uses its Dexterity modifier instead of its Strength modifier for Climb checks. It can always choose to take 10 on a Climb check, even if rushed or threatened.

TARRASQUE

Colossal Magical Beast
Hit Dice: 48d10+594 (858 hp)
Initiative: +7
Speed: 20 ft. (4 squares)
Armor Class: 35 (–8 size, +3 Dex, +30 natural), touch 5, flat-footed 32
Base Attack/Grapple: +48/+81
Attack: Bite +57 melee (4d8+17/18–20/×3)
Full Attack: Bite +57 melee (4d8+17/18–20/×3) and 2 horns +52 melee (1d10+8) and 2 claws +52 melee (1d12+8) and tail slap +52 melee (3d8+8)
Space/Reach: 30 ft./20 ft.
Special Attacks: Augmented critical, frightful presence, improved grab, rush, swallow whole
Special Qualities: Carapace, damage reduction 15/epic, immunity to fire, poison, disease, energy drain, and ability damage, regeneration 40, scent, spell resistance 32
Saves: Fort +38, Ref +29, Will +20
Abilities: Str 45, Dex 16, Con 35, Int 3, Wis 14, Cha 14
Skills: Listen +17, Search +9, Spot +17, Survival +14 (+16 following tracks)

Feats: Alertness, Awesome Blow, Blind-Fight, Cleave, Combat Reflexes, Dodge, Great Cleave, Improved Bull Rush, Improved Initiative, Iron Will, Power Attack, Toughness (6)
Environment: Any
Organization: Solitary
Challenge Rating: 20
Treasure: None
Alignment: Always neutral
Advancement: 49+ HD (Colossal)
Level Adjustment: —

This scaly biped seems about as tall as a five-story building. It carries itself like a bird of prey, leaning well forward and using its powerful, lashing tail for balance. It has two horns on its head and a thick, reflective carapace on its back.

The legendary tarrasque—fortunately, only one exists—is possibly the most dreaded monster of all (except for the largest dragons). None can predict where and when the creature will strike next.

The location of the tarrasque's lair is a mystery, and the beast remains dormant much of the time. Its torporous slumber usually lasts 6d4 months before it leaves its lair for a brief hunting foray lasting 1d3 days. Once every decade or so, the monster is particularly active, staying awake for 1d2 weeks. Thereafter, it slumbers for at least 4d6 years unless disturbed.

When active, the tarrasque is a perfect engine of destruction. It rampages across the land eating everything in its path, including plants, animals, humanoids, and even towns. Nothing is safe, and entire communities prefer to flee the ravening tarrasque rather than face its power.

Many legends surround the tarrasque's origins and purpose. Some hold it to be an abomination unleashed by ancient, forgotten gods to punish all of nature, while others tell of a conspiracy between evil wizards or merciless elemental powers. These tales are mere speculation, however, and the creature's true nature will probably remain a mystery. The tarrasque isn't in the habit of explaining itself, and it rarely leaves any living witnesses in its wake.

The tarrasque is 70 feet long and 50 feet tall, and it weighs about 130 tons.

The tarrasque cannot speak.

Tarrasque

TARRASQUE

COMBAT

The tarrasque attacks with its claws, teeth, horns, and tail.

The tarrasque's natural weapons are treated as epic weapons for the purpose of overcoming damage reduction.

Augmented Critical (Ex): The tarrasque's bite threatens a critical hit on a natural attack roll of 18–20, dealing triple damage on a successful critical hit.

Frightful Presence (Su): The tarrasque can inspire terror by charging or attacking. Affected creatures must succeed on a DC 36 Will save or become shaken, remaining in that condition as long as they remain with 60 feet of the tarrasque. The save DC is Charisma-based.

Improved Grab (Ex): To use this ability, the tarrasque must hit a Huge or smaller opponent with its bite attack. It can then attempt to start a grapple as a free action without provoking an attack of opportunity. If it wins the grapple check, it establishes a hold and can try to swallow the foe the following round.

Rush (Ex): Once per minute, the normally slow-moving tarrasque can move at a speed of 150 feet.

Swallow Whole (Ex): The tarrasque can try to swallow a grabbed opponent of Huge or smaller size by making a successful grapple check. Once inside, the opponent takes 2d8+8 points of crushing damage plus 2d8+6 points of acid damage per round from the tarrasque's digestive juices. A swallowed creature can cut its way out by dealing 50 points of damage to the tarrasque's digestive tract (AC 25). Once the creature exits, muscular action closes the hole; another swallowed opponent must cut its own way out.

The tarrasque's gullet can hold 2 Huge, 8 Large, 32 Medium, 128 Small, or 512 Tiny or smaller creatures.

Carapace (Ex): The tarrasque's armorlike carapace is exceptionally tough and highly reflective, deflecting all rays, lines, cones, and even *magic missile* spells. There is a 30% chance of reflecting any such effect back at the caster; otherwise, it is merely negated. Check for reflection before rolling to overcome the creature's spell resistance.

Regeneration (Ex): No form of attack deals lethal damage to the tarrasque. The tarrasque regenerates even if it fails a saving throw against a *disintegrate* spell or a death effect. If the tarrasque fails its save against a spell or effect that would kill it instantly (such as those mentioned above), the spell or effect instead deals nonlethal damage equal to the creature's full normal hit points +10 (or 868 hp). The tarrasque is immune to effects that produce incurable or bleeding wounds, such as mummy rot, a sword with the wounding special ability, or a clay golem's cursed wound ability. The tarrasque can be slain only by raising its nonlethal damage total to its full normal hit points +10 (or 868 hit points) and using a *wish* or *miracle* spell to keep it dead.

If the tarrasque loses a limb or body part, the lost portion regrows in 1d6 minutes (the detached piece dies and decays normally). The creature can reattach the severed member instantly by holding it to the stump.

Skills: The tarrasque has a +8 racial bonus on Listen and Spot checks.

TENDRICULOS

Huge Plant
Hit Dice: 9d8+54 (94 hp)
Initiative: –1
Speed: 20 ft. (4 squares)
Armor Class: 16 (–2 size, –1 Dex, +9 natural), touch 7, flat-footed 16
Base Attack/Grapple: +6/+23
Attack: Bite +13 melee (2d8+9) and 2 tendrils +8 melee (1d6+4)
Full Attack: Bite +13 melee (2d8+9) and 2 tendrils +8 melee (1d6+4)
Space/Reach: 15 ft./15 ft.
Special Attacks: Improved grab, paralysis, swallow whole
Special Qualities: Low-light vision, plant traits, regeneration 10
Saves: Fort +12, Ref +2, Will +4
Abilities: Str 28, Dex 9, Con 22, Int 3, Wis 8, Cha 3
Skills: Hide +9, Listen +1, Move Silently +1, Spot +1
Feats: Alertness, Iron Will, Power Attack, Stealthy
Environment: Temperate forests
Organization: Solitary
Challenge Rating: 6
Treasure: 1/10th coins; 50% goods; 50% items
Alignment: Always neutral
Advancement: 10–16 HD (Huge); 17–27 HD (Gargantuan)
Level Adjustment: —

Tendriculos

This creature looks like a mound of vegetation supported by vines and branches. The mass has a huge opening filled with "teeth" of sharp branches and long thorns.

The tendriculos is a plant that may have been mutated by foul magic, or may have originated on another plane of existence—or possibly both of these theories are true.

A tendriculos can rear up to a height of 15 feet. It weighs about 3,500 pounds.

The tendriculos is best known for its ability to grow and regrow its vegetable body extremely rapidly. Whole new leaves and vines appear in just a few minutes. A tendriculos accomplishes this by consuming vast quantities of meat.

Animals and other plant creatures are unnerved by the presence of a tendriculos; they avoid it and any place it has been within the last 24 hours.

COMBAT

Prowling deep forests or waiting in vegetated areas (looking like nothing more than a small hillock), a tendriculos attacks savagely, showing no fear. It attempts to swallow as much flesh as it can, as quickly as it can.

Improved Grab (Ex): To use this ability, a tendriculos must hit a creature at least one size smaller than itself with its bite attack. It can then attempt to start a grapple as a free action without provoking an attack of opportunity. If it wins the grapple check, it establishes a hold and can try to swallow the opponent in the following round.

A tendriculos can also use its improved grab ability on a tendril

241

attack. If it wins the grapple check, it establishes a hold, picks up the opponent, and transfers it to the mouth as a free action, automatically dealing bite damage.

Swallow Whole/Paralysis (Ex): A tendriculos can try to swallow a grabbed opponent by making a successful grapple check. Once inside the plant's mass, the opponent must succeed on a DC 20 Fortitude save or be paralyzed for 3d6 rounds by the tendriculos's digestive juices, taking 2d6 points of acid damage per round. A new save is required each round inside the plant. The save DC is Constitution-based.

A swallowed creature that avoids paralysis can climb out of the mass with a successful grapple check. This returns it to the plant's maw, where another successful grapple check is needed to get free. A swallowed creature can also cut its way out by using a light slashing or piercing weapon to deal 25 points of damage to the tendriculos's interior (AC 14). Once the creature exits, the plant's regenerative capacity closes the hole; another swallowed opponent must cut its own way out.

A Huge tendriculos's interior can hold 2 Large, 8 Medium, 32 Small, 128 Tiny, or 512 Diminutive or smaller opponents.

Regeneration (Ex): Bludgeoning weapons and acid deal normal damage to a tendriculos.

A tendriculos that loses part of its body mass can regrow it in 1d6 minutes. Holding the severed portion against the mass enables it to reattach instantly.

THOQQUA

Medium Elemental (Earth, Extraplanar, Fire)

Hit Dice: 3d8+3 (16 hp)

Initiative: +1

Speed: 30 ft. (6 squares), burrow 20 ft.

Armor Class: 18 (+1 Dex, +7 natural), touch 11, flat-footed 17

Base Attack/Grapple: +2/+4

Attack: Slam +4 melee (1d6+3 plus 2d6 fire)

Full Attack: Slam +4 melee (1d6+3 plus 2d6 fire)

Space/Reach: 5 ft./5 ft.

Special Attacks: Heat, burn

Special Qualities: Darkvision 60 ft., elemental traits, immunity to fire, tremorsense 60 ft., vulnerability to cold

Saves: Fort +4, Ref +2, Will +2

Abilities: Str 15, Dex 13, Con 13, Int 6, Wis 12, Cha 10

Skills: Listen +5, Move Silently +3, Survival +3

Feats: Alertness, Track

Environment: Elemental Plane of Fire

Organization: Solitary or pair

Challenge Rating: 2

Treasure: None

Alignment: Usually neutral

Advancement: 4–9 HD (Large)

Level Adjustment: —

This creature has a sinuous body that is segmented like an earthworm's. The whole body glows with orange-white heat.

The thoqqua is a wormlike monster with a body hot enough to melt solid rock. It has a choleric mood and a foul temper. Although native to the Elemental Plane of Fire, it is also known to inhabit the Elemental Plane of Earth.

Thoqqua

A thoqqua spends most of its time burrowing through rock looking for minerals to eat. It burrowing leaves behind a usable tunnel, albeit a small one with blistering hot walls.

A thoqqua is about 1 foot in diameter and 4 to 5 feet long. It weighs about 200 pounds.

COMBAT

When a thoqqua is disturbed, its first instinct is to attack. Its favored tactic is to spring directly at a foe, either by bursting out of the rock or by coiling up its body and launching itself like a spring. (Treat this as a charge, even though the thoqqua does not need to move 10 feet before attacking.)

Heat (Ex): Merely touching or being touched by a thoqqua automatically deals 2d6 fire damage.

Burn (Ex): When a thoqqua hits with its slam attack, the opponent must succeed on a DC 12 Reflex save or catch fire. The save DC is Constitution-based. The flame burns for 1d4 rounds if not extinguished sooner. A burning creature can use a full-round action to put out the flame (see Catching on Fire, page 303 of the *Dungeon Master's Guide*).

TITAN

Huge Outsider (Chaotic, Extraplanar)

Hit Dice: 20d8+280 (370 hp)

Initiative: +1

Speed: 40 ft. in half-plate armor (8 squares); base speed 60 ft.

Armor Class: 38 (–2 size, +19 natural, +11 +4 *half-plate armor*), touch 8, flat-footed 38

Base Attack/Grapple: +20/+44

Attack: Gargantuan +3 *adamantine warhammer* +37 melee (4d6+27/×3) or +3 javelin +22 ranged (2d6+19) or slam +34 (1d8+16)

Full Attack: Gargantuan +3 *adamantine warhammer* +37/+32/+27/+22 melee (4d6+27/×3) or +3 javelin +22 ranged (2d6+19) or 2 slams +34 (1d8+16)

Space/Reach: 15 ft./15 ft.

Special Attacks: Oversized weapon, spell-like abilities

Special Qualities: Damage reduction 15/lawful, darkvision 60 ft., spell resistance 32

Saves: Fort +26, Ref +13, Will +21

Abilities: Str 43, Dex 12, Con 39, Int 21, Wis 28, Cha 24

Skills: Balance +7, Bluff +19, Climb +22, Concentration +37, Craft (any one) +28, Diplomacy +11, Disguise +7 (+9 acting), Heal +20, Intimidate +32, Jump +38, Knowledge (any one) +28, Listen +32, Perform (oratory) +30, Sense Motive +32, Search +28, Spellcraft +17, Spot +32, Survival +9 (+11 following tracks), Swim +16

Titan

Titan illus. by J. Jarvis

Feats: Awesome Blow, Blind-Fight, Cleave, Improved Bull Rush, Improved Sunder, Power Attack, Quicken Spell-Like Ability (*chain lightning*)

Environment: Olympian Glades of Arborea
Organization: Solitary or pair
Challenge Rating: 21
Treasure: Double standard plus +4 *half-plate armor* and Gargantuan +3 *adamantine warhammer*
Alignment: Always chaotic (any)
Advancement: 21–30 HD (Huge); 31–60 HD (Gargantuan)
Level Adjustment: —

This being looks like a giant-sized human of great physical strength and beauty. It carries an enormous warhammer. It seems very lively and self-assured.

Titans are statuesque beings of heroic proportions. They have agile minds and powerful bodies. Many come from the plane of Arborea.

Titans favor heavy armor crafted in ancient designs. They wear rare and valuable jewelry and generally make themselves seem beautiful and overpowering.

Titans are wild and chaotic, masters of their own fates. They are closer to the wellsprings of life than mere mortals and so revel in existence. They are prone to more pronounced emotions than humans and can experience deitylike fits of rage. Many titans are powerful servants of good, but in ages past the race of titans rebelled against the deities themselves, and a number of titans turned to evil. An evil titan is an indomitable tyrant who often masters entire kingdoms of mortals.

A titan is about 25 feet tall and weighs about 14,000 pounds.

Titans speak Abyssal, Common, Celestial, Draconic, and Giant.

COMBAT

Titans can wreak havoc with their massive warhammers, which are sometimes referred to as "mauls of the titans." In addition to their considerable battle prowess, titans possess great speed and considerable magical power.

A titan's natural weapons, as well as any weapons it wields, are treated as chaotic-aligned for the purpose of overcoming damage reduction.

Oversized Weapon (Ex): A titan wields a great, two-handed warhammer (big enough for Gargantuan creatures) without penalty.

Spell-Like Abilities:
At will—*chain lightning* (DC 23), *charm monster* (DC 21), *cure critical wounds* (DC 21), *fire storm* (DC 24), *greater dispel magic*, *hold monster* (DC 22), *invisibility*, *invisibility purge*, *levitate*, *persistent image* (DC 22), *polymorph* (humanoid forms only, duration 1 hour); 3/day—*etherealness*, *word of chaos* (DC 22), *summon nature's ally IX*; 1/day—*gate*, *maze*, *meteor swarm* (DC 26). Caster level 20th. The save DCs are Charisma-based.

In addition, titans of good or neutral alignment can use the following additional spell-like abilities: At will—*daylight*, *holy smite* (DC 21), *remove curse* (DC 21); 1/day—*greater restoration*. Caster level 20th. The save DCs are Charisma-based.

Titans of evil alignment can use the following additional spell-like abilities: At will—*bestow curse* (DC 21), *deeper darkness*, *unholy blight* (DC 21); 1/day—*Bigby's crushing hand* (DC 26). Caster level 20th. The save DCs are Charisma-based.

TACTICS ROUND-BY-ROUND

Titans enjoy combat and usually close with their foes. If that proves ineffective, they swiftly back off and pelt the foe with spell-like abilities and magical effects. Because of a titan's Quicken Spell-Like Ability feat, it can use *chain lightning* as a free action, and frequently attacks in melee while lashing out with this ability at the same time.

Prior to combat: Invisibility purge or invisibility.

Round 1: Charge and attempt to sunder the weapon of the most dangerous foe. Hurl *chain lightning* at opponents standing away from the fight.

Round 2: Full attack against the disarmed opponent, and hurl *chain lightning* at other opponents.

Round 3: Back away from first opponent and use *maze* or *meteor swarm* on any spellcaster causing trouble.

Round 4: Sunder the weapon of the next most effective combatant, or use *greater dispel magic* on all nearby opponents.

Round 5: Full attack against any nearby opponent, or use *fire storm*. Use another quickened *chain lightning* if foes seem really dangerous.

A titan usually reserves its *gate* and *etherealness* abilities to escape a fight that is not going well.

TOJANIDA

This creature resembles a snapping turtle. It has a spindle-shaped shell made up of hexagonal plates and a narrow head with jaws that open horizontally rather than vertically. A seemingly random array of crablike claws and paddles sprout from openings at both ends of the creature's shell.

Tojanida

Tojanidas are omnivores from the Elemental Plane of Water. Though they seem clumsy and innocuous at first glance, they are nimble swimmers and capable fighters.

A tojanida's shell is blue-green in color. Inside the shell is a fleshy body from which extend seven stalks. Four of these stalks

	Juvenile Tojanida Small Outsider (Extraplanar, Water)	Adult Tojanida Medium Outsider (Extraplanar, Water)	Elder Tojanida Large Outsider (Extraplanar, Water)
Hit Dice:	3d8+6 (19 hp)	7d8+14 (45 hp)	15d8+60 (127 hp)
Initiative:	+1	+1	+1
Speed:	10 ft. (2 squares), swim 90 ft.	10 ft. (2 squares), swim 90 ft.	10 ft. (2 squares), swim 90 ft.
Armor Class:	22 (+1 size, +1 Dex, +10 natural), touch 12, flat-footed 21	23 (+1 Dex, +12 natural), touch 11, flat-footed 22	24 (−1 size, +1 Dex, +14 natural), touch 10, flat-footed 23
Base Attack/Grapple:	+3/+1	+7/+10	+15/+25
Attack:	Bite +6 melee (2d6+2)	Bite +10 melee (2d8+3)	Bite +20 melee (4d6+6)
Full Attack:	Bite +6 melee (2d6+2) and 2 claws +1 melee (1d4+1)	Bite +10 melee (2d8+3) and 2 claws +5 melee (1d6+1)	Bite +20 melee (4d6+6) and 2 claws +15 melee (1d8+3)
Space/Reach:	5 ft./5 ft.	5 ft./5 ft.	10 ft./5 ft.
Special Attacks:	Improved grab, ink cloud	Improved grab, ink cloud	Improved grab, ink cloud
Special Qualities:	All-around vision, darkvision 60 ft., immunity to acid and cold, resistance to electricity 10 and fire 10	All-around vision, darkvision 60 ft., immunity to acid and cold, resistance to electricity 10 and fire 10	All-around vision, darkvision 60 ft., immunity to acid and cold, resistance to electricity 10 and fire 10
Saves:	Fort +5, Ref +4, Will +4	Fort +7, Ref +6, Will +6	Fort +13, Ref +10, Will +10
Abilities:	Str 14, Dex 13, Con 15, Int 10, Wis 12, Cha 9	Str 16, Dex 13, Con 15, Int 10, Wis 12, Cha 9	Str 22, Dex 13, Con 19, Int 10, Wis 12, Cha 9
Skills:	Diplomacy +1, Escape Artist +7, Hide +11, Knowledge (the planes) +6, Listen +7, Search +6, Spot +9, Sense Motive +7, Survival +1 (+3 other planes and following tracks), Swim +10, Use Rope +1 (+3 with bindings)	Diplomacy +1, Escape Artist +11, Hide +11, Knowledge (the planes) +6, Listen +11, Search +14, Sense Motive +11, Spot +15, Survival +1 (+3 other planes and following tracks), Swim +11, Use Rope+1 (+3 with bindings)	Escape Artist +19, Hide +15, Intimidate +17, Knowledge (the Planes) +18, Listen +21, Search +22, Sense Motive +17, Spot +25, Survival +1 (+3 other planes and following tracks), Swim +14, Use Rope+1 (+3 with bindings)
Feats:	Blind-Fight, Dodge	Blind-Fight, Dodge, Power Attack	Alertness, Blind-Fight, Cleave, Dodge, Improved Sunder, Power Attack
Environment:	Elemental Plane of Water	Elemental Plane of Water	Elemental Plane of Water
Organization:	Solitary or clutch (2–4)	Solitary or clutch (2–4)	Solitary or clutch (2–4)
Challenge Rating:	3	5	9
Treasure:	Standard	Standard	Standard
Alignment:	Always neutral	Always neutral	Always neutral
Advancement:	4–6 HD (Small)	8–14 HD (Medium)	16–24 HD (Large); 25–45 HD (Huge)
Level Adjustment:	—	—	—

have paddles for locomotion, two are tipped with claws, and one bears the creature's head. Eight vents in the shell, four at each end, allow the tojanida to thrust its stalks out in whatever configuration it finds convenient.

A juvenile tojanida is up to 25 years old. It has a shell about 3 feet long, and it weighs about 60 pounds. An adult is aged 26 to 80. Its shell is about 6 feet long, and it weighs about 220 pounds. An elder can reach 150 years of age. It has a shell about 9 feet long, and it weighs about 500 pounds.

Tojanidas speak Aquan and can be loquacious, but usually only on the subject of food.

COMBAT

Tojanidas are fairly even-tempered but can be ferocious if molested. They are very jealous of their food supply and become testy if they suspect a newcomer is trying to beat them to a meal.

Improved Grab (Ex): To use this ability, a tojanida must hit with a bite or claw attack. It can then attempt to start a grapple as a free action without provoking an attack of opportunity. Underwater, a tojanida can tow a grabbed victim of its own size or smaller at its swim speed (but it cannot run). A favorite tactic is to grab a single opponent, then withdraw, hauling the opponent away from its allies.

Ink Cloud (Ex): A tojanida can emit a spherical cloud of jet-black ink with a radius of 30 feet once per minute as a free action. The effect is otherwise similar to *fog cloud* cast by an individual of a level equal to the tojanida's Hit Dice. Out of water, the ink emerges in a stream up to 30 feet long, which a tojanida can squirt into an opponent's eyes. The affected creature must succeed on a Reflex save or be blinded for 1 round. The save DC is 13 against a juvenile, 15 against an adult, and 21 against an elder. The save DCs are Constitution based.

All-Around Vision (Ex): The multiple apertures in a tojanida's shell allow it to look in any direction, bestowing a +4 racial bonus on Spot and Search checks. Opponents gain no flanking bonuses when attacking a tojanida.

Skills: A tojanida has a +8 racial bonus on any Swim check to perform some special action or avoid a hazard. It can always choose to take 10 on a Swim check, even if distracted or endangered. It can use the run action while swimming, provided it swims in a straight line.

TREANT

Huge Plant
Hit Dice: 7d8+35 (66 hp)
Initiative: −1
Speed: 30 ft. (6 squares)
Armor Class: 20 (−2 size, −1 Dex, +13 natural), touch 7, flat-footed 20
Base Attack/Grapple: +5/+22
Attack: Slam +12 melee (2d6+9)
Full Attack: 2 slams +12 melee (2d6+9)
Space/Reach: 15 ft./15 ft.

Special Attacks: Animate trees, double damage against objects, trample 2d6+13

Special Qualities: Damage reduction 10/slashing, low-light vision, plant traits, vulnerability to fire

Saves: Fort +10, Ref +1, Will +7

Abilities: Str 29, Dex 8, Con 21, Int 12, Wis 16, Cha 12

Skills: Diplomacy +3, Hide –9*, Intimidate +6, Knowledge (nature) +6, Listen +8, Sense Motive +8, Spot +8, Survival +8 (+10 aboveground)

Feats: Improved Sunder, Iron Will, Power Attack

Environment: Temperate forests

Organization: Solitary or grove (4–7)

Challenge Rating: 8

Treasure: Standard

Alignment: Usually neutral good

Advancement: 8–16 HD (Huge); 17–21 HD (Gargantuan)

Level Adjustment: +5

This tall being looks much like an animated tree. Its skin is thick and brown, with a barklike texture. Its arms are gnarled like branches, and its legs look like the split trunk of a tree. Above the eyes and along the head are dozens of smaller branches from which hang great leaves.

Treants combine features of trees and humans. They are peaceful by nature but deadly when angered. They hate evil and the unrestrained use of fire, considering themselves guardians of the trees.

A treant's leaves are deep green in the spring and summer. In the fall and winter the leaves change to yellow, orange, or red, but they rarely fall out. A treant's legs fit together when closed to look like the trunk of a tree, and a motionless treant is nearly indistinguishable from a tree.

A treant is about 30 feet tall, with a "trunk" about 2 feet in diameter. It weighs about 4,500 pounds.

Treants speak their own language, plus Common and Sylvan. Most also can manage a smattering of just about all other humanoid tongues—at least enough to say "Get away from my trees!"

COMBAT

Treants prefer to watch potential foes carefully before attacking. They often charge suddenly from cover to trample the despoilers of forests. If sorely pressed, they animate trees as reinforcements.

Animate Trees (Sp): A treant can animate trees within 180 feet at will, controlling up to two trees at a time. It takes 1 full round for a normal tree to uproot itself. Thereafter it moves at a speed of 10 feet and fights as a treant in all respects. Animated trees lose their ability to move if the treant that animated them is incapacitated or moves out of range. The ability is otherwise similar to *liveoak* (caster level 12th). Animated trees have the same vulnerability to fire that a treant has.

Double Damage against Objects (Ex): A treant or animated tree that makes a full attack against an object or structure deals double damage.

Trample (Ex): Reflex DC 22 half. The save DC is Strength-based.

Skills: *Treants have a +16 racial bonus on Hide checks made in forested areas.

Treant

Medium Outsider (Native, Water)

Hit Dice: 3d8+3 (16 hp)

Initiative: +0

Speed: 5 ft. (1 square), swim 40 ft.

Armor Class: 16 (+6 natural), touch 10, flat-footed 16

Base Attack/Grapple: +3/+4

Attack: Trident +4 melee (1d8+1) or heavy crossbow +3 ranged (1d10/19–20)

Full Attack: Trident +4 melee (1d8+1) or heavy crossbow +3 ranged (1d10/19–20)

Space/Reach: 5 ft./5 ft.

Special Attacks: Spell-like abilities

Special Qualities: Darkvision 60 ft.

Saves: Fort +4, Ref +3, Will +4

Abilities: Str 12, Dex 10, Con 12, Int 13, Wis 13, Cha 11

Skills: Craft (any one) +7, Diplomacy +2, Hide +6, Listen +7, Move Silently +6, Ride +6, Search +7, Sense Motive +7, Spot +7, Survival +7 (+9 following tracks), Swim +9

Feats: Mounted Combat, Ride-By Attack

Environment: Temperate aquatic

Organization: Company (2–5), squad (6–11), or band (20–80)

Challenge Rating: 2

Treasure: Standard

Alignment: Usually neutral good

Advancement: 4–9 HD (Medium)

Level Adjustment: +2

This being is roughly human-sized. Its lower half ends in two finned legs, while its torso, head, and arms are human.

Tritons are thought to originate from the Elemental Plane of Water, but have migrated to the Material Plane for some unknown purpose. They are sea dwellers, preferring warm waters but able to tolerate colder depths.

A triton has silvery skin that fades into silver-blue scales on the lower half of its body. A triton's hair is deep blue or blue-green.

Tritons form communities, either in great undersea castles built of rock, coral, and other natural materials or in finely sculpted caverns. A hunter-gatherer people, tritons take from the sea's vast bounty only what they need to survive. They are naturally suspicious of surface dwellers and prefer not to deal with them if possible. However, tritons deal harshly with beings who intentionally invade their communities, capturing the intruders and setting them adrift without any possessions at least 10 miles from any shoreline, left "to the mercy of the sea."

Tritons are the natural enemy of the cruel and evil sahuagin. The two cannot coexist peacefully: Wars between them are prolonged, bloody affairs that sometimes interfere with shipping and maritime trade.

A triton is about the same size and weight as a human.

Tritons speak Common and Aquan.

Illus. by T. Diterlizzi

COMBAT

The reclusive tritons prefer to avoid combat, but they fiercely defend their homes. They attack with either melee or ranged weapons as the circumstances warrant. When encountered outside their lair, they are 90% likely to be mounted on friendly sea creatures such as porpoises.

Spell-Like Abilities: 1/day—*summon nature's ally IV.* Caster level 7th. Tritons often choose water elementals for their companions.

Skills: A triton has a +8 racial bonus on any Swim check to perform some special action or avoid a hazard. It can always choose to take 10 on a Swim check, even if distracted or endangered. It can use the run action while swimming, provided it swims in a straight line.

Triton

TROGLODYTE

Medium Humanoid (Reptilian)

Hit Dice: 2d8+4 (13 hp)

Initiative: –1

Speed: 30 ft. (6 squares)

Armor Class: 15 (–1 Dex, +6 natural), touch 9, flat-footed 15

Base Attack/Grapple: +1/+1

Attack: Club +1 melee (1d6) or claw +1 melee (1d4) or javelin +1 ranged (1d6)

Full Attack: Club +1 melee (1d6) and claw –1 melee (1d4) and bite –1 melee (1d4); or 2 claws +1 melee (1d4) and bite –1 melee (1d4); or javelin +1 ranged (1d6)

Space/Reach: 5 ft./5 ft.

Special Attacks: Stench

Special Qualities: Darkvision 90 ft.

Saves: Fort +5, Ref –1, Will +0

Abilities: Str 10, Dex 9, Con 14, Int 8, Wis 10, Cha 10

Skills: Hide +5*, Listen +3

Feats: Multiattack[B], Weapon Focus (javelin)

Environment: Underground

Organization: Clutch (2–5), squad (6–11 plus 1–2 monitor lizards), or band (20–80 plus 20% noncombatants plus 3–13 monitor lizards)

Challenge Rating: 1

Treasure: 50% coins; 50% goods; 50% items

Alignment: Usually chaotic evil

Advancement: By character class

Level Adjustment: +2

This reptilian creature looks somewhat humanoid. It is a little shorter than a human. It has spindly but muscular arms and walks erect on its squat legs, trailing a long, slender tail. Its head is lizardlike and crowned with a frill that extends from the forehead to the base of the neck. Its eyes are black and beady.

Troglodytes are revolting lizard creatures as evil as the foulest of demons. They are very warlike and savor the taste of their enemies—especially humanoids.

Troglodytes are not especially intelligent, but their ferocity and natural cunning more than compensate for this deficiency. They often launch bloody raids against humanoid settlements or ambush caravans in warm climates. They guard their lairs aggressively, lashing out at anyone who comes too near.

A troglodyte stands about 5 feet tall and weighs about 150 pounds.

Troglodytes speak Draconic.

COMBAT

Half of a group of troglodytes are armed only with claws and teeth; the rest carry one or two javelins and clubs. They normally conceal themselves, launch a volley of javelins, then close to attack. If the battle goes against them, they retreat and attempt to hide.

Stench (Ex): When a troglodyte is angry or frightened, it secretes an oily, musklike chemical that nearly every form of animal life finds offensive. All living creatures (except troglodytes) within 30 feet of a troglodyte must succeed on a DC 13 Fortitude save or be sickened for 10 rounds. The save DC is Constitution-based. Creatures that successfully save cannot be affected by the same troglodyte's stench for 24 hours. A *delay poison* or *neutralize poison* spell removes the effect from the sickened creature. Creatures with immunity to poison are unaffected, and creatures resistant to poison receive their normal bonus on their saving throws.

Skills: The skin of a troglodyte changes color somewhat, allowing it to blend in with its surroundings like a chameleon and providing a +4 racial bonus on Hide checks. *In rocky or underground settings, this bonus improves to +8.

TROGLODYTE SOCIETY

Troglodyte tribes are ruled by the largest and fiercest among them, with subchieftains who have distinguished themselves in battle. Trogs like to lair near humanoid settlements to prey on inhabitants and their livestock. They raid on moonless nights when their darkvision and coloration are most effective.

Troglodyte

Troglodytes prize steel above all else. Though individuals usually have no wealth, a lair may contain valuable items casually discarded, pushed into corners, or mixed in with refuse. The lair is usually a large cave with smaller caves for the hatchlings and eggs. A lair has hatchlings equal to one-fifth the number of adults and eggs equal to one-tenth.

Troglodytes revere Laogzed, a vile deity who resembles a cross between a toad and a lizard.

TROGLODYTE CHARACTERS

Troglodyte characters possess the following racial traits.

— —2 Dexterity, +4 Constitution, —2 Intelligence.
—Medium size.
—A troglodyte's base land speed is 30 feet.
—Darkvision out to 90 feet.
—Racial Hit Dice: A troglodyte begins with two levels of humanoid, which provide 2d8 Hit Dice, a base attack bonus of +1, and base saving throw bonuses of Fort +3, Ref +0, and Will +0.
—Racial Skills: A troglodyte's humanoid levels give it skill points equal to 5 × (2 + Int modifier, minimum 1). Its class skills are Hide and Listen. Troglodytes have a +4 racial bonus on Hide checks (+8 in rocky or underground surroundings).
—Racial Feats: A troglodyte's humanoid levels give it one feat. A troglodyte receives Multiattack as a bonus feat.
— +6 natural armor bonus.
—Natural Weapons: 2 claws (1d4) and bite (1d4).
—Special Attacks (see above): Stench.
—Automatic Languages: Draconic. Bonus Languages: Common, Giant, Goblin, Orc.
—Favored Class: Cleric.
—Level adjustment +2.

This big, bipedal creature is about one and a half times as tall as a human but very thin. It has long and ungainly arms and legs The legs end in great three-toed feet, the arms in wide, powerful hands with sharpened claws. The hide is rubbery, and its hair is thick and ropy, and seems to writhe with its own energy.

Trolls are horrid carnivores found in all climes, from arctic wastelands to tropical jungles. Most creatures avoid these beasts, who know no fear and attack unceasingly when hungry.

Trolls have ravenous appetites, devouring everything from grubs to bears and humanoids. They often lair near settlements and hunt the inhabitants until they devour every last one.

Trolls walk upright but hunched forward with sagging shoulders. Their gait is uneven, and when they run, their arms dangle and drag along the ground. For all this seeming awkwardness, trolls are very agile.

A typical adult troll stands 9 feet tall and weighs 500 pounds. Females are slightly larger than males. A troll's rubbery hide is moss green, mottled green and gray, or putrid gray. The hair is usually greenish black or iron gray.

Trolls speak Giant.

COMBAT

Trolls have no fear of death: They launch themselves into combat without hesitation, flailing wildly at the closest opponent. Even when confronted with fire, they try to get around the flames and attack.

Rend (Ex): If a troll hits with both claw attacks, it latches onto the opponent's body and tears the flesh. This attack automatically deals an additional 2d6+9 points of damage.

	Troll	Troll Hunter, 6th-Level Ranger
	Large Giant	Large Giant
Hit Dice:	6d8+36 (63 hp)	6d8+6d8+72 (130 hp)
Initiative:	+2	+1
Speed:	30 ft. (6 squares)	30 ft. (6 squares)
Armor Class:	16 (—1 size, +2 Dex, +5 natural), touch 11, flat-footed 14	21 (—1 size, +1 Dex, +6 natural, +5 *+1 chain shirt*), touch 10, flat-footed 20
Base Attack/Grapple:	+4/+14	+10/+21
Attack:	Claw +9 melee (1d6+6)	Claw +16 melee (1d6+7) or +1 *battleaxe* +17 melee (2d6+8/×3) or javelin +10 ranged (1d8+7)
Full Attack:	2 claws +9 melee (1d6+6) and bite +4 melee (1d6+3)	2 claws +16 melee (1d6+7) and bite +11 melee (1d6+3); or +1 *battleaxe* +17/+12 melee (2d6+8/×3) and claw +12 melee (1d6+3) and bite +12 (1d6+3); or javelin +10 ranged (1d8+7)
Space/Reach:	10 ft./10 ft.	10 ft./10 ft.
Special Attacks:	Rend 2d6+9	Rend 2d6+10, spells
Special Qualities:	Darkvision 90 ft., low-light vision, regeneration 5, scent	Darkvision 90 ft., favored enemy elves (+4), favored enemy humans (+2), low-light vision, regeneration 5, scent, wild empathy
Saves:	Fort +11, Ref +4, Will +3	Fort +16, Ref +8, Will +8
Abilities:	Str 23, Dex 14, Con 23, Int 6, Wis 9, Cha 6	Str 25, Dex 12, Con 22, Int 10, Wis 15, Cha 10
Skills:	Listen +5, Spot +6	Knowledge (nature) +6, Knowledge (dungeoneering) +6, Listen +13, Move Silently +9, Search +6, Spot +13, Survival +11 (+13 above- or underground and following tracks)
Feats:	Alertness, Iron Will, Track	Alertness, Cleave, Endurance[B], Improved Natural Armor, Improved Two-Weapon Fighting[B], Iron Will, Power Attack, Track[B], Two-Weapon Fighting[B]
Environment:	Cold mountains (Scrag: Cold aquatic)	Cold mountains
Organization:	Solitary or gang (2—4)	Solitary
Challenge Rating:	5	11
Treasure:	Standard	Standard
Alignment:	Usually chaotic evil	Usually chaotic evil
Advancement:	By character class	—
Level Adjustment:	+5	+5

Troll

bonus on grapple checks, lifting and carrying limits double those of Medium characters.

—Space/Reach: 10 feet/10 feet.

—A troll's base land speed is 30 feet.

—Darkvision out to 60 feet and low-light vision.

—Racial Hit Dice: A troll begins with six levels of giant, which provide 6d8 Hit Dice, a base attack bonus of +4, and base saving throw bonuses of Fort +5, Ref +2, and Will +2.

—Racial Skills: A troll's giant levels give it skill points equal to 9 × (2 + Int modifier, minimum 1). Its class skills are Listen and Spot.

—Racial Feats: A troll's giant levels give it three feats.

— +5 natural armor bonus.

—Natural Weapons: Claw (1d6) and bite (1d6).

—Special Attacks (see above): Rend, damage 2d6 + 1-1/2 times Str modifier.

—Special Qualities: Regeneration 5, scent.

—Automatic Languages: Giant. Bonus Languages: Common, Orc.

—Favored Class: Fighter.

—Level adjustment +5.

UMBER HULK

This hulking, powerfully built creature looks something like a cross between a great ape and a beetle. The low, rounded head is dominated by a massive pair of mandibles and rows of triangular teeth. It has two big compound eyes like a beetle's, with two smaller eyes like an ape's in between. Armor plates cover virtually all of its chitinous body, whose scattered feelers resemble sparse hair.

Umber hulks are massive creatures that dwell deep beneath the earth. Ripping through rock as though it were light underbrush, they rampage continuously, leaving destruction in their wake.

Regeneration (Ex): Fire and acid deal normal damage to a troll. If a troll loses a limb or body part, the lost portion regrows in 3d6 minutes. The creature can reattach the severed member instantly by holding it to the stump.

SCRAG

These cousins of the troll have the aquatic subtype. They dwell in any body of water in any climate. They have a base land speed of 20 feet and a swim speed of 40 feet and are found only in aquatic environments. They regenerate only if mostly immersed in water.

TROLL HUNTER

Some trolls, more cunning than most, are not satisfied with merely eating civilized beings but train to hunt them relentlessly. These troll hunters are fearsome rangers who focus on slaying and devouring humanoid prey.

Combat

A troll hunter makes full use of its scent ability to track its favored enemies and generally prefers to hunt in darkness.

The troll hunter uses its limited repertoire of spells to protect itself from damaging forms of energy and to immobilize enemies.

Typical Ranger Spells Prepared (2; save DC 12 + spell level): 1st—*entangle, resist energy.*

TROLLS AS CHARACTERS

Troll characters possess the following racial traits.

— +12 Strength, +4 Dexterity, +12 Constitution, –4 Intelligence (minimum 3), –2 Wisdom, –4 Charisma.

—Large size. –1 penalty to Armor Class, –1 penalty on attack rolls, –4 penalty on Hide checks, +4

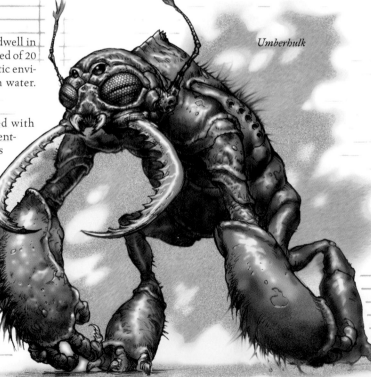

Umberhulk

	Umber Hulk Large Aberration	Truly Horrid Umber Hulk Huge Aberration
Hit Dice:	8d8+35 (71 hp)	20d8 + 180 (270 hp)
Initiative:	+1	+0
Speed:	20 ft. (4 squares), burrow 20 ft.	20 ft. (4 squares), burrow 20 ft.
Armor Class:	18 (−1 size, +1 Dex, +8 natural), touch 10, flat-footed 17	22 (−2 size, +14 natural), touch 8, flat-footed 24
Base Attack/Grapple:	+6/+16	+15/+36
Attack:	Claw +11 melee (2d4+6)	Claw +26 melee (3d6+13)
Full Attack:	2 claws +11 melee (2d4+6) and bite +9 melee (2d8+3)	2 claws +26 melee (3d6+13) and bite +24 melee (4d6+6)
Space/Reach:	10 ft./10 ft.	15 ft/15 ft.
Special Attacks:	Confusing gaze	Confusing gaze
Special Qualities:	Darkvision 60 ft., tremorsense 60 ft.	Darkvision 60 ft., tremorsense 60 ft.
Saves:	Fort +8, Ref +3, Will +6	Fort +17, Ref +6, Will +15
Abilities:	Str 23, Dex 13, Con 19, Int 11, Wis 11, Cha 13	Str 36, Dex 10, Con 29, Int 10, Wis 13, Cha 15
Skills:	Climb +12, Jump +5, Listen +11	Climb +23, Jump +15, Listen +21, Sense Motive +5
Feats:	Great Fortitude, Multiattack, Toughness	Great Fortitude, Improved Natural Attack (claw), Improved Natural Armor ×3, Iron Will, Multiattack
Environment:	Underground	Underground
Organization:	Solitary or cluster (2–4)	Solitary
Challenge Rating:	7	14
Treasure:	Standard	Standard
Alignment:	Usually chaotic evil	Usually chaotic evil
Advancement:	9–12 HD (Large); 13–24 HD (Huge)	—
Level Adjustment:	—	—

An umber hulk stands roughly 8 feet tall and measures nearly 5 feet across, weighing about 800 pounds. An umber hulk can burrow through solid rock at a speed of 5 feet. It does not leave a usable tunnel unless it chooses to.

Umber hulks speak Terran.

COMBAT

An umber hulk can deliver blows powerful enough to crush almost any enemy. In addition, its mandibles are strong enough to bite through armor or exoskeletons with ease.

Despite its great bulk, an umber hulk is intelligent. When brute force won't overcome an enemy, it is more than capable of outthinking those who assume it to be a stupid beast. Umber hulks often use their tunneling ability to create deadfalls and pits for the unwary.

Confusing Gaze (Su): *Confusion* as the spell, 30 feet, caster level 8th, Will DC 15 negates. The save DC is Charisma-based.

TRULY HORRID UMBER HULK

Umber hulks have been known to grow to tremendous size and strength. The truly horrid umber hulk stands more than 16 feet in height and weighs about 8,000 pounds. Phenomenally powerful, the truly horrid umber hulk is a loner that is feared even by its own kind. It is occasionally found in the service of evil dragons or sorcerers, guarding their lairs.

The Will save DC is 22 against the truly horrid umber hulk's confusing gaze, due to its higher Hit Dice and Charisma score.

UNICORN

This powerful, equine creature has a gleaming white coat and big, lively eyes. Long, silky white hair hangs down in a mane and forelock. A single ivory-colored horn, about 2 feet long, grows from the center of the forehead. The hooves are cloven.

These fierce, noble beasts shun contact with all but sylvan creatures (dryads, pixies, and the like), showing themselves only to defend their woodland homes.

Unicorn

A unicorn has deep sea-blue, violet, brown, or fiery gold eyes. Males sport a white beard.

Unicorns mate for life, making their homes in open dells or glades in the forests they protect. Good and neutral travelers may pass freely through and even hunt for food in a unicorn's forest, but evil creatures do so at great risk. Likewise, a unicorn will attack any being it discovers killing for sport in its territory or damaging the forest maliciously.

Lone unicorns occasionally allow themselves to be tamed and ridden by good human or elven maidens of pure heart. Such a unicorn, if treated kindly, is the maiden's loyal steed and protector for life, even accompanying her beyond its forest.

A unicorn's horn is renowned for its healing properties. Evil and unscrupulous beings sometimes hunt a unicorn for its horn, which can fetch up to 2,000 gp, for use in various healing potions and devices. Most good creatures refuse to traffic in such things.

A typical adult unicorn grows to 8 feet in length, stands 5 feet high at the shoulder, and weighs 1,200 pounds. Females are slightly smaller and slimmer than males.

Unicorns speak Sylvan and Common.

COMBAT

Unicorns normally attack only when defending themselves or their forests. They either charge, impaling foes with their horns like lances, or strike with their hooves. The horn is a +3 magic weapon, though its power fades if removed from the unicorn.

Magic Circle against Evil (Su): This ability continuously duplicates the effect of the spell. A unicorn cannot suppress this ability.

Spell-Like Abilities: Unicorns can use *detect evil* at will as a free action. Once per day a unicorn can use *greater teleport* to move anywhere within its home. It cannot teleport beyond the forest boundaries nor back from outside.

A unicorn can use *cure light wounds* three times per day and *cure moderate wounds* once per day (caster level 5th) by touching a wounded creature with its horn. Once per

249

	Unicorn	Celestial Charger, 7th-Level Cleric
	Large Magical Beast	Large Magical Beast
Hit Dice:	4d10+20 (42 hp)	8d10+7d8+75 (155 hp)
Initiative:	+3	+4
Speed:	60 ft. (12 squares)	60 ft. (12 squares)
Armor Class:	18 (−1 size, +3 Dex, +6 natural), touch 12, flat-footed 15	24 (−1 size, +4 Dex, +6 natural, +5 *bracers of armor +5*), touch 13, flat-footed 20
Base Attack/Grapple:	+4/+13	+13/+24
Attack:	Horn +11 melee (1d8+8)	Horn +22 melee (1d8+10)
Full Attack:	Horn +11 melee (1d8+8) and 2 hooves +3 melee (1d4+2)	Horn +22 melee (1d8+10) and 2 hooves +14 melee (1d4+3)
Space/Reach:	10 ft./5 ft.	10 ft./5 ft.
Special Attacks:	—	Turn undead 13/day, smite evil, spells
Special Qualities:	Darkvision 60 ft., magic circle against evil, spell-like abilities, immunity to poison, charm, and compulsion, low-light vision, scent, wild empathy	Damage reduction 10/magic, darkvision 60 ft., immunity to poison, charm, and compulsion, low-light vision, magic circle against evil, resistance to acid 10, cold 10, and electricity 10, scent, spell-like abilities, spell resistance 20, wild empathy
Saves:	Fort +9, Ref +7, Will +6	Fort +16, Ref +12, Will +15
Abilities:	Str 20, Dex 17, Con 21, Int 10, Wis 21, Cha 24	Str 24, Dex 18, Con 20, Int 13, Wis 27, Cha 22
Skills:	Jump +21, Listen +11, Move Silently +9, Spot +11, Survival +8*	Concentration +11, Knowledge (nature) +9, Knowledge (religion) +8, Listen +15, Move Silently +12, Spellcraft +5, Spot +15, Survival +15 (+17 aboveground)*
Feats:	Alertness, Skill Focus (Survival)	Alertness, Combat Casting, Extra Turning, Improved Turning, Run, Skill Focus (Survival)
Environment:	Temperate forests	Seven Mounting Heavens of Celestia
Organization:	Solitary, pair, or grace (3–6)	Solitary
Challenge Rating:	3	13
Treasure:	None	None
Alignment:	Always chaotic good	Always chaotic good
Advancement:	5–8 HD (Large)	By character class
Level Adjustment:	+4 (cohort)	+8 (cohort)

day it can use *neutralize poison* (DC 21, caster level 8th) with a touch of its horn. The save DC is Charisma-based.

Wild Empathy (Ex): This power works like the druid's wild empathy class feature, except that a unicorn has a +6 racial bonus on the check.

Skills: Unicorns have a +4 racial bonus on Move Silently checks.

*Unicorns have a +3 competence bonus on Survival checks within the boundaries of their forest.

CELESTIAL CHARGER

A celestial unicorn is a champion for good, the fierce enemy of evil beings that would destroy woodlands and their inhabitants. It is a dedicated follower of Ehlonna.

The celestial charger described here is an 8 HD celestial unicorn with seven levels of cleric.

Combat

The save DC for this celestial charger's *neutralize poison* ability (DC 20) is adjusted for its greater Hit Dice and altered Charisma score.

A celestial charger's natural weapons are treated as magic weapons for the purpose of overcoming damage reduction.

Smite Evil (Su): Once per day a celestial charger can make a normal melee attack to deal 15 points of extra damage against an evil foe.

Cleric Spells Prepared (6/7/6/5/4; save DC 18 + spell level): 0—*detect magic, detect poison* (2), *light, virtue* (2); 1st—*bless* (2), *calm animals*, *obscuring mist, remove fear, sanctuary, shield of faith*; 2nd—*aid* (2), *animal messenger, lesser restoration, remove paralysis, shield other*; 3rd—*prayer, protection from energy, remove curse, searing light* (2); 4th—*air walk, divine power, holy smite*, *restoration*.

*Domain spell. Domains: Animal and Good.

VAMPIRE

Forever anchored to their coffins and the unholy earth of their graves, these nocturnal predators scheme constantly to strengthen themselves and fill the world with their foul progeny.

Vampires appear just as they did in life, although their features are often hardened and feral, with the predatory look of wolves. Like liches, they often embrace finery and decadence and may assume the guise of nobility. Despite their human appearance, vampires can be easily recognized, for they cast no shadows and throw no reflections in mirrors.

Vampires speak any languages they knew in life.

SAMPLE VAMPIRE

This sinister-looking warrior has pale skin, haunting red eyes, and a feral cast to his features. He wears chain armor and holds a spiked chain in his clawed hands.

This example uses a 5th-level human fighter as the base creature.

Vampire, 5th-Level Human Fighter
Medium Undead (Augmented Humanoid)
Hit Dice: 5d12 (32 hp)
Initiative: +7
Speed: 30 ft. (6 squares)
Armor Class: 23 (+3 Dex, +6 natural, +4 masterwork chain shirt), touch 13, flat-footed 20
Base Attack/Grapple: +5/+11
Attack: Slam +11 melee (1d6+9 plus energy drain) or +1 *spiked chain* +13 melee (2d4+12) or masterwork shortbow +9 ranged (1d6/×3)
Full Attack: Slam +11 melee (1d6+9 plus energy drain) or +1 *spiked chain* +13 melee (2d4+12) or masterwork shortbow +9 ranged (1d6/×3)

Space/Reach: 5 ft./5 ft. (10 ft. with spiked chain)

Special Attacks: Blood drain, children of the night, create spawn, dominate, energy drain

Special Qualities: Alternate form, damage reduction 10/silver and magic, darkvision 60 ft., fast healing 5, gaseous form, resistance to cold 10 and electricity 10, spider climb, undead traits, vampire weaknesses

Saves: Fort +4, Ref +6, Will +4

Abilities: Str 22, Dex 17, Con —, Int 12, Wis 16, Cha 12

Skills: Bluff +9, Climb +10, Hide +10, Listen +17, Move Silently +10, Ride +11, Search +9, Sense Motive +11, Spot +17

Feats: Alertness[B], Blind-Fight, Combat Reflexes[B], Dodge[B], Exotic Weapon Proficiency (spiked chain), Improved Initiative[B], Lightning Reflexes[B], Mobility, Power Attack, Weapon Focus (spiked chain), Weapon Specialization (spiked chain)

Environment: Temperate plains

Organization: Solitary

Challenge Rating: 7

Treasure: Double standard

Alignment: Always evil (any)

Advancement: By character class

Level Adjustment: +5

Combat

This vampire's slam attack is treated as a magic weapon for the purpose of overcoming damage reduction.

The DC is 13 for the Will save against this vampire's domination ability, and for the Fortitude save to remove a negative level caused by its energy drain.

Possessions: +1 spiked chain, masterwork chain shirt, *potion of haste.*

SAMPLE ELITE VAMPIRE

This example uses a half-elf 9th-level monk/4th-level shadowdancer as the base creature.

Elite Vampire, 13th-Level Half-Elf Monk/Shadowdancer

Medium Undead (Augmented Humanoid)

Hit Dice: 13d12 (90 hp)

Initiative: +8

Speed: 60 ft. (12 squares)

Armor Class: 32 (+4 Dex, +6 natural, +6 Wis, +1 intrinsic, *bracers of armor +3, ring of protection +2),* touch 23, flat-footed 32

Base Attack/Grapple: +9/+14

Attack: Unarmed strike +14 melee (1d10+5 plus energy drain) or +2 *keen kama* +16 melee (1d6+7) or +1 *frost sling* +14 ranged (1d4+1 plus 1d6 cold)

Full Attack: Unarmed strike +14/+14/+9 melee (1d10+5 plus energy drain) or +2 *keen kama* +16/+16/+11 melee (1d6+7) or +1 *frost sling* +14 ranged (1d4+1 plus 1d6 cold)

Space/Reach: 5 ft./5 ft.

Special Attacks: Blood drain, children of the night, create spawn, dominate, energy drain, flurry of blows, ki strike (magic), *shadow illusion, summon shadow*

Special Qualities: Alternate form, damage reduction 10/silver and magic, darkvision 60 ft., fast healing 5, gaseous form, half-elf traits, hide in

plain sight, improved evasion, purity of body, resistance to cold 10 and electricity 10, *shadow jump* 20 ft., slow fall 40 ft., spider climb, still mind, uncanny dodge (Dex bonus to AC), undead traits, vampire weaknesses, wholeness of body

Saves: Fort +7, Ref +16, Will +13

Abilities: Str 20, Dex 19, Con —, Int 12, Wis 22, Cha 12

Skills: Balance +22, Bluff +9, Climb +9, Hide +28, Jump +23, Listen +16, Move Silently +28, Perform (wind instruments) +7, Search +9, Sense Motive +14, Spot +16, Tumble +22

Feats: Alertness, Blind-Fight, Combat Reflexes, Deflect Arrows[B], Dodge, Improved Initiative, Improved Disarm[B], Lightning Reflexes, Mobility, Spring Attack, Stunning Fist[B]

Environment: Temperate forests

Organization: Solitary

Challenge Rating: 15

Treasure: Double standard

Alignment: Always evil (any)

Advancement: By character class

Level Adjustment: +8

Combat

This vampire's unarmed strikes are treated as magic weapons for the purpose of overcoming damage reduction.

The DC is 17 for the Will save against this vampire's domination ability, and for the Fortitude save to remove a negative level caused by its energy drain.

Flurry of Blows (Ex): Use the full attack action to make one extra attack per round with an unarmed strike or a special monk weapon at her highest base attack, making the extra attack either with her +2 *keen kama* or unarmed.

Ki Strike (Su): Deal damage to creatures with damage reduction using unarmed strike as though with a magic weapon.

Shadow Illusion (Sp): Create visual illusions from shadows as *silent image* once per day.

Summon Shadow (Sp): Summon one shadow companion, which cannot be turned, rebuked, or commanded by others. If the shadow is destroyed or dismissed, the shadowdancer must succeed on a DC 15 Fortitude save or lose 800 XP (400 XP on a successful save). A new shadow cannot be summoned for a year and a day.

Half-Elf Traits (Ex): Immunity to *sleep* spells and effects; +2 racial bonus on saves against enchantment spells or effects; low-light vision (can see twice as far as a human in low-light conditions); +1 racial bonus on Listen, Spot, and Search checks (already figured into the statistics given here); +2 racial bonus on Diplomacy and Gather Information checks.

Hide in Plain Sight (Su): Can use the Hide skill even while being observed as long as within 10 feet of a shadow.

Improved Evasion (Ex): If the vampire makes a successful Reflex saving throw against an attack that normally deals half damage on a successful save, she instead takes no damage. In addition, she takes only half damage on a failed save.

Vampires

251

Purity of Body (Ex): Immunity to all diseases except for magical diseases such as mummy rot and lycanthropy.

Shadow Jump (Sp): Travel instantaneously between shadows as a *dimension door* spell, up to 20 feet per day.

Slow Fall (Ex): A monk within arm's reach of a wall takes damage as if the fall were 40 feet shorter than it actually is.

Still Mind (Ex): +2 bonus on saves against enchantment spells and effects.

Wholeness of Body (Su): Cure up to 18 hit points of her own wounds each day.

Possessions: +2 keen kama, +1 frost sling, 10 +1 sling bullets, ring of protection +2, bracers of armor +3, periapt of Wisdom +4.

CREATING A VAMPIRE

"Vampire" is an acquired template that can be added to any humanoid or monstrous humanoid creature (referred to hereafter as the base creature).

A vampire uses all the base creature's statistics and special abilities except as noted here.

Size and Type: The creature's type changes to undead (augmented humanoid or monstrous humanoid). Do not recalculate base attack bonus, saves, or skill points. Size is unchanged.

Hit Dice: Increase all current and future Hit Dice to d12s.

Speed: Same as the base creature. If the base creature has a swim speed, the vampire retains the ability to swim and is not vulnerable to immersion in running water (see below).

Armor Class: The base creature's natural armor bonus improves by +6.

Attack: A vampire retains all the attacks of the base creature and also gains a slam attack if it didn't already have one. If the base creature can use weapons, the vampire retains this ability. A creature with natural weapons retains those natural weapons. A vampire fighting without weapons uses either its slam attack or its primary natural weapon (if it has any). A vampire armed with a weapon uses its slam or a weapon, as it desires.

Full Attack: A vampire fighting without weapons uses either its slam attack (see above) or its natural weapons (if it has any). If armed with a weapon, it usually uses the weapon as its primary attack along with a slam or other natural weapon as a natural secondary attack.

Damage: Vampires have slam attacks. If the base creature does not have this attack form, use the appropriate damage value from the table below according to the vampire's size. Creatures that have other kinds of natural weapons retain their old damage values or use the appropriate value from the table below, whichever is better.

Size	Damage
Fine	1
Diminutive	1d2
Tiny	1d3
Small	1d4
Medium	1d6
Large	1d8
Huge	2d6
Gargantuan	2d8
Colossal	4d6

Special Attacks: A vampire retains all the special attacks of the base creature and gains those described below. Saves have a DC of 10 + 1/2 vampire's HD + vampire's Cha modifier unless noted otherwise.

Blood Drain (Ex): A vampire can suck blood from a living victim with its fangs by making a successful grapple check. If it pins the foe, it drains blood, dealing 1d4 points of Constitution drain each round the pin is maintained. On each such successful attack, the vampire gains 5 temporary hit points.

Children of the Night (Su): Vampires command the lesser creatures of the world and once per day can call forth 1d6+1 rat swarms, 1d4+1 bat swarms, or a pack of 3d6 wolves as a standard action. (If the base creature is not terrestrial, this power might summon other creatures of similar power.) These creatures arrive in 2d6 rounds and serve the vampire for up to 1 hour.

Dominate (Su): A vampire can crush an opponent's will just by looking onto his or her eyes. This is similar to a gaze attack, except that the vampire must use a standard action, and those merely looking at it are not affected. Anyone the vampire targets must succeed on a Will save or fall instantly under the vampire's influence as though by a *dominate person* spell (caster level 12th). The ability has a range of 30 feet.

Create Spawn (Su): A humanoid or monstrous humanoid slain by a vampire's energy drain rises as a vampire spawn (see the Vampire Spawn entry, page 253) 1d4 days after burial.

If the vampire instead drains the victim's Constitution to 0 or lower, the victim returns as a spawn if it had 4 or less HD and as a vampire if it had 5 or more HD. In either case, the new vampire or spawn is under the command of the vampire that created it and remains enslaved until its master's destruction. At any given time a vampire may have enslaved spawn totaling no more than twice its own Hit Dice; any spawn it creates that would exceed this limit are created as free-willed vampires or vampire spawn. A vampire that is enslaved may create and enslave spawn of its own, so a master vampire can control a number of lesser vampires in this fashion. A vampire may voluntarily free an enslaved spawn in order to enslave a new spawn, but once freed, a vampire or vampire spawn cannot be enslaved again.

Energy Drain (Su): Living creatures hit by a vampire's slam attack (or any other natural weapon the vampire might possess) gain two negative levels. For each negative level bewtowed, the vampire gains 5 temporary hit points. A vampire can use its energy drain ability once per round.

Special Qualities: A vampire retains all the special qualities of the base creature and gains those described below.

Alternate Form (Su): A vampire can assume the shape of a bat, dire bat, wolf, or dire wolf as a standard action. This ability is similar to a *polymorph* spell cast by a 12th-level character, except that the vampire does not regain hit points for changing form and must choose from among the forms mentioned here. While in its alternate form, the vampire loses its natural slam attack and dominate ability, but it gains the natural weapons and extraordinary special attacks of its new form. It can remain in that form until it assumes another or until the next sunrise. (If the base creature is not terrestrial, this power might allow other forms.)

Damage Reduction (Su): A vampire has damage reduction 10/silver and magic. A vampire's natural weapons are treated as magic weapons for the purpose of overcoming damage reduction.

Fast Healing (Ex): A vampire heals 5 points of damage each round so long as it has at least 1 hit point. If reduced to 0 hit points in combat, it automatically assumes gaseous form and attempts to escape. It must reach its coffin home within 2 hours or be utterly destroyed. (It can travel up to nine miles in 2 hours.) Any additional damage dealt to a vampire forced into gaseous form has no effect. Once at rest in its coffin, a vampire is helpless. It regains 1 hit point after 1 hour, then is no longer helpless and resumes healing at the rate of 5 hit points per round.

Gaseous Form (Su): As a standard action, a vampire can assume gaseous form at will as the spell (caster level 5th), but it can remain gaseous indefinitely and has a fly speed of 20 feet with perfect maneuverability.

Resistances (Ex): A vampire has resistance to cold 10 and electricity 10.

Spider Climb (Ex): A vampire can climb sheer surfaces as though with a *spider climb* spell.

Turn Resistance (Ex): A vampire has +4 turn resistance.

Abilities: Increase from the base creature as follows: Str +6, Dex +4, Int +2, Wis +2, Cha +4. As an undead creature, a vampire has no Constitution score.

Skills: Vampires have a +8 racial bonus on Bluff, Hide, Listen, Move Silently, Search, Sense Motive, and Spot checks. Otherwise same as the base creature.

Feats: Vampires gain Alertness, Combat Reflexes, Dodge, Improved Initiative, and Lightning Reflexes, assuming the base creature meets the prerequisites and doesn't already have these feats.

Environment: Any, usually same as base creature.

Organization: Solitary, pair, gang (3–5), or troupe (1–2 plus 2–5 vampire spawn)

Challenge Rating: Same as the base creature +2.

Treasure: Double standard.

Alignment: Always evil (any).

Advancement: By character class.

Level Adjustment: Same as the base creature +8.

Vampire Weaknesses

For all their power, vampires have a number of weaknesses.

Repelling a Vampire: Vampires cannot tolerate the strong odor of garlic and will not enter an area laced with it. Similarly, they recoil from a mirror or a strongly presented holy symbol. These things don't harm the vampire—they merely keep it at bay. A recoiling vampire must stay at least 5 feet away from a creature holding the mirror or holy symbol and cannot touch or make melee attacks against the creature holding the item for the rest of the encounter. Holding a vampire at bay takes a standard action.

Vampires are also unable to cross running water, although they can be carried over it while resting in their coffins or aboard a ship. They are utterly unable to enter a home or other building unless invited in by someone with the authority to do so. They may freely enter public places, since these are by definition open to all.

Slaying a Vampire: Reducing a vampire's hit points to 0 or lower incapacitates it but doesn't always destroy it (see the note on fast healing). However, certain attacks can slay vampires.

Exposing any vampire to direct sunlight disorients it: It can take only a single move action or attack action and is destroyed utterly in the next round if it cannot escape. Similarly, immersing a vampire in running water robs it of one-third of its hit points each round until it is destroyed at the end of the third round of immersion.

Driving a wooden stake through a vampire's heart instantly slays the monster. However, it returns to life if the stake is removed, unless the body is destroyed. A popular tactic is to cut off the creature's head and fill its mouth with holy wafers (or their equivalent).

Vampire Characters

Vampires are always evil, which causes characters of certain classes to lose some class abilities, as noted in Chapter 3 of the *Player's Handbook*. In addition, certain classes take additional penalties.

Clerics: Vampire clerics lose their ability to turn undead but gain the ability to rebuke undead. This ability does not affect the vampire's controller or any other vampires that a master controls.

A vampire cleric has access to two of the following domains: Chaos, Destruction, Evil, or Trickery.

Sorcerers and Wizards: Vampire sorcerers and wizards retain their class abilities, but if a character has a familiar other than a rat or bat, the link between them is broken, and the familiar shuns its former companion. The character can summon another familiar, but it must be a rat or bat.

VAMPIRE SPAWN

Medium Undead

Hit Dice: 4d12+3 (29 hp)

Initiative: +6

Speed: 30 ft. (6 squares)

Armor Class: 15 (+2 Dex, +3 natural), touch 12, flat-footed 13

Base Attack/Grapple: +2/+5

Attack: Slam +5 melee (1d6+4 plus energy drain)

Full Attack: Slam +5 melee (1d6+4 plus energy drain)

Space/Reach: 5 ft./5 ft.

Special Attacks: Blood drain, domination, energy drain

Special Qualities: +2 turn resistance, damage reduction 5/silver, darkvision 60 ft., fast healing 2, gaseous form, resistance to cold 10 and electricity 10, spider climb, undead traits

Saves: Fort +1, Ref +5, Will +5

Abilities: Str 16, Dex 14, Con —, Int 13, Wis 13, Cha 14

Skills: Bluff +6, Climb +8, Craft or Profession (any one) +4, Diplomacy +4, Hide +10, Jump +8, Listen +11, Move Silently +10, Search +8, Sense Motive +11, Spot +11

Feats: Alertness[B], Improved Initiative[B], Lightning Reflexes[B], Skill Focus (selected Craft or Profession skill), Toughness

Environment: Any

Organization: Solitary or pack (2–5)

Challenge Rating: 4

Treasure: Standard

Alignment: Always evil (any)

Advancement: —

Level Adjustment: —

This feral-looking creature virtually drips with evil. Its garb is noble-looking, though in a state of disrepair. Its dark red mouth is dominated by a pair of vicious-looking canine teeth.

Vampire spawn

Vampire spawn are undead creatures that come into being when vampires slay mortals. Like their creators, spawn remain bound to their coffins and to the soil of their graves.

Vampire spawn appear much as they did in life, although their features are often hardened, with a predatory look.

Vampire spawn speak Common.

COMBAT

Vampire spawn use their inhuman strength when engaging mortals, hammering their foes with powerful blows and dashing them against rocks or walls. They also use their gaseous form and flight abilities to strike where opponents are most vulnerable.

Blood Drain (Ex): A vampire spawn can suck blood from a living victim with its fangs by making a successful grapple check. If it pins the foe, it drains blood, dealing 1d4 points of Constitution drain each round. On each such successful drain attack, the vampire spawn gains 5 temporary hit pints.

Domination (Su): A vampire spawn can crush an opponent's will just by looking onto his or her eyes. This is similar to a gaze attack, except that the vampire must take a standard action, and those merely looking at it are not affected. Anyone the vampire targets must succeed on a DC 14 Will save or fall instantly under the vampire's influence as though by a *dominate person* spell from a 5th-level caster. The ability has a range of 30 feet. The save DC is Charisma-based.

Energy Drain (Su): Living creatures hit by a vampire spawn's slam attack gain one negative level. The DC is 14 for the Fortitude save to remove a negative level. The save DC is Charisma-based. For each such negative level bestowed, the vampire spawn gains 5 temporary hit points.

Fast Healing (Ex): A vampire spawn heals 2 points of damage each round so long as it has at least 1 hit point. If reduced to 0 hit points in combat, it automatically assumes gaseous form and attempts to escape. It must reach its coffin home within 2 hours or be utterly destroyed. (It can travel up to nine miles in 2 hours.) Once at rest in its coffin, it is helpless. It regains 1 hit point after 1 hour, then is no longer helpless and resumes healing at the rate of 2 hit points per round.

Gaseous Form (Su): As a standard action, a vampire spawn can assume *gaseous form* at will as the spell (caster level 6th), but it can remain gaseous indefinitely and has a fly speed of 20 feet with perfect maneuverability.

Spider Climb (Ex): A vampire spawn can climb sheer surfaces as though with a *spider climb* spell.

Skills: Vampire spawn have a +4 racial bonus on Bluff, Hide, Listen, Move Silently, Search, Sense Motive, and Spot checks.

VAMPIRE SPAWN WEAKNESSES

Vampire spawn are vulnerable to all attacks and effects that repel or slay vampires. For details, see the Vampire entry.

VARGOUILLE

Small Outsider (Evil, Extraplanar)
Hit Dice: 1d8+1 (5 hp)
Initiative: +1
Speed: Fly 30 ft. (good) (6 squares)
Armor Class: 12 (+1 size, +1 Dex), touch 11, flat-footed 11
Base Attack/Grapple: +1/–3
Attack: Bite +3 melee (1d4 plus poison)
Full Attack: Bite +3 melee (1d4 plus poison)
Space/Reach: 5 ft./5 ft.
Special Attacks: Shriek, kiss, poison
Special Qualities: Darkvision 60 ft.
Saves: Fort +3, Ref +3, Will +3
Abilities: Str 10, Dex 13, Con 12, Int 5, Wis 12, Cha 8
Skills: Hide +9, Intimidate +3, Listen +5, Move Silently +5, Spot +5
Feats: Weapon Finesse
Environment: Tarterian Depths of Carceri
Organization: Cluster (2–5) or mob (6–11)

Challenge Rating: 2
Treasure: None
Alignment: Always neutral evil
Advancement: 2–3 HD (Small)
Level Adjustment: —

This creature looks like a hideous, distorted human head suspended from leathery wings. In place of hair, it is crowned with writhing tendrils, and its eyes burn with a menacing green flame.

These revolting creatures come into the world from the deepest pits of the plane of Carceri. They haunt graveyards, ruins, and other places of death and decay.

A vargouille is slightly larger than a human head, about 18 inches high, with a wingspan of 4 feet. It weighs about 10 pounds.

Vargouilles speak Infernal.

COMBAT

Vargouilles attack by biting with their jagged teeth. Their special attacks make them even more dangerous.

A vargouille's natural weapons, as well as any weapons it wields, are treated as evil-aligned for the purpose of overcoming damage reduction.

Vargouille

Shriek (Su): Instead of biting, a vargouille can open its distended mouth and let out a terrible shriek. Those within 60 feet (except other vargouilles) who hear the shriek and can clearly see the creature must succeed on a DC 12 Fortitude save or be paralyzed with fear for 2d4 rounds or until the monster attacks them, goes out of range, or leaves their sight. A paralyzed creature is susceptible to the vargouille's kiss (see below). A creature that successfully saves cannot be affected again by the same vargouille's shriek for 24 hours. The shriek is a mind-affecting fear effect. The save DC is Constitution-based and includes a +1 racial bonus.

Kiss (Su): A vargouille can kiss a paralyzed target with a successful melee touch attack. An affected opponent must succeed on a DC 15 Fortitude save or begin a terrible transformation that turns the creature into a vargouille within 24 hours (and often much sooner; roll 1d6 separately for each phase of the transformation). First, over a period of 1d6 hours, all the victim's hair falls out. Within another 1d6 hours thereafter, the ears grow into leathery wings, tentacles sprout on the chin and scalp, and the teeth become long, pointed fangs. During the next 1d6 hours, the victim takes Intelligence drain and Charisma drain equal to 1 point per hour (to a minimum of 3). The transformation is complete 1d6 hours later, when the head breaks free of the body (which promptly dies) and becomes a vargouille.

Illus. by C. Arellano

VARGOUILLE

This transformation is interrupted by sunlight, and even a *daylight* spell can delay death, but to reverse the transformation requires *remove disease*. The save DC is Constitution-based and includes a +4 racial bonus.

Poison (Ex): Injury, Fortitude DC 12 or be unable to heal the vargouille's bite damage naturally or magically. A *neutralize poison* or *heal* spell removes the effect, while *delay poison* allows magical healing. The save DC is Constitution-based and includes a +1 racial bonus.

WIGHT

Medium Undead
Hit Dice: 4d12 (26 hp)
Initiative: +1
Speed: 30 ft. (6 squares)
Armor Class: 15 (+1 Dex, +4 natural), touch 11, flat-footed 14
Base Attack/Grapple: +2/+3
Attack: Slam +3 melee (1d4+1 plus energy drain)
Full Attack: Slam +3 melee (1d4+1 plus energy drain)
Space/Reach: 5 ft./5 ft.
Special Attacks: Create spawn, energy drain
Special Qualities: Darkvision 60 ft., undead traits
Saves: Fort +1, Ref +2, Will +5
Abilities: Str 12, Dex 12, Con —, Int 11, Wis 13, Cha 15
Skills: Hide +8, Listen +7, Move Silently +16, Spot +7
Feats: Alertness, Blind-Fight
Environment: Any
Organization: Solitary, pair, gang (3–5), or pack (6–11)
Challenge Rating: 3
Treasure: None
Alignment: Always lawful evil
Advancement: 5–8 HD (Medium)
Level Adjustment: —

This creature resembles a human corpse. Its wild, frantic eyes burn with malevolence. The leathery, desiccated flesh is drawn tight across its bones, and the teeth have grown into sharp, jagged needles.

Wights are undead creatures given a semblance of life through sheer violence and hatred. A wight's appearance is a weird and twisted reflection of the form it had in life.

Wights lurk in barrow-mounds, catacombs, and other places thick with the aura of death, where they nurture their hatred. They seek to destroy all life, filling graveyards with their victims and populating the world with their horrid progeny.

A wight is about the height and weight of a human.

Wights speak Common.

Wight

COMBAT

Wights attack by hammering with their fists.

Create Spawn (Su): Any humanoid slain by a wight becomes a wight in 1d4 rounds. Spawn are under the command of the wight that created them and remain enslaved until its death. They do not possess any of the abilities they had in life.

Energy Drain (Su): Living creatures hit by a wight's slam attack gain one negative level. The DC is 14 for the Fortitude save to remove a negative level. The save DC is Charisma-based. For each such negative level bestowed, the wight gains 5 temporary hit points.

Skills: Wights have a +8 racial bonus on Move Silently checks.

WILL-O'-WISP

Small Aberration (Air)
Hit Dice: 9d8 (40 hp)
Initiative: +13
Speed: Fly 50 ft. (perfect) (10 squares)
Armor Class: 29 (+1 size, +9 Dex, +9 deflection), touch 29, flat-footed 20
Base Attack/Grapple: +6/−3
Attack: Shock +16 melee touch (2d8 electricity)
Full Attack: Shock +16 melee touch (2d8 electricity)
Space/Reach: 5 ft./5 ft.
Special Attacks: —
Special Qualities: Darkvision 60 ft., immunity to magic, natural invisibility
Saves: Fort +3, Ref +12, Will +9
Abilities: Str 1, Dex 29, Con 10, Int 15, Wis 16, Cha 12
Skills: Bluff +13, Diplomacy +3, Disguise +1 (+3 acting), Intimidate +3, Listen +17, Search +14, Spot +17, Survival +3 (+5 following tracks)
Feats: Alertness, Blind-Fight, Dodge, Improved Initiative, Weapon Finesse[B]
Environment: Temperate marshes
Organization: Solitary, pair, or string (3–4)
Challenge Rating: 6
Treasure: 1/10 coins; 50% goods; 50% items
Alignment: Usually chaotic evil
Advancement: 10–18 HD (Small)
Level Adjustment: —

This creature seems to be nothing but a faintly glowing sphere of light.

Will-o'-wisps are evil creatures that feed on the powerful emotions associated with panic, horror, and death. They delight in luring travelers into deadly peril, then absorbing the resulting emanations.

Will-o'-wisps can be yellow, white, green, or blue. They are easily mistaken for lanterns, especially in the foggy marshes and swamps where they reside.

A will-o'-wisp's body is a globe of spongy material about 1 foot across and weighing about 3 pounds, and its glowing body sheds as much light as a torch.

Will-o'-wisps speak Common and Auran. They have no vocal apparatus but can vibrate to create a voice with a ghostly sound.

COMBAT

Will-o'-wisps usually avoid combat. They prefer to confuse and bewilder adventurers, luring them into morasses or other hazardous places. When they are forced to fight, they loose small electrical shocks, which act as melee touch attacks.

Immunity to Magic (Ex): A will-o'-wisp is immune to most spells or spell-like abilities that allow spell resistance, except *magic missile* and *maze*.

Natural Invisibility (Ex): A startled or frightened will-o'-wisp can extinguish its glow, effectively becoming invisible as the spell.

WINTER WOLF

Large Magical Beast (Cold)
Hit Dice: 6d10+18 (51 hp)
Initiative: +5
Speed: 50 ft. (10 squares)
Armor Class: 15 (–1 size, +1 Dex, +5 natural), touch 10, flat-footed 14
Base Attack/Grapple: +6/+14
Attack: Bite +9 melee (1d8+6 plus 1d6 cold)
Full Attack: Bite +9 melee (1d8+6 plus 1d6 cold)
Space/Reach: 10 ft./5 ft.
Special Attacks: Breath weapon, freezing bite, trip
Special Qualities: Darkvision 60 ft., immunity to cold, low-light vision, scent, vulnerability to fire
Saves: Fort +8, Ref +6, Will +3
Abilities: Str 18, Dex 13, Con 16, Int 9, Wis 13, Cha 10
Skills: Hide –1*, Listen +6, Move Silently +7, Spot +6, Survival +1*
Feats: Alertness, Improved Initiative, Track
Environment: Cold forests
Organization: Solitary, pair, or pack (3–5)
Challenge Rating: 5
Treasure: 1/10 coins; 50% goods; 50% items
Alignment: Usually neutral evil
Advancement: 7–9 HD (Large); 10–18 HD (Huge)
Level Adjustment: +3 (cohort)

This creature looks like a white wolf with icy blue eyes. It stands as tall as a horse, and its breath smokes with cold.

Dangerous predators of the tundra and other chill regions, winter wolves pursue prey relentlessly. They rarely give up the chase until they bring down their quarry.

Winter wolves are more intelligent than their smaller cousins and sometimes associate with other evil creatures of their cold homelands, such as frost giants, whom they serve as scouts, hunters, and trackers.

A winter wolf grows about 8 feet long and stands about 4-1/2 feet at the shoulder. It weighs about 450 pounds.

Winter wolves can speak Giant and Common.

COMBAT

Winter wolves typically hunt in packs. Their size, cunning, and formidable breath weapon allow them to hunt and kill creatures much larger than themselves. A pack usually circles an opponent, each wolf attacking in turn to exhaust it. If they're in a hurry, white wolves try to pin their foes.

Breath Weapon (Su): 15-foot cone, once every 1d4 rounds, damage 4d6 cold, Reflex DC 16 half. The save DC is Constitution-based.

Freezing Bite (Su): A winter wolf deals an extra 1d6 points of cold damage every time it bites an opponent, as if its bite were a frost weapon.

Winter wolf

Trip (Ex): A winter wolf that hits with a bite attack can attempt to trip the opponent (+8 check modifier) as a free action without making a touch attack or provoking an attack of opportunity. If the attempt fails, the opponent cannot react to trip the winter wolf.

Skills: Winter wolves have a +1 racial bonus on Listen, Move Silently, and Spot checks.

Winter wolves have a +2 racial bonus on Hide checks. *Their natural coloration grants them a +7 racial bonus on Hide checks in areas of snow and ice.

A winter wolf has a +4 racial bonus on Survival checks when tracking by scent.

WORG

Medium Magical Beast
Hit Dice: 4d10+8 (30 hp)
Initiative: +2
Speed: 50 ft. (10 squares)
Armor Class: 14 (+2 Dex, +2 natural), touch 12, flat-footed 12
Base Attack/Grapple: +4/+7
Attack: Bite +7 melee (1d6+4)
Full Attack: Bite +7 melee (1d6+4)
Space/Reach: 5 ft./5 ft.
Special Attacks: Trip
Special Qualities: Darkvision 60 ft., low-light vision, scent
Saves: Fort +6, Ref +6, Will +3
Abilities: Str 17, Dex 15, Con 15, Int 6, Wis 14, Cha 10
Skills: Hide +4, Listen +6, Move Silently +6, Spot +6, Survival +2*

Feats: Alertness, Track
Environment: Temperate plains
Organization: Solitary, pair, or pack (6–11)
Challenge Rating: 2
Treasure: 1/10 coins; 50% goods; 50% items
Alignment: Usually neutral evil
Advancement: 5–6 HD (Medium); 7–12 HD (Large)
Level Adjustment: +1 (cohort)

This beast looks like a dark-colored wolf with a malevolent intelligence in its face and eyes.

Worgs are sinister wolves that have attained some intelligence and an evil disposition. They sometimes associate with other evil beings, particularly goblins, whom they serve as mounts and guardians.

Worgs usually live and hunt in packs. Their favored prey is large herbivores. Although they typically stalk and kill young, sick, or weak animals, they don't hesitate to hunt humanoids, particularly when game is scarce. Worgs may stalk humanoid prey for hours or even days before attacking, and choose the most advantageous terrain and time of day to do so (during the predawn hours, for example).

A typical worg has gray or black fur, grows to 5 feet long and stands 3 feet tall at the shoulder. It weighs 300 pounds.

More intelligent than their smaller cousins, worgs speak their own language. Some can also speak Common and Goblin.

COMBAT

Mated pairs or packs work together to bring down large game, while lone worgs usually chase down creatures smaller than themselves. Both often use hit-and-run tactics to exhaust their quarry. A pack usually circles a larger opponent: Each wolf attacks in turn, biting and retreating, until the creature is exhausted, at which point the pack moves in for the kill. If they get impatient or heavily outnumber the opponent, worgs attempt to pin it.

Trip (Ex): A worg that hits with a bite attack can attempt to trip the opponent (+3 check modifier) as a free action without making a touch attack or provoking an attack of opportunity. If the attempt fails, the opponent cannot react to trip the worg.

Skills: A worg has a +1 racial bonus on Listen, Move Silently, and Spot checks, and a +2 racial bonus on Hide checks.

*A worg has a +4 racial bonus on Survival checks when tracking by scent.

WRAITH

This creature is a sinister, spectral figure robed in darkness. It has no visible features or appendages, except for the glowing red pinpoints of its eyes.

Wraiths are incorporeal creatures born of evil and darkness. They despise all living things, as well as the light that nurtures them.

In some cases, the grim silhouette of a wraith might appear armored or outfitted with weapons. This appearance does not affect the creature's AC or combat abilities but only reflects the shape it had in life.

Worgs

A wraith is about as tall as a human, while a dread wraith is roughly the size of an ogre. Since both are incorporeal, they are weightless.

Wraiths speak Common and Infernal.

COMBAT

Both the wraith and the dread wraith share the following abilities.

Unnatural Aura (Su): Animals, whether wild or domesticated, can sense the unnatural presence of a wraith at a distance of 30 feet. They will not willingly approach nearer than that and panic if forced to do so; they remain panicked as long as they are within that range.

Daylight Powerlessness (Ex): Wraiths are utterly powerless in natural sunlight (not merely a *daylight* spell) and flee from it.

Wraith

WRAITH

Close combat with a wraith is dangerous, thanks to its deadly touch.

Constitution Drain (Su): Living creatures hit by a wraith's incorporeal touch attack must succeed on a DC 14 Fortitude save or take 1d6 points of Constitution drain. The save DC is Charisma-based. On each such successful attack, the wraith gains 5 temporary hit points.

Create Spawn (Su): Any humanoid slain by a wraith becomes a wraith in 1d4 rounds. Its body remains intact and inanimate, but its spirit is torn free from its corpse and transformed. Spawn are under the command of the wraith that created them and remain enslaved until its death. They do not possess any of the abilities they had in life.

DREAD WRAITH

The oldest and most malevolent wraiths lurk in the depths of forgotten temples and other forsaken places. They can sense the approach of living creatures, and hunger for them. Despite its size, the dread wraith possesses unearthly quickness, and makes use of its Spring Attack feat and natural reach to strike with deadly effect and melt back into the shadows—or the walls.

Lifesense (Su): A dread wraith notices and locates living creatures within 60 feet, just as if it possessed the blindsight ability. It also senses the strength of their life force automatically, as if it had cast *deathwatch*.

Constitution Drain (Su): Living creatures hit by a dread wraith's incorporeal touch attack must succeed on a DC 25 Fortitude save or take 1d8 points of Constitution drain. The save DC is Charisma-based. On each such successful attack, the dread wraith gains 5 temporary hit points.

Create Spawn (Su): Any humanoid slain by a dread wraith becomes a wraith in 1d4 rounds. Its body remains intact and inanimate, but its spirit is torn free from its corpse and transformed. Spawn are under the command of the wraith that created them and remain enslaved until its death. They do not possess any of the abilities they had in life.

	Wraith	Dread Wraith
	Medium Undead (Incorporeal)	Large Undead (Incorporeal)
Hit Dice:	5d12 (32 hp)	16d12 (104 hp)
Initiative:	+7	+13
Speed:	Fly 60 ft. (good) (12 squares)	Fly 60 ft. (good) (12 squares)
Armor Class:	15 (+3 Dex, +2 deflection), touch 15, flat-footed 12	25 (−1 size, +9 Dex, +7 deflection), touch 25, flat-footed 16
Base Attack/Grapple:	+2/—	+8/—
Attack:	Incorporeal touch +5 melee (1d4 plus 1d6 Constitution drain)	Incorporeal touch +16 melee (2d6 plus 1d8 Constitution drain)
Full Attack:	Incorporeal touch +5 melee (1d4 plus 1d6 Constitution drain)	Incorporeal touch +16 melee (2d6 plus 1d8 Constitution drain)
Space/Reach:	5 ft./5 ft.	10 ft./10 ft.
Special Attacks:	Constitution drain, create spawn	Constitution drain, create spawn
Special Qualities:	Darkvision 60 ft., daylight powerlessness, incorporeal traits, +2 turn resistance, undead traits, unnatural aura	Darkvision 60 ft., daylight powerlessness, incorporeal traits, lifesense 60 ft., undead traits, unnatural aura
Saves:	Fort +1, Ref +4, Will +6	Fort +5, Ref +14, Will +14
Abilities:	Str —, Dex 16, Con —, Int 14, Wis 14, Cha 15	Str —, Dex 28, Con —, Int 17, Wis 18, Cha 24
Skills:	Diplomacy +6, Hide +11, Intimidate +10, Listen +12, Search +10, Sense Motive +8, Spot +12, Survival +2 (+4 following tracks)	Diplomacy +9, Hide +24, Intimidate +26, Knowledge (religion) +22, Listen +25, Search +22, Sense Motive +23, Spot +25, Survival +4 (+6 following tracks)
Feats:	Alertness[B], Blind-Fight, Combat Reflexes, Improved Initiative[B]	Alertness[B], Blind-Fight, Combat Reflexes, Dodge, Improved Initiative[B], Improved Natural Attack (incorporeal touch), Mobility, Spring Attack
Environment:	Any	Any
Organization:	Solitary, gang (2–5), or pack (6–11)	Solitary
Challenge Rating:	5	11
Treasure:	None	None
Alignment:	Always lawful evil	Always lawful evil
Advancement:	6–10 HD (Medium)	17–32 HD (Large)
Level Adjustment:	—	—

WYVERN

Large Dragon
Hit Dice: 7d12+14 (59 hp)
Initiative: +1
Speed: 20 ft. (4 squares), fly 60 ft. (poor)
Armor Class: 18 (−1 size, +1 Dex, +8 natural), touch 10, flat-footed 17
Base Attack/Grapple: +7/+15
Attack: Sting +10 melee (1d6+4 plus poison) or talon +10 melee (2d6+4) or bite +10 melee (2d8+4)
Full Attack: Sting +10 melee (1d6+4 plus poison) and bite +8 melee (2d8+4) and 2 wings +8 melee (1d8+2) and 2 talons +8 melee (2d6+4)
Space/Reach: 10 ft./5 ft.
Special Attacks: Poison, improved grab
Special Qualities: Darkvision 60 ft., immunity to *sleep* and paralysis, low-light vision, scent
Saves: Fort +7, Ref +6, Will +6
Abilities: Str 19, Dex 12, Con 15, Int 6, Wis 12, Cha 9
Skills: Hide +7, Listen +13, Move Silently +11, Spot +16
Feats: Ability Focus (poison), Alertness, Flyby Attack, Multiattack[B]
Environment: Warm hills
Organization: Solitary, pair, or flight (3–6)
Challenge Rating: 6
Treasure: Standard
Alignment: Usually neutral
Advancement: 8–10 HD (Huge); 11–21 HD (Gargantuan)
Level Adjustment: —

This two-legged lizard is bigger than an ogre. It has a long tail tipped with a thick knot of cartilage from which a stinger protrudes much like that of a scorpion. It has leathery bat wings and huge jaws filled with long, sharp teeth.

A distant cousin to the true dragons, the wyvern is a huge flying lizard with a poisonous stinger in its tail.

A wyvern does not have a strong odor, although its lair might smell of a recent kill.

A wyvern's body is 15 feet long, and dark brown to gray; half that length is tail. Its wingspan is about 20 feet. A wyvern weighs about one ton.

Wyverns speak Draconic, but usually don't bother with anything more elaborate than a loud hiss or a deep-throated growl much like that of a bull alligator.

COMBAT

Wyverns are rather stupid but always aggressive: They attack nearly anything that isn't obviously more powerful than themselves. A wyvern dives from the air, snatching the opponent with its talons and stinging it to death.

A wyvern can slash with its talons only when making a flyby attack.

Improved Grab (Ex): To use this ability, a wyvern must hit with its talons. It can then attempt to start a grapple as a free action without provoking an attack of opportunity. If it wins the grapple check, it establishes a hold and stings.

Poison (Ex): Injury, Fortitude DC 17, initial and secondary damage 2d6 Con. The save DC is Constitution-based.

Skills: Wyverns have a +3 racial bonus on Spot checks.

Wyvern

XILL

Medium Outsider (Extraplanar)
Hit Dice: 5d8+10 (32 hp)
Initiative: +7
Speed: 40 ft. (8 squares)
Armor Class: 20 (+3 Dex, +7 natural), touch 13, flat-footed 17
Base Attack/Grapple: +5/+7
Attack: Short sword +7 melee (1d6+2/19–20) or claw +7 melee (1d4+2) or longbow +8 ranged (1d8/×3)
Full Attack: 2 short swords +5 melee (1d6+2/19–20, 1d6+1/19–20) and 2 claws +5 melee (1d4+1); or 4 claws +5 melee (1d4+2, 1d4+1); or 2 longbows +4 ranged (1d8/×3)
Space/Reach: 5 ft./5 ft.
Special Attacks: Implant, improved grab, paralysis
Special Qualities: Darkvision 60 ft., planewalk, spell resistance 21
Saves: Fort +6, Ref +7, Will +5
Abilities: Str 15, Dex 16, Con 15, Int 12, Wis 12, Cha 11
Skills: Balance +13, Climb +10, Diplomacy +2, Escape Artist +11, Intimidate +8, Listen +9, Move Silently +11, Sense Motive +8, Spot +9, Tumble +11, Use Rope +3 (+5 with bindings)
Feats: Improved Initative, Multiattack[B], Multiweapon Fighting

Xill

Environment: Ethereal Plane
Organization: Solitary or gang (2–5)
Challenge Rating: 6
Treasure: Standard
Alignment: Always lawful evil
Advancement: 6–8 HD (Medium); 9–15 HD (Large)
Level Adjustment: +4

This quasi-reptilian creature has four arms, bright red scales, and dark, penetrating eyes. It is not quite as tall as a human.

Malevolent in the extreme, xills are known for brutality and totalitarianism. They combine a healthy dose of evil with a keen love of cruelty.

Some xills are barbaric and fierce; others are more civilized creatures who rely on brutal order.

A xill stands 4 to 5 feet tall and weighs about 100 pounds.

Xills speak Infernal.

COMBAT

Xills are dangerous opponents, attacking with all four limbs. More civilized ones use weapons, usually fighting with two at a time so as to leave two claws free for grab attacks.

Xills typically lie in wait on the Ethereal Plane for suitable prey to happen by, then ambush it using their planewalk ability. They make full use of their Tumble skill in combat: Usually, one or two distract physically powerful enemies by attacking, then assuming a defensive stance while their fellows maneuver to advantage.

Implant (Ex): As a standard action, a xill can lay eggs inside a paralyzed creature. The young emerge about 90 days later, literally devouring the host from inside. A *remove disease* spell rids a victim of the egg, as does a DC 25 Heal check. If the check fails, the healer can try again, but each attempt (successful or not) deals 1d4 points of damage to the patient.

Improved Grab (Ex): To use this ability, a xill must hit with one or more claw attacks. It can then attempt to start a grapple as a free action without provoking an attack of opportunity. It receives a +2 bonus on the grapple check for each claw that hits. If it wins the grapple check and maintains the hold in the next round, it automatically bites the foe at that time. The bite deals no damage but injects a paralyzing venom.

Paralysis (Ex): Those bitten by a xill must succeed on a DC 14 Fortitude save or be paralyzed for 1d4 hours. The save DC is Constitution-based.

Planewalk (Su): These planar travelers like to slip between the folds of space to attack enemies as though from thin air. They can cross from the Ethereal Plane with a move action but take 2 rounds to cross back, during which time they are immobile. As a xill fades away, it becomes harder to hit: Opponents have a 20% miss chance in the first round and a 50% miss chance in the second. A xill can planewalk with a willing or helpless creature.

XILL CHARACTERS

A gang of xills is often led by a cleric. A xill cleric has access to two of the following domains: Evil, Law, Strength, or Travel.

XORN

This bizarre creature has a wide body made of a pebbly, stonelike material. It has a large, powerful mouth on top of its head, with three long arms, tipped with sharp talons, symmetrically positioned around it. Between the arms are large, stone-lidded eyes that see in all directions. At its base are three thick, short legs, each directly beneath an eye.

Xorns are scavengers from the Elemental Plane of Earth.

Minor xorns are about 3 feet tall and wide and weigh about 120 pounds. Average xorns are about 5 feet tall and wide, weighing about 600 pounds. Elder xorns are about 8 feet tall and wide and weigh about 9,000 pounds.

Xorns speak Common and Terran.

COMBAT

Xorns do not attack fleshly beings except to defend themselves or their property, since they cannot digest meat. Xorns are indifferent to creatures of the Material Plane—with the sole exception of anyone carrying a significant amount of precious metals or minerals, which xorns eat. They can smell food up to 20 feet away. A xorn can be quite aggressive when seeking food, especially on the Material Plane, where such sustenance is harder to find than it is on its native plane.

Xorn

A xorn's favorite mode of attack is to wait just beneath a stone surface until a foe comes within reach, then emerge suddenly. Groups of xorns often send one of their number to the surface to negotiate for food while the remainder position themselves for a surprise attack.

All-Around Vision (Ex): A xorn's symmetrically placed eyes allow it to look in any direction, providing a +4 racial bonus on Spot and Search checks. A xorn can't be flanked.

Earth Glide (Ex): A xorn can glide through stone, dirt, or almost any other sort of earth except metal as easily as a fish swims through water. Its burrowing leaves behind no tunnel or hole, nor does it create any ripple or other signs of its presence. A *move earth* spell cast on an area containing a burrowing xorn flings the xorn back 30 feet, stunning the creature for 1 round unless it succeeds on a DC 15 Fortitude save.

YETH HOUND

Medium Outsider (Extraplanar, Evil)
Hit Dice: 3d8+6 (19 hp)
Initiative: +6
Speed: 40 ft. (8 squares), fly 60 ft. (good)
Armor Class: 20 (+2 Dex, +8 natural), touch 12, flat-footed 18
Base Attack/Grapple: +3/+6
Attack: Bite +6 melee (1d8+4)
Full Attack: Bite +6 melee (1d8+4)
Space/Reach: 5 ft./5 ft.
Special Attacks: Bay, trip
Special Qualities: Damage reduction 10/silver, darkvision 60 ft., flight, scent
Saves: Fort +5, Ref +5, Will +5
Abilities: Str 17, Dex 15, Con 15, Int 6, Wis 14, Cha 10
Skills: Listen +11, Spot +11, Search +7, Survival +11 (+13 following tracks)*
Feats: Improved Initiative, Track

	Minor Xorn Small Outsider (Extraplanar, Earth)	Average Xorn Medium Outsider (Extraplanar, Earth)	Elder Xorn Large Outsider (Extraplanar, Earth)
Hit Dice:	3d8+9 (22 hp)	7d8+17 (48 hp)	15d8+63 (130 hp)
Initiative:	+0	+0	+0
Speed:	20 ft. (4 squares), burrow 20 ft.	20 ft. (4 squares), burrow 20 ft.	20 ft. (4 squares), burrow 20 ft.
Armor Class:	23 (+1 size, +12 natural), touch 11, flat-footed 23	24 (+14 natural), touch 10, flat-footed 24	25 (–1 size, +16 natural), touch 9, flat-footed 25
Attack:	Bite +6 melee (2d8+2)	Bite +10 melee (4d6+3)	Bite +21 melee (4d8+7)
Full Attack:	Bite +6 melee (2d8+2) and 3 claws +4 melee (1d3+1)	Bite +10 melee (4d6+3) and 3 claws +8 melee (1d4+1)	Bite +21 melee (4d8+7) and 3 claws +19 melee (1d6+3)
Space/Reach:	5 ft./5 ft.	5 ft./5 ft.	10 ft./10 ft.
Special Attacks:	—	—	
Special Qualities:	All-around vision, earth glide, damage reduction 5/bludgeoning, darkvision 60 ft., immunity to cold and fire, resistance to electricity 10, tremorsense 60 ft.	All-around vision, earth glide, damage reduction 5/bludgeoning, darkvision 60 ft., immunity to cold and fire, resistance to electricity 10, tremorsense 60 ft.	All-around vision, earth glide, damage reduction 5/bludgeoning, darkvision 60 ft., immunity to cold and fire, resistance to electricity 10, tremorsense 60 ft.
Saves:	Fort +5, Ref +3, Will +3	Fort +7, Ref +5, Will +5	Fort +13, Ref +9, Will +9
Abilities:	Str 15, Dex 10, Con 15, Int 10, Wis 11, Cha 10	Str 17, Dex 10, Con 15, Int 10, Wis 11, Cha 10	Str 25, Dex 10, Con 19, Int 10, Wis 11, Cha 10
Skills:	Hide +10, Intimidate +3, Knowledge (dungeoneering) +6, Listen +6, Move Silently +3, Search +6, Spot +8, Survival +6 (+8 following tracks or underground)	Hide +10, Intimidate +10, Knowledge (dungeoneering) +10, Listen +10, Move Silently +10, Search +10, Spot +10, Survival+10 (+12 following tracks or underground)	Hide +14, Intimidate +18, Knowledge (dungeoneering) +18, Listen +18, Move Silently +18, Search +22, Spot +22, Survival+18 (+20 following tracks or underground)
Feats:	Multiattack, Toughness Power Attack, Toughness	Cleave[B], Multiattack, Cleave, Improved Bull Rush, Multiattack, Power Attack, Toughness	Awesome Blow, Cleave[B], Great
Environment:	Elemental Plane of Earth	Elemental Plane of Earth	Elemental Plane of Earth
Organization:	Solitary, pair, or cluster (3–5)	Solitary, pair, or cluster (3–5)	Solitary, pair, or party (6–11)
Challenge Rating:	3	6	8
Treasure:	None	None	None
Alignment:	Usually neutral	Usually neutral	Usually neutral
Advancement:	4–6 HD (Small)	8–14 HD (Medium)	16–21 HD (Large); 22–45 HD (Huge)
Level Adjustment:	—		

Environment: Gray Waste of Hades
Organization: Solitary, pair, or pack (6–11)
Challenge Rating: 3
Treasure: None
Alignment: Always neutral evil
Advancement: 4–6 HD (Medium); 7–9 HD (Large)
Level Adjustment: +3 (cohort)

A yeth hound's natural weapons, as well as any weapons it wields, are treated as evil-aligned for the purpose of overcoming damage reduction.

This creature looks something like an oversized greyhound with dull black fur. Its eyes glow cherry red.

These fearsome flying hounds glide low over the countryside at night, seeking likely prey.

A yeth hound stands 5 feet tall at the shoulder and weighs about 400 pounds.

Yeth hounds cannot speak, but understand Infernal.

COMBAT

Yeth hounds hunt only at night. They fear the sun and never venture out in daylight, even if their lives depend on it.

Yeth hound

Illus. by S. Wood

Bay (Su): When a yeth hound howls or barks, all creatures except other evil outsiders within a 300-foot spread must succeed on a DC 11 Will save or become panicked for 2d4 rounds. This is a sonic mind-affecting fear effect. Whether or not the save is successful, an affected creature is immune to the same hound's bay for 24 hours. The save DC is Charisma-based.

Trip (Ex): A yeth hound that hits with its bite attack can attempt to trip the opponent (+3 check modifier) as a free action without making a touch attack or provoking an attack of opportunity. If the attempt fails, the opponent cannot react to trip the yeth hound.

Flight (Su): A yeth hound can cease or resume flight as a free action.

Skills: *A yeth hound has a +4 racial bonus on Survival checks when tracking by scent.

YRTHAK

Huge Magical Beast
Hit Dice: 12d10+36 (102 hp)
Initiative: +6
Speed: 20 ft. (4 squares), fly 60 ft. (average)
Armor Class: 18 (−2 size, +2 Dex, +8 natural), touch 10, flat-footed 16
Base Attack/Grapple: +12/+25
Attack: Bite +15 melee (2d8+5) or sonic lance +12 ranged touch (6d6)
Full Attack: Bite +15 melee (2d8+5) and 2 claws +13 melee (1d6+2); or sonic lance +12 ranged touch (6d6)
Space/Reach: 15 ft./10 ft.
Special Attacks: Sonic lance, explosion
Special Qualities: Blindsight 120 ft., immunities, vulnerability to sonic
Saves: Fort +11, Ref +10, Will +5
Abilities: Str 20, Dex 14, Con 17, Int 7, Wis 13, Cha 11
Skills: Listen +12, Move Silently +10
Feats: Endurance, Flyby Attack, Improved Initiative, Multiattack, Snatch
Environment: Temperate mountains
Organization: Solitary or clutch (2–4)
Challenge Rating: 9
Treasure: None
Alignment: Often neutral
Advancement: 13–16 HD (Huge); 17–36 HD (Gargantuan)
Level Adjustment: —

Yrthak

This creature resembles an eyeless, yellow-green flying reptile with fleshy wings, a long tail, and a large fin on its back. It has single hornlike protrusion on its crocodilian head.

A strange predator from desolate wastelands, the yrthak terrorizes the area it inhabits as an always hungry dragon might.

A yrthak is blind. It senses sound and movement by means of a special organ on its long tongue. It emits powerfully focused beams of sound from the protrusion on its head. The creature is a yellowish-green color, with the wings and fin being more yellow and the head and body more green. The teeth are yellow.

Yrthaks are crafty and devious. They are omnivorous but prefer meat. An yrthak keeps a nest high in its isolated mountain lair and may travel for days in search of food, returning only infrequently. Yrthaks are sometimes seen swooping 100 feet or more above the ground, attempting to sense prey.

A yrthak is about 20 feet long, with a wingspan of 40 feet. It weighs about 5,000 pounds.

Despite their intelligence, yrthaks do not speak.

COMBAT

A yrthak prefers to attack from the air, strafing the ground with sonic attacks or snatching up and dropping prey (eventually landing to devour the flattened mess).

Sonic Lance (Su): Once every 2 rounds, a yrthak can focus sonic energy in a ray up to 60 feet long. This is a ranged touch attack that deals 6d6 points of damage to a single target.

Explosion (Su): A yrthak can fire its sonic lance at the ground, a large rock, a stone wall, or the like to create an explosion of shattered stone. This attack deals 2d6 points of piercing damage to all within 10 feet of the effect's center.

This counts as a use of the sonic lance attack and thus is usable only once every 2 rounds, and never on the round following a sonic lance attack.

Blindsight (Ex): A yrthak can ascertain all foes within 120 feet. Beyond that range it is considered blinded. Yrthaks are invulnerable to gaze attacks, visual effects of spells such as illusions, and other attack forms that rely on sight.

A yrthak whose sense of hearing is impaired is effectively blinded, treating all targets as having total concealment.

Immunities: Yrthaks have immunity to gaze attacks, visual effects, illusions, and other attack forms that rely on sight.

Skills: Yrthaks have a +4 racial bonus on Listen checks.

YUAN-TI

The yuan-ti are descended from humans whose bloodlines have been mingled with those of snakes. Their evilness, cunning, and ruthlessness are legendary.

Yuan-ti constantly scheme to advance their own dark agendas. They are calculating and suave enough to form alliances with other evil creatures when necessary, but they always put their own interests first.

All yuan-ti possess some snakelike features, and many have snake body parts.

Yuan-ti speak their own language, plus Common, Draconic, and Abyssal.

COMBAT

Yuan-ti are geniuses and fight as such. They plan elaborate traps and utilize their surroundings superbly in combat, preferring ambushes to direct confrontation. They also prefer ranged attacks and spells to melee.

In a mixed group, the least valuable and powerful attack first. This means that the purebloods go before the halfbloods, which go before the abominations. The group leader may order particular members forward before others if that makes for better strategy.

Alternate Form (Sp): All yuan-ti can assume the form of a Tiny to Large viper (see the Snake entry, page 280) as a psionic ability. This ability is similar to a *polymorph* spell (caster level 19th), but a yuan-ti does not regain any hit points for changing form, and it can only assume viper forms. The yuan-ti loses its natural weapons (if any) and gains the natural weapon of the viper form it assumes. If the yuan-ti has a poisonous bite of its own, it uses its own or the viper's poison, whichever is more potent.

Detect Poison (Sp): All yuan-ti have the psionic ability to *detect poison* as the spell (caster level 6th).

YUAN-TI CHARACTERS

The favored class for yuan-ti purebloods and halfbloods is ranger. Yuan-ti abominations favor the cleric class. Yuan-ti clerics worship Merrshaulk. A yuan-ti cleric has access to two of the following domains: Chaos, Evil, Destruction, or Plant.

YUAN-TI SOCIETY

The yuan-ti are devout worshipers of evil. They also hold all reptiles in high esteem. The center of yuan-ti life is the temple, and their rituals often involve bloody sacrifices. They tend toward isolated, old ruins but have been known to build even underneath human cities. Yuan-ti are always secretive about the location of a city or temple. Their architecture favors curves, with ramps and poles replacing stairs.

The abominations rule over the yuan-ti and are the temple leaders, with the high priest above all. Purebloods take care of all outside negotiations, always pretending to be human.

The chief deity of the yuan-ti is Merrshaulk, who prompted and directed the formation of the line.

YUAN-TI PUREBLOOD

Medium Monstrous Humanoid

Hit Dice: 4d8 (18 hp)

Initiative: +5

Speed: 30 ft. (6 squares)

Armor Class: 17 (+1 Dex, +1 natural, +3 masterwork studded leather, +2 masterwork heavy shield), touch 11, flat-footed 16

Base Attack/Grapple: +4/+4

Attack: Masterwork scimitar +5 melee (1d6/18–20) or masterwork longbow +6 ranged (1d8/×3)

Full Attack: Masterwork scimitar +5 melee (1d6/18–20) or masterwork longbow +6 ranged (1d8/×3)

Space/Reach: 5 ft./5 ft.

Special Attacks: Spell-like abilities

Special Qualities: Alternate form, darkvision 60 ft., *detect poison*, spell resistance 14

Saves: Fort +1, Ref +5, Will +4

Abilities: Str 11, Dex 13, Con 11, Int 12, Wis 10, Cha 12

Skills: Concentration +7, Disguise +4*, Hide +3, Knowledge (any one) +5, Listen +4, Spot +4

Feats: Alertness[B], Blind-Fight[B], Dodge, Improved Initiative

Environment: Warm forests

Organization: Solitary, pair, gang (3–4), troupe (2–13 purebloods, 2–5 halfbloods, and 2–4 abominations), or tribe (20–160 purebloods, 10–80 halfbloods, and 10–40 abominations)

Challenge Rating: 3

Treasure: Double standard

Alignment: Usually chaotic evil

Advancement: By character class

Level Adjustment: +2

Yuan-ti

This being looks much like a slim-hipped, lithe human with sharp features and unblinking eyes. A closer look, however, reveals a forked tongue, pointed teeth, and scaly patches on the neck and limbs.

Yuan-ti purebloods appear human at first glance, with only very subtle snakelike features.

A pureblood is about the same height and weight as a human.

Combat

Purebloods are the least intelligent of the yuan-ti, though they still pride themselves on being more intelligent than humans. Purebloods often disguise themselves as humans and work among them as spies for their abomination masters.

Spell-Like Abilities: 1/day—*animal trance* (DC 13), *cause fear* (DC 12), *charm person* (DC 12), *darkness*, *entangle* (DC 12). Caster level 4th. The save DCs are Charisma-based.

Skills: *A pureblood gains a +5 racial bonus on Disguise checks when impersonating a human.

Yuan-Ti Purebloods as Characters

Yuan-ti pureblood characters possess the following racial traits.

— +2 Dexterity, +2 Intelligence, +2 Charisma.

—Medium size.

—A yuan-ti pureblood's base land speed is 30 feet.

—Darkvision out to 60 feet.

—Racial Hit Dice: A yuan-ti pureblood begins with four levels of monstrous humanoid, which provide 4d8 Hit Dice, a base attack bonus of +4, and base saving throw bonuses of Fort +1, Ref +4, and Will +4.

—Racial Skills: A yuan-ti pureblood's monstrous humanoid levels give it skill points equal to 7 × (2 + Int modifier). Its class skills are Concentration, Disguise, Hide, Knowledge (any), Listen and Spot.

—Racial Feats: A yuan-ti pureblood's monstrous humanoid levels give it two feats. Yuan-ti purebloods receive Alertness and Blind-Fight as bonus feats.

— +1 natural armor bonus.

—Special Attacks (see above): Spell-like abilities.

—Special Qualities (see above): *Alternate form, detect poison, spell resistance equal to class levels + 14.*

—Automatic Languages: Yuan-ti, Common. Bonus Languages: Abyssal, Draconic.

—Favored Class: Ranger.

—Level adjustment +2.

YUAN-TI HALFBLOOD

Medium Monstrous Humanoid
Hit Dice: 7d8+7 (38 hp)
Initiative: +5
Speed: 30 ft. (6 squares)
Armor Class: 20 (+1 Dex, +4 natural, +3 masterwork studded leather, +2 masterwork heavy shield), touch 11, flat-footed 19
Base Attack/Grapple: +7/+9
Attack: Masterwork scimitar +10 melee (1d6+2/18–20) or masterwork composite longbow (+2 Str bonus) +9 ranged (1d8+2/×3)
Full Attack: Masterwork scimitar +10/+5 melee (1d6+2/18–20) and bite +4 melee (1d6+1 plus poison); or masterwork composite longbow (+2 Str bonus) +9/+4 ranged (1d8+2/×3)
Space/Reach: 5 ft./5 ft.
Special Attacks: Poison, *produce acid,* spell-like abilities
Special Qualities: *Alternate form, chameleon power,* darkvision 60 ft., *detect poison,* scent, spell resistance 16
Saves: Fort +3, Ref +6, Will +9
Abilities: Str 15, Dex 13, Con 13, Int 18, Wis 18, Cha 16
Skills: Concentration +11, Craft or Knowledge (any two) +14, Hide +10*, Listen +16, Spot +16
Feats: Alertness[B], Blind-Fight[B], Combat Expertise, Dodge, Improved Initiative
Environment: Warm forests
Organization: Solitary, pair, gang (3–4), troupe (2–13 purebloods, 2–5 halfbloods, and 2–4 abominations), or tribe (20–160 purebloods, 10–80 halfbloods, and 10–40 abominations)
Challenge Rating: 5
Treasure: Double standard
Alignment: Usually chaotic evil
Advancement: By character class
Level Adjustment: +5

This being has the body of a lithe human with sharp features and unblinking eyes. Its skin is covered with gleaming scales, and a serpent's head, complete with long fangs and forked tongue, rises from its shoulders.

Like purebloods, yuan-ti halfbloods appear mostly human, but they always have obvious snake features. The snakelike features of a halfblood may reflect any of a variety of venomous snakes, so a halfblood may have a cobra's hood or a diamondback's distinctive scale pattern. These features are usually consistent within a single troupe of yuan-ti, and often mark a troupe's status within a tribe.

A halfblood is about the same height and weight as a human.

Combat

Halfbloods typically hang back out of melee while any purebloods accompanying them wade in, using their *chameleon power* to hide while softening up opponents with their spell-like abilities. If the

purebloods all fall, the halfbloods wade into melee in their stead.

Poison (Ex): Injury, Fortitude DC 14, initial and secondary damage 1d6 Con. The save DC is Constitution-based.

Produce Acid (Sp): A yuan-ti halfblood has the psionic power to exude acid from its body, dealing 3d6 points of acid damage to the next creature it touches, including a creature hit by its bite attack. If the yuan-ti is grappling or pinning a foe when it uses this power, its grasp deals 5d6 points of acid damage. The acid becomes inert when it leaves the yuan-ti's body, and the yuan-ti is immune to its effects.

Spell-Like Abilities: 3/day—*animal trance* (DC 15), *cause fear* (DC 14), *entangle* (DC 14); 1/day—*deeper darkness, neutralize poison* (DC 17), *suggestion* (DC 16). Caster level 8th. The save DCs are Charisma-based.

Chameleon Power (Sp): A yuan-ti halfblood can psionically change the coloration of itself and its equipment to match its surroundings, granting it a +10 circumstance bonus on Hide checks.

Skills: *Yuan-ti halfbloods using *chameleon power* gain a +10 circumstance bonus on Hide checks.

Halfblood Variants

The statistics above reflect the most common form of a yuan-ti halfblood, with the head and scaly skin of a serpent but otherwise human features. The curse of the yuan-ti produces a wide variety of halfbloods, however, manifesting their serpentine nature in different ways. To generate a random yuan-ti halfblood, roll d% and consult the following table.

d%	Halfblood Variety
01–40	As described above
41–60	Human head, but arms are snakes (two bite attacks instead of one, damage 1d4+2 plus poison)
61–80	Snake tail in addition to human legs (speed 30 ft., swim 15 ft., can constrict Small or smaller creatures for 1d4+3 points of damage)
81–00	Snake tail instead of human legs (speed 20 ft., climb 15 ft., swim 15 ft., can constrict Medium or smaller creatures for 1d6+3 points of damage)

Constrict (Ex): A halfblood with a snake tail deals extra damage (1d4+3 if it also has legs, or 1d6+3 if it does not) with a successful grapple check against a creature small enough for it to constrict.

YUAN-TI ABOMINATION

Large Monstrous Humanoid
Hit Dice: 9d8+27 (67 hp)
Initiative: +5
Speed: 30 ft. (6 squares), climb 20 ft., swim 20 ft.
Armor Class: 22 (–1 size, +1 Dex, +10 natural, +2 masterwork heavy shield), touch 10, flat-footed 21
Base Attack/Grapple: +9/+17
Attack: Masterwork scimitar +13 melee (1d8+4/18–20) or masterwork composite longbow (+4 Str bonus) +10 ranged (2d6+4/×3)
Full Attack: Masterwork scimitar +13/+8 melee (1d8+4/18–20) and bite +7 melee (2d6+3 plus poison); or masterwork composite longbow (+4 Str bonus) +10/+5 ranged (2d6+4/×3)
Space/Reach: 10 ft./10 ft.
Special Attacks: *Aversion,* constrict 1d6+6, improved grab, poison, *produce acid,* spell-like abilities
Special Qualities: *Alternate form, chameleon power,* darkvision 60 ft., *detect poison,* scent, spell resistance 18
Saves: Fort +6, Ref +7, Will +11
Abilities: Str 19, Dex 13, Con 17, Int 20, Wis 20, Cha 18
Skills: Concentration +15, Craft or Knowledge (any two) +17, Hide +8*, Listen +19, Move Silently +12, Spot +19
Feats: Alertness[B], Blind-Fight[B], Combat Expertise, Dodge, Improved Initiative, Mobility

264

YUAN-TI

Environment: Warm forests
Organization: Solitary, pair, gang (3–4), troupe (2–13 purebloods, 2–5 halfbloods, and 2–4 abominations), or tribe (20–160 purebloods, 10–80 halfbloods, and 10–40 abominations)
Challenge Rating: 7
Treasure: Double standard
Alignment: Usually chaotic evil
Advancement: By character class
Level Adjustment: +7

This creature looks like a big serpent, except that its eyes betray a baleful intelligence and it has two burly, humanoid arms.

Yuan-ti abominations are monstrous snakes with humanlike arms. The snakelike features of an abomination may reflect any of a variety of venomous snakes, so an abomination may have a black mamba's glossy scales or a viper's wedge-shaped head. These features are usually consistent within a single troupe of yuan-ti, and often mark a troupe's status within a tribe.

A yuan-ti abomination is 8 to 12 feet long and weighs 200 to 300 pounds.

Combat

Abominations are the masterminds of yuan-ti society, and urge their lesser kin into battle from the rear. While their underlings fight, the abominations watch the proceedings carefully, identifying the most dangerous foes and their most worrisome abilities, then try to neutralize those enemies with their extensive spell-like and psionic abilities.

Aversion (Sp): A yuan-ti abomination can psionically create a compulsion effect targeting one creature within 30 feet. The target must succeed on a DC 22 Will save or gain an aversion to snakes for 10 minutes. Affected creatures must stay at least 20 feet away from any snake or yuanti, alive or dead; if already within 20 feet, they move away. A subject unable to move away, or one attacked by snakes or yuan-ti, is overcome with revulsion. This revulsion reduces the creature's Dexterity score by 4 points until the effect wears off or the subject is no longer within 20 feet of a snake or yuan-ti. This ability is otherwise similar to *antipathy* as the spell (caster level 16th). The save DC is Charisma-based.

Constrict (Ex): An abomination deals 1d6+6 points of damage with a successful grapple check.

Improved Grab (Ex): To use this ability, an abomination must hit a Large or smaller creature with its bite attack. It can then attempt to start a grapple as a free action without provoking an attack of opportunity. If it wins the grapple check, it establishes a hold and can constrict.

Poison (Ex): Injury, Fortitude DC 17, initial and secondary damage 1d6 Con. The save DC is Constitution-based.

Produce Acid (Sp): An abomination has the psionic ability to exude acid from its body, dealing 3d6 points of acid damage to the next creature it touches, including a creature hit by its bite attack. If the yuan-ti is grappling, constricting, or pinning a foe when it uses this power, its grasp deals 5d6 points of acid damage. The acid becomes inert when it leaves the yuan-ti's body, and the yuan-ti is immune to its effects.

Spell-Like Abilities: At will—*animal trance* (DC 16), *entangle* (DC 15); 3/day—*deeper darkness, neutralize poison* (DC 18), *suggestion* (DC 17); 1/day—*baleful polymorph* (DC 19; into snake form only), *fear* (DC 18). Caster level 10th. The save DCs are Charisma-based.

Chameleon Power (Sp): A yuan-ti abomination can psionically change the coloration of itself and its equipment to match its surroundings, granting it a +10 circumstance bonus on Hide checks.

Skills: A yuan-ti abomination can always choose to take 10 on a Climb checks, even if rushed or threatened.

A yuan-ti abomination has a +8 racial bonus on any Swim check to perform some special action or avoid a hazard. It can always choose to take 10 on a Swim check, even if distracted or endangered. It can use the run action while swimming, provided it swims in a straight line.

*Yuan-ti abominations using *chameleon power* gain a +10 circumstance bonus on Hide checks.

ZOMBIE

Zombies are corpses reanimated through dark and sinister magic. These mindless automatons shamble about, doing their creator's bidding without fear or hesitation.

Zombies are not pleasant to look upon. Drawn from their graves, half decayed and partially consumed by worms, they wear the tattered remains of their burial clothes. A rank odor of death hangs heavy in the air around them.

Because of their utter lack of intelligence, the instructions given to a newly created zombie must be very simple, such as "Kill anyone who enters this room."

CREATING A ZOMBIE

"Zombie" is an acquired template that can be added to any corporeal creature (other than an undead) that has a skeletal system (referred to hereafter as the base creature).

Size and Type: The creature's type changes to undead. It retains any subtypes except alignment subtypes (such as good) and subtypes that indicate kind (such as goblinoid or reptilian). It does not gain the augmented subtype. It uses all the base creature's statistics and special abilities except as noted here.

Hit Dice: Drop any Hit Dice from class levels (to a minimum of 1), double the number of Hit Dice left, and raise them to d12s. If the base creature has more than 10 Hit Dice (not counting those gained with experience), it can't be made into a zombie with the *animate dead* spell.

Speed: If the base creature can fly, its maneuverability rating drops to clumsy.

Zombie

Armor Class: Natural armor bonus increases by a number based on the zombie's size:

Tiny or smaller	+0
Small	+1
Medium	+2
Large	+3
Huge	+4
Gargantuan	+7
Colossal	+11

Base Attack: A zombie has a base attack bonus equal to 1/2 its Hit Dice.

Attacks: A zombie retains all the natural weapons, manufactured weapon attacks, and weapon proficiencies of the base creature. A zombie also gains a slam attack.

Damage: Natural and manufactured weapons deal damage normally. A slam attack deals damage depending on the zombie's size. (Use the base creature's slam damage if it's better.)

Fine	1
Diminutive	1d2
Tiny	1d3
Small	1d4
Medium	1d6
Large	1d8
Huge	2d6
Gargantuan	2d8
Colossal	4d6

Special Attacks: A zombie retains none of the base creature's special attacks.

Special Qualities: A zombie loses most special qualities of the base creature. It retains any extraordinary special qualities that improve its melee or ranged attacks. A zombie gains the following special quality.

Single Actions Only (Ex): Zombies have poor reflexes and can perform only a single move action or attack action each round. A zombie can move up to its speed and attack in the same round, but only if it attempts a charge.

Saves: Base save bonuses are Fort +1/3 HD, Ref +1/3 HD, and Will +1/2 HD + 2.

Abilities: A zombie's Strength increases by +2, its Dexterity decreases by 2, it has no Constitution or Intelligence score, its Wisdom changes to 10, and its Charisma changes to 1.

Skills: A zombie has no skills.

Feats: A zombie loses all feats of the base creature and gains Toughness.

Environment: Any land and underground.

Organization: Any.

Challenge Rating: Depends on Hit Dice, as follows:

Hit Dice	Challenge Rating
1/2	1/8
1	1/4
2	1/2
4	1
6	2
8–10	3
12–14	4
15–16	5
18–20	6

Treasure: None.

Alignment: Always neutral evil.

Advancement: As base creature, but double Hit Dice (maximum 20), or — if the base creature advances by character class.

Level Adjustment: —.

	Kobold Zombie Small Undead	Human Commoner Zombie Medium Undead	Troglodyte Zombie Medium Undead
Hit Dice:	2d12+3 (16 hp)	2d12+3 (16 hp)	4d12+3 (29 hp)
Initiative:	+0	−1	−2
Speed:	30 ft. (6 squares; can't run)	30 ft. (6 squares; can't run)	30 ft. (6 squares; can't run)
Armor Class:	13 (+1 size, +2 natural), touch 11, flat-footed 13	11 (−1 Dex, +2 natural), touch 9, flat-footed 11	16 (−2 Dex, +8 natural), touch 8, flat-footed 16
Base Attack/Grapple:	+1/−4	+1/+2	+2/+3
Attack:	Spear +1 melee (1d6−1/×3) or slam +1 melee (1d4−1) or light crossbow +2 ranged (1d6/19–20)	Slam +2 melee (1d6+1) or club +2 melee (1d6+1)	Greatclub +3 melee (1d10+1) or bite +3 melee (1d4+1) or slam +3 melee (1d6+1) or javelin +0 ranged (1d6+1)
Full Attack:	Spear +0 melee (1d6−1/×3) or slam +0 melee (1d4−1) or light crossbow +1 ranged (1d6/19–20)	Slam +2 melee, (1d6+1) or club +2 melee (1d6+1)	Greatclub +3 melee (1d10+1) or bite +3 melee (1d4+1) or slam +3 melee (1d6+1) or javelin +0 ranged (1d6+1)
Space/Reach:	5 ft./5 ft.	5 ft./5 ft	5 ft./5 ft
Special Attacks:	—	—	—
Special Qualities:	Single actions only, damage reduction 5/slashing, darkvision 60 ft., undead traits	Single actions only, damage reduction 5/slashing, darkvision 60 ft., undead traits	Single actions only, damage reduction 5/slashing, darkvision 60 ft., undead traits
Saves:	Fort +0, Ref +0, Will +3	Fort +0, Ref −1, Will +3	Fort +1, Ref −1, Will +4
Abilities:	Str 8, Dex 11, Con —, Int —, Wis 10, Cha 1	Str 12, Dex 8, Con —, Int —, Wis 10, Cha 1	Str 12, Dex 7, Con —, Int —, Wis 10, Cha 1
Skills:	—	—	—
Feats:	Toughness	Toughness	Toughness
Environment:	Temperate forests	Any	Underground
Organization:	Any	Any	Any
Challenge Rating:	1/2	1/2	1
Treasure:	None	None	None
Alignment:	Always neutral evil	Always neutral evil	Always neutral evil
Advancement:	None	None	None
Level Adjustment:			

	Bugbear Zombie Medium Undead	Ogre Zombie Large Undead	Minotaur Zombie Large Undead
Hit Dice:	6d12+3 (42 hp)	8d12+3 (55 hp)	12d8+3 (81 hp)
Initiative:	+0	−2	−1
Speed:	30 ft. (6 squares; can't run)	40 ft. (8 squares; can't run)	30 ft. (6 squares; can't run)
Armor Class:	16 (+5 natural, +1 light wooden shield), touch 10, flat-footed 16	15 (−1 size, −2 Dex, +8 natural) touch 7, flat-footed 15	16 (−1 size, −1 Dex, +8 natural) touch 8, flat-footed 16
Base Attack/Grapple:	+3/+6	+4/+14	+6/+15
Attack:	Morningstar +6 melee (1d8+3) or slam +6 melee (1d6+3) or javelin +3 ranged (1d6+2)	Greatclub +9 melee (2d8+9) or slam +9 melee (1d8+9) or javelin +1 ranged (1d8+6)	Greataxe +10 melee (3d6+7/×3) or gore +10 melee (1d8+5) or slam +10 melee (1d8+5)
Full Attack:	Morningstar +6 melee (1d8+3) or slam +6 melee (1d6+3) or javelin +3 ranged (1d6+2)	Greatclub +9 melee (2d8+9) or slam +6 melee (1d8+9) or javelin +1 ranged (1d8+6)	Greataxe +10 melee (3d6+7/×3) or gore +10 melee (1d8+5) or slam +10 melee (1d8+5)
Space/Reach:	5 ft./5 ft.	10 ft./10 ft.	10 ft./10 ft.
Special Attacks:	—	—	—
Special Qualities:	Single actions only, damage reduction 5/slashing, darkvision 60 ft., undead traits	Single actions only, damage reduction 5/slashing, darkvision 60 ft., undead traits	Single actions only, damage reduction 5/slashing, darkvision 60 ft., undead traits
Saves:	Fort +2, Ref +2, Will +5	Fort +2, Ref +0, Will +6	Fort +4, Ref +3, Will +8
Abilities:	Str 17, Dex 10, Con —, Int —, Wis 10, Cha 1	Str 23, Dex 6, Con —, Int —, Wis 10, Cha 1	Str 21, Dex 8, Con —, Int —, Wis 10, Cha 1
Skills:	—	—	—
Feats:	Toughness	Toughness	Toughness
Environment:	Temperate mountains	Temperate hills	Underground
Organization:	Any	Any	Any
Challenge Rating:	2	3	4
Treasure:	None	None	None
Alignment:	Always neutral evil	Always neutral evil	Always neutral evil
Advancement:	None	None	None
Level Adjustment:	—	—	—

	Wyvern Zombie Large Undead	Umber Hulk Zombie Large Undead	Gray Render Zombie Large Undead
Hit Dice:	14d12+3 (94 hp)	16d12+3 (107 hp)	20d8+3 (133 hp)
Initiative:	+0	+0	−1
Speed:	20 ft. (4 squares; can't run), fly 60 ft. (poor)	20 ft. (4 squares; can't run), burrow 20 ft.	30 ft. (6 squares; can't run)
Armor Class:	20 (−2 size, +12 natural), touch 8, flat-footed 20	19 (−1 size, +10 natural) touch 0, flat-footed 19	16 (−1 size, −1 Dex, +8 natural) touch 8, flat-footed 16
Base Attack/Grapple:	+7/+16	+8/+19	+10/+21
Attack:	Slam +11 melee (2d6+7) or talons +11 melee (2d6+5)	Claw +14 melee (2d4+7) or bite +14 melee (2d8+3)	Bite +16 melee (2d6+7) or slam +16 melee (1d8+10)
Full Attack:	Slam +11 melee (2d6+7) or talons +11 melee (2d6+5)	Claw +14 melee (2d4+7) or bite +14 melee (2d8+3)	Bite +16 melee (2d6+7) or slam +16 melee (1d8+10)
Space/Reach:	10 ft./5 ft.	10 ft./10 ft.	10 ft./10 ft.
Special Attacks:			
Special Qualities:	Single actions only, damage reduction 5/slashing, darkvision 60 ft., undead traits	Single actions only, damage reduction 5/slashing, darkvision 60 ft., undead traits	Single actions only, damage reduction 5/slashing, darkvision 60 ft., undead traits
Saves:	Fort +4, Ref +4, Will +9	Fort +5, Ref +5, Will +10	Fort +6, Ref +5, Will +12
Abilities:	Str 21, Dex 10, Con —, Int —, Wis 10, Cha 1	Str 25, Dex 11, Con —, Int —, Wis 10, Cha 1	Str 25, Dex 8, Con —, Int —, Wis 10, Cha 1
Skills:	—	—	—
Feats:	Toughness	Toughness	Toughness
Environment:	Warm hills	Underground	Temperate marshes
Organization:	Any	Any	Any
Challenge Rating:	4	5	6
Treasure:	None	None	None
Alignment:	Always neutral evil	Always neutral evil	Always neutral evil
Advancement:	16–20 HD (Huge)	18–20 HD (Large)	None
Level Adjustment:	—	—	

CHAPTER 2: ANIMALS

This chapter provides statistics and basic information for many common kinds of mundane animals. These creatures generally operate on instinct, driven by simple needs such as food and reproduction. Most animals, even predators, do not attack unless they or their young are threatened.

Animals are not capable of detailed reasoning, although with the Handle Animal skill it is possible to tame an animal and teach it to perform certain tricks.

Some herbivorous animals do not normally use their natural weapons to attack. As such, their natural weapons are treated as secondary attacks. The animal's attack and damage entries note this fact, with an explanatory footnote.

Animal Traits: An animal possesses the following traits (unless otherwise noted in a creature's entry).

—Intelligence score of 1 or 2 (no creature with an Intelligence score of 3 or higher can be an animal).

—Low-light vision.

—*Alignment:* Always neutral. Animals are not governed by a human sense of morality.

—*Treasure:* None. Animals never possess treasure.

APE

Large Animal
Hit Dice: 4d8+11 (29 hp)
Initiative: +2
Speed: 30 ft. (6 squares), climb 30 ft.
Armor Class: 14 (−1 size, +2 Dex, +3 natural), touch 11, flat-footed 12
Base Attack/Grapple: +3/+12
Attack: Claws +7 melee (1d6+5)
Full Attack: 2 claws +7 melee (1d6+5) and bite +2 melee (1d6+2)
Space/Reach: 10 ft./10 ft.
Special Attacks: —
Special Qualities: Low-light vision, scent
Saves: Fort +6, Ref +6, Will +2
Abilities: Str 21, Dex 15, Con 14, Int 2, Wis 12, Cha 7
Skills: Climb +14, Listen +6, Spot +6
Feats: Alertness, Toughness
Environment: Warm forests
Organization: Solitary, pair, or company (3–5)
Challenge Rating: 2
Advancement: 5–8 HD (Large)
Level Adjustment: —

These powerful omnivores resemble gorillas but are far more aggressive; they kill and eat anything they can catch. An adult male ape is 5-1/2 to 6 feet tall and weighs 300 to 400 pounds.

Combat

An ape often precedes an attack with a display of aggression, hoping to intimidate potential foes.

Skills: Apes have a +8 racial bonus on Climb checks and can always choose to take 10 on Climb checks, even if rushed or threatened.

BABOON

Medium Animal
Hit Dice: 1d8+1 (5 hp)
Initiative: +2
Speed: 40 ft. (8 squares), climb 30 ft.
Armor Class: 13 (+2 Dex, +1 natural), touch 12, flat-footed 11
Base Attack/Grapple: +0/+2
Attack: Bite +2 melee (1d6+3)
Full Attack: Bite +2 melee (1d6+3)
Space/Reach: 5 ft./5 ft.
Special Attacks: —
Special Qualities: Low-light vision, scent
Saves: Fort +3, Ref +4, Will +1
Abilities: Str 15, Dex 14, Con 12, Int 2, Wis 12, Cha 4
Skills: Climb +10, Listen +5, Spot +5
Feats: Alertness
Environment: Warm plains
Organization: Solitary or troop (10–40)
Challenge Rating: 1/2
Advancement: 2–3 HD (Medium)
Level Adjustment: —

Baboons are powerful and aggressive primates adapted to life on the ground. They prefer open spaces but climb trees to find safe places to rest overnight. A typical baboon is the size of a big dog. Males can be 2 to 4 feet long and weigh as much as 90 pounds.

Combat

Baboons usually attack in groups.

Skills: Baboons have a +8 racial bonus on Climb checks and can always choose to take 10 on Climb checks, even if rushed or threatened.

BADGER

Small Animal
Hit Dice: 1d8+2 (6 hp)
Initiative: +3
Speed: 30 ft. (6 squares), burrow 10 ft.
Armor Class: 15 (+1 size, +3 Dex, +1 natural), touch 14, flat-footed 12
Base Attack/Grapple: +0/−5
Attack: Claw +4 melee (1d2−1)
Full Attack: 2 claws +4 melee (1d2−1) and bite −1 melee (1d3−1)
Space/Reach: 5 ft./5 ft.
Special Attacks: Rage
Special Qualities: Low-light vision, scent
Saves: Fort +4, Ref +5, Will +1
Abilities: Str 8, Dex 17, Con 15, Int 2, Wis 12, Cha 6
Skills: Escape Artist +7, Listen +3, Spot +3
Feats: Track[B], Weapon Finesse
Environment: Temperate forests
Organization: Solitary, pair, or cete (3–5)
Challenge Rating: 1/2
Advancement: 2 HD (Small)
Level Adjustment: —

The badger is a furry animal with a squat, powerful body. Its strong forelimbs are armed with long claws for digging.

An adult badger is 2 to 3 feet long and weighs 25 to 35 pounds.

Combat

Badgers attack with their sharp claws and teeth.

Rage (Ex): A badger that takes damage in combat flies into a berserk rage on its next turn, clawing and biting madly until either it or its opponent is dead. It gains +4 to Strength, +4 to Constitution, and −2 to Armor Class. The creature cannot end its rage voluntarily.

Skills: A badger has a +4 racial bonus on Escape Artist checks.

BAT

Diminutive Animal
Hit Dice: 1/4 d8 (1 hp)
Initiative: +2
Speed: 5 ft (1 square), fly 40 ft. (good)
Armor Class: 16 (+4 size, +2 Dex), touch 16, flat-footed 14
Base Attack/Grapple: +0/−17
Attack: —

Full Attack: —
Space/Reach: 1 ft./0 ft.
Special Attacks: —
Special Qualities: Blindsense 20 ft., low-light vision
Saves: Fort +2, Ref +4, Will +2
Abilities: Str 1, Dex 15, Con 10, Int 2, Wis 14, Cha 4
Skills: Hide +14, Listen +8*, Move Silently +6, Spot +8*
Feats: Alertness
Environment: Temperate deserts
Organization: Colony (10–40) or crowd (10–50)
Challenge Rating: 1/10
Advancement: —
Level Adjustment: —

Bats are nocturnal flying mammals. The statistics presented here describe small, insectivorous bats.

Combat

Blindsense (Ex): A bat notices and locates creatures within 20 feet. Opponents still have 100% concealment against a creature with blindsense.

Skills: *A bat has a +4 racial bonus on Spot and Listen checks. These bonuses are lost if its blindsense is negated.

BEAR, BLACK
Medium Animal
Hit Dice: 3d8+6 (19 hp)
Initiative: +1
Speed: 40 ft. (8 squares)
Armor Class: 13 (+1 Dex, +2 natural), touch 11, flat-footed 12
Base Attack/Grapple: +2/+6
Attack: Claw +6 melee (1d4+4)
Full Attack: 2 claws +6 melee (1d4+4) and bite +1 melee (1d6+2)
Space/Reach: 5 ft./5 ft.
Special Attacks: —
Special Qualities: Low-light vision, scent
Saves: Fort +5, Ref +4, Will +2
Abilities: Str 19, Dex 13, Con 15, Int 2, Wis 12, Cha 6
Skills: Climb +4, Listen +4, Spot +4, Swim +8
Feats: Endurance, Run
Environment: Temperate forests
Organization: Solitary or pair
Challenge Rating: 2
Advancement: 4–5 HD (Medium)
Level Adjustment: —

The black bear is a forest-dwelling omnivore that usually is not dangerous unless an interloper threatens its cubs or food supply.
Black bears can be pure black, blond, or cinnamon in color and are rarely more than 5 feet long.

Combat
Black bears rip prey with their claws and teeth.
Skills: A black bear has a +4 racial bonus on Swim checks.

BEAR, BROWN
Large Animal
Hit Dice: 6d8+24 (51 hp)
Initiative: +1
Speed: 40 ft. (8 squares)
Armor Class: 15 (–1 size, +1 Dex, +5 natural), touch 10, flat-footed 14
Base Attack/Grapple: +4/+16
Attack: Claw +11 melee (1d8+8)
Full Attack: 2 claws +11 melee (1d8+8) and bite +6 melee (2d6+4)
Space/Reach: 10 ft./5 ft.
Special Attacks: Improved grab

Special Qualities: Low-light vision, scent
Saves: Fort +9, Ref +6, Will +3
Abilities: Str 27, Dex 13, Con 19, Int 2, Wis 12, Cha 6
Skills: Listen +4, Spot +7, Swim +12
Feats: Endurance, Run, Track
Environment: Cold forests
Organization: Solitary or pair
Challenge Rating: 4
Advancement: 7–10 HD (Large)
Level Adjustment: —

These massive carnivores weigh more than 1,800 pounds and stand nearly 9 feet tall when they rear up on their hind legs. They are bad-tempered and territorial. The brown bear's statistics can be used for almost any big bear, including the grizzly.

Combat
A brown bear attacks mainly by tearing at opponents with its claws.
Improved Grab (Ex): To use this ability, a brown bear must hit with a claw attack. It can then attempt to start a grapple as a free action without provoking an attack of opportunity.
Skills: A brown bear has a +4 racial bonus on Swim checks.

BEAR, POLAR
Large Animal
Hit Dice: 8d8+32 (68 hp)
Initiative: +1
Speed: 40 ft. (8 squares), swim 30 ft.
Armor Class: 15 (–1 size, +1 Dex, +5 natural), touch 10, flat-footed 14
Base Attack/Grapple: +6/+18
Attack: Claw +13 (1d8+8)
Full Attack: 2 claws +13 melee (1d8+8) and bite +8 melee (2d6+4)
Space/Reach: 10 ft./5 ft.
Special Attacks: Improved grab
Special Qualities: Low-light vision, scent
Saves: Fort +10, Ref +7, Will +3
Abilities: Str 27, Dex 13, Con 19, Int 2, Wis 12, Cha 6
Skills: Hide –2*, Listen +5, Spot +7, Swim +16
Feats: Endurance, Run, Track
Environment: Cold plains
Organization: Solitary or pair
Challenge Rating: 4
Advancement: 9–12 HD (Large)
Level Adjustment: —

These long, lean carnivores are slightly taller than brown bears.

Combat
Polar bears fight just as brown bears do.
Improved Grab (Ex): To use this ability, a polar bear must hit with a claw attack. It can then attempt to start a grapple as a free action without provoking an attack of opportunity.
Skills: A polar bear has a +8 racial bonus on any Swim check to perform some special action or avoid a hazard. It can always choose to take 10 on a Swim check, even if distracted or endangered. It can use the run action while swimming, provided it swims in a straight line.
*A polar bear's white coat bestows a +12 racial bonus on Hide checks in snowy areas.

BISON
Large Animal
Hit Dice: 5d8+15 (37 hp)
Initiative: +0
Speed: 40 ft. (8 squares)

Armor Class: 13 (−1 size, +4 natural), touch 9, flat-footed 13
Base Attack/Grapple: +3/+13
Attack: Gore +8 melee (1d8+9)
Full Attack: Gore +8 melee (1d8+9)
Space/Reach: 10 ft./5 ft.
Special Attacks: Stampede
Special Qualities: Low-light vision, scent
Saves: Fort +7, Ref +4, Will +1
Abilities: Str 22, Dex 10, Con 16, Int 2, Wis 11, Cha 4
Skills: Listen +7, Spot +5
Feats: Alertness, Endurance
Environment: Temperate plains
Organization: Solitary or herd (6–30)
Challenge Rating: 2
Advancement: 6–7 HD (Large)
Level Adjustment: —

These herd animals can be aggressive when protecting young and during the mating season, but they generally prefer flight to fighting.

A bison stands more than 6 feet tall at the shoulder and is 9 to 12 feet long. It weigh 1,800 to 2,400 pounds. The bison's statistics can be used for almost any large herd animal.

Combat

Stampede (Ex): A frightened herd of bison flees as a group in a random direction (but always away from the perceived source of danger). They literally run over anything of Large size or smaller that gets in their way, dealing 1d12 points of damage for each five bison in the herd (Reflex DC 18 half). The save DC is Strength-based.

BOAR

Medium Animal
Hit Dice: 3d8+12 (25 hp)
Initiative: +0
Speed: 40 ft. (8 squares)
Armor Class: 16 (+6 natural), touch 10, flat-footed 16
Base Attack/Grapple: +2/+4
Attack: Gore +4 melee (1d8+3)
Full Attack: Gore +4 melee (1d8+3)
Space/Reach: 5 ft./5 ft.
Special Attacks: Ferocity
Special Qualities: Low-light vision, scent
Saves: Fort +6, Ref +3, Will +2
Abilities: Str 15, Dex 10, Con 17, Int 2, Wis 13, Cha 4
Skills: Listen +7, Spot +5
Feats: Alertness, Toughness
Environment: Temperate forests
Organization: Solitary or herd (5–8)
Challenge Rating: 2
Advancement: 4–5 HD (Medium)
Level Adjustment: —

Though not carnivores, these wild swine are bad-tempered and usually charge anyone who disturbs them.

A boar is covered in coarse, grayish-black fur. Adult males are about 4 feet long and 3 feet high at the shoulder.

Combat

Ferocity (Ex): A boar is such a tenacious combatant that it continues to fight without penalty even while disabled or dying.

CAMEL

Large Animal
Hit Dice: 3d8+6 (19 hp)
Initiative: +3
Speed: 50 ft. (10 squares)

Armor Class: 13 (−1 size, +3 Dex, +1 natural) touch 12, flat-footed 10
Base Attack/Grapple: +2/+10
Attack: Bite +0 melee (1d4+2*)
Full Attack: Bite +0 melee* (1d4+2*)
Space/Reach: 10 ft./5 ft.
Special Attacks: —
Special Qualities: Low-light vision, scent
Saves: Fort +5, Ref +6, Will +1
Abilities: Str 18, Dex 16, Con 14, Int 2, Wis 11, Cha 4
Skills: Listen +5, Spot +5
Feats: Alertness, Endurance
Environment: Warm deserts
Organization: Domesticated or herd (6–30)
Challenge Rating: 1
Advancement: —
Level Adjustment: —

Camels are known for their ability to travel long distances without food or water.

The statistics presented here are for the dromedary, or one-humped camel, which thrives in warm deserts. A dromedary stands about 7 feet tall at the shoulder, with its hump rising 1 foot higher.

The two-humped, or Bactrian, camel is suited to cooler, rocky areas. It is stockier, slower (speed 40 feet), and has a higher Constitution score (16).

Carrying Capacity: A light load for a camel is up to 300 pounds; a medium load, 301–600 pounds; and a heavy load, 601–900 pounds. A camel can drag 4,500 pounds.

Combat

*A camel's bite is treated as a secondary attack and adds only half the camel's Strength bonus to the damage roll.

CAT

Tiny Animal
Hit Dice: 1/2 d8 (2 hp)
Initiative: +2
Speed: 30 ft. (6 squares)
Armor Class: 14 (+2 size, +2 Dex), touch 14, flat-footed 12
Base Attack/Grapple: +0/−12
Attack: Claw +4 melee (1d2−4)
Full Attack: 2 claws +4 melee (1d2−4) and bite −1 melee (1d3−4)
Space/Reach: 2-1/2 ft./0 ft.
Special Attacks: —
Special Qualities: Low-light vision, scent
Saves: Fort +2, Ref +4, Will +1
Abilities: Str 3, Dex 15, Con 10, Int 2, Wis 12, Cha 7
Skills: Balance +10, Climb +6, Hide +14*, Jump +10, Listen +3, Move Silently +6, Spot +3
Feats: Weapon Finesse
Environment: Temperate plains
Organization: Domesticated or solitary
Challenge Rating: 1/4
Advancement: —
Level Adjustment: —

The statistics presented here describe a common housecat.

Combat

Cats prefer to sneak up on their prey.

Skills: Cats have a +4 racial bonus on Climb, Hide, and Move Silently checks and a +8 racial bonus on Jump checks. Cats have a +8 racial bonus on Balance checks. They use their Dexterity modifier instead of their Strength modifier for Climb and Jump checks.
*In areas of tall grass or heavy undergrowth, the Hide bonus rises to +8.

CHEETAH

Medium Animal
Hit Dice: 3d8+6 (19 hp)
Initiative: +4
Speed: 50 ft. (10 squares)
Armor Class: 15 (+4 Dex, +1 natural), touch 14, flat-footed 11
Base Attack/Grapple: +2/+5
Attack: Bite +6 melee
Full Attack: Bite +6 melee (1d6+3) and 2 claws +1 melee (1d2+1)
Space/Reach: 5 ft./5 ft.
Special Attacks: Trip
Special Qualities: Low-light vision, scent, sprint
Saves: Fort +5, Ref +7, Will +2
Abilities: Str 16, Dex 19, Con 15, Int 2, Wis 12, Cha 6
Skills: Hide +6, Listen +4, Move Silently +6, Spot +4
Feats: Alertness, Weapon Finesse
Environment: Warm plains
Organization: Solitary, pair, or family (3–5)
Challenge Rating: 2
Advancement: 4–5 HD (Medium)
Level Adjustment: —

Cheetahs are swift feline predators of the plains. A cheetah is 3 to 5 feet long and weighs 110 to 130 pounds.

Combat

Cheetahs make sudden sprints to bring down prey.

Trip (Ex): A cheetah that hits with a claw or bite attack can attempt to trip the opponent (+3 check modifier) as a free action without making a touch attack or provoking an attack of opportunity. If the attempt fails, the opponent cannot react to trip the cheetah.

Sprint (Ex): Once per hour, a cheetah can move ten times its normal speed (500 feet) when it makes a charge.

CROCODILE

Medium Animal
Hit Dice: 3d8+9 (22 hp)
Initiative: +1
Speed: 20 ft. (4 squares), swim 30 ft.
Armor Class: 15 (+1 Dex, +4 natural), touch 11, flat-footed 14
Base Attack/Grapple: +2/+6
Attack: Bite +6 melee (1d8+6) or tail slap +6 melee (1d12+6)
Full Attack: Bite +6 melee (1d8+6) or tail slap +6 melee (1d12+6)
Space/Reach: 5 ft./5 ft.
Special Attacks: Improved grab
Special Qualities: Hold breath, low-light vision
Saves: Fort +6, Ref +4, Will +2
Abilities: Str 19, Dex 12, Con 17, Int 1, Wis 12, Cha 2
Skills: Hide +7*, Listen +4, Spot +4, Swim +12
Feats: Alertness, Skill Focus (Hide)
Environment: Warm marshes
Organization: Solitary or colony (6–11)
Challenge Rating: 2
Advancement: 4–5 HD (Medium)
Level Adjustment: —

Crocodiles are aggressive predators 11 to 12 feet long. They lie mostly submerged in rivers or marshes, with only their eyes and nostrils showing, waiting for prey to come within reach.

Combat

Improved Grab (Ex): To use this ability, a crocodile must hit with its bite attack. It can then attempt to start a grapple as a free action without provoking an attack of opportunity. If it wins the grapple check, the crocodile establishes a hold on the opponent with its mouth and drags it into deep water, attempting to pin it to the bottom.

Hold Breath (Ex): A crocodile can hold its breath for a number of rounds equal to 4 × its Constitution score before it risks drowning.

Skills: A crocodile has a +8 racial bonus on any Swim check to perform some special action or avoid a hazard. It can always choose to take 10 on a Swim check, even if distracted or endangered. It can use the run action while swimming, provided it swims in a straight line.

*A crocodile gains a +4 racial bonus on Hide checks when in the water. Further, a crocodile can lie in the water with only its eyes and nostrils showing, gaining a +10 cover bonus on Hide checks.

CROCODILE, GIANT

Huge Animal
Hit Dice: 7d8+28 (59 hp)
Initiative: +1
Speed: 20 ft. (4 squares), swim 30 ft.
Armor Class: 16 (–2 size, +1 Dex, +7 natural), touch 9, flat-footed 15
Base Attack/Grapple: +5/+21
Attack: Bite +11 melee (2d8+12) or tail slap +11 melee (1d12+12)
Full Attack: Bite +11 melee (2d8+12) or tail slap +11 melee (1d12+12)
Space/Reach: 15 ft./10 ft.
Special Attacks: Improved grab
Special Qualities: Hold breath, low-light vision
Saves: Fort +9, Ref +6, Will +3
Abilities: Str 27, Dex 12, Con 19, Int 1, Wis 12, Cha 2
Skills: Hide +1*, Listen +5, Spot +5, Swim +16
Feats: Alertness, Endurance, Skill Focus (Hide)
Environment: Warm marshes
Organization: Solitary or colony (6–11)
Challenge Rating: 4
Advancement: 8–14 HD (Huge)
Level Adjustment: —

These huge creatures usually live in salt water and can be more than 20 feet long.

Giant crocodiles fight and behave like their smaller cousins.

DOG

Small Animal
Hit Dice: 1d8+2 (6 hp)
Initiative: +3
Speed: 40 ft. (8 squares)
Armor Class: 15 (+1 size, +3 Dex, +1 natural), touch 14, flat-footed 12
Base Attack/Grapple: +0/–3
Attack: Bite +2 melee (1d4+1)
Full Attack: Bite +2 melee (1d4+1)
Space/Reach: 5 ft./5 ft.
Special Attacks: —
Special Qualities: Low-light vision, scent
Saves: Fort +4, Ref +5, Will +1
Abilities: Str 13, Dex 17, Con 15, Int 2, Wis 12, Cha 6
Skills: Jump +7, Listen +5, Spot +5, Survival +1*
Feats: Alertness, Track[B]
Environment: Temperate plains
Organization: Solitary or pack (5–12)
Challenge Rating: 1/3
Advancement: —
Level Adjustment: —

The statistics presented here describe a fairly small dog of about 20 to 50 pounds in weight. They also can be used for small wild canines such as coyotes, jackals, and African wild dogs.

Combat

Dogs generally hunt in packs, chasing and exhausting prey until they can drag it down.

Skills: Dogs have a +4 racial bonus on Jump checks. *Dogs have a +4 racial bonus on Survival checks when tracking by scent.

DOG, RIDING

Medium Animal
Hit Dice: 2d8+4 (13 hp)
Initiative: +2
Speed: 40 ft. (8 squares)
Armor Class: 16 (+2 Dex, +4 natural), touch 12, flat-footed 14
Base Attack/Grapple: +1/+3
Attack: Bite +3 melee (1d6+3)
Full Attack: Bite +3 melee (1d6+3)
Space/Reach: 5 ft./5 ft.
Special Attacks: —
Special Qualities: Low-light vision, scent
Saves: Fort +5, Ref +5, Will +1
Abilities: Str 15, Dex 15, Con 15, Int 2, Wis 12, Cha 6
Skills: Jump +8, Listen +5, Spot +5, Swim +3, Survival +1*
Feats: Alertness, Track[B]
Environment: Temperate plains
Organization: Solitary or pack (5–12)
Challenge Rating: 1
Advancement: —
Level Adjustment: —

This category includes working breeds such as collies, huskies, and St. Bernards.

Carrying Capacity: A light load for a riding dog is up to 100 pounds; a medium load, 101–200 pounds; and a heavy load, 201–300 pounds. A riding dog can drag 1,500 pounds.

Combat

If trained for war, these animals can make trip attacks just as wolves do (see the Wolf entry). A riding dog can fight while carrying a rider, but the rider cannot also attack unless he or she succeeds on a Ride check.

Skills: Riding dogs have a +4 racial bonus on Jump checks.
*Riding dogs have a +4 racial bonus on Survival checks when tracking by scent.

DONKEY

Medium Animal
Hit Dice: 2d8+2 (11 hp)
Initiative: +1
Speed: 30 ft. (6 squares)
Armor Class: 13 (+1 Dex, +2 natural), touch 11, flat-footed 12
Base Attack/Grapple: +1/+1
Attack: Bite +1 melee (1d2)
Full Attack: Bite +1 melee (1d2)
Space/Reach: 5 ft./5 ft.
Special Attacks: —
Special Qualities: Low-light vision, scent
Saves: Fort +4, Ref +4, Will +0
Abilities: Str 10, Dex 13, Con 12, Int 2, Wis 11, Cha 4
Skills: Balance +3, Listen +3, Spot +2
Feats: Endurance
Environment: Temperate deserts
Organization: Solitary
Challenge Rating: 1/6
Advancement: —
Level Adjustment: —

These long-eared, horselike creatures are surefooted and sturdy. The statistics presented here could also describe burros.

Carrying Capacity: A light load for a donkey is up to 50 pounds; a medium load, 51–100 pounds; and a heavy load, 101–150 pounds. A donkey can drag 750 pounds.

Combat

A donkey bites only when it has no way to escape.

Skills: Donkeys have a +2 racial bonus on Balance checks.

EAGLE

Small Animal
Hit Dice: 1d8+1 (5 hp)
Initiative: +2
Speed: 10 ft. (2 squares), fly 80 ft. (average)
Armor Class: 14 (+1 size, +2 Dex, +1 natural), touch 13, flat-footed 12
Base Attack/Grapple: +0/−4
Attack: Talons +3 melee (1d4)
Full Attack: 2 talons +3 melee (1d4) and bite −2 melee (1d4)
Space/Reach: 5 ft./5 ft.
Special Attacks: —
Special Qualities: Low-light vision
Saves: Fort +3, Ref +4, Will +2
Abilities: Str 10, Dex 15, Con 12, Int 2, Wis 14, Cha 6
Skills: Listen +2, Spot +14
Feats: Weapon Finesse
Environment: Temperate mountains
Organization: Solitary or pair
Challenge Rating: 1/2
Advancement: 2–3 HD (Medium)
Level Adjustment: —

These birds of prey inhabit nearly every terrain and climate, though they all prefer high, secluded nesting spots.

A typical eagle is about 3 feet long and has a wingspan of about 7 feet. The statistics presented here can describe any similar-sized, diurnal bird of prey.

Combat

Eagles dive at prey, raking with their powerful talons.

Skills: Eagles have a +8 racial bonus on Spot checks.

ELEPHANT

Huge Animal
Hit Dice: 11d8+55 (104 hp)
Initiative: +0
Speed: 40 ft. (8 squares)
Armor Class: 15 (−2 size, +7 natural), touch 8, flat-footed 15
Base Attack/Grapple: +8/+26
Attack: Gore +16 melee (2d8+15)
Full Attack: Slam +16 melee (2d6+10) and 2 stamps +11 melee (2d6+5); or gore +16 melee (2d8+15)
Space/Reach: 15 ft./10 ft.
Special Attacks: Trample 2d8+15
Special Qualities: Low-light vision, scent
Saves: Fort +12, Ref +7, Will +6
Abilities: Str 30, Dex 10, Con 21, Int 2, Wis 13, Cha 7
Skills: Listen +12, Spot +10
Feats: Alertness, Endurance, Iron Will, Skill Focus (Listen)
Environment: Warm plains
Organization: Solitary or herd (6–30)
Challenge Rating: 7
Advancement: 12–22 HD (Huge)
Level Adjustment: —

Massive herbivores of tropical lands, elephants are unpredictable creatures but nevertheless are sometimes used as mounts or beasts of burden.

This entry describes an African elephant. Indian elephants are slightly smaller and weaker (Strength 28), but more readily trained (Wisdom 15). These statistics can also represent prehistoric creatures such as mammoths and mastodons.

Combat

Elephants tend to charge at threatening creatures.

Trample (Ex): Reflex half DC 25. The save DC is Strength-based.

HAWK

Tiny Animal
Hit Dice: 1d8 (4 hp)
Initiative: +3
Speed: 10 ft. (2 squares), fly 60 ft. (average)
Armor Class: 17 (+2 size, +3 Dex, +2 natural), touch 15, flat-footed 14
Base Attack/Grapple: +0/−10
Attack: Talons +5 melee (1d4−2)
Full Attack: Talons +5 melee (1d4−2)
Space/Reach: 2-1/2 ft./0 ft.
Special Attacks: —
Special Qualities: Low-light vision
Saves: Fort +2, Ref +5, Will +2
Abilities: Str 6, Dex 17, Con 10, Int 2, Wis 14, Cha 6
Skills: Listen +2, Spot +14
Feats: Weapon Finesse
Environment: Temperate forests
Organization: Solitary or pair
Challenge Rating: 1/3
Advancement: —
Level Adjustment: —

These creatures are similar to eagles but slightly smaller: 1 to 2 feet long, with wingspans of 6 feet or less.

Combat

Hawks combine both talons into a single attack.

Skills: Hawks have a +8 racial bonus on Spot checks.

HORSE

Horses are widely domesticated for riding and as beasts of burden.

Combat

A horse not trained for war does not normally use its hooves to attack. Its hoof attack is treated as a secondary attack and adds only half the horse's Strength bonus to damage. (These secondary attacks are noted with an asterisk in the Attack and Full Attack entries for the heavy horse and the light horse.)

Horse, Heavy

Large Animal
Hit Dice: 3d8+6 (19 hp)
Initiative: +1
Speed: 50 ft. (10 squares)
Armor Class: 13 (−1 size, +1 Dex, +3 natural), touch 10, flat-footed 12
Base Attack/Grapple: +2/+9
Attack: Hoof −1 melee (1d6+1*)
Full Attack: 2 hooves −1 melee (1d6+1*)
Space/Reach: 10 ft./5 ft.
Special Attacks: —
Special Qualities: Low-light vision, scent
Saves: Fort +5, Ref +4, Will +2
Abilities: Str 16, Dex 13, Con 15, Int 2, Wis 12, Cha 6
Skills: Listen +4, Spot +4
Feats: Endurance, Run
Environment: Temperate plains

Organization: Domesticated
Challenge Rating: 1
Advancement: —
Level Adjustment: —

The statistics presented here describe large breeds of working horses such as Clydesdales. These animals are usually ready for heavy work by age three. A heavy horse cannot fight while carrying a rider.

Carrying Capacity: A light load for a heavy horse is up to 200 pounds; a medium load, 201–400 pounds; and a heavy load, 401–600 pounds. A heavy horse can drag 3,000 pounds.

Horse, Light

Large Animal
Hit Dice: 3d8+6 (19 hp)
Initiative: +1
Speed: 60 ft. (12 squares)
Armor Class: 13 (−1 size, +1 Dex, +3 natural), touch 10, flat-footed 12
Base Attack/Grapple: +2/+8
Attack: Hoof −2 melee (1d4+1*)
Full Attack: 2 hooves −2 melee (1d4+1*)
Space/Reach: 10 ft./5 ft.
Special Attacks: —
Special Qualities: Low-light vision, scent
Saves: Fort +5, Ref +4, Will +2
Abilities: Str 14, Dex 13, Con 15, Int 2, Wis 12, Cha 6
Skills: Listen +4, Spot +4
Feats: Endurance, Run
Environment: Temperate plains
Organization: Domesticated or herd (6–30)
Challenge Rating: 1
Advancement: —
Level Adjustment: —

The statistics presented here describe smaller breeds of working horses such as quarter horses and Arabians as well as wild horses. These animals are usually ready for useful work by age two. A light horse cannot fight while carrying a rider.

Carrying Capacity: A light load for a light horse is up to 150 pounds; a medium load, 151–300 pounds; and a heavy load, 301–450 pounds. A light horse can drag 2,250 pounds.

Warhorse, Heavy

Large Animal
Hit Dice: 4d8+12 (30 hp)
Initiative: +1
Speed: 50 ft. (10 squares)
Armor Class: 14 (−1 size, +1 Dex, +4 natural), touch 10, flat-footed 13
Base Attack/Grapple: +3/+11
Attack: Hoof +6 melee (1d6+4)
Full Attack: 2 hooves +6 melee (1d6+4) and bite +1 melee (1d4+2)
Space/Reach: 10 ft./5 ft.
Special Attacks: —
Special Qualities: Low-light vision, scent
Saves: Fort +7, Ref +5, Will +2
Abilities: Str 18, Dex 13, Con 17, Int 2, Wis 13, Cha 6
Skills: Listen +5, Spot +4
Feats: Endurance, Run
Environment: Temperate plains
Organization: Domesticated
Challenge Rating: 2
Advancement: —
Level Adjustment: —

These animals are similar to heavy horses but are trained and bred for strength and aggression. A heavy warhorse can fight while carrying a rider, but the rider cannot also attack unless he or she succeeds on a Ride check.

Carrying Capacity: A light load for a heavy warhorse is up to 300 pounds; a medium load, 301–600 pounds; and a heavy load, 601–900 pounds. A heavy warhorse can drag 4,500 pounds.

Warhorse, Light

Large Animal
Hit Dice: 3d8+9 (22 hp)
Initiative: +1
Speed: 60 ft. (12 squares)
Armor Class: 14 (–1 size, +1 Dex, +4 natural), touch 10, flat-footed 13
Base Attack/Grapple: +2/+9
Attack: Hoof +4 melee (1d4+3)
Full Attack: 2 hooves +4 melee (1d4+3) and bite –1 melee (1d3+1)
Space/Reach: 10 ft./5 ft.
Special Attacks: —
Special Qualities: Low-light vision, scent
Saves: Fort +6, Ref +4, Will +2
Abilities: Str 16, Dex 13, Con 17, Int 2, Wis 13, Cha 6
Skills: Listen +4, Spot +4
Feats: Endurance, Run
Environment: Temperate plains
Organization: Domesticated
Challenge Rating: 1
Advancement: —
Level Adjustment: —

These animals or similar to light horses but are trained and bred for strength and aggression. They usually are not ready for warfare before age three. A light warhorse can fight while carrying a rider, but the rider cannot also attack unless he or she succeeds on a Ride check.

Carrying Capacity: A light load for a light warhorse is up to 230 pounds; a medium load, 231–460 pounds; and a heavy load, 461–690 pounds. A light warhorse can drag 3,450 pounds.

HYENA

Medium Animal
Hit Dice: 2d8+4 (13 hp)
Initiative: +2
Speed: 50 ft. (10 squares)
Armor Class: 14 (+2 Dex, +2 natural), touch 12, flat-footed 12
Base Attack/Grapple: +1/+3
Attack: Bite +3 melee (1d6+3)
Full Attack: Bite +3 melee (1d6+3)
Space/Reach: 5 ft./5 ft.
Special Attacks: Trip
Special Qualities: Low-light vision, scent
Saves: Fort +5, Ref +5, Will +1
Abilities: Str 14, Dex 15, Con 15, Int 2, Wis 13, Cha 6
Skills: Hide +3*, Listen +6, Spot +4
Feats: Alertness
Environment: Warm deserts
Organization: Solitary, pair, or pack (7–16)
Challenge Rating: 1
Advancement: 3 HD (Medium); 4–5 HD (Large)
Level Adjustment: —

Hyenas are pack hunters infamous for their cunning and their unnerving vocalizations. The statistics presented here are for a striped hyena, which is about 3 feet long and weighs about 120 pounds.

Combat

A favorite tactic is to send a few individuals against the foe's front while the rest of the pack circles and attacks from the flanks or rear.

Trip (Ex): A hyena that hits with its bite attack can attempt to trip the opponent (+2 check modifier) as a free action without making a touch attack or provoking an attack of opportunity. If the attempt fails, the opponent cannot react to trip the hyena.

Skills: *Hyenas have a +4 racial bonus on Hide checks in areas of tall grass or heavy undergrowth.

LEOPARD

Medium Animal
Hit Dice: 3d8+6 (19 hp)
Initiative: +4
Speed: 40 ft (8 squares), climb 20 ft.
Armor Class: 15 (+4 Dex, +1 natural), touch 14, flat-footed 11
Base Attack/Grapple: +2/+5
Attack: Bite +6 melee (1d6+3)
Full Attack: Bite +6 melee (1d6+3) and 2 claws +1 melee (1d3+1)
Space/Reach: 5 ft./5 ft.
Special Attacks: Improved grab, pounce, rake 1d3+1
Special Qualities: Low-light vision, scent
Saves: Fort +5, Ref +7, Will +2
Abilities: Str 16, Dex 19, Con 15, Int 2, Wis 12, Cha 6
Skills: Balance +12, Climb +11, Hide +8*, Jump +11, Listen +6, Move Silently +8, Spot +6
Feats: Alertness, Weapon Finesse
Environment: Warm forests
Organization: Solitary or pair
Challenge Rating: 2
Advancement: 4–5 HD (Medium)
Level Adjustment: —

These jungle cats are about 4 feet long and weigh about 120 pounds. They usually hunt at night.

The statistics presented here can describe any feline of similar size, such as jaguars, panthers, and mountain lions.

Combat

Improved Grab (Ex): To use this ability, a leopard must hit with its bite attack. It can then attempt to start a grapple as a free action without provoking an attack of opportunity. If it wins the grapple check, it establishes a hold and can rake.

Pounce (Ex): If a leopard charges a foe, it can make a full attack, including two rake attacks.

Rake (Ex): Attack bonus +6 melee, damage 1d3+1.

Skills: Leopards have a +8 racial bonus on Jump checks and a +4 racial bonus on Hide and Move Silently checks.

Leopards have a +8 racial bonus on Balance and Climb checks. A leopard can always choose to take 10 on a Climb check, even if rushed or threatened.

LION

Large Animal
Hit Dice: 5d8+10 (32 hp)
Initiative: +3
Speed: 40 ft. (8 squares)
Armor Class: 15 (–1 size, +3 Dex, +3 natural), touch 12, flat-footed 12
Base Attack/Grapple: +3/+12
Attack: Claw +7 melee (1d4+5)
Full Attack: 2 claws +7 melee (1d4+5) and bite +2 melee (1d8+2)
Space/Reach: 10 ft./5 ft.
Special Attacks: Pounce, improved grab, rake 1d4+2
Special Qualities: Low-light vision, scent
Saves: Fort +6, Ref +7, Will +2

Abilities: Str 21, Dex 17, Con 15, Int 2, Wis 12, Cha 6
Skills: Balance +7, Hide +3*, Listen +5, Move Silently +11, Spot +5
Feats: Alertness, Run
Environment: Warm plains
Organization: Solitary, pair, or pride (6–10)
Challenge Rating: 3
Advancement: 6–8 HD (Large)
Level Adjustment: —

The statistics presented here describe a male African lion, which is 5 to 8 feet long and weighs 330 to 550 pounds. Females are slightly smaller but use the same statistics.

Combat

Pounce (Ex): If a lion charges a foe, it can make a full attack, including two rake attacks.

Improved Grab (Ex): To use this ability, a lion must hit with its bite attack. It can then attempt to start a grapple as a free action without provoking an attack of opportunity. If it wins the grapple check, it establishes a hold and can rake.

Rake (Ex): Attack bonus +7 melee, damage 1d4+2.

Skills: Lions have a +4 racial bonus on Balance, Hide, and Move Silently checks. *In areas of tall grass or heavy undergrowth, the Hide bonus improves to +12.

LIZARD

Tiny Animal
Hit Dice: 1/2 d8 (2 hp)
Initiative: +2
Speed: 20 ft. (4 squares), climb 20 ft.
Armor Class: 14 (+2 size, +2 Dex), touch 14, flat-footed 12
Base Attack/Grapple: +0/–12
Attack: Bite +4 melee (1d4–4)
Full Attack: Bite +4 melee (1d4–4)
Space/Reach: 2-1/2 ft./0 ft.
Special Attacks: —
Special Qualities: Low-light vision
Saves: Fort +2, Ref +4, Will +1
Abilities: Str 3, Dex 15, Con 10, Int 1, Wis 12, Cha 2
Skills: Balance +10, Climb +12, Hide +10, Listen +3, Spot +3
Feats: Weapon Finesse
Environment: Warm forests
Organization: Solitary
Challenge Rating: 1/6
Advancement: —
Level Adjustment: —

The statistics presented here describe small, nonvenomous lizards of perhaps a foot or two in length, such as an iguana.

Combat

Lizards prefer flight to combat, but they can bite painfully if there is no other option.

Skills: Lizards have a +8 racial bonus on Balance checks. They also have a +8 racial bonus on Climb checks and can always choose to take 10 on Climb checks, even if rushed or threatened. Lizards use their Dexterity modifier instead of their Strength modifier for Climb checks.

LIZARD, MONITOR

Medium Animal
Hit Dice: 3d8+9 (22 hp)
Initiative: +2
Speed: 30 ft. (6 squares), swim 30 ft.
Armor Class: 15 (+2 Dex, +3 natural), touch 12, flat-footed 13
Base Attack/Grapple: +2/+5

Attack: Bite +5 melee (1d8+4)
Full Attack: Bite +5 melee (1d8+4)
Space/Reach: 5 ft./5 ft.
Special Attacks: —
Special Qualities: Low-light vision
Saves: Fort +8, Ref +5, Will +2
Abilities: Str 17, Dex 15, Con 17, Int 1, Wis 12, Cha 2
Skills: Climb +7, Hide +6*, Listen +4, Move Silently +6, Spot +4, Swim +11
Feats: Alertness, Great Fortitude
Environment: Warm forests
Organization: Solitary
Challenge Rating: 2
Advancement: 4–5 HD (Medium)
Level Adjustment: —

This category includes fairly large, carnivorous lizards from 3 to 5 feet long.

Combat

Monitor lizards can be aggressive, using their powerful jaws to tear at prey or enemies.

Skills: A monitor lizard has a +8 racial bonus on any Swim check to perform some special action or avoid a hazard. It can always choose to take 10 on a Swim check, even if distracted or endangered. It can use the run action while swimming, provided it swims in a straight line.

Monitor lizards have a +4 racial bonus on Hide and Move Silently checks. *In forested or overgrown areas, the Hide bonus improves to +8.

MANTA RAY

Large Animal (Aquatic)
Hit Dice: 4d8 (18 hp)
Initiative: +0
Speed: Swim 30 ft. (6 squares)
Armor Class: 12 (–1 size, +3 natural), touch 9, flat-footed 12
Base Attack/Grapple: +3/+9
Attack: Ram –1 melee* (1d6+1)
Full Attack: Ram –1 melee* (1d6+1)
Space/Reach: 10 ft./5 ft.
Special Attacks: —
Special Qualities: Low-light vision
Saves: Fort +4, Ref +4, Will +2
Abilities: Str 15, Dex 11, Con 10, Int 1, Wis 12, Cha 2
Skills: Listen +7, Spot +6, Swim +10
Feats: Alertness, Endurance
Environment: Warm aquatic
Organization: Solitary or school (2–5)
Challenge Rating: 1
Advancement: 5–6 HD (Medium)
Level Adjustment: —

These fish are nonaggressive and generally avoid contact with other creatures. They filter plankton and similar small organisms from the water through their gaping, toothless maws.

Combat

*If threatened, a manta ray uses its size and weight to ram opponents. This is treated as a secondary attack.

Skills: A manta ray has a +8 racial bonus on any Swim check to perform some special action or avoid a hazard. It can always choose to take 10 on a Swim check, even if distracted or endangered. It can use the run action while swimming, provided it swims in a straight line.

MONKEY

Tiny Animal
Hit Dice: 1d8 (4 hp)
Initiative: +2
Speed: 30 ft. (6 squares), climb 30 ft.
Armor Class: 14 (+2 size, +2 Dex), touch 14, flat-footed 12
Base Attack/Grapple: +0/−12
Attack: Bite +4 melee (1d3−4)
Full Attack: Bite +4 melee (1d3−4)
Space/Reach: 2-1/2 ft./0 ft.
Special Attacks: —
Special Qualities: Low-light vision
Saves: Fort +2, Ref +4, Will +1
Abilities: Str 3, Dex 15, Con 10, Int 2, Wis 12, Cha 5
Skills: Balance + 10, Climb +10, Hide +10, Listen +3, Spot +3
Feats: Weapon Finesse
Environment: Warm forests
Organization: Troop (10–40)
Challenge Rating: 1/6
Advancement: 2–3 HD (Small)
Level Adjustment: —

The statistics presented here can describe any arboreal monkey that is no bigger than a housecat, such as a colobus or capuchin.

Combat

Monkeys generally flee into the safety of the trees, but if cornered can fight ferociously.

Skills: Monkeys have a +8 racial bonus on Balance and Climb checks. They can always choose to take 10 on Climb checks, even if rushed or threatened. They use their Dexterity modifier instead of their Strength modifier for Climb checks.

MULE

Large Animal
Hit Dice: 3d8+9 (22 hp)
Initiative: +1
Speed: 30 ft. (6 squares)
Armor Class: 13 (−1 size, +1 Dex, +3 natural), touch 10, flat-footed 12
Base Attack/Grapple: +2/+9
Attack: Hoof +4 melee (1d4+3)
Full Attack: 2 hooves +4 melee (1d4+3)
Space/Reach: 10 ft./5 ft.
Special Attacks: —
Special Qualities: Low-light vision, scent
Saves: Fort +6, Ref +4, Will +1
Abilities: Str 16, Dex 13, Con 17, Int 2, Wis 11, Cha 6
Skills: Listen +6, Spot +6
Feats: Alertness, Endurance
Environment: Warm plains
Organization: Domesticated
Challenge Rating: 1
Advancement: —
Level Adjustment: —

Mules are sterile crossbreeds of donkeys and horses. A mule is similar to a light horse, but slightly stronger and more agile.

Combat

A mule's powerful kick can be dangerous.

Carrying Capacity: A light load for a mule is up to 230 pounds; a medium load, 231–460 pounds; and a heavy load, 461–690 pounds. A mule can drag 3,450 pounds.

Skills: Mules have a +2 racial bonus on Dexterity checks to avoid slipping or falling.

OCTOPUS

Small Animal (Aquatic)
Hit Dice: 2d8 (9 hp)
Initiative: +3
Speed: 20 ft. (4 squares), swim 30 ft.
Armor Class: 16 (+1 size, +3 Dex, +2 natural), touch 14, flat-footed 13
Base Attack/Grapple: +1/+2
Attack: Arms +5 melee (0)
Full Attack: Arms +5 melee (0) and bite +0 melee (1d3)
Space/Reach: 5 ft./5 ft.
Special Attacks: Improved grab
Special Qualities: Ink cloud, jet, low-light vision
Saves: Fort +3, Ref +6, Will +1
Abilities: Str 12, Dex 17, Con 11, Int 2, Wis 12, Cha 3
Skills: Escape Artist +13, Hide +11, Listen +2, Spot +5, Swim +9
Feats: Weapon Finesse
Environment: Warm aquatic
Organization: Solitary
Challenge Rating: 1
Advancement: 3–6 HD (Medium)
Level Adjustment: —

These bottom-dwelling sea creatures are dangerous only to their prey. If disturbed, they usually try to escape.

Combat

Improved Grab (Ex): To use this ability, an octopus must hit an opponent of any size with its arms attack. It can then attempt to start a grapple as a free action without provoking an attack of opportunity. If it wins the grapple check, it establishes a hold and automatically deals bite damage.

Ink Cloud (Ex): An octopus can emit a cloud of jet-black ink 10 feet high by 10 feet wide by 10 feet long once per minute as a free action. The cloud provides total concealment, which the octopus normally uses to escape a losing fight. All vision within the cloud is obscured.

Jet (Ex): An octopus can jet backward once per round as a full-round action, at a speed of 200 feet. It must move in a straight line, but does not provoke attacks of opportunity while jetting.

Skills: An octopus can change colors, giving it a +4 racial bonus on Hide checks.

An octopus also can squeeze and contort its body, giving it a +10 racial bonus on Escape Artist checks.

An octopus has a +8 racial bonus on any Swim check to perform some special action or avoid a hazard. It can always choose to take 10 on a Swim check, even if distracted or endangered. It can use the run action while swimming, provided it swims in a straight line.

OCTOPUS, GIANT

Large Animal (Aquatic)
Hit Dice: 8d8+11 (47 hp)
Initiative: +2
Speed: 20 ft. (4 squares), swim 30 ft.
Armor Class: 18 (−1 size, +2 Dex, +7 natural), touch 11, flat-footed 16
Base Attack/Grapple: +6/+15
Attack: Tentacle +10 melee (1d4+5)
Full Attack: 8 tentacles +10 melee (1d4+5) and bite +5 melee (1d8+2)
Space/Reach: 10 ft./10 ft. (20 ft. with tentacle)
Special Attacks: Improved grab, constrict
Special Qualities: Ink cloud, jet, low-light vision
Saves: Fort +7, Ref +8, Will +3
Abilities: Str 20, Dex 15, Con 13, Int 2, Wis 12, Cha 3
Skills: Escape Artist +12, Hide +12, Listen +4, Spot +6, Swim +13
Feats: Alertness, Skill Focus (Hide), Toughness

Environment: Warm aquatic
Organization: Solitary
Challenge Rating: 8
Advancement: 9–12 HD (Large); 13–24 HD (Huge)
Level Adjustment: —

These creatures are aggressive and territorial hunters, with arms reaching 10 feet or more in length. Their tentacles are studded with barbs and sharp-edged suckers.

Combat

An opponent can attack a giant octopus's tentacles with a sunder attempt as if they were weapons. A giant octopus's tentacles have 10 hit points each. If a giant octopus is currently grappling a target with the tentacle that is being attacked, it usually uses another limb to make its attack of opportunity against the opponent making the sunder attempt. Severing one of a giant octopus's tentacles deals 5 points of damage to the creature. A giant octopus usually withdraws from combat if it loses four tentacles. The creature regrows severed limbs in 1d10+10 days.

Constrict (Ex): A giant octopus deals 2d8+6 points of damage with a successful grapple check.

Improved Grab (Ex): To use this ability, a giant octopus must hit an opponent of any size with a tentacle attack. It can then attempt to start a grapple as a free action without provoking an attack of opportunity. If it wins the grapple check, it establishes a hold and can constrict.

Ink Cloud (Ex): A giant octopus can emit a cloud of jet-black ink 20 feet high by 20 feet wide by 20 feet long once per minute as a free action. The cloud provides total concealment, which the octopus normally uses to escape a losing fight. All vision within the cloud is obscured.

Jet (Ex): A giant octopus can jet backward once per round as a full-round action, at a speed of 200 feet. It must move in a straight line, but does not provoke attacks of opportunity while jetting.

Skills: A giant octopus can change colors, giving it a +4 racial bonus on Hide checks.

A giant octopus also can squeeze and contort its body, giving it a +10 racial bonus on Escape Artist checks.

A giant octopus has a +8 racial bonus on any Swim check to perform some special action or avoid a hazard. It can always choose to take 10 on a Swim check, even if distracted or endangered. It can use the run action while swimming, provided it swims in a straight line.

OWL

Tiny Animal
Hit Dice: 1d8 (4 hp)
Initiative: +3
Speed: 10 ft. (2 squares), fly 40 ft. (average)
Armor Class: 17 (+2 size, +3 Dex, +2 natural), touch 15, flat-footed 14
Base Attack/Grapple: +0/–11
Attack: Talons +5 melee (1d4–3)
Full Attack: Talons +5 melee (1d4–3)
Space/Reach: 2-1/2 ft./0 ft.
Special Attacks: —
Special Qualities: Low-light vision
Saves: Fort +2, Ref +5, Will +2
Abilities: Str 4, Dex 17, Con 10, Int 2, Wis 14, Cha 4
Skills: Listen +14, Move Silently +17, Spot +6*
Feats: Weapon Finesse
Environment: Temperate forests
Organization: Solitary
Challenge Rating: 1/4
Advancement: 2 HD (Small)
Level Adjustment: —

The statistics presented here describe nocturnal birds of prey from 1 to 2 feet long, with wingspans up to 6 feet. They combine both talons into a single attack.

Combat

Owls swoop quietly down onto prey, attacking with their powerful talons.

Skills: Owls have a +8 racial bonus on Listen checks and a +14 racial bonus on Move Silently checks. *They have a +8 racial bonus on Spot checks in areas of shadowy illumination.

PONY

Medium Animal
Hit Dice: 2d8+2 (11 hp)
Initiative: +1
Speed: 40 ft. (8 squares)
Armor Class: 13 (+1 Dex, +2 natural), touch 11, flat-footed 12
Base Attack/Grapple: +1/+2
Attack: Hoof –3 melee (1d3*)
Full Attack: 2 hooves –3 melee (1d3*)
Space/Reach: 5 ft./5 ft.
Special Attacks: —
Special Qualities: Low-light vision, scent
Saves: Fort +4, Ref +4, Will +0
Abilities: Str 13, Dex 13, Con 12, Int 2, Wis 11, Cha 4
Skills: Listen +5, Spot +5
Feats: Endurance
Environment: Temperate plains
Organization: Solitary
Challenge Rating: 1/4
Advancement: —
Level Adjustment: —

The statistics presented here describe a small horse, under 5 feet tall at the shoulder. Ponies are otherwise similar to light horses and cannot fight while carrying a rider.

Combat

*A pony not trained for war does not normally use its hooves to attack but rather to run. Its hoof attack is treated as a secondary attack and adds only half the pony's Strength bonus to damage.

Carrying Capacity: A light load for a pony is up to 75 pounds; a medium load, 76–150 pounds; and a heavy load, 151–225 pounds. A pony can drag 1,125 pounds.

PONY, WAR

Medium Animal
Hit Dice: 2d8+4 (13 hp)
Initiative: +1
Speed: 40 ft. (8 squares)
Armor Class: 13 (+1 Dex, +2 natural), touch 11, flat-footed 12
Base Attack/Grapple: +1/+3
Attack: Hoof +3 melee (1d3+2)
Full Attack: 2 hooves +3 melee (1d3+2)
Space/Reach: 5 ft./5 ft.
Special Attacks: —
Special Qualities: Low-light vision, scent
Saves: Fort +5, Ref +4, Will +0
Abilities: Str 15, Dex 13, Con 14, Int 2, Wis 11, Cha 4
Skills: Listen +5, Spot +5
Feats: Endurance
Environment: Temperate plains
Organization: Domesticated
Challenge Rating: 1/2
Advancement: —
Level Adjustment: —

Warponies are bred for strength and aggression, and are similar to light warhorses.

Combat

A warpony can fight while carrying a rider, but the rider cannot also attack unless he or she succeeds on a Ride check.

Carrying Capacity: A light load for a warpony is up to 100 pounds; a medium load, 101–200 pounds; and a heavy load, 201–300 pounds. A warpony can drag 1,500 pounds.

PORPOISE

Medium Animal
Hit Dice: 2d8+2 (11 hp)
Initiative: +3
Speed: Swim 80 ft. (16 squares)
Armor Class: 15 (+3 Dex, +2 natural), touch 13, flat-footed 12
Base Attack/Grapple: +1/+1
Attack: Slam +4 melee (2d4)
Full Attack: Slam +4 melee (2d4)
Space/Reach: 5 ft./5 ft.
Special Attacks: —
Special Qualities: Blindsight 120 ft., hold breath, low-light vision
Saves: Fort +4, Ref +6, Will +1
Abilities: Str 11, Dex 17, Con 13, Int 2, Wis 12, Cha 6
Skills: Listen +8*, Spot +7*, Swim +8
Feats: Weapon Finesse
Environment: Temperate aquatic
Organization: Solitary, pair, or school (3–20)
Challenge Rating: 1/2
Advancement: 3–4 HD (Medium); 5–6 HD (Large)
Level Adjustment: —

Porpoises are mammals that tend to be playful, friendly, and helpful.

A typical porpoise is 4 to 6 feet long and weighs 110 to 160 pounds. The statistics presented here can describe any small whale of similar size.

Combat

Blindsight (Ex): Porpoises can "see" by emitting high-frequency sounds, inaudible to most other creatures, that allow them to locate objects and creatures within 120 feet. A *silence* spell negates this and forces the porpoise to rely on its vision, which is approximately as good as a human's.

Hold Breath (Ex): A porpoise can hold its breath for a number of rounds equal to 6 × its Constitution score before it risks drowning.

Skills: A porpoise has a +8 racial bonus on any Swim check to perform some special action or avoid a hazard. It can always choose to take 10 on a Swim check, even if distracted or endangered. It can use the run action while swimming, provided it swims in a straight line.

*A porpoise has a +4 racial bonus on Spot and Listen checks. These bonuses are lost if its blindsight is negated.

RAT

Tiny Animal
Hit Dice: 1/4 d8 (1 hp)
Initiative: +2
Speed: 15 ft. (3 squares), climb 15 ft., swim 15 ft.
Armor Class: 14 (+2 size, +2 Dex), touch 14, flat-footed 12
Base Attack/Grapple: +0/–12
Attack: Bite +4 melee (1d3–4)
Full Attack: Bite +4 melee (1d3–4)
Space/Reach: 2-1/2 ft./0 ft.
Special Attacks: —
Special Qualities: Low-light vision, scent
Saves: Fort +2, Ref +4, Will +1
Abilities: Str 2, Dex 15, Con 10, Int 2, Wis 12, Cha 2
Skills: Balance +10, Climb +12, Hide +14, Move Silently +10, Swim +10
Feats: Weapon Finesse
Environment: Any
Organization: Plague (10–100)
Challenge Rating: 1/8
Advancement: —
Level Adjustment: —

These omnivorous rodents thrive almost anywhere.

Combat

Rats usually run away. They bite only as a last resort.

Skills: Rats have a +4 racial bonus on Hide and Move Silently checks, and a +8 racial bonus on Balance, Climb, and Swim checks.

A rat can always choose to take 10 on Climb checks, even if rushed or threatened.

A rat uses its Dexterity modifier instead of its Strength modifier for Climb and Swim checks.

A rat has a +8 racial bonus on any Swim check to perform some special action or avoid a hazard. It can always choose to take 10 on a Swim check, even if distracted or endangered. It can use the run action while swimming, provided it swims in a straight line.

RAVEN

Tiny Animal
Hit Dice: 1/4 d8 (1 hp)
Initiative: +2
Speed: 10 ft. (2 squares), fly 40 ft. (average)
Armor Class: 14 (+2 size, +2 Dex), touch 14, flat-footed 12
Base Attack/Grapple: +0/–13
Attack: Claws +4 melee (1d2–5)
Full Attack: Claws +4 melee (1d2–5)
Space/Reach: 2-1/2 ft./0 ft.
Special Attacks: —
Special Qualities: Low-light vision
Saves: Fort +2, Ref +4, Will +2
Abilities: Str 1, Dex 15, Con 10, Int 2, Wis 14, Cha 6
Skills: Listen +3, Spot +5
Feats: Weapon Finesse
Environment: Temperate forests
Organization: Solitary
Challenge Rating: 1/6
Advancement: —
Level Adjustment: —

These glossy black birds are about 2 feet long and have wingspans of about 4 feet. They combine both claws into a single attack.

The statistics presented here can describe most nonpredatory birds of similar size.

RHINOCEROS

Large Animal
Hit Dice: 8d8+40 (76 hp)
Initiative: +0
Speed: 30 ft. (6 squares)
Armor Class: 16 (–1 size, +7 natural), touch 9, flat-footed 16
Base Attack/Grapple: +6/+18
Attack: Gore +13 melee (2d6+12)
Full Attack: Gore +13 melee (2d6+12)
Space/Reach: 10 ft./5 ft.
Special Attacks: Powerful charge
Special Qualities: Low-light vision
Saves: Fort +11, Ref +6, Will +3
Abilities: Str 26, Dex 10, Con 21, Int 2, Wis 13, Cha 2

Skills: Listen +14, Spot +3
Feats: Alertness, Endurance, Improved Natural Attack (gore)
Environment: Warm plains
Organization: Solitary or herd (2–12)
Challenge Rating: 4
Advancement: 9–12 HD (Large); 13–24 HD (Huge)
Level Adjustment: —

The rhinoceros is infamous for its bad temper and willingness to charge intruders.

The statistics presented here are based on the African black rhino, which is 6 to 14 feet long, 3 to 6 feet high at the shoulder, and weighs up to 6,000 pounds. These statistics can describe any herbivore of similar size and similar natural weapons (antlers, horns, tusks, or the like).

Combat

When it is harassed or annoyed, a rhinoceros lowers its head and charges.

Powerful Charge (Ex): A rhinoceros deals 4d6+24 points of damage when it makes a charge.

SHARK

These carnivorous fish are aggressive and liable to make unprovoked attacks against anything that approaches them.

Smaller sharks are from 5 to 8 feet long and not usually dangerous to creatures other than their prey. Large sharks can reach around 15 feet in length and are a serious threat. Huge sharks are true monsters, like great whites, that can exceed 20 feet in length.

Combat

Sharks circle and observe potential prey, then dart in and bite with their powerful jaws.

Blindsense (Ex): A shark can locate creatures underwater within a 30-foot radius. This ability works only when the shark is underwater.

Keen Scent (Ex): A shark can notice creatures by scent in a 180-foot radius and detect blood in the water at ranges of up to a mile.

Skills: A shark has a +8 racial bonus on any Swim check to perform some special action or avoid a hazard. It can always choose to take 10 on a Swim check, even if distracted or endangered. It can use the run action while swimming, provided it swims in a straight line.

SNAKE

Snakes usually are not aggressive and flee when confronted.

Skills: Snakes have a +4 racial bonus on Hide, Listen, and Spot checks and a +8 racial bonus on Balance and Climb checks.

A snake can always choose to take 10 on a Climb check, even if rushed or threatened.

Snakes use either their Strength modifier or Dexterity modifier for Climb checks, whichever is higher.

A snake has a +8 racial bonus on any Swim check to perform some special action or avoid a hazard. It can always choose to take 10 on a Swim check, even if distracted or endangered. It can use the run action while swimming, provided it swims in a straight line.

Constrictor Snake

Medium Animal
Hit Dice: 3d8+6 (19 hp)
Initiative: +3
Speed: 20 ft. (4 squares), climb 20 ft., swim 20 ft.
Armor Class: 15 (+3 Dex, +2 natural), touch 13, flat-footed 12
Base Attack/Grapple: +2/+5
Attack: Bite +5 melee (1d3+4)
Full Attack: Bite +5 melee (1d3+4)
Space/Reach: 5 ft./5 ft.
Special Attacks: Constrict 1d3+4, improved grab
Special Qualities: Scent
Saves: Fort +4, Ref +6, Will +2
Abilities: Str 17, Dex 17, Con 13, Int 1, Wis 12, Cha 2
Skills: Balance +11, Climb +14, Hide +10, Listen +7, Spot +7, Swim +11
Feats: Alertness, Toughness
Environment: Warm forests
Organization: Solitary
Challenge Rating: 2
Advancement: 4–5 HD (Medium); 6–10 HD (Large)
Level Adjustment: —

Constrictor snakes usually are not aggressive and flee when confronted. They hunt for food but do not attempt to make a meal out of any creature that is too large to constrict.

Combat

Constrictor snakes hunt by grabbing prey with their mouths and

	Shark, Medium	Shark, Large	Shark, Huge
	Medium Animal (Aquatic)	Large Animal (Aquatic)	Huge Animal (Aquatic)
Hit Dice:	3d8+3 (16 hp)	7d8+7 (38 hp)	10d8+20 (65 hp)
Initiative:	+2	+6	+6
Speed:	Swim 60 ft. (12 squares)	Swim 60 ft. (12 squares)	Swim 60 ft. (12 squares)
Armor Class:	15 (+2 Dex, +3 natural), touch 12, flat-footed 13	15 (–1 size, +2 Dex, +4 natural), touch 11, flat-footed 13	15 (–2 size, +2 Dex, +5 natural), touch 10, flat-footed 13
Base Attack/Grapple:	+2/+3	+5/+12	+7/+20
Attack:	Bite +4 melee (1d6+1)	Bite +7 melee (1d8+4)	Bite +10 melee (2d6+7)
Full Attack:	Bite +4 melee (1d6+1)	Bite +7 melee (1d8+4)	Bite +10 melee (2d6+7)
Space/Reach:	5 ft./5 ft.	10 ft./5 ft.	15 ft./10 ft.
Special Attacks:	—	—	—
Special Qualities:	Blindsense, keen scent	Blindsense, keen scent	Blindsense, keen scent
Saves:	Fort +4, Ref +5, Will +2	Fort +8, Ref +7, Will +3	Fort +11, Ref +9, Will +4
Abilities:	Str 13, Dex 15, Con 13, Int 1, Wis 12, Cha 2	Str 17, Dex 15, Con 13, Int 1, Wis 12, Cha 2	Str 21, Dex 15, Con 15, Int 1, Wis 12, Cha 2
Skills:	Listen +6, Spot +6, Swim +9	Listen +8, Spot +7, Swim +11	Listen +10, Spot +10, Swim +13
Feats:	Alertness, Weapon Finesse	Alertness, Great Fortitude, Improved Initiative	Alertness, Great Fortitude, Improved Initiative, Iron Will
Environment:	Cold aquatic	Cold aquatic	Cold aquatic
Organization:	Solitary, school (2–5), or pack (6–11)	Solitary, school (2–5), or pack (6–11)	Solitary, school (2–5), or pack (6–11)
Challenge Rating:	1	2	4
Advancement:	4–6 HD (Medium)	8–9 HD (Large)	11–17 HD (Huge)
Level Adjustment:	—		

	Snake, Tiny Viper Tiny Animal	Snake, Small Viper Small Animal
Hit Dice:	1/4 d8 (1 hp)	1d8 (4 hp)
Initiative:	+3	+3
Speed:	15 ft. (3 squares), climb 15 ft., swim 15 ft.	20 ft. (4 squares), climb 20 ft., swim 20 ft.
Armor Class:	17 (+2 size, +3 Dex, +2 natural), touch 15, flat-footed 14	17 (+1 size, +3 Dex, +3 natural), touch 14, flat-footed 14
Base Attack/Grapple:	+0/−11	+0/−6
Attack:	Bite +5 melee (1 plus poison)	Bite +4 melee (1d2−2 plus poison)
Full Attack:	Bite +5 melee (1 plus poison)	Bite +4 melee (1d2−2 plus poison)
Space/Reach:	2-1/2 ft./0 ft.	5 ft./5 ft.
Special Attacks:	Poison	Poison
Special Qualities:	Scent	Scent
Saves:	Fort +2, Ref +5, Will +1	Fort +2, Ref +5, Will +1
Abilities:	Str 4, Dex 17, Con 11, Int 1, Wis 12, Cha 2	Str 6, Dex 17, Con 11, Int 1, Wis 12, Cha 2
Skills:	Balance +11, Climb +11, Hide +15, Listen +6, Spot +6, Swim +5	Balance +11, Climb +11, Hide +11, Listen +7, Spot +7, Swim +6
Feats:	Weapon Finesse	Weapon Finesse
Environment:	Temperate marshes	Temperate marshes
Organization:	Solitary	Solitary
Challenge Rating:	1/3	1/2
Advancement:	—	—
Level Adjustment:	—	—

	Snake, Medium Viper Medium Animal	Snake, Large Viper Large Animal	Snake, Huge Viper Huge Animal
Hit Dice:	2d8 (9 hp)	3d8 (13 hp)	6d8+6 (33 hp)
Initiative:	+3	+7	+6
Speed:	20 ft. (4 squares), climb 20 ft., swim 20 ft.	20 ft. (4 squares), climb 20 ft., swim 20 ft.	20 ft. (4 squares), climb 20 ft., swim 20 ft.
Armor Class:	16 (+3 Dex, +3 natural), touch 13, flat-footed 13	15 (−1 size, +3 Dex, +3 natural), touch 12, flat-footed 12	15 (−2 size, +2 Dex, +5 natural), touch 10, flat-footed 15
Base Attack/Grapple:	+1/+0	+2/+6	+4/+15
Attack:	Bite +4 melee (1d4−1 plus poison)	Bite +4 melee (1d4 plus poison)	Bite +6 melee (1d6+4 plus poison)
Full Attack:	Bite +4 melee (1d4−1 plus poison)	Bite +4 melee (1d4 plus poison)	Bite +6 melee (1d6+4 plus poison)
Space/Reach:	5 ft./5 ft.	10 ft./5 ft.	15 ft./10 ft.
Special Attacks:	Poison	Poison	Poison
Special Qualities:	Scent	Scent	Scent
Saves:	Fort +3, Ref +6, Will +1	Fort +3, Ref +6, Will +2	Fort +6, Ref +7, Will +3
Abilities:	Str 8, Dex 17, Con 11, Int 1, Wis 12, Cha 2	Str 10, Dex 17, Con 11, Int 1, Wis 12, Cha 2	Str 16, Dex 15, Con 13, Int 1, Wis 12, Cha 2
Skills:	Balance +11, Climb +11, Hide +12, Listen +5, Spot +5, Swim +7	Balance +11, Climb +11, Hide +8, Listen +5, Spot +6, Swim +8	Balance +10, Climb +11, Hide +3, Listen +7, Spot +7, Swim +11
Feats:	Weapon Finesse	Improved Initiative, Weapon Finesse	Improved Initiative, Run, Weapon Focus (bite)
Environment:	Temperate marshes	Temperate marshes	Temperate marshes
Organization:	Solitary	Solitary	Solitary
Challenge Rating:	1	2	3
Advancement:	—	—	7–18 HD (Huge)
Level Adjustment:	—	—	—

then squeezing it with their powerful bodies.

Constrict (Ex): On a successful grapple check, a constrictor snake deals 1d3+4 points of damage.

Improved Grab (Ex): To use this ability, a constrictor snake must hit with its bite attack. It can then attempt to start a grapple as a free action without provoking an attack of opportunity. If it wins the grapple check, it establishes a hold and can constrict.

Constrictor Snake, Giant

Huge Animal
Hit Dice: 11d8+14 (63 hp)
Initiative: +3
Speed: 20 ft. (4 squares), climb 20 ft., swim 20 ft.
Armor Class: 15 (−2 size, +3 Dex, +4 natural), touch 11, flat-footed 12
Base Attack/Grapple: +8/+23

Attack: Bite +13 melee (1d8+10)
Full Attack: Bite +13 melee (1d8+10)
Space/Reach: 15 ft./10 ft.
Special Attacks: Constrict 1d8+10, improved grab
Special Qualities: Scent
Saves: Fort +8, Ref +10, Will +4
Abilities: Str 25, Dex 17, Con 13, Int 1, Wis 12, Cha 2
Skills: Balance +11, Climb +17, Hide +10, Listen +9, Spot +9, Swim +16
Feats: Alertness, Endurance, Skill Focus (Hide), Toughness
Environment: Warm forests
Organization: Solitary
Challenge Rating: 5
Advancement: 12–16 HD (Huge); 17–33 HD (Gargantuan)
Level Adjustment: —

Giant constrictor snakes are more aggressive than their smaller cousins, principally because they need a great amount of food to survive.

Viper Snake

These creatures range widely in size. They are not particularly aggressive, but will often lash out with a bite attack before attempting to retreat.

Combat

Viper snakes rely on their venomous bite to kill prey and defend themselves.

Poison (Ex): A viper snake has a poisonous bite that deals initial and secondary damage of 1d6 Con. The save DC varies by the snake's size, as shown on the table below. The save DCs are Constitution-based.

Size	Fort DC
Tiny	10
Small	10
Medium	11
Large	11
Huge	14

SQUID

Medium Animal (Aquatic)
Hit Dice: 3d8 (13 hp)
Initiative: +3
Speed: Swim 60 ft. (12 squares)
Armor Class: 16 (+3 Dex, +3 natural), touch 13, flat-footed 13
Base Attack/Grapple: +2/+8*
Attack: Arms +4 melee (0)
Full Attack: Arms +4 melee (0) and bite –1 melee (1d6+1)
Space/Reach: 5 ft./5 ft.
Special Attacks: Improved grab
Special Qualities: Ink cloud, jet, low-light vision
Saves: Fort +3, Ref +6, Will +2
Abilities: Str 14, Dex 17, Con 11, Int 1, Wis 12, Cha 2
Skills: Listen +7, Spot +7, Swim +10
Feats: Alertness, Endurance
Environment: Temperate aquatic
Organization: Solitary or school (6–11)
Challenge Rating: 1
Advancement: 4–6 HD (Medium); 7–11 HD (Large)
Level Adjustment: —

These free-swimming mollusks are fairly aggressive. They are more feared than sharks in some locales.

Combat

Improved Grab (Ex): To use this ability, a squid must hit an opponent of any size with its arms attack. It can then attempt to start a grapple as a free action without provoking an attack of opportunity. If it wins the grapple check, it establishes a hold and automatically deals bite damage.

*A squid has a +4 racial bonus on grapple checks.

Ink Cloud (Ex): A squid can emit a cloud of jet-black ink 10 feet high by 10 feet wide by 10 feet long once per minute as a free action. The cloud provides total concealment, which the squid normally uses to escape a losing fight. All vision within the cloud is obscured.

Jet (Ex): A squid can jet backward once per round as a full-round action, at a speed of 240 feet. It must move in a straight line, but does not provoke attacks of opportunity while jetting.

Skills: A squid has a +8 racial bonus on any Swim check to perform some special action or avoid a hazard. It can always choose to take 10 on a Swim check, even if distracted or endangered. It can use the run action while swimming, provided it swims in a straight line

SQUID, GIANT

Huge Animal (Aquatic)
Hit Dice: 12d8+18 (72 hp)
Initiative: +3
Speed: Swim 80 ft. (16 squares)
Armor Class: 17 (–2 size, +3 Dex, +6 natural), touch 11, flat-footed 14
Base Attack/Grapple: +9/+29
Attack: Tentacle +15 melee (1d6+8)
Full Attack: 10 tentacles +15 melee (1d6+8) and bite +10 melee (2d8+4)
Space/Reach: 15 ft./15 ft. (30 ft. with tentacle)
Special Attacks: Constrict 1d6+8, improved grab
Special Qualities: Ink cloud, jet, low-light vision
Saves: Fort +9, Ref +11, Will +5
Abilities: Str 26, Dex 17, Con 13, Int 1, Wis 12, Cha 2
Skills: Listen +10, Spot +11, Swim +16
Feats: Alertness, Diehard, Endurance, Toughness (2)
Environment: Temperate aquatic
Organization: Solitary
Challenge Rating: 9
Advancement: 13–18 HD (Huge); 19–36 HD (Gargantuan)
Level Adjustment: —

These voracious creatures can have bodies more than 20 feet long and attack almost anything they meet.

Combat

An opponent can attack a giant squid's tentacles with a sunder attempt as if they were weapons. A giant squid's tentacles have 10 hit points each. If a giant squid is currently grappling a target with the tentacle that is being attacked, it usually uses another limb to make its attack of opportunity against the opponent making the sunder attempt. Severing one of a giant squid's tentacles deals 5 points of damage to the creature. A giant squid usually withdraws from combat if it loses five tentacles. The creature regrows severed limbs in 1d10+10 days.

Constrict (Ex): A giant squid deals 1d6+8 points of damage with a successful grapple check.

Improved Grab (Ex): To use this ability, a giant squid must hit an opponent of any size with a tentacle attack. It can then attempt to start a grapple as a free action without provoking an attack of opportunity. If it wins the grapple check, it establishes a hold and can constrict.

*A giant squid has a +4 racial bonus on grapple checks.

Ink Cloud (Ex): A giant squid can emit a cloud of jet-black ink 20 feet high by 20 feet wide by 20 feet long once per minute as a free action. The cloud provides total concealment, which the squid normally uses to escape a losing fight. All vision within the cloud is obscured.

Jet (Ex): A giant squid can jet backward once per round as a full-round action, at a speed of 320 feet. It must move in a straight line, but does not provoke attacks of opportunity while jetting.

Skills: A giant squid has a +8 racial bonus on any Swim check to perform some special action or avoid a hazard. It can always choose to take 10 on a Swim check, even if distracted or endangered. It can use the run action while swimming, provided it swims in a straight line.

TIGER

Large Animal
Hit Dice: 6d8+18 (45 hp)
Initiative: +2
Speed: 40 ft. (8 squares)
Armor Class: 14 (–1 size, +2 Dex, +3 natural), touch 11, flat-footed 12
Base Attack/Grapple: +4/+14

Attack: Claw +9 melee (1d8+6)

Full Attack: 2 claws +9 melee (1d8+6) and bite +4 melee (2d6+3)

Space/Reach: 10 ft./5 ft.

Special Attacks: Improved grab, pounce, rake 1d8+3

Special Qualities: Low-light vision, scent

Saves: Fort +8, Ref +7, Will +3

Abilities: Str 23, Dex 15, Con 17, Int 2, Wis 12, Cha 6

Skills: Balance +6, Hide +3*, Listen +3, Move Silently +9, Spot +3, Swim +11

Feats: Alertness, Improved Natural Attack (bite), Improved Natural Attack (claw)

Environment: Warm forests

Organization: Solitary

Challenge Rating: 4

Advancement: 7–12 HD (Large); 13–18 HD (Huge)

Level Adjustment: —

These great cats stand more than 3 feet tall at the shoulder and are about 9 feet long. They weigh from 400 to 600 pounds.

Combat

Improved Grab (Ex): To use this ability, a tiger must hit with a claw or bite attack. It can then attempt to start a grapple as a free action without provoking an attack of opportunity. If it wins the grapple check, it establishes a hold and can rake.

Pounce (Ex): If a tiger charges a foe, it can make a full attack, including two rake attacks.

Rake (Ex): Attack bonus +9 melee, damage 1d8+3.

Skills: Tigers have a +4 racial bonus on Balance, Hide, and Move Silently checks. *In areas of tall grass or heavy undergrowth, the Hide bonus improves to +8.

TOAD

Diminutive Animal

Hit Dice: 1/4 d8 (1 hp)

Initiative: +1

Speed: 5 ft. (1 square)

Armor Class: 15 (+4 size, +1 Dex), touch 15, flat-footed 14

Base Attack/Grapple: +0/−17

Attack: —

Full Attack: —

Space/Reach: 1 ft./0 ft.

Special Attacks: —

Special Qualities: Amphibious, low-light vision

Saves: Fort +2, Ref +3, Will +2

Abilities: Str 1, Dex 12, Con 11, Int 1, Wis 14, Cha 4

Skills: Hide +21, Listen +4, Spot +4

Feats: Alertness

Environment: Temperate marshes

Organization: Swarm (10–100)

Challenge Rating: 1/10

Advancement: —

Level Adjustment: —

These diminutive amphibians are innocuous and beneficial, since they eat insects.

Skills: A toad's coloration gives it a +4 racial bonus on Hide checks.

WEASEL

Tiny Animal

Hit Dice: 1/2 d8 (2 hp)

Initiative: +2

Speed: 20 ft. (4 squares), climb 20 ft.

Armor Class: 14 (+2 size, +2 Dex), touch 14, flat-footed 12

Base Attack/Grapple: +0/−12

Attack: Bite +4 melee (1d3−4)

Full Attack: Bite +4 melee (1d3−4)

Space/Reach: 2-1/2 ft./0 ft.

Special Attacks: Attach

Special Qualities: Low-light vision, scent

Saves: Fort +2, Ref +4, Will +1

Abilities: Str 3, Dex 15, Con 10, Int 2, Wis 12, Cha 5

Skills: Balance +10, Climb +10, Hide +11, Move Silently +8, Spot +3

Feats: Weapon Finesse

Environment: Temperate hills

Organization: Solitary

Challenge Rating: 1/4

Advancement: —

Level Adjustment: —

These little mammals are aggressive predators but usually confine themselves to smaller prey. The statistics presented here can also apply to ferrets.

Combat

Attach (Ex): If a weasel hits with a bite attack, it uses its powerful jaws to latch onto the opponent's body and automatically deals bite damage each round it remains attached. An attached weasel loses its Dexterity bonus to Armor Class and has an AC of 12.

An attached weasel can be struck with a weapon or grappled itself. To remove an attached weasel through grappling, the opponent must achieve a pin against the creature.

Skills: Weasels have a +4 racial bonus on Move Silently checks and a +8 racial bonus on Balance and Climb checks. They use their Dexterity modifier for Climb checks. A weasel can always choose to take 10 on a Climb check, even if rushed or threatened.

WHALE

Some varieties of these seagoing mammals are among the largest animals known. Relatively small whales (such as the orca presented here) can be vicious predators, attacking virtually anything they detect.

Blindsight (Ex): Whales can "see" by emitting high-frequency sounds, inaudible to most other creatures, that allow them to locate objects and creatures within 120 feet. A *silence* spell negates this and forces the whale to rely on its vision, which is approximately as good as a human's.

Hold Breath (Ex): A whale can hold its breath for a number of rounds equal to 8 × its Constitution score before it risks drowning.

Skills: A whale has a +8 racial bonus on any Swim check to perform some special action or avoid a hazard. It can always choose to take 10 on a Swim check, even if distracted or endangered. It can use the run action while swimming, provided it swims in a straight line.

*A whale has a +4 racial bonus on Spot and Listen checks. These bonuses are lost if its blindsight is negated.

Baleen Whale

Gargantuan Animal

Hit Dice: 12d8+78 (132 hp)

Initiative: +1

Speed: Swim 40 ft. (8 squares)

Armor Class: 16 (−4 size, +1 Dex, +9 natural), touch 7, flat-footed 15

Base Attack/Grapple: +9/+33

Attack: Tail slap +17 melee (1d8+18)

Full Attack: Tail slap +17 melee (1d8+18)

Space/Reach: 20 ft./15 ft.

Special Attacks: —

Special Qualities: Blindsight 120 ft., hold breath, low-light vision

Saves: Fort +14, Ref +9, Will +5

Abilities: Str 35, Dex 13, Con 22, Int 2, Wis 12, Cha 6

Skills: Listen +15*, Spot +14*, Swim +20

Feats: Alertness, Diehard, Endurance, Toughness (2)
Environment: Warm aquatic
Organization: Solitary
Challenge Rating: 6
Advancement: 13–18 HD (Gargantuan); 19–36 HD (Colossal)
Level Adjustment: —

The statistics here describe a plankton-feeding whale between 30 and 60 feet long, such as gray, humpback, and right whales.

These massive creatures are surprisingly gentle. If harassed or provoked, they are as likely to flee as they are to retaliate.

Cachalot Whale

Gargantuan Animal
Hit Dice: 12d8+87 (141 hp)
Initiative: +1
Speed: Swim 40 ft. (8 squares)
Armor Class: 16 (–4 size, +1 Dex, +9 natural), touch 7, flat-footed 15
Base Attack/Grapple: +9/+33
Attack: Bite +17 melee (4d6+12)
Full Attack: Bite +17 melee (4d6+12) and tail slap +12 melee (1d8+6)
Space/Reach: 20 ft./15 ft.
Special Attacks: —
Special Qualities: Blindsight 120 ft., hold breath, low-light vision
Saves: Fort +15, Ref +9, Will +6
Abilities: Str 35, Dex 13, Con 24, Int 2, Wis 14, Cha 6
Skills: Listen +15*, Spot +14*, Swim +20
Feats: Alertness, Diehard, Endurance, Improved Natural Attack (bite), Toughness
Environment: Temperate aquatic
Organization: Solitary or pod (6–11)
Challenge Rating: 7
Advancement: 13–18 HD (Gargantuan); 19–36 HD (Colossal)
Level Adjustment: —

Also known as sperm whales, these creatures can be up to 60 feet long. They prey on giant squids.

Orca

Huge Animal
Hit Dice: 9d8+48 (88 hp)
Initiative: +2
Speed: Swim 50 ft. (10 squares)
Armor Class: 16 (–2 size, +2 Dex, +6 natural), touch 10, flat-footed 14
Base Attack/Grapple: +6/+22
Attack: Bite +12 melee (2d6+12)
Full Attack: Bite +12 melee (2d6+12)
Space/Reach: 15 ft./10 ft.
Special Attacks: —
Special Qualities: Blindsight 120 ft., hold breath, low-light vision
Saves: Fort +11, Ref +8, Will +5
Abilities: Str 27, Dex 15, Con 21, Int 2, Wis 14, Cha 6
Skills: Listen +14*, Spot +14*, Swim +16
Feats: Alertness, Endurance, Run, Toughness
Environment: Cold aquatic
Organization: Solitary or pod (6–11)
Challenge Rating: 5
Advancement: 10–13 HD (Huge); 14–27 HD (Gargantuan)
Level Adjustment: —

These ferocious creatures are about 30 feet long. They eat fish, squid, seals, and other whales.

WOLF

Medium Animal
Hit Dice: 2d8+4 (13 hp)
Initiative: +2
Speed: 50 ft. (10 squares)
Armor Class: 14 (+2 Dex, +2 natural), touch 12, flat-footed 12
Base Attack/Grapple: +1/+2
Attack: Bite +3 melee (1d6+1)
Full Attack: Bite +3 melee (1d6+1)
Space/Reach: 5 ft./5 ft.
Special Attacks: Trip
Special Qualities: Low-light vision, scent
Saves: Fort +5, Ref +5, Will +1
Abilities: Str 13, Dex 15, Con 15, Int 2, Wis 12, Cha 6
Skills: Hide +2, Listen +3, Move Silently +3, Spot +3, Survival +1*
Feats: Track[B], Weapon Focus (bite)
Environment: Temperate forests
Organization: Solitary, pair, or pack (7–16)
Challenge Rating: 1
Advancement: 3 HD (Medium); 4–6 HD (Large)
Level Adjustment: —

Wolves are pack hunters known for their persistence and cunning.

Combat

A favorite tactic is to send a few individuals against the foe's front while the rest of the pack circles and attacks from the flanks or rear.

Trip (Ex): A wolf that hits with a bite attack can attempt to trip the opponent (+1 check modifier) as a free action without making a touch attack or provoking an attack of opportunity. If the attempt fails, the opponent cannot react to trip the wolf.

Skills: *Wolves have a +4 racial bonus on Survival checks when tracking by scent.

WOLVERINE

Medium Animal
Hit Dice: 3d8+15 (28 hp)
Initiative: +2
Speed: 30 ft. (6 squares), burrow 10 ft., climb 10 ft.
Armor Class: 14 (+2 Dex, +2 natural), touch 12, flat-footed 12
Base Attack/Grapple: +2/+4
Attack: Claw +4 melee (1d4+2)
Full Attack: 2 claws +4 melee (1d4+2) and bite –1 melee (1d6+1)
Space/Reach: 5 ft./5 ft.
Special Attacks: Rage
Special Qualities: Low-light vision, scent
Saves: Fort +7, Ref +5, Will +2
Abilities: Str 14, Dex 15, Con 19, Int 2, Wis 12, Cha 10
Skills: Climb +10, Listen +6, Spot +6
Feats: Alertness, Toughness, Track[B]
Environment: Cold forests
Organization: Solitary
Challenge Rating: 2
Advancement: 4–5 HD (Large)
Level Adjustment: —

These creatures are similar to badgers but are bigger, stronger, and even more ferocious.

COMBAT

Rage (Ex): A wolverine that takes damage in combat flies into a berserk rage on its next turn, clawing and biting madly until either it or its opponent is dead. It gains +4 to Strength, +4 to Constitution, and –2 to Armor Class. The creature cannot end its rage voluntarily.

Skills: Wolverines have a +8 racial bonus on Climb checks and can always choose to take 10 on Climb checks, even if rushed or threatened.

CHAPTER 3: VERMIN

This chapter provides statistics and basic information for several kinds of monstrous vermin. These creatures operate on instinct, driven by simple needs such as food and reproduction.

Except where noted, vermin attack only when hungry or threatened.

Vermin Traits: Vermin possess the following traits (unless otherwise noted in a creature's entry).

—Mindless: No Intelligence score, and immunity to all mind-affecting effects (charms, compulsions, phantasms, patterns, and morale effects).

—Darkvision out to 60 feet.

—Alignment: Always neutral. Vermin are not governed by a human sense of morality.

—Treasure: Vermin generally possess no treasure. For those that do, this treasure consists of possessions formerly owned by a creature that the monster has killed.

GIANT ANT

Giant ants are among the hardiest and most adaptable vermin. Soldiers and workers are about 6 feet long, while queens can grow to a length of 9 feet.

Acid Sting (Ex): A giant soldier ant has a stinger and an acid-producing gland in its abdomen. If it successfully grabs an opponent, it can attempt to sting each round (+3 attack bonus). A hit with the sting attack deals 1d4+1 points of piercing damage and 1d4 points of acid damage.

Improved Grab (Ex): To use this ability, a giant ant must hit with its bite attack. A giant soldier ant that wins the ensuing grapple check establishes a hold and can sting.

Skills: *Giant ants have a +4 racial bonus on Survival checks when tracking by scent and a +8 racial bonus on Climb checks. A giant ant can always choose to take 10 on Climb checks, even if rushed or threatened.

GIANT BEE

Medium Vermin
Hit Dice: 3d8 (13 hp)
Initiative: +2
Speed: 20 ft. (4 squares), fly 80 ft. (good)

Armor Class: 14 (+2 Dex, +2 natural), touch 12, flat-footed 12
Base Attack/Grapple: +2/+2
Attack: Sting +2 melee (1d4 plus poison)
Full Attack: Sting +2 melee (1d4 plus poison)
Space/Reach: 5 ft./5 ft.
Special Attacks: Poison
Special Qualities: Darkvision 60 ft., vermin traits
Saves: Fort +3, Ref +3, Will +2
Abilities: Str 11, Dex 14, Con 11, Int —, Wis 12, Cha 9
Skills: Spot +5, Survival +1*
Feats: —
Environment: Temperate plains
Organization: Solitary, buzz (2–5), or hive (11–20)
Challenge Rating: 1
Treasure: No coins; 1/4 goods (honey only); no items
Advancement: 4–6 HD (Medium); 7–9 HD (Large)
Level Adjustment: —

Although many times larger, growing to a length of about 5 feet, giant bees behave generally the same as their smaller cousins.

Giant bees are usually not aggressive except when defending themselves or their hive.

Poison (Ex): Injury, Fortitude DC 11, initial and secondary damage 1d4 Con. The save DC is Constitution-based.

A giant bee that successfully stings another creature pulls away, leaving its stinger in the creature. The bee then dies.

Skills: Giant bees have a +4 racial bonus on Spot checks. *They also have a +4 racial bonus on Survival checks to orient themselves.

GIANT BOMBARDIER BEETLE

Medium Vermin
Hit Dice: 2d8+4 (13 hp)
Initiative: +0
Speed: 30 ft. (6 squares)
Armor Class: 16 (+6 natural), touch 10, flat-footed 16
Base Attack/Grapple: +1/+2
Attack: Bite +2 melee (1d4+1)
Full Attack: Bite +2 melee (1d4+1)
Space/Reach: 5 ft./5 ft.
Special Attacks: Acid spray
Special Qualities: Darkvision 60 ft., vermin traits

	Giant Ant, Worker Medium Vermin	Giant Ant, Soldier Medium Vermin	Giant Ant, Queen Large Vermin
Hit Dice:	2d8 (9 hp)	2d8+2 (11 hp)	4d8+4 (22 hp)
Initiative:	+0	+0	−1
Speed:	50 ft. (10 squares), climb 20 ft.	50 ft. (10 squares), climb 20 ft.	40 ft. (8 squares)
Armor Class:	17 (+7 natural), touch 10, flat-footed 17	17 (+7 natural), touch 10, flat-footed 17	17 (−1 size, −1 Dex, +9 natural), touch 8, flat-footed 17
Base Attack/Grapple:	+1/+1	+1/+3	+3/+10
Attack:	Bite +1 melee (1d6)	Bite +3 melee (2d4+3)	Bite +5 melee (2d6+4)
Full Attack:	Bite +1 melee (1d6)	Bite +3 melee (2d4+3)	Bite +5 melee (2d6+4)
Space/Reach:	5 ft./5 ft.	5 ft./5 ft.	10 ft./5 ft.
Special Attacks:	Improved grab	Improved grab, acid sting	Improved grab
Special Qualities:	Scent, vermin traits	Scent, vermin traits	Scent, vermin traits
Saves:	Fort +3, Ref +0, Will +0	Fort +4, Ref +0, Will +1	Fort +5, Ref +0, Will +2
Abilities:	Str 10, Dex 10, Con 10, Int —, Wis 11, Cha 9	Str 14, Dex 10, Con 13, Int —, Wis 13, Cha 11	Str 16, Dex 9, Con 13, Int —, Wis 13, Cha 11
Skills:	Climb +8	Climb +10	—
Feats:	Track[B]	Track[B]	Track[B]
Environment:	Temperate plains	Temperate plains	Temperate plains
Organization:	Gang (2–6) or crew (6–11 plus 1 giant ant soldier)	Solitary or gang (2–4)	Hive (1 plus 10–100 workers and 5–20 soldiers)
Challenge Rating:	1	2	2
Treasure:	None	None	1/10 coins; 50% goods; 50% items
Advancement:	3–4 HD (Medium); 5–6 HD (Large)	3–4 HD (Medium); 5–6 HD (Large)	5–6 HD (Large); 7–8 HD (Huge)
Level Adjustment:	—	—	—

Saves: Fort +5, Ref +0, Will +0
Abilities: Str 13, Dex 10, Con 14, Int —, Wis 10, Cha 9
Skills: —
Feats: —
Environment: Warm forests
Organization: Cluster (2–5) or click (6–11)
Challenge Rating: 2
Advancement: 3–4 HD (Medium); 5–6 HD (Large)
Level Adjustment: —

These creatures feed primarily on carrion and offal, gathering heaps of the stuff in which to build nests and lay eggs. A giant bombardier beetle is about 6 feet long.

Giant bombardier beetles normally attack only to defend themselves, their nests, or their eggs.

Acid Spray (Ex): When attacked or disturbed, the creature can release a 10-foot cone of acidic vapor once per round. Those within the cone must succeed on a DC 13 Fortitude save or take 1d4+2 points of acid damage. The save DC is Constitution-based.

GIANT FIRE BEETLE

Small Vermin
Hit Dice: 1d8 (4 hp)
Initiative: +0
Speed: 30 ft. (6 squares)
Armor Class: 16 (+1 size, +5 natural), touch 11, flat-footed 16
Base Attack/Grapple: +0/−4
Attack: Bite +1 melee (2d4)
Full Attack: Bite +1 melee (2d4)
Space/Reach: 5 ft./5 ft.
Special Attacks: —
Special Qualities: Darkvision 60 ft., vermin traits
Saves: Fort +2, Ref +0, Will +0
Abilities: Str 10, Dex 11, Con 11, Int —, Wis 10, Cha 7
Skills: —
Feats: —
Environment: Warm plains
Organization: Cluster (2–5) or colony (6–11)
Challenge Rating: 1/3
Advancement: 2–3 HD (Small)
Level Adjustment: —

These luminous nocturnal insects are prized by miners and adventurers. They have two glands, one above each eye, that produce a red glow. The glands' luminosity persists for 1d6 days after removal from the beetle, illuminating a roughly circular area with a 10-foot radius. Giant fire beetles are about 2 feet long.

GIANT STAG BEETLE

Large Vermin
Hit Dice: 7d8+21 (52 hp)
Initiative: +0
Speed: 20 ft. (4 squares)
Armor Class: 19 (−1 size, +10 natural), touch 9, flat-footed 19
Base Attack/Grapple: +5/+15
Attack: Bite +10 melee (4d6+9)
Full Attack: Bite +10 melee (4d6+9)
Space/Reach: 10 ft./5 ft.
Special Attacks: Trample 2d8+3
Special Qualities: Darkvision 60 ft., vermin traits
Saves: Fort +8, Ref +2, Will +2
Abilities: Str 23, Dex 10, Con 17, Int —, Wis 10, Cha 9
Skills: —
Feats: —
Environment: Temperate forests
Organization: Cluster (2–5) or mass (6–11)
Challenge Rating: 4

Alignment: Always neutral
Advancement: 8–10 HD (Large); 11–21 HD (Huge)
Level Adjustment: —

These creatures are serious pests that greedily devour cultivated crops. A single beetle can strip an entire farm in short order. An adult giant stag beetle is about 10 feet long.

Trample (Ex): Reflex half DC 19. The save DC is Strength-based.

GIANT PRAYING MANTIS

Large Vermin
Hit Dice: 4d8+8 (26 hp)
Initiative: −1
Speed: 20 ft. (4 squares), fly 40 ft. (poor)
Armor Class: 14 (−1 size, −1 Dex, +6 natural), touch 8, flat-footed 14
Base Attack/Grapple: +3/+11
Attack: Claws +6 melee (1d8+4)
Full Attack: Claws +6 melee (1d8+4) and bite +1 melee (1d6+2)
Space/Reach: 10 ft (4 squares)./5 ft.
Special Attacks: Improved grab
Special Qualities: Darkvision 60 ft., vermin traits
Saves: Fort +6, Ref +0, Will +3
Abilities: Str 19, Dex 8, Con 15, Int —, Wis 14, Cha 11
Skills: Hide −1*, Spot +6
Feats: —
Environment: Temperate forests
Organization: Solitary
Challenge Rating: 3
Advancement: 5–8 HD (Large); 9–12 HD (Huge)
Level Adjustment: —

This patient carnivore remains completely still as it waits for prey to come near.

Improved Grab (Ex): To use this ability, a giant praying mantis must hit with its claws attack. If it wins the ensuing grapple check, it establishes a hold and makes a bite attack as a primary attack (at its full +6 attack bonus).

Skills: A giant praying mantis has a +4 racial bonus on Hide and Spot checks. *Because of its camouflage, the Hide bonus increases to +12 when a mantis is surrounded by foliage.

GIANT WASP

Large Vermin
Hit Dice: 5d8+10 (32 hp)
Initiative: +1
Speed: 20 ft. (4 squares), fly 60 ft. (good)
Armor Class: 14 (−1 size, +1 Dex, +4 natural), touch 10, flat-footed 13
Base Attack/Grapple: +3/+11
Attack: Sting +6 melee (1d3+6 plus poison)
Full Attack: Sting +6 melee (1d3+6 plus poison)
Space/Reach: 10 ft./5 ft.
Special Attacks: Poison
Special Qualities: Darkvision 60 ft., vermin traits
Saves: Fort +6, Ref +2, Will +2
Abilities: Str 18, Dex 12, Con 14, Int —, Wis 13, Cha 11
Skills: Spot +9, Survival +1*
Feats: —
Environment: Temperate forests
Organization: Solitary, swarm (2–5), or nest (11–20)
Challenge Rating: 3
Advancement: 6–8 HD (Large); 9–15 HD (Huge)
Level Adjustment: —

Giant wasps attack when hungry or threatened, stinging their prey to death. They take dead or incapacitated opponents back to their lairs as food for their unhatched young.

	Monstrous Centipede, Tiny Tiny Vermin	Monstrous Centipede, Small Small Vermin	Monstrous Centipede, Medium Medium Vermin
Hit Dice:	1/4 d8 (1 hp)	1/2 d8 (2 hp)	1d8 (4 hp)
Initiative:	+2	+2	+2
Speed:	20 ft. (4 squares), climb 20 ft.	30 ft. (6 squares), climb 30 ft..	40 ft. (8 squares), climb 40 ft.
Armor Class:	14 (+2 size, +2 Dex), touch 14, flat-footed 12	14 (+1 size, +2 Dex, +1 natural), touch 13, flat-footed 12	14 (+2 Dex, +2 natural), touch 12, flat-footed 12
Base Attack/Grapple:	+0/–13	+0/–7	+0/–1
Attack:	Bite +4 melee (1d3–5 plus poison)	Bite +3 melee (1d4–3 plus poison)	Bite +2 melee (1d6–1 plus poison)
Full Attack:	Bite +4 melee (1d3–5 plus poison)	Bite +3 melee (1d4–3 plus poison)	Bite +2 melee (1d6–1 plus poison)
Space/Reach:	2-1/2 ft./0 ft.	5 ft./5 ft.	5 ft./5 ft.
Special Attacks:	Poison	Poison	Poison
Special Qualities:	Darkvision 60 ft., vermin traits	Darkvision 60 ft., vermin traits	Darkvision 60 ft., vermin traits
Saves:	Fort +2, Ref +2, Will +0	Fort +2, Ref +2, Will +0	Fort +2, Ref +2, Will +0
Abilities:	Str 1, Dex 15, Con 10, Int —, Wis 10, Cha 2	Str 5, Dex 15, Con 10, Int —, Wis 10, Cha 2	Str 9, Dex 15, Con 10, Int —, Wis 10, Cha 2
Skills:	Climb +10, Hide +18, Spot +4	Climb +10, Hide +14, Spot +4	Climb +10, Hide +10, Spot +4
Feats:	Weapon Finesse[B]	Weapon Finesse[B]	Weapon Finesse[B]
Environment:	Underground	Underground	Underground
Organization:	Colony (8–16)	Colony (2–5) or swarm (6–11)	Solitary or colony (2–5)
Challenge Rating:	1/8	1/4	1/2
Advancement:	—	—	—
Level Adjustment:	—	—	—

	Monstrous Centipede, Large Large Vermin	Monstrous Centipede, Huge Huge Vermin
Hit Dice:	3d8 (13 hp)	6d8+6 (33 hp)
Initiative:	+2	+2
Speed:	40 ft. (8 squares), climb 40 ft.	40 ft. (8 squares), climb 40 ft.
Armor Class:	14 (–1 size, +2 Dex, +3 natural), touch 11, flat-footed 12	16 (–2 size, +2 Dex, +6 natural), touch 10, flat-footed 14
Base Attack/Grapple:	+2/+7	+4/+15
Attack:	Bite +3 melee (1d8+1 plus poison)	Bite +5 melee (2d6+4 plus poison)
Full Attack:	Bite +3 melee (1d8+1 plus poison)	Bite +5 melee (2d6+4 plus poison)
Space/Reach:	10 ft./5 ft.	15 ft./10 ft.
Special Attacks:	Poison	Poison
Special Qualities:	Darkvision 60 ft., vermin traits	Darkvision 60 ft., vermin traits
Saves:	Fort +3, Ref +3, Will +1	Fort +6, Ref +4, Will +2
Abilities:	Str 13, Dex 15, Con 10, Int —, Wis 10, Cha 2	Str 17, Dex 15, Con 12, Int —, Wis 10, Cha 2
Skills:	Climb +10, Hide +6, Spot +4	Climb +11, Hide +2, Spot +4
Feats:	Weapon Finesse[B]	—
Environment:	Underground	Underground
Organization:	Solitary or colony (2–5)	Solitary or colony (2–5)
Challenge Rating:	1	2
Advancement:	4–5 HD (Large)	7–11 HD (Huge)
Level Adjustment:	—	—

	Monstrous Centipede, Gargantuan Gargantuan Vermin	Monstrous Centipede, Colossal Colossal Vermin
Hit Dice:	12d8+12 (66 hp)	24d8+24 (132 hp)
Initiative:	+2	+1
Speed:	40 ft. (8 squares), climb 40 ft.	40 ft. (8 squares), climb 40 ft.
Armor Class:	18 (–4 size, +2 Dex, +10 natural), touch 8, flat-footed 16	20 (–8 size, +2 Dex, +16 natural), touch 4, flat-footed 18
Base Attack/Grapple:	+9/+27	+18/+42
Attack:	Bite +11 melee (2d8+9 plus poison)	Bite +18 melee (4d6+12 plus poison)
Full Attack:	Bite +11 melee (2d8+9 plus poison)	Bite +18 melee (4d6+12 plus poison)
Space/Reach:	20 ft./15 ft.	30 ft./20 ft.
Special Attacks:	Poison	Poison
Special Qualities:	Darkvision 60 ft., vermin traits	Darkvision 60 ft., vermin traits
Saves:	Fort +9, Ref +6, Will +4	Fort +15, Ref +9, Will +8
Abilities:	Str 23, Dex 15, Con 12, Int —, Wis 10, Cha 2	Str 27, Dex 13, Con 12, Int —, Wis 10, Cha 2
Skills:	Climb +14, Hide –2, Spot +4	Climb +16, Hide –7, Spot +4
Feats:	—	—
Environment:	Underground	Underground
Organization:	Solitary	Solitary
Challenge Rating:	6	9
Advancement:	17–23 HD (Gargantuan)	25–48 HD (Colossal)
Level Adjustment:	—	—

	Monstrous Scorpion, Tiny Tiny Vermin	Monstrous Scorpion, Small Small Vermin	Monstrous Scorpion, Medium Medium Vermin
Hit Dice:	1/2 d8+2 (4 hp)	1d8+2 (6 hp)	2d8+4 (13 hp)
Initiative:	+0	+0	+0
Speed:	20 ft. (4 squares)	30 ft. (6 squares)	40 ft. (8 squares)
Armor Class:	14 (+2 size, +2 natural), touch 12, flat-footed 14	14 (+1 size, +3 natural), touch 11, flat-footed 14	14 (+4 natural), touch 10, flat-footed 14
Base Attack/Grapple:	+0/−8	+0/−4	+1/+2
Attack:	Claw +2 melee (1d2−4)	Claw +1 melee (1d3−1)	Claw +2 melee (1d4+1)
Full Attack:	2 claws +2 melee (1d2−4) and sting −3 melee (1d2−4 plus poison)	2 claws +1 melee (1d3−1) and sting −4 melee (1d3−1 plus poison)	2 claws +2 melee (1d4+1) and sting −3 melee (1d4 plus poison)
Space/Reach:	2-1/2 ft./0 ft.	5 ft./5 ft.	5 ft./5 ft.
Special Attacks:	Constrict 1d2−4, improved grab, poison	Constrict 1d3−1, improved grab, poison	Constrict 1d4+1, improved grab, poison
Special Qualities:	Darkvision 60 ft., tremorsense 60 ft., vermin traits	Darkvision 60 ft., tremorsense 60 ft., vermin traits	Darkvision 60 ft., tremorsense 60 ft., vermin traits
Saves:	Fort +4, Ref +0, Will +0	Fort +4, Ref +0, Will +0	Fort +5, Ref +0, Will +0
Abilities:	Str 3, Dex 10, Con 14, Int —, Wis 10, Cha 2	Str 9, Dex 10, Con 14, Int —, Wis 10, Cha 2	Str 13, Dex 10, Con 14, Int —, Wis 10, Cha 2
Skills:	Climb +0, Hide +12, Spot +4	Climb +3, Hide +8, Spot +4	Climb +5, Hide +4, Spot +4
Feats:	Weapon Finesse[B]	Weapon Finesse[B]	—
Environment:	Warm deserts	Warm deserts	Warm deserts
Organization:	Colony (8–16)	Colony (2–5) or swarm (6–11)	Solitary or colony (2–5)
Challenge Rating:	1/4	1/2	1
Alignment:	Always neutral	Always neutral	Always neutral
Advancement:	—	—	3–4 HD (Medium)
Level Adjustment:	—	—	

	Monstrous Scorpion, Large Large Vermin	Monstrous Scorpion, Huge Huge Vermin
Hit Dice:	5d8+10 (32 hp)	10d8+30 (75 hp)
Initiative:	+0	+0
Speed:	50 ft. (10 squares)	50 ft. (10 squares)
Armor Class:	16 (−1 size, +7 natural), touch 9, flat-footed 16	20 (−2 size, +12 natural), touch 8, flat-footed 20
Base Attack/Grapple:	+3/+11	+7/+21
Attack:	Claw +6 melee (1d6+4)	Claw +11 melee (1d8+6)
Full Attack:	2 claws +6 melee (1d6+4) and sting +1 melee (1d6+2 plus poison)	2 claws +11 melee (1d8+6) and sting +6 melee (2d4+3 plus poison)
Space/Reach:	10 ft./5 ft.	15 ft./10 ft.
Special Attacks:	Constrict 1d6+4, improved grab, poison	Constrict 1d8+6, improved grab, poison
Special Qualities:	Darkvision 60 ft., tremorsense 60 ft., vermin traits	Darkvision 60 ft., tremorsense 60 ft., vermin traits
Saves:	Fort +6, Ref +1, Will +1	Fort +10, Ref +3, Will +3
Abilities:	Str 19, Dex 10, Con 14, Int —, Wis 10, Cha 2	Str 23, Dex 10, Con 16, Int —, Wis 10, Cha 2
Skills:	Climb +8, Hide +0, Spot +4	Climb +10, Hide −4, Spot +4
Feats:	—	—
Environment:	Warm deserts	Warm deserts
Organization:	Solitary or colony (2–5)	Solitary or colony (2–5)
Challenge Rating:	3	7
Treasure:	1/10 coins; 50% goods; 50% items	1/10 coins; 50% goods; 50% items
Advancement:	6–9 HD (Large)	11–19 HD (Huge)
Level Adjustment:	—	—

Poison (Ex): Injury, Fortitude DC 14, initial and secondary damage 1d6 Dex. The save DC is Constitution-based.

Skills: Giant wasps have a +8 racial bonus on Spot checks. *They also have a +4 racial bonus on Survival checks to orient themselves.

MONSTROUS CENTIPEDE

Monstrous centipedes tend to attack anything that resembles food, biting with their jaws and injecting their poison.

Size	Fort DC	Damage	Size	Fort DC	Damage
Tiny	10	1 Dex	Huge	14	1d6 Dex
Small	10	1d2 Dex	Gargantuan	17	1d8 Dex
Medium	10	1d3 Dex	Colossal	23	2d6 Dex
Large	11	1d4 Dex			

Poison (Ex): A monstrous centipede has a poisonous bite. The details vary by the centipede's size, as shown on the table above. The save DCs are Constitution-based. The indicated damage is both initial and secondary damage.

Skills: Monstrous centipedes have a +4 racial bonus on Spot checks, and a +8 racial bonus on Climb and Hide checks. They can use either their Strength or Dexterity modifier for Climb checks, whichever is higher. Monstrous scorpions can take 10 on Climb checks, even if threatened or distracted.

MONSTROUS SCORPION

Monstrous scorpions are likely to attack any creature that approaches, and they usually charge when attacking prey.

Constrict (Ex): A monstrous scorpion deals automatic claw damage on a successful grapple check.

Improved Grab (Ex): To use this ability, a monstrous scorpion must hit with a claw attack. A monstrous scorpion can use either its Strength modifier or Dexterity modifier for grapple checks, whichever is better.

	Monstrous Scorpion, Gargantuan Gargantuan Vermin	Monstrous Scorpion, Colossal Colossal Vermin
Hit Dice:	20d8+60 (150 hp)	40d8+120 (300 hp)
Initiative:	+0	−1
Speed:	50 ft. (10 squares)	50 ft. (10 squares)
Armor Class:	24 (−4 size, +18 natural), touch 6, flat-footed 24	26 (−8 size, −1 Dex, +25 natural), touch 1, flat-footed 26
Base Attack/Grapple:	+15/+37	+30/+58
Attack:	Claw +21 melee (2d6+10)	Claw +34 melee (2d8+12)
Full Attack:	2 claws +21 melee (2d6+10) and sting +16 melee (2d6+5 plus poison)	2 claws +34 melee (2d8+12) and sting +29 melee (2d8+6 plus poison)
Space/Reach:	20 ft./15 ft.	40 ft./30 ft.
Special Attacks:	Constrict 2d6+10, improved grab, poison	Constrict 2d8+12, improved grab, poison
Special Qualities:	Darkvision 60 ft., tremorsense 60 ft., vermin traits	Darkvision 60 ft., tremorsense 60 ft., vermin traits
Saves:	Fort +15, Ref +6, Will +6	Fort +25, Ref +12, Will +13
Abilities:	Str 31, Dex 10, Con 16, Int —, Wis 10, Cha 2	Str 35, Dex 8, Con 16, Int —, Wis 10, Cha 2
Skills:	Climb +14, Hide −8, Spot +4	Climb +16, Hide −12, Spot +4
Feats:	—	
Environment:	Warm deserts	Warm deserts
Organization:	Solitary	Solitary
Challenge Rating:	10	12
Treasure:	1/10 coins; 50% goods; 50% items	1/10 coins; 50% goods; 50% items
Advancement:	21–39 HD (Gargantuan)	41–60 HD (Colossal)
Level Adjustment:	—	

Poison (Ex): A monstrous scorpion has a poisonous sting. The details vary by the scorpion's size, as follows. The save DCs are Constitution-based. The indicated damage is initial and secondary damage.

Size	Fort DC	Damage	Size	Fort DC	Damage
Tiny	12	1 Con	Huge	18	1d6 Con
Small	12	1d2 Con	Gargantuan	23	1d8 Con
Medium	13	1d3 Con	Colossal	33	1d10 Con
Large	14	1d4 Con			

Skills: A monstrous scorpion has a +4 racial bonus on Climb, Hide, and Spot checks.

MONSTROUS SPIDER

All monstrous spiders are aggressive predators that use their poisonous bites to subdue or kill prey.

Monstrous spiders come in two general types: hunters and web-spinners. Hunters rove about, while web-spinners usually attempt to trap prey. Hunting spiders can spin webs to use as lairs, but cannot use their webs as weapons the way web-spinners can. A hunting spider has a base land speed 10 feet faster than the figures given in the statistics blocks.

Poison (Ex): A monstrous spider has a poisonous bite. The details vary by the spider's size, as shown on the table below. The save DCs are Constitution-based. The indicated damage is initial and secondary damage.

Size	Fort DC	Damage	Size	Fort DC	Damage
Tiny	10	1d2 Str	Huge	16	1d8 Str
Small	10	1d3 Str	Gargantuan	20	2d6 Str
Medium	12	1d4 Str	Colossal	28	2d8 Str
Large	13	1d6 Str			

Web (Ex): Both types of monstrous spiders often wait in their webs or in trees, then lower themselves silently on silk strands and leap onto prey passing beneath. A single strand is strong

	Monstrous Spider, Tiny Tiny Vermin	Monstrous Spider, Small Small Vermin	Monstrous Spider, Medium Medium Vermin
Hit Dice:	1/2 d8 (2 hp)	1d8 (4 hp)	2d8+2 (11 hp)
Initiative:	+3	+3	+3
Speed:	20 ft. (4 squares), climb 10 ft.	30 ft. (6 squares), climb 20 ft.	30 ft. (6 squares), climb 20 ft.
Armor Class:	15 (+2 size, +3 Dex), touch 15, flat-footed 12	14 (+1 size, +3 Dex), touch 14, flat-footed 11	14 (+3 Dex, +1 natural), touch 13, flat-footed 11
Base Attack/Grapple:	+0/−12	+0/−6	+1/+1
Attack:	Bite +5 melee (1d3−4 plus poison)	Bite +4 melee (1d4−2 plus poison)	Bite +4 melee (1d6 plus poison)
Full Attack:	Bite +5 melee (1d3−4 plus poison)	Bite +4 melee (1d4−2 plus poison)	Bite +4 melee (1d6 plus poison)
Space/Reach:	2-1/2 ft./0 ft.	5 ft./5 ft.	5 ft./5 ft.
Special Attacks:	Poison, web	Poison, web	Poison, web
Special Qualities:	Darkvision 60 ft., tremorsense 60 ft., vermin traits	Darkvision 60 ft., tremorsense 60 ft., vermin traits	Darkvision 60 ft., tremorsense 60 ft., vermin traits
Saves:	Fort +2, Ref +3, Will +0	Fort +2, Ref +3, Will +0	Fort +4, Ref +3, Will +0
Abilities:	Str 3, Dex 17, Con 10, Int —, Wis 10, Cha 2	Str 7, Dex 17, Con 10, Int —, Wis 10, Cha 2	Str 11, Dex 17, Con 12, Int —, Wis 10, Cha 2
Skills:	Climb +11, Hide +15*, Jump −4*, Spot +4*	Climb +11, Hide +11*, Jump −2*, Spot +4*	Climb +11, Hide +7*, Jump +0*, Spot +4*
Feats:	Weapon Finesse[B]	Weapon Finesse[B]	Weapon Finesse[B]
Environment:	Temperate forests	Temperate forests	Temperate forests
Organization:	Colony (8–16)	Colony (2–5) or swarm (6–11)	Solitary or colony (2–5)
Challenge Rating:	1/4	1/2	1
Treasure:	None	None	1/10 coins; 50% goods; 50% items
Advancement:	—	—	3 HD (Medium)
Level Adjustment:	—	—	—

enough to support the spider and one creature of the same size.

Web-spinners can throw a web eight times per day. This is similar to an attack with a net but has a maximum range of 50 feet, with a range increment of 10 feet, and is effective against targets up to one size category larger than the spider.

An entangled creature can escape with a successful Escape Artist check or burst it with a Strength check. Both are standard actions whose DCs are given in the table below. The check DCs are Constitution-based, and the Strength check DC includes a +4 racial bonus.

Web-spinners often create sheets of sticky webbing from 5 to 60 feet square, depending on the size of the spider. They usually position these sheets to snare flying creatures but can also try to trap prey on the ground. Approaching creatures must succeed on a DC 20 Spot check to notice a web; otherwise they stumble into it and become trapped as though by a successful web attack. Attempts to escape or burst the webbing gain a +5 bonus if the trapped creature has something to walk on or grab while pulling free. Each 5-foot section has the hit points given on the table, and sheet webs have damage reduction 5/—.

A monstrous spider can move across its own web at its climb speed and can pinpoint the location of any creature touching its web.

Size	Escape Artist DC	Break DC	Hit Points
Tiny	10	14	2
Small	10	14	4
Medium	12	16	6
Large	13	17	12
Huge	16	20	14
Gargantuan	20	24	16
Colossal	28	32	18

Tremorsense (Ex): A monstrous spider can detect and pinpoint any creature or object within 60 feet in contact with the ground, or within any range in contact with the spider's webs.

Skills: Monstrous spiders have a +4 racial bonus on Hide and Spot checks and a +8 racial bonus on Climb checks. A monstrous spider can always choose to take 10 on Climb checks, even if rushed or threatened. Monstrous spiders use either their Strength or Dexterity modifier for Climb checks, whichever is higher.

*Hunting spiders have a +10 racial bonus on Jump checks and a +8 racial bonus on Spot checks. Web-spinning spiders have a +8 racial bonus on Hide and Move Silently checks when using their webs.

	Monstrous Spider, Large Large Vermin	Monstrous Spider, Huge Huge Vermin
Hit Dice:	4d8+4 (22 hp)	8d8+16 (52 hp)
Initiative:	+3	+3
Speed:	30 ft. (6 squares), climb 20 ft.	30 ft. (6 squares), climb 20 ft.
Armor Class:	14 (−1 size, +3 Dex, +2 natural), touch 12, flat-footed 11	16 (−2 size, +3 Dex, +5 natural), touch 11, flat-footed 13
Base Attack/Grapple:	+3/+9	+6/+18
Attack:	Bite +4 melee (1d8+3 plus poison)	Bite +9 melee (2d6+6 plus poison)
Full Attack:	Bite +4 melee (1d8+3 plus poison)	Bite +9 melee (2d6+6 plus poison)
Space/Reach:	10 ft./5 ft.	15 ft./10 ft.
Special Attacks:	Poison, web	Poison, web
Special Qualities:	Darkvision 60 ft., tremorsense 60 ft., vermin traits	Darkvision 60 ft., tremorsense 60 ft., vermin traits
Saves:	Fort +5, Ref +4, Will +1	Fort +8, Ref +5, Will +2
Abilities:	Str 15, Dex 17, Con 12, Int —, Wis 10, Cha 2	Str 19, Dex 17, Con 14, Int —, Wis 10, Cha 2
Skills:	Climb +11, Hide +3*, Jump +2*, Spot +4*	Climb +12, Hide −1*, Jump +4*, Spot +4*
Feats:	—	—
Environment:	Temperate forests	Temperate forests
Organization:	Solitary or colony (2–5)	Solitary or colony (2–5)
Challenge Rating:	2	5
Treasure:	1/10 coins; 50% goods; 50% items	1/10 coins; 50% goods; 50% items
Advancement:	5–7 HD (Large)	9–15 HD (Huge)
Level Adjustment:	—	—

	Monstrous Spider, Gargantuan Gargantuan Vermin	Monstrous Spider, Colossal Colossal Vermin
Hit Dice:	16d8+32 (104 hp)	32d8+64 (208 hp)
Initiative:	+3	+2
Speed:	30 ft. (6 squares), climb 20 ft.	30 ft. (6 squares), climb 20 ft.
Armor Class:	19 (−4 size, +3 Dex, +10 natural), touch 9, flat-footed 16	22 (−8 size, +2 Dex, +18 natural), touch 4, flat-footed 20
Base Attack/Grapple:	+12/+31	+24/+50
Attack:	Bite +15 melee (2d8+10 plus poison)	Bite +26 melee (4d6+15 plus poison)
Full Attack:	Bite +15 melee (2d8+10 plus poison)	Bite +26 melee (4d6+15 plus poison)
Space/Reach:	20 ft./15 ft.	40 ft./30 ft.
Special Attacks:	Poison, web	Poison, web
Special Qualities:	Darkvision 60 ft., tremorsense 60 ft., vermin traits	Darkvision 60 ft., tremorsense 60 ft., vermin traits
Saves:	Fort +12, Ref +8, Will +5	Fort +20, Ref +12, Will +10
Abilities:	Str 25, Dex 17, Con 14, Int —, Wis 10, Cha 2	Str 31, Dex 15, Con 14, Int —, Wis 10, Cha 2
Skills:	Climb +14, Hide −5*, Jump +7*, Spot +4*	Climb +16, Hide −10*, Jump +10*, Spot +7*
Feats:	—	—
Environment:	Temperate forests	Temperate forests
Organization:	Solitary	Solitary
Challenge Rating:	8	11
Treasure:	1/10 coins; 50% goods; 50% items	1/10 coins; 50% goods; 50% items
Advancement:	17–31 HD (Gargantuan)	33–60 HD (Colossal)
Level Adjustment:	—	—

CHAPTER 4: IMPROVING MONSTERS

Each of the monster entries in Chapters 1 through 3 describes a typical creature of its kind. However, there are several methods by which extraordinary or unique monsters can be created using a typical creature as the foundation: by adding character classes, increasing a monster's Hit Dice, or by adding a template to a monster. These methods are not mutually exclusive—it's possible for a monster with a template (a half-dragon lammasu, for example) to be improved by both increasing its Hit Dice and adding character class levels.

Class Levels: Intelligent creatures that are reasonably humanoid in shape most commonly advance by adding class levels. Creatures that fall into this category have an entry of "By character class" in their Advancement line. When a monster adds a class level, that level usually represents an increase in experience and learned skills and capabilities.

Increased Hit Dice: Intelligent creatures that are not humanoid in shape, and nonintelligent monsters, can advance by increasing their Hit Dice. Creatures with increased Hit Dice are usually superior specimens of their race, bigger and more powerful than their run-of-the-mill fellows.

Templates: Both intelligent and nonintelligent creatures with an unusual heritage (such as draconic or fiendish blood) or an inflicted change in their essential nature (undeath or lycanthropy) may be modified with a template. Templates usually result in tougher monsters with capabilities that differ from those of their common kin.

Each of these three methods for improving monsters is discussed in more detail below.

ABILITY SCORE ARRAYS

Monsters are assumed to have completely average (or standard) ability scores—a 10 or an 11 in each ability, as modified by their racial bonuses. However, improved monsters are individuals and often have better than normal ability scores, and usually make use of either the elite array or the nonelite array of ability scores.

Monsters who improve by adding a template, and monsters who improve by increasing their Hit Dice, may use any of the three arrays (standard, nonelite, or elite). Any monster unique enough to be improved could easily be considered elite.

Elite Array: The elite array is 15, 14, 13, 12, 10, 8. These numbers result in modifying the standard scores by +4, +4, +2, +2, +0, and −2. While the monster has one weakness compared to a typical member of its race, it is significantly better overall. The elite array is most appropriate for monsters who add levels in a player character class. A player who wants to play a monster out of this book as a player character but doesn't want to roll its ability scores should use the elite array.

Nonelite Array: The nonelite array is 13, 12, 11, 10, 9, 8. These numbers result in modifying the standard scores by +2, +2, +0, +0, −2, and −2. The nonelite array does not necessarily make a monster better than normal, but it does customize the monster as an individual with strengths and weaknesses compared to a typical member of its race. The nonelite array is most appropriate for monsters who add class levels in a NPC class such as warrior or adept.

Ability Score Improvement: Whenever a monster reaches a number of Hit Dice divisible by 4, it improves one ability score by 1 point. For example, a lammasu of 7 Hit Dice increased to 14 Hit Dice gains an ability score improvement at 8 HD and another one at 12 HD. Monsters do not gain ability score increases for levels they "already reached" with their racial Hit Dice, since these adjustments are included in their basic ability scores.

MONSTERS AND CLASS LEVELS

If a creature acquires a character class, it follows the rules for multiclass characters described on pages 59–60 of the *Player's Handbook*. The creature's Hit Dice equal the number of class levels it has plus its racial Hit Dice. For example, an ogre normally has 4 HD. If it picks up one level of barbarian, it becomes a creature of 5 Hit Dice: 4d8 HD for its ogre levels, plus 1d12 HD for its barbarian level. A creature's "monster class" is always a favored class, and the creature never takes XP penalties for having it. Additional Hit Dice gained from taking levels in a character class never affect a creature's size.

Humanoids and Class Levels: Creatures with 1 or less HD replace their monster levels with their character levels. For example, a goblin sorcerer loses its humanoid attack bonus, saving throw bonuses, skills, and feats, and gains the attack bonus, save bonuses, skills, feats, and other class abilities of a 1st-level sorcerer.

Level Adjustment and Effective Character Level: To determine the effective character level (ECL) of a monster character, add its level adjustment to its racial Hit Dice and character class levels. The monster is considered to have experience points equal to the minimum needed to be a character of its ECL. For example, a 4th-level minotaur barbarian has an ECL of 12 (6 for its minotaur HD, 4 for its class levels, and 2 for its level adjustment). As the equivalent of a 12th-level character, it has 66,000 XP, and must reach a total of 78,000 XP to become 13th level and add another class level.

TABLE 4–1: CREATURE IMPROVEMENT BY TYPE

	Hit Die	Attack Bonus	Good Saving Throws	Skill Points*
Aberration	d8	HD ×3/4 (as cleric)	Will	2 + Int mod per HD
Animal	d8	HD ×3/4 (as cleric)	Fort, Ref (and sometimes Will)	2 + Int mod per HD
Construct	d10	HD ×3/4 (as cleric)	—	2 + Int mod per HD**
Dragon	d12	HD (as fighter)	Fort, Ref, Will	6 + Int mod per HD
Elemental	d8	HD ×3/4 (as cleric)	Ref (Air, Fire), or Fort (Earth, Water)	2 + Int mod per HD
Fey	d6	HD ×1/2 (as wizard)	Ref, Will	6 + Int mod per HD
Giant	d8	HD ×3/4 (as cleric)	Fort	2 + Int mod per HD
Humanoid	d8	HD ×3/4 (as cleric)	Varies (any one)	2 + Int mod per HD
Magical beast	d10	HD (as fighter)	Fort, Ref	2 + Int mod per HD
Monstrous humanoid	d8	HD (as fighter)	Ref, Will	2 + Int mod per HD
Ooze	d10	HD ×3/4 (as cleric)	—	2 + Int mod per HD**
Outsider	d8	HD (as fighter)	Fort, Ref, Will	8 + Int mod per HD
Plant	d8	HD ×3/4 (as cleric)	Fort	2 + Int mod per HD**
Undead	d12	HD ×1/2 (as wizard)	Will	4 + Int mod per HD**
Vermin	d8	HD ×3/4 (as cleric)	Fort	2 + Int mod per HD**

All types have a number of feats equal to 1 + 1 per 3 Hit Dice.

* As long as a creature has an Intelligence of at least 1, it gains a minimum of 1 skill point per Hit Die.

** Creatures with an Intelligence score of "—" gain no skill points or feats.

If you choose to equip a monster with gear, use its ECL as its character level for purposes of determining how much equipment it can purchase. Generally, only monsters with an Advancement entry of "By character class" receive NPC gear; other creatures adding character levels should be treated as monsters of the appropriate CR and assigned treasure, not equipment.

Feat Acquisition and Ability Score Increases: A monster's total Hit Dice, not its ECL, govern its acquisition of feats and ability score increases. For example, a 1st-level minotaur barbarian has a total of 7 HD. It has three feats (for its 1st, 3rd, and 6th HD). When it gains 2nd level as a barbarian, it becomes a creature of 8 Hit Dice and improves one ability score by 1 point. When it adds its 3rd level of barbarian, the minotaur becomes a creature of 9 Hit Dice and gains its fourth feat.

INCREASING HIT DICE

As its Hit Dice increase, a creature's attack bonuses and saving throw modifiers might improve. It gains more feats and skills, depending on its type, as shown on Table 4–1.

Saving throw bonuses are given on Table 3–1: Base Save and Base Attack Bonuses, page 22 of the *Player's Handbook*. A "good" saving throw uses the higher of the listed values.

Note that if a creature acquires a character class, it improves according to its class, not its type.

See the sidebar on page 292 for an example of how to adjust the statistics for a creature whose Hit Dice have been increased.

SIZE INCREASES

A creature may become larger when its Hit Dice are increased (the new size is noted parenthetically in the monster's Advancement entry).

A size increase affects any special ability the creature has that is affected by size, such as improved grab. Increased size also affects a creature's ability scores, AC, attack bonuses, and damage values as indicated on Tables 4–2 and 4–3.

TABLE 4–2: CHANGES TO STATISTICS BY SIZE

Old Size*	New Size	Str	Dex	Con	Natural Armor	AC/ Attack
Fine	Diminutive	Same	–2	Same	Same	–4
Diminutive	Tiny	+2	–2	Same	Same	–2
Tiny	Small	+4	–2	Same	Same	–1
Small	Medium	+4	–2	+2	Same	–1
Medium	Large	+8	–2	+4	+2	–1
Large	Huge	+8	–2	+4	+3	–1
Huge	Gargantuan	+8	Same	+4	+4	–2
Gargantuan	Colossal	+8	Same	+4	+5	–4

*-Repeat the adjustment if the creature moves up more than one size. For example, if a creature advances from Medium to Huge size, it gains +16 to Strength, –4 to Dexterity, and –2 to attack bonus and Armor Class.

TABLE 4–3: INCREASED DAMAGE BY SIZE

Old Damage (Each)*	New Damage
1d2	1d3
1d3	1d4
1d4	1d6
1d6	1d8
1d8	2d6
1d10	2d8
2d6	3d6
2d8	3d8

* Repeat the adjustment if the creature moves up more than one size category. For example, if a Medium creature with two claw attacks dealing 1d4 points of damage each advances from Medium to Huge, the damage dealt by each of its claw attacks increases to 1d8.

TEMPLATES

Certain creatures are created by adding a template to an existing creature. A templated creature can represent a freak of nature, the individual creation of a single experimenter, or the first generation of offspring from parents of different species.

ACQUIRED AND INHERITED TEMPLATES

Some templates can be added to creatures anytime. A monster or character may become a ghost after death. A spellcaster of at least 11th level can become a lich. Those with 5 or more HD killed by vampires may become vampires. Templates such as these are referred to as acquired templates, indicating that the creature did not always have the attributes of the template.

Other templates, known as inherited templates, are part of a creature from the beginning of its existence. Examples include the celestial, fiendish, half-celestial, half-dragon, and half-fiend templates—all assume the creature was born with the template.

It's possible for a certain kind of template to be of either type. The lycanthrope template, for instance, is inherited for a creature that was born with the affliction. It can also be acquired by a creature that is bitten by a natural lycanthrope.

READING A TEMPLATE

A template's description provides a set of instructions for altering an existing creature, known as the base creature.

The changes that a template might cause to each line of a creature's statistics block are discussed below. Generally, if a template does not cause a change to a certain statistic, that entry is missing from the template description. For clarity, the entry for a statistic or attribute that is not changed is sometimes given as "Same as the base creature."

Size and Type: Templates often change a creature's type, and may change the creature's size.

If a template changes the base creature's type, the creature also acquires the augmented subtype (see page 306) unless the template description indicates otherwise. The augmented subtype is always paired with the creature's original type. For example, a unicorn with the half-celestial template is an outsider with the augmented magical beast subtype. Unless a template indicates otherwise, the new creature has the traits of the new type but the features of the original type. The example half-celestial unicorn has outsider traits (darkvision out to 60 feet, no soul) and magical beast features (10-sided Hit Dice, base attack bonus equal to total Hit Dice, good Fortitude and Reflex saves, and so on).

If a template changes a creature's size, use Table 4–2 to calculate changes to natural armor, Armor Class, attack rolls, and grapple bonus.

Hit Dice and Hit Points: Most templates do not change the number of Hit Dice a monster has, but some do.

Some templates change the size of a creature's Hit Dice (usually by changing the creature type). A few templates change previously acquired Hit Dice, and continue to change Hit Dice gained with class levels, but most templates that change Hit Dice change only the creature's original HD and leave class Hit Dice unchanged.

If the Hit Dice entry in a template description is missing, Hit Dice and hit points do not change unless the creature's Constitution modifier changes.

Initiative: If a template changes the monster's Dexterity, or if it adds or removes the Improved Initiative feat, this entry changes.

Speed: If a template modifies a creature's speed, the template states how that happens. More commonly, a template adds a new movement mode, such as a fly speed.

Armor Class: If a template changes the creature's size, see Table 4–2 to determine its new Armor Class and to see whether its natural armor changes. In some cases, such as with the ghost template, the method of determining Armor Class changes radically; the template description explains how to adjust the creature's AC.

Base Attack/Grapple: Templates usually do not change a creature's base attack bonus. If a template modifies a creature's base attack bonus, the template description states how that happens. Changes to a creature's Strength score can change a creature's grapple bonus, as can changes to its size; see Table 7–1, page 314.

Attack and Full Attack: Most templates do not change a creature's attack bonus or modes of attack, even when the creature's type changes (the creature's base attack bonus is the same as a creature of the original type). Of course, any change in ability scores may affect attack bonuses. If Strength or Dexterity changes, use the new modifier to determine attack bonuses. A change in a monster's size also changes its attack bonus; see Table 4–2.

Damage: Damage changes with Strength. If the creature uses a two-handed weapon or has a single natural weapon, it adds 1-1/2 times its Strength bonus to the damage. If it has more than a single attack, such as a character with two weapons or a monster with claws and a bite, then it adds its Strength bonus to damage rolls for the primary attack and 1/2 its Strength bonus to all secondary attacks.

Space/Reach: A template may change this entry if it changes the monster's size. The typical space and reach for monsters of each size is given on Table 7–1: Creature Sizes (page 314). Note that this table does not take into account special situations such as a roper's strands.

Special Attacks: A template may add or remove special attacks. The template description gives the details of any special attacks a template provides, including how to determine saving throw DCs, if applicable.

Special Qualities: A template may add or remove special qualities. The template description gives the details of any special qualities a template provides, including how to determine saving throw DCs, if applicable. Even if the special qualities entry is missing from a template description, the creature still gains any qualities associated with its new type (see Chapter 7: Glossary).

Base Saves: As with attacks, changing a monster's type does not always change its base saving throw bonuses. You only need to adjust them for new modifiers for Constitution, Dexterity, or

EXAMPLE OF MONSTER ADVANCEMENT

An otyugh is a Large aberration with an advancement of 7–8 HD (Large) and 9–18 HD (Huge). Creating a more powerful otyugh with 15 HD requires the following adjustments.

ADVANCING AN OTYUGH FROM 6 HD TO 15 HD

	Old Statistics	New Statistics	Notes
Size/Type:	Large Aberration	Huge Aberration	New size due to 15 HD.
Hit Dice:	6d8+9 (36 hp)	15d8+48 (115 hp)	Constitution increases from 13 to 17 for becoming Huge. The otyugh keeps its Toughness feat.
Initiative:	+0	+3	Dexterity decreases from 10 to 8 for becoming Huge; Improved Initiative added as a new feat (one of two from gaining +9 HD).
Speed:	20 ft. (4 squares)	20 ft. (4 squares)	No change.
Armor Class:	17 (–1 size, +8 natural), touch 9, flat-footed 17	19 (–2 size, –1 Dex, +12 natural), touch 7, flat-footed 19	Natural armor increases by +4 for becoming Huge, but size modifier reduces AC –1.
Base Attack/Grapple:	+4/+8	+11/+23	Base attack bonus for a 15 HD aberration is +11. For grapple bonus add + 4 (Strength 19), +8 (Huge size).
Attack:	Tentacle +4 melee (1d6)	Tentacle +14 melee (1d8+4)	Base attack bonus for a 15 HD aberration is +11 + 4 (Strength 19) –2 (Huge size), for a primary attack bonus of +13. The otyugh keeps its Weapon Focus feat. The size increase improves the damage die from d6 to d8, and Strength 19 adds a +4 bonus to damage rolls.
Full Attack:	2 tentacles +4 melee (1d6), bite –2 melee bite –2 melee (1d4)	2 tentacles +14 melee (1d8+4), bite +11 melee (1d6+2)	As above. The otyugh added the Multiattack feat, so its secondary bite attack is at –2 instead of –5. The size increase improves the bite damage from 1d4 to 1d6, and the otyugh adds half its Strength bonus to the secondary attack.
Space/Reach:	10 ft./10 ft. (15 ft. with tentacle)	15 ft./15 ft. (25 ft. with tentacle)	Increased space and reach for Huge size.
Special Attacks:	Constrict (1d6), disease, improved grab	Constrict (1d8+4), disease, improved grab	The otyugh can grab and constrict creatures of up to Large size; thanks to the otyugh's increased Hit Dice and Constitution, the save DC against its disease is now 20.
Special Qualities:	Scent	Scent	No change.
Saves:	Fort +3, Ref +2, Will +6	Fort +10, Ref +4, Will +10	At 15 HD, normal saves have a +5 bonus and good saves have a +9 bonus, adjusted for ability scores. The otyugh added the Great Fortitude feat.
Abilities:	Str 11, Dex 10, Con 13, Int 5, Wis 12, Cha 6	Str 19, Dex 8, Con 17, Int 5, Wis 12, Cha 6	Strength increases by +8, Dexterity decreases by –2, Constitution increases by +4.
Skills:	Hide –1*, Listen +6, Spot +6	Hide –3*, Listen +9, Spot +9	Adding 9 HD raises maximum skill rank to 18 and adds 9 skill points. (+3 to Hide, +3 to Listen, +3 to Spot). Hide skill size penalty increases from –4 to –8 because of Huge size. Skill scores adjusted for ability scores.
Feats:	Alertness, Toughness, Weapon Focus (tentacle)	Alertness, Great Fortitude, Improved Initiative, Multiattack, Toughness, Weapon Focus (tentacle)	Increasing from 6 to 15 HD gives the otyugh six feats instead of three. Added Great Fortitude, Improved Initiative, and Multiattack.

Wisdom. A template may, however, state that a monster has a different "good" saving throw—see Table 4-1.

Abilities: If a template changes one or more ability scores, these changes are noted here.

Skills: As with attacks, changing a monster's type does not always change its skill points. Most templates don't change the number of Hit Dice a creature has, so you don't need to adjust skills in that case unless the key abilities for those skills have changed, or the template gives a bonus on one or more skills, or unless the template gives a feat that provides a bonus on a skill check.

Some templates change how skill points are determined, but this change usually only affects skill points gained after the template is applied. Treat skills listed in the base creature's description as class skills, as well as any new skills provided by the template.

Feats: Since most templates do not change the number of Hit Dice a creature has, a template will not change the number of feats the creature has. Some templates grant one or more bonus feats.

Environment: Usually the same as the base creature.

Organization: Usually the same as the base creature.

Challenge Rating: Most templates increase the creature's Challenge Rating. A template might provide a modifier to be added to the base creature's CR, or it might specify a range of modifiers depending on the base creature's original Hit Dice or CR.

Treasure: Usually the same as the base creature.

Alignment: Usually the same as the base creature, unless the template is associated with a certain alignment (such as the celestial and fiendish templates, and any template that changes a creature's type to undead).

Advancement: Usually the same as the base creature.

Level Adjustment: This entry is a modifier to the base creature's level adjustment. Any level adjustment is meaningless unless the creature retains a high enough Intelligence (minimum 3) to gain class levels after applying the template.

ADDING A TEMPLATE, STEP-BY-STEP

All the templates presented in this book include at least one example of the template applied to a creature. To apply a template to a creature yourself, follow the steps outlined below.

If the template changes the base creature's size, use Table 4-2 to determine changes to natural armor, Armor Class, and attack rolls. Check the text of the template to see if you apply size modifiers to Strength, Dexterity, and Constitution. The template's Abilities entry may already account for those adjustments.

Add all ability score modifiers, from size and from the Abilities entry, to the base creature's ability scores.

When you know the new Constitution modifier and any change to Hit Die size, recalculate the templated monster's hit points. See Hit Dice and Hit Points, above.

The new Constitution modifier also modifies the creature's Fortitude saving throw modifier and any skill modifier for Concentration checks. Check for Great Fortitude or any other feat that affects the Fortitude saving throw modifier and apply the change now.

When you know the new Dexterity modifier, recalculate the creature's modifier on initiative checks and Armor Class. Apply modifiers for size and natural armor at this time. Check for Improved Initiative and any other feat that affects Initiative and apply the change now.

Check to see if either the base creature or the templated creature uses Weapon Finesse with one or more of its attacks. If it does, use the new Dexterity modifier to recalculate the attack bonus. Apply any size modifiers at the same time.

The new Dexterity modifier also modifies the Reflex saving throw modifier and the modifiers of any skills with Dexterity as the key ability. Check for Lightning Reflexes or any other feat that affects the Reflex saving throw modifier and apply the change now.

When you know the new Strength modifier, check to see if

either the base creature or the templated creature has Weapon Finesse. For all attacks that do not use Weapon Finesse, use the new Strength modifier to recalculate attack bonus. Apply any size modifiers at the same time.

The new Strength modifier affects damage and any modifiers for skills with Strength as the key ability.

When you know the new Intelligence modifier, recalculate skill modifiers for any skills that use Intelligence as the key ability.

When you know the new Wisdom modifier, recalculate the Will saving throw modifier and the modifiers for any skills that use Wisdom as the key ability. Check for Iron Will or any other feat that affects the Will saving throw modifier and apply the change now.

For all special abilities of the base creature that remain, recalculate saving throw DCs (the template description tells how to calculate the DCs for any special abilities the template provides). The formula for most save DCs is 10 + 1/2 the creature's Hit Dice + the relevant ability score modifier of the creature using the ability. Typically, each ability is associated with certain kinds of abilities, as follows.

Strength: Any application of force, crushing, binding, or constriction.

Dexterity: Movement, movement restrictions, hitting with a missile, entanglement.

Constitution: Almost anything that comes from the creature's body, including poison attacks and breath weapons.

Intelligence: Illusion effects.

Wisdom: Mental or perception effects (except charms and compulsions; see Charisma).

Charisma: A creature's Charisma modifier affects the save DC for any spell-like abilities it has. Use Charisma for anything pitting the creature's will against an opponent, such as gaze attacks, charms, compulsions, and energy drain effects. Also use Charisma for any DC that normally would be based on an ability score the creature does not have. For example, undead have no Constitution score, so any poison attack an undead creature has would use Charisma to determine the save DC.

Add any new special abilities granted by the template.

Add any skill bonuses given by the template.

Add any feats given by the template that are not already taken into account.

Update the Challenge Rating as instructed by the template.

Adding More Than One Template

In theory, there's no limit to the number of templates you can add to a creature. To add more than one template, just apply each template one at a time. Always apply inherited templates before applying acquired templates. Whenever you add multiple templates, pay attention to the creature's type—you may add a template that makes the creature ineligible for other templates you might want to add. For example, a vampire cannot become a lich and vice versa.

ADVANCED MONSTER CHALLENGE RATING

When you add higher ability scores, class levels, more Hit Dice, or a template to a monster, you make it a more challenging opponent for your players.

When adding class levels to a creature with 1 or less HD, you advance the creature like a character. Otherwise, use the following guidelines.

ADDING CLASS LEVELS

If you are advancing a monster by adding player character class levels, decide if the class levels directly improve the monster's existing capabilities.

When adding class levels to a creature, you should give it typical ability scores appropriate for that class. Most creatures in this book are built using the standard array of ability scores: 11, 11, 11, 10, 10, 10, adjusted by racial modifiers. If you give a creature a PC class, such as fighter or druid, use the elite array of ability scores before racial adjustments: 15, 14, 13, 12, 10, 8. For example, the troll hunter (in the Troll entry) is a ranger and uses the elite array, which is then modified by the troll's racial adjustments (Str +12, Dex +4, Con +12, Int −4, Wis −2, Cha −4). Creatures with NPC classes, such as adept or warrior, use the nonelite array of 13, 12, 11, 10, 9, 8. The orc warrior presented in this book is an example.

Estimating CR: Assigning a Challenge Rating is a subjective judgment, not an exact science—meaning that you have control over what the CR of an monster with class levels should be. If you find a class combination that improves a monster's capabilities significantly—or not as significantly as this guideline supposes—you should modify its CR as seems logical. Err on the side of overestimating: If a monster has a higher Challenge Rating than it deserves, it's less likely to kill off an entire party than if you had erred in the other direction.

Associated Class Levels

Class levels that increase a monster's existing strengths are known as associated class levels. Each associated class level a monster has increases its CR by 1.

Barbarian, fighter, paladin, and ranger are associated classes for a creature that relies on its fighting ability. For example, if you add a level of fighter, barbarian, ranger, or paladin to a frost giant, this directly improves the monster's existing strengths and is therefore an associated class level.

Rogue and ranger are associated classes for a creature that relies on stealth to surprise its foes, or on skill use to give itself an advantage. The babau demon, for example, is "sneaky and sly" and has sneak attack as a special ability. Rogue is an associated class for this creature.

A spellcasting class is an associated class for a creature that already has the ability to cast spells as a character of the class in question, since the monster's levels in the spellcasting class stack with its innate spellcasting ability. A rakshasa, for example, casts spells as a 7th-level sorcerer. If it picks up a level of sorcerer, it casts spells as an 8th-level sorcerer.

Nonassociated Class Levels

If you add a class level that doesn't directly play to a creature's strength (such as adding a sorcerer level to a frost giant), the class level is considered nonassociated, and things get a little more complicated. Adding a nonassociated class level to a monster increases its CR by 1/2 per level until one of its nonassociated class levels equals its original Hit Dice. At that point, each additional level of the same class or a similar one is considered associated and increases the monster's CR by 1.

For example, frost giants have 14 HD. After you add 14 levels of sorcerer to a frost giant (and +7 to its CR), any further sorcerer class levels are considered associated. Adding one more sorcerer level increases this particular frost giant's CR by 1.

Levels in NPC classes are always treated as nonassociated.

ADDING HIT DICE

When you improve a monster by adding Hit Dice, use Table 4–4 to determine the effect on the creature's CR. Keep in mind that many monsters that advance by adding Hit Dice also increase in size. Do not stack this CR increase with any increase from class levels.

In general, once you've doubled a creature's CR, you should closely watch any additional increases in its abilities. Adding Hit Dice to a creature improves several of its abilities, and radical increases might not follow this progression indefinitely. Compare the monster's improved attack bonus, saving throw bonuses, and

TABLE 4–4: IMPROVED MONSTER CR INCREASE

Creature's Original Type	CR Increase
Aberration, construct, elemental, fey, giant, humanoid, ooze, plant, undead, vermin	+1 per 4 HD added
Animal, magical beast, monstrous humanoid	+1 per 3 HD added
Dragon, outsider, nonassociated class levels	+1 per 2 HD or 2 levels added
Directly associated class levels	+1 per level added
Other Modifiers:	
Size increased to Large or larger	+1 to CR
Monster's ability scores based on elite array*	+1 to CR
Monster possesses special attacks or qualities that significantly improve combat effectiveness	+2 to CR
Monster possesses special attacks or qualities that improve combat effectiveness in a minor way	+1 to CR
Template added	+ template CR modifier

* Do not apply this increase if you advance a monster by class levels. (Monsters advanced by class levels are assumed to use the elite array.)

any DCs of its special abilities from the HD increase to typical characters of the appropriate level and adjust the CR accordingly.

INCREASING SIZE

Generally, increasing a monster's size increases its combat effectiveness. Large creatures gain increased Strength, reach, and other benefits. Apply this modifier if you increase a creature beyond Medium and in conjunction with any other increases.

Be careful, though. Monsters that benefit from a smaller size may actually lose effectiveness because of a size increase. A grig, for example, gains AC and attack bonuses for being Tiny, and reduced Dexterity from a size increase actually hurts its Weapon Finesse capability. Monsters that don't benefit from size increases don't advance in that manner for this reason.

ADDING SPECIAL ABILITIES

You can add any sort of spell-like, supernatural, or extraordinary ability to a creature. As with a class level, you should determine how much, or how little, this ability adds to the creature's existing repertoire. A suite of abilities that work together should be treated as a single modifier for this purpose. If the ability (or combination of abilities) significantly increases the monster's combat effectiveness, increase its CR by 2. Minor abilities increase the creature's CR by 1, and truly trivial abilities may not increase CR at all. If the special abilities a monster gains are not tied to a class or Hit Die increase, this CR increase stacks.

A significant special attack is one that stands a good chance of incapacitating or crippling a character in one round; the troll's rend ability, while it is dangerous, does not make it significantly more dangerous than it already is, but an umber hulk's confusing gaze can take characters out of the fight every round. A significant special quality is one that seriously diminishes the monster's vulnerability to common attacks, such as spell resistance or an undead creature's immunities. Do not add this factor twice if a monster has both special attacks and special qualities.

Make sure to "scale" your evaluation of these abilities by the monster's current CR. Giving a CR 15 monster built for melee combat the ability to cast *bull's strength* once per day is pretty trivial, taken all by itself. It probably wouldn't bump the CR at all, or at best, by 1. If you give a melee combat monster of CR 1 the same ability, however, that's fairly significant: Increase the CR by 2.

Adding lots of abilities is always problematic. Monsters usually only spend a short period of time "on screen" in any adventure. If you give a monster more special abilities than it can reliably use in a single encounter, you may just be increasing complexity for no real improvement.

CHAPTER 5: MAKING MONSTERS

All the really great monsters, in the D&D game and in literature, have one thing in common—you can sum up what they're all about in just a few words. That's the first and most essential item in any monster recipe—a solid and fairly simple statement of what the monster is all about.

THE MONSTER'S CONCEPT

Before you begin assigning statistics and other particulars, take some time to think about the basic nature, or concept, of your monster.

Think about the following when working on your concept:

—What do you expect the creature to do in the game? (Is it a friend or a foe of the PCs? Does it depend primarily on physical abilities or mental abilities? Is it meant to be encountered once, or on a recurring basis?)

—Where does it live? (A monster that lives underground may have characteristics not shared by monsters that inhabit the wilderness, and vice versa.)

—How does it live? (Is it a predator that relies on its own strength and speed, or is it intelligent enough to get other creatures to do its bidding?)

—Does it have any particular enemies or favorite prey?

After you have an idea of what your monster is about, you'll have a much easier time making your creature's type, ability scores, feats, skills, and special powers fit your concept. It's okay to model your new monster on a creature that's already in the game—you'll have less work to do, and your monster will be easier to use. You'll find that a short menu of special abilities tightly wedded to your concept makes the best monster, and it makes the monster much easier to use.

DETERMINING THE MONSTER'S TYPE

Once you have your monster's concept figured out, it's time to pick a creature type that fits the concept. Use the following information to determine the most appropriate type for your monster (perhaps refining your concept as you go).

Aberration: An aberration has a bizarre anatomy, strange abilities, an alien mindset, or any combination of the three. This type works best for creatures that are just plain weird. Aberrations have average combat ability and hit points, but generally poor saving throws.

If you want your aberration to be a tough customer in combat, you'll need to give it some sort of special attack ability. For example, a carrion crawler has eight paralyzing tentacle attacks, while an umber hulk has a gaze that causes confusion.

Animal: An animal is a living, nonhuman creature, usually a vertebrate with no magical abilities and no innate capacity for language or culture. Animals have average combat ability, average hit points, and average saving throws.

If your creature ever lived on Earth, and it's not an insect of some kind, it's probably an animal.

Construct: A construct is an animated object or artificially constructed creature. Constructs have average combat ability and hit points, and very poor saving throws, but they have immunity to many attack forms.

Use this type for any creature that was built or made rather than born or hatched.

Dragon: A dragon is a reptilelike creature, usually winged, with magical or unusual abilities. This type is exceptionally powerful, combining good combat ability, hit points, and saving throws.

Use the dragon type for variations on the basic dragon design (a flying reptile with supernatural abilities). If your creature is essentially just a flying reptile (such as a pterodactyl), the animal or magical beast type may be more suitable.

Elemental: An elemental is a being composed of one of the four classical elements: air, earth, fire, or water. Elementals have average combat ability and hit points and poor saving throws, but have immunity to some forms of attack.

Use the elemental type for a creature from the elemental planes that is more element than creature. If your creature is a native of the elemental planes but more like a living creature than the incarnation of an element, you should probably use the outsider type.

Fey: A fey is a creature with supernatural abilities and connections to nature or to some other force or place. Fey are usually human-shaped. Fey have poor combat ability and hit points and average saving throws. If you want to create a tough fey, you will need to assign formidable physical ability scores and special attacks or defenses to make the creature survivable.

Fey creatures include fairies and many sylvan creatures. They could also include evil creatures such as the sidhe and unseelie fairies.

Giant: A giant is a humanoid-shaped creature of great strength, usually of at least Large size. Giants have average combat ability and hit points, and poor saving throws, but their size and physical ability scores usually make them very dangerous combatants.

If your creature is humanoid-shaped and at least as big as an ogre, it's probably a giant, especially if it doesn't have a lot of special abilities.

Humanoid: A humanoid usually has two arms, two legs, and one head, or a humanlike torso, arms, and a head. Humanoids have few or no supernatural or extraordinary abilities, but most can speak and usually have well-developed societies. They usually are Small or Medium. Every humanoid creature also has a subtype, such as elf, goblinoid, or reptilian.

Humanoids with 1 Hit Die exchange the features of their humanoid Hit Die for the class features of a PC or NPC class. Humanoids of this sort are presented as 1st-level warriors, which means that they have average combat ability and poor saving throws.

Humanoids with more than 1 Hit Die (for example, gnolls and bugbears) are the only humanoids who make use of the features of the humanoid type. Humanoids have average combat ability and hit points, but poor saving throws.

Magical Beast: A magical beast is similar to an animal but can have an Intelligence score higher than 2. Magical beasts usually have supernatural or extraordinary abilities, but sometimes are merely bizarre in appearance or habits. Magical beasts have good combat ability and hit points, and average saving throws.

If your creature resembles an animal but is intelligent or has supernatural or spell-like abilities, it's probably a magical beast. You can also use this type for animallike creatures that combine the features of two or more animals, or are similar to animals but just tougher.

Monstrous Humanoid: Monstrous humanoids are similar to humanoids, but with monstrous or animalistic features. They often have magical abilities as well. Monstrous humanoids have good combat ability and average hit points and saving throws.

Use this type for just about anything that combines elements of human and animal or monster anatomy, unless it is weird enough to qualify as an aberration. Monstrous humanoids might also include otherwise humanoid creatures with odd vulnerabilities or abilities you wouldn't normally find in a humanoid.

Ooze: An ooze is an amorphous or mutable creature, usually mindless. Oozes have average combat ability, good hit points, and very poor saving throws, but they have immunity to many forms of attack.

If your creature has a bizarre physiology that takes the form of a mindless, amorphous blob, it's an ooze. Otherwise, it's probably an aberration.

Outsider: An outsider is at least partially composed of the essence (but not necessarily the material) of some plane other than the Material Plane. Some creatures start out as some other type and become outsiders when they attain a higher (or lower) state of spiritual existence. Outsiders have good combat ability, average hit points, and good saving throws.

If your creature comes from another plane and it's not an elemental, it's an outsider.

Plant: This type comprises vegetable creatures. Note that regular plants, such as one finds growing in gardens and fields, lack Wisdom and Charisma scores and thus are not creatures, but objects, even though they are alive. Plant creatures have average combat ability and hit points and poor saving throws, but have immunity to many forms of attack.

Undead: Undead are once-living creatures animated by spiritual or supernatural forces. Undead have poor combat ability, average hit points, and poor saving throws, but have immunity to many forms of attack. If you want to create an undead creature with formidable combat abilities, you will need to give it high Strength or Dexterity, or provide it with dangerous special attacks and defenses.

If it's dead, but still kicking, it's undead (although it could be a construct if it's just a collection of parts animated through an arcane process). If the creature has energy drain or ability drain capability, it is more likely undead than a construct.

Vermin: This type includes insects, arachnids, other arthropods, worms, and similar invertebrates. Vermin have average combat ability and hit points and poor saving throws, but are often mindless and therefore have immunity to mind-affecting effects (charms, compulsions, phantasms, patterns, and morale effects).

Use this type for giant bugs and other mindless invertebrates. If your creature has an Intelligence score and you've considered the vermin type, it's probably a magical beast or an aberration instead.

TARGET CHALLENGE RATING

Before you get too far into designing your monster, you should decide about how tough a monster you're trying to build by picking a target CR. Challenge rating measures the level of characters the monster will be best suited to oppose. As you assign the monster's Hit Dice, Armor Class, attack bonus, special attacks, save DCs, and other characteristics, you will want to keep your target CR in mind.

For example, if you want to create a monster to challenge a party of 2nd-level characters, you probably don't want to create a monster with an Armor Class of 25. A strong and capable 2nd-level fighter might have an attack bonus of +6 or so, which means that the best character in the party will hit your monster only on a natural 19 or 20. The clerics, rogues, and other characters in the party will only hit on a natural 20.

If you are interested in creating your own monsters for a particular game or campaign, you have an advantage: You know exactly what characters your monsters will face. You can examine your players' character sheets and check the attack bonus, Armor Class, and saving throws of the characters you expect your monster to fight. If you don't want to tailor your monster to a particular group of characters, you can use the NPC tables in Chapter 4 of the *Dungeon Master's Guide* to see how characters of a level equal to your target CR can handle different monster attacks and defenses.

As you proceed through the steps of creating your monster, use your target CR to guide your decisions about what value to assign. Your final monster design may or may not match the target CR, but you will be much less likely to create a monster that never misses or can't be hit.

CREATING THE MONSTER

All the other elements of the monster recipe serve to put your concept into words and numbers so you can use the monster in play. The steps below are not presented in the same order as a monster entry, because some items that appear late in a monster entry (for example, the monster's ability scores) affect decisions you might make about items that precede them.

CREATURE TYPE

A creature's type defines what the creature is like and what it can do in the much the same way as a character's class defines the character's abilities. A creature's type determines the size of its Hit Dice and how magic affects the creature; for example, the *hold animal* spell affects only creatures of the animal type.

Type, along with size, helps determine the monster's ability scores and damage values. Consider your concept for the monster, and choose the type that best matches that concept. Full descriptions of each type's features and traits appear in Chapter 7: Glossary.

SIZE

A creature's size affects its combat abilities in numerous ways. In general, the bigger the creature, the nastier it is. When assigning a size to your monster, think about your monster concept. Does the creature need to be really strong and tough? Does it have a voracious appetite? If so, it should be big. Is the creature sneaky, agile, and easy to overlook? If so, it should be smaller.

It's important to remember that a creature's total volume is what determines its size. If a creature is significantly denser or less dense than a regular animal, then its weight is a poor indicator of size. For example, the ghost of a human weighs nothing but is size Medium.

A creature's size should influence its ability scores and its number of Hit Dice. Table 5–1 shows suggested ability scores, Hit Dice, and natural weapon damage for monsters of various sizes. These are guidelines, not hard-and-fast requirements. Many creatures in this book do not adhere to the guidelines on the table.

The column headers on Table 5–1 are defined below.

Minimum CR: This column gives the minimum target CR you should assign to a creature of this size. This reflects the size-based suggestions for number of HD, Strength, and damage capability. For example, if you are creating a Gargantuan creature, you should plan on a final CR of 6 or higher.

Str, Dex, Con: These numbers are typical values for a creature of the indicated size. The creature's type influences which end of the given range a monster falls into; for example, since giants are often at the high end of the Strength range for their size, a Large giant's Strength score should be closer to 27 than 18.

TABLE 5–1: CREATURE SIZE, ABILITY SCORES, AND DAMAGE

Size	Minimum CR	Str	Dex	Con	Minimum HD	Maximum HD	Slam or Tentacle	Bite	Claw or Sting	Gore or Tail
Fine	–	1	16–27	2–11	—	2	—	1	—	—
Diminutive	–	1	14–25	4–13	—	4	1	1d2	1	1
Tiny	–	2–5	12–23	4–15	—	6	1	1d3	1d2	1d2
Small	–	4–11	10–21	6–17	1/2	—	1d3	1d4	1d3	1d4
Medium	–	8–19	8–19	8–19	1	—	1d4	1d6	1d4	1d6
Large	2	18–27	6–17	10–23	2	—	1d6	1d8	1d6	1d8
Huge	4	24–33	4–15	12–27	4	—	1d8	2d6	1d8	2d6
Gargantuan	6	30–41	4–13	14–31	12	—	2d6	2d8	2d6	2d8
Colossal	10	36–49	2–11	18–39	24	—	2d8	4d6	2d8	4d6

Ability score guidelines for some creature types are given below.

Elemental: Air and fire elementals often have high Dexterity scores for their size; earth and water elementals often have high Constitution scores.

Fey: Fey often have high Dexterity scores for their size.

Giant: Giants often have high Strength and Constitution scores for their size.

Magical Beast: Magical beasts often have high Dexterity scores for their size.

Ooze: Oozes often have low Dexterity and high Constitution scores for their size.

Outsider: Outsiders may be supernaturally quick and agile, despite their size. Outsiders have the Dexterity range of a creature three sizes smaller than their actual size.

Plant: Plants often have low Dexterity and high Constitution scores for their size.

Undead: Undead often have high Strength and Dexterity scores for their size.

Minimum HD: Creatures of size Small or larger should be assigned a certain number of Hit Dice as a minimum to reflect their mass. A Gargantuan creature with 2 Hit Dice would be larger than an elephant, but would have the hit points of a wolf.

Maximum HD: Creatures of size Tiny or smaller shouldn't have a very large number of Hit Dice, simply because they don't have the necessary body mass to have the sort of innate toughness that a large number of racial Hit Dice would suggest. If you want to create very small creatures with lots of Hit Dice, you might be better off to keep the creature's racial Hit Dice low and assign it some number of character class levels instead.

Slam or Tentacle: The suggested damage value for any blunt attack the creature might have (punches, constriction, slaps, and the like).

Bite: The suggested damage value for any attack the creature delivers with its mouth or teeth.

Claw or Sting: The suggested damage value for any attack the creature makes by scratching, tearing, raking, or poking with an appendage.

Gore or Tail: The suggested damage value for any attack the creature makes with horns, antlers, or a head butt. A tail slap or tail whip falls in this category, too.

SUBTYPE

A monster associated with an element, form of energy, or the like also gets a parenthetical subtype. Applying a subtype can indicate a subgroup within a larger type, such as undead (incorporeal). Some subtypes link creatures that share characteristics, such as humanoid (goblinoid). Other subtypes categorize members of different types that share common characteristics For example, white dragons and frost giants belong to the dragon and giant types, respectively, but they are also of the cold subtype.

Some common subtypes that affect a creature's abilities are briefly described below. Details are given in Chapter 7: Glossary.

Air: The creature (usually an elemental or outsider) possesses an innate bond to the Elemental Plane of Air.

Angel: The creature belongs to one of the angel races and shares common characteristics with other angels.

Aquatic: The creature breathes water, not air.

Archon: The creature belongs to one of the archon races and shares common characteristics with other archons.

Augmented: The creature's type has been changed by a template.

Baatezu: The creature is a devil that belongs to the baatezu race and shares common characteristics with other baatezu.

Chaos: The creature (usually an outsider) possesses an innate bond to the chaotic-aligned Outer Planes, which determines how it is affected by certain spells.

Cold: The creature has immunity to cold, but is vulnerable to fire attacks.

Earth: The creature (usually an elemental or outsider) possesses an innate bond to the Elemental Plane of Earth.

Eladrin: The creature is a celestial that belongs to the eladrin race and shares common characteristics with other eladrins.

Evil: The creature (usually an outsider) possesses an innate bond to the evil-aligned Outer Planes, which determines how it is affected by certain spells.

Extraplanar: The creature (usually an elemental or outsider) is not native to the Material Plane, which determines how it is affected by spells that banish or dismiss extraplanar creatures.

Fire: The creature has immunity to fire, but is vulnerable to cold attacks.

Goblinoid: The creature belongs to one of the goblin races.

Good: The creature (usually an outsider) possesses an innate bond to the good-aligned Outer Planes, which determines how it is affected by certain spells.

Guardinal: The creature is a celestial that belongs to the guardinal race and shares common characteristics with other guardinals.

Incorporeal: The creature is completely intangible on the Material Plane and can pass through solid objects.

Lawful: The creature (usually an outsider) possesses an innate bond to the lawful-aligned Outer Planes, which determines how it is affected by certain spells.

Native: Despite its outsider type, the creature is actually a native of the Material Plane.

Reptilian: The creature is a humanoid with reptilelike characteristics.

Shapechanger: The creature possesses an innate ability to change shape or assume an alternate form.

Swarm: The creature is actually a swarm of hundreds or thousands of very small creatures.

Tanar'ri: The creature is a demon that belongs to the tanar'ri race and shares common characteristics with other tanar'ri.

Water: The creature (usually an elemental or outsider) possesses an innate bond to the Elemental Plane of Water.

HIT DICE

This entry in a statistics block provides the number and size (number of sides) of Hit Dice and any bonus hit points. The size of the dice is derived from the creature's type. The number of bonus hit points is a function of the creature's Hit Dice and Constitution score.

A parenthetical listing of the creature's average hit points follows the Hit Dice listing. To calculate a creature's average hit points, take the average value of each Hit Die, apply the creature's Constitution modifier (a creature always has at least 1 hit point per Hit Die), multiply by the number of Hit Dice, and round down.

AVERAGE HIT DIE VALUES

Die Size	Average
1d4	2.5
1d6	3.5
1d8	4.5
1d10	5.5
1d12	6.5

Hit Dice and Target CR: In general, a creature's Hit Dice should be equal to or greater than the target CR you've set for the creature, but not more than three times the target CR. For example, if you are designing a CR 5 monster, you should probably assign at least 5 Hit Dice, but not more than 15 Hit Dice. If your monster has too few Hit Dice for its Challenge Rating, it won't have staying power comparable to other monsters of that CR. If your monster has too many Hit Dice, not only will it have more hit points than a creature of that CR should have, but it will also have a better attack bonus and saving throws than expected, because those numbers are determined by the creature's Hit Dice.

Obviously, many monsters break this rule, usually by falling 1 or 2 Hit Dice short of their CR. That's okay, provided that the monster has special attacks or qualities that make it a suitable challenge at its CR.

ABILITY SCORES

In this entry, a creature's ability scores are presented in this order: Str, Dex, Con, Int, Wis, Cha.

Assigning Abilities: Physical abilities (Strength, Dexterity, and Constitution) are largely a function of a creature's type and size, as shown on Table 5–1. In general, the bigger a creature gets, the higher its Strength and Constitution scores and the lower its Dexterity. Exceptions abound.

The remaining abilities (Intelligence, Wisdom, and Charisma) are seldom related to size. You'll need to assign values to these abilities to match your concept.

Intelligence: Reflects how well the creature learns and reasons. In most cases, it affects how many skills and feats the creature has. A creature needs an Intelligence score of at least 3 to speak a language; anything lower makes the creature no smarter than a typical animal. An Intelligence score of 4 to 7 represents a limited ability to reason and a certain low cunning. An Intelligence score of 8 or 9 approaches the typical human range. A score of 10 or 11 covers the human norm. A score of 12 to 19 reflects above-average to genius-level Intelligence. A score of 20 or higher represents superhuman intellect.

Wisdom: Reflects the creature's level of perception and strength of will. A creature can have a very low Intelligence score and still be very wise. A Wisdom score of 3 or lower indicates a creature that is barely sentient. A score of 4 to 6 represents Wisdom equivalent to that of an unusually foolhardy or unperceptive human. A score of 16 to 18 reflects acute senses and unusual guile. A score of 20 or higher represents superhuman perceptiveness.

Charisma: Reflects the creature's sense of self and ability to influence other creatures for good or for ill (a particularly scary creature often has a high Charisma score). A creature can have a very low Intelligence score and still be very charismatic. A Charisma score of 3 or lower indicates a creature that is barely sentient. A score of 4 to 6 represents Charisma equivalent to that of a strikingly sullen, crass, or retiring human. A score of 16 to 18 reflects an unusually strong presence and force of personality. A score of 20 or higher represents superhuman Charisma.

Nonabilities: Some creatures lack one or more ability scores. In most cases, a nonability is an advantage for the creature. Note that all creatures must have both a Wisdom score and a Charisma score. Anything that lacks Wisdom or Charisma is an object, not a creature (though it may be alive, such as a tree or a sponge).

INITIATIVE

This entry gives the creature's modifier to initiative rolls. The bonus is most commonly derived from the creature's Dexterity modifier and the Improved Initiative feat (if the creature has it).

SPEED

This entry gives the creature's base land speed in feet per move action. All speeds must be evenly divisible by 5 feet. Most creatures have base land speeds of between 20 and 40 feet. Larger creatures and quadrupeds tend to be faster, and predators or creatures noted for their fast movement could have a speed of up to 60 to 80 feet. Compare the speeds of monsters similar to your monster concept to pick a suitable value. See Table 5–2 for some guidelines and suggestions.

If the creature has other modes of movement, list all that apply after the base land speed in alphabetical order. If the creature wears armor that reduces its speed, it's helpful to give its reduced movement rate in a parenthetical note following the base land speed.

ARMOR CLASS

All creatures start with a base Armor Class of 10, which is modified by the creature's size, Dexterity, armor (including natural armor), and shield. Some creatures, such as incorporeal monsters, may also have a deflection bonus to their Armor Class.

Consider the creature's anatomy and overall toughness when you choose an Armor Class for your monster. The table below shows some typical values for natural armor.

Touch Armor Class: To figure your monster's Armor Class against touch attacks, add only its size modifier, Dexterity modifier, and deflection bonus (if any) to its base AC of 10.

Flat-Footed Armor Class: To figure your monster's Armor Class when it is caught flat-footed, include all the normal elements except the creature's Dexterity bonus.

Don't forget to include the creature's size modifier in your final Armor Class calculation. If the creature wears armor, its natural armor bonus stacks with the bonus provided by its armor. For example, a centaur is a Large creature with a Dexterity score of 14 (+2 bonus to AC) and +2 natural armor. If the centaur carries a heavy shield and wears a chain shirt, its Armor Class is 19 (–1 size, +2 Dex, +2 natural, +2 heavy shield, +4 chain shirt).

Armor Class and Target CR: Too high an Armor Class may make your monster unbeatable at the Challenge Rating you're aiming for. Too low, and the monster won't be a challenge at all. A good rule of thumb is to arrange the components of a creature's AC to arrive at a total Armor Class equal to 13 + target CR. For example, if you'd like your monster to be about CR 8, you should aim for AC 21. Naturally, you can choose to make a monster somewhat more soft-skinned if it has other defenses (damage reduction, for example), or you might choose to make your monster an unusually tough target for its CR by giving it "extra" armor.

TABLE 5–2: TYPICAL SPEEDS

Type	Slow	Normal	Fast	Example Creature
Tiny or Small biped	15 ft.	20 ft.	30 ft.	Halfling (20 ft.)
Medium biped	20 ft.	30 ft.	40 ft.	Human (30 ft.)
Large or Huge biped	30 ft.	40 ft.	50 ft.	Ogre (40 ft.)
Tiny quadruped	15 ft.	20 ft.	30 ft.	Cat (30 ft.)
Small quadruped	30 ft.	40 ft.	50 ft.	Dog (40 ft.)
Medium quadruped	30 ft.	40 ft.	50 ft.	Wolf (50 ft.)
Large or Huge quadruped	30 ft.	50 ft.	60 ft.	Unicorn (60 ft.)
Tiny or Small flier	40 ft.	50 ft.	60 ft.	Raven (40 ft.)
Medium flier	40 ft.	60 ft.	90 ft.	Gargoyle (60 ft.)
Large or Huge flier	60 ft.	80 ft.	120 ft.	Griffon (80 ft.)
Swimmer	40 ft.	60 ft.	80 ft.	Water naga (50 ft.)

TABLE 5–3: TYPICAL NATURAL ARMOR VALUES

Type	Bonus	Example Creature
Normal skin	+0	Human
Thick skin or fur	+1 to +3	Baboon (+1)
		Black bear (+2)
		Shark (+3)
Tough hide	+4 to +7	Crocodile (+4)
		Polar bear (+5)
		Boar (+6)
		Rhinoceros (+7)
Scales	+5 to +10 or more	Dragon (varies)
Exoskeleton	+2 to +11 or more	Giant bee (+2)
		Chuul (+10)
		Remorhaz (+11)
Shell or carapace	+10 to +12 or more	Juvenile tojanida (+10)
		Bulette (+12)
Very tough hide	+8 to +15 or more	Otyugh (+8)
		Kraken (+14)
		Ravid (+15)

ATTACK

Decide what attack forms the creature uses in melee and ranged combat and determine the monster's attack bonus with each attack. The attacks you might decide to give a creature include:

—Melee weapon (possibly multiple melee weapons)
—Ranged weapon
—Bite
—Claw or tentacle
—Slam
—Gore
—Touch attack

Attack Bonus: A creature's attack bonus consists of the following components: base attack bonus (as determined by the creature's type and Hit Dice), size modifier, and Strength modifier for melee attacks or Dexterity modifier for ranged attacks. You may select feats or equipment for the monster that alter the creature's attack bonus with a particular weapon; for example, if you give the monster a +2 *longsword*, you will increase its attack bonus with that weapon by 2 points. Similarly, Weapon Focus or Weapon Finesse might alter the creature's attack bonus.

The Attack entry in a statistics block gives the attack and damage bonus for each of the monster's attacks, if the monster decides to use a standard action to make a single attack. You do not need to account for secondary weapons or multiple attacks with the same weapon when you describe the monster's individual attack options here—any weapon the monster uses to make a single attack as a standard action gets the monster's full attack bonus and damage bonus for Strength.

Damage: Assign damage values to each of the creature's natural attacks. The base damage value depends on the creature's size and the type of attack, as shown on Table 5–1.

Particularly tough or weak creatures might have higher or lower damage values. In general, you can vary the power of a monster's attacks by moving up or down one or two lines on the table. For example, a Medium monster's bite usually has a damage value of 1d6, but it could be as little as 1d3 or as much as 2d6. Use the 1d3 value for a creature with a very small or weak mouth, or the 2d6 value to represent a creature with large or very powerful mouth.

Natural Weapons: A creature's attack gets the creature's full damage bonus from Strength, or 1-1/2 times the Strength bonus if it is the creature's sole natural weapon.

If any of the creature's attacks also have some special effect other than damage (poison, disease, energy drain, paralyzation, and so forth), note it after the attack's hit point damage—for example, sting (1d6 plus poison).

Critical Hits: Unless you decide otherwise, a creature's natural attack threatens a critical hit on a roll of natural 20 and deals double damage if a critical hit is confirmed. Very few monsters have better than normal threat ranges or critical multipliers with their natural weapons.

Weapon-Using Creatures: Creatures that use weapons follow all the rules that characters do; two-handed weapons gain 1-1/2 times the creature's Strength bonus on damage rolls.

Attack Bonus and Target CR: Much like Armor Class, a monster's attack bonus may make it unplayable at the Challenge Rating you intend. A monster without a high enough attack bonus poses no threat to the PCs, and a monster with too high an attack bonus never misses.

As a guideline, arrange the components of a monster's attack bonus so that its attack bonus with its primary weapon is equal to (target CR × 1.5) + 2. For example, if you are building a CR 5 monster, an appropriate attack bonus would be (5 × 1.5) + 2, or 9.5, which comes out to an attack bonus of +9 or +10. This guideline works best for monsters with few special attacks; if you expect your monster will rely on special attacks rather than pure melee ability, a better guideline would be an attack bonus equal to (target

CR × 1.5) – 1. A CR 5 monster of this sort would have an attack bonus of +6 or +7.

Manipulating your monster's attack bonus to fit the CR you have in mind is not quite as easy as manipulating Armor Class. You can change the creature's Hit Dice, since base attack bonus is derived from Hit Dice, but doing this will change several other characteristics. The best way to fine-tune your monster at this step is to change its Strength score (or Dexterity, for ranged attacks), but watch out for creating ability scores that seem unusually low or high for a creature of the given size and type.

FULL ATTACK

In this step, you'll determine the monster's attack routine when it uses a full-round action to make a full attack. This is based on the individual attacks the monster has available to it (see Attack, above), but you need to account for the difference between primary and secondary attacks.

Natural Weapons: In general, a creature attacks once with each natural weapon it has. For most monsters, that will be two claws and a bite (or the other way around). Decide which of the monster's natural weapons is its primary weapon. A monster many have two or more primary weapons if it has two or more of the same natural attack—for example, a treant attacks with two slams, one for each limb, and both are primary natural weapons.

Primary weapons use a creature's full attack bonus, no matter how many primary weapons it has. The monster applies its full Strength bonus on damage rolls with its primary natural weapons, or 1-1/2 times its Strength bonus if the monster has only one primary natural weapon (for example, a wolf's bite).

All other natural weapons are secondary attacks. Reduce the creature's attack bonus by 5 for all such attacks, no matter how many there are. Creatures with the Multiattack feat take only a –2 penalty on secondary attacks. A monster applies 1/2 its Strength bonus on damage rolls with its secondary natural weapons.

Manufactured Weapons: Creatures that use weapons follow all the rules characters that do, including multiple attacks with the same weapon and penalties for using two weapons at once.

Natural and Manufactured Weapons: If a creature has both a manufactured weapon and natural weapons, it usually uses its manufactured weapon as its primary attack (and receives multiple attacks with that weapon, if its base attack bonus is +6 or higher), and uses its natural weapons as secondary attacks (–5 penalty on attack rolls, and 1/2 Strength bonus on damage rolls). While a humanoid fighting with two weapons takes a –2 penalty (or worse) on its primary attack, a monster fighting with a hand-held weapon and a natural weapon at the same times does not take this penalty—the natural weapon is a secondary attack, and that's all.

SPECIAL ATTACKS

Decide what special attacks (if any) your monster has. A special attack is anything the creature uses offensively to harm or hinder another creature. Common special attacks include:

—Ability damage (temporary)
—Ability drain (permanent)
—Breath weapon
—Change shape
—Constrict
—Cursed wound
—Disease
—Energy drain (negative levels)
—Fear
—Gaze
—Improved grab
—Paralysis
—Poison

—Pounce
—Powerful charge
—Psionics
—Ray
—Rend
—Roar
—Sonic attack
—Spells
—Spell-like abilities
—Summon
—Swallow whole
—Trample
—Wounding

Most of these special attacks are described in detail in Chapter 7: Glossary. A number of monsters possess unusual special attacks that are less common (for example, the mind flayer's *mind blast* and extract attacks). In general, one or two special attacks for any monster is enough—monsters usually don't get the chance to use more than a couple of special abilities in the course of a single encounter, so creating a number of special attacks simply makes the monster more difficult to use in play.

Each special attack should include the type of saving throw the attack allows (if any) and the DC of the save. The saving throw type depends on the nature of the attack, as follows:

—Fortitude saving throws apply to attacks on the defender's vitality: poison, magic that causes instant death, level draining, or magic that causes physical transformation.

—Reflex saving throws apply to massive attacks such as a wizard's *fireball* or a damage-dealing breath weapon.

—Will saving throws apply to mental influence and domination as well as any magical effect that doesn't fall into one of the previous two categories.

Calculating Saving Throw DCs

The formula for save DCs is: 10 + 1/2 the creature's Hit Dice + relevant ability score modifier. The relevant ability score depends on the type of attack, as follows:

Strength: Any application of force, crushing, binding, or constriction. Example: trample.

Dexterity: Movement, movement restrictions, hitting with a missile, entanglement. Example: entangle.

Constitution: Almost anything that comes from the creature's body, such as poison or breath weapons. Examples: breath weapon, poison.

Intelligence: Usually not used to determine save DCs for monsters' special attacks. Possible uses: illusion effects.

Wisdom: Usually not used to determine save DCs for monsters'

special attacks. Possible uses: Mental or perception effects (except charms and compulsions; see Charisma).

Charisma: Use Charisma for anything pitting the creature's will against an opponent: gaze attacks, charms, compulsions, or energy drain. The creature's Charisma modifier affects the save DC for any spell-like abilities it has (no matter what form they take).

Also use Charisma for any DC that normally would be based on an ability score the creature does not have. For example, undead creatures have no Constitution score, so any poison attacks they have would use Charisma to determine the save DC.

SPECIAL QUALITIES

A special quality is any ability a creature can use to protect itself. The Special Qualities entry also is the catch-all for anything the creature might do or have that does not logically belong somewhere else. Common special qualities include:

—Blindsense
—Blindsight
—Damage reduction
—Fast healing
—Frightful presence
—Immunity to energy or a certain attack form
—Regeneration
—Resistance to energy
—Scent
—Spell immunity
—Spell resistance
—Subtype features (for example, cold subtype)
—Tremorsense
—Turn resistance
—Type traits (for example, construct traits)

These abilities are described in Chapter 7: Glossary. A number of monsters have less common special qualities that are not listed here. As with special attacks, limit the number of special qualities you give a monster, because you'll have an easier time running the monster in play.

SAVING THROWS

Determine the creature's saving throw bonuses. The creature's base saving throw bonuses depend on its type and Hit Dice. Include all adjustments that apply to each save, provided they apply all the time (such as ability score modifiers and racial bonuses). Conditional saving throw bonuses should be noted in the creature's Special Qualities entry and explained in the creature's description.

Saving Throws and Target CR: In general, a creature's good saving throw bonus should be around (target CR × 1.5), while its

---

BEHIND THE CURTAIN: SPELL RESISTANCE AND DAMAGE REDUCTION

Too much spell resistance or damage reduction can make a monster virtually unbeatable at the Challenge Rating you're aiming for. Too little, and the monster might as well not have any at all, since any character will have the caster level or magic weaponry necessary to penetrate the creature's defense.

Spell Resistance: If you choose to give your monster this ability, you'll probably want to set the resistance number equal to the creature's CR + 11. This means that a character of a level equal to the creature's will have a 50% chance to overcome the monster's spell resistance (barring the Spell Penetration feat). For example, a 12th-level character has a 50% chance to overcome spell resistance 23, so 23 is a good spell resistance number for a CR 12 creature.

You may need to adjust a creature's spell resistance number after you finally settle on a CR for the creature.

If you want a highly magic-resistant creature, set the monster's spell resistance higher than CR + 11. For lesser resistance, set the spell

resistance lower. For each point of difference, you'll change the chance of successfully overcoming spell resistance by 5%. For example, a 12th-level caster has a 45% chance to overcome spell resistance 24, and no chance to overcome spell resistance 33.

Damage Reduction: Assigning a damage reduction value can be tricky. Setting the value too high can make a creature virtually immune to physical attacks, On the other hand, most player characters carry some magic weapons, so setting the value too low can result in an ineffective ability.

Target CR	Recommended Damage Reduction
0–2	None
3–5	5
6–13	10
14–20	15

Remember, even if player characters can hurt the monster, lesser creatures in the game world often cannot hurt the creature, nor can the player character's cohorts or any creatures they summon.

poor saving throws should be roughly equal to its target CR. For example, if you are designing a CR 6 monster, a good save bonus of +9 and a poor save bonus of +6 should give the monster a decent chance to save against the player characters' attacks without making their attacks ineffective.

The easiest way to manipulate a creature's save bonuses is to assign a feat that increases a save bonus (for example, Iron Will). If you don't want to give the monster the feat, but you still want to increase the save bonus, then you need to adjust the ability score from which the save bonus is derived.

SKILLS

Assign whatever skills you think the creature ought to have. The number of skill points a creature has depends on its type, Hit Dice, and Intelligence; see Table 5–4. Assume that any skill you choose for the creature is a class skill, and each rank costs 1 skill point. The maximum rank for any skill is the creature's Hit Dice + 3. A creature with less than 1 Hit Die is treated as having 1 Hit Die for the purpose of determining skill points and maximum skill rank.

TABLE 5–4: SKILL POINTS BY MONSTER TYPE

Type	Skill Points
Aberration	(2 + Int modifier, minimum 1) × (HD+3)
Animal	(2 + Int modifier, minimum 1) × (HD+3)
Construct*	(2 + Int modifier, minimum 1) × (HD+3)
Dragon	(6 + Int modifier, minimum 1) × (HD+3)
Elemental	(2 + Int modifier, minimum 1) × (HD+3)
Fey	(6 + Int modifier, minimum 1) × (HD+3)
Giant	(2 + Int modifier, minimum 1) × (HD+3)
Humanoid**	(2 + Int modifier, minimum 1) × (HD+3)
Magical beast	(2 + Int modifier, minimum 1) × (HD+3)
Monstrous humanoid	(2 + Int modifier, minimum 1) × (HD+3)
Ooze*	(2 + Int modifier, minimum 1) × (HD+3)
Outsider	(8 + Int modifier, minimum 1) × (HD+3)
Plant*	(2 + Int modifier, minimum 1) × (HD+3)
Undead*	(4 + Int modifier, minimum 1) × (HD+3)
Vermin*	(2 + Int modifier, minimum 1) × (HD+3)

* Mindless creatures receive no skill points or feats.
** Or by character class.

It is important to consider your concept when assigning skills. Creatures that live by hunting need Hide, Spot, and Listen, and probably Move Silently. Creatures that use spells or spell-like abilities need Concentration and probably Spellcraft. Creatures that do not have a climb or swim speed may benefit from Climb or Swim. Skills such as Balance and Escape Artist can be useful for almost any creature.

A creature's final skill modifier consists of: skill ranks + ability modifier + size modifier (for Hide) + movement mode modifier (for Climb, Jump, or Swim) + racial bonuses (if any) + synergy bonuses (if any) + armor check modifier (if any). You may decide to purchase feats that change the creature's skill modifiers, too.

Conditional Bonuses: If the creature has conditional ability adjustments, do not apply them in the Skills entry. Instead, mark the skill modifier with an asterisk and note the conditional modifier in the creature's description.

Racial Skill Bonuses: Often a creature will need a better skill modifier than its abilities and skill points allow. In such cases, it's a good idea to assign it a racial bonus (which is effective all the time), or a specific circumstance bonus. For example, most big cats get bonuses on Hide and Move Silently checks, and even larger conditional bonuses on Hide and Move Silently checks when they're in the right terrain. They'd have a hard time surviving as predators without them.

FEATS

All monsters have a number of feats equal to 1 + (1 per 3 HD). Monsters must meet the prerequisites for feats, just as characters must. If your creature concept begs for a feat for which the crea-

ture does not qualify, consider altering the creature so that it qualifies for the feat, or assign the feat as a bonus feat. (It is acceptable for a creature to have a bonus feat for which it does not meet the prerequisites.)

Assign feats with your creature concept in mind, just as you did for skills. For example, spellcasting creatures can benefit from Combat Casting. Creatures that depend on their senses to locate prey or alert them to danger can benefit from Alertness. Creatures that attack from ambush can use Improved Initiative. Any creature can benefit from the feats that improve saving throws (Great Fortitude, Lightning Reflexes, and Iron Will).

Weak creatures can often benefit from Weapon Finesse, which allows a creature to use its Dexterity bonus on melee attacks (very useful for Small, Tiny, and Diminutive creatures). Likewise, very big or strong creatures benefit from Power Attack, which allows them to convert points from their attack bonus into extra damage.

SPACE/REACH

This entry describes how much space the creature takes up on the battle grid and needs to fight effectively, as well as how close it has to be to an opponent to threaten that opponent.

A creature's Space/Reach entry depends on its size, as shown on Table 7–1: Creature Sizes (page 314). A creature's space is always a square area, no matter what the creature's shape or anatomy is like. For example, an ogre and a horse have the same space figure (10 feet), because they're both Large creatures.

Tall creatures (bipeds, usually) have a longer reach than long creatures. For example, a horse has a reach of 5 feet, but an ogre has a reach of 10 feet because it is taller.

Some creatures have exceptional reach due to a particular weapon choice or a quirk of anatomy. It's all right to assign a special reach figure that applies to a particular attack (such as the roper's strands).

ENVIRONMENT

Consider where the creature lives and choose a preferred climate (warm, temperate, or cold) and terrain (plains, hills, forest, marsh, mountains, or desert). Your monster is not restricted to that combination of climate and terrain, but it's the setting the monster is most likely to be encountered in.

Creatures that have no place in the natural environment (particularly constructs and undead) usually have an entry of "Any." Extraplanar outsiders should be assigned a plane of origin.

TREASURE

Most creatures will have no treasure (None) or standard treasure. Very intelligent creatures might have double or triple treasure. Some creatures may collect only certain types of treasure. See Table 3–5, page 52 of the *Dungeon Master's Guide.*

ALIGNMENT

What alignment does your monster have? Choose lawful, neutral, or chaotic, followed by good, neutral, or evil. All alignments have a qualifier: always, usually, or often. See page 305 for details.

SKILLS THE QUICK WAY

Instead of fretting about each skill point, an easy way to assign skills to a monster is to simply buy a number of skills, all at the creature's maximum ranks. The number of individual skills a creature can choose this way is equal to its Intelligence modifier plus the base number of skill points a creature of its type receives per HD. For example, undead have skill points equal to (4 + Int modifier) at each HD, so an undead creature with an Intelligence score of 15 (Int modifier +2) could simply select six skills at maximum rank.

ADVANCEMENT

This entry provides a measure of how tough the creature can get if you decide to increase its Hit Dice. In general, a creature should be able to have up to three times its original Hit Dice (that is, a 3 HD creature should be able to advance up to 9 HD).

Most creatures will get larger if you add a lot of Hit Dice, so you should pick a break point at which the creature's size changes. For example, the Advancement entry for a Large plant creature with 3 Hit Dice might read: 4–5 HD (Large); 6–9 HD (Huge). See Table 5–1 for guidelines on size and Hit Dice.

Some monster types don't have obvious break points between size categories. In these cases, you probably want to set the break point between sizes at 1/2 the maximum Hit Dice to be added. For example, a Large aberration with 4 HD could advance to 12 HD. Since you're adding up to 8 Hit Dice, the creature's Advancement entry might read: 5–8 HD (Large); 9–12 (Huge).

CHALLENGE RATING

This shows what level of party for which the creature would make a good encounter of moderate difficulty. A party of four fresh characters (full hit points, full spells, and an assortment of equipment appropriate to their levels) should be able to win the encounter with some damage, but no casualties, given reasonable luck. This victory should consume no more than 20% of the party resources (hit points, spells, and consumable magic items).

Assigning an appropriate Challenge Rating can be difficult. The two basic tools for determining CR are comparing and playtesting.

Comparing CR

The simplest and quickest way to estimate your monster's Challenge Rating is to compare it to similar monsters in an appropriate CR range. Begin with the target CR you used in constructing your monster. Use the list of Monsters by Challenge Rating (see page 318) to compile a list of monsters whose CRs match your monster's CR, plus or minus 1. For example, if your target CR is 7, you should closely examine monsters of CR 6, 7, and 8.

To narrow your list, look for monsters with similar types or similar methods (bruisers, spell-like ability users, special attack users, and so on). Once you've reduced your list of comparable monsters to a manageable number, see how your monster compares to the others, using the following checklist:

—Does your monster have more or less Hit Dice?

—Does your monster have a better or worse Armor Class?

—Does your monster have a higher or lower attack bonus?

—Does your monster deal more or less damage?

—Does your monster have more deadly special attacks?

—Does your monster have spell-like abilities whose highest spell level is lower or higher than the spell-like abilities of comparable monsters?

—Does your monster have special defenses the other monsters don't have?

If your monster is clearly superior to most of the comparable monsters, your target CR is probably too low. Try adjusting the CR up by 1 or 2, then find a new list of monsters that should be comparable at the new CR and see how your monster stacks up. If your monster is clearly not as tough as most of the comparable monsters, reduce your CR by 1 or 2 and find a new list of comparable monsters to check your monster against.

Playtesting CR

The best way to set a monster's CR is to see how it handles in play. This can be time-consuming, but it probably gives you the best information about how challenging your monster is.

To playtest a monster's CR, use the following procedure:

1. Create a "playtest party" consisting of four characters whose level equals your monster's target CR + 2. Each character should be built using the standard ability score array and equipment for a PC of their level. Include a fighter, rogue, cleric, and wizard if possible. You can use copies of your players' characters for this, but if your PCs are unusual, your results will be skewed.

2. Create a representative encounter for the monster that uses two of the creatures (two monsters of CR X is an appropriate encounter for four PCs of level X+2). For simple monsters, a room and a door should suffice, but if your monster is built to ambush parties or make good use of a particular terrain, you should probably check the monster in the sort of environment you expect to use when you employ the monster in a real game session.

3. Allow the PCs to begin the encounter with spells or effects whose duration is measured at 10 minutes per level or longer in effect.

4. Assign all combatants an initiative roll of 10, modified by their normal initiative modifiers (for playtests, you want everyone to take 10 on their initiative roll).

5. Run the encounter several times and try different tactics and setups for the monsters.

If your proposed CR is appropriate, the PCs should be able to win the encounter with some damage, given reasonable luck. This victory should consume no more than 20% of the party resources (hit points, spells, and consumable magic items). In the case of high-CR monsters (say, 11 or more), an occasional PC death is not out of line with the monster's CR, since parties of that level can usually bring dead characters back to life pretty easily.

If your monster seems too dangerous, try the encounter again with a single monster; this lets you see how the monster looks as a solitary combatant whose CR is equal to the party's level. If the party handles the monster with no trouble, try increasing the number of monsters to three or four (which would effectively lower the monster's CR by 1 or 2). You may need to adjust the party's level and try the monster again at its new CR.

Monster Function and Challenge Rating

A quick and dirty way to double-check your CR assignment is to compare your monster's Hit Dice against its CR. Depending on their function, monsters need a high number of Hit Dice for their CR, a low amount of Hit Dice for their CR, or an average amount.

Evaluate your monster and decide what its basic function is: battler, ambusher, magic user, special attack user, or multiple threat.

Battler: The monster uses sheer combat skill to threaten the party and has few special abilities. Examples: dire animal (any), giant (any), gray render, minotaur, shambling mound, worg. A battler's CR should be from 1/3 its HD to 2/3 its HD.

Ambusher: The monster depends on stealth or surprise attacks to threaten the party. Examples: assassin vine, choker, derro, mimic, phase spider, roper. An ambusher's CR should be from 1/2 its HD to its HD.

Magic User: The monster's best attacks are its spells or spell-like abilities. Examples: aboleth, lamia, lillend, mind flayer, nymph. A magic user's CR should be from about its HD to its HD +2, provided the spells it can employ would be appropriate for a spellcasting character whose level is about the same as the monster's Hit Dice. (If they're less than expected, your monster is probably better described as an ambusher or battler.)

Special Attack User: The monster is dangerous because of a special attack it can employ. Examples: basilisk, dragon (any), harpy, medusa, wraith, vampire. A special attack user's CR should be from 2/3 its HD to its HD.

Multiple Threat: The monster combines two or more of the previous functions. For example, many demons and devils combine battler and magic user functions, while a mind flayer combines magic user and special attack user functions. Dragons with significant spellcasting ability frequently combine battler, magic user, and special attack user functions. A multiple threat's CR should be from about 3/4 its HD to its HD +2.

CHAPTER 6: MONSTER SKILLS AND FEATS

This chapter provides descriptions of one skill, Control Shape, and a number of feats that are typically used only by monsters.

CONTROL SHAPE (WIS)

Any character who has contracted lycanthropy and is aware of his condition can learn Control Shape as a class skill. (An afflicted lycanthrope not yet aware of his condition can attempt Control Shape checks untrained.) This skill determines whether an afflicted lycanthrope can control his shape. A natural lycanthrope does not need this skill, since it has full control over its shape.

Check (Involuntary Change): An afflicted character must make a check at moonrise each night of the full moon to resist involuntarily assuming animal form. An injured character must also check for an involuntary change after accumulating enough damage to reduce his hit points by one-quarter and again after each additional one-quarter lost.

Involuntary Change	Control Shape DC
Resist involuntary change	25

On a failed check, the character must remain in animal form until the next dawn, when he automatically returns to his base form. A character aware of his condition may make one attempt to return to humanoid form (see below), but if he fails, he remains in animal form until the next dawn.

Retry (Involuntary Change): Check to resist an involuntary change once each time a triggering event occurs.

Check (Voluntary Change): In addition, an afflicted lycanthrope aware of his condition may attempt to use this skill voluntarily in order to change to animal form, assume hybrid form, or return to humanoid form, regardless of the state of the moon or whether he has been injured.

Involuntary Change	Control Shape DC
Return to humanoid form (full moon*)	25
Return to humanoid form (not full moon)	20
Assume hybrid form	15
Voluntary change to animal form (full moon)	15
Voluntary change to animal form (not full moon)	20

* For game purposes, the full moon lasts three days every month.

Retry (Voluntary Change): A character can retry voluntary changes to animal form or hybrid form as often as he likes. Each attempt is a standard action. However, on a failed check to return to humanoid form, the character must remain in animal or hybrid form until the next dawn, when he automatically returns to humanoid form.

Special: An afflicted lycanthrope cannot attempt a voluntary change until it becomes aware of its condition (see Lycanthropy as an Affliction, page 178).

ABILITY FOCUS [GENERAL]

Choose one of the creature's special attacks. This attack becomes more potent than normal.

Prerequisite: Special attack.

Benefit: Add +2 to the DC for all saving throws against the special attack on which the creature focuses.

Special: A creature can gain this feat multiple times. Its effects do not stack. Each time the creature takes the feat, it applies to a different special attack.

AWESOME BLOW [GENERAL, FIGHTER]

The creature can choose to deliver blows that send its smaller opponents flying like bowling pins.

Prerequisites: Str 25, Power Attack, Improved Bull Rush, size Large or larger.

Benefit: As a standard action, the creature may choose to subtract 4 from its melee attack roll and deliver an awesome blow. If the creature hits a corporeal opponent smaller than itself with an awesome blow, its opponent must succeed on a Reflex save (DC = damage dealt) or be knocked flying 10 feet in a direction of the attacking creature's choice and fall prone. The attacking creature can only push the opponent in a straight line, and the opponent can't move closer to the attacking creature than the square it started in. If an obstacle prevents the completion of the opponent's move, the opponent and the obstacle each take 1d6 points of damage, and the opponent stops in the space adjacent to the obstacle.

CRAFT CONSTRUCT [ITEM CREATION]

The creature can create golems and other magic automatons that obey its orders.

Prerequisites: Craft Magic Arms and Armor, Craft Wondrous Item.

Benefit: A creature with this feat can create any construct whose prerequisites it meets. Enchanting a construct takes one day for each 1,000 gp in its market price. To enchant a construct, a spellcaster must spend 1/25 the item's price in XP and use up raw materials costing half of this price (see the Golem, Homunculus, and Shield Guardian monster entries for details).

A creature with this feat can repair constructs that have taken damage. In one day of work, the creature can repair up to 20 points of damage by expending 50 gp per point of damage repaired.

A newly created construct has average hit points for its Hit Dice.

EMPOWER SPELL-LIKE ABILITY [GENERAL]

The creature can use a spell-like ability with greater effect than normal.

Prerequisite: Spell-like ability at caster level 6th or higher.

Benefit: Choose one of the creature's spell-like abilities, subject to the restrictions below. The creature can use that ability as an empowered spell-like ability three times per day (or less, if the ability is normally usable only once or twice per day).

When a creature uses an empowered spell-like ability, all variable, numeric effects of the spell-like ability are increased by one-half. An empowered spell-like ability does half again as much damage as normal, cures half again as many hit points, affects half again as many targets, and so on as appropriate. For example, a night hag's empowered *magic missile* deals 1-1/2 times normal damage (roll 1d4+1 and multiply the result by 1-1/2 for each missile). Saving throws and opposed rolls (such as the one made when a character casts *dispel magic*) are not affected. Spell-like abilities without random variables are not affected.

The creature can only select a spell-like ability duplicating a spell with a level less than or equal to half its caster level (round down) −2. For a summary, see the table in the description of the Quicken Spell-Like Ability feat. For example, a creature that uses its spell-like abilities as a 13th-level caster can only empower spell-like abilities duplicating spells of 4th level or lower.

Special: This feat can be taken multiple times. Each time it is taken, the creature can apply it to a different one of its spell-like abilites.

FLYBY ATTACK [GENERAL]

The creature can attack on the wing.

Prerequisite: Fly speed.

Benefit: When flying, the creature can take a move action (including a dive) and another standard action at any point during the move. The creature cannot take a second move action during a round when it makes a flyby attack.

Normal: Without this feat, the creature takes a standard action either before or after its move.

HOVER [GENERAL]

The creature can come to a halt in midair.

Prerequisite: Fly speed.

Benefit: When flying, the creature can halt its forward motion and hover in place as a move action. It can then fly in any direction, including straight down or straight up, at half speed, regardless of its maneuverability.

If a creature begins its turn hovering, it can hover in place for the turn and take a full-round action. A hovering creature cannot make wing attacks, but it can attack with all other limbs and appendages it could use in a full attack. The creature can instead use a breath weapon or cast a spell instead of making physical attacks, if it could normally do so.

If a creature of Large size or larger hovers within 20 feet of the ground in an area with lots of loose debris, the draft from its wings creates a hemispherical cloud with a radius of 60 feet. The winds so generated can snuff torches, small campfires, exposed lanterns, and other small, open flames of nonmagical origin. Clear vision within the cloud is limited to 10 feet. Creatures have concealment at 15 to 20 feet (20% miss chance). At 25 feet or more, creatures have total concealment (50% miss chance, and opponents cannot use sight to locate the creature).

Those caught in the cloud must succeed on a Concentration check (DC 10 + 1/2 creature's HD) to cast a spell.

Normal: Without this feat, a creature must keep moving while flying unless it has perfect maneuverability.

IMPROVED NATURAL ARMOR [GENERAL]

The creature's natural armor is thicker and harder than that of others of its kind.

Prerequisites: Natural armor, Con 13.

Benefit: The creature's natural armor bonus increases by 1.

Special: A creature can gain this feat multiple times. Each time the creature takes the feat, its natural armor bonus increases by another point.

IMPROVED NATURAL ATTACK [GENERAL]

The creature's natural attacks are more dangerous than its size and type would otherwise dictate.

Prerequisite: Natural weapon, base attack bonus +4.

Benefit: Choose one of the creature's natural attack forms. The damage for this natural weapon increases by one step, as if the creature's size had increased by one category: 1d2, 1d3, 1d4, 1d6, 1d8, 2d6, 3d6, 4d6, 6d6, 8d6, 12d6. A weapon or attack that deals 1d10 points of damage increases as follows: 1d10, 2d8, 3d8, 4d8, 6d8, 8d8, 12d8.

MULTIATTACK [GENERAL]

The creature is adept at using all its natural weapons at once.

Prerequisite: Three or more natural attacks.

Benefit: The creature's secondary attacks with natural weapons take only a –2 penalty.

Normal: Without this feat, the creature's secondary attacks with natural weapons take a –5 penalty.

MULTIWEAPON FIGHTING [GENERAL]

A creature with three or more hands can fight with a weapon in each hand. The creature can make one extra attack each round with each extra weapon.

Prerequisites: Dex 13, three or more hands.

Benefit: Penalties for fighting with multiple weapons are reduced by 2 with the primary hand and reduced by 6 with off hands.

Normal: A creature without this feat takes a –6 penalty on attacks made with its primary hand and a –10 penalty on attacks made with its off hands. (It has one primary hand, and all the others are off hands.) See Two-Weapon Fighting, page 160 of the *Player's Handbook*.

Special: This feat replaces the Two-Weapon Fighting feat for creatures with more than two arms.

QUICKEN SPELL-LIKE ABILITY [GENERAL]

The creature can employ a spell-like ability with a moment's thought.

Prerequisite: Spell-like ability at caster level 10th or higher.

Benefit: Choose one of the creature's spell-like abilities, subject to the restrictions described below. The creature can use that ability as a quickened spell-like ability three times per day (or less, if the ability is normally usable only once or twice per day).

Using a quickened spell-like ability is a free action that does not provoke an attack of opportunity. The creature can perform another action—including the use of another spell-like ability—in the same round that it uses a quickened spell-like ability. The creature may use only one quickened spell-like ability per round.

The creature can only select a spell-like ability duplicating a spell with a level less than or equal to half its caster level (round down) –4. For a summary, see the table below. For example, a creature that uses its spell-like abilities as a 15th-level caster can only quicken spell-like abilities duplicating spells of 3rd level or lower. In addition, a spell-like ability that duplicates a spell with a casting time greater than 1 full round cannot be quickened.

Normal: Normally the use of a spell-like ability requires a standard action and provokes an attack of opportunity unless noted otherwise.

Special: This feat can be taken multiple times. Each time it is taken, the creature can apply it to a different one of its spell-like abilities.

EMPOWER AND QUICKEN SPELL-LIKE ABILITY

Spell Level	Caster Level to Empower	Caster Level to Quicken
0	4th	8th
1st	6th	10th
2nd	8th	12th
3rd	10th	14th
4th	12th	16th
5th	14th	18th
6th	16th	20th
7th	18th	—
8th	20th	—
9th	—	—

SNATCH [GENERAL]

The creature can grab opponents much smaller than itself and hold them in its mouth or claw.

Prerequisite: Size Huge or larger.

Benefits: The creature can choose to start a grapple when it hits with a claw or bite attack, as though it had the improved grab special attack. If the creature gets a hold on a creature three or more sizes smaller, it squeezes each round for automatic bite or claw damage. A snatched opponent held in the creature's mouth is not allowed a Reflex save against the creature's breath weapon, if it has one.

The creature can drop a creature it has snatched as a free action or use a standard action to fling it aside. A flung creature travels 1d6×10 feet, and takes 1d6 points of damage per 10 feet traveled. If the creature flings a snatched opponent while flying, the opponent takes this amount or falling damage, whichever is greater.

WINGOVER [GENERAL]

The creature can change direction quickly while flying.

Prerequisite: Fly speed.

Benefits: A flying creature with this feat can change direction quickly once each round as a free action. This feat allows it to turn up to 180 degrees regardless of its maneuverability, in addition to any other turns it is normally allowed. A creature cannot gain altitude during a round when it executes a wingover, but it can dive. The change of direction consumes 10 feet of flying movement.

CHAPTER 7: GLOSSARY

This chapter provides definitions and descriptions of monster characteristics. If you come across a term earlier in this book that you're not familiar with, this is the place to find out more.

Aberration Type: An aberration has a bizarre anatomy, strange abilities, an alien mindset, or any combination of the three.

Features: An aberration has the following features.
—d8 Hit Dice.
—Base attack bonus equal to 3/4 total Hit Dice (as cleric).
—Good Will saves.
—Skill points equal to (2 + Int modifier, minimum 1) per Hit Die, with quadruple skill points for the first Hit Die.

Traits: An aberration possesses the following traits (unless otherwise noted in a creature's entry).
—Darkvision out to 60 feet.
—Proficient with its natural weapons. If generally humanoid in form, proficient with all simple weapons and any weapon it is described as using.
—Proficient with whatever type of armor (light, medium, or heavy) it is described as wearing, as well as all lighter types. Aberrations not indicated as wearing armor are not proficient with armor. Aberrations are proficient with shields if they are proficient with any form of armor.
—Aberrations eat, sleep, and breathe.

Ability Score Loss (Su): Some attacks reduce the opponent's score in one or more abilities. This loss can be temporary (ability damage) or permanent (ability drain).

Ability Damage: This attack damages an opponent's ability score. The creature's descriptive text gives the ability and the amount of damage. If an attack that causes ability damage scores a critical hit, it deals twice the indicated amount of damage (if the damage is expressed as a die range, roll two dice). Ability damage returns at the rate of 1 point per day for each affected ability.

Ability Drain: This effect permanently reduces a living opponent's ability score when the creature hits with a melee attack. The creature's descriptive text gives the ability and the amount drained. If an attack that causes ability drain scores a critical hit, it drains twice the indicated amount (if the damage is expressed as a die range, roll two dice). Unless otherwise specified in the creature's description, a draining creature gains 5 temporary hit points (10 on a critical hit) whenever it drains an ability score no matter how many points it drains. Temporary hit points gained in this fashion last for a maximum of 1 hour.

Some ability drain attacks allow a Fortitude save (DC 10 + 1/2 draining creature's racial HD + draining creature's Cha modifier; the exact DC is given in the creature's descriptive text). If no saving throw is mentioned, none is allowed.

Alternate Form (Su): A creature with this special quality has the ability to assume one or more specific alternate forms. This ability works much like the *polymorph* spell, except that the creature is limited to the forms specified, and does not regain any hit points for changing its form. Assuming an alternate form results in the following changes to the creature:
—The creature retains the type and subtype of its original form. It gains the size of its new form.
—The creature loses the natural weapons, natural armor, movement modes, and extraordinary special attacks of its original form.
—The creature gains the natural weapons, natural armor, movement modes, and extraordinary special attacks of its new form.
—The creature retains the special qualities of its original form. It does not gain any special qualities of its new form.
—The creature retains the spell-like abilities and supernatural attacks of its old form (except for breath weapons and gaze attacks). It does not gain the spell-like abilities or supernatural attacks of its new form.
—The creature gains the physical ability scores (Str, Dex, Con) of its new form. It retains the mental ability scores (Int, Wis, Cha) of its original form.
—The creature retains its hit points and save bonuses, although its save modifiers may change due to a change in ability scores.
—The creature retains any spellcasting ability it had in its original form, although it must be able to speak intelligibly to cast spells with verbal components and it must have humanlike hands to cast spells with somatic components.
—The creature is effectively camouflaged as a creature of its new form, and it gains a +10 bonus on Disguise checks if it uses this ability to create a disguise.

Air Subtype: This subtype usually is used for elementals and outsiders with a connection to the Elemental Plane Air. Air creatures always have fly speeds and usually have perfect maneuverability (see the section on Movement, page 311).

Alignment: This line in a monster entry gives the alignment that the creature is most likely to have. Every entry includes a qualifier that indicates how broadly that alignment applies to all monsters of that kind.

Always: The creature is born with the indicated alignment. The creature may have a hereditary predisposition to the alignment or come from a plane that predetermines it. It is possible for individuals to change alignment, but such individuals are either unique or rare exceptions.

Usually: The majority (more than 50%) of these creatures have the given alignment. This may be due to strong cultural influences, or it may be a legacy of the creatures' origin. For example, most elves inherited their chaotic good alignment from their creator, the deity Corellon Larethian.

Often: The creature tends toward the given alignment, either by nature or nurture, but not strongly. A plurality (40–50%) of individuals have the given alignment, but exceptions are common.

Angel Subtype: Angels are a race of celestials, or good outsiders, native to the good-aligned Outer Planes. In the D&D cosmology, these planes are the Seven Mounting Heavens of Celestia, the Twin Paradises of Bytopia, the Olympian Glades of Arborea, the Blessed Fields of Elysium, and the Wilderness of the Beastlands.

Traits: An angel possesses the following traits (unless otherwise noted in a creature's entry).
—Darkvision out to 60 feet and low-light vision.
—Immunity to acid, cold, and petrification.
—Resistance to electricity 10 and fire 10.
—+4 racial bonus on saves against poison.
—Protective Aura (Su): Against attacks made or effects created by evil creatures, this ability provides a +4 deflection bonus to AC and a +4 resistance bonus on saving throws to anyone within 20 feet of the angel. Otherwise, it functions as a *magic circle against evil* effect and a *lesser globe of invulnerability*, both with a radius of 20 feet (caster level equals angel's HD). (The defensive benefits from the circle are not included in an angel's statistics block.)
—Tongues (Su): All angels can speak with any creature that has a language, as though using a *tongues* spell (caster level equal to angel's Hit Dice). This ability is always active.

Animal Type: An animal is a living, nonhuman creature, usually a vertebrate with no magical abilities and no innate capacity for language or culture.

Features: An animal has the following features (unless otherwise noted in a creature's entry).

—d8 Hit Dice.

—Base attack bonus equal to 3/4 total Hit Dice (as cleric).

—Good Fortitude and Reflex saves (certain animals have different good saves).

—Skill points equal to (2 + Int modifier, minimum 1) per Hit Die, with quadruple skill points for the first Hit Die.

Traits: An animal possesses the following traits (unless otherwise noted in a creature's entry).

—Intelligence score of 1 or 2 (no creature with an Intelligence score of 3 or higher can be an animal).

—Low-light vision.

—Alignment: Always neutral.

—Treasure: None.

—Proficient with its natural weapons only. A noncombative herbivore uses its natural weapons as a secondary attack. Such attacks are made with a −5 penalty on the creature's attack rolls, and the animal receives only 1/2 its Strength modifier as a damage adjustment.

—Proficient with no armor unless trained for war.

—Animals eat, sleep, and breathe.

Aquatic Subtype: These creatures always have swim speeds and thus can move in water without making Swim checks. An aquatic creature can breathe underwater. It cannot also breathe air unless it has the amphibious special quality.

Archon Subtype: Archons are a race of celestials, or good outsiders, native to the Seven Mounting Heavens of Celestia.

Traits: An archon possesses the following traits (unless otherwise noted in a creature's entry).

—Darkvision out to 60 feet and low-light vision.

—Aura of Menace (Su): A righteous aura surrounds archons that fight or get angry. Any hostile creature within a 20-foot radius of an archon must succeed on a Will save to resist its effects. The save DC varies with the type of archon, is Charisma-based, and includes a +2 racial bonus. Those who fail take a −2 penalty on attacks, AC, and saves for 24 hours or until they successfully hit the archon that generated the aura. A creature that has resisted or broken the effect cannot be affected again by the same archon's aura for 24 hours.

—Immunity to electricity and petrification.

—+4 racial bonus on saves against poison.

—Magic Circle against Evil (Su): A magic circle against evil effect always surrounds an archon (caster level equals the archon's Hit Dice). (The defensive benefits from the circle are not included in an archon's statistics block.)

—Teleport (Su): Archons can use greater teleport at will, as the spell (caster level 14th), except that the creature can transport only itself and up to 50 pounds of objects.

—Tongues (Su): All archons can speak with any creature that has a language, as though using a *tongues* spell (caster level 14th). This ability is always active.

Augmented Subtype: A creature receives this subtype whenever something happens to change its original type. Some creatures (those with an inherited template) are born with this subtype; others acquire it when they take on an acquired template. The augmented subtype is always paired with the creature's original type. For example, a wizard's raven familiar is a magical beast (augmented animal). A creature with the augmented subtype usually has the traits of its current type, but the features of its original type. For example, a wizard's raven familiar has an animal's features and the traits of a magical beast.

Baatezu Subtype: Many devils belong to the race of evil outsiders known as the baatezu.

Traits: A baatezu possesses the following traits (unless otherwise noted in a creature's entry).

—Immunity to fire and poison.

—Resistance to acid 10 and cold 10.

—See in Darkness (Su): All baatezu can see perfectly in darkness of any kind, even that created by a *deeper darkness* spell.

—Summon (Sp): Baatezu share the ability to summon others of their kind (the success chance and type of baatezu summoned are noted in each monster description).

—Telepathy.

Blindsense (Ex): Using nonvisual senses, such as acute smell or hearing, a creature with blindsense notices things it cannot see. The creature usually does not need to make Spot or Listen checks to pinpoint the location of a creature within range of its blindsense ability, provided that it has line of effect to that creature. Any opponent the creature cannot see still has total concealment against the creature with blindsense, and the creature still has the normal miss chance when attacking foes that have concealment. Visibility still affects the movement of a creature with blindsense. A creature with blindsense is still denied its Dexterity bonus to Armor Class against attacks from creatures it cannot see.

Blindsight (Ex): This ability is similar to blindsense, but is far more discerning. Using nonvisual senses, such as sensitivity to vibrations, keen smell, acute hearing, or echolocation, a creature with blindsight maneuvers and fights as well as a sighted creature. Invisibility, darkness, and most kinds of concealment are irrelevant, though the creature must have line of effect to a creature or object to discern that creature or object. The ability's range is specified in the creature's descriptive text. The creature usually does not need to make Spot or Listen checks to notice creatures within range of its blindsight ability. Unless noted otherwise, blindsight is continuous, and the creature need do nothing to use it. Some forms of blindsight, however, must be triggered as a free action. If so, this is noted in the creature's description. If a creature must trigger its blindsight ability, the creature gains the benefits of blindsight only during its turn.

Breath Weapon (Su): A breath weapon attack usually deals damage and is often based on some type of energy (such as fire). Such breath weapons allow a Reflex save for half damage (DC 10 + 1/2 breathing creature's racial HD + breathing creature's Con modifier; the exact DC is given in the creature's descriptive text). A creature is immune to its own breath weapon unless otherwise noted. Some breath weapons allow a Fortitude save or a Will save instead of a Reflex save.

Change Shape (Su): A creature with this special quality has the ability to assume the appearance of a specific creature or type of creature (usually a humanoid), but retains most of its own physical qualities. A creature cannot change shape to a form more than one size category smaller or larger than its original form. Changing shape results in the following changes to the creature:

—The creature retains the type and subtype of its original form. It gains the size of its new form.

—The creature loses the natural weapons, movement modes, and extraordinary special attacks of its original form.

—The creature gains the natural weapons, movement modes, and extraordinary special attacks of its new form.

—The creature retains all other special attacks and qualities of its original form, except for breath weapons and gaze attacks.

—The creature retains the ability scores of its original form.

—The creature retains its hit points and saves.

—The creature retains any spellcasting ability it had in its original form, although it must be able to speak intelligibly to cast spells with verbal components and it must have humanlike hands to cast spells with somatic components.

—The creature is effectively camouflaged as a creature of its new form, and gains a +10 bonus on Disguise checks if it uses this ability to create a disguise.

Chaotic Subtype: A subtype usually applied only to outsiders native to the chaotic-aligned Outer Planes. Most creatures that have this subtype also have chaotic alignments; however, if their alignments change they still retain the subtype. Any effect that depends on alignment affects a creature with this subtype as if the creature has a chaotic alignment, no matter what its alignment actually is. The creature also suffers effects according to its actual alignment. A creature with the chaotic subtype overcomes damage reduction as if its natural weapons and any weapons it wields were chaotic-aligned (see Damage Reduction, below).

Class Skills: Any skill in which a monster has acquired at least one rank or in which the creature has a racial bonus is considered a class skill for that kind of creature. Some monsters, such as the true dragons, have their class skills explicitly listed. Other monsters' class skills can be determined from their statistics blocks.

Creatures with a Swim speed always have Swim as a class skill. Creatures with a Climb speed always have Climb as a class skill. Skills listed in an entry merely because of synergy with another skill are not class skills. For example, a marilith's class skills are Bluff, Concentration, Diplomacy, Hide, Intimidate, Listen, Move Silently, Search, Sense Motive, Spellcraft, Spot, and Use Magic Device. Even though Disguise and Survival are mentioned in the creature's statistics block, their presence is exclusively due to the synergy benefit granted by Bluff and Search.

Cold Subtype: A creature with the cold subtype has immunity to cold. It has vulnerability to fire, which means it takes half again as much (+50%) damage as normal from fire, regardless of whether a saving throw is allowed, or if the save is a success or failure.

Constrict (Ex): A creature with this special attack can crush an opponent, dealing bludgeoning damage, after making a successful grapple check. The amount of damage is given in the creature's entry. If the creature also has the improved grab ability (see page 310), it deals constriction damage in addition to damage dealt by the weapon used to grab.

Construct Type: A construct is an animated object or artificially constructed creature.

Features: A construct has the following features.
—10-sided Hit Dice.
—Base attack bonus equal to 3/4 total Hit Dice (as cleric).
—No good saving throws.
—Skill points equal to (2 + Int modifier, minimum 1) per Hit Die, with quadruple skill points for the first Hit Die, if the construct has an Intelligence score. However, most constructs are mindless and gain no skill points or feats.

Traits: A construct possesses the following traits (unless otherwise noted in a creature's entry).
—No Constitution score.
—Low-light vision.
—Darkvision out to 60 feet.
—Immunity to all mind-affecting effects (charms, compulsions, phantasms, patterns, and morale effects).
—Immunity to poison, sleep effects, paralysis, stunning, disease, death effects, and necromancy effects.
—Cannot heal damage on their own, but often can be repaired by exposing them to a certain kind of effect (see the creature's description for details) or through the use of the Craft Construct feat (see page 303). A construct with the fast healing special quality still benefits from that quality.
—Not subject to critical hits, nonlethal damage, ability damage, ability drain, fatigue, exhaustion, or energy drain.

—Immunity to any effect that requires a Fortitude save (unless the effect also works on objects, or is harmless).
—Not at risk of death from massive damage (see page 145 of the *Player's Handbook*). Immediately destroyed when reduced to 0 hit points or less.
—Since it was never alive, a construct cannot be raised or resurrected.
—Because its body is a mass of unliving matter, a construct is hard to destroy. It gains bonus hit points based on size, as shown on the following table.

Construct Size	Bonus Hit Points	Construct Size	Bonus Hit Points
Fine	—	Large	30
Diminutive	—	Huge	40
Tiny	—	Gargantuan	60
Small	10	Colossal	80
Medium	20		

—Proficient with its natural weapons only, unless generally humanoid in form, in which case proficient with any weapon mentioned in its entry.
—Proficient with no armor.
—Constructs do not eat, sleep, or breathe.

Damage Reduction (Ex or Su): A creature with this special quality ignores damage from most weapons and natural attacks. Wounds heal immediately, or the weapon bounces off harmlessly (in either case, the opponent knows the attack was ineffective). The creature takes normal damage from energy attacks (even nonmagical ones), spells, spell-like abilities, and supernatural abilities. A certain kind of weapon can sometimes damage the creature normally, as noted below.

The entry indicates the amount of damage ignored (usually 5 to 15 points) and the type of weapon that negates the ability. For example, the werewolf's entry reads "damage reduction 10/silver": Each time a foe hits a werewolf with a weapon, the damage dealt by that attack is reduced by 10 points (to a minimum of 0). However, a silvered weapon deals full damage.

Some monsters are vulnerable to piercing, bludgeoning, or slashing damage. For example, skeletons have damage reduction 5/bludgeoning. When hit with slashing or piercing weapons, the damage dealt by each attack is reduced by 5 points, but bludgeoning weapons deal full damage.

Some monsters are vulnerable to certain materials, such as alchemical silver, adamantine, or cold-forged iron. Attacks from weapons that are not made of the correct material have their damage reduced, even if the weapon has an enhancement bonus. Examples: the werewolf's damage reduction 10/silver, the iron golem's damage reduction 15/adamantine, and the nymph's damage reduction 10/cold iron.

Some monsters are vulnerable to magic weapons. Any weapon with at least a +1 magical enhancement bonus on attack and damage rolls overcomes the damage reduction of these monsters. Such creatures' natural weapons (but not their attacks with weapons) are treated as magic weapons for the purpose of overcoming damage reduction. For example, the gargoyle has damage reduction 10/magic and can strike as a magic weapon for the purpose of overcoming damage reduction.

A few very powerful monsters, such as the solar and the tarrasque, are vulnerable only to epic weapons; that is, magic weapons with at least a +6 enhancement bonus. Such creatures' natural weapons are also treated as epic weapons for the purpose of overcoming damage reduction.

Some monsters are vulnerable to chaotic-, evil-, good-, or lawful-aligned weapons. When a cleric casts *align weapon*, affected weapons might gain one or more of these properties, and certain magic weapons have these properties as well. For example, many tanar'ri demons and baatezu devils have damage reduction 10/good, while many celestials have damage reduction 10/evil. A creature with an alignment subtype (chaotic, evil, good, or lawful) can overcome this type of damage reduction with its natural weapons and weapons it wields as if the weapons or natural weapons had an alignment (or alignments) that match the subtype(s) of the creature. A bearded devil, for instance, has the evil and lawful subtypes, and thus can overcome damage reduction as if its weapons and natural weapons were evil-aligned and lawful-aligned.

When a damage reduction entry has a dash (–) after the slash, no weapon negates the damage reduction.

A few creatures are harmed by more than one kind of weapon. The babau demon, for example, has damage reduction 10/cold iron or good. Either kind of weapon—cold iron or good—overcomes its damage reduction.

A few other creatures require combinations of different types of attacks to overcome their damage reduction. The ghaele eladrin has damage reduction 10/evil and cold iron, meaning that a weapon must be made of cold-forged iron and be evil-aligned in order to overcome the ghaele's damage reduction. A lich has damage reduction 15/bludgeoning and magic, meaning that only bludgeoning weapons with at least a +1 enhancement bonus deal full damage to it. A weapon that falls into one category but not the other is of no help in overcoming the creature's damage reduction—a magic sword or a nonmagical mace is no better at harming a lich than any other weapon.

Dragon Type: A dragon is a reptilelike creature, usually winged, with magical or unusual abilities.

Features: A dragon has the following features.
—12-sided Hit Dice.
—Base attack bonus equal to total Hit Dice (as fighter).
—Good Fortitude, Reflex, and Will saves.
—Skill points equal to (6 + Int modifier, minimum 1) per Hit Die, with quadruple skill points for the first Hit Die.

Traits: A dragon possesses the following traits (unless otherwise noted in the description of a particular kind).
—Darkvision out to 60 feet and low-light vision.
—Immunity to magic sleep effects and paralysis effects.
—Proficient with its natural weapons only unless humanoid in form (or capable of assuming humanoid form), in which case proficient with all simple weapons and any weapons mentioned in its entry.
—Proficient with no armor.
—Dragons eat, sleep, and breathe.

Earth Subtype: This subtype usually is used for elementals and outsiders with a connection to the Elemental Plane of Earth. Earth creatures usually have burrow speeds, and most earth creatures can burrow through solid rock.

Effective Character Level (ECL): This number represents a creature's overall power relative to that of a character from the *Player's Handbook.* A creature with an ECL of 10 is roughly equivalent to a 10th-level character. A creature's ECL is the sum of its Hit Dice (including class levels) and level adjustment. For instance, a minotaur has 6 HD and a +2 level adjustment. It is the equivalent of an 8th-level character.

Eladrin Subtype: Eladrins are a race of celestials, or good outsiders, native to the the Olympian Glades of Arborea.

Traits: An eladrin possesses the following traits (unless otherwise noted in a creature's entry).
—Darkvision out to 60 feet and low-light vision.
—Immunity to electricity and petrification.
—Resistance to cold 10 and fire 10.
—Tongues (Su): All eladrins can speak with any creature that has a language, as though using a *tongues* spell (caster level 14th). This ability is always active.

Elemental Type: An elemental is a being composed of one of the four classical elements: air, earth, fire, or water.

Features: An elemental has the following features.
—8-sided Hit Dice.
—Base attack bonus equal to 3/4 total Hit Dice (as cleric).
—Good saves depend on the element: Fortitude (earth, water) or Reflex (air, fire).
—Skill points equal to (2 + Int modifier, minimum 1) per Hit Die, with quadruple skill points for the first Hit Die.

Traits: An elemental possesses the following traits (unless otherwise noted in a creature's entry).
—Darkvision out to 60 feet.
—Immunity to poison, sleep effects, paralysis, and stunning.
—Not subject to critical hits or flanking.
—Unlike most other living creatures, an elemental does not have a dual nature—its soul and body form one unit. When an elemental is slain, no soul is set loose. Spells that restore souls to their bodies, such as *raise dead, reincarnate,* and *resurrection,* don't work on an elemental. It takes a different magical effect, such as *limited wish, wish, miracle,* or *true resurrection,* to restore it to life.
—Proficient with natural weapons only, unless generally humanoid in form, in which case proficient with all simple weapons and any weapons mentioned in its entry.
—Proficient with whatever type of armor (light, medium, or heavy) that it is described as wearing, as well as all lighter types. Elementals not indicated as wearing armor are not proficient with armor. Elementals are proficient with shields if they are proficient with any form of armor.
—Elementals do not eat, sleep, or breathe.

Energy Drain (Su): This attack saps a living opponent's vital energy and happens automatically when a melee or ranged attack hits. Each successful energy drain bestows one or more negative levels (the creature's description specifies how many). If an attack that includes an energy drain scores a critical hit, it drains twice the given amount. Unless otherwise specified in the creature's description, a draining creature gains 5 temporary hit points (10 on a critical hit) for each negative level it bestows on an opponent. These temporary hit points last for a maximum of 1 hour.

An affected opponent takes a –1 penalty on all skill checks and ability checks, attack rolls, and saving throws, and loses one effective level or Hit Die (whenever level is used in a die roll or calculation) for each negative level. A spellcaster loses one spell slot of the highest level of spells she can cast and (if applicable) one prepared spell of that level; this loss persists until the negative level is removed.

Negative levels remain until 24 hours have passed or until they are removed with a spell, such as *restoration.* If a negative level is not removed before 24 hours have passed, the affected creature must attempt a Fortitude save (DC 10 + 1/2 draining creature's racial HD + draining creature's Cha modifier; the exact DC is given in the creature's descriptive text). On a success, the negative level goes away with no harm to the creature. On a failure, the negative level goes away, but the creature's level is also reduced by one. A separate saving throw is required for each negative level.

Environment: This entry in a statistics block describes the type of climate and terrain where the creature is typically found. This is a preference, but is not exclusionary. Note that these environments can also exist in portions of dungeons due to magical effects or other supernatural interference, or as features in dungeons or other environment areas. Chapter 5 of the *Dungeon Master's Guide* has details on climate and terrain types.

Evil Subtype: A subtype usually applied only to outsiders native to the evil-aligned Outer Planes. Evil outsiders are also called fiends. Most creatures that have this subtype also have evil alignments; however, if their alignments change, they still retain the subtype. Any effect that depends on alignment affects a creature with this subtype as if the creature has an evil alignment, no matter what its alignment actually is. The creature also suffers effects according to its actual alignment. A creature with the evil subtype overcomes damage reduction as if its natural weapons and any weapons it wields were evil-aligned (see Damage Reduction, above).

Extraplanar Subtype: A subtype applied to any creature when it is on a plane other than its native plane. A creature that travels the planes can gain or lose this subtype as it goes from plane to plane. This book assumes that encounters with creatures take place on the Material Plane, and every creature whose native plane is not the Material Plane has the extraplanar subtype (but would not have when on its home plane). Every extraplanar creature in this book has a home plane mentioned in its description. These home planes are taken from the Great Wheel cosmology of the D&D game (see Chapter 5 of the *Dungeon Master's Guide*). If your campaign uses a different cosmology, you will need to assign different home planes to extraplanar creatures.

Creatures not labeled as extraplanar are natives of the Material Plane, and they gain the extraplanar subtype if they leave the Material Plane. No creature has the extraplanar subtype when it is on a transitive plane; the transitive planes in the D&D cosmology are the Astral Plane, the Ethereal Plane, and the Plane of Shadow.

Fast Healing (Ex): A creature with the fast healing special quality regains hit points at an exceptionally fast rate, usually 1 or more hit points per round, as given in the creature's entry (for example, a vampire has fast healing 5). Except where noted here, fast healing is just like natural healing (see page 146 of the *Player's Handbook*). Fast healing does not restore hit points lost from starvation, thirst, or suffocation, and it does not allow a creature to regrow lost body parts. Unless otherwise stated, it does not allow lost body parts to be reattached.

Favored Class: A monster that takes levels in a class (or more than one class) has a favored class, just as player characters do. In addition, a monster's racial Hit Dice also count as a favored class, in effect: If the monster becomes a multiclass character, neither its favored class nor its racial Hit Dice count when determining whether the creature takes an experience point penalty.

Fear (Su or Sp): Fear attacks can have various effects.

Fear Aura (Su): The use of this ability is a free action. The aura can freeze an opponent (such as a mummy's despair) or function like the *fear* spell (for example, the aura of a lich). Other effects are possible. A fear aura is an area effect. The descriptive text gives the size and kind of area.

Fear Cones (Sp) and Rays (Su): These effects usually work like the *fear* spell.

If a fear effect allows a saving throw, it is a Will save (DC 10 + 1/2 fearsome creature's racial HD + creature's Cha modifier; the exact DC is given in the creature's descriptive text). All fear attacks are mind-affecting fear effects.

Fey Type: A fey is a creature with supernatural abilities and connections to nature or to some other force or place. Fey are usually human-shaped.

Features: A fey has the following features.
—6-sided Hit Dice.
—Base attack bonus equal to 1/2 total Hit Dice (as wizard).
—Good Reflex and Will saves.
—Skill points equal to (6 + Int modifier, minimum 1) per Hit Die, with quadruple skill points for the first Hit Die.

Traits: A fey possesses the following traits (unless otherwise noted in a creature's entry).

—Low-light vision.
—Proficient with all simple weapons and any weapons mentioned in its entry.
—Proficient with whatever type of armor (light, medium, or heavy) that it is described as wearing, as well as all lighter types. Fey not indicated as wearing armor are not proficient with armor. Fey are proficient with shields if they are proficient with any form of armor.
—Fey eat, sleep, and breathe.

Fire Subtype: A creature with the fire subtype has immunity to fire. It has vulnerability to cold, which means it takes half again as much (+50%) damage as normal from cold, regardless of whether a saving throw is allowed, or if the save is a success or failure.

Flight (Ex or Su): A creature with this ability can cease or resume flight as a free action. If the ability is supernatural, it becomes ineffective in an antimagic field, and the creature loses its ability to fly for as long as the antimagic effect persists.

Frightful Presence (Ex): This special quality makes a creature's very presence unsettling to foes. It takes effect automatically when the creature performs some sort of dramatic action (such as charging, attacking, or snarling). Opponents within range who witness the action may become frightened or shaken.

Actions required to trigger the ability are given in the creature's descriptive text. The range is usually 30 feet, and the duration is usually 5d6 rounds.

This ability affects only opponents with fewer Hit Dice or levels than the creature has. An affected opponent can resist the effects with a successful Will save (DC 10 + 1/2 frightful creature's racial HD + frightful creature's Cha modifier; the exact DC is given in the creature's descriptive text). An opponent that succeeds on the saving throw is immune to that same creature's frightful presence for 24 hours. Frightful presence is a mind-affecting fear effect.

Gaze (Su): A gaze special attack takes effect when opponents look at the creature's eyes. The attack can have almost any sort of effect: petrification, death, charm, and so on. The typical range is 30 feet, but check the creature's entry for details.

The type of saving throw for a gaze attack varies, but it is usually a Will or Fortitude save (DC 10 + 1/2 gazing creature's racial HD + gazing creature's Cha modifier; the exact DC is given in the creature's descriptive text). A successful saving throw negates the effect. A monster's gaze attack is described in abbreviated form in its description.

Each opponent within range of a gaze attack must attempt a saving throw each round at the beginning of his or her turn in the initiative order. Only looking directly at a creature with a gaze attack leaves an opponent vulnerable. Opponents can avoid the need to make the saving throw by not looking at the creature, in one of two ways.

Averting Eyes: The opponent avoids looking at the creature's face, instead looking at its body, watching its shadow, tracking it in a reflective surface, and so on. Each round, the opponent has a 50% chance to not need to make a saving throw against the gaze attack. The creature with the gaze attack, however, gains concealment against that opponent.

Wearing a Blindfold: The opponent cannot see the creature at all (also possible to achieve by turning one's back on the creature or shutting one's eyes). The creature with the gaze attack gains total concealment against the opponent.

A creature with a gaze attack can actively gaze as an attack action by choosing a target within range. That opponent must attempt a saving throw but can try to avoid this as described above. Thus, it is possible for an opponent to save against a creature's gaze twice during the same round, once before the opponent's action and once during the creature's turn.

Gaze attacks can affect ethereal opponents. A creature is immune to gaze attacks of others of its kind unless otherwise noted. Allies of a creature with a gaze attack might be affected. All the creature's allies are considered to be averting their eyes from the creature with the gaze attack, and have a 50% chance to not need to make a saving throw against the gaze attack each round. The creature also can veil its eyes, thus negating its gaze ability.

Giant Type: A giant is a humanoid-shaped creature of great strength, usually of at least Large size.

Features: A giant has the following features.

—8-sided Hit Dice.

—Base attack bonus equal to 3/4 total Hit Dice (as cleric).

—Good Fortitude saves.

—Skill points equal to (2 + Int modifier, minimum 1) per Hit Die, with quadruple skill points for the first Hit Die.

Traits: A giant possesses the following traits (unless otherwise noted in a creature's entry).

—Low-light vision.

—Proficient with all simple and martial weapons, as well as any natural weapons.

—Proficient with whatever type of armor (light, medium or heavy) it is described as wearing, as well as all lighter types. Giants not described as wearing armor are not proficient with armor. Giants are proficient with shields if they are proficient with any form of armor.

—Giants eat, sleep, and breathe.

Goblinoid Subtype: Goblinoids are stealthy humanoids who live by hunting and raiding and who all speak Goblin.

Good Subtype: A subtype usually applied only to outsiders native to the good-aligned Outer Planes. Most creatures that have this subtype also have good alignments; however, if their alignments change, they still retain the subtype. Any effect that depends on alignment affects a creature with this subtype as if the creature has a good alignment, no matter what its alignment actually is. The creature also suffers effects according to its actual alignment. A creature with the good subtype overcomes damage reduction as if its natural weapons and any weapons it wields were good-aligned (see Damage Reduction, above).

Guardinal Subtype: Guardinals are a race of celestials, or good outsiders, native to the the Blessed Fields of Elysium.

Traits: A guardinal possesses the following traits (unless otherwise noted in a creature's entry).

—Darkvision out to 60 feet and low-light vision.

—Immunity to electricity and petrification.

—Resistance to cold 10 and sonic 10.

—Lay on Hands (Su): As the paladin class feature, except that each day, a guardinal can heal an amount of damage equal to its full normal hit points.

— +4 racial bonus on saves against poison.

—Speak with Animals (Su): This ability works like *speak with animals* (caster level 8th) but is a free action and does not require sound.

Humanoid Type: A humanoid usually has two arms, two legs, and one head, or a humanlike torso, arms, and a head. Humanoids have few or no supernatural or extraordinary abilities, but most can speak and usually have well-developed societies. They usually are Small or Medium. Every humanoid creature also has a subtype, such as elf, goblinoid, or reptilian.

Humanoids with 1 Hit Die exchange the features of their humanoid Hit Die for the class features of a PC or NPC class. Humanoids of this sort are presented as 1st-level warriors, which means that they have average combat ability and poor saving throws.

Humanoids with more than 1 Hit Die (for example, gnolls and bugbears) are the only humanoids who make use of the features of the humanoid type.

Features: A humanoid has the following features (unless otherwise noted in a creature's entry).

—8-sided Hit Dice, or by character class.

—Base attack bonus equal to 3/4 total Hit Dice (as cleric).

—Good Reflex saves (usually; a humanoid's good save varies).

—Skill points equal to (2 + Int modifier, minimum 1) per Hit Die, with quadruple skill points for the first Hit Die, or by character class.

Traits: A humanoid possesses the following traits (unless otherwise noted in a creature's entry).

—Proficient with all simple weapons, or by character class.

—Proficient with whatever type of armor (light, medium, or heavy) it is described as wearing, or by character class. If a humanoid does not have a class and wears armor, it is proficient with that type of armor and all lighter types. Humanoids not indicated as wearing armor are not proficient with armor. Humanoids are proficient with shields if they are proficient with any form of armor.

—Humanoids breathe, eat, and sleep.

Improved Grab (Ex): If a creature with this special attack hits with a melee weapon (usually a claw or bite attack), it deals normal damage and attempts to start a grapple as a free action without provoking an attack of opportunity (see Grapple, page 155 of the *Player's Handbook*). No initial touch attack is required.

Unless otherwise noted, improved grab works only against opponents at least one size category smaller than the creature. The creature has the option to conduct the grapple normally, or simply use the part of its body it used in the improved grab to hold the opponent. If it chooses to do the latter, it takes a –20 penalty on grapple checks, but is not considered grappled itself; the creature does not lose its Dexterity bonus to AC, still threatens an area, and can use its remaining attacks against other opponents.

A successful hold does not deal any extra damage unless the creature also has the constrict special attack. If the creature does not constrict, each successful grapple check it makes during successive rounds automatically deals the damage indicated for the attack that established the hold. Otherwise, it deals constriction damage as well (the amount is given in the creature's descriptive text).

When a creature gets a hold after an improved grab attack, it pulls the opponent into its space. This act does not provoke attacks of opportunity. It can even move (possibly carrying away the opponent), provided it can drag the opponent's weight.

Incorporeal Subtype: An incorporeal creature has no physical body. It can be harmed only by other incorporeal creatures, magic weapons or creatures that strike as magic weapons, and spells, spell-like abilities, or supernatural abilities. It is immune to all nonmagical attack forms. Even when hit by spells or magic weapons, it has a 50% chance to ignore any damage from a corporeal source (except for positive energy, negative energy, force effects such as *magic missile*, or attacks made with *ghost touch* weapons). Although it is not a magical attack, holy water can affect incorporeal undead, but a hit with holy water has a 50% chance of not affecting an incorporeal creature.

An incorporeal creature has no natural armor bonus but has a deflection bonus equal to its Charisma bonus (always at least +1, even if the creature's Charisma score does not normally provide a bonus).

An incorporeal creature can enter or pass through solid objects, but must remain adjacent to the object's exterior, and so cannot pass entirely through an object whose space is larger than its own. It can sense the presence of creatures or objects within a square adjacent to its current location, but enemies have total concealment (50% miss chance) from an incorporeal creature that is inside an object. In order to see farther from the object it is in and attack normally, the incorporeal creature must emerge. An incorporeal creature inside an object has total cover, but when it attacks a creature outside the object it only has cover, so a creature outside with a readied action could strike at it as it attacks. An incorporeal creature cannot pass through a force effect.

An incorporeal creature's attacks pass through (ignore) natural armor, armor, and shields, although deflection bonuses and force effects (such as *mage armor*) work normally against it. Incorporeal creatures pass through and operate in water as easily as they do in air. Incorporeal creatures cannot fall or take falling damage. Incorporeal creatures cannot make trip or grapple attacks, nor can they be tripped or grappled. In fact, they cannot take any physical action that would move or manipulate an opponent or its equipment, nor are they subject to such actions. Incorporeal creatures have no weight and do not set off traps that are triggered by weight.

An incorporeal creature moves silently and cannot be heard with Listen checks if it doesn't wish to be. It has no Strength score, so its Dexterity modifier applies to both its melee attacks and its ranged attacks. Nonvisual senses, such as scent and blindsight, are either ineffective or only partly effective with regard to incorporeal creatures. Incorporeal creatures have an innate sense of direction and can move at full speed even when they cannot see.

Lawful: A subtype usually applied only to outsiders native to the lawful-aligned Outer Planes. Most creatures that have this subtype also have lawful alignments; however, if their alignments change, they still retain the subtype. Any effect that depends on alignment affects a creature with this subtype as if the creature has a lawful alignment, no matter what its alignment actually is. The creature also suffers effects according to its actual alignment. A creature with the lawful subtype overcomes damage reduction as if its natural weapons and any weapons it wields were lawful-aligned (see Damage Reduction, above).

Level Adjustment: Certain monsters can used as the basis for interesting, viable player characters. These creatures have a level adjustment entry, which is a number that is added to the creature's total Hit Dice to arrive at its effective character level. A creature with multiple special abilities is more powerful as a player character than its Hit Dice alone would indicate. For example, a drow elf has spell resistance, bonuses to its ability scores, and spell-like abilities. Its level adjustment of +2 indicates that a 1st-level drow wizard is the equivalent of a 3rd-level character.

Some creatures' level adjustment entries include the word "(cohort)." Although these creatures may be problematic as PCs, they make good companions for a character who has taken the Leadership feat. Some other creatures aren't intended for use as PCs or cohorts but can become companions through the use of the Improved Familiar feat. In these cases, the level adjustment entry is a dash followed by the words "(Improved Familiar)."

Level adjustment is not the same thing as an adjustment to a creature's Challenge Rating because of some special qualities it possesses. Challenge Rating reflects how difficult an opponent is to fight in a limited number of encounters. Level adjustment shows how powerful a creature is as a player character or cohort in campaign play. For instance, a drow receives a +1 adjustment to its Challenge Rating to account for its special abilities, indicating that it's tougher in a fight than its Hit Dice would suggest, but its level adjustment is +2 to balance its abilities over long-term play.

Low-Light Vision (Ex): A creature with low-light vision can see twice as far as a human in starlight, moonlight, torchlight, and similar conditions of shadowy illumination. It retains the ability to distinguish color and detail under these conditions.

Magical Beast Type: Magical beasts are similar to animals but can have Intelligence scores higher than 2. Magical beasts usually have supernatural or extraordinary abilities, but sometimes are merely bizarre in appearance or habits.

Features: A magical beast has the following features.
—10-sided Hit Dice.
—Base attack bonus equal to total Hit Dice (as fighter).
—Good Fortitude and Reflex saves.
—Skill points equal to (2 + Int modifier, minimum 1) per Hit Die, with quadruple skill points for the first Hit Die.

Traits: A magical beast possesses the following traits (unless otherwise noted in a creature's entry).
—Darkvision out to 60 feet and low-light vision.
—Proficient with its natural weapons only.
—Proficient with no armor.
—Magical beasts eat, sleep, and breathe.

Manufactured Weapons: Some monsters employ manufactured weapons when they attack. Creatures that use swords, bows, spears, and the like follow the same rules as characters, including those for additional attacks from a high base attack bonus and two-weapon fighting penalties. This category also includes "found items," such as rocks and logs, that a creature wields in combat—in essence, any weapon that is not intrinsic to the creature.

Some creatures combine attacks with natural and manufactured weapons when they make a full attack. When they do so, the manufactured weapon attack is considered the primary attack unless the creature's description indicates otherwise (using the manufactured weapon consumes most of the creature's attention), and any natural weapons the creature also uses are considered secondary natural attacks. These secondary attacks do not interfere with the primary attack as attacking with an off-hand weapon does, but they take the usual –5 penalty (or –2 with the Multiattack feat) for such attacks, even if the natural weapon used is normally the creature's primary natural weapon.

Monstrous Humanoid Type: Monstrous humanoids are similar to humanoids, but with monstrous or animalistic features. They often have magical abilities as well.

Features: A monstrous humanoid has the following features.
—8-sided Hit Dice.
—Base attack bonus equal to total Hit Dice (as fighter).
—Good Reflex and Will saves.
—Skill points equal to (2 + Int modifier, minimum 1) per Hit Die, with quadruple skill points for the first Hit Die.

Traits: A monstrous humanoid possesses the following traits (unless otherwise noted in a creature's entry).
—Darkvision out to 60 feet.
—Proficient with all simple weapons and any weapons mentioned in its entry.
—Proficient with whatever type of armor (light, medium, or heavy) it is described as wearing, as well as all lighter types. Monstrous humanoids not indicated as wearing armor are not proficient with armor. Monstrous humanoids are proficient with shields if they are proficient with any form of armor.
—Monstrous humanoids eat, sleep, and breathe.

Movement Modes: Creatures may have modes of movement other than walking and running. These are natural, not magical, unless specifically noted in a monster description.

Burrow: A creature with a burrow speed can tunnel through dirt, but not through rock unless the descriptive text says otherwise. Creatures cannot charge or run while burrowing. Most burrowing creatures do not leave behind tunnels other creatures can use (either because the material they tunnel through fills in behind them or because they do not actually dislocate any material when burrowing); see the individual creature descriptions for details.

Climb: A creature with a climb speed has a +8 racial bonus on all Climb checks. The creature must make a Climb check to climb any wall or slope with a DC of more than 0, but it always can choose to take 10 (see Checks without Rolls, page 65 of the *Player's Handbook*), even if rushed or threatened while climbing. The creature climbs at the given speed while climbing. If it chooses an accelerated climb (see the Climb skill, page 69 of the *Player's Handbook*), it moves at double the given climb speed (or its base land speed, whichever is lower) and makes a single Climb check at a −5 penalty. Creatures cannot run while climbing. A creature retains its Dexterity bonus to Armor Class (if any) while climbing, and opponents get no special bonus on their attacks against a climbing creature.

Fly: A creature with a fly speed can move through the air at the indicated speed if carrying no more than a light load; see Carrying Capacity, page 161 of the *Player's Handbook*. (Note that medium armor does not necessarily constitute a medium load.) All fly speeds include a parenthetical note indicating maneuverability, as follows:

—Perfect: The creature can perform almost any aerial maneuver it wishes. It moves through the air as well as a human moves over smooth ground.

—Good: The creature is very agile in the air (like a housefly or a hummingbird), but cannot change direction as readily as those with perfect maneuverability.

—Average: The creature can fly as adroitly as a small bird.

—Poor: The creature flies as well as a very large bird.

—Clumsy: The creature can barely maneuver at all.

A creature that flies can make dive attacks. A dive attack works just like a charge, but the diving creature must move a minimum of 30 feet and descend at least 10 feet. It can make only claw or talon attacks, but these deal double damage. A creature can use the run action while flying, provided it flies in a straight line.

For more information, see Tactical Aerial Movement, page 20 of the *Dungeon Master's Guide*.

Swim: A creature with a swim speed can move through water at its swim speed without making Swim checks. It has a +8 racial bonus on any Swim check to perform some special action or avoid a hazard. The creature can always can choose to take 10 on a Swim check, even if distracted or endangered. The creature can use the run action while swimming, provided it swims in a straight line.

Native Subtype: A subtype applied only to outsiders. These creatures have mortal ancestors or a strong connection to the Material Plane and can be raised, reincarnated, or resurrected just as other living creatures can be. Creatures with this subtype are native to the Material Plane (hence the subtype's name).

Unlike true outsiders, native outsiders need to eat and sleep.

Natural Weapons: Natural weapons are weapons that are physically a part of a creature. A creature making a melee attack with a natural weapon is considered armed and does not provoke attacks of opportunity. Likewise, it threatens any space it can reach.

Creatures do not receive additional attacks from a high base attack bonus when using natural weapons. The number of attacks a creature can make with its natural weapons depends on the type of the attack—generally, a creature can make one bite attack, one attack per claw or tentacle, one gore attack, one sting attack, or one slam attack (although Large creatures with arms or armlike limbs can make a slam attack with each arm). Refer to the individual monster descriptions.

Unless otherwise noted, a natural weapon threatens a critical hit on a natural attack roll of 20.

When a creature has more than one natural weapon, one of them (or sometimes a pair or set of them) is the primary weapon. All the creature's remaining natural weapons are secondary.

The primary weapon is given in the creature's Attack entry, and the primary weapon or weapons is given first in the creature's Full Attack entry. A creature's primary natural weapon is its most effective natural attack, usually by virtue of the creature's physiology, training, or innate talent with the weapon. An attack with a primary natural weapon uses the creature's full attack bonus. Attacks with secondary natural weapons are less effective and are made with a −5 penalty on the attack roll, no matter how many there are. (Creatures with the Multiattack feat take only a −2 penalty on secondary attacks.) This penalty applies even when the creature makes a single attack with the secondary weapon as part of the attack action or as an attack of opportunity.

Natural weapons have types just as other weapons do. The most common are summarized below.

Bite: The creature attacks with its mouth, dealing piercing, slashing, and bludgeoning damage.

Claw or Talon: The creature rips with a sharp appendage, dealing piercing and slashing damage.

Gore: The creature spears the opponent with an antler, horn, or similar appendage, dealing piercing damage.

Slap or Slam: The creature batters opponents with an appendage, dealing bludgeoning damage.

Sting: The creature stabs with a stinger, dealing piercing damage. Sting attacks usually deal damage from poison in addition to hit point damage.

Tentacle: The creature flails at opponents with a powerful tentacle, dealing bludgeoning (and sometimes slashing) damage.

Nonabilities: Some creatures lack certain ability scores. These creatures do not have an ability score of 0—they lack the ability altogether. The modifier for a nonability is +0. Other effects of nonabilities are detailed below.

Strength: Any creature that can physically manipulate other objects has at least 1 point of Strength.

A creature with no Strength score can't exert force, usually because it has no physical body (a spectre, for example) or because it doesn't move (a shrieker). The creature automatically fails Strength checks. If the creature can attack, it applies its Dexterity modifier to its base attack bonus instead of a Strength modifier.

Dexterity: Any creature that can move has at least 1 point of Dexterity.

A creature with no Dexterity score can't move (a shrieker, for example). If it can perform actions (such as casting spells), it applies its Intelligence modifier to initiative checks instead of a Dexterity modifier. The creature automatically fails Reflex saves and Dexterity checks.

Constitution: Any living creature has at least 1 point of Constitution.

A creature with no Constitution has no body (a spectre, for example) or no metabolism (a golem). It is immune to any effect that requires a Fortitude save unless the effect works on objects or is harmless. For example, a zombie is unaffected by any type of poison but is susceptible to a *disintegrate* spell. The creature is also immune to ability damage, ability drain, and energy drain, and automatically fails Constitution checks. A creature with no Constitution cannot tire and thus can run indefinitely without tiring (unless the creature's description says it cannot run).

Intelligence: Any creature that can think, learn, or remember has at least 1 point of Intelligence.

A creature with no Intelligence score is mindless, an automaton operating on simple instincts or programmed instructions. It has immunity to mind-affecting effects (charms, compulsions, phantasms, patterns, and morale effects) and automatically fails Intelligence checks.

Mindless creatures do not gain feats or skills, although they may have bonus feats or racial skill bonuses.

Wisdom: Any creature that can perceive its environment in any fashion has at least 1 point of Wisdom.

Anything with no Wisdom score is an object, not a creature. Anything without a Wisdom score also has no Charisma score.

Charisma: Any creature capable of telling the difference between itself and things that are not itself has at least 1 point of Charisma.

Anything with no Charisma score is an object, not a creature. Anything without a Charisma score also has no Wisdom score.

Ooze Type: An ooze is an amorphous or mutable creature, usually mindless.

Features: An ooze has the following features.
—10-sided Hit Dice.
—Base attack bonus equal to 3/4 total Hit Dice (as cleric).
—No good saving throws.
—Skill points equal to (2 + Int modifier, minimum 1) per Hit Die, with quadruple skill points for the first Hit Die, if the ooze has an Intelligence score. However, most oozes are mindless and gain no skill points or feats.

Traits: An ooze possesses the following traits (unless otherwise noted in a creature's entry).
—Mindless: No Intelligence score, and immunity to all mind-affecting effects (charms, compulsions, phantasms, patterns, and morale effects).
—Blind (but have the blindsight special quality), with immunity to gaze attacks, visual effects, illusions, and other attack forms that rely on sight.
—Immunity to poison, sleep effects, paralysis, polymorph, and stunning.
—Some oozes have the ability to deal acid damage to objects. In such a case, the amount of damage is equal to 10 + 1/2 ooze's HD + ooze's Con modifier per full round of contact.
—Not subject to critical hits or flanking.
—Proficient with its natural weapons only.
—Proficient with no armor.
—Oozes eat and breathe, but do not sleep.

Outsider Type: An outsider is at least partially composed of the essence (but not necessarily the material) of some plane other than the Material Plane. Some creatures start out as some other type and become outsiders when they attain a higher (or lower) state of spiritual existence.

Features: An outsider has the following features.
—8-sided Hit Dice.
—Base attack bonus equal to total Hit Dice (as fighter).
—Good Fortitude, Reflex, and Will saves.
—Skill points equal to (8 + Int modifier, minimum 1) per Hit Die, with quadruple skill points for the first Hit Die.

Traits: An outsider possesses the following traits (unless otherwise noted in a creature's entry).
—Darkvision out to 60 feet.
—Unlike most other living creatures, an outsider does not have a dual nature—its soul and body form one unit. When an outsider is slain, no soul is set loose. Spells that restore souls to their bodies, such as *raise dead*, *reincarnate*, and *resurrection*, don't work on an outsider. It takes a different magical effect, such as *limited wish*, *wish*, *miracle*, or *true resurrection* to restore it to life. An outsider with the native subtype (see page 312) can be raised, reincarnated, or resurrected just as other living creatures can be.
—Proficient with all simple and martial weapons and any weapons mentioned in its entry.
—Proficient with whatever type of armor (light, medium, or heavy) it is described as wearing, as well as all lighter types. Outsiders not indicated as wearing armor are not proficient with armor. Outsiders are proficient with shields if they are proficient with any form of armor.
—Outsiders breathe, but do not need to eat or sleep (although they can do so if they wish). Native outsiders breathe, eat, and sleep.

Paralysis (Ex or Su): This special attack renders the victim immobile. Paralyzed creatures cannot move, speak, or take any physical actions. The creature is rooted to the spot, frozen and helpless. Paralysis works on the body, and a character can usually resist it with a Fortitude saving throw (the DC is given in the creature's description). Unlike *hold person* and similar effects, a paralysis effect does not allow a new save each round. A winged creature flying in the air at the time that it is paralyzed cannot flap its wings and falls. A swimmer can't swim and may drown.

Plant Type: This type comprises vegetable creatures. Note that regular plants, such as one finds growing in gardens and fields, lack Wisdom and Charisma scores (see Nonabilities, above) and are not creatures, but objects, even though they are alive.

Features: A plant creature has the following features.
—8-sided Hit Dice.
—Base attack bonus equal to 3/4 total Hit Dice (as cleric).
—Good Fortitude saves.
—Skill points equal to (2 + Int modifier, minimum 1) per Hit Die, with quadruple skill points for the first Hit Die, if the plant creature has an Intelligence score. However, some plant creatures are mindless and gain no skill points or feats.

Traits: A plant creature possesses the following traits (unless otherwise noted in a creature's entry).
—Low-light vision.
—Immunity to all mind-affecting effects (charms, compulsions, phantasms, patterns, and morale effects).
—Immunity to poison, sleep effects, paralysis, polymorph, and stunning.
—Not subject to critical hits.
—Proficient with its natural weapons only.
—Proficient with no armor.
—Plants breathe and eat, but do not sleep.

Poison (Ex): Poison attacks deal initial damage, such as ability damage (see page 305) or some other effect, to the opponent on a failed Fortitude save. Unless otherwise noted, another saving throw is required 1 minute later (regardless of the first save's result) to avoid secondary damage. A creature's descriptive text provides the details.

A creature with a poison attack is immune to its own poison and the poison of others of its kind.

The Fortitude save DC against a poison attack is equal to 10 + 1/2 poisoning creature's racial HD + poisoning creature's Con modifier (the exact DC is given in the creature's descriptive text). A successful save avoids (negates) the damage.

Pounce (Ex): When a creature with this special attack makes a charge, it can follow with a full attack—including rake attacks if the creature also has the rake ability.

Powerful Charge (Ex): When a creature with this special attack makes a charge, its attack deals extra damage in addition to the normal benefits and hazards of a charge. The amount of damage from the attack is given in the creature's description.

Psionics (Sp): These are spell-like abilities that a creature generates with the power of its mind. Psionic abilities are usually usable at will.

Racial Hit Dice: The Hit Dice a monster has by virtue of what type of creature it is. Hit Dice gained from taking class levels are not racial Hit Dice. For example, the mind flayer sorcerer described in this book is a 17 HD creature because of its nine levels of sorcerer, but it has 8 racial Hit Dice (the same number as a typical mind flayer without any class levels).

Rake (Ex): A creature with this special attack gains extra natural attacks when it grapples its foe. Normally, a monster can attack with only one of its natural weapons while grappling, but a monster with the rake ability usually gains two additional claw attacks that it can use only against a grappled foe. Rake attacks are not subject to the usual –4 penalty for attacking with a natural weapon in a grapple.

A monster with the rake ability must begin its turn grappling to use its rake—it can't begin a grapple and rake in the same turn.

Ray (Su or Sp): This form of special attack works like a ranged attack (see Aiming a Spell, page 175 of the *Player's Handbook*). Hitting with a ray attack requires a successful ranged touch attack roll, ignoring armor, natural armor, and shield and using the creature's ranged attack bonus. Ray attacks have no range increment. The creature's descriptive text specifies the maximum range, effects, and any applicable saving throw.

Regeneration (Ex): A creature with this ability is difficult to kill. Damage dealt to the creature is treated as nonlethal damage. The creature automatically heals nonlethal damage at a fixed rate per round, as given in the entry (for example, a troll has regeneration 5). Certain attack forms, typically fire and acid, deal lethal damage to the creature, which doesn't go away. The creature's descriptive text describes the details.

A regenerating creature that has been rendered unconscious through nonlethal damage can be killed with a coup de grace (see page 153 of the *Player's Handbook*). The attack cannot be of a type that automatically converts to nonlethal damage.

Attack forms that don't deal hit point damage (for example, most poisons and disintegration) ignore regeneration. Regeneration also does not restore hit points lost from starvation, thirst, or suffocation.

Regenerating creatures can regrow lost portions of their bodies and can reattach severed limbs or body parts; details are in the creature's descriptive text. Severed parts that are not reattached wither and die normally.

A creature must have a Constitution score to have the regeneration ability.

Reptilian Subtype: These creatures are scaly and usually cold-blooded. The reptilian subtype is only used to describe a set of humanoid races, not all animals and monsters that are truly reptiles.

Resistance to Energy (Ex): A creature with this special quality ignores some damage of the indicated type each time it takes damage of that kind (commonly acid, cold, fire, or electricity). The entry indicates the amount and type of damage ignored. For example, a lillend has resistance to fire 10, so it ignores the first 10 points of fire damage dealt to it anytime it takes fire damage.

Scent (Ex): This special quality allows a creature to detect approaching enemies, sniff out hidden foes, and track by sense of smell. Creatures with the scent ability can identify familiar odors just as humans do familiar sights.

The creature can detect opponents within 30 feet by sense of smell. If the opponent is upwind, the range increases to 60 feet; if downwind, it drops to 15 feet. Strong scents, such as smoke or rotting garbage, can be detected at twice the ranges noted above. Overpowering scents, such as skunk musk or troglodyte stench, can be detected at triple normal range.

When a creature detects a scent, the exact location of the source is not revealed—only its presence somewhere within range. The creature can take a move action to note the direction of the scent. Whenever the creature comes within 5 feet of the source, the creature pinpoints the source's location.

A creature with the Track feat and the scent ability can follow tracks by smell, making a Wisdom (or Survival) check to find or follow a track. The typical DC for a fresh trail is 10 (no matter what kind of surface holds the scent). This DC increases or decreases depending on how strong the quarry's odor is, the number of creatures, and the age of the trail. For each hour that the trail is cold, the DC increases by 2. The ability otherwise follows the rules for the Track feat. Creatures tracking by scent ignore the effects of surface conditions and poor visibility.

Shapechanger Subtype: A shapechanger has the supernatural ability to assume one or more alternate forms. Many magical effects allow some kind of shape shifting, and not every creature that can change shapes has the shapechanger subtype.

Traits: A shapechanger possesses the following traits (unless otherwise noted in a creature's entry).

—Proficient with its natural weapons, with simple weapons, and with any weapons mentioned in the creature's description.

—Proficient with any armor mentioned in the creature's description, as well as all lighter forms. If no form of armor is mentioned, the shapechanger is not proficient with armor. A shapechanger is proficient with shields if it is proficient with any type of armor.

Size: The nine size categories are (in ascending order) Fine, Diminutive, Tiny, Small, Medium, Large, Huge, Gargantuan, and Colossal. A creature's size provides a modifier to its Armor Class and attack bonus, a modifier on grapple checks it attempts, and a modifier on Hide checks. Table 7–1: Creature Sizes provides a summary of the attributes that apply to each size category.

Sonic Attacks (Su): Unless otherwise noted, a sonic attack follows the rules for spreads (see Aiming a Spell, page 175 of the *Player's Handbook*). The range of the spread is measured from the creature using the sonic attack. Once a sonic attack has taken effect, deafening the subject or stopping its ears does not end the effect. Stopping one's ears ahead of time allows opponents to avoid having to make saving throws against mind-affecting sonic attacks, but not other kinds of sonic attacks (such as those that

TABLE 7–1: CREATURE SIZES

Size Category	AC/Attack Modifier	Grapple Modifier	Hide Modifier	Dimension*	Weight**	Space (in squares)	Reach (Tall) (in squares)	Reach (Long) (in squares)
Fine	+8	–16	+16	6 in. or less	1/8 lb. or less	1/2 ft. (1/100)	0 ft. (0)	—
Diminutive	+4	–12	+12	6 in.–1 ft.	1/8 lb. – 1 lb.	1 ft. (1/25)	0 ft. (0)	—
Tiny	+2	–8	+8	1 ft.–2 ft.	1 – 8 lb.	2-1/2 ft. (1/4)	0 ft. (0)	—
Small	+1	–4	+4	2 ft.–4 ft.	8 – 60 lb.	5 ft. (1)	5 ft. (1)	—
Medium	+0	+0	+0	4 ft.–8 ft.	60 – 500 lb.	5 ft. (1)	5 ft. (1)	5 ft. (1)
Large	–1	+4	–4	8 ft.–16 ft.	500 – 4,000 lb.	10 ft. (2 × 2)	10 ft. (2)	5 ft. (1)
Huge	–2	+8	–8	16 ft.–32 ft.	2 – 16 tons	15 ft. (3 × 3)	15 ft. (3)	10 ft. (2)
Gargantuan	–4	+12	–12	32 ft.–64 ft.	16 – 125 tons	20 ft. (4 × 4)	20 ft. (4)	15 ft. (3)
Colossal	–8	+16	–16	64 ft. or more	125 tons or more	30 ft.+ (6 × 6+)	30 ft.+ (6+)	20 ft.+ (4+)

* Biped's height, quadruped's body length (nose to base of tail).

**Assumes that the creature is roughly as dense as a regular animal. A creature made of stone will weigh considerably more. A gaseous creature will weigh much less.

deal damage). Stopping one's ears is a full-round action and requires wax or other soundproof material to stuff into the ears.

Special Abilities: A special ability is either extraordinary (Ex), spell-like (Sp), or supernatural (Su).

Extraordinary: Extraordinary abilities are nonmagical, don't become ineffective in an *antimagic field*, and are not subject to any effect that disrupts magic. Using an extraordinary ability is a free action unless otherwise noted.

Spell-Like: Spell-like abilities are magical and work just like spells (though they are not spells and so have no verbal, somatic, material, focus, or XP components). They go away in an *antimagic field* and are subject to spell resistance if the spell the ability resembles or duplicates would be subject to spell resistance.

A spell-like ability usually has a limit on how often it can be used. A spell-like ability that can be used at will has no use limit. Using a spell-like ability is a standard action unless noted otherwise, and doing so while threatened provokes attacks of opportunity. It is possible to make a Concentration check to use a spell-like ability defensively and avoid provoking an attack of opportunity, just as when casting a spell. A spell-like ability can be disrupted just as a spell can be. Spell-like abilities cannot be used to counterspell, nor can they be counterspelled.

For creatures with spell-like abilities, a designated caster level defines how difficult it is to dispel their spell-like effects and to define any level-dependent variables (such as range and duration) the abilities might have. The creature's caster level never affects which spell-like abilities the creature has; sometimes the given caster level is lower than the level a spellcasting character would need to cast the spell of the same name. If no caster level is specified, the caster level is equal to the creature's Hit Dice.

The saving throw (if any) against a spell-like ability is 10 + the level of the spell the ability resembles or duplicates + the creature's Cha modifier.

Some spell-like abilities duplicate spells that work differently when cast by characters of different classes—for example, *true seeing*. A monster's spell-like abilities are presumed to be the sorcerer/wizard versions. If the spell in question is not a sorcerer/wizard spell, then default to cleric, druid, bard, paladin, and ranger, in that order.

Supernatural: Supernatural abilities are magical and go away in an *antimagic field* but are not subject to spell resistance. Supernatural abilities cannot be dispelled. Using a supernatural ability is a standard action unless noted otherwise. Supernatural abilities may have a use limit or be usable at will, just like spell-like abilities. However, supernatural abilities do not provoke attacks of opportunity and never require Concentration checks. Unless otherwise noted, a supernatural ability has an effective caster level equal to the creature's Hit Dice.

The saving throw (if any) against a supernatural ability is 10 + 1/2 the creature's HD + the creature's ability modifier (usually Charisma).

Spell Immunity (Ex): A creature with spell immunity avoids the effects of spells and spell-like abilities that directly affect it. This works exactly like spell resistance, except that it cannot be overcome. Sometimes spell immunity is conditional or applies to only spells of a certain kind or level. Spells that do not allow spell resistance are not affected by spell immunity.

Spell Resistance (Ex): A creature with spell resistance can avoid the effects of spells and spell-like abilities that directly affect it. To determine if a spell or spell-like ability works against a creature with spell resistance, the caster must make a caster level check (1d20 + caster level). If the result equals or exceeds the creature's spell resistance, the spell works normally, although the creature is still allowed a saving throw.

Spells: Sometimes a creature can cast arcane or divine spells just as a member of a spellcasting class can (and can activate magic items accordingly). Such creatures are subject to the same spellcasting rules that characters are, except as follows.

A spellcasting creature that lacks hands or arms can provide any somatic component a spell might require by moving its body. Such a creature also does need material components for its spells. The creature can cast the spell by either touching the required component (but not if the component is in another creature's possession) or having the required component on its person. Sometimes spellcasting creatures utilize the Eschew Materials feat to avoid fussing with noncostly components.

A spellcasting creature is not actually a member of a class unless its entry says so, and it does not gain any class abilities. For example, a creature that casts arcane spells as a sorcerer cannot acquire a familiar. A creature with access to cleric spells must prepare them in the normal manner and receives domain spells if noted, but it does not receive domain granted powers unless it has at least one level in the cleric class.

Summon (Sp): A creature with the *summon* ability can summon specific other creatures of its kind much as though casting a *summon monster* spell, but it usually has only a limited chance of success (as specified in the creature's entry). Roll d%: On a failure, no creature answers the summons. Summoned creatures automatically return whence they came after 1 hour. A creature that has just been summoned cannot use its own summon ability for 1 hour.

Most creatures with the ability to summon do not use it lightly, since it leaves them beholden to the summoned creature. In general, they use it only when necessary to save their own lives.

An appropriate spell level is given for each summoning ability for purposes of Concentration checks and attempts to dispel the summoned creature. As stated on page 37 of the *Dungeon Master's Guide*, no experience points are awarded for summoned monsters.

Swallow Whole (Ex): If a creature with this special attack begins its turn with an opponent held in its mouth (see Improved Grab, page 310), it can attempt a new grapple check (as though attempting to pin the opponent). If it succeeds, it swallows its prey, and the opponent takes bite damage. Unless otherwise noted, the opponent can be up to one size category smaller than the swallowing creature.

Being swallowed has various consequences, depending on the creature doing the swallowing. A swallowed creature is considered to be grappled, while the creature that did the swallowing is not. A swallowed creature can try to cut its way free with any light slashing or piercing weapon (the amount of cutting damage required to get free is noted in the creature description), or it can just try to escape the grapple. The Armor Class of the interior of a creature that swallows whole is normally 10 + 1/2 its natural armor bonus, with no modifiers for size or Dexterity. If the swallowed creature escapes the grapple, success puts it back in the attacker's mouth, where it may be bitten or swallowed again.

Swarm Subtype: A swarm is a collection of Fine, Diminutive, or Tiny creatures that acts as a single creature. A swarm has the characteristics of its type, except as noted here. A swarm has a single pool of Hit Dice and hit points, a single initiative modifier, a single speed, and a single Armor Class. A swarm makes saving throws as a single creature.

A single swarm occupies a square (if it is made up of nonflying creatures) or a cube (of flying creatures) 10 feet on a side, but its reach is 0 feet, like its component creatures. In order to attack, it moves into an opponent's space, which provokes an attack of opportunity. It can occupy the same space as a creature of any size, since it crawls all over its prey. A swarm can move through squares occupied by enemies and vice versa without impediment, although the swarm provokes an attack of opportunity if it does so. A swarm can move through cracks or holes large enough for its component creatures.

A swarm of Tiny creatures consists of 300 nonflying creatures or 1,000 flying creatures. A swarm of Diminutive creatures consists of 1,500 nonflying creatures or 5,000 flying creatures. A swarm of Fine creatures consists of 10,000 creatures, whether they are flying or not. Swarms of nonflying creatures include many more creatures than could normally fit in a 10-foot square based on their normal space, because creatures in a swarm are packed tightly together and generally crawl over each other and their prey when moving or attacking. Larger swarms are represented by multiples of single swarms. (A swarm of 15,000 centipedes is ten centipede swarms, each swarm occupying a 10-foot square.) The area occupied by a large swarm is completely shapeable, though the swarm usually remains in contiguous squares.

Traits: A swarm has no clear front or back and no discernable anatomy, so it is not subject to critical hits or flanking. A swarm made up of Tiny creatures takes half damage from slashing and piercing weapons. A swarm composed of Fine or Diminutive creatures is immune to all weapon damage.

Reducing a swarm to 0 hit points or lower causes it to break up, though damage taken until that point does not degrade its ability to attack or resist attack. Swarms are never staggered or reduced to a dying state by damage. Also, they cannot be tripped, grappled, or bull rushed, and they cannot grapple an opponent.

A swarm is immune to any spell or effect that targets a specific number of creatures (including single-target spells such as *disintegrate*), with the exception of mind-affecting effects (charms, compulsions, phantasms, patterns, and morale effects) if the swarm has an Intelligence score and a hive mind. A swarm takes half again as much damage (+50%) from spells or effects that affect an area, such as splash weapons and many evocation spells.

Swarms made up of Diminutive or Fine creatures are susceptible to high winds such as that created by a *gust of wind* spell. For purposes of determining the effects of wind on a swarm, treat the swarm as a creature of the same size as its constituent creatures (see Winds, page 95 of the *Dungeon Master's Guide*). For example, a swarm of locusts (a swarm of Diminutive creatures) can be blown away by a severe wind. Wind effects deal 1d6 points of nonlethal damage to a swarm per spell level (or Hit Dice of the originating creature, in the case of effects such as an air elemental's whirlwind). A swarm rendered unconscious by means of nonlethal damage becomes disorganized and dispersed, and does not reform until its hit points exceed its nonlethal damage.

Swarm Attack: Creatures with the swarm subtype don't make standard melee attacks. Instead, they deal automatic damage to any creature whose space they occupy at the end of their move, with no attack roll needed. Swarm attacks are not subject to a miss chance for concealment or cover. A swarm's statistics block has "swarm" in the Attack and Full Attack entries, with no attack bonus given. The amount of damage a swarm deals is based on its Hit Dice, as shown below.

Swarm HD	Swarm Base Damage
1–5	1d6
6–10	2d6
11–15	3d6
16–20	4d6
21 or more	5d6

A swarm's attacks are nonmagical, unless the swarm's description states otherwise. Damage reduction sufficient to reduce a swarm attack's damage to 0, being incorporeal, and other special abilities usually give a creature immunity (or at least resistance) to damage from a swarm. Some swarms also have acid, poison, blood drain, or other special attacks in addition to normal damage.

Swarms do not threaten creatures in their square, and do not make attacks of opportunity with their swarm attack. However, they distract foes whose squares they occupy, as described below.

Distraction (Ex): Any living creature vulnerable to a swarm's damage that begins its turn with a swarm in its square is nauseated for 1 round; a Fortitude save (DC 10 + 1/2 swarm's HD + swarm's Con modifier; the exact DC is given in a swarm's description) negates the effect. Spellcasting or concentrating on spells within the area of a swarm requires a Concentration check (DC 20 + spell level). Using skills that involve patience and concentration requires a DC 20 Concentration check.

Tanar'ri Subtype: Many demons belong to the race of evil outsiders known as the tanar'ri.

Traits: A tanar'ri possesses the following traits (unless otherwise noted in a creature's entry).
—Immunity to electricity and poison.
—Resistance to acid 10, cold 10, and fire 10.
—*Summon (Sp):* Tanar'ri share the ability to summon others of their kind (the success chance and type of tanar'ri summoned are noted in each monster description).
—Telepathy.

Telepathy (Su): A creature with this ability can communicate telepathically with any other creature within a certain range (specified in the creature's entry, usually 100 feet) that has a language. It is possible to address multiple creatures at once telepathically, although maintaining a telepathic conversation with more than one creature at a time is just as difficult as simultaneously speaking and listening to multiple people at the same time.

Some creatures (such as the pseudodragon) have a limited form of telepathy, while others (such as the formian queen) have a more powerful form of the ability.

Trample (Ex): As a full-round action, a creature with this special attack can move up to twice its speed and literally run over any opponents at least one size category smaller than itself. The creature merely has to move over the opponents in its path; any creature whose space is completely covered by the trampling creature's space is subject to the trample attack.

If a target's space is larger than 5 feet, it is only considered trampled if the trampling creature moves over all the squares it occupies. If the trampling creature moves over only some of a target's space, the target can make an attack of opportunity against the trampling creature at a –4 penalty. A trampling creature that accidentally ends its movement in an illegal space returns to the last legal position it occupied, or the closest legal position, if there's a legal position that's closer.

A trample attack deals bludgeoning damage (the creature's slam damage + 1-1/2 times its Str modifier). The creature's descriptive text gives the exact amount.

Trampled opponents can attempt attacks of opportunity, but these take a –4 penalty. If they do not make attacks of opportunity, trampled opponents can attempt Reflex saves to take half damage. The save DC against a creature's trample attack is 10 + 1/2 creature's HD + creature's Str modifier (the exact DC is given in the creature's descriptive text). A trampling creature can only deal trampling damage to each target once per round, no matter how many times its movement takes it over a target creature.

Tremorsense (Ex): A creature with tremorsense is sensitive to vibrations in the ground and can automatically pinpoint the location of anything that is in contact with the ground. Aquatic creatures with tremorsense can also sense the location of creatures moving through water. The ability's range is specified in the creature's descriptive text.

Treasure: This entry in a monster description describes how much wealth a creature owns. (See pages 52–56 of the *Dungeon Master's Guide* for details about treasure, particularly Tables 3–5, through 3–8.) In most cases, a creature keeps valuables in its home or lair and has no treasure with it when it travels. Intelligent creatures that own useful, portable treasure (such as magic items) tend to carry and use these, leaving bulky items at home.

Treasure can include coins, goods, and items. Creatures can have varying amounts of each, as follows.

Standard: Refer to Table 3–5 in the *Dungeon Master's Guide* and roll d% once for each type of treasure (Coins, Goods, Items) on the Level section of the table that corresponds to the creature's Challenge Rating (for groups of creatures, use the Encounter Level for the encounter instead).

Some creatures have double, triple, or even quadruple standard treasure; in these cases, roll for each type of treasure two, three, or four times.

None: The creature collects no treasure of its own.

Nonstandard: Some creatures have quirks or habits that affect the types of treasure they collect. These creatures use the same treasure tables, but with special adjustments.

Fractional Coins: Roll on the Coins column in the section corresponding to the creature's Challenge Rating, but divide the result as indicated.

% Goods or Items: The creature has goods or items only some of the time. Before checking for goods or items, roll d% against the given percentage. On a success, make a normal roll on the appropriate Goods or Items column (which may still result in no goods or items).

Double Goods or Items: Roll twice on the appropriate Goods or Items column.

Parenthetical Notes: Some entries for goods or items include notes that limit the types of treasure a creature collects.

When a note includes the word "no," it means the creature does not collect or cannot keep that thing. If a random roll generates such a result, treat the result as "none" instead. For example, if a creature's "items" entry reads "no flammables," and a random roll generates a scroll, the creature instead has no item at all (the scroll burned up, or the creature left it behind).

When a note includes the word "only," the creature goes out of its way to collect treasure of the indicated type. If an entry for goods indicates "gems only," roll on the appropriate Goods column and treat any "art" result as "gems" instead.

It's sometimes necessary to reroll until the right sort of item appears. For example, if a creature's items entry reads "nonflammables only," roll normally on the appropriate Items column. If you get a flammable item, reroll on the same portion of the table until you get a nonflammable one. If the table you rolled on contains only flammable items, back up a step and reroll until you get to a table that can give you an appropriate item.

Turn Resistance (Ex): A creature with this special quality (usually an undead) is less easily affected by clerics or paladins (see Turn or Rebuke Undead, page 159 of the *Player's Handbook*). When resolving a turn, rebuke, command, or bolster attempt, add the indicated number to the creature's Hit Dice total. For example, a shadow has 3 Hit Dice and +2 turn resistance. Attempts to turn, rebuke, command, or bolster treat the shadow as though it had 5 Hit Dice, though it is a 3 HD creature for any other purpose.

Undead Type: Undead are once-living creatures animated by spiritual or supernatural forces.

Features: An undead creature has the following features.
—12-sided Hit Dice.
—Base attack bonus equal to 1/2 total Hit Dice (as wizard).
—Good Will saves.
—Skill points equal to (4 + Int modifier, minimum 1) per Hit Die, with quadruple skill points for the first Hit Die, if the undead

creature has an Intelligence score. However, many undead are mindless and gain no skill points or feats.

Traits: An undead creature possesses the following traits (unless otherwise noted in a creature's entry).
—No Constitution score.
—Darkvision out to 60 feet.
—Immunity to all mind-affecting effects (charms, compulsions, phantasms, patterns, and morale effects).
—Immunity to poison, sleep effects, paralysis, stunning, disease, and death effects.
—Not subject to critical hits, nonlethal damage, ability drain, or energy drain. Immune to damage to its physical ability scores (Strength, Dexterity, and Constitution), as well as to fatigue and exhaustion effects.
—Cannot heal damage on its own if it has no Intelligence score, although it can be healed. Negative energy (such as an *inflict* spell) can heal undead creatures. The fast healing special quality works regardless of the creature's Intelligence score.
—Immunity to any effect that requires a Fortitude save (unless the effect also works on objects or is harmless).
—Uses its Charisma modifier for Concentration checks.
—Not at risk of death from massive damage, but when reduced to 0 hit points or less, it is immediately destroyed.
—Not affected by *raise dead* and *reincarnate* spells or abilities. *Resurrection* and *true resurrection* can affect undead creatures. These spells turn undead creatures back into the living creatures they were before becoming undead.
—Proficient with its natural weapons, all simple weapons, and any weapons mentioned in its entry.
—Proficient with whatever type of armor (light, medium, or heavy) it is described as wearing, as well as all lighter types. Undead not indicated as wearing armor are not proficient with armor. Undead are proficient with shields if they are proficient with any form of armor.
—Undead do not breathe, eat, or sleep.

Vermin Type: This type includes insects, arachnids, other arthropods, worms, and similar invertebrates.

Features: Vermin have the following features.
—8-sided Hit Dice.
—Base attack bonus equal to 3/4 total Hit Dice (as cleric).
—Good Fortitude saves.
—Skill points equal to (2 + Int modifier, minimum 1) per Hit Die, with quadruple skill points for the first Hit Die, if the vermin has an Intelligence score. However, most vermin are mindless and gain no skill points or feats.

Traits: Vermin possess the following traits (unless otherwise noted in a creature's entry).
—Mindless: No Intelligence score, and immunity to all mind-affecting effects (charms, compulsions, phantasms, patterns, and morale effects).
—Darkvision out to 60 feet.
—Proficient with their natural weapons only.
—Proficient with no armor.
—Vermin breathe, eat, and sleep.

Vulnerability to Energy: Some creatures have vulnerability to a certain kind of energy effect (typically either cold or fire). Such a creature takes half again as much (+50%) damage as normal from the effect, regardless of whether a saving throw is allowed, or if the save is a success or failure.

Water Subtype: This subtype usually is used for elementals and outsiders with a connection to the Elemental Plane of Water. Creatures with the water subtype always have swim speeds and can move in water without making Swim checks. A water creature can breathe underwater and usually can breathe air as well.

MONSTERS RANKED BY CHALLENGE RATINGS

Bat 1/10
Toad 1/10

Monstrous centipede,
   Tiny 1/8
Rat 1/8

Donkey 1/6
Lizard 1/6
Monkey 1/6
Raven 1/6

Cat 1/4
Kobold 1/4
Monstrous centipede,
   Small 1/4
Monstrous scorpion, Tiny . 1/4
Monstrous spider, Tiny . . . 1/4
Owl 1/4
Pony 1/4
Weasel 1/4
Zombie, kobold 1/4

Dire rat 1/3
Dog 1/3
Giant fire beetle 1/3
Goblin 1/3
Hawk 1/3
Skeleton, human warrior . . 1/3
Snake, Tiny viper 1/3

Aasimar (planetouched) . . . 1/2
Animated object, Tiny 1/2
Baboon 1/2
Badger 1/2
Dwarf (any but duergar) . . 1/2
Eagle 1/2
Elf (any but drow) 1/2
Fiendish dire rat 1/2
Formian worker 1/2
Gnome
   (any but svirfneblin) 1/2
Halfling (any) 1/2
Hobgoblin 1/2
Locathah 1/2
Merfolk 1/2
Monstrous centipede,
   Medium 1/2
Monstrous scorpion, Small . 1/2
Monstrous spider, Small . . . 1/2
Orc 1/2
Pony, war 1/2
Porpoise 1/2
Snake, Small viper 1/2
Stirge 1/2
Tiefling (planetouched) . . . 1/2
Zombie, human commoner 1/2

Animated object, Small 1
Camel 1
Darkmantle 1
Dog, riding 1
Dwarf, duergar 1
Elemental, Small (any) 1
Elf, drow 1
Ghoul 1
Giant ant, worker 1
Giant bee 1
Githyanki 1

Githzerai 1
Gnoll 1
Gnome, svirfneblin 1
Grig (sprite) 1
Grimlock 1
Homunculus 1
Horse, heavy 1
Horse, light 1
Horse, light war 1
Hyena 1
Krenshar 1
Lemure (devil) 1
Lizardfolk 1
Manta ray 1
Monstrous centipede,
   Large 1
Monstrous scorpion,
   Medium 1
Monstrous spider,
   Medium 1
Mule 1
Nixie (sprite) 1
Octopus 1
Pseudodragon 1
Shark, Medium 1
Shrieker (fungus) 1
Skeleton, wolf 1
Snake, Medium viper 1
Spider swarm 1
Squid 1
Troglodyte 1
Wolf 1
Zombie, troglodyte 1

Animated object, Medium . . . 2
Ape 2
Archon, lantern 2
Azer 2
Bat swarm 2
Bear, black 2
Bison 2
Blink dog 2
Boar 2
Bugbear 2
Cheetah 2
Choker 2
Crocodile 2
Devil, imp 2
Dire badger 2
Dire bat 2
Dire weasel 2
Dretch (demon) 2
Giant ant, queen 2
Giant ant, soldier 2
Giant bombardier beetle 2
Hippogriff 2
Horse, heavy war 2
Kuo-toa 2
Leopard 2
Lizard, monitor 2
Monstrous centipede, Huge . 2
Monstrous spider, Large 2
Quasit (demon) 2
Rat swarm 2
Sahuagin 2
Satyr 2

Shark, Large 2
Shocker lizard 2
Skeleton, owlbear 2
Skum 2
Snake, constrictor 2
Snake, Large viper 2
Thoqqua 2
Triton 2
Vargouille 2
Wererat (lycanthrope) 2
Wolverine 2
Worg 2
Zombie, bugbear 2

Allip 3
Animated object, Large 3
Ankheg 3
Arrowhawk, juvenile 3
Assassin vine 3
Centaur 3
Cockatrice 3
Deinonychus (dinosaur) 3
Derro 3
Dire ape 3
Dire wolf 3
Doppelganger 3
Dryad 3
Eagle, giant 3
Elemental, Medium (any) . . . 3
Ethereal filcher 3
Ethereal marauder 3
Ettercap 3
Formian, warrior 3
Gelatinous cube (ooze) 3
Ghast 3
Giant praying mantis 3
Giant wasp 3
Grick 3
Hell hound 3
Howler 3
Lion 3
Locust swarm 3
Magmin 3
Mephit (any) 3
Monstrous scorpion, Large . . 3
Ogre 3
Ogre, merrow 3
Owl, giant 3
Pegasus 3
Phantom fungus 3
Rust monster 3
Salamander, flamebrother . . . 3
Shadow 3
Skeleton, troll 3
Snake, Huge viper 3
Tojanida, juvenile 3
Unicorn 3
Violet fungus 3
Werewolf (lycanthrope) 3
Wight 3
Xorn, minor 3
Yeth hound 3
Yuan-ti, pureblood 3
Zombie, ogre 3

Aranea 4
Archon, hound 4

Barghest 4
Bear, brown 4
Bear, polar 4
Carrion crawler 4
Celestial lion 4
Crocodile, giant 4
Dire boar 4
Dire wolverine 4
Displacer beast 4
Gargoyle 4
Giant stag beetle 4
Gray ooze 4
Griffon 4
Harpy 4
Hydra, five-headed 4
Janni (genie) 4
Mimic 4
Minotaur 4
Otyugh 4
Owlbear 4
Pixie (sprite) 4
Rhinoceros 4
Sea cat 4
Sea hag 4
Shark, Huge 4
Skeleton, chimera 4
Swarm, Centipede 4
Tiger 4
Vampire spawn 4
Wereboar (lycanthrope) 4
Zombie, minotaur 4
Zombie, wyvern 4

Achaierai 5
Animated object, Huge 5
Arrowhawk, adult 5
Barghest, greater 5
Basilisk 5
Bearded devil (barbazu) 5
Cloaker 5
Dire lion 5
Djinni (genie) 5
Elemental, Large (any) 5
Gibbering mouther 5
Green hag 5
Hieracosphinx 5
Hydra, six-headed 5
Manticore 5
Monstrous spider, Huge 5
Mummy 5
Nightmare 5
Ochre jelly (ooze) 5
Orca 5
Phase spider 5
Rast 5
Ravid 5
Shadow mastiff 5
Skeleton, ettin 5
Snake, giant constrictor 5
Spider eater 5
Pixie (with *Otto's Irresistible*
   Dance) (sprite) 5
Tojanida, adult 5
Troll 5
Troll, scrag 5
Werebear (lycanthrope) 5

DRAGON CRS BY AGE AND COLOR

Age	White	Black	Brass	Green	Blue	Copper	Bronze	Red	Silver	Gold
Wyrmling	2	3	3	3	3	3	3	4	4	5
Very young	3	4	4	4	4	5	5	5	5	7
Young	4	5	6	5	6	7	7	7	7	9
Juvenile	6	7	8	8	8	9	9	10	10	11
Young adult	8	9	10	11	11	11	12	13	13	14
Adult	10	11	12	13	14	14	15	15	15	16
Mature adult	12	14	15	16	16	16	17	18	18	19
Old	15	16	17	18	18	19	19	20	20	21
Very old	17	18	19	19	19	20	20	21	21	22
Ancient	18	19	20	21	21	22	22	23	23	24
Wyrm	19	20	21	22	23	23	23	24	24	25
Great wyrm	21	22	23	24	25	25	25	26	26	27

find adventure
WITHOUT A
Dungeon Master

Leave your dice bag behind. For this trek into the exciting **Dungeons & Dragons**® world, all you need is your imagination. Join Regdar, Lidda, Jozan, Mialee, and other familiar characters as they burst out of the core rulebooks and onto the pages of this action-packed novel series. So, pick up a **Dungeons & Dragons** novel at your favorite hobby or bookstore. And enjoy keeping all the experience for yourself.

DUNGEONS & DRAGONS NOVELS

www.wizards.com/books

DRAGON CRS BY AGE AND COLOR

Age	White	Black	Brass	Green	Blue	Copper	Bronze	Red	Silver	Gold
Wyrmling	2	3	3	3	3	3	3	4	4	5
Very young	3	4	4	4	4	5	5	5	5	7
Young	4	5	6	5	6	7	7	7	7	9
Juvenile	6	7	8	8	8	9	9	10	10	11
Young adult	8	9	10	11	11	11	12	13	13	14
Adult	10	11	12	13	14	14	15	15	15	16
Mature adult	12	14	15	16	16	16	17	18	18	19
Old	15	16	17	18	18	19	19	20	20	21
Very old	17	18	19	19	19	20	20	21	21	22
Ancient	18	19	20	21	21	22	22	23	23	24
Wyrm	19	20	21	22	23	23	23	24	24	25
Great wyrm	21	22	23	24	25	25	25	26	26	27

find adventure
WITHOUT A
Dungeon Master

Leave your dice bag behind. For this trek into the exciting **Dungeons & Dragons**® w
all you need is your imagination. Join Regdar, Lidda, Jozan, Mialee, and other familiar chara
as they burst out of the core rulebooks and onto the pages of this action-packed novel s
So, pick up a **Dungeons & Dragons** novel at your favorite hobby or books
And enjoy keeping all the experience for yourself.

DUNGEONS & DRAGONS NOVELS

www.wizards.com/books

DRAGON CRS BY AGE AND COLOR

Age	White	Black	Brass	Green	Blue	Copper	Bronze	Red	Silver	Gold
Wyrmling	2	3	3	3	3	3	3	4	4	5
Very young	3	4	4	4	4	5	5	5	5	7
Young	4	5	6	5	6	7	7	7	7	9
Juvenile	6	7	8	8	8	9	9	10	10	11
Young adult	8	9	10	11	11	11	12	13	13	14
Adult	10	11	12	13	14	14	15	15	15	16
Mature adult	12	14	15	16	16	16	17	18	18	19
Old	15	16	17	18	18	19	19	20	20	21
Very old	17	18	19	19	19	20	20	21	21	22
Ancient	18	19	20	21	21	22	22	23	23	24
Wyrm	19	20	21	22	23	23	23	24	24	25
Great wyrm	21	22	23	24	25	25	25	26	26	27

find adventure
WITHOUT A
Dungeon Maste

Leave your dice bag behind. For this trek into the exciting **Dungeons & Dragons®** w
all you need is your imagination. Join Regdar, Lidda, Jozan, Mialee, and other familiar chara
as they burst out of the core rulebooks and onto the pages of this action-packed novel s
So, pick up a **Dungeons & Dragons** novel at your favorite hobby or books
And enjoy keeping all the experience for yourself.

DUNGEONS & DRAGONS NOVELS

www.wizards.com/books

DRAGON CRS BY AGE AND COLOR

Age	White	Black	Brass	Green	Blue	Copper	Bronze	Red	Silver	Gold
Wyrmling	2	3	3	3	3	3	3	4	4	5
Very young	3	4	4	4	4	5	5	5	5	7
Young	4	5	6	5	6	7	7	7	7	9
Juvenile	6	7	8	8	8	9	9	10	10	11
Young adult	8	9	10	11	11	11	12	13	13	14
Adult	10	11	12	13	14	14	15	15	15	16
Mature adult	12	14	15	16	16	16	17	18	18	19
Old	15	16	17	18	18	19	19	20	20	21
Very old	17	18	19	19	19	20	20	21	21	22
Ancient	18	19	20	21	21	22	22	23	23	24
Wyrm	19	20	21	22	23	23	23	24	24	25
Great wyrm	21	22	23	24	25	25	25	26	26	27

find adventure
WITHOUT A
Dungeon Master

Leave your dice bag behind. For this trek into the exciting **Dungeons & Dragons®** w
all you need is your imagination. Join Regdar, Lidda, Jozan, Mialee, and other familiar chara
as they burst out of the core rulebooks and onto the pages of this action-packed novel se
So, pick up a **Dungeons & Dragons** novel at your favorite hobby or books
And enjoy keeping all the experience for yourself.

DUNGEONS & DRAGONS NOVELS

www.wizards.com/books

Weretiger (lycanthrope) 5	Giant, hill 7	Tyrannosaurus (dinosaur) 8	Half-dragon celestial
Winter wolf 5	Golem, flesh 7	Xorn, elder 8	lammasu 11

Weretiger (lycanthrope) 5
Winter wolf 5
Wraith 5
Yuan-ti, halfblood 5
Zombie, umber hulk 5

Annis (hag) 6
Baleen whale 6
Belker 6
Bralani (eladrin) 6
Chain devil (kyton) 6
Demon, babau 6
Digester 6
Megaraptor (dinosaur) 6
Ettin 6
Gauth (beholder) 6
Girallon 6
Half-black dragon, 4th-level
   human fighter 6
Hydra, five-headed cryo- 6
Hydra, five-headed pyro- 6
Hydra, seven-headed 6
Lamia 6
Monstrous centipede,
   Gargantuan 6
Salamander, average 6
Shambling mound 6
Skeleton,
   advanced megaraptor 6
Tendriculos 6
Will-o'-wisp 6
Wyvern 6
Xill 6
Xorn, average 6
Zombie, gray render 6

Aboleth 7
Animated object,
   Gargantuan 7
Black pudding (ooze) 7
Bulette 7
Cachalot whale 7
Chaos beast 7
Chimera 7
Chuul 7
Criosphinx 7
Dire bear 7
Dragonne 7
Drider 7
Elasmosaurus (dinosaur) 7
Elemental, Huge (any) 7
Elephant 7
Formian, taskmaster 7
Ghost,
   5th-level human fighter . . . 7

Giant, hill 7
Golem, flesh 7
Hellcat (devil) 7
Hydra, eight-headed 7
Hydra, six-headed cryo- . . . 7
Hydra, six-headed pyro- . . . 7
Invisible stalker 7
Lillend 7
Medusa 7
Monstrous scorpion, Huge . . 7
Naga, water 7
Nymph 7
Ogre barbarian 7
Phasm 7
Remorhaz 7
Skeleton, cloud giant 7
Slaad, red 7
Spectre 7
Succubus (demon) 7
Umber hulk 7
Vampire, 5th-level
   human fighter 7
Yuan-ti, abomination 7

Arrowhawk, elder 8
Athach 8
Behir 8
Bodak 8
Destrachan 8
Dire tiger 8
Djinni noble (genie) 8
Efreeti (genie) 8
Erinyes (devil) 8
Giant, stone 8
Gorgon 8
Gray render 8
Gynosphinx 8
Hellwasp swarm 8
Hydra, nine-headed 8
Hydra, seven-headed cryo- . . 8
Hydra, seven-headed pyro- . . 8
Lammasu 8
Mind flayer 8
Mohrg 8
Monstrous spider,
   Gargantuan 8
Naga, dark 8
Octopus, giant 8
Ogre mage 8
Shield guardian 8
Skeleton, young adult
   red dragon 8
Shadow, greater 8
Slaad, blue 8
Treant 8

Tyrannosaurus (dinosaur) 8
Xorn, elder 8

Androsphinx 9
Avoral (guardinal) 9
Bone devil (osyluth) 9
Delver 9
Dire shark 9
Dragon turtle 9
Elemental, greater (any) 9
Giant, frost 9
Giant, elder stone 9
Half-fiend, 7th-level
   human cleric 9
Hydra, eight-headed cryo- . . . 9
Hydra, eight-headed pyro- . . . 9
Hydra, ten-headed 9
Monstrous centipede,
   Colossal 9
Naga, spirit 9
Nessian warhound
   (hell hound) 9
Night hag 9
Roc 9
Slaad, green 9
Squid, giant 9
Tojanida, elder 9
Triceratops (dinosaur) 9
Vrock (demon) 9
Yrthak 9
Zelekhut (inevitable) 9

Animated object, Colossal . . . 10
Bebilith (demon) 10
Couatl 10
Formian, myrmarch 10
Giant, fire 10
Golem, clay 10
Hydra, eleven-headed 10
Hydra, nine-headed cryo- . . . 10
Hydra, nine-headed pyro- . . . 10
Monstrous scorpion,
   Gargantuan 10
Naga, guardian 10
Rakshasa 10
Salamander, noble 10
Slaad, gray 10

Barbed devil (hamatula) 11
Cauchemar (nightmare) 11
Devourer 11
Elemental, elder (any) 11
Giant, cloud 11
Golem, stone 11
Half-celestial, 9th-level
   human paladin 11

Half-dragon celestial
   lammasu 11
Harpy archer 11
Hill giant dire wereboar
   (lycanthrope) 11
Hezrou (demon) 11
Hydra, ten-headed cryo- . . . 11
Hydra, ten-headed pyro- 11
Hydra, twelve-headed 11
Monstrous spider, Colossal . . 11
Retriever (demon) 11
Troll hunter 11
Wraith, dread 11

Basilisk, Abyssal greater 12
Black pudding, elder (ooze) . 12
Displacer beast pack lord . . . 12
Frost worm 12
Hydra, eleven-headed cryo- . . 12
Hydra, eleven-headed pyro- . . 12
Kolyarut (inevitable) 12
Kraken 12
Leonal (guardinal) 12
Monstrous scorpion,
   Colossal 12
Purple worm 12
Roper 12

Beholder 13
Celestial charger (unicorn) . . 13
Ghaele (eladrin) 13
Glabrezu (demon) 13
Giant, storm 13
Golem, iron 13
Hydra, twelve-headed cryo- . 13
Hydra, twelve-headed pyro-. 13
Ice devil (gelugon) 13
Lich, 11th-level
   human wizard 13
Mummy lord 13
Slaad, death 13

Archon, trumpet 14
Astral deva (angel) 14
Nalfeshnee (demon) 14
Nightwing (nightshade) . . . 14
Umber hulk, truly horrid . . . 14
Werewolf lord (lycanthrope) . 14

Marut (inevitable) 15
Vampire, half-elf
   Mnk 9/Shd 4 15

Archon, hound hero 16
Horned devil (cornugon) . . . 16
Golem, greater stone 16
Nightwalker (nightshade) . . . 16
Planetar (angel) 16

Aboleth mage 17
Formian, queen 17
Giant, frost jarl 17
Marilith (demon) 17
Mind flayer sorcerer 17

Nightcrawler (nightshade) . . 18

Balor (demon) 20
Pit fiend (devil) 20
Tarrasque 20

Titan 21

Solar (angel) 23

DRAGON CRS BY AGE AND COLOR

Age	White	Black	Brass	Green	Blue	Copper	Bronze	Red	Silver	Gold
Wyrmling	2	3	3	3	3	3	3	4	4	5
Very young	3	4	4	4	4	5	5	5	5	7
Young	4	5	6	5	6	7	7	7	7	9
Juvenile	6	7	8	8	8	9	9	10	10	11
Young adult	8	9	10	11	11	11	12	13	13	14
Adult	10	11	12	13	14	14	15	15	15	16
Mature adult	12	14	15	16	16	16	17	18	18	19
Old	15	16	17	18	18	19	19	20	20	21
Very old	17	18	19	19	19	20	20	21	21	22
Ancient	18	19	20	21	21	22	22	23	23	24
Wyrm	19	20	21	22	23	23	23	24	24	25
Great wyrm	21	22	23	24	25	25	25	26	26	27

find adventure
WITHOUT A
Dungeon Master

Leave your dice bag behind. For this trek into the exciting **Dungeons & Dragons**® world, all you need is your imagination. Join Regdar, Lidda, Jozan, Mialee, and other familiar characters as they burst out of the core rulebooks and onto the pages of this action-packed novel series. So, pick up a **Dungeons & Dragons** novel at your favorite hobby or bookstore. And enjoy keeping all the experience for yourself.

DUNGEONS & DRAGONS NOVELS

www.wizards.com/books

Weretiger (lycanthrope) 5
Winter wolf 5
Wraith 5
Yuan-ti, halfblood 5
Zombie, umber hulk 5

Annis (hag) 6
Baleen whale 6
Belker 6
Bralani (eladrin) 6
Chain devil (kyton) 6
Demon, babau 6
Digester 6
Megaraptor (dinosaur) 6
Ettin 6
Gauth (beholder) 6
Girallon 6
Half-black dragon, 4th-level
    human fighter 6
Hydra, five-headed cryo- 6
Hydra, five-headed pyro- 6
Hydra, seven-headed 6
Lamia 6
Monstrous centipede,
    Gargantuan 6
Salamander, average 6
Shambling mound 6
Skeleton,
    advanced megaraptor 6
Tendriculos 6
Will-o'-wisp 6
Wyvern 6
Xill 6
Xorn, average 6
Zombie, gray render 6

Aboleth 7
Animated object,
    Gargantuan 7
Black pudding (ooze) 7
Bulette 7
Cachalot whale 7
Chaos beast 7
Chimera 7
Chuul 7
Criosphinx 7
Dire bear 7
Dragonne 7
Drider 7
Elasmosaurus (dinosaur) 7
Elemental, Huge (any) 7
Elephant 7
Formian, taskmaster 7
Ghost,
    5th-level human fighter . . . 7

Giant, hill 7
Golem, flesh 7
Hellcat (devil) 7
Hydra, eight-headed 7
Hydra, six-headed cryo- 7
Hydra, six-headed pyro- 7
Invisible stalker 7
Lillend 7
Medusa 7
Monstrous scorpion, Huge . . . 7
Naga, water 7
Nymph 7
Ogre barbarian 7
Phasm 7
Remorhaz 7
Skeleton, cloud giant 7
Slaad, red 7
Spectre 7
Succubus (demon) 7
Umber hulk 7
Vampire, 5th-level
    human fighter 7
Yuan-ti, abomination 7

Arrowhawk, elder 8
Athach 8
Behir 8
Bodak 8
Destrachan 8
Dire tiger 8
Djinni noble (genie) 8
Efreeti (genie) 8
Erinyes (devil) 8
Giant, stone 8
Gorgon 8
Gray render 8
Gynosphinx 8
Hellwasp swarm 8
Hydra, nine-headed 8
Hydra, seven-headed cryo- . . . 8
Hydra, seven-headed pyro- . . . 8
Lammasu 8
Mind flayer 8
Mohrg 8
Monstrous spider,
    Gargantuan 8
Naga, dark 8
Octopus, giant 8
Ogre mage 8
Shield guardian 8
Skeleton, young adult
    red dragon 8
Shadow, greater 8
Slaad, blue 8
Treant 8

Tyrannosaurus (dinosaur) 8
Xorn, elder 8

Androsphinx 9
Avoral (guardinal) 9
Bone devil (osyluth) 9
Delver 9
Dire shark 9
Dragon turtle 9
Elemental, greater (any) 9
Giant, frost 9
Giant, elder stone 9
Half-fiend, 7th-level
    human cleric 9
Hydra, eight-headed cryo- . . . 9
Hydra, eight-headed pyro- . . . 9
Hydra, ten-headed 9
Monstrous centipede,
    Colossal 9
Naga, spirit 9
Nessian warhound
    (hell hound) 9
Night hag 9
Roc 9
Slaad, green 9
Squid, giant 9
Tojanida, elder 9
Triceratops (dinosaur) 9
Vrock (demon) 9
Yrthak 9
Zelekhut (inevitable) 9

Animated object, Colossal . . 10
Bebilith (demon) 10
Couatl 10
Formian, myrmarch 10
Giant, fire 10
Golem, clay 10
Hydra, eleven-headed 10
Hydra, nine-headed cryo- . . 10
Hydra, nine-headed pyro- . . 10
Monstrous scorpion,
    Gargantuan 10
Naga, guardian 10
Rakshasa 10
Salamander, noble 10
Slaad, gray 10

Barbed devil (hamatula) . . . 11
Cauchemar (nightmare) . . . 11
Devourer 11
Elemental, elder (any) 11
Giant, cloud 11
Golem, stone 11
Half-celestial, 9th-level
    human paladin 11

Half-dragon celestial
    lammasu 11
Harpy archer 11
Hill giant dire wereboar
    (lycanthrope) 11
Hezrou (demon) 11
Hydra, ten-headed cryo- . . . 11
Hydra, ten-headed pyro- . . . 11
Hydra, twelve-headed 11
Monstrous spider, Colossal . 11
Retriever (demon) 11
Troll hunter 11
Wraith, dread 11

Basilisk, Abyssal greater 12
Black pudding, elder (ooze) . 12
Displacer beast pack lord . . . 12
Frost worm 12
Hydra, eleven-headed cryo- . 12
Hydra, eleven-headed pyro- . 12
Kolyarut (inevitable) 12
Kraken 12
Leonal (guardinal) 12
Monstrous scorpion,
    Colossal 12
Purple worm 12
Roper 12

Beholder 13
Celestial charger (unicorn) . . 13
Ghaele (eladrin) 13
Glabrezu (demon) 13
Giant, storm 13
Golem, iron 13
Hydra, twelve-headed cryo- . 13
Hydra, twelve-headed pyro- . 13
Ice devil (gelugon) 13
Lich, 11th-level
    human wizard 13
Mummy lord 13
Slaad, death 13

Archon, trumpet 14
Astral deva (angel) 14
Nalfeshnee (demon) 14
Nightwing (nightshade) 14
Umber hulk, truly horrid . . . 14
Werewolf lord (lycanthrope) . 14

Marut (inevitable) 15
Vampire, half-elf
    Mnk 9/Shd 4 15

Archon, hound hero 16
Horned devil (cornugon) . . . 16
Golem, greater stone 16
Nightwalker (nightshade) . . . 16
Planetar (angel) 16

Aboleth mage 17
Formian, queen 17
Giant, frost jarl 17
Marilith (demon) 17
Mind flayer sorcerer 17

Nightcrawler (nightshade) . . 18

Balor (demon) 20
Pit fiend (devil) 20
Tarrasque 20

Titan 21

Solar (angel) 23

DRAGON CRS BY AGE AND COLOR

Age	White	Black	Brass	Green	Blue	Copper	Bronze	Red	Silver	Gold
Wyrmling	2	3	3	3	3	3	3	4	4	5
Very young	3	4	4	4	4	5	5	5	5	7
Young	4	5	6	5	6	7	7	7	7	9
Juvenile	6	7	8	8	8	9	9	10	10	11
Young adult	8	9	10	11	11	11	12	13	13	14
Adult	10	11	12	13	14	14	15	15	15	16
Mature adult	12	14	15	16	16	16	17	18	18	19
Old	15	16	17	18	18	19	19	20	20	21
Very old	17	18	19	19	19	20	20	21	21	22
Ancient	18	19	20	21	21	22	22	23	23	24
Wyrm	19	20	21	22	23	23	23	24	24	25
Great wyrm	21	22	23	24	25	25	25	26	26	27

find adventure
WITHOUT A
Dungeon Maste

Leave your dice bag behind. For this trek into the exciting **Dungeons & Dragons**® all you need is your imagination. Join Regdar, Lidda, Jozan, Mialee, and other familiar cha as they burst out of the core rulebooks and onto the pages of this action-packed novel So, pick up a **Dungeons & Dragons** novel at your favorite hobby or book And enjoy keeping all the experience for yourself.

DUNGEONS & DRAGONS NOVELS

www.wizards.com/books

Weretiger (lycanthrope) 5
Winter wolf 5
Wraith 5
Yuan-ti, halfblood 5
Zombie, umber hulk 5

Annis (hag) 6
Baleen whale 6
Belker 6
Bralani (eladrin) 6
Chain devil (kyton) 6
Demon, babau 6
Digester 6
Megaraptor (dinosaur) 6
Ettin 6
Gauth (beholder) 6
Girallon 6
Half-black dragon, 4th-level
    human fighter 6
Hydra, five-headed cryo- 6
Hydra, five-headed pyro- 6
Hydra, seven-headed 6
Lamia 6
Monstrous centipede,
    Gargantuan 6
Salamander, average 6
Shambling mound 6
Skeleton,
    advanced megaraptor 6
Tendriculos 6
Will-o'-wisp 6
Wyvern 6
Xill 6
Xorn, average 6
Zombie, gray render 6

Aboleth 7
Animated object,
    Gargantuan 7
Black pudding (ooze) 7
Bulette 7
Cachalot whale 7
Chaos beast 7
Chimera 7
Chuul 7
Criosphinx 7
Dire bear 7
Dragonne 7
Drider 7
Elasmosaurus (dinosaur) . . . 7
Elemental, Huge (any) 7
Elephant 7
Formian, taskmaster 7
Ghost,
    5th-level human fighter . . . 7

Giant, hill 7
Golem, flesh 7
Hellcat (devil) 7
Hydra, eight-headed 7
Hydra, six-headed cryo- 7
Hydra, six-headed pyro- 7
Invisible stalker 7
Lillend 7
Medusa 7
Monstrous scorpion, Huge . . . 7
Naga, water 7
Nymph 7
Ogre barbarian 7
Phasm 7
Remorhaz 7
Skeleton, cloud giant 7
Slaad, red 7
Spectre 7
Succubus (demon) 7
Umber hulk 7
Vampire, 5th-level
    human fighter 7
Yuan-ti, abomination 7

Arrowhawk, elder 8
Athach 8
Behir 8
Bodak 8
Destrachan 8
Dire tiger 8
Djinni noble (genie) 8
Efreeti (genie) 8
Erinyes (devil) 8
Giant, stone 8
Gorgon 8
Gray render 8
Gynosphinx 8
Hellwasp swarm 8
Hydra, nine-headed 8
Hydra, seven-headed cryo- . . 8
Hydra, seven-headed pyro- . . 8
Lammasu 8
Mind flayer 8
Mohrg 8
Monstrous spider,
    Gargantuan 8
Naga, dark 8
Octopus, giant 8
Ogre mage 8
Shield guardian 8
Skeleton, young adult
    red dragon 8
Shadow, greater 8
Slaad, blue 8
Treant 8

Tyrannosaurus (dinosaur) . . . 8
Xorn, elder 8

Androsphinx 9
Avoral (guardinal) 9
Bone devil (osyluth) 9
Delver 9
Dire shark 9
Dragon turtle 9
Elemental, greater (any) 9
Giant, frost 9
Giant, elder stone 9
Half-fiend, 7th-level
    human cleric 9
Hydra, eight-headed cryo- . . . 9
Hydra, eight-headed pyro- . . . 9
Hydra, ten-headed 9
Monstrous centipede,
    Colossal 9
Naga, spirit 9
Nessian warhound
    (hell hound) 9
Night hag 9
Roc 9
Slaad, green 9
Squid, giant 9
Tojanida, elder 9
Triceratops (dinosaur) 9
Vrock (demon) 9
Yrthak 9
Zelekhut (inevitable) 9

Animated object, Colossal . . 10
Bebilith (demon) 10
Couatl 10
Formian, myrmarch 10
Giant, fire 10
Golem, clay 10
Hydra, eleven-headed 10
Hydra, nine-headed cryo- . . . 10
Hydra, nine-headed pyro- . . . 10
Monstrous scorpion,
    Gargantuan 10
Naga, guardian 10
Rakshasa 10
Salamander, noble 10
Slaad, gray 10

Barbed devil (hamatula) . . . 11
Cauchemar (nightmare) . . . 11
Devourer 11
Elemental, elder (any) 11
Giant, cloud 11
Golem, stone 11
Half-celestial, 9th-level
    human paladin 11

Half-dragon celestial
    lammasu 11
Harpy archer 11
Hill giant dire wereboar
    (lycanthrope) 11
Hezrou (demon) 11
Hydra, ten-headed cryo- . . . 11
Hydra, ten-headed pyro- . . . 11
Hydra, twelve-headed 11
Monstrous spider, Colossal . 11
Retriever (demon) 11
Troll hunter 11
Wraith, dread 11

Basilisk, Abyssal greater 12
Black pudding, elder (ooze) . 12
Displacer beast pack lord . . . 12
Frost worm 12
Hydra, eleven-headed cryo- . . 12
Hydra, eleven-headed pyro- . 12
Kolyarut (inevitable) 12
Kraken 12
Leonal (guardinal) 12
Monstrous scorpion,
    Colossal 12
Purple worm 12
Roper 12

Beholder 13
Celestial charger (unicorn) . . 13
Ghaele (eladrin) 13
Glabrezu (demon) 13
Giant, storm 13
Golem, iron 13
Hydra, twelve-headed cryo- . . 13
Hydra, twelve-headed pyro- . . 13
Ice devil (gelugon) 13
Lich, 11th-level
    human wizard 13
Mummy lord 13
Slaad, death 13

Archon, trumpet 14
Astral deva (angel) 14
Nalfeshnee (demon) 14
Nightwing (nightshade) 14
Umber hulk, truly horrid 14
Werewolf lord (lycanthrope) . 14

Marut (inevitable) 15
Vampire, half-elf
    Mnk 9/Shd 4 15

Archon, hound hero 16
Horned devil (cornugon) . . . 16
Golem, greater stone 16
Nightwalker (nightshade) . . . 16
Planetar (angel) 16

Aboleth mage 17
Formian, queen 17
Giant, frost jarl 17
Marilith (demon) 17
Mind flayer sorcerer 17

Nightcrawler (nightshade) . . 18

Balor (demon) 20
Pit fiend (devil) 20
Tarrasque 20

Titan 21

Solar (angel) 23

DRAGON CRS BY AGE AND COLOR

Age	White	Black	Brass	Green	Blue	Copper	Bronze	Red	Silver	Gold
Wyrmling	2	3	3	3	3	3	3	4	4	5
Very young	3	4	4	4	4	5	5	5	5	7
Young	4	5	6	5	6	7	7	7	7	9
Juvenile	6	7	8	8	8	9	9	10	10	11
Young adult	8	9	10	11	11	11	12	13	13	14
Adult	10	11	12	13	14	14	15	15	15	16
Mature adult	12	14	15	16	16	16	17	18	18	19
Old	15	16	17	18	18	19	19	20	20	21
Very old	17	18	19	19	19	20	20	21	21	22
Ancient	18	19	20	21	21	22	22	23	23	24
Wyrm	19	20	21	22	23	23	23	24	24	25
Great wyrm	21	22	23	24	25	25	25	26	26	27

find adventure
WITHOUT A
Dungeon Master

Leave your dice bag behind. For this trek into the exciting **Dungeons & Dragons**® w
all you need is your imagination. Join Regdar, Lidda, Jozan, Mialee, and other familiar chara
as they burst out of the core rulebooks and onto the pages of this action-packed novel se
So, pick up a **Dungeons & Dragons** novel at your favorite hobby or books
And enjoy keeping all the experience for yourself.

DUNGEONS & DRAGONS NOVELS

www.wizards.com/books

Weretiger (lycanthrope) 5
Winter wolf 5
Wraith 5
Yuan-ti, halfblood 5
Zombie, umber hulk 5

Annis (hag) 6
Baleen whale 6
Belker 6
Bralani (eladrin) 6
Chain devil (kyton) 6
Demon, babau 6
Digester 6
Megaraptor (dinosaur) 6
Ettin 6
Gauth (beholder) 6
Girallon 6
Half-black dragon, 4th-level
   human fighter 6
Hydra, five-headed cryo- 6
Hydra, five-headed pyro- 6
Hydra, seven-headed 6
Lamia 6
Monstrous centipede,
   Gargantuan 6
Salamander, average 6
Shambling mound 6
Skeleton,
   advanced megaraptor 6
Tendriculos 6
Will-o'-wisp 6
Wyvern 6
Xill 6
Xorn, average 6
Zombie, gray render 6

Aboleth 7
Animated object,
   Gargantuan 7
Black pudding (ooze) 7
Bulette 7
Cachalot whale 7
Chaos beast 7
Chimera 7
Chuul 7
Criosphinx 7
Dire bear 7
Dragonne 7
Drider 7
Elasmosaurus (dinosaur) 7
Elemental, Huge (any) 7
Elephant 7
Formian, taskmaster 7
Ghost,
   5th-level human fighter . . . 7

Giant, hill 7
Golem, flesh 7
Hellcat (devil) 7
Hydra, eight-headed 7
Hydra, six-headed cryo- 7
Hydra, six-headed pyro- 7
Invisible stalker 7
Lillend 7
Medusa 7
Monstrous scorpion, Huge . . . 7
Naga, water 7
Nymph 7
Ogre barbarian 7
Phasm 7
Remorhaz 7
Skeleton, cloud giant 7
Slaad, red 7
Spectre 7
Succubus (demon) 7
Umber hulk 7
Vampire, 5th-level
   human fighter 7
Yuan-ti, abomination 7

Arrowhawk, elder 8
Athach 8
Behir 8
Bodak 8
Destrachan 8
Dire tiger 8
Djinni noble (genie) 8
Efreeti (genie) 8
Erinyes (devil) 8
Giant, stone 8
Gorgon 8
Gray render 8
Gynosphinx 8
Hellwasp swarm 8
Hydra, nine-headed 8
Hydra, seven-headed cryo- . . . 8
Hydra, seven-headed pyro- . . . 8
Lammasu 8
Mind flayer 8
Mohrg 8
Monstrous spider,
   Gargantuan 8
Naga, dark 8
Octopus, giant 8
Ogre mage 8
Shield guardian 8
Skeleton, young adult
   red dragon 8
Shadow, greater 8
Slaad, blue 8
Treant 8

Tyrannosaurus (dinosaur) . . . 8
Xorn, elder 8

Androsphinx 9
Avoral (guardinal) 9
Bone devil (osyluth) 9
Delver 9
Dire shark 9
Dragon turtle 9
Elemental, greater (any) 9
Giant, frost 9
Giant, elder stone 9
Half-fiend, 7th-level
   human cleric 9
Hydra, eight-headed cryo- . . . 9
Hydra, eight-headed pyro- . . . 9
Hydra, ten-headed 9
Monstrous centipede,
   Colossal 9
Naga, spirit 9
Nessian warhound
   (hell hound) 9
Night hag 9
Roc 9
Slaad, green 9
Squid, giant 9
Tojanida, elder 9
Triceratops (dinosaur) 9
Vrock (demon) 9
Yrthak 9
Zelekhut (inevitable) 9

Animated object, Colossal . . 10
Bebilith (demon) 10
Couatl 10
Formian, myrmarch 10
Giant, fire 10
Golem, clay 10
Hydra, eleven-headed 10
Hydra, nine-headed cryo- . . . 10
Hydra, nine-headed pyro- . . . 10
Monstrous scorpion,
   Gargantuan 10
Naga, guardian 10
Rakshasa 10
Salamander, noble 10
Slaad, gray 10

Barbed devil (hamatula) 11
Cauchemar (nightmare) 11
Devourer 11
Elemental, elder (any) 11
Giant, cloud 11
Golem, stone 11
Half-celestial, 9th-level
   human paladin 11

Half-dragon celestial
   lammasu 11
Harpy archer 11
Hill giant dire wereboar
   (lycanthrope) 11
Hezrou (demon) 11
Hydra, ten-headed cryo- 11
Hydra, ten-headed pyro- 11
Hydra, twelve-headed 11
Monstrous spider, Colossal . . 11
Retriever (demon) 11
Troll hunter 11
Wraith, dread 11

Basilisk, Abyssal greater 12
Black pudding, elder (ooze) . . 12
Displacer beast pack lord . . . 12
Frost worm 12
Hydra, eleven-headed cryo- . . 12
Hydra, eleven-headed pyro- . . 12
Kolyarut (inevitable) 12
Kraken 12
Leonal (guardinal) 12
Monstrous scorpion,
   Colossal 12
Purple worm 12
Roper 12

Beholder 13
Celestial charger (unicorn) . . 13
Ghaele (eladrin) 13
Glabrezu (demon) 13
Giant, storm 13
Golem, iron 13
Hydra, twelve-headed cryo- . . 13
Hydra, twelve-headed pyro- . . 13
Ice devil (gelugon) 13
Lich, 11th-level
   human wizard 13
Mummy lord 13
Slaad, death 13

Archon, trumpet 14
Astral deva (angel) 14
Nalfeshnee (demon) 14
Nightwing (nightshade) 14
Umber hulk, truly horrid 14
Werewolf lord (lycanthrope) . . 14

Marut (inevitable) 15
Vampire, half-elf
   Mnk 9/Shd 4 15

Archon, hound hero 16
Horned devil (cornugon) 16
Golem, greater stone 16
Nightwalker (nightshade) . . . 16
Planetar (angel) 16

Aboleth mage 17
Formian, queen 17
Giant, frost jarl 17
Marilith (demon) 17
Mind flayer sorcerer 17

Nightcrawler (nightshade) . . . 18

Balor (demon) 20
Pit fiend (devil) 20
Tarrasque 20

Titan 21

Solar (angel) 23

DRAGON CRS BY AGE AND COLOR

Age	White	Black	Brass	Green	Blue	Copper	Bronze	Red	Silver	Gold
Wyrmling	2	3	3	3	3	3	3	4	4	5
Very young	3	4	4	4	4	5	5	5	5	7
Young	4	5	6	5	6	7	7	7	7	9
Juvenile	6	7	8	8	8	9	9	10	10	11
Young adult	8	9	10	11	11	11	12	13	13	14
Adult	10	11	12	13	14	14	15	15	15	16
Mature adult	12	14	15	16	16	16	17	18	18	19
Old	15	16	17	18	18	19	19	20	20	21
Very old	17	18	19	19	19	20	20	21	21	22
Ancient	18	19	20	21	21	22	22	23	23	24
Wyrm	19	20	21	22	23	23	23	24	24	25
Great wyrm	21	22	23	24	25	25	25	26	26	27

find adventure
WITHOUT A
Dungeon Master

Leave your dice bag behind. For this trek into the exciting **Dungeons & Dragons**® w
all you need is your imagination. Join Regdar, Lidda, Jozan, Mialee, and other familiar chara
as they burst out of the core rulebooks and onto the pages of this action-packed novel s
So, pick up a **Dungeons & Dragons** novel at your favorite hobby or books
And enjoy keeping all the experience for yourself.

DUNGEONS & DRAGONS NOVELS

www.wizards.com/books